CROSS-BORDER LITIGATION IN EUROPE

This substantial and original book examines how the EU Private International Law ('PIL') framework is functioning and considers its impact on the administration of justice in cross-border cases within the EU. It grew out of a major project (ie EUPILLAR: European Union Private International Law: Legal Application in Reality) financially supported by the EU Civil Justice Programme. The research was led by the Centre for Private International Law at the University of Aberdeen and involved partners from the Universities of Freiburg, Antwerp, Wroclaw, Leeds, Milan and Madrid (Complutense).

The contributors address the specific features of cross-border disputes in the EU by undertaking a comprehensive analysis of the Court of Justice of the EU (CJEU) and national case law on the Brussels I, Rome I and II, Brussels IIa and Maintenance Regulations. Part I discusses the development of the EU PIL framework. Part II contains the national reports from 26 EU Member States. Parts III (civil and commercial) and IV (family law) contain the CJEU case law analysis and several cross-cutting chapters. Part V briefly sets the agenda for an institutional reform which is necessary to improve the effectiveness of the EU PIL regime. This comprehensive research-project book will be of interest to researchers, students, legal practitioners, judges and policy-makers who work, or are interested, in the field of private international law.

Volume 20 in the series Studies in Private International Law

Studies in Private International Law

Recent titles in the series

Cross-Border Litigation in Europe

Edited by
Paul Beaumont, Mihail Danov,
Katarina Trimmings and Burcu Yüksel

·HART·

OXFORD · LONDON · NEW YORK · NEW DELHI · SYDNEY

HART PUBLISHING
Bloomsbury Publishing Plc
Kemp House, Chawley Park, Cumnor Hill, Oxford, OX2 9PH, UK

HART PUBLISHING, the Hart/Stag logo, BLOOMSBURY and the Diana logo are
trademarks of Bloomsbury Publishing Plc
First published in Great Britain 2017

First published in hardback, 2017
Paperback edition, 2020

A catalogue record for this book is available from the British Library.

Library of Congress Cataloging-in-Publication Data

Names: Beaumont, Paul, editor. | Danov, Mihail, editor. | Trimmings, Katarina, editor. |
Yüksel, Burcu, editor.

Title: Cross-border litigation in Europe / Edited by Paul Beaumont, Mihail Danov,
Katarina Trimmings and Burcu Yüksel.

Description: Portland, Oregon : Hart Publishing, 2017. | Series: Studies in private international law ;
volume 20 | Includes bibliographical references and index.

Identifiers: LCCN 2017040712 (print) | LCCN 2017041726 (ebook) | ISBN 9781782256779 (Epub) |
ISBN 9781782256762 (hardback)

Subjects: LCSH: Conflict of laws—European Union countries. | Civil law—European Union
countries. | Judicial assistance—European Union countries. | Judgments, Foreign—European
Union countries. | Jurisdiction—European Union countries. | Torts—European Union countries.

Classification: LCC KJE982 (ebook) | LCC KJE982 .C76 2017 (print) | DDC 340.9/3094—dc23

LC record available at https://lccn.loc.gov/2017040712

ISBN: HB: 978-1-78225-676-2
PB: 978-1-50993-692-2
ePDF: 978-1-78225-678-6
ePub: 978-1-78225-677-9

Typeset by Compuscript Ltd, Shannon

To find out more about our authors and books visit www.hartpublishing.co.uk. Here you will find
extracts, author information, details of forthcoming events and the option to sign up for our newsletters.

SERIES EDITOR'S PREFACE

As one of the editors of the book it does not seem appropriate for me to write a Series Editor's Preface which focuses on commending the merits of the book to potential readers. So I will take the opportunity to thank people who were involved personally.

The Centre for Private International Law, at the University of Aberdeen, began its life on 1 January 2012. I am proud of the hard work and devotion to the subject by the team of academic staff and research students in the Centre. This book arose out of the EUPILLAR project which was led by the Centre and involved several of its key members, notably my tireless fellow editors (Dr Katarina Trimmings and Dr Burcu Yüksel) and Dr Jonathan Fitchen. It was a privilege to co-author the two major chapters on the case law of the Court of Justice of the European Union on the five EUPILLAR Regulations (Brussels I, Rome I and II with Dr Yüksel and Brussels IIa and Maintenance with Dr Trimmings) and we hope that the systematic analysis and critique of that case law will help to guide the future work of national courts and the CJEU in interpreting the Regulations and the EU legislature when it revises them.

EUPILLAR could not have happened without the very generous financial support from the EU Commission and I want to thank those who were involved in selecting this project. One key member of the Commission unit that is responsible for private international law gave an excellent paper at the initial project conference at the University of Aberdeen. Her name is Dr Karen Vandekerckhove and she has since been promoted to head another unit in the Commission but her loss to the development of private international law in the EU and globally (through her work representing the EU in the Hague Conference on Private International Law) will be immense. I had the privilege, as a member of the UK delegation, of seeing Karen expertly carry out the Commission's negotiation of the Maintenance, Brussels Ia and Succession Regulations in Brussels and for the last few years I have been an expert adviser to the Commission as she brilliantly led the EU's negotiation team in the revived Judgments Project at the Hague Conference on Private International Law.

Another ex-member of the Commission unit responsible for private international law and for many years a Scottish civil servant, who represented Scotland and the UK on many issues of private international law in the Council of the European Union and in the Hague Conference on Private International Law, Peter Beaton, was one of the many willing volunteers to be interviewed for the EUPILLAR project. Sadly he died suddenly earlier this year but not before he had consented to the use of the transcript of his interview for the project and therefore it is reflected in various places anonymously in this book. He had no objection to people knowing that he participated in the project by being an interviewee. I worked with Peter very closely for many years in my role as consultant to the Scottish and UK Governments on private international law. He was a lovely man to spend time with: a passionate Scot, huge enthusiast about private international law and trying to improve it in Scotland, the UK, the EU and throughout the world, and someone who loved life (especially good food, wine and stimulating conversation). He will be greatly missed.

EUPILLAR would have been impossible without the lead partners from several European Universities. First, many thanks are due to Dr Mihail Danov (now of the University of Exeter) as one of my fellow editors of the book and as the inspirational co-author with me of several chapters in the book and of two journal articles that were written during the project and are referred to several times in the book. Professor Stefania Bariatti (Milan) is a long-time colleague who I have enjoyed working with on many projects and has a vast and intricate knowledge of private international law; Professor Dr Jan von Hein (Freiburg) is a new colleague who proved to be easy to work with and, as expected, excellent; and Professors Carmen Otero García-Castrillon (Madrid), Thalia Kruger (Antwerp) and Agnieszka Frąckowiak-Adamska (Wroclaw) have all kindly hosted me in their Universities and did excellent work on the project. I am very pleased that these distinguished colleagues are taking EUPILLAR 2 forward with EU funding from the Civil Justice programme that is no longer available for UK applicants.

Thanks are also due to the many national reporters who have made this book a much more comprehensive analysis of how the EUPILLAR Regulations are operating in the EU. Some of them are good friends, some are leading lights in our discipline (the two categories overlap)—notably Professors Bea Verschraegen, Monica Pauknerová, Horatia Muir Watt, Aukje Van Hoek and Michael Bogdan and the seemingly ageless Judge Gustaf Möller—and all played an invaluable role.

It is a great pleasure to thank those who wrote cross-cutting chapters in the book having been given access to the EUPILLAR database and the national reports. These guests have provided stimulating critical insights from their analysis of the data and from their own expertise. They are Michael Wilderspin (Commission Legal Service), Professor Zheng Sophia Tang (Newcastle), Professor Paul Torremans (Nottingham), Dr Jonathan Fitchen (Aberdeen), Dr Ruth Lamont (Manchester), Dr Lara Walker (Sussex) and Dr Stephen Dnes (Dundee).

It is a delight to have the chance to thank Sinead Moloney, Tom Adams and the other members of the Hart team who work efficiently and well not only on this book but also on all the books in the Series.

Finally, I want to take the opportunity to thank Professor Jonathan Harris QC (King's College, London) for the excellent collaboration we enjoyed together as fellow editors of the Hart Studies in Private International Law from its inception. We worked together on nearly twenty volumes in the Series. Jonathan is a tireless enthusiast for private international law and for the development of the discipline. He has always been particularly keen to help early career scholars and many of the volumes in the Series have been written by such scholars. He will be missed by the Series but he has moved on to work with the OUP Private International Law Series in order to continue to help the development of private international law. I wish him well.

Paul Beaumont, University of Aberdeen

EDITORS' PREFACE

This substantial and original book grew out of a major research project (ie EUPILLAR: European Union Private International Law: Legal Application in Reality). The research consortium was led by Professor Paul Beaumont from the Centre for Private International Law at the University of Aberdeen between 2014 and 2016, and involved Professor Stefania Bariatti, Professor Jan von Hein, Professor Carmen Otero García-Castrillón, Dr Thalia Kruger, Dr Agnieszka Frąckowiak-Adamska, Dr Katarina Trimmings, Dr Burcu Yüksel and Dr Mihail Danov as research collaborators. The Project examined the case law and legal practice on the main EU private international law instruments (ie the Brussels I, Rome I and II, Brussels IIa and Maintenance Regulations) in the Court of Justice of the European Union (CJEU) and in Germany, Belgium, Poland, Great Britain, Italy and Spain. In order to consider whether the selected Member States' courts and the CJEU can appropriately deal with the relevant cross-border issues arising in the EU context and to propose ways to improve the effectiveness of the EU private international Law (EU PIL) framework, the research teams analysed over 2300 judgments and conducted interviews with over 180 participants—representatives of the EU institutions, members of the CJEU, national judges and legal practitioners across the EU. We are very thankful and much indebted to the interview respondents from Belgium, England and Wales, Germany, Italy, Poland, Scotland, Spain and the EU institutions for kindly taking part in this Project, providing us with very many useful insights.

Building on this empirical research, this book addresses cross-border civil, commercial and family law issues in the EU by a comprehensive analysis of the CJEU and national case law on the Brussels I, Rome I and II, Brussels IIa and Maintenance Regulations. Part I discusses the development of the EU PIL framework. Part II contains the national reports from all EU Member States apart from Denmark and Estonia. Parts III (civil and commercial) and IV (family law) analyse the CJEU case law on the relevant EU PIL Regulations along with several cross-cutting chapters taking account of the data from the national reports. Part V briefly addresses some theoretical issues and some practical challenges in cross-border litigation in the EU, and sets the agenda for an institutional reform which is necessary to improve the effectiveness of the EU PIL regime.

The EUPILLAR study would not have materialised without the financial support from the EU Commission's Civil Justice Programme to whom we are eternally grateful. We would also like to thank the key research collaborators and their teams for their great efforts to realise this project book, the authors of the national reports and of the cross-cutting chapters for their invaluable contributions to the book, and the speakers and the attendees of the EUPILLAR Project conferences held in Aberdeen and in London for their help with the project. The gratitude is further extended to the anonymous referees who reviewed the chapters in this book. We remain indebted to Hart Publishing for producing this book and supporting us throughout the years. We are also very grateful for the support of our families.

Paul Beaumont, Katarina Trimmings and
Burcu Yüksel (University of Aberdeen)
Mihail Danov (University of Exeter)

TABLE OF CONTENTS

**Part III: Litigating Cross-border Civil and Commercial
Disputes—A Europe of Law and Justice**

Part IV: Litigating Cross-border Family Law Disputes—A Europe of Law and Justice

Part V: Conclusion

CONTRIBUTORS LIST

Archontaki, Aspasia	Attorney-at-Law PhD
Bariatti, Stefania	University of Milan
Beaumont, Paul	University of Aberdeen
Bernasconi, Sara	University of Milan
Boden, Didier	Université Paris 1 Panthéon-Sorbonne
Bogdan, Michael	University of Lund
Burdova, Katarina	Comenius University (Bratislava)
Calleja, Calvin	GANADO Advocates
Camara, Céline	Max Planck Institute
Corneloup, Sabine	Université Paris 2 Panthéon-Assas
Correia, Raquel	Formerly of the Portuguese Permanent Representation to the EU
Cremona, Antoine G	GANADO Advocates
Danov, Mihail	University of Exeter
De Almeida, João Gomes	University of Lisbon
Dittmers, Hannah	Albert-Ludwigs-University of Freiburg
Dnes, Stephen	University of Dundee
Dobre, Alexandra Ema	European Court of Justice
Fitchen, Jonathan	University of Aberdeen
Frąckowiak-Adamska, Agnieszka	University of Wroclaw
García-Castrillón Otero, Carmen	Complutense University (Madrid)
Grygar, Jiří	Regional Court in Prague, Judge
Guzewicz, Agnieszka	University of Wroclaw
Harding, Maebh	University of Warwick
Hatzimihail, Nikitas E	University of Cyprus
Heindler, Florian	Sigmund Freud University Vienna
Heymann, Jeremy	Université de Lyon
Ilie, Lucian	Lazareff Le Bars (Paris)
Kraljić, Suzana	University of Maribor
Kruger, Thalia	University of Antwerp
Kucina, Irēna	Ministry of Justice, Latvia
Kunda, Ivana	University of Rijeka
Lamont, Ruth	University of Manchester
Maltez, Susana	University of Lisbon
Marchetti, Filippo	University of Milan
Maunsbach, Ulf	University of Lund
Mifsud-Bonnici, Clement	GANADO Advocates
Möller, Gustaf	Krogerus

Muir Watt, Horatia	SciencesPo Paris
Nagy, Csongor Istvan	University of Szeged
Oliveira, Elsa Dias	University of Lisbon
Pauknerová, Monika	Charles University Prague
Petelski, Łukasz	University of Wroclaw
Petrov, Anton	Djingov, Gouginski, Kyutchukov & Velichkov
Praneviciene, Kristina	Vytautas Magnus University
Simsive, Paata	Member of Piraeus Bar Association
Sindres, David	Université d'Angers
Smeureanu, Ileana M	Jones Day (Paris)
Sumner, Ian	Voorts Legal Services
Tang, Zheng Sophia	Newcastle University
Teles, Eugénia Galvão	University of Lisbon
Torremans, Paul	University of Nottingham
Trimmings, Katarina	University of Aberdeen
Tsenova, Teodora	Djingov, Gouginski, Kyutchukov & Velichkov, Institute of Private International Law in Sofia
Ulrix, Eline	Allen & Overy
Usunier, Laurence	Université de Cergy-Pontoise
Van der Plas, Cathalijne	FLORENT Advocaten
Van Hoek Aukje	University of Amsterdam
Verschraegen, Bea	University of Vienna
Viarengo, Ilaria	University of Milan
Villata, Francesca C	University of Milan
Von Hein, Jan	University of Freiburg
Vozaryova, Miroslava	Comenius University (Bratislava)
Walker, Lara	University of Sussex
Wilderspin, Michael	European Commission
Yüksel, Burcu	University of Aberdeen
Zavadilová, Marta	Ministry of Justice, Czech Republic

1

Introduction: Research Aims and Methodology

PAUL BEAUMONT AND MIHAIL DANOV

I. Legislative Developments and Theoretical Framework

It is well established that the European Union has created an internal market between its Member States based on free movement of goods, services, capital and persons across its internal borders.[1] The intentional preservation of the diverse nature of the EU Member States' legal systems[2] has justified the adoption of EU private international law ('PIL') instruments[3] to support the effective functioning of the internal market[4] and to help create an area of freedom, security and justice[5] that is designed to 'facilitate the sound administration of justice.'[6] The Treaty on the Functioning of the European Union (TFEU)[7] creates a legislative competence for the EU to take measures aimed at ensuring 'effective access to justice'[8] in cross-border cases. It has been submitted that the EU PIL framework is the foundation of EU civil justice,[9] which—according to the EU Charter of Fundamental Rights—is set to guarantee the 'right to an effective remedy'.[10] To this end, the EU PIL framework has an important role to play with a view to allocating jurisdiction between the EU Member States' courts and enabling national judges to determine the applicable substantive laws in

---

[1] See Art 26 TFEU.

[2] See Art 67(1) TFEU which says that the Union's area of freedom, security and justice has 'respect for fundamental rights and the different legal systems and traditions of the Member States.'

[3] Notably Council Reg 1215/2012 ('Brussels Ia') [2012] OJ L351/1; Council Reg 2201/2003 ('Brussels IIa') [2003] OJ L338/1; Council Reg 4/2009 ('Maintenance Regulation') [2009] OJ L7/1; Council Reg 593/2008 ('Rome I') [2008] OJ L177/6; and Council Reg 864/2007 ('Rome II') [2007] OJ L199/40 (the EUPILLAR Regulations).

[4] See Art 81(2) TFEU. See more M Danov and P Beaumont, 'Measuring the Effectiveness of the EU Civil Justice Framework: Theoretical and Methodological Challenges' (2015/2016) 17 *Yearbook of Private International Law* 151–80.

[5] See Arts 67(1) and (4) and 81 TFEU.

[6] Recital 16 to Brussels Ia.

[7] [2012] OJ C326/47.

[8] Art 81(2)(e) TFEU. See also Art 67(4) TFEU and Recital 1 to Brussels Ia.

[9] P Beaumont and M Danov, 'The EU Civil Justice Framework and Private Law: "Integration through [Private International] Law"' (2015) 22 *Maastricht Journal of European and Comparative Law* 706–31.

[10] Art 47(1) and (2) of the Charter of Fundamental Human Rights. See also Recital 38 to Brussels Ia.

cross-border cases. What is the impact of these legislative developments on the definition of EU PIL? The traditional view is that:

> [C]lassical private international law ... is generally understood by both courts and scholars to define the competent court, applicable law, and status of foreign judgments in transnational settings without regard for the final result in terms of individual rights and obligations or indeed wider policy concerns.[11]

That said, the EU legislative developments in the area of PIL strongly suggest that a broader definition of EU PIL is to be adopted.[12] In particular, the litigants' rights to an effective remedy and to a fair trial in disputes with an international element are safeguarded by the most important PIL instrument, Brussels Ia.[13] The importance of the right to effective remedies in cross-border cases is seen in the EU Justice Agenda 2020.[14] These examples strongly suggest that the EU civil justice system aims to facilitate private parties' effective access to remedies in cross-border cases.

An analysis of the effectiveness of EU PIL needs to consider the context in which the relevant rules are applied by the judges who have the task to disseminate justice in cross-border cases across the EU. It is well established that 'there cannot be law without a legal system; legality necessarily finds its source in a legal system. What makes a norm or set of norms legal is their belonging to a legal system ...'[15] In other words, the implications of the EU civil justice system must be carefully considered when analysing the effectiveness of the EU PIL instruments because it provides the institutional architecture within which the PIL rules are functioning. That said, it is somewhat surprising that a recent book on *Human Rights and Private International Law*[16] which devoted six chapters to the right to a fair trial, failed to include a chapter dealing with the right to an effective remedy. Bearing the recent EU legislative developments in mind, this is a significant omission. The importance of the right to an effective remedy was captured by Calliess[17] who stated that:

> [A]fter World War II it became generally accepted that *the right to effective access to justice* is a *human right*, which is granted to everyone, including foreigners ... In modern times of globalization, where communication, transactions, and migration across borders have transformed from exceptional to

---

[11] H Muir Watt, 'Theorizing Private International Law' in A Orford, F Hoffman and M Clark (eds), *The Oxford Handbook of the Theory of International Law* (Oxford, Oxford University Press, 2016) 862, 862–63.

[12] Modern PIL also includes judicial and administrative co-operation particularly in family law (see the use of Central Authorities (CAs) in Brussels IIa and Maintenance). This was not the focus of the EUPILLAR research as no interviews were conducted with CAs. For the results of empirical research on the work of the CAs in Brussels IIa see P Beaumont, L Walker and J Holliday, 'Conflicts of EU Courts on Child Abduction: The Reality of Article 11(6)–(8) Brussels IIa Proceedings across the EU' (2016) 12 *Journal of Private International Law* 211–60 and on Maintenance see P Beaumont, B Hess, S Spancken and L Walker (eds), *Recovery of Maintenance in the EU and Worldwide* (Oxford, Hart Publishing, 2014) and L Walker, *Maintenance and Child Support in Private International Law* (Oxford, Hart Publishing, 2015).

[13] Recital 38 to Brussels Ia. See also J Lonbay and A Biondi (eds), *Remedies for Breach of EC Law* (Oxford, John Wiley & Sons, 1997).

[14] Commission Communication, The Strasbourg Programme—The EU Justice Agenda for 2020—Strengthening Trust, Mobility and Growth within the Union, COM(2014) 144 final, para 4.1(ii).

[15] T Schultz, *Transnational Legality: Stateless Law and International Arbitration* (Oxford, Oxford University Press, 2014) 104.

[16] J Fawcett, M Ni Shuilleabhain and S Shah, *Human Rights and Private International Law* (Oxford, Oxford University Press, 2016).

[17] G-P Calliess, 'Introduction' in G-P Calliess (ed), *Rome Regulations* (Alphen aan den Rijn, Wolters Kluwer, 2015) 1.

mundane phenomena, the pressing question is no longer *if* the state has to grant access to justice in international situations as well, but *how* the right can be implemented effectively.[18]

Therefore, the lack of a systematic analysis of the way the current EU PIL framework shapes litigants' strategies and affects parties' effective access to remedies in cross-border cases indicate that the research findings of the EUPILLAR project are needed. The significance of the right to an effective remedy is patently reflected in Council Directive 2002/8/EC[19] which states that: 'Neither the lack of resources of a litigant, whether acting as claimant or as defendant, nor the difficulties flowing from a dispute's cross-border dimension should be allowed to hamper effective access to justice.'[20] This demonstrates that the EU policy-makers are mindful that the high litigation costs, which may be inflated by a greater level of complexity in cross-border cases, may hinder the litigants' effective access to remedies in disputes with an international element. Therefore, there are two important features of the EU legal landscape in relation to PIL which must be considered in a cross-border context.

First, justice in cross-border cases is to be dispensed by the national judges who will apply the relevant EU PIL instruments in disputes with an international element. As a result, the EU Member States' courts form an important and integral part of the EU civil justice system, which shapes the development of the EU PIL rules, in cross-border cases. Since the effectiveness of EU civil justice is dependent on the adequate application of EU PIL instruments by national courts, any analysis of the effectiveness of the current framework must take account of the practice of Member States' courts.[21] Indeed, the current EU policies may well reflect Member States' governmental interests, but their implementation[22] is dependent on the active role of private parties,[23] decisions of national judges and the effectiveness of the current institutional framework.[24] Moreover, given the level of diversity across the EU, there may be problems with a somewhat inconsistent application of the EU PIL instruments as well as with the ability of the different EU Member States' courts to apply foreign law(s).[25] Furthermore, the different levels of efficiency which characterise the various Member States' legal systems[26] might suggest that, depending on where the litigation takes

---

[18] ibid 4—the emphasis is in the original.

[19] Council Dir 2002/8/EC of 27 January 2003 to improve access to justice in cross-border disputes by establishing minimum common rules relating to legal aid for such disputes [2003] OJ L26/14. See J Monar, 'The Area of Freedom, Security and Justice' in A von Bogdany and J Bast (eds), *Principles of European Constitutional Law* revised 2nd edn (Oxford, Hart Publishing, 2010) 551, 561–62.

[20] Recital 6 to Council Dir 2002/8/EC.

[21] D Chalmers, 'The Positioning of EU Judicial Politics within the United Kingdom' [2000] *West European Politics* 169, 171.

[22] S Milio, *From Policy to Implementation in the European Union: The Challenge of a Multi-Level Governance System* (London, IB Tauris Publishers, 2010).

[23] FW Scharpf, *Community and Autonomy: Institutions, Policies and Legitimacy in Multilevel Europe* (Campus Verlag—Publication Series of the Max Planck Institute, 2010) 363. See also RD Kelemen, 'The Structure and Dynamics of EU Federalism' [2003] *Comparative Political Studies* 184, 201–02.

[24] F Snyder, 'The Effectiveness of European Community Law: Institutions, Processes, Tools and Techniques' [1993] *Modern Law Review* 19; and Danov and Beaumont, above n 4 at 173–78.

[25] *Sheraleen Boyd Munro v Ian Munro* [2007] EWHC 3315 (Fam) [5–6]. See also R Fentiman, 'Methods and Approaches—Choice of Law in Europe: Uniformity and Integration' (2007–2008) 82 *Tulane Law Review* 2021, 2035–36. Considered further in Danov and Beaumont, above n 4 at 158–59.

[26] See also G Palumbo and others, 'The Economics of Civil Justice: New Cross-country Data and Empirics' (2013) *OECD Economics Department Working Papers, No 1060*, OECD Publishing, available at http://dx.doi.org/10.1787/5k41w04ds6kf-en.

place, the parties may face different types of problems in disputes with an international element. Could there be litigation tactics, which are designed under the EU PIL, with a view to exploiting the deficiencies of some national judicial systems? Could strategic litigants exploit the weakness of the institutional architecture in relation to the EU PIL framework, impairing parties' effective access to remedies in disputes with an international element? Should the institutional architecture be revised, in order to facilitate private parties' access to effective remedies in cross-border cases, considering the specific characteristics of the EU Member States' judicial systems?

Second, despite the fact that it is the EU Member States' courts that apply the EU PIL instruments, the Court of Justice of the European Union (CJEU) plays an important role in supporting the national judges by interpreting the relevant PIL instruments. It is a real issue that '[i]n the case of references for a preliminary ruling, the average duration amounted to 15 months …'[27] A consequence of the slowness of the preliminary reference process may explain why some of the Member States' judges are unwilling to refer a case to the CJEU, considering it as a measure of last resort.[28] The issue is not new and it was identified over 15 years ago in a Report from January 2000,[29] the Working Party for the European Commission noted:

> *Judicial cooperation in civil matters* ([now Article 81 TFEU] Article 65—ex Article 73m—of the EC Treaty) gives rise to very specific issues of private international law which, by their nature, differ from those normally encountered in [EU] law.

> … the Working Party considers that preliminary questions concerning judicial cooperation should be withdrawn from the Court of Justice and assigned to a [Union] court with members drawn from specialist private international lawyers. An appeal to the Court of Justice on a point of general legal interest, at the request of the Commission, would be retained.[30]

The institutional architecture is even more of an issue in an already significantly enlarged European Union. In particular, the ability of the CJEU to effectively interpret the growing number of PIL instruments must be considered when making an evaluation of the capacity of the EU Member States' courts to consistently and uniformly apply the private international law instruments, 'do[ing] justice in individual cases'[31] with an international element.

Therefore, an analysis of the EU Member States' practice and the CJEU work in PIL will indicate whether the current EU civil justice framework achieves its objective to provide effective remedies for parties in cross-border disputes. And, if not, suggestions will be made as to how the institutional architecture should be revised. In this context, as an interview respondent, a judge from England and Wales noted, one might contemplate whether there is a case 'for specialist judges in the area of civil litigation'[32] sitting at the CJEU. To this end, it will be important to define the main aspects of the right to an effective remedy which

---

[27] Court of Justice of the European Union, Press Release No 27/15, Luxembourg, 3 March 2015. See also: Court of Justice of the European Union, *Annual Report 2014*, Luxembourg 2015.

[28] eg *I (A Child) (Contact Application: Jurisdiction), Re* [2009] UKSC 10 [35, 76 and 92]; *Cooper Tire and Rubber Co Europe Ltd v Shell Chemicals UK Ltd* [2010] EWCA Civ 864 [46]; *M v M* [2013] EWCA Civ 1255 [50]; *Canyon Offshore Ltd v GDF Suez E&P Nederland BV* [2014] EWHC 3801 (Comm) [54]; and *Lady Christine Brownlie v Four Seasons Holdings Incorporated* [2015] EWCA Civ 665 [92].

[29] Report by the Working Party on the Future of European Communities' Court System, January 2001, available at http://ec.europa.eu/dgs/legal_service/pdf/due_en.pdf.

[30] ibid 32–33—the emphasis is in the original.

[31] Recital 14 to the Rome II Reg.

[32] EUPILLAR—England and Wales—Interview Transcripts No 19.

must be considered when making the analysis of the EU PIL framework, specifying how the regime is functioning.[33]

There are two important elements of the right to an effective remedy which must be considered in cross-border cases.[34] First, the allocation of jurisdiction before a competent court will be important for the party's access to a remedy in cross-border cases. In this context, the local procedural rules and efficiency of the national judicial system may be considered by potential litigants along with the ability of the judges to deal with cross-border cases as well as the enforceability of the rendered judgment. Second, the applicable law should determine a party's entitlement to an effective remedy and ascertain the other party's liability. One of our aims is to consider how the EU PIL framework is functioning in different EU Member States, in order to identify the various problems which may impair litigants' access to remedies in different Member States.

In making the analysis of the EU PIL rules, it would be particularly important to consider the factors which could impact on the triangular relationship between the relevant set of jurisdiction rules, the choice-of-law rules and the parties access to desired legal remedies (presupposing the recognition and enforcement of foreign judgments) in cross-border cases. In theory, the 'barriers to conflict resolution'[35] have been considered in three broad categories: tactical and strategic; psychological; and organisational and institutional.[36] Could the insufficient experience of some EU Member States' judges (and litigators) in applying the EU PIL rules adversely affect parties' access to remedies in cross-border cases? How would the various deficiencies in the way some of the national judicial systems are functioning impact on litigants' strategies and settlement dynamics in the different EU Member States? How could the various delaying strategies, exploiting the weaknesses of the EU PIL framework, impact on the parties' access to remedies in cross-border cases?

II. Other Relevant Studies and Project Research Aims

A number of recently completed projects touched upon aspects which are relevant to the application of the EU PIL instruments as well as on the factors affecting the parties' decision where to sue in cross-border cases. In this sub-section, some of the recent projects will be briefly considered, in order to reinforce the unique nature of the EUPILLAR project.

A research project, led by Kacevska, aimed to identify issues with the application and implementation of the EU law rules in the area of civil justice. The study was undertaken in five Member States—Germany, Hungary, Latvia, Sweden and UK.[37] It was concluded that:

> … difficulties with the application of the EU law at the national level are closely related and sometimes directly caused by the *problems at the EU level*. The most noticeable shortcomings of the

---

[33] Directorate General Human Rights and Rule of Law Council of Europe, *Guide to Good Practice in respect of Domestic Remedies*, available at www.echr.coe.int/Documents/Pub_coe_domestics_remedies_ENG.pdf, adopted by the Committee of Ministers on 18 September 2013, 11–13.

[34] See more in Ch 32 below.

[35] K Arrow et al (eds), *Barriers to Conflict Resolution* (London, WW Norton & Company, 1995).

[36] RH Mnookin and L Ross, 'Introduction' in Arrow et al (eds), ibid, 1, 6–24.

[37] I Kacevska et al, *Recommendations and Guidelines—Effective adoption, transposition, implementation and application of European Union legislation in the area of civil justice* (Riga, 2015) available at www.kacevska.lv/upload/Vadlinijas_anglu.pdf.

EU law itself are identified by Recommendations and Guidelines and include overall fragmentation of the EU law in the area of civil justice and uneven drafting of the EU acts. The roots of those
shortcomings to a large extent lay within [the] overly politicized, slow and not sufficiently transparent adoption process of the EU instruments. Additionally, the Commission as the main controlling
body over correct application of the EU law in Member States could have been more active in the
area of civil justice.[38]

Although the scope of Kacevska's project was much broader, it inter alia concluded that
'the Brussels I*bis* Regulation is a very powerful instrument in the hands of practitioners.'[39]
That said, their analysis stopped a long way short of considering how the current EU PIL
framework would shape the litigants' strategies and affect the parties' access to remedies in
cross-border cases.

The factors, affecting the litigants' choice of London as a litigation venue in cross-border
cases, were identified in a recent study commissioned by the UK Ministry of Justice and
undertaken by the British Institute of International and Comparative Law ('BIICL').[40] The
BIICL report has noted that:

It is difficult to make precise statements about the value of commercial claims brought to the
English courts and the extent to which they involve foreign parties, as data is not routinely collected.
However, the Rolls Building courts were able to provide some indicative data.[…] The most comprehensive available data on foreign litigants comes from the Admiralty and Commercial Courts.
This suggested that since 2010, around 80% of all Commercial Court cases each year have involved
at least one foreign party … In almost 50% of all cases, all parties are foreign … No reliable similar
data exists for the Chancery or Technology and Construction Court (TCC).[41]

The BIICL report's indicative data demonstrates that 'London is a centre for high value
commercial litigation and that foreign parties are frequent litigants.'[42] On this basis, the
BIICL study has identified the experience of the English judges as being one of the most
important factors which influences parties' decisions where to sue in cross-border cases.
Choice-of-court agreements in combination with choice of law clauses were outlined as the
second most important factor. This research finding of the BIICL report is in line with the
survey data published by the Oxford Institute of European and Comparative Law and
the Oxford Centre for Socio-Legal-Studies.[43] That said, it is open for discussion whether
choice-of-court and choice-of-law agreements would have been included if it were not for
the other factors. After all, English judges are best placed to apply English law.

---

[38] ibid, 85—the emphasis in the original. The suggestion that the Commission could more actively ensure that
EU civil justice is correctly applied is worth following up with further research on whether more use should be
made by the Commission of its power to initiate legal proceedings in the CJEU against Member States that have
failed to correctly apply EU civil justice law (see Arts 258 and 260 TFEU). This has not been a specific part of the
research for this book but we believe the Commission should fund research on this matter to enable it to do due
diligence in assessing its effectiveness as the guardian of the Treaties in the civil justice area.

[39] Kacevska, above n 37 [118].

[40] E Lein et al, 'Factors Influencing International Litigants' Decisions to Bring Commercial Claims to the
London Based Courts ('BIICL Report')', available at www.gov.uk/government/uploads/system/uploads/attach-
ment_data/file/396343/factors-influencing-international-litigants-with-commercial-claims.pdf.

[41] ibid, 10.

[42] ibid.

[43] 'Civil Justice Systems in Europe: Implications for Choice of Forum and Choice of Contract Law—A Business Survey—Final Results' (Oxford, 2008), available at www.fondation-droitcontinental.org/fr/wp-content/
uploads/2013/12/oxford_civil_justice_survey_-_summary_of_results_final.pdf.

The other important factors, which were outlined in the BIICL report as influencing the litigants' decision to sue in England, included: 'efficient remedies; ... procedural effectiveness; ... neutrality of the forum; ... market practice; ... English language; ... effective UK-based counsel; ... speed; and ... enforceability of judgments in foreign jurisdictions.'[44] It was noted that there is 'increasing competition in the international dispute resolution market with other jurisdictions marketing themselves to attract disputes traditionally adjudicated in London.'[45] However, the BIICL project failed to consider how the EU model of administration of justice in cross-border cases affected the parties' effective access to justice in cross-border cases. It would be particularly important to consider how the parties' strategies, devised under the current EU PIL, impact on the litigants' access to remedies in cross-border cases. Given the high number of settlements in England and Wales,[46] this may be another important factor in the forum selection process. This poses the questions what are the aspects which might impact on the settlement dynamics in disputes with an international element.

If parties' effective access to a remedy in cross-border cases could be impaired by the way the EU PIL framework is functioning across the EU, then the whole EU justice framework would be ineffective. An ineffective EU civil justice system has an impact on litigants' strategies and the relevant settlement dynamics, making it harder for parties (or for certain parties which have no access to finance) to obtain effective remedies in cross-border cases. The role of the national judicial system is particularly important for devising an EU PIL framework which promotes a more effectively functioning EU civil justice system. That said, in theory, Dammann and Hansmann[47] have submitted that:

> Effective courts are central to sustained economic development. Badly performing courts burden not only litigants, but also nations as a whole ... An obvious implication is that countries with underperforming courts should reform them. Yet experience has shown reform to be both difficult and slow, ... especially where the independence and integrity of the judiciary are in question.
>
> There is, however, another approach to dealing with a dysfunctional court system-one that can go hand in hand with domestic judicial reform. The law can enable litigants from countries with ineffective judicial systems to have their cases adjudicated in the courts of other nations that have better-functioning judicial systems.[48]

In other words, devising an appropriately functioning EU PIL framework, which factors in the deficiencies of some of the EU Member States' judicial systems, may be another way to improve the effectiveness of the EU PIL framework. The choice of a policy option in this context very much depends on the type of problems impacting on the effectiveness of the EU PIL framework. In this context, the EUPILLAR project aims to provide answers to the following research questions: (1) Do national courts deal appropriately with harmonised PIL instruments? (2) Does the CJEU deal appropriately with PIL issues? (3) Is the institutional architecture in the EU suited to providing an 'effective remedy' for cross-border litigants whose rights have been violated?[49] (4) Is there a need for reform? If so, what should

---

[44] E Lein et al, above n 40, 15.
[45] ibid, 2 and 11.
[46] See more in Ch 40 below.
[47] J Dammann and H Hansmann, 'Globalizing Commercial Litigation' [2008–2009] *Cornell Law Review* 1.
[48] ibid, 3.
[49] Compare Art 47(1) of the Charter for Fundamental Rights.

be the direction of any potential reform? In other words, our research findings should help to indicate how the EU civil justice framework should evolve, so that 'a Europe of law and justice'[50] can be created.

III. Assessing the Effectiveness of EU PIL: Legislative Objectives and Issues in a Cross-border Context[51]

The need to assess the effectiveness of the EU PIL framework was identified in the Stockholm Programme which stated that '[t]here has to be an evaluation of the effectiveness of the legal instruments adopted at Union level. Evaluation is also necessary to determine any obstacles to the proper functioning of the European judicial area'.[52] However, it is less clear what a study of the effectiveness of EU PIL should consider. An analysis of the relevant case law indicated that the PIL issues are often argued by the parties in cross-border disputes.[53] This reiterates the importance of a review of the PIL case law under the current institutional architecture for the interpretation and application of PIL legislative instruments to be undertaken in different jurisdictions. The effectiveness of the current EU PIL framework is central to the litigants' effective access to remedies under the EU Civil Justice regime.

As a part of the analysis of the EU PIL framework, as noted elsewhere,[54] it is best to use the criterion of effectiveness which 'refers to the relationship between the anticipated effects of a policy and those that actually emerge in social reality.'[55] It should be noted that the adopted approach takes account of the recent public international law literature which has 'introduce[d] a sophisticated and complex theoretical model for assessing international court effectiveness ...'[56] The various approaches to the evaluation of effectiveness of international courts in public international law have been summarised in the *Oxford Handbook of International Adjudication* by Helfer as follows:

> ... the principal function of [international courts ('ICs')] was to provide a judicial forum to assist nation states in settling their disputes ...

> Recent scholarship on IC effectiveness analyses these functions from a range of vantage points. Some studies focus on developing typologies to categorize the multiple roles that ICs perform. Others assess empirically whether a particular IC, or the international judicial system in general, is successful in achieving one or more identified objectives. Yet another group of studies makes normative claims about which goals international judges ought to prioritize, regardless of the tasks that they in fact perform.[57]

---

[50] European Council, The Stockholm Programme—An open and secure Europe serving and protecting the citizens, [2010] OJ C115/1.

[51] See more in Danov and Beaumont, above n 4.

[52] The Stockholm Programme, above n 50, p 6.

[53] Beaumont and Danov, above n 9.

[54] Danov and Beaumont, above n 4.

[55] See also F Varone, B Rihoux and A Marx, 'A New Method for Policy Evaluation? Longstanding Challenges and the Possibilities of Qualitative Comparative Analysis (QCA)' in B Rihoux and H Grimm (eds), *Innovative Comparative Methods for Policy Analysis* (New York, Springer, 2006) 213, 215.

[56] Y Shany, *Assessing the Effectiveness of International Courts* (Oxford, Oxford University Press, 2014) 6.

[57] LR Helfer, 'The Effectiveness of International Adjudication' in CPR Romano, KJ Alter and Y Shany (eds), *The Oxford Handbook of International Adjudication* (Oxford, Oxford University Press, 2014) 464, 465.

Before considering whether the objectives—which are set in the recitals to the harmonised PIL instruments—are effectively pursued in the EU, the EUPILLAR study had to first identify the objectives of EU PIL. To this end, there was a need to devise a theoretical model which aimed to investigate the relationship between the allocation of jurisdiction and identification of applicable law, on the one hand, and the available remedy and its accessibility, on the other hand.[58] It is well established that the EU PIL Regulations have an important role to play in providing effective access to available remedies for litigants in such cases.[59]

For the purposes of assessing the effectiveness of the current private international law framework, it was important to consider how effectively the parties' *entitlement to remedy* could be determined by the governing law(s). The application of Rome I and Rome II would need to be relied upon by the courts when determining litigants' *entitlement to remedies* in cross-border cases. Although one of the important objectives of the Rome I and II Regulations is to have the same law applied irrespective of where the parties litigate,[60] the cost of applying the foreign laws, due to the relevant rules of evidence, will be different. For example, in Germany, the content of the foreign laws would have to be determined *ex officio* by the German judge.[61] In England, there is a presumption that the foreign law is the same as English law. The presumption may be rebutted, if a party proves that the content of the foreign law is different.[62] This may increase the litigation costs in such jurisdictions.

Although the cost of proving the foreign law should not be overstated with regard to high value claims which would normally involve sophisticated parties, the cross-border litigation costs which are inflated by the evidential rules regarding proof of foreign laws and/or ability of the judges to apply the foreign law might affect the parties' access to effective remedies in certain types of cross-border disputes. However, an even bigger issue is the ability of national judges to apply foreign law.[63] This appears to be an issue not only in some of the new Member States, but also in some of the courts in Germany,[64] which happens to be one of the leading jurisdictions in the EU. Although one solution to this problem could be further training for national judges and legal practitioners, another approach might be for the EU to start considering setting up specialised national courts where the cross-border cases are to be dealt with.

A case for more far reaching reform would be strengthened if the access of parties to a remedy is impaired by the tactics of those seeking to deny a party a remedy based on the weaknesses/deficiencies of the current EU PIL regime and the relevant institutional framework. The access to a remedy in cross-border cases may often depend on establishing jurisdiction before a court where an effective remedy may be obtained through litigation and/or alternative dispute resolution (ADR) settlement within a reasonable time.[65] In this context, the specific characteristics of the EU Member States' national systems for administration of justice may also have an impact on the cross-border litigation pattern across the EU. Any evaluation of the effectiveness of the PIL framework, which is the foundation of the

---

[58] Danov and Beaumont, above n 4.

[59] Art 47(1) and (2) of the Charter of Fundamental Human Rights. See also Recital 38 to Brussels Ia; Art 81(2)(e) TFEU; Art 67(4) TFEU: and Recital 1 to Brussels Ia.

[60] Recital 6 to Rome I and Rome II.

[61] See Ch 7 below.

[62] See more in Ch 35 below.

[63] Danov and Beaumont, above n 4.

[64] See Ch 7 below.

[65] See Chs 32, 35 and 40 below.

EU civil justice system, should factor in the 'institutional arrangements and traditions that we have'[66] in the EU.[67] Access to remedies may be impaired, for example, because the cross-border litigation is 'time-consuming and costly'[68] or because the EU civil justice framework fails to 'avoid abusive litigation tactics'[69] which may exploit the slowness of some EU Member States' judicial systems, inflating litigation costs. The litigants' access to remedies may be also hindered, for example, by lack of experience of national judges and local lawyers. Given the diverse nature of the EU (which has now expanded to integrate not only a number of Member States representing the two major legal traditions—the common law and the civil law,[70] but also some of the former communist countries),[71] there may be various types of difficulties in the implementation of the EU PIL regime across Europe. The diverse nature of the Union indicates that the creation of 'a Europe of law and justice'[72] presupposes for the EU policy-makers to address entirely different problems which appear to affect the cross-border litigation pattern in the different Member States.

EU PIL is designed to 'enhance access to justice'[73] and remedies in cross-border cases by pursuing the following objectives: (1) to set up jurisdictional rules which are unified[74] and highly predictable;[75] (2) to create effective mechanisms dealing with parallel proceedings;[76] (3) to ensure that the same law is applied regardless of which court in the EU hears the case (while recognising that this objective will only be followed by some Member States in relation to family law matters)[77] and (4) to ensure that judgments given in a Member State are swiftly recognised and enforced across Europe.[78] The foregoing objectives mean that an evaluation research project[79] in relation to EU PIL has to consider how effectively these aims are being pursued across a significantly enlarged and diverse European Union.

Hence EUPILLAR was a collaborative research study involving almost all the EU Member States.[80]

IV. Research Methodology[81]

The research methodology was designed to provide us with data which reflect how the current private international law regime is shaping the private litigants' strategies in

---

[66] AT von Mehren, 'Conflict of Laws in a Federal System: Some Perspectives' (1969) 18 *International and Comparative Law Quarterly* 681, 684.

[67] Danov and Beaumont, above n 4.

[68] Recital 26 to Brussels Ia.

[69] Recital 22 to Brussels Ia.

[70] P Legrand, 'Against a European Civil Code' [1997] *Modern Law Review* 44.

[71] Danov and Beaumont, above n 4.

[72] The Stockholm Programme, above n 50.

[73] Recital 1 to Brussels Ia.

[74] Recital 4 to Brussels Ia and Recital 12 to Brussels IIa.

[75] Recital 15 to Brussels Ia.

[76] Recital 21 to Brussels Ia.

[77] Recital 6 to Rome II, Recital 6 to Rome I, Recital 3 to the EC Council Decision Concluding the Hague Maintenance Protocol and Recital 9 to Rome III.

[78] Recital 4 to Brussels Ia. See Art 19 of Brussels IIa.

[79] See Varone, Rihoux and Marx, above n 55.

[80] The project was funded by the European Commission, led by the University of Aberdeen with the main partners being the Universities of Antwerp, Freiburg, Leeds, Milan, Complutense Madrid, and Wroclaw.

[81] See more in Danov and Beaumont, above n 4.

the EU. Also, bearing in mind the EU policy makers' objectives, the data have to enable the EUPILLAR study on effectiveness to weigh up how the parties' strategies affect litigants' access to remedies and settlement negotiations in cross-border cases. A mix of research methods was used in the EU Member States—Belgium, England and Wales, Germany, Italy, Poland, Scotland and Spain—chosen for in-depth analysis. These places reflect the diversity of legal traditions within the EU (civil law, common law, mixed legal systems, post-communist, federal, quasi-federal, non-unified and unitary), have a large number of persons engaging in cross-border transactions and have a large number of immigrants and/or emigrants taking advantage of free movement of persons.

To this end, the research teams compiled 'datasets'[82] for the identified PIL cases for the period since 1 March 2002 (entry into force of the Brussels I Regulation). The Member States' datasets include the following information: the harmonised PIL instrument; the Member State court; the year when the proceedings were initiated; the remedy sought (declaratory, injunctive, monetary); the value of the claim; the domicile (or habitual residence) of the claimants to help to measure the mobility of the claimants (eg corporations; small and medium-sized enterprises (SMEs); consumers; family members); the PIL issue raised and addressed (eg the relevant jurisdictional rule(s), the national law(s) applied); important factors influencing the judgment (eg choice of court/law agreements, etc); and the date of the judgment. Since the CJEU has an important role to play when it comes to the interpretation of the harmonised EU PIL instruments, a separate dataset for the preliminary references before the CJEU was compiled by the University of Aberdeen.

That said, bearing in mind the objectives of the study, it was considered that any quantitative data is bound to be insufficient to determine whether the EU policy makers' objectives are effectively pursued. First, it would be unlikely for all the judgments in cross-border cases to be reported or be accessible to researchers through electronic databases. Second, any search engine would not detect the cases in which the court, for whatever reason, did not refer to the relevant PIL mechanisms.[83] Third, any judgments on preliminary PIL issues (especially the ones where a reference to the CJEU was made) are likely to be rendered in cases where the jurisdictional and/or choice-of-law aspects have been heavily contested by the parties. Making a case for reform on this basis would be like 'generalizing about war from the details of the most bloody and hard fought battles.'[84] Fourth, any analysis based only on datasets including information about the PIL judgments would hardly factor in the way PIL shapes the litigants' strategies in cases which do not end in judgments, which appear to be quite common in some of the leading jurisdictions.[85]

Therefore, it was considered important to do qualitative research interviews involving legal practitioners. As a part of this process, the EUPILLAR research teams discussed with legal practitioners key questions concerning cross-border litigation. Legal practitioners

---

[82] For those purposes, a dataset is defined as 'a collection of data that someone has organised in a form that is susceptible to empirical analysis.' See L Epstein and AD Martin, *An Introduction to Empirical Legal Research* (Oxford, Oxford University Press, 2014) 66. The EUPILLAR database is available on the University of Aberdeen Centre for Private International Law website at www.abdn.ac.uk/law/research/eupillar-database-559.php.

[83] eg *Emerald Supplies Ltd & Others v British Airways v Air Canada & Others* [2014] EWHC 3513 (Ch).

[84] H Genn, 'Preliminary Analysis of Costs Data', *Review of Civil Litigation Costs*, Seminar 26 June 2009, available at www.ucl.ac.uk/laws/judicial-institute/events/Jackson_Costs_Review_Preliminary_Analysis_of_Costs_Data_.pdf.

[85] eg England and Wales. See H Genn, *Judging Civil Justice* (Cambridge, Cambridge University Press, 2010) 21.

were well placed to provide us with information about the litigation strategies, use of ADR and settlement dynamics.[86]

Central to the process of conducting qualitative interviews with legal practitioners was drawing up a sampling framework[87] to select interview participants which took account of the national characteristics. Although an indicative list of interview questions was created setting out a structure to the interviews, the interviewer and/or interviewee was always free to depart from the structure if the participants' viewpoints and experience were thereby better expressed. The interview questions focused on key areas: 1) General questions about cross-border disputes; 2) Interpretation of the EU Regulations; 3) Jurisdictional issues; 4) Applicable law issues; 5) Procedural issues; 6) Settlement; and 7) Alternative Dispute Resolution.

Where large data sets are produced, the way the data are organised is central to an effective and comparative data analysis.[88] In view of this, data were organised around the following themes: 1) Parties (eg legal entities, individuals) and their relationship (eg contractual, non-contractual, matrimonial); 2) Remedies and their value; 3) Legal landscape (eg first-seised-rule, different procedures, different length of proceedings, preliminary rulings); 4) Litigants' strategies (eg where to sue, jurisdictional challenges, negative declarations, parallel proceedings, legal uncertainty, costs, legal aid, litigation funders); and 5) Settlement dynamics—factors affecting the settlement negotiations and the use of ADR mechanisms (eg cost shifting, level of uncertainty).

The aim of the data analysis was to try to identify how the litigants' tactics in cross-border cases are affected by the EU PIL regime, taking into account the remedy which the parties seek to obtain. It was particularly important to consider how the litigants' strategies, devised under the current EU PIL, impact on any settlement dynamics which ultimately affect the parties' access to remedies in disputes with an international element. The analysis of the collected data further aimed to indicate whether different strategies might be employed by the parties depending on the remedy they seek to obtain (and the remedy's value) in different types of PIL cases. The qualitative data should further indicate whether/how the weaknesses of the current EU PIL framework are exploited by the strategic litigants in the various PIL cases. Therefore, the EUPILLAR project aimed to evaluate the effectiveness of the EU PIL framework by considering the way it shapes the litigants' strategies in different types of cross-border cases.

In addition to the in-depth analysis of the EUPILLAR Regulations in the sampled Member States,[89] national reports were obtained on the application of those Regulations in almost all the other Member States.[90]

---

[86] Compare SC Salop and LJ White, 'Private Antitrust Litigation: An Introduction and Framework' in LJ White (ed), *Private Antitrust Litigation: New Evidence, New Learning* (Cambridge MA, MIT Press, 1988) 3, 16.

[87] A Wilmot, 'Designing sampling strategies for qualitative social research: with particular reference to the Office for National Statistics' qualitative respondent register' (2005), Paper on qualitative sampling strategies presented to QUEST 2005, Office of National Statistics, available at www.ons.gov.uk/ons/guide-method/method-quality/general-methodology/data-collection-methodology/reports-and-publications/index.html?format=print.

[88] P Bazeley, 'Analysing Qualitative Data: More Than "Identifying Themes"' [2009] *Malaysian Journal of Qualitative Research* 6.

[89] M Adams and J Bomhoff, 'Comparing Law; Practice and Theory' in M Adams and J Bomhoff (eds), *Practice and Theory in Comparative Law* (Cambridge, Cambridge University Press, 2012) 1, 6–9.

[90] These reports are published in Part II of this book and come from all the Member States except Denmark (which only applies Brussels Ia and Maintenance and even then only by international agreements with the rest of the EU) and Estonia.

A central aspect in the analysis of the collected data was the question whether the institutional architecture in the EU is suited to provide effective remedies for cross-border litigants in cross-border cases, identifying the problems (if any) with the way it is functioning across the EU. The principles of legal certainty (and predictability of the outcome) needed to be considered, along with the relevant legislative and institutional framework in civil and commercial matters as well as in family law matters. In this context, it is important to consider how the current PIL framework affects the strategies of the litigants who seek remedies in cases with an international element, addressing such questions as: How would the litigants' strategies impact costs and settlement dynamics? How would delay (and the excessive delay) impact settlements/remedies? The specific issues in contractual, non-contractual, intellectual property (IP), competition law disputes with an international element should be discussed when assessing the effectiveness of the current PIL framework whilst considering whether ADR might be an appropriate solution at least in some cross-border civil and commercial law cases. Moreover, given the specific litigation pattern in the family law disputes, it will be important to consider the operation of the Brussels IIa Regulation in cross-border divorce disputes as well as in parental responsibility proceedings and child abduction cases with an international element. In the light of the research findings, one should consider whether ADR might be an appropriate tool for resolving cross-border family law disputes.

In other words, an analysis of the empirical data should indicate what the major weaknesses under the current institutional framework are. In this context, the following questions are to be addressed: Are there effective remedies for those who need them in cross-border cases? If there are any issues, should they be addressed at Member State level? Or should there rather be a comprehensive reform at EU level? Should there be any 'codification of the existing instruments … in the area of conflict of laws'?[91] Should there be any reform of the Union's judicial and legislative system?

V. Value Added by the Project

The project has tried to develop a novel theoretical and methodological framework[92] for research in PIL with a view to assessing the effectiveness of the EU PIL framework. Applying a consistent research design allowed the EUPILLAR research teams in the sampled jurisdictions to create relevant datasets and research resources. Indeed, the EUPILLAR database[93] of the cases before national courts in the sampled Member States and all the preliminary references on the EUPILLAR instruments before the CJEU should appeal to legal practitioners and researchers across the EU and beyond.

This book gives an independent and critical analysis of how the EU PIL instruments have been interpreted by the CJEU and by the national courts in the Member States of the EU. It is hoped that these critiques will help the CJEU and national courts to perform even better

---

[91] The EU Justice Agenda for 2020—Strengthening Trust, Mobility and Growth within the Union, COM(2014) 144 final [4.2].

[92] Danov and Beaumont, above n 4.

[93] The EUPILLAR Database, above n 82.

in their interpretations and applications of EU PIL in the future. The book provides information on how cross-border private litigation functions at the moment, but as will become clear this can only be a partial understanding due to the inevitably incomplete nature of the data obtained from the analysis of available judgments and from the qualitative interviews in the sampled Member States. Obviously, the picture is much more incomplete from the other national reports where qualitative interviews were not possible and much less time and resource was available for in-depth research and analysis of the national case law on the EU PIL instruments.

Nevertheless there is enough useful data from the study to offer some proposals as to how the EU institutional framework could be developed in the future to better handle PIL. In particular, the case law data along with qualitative interviews conducted in Belgium, Germany, Great Britain, Italy, Poland and Spain did help the researchers to identify how the EU PIL shapes the litigants' strategies. On this basis, the research team carefully considered the way the parties' strategies which are devised under the current EU PIL framework affected the private parties' access to desired legal remedies in cross-border cases. This allowed the researchers to consider how the litigants' tactical manoeuvring impacts the settlement dynamics and parties' effective access to remedies. Therefore, a major contribution of this project is the theoretical framework which allowed the researchers to consider the context in which the EU PIL rules are being applied by judges who aim to dispense justice, providing effective remedies for litigants in cross-border cases.

The EUPILLAR project may demonstrate that the current EU model of administration of justice in cross-border cases shapes the litigants' strategies which, as the data suggest,[94] vary depending on the strength of the claimant's claim as well as on the desired legal remedy and its value. A level of legal certainty and predictability of the outcome of private disputes is a means to reduce litigation costs and facilitate litigants' effective access to justice.[95] In other words, the EU PIL instruments, being the foundation of the EU civil justice regime,[96] should be providing litigants with effective access to remedies enabling the EU Member States' judges to 'do justice in individual cases.'[97] Since the current EU PIL regime aims to set the scene for national judges to provide effective remedies for parties in cross-border cases in the EU, the researchers carefully considered how its weaknesses along with the deficiencies of the national judicial systems could be exploited by the parties to gain a tactical or negotiating advantage, impairing their opponents' effective access to remedies in cross-border cases. Furthermore, an analysis of the relationship between cross-border litigation and ADR/settlements has allowed the researchers to consider the way in which cross-border litigation proceedings—based on the EU PIL framework—impact on out-of-court dispute resolution, promoting and shaping the ADR/settlement negotiations. On this basis, the researchers make a case for an institutional reform which is needed to improve parties' effective access to remedies in cross-border cases.

---

[94] See more in Pt II of the book.
[95] Recital 1 to Brussels Ia.
[96] Danov and Beaumont, above n 4 and Beaumont and Danov, above n 9.
[97] Recital 14 to the Rome II Reg.

VI. Structure of the Book

The project research findings are presented in this book which aims to highlight the specific problems with regard to the application of Brussels I, Brussels IIa, the Maintenance Regulation, Rome I and Rome II (the EUPILLAR Regulations) in the EU. The book consists of five parts. The first part sets the scene by considering how the EU shapes the development of the private international law (PIL) framework. In this context, the European Union competence to legislate in the area of PIL is presented, with particular attention being paid to the practical working of law reform at EU level. Further, the judicial activities of the CJEU in PIL are outlined, discussing inter alia the effectiveness of law-making by the EU institutions in terms of the clarity of the legislation and of prescribing the intended interpretation (eg recitals compared to explanatory reports). Another chapter from Part I examines implementation and procedural issues in relation to the EUPILLAR Regulations. In Part II, the national reports which consider the way the PIL framework is functioning in different EU Member States are presented with a view to identifying the issues which require to be carefully considered in the subsequent Parts of the book. In Part III and Part IV, the relevant empirical data are analysed with regard to cross-border civil and commercial disputes and cross-border family law disputes along with a very thorough analysis of all the case law by the CJEU on the EUPILLAR instruments. In Part V, some conclusions are drawn with a view to specifying the way forward.

Part I

Shaping the Development of the Private International Law Framework

2

EU Competence to Legislate in the Area of Private International Law and Law Reforms at the EU Level

JAN VON HEIN

I. EU Competence to Legislate in the Area of Private International Law

A. Introduction

Genuinely European sources of private international law (PIL) were of minor importance during the twentieth century because the European Community (EC) did not have a specific competence to legislate in the field of conflict of laws before 1999. Nevertheless, the Member States of the EC had concluded two important treaties among themselves, namely the Brussels Convention of 1968 on jurisdiction and the recognition and enforcement of judgments in civil and commercial matters[1] and the Rome Convention of 1980 on the law applicable to contractual obligations.[2] In addition, some directives on consumer protection based on ex-Article 95 Treaty establishing the European Community (TEC) (now Article 114 Treaty on the Functioning of the European Union (TFEU)) contained special conflicts provisions that served the purpose of shielding consumers from choice-of-law clauses designating a third State's law (see below section II.D). In 1999, however, the Treaty of Amsterdam[3] conferred a genuine competence on the EC legislature to pass legal

---

[1] Brussels Convention of 27 September 1968 on Jurisdiction and the Enforcement of Judgments in Civil and Commercial Matters, [1972] OJ L299/32.

[2] Convention on the Law Applicable to Contractual Obligations of 19 June 1980, (Consolidated Version), [1998] OJ C27/34.

[3] Treaty of Amsterdam amending the Treaty on European Union, the Treaties establishing the European Communities and certain related acts, [1997] OJ C340/1.

instruments on PIL (ex-Article 65 TEC). In its current version—as amended by the Treaty of Lisbon[4]—the provision, which is now numbered as Article 81 TFEU, reads as follows:

JUDICIAL COOPERATION IN CIVIL MATTERS

Article 81

1. The Union shall develop judicial cooperation in civil matters having cross-border implications, based on the principle of mutual recognition of judgments and of decisions in extrajudicial cases. Such cooperation may include the adoption of measures for the approximation of the laws and regulations of the Member States.

2. For the purposes of paragraph 1, the European Parliament and the Council, acting in accordance with the ordinary legislative procedure, shall adopt measures, particularly when necessary for the proper functioning of the internal market, aimed at ensuring:

(a)   the mutual recognition and enforcement between Member States of judgments and of decisions in extrajudicial cases;
(b)   the cross-border service of judicial and extrajudicial documents;
(c)   the compatibility of the rules applicable in the Member States concerning conflict of laws and of jurisdiction;
(d)   cooperation in the taking of evidence;
(e)   effective access to justice;
(f)   the elimination of obstacles to the proper functioning of civil proceedings, if necessary by promoting the compatibility of the rules on civil procedure applicable in the Member States;
(g)   the development of alternative methods of dispute settlement;
(h)   support for the training of the judiciary and judicial staff.

3. Notwithstanding paragraph 2, measures concerning family law with cross-border implications shall be established by the Council, acting in accordance with a special legislative procedure. The Council shall act unanimously after consulting the European Parliament.

The Council, on a proposal from the Commission, may adopt a decision determining those aspects of family law with cross-border implications which may be the subject of acts adopted by the ordinary legislative procedure. The Council shall act unanimously after consulting the European Parliament.

The proposal referred to in the second subparagraph shall be notified to the national Parliaments. If a national Parliament makes known its opposition within six months of the date of such notification, the decision shall not be adopted. In the absence of opposition, the Council may adopt the decision.

Since the EU was endowed with a competence in the field of conflict of laws, a sizeable number of legal instruments have been passed, although not all of them are applicable in all Member States of the Union (see below section III). Denmark does not participate in the judicial cooperation in civil matters and does not have the right to opt into such measures (see below section III). The UK and Ireland do not participate automatically in measures of judicial cooperation, but they enjoy the right to opt into such legal acts if they so wish (see below section III).With regard to choice of law in the narrow sense, the following Regulations must be mentioned: first, in 2007, the Rome II Regulation on the law applicable to

---

[4] Treaty of Lisbon amending the Treaty on European Union and the Treaty establishing the European Community, [2007] OJ C306/1.

non-contractual obligations was enacted,[5] which was followed in 2008 by the Rome I Regulation on the law applicable to contractual obligations that transformed the former Rome Convention into a genuinely EC legal instrument.[6] In 2010, the so-called Rome III Regulation determining the law applicable to divorce and legal separation[7] was passed as an act of enhanced cooperation (see below section II.C).

Whereas the Rome I, II and III Regulations are all exclusively devoted to choice of law, there are other Regulations that are exclusively focused on international civil procedure. The most well-known and arguably most important Regulations of the second type are the Brussels Regulation, which transformed the Brussels Convention of 1968 into a genuinely unionised legal instrument and which was recast as the Brussels I*bis* Regulation in 2012,[8] as well as the Brussels II*bis* Regulation.[9] The Brussels I*bis* Regulation focuses on jurisdiction, recognition and enforcement of foreign judgments in civil and commercial matters, the Brussels II*bis* Regulation deals with jurisdiction, recognition and enforcement in matrimonial matters and matters of parental responsibility. Both instruments are supplemented by various Regulations dealing with specific types of decisions or establishing special procedures. These include the Regulation on the European Order for Uncontested Claims,[10] the Regulation on the European Order for Payment,[11] the Small Claims Regulation,[12] the Regulation on the European Account Preservation Order[13] and the Regulation on Mutual Recognition of Protection Measures in Civil Matters.[14] In addition, matters of international judicial assistance (international service of documents, cross-border taking of evidence) are governed by two specific regulations, namely the Service of Process and the Taking of Evidence Regulation.[15]

---

[5] Reg (EC) No 864/2007 of the European Parliament and of the Council of 11 July 2007 on the law applicable to non-contractual obligations (Rome II), [2007] OJ L199/40.

[6] Reg (EC) No 593/2008 of the European Parliament and of the Council of 17 June 2008 on the law applicable to contractual obligations (Rome I), [2008] OJ L177/6.

[7] Council Reg (EU) No 1259/2010 of 20 December 2010 implementing enhanced cooperation in the area of the law applicable to divorce and legal separation, [2010] OJ L343/10.

[8] Reg (EU) No 1215/2012 of the European Parliament and of the Council of 12 December 2012 on jurisdiction and the recognition and enforcement of judgments in civil and commercial matters, [2012] OJ L351/1.

[9] Council Reg (EC) No 2201/2003 of 27 November 2003 concerning jurisdiction and the recognition and enforcement of judgments in matrimonial matters and the matters of parental responsibility, repealing Reg (EC) No 1347/2000, [2003] OJ L338/1. See now the Commission Proposal for a recast of Brussels II*bis* (COM(2016) 411) of 30 June 2016.

[10] Reg (EC) No 805/2004 of the European Parliament and of the Council of 21 April 2004 creating a European Enforcement Order for uncontested claims, [2004] OJ L143/15.

[11] Reg (EC) No 1896/2006 of the European Parliament and of the Council of 12 December 2006 creating a European order for payment procedure, [2006] OJ L399/1.

[12] Reg (EC) No 861/2007 of the European Parliament and of the Council of 11 July 2007 establishing a European Small Claims Procedure, [2007] OJ L199/1.

[13] Reg (EU) No 655/2014 of the European Parliament and of the Council of 15 May 2014 establishing a European Account Preservation Order procedure to facilitate cross-border debt recovery in civil and commercial matters, [2014] OJ L189/59.

[14] Reg (EU) No 606/2013 of the European Parliament and of the Council of 12 June 2013 on mutual recognition of protection measures in civil matters, [2013] OJ L181/4.

[15] Reg (EC) No 1393/2007 of the European Parliament and of the Council of 13 November 2007 on the service in the Member States of judicial and extrajudicial documents in civil or commercial matters (service of documents), and repealing Council Reg (EC) No 1348/2000, [2007] OJ L 324/79; Council Reg (EC) No 1206/2001 of 28 May 2001 on cooperation between the courts of the Member States in the taking of evidence in civil or commercial matters, [2001] OJ L174/1.

Finally, several combined Regulations have been passed that contain rules on both choice of law and international civil procedure. Regulations of this third type are the Insolvency Regulation[16] and the Succession Regulation.[17] In addition, two Regulations on matrimonial property[18] and the property consequences of registered partnerships[19] that have recently been passed as acts of enhanced cooperation (see section II.C) combine both choice of law and international civil procedure as well. A mutual interdependence between choice of law and jurisdiction and enforcement can also be observed in the Maintenance Regulation.[20] In contrast to the Insolvency and Succession Regulations, however, the Maintenance Regulation only contains a detailed set of rules as regards international civil procedure. As far as choice of law is concerned, Article 15 of the Maintenance Regulation merely provides a reference to the Hague Protocol on the law applicable to maintenance obligations[21] and, in substance, does not itself contain any specifically EU choice-of-law rules. The Hague Protocol is a convention that was concluded by the EU (except for the UK and Denmark) and has thus become a genuine part of EU law (see below section II.B).

B. Legislation by Way of Regulations

At first, the wording of ex Article 65(b) TEC, which merely spoke of '*promoting* the compatibility of the rules applicable in the Member States concerning the conflict of laws and of jurisdiction', gave rise to doubts whether the EC actually had acquired the competence to unify PIL by way of directly applicable Regulations (cf now Article 288 TFEU) or whether it was rather limited to harmonising national rules by way of Directives, which would then have to be implemented into the domestic legislation on conflict of laws.[22] The latter approach is the preferred mode of legislation in the field of substantive EU private law in order to facilitate the integration of EU rules into the various domestic legal systems. It soon became clear, however, that the Regulation was to become the instrument of choice

---

[16] Council Reg (EC) No 1346/2000 of 29 May 2000 on insolvency proceedings, [2000] OJ L 160/1; now replaced by a recast version, cf [2015] OJ L141/19.

[17] Reg (EU) No 650/2012 of the European Parliament and of the Council of 4 July 2012 on jurisdiction, applicable law, recognition and enforcement of decisions and acceptance and enforcement of authentic instruments in matters of succession and on the creation of a European Certificate of Succession, [2012] OJ L201/107.

[18] Council Reg (EU) 2016/1103 of 24 June 2016 implementing enhanced cooperation in the area of jurisdiction, applicable law and the recognition and enforcement of decisions in matters of matrimonial property regimes, [2016] OJ L183/1.

[19] Council Reg (EU) 2016/1104 of 24 June 2016 implementing enhanced cooperation in the area of jurisdiction, applicable law and the recognition and enforcement of decisions in matters of the property consequences of registered partnerships, [2016] OJ L183/30.

[20] Council Reg (EC) No 4/2009 of 18 December 2008 on jurisdiction, applicable law, recognition and enforcement of decisions and cooperation in matters relating to maintenance obligations, [2009] OJ L7/1.

[21] Hague Protocol of 23 November 2007 on the law applicable to maintenance obligations, [2009] OJ L331/19.

[22] See Y Lequette, 'De Bruxelles à La Haye: réflexions critiques sur la compétence communautaire en matière de droit international privé', in T Azzi (ed), *Liber Amicorum Gaudemet-Tallon* (Paris, Dalloz, 2008) 515; for comprehensive analyses of ex Art 65 TEC, cf also J Basedow, 'The Communitarization of the Conflict of Laws under the Treaty of Amsterdam' (2000) 37 *Common Market Law Review* 687; C Kohler, 'Interrogations sur les sources du droit international privé européen après le traité d'Amsterdam' (1999) 88 *Revue critique droit international privé* 1; H Schack, 'Die EG-Kommission auf dem Holzweg von Amsterdam' (1999) 7 *Zeitschrift für Europäisches Privatrecht* 805.

for EU legislation on PIL because enacting directly applicable choice-of-law rules is clearly the most effective way to guarantee international harmony of decisions among the Member States.[23] The more stringent wording of Article 81(2)(c) TFEU, that the EU legislature shall adopt measures that are not only aimed at 'promoting', but at '*ensuring … the compatibility*' (emphasis added) of choice-of-law rules has confirmed this approach.

C. Legislation in Relations with Third States

Moreover, the competence of the EU to enact choice-of-law rules that are universally applicable, ie regardless of whether they concern only intra-EU conflicts or relations with third States, was controversial at first. Creating universally applicable choice-of-law rules was criticised by some writers as being incompatible with the limitations apparently imposed by the original wording of the competence clause, which referred to the internal market (Articles 61(c), 65(b) and 67 EC).[24] Nevertheless, both the Rome II and Rome I Regulations apply in all 'situations involving a conflict of laws', without limiting their scope to conflicts between the laws of Member States (Article 1(1) of Rome II and Rome I). In addition, Article 3 of Rome II and Article 2 of Rome I lay down the principle of universal application, ie that any law specified by the Regulation shall be applied whether or not it is the law of a Member State. This approach has been followed in all subsequent Regulations as well. The Treaty of Lisbon modified the wording of the provision in this regard; pursuant to Article 81(2) TFEU, the Union 'shall adopt measures, *particularly* when necessary for the proper functioning of the internal market' (emphasis added), thus clarifying that a connection to the internal market is not a strictly indispensable requirement for EU legislation in this field.[25] Apart from that, having two sets of conflicts rules for intra-EU cases on the one hand and cases involving a third-State element would have increased the complexity of the conflict of laws considerably, thus leading to higher costs of litigation.[26] Therefore, creating universally

---

[23] European Commission, Green Paper of 14 January 2003, COM(2002) 654, 19; see also J Basedow, 'The Communitarisation of Private International Law' (2009) 73 *Rabels Zeitschrift* 455, 460; H Dohrn, *Die Kompetenzen der Europäischen Gemeinschaft im Internationalen Privatrecht* (Tubingen, Mohr Siebeck, 2004) 136; B von Hoffmann, 'Relevance of European Community Law' in B von Hoffmann (ed), *European Private International Law* (Nijmegen, Ars Aequi Libri, 1998) 19, 31; HJ Sonnenberger, 'Grenzen der Verweisung durch europäisches internationales Privatrecht' (2011) 31 *Praxis des internationalen Privat- und Verfahrensrecht* 325, 326; R Wagner, 'EU-Kompetenz in der justiziellen Zusammenarbeit in Zivilsachen' (2016) 80 *Rabels Zeitschrift* 521, 538.

[24] Especially in the UK, see, eg, P Beaumont, 'Private International Law of the European Union: Competence Questions Arising From the Proposed Rome II Regulation On Choice of Law in Non-Contractual Obligations' in R Brand (ed), *Private Law, Private International Law & Judicial Cooperation in the EU-US Relationship*, (Qatar, CILE Studies 2, 2005) 15, 22 et seq; A Dickinson, 'European Private International Law: Embracing New Horizons or Mourning the Past?' (2005) 1 *Journal of Private International Law* 197, 222–27; for a more favourable attitude towards universal application, see JM Carruthers and EB Crawford, 'Variations on a Theme of Rome II—Part I' (2005) 9 *Edinburgh Law Review* 65, 70.

[25] See HP Mansel, K Thorn and R Wagner, 'Europäisches Kollisionsrecht 2009: Hoffnungen durch den Vertrag von Lissabon' (2010) 30 *Praxis des internationalen Privat- und Verfahrensrecht* 1, 25; WH Roth, 'Europäische Kollisionsrechtsvereinheitlichung: Überblick—Kompetenzen—Grundfragen' (2011) 22 *Europäisches Wirtschafts- und Steuerrecht* 314, 318.

[26] See T Domej, 'Das Verhältnis nach „außen": Europäische v Drittstaatensachverhalte' in J von Hein and G Rühl (eds), *Kohärenz im Internationalen Privat- und Verfahrensrecht der Europäischen Union* (Tubingen, Mohr Siebeck, 2016) 90 et seq.

applicable choice-of-law rules is also compatible with the principles of subsidiarity and proportionality.[27]

D. Particular Restrictions with Regard to Matters of Family Law

Particular procedural requirements have to be observed pursuant to Article 81(3) TFEU with regard to legislation in the field of international family law.[28] Whereas, under the ordinary legislative procedure (Article 81(2) in conjunction with Article 294 TFEU), the European Parliament has the right of co-decision and the Council may adopt a measure with a qualified majority, Parliament merely has a right to be consulted on legislation dealing with cross-border issues of family law and the Council may only adopt a measure in this area by a unanimous vote (Article 81(3) TFEU). This amounts to strengthening the role of the Member States in the legislative procedure considerably, because family law is frequently regarded as an important part of their 'cultural identity'.[29] The special legislative procedure is, however, not strictly mandatory; under the conditions provided for in Article 81(3) TFEU (the so-called 'passerelle'-clause), the Council may, on a proposal from the Commission, adopt a decision determining those aspects of family law with cross-border implications which may be the subject of acts adopted by the ordinary legislative procedure. The Council shall act unanimously after consulting the European Parliament. This procedure is only available, however, if not a single national Parliament objects.[30]

Against this background, the question whether a proposal for legislation concerns family law becomes decisive from a political point of view. This was particularly controversial with regard to the Succession Regulation.[31] At the end of the day, the opinion prevailed that the law of succession should be classified as falling under civil matters in general rather than under family law. Although the property of the deceased will, from a sociological perspective, in most cases be inherited by his descendants or other relatives, the law of succession is, from a technical point of view, a part of general civil law, because the deceased may well have decided to appoint persons to whom he is not related as heirs.[32]

E. Distinction between Private International Law and Substantive Law

i. Introduction

Drawing the line between competences aimed at harmonising PIL, on the one hand, and substantive law, on the other, can occasionally be a difficult matter. This problem has arisen in three contexts: first, defining the content of public policy at the Union level; second, regulating the borderline area between actually applying foreign law and merely taking its

---

[27] For a contrary view, cf CF Majer, 'Die Geltung der EU-Erbrechtsverordnung für reine Drittstaatensachverhalte' (2011) 18 *Zeitschrift für Erbrecht und Vermögensnachfolge* 445, 448.

[28] For a detailed description, see Wagner, above n 23, 526 et seq.

[29] See M Stürner, 'Die justizielle Zusammenarbeit im Privatrecht der EU' (2015) 37 *Jura* 813, 821.

[30] Wagner, above n 23, 527 (stating that the procedure is so complicated that it has never been used so far).

[31] See C Stumpf, 'EG-Rechtssetzungskompetenzen im Erbrecht' (2007) 42 *Europarecht* 291.

[32] See Recital 2 to the Succession Reg and the Commission Proposal COM(2009) 154 final, 3; see also Roth, above n 25, 320.

content into account while applying the forum's (or another state's) substantive law; third, distinguishing between acts aiming at the harmonisation of PIL and those aimed primarily at unifying substantive law.

ii. Public Policy

The Commission's proposal for a Rome II Regulation of 2003 contained both a general public policy clause with regard to the forum's law (Article 22) as well as a specific provision on Community public policy (Article 23(1)).[33] The Commission went even further by adding a new Article 24 on non-compensatory damages. This provision read as follows: 'The application of a provision of the law designated by this Regulation which has the effect of causing non-compensatory damages, such as exemplary or punitive damages, to be awarded shall be contrary to Community public policy.'[34]

The idea of defining 'public policy' on this sensitive issue, which might be of a prejudicial character with regard to the future Communitarisation of substantive tort law, met with strong opposition from the UK. The European Union Committee of the House of Lords pointed out

> that Article 24 moves away from dealing simply with conflict of laws/choice of law rules, and addresses an aspect of the substantive law applicable in tortious and other actions. Article 24 would effect a harmonisation of part of the substantive law of damages. … [W]e do not believe that the Community has the *vires* to do this under Articles 61 and 65 of the EC Treaty.[35]

At the end of the day, the final Rome II Regulation merely contains a general clause on the public policy 'of the forum' (Article 26 Rome II). Recital 32 clarifies that courts remain free to consider non-compensatory exemplary or punitive damages of an excessive nature as being contrary to their public policy.

Like the Rome II Regulation, the Rome I Regulation (Article 21), the Succession Regulation (Article 35) and the Matrimonial Property Regulation (Article 31) confine themselves to general clauses on public policy. The Rome III Regulation, in contrast, contains not only a general provision (Article 12 Rome III), but also a specific public policy clause in Article 10, which reads:

> Where the law applicable pursuant to Article 5 or 8 makes no provision for divorce or does not grant one of the spouses equal access to divorce or legal separation on grounds of their sex, the law of the forum shall apply.

It is highly controversial whether this provision should be construed as implying an abstract control of a foreign law or whether, in line with the traditional approach to public policy, it is merely designed to prevent discriminatory results.[36] The Higher Regional Court of

---

[33] Original Proposal by the EC Commission of 22 July 2003, COM(2003), 427 final.

[34] Explanatory Memorandum of 2003, COM(2003), 427 final, 29.

[35] House of Lords, European Union Committee, Eighth Report, 2004, para 164.

[36] For more comprehensive accounts of this discussion, see E Lein, 'Art 8 Rome III' in GP Calliess (ed), *Rome Regulations—Commentary* 2nd edn (Alphen aan den Rijn, Kluwer, 2015), paras 23–27; LM Möller, 'No Fear of Talaq: a Reconsideration of Muslim Divorce Laws in Light of the Rome III Regulation' (2014) 10 *Journal of Private International Law* 461, with further references.

Munich recently asked the CJEU for a clarification of this issue,[37] but the Court rejected the request for a preliminary ruling as inadmissible.[38]

iii. Taking Foreign Law into Account

One has to grant the Union a competence, however, to pass legislation in a border area between choice of law in a technical sense and issues related to applying the designated law. An example of this approach can be found in Article 17 of the Rome II Regulation. Following the *local data* theory pioneered by *Ehrenzweig*,[39] Article 17 merely obliges the court to take foreign rules of safety and conduct into account as matters of fact, not to apply them as rules of law.[40] In addition, Article 32 of the Succession Regulation provides for a substantive solution to the classic problem of adaptation that arises from contradictory presumptions related to the time of death.[41] In contrast, the CJEU has recently decided that Article 9(3) Rome I, which relates only to third-State mandatory rules found in the law at the place of performance, merely harmonises conflict-of-law rules concerning contractual obligations and does not preclude Member State courts from taking into account other third-State mandatory rules when they apply their own substantive law.[42] Already with regard to the Rome Convention of 1980, it was generally held that the reservations entered against its Article 7(1) did not bar courts in the states concerned from taking into account foreign mandatory laws.[43]

iv. Uniform Substantive Law

Finally, the delineation between PIL and substantive law can become difficult with regard to acts aimed at unifying primarily substantive law, but which also contain some unilateral choice-of-law rules that define the spatial reach of the uniform substantive provisions. This problem was very controversial after the European Commission had presented its proposal for a uniform European Sales Law,[44] which was withdrawn at the end of 2014. While the Commission tried to argue that its proposal had nothing at all to do with PIL and could thus be based exclusively on Article 114 TFEU, critics argued that creating an optional contractual regime that could only apply by virtue of a parties' choice in cross-border cases must be based on Article 352 TFEU.[45]

---

[37] OLG München (2016) *IPRax* 158.

[38] Case C-281/15 *Sahyouni* ECLI:EU:C:2016:343; a new request has been made by OLG München (2016) *BeckRS* no 12020 CJEU pending case C-372/16 *Sahyouni*.

[39] AE Ehrenzweig, 'Local and Moral Data in the Conflict of Laws: Terra Incognita' (1966) 16 *Buffalo Law Review* 55.

[40] JJ Fawcett, JM Carruthers and P North, *Cheshire, North and Fawcett's, Private International Law* 14th edn (Oxford, Oxford University Press, 2008) 855.

[41] cf P Wautelet, 'Art 32 Succession Regulation' in A Bonomi and P Wautelet (eds), *Le droit européen des successions* 2nd edn (Brussels, Larcier, 2016), para 15 ('une règle matérielle: neutralisation des droits successoraux').

[42] Case C-135/15 *Nikiforidis* ECLI:EU:C:2016:774 para 52.

[43] See K Schurig, '§ 2. Interessen' in G Kegel and K Schurig (eds), *Internationales Privatrecht* 9th edn (Munich, CH Beck, 2004) 155.

[44] COM(2011) 635 final.

[45] For a survey of this controversy, see J von Hein, 'Einheitsrechtliche Anwendungsnormen und Internationales Vertragsrecht' in N Witzleb, R Ellger, P Mankowski, H Merkt and O Remien (eds), *Festschrift für Dieter Martiny* (Tubingen, Mohr Siebeck, 2014) 365–90, with comprehensive references.

As far as its external competence is concerned, the EU takes a less strict approach. Thus, it was the EU—and not its Member States—which signed the Capetown Convention on security rights in mobile equipment in 2009.[46] Although this convention is primarily aimed at creating uniform substantive law—an international security right—the EU regarded the special, unilateral choice of law rule in Article 3 of the Capetown Convention as well as the supplemental reference to the law applicable pursuant to the lex fori's PIL (Article 5(2) and (3) of the Capetown Convention) as sufficient in order to claim an exclusive competence for itself.[47]

F. Subsidiarity and Proportionality

Moreover, the Union has to comply with the general limitations of its competence flowing from principles of subsidiarity and proportionality (Article 5 Treaty on European Union (TEU)) when legislating in the field of private international law.[48] Yet so far, these requirements have not appeared as serious obstacles to further unification in this area. The mere fact that jurisdiction and the recognition and enforcement of Member State judgments have been unified by Brussels I*bis* and II*bis*, acts which no longer presuppose any kind of choice-of-law control in the requested States, does not render the unification of choice-of-law rules superfluous. On the contrary, the unification of choice-of-law rules as well is required in order to deter forum shopping and to ensure an international harmony of decisions.[49] Transforming already existing Conventions on PIL (such as the Rome Convention of 1980) into EU Regulations is compatible with the principle of subsidiarity because, even if the substantive content of most rules remains the same, the instrument of a Regulation offers significant practical advantages compared with a traditional Convention (amendments in the future are much easier because there is no need for lengthy procedures of ratification, the CJEU acquires a direct competence for interpreting the legal act, etc).[50] That being said, regulatory self-restraint has turned out to be a wise strategy for the EU in areas which are already covered by up-to-date and comprehensive Hague Conventions, such as the choice-of-law rules contained in the Convention on the protection of children,[51] the Convention on the protection of vulnerable adults or the Hague Protocol on the law applicable to maintenance claims.

---

[46] Council Decision 2009/370/EC of 6 April 2009, [2009] OJ L121/3.

[47] Recital 5 to Council Decision 2009/370/EC (ibid).

[48] See J Heymann, 'Importing Proportionality to the Conflict of Laws' in H Muir Watt and D Fernández Arroyo (eds), *Private International Law and Global Governance* (Oxford, Oxford University Press, 2014) 277; K Kreuzer, 'Was gehört in den allgemeinen Teil eines Europäischen Kollisionsrechtes?' in B Jud, W Rechberger, G Reichelt (eds), *Kollisionsrecht in der Europäischen Union* (Wien, Sramek, 2008) 1, 5; J Meeusen, 'A SWOT Analysis of EU Private International Law' in M Piers, H Storme and J Verhellen (eds), *Liber Amicorum Johan Erauw* (Mortsel, Intersentia, 2014) 139, 140–42; A Mills, 'Federalism in the European Union and the United States: Subsidiarity, Private Law, and the Conflict of Laws' (2010) 32 *University of Pennsylvania Journal of International Law* 369; Roth, above n 25. 319; Sonnenberger, above n 23, 326.

[49] Roth, above n 25, 319.

[50] Roth, above n 25, 319; M Weller, *Europäisches Kollisionsrecht* (Baden-Baden, Nomos, 2015) para 37.

[51] Whereas parts of the Hague 1996 Protection of Children Convention are implemented into EU law by specific provisions in the Brussels II*bis* Regulation, other parts are given effect to in EU law through the general provisions on the relationship with the 1996 Convention in Arts 61 and 62(1) of Brussels II*bis*.

II. Legal Sources of EU Private International Law

A. EU Regulations on Private International Law

Apart from the already mentioned (above section I.A) EU Regulations that are directly aimed at creating rules of PIL, special conflicts rules may be found in Regulations dealing primarily with substantive private law that are not based on Article 81(2)(c) TFEU, but rather on Article 114 TFEU or its predecessors, for example in the Flight Delay Regulation.[52] The compensation claims granted to the airline passengers according to this Regulation also apply if the contract of carriage is subject to the law of a third State pursuant to Article 5 of the Rome I Regulation;[53] it is only necessary that the territorial-personal conditions of application of the Flight Delay Regulation itself are fulfilled. This is justified by Article 23 of the Rome I Regulation, which states that the Regulation does not affect the applicability of any provision of EU law, 'which, in relation to particular matters, lays down conflict-of-law rules relating to contractual obligations'.

B. International Conventions

Following the *ERTA*-case-law of the CJEU,[54] that has been codified by the Lisbon Treaty in Articles 3(2) and 216(1) TFEU, the EU has the exclusive competence to conclude a Convention 'when its conclusion is provided for in a legislative act of the Union or is necessary to enable the Union to exercise its internal competence, or in so far as its conclusion may affect common rules or alter their scope'.[55] This doctrine applies in the field of PIL as well. Thus, the Lugano Convention of 2007 was concluded by the EU and not its Member States (except for Denmark).[56] Since the EU joined the Hague Conference in 2007, the EU may also conclude or approve Hague Conventions.[57] Therefore, the Hague Convention on Choice of Court Agreements 2005 was approved by the EU (except for Denmark) and not its Member States;[58] the same applies to the Hague Protocol on Maintenance, which,

---

[52] Reg (EC) No 261/2004 of the European Parliament and of the Council of 11 February 2004 establishing common rules on compensation and assistance to passengers in the event of denied boarding and of cancellation or long delay of flights, and repealing Reg (EEC) No 295/91, [2004] OJ L 46/1.

[53] Bundesgerichtshof 18 January 2011, *Entscheidungen des Bundesgerichtshofs in Zivilsachen [BGHZ]* 188, 85, para 33, referring to the former Art 28 of the Introductory Law to the German Civil Code (EGBGB), which corresponded to Art 4 of the Rome Convention.

[54] Case 22/70 *Commission v Council* [1971] ECR 263— *ERTA*.

[55] See A Mills, 'Private International Law and EU External Relations: Think Local Act Global, or Think Global Act Local?' (2016) 65(3) *International and Comparative Law Quarterly* 541.

[56] Opinion 1/03, [2006] ECR I-1145; on this opinion, see the contributions in: F Pocar (ed), *The External Competence of the European Union and Private International Law* (CEDAM, 2007); see also the case notes by J A Bischoff (2006) 17 *Europäische Zeitschrift für Wirtschaftsrecht* 295–301; N Lavranos (2006) 43 *Common Market Law Review* 1087–100; UG Schroeter (2006) 3 *GPR—Zeitschrift für Gemeinschaftsprivatrecht* 203–05.

[57] See JA Bischoff, *Die Europäische Gemeinschaft und die Konventionen des einheitlichen Privatrechts* (Tubingen, Mohr Siebeck, 2010); A Schulz, 'Die EU und die Haager Konferenz für Internationales Privatrecht' in J von Hein and G Rühl (eds), *Kohärenz im Internationalen Privat- und Verfahrensrecht der Europäischen Union* (Tübingen, Mohr Siebeck, 2016) 110.

[58] Council Decision 2014/887/EU [2014] OJ L 353/5.

however, was not joined by the UK and Denmark;[59] and the Hague Maintenance Convention 2007 (except for Denmark).[60] Conventions that have been concluded directly by the EU become a part of EU law, meaning that the CJEU has the final say on their interpretation.[61]

Problems may arise with regard to Hague Conventions which have been concluded by the Member States themselves but which are nevertheless closely integrated into the EU framework, in particular the Brussels II*bis* Regulation. The Hague Convention on the Protection of Children, for example, could only be ratified by the Member States after they were empowered to do so by the EU.[62] This approach was necessary because the Member States had retained a competence with regard to choice of law in matters related to the protection of children, whereas the EU had acquired an exclusive competence for the procedural aspects in this area after the enactment of the Brussels II*bis* Regulation (a so-called 'mixed' Convention).[63] Yet under the Hague Convention on the Protection of Children, only sovereign States could join this treaty. While it is undisputed that the procedural rules of the Convention have become secondary Union law after the accession of the EU's Member States,[64] it is questionable whether this is also true for its choice-of-law rules.[65]

With regard to the Hague Convention on Child Abduction, the CJEU has opted for a quite extensive reading of the Union's competences. In its Opinion 1/13, the Court held that

> because of the overlap and the close connection between the provisions of Regulation 2201/2003 and those of the Convention, in particular between Article 11 of the Regulation and Chapter III of the Convention, the provisions of the Convention may have an effect on the meaning, scope and effectiveness of the rules laid down in Regulation No 2201/2003.[66]

Thus, the CJEU affirmed that the exclusive competence of the EU encompasses the acceptance of the accession of a third State to the Convention on Child Abduction.[67]

Claiming an exclusive competence for the EU would be inappropriate in cases where only one or a few Member States are actually interested in concluding a specific agreement of limited importance with third States (Recital 42 to Rome I). These particular questions are dealt with in special Regulations concerning the conclusion of such treaties with regard to the private international law of obligations[68] and matters of family law.[69]

---

[59] Council Decision 2009/941/EC [2009] OJ L331/17.

[60] Council Decision 2011/432/EU [2011] OJ L192/39.

[61] cf Case C-533/08 *TNT Express v AXA* [2010] ECR I-4107, [60].

[62] [2008] OJ L151/36.

[63] Memorandum of the German Government on the Convention on the Protection of Children, BT-Drucks. 16/12068, 28, 30; see Schulz, above n 57, 118 et seq.

[64] Memorandum of the German Government (above n 63) 34; B Hess, *Europäisches Zivilprozessrecht* (Heidelberg, CF Müller 2010) § 5 Rn 41.

[65] This seems to be the position taken by the German Government (above n 63) 34 ('insofar' as the competence of the EU is concerned); for a contrary view, see D Schäuble, 'Die gesetzliche Vertretung Minderjähriger in der notariellen Praxis in Fällen mit Auslandsbezug' (2016) 82 *Zeitschrift für das Notariat in Baden-Württemberg* 5, 8.

[66] Opinion 1/13, ECLI:EU:C:2014:2303 [85]; on this opinion, see P Beaumont, 'A Critical Analysis of the Judicial Activism of the Court of Justice of the European Union in Opinion 1/13' *Aberdeen Centre for Private International Law Working Paper* No 2015/1, available at www.abdn.ac.uk/law/research/working-papers-455.php.

[67] Opinion 1/13, ECLI:EU:C:2014:2303 [90].

[68] Reg (EC) 662/2009 of 13 July 2009 establishing a procedure for the negotiation and conclusion of agreements between Member States and third countries on particular matters concerning the law applicable to contractual and non-contractual obligations, [2009] OJ L200/25.

[69] Reg (EC) 664/2009 of 13 July 2009 establishing a procedure for the negotiation and conclusion of agreements between Member States and third countries concerning jurisdiction, recognition and enforcement of judgments and decisions in matrimonial matters, matters of personal responsibility and matters relating to maintenance obligations, and the law applicable to matters relating to maintenance obligations, [2009] OJ L200/46.

C. Acts of Enhanced Cooperation

The Rome III Regulation on Divorce is the first test-case for adopting PIL Regulations under enhanced cooperation pursuant to Article 20 TEU in conjunction with Articles 326–334 TFEU. Recently, the Regulations on Matrimonial Property and the Property Consequences of Registered Partnerships have been adopted in the same fashion. Enhanced cooperation allows at least nine Member States to use the legislative procedures of the EU to reach a deeper level of integration.[70] Thus, it constitutes an important alternative to the traditional conclusion of international Conventions. Enhanced cooperation may only be deployed as a remedy of last resort, after attempts at reaching the required majority in the Council to adopt a Regulation under the normal Treaty rules have failed. Other parts of the *acquis* and the internal market must not be infringed upon. For further details of the procedure, see Article 329 et seq TFEU.

It is controversial among academics whether enhanced cooperation should be regarded as positive or negative.[71] The potential disadvantages of this method consist in a further fragmentation of EU PIL and a throwback to an intergovernmental approach to law-making in the EU.[72] In particular, fears have been voiced that the availability of enhanced cooperation might weaken the pressure to reach a consensus or a qualified majority in the course of the special or ordinary legislative procedure.[73] The threshold of nine participating States necessary for a coalition of the willing is regarded by some as too low for a Union that now consists of 28 Member States.[74] Critics point to the Hague Conference as the better forum for intergovernmental law-making, which has the added advantage of allowing for the accession of third States.[75]

These concerns must be weighed against significant advantages of enhanced cooperation, of which the most important is that the speed of integration can no longer be blocked by a minority of reluctant Member States.[76] Reverting to treaties as an instrument of intergovernmental law-making fails to convince because this approach would be fraught with all the well-known drawbacks (slow procedures of ratification, no direct competence of the CJEU for interpretation, etc) that have led to the transformation of the Brussels and

---

[70] For a closer analysis, see A Fiorini, 'Harmonizing the Law Applicable to Divorce and Legal Separation—Enhanced Cooperation as the Way Forward?' (2010) 59(4) *International and Comparative Law Quarterly* 1143, 1147 et seq; C Lignier and A Geier, 'Die verstärkte Zusammenarbeit in der Europäischen Union' (2015) 79 *Rabels Zeitschrift* 546; C Thomale, "Verstärkte Zusammenarbeit als Einigungsersatz?—Eine Gegenrede am Beispiel des Europäischen Privat- und Gesellschaftsrechts" (2015) 23 *Zeitschrift für Europäisches Privatrecht* 517; D Trüten, *Die Entwicklung des Internationalen Privatrechts in der Europäischen Union* (Baden-Baden/Bern, Nomos/Stämpfli, 2015) 626 et seq.

[71] For critical assessments, see NA Baarsma, 'European Choice of Law on Divorce (Rome III): Where did it go Wrong?" (2009) 27 *Nederlands Internationaal Privaatrecht* 9; T Brand, 'Abschied vom einheitlichen EU-Recht' (2011) 89 *Deutsche Richterzeitung* 56; Fiorini, ibid 1143 et seq; JJ Kuipers, 'The Law Applicable to Divorce as Test Ground for Enhanced Cooperation' (2012) 18 *European Law Journal* 201; Lignier and Geier, above n 70, 573 et seq; Trüten, ibid 630; Thomale, ibid 526 et seq.

[72] See Brand, ibid 56; Trüten, above n70, 631.

[73] Baarsma, above n 71, 14; Brand, above n 71, 56; Fiorini, above n 70, 1157 et seq; Kuipers, above n 71, 215 et seq.

[74] Kuipers, above n 71, 213.

[75] ibid 215.

[76] See R Wagner, 'Fünfzehn Jahre justizielle Zusammenarbeit in Zivilsachen' (2014) 34 *Praxis des internationalen Privat- und Verfahrensrecht* 217, 224: enhanced cooperation is 'better than nothing'; see also P Winkler von Mohrenfels, 'Die Rom III-VO und die Parteiautonomie' in H Kronke and K Thorn (eds), *Festschrift für Bernd von Hoffmann* (Bielefeld, Gieseking, 2011) 527, 534: 'A bird in the hand is worth two in the bush.'

Rome Conventions into Regulations.[77] The risk of a fragmentation of EU PIL is reduced by the possibility of other Member States joining at a later stage.[78] Contrary to pessimistic expectations,[79] Greece, Lithuania and Estonia have already joined the Rome III Regulation, which will soon be in force in 17 States, ie a clear majority of Member States.[80] The Regulations on Matrimonial Property and the Property of Registered Partnerships will apply in even more, namely 19 Member States (see Recital 11 to each Regulation).[81]

D. Directives

In addition to EU Regulations, rules of PIL are occasionally found in EU Directives, notably those on consumer protection based on Article 114 TFEU or one of its predecessors. These rules usually require Member States to ensure that consumers are not deprived of the protection granted by the relevant Directive if the contract has a close connection with the territory of the Member States.[82] Of course, in the light of Articles 3(4) and 6(2) of Rome I, it is open to debate whether such rules are still necessary.[83] The recently enacted Consumer Rights Directive[84] has answered this question in the negative. It contains no specific choice-of-law rule, but simply refers to the protection granted to consumers by the Rome I Regulation in Recital 58. Apart from that, the question as to whether the so-called E-Commerce-Directive[85] enshrines a principle of 'country of origin' for choice of law has been answered in the negative by the CJEU in its *eDate*-decision.[86]

E. Primary EU law

A further source of EU PIL, at least in a broad sense, is EU primary law as interpreted by the CJEU. By their nature, neither the founding treaties nor the TFEU or the TEU contain

---

[77] Fiorini, above n 70, 1151.

[78] Baarsma, above n 71, 14.

[79] Kuipers, above n 71, 228 considered it as 'not likely' that other States would ever join Rome III.

[80] [2012] OJ L323/18 (Lithuania); [2014] OJ L23/41 (Greece); [2016] OJ L216/23 (Estonia).

[81] In addition to the original 18 participating States, Estonia announced its intention to take part in the cooperation after its adoption, see the press release issued by the European Council, www.consilium.europa.eu/en/press/press-releases/2016/06/09-property-regimes-for-international-couples/.

[82] Council Dir (EEC) No 13/1993 of 5 April 1993 on unfair terms in consumer contracts, [1993] OJ L95/29; Dir (EC) No 44/1999 of the European Parliament and of the Council of 25 May 1999 on certain aspects of the sale of consumer goods and associated guarantees, [1999] OJ L171/12; Dir (EC) No 65/2002 of the European Parliament and of the Council of 23 September 2002 concerning the distance marketing of consumer financial services and amending Council Dir 90/619/EEC and Dirs 97/7/EC and 98/27/EC, [2002] OJ L271/16; Dir (EC) No 48/2008 of the European parliament and of the Council of 23 April 2008 on credit agreements for consumers and repealing Council Dir 87/102/EEC, [2008] OJ L133/66.

[83] For a detailed analysis, see EM Kieninger, 'Der grenzüberschreitende Verbrauchervertrag zwischen Richtlinienkollisionsrecht und Rom I-Verordnung. Nach der Reform ist vor der Reform' in D Baetge, J von Hein and M von Hinden (eds), *Festschrift für Jan Kropholler* (Tübingen, Mohr Siebeck, 2008) 499; S Leible, 'Brauchen wir noch Art 46b EGBGB?', *Festschrift für Bernd von Hoffmann*, above n 76, 230.

[84] Dir (EU) No 83/2011 of the European Parliament and of the Council of 25 October 2011 on consumer right, amending Council Dir 93/13/EEC and Dir 1999/44/EC of the European Parliament and of the Council and repealing Council Dir 85/577/EEC and Dir 97/7/EC of the European Parliament and of the Council, [2011] OJ L304/64.

[85] Dir 2000/31/EC of 8 June 2000 on certain legal aspects of information society services, in particular electronic commerce, in the Internal Market (Dir on electronic commerce), [2000] OJ L178/1.

[86] C-509/09 *eDate* and C-161/10 *Martinez*, ECLI:EU:C: 2011:685, [61]–[63].

choice-of-law rules in a technical sense.[87] However, the basic freedoms guaranteed by the TFEU have had a profound impact on domestic choice-of-law rules, particularly on the law of names. Here, the CJEU has developed a principle of recognition that requires Member States to restrict nationality as a connecting factor and to accept a name that a person has lawfully acquired in another Member State provided the result does not violate domestic public policy.[88] This approach is problematic because the CJEU openly admits that the EU has no competence for the substantive law of names;[89] it nevertheless proceeds on the basis that even where Member States make use of their competence, they must respect the guarantee of free movement under Article 21 TFEU.[90] Yet, the very detailed judicial examination of Member States' public policy on the law of names, especially insofar as titles of nobility are concerned,[91] comes dangerously close to usurping a substantive competence that Member States have not yet not conferred on the EU; moreover, this case-law in effect circumvents the requirement of unanimity that would be necessary to harmonise choice of law rules for family matters under Article 81(3) TFEU (see above section I.D).

Despite the growing Europeanisation of PIL a general Regulation concerning the law applicable to companies, which might be based on Article 81(2)(c) TFEU, is still missing.[92] Nevertheless, the CJEU's reasoning in *Centros* and other decisions (*Überseering, InspireArt*, etc) forced some Member States to abandon the real seat theory, at least with regard to companies migrating from one Member State that adheres to the incorporation theory to another Member State.[93]

III. Territorial Scope of EU Legislation on Private International Law

The territorial scope of EU PIL Regulations is, generally speaking, defined in accordance with Article 52 TEU in conjunction with Article 355 TFEU. Particular restrictions have to be observed with regard to Denmark, the United Kingdom and Ireland (see above section I.A). Although the recast of the Protocol concerning the legal position of Denmark under the Lisbon Treaty would have allowed an opt-in with regard to the judicial cooperation in civil matters,[94] the Danish population voted against such a possibility in a

---

[87] cf however, the recent monograph by R Westrik, *Hidden Civil Law* (Paris, Paris Legal Pusblishers, 2016).

[88] Case C-148/02 *Garcia Avello* [2003] ECR I-11613; Case C-353/06 *Grunkin Paul* [2008] ECR I-7639; Case C-208/09 *Sayn-Wittgenstein* [2010] ECR I-13693; Case C-391/09 *(Runevič-Vardyn)* [2011] ECR I-3787; Case C-438/14, *Bogendorff von Wolffersdorff* ECLI:EU:C:2016:401.

[89] *Bogendorff von Wolffersdorff*, ibid [32].

[90] ibid [32].

[91] Case C-208/09 *Sayn-Wittgenstein* [2010] ECR I-13693; *Bogendorff von Wolffersdorff*, ibid.

[92] See J von Hein, 'Corporations in European Private International Law—From Case-Law to Codification?' (2015) 17 *Japanese Yearbook of Private International Law* 90, with further references.

[93] Case C-212/97 *Centros* [1999] ECR I-1459; Case C-208/00 *Überseering* [2002] ECR I-9919; Case C-167/01 *Inspire Art Ltd* [2003] ECR I-10159; but cf. the more restrictive approach in Case C-210/06 *CARTESIO* [2009] ECR I-9641 and Case C-378/10 *VALE* ECLI:EU:C:2012:440.

[94] Trüten, above n 70, 625.

referendum on 4 December 2015.[95] However, some Regulations enacted under Article 81 TFEU have been extended to Denmark by way of bilateral treaties between the EU and the Kingdom (Brussels I*bis*, some aspects of the Maintenance Regulation and the Service Regulation). The UK and Ireland both participate in the vast majority of the private international law Regulations; both Member States have refrained from opting into the Succession Regulation, the Rome III Regulation, the Matrimonial Property Regulation and the Regulation on the Property of Registered Partnerships. The UK and Ireland have at times made different choices. Ireland, for example, is party to the EU Maintenance Regulation and the Hague Protocol on the law applicable to maintenance regulation, whereas the UK decided to opt into the EU Maintenance Regulation only. On 23 June 2016, the voters in the United Kingdom decided by a slim majority to leave the EU. The consequences of the 'Brexit' on EU PIL are not yet settled.[96] Details will depend on the negotiations following the UK's request for a withdrawal under Article 50 TEU.

IV. Law Reforms at EU Level

There is an ongoing debate on the question of a future comprehensive codification of EU PIL[97] or the comparatively more modest approach of enacting a so-called 'Rome 0'-Regulation on general principles of PIL.[98] As the TFEU distinguishes between matters of PIL in general, which are subject to the general legislative procedure (Article 81(1) and (2)(c) TFEU) and matters relating to family law which are subject to the special procedure laid down in Article 81(3) TFEU (see above section I.D), the adoption of a comprehensive EU Code on PIL would require compliance with the general legislative procedure as regards, for example, contract, tort as well as succession law, while adherence to the special procedure of Article 81(3) TFEU would be required as regards family law.[99] Difficulties, however, would arise as far as the general part of an EU Code on PIL is concerned.[100] A single provision on *renvoi* intended to cover, for example, contract and tort law as well as family law, would

---

[95] HP Mansel, K Thorn and R Wagner, 'Europäisches Kollisionsrecht 2015: Neubesinnung' (2016) 36 *Praxis des internationalen Privat- und Verfahrensrecht* 1, 3.

[96] On the impact of Brexit on private international law in general, see J Basedow, 'Brexit und das Privat- und Wirtschaftsrecht' (2016) 24 *Zeitschrift für Europäisches Privatrecht* 567; A Dickinson, 'Back to the Future: the UK's EU Exit and the Conflict of Laws' (2016) 12 *Journal of Private International Law* 195; B Hess, 'Back to the Past: BREXIT und das europäische internationale Privat- und Verfahrensrecht' (2016) 36 *Praxis des internationalen Privat- und Verfahrensrecht* 409.

[97] M Czepelak, 'Would we like to have a European Code of Private International Law?' (2010) 18 *European Review of Private Law* 705; EM Kieninger, 'Das Europäische IPR vor der Kodifikation?', *Festschrift für Bernd von Hoffmann*, above n 76, 184; X Kramer, *A European Framework for Private International Law: Current Gaps and Future Perspectives*, 2012 (available at www.europarl.europa.eu/document/activities/cont/201212/20121219ATT 58300/20121219ATT58300EN.pdf); P Lagarde, 'Embryon de Règlement portant Code européen de droit international privé' (2011) 75 *Rabels Zeitschrift* 673; G Rühl and J von Hein, 'Towards a European Code on Private International Law?' (2015) 79 *Rabels Zeitschrift* 701, all with further references.

[98] S Leible and M Müller, 'The Idea of a "Rome 0 Regulation"' (2012/2013) 14 *Yearbook of Private International Law* 137.

[99] cf, R Wagner, 'Do we need a Rome 0 Regulation?' (2014) 61 *Netherlands International Law Review* 225, 233 et seq.

[100] cf Rühl and von Hein, above n 97, 732–35; Wagner, ibid 234 et seq.

arguably have to comply with both legislative procedures.[101] The problems inherent in Article 81 TFEU are exacerbated by the special position of Denmark, the UK and Ireland with regard to judicial cooperation in civil matters (see above section III). Finally, the Rome III Regulation, the Matrimonial Property Regulation and the Regulation on the Property of Registered Partnerships provide challenges for a comprehensive codification because they are measures of enhanced cooperation (see above section II.C). It is doubtful whether those Member States which have so far been reluctant to join Rome III, notably Sweden or the Netherlands, and other Member States who are reluctant to join the Matrimonial Property Regulation and the Regulation on the Property of Registered Partnerships, notably Ireland and Poland, would be enthusiastic about the prospect of codifying international family law in the context of a comprehensive Code.[102] The latter aspect leads to the question whether an EU code of PIL could itself be passed as a measure of enhanced cooperation.[103] However, according to Article 327 TFEU '[a]ny enhanced cooperation shall respect the competences, rights and obligations of those Member States which do not participate in it'. Thus, it is hard to see how matters already governed by the *acquis communautaire* in PIL could be integrated into a comprehensive code without infringing upon the rights and obligations of those Member States which participate in the existing Regulations but prefer not to join a comprehensive Code.[104]

In view of the above-mentioned difficulties, the only legislative competence for a comprehensive Code would probably be Article 352(1) TFEU.[105] It must be emphasised, however, that the threshold for invoking this provision is rather high. To begin with, a certain legislative action must 'prove necessary ... to attain one of the objectives set out in the Treaties'. In addition, Article 352(1) TFEU requires unanimity in the Council. Whether an EU Code on PIL would actually meet these thresholds is unclear.[106]

---

[101] cf Wagner, ibid 234 et seq.
[102] Rühl and von Hein, above n 97, 734.
[103] Kramer, above n 97, paras 8.3. et seq.
[104] Kramer, ibid paras 8.3. et seq; Rühl and von Hein, above n 97, 734.
[105] Rühl and von Hein, above n 97, 735.
[106] Rühl and von Hein, ibid.

3

An Analysis of the Effectiveness of the EU Institutions in Making and Interpreting EU Private International Law Regulations

BURCU YÜKSEL[*]

I. Introduction

The institutional framework of the European Union ('EU') is prescribed by the rules provided for under Title III of the Treaty on EU ('TEU').[1] Pursuant to these rules, the EU has a unique institutional set up having three main institutions involved in EU legislation, namely the European Parliament representing the EU's citizens, the Council of the EU representing the governments of individual Member States, and the European Commission representing the interests of the Union as a whole.[2] After new laws are adopted, the Court of Justice of the EU ('CJEU' or 'Court') plays a vital role to ensure that laws are interpreted and applied in the same manner in every EU Member State and also that the Member States and EU institutions abide by EU law.[3]

As part of EU law, EU Private International Law ('PIL') has been developed under this unique institutional framework which requires a certain degree of interaction between the EU institutions of the Commission, Council, Parliament and CJEU. The effectiveness of the EU PIL framework as a whole is dependent, by and large, on the effectiveness of each of these institutions in their roles and also on the quality of the interaction between them.

The purpose of this chapter is to analyse the effectiveness of EU institutions in making and interpreting EU PIL regulations by focusing on certain selected issues.[4] The chapter

---

[*] The author would like to thank Professor Paul Beaumont for his valuable comments and suggestions on an earlier version of this chapter. All errors and omissions that remain are the author's.
[1] Consolidated version of the Treaty on European Union [2012] OJ C326/13.
[2] See www.europa.eu/european-union/about-eu/institutions-bodies_en.
[3] See www.europa.eu/european-union/about-eu/institutions-bodies/court-justice_en.
[4] The EU institutional issues selected to be examined in this chapter are not peculiar only to the area of PIL but are also relevant to other areas of law. However, in consistent with the subject matter of the EUPILLAR Project, this chapter deals with these institutional issues from a PIL perspective.

builds on empirical evidence gathered from 16 interviews[5] conducted with participants in the Commission,[6] the Council,[7] the European Parliament,[8] and with current Judges, Advocates General ('AGs') and Legal Secretaries in the CJEU.[9] All interviewees have been involved in making or interpreting at least one of the EU PIL regulations that are examined within the scope of the EUPILLAR Project, namely the Brussels I, Rome I, Rome II, Brussels IIa and Maintenance Regulations. The chapter also builds on a comprehensive case law analysis on 104 CJEU judgments concerning these regulations given between 2002 and 2015.[10] In this respect, the chapter aims to give a different angle to the academic debate on the EU institutional issues from the perspective of the insiders' of the Commission, the Council, the Parliament and the CJEU whilst taking account of outside perspectives in the interests of balance.

II. Effectiveness of the EU Legislature in Making EU Private International Law Regulations

A. An Overview of the Roles of the Commission, Council and Parliament in Law-making

Policies and laws that apply throughout the EU are produced by the unique law-making mechanism set up under Title III of the TEU through the ordinary legislative procedure.[11] It is for the Commission to propose new laws and for the Parliament and the Council to adopt them.[12]

The European Commission is the politically independent executive authority of the EU. As part of its mission defined under Article 17 of the TEU, the Commission prepares proposals for new EU legislation to be adopted. The Council of the EU is, together with the European Parliament, the main decision-making body of the EU.[13] As part of its

---

[5] The interviewees were selected from a long list of potential interviewees prepared on the basis of the interviewees' expertise and experience in the field of EU PIL. The EUPILLAR team is extremely grateful for the time given up by the interviewees to help with this research. The interviews were semi-structured and recorded (except one interview). Each interviewee was given the interview questions in advance (one set of questions for the interviewees involved in the Commission, Council and European Parliament and a different set of questions for the interviewees from the CJEU). The interviews allowed for spontaneous additional responses from interviewees and for spontaneous follow up questions by the interviewer.

[6] EUPILLAR_EU 1, EUPILLAR_EU 8, EUPILLAR_EU 9, EUPILLAR_EU 12. These interviews were with current or past officials in the Commission.

[7] EUPILLAR_EU 2, EUPILLAR_EU 10, EUPILLAR_EU 11, EUPILLAR_EU 12, EUPILLAR_EU 13, EUPILLAR_EU 14, EUPILLAR_EU 16. These interviews were with participants from several Member States who had represented their States in one or more of the Council Working Parties that negotiated at least one of the EU PIL regulations that are examined within the scope of the EUPILLAR Project.

[8] EUPILLAR_EU 15. The interview was with an official of the European Parliament.

[9] EUPILLAR_EU 3, EUPILLAR_EU 4, EUPILLAR_EU 5, EUPILLAR_EU 6, EUPILLAR_EU 7.

[10] See chs 33 and 41, and also the EUPILLAR Database available at https://w3.abdn.ac.uk/clsm/eupillar/#/home.

[11] www.europa.eu/european-union/about-eu/institutions-bodies_en. For issues related to the ordinary legislative procedure, see s II.B.i below.

[12] www.europa.eu/european-union/about-eu/institutions-bodies_en.

[13] www.europa.eu/european-union/about-eu/institutions-bodies/council-eu_en.

mission defined under Article 16 of the TEU, the Council negotiates and adopts EU legislation on the basis of proposals submitted by the Commission. The European Parliament is the directly-elected EU institution which, jointly with the Council, exercises legislative functions as part of its mission defined under Article 14 of the TEU. The Parliament has been much more effective in EU law-making as the introduction of the ordinary legislative procedure put Parliament on an equal footing with the Council.

B. Selected Issues in Law-making Process and Ways Forward for the EU Legislature

i. *Ordinary Legislative Procedure*

The ordinary legislative procedure, which renamed the co-decision procedure that had been originally introduced by the Maastricht Treaty on European Union[14] and extended by the Amsterdam Treaty,[15] became the main legislative procedure of the EU's decision-making system with the Lisbon Treaty[16] and was extended therein to further areas.[17] Pursuant to Article 289 of the Treaty on the Functioning of the EU ('TFEU'),[18] the ordinary legislative procedure consists in the joint adoption by the European Parliament and the Council of a regulation, directive or decision on a proposal from the Commission, and it is carried out as defined in Article 294. Most of the EU PIL instruments have been drawn up under this procedure. However, for family law, the special legislative procedure applies.

The Council is in the lead of the negotiations on a Commission proposal on EU PIL and is also the critical actor.[19] As regards the EU PIL regulations, there have been many issues where the Council strongly departed from the Commission's proposal, such as arbitration and the non-extension of EU jurisdiction rules to non-EU defendants in the Brussels I Recast.[20] The Council has also made a key difference on certain issues that reflected in the final version of the regulations, such as the consumer provisions in Rome I which were the result of negotiations between the Portuguese Presidency at that time and the European Parliament.[21] The Parliament has had considerable influence on the Brussels I Recast as well particularly in relation to the abolition of exequatur in the final version of the Regulation and the complete exclusion of arbitration from the Regulation against the Commission's proposal.[22] In relation to Rome II, which was the first PIL regulation in which the Parliament was involved with the co-decision procedure, the Parliament emphasised party autonomy which to a certain extent changed the emphasis of the instrument compared with the original approach of the Commission.[23]

---

[14] [1992] OJ C191/1.

[15] [1997] OJ C340/1.

[16] [2007] OJ C306/01.

[17] www.europarl.europa.eu/aboutparliament/en/20150201PVL00004/Powers-and-procedures.

[18] [2012] OJ C 326/47.

[19] EUPILLAR_EU 14, EUPILLAR_EU 16.

[20] EUPILLAR_EU 14.

[21] EUPILLAR_EU 15. See also the creation of flexibility in the objective applicable law rules in Arts 4–8 of Rome I by the inclusion of escape clauses.

[22] EUPILLAR_EU 15. For the Report of the Parliament on the proposal for the Brussels I Recast Regulation, see www.europarl.europa.eu/sides/getDoc.do?type=REPORT&reference=A7-2012-0320&language=EN.

[23] EUPILLAR_EU 15.

The efficiency of the ordinary legislative procedure in non-family law matters requires a good interaction between the Council and Parliament. However, the interview data indicate that there is a tension between the Council and the Parliament which risks undermining the effectiveness of the procedure and also of the EU PIL regulations. The interviewees from the Council indicated that the Council is still not so comfortable with the more and more active involvement of the European Parliament as the Council was used to playing the main role in law-making.[24] It was further added that some Member States feel that after they spend a lot of time and effort to achieve a certain result in the Council, something may come in the Parliament which can completely destroy this delicate balance that they have achieved.[25] In this sense, from a political and technical point of view, some interviewees assessed that the Parliament's increasing active involvement leads to difficulties.[26] The issue of defamation in the co-decision of Rome II is indeed a clear example of that which remained as a failure since the Parliament did not manage to get a provision on the issue into Rome II even though the rapporteur tried very hard and it went to conciliation.[27]

Although the tension between the Council and the European Parliament which is apparent in the ordinary legislative procedure requires further discussions, beyond the scope of this chapter, it is suggested that the Commission's efforts can be very helpful to reduce this tension and to find a workable solution. The main impact of the Commission in the ordinary legislative process is putting things on the table.[28] However, the Commission also act as a very important player in the negotiations and tries to broker a compromise between the Council and the Parliament when they are in co-decision.[29]

ii. Qualified Majority and Unanimity Requirements

The Council acts by a qualified majority, except where the Treaties provide otherwise.[30] The qualified majority is defined under Article 16(4) of the TEU as from 1 November 2014 as 'at least 55% of the members of the Council, comprising at least fifteen of them and representing Member States comprising at least 65% of the population of the Union.' On a number of matters which the Member States consider to be sensitive including the family law provisions in the field of justice and home affairs, the Council acts unanimously pursuant to Article 81(3) of the TFEU.

The interview data indicate that both the qualified majority requirement and unanimity have certain effects undermining the effectiveness of the legislative process. In the field of commercial law although matters are less sensitive and less controversial, it is still not easy to reach agreement on EU legislation because of the qualified majority requirement.[31] In the field of family law, unanimity seems to cause major issues, as demonstrated recently by the two important proposals of the Commission for Council Regulations on jurisdiction and applicable law for matrimonial property regimes and the property consequences of

---

[24] EUPILLAR_EU 2.
[25] ibid.
[26] EUPILLAR_EU 2, EUPILLAR_EU 14.
[27] EUPILLAR_EU 15.
[28] EUPILLAR_EU 1, EUPILLAR_EU 8, EUPILLAR_EU 9.
[29] EUPILLAR_EU 8.
[30] Art 16(3) of the TEU.
[31] EUPILLAR_EU 1.

registered partnerships.[32] The politically sensitive nature of these proposals, mainly linked to the fact that the institutions of same sex marriages and/or registered partnerships were not known in a number of Member States, caused difficulties for those Member States and eventually the Council concluded that it would not be possible, within a reasonable period of time, to reach a unanimous agreement on the original Commission proposals.[33] Later on, a final text was adopted in June 2016 by the Council on the basis of enhanced cooperation for a Regulation covering the property arrangements of spouses.[34]

As demonstrated by this recent experience of the EU, in the field of family law, it may be extremely difficult to accommodate the views of some of the more liberal Member States with those of the more conservative Member States[35] and to find common ground between different Member States' positions.[36] Given that the unanimity requirement at the moment allows the possibility that one Member State with a very small population may block the whole process while all the other Member States reach an agreement,[37] it is doubtful whether the unanimity requirement in the field of family law actually serves the best interests of the EU. Unanimity makes both the adoption of new legislation and the reform of existing legislation very hard.[38] As one of the interviewees noted, if unanimity cannot be achieved, then enhanced cooperation can be utilised.[39] However, the downside of enhanced cooperation is that it results in limiting the territorial scope of application of the regulations.[40]

iii. Interpretation Tools

Interpretation tools, such as recitals to the regulations, explanatory reports, preparatory documents, are used by the judicial actors, particularly by the courts of Member States and the CJEU, to ascertain the intention of the EU legislature on a particular matter. As the interviews conducted with the members of the CJEU indicate, the Court does an in-depth analysis in ascertaining the intention of the EU legislature when interpreting Regulations

---

[32] EUPILLAR_EU 1, EUPILLAR_EU 2, EUPILLAR_EU 8, EUPILLAR_EU 11, EUPILLAR_EU 15.

[33] See www.europarl.europa.eu/legislative-train/theme-area-of-justice-and-fundamental-rights/file-matrimonial-property-regimes-and-consequences-of-registered-partnerships.

[34] See Council Reg (EU) 2016/1103 of 24 June 2016 implementing enhanced cooperation in the area of jurisdiction, applicable law and the recognition and enforcement of decisions in matters of matrimonial property regimes [2016] OJ L183/1 (see Recital 11 for the 18 Member States who wanted to participate in the enhanced cooperation) building on Council Dec (EU) 2016/954 of 9 June 2016 authorising enhanced cooperation in the area of jurisdiction, applicable law and the recognition and enforcement of decisions on the property regimes of international couples, covering both matters of matrimonial property regimes and the property consequences of registered partnerships [2016] OJ L159/16. For registered partners, see the Commission Proposal for a Council Reg on jurisdiction, applicable law and the recognition and enforcement of decisions in matters of the property consequences of registered partnerships under enhanced cooperation—COM(2016) 107 final.

[35] EUPILLAR_EU 1.

[36] EUPILLAR_EU 8.

[37] EUPILLAR_EU 1, EUPILLAR_EU 8.

[38] The Commission's Proposal for the Recast of Brussels IIa (Proposal for a Council Reg on jurisdiction, the recognition and enforcement of decisions in matrimonial matters and the matters of parental responsibility, and on international child abduction (recast) COM/2016/0411 final) contains no proposals in relation to jurisdiction for divorce and legal separation at least partly because of the fear of not obtaining unanimity in the Council due to different views on same sex marriage as in the context of matrimonial property, see above n 34.

[39] EUPILLAR_EU 1. This was the outcome in matrimonial property, above n 34, and in the Rome III Reg on the Law Applicable to Divorce and Legal Separation [2010] OJ L343/10.

[40] EUPILLAR_EU 8.

even if sometimes this cannot be seen from the judgment;[41] and in the process of deliberation, it duly examines all the materials which could be useful.[42] Cabinet work, preparatory
work, parliamentary debates, the instrument itself, recitals, first proposal of the Commission and the opinions on it are taken into account by the Court.[43] Given this function of
the interpretation tools, it is crucial for the legislature to express its correct intention in the
law-making process through these tools.

There is no doubt that the explanatory reports were an excellent feature of the early
success of PIL in the EU in relation to the Brussels,[44] Rome[45] and Lugano Conventions.[46]
A careful case law analysis of the Member States' courts and the CJEU demonstrates that
the explanatory reports are actually still very useful in relation to the successor regulations of these conventions.[47] They are also very helpful to academics and practitioners.[48]
Even the explanatory reports of the conventions that never entered into force, such as the
Virgos-Schmit Report[49] and the Borrás Report,[50] are still being referred to a lot.[51] As stated
in the interviews, although the idea behind having no explanatory report was that what
is in the text is supposed to be self-explanatory, the wide use of the explanatory reports
indicates that in many respects the text on its own is not self-explanatory.[52] Thus, there
is a strong need to re-introduce the explanatory reports to the law-making process. Well
drafted explanatory reports can considerably enhance the effectiveness of the PIL framework in the EU. The interviews conducted with the members of the CJEU also indicate
that the explanatory reports on the previous PIL conventions are very helpful,[53] and something comparable could be very helpful for PIL regulations as well.[54] There seem to be no
legal obstacles to having explanatory reports in relation to regulations. Obstacles seem to
be mostly practical and procedural especially at the institutional level. Some interviewees
stated that having an official explanatory report would be a very complex procedure since it
would have to be agreed and approved by both Council and Parliament which is considered

---

[41] This might be due to the budget considerations in relation to translation costs mentioned in EUPILLAR_EU
6 that all the references to case law increase the length of the judgments and the Court is trying to reduce unnecessary length without affecting the understanding of the reasoning of the judgment.

[42] EUPILLAR_EU 3.

[43] EUPILLAR_EU 6. However, some interviewees from the EU legislative institutions expressed some concerns
that they have the impression that sometimes the Court first looks and tries to find a result and then it justifies that
result with the interpretation tools and cites them so long as they are helpful for this justification: EUPILLAR_EU
10, EUPILLAR_EU 11, EUPILLAR_EU 14 and EUPILLAR_EU 15 are also in the same line. For a detailed analysis
on how well the CJEU uses the interpretation tools, see chs 33 and 41.

[44] Convention on jurisdiction and the enforcement of judgments in civil and commercial matters, consolidated
version, [1998] OJ C27/1.

[45] 80/934/EEC: Convention on the law applicable to contractual obligations [1980] OJ L66/1.

[46] 88/592/EEC: Convention on jurisdiction and the enforcement of judgments in civil and commercial matters
[1988] OJ L319/9.

[47] For the specific examples, see chs 5–30, and chs 33 and 41.

[48] EUPILLAR_EU 15.

[49] M Virgos and E Schmit, Report on the Convention on the Insolvency Proceedings, EC Doc of 8 July
1996-6500/1/96.

[50] A Borrás, Explanatory Report on the Convention on Jurisdiction and the Recognition and Enforcement of
Judgments in Matrimonial Matters, [1998] OJ 221/27.

[51] EUPILLAR_EU 1, EUPILLAR_EU 9.

[52] EUPILLAR_EU 1.

[53] EUPILLAR_EU 3, EUPILLAR_EU 4.

[54] EUPILLAR_EU 4.

to be very difficult to achieve,[55] and that the authorship of the explanatory reports may cause difficulties.[56] In response to these concerns, it is suggested that the Council (and also the European Parliament for non-family law matters) should agree to the appointment of a rapporteur or rapporteurs who would attend all the relevant meetings in the Council (and also in the European Parliament on non-family law matters) where the Commission's proposals are discussed and then that person(s) would prepare an explanatory report. The Hague Conference system can be a model for the EU in this regard and the explanatory report could be written after the adoption of the instrument.[57] This may not be an ideal solution in terms of time-frame but seems to be working in the Hague Conference system. Therefore, after the adoption of the instrument by the Council (and European Parliament for non-family law matters), the rapporteur could submit a draft report to the Council (and European Parliament for non-family law matters) for it to be amended before its final approval by the Council (and European Parliament for non-family law matters). Although the report would be a work of the rapporteur as the author, through this suggested procedure, it would be a document reflecting a collective view. This suggested procedure might be realised in the future for the Recast of the EU PIL regulations.

In the absence of the explanatory reports, best practice guides prepared by the Commission carefully, in co-operation with various experts and the European Judicial Network ('EJN'), can serve a useful function although they are not as authoritative as an explanatory report.[58] As regards best practice guides, the challenge seems to be that they should be drafted in a way to add an explanatory value, rather than merely repeating what the legislation says.[59]

Recitals are useful tools so far as they explain the purpose of articles in regulations. In cases where there is a gap in the rules or where the text is ambiguous, they are helpful to gather some information in order to resolve the problems arising from that gap or ambiguity.[60] However, as indicated in the interviews, when texts which should be in an article are placed into recitals, this poses a problem considering that recitals, as opposed to articles, are not binding. In addition, in the absence of explanatory reports, texts which previously would have been in the explanatory reports are being placed into recitals[61] while recitals cannot indeed replace an explanatory report.[62] As the interviewees explained, in some difficult cases, recitals reflect contradictory positions, which does not help very much to understand what the actual intention of the legislature was.[63] In others, they replace what was to have been a provision in the text which could not be agreed[64] and this shows that they are sometimes the result of a compromise.[65] They can become extremely political since some states or the European Parliament can insist on having certain issues in the recital,

---

[55] EUPILLAR_EU 2, EUPILLAR_EU 8.
[56] EUPILLAR_EU 16.
[57] EUPILLAR_EU 13.
[58] EUPILLAR_EU 2.
[59] EUPILLAR_EU 9.
[60] EUPILLAR_EU 10.
[61] EUPILLAR_EU 1, EUPILLAR_EU 11.
[62] EUPILLAR_EU 9.
[63] EUPILLAR_EU 8.
[64] EUPILLAR_EU 12.
[65] EUPILLAR_EU 9, EUPILLAR_EU 16.

even if it has almost nothing to do with the regulation itself or the provision in question.[66] Definitions are sometimes given in recitals, such as Recitals 9, 22 and 30 to the Rome I Regulation.[67] As a result, recitals in the EU PIL regulations get quite lengthy, such as Recital 12 of the Brussels I Recast consisting of four paragraphs. Re-introducing the explanatory reports to the law-making process can also be helpful to deal with some of these problems.

Preparatory documents, such as Green Papers, answers to Green Papers and proposals on the Explanatory Memorandum, are also useful tools. Although they are publicly available, they can be made more easily accessible[68] and can be published in a systematic way after the negotiations are completed.[69] On the other hand, some concerns were expressed in the interviews that this suggestion can be useful for academics in writing their research papers but not much use for judges, who do not have much time to resolve the cases, as this may overload them with information and may lead to some confusion when giving the decision.[70]

iv. Review Clauses

Review clauses in EU legislation are used to ensure that legislation is reviewed within a set period of time. For the Brussels I,[71] Rome I,[72] Rome II,[73] Brussels IIa,[74] and Maintenance Regulations,[75] this time frame was usually set as five years after their entry into force and the responsibility to submit a report on the application of the Regulations, where needed accompanied by proposals for adaptions to the Regulations, to the European Parliament, the Council and the Economic and Social Committee was assigned to the Commission.[76]

Although the review clauses are useful to monitor the operation and effectiveness of the regulations in practice, the interview data indicate that their practical and legal value is being questioned. Three main reasons were given at the interviews. One of them is that the time-frame for the review is often not sufficiently long enough to see the operation and effectiveness of the regulations in practice.[77] This was particularly the case with Rome I and Rome II as there have been only a few cases on these regulations.[78] In addition, as an interviewee pointed out, in most cases there is often a timeline between the nominal entry into force and the date of application of the regulations which results in an obligation for the Commission to produce a report when there are practically no data.[79] The second reason

---

[66] EUPILLAR_EU 2.
[67] This point was made by F Garcimartín during his presentation entitled 'A Perspective on Rome I' at the Kick-Off Workshop on 'Cross-Border Litigation in Europe: European and British Perspectives on the Private International Law Legislative Framework, Juridical Experience and Practice' (Aberdeen, 17 April 2015).
[68] EUPILLAR_EU 1.
[69] EUPILLAR_EU 9, EUPILLAR_EU 13, EUPILLAR_EU 15, EUPILLAR_EU 16.
[70] EUPILLAR_EU 10.
[71] See Art 73.
[72] See Art 27.
[73] See Art 30.
[74] See Art 65 which requires the first review to be no later than 1 January 2012 and then every five years.
[75] See Art 74.
[76] Brussels I was reviewed and the Brussels I Recast was adopted in 2012. Brussels IIa is currently under review.
[77] EUPILLAR_EU 1, EUPILLAR_EU 9, EUPILLAR_EU 10, EUPILLAR_EU 11, EUPILLAR_EU 14, EUPILLAR_EU 16.
[78] EUPILLAR_EU 10.
[79] EUPILLAR_EU 1.

is that it is known that the review clauses can also be used, during the negotiations, to help broker a compromise,[80] and in this sense they are becoming less to do with the need for review and more to do with achieving a political agreement.[81] The third reason is that the Commission in any case can review the regulations whenever it thinks necessary even when there is no review clause that obliges it to do so.[82]

As well expressed by an interviewee, the regulations should be reviewed when there is a real objective necessity.[83] Indeed, there would not be any need for the review clauses if there would be a pattern which the EU could rely on that legislation would be, at the appropriate time, properly reviewed. In establishing such a pattern, the Commission can consistently prepare for revision of each of the instruments with thorough academic reports and thorough Green Papers to get proper consultation, and then make its proposal. However, given the political functions that the review clauses serve, they will probably continue to be used in the regulations. At least, a longer and more realistic time-frame can be set up in the regulations so that sufficient data as regards the operation of the regulations can come into being and be collected.[84] This will also help review clauses not to be devalued when the Commission may not be able to produce anything valuable because the time-frame is far too short,[85] which was the case with Rome I and Rome II.

v. Research to Prepare Evidence-based Law Reform

For the efficiency of the EU PIL framework, it is important for the EU institutions to do the necessary research to prepare evidence-based law reform in relation to the regulations.

On the part of the Commission, the interviewees assessed that the Commission is overall doing a good job as is reflected in commissioning academic research, preparing Green Papers, organising expert meetings and using expert groups.[86] As indicated at the interviews, good preparation by the Commission also increases the Commission's chance of succeeding in the Council.[87] In this regard, it is very important for the Commission to do the necessary research to prepare evidence-based law reform in relation to the EU PIL regulations. However, in addition to funding to do that, the workload of the officials of the Commission may also be an issue on this point. An interviewee explained that, during the periods when the Commission tries to produce too much legislation too quickly, such as the case in the last Commission when Commissioner Viviane Reding was Commissioner, then the officials in DG Justice are placed under very heavy pressure to do a good job in difficult circumstances.[88]

As regards impact assessment, the main problem revealed at the interviews is the response rate that the Commission receives to public consultations since in many respects

---

[80] EUPILLAR_EU 9, EUPILLAR_EU 16.
[81] EUPILLAR_EU 2, EUPILLAR_EU 13.
[82] EUPILLAR_EU 2, EUPILLAR_EU 13.
[83] EUPILLAR_EU 1.
[84] EUPILLAR_EU 9, EUPILLAR_EU 12, EUPILLAR_EU 15.
[85] EUPILLAR_EU 14.
[86] EUPILLAR_EU 1, EUPILLAR_EU 2. The interviewees were of the opinion that as regards Brussels I, an appreciable amount of research was done, whereas that was not the case with Brussels IIa, Rome I and Rome II.
[87] EUPILLAR_EU 2.
[88] EUPILLAR_EU 1.

it is disappointingly low.[89] Considering that in particular judges and practitioners are often reluctant to comment whereas lobby groups whose views are well-known but not necessarily particularly representative give a lot of input,[90] it does not seem an easy task to ensure the balance in reflecting the divergent views of the different stakeholders in this process as pointed out by the interviewees. In addition, although Expert Groups are helpful as regards the technicalities, different experts have their own schools of thought.[91] In respect of getting evidence, the Commission seems to face difficulties to collect reliable data from the Member States[92] because the Member States actually do not collect data.[93] As a result, in the process of impact assessment, the legislator grapples with detecting the right problems.[94] This makes a strong case for requiring more precise reporting requirements from Member States,[95] perhaps even in EU PIL regulations themselves,[96] as suggested at the interviews, although this may not be welcomed by the Member States due to certain considerations including the cost.[97]

On the part of the European Parliament, it is known that the Legal Affairs Committee has been commissioning studies which are particularly helpful in the reform of the EU PIL regulations.[98] As pointed out at the interviews, the Parliament has reports from experts either at hearings or at workshops and in this sense it seems to be better equipped now in terms of research and legislating on the basis of evidence.[99] The Parliament can also do their own impact assessments, including ex post impact assessments,[100] although based on the interview data, it would be welcome if the Parliament would be obliged to produce their own impact assessment if it goes beyond the Commission's proposal.[101]

III. Effectiveness of the Court of Justice of the EU in Interpreting EU Private International Law Regulations

A. An Overview of the Role of the Court of Justice of the EU

The CJEU is the judicial authority of the EU.[102] As set out in Article 19(1) of the TEU, its mission is to ensure that the law is observed in the interpretation and application of the Treaties. Pursuant to Article 19(3)(b) of the TEU, the CJEU, as part of its mission, gives

---

[89] EUPILLAR_EU 1, as explained by the interviewee, the Commission got 18 responses for Rome I.
[90] ibid.
[91] ibid.
[92] ibid.
[93] EUPILLAR_EU 8, EUPILLAR_EU 9.
[94] EUPILLAR_EU 9.
[95] EUPILLAR_EU 1.
[96] EUPILLAR_EU 8.
[97] EUPILLAR_EU 1, EUPILLAR_EU 8.
[98] For these commissioned external studies, see www.europarl.europa.eu/committees/en/juri/reports. html?action=0.
[99] EUPILLAR_EU 15.
[100] ibid.
[101] EUPILLAR_EU 2.
[102] www.curia.europa.eu/jcms/jcms/Jo2_6999/.

preliminary rulings, at the request of courts or tribunals of the Member States, on the interpretation of Union law or the validity of acts adopted by the institutions.

This function of the CJEU to give preliminary rulings is of significant importance in order to ensure the uniform application of the EU PIL regulations. It is known that, since 2002, the EU has been deliberately forming its PIL framework through regulations[103] which are binding on and directly applicable in all Member States pursuant to Article 288 of the TFEU. There is no doubt that, for the efficiency of this framework, it is not sufficient to adopt harmonised PIL rules that reflect the agreed approaches of Member States. True harmony also requires their uniform interpretation and application by the national courts of the Member States sharing different legal traditions and heritages and having their own domestic legal concepts and definitions. Although recitals may be of guidance for the uniform interpretation and application of the provisions, each national court and ultimately the CJEU decide the weight attributed to them when determining the meaning of the articles in the legislation. Therefore, the need for an autonomous Union meaning for EU legal concepts still remains.[104] It is for the CJEU to give definitive and clear interpretations to make the regulations fully effective, which increases legal certainty and predictability, and for the courts of Member States to follow an approach consistent with that in order to deal appropriately with harmonised PIL instruments.[105]

B. Selected Issues in Judicial Process and Ways Forward for the Court of Justice of the EU

i. *The Adequacy of the Current System of Preliminary References*

The interview data indicate that the current system of preliminary references is adequate in general.[106] However, its adequacy can be further strengthened if the national courts use this mechanism more appropriately. The national courts should not be too reluctant to make preliminary reference requests to the CJEU, but on the other hand they should not refer the straightforward cases, which they can decide themselves, to the CJEU either. In addition, the EUPILLAR case law data demonstrate that very low value claims can end up being ruled upon by the CJEU,[107] which does not seem to be really cost and time effective and proportionate to involve so much high level judicial manpower over such a long period to resolve small claims. This kind of case being referred to the CJEU is increasing the workload of the CJEU whereas the CJEU needs to have sufficient time to interpret novel and difficult questions of interpretation.

---

[103] See eg Green Paper on the Conversion of the Rome Convention of 1980 on the Law Applicable to Contractual Obligations into a Community Instrument and Its Modernisation ('Green Paper'), COM (2002) 654 final, 16.

[104] That is the position unless the instrument expressly refers back to the national PIL rules as being applicable, see eg Art 6(1) of the Brussels I Recast referring to national law.

[105] It is nevertheless to be noted that the CJEU may occasionally decide not to give an autonomous interpretation to a term, see eg Art 7(1)(a) Brussels I Recast in relation to the meaning of 'place of performance' and Case 12-76 *Tessili v Dunlop* [1976] ECR 01473.

[106] EUPILLAR_EU 3, EUPILLAR_EU 4, EUPILLAR_EU 5.

[107] See eg C-469/12 *Krejci Lager & Umschlagbetriebs GmbH v Olbrich Transport und Logistik GmbH* where the value in question was EUR 325, and C-45/13 *Armin Maletic and Marianne Maletic v lastminute.com Gmbh and TUI Österreich GmbH* where the claim was EUR 1,201.38. On these cases, see ch 33.

The interview data indicate that receiving a new reference from national courts on the same or similar issue may give the opportunity to the Court to address the criticism received in a previous reference.[108] Thus, this should be something that the national courts take into account in their decision on whether or not to make a request for a preliminary ruling to the CJEU on a matter that has been previously referred to it.

ii. The Style and Reasoning of the CJEU's Judgments

a. Dissenting and Concurring Opinions in the Judgments

The judgments of the CJEU do not include dissenting and concurring opinions. It is known that there has been a lot of discussion about whether or not dissenting and concurring opinions should be permitted in the Court, and there are divergent views on the issue.[109]

It would help to enhance the development of a more nuanced approach to the interpretation of EU law if dissenting and concurring opinions were permitted in the Court. There is a longstanding concern that collegial judgments can produce a lack of clarity as the tendency is for the reasoning to reflect what can be agreed as to the reasoning by all the judges after a majority has determined what will be the Court's conclusion in the case.[110] However, the interview data indicate that, due to some practical and also political reasons, the view of the members of the Court is different. The reasons given at the interviews against permitting dissenting and concurring opinions are as follows: dissenting opinions coming from a judge from a certain country could lead to certain speculations;[111] a dissenting opinion could lessen the authority of the judgment itself;[112] the mandate of the judges is renewable and there might be a problem with their independence, so the value of the dissenting opinion could be also reduced by this;[113] because of the system of the reappointment, the judges could be placed in a very uncomfortable situation;[114] and the Court is responsible for dealing with cases other than PIL which are much more sensitive from the national point of view.[115]

Some of these answers raise serious concerns in relation to the reappointment system. These concerns need to be addressed at the institutional level in order to protect the judges from any possible external pressure. There have been proposals on this issue that offer solutions to these concerns, such as revising the rules on the appointment of judges in the Treaty so as to provide one longer and non-renewable fixed term appointment;[116] and providing for the possibility of publishing the dissenting opinions anonymously.[117]

---

[108] EUPILLAR_EU 4. On this issue, see also s III.B.v below.

[109] On this issue, see generally M Adams, H de Waele, J Meeusen and G Straetmans (eds), *Judging Europe's Judges* (Oxford, Hart Publishing, 2013) and in particular J Weiler, 'Epilogue: Judging the Judges—Apology and Critique' in ibid, 235–53; R Raffeaelli, 'Dissenting opinions in the Supreme Courts of the Member States', European Parliament Committee on Legal Affairs, PE 462.470, 2012, 33–39.

[110] See Weiler, ibid, 252.

[111] EUPILLAR_EU 3.

[112] ibid.

[113] EUPILLAR_EU 4.

[114] EUPILLAR_EU 5.

[115] ibid.

[116] Currently, pursuant to Art 19(2) of the TEU and Art 223 of the TFEU, the Judges and the AGs of the Court of Justice and the Judges of the General Court are appointed by common accord of the governments of the Member States for six years, and this is renewable.

[117] For these suggestions, see eg Weiler, above n 109, 252, and Raffeaelli, above n 109, 37.

b. AG's Opinion

Pursuant to Article 252 of the TFEU, the CJEU is assisted by an AG who makes reasoned submissions on cases that require his or her involvement. Although the Court is not bound by the AG's Opinion, the EUPILLAR case law data demonstrate that it follows the Opinion in a large number of cases.[118] In this regard, the Opinions of AGs are quite influential.[119] There are a relatively large number of cases where the Court, after hearing the AG, gave judgment without an Opinion,[120] although in some of these cases an Opinion would be helpful.[121]

There are a small number of cases where the Court did not follow the AG's Opinion. The interview data indicate that although there are no methodological differences in the interpretation by the Court and the AGs,[122] as well expressed by an interviewee, 'there is a difference between how the Court writes a judgment (and why it's written that way) and how an AG writes an Opinion (and why that is written that way)'.[123] In this regard, the interviewees made the following points: the AG writes his Opinion alone whereas the Court decides in a colloquium which results in the judgments being a compromise,[124] the AG gives an opinion whereas the Court has to decide a case,[125] and the analysis of an AG is much more in depth and thorough since the AGs do not have the same restraints as the Court in reaching the final decision.[126]

It is interesting to note that, as indicated by the EUPILLAR interview and case law data, in cases where the Court agrees with the AG, the Court refers to the AG's Opinion whereas where the Court disagrees with the AG, the Court does not discuss in the judgment the reasons why it disagrees with the AG.[127] The interview data indicate two main reasons for this practice. One of them is that, as a sign of respect, the judges avoid openly criticising either opinions of AGs or of the EU institutions.[128] The second one is a budget issue in relation to translation costs, since it is an external service and the longer the judgment gets, the more expensive it becomes.[129]

As expressed by an interviewee, it is neither the task of the Court to deliver an explicit explanation nor is this the function of the Court's judgments, but the language of a Court's judgment should be clear to such an extent that it is clear why the Court disagrees with the AG's Opinion. However, if the judgments were to explain the reasons why the Court disagrees with the AG and does not follow the AG's Opinion, this could help to enhance the development of a more nuanced approach to the interpretation of EU law. As an

---

[118] See chs 33 and 41.

[119] For a recent study which aims to measure the influence of the AG on the CJEU, see C Arrebola, AJ Mauricio and HJ Portilla, 'An Econometric Analysis of the Influence of the Advocate General on the Court of Justice of the European Union' University of Cambridge Faculty of Law Legal Studies, Research Paper Series, Paper No 3/2016.

[120] The Court may do so if it is decided that the case raises no new question of law, see www.curia.europa.eu/jcms/jcms/Jo2_7024/en/.

[121] See chs 33 and 41.

[122] EUPILLAR_EU 4.

[123] EUPILLAR_EU 7.

[124] EUPILLAR_EU 3.

[125] EUPILLAR_EU 4.

[126] EUPILLAR_EU 5.

[127] EUPILLAR_EU 9, EUPILLAR_EU 3. For these cases, see also chs 33 and 41.

[128] EUPILLAR_EU 6.

[129] ibid.

interviewee explained, it is possible to do so since the current rule is a non-written rule so that it could be changed at any moment.[130]

iii. *The Length of the Proceedings in the CJEU*

The length of the proceedings is an important parameter for accessing justice. Excessive delays in proceedings could raise a concern in the light of Article 6(1) of the European Convention on Human Rights,[131] which requires 'a fair and public hearing within a reasonable time'.

The EUPILLAR case law data demonstrate that there are a few cases where there is a significant delay before the CJEU (such as C-213/10 *F-Tex SIA v Lietuvos-Anglijos UAB 'Jadecloud-Vilma'*[132] decided in 23 months, C-406/09 *Realchemie Nederland BV v Bayer CropScience AG*[133] decided in 24 months, C-543/10 *Refcomp SpA v Axa Corporate Solutions Assurance SA and Others*[134] decided in 26 months and most notably C-180/06 *Renate Ilsinger v Martin Dreschers*[135] decided in 37 months),[136] which is called a 'Luxembourg torpedo' by some lawyers.[137] The length of the procedure raises serious concerns relating to the delay in justice that can arise before national courts of the EU where a significant additional time is taken to deal with a preliminary reference to the CJEU. However, it is to be acknowledged that the statistics in the Annual Report of 2015 of the CJEU[138] show improvements on this issue which states that the average duration of proceedings is 15.6 months.[139]

The interviewees expressed that it would be useful to shorten the length of the procedure, but it is not possible to significantly shorten it despite all endeavours of the members of the Court and the improvements in the institution, because translating the documents into all 24 official languages does take a lot of time.[140] It was stated at the interviews that the real procedure itself, ie deciding the order, the hearing, the deliberation, and delivering the judgment, takes generally just six or eight months.[141] As one of the interviewees explained, an AG has nine weeks after the hearing to present an Opinion, but in reality, it is only four or five weeks for the AG and the rest is for the translation.[142] This reveals that further improvements are needed on the issue of translation at the institutional level since translating all documents into all 24 official languages causes considerable delay and cost. One suggestion

---

[130] EUPILLAR_EU 3.
[131] The Convention for the Protection of Human Rights and Fundamental Freedoms.
[132] EU:C:2012:215.
[133] [2011] ECR I-09773.
[134] EU:C:2013:62.
[135] [2009] ECR I-03961.
[136] See ch 33.
[137] See eg A Dickinson, 'Trust and Confidence in the European Community Supreme Court?' available at www.conflictoflaws.net/2008/guest-editorial-dickinson-on-trust-and-confidence-in-the-european-community-supreme-court/.
[138] http://curia.europa.eu/jcms/upload/docs/application/pdf/2016-10/qdaq16001enn.pdf.
[139] See ibid 28.
[140] EUPILLAR_EU 3, EUPILLAR_EU 4, EUPILLAR_EU 5.
[141] EUPILLAR_EU 3.
[142] EUPILLAR_EU 5.

that might be discussed in this context is that the Court should work primarily in three languages, which are English, French and German.[143]

On the other hand, preliminary rulings are dealt with by the CJEU swiftly under the urgent preliminary ruling procedure, ie the PPU, which was established in 2008.[144] As stated in the Annual Report of 2015, the average duration of the urgent preliminary ruling procedure is 1.9 months.[145] The CJEU has applied this procedure in a very commendable way to sensitive cases under the Brussels IIa Regulation.[146] The case of C-376/14 PPU *C* concerning the concept of the wrongful removal or retention of a child within the meaning of Brussels IIa and the procedure to be followed when a court is seised, on the basis of the 1980 Hague Convention, of an application for return of a child who has allegedly been wrongfully removed or retained in another Member State, is one example where the CJEU delivered its judgment in about two months under the urgent preliminary ruling procedure.

It is to be noted that the urgent preliminary ruling procedure seems to work well at the moment because the number of PPU cases is low for now and the CJEU has taken different organisational measures in order to be sufficiently prepared to deal with these cases.[147] However, the interviews indicate that time constraint is an issue for the members of the Court and that there is a real issue if the number of PPU cases increases significantly. As explained by the interviewees, there is only one chamber of five judges and one AG per year dealing with PPU cases as well as their ordinary duties,[148] and whereas the work and the quality of analysis is the same, the judges and the AG need to be much quicker in PPU.[149] This usually results in the AG having to leave aside other cases to concentrate entirely on the PPU,[150] and the judges have to give their decision quickly without having much opportunity to think it over.[151] When the efficiency of the PPU is assessed from this point of view, as one of the interviewees pointed out, the PPU has risks because it is a preliminary ruling procedure which has an erga omnes effect but which has to be dealt with very quickly.[152]

---

[143] For this suggestion made by Hartley, see T Hartley, 'Balance of Competences in the European Union: The Court of Justice of the EU' available at www.gov.uk/government/uploads/system/uploads/attachment_data/file/279275/professor-trevor-hartley-evidence.pdf, 5.

[144] The procedure is applicable in the areas relating to the area of freedom, security and justice. There is no list of situations that the procedure applies to. However, the procedure might be applied in the cases such as where the question raised is with regard to a person in custody or deprived of his liberty and the answer is decisive as to the assessment of that person's legal situation or, in proceedings concerning parental authority or custody of children. For the application of this procedure, 'the request must set out the matters of fact and law which establish the urgency and, in particular, the risks involved in following the normal preliminary ruling procedure.' For this and more information on the urgent preliminary ruling procedure, see Notices from European Union Institutions, Bodies, Offices and Agency- Court of Justice of the European Union, Information Note on References From National Courts For A Preliminary Ruling ([2008] OJ C160/1), 37.

[145] See the Annual Report of 2015, above n 138, 28.

[146] See ch 41.

[147] EUPILLAR_EU 4.

[148] EUPILLAR_EU 5, EUPILLAR_EU 7.

[149] EUPILLAR_EU 5.

[150] ibid.

[151] EUPILLAR_EU 3.

[152] ibid. On the issue of the PPU, see also the article written by a CJEU Judge, A Rosas, 'Justice in Haste, Justice Denied? The European Court of Justice and the Area of Freedom, Security and Justice' (2009) 11 *Cambridge Yearbook of European Legal Studies* 1.

iv. Establishment of Specialised Chambers

The CJEU does not have specialised chambers for any field of law. Like the issue of dissenting and concurring opinions, there has been a lot of discussion also about specialisation in the Court and there are divergent views on it.

Given that greater specialisation of courts dealing with PIL issues would help to ensure a higher quality of decision-making and greater efficiency in doing so, this specialisation would be welcome also in the CJEU by the establishment of a dedicated chamber on PIL. Although the CJEU generally interprets the EU PIL regulations well, there are several controversial decisions where the Court's interpretations do not reflect the intention of the EU legislature.[153] There is no doubt that the members of the Court are good jurists as the Treaty under Article 253 requires as to the specification of the members[154] and, as expressed at the interviews, they all learn and are ready to learn all the time.[155] However, considering the significant variety of issues that are being referred to the CJEU and the limited time that the members of the Court have to decide a case, specialisation could offer a better solution for the CJEU in dealing with preliminary rulings and it could also increase the effectiveness of the CJEU in the development of EU law.

This view is not shared by the CJEU interviewees though, who all expressed that there should not be a specialised chamber, in any field, in the Court, and that the Court needs a general approach. The reasons given at the interviews against establishing specialised chambers are as follows: from an organisational point of view, PIL cases are not numerous and therefore a specialised chamber on PIL does not seem necessary;[156] it is generally difficult to define the limits of PIL as every case that the Court deals with concerning the EU PIL regulations affects also material law, private law in general, civil procedure of a Member State, and some principles of civil procedure which have been developed in the EU;[157] specialised chambers in courts such as the CJEU would not help and on the contrary there must be a more general view on the issue which the Court takes;[158] a judge of the CJEU must deal with several types of cases;[159] and a specialist service is asked where necessary.[160] As further clarified by an interviewee, the Court needs and has specialists in various fields of EU law but the Court's approach is for each Judge and AG to become a generalist.[161] The interviewee also noted that there are not specialised courts in many Member States but jurisdiction works nonetheless and that the Court's system reflects the system in many Member States.[162] Another interviewee stated that the Court cannot afford to have specialised jurisdiction with the Court of Justice of 28 Judges and 11 AGs.[163] One disadvantage of such a specialised system from the perspective of the member of the Court is that one can always expect from an AG who specialises in a certain area of law what he or she would

---

[153] See chs 33 and 41.
[154] EUPILLAR_EU 6.
[155] EUPILLAR_EU 5.
[156] EUPILLAR_EU 6.
[157] EUPILLAR_EU 3.
[158] ibid.
[159] EUPILLAR_EU 6.
[160] ibid.
[161] EUPILLAR_EU 4.
[162] ibid.
[163] EUPILLAR_EU 5.

write in his or her opinion, however the essence of the role of AG is that the AGs should sometimes provoke the discussion and suggest the departure from the well-established case law in some areas.[164] It was also stated that it is important for all chambers of the Court, if possible, to be composed in a way which reflects judicial diversity.[165]

One of the difficulties establishing specialist chambers, as expressed by an interviewee, is that the Court cannot arrange to have specialist chambers because the Court has no control over whether the judges and AGs who are sent to serve to the Court are specialists in a particular area.[166] As the interviewee rightly further pointed out:

> [T]he Member States nominate people who fulfil the Treaty criteria in the sense that they are qualified to sit in the highest jurisdiction in their own Member State; but there is no way that the Court can ensure that it gets from Member States a new Judge or a new Advocate General with a particular legal background.[167]

There has been a suggestion that a Judicial Appointments committee should be established to make appointments to the CJEU[168] which might help to overcome the difficulty addressed by the interviewee.

It is known that the issue of establishing specialised chambers has been discussed by the Court on various occasions and has been rejected. It would be ideal if references concerning the EU PIL regulations could be dealt with by a specialist chamber with at least one AG being a specialist in PIL and by at least five judges being specialists in or specially trained in PIL with supporting specialist Legal Secretaries. However, one might validly argue against establishing such a specialised system in the Court for any field of law. Considering this with the view of the members of the Court not favouring a specialised system, it is to be acknowledged that specialisation in the Court by establishing specialist chambers with one having a remit for PIL does not seem to be realistic to achieve in the short to medium term. There has been another suggestion, which could perhaps be realised more easily and quicker, that a private-law section should be established within the CJEU and cases concerning private law (including PIL) should be allocated to that section and heard by judges with experience in that area.[169] Such a solution would also help to address the critiques about the Court's controversial interpretations on the EU PIL regulations that were given by the chambers whose members mostly have a public law or European law background.[170]

v. Openness of the CJEU to Criticism

The reasoning of the CJEU in some cases and the quality of the judgments, particularly where the Court has interpreted PIL instruments, are sometimes criticised.[171] The criticism of the CJEU is not just from academics but also, to some extent, from the officials of the

---

[164] ibid.
[165] EUPILLAR_EU 7.
[166] ibid.
[167] ibid.
[168] For this suggestion made by Hartley, see Hartley, above n 143, 6.
[169] ibid.
[170] For this critique, see eg Dickinson, above n 137.
[171] See eg ibid.

EU legislative institutions as to how well the CJEU ensures that the will of the EU legislature is discerned and respected.[172]

The EUPILLAR case law data show that the CJEU, overall, interprets the EU PIL regulations well, although there are issues where the CJEU needs to re-consider its existing interpretations and change some of them.[173] On this point, it is reassuring that the Court is very open to listen to critical analysis of judgments in all fields of law, as indicated by the interviewees from the Court.[174] Some interviewees expressed the view that the Judges and AGs read academic writings concerning their judgments, and if another case of the same type arrives at the CJEU, they work on all the critiques on the former judgment very well, take note of them and sometimes follow some theoretical approaches.[175] The *West Tankers* case[176] was given as an example at the interviews. An interviewee explained that, in the *Gazprom* case,[177] even if it is not directly seen from the judgment, the CJEU took into account the lessons learnt from *West Tankers*, quoted directly several paragraphs of the *West Tankers* judgment and tried to explain a little further what it said in the *West Tankers* case.[178] More evidence of this willingness to learn from external critiques in the AG's Opinions and in the judgments of the CJEU would be welcome.[179]

IV. Conclusion

The EU institutions of the Commission, the Council, the European Parliament and the CJEU play a significant role in the effectiveness of the EU PIL framework. Empirical evidence that this chapter relies on indicates that the EU legislature and the CJEU overall do a very good job in making and interpreting the EU PIL regulations respectively under their own institutional dynamics. However, there is still scope for further improvements at the institutional level, as put forward by this chapter.

As regards the legislative activity, enhancing the quality of the interaction between the Council and Parliament in the ordinary legislative procedure, reviewing the usefulness of the qualified majority requirement in non-family law matters and of unanimity in family law matters, enhancing the appropriate use of interpretation tools and considering re-introduction of the explanatory report to the system, reviewing the usefulness of the review clauses in the regulations and conducting thorough research to prepare evidence-based law reform are needed for a more effective and efficient EU law-making system.

---

[172] EUPILLAR_EU 10, EUPILLAR_EU 11, EUPILLAR_EU 14, EUPILLAR_EU 15, EUPILLAR_EU 16. On this issue, see also chs 33 and 41.

[173] See chs 33 and 41.

[174] EUPILLAR_EU 3, EUPILLAR_EU 4, EUPILLAR_EU 5, EUPILLAR_EU 6, EUPILLAR_EU 7.

[175] EUPILLAR_EU 3, EUPILLAR_EU 4, EUPILLAR_EU 5, EUPILLAR_EU 6.

[176] C-185/07 *Allianz SpA, formerly Riunione Adriatica di Sicurtà SpA, Generali Assicurazioni Generali SpA v West Tankers Inc* [2009] ECR I-00663.

[177] C-536/13 '*Gazprom*' *OAO v Lietuvos Respublika*.

[178] EUPILLAR_EU 3.

[179] Looking at the issue from another perspective, we, the academics, should also be open to revise the well-established academic doctrines and be more aware of the real life problems coming from PIL that practitioners and the CJEU are facing, as stated by one of the interviewees: EUPILLAR_EU 5.

As regards the judicial activity, several things could be done to enhance the effectiveness of the CJEU. First, the style and the reasoning of the judgments can be further improved particularly by permitting individual opinions and providing clear reasons why there is a disagreement with the AG. Second, the usefulness of translating all the documents into all official languages, which seems to create pressure on the Court to keep costs down and increases the length of time it takes to give its rulings, needs to be re-considered. Third, a certain degree of specialisation within the CJEU can be established through a private law section to which cases concerning private law (including PIL) would be allocated. Fourth, the protection of the members of the Court from any unfair external pressure needs to be increased by making appointments for a fixed and non-renewable term. Last but not least, more education and legal training, and a more efficient network and open dialogue among the EU institutions themselves and between the EU institutions and national judges, practitioners and academics, are also welcome to further improve the effectiveness of the EU PIL framework.

4

Unharmonised Procedural Rules: Is there a Case for Further Harmonisation at EU Level?

JONATHAN FITCHEN

I. Introduction

The basic premise of this chapter is that the EU has already partially harmonised national procedural rules by means of its private international law (hereafter PIL) Regulations. This premise is derived from the proposition that 'private international law' (which name should usually be understood to be interchangeable with 'conflict of laws' in this chapter), if considered in broad functional terms, is part of a legal system's procedural law:[1] it follows that when the EU harmonises aspects of PIL it also thereby harmonises aspects of domestic civil procedure law. This assumed premise leads to a central question concerning whether there is a compelling political or legal case for the EU to engage in further harmonisation of Member State civil procedure concerning the Regulations examined by this study, or even of the subject of EU PIL in general. If either part of the preceding question is answered in the affirmative the next question concerns the possibilities of further harmonisation and necessitates an examination of the related questions of what should be harmonised and how this harmonisation should be effected within the EU's legislative competence. This chapter addresses these issues in four substantive parts and concludes that logic and evidence both indicate a compelling need for further reform. The novel aspect of this chapter is that its suggested reforms (reform of the procedure by which preliminary references can be referred to the Court of Justice of the European Union (CJEU), and, the creation of an intra-EU forum for the curation and improvement of EU PIL) diverge from the reform suggestions usually encountered and focus on relatively simple and inexpensive methods by which the targeted or general curation of the Regulations that constitute EU PIL and its procedures may be achieved.

---

[1] This suggestion may strike those used to different national conceptions of the nature and scope of legal procedure as odd. For the purposes of this study, and also for the purposes of conceptualising the European Union law relating thereunto, a wider 'functional' view is suggested.

II. To What Extent has the EU already Harmonised National Procedural Rules?

In the course of setting out its legislative interventions in private international law, the EU has necessarily been involved in the consequential amendment of domestic rules of civil procedure of the Member States subject to its harmonising legislation. The essential points to note from the foregoing sentence are the necessity and consequentiality that have informed the EU's adjustments of national procedural rules by means of PIL harmonisation. The EU has not used PIL harmonisations (or any other harmonisation competence) to implement a general plan specifically aimed at the general reform of the civil procedure laws of Member State legal systems: although such a general plan has certain atavistic attractions for academic lawyers, it also has a vast scope, many notionally equivalent candidate donors and, arguably, pre-supposes the prior unification of Member State laws and legal systems. Even the scope of the subject of civil procedure reform across the European Union's own legal instruments and laws is huge; EU procedural law not only concerns PIL Regulations, but other diverse aspects of civil procedure law which interact with domestic civil procedure laws across all 28 Member States.[2] This chapter is however restricted to a consideration of certain EU PIL Regulations by the terms of the present study.

The EU PIL harmonisation that has occurred to date has been consequential upon, and incidental to, legislative reform of legal issues that the EU has, at different times, identified as deserving of its legislative intervention via a new or updated PIL Convention or Regulation.[3] This observation is not meant to diminish the EU's accomplishments, but rather to invite a proper appreciation of the current position and, more importantly, to set the suggestion of further harmonisation of national procedural rules in context: a specific EU plan to harmonise the civil procedure rules touching EU PIL would mark a departure from, and not a continuation of, its earlier incidental legislative interventions into the reform of domestic PIL and civil procedure.

The approach to the harmonisation of PIL taken by the EU to date, and hence to the direct and incidental harmonisation of domestic civil procedure rules, is most simply exemplified by the original plan of action concerning the first example of such European harmonisation; the Brussels Convention on jurisdiction and the enforcement of judgments in civil

---

[2] For further detail on the unrestricted scope of this area of law see generally, E Storskrubb, *Civil Procedure and EU Law: A Policy Area Uncovered* (Oxford, Oxford University Press, 2008); B Hess, 'The State of the Civil Justice Union' in B Hess, M Bergström, E Storskrubb, *EU Civil Justice—Current Issues and Future Outlook* (Oxford, Hart Publishing, 2016) (hereafter, Hess, Bergström and Storskrubb). For an introduction to the EU law concerning a number of matters not addressed in this chapter (including service of proceedings, taking of evidence and cooperation in civil matters) see D McClean, *International Co-operation In Civil And Criminal Matters* 3rd edn (Oxford, Oxford University Press, 2012). See also the comment by E Guinchard (2011) 47(4) *RTD eur* 871, on the Commission proposal for what would become Reg (EU) No 655/2014 of the European Parliament and of the Council of 15 May 2014 establishing a European Account Preservation Order procedure to facilitate cross-border debt recovery in civil and commercial matters [2014] OJ L189/59.

[3] See P Beaumont and M Danov, 'The EU Civil Justice Framework and Private Law: "Integration through (Private International) Law' (2015) 22(5) *Maastricht Journal of European and Comparative Law* 706–31 also M Danov and P Beaumont, 'Measuring the Effectiveness of the EU Civil Justice Framework: Theoretical and Methodological Challenges' (2015–16) XVII *Yearbook of Private International Law* 151–80.

and commercial matters of 1968.[4] This Convention was intended to replace and to improve the incomplete and, where present, sometimes threadbare patchwork of earlier bilateral arrangements between the Member States by introducing a single European system that, in accordance with Article 220 EEC, would allow the simplification of the formalities concerning the cross-border recognition and enforcement of civil and commercial judgments between the original six EEC Member States. To achieve the central goal of expedited and mutual recognition and enforcement of judgments, it was deemed necessary to also provide a common set of rules governing the international jurisdiction of Member State courts in civil and commercial matters. If the jurisdiction of the EEC court that created the incoming judgment was accepted, there would be fewer legitimate reasons to obstruct the *exequatur* concerning the resulting judgment when it was produced in the Member State addressed. Thus the Convention set out the essential and overriding imperative rules and procedures necessary for it to so operate in Member State legal systems. These rules affected existing rules of domestic civil procedure by diverting matters concerning qualifying judgments away from existing domestic procedures, as laid down in civil procedure rules or earlier bilateral conventions, and towards the new rules and procedures set out in the Convention. The new rules, inter alia, repressed certain exorbitant peculiarities of jurisdiction, introduced a harmonised *exequatur* procedure and restricted former domestic possibilities for raising procedural or substantive objections to incoming 'Convention judgments': thus the Convention dispensed with now redundant reciprocity, forbade any *revision au fond* concerning the incoming judgment, set a procedure for *exequatur* and restricted the bases on which that *exequatur* could be refused, limited or postponed to the circumstances expressly permitted by the Convention.

To the extent that Convention provisions overrode and reformulated the domestic possibilities previously available to the domestic court, or to judgment debtors/creditors, they may be regarded as a form of procedural harmonisation incidental to the main purpose of the Convention. However, the drafters of the Convention were motivated by the desire to quickly achieve a simplification of the cross-border transmission of civil and commercial judgments so they only provided such overriding procedural provisions as seemed necessary to allow the Convention to operate. In this sense the design and execution of the Brussels Convention may be said to resemble the design brief apocryphally attributed to the US Army's Jeep by containing, 'Just Enough Essential (civil) Procedure'. The design of the Brussels Convention was thus intentionally partial and directed solely to the operation of its own essential provisions: what seemed to be non-essential aspects of civil procedure were left to the procedural law of each Member State.[5] The Convention did not seek to govern non-civil and commercial matters which were outside its scope, and nor did it attempt to replace or influence the varied domestic civil procedure rules of the Member States concerning any matter excluded from the Convention's temporal or material scope.

The Brussels Convention established the basic subsequent pattern for the EU's sectoral approach to the harmonisation of discrete areas of PIL that, except for the change to Regulation form, continues to the present day. Despite the improvement of now proceeding

---

[4] See P Jenard, Report on the Convention on jurisdiction and the enforcement of judgments in civil and commercial matters [1979] OJ C59/1.

[5] See Art 33 of the Brussels Convention echoed by Art 40 of the Brussels I Regulation and by Art 41(1) of the Brussels Ia Regulation.

via directly applicable and periodically reviewable EU Regulations, the EU has essentially remained true to the same modus operandi concerning the PIL Regulations that concern this study. Though changes in the legislative procedure and legal base over the years render the following summary somewhat impressionistic, the basic process seems to begin with the identification of a threat to the operation of an important aspect of the European Union that resides within the diverse, and hence uncertain or unpredictable, private international laws operating within the EU. This leads to the issuance of a corrective legislative proposal and to initial consultations followed by the preparation of a draft measure which, eventually, is referred for detailed negotiations to expert representatives from the Member States and the EU. If all necessary agreements are reached, the final agreed text will lead to a new EU PIL measure.[6] The original development of the 1968 Brussels Convention exemplifies this modernistic process.

The subsequent development of what for ease of reference will be called 'the Brussels I regime' also exemplifies the typical modernising approach to the improvement of an existing measure of EU PIL in light of integrative developments within the EU and also to remedy earlier defects or to reflect subsequent events. After various adjustments at the point of new accessions, the Brussels Convention[7] was developed into the Brussels I Regulation which, inter alia, automated the recognition of judgments and simplified the *exequatur* process.[8] The latest development of these provisions resulted from the recasting of the Brussels I Regulation.[9] The Brussels Ia Regulation has, inter alia, abolished the foreign *exequatur* requirement and added automatic enforcement of judgments to the automatic recognition introduced by its forerunner.[10]

Similar developmental trends can be discerned in relation to the far murkier legislative history of the Brussels II regime:[11] the first attempt at what would become the

---

[6] For an example of what may occur if such agreement is *not* forthcoming see, Council Reg (EU) 2016/1103 of 24 June 2016 implementing enhanced cooperation in the area of jurisdiction, applicable law and the recognition and enforcement of decisions in matters of matrimonial property regimes, [2016] OJ L183/1 and Council Reg (EU) 2016/1104 of 24 June 2016 implementing enhanced cooperation in the area of jurisdiction, applicable law and the recognition and enforcement of decisions in matters of the property consequences of registered partnerships, [2016] OJ L183/30. Also see the Proposal for a Council Decision authorising enhanced cooperation in the area of jurisdiction, applicable law and the recognition and enforcement of decisions on the property regimes of international couples, covering both matters of matrimonial property regimes and the property consequences of registered partnerships Brussels, 2.3.2016 COM(2016) 108 final and also the draft Regs associated with this Decision on Enhanced Cooperation between 17 Member States, Brussels, 2.3.2016 COM(2016) 107 final and Brussels, 2.3.2016 COM(2016) 106 final.

[7] The original pre-Accession Convention 1968 Brussels Convention on jurisdiction and the enforcement of judgments in civil and commercial matters (Consolidated version) [1972] OJ L 299/32 see http://eur-lex.europa.eu/legal-content/EN/ALL/?uri=CELEX:41968A0927(01). For a version taking account of the various Accession Conventions, before the Brussels Convention was largely replaced by the Brussels I Reg, see [1998] OJ C27/1.

[8] See Council Reg (EC) No 44/2001 of 22 December 2000 on jurisdiction and the recognition and enforcement of judgments in civil and commercial matters, [2001] OJ L12/1.

[9] Concerning recasting as a technique see http://ec.europa.eu/dgs/legal_service/recasting_en.htm.

[10] Reg (EU) No 1215/2012 of the European Parliament and of the Council of 12 December 2012 on jurisdiction and the recognition and enforcement of judgments in civil and commercial matters, [2012] OJ L351/1.

[11] For an attempt to navigate through the considerable early uncertainties, see P McEleavy, 'The Brussels II Regulation: How The European Community Has Moved Into Family Law' (2002) *International and Comparative Law Quarterly* 883 at 888; also P McEleavy, 'Private International Law: Brussels II bis: Matrimonial Matters, Parental Responsibility, Child Abduction And Mutual Recognition' (2004) *International and Comparative Law Quarterly* 503 at 504–05. See also the legislative history in the Commission's Brussels IIa recasting proposal http://ec.europa.eu/justice/civil/files/family-matters/brussels2_regulation_en.pdf.

Brussels II regime was a European Convention on Jurisdiction, Recognition and Enforcement of Judgments in Matrimonial Matters,[12] this was swiftly transformed into the first Brussels II Regulation[13] and, in turn, was upgraded to the Brussels IIa Regulation by 2003.[14] The European Commission is currently proposing a recasting of the Brussels IIa Regulation that, if adopted, would, inter alia, abolish the existing *exequatur* requirement; encourage the concentration of some 'family law' cases in expert courts; re-emphasise the importance of hearing the child (to reduce the likelihood of refusals of recognition predicated on a failure to do so); and improve the actual enforcement of decisions on parental responsibility.[15] Each of these proposals would develop the existing Brussels IIa Regulation and also affect current Member State procedures relating thereunto.

Though neither of the applicable law Regulations considered by this project have yet undergone a recasting exercise, the legislative development of the Rome I Regulation followed aspects of the trend sketched above by proceeding from a convention between EEC States[16] to an EU Regulation.[17] Though the determination of the applicable law for non-contractual obligations was dropped from the 1980 Rome Convention, the Rome II Regulation of 2007 can also trace its origins to the preliminary work undertaken within the EEC in the run up to the 1980 Rome Convention and to the intergovernmental work done under the EU justice and home affairs pillar in the 1990s.[18] Both the Rome I and Rome II Regulations contain review clauses directed to the preparation of reports concerning specific issues: reports have been received by the Commission but seemingly with little immediate prospect of significant change for either Regulation.[19]

A. Advantages of the Existing Approach

The immediate advantage of this method of proceeding by laying down imperative provisions and only affecting the essential procedural rules is that it reduces the scope and complexity of the matters to be addressed during negotiations involving the Member States, the European Commission and the European Parliament. It also ostensibly accommodates existing diversity in areas of domestic civil procedure that seem non-essential for the intended operation of the given EU Regulation. The benefits of such a pragmatic approach

---

[12] See Council Act of 28 May 1998 drawing up, on basis of Art K.3 of the Treaty on European Union, the Convention on Jurisdiction and the Recognition and Enforcement of Judgments in Matrimonial Matters, [1998] OJ C221/01 (and see [1998] OJ C 221/02-05 for further information on the Convention).

[13] Council Reg (EC) No 1347/2000 of 29 May 2000 on jurisdiction and the recognition and enforcement of judgments in matrimonial matters and in matters of parental responsibility for children of both spouses, [2000] OJ L160/19.

[14] Council Reg (EC) No 2201/2003 of 27 November 2003 concerning jurisdiction and the recognition and enforcement of judgments in matrimonial matters and the matters of parental responsibility, repealing Reg (EC) No 1347/2000 [2003] OJ L338/01.

[15] COM(2016) 411 final.

[16] 1980 Rome Convention on the law applicable to contractual obligations (consolidated version), [1998] OJ C27/34.

[17] Reg (EC) No 593/2008 of the European Parliament and of the Council of 17 June 2008 on the law applicable to contractual obligations (Rome I) [2008] OJ L177/6–16. The Rome II Reg of 2007 is also yet to be recast.

[18] Reg (EC) No 864/2007 of the European Parliament and of the Council of 11 July 2007 on the law applicable to non-contractual obligations (Rome II) [2007] OJ L199/40.

[19] See Art 27 of Rome I and Art 30 of Rome II. The reports may be accessed from http://ec.europa.eu/justice/civil/document/index_en.htm.

to the creation and the drafting of a new EU PIL instrument were obvious even when the negotiations only involved the original six Member States; as current negotiations now involve 25 to 28 Member States; such an approach is essential if a new or recast EU PIL Regulation is ever to progress to final approval.

The EU's minimalist and sectoral approach to procedural harmonisation has two further practical advantages: first, the relative ease and speed of national implementation, and, second, the accommodation of other non-EU PIL provisions in Member State legal systems. The last advantage concerns an important limiting factor on the current harmonisation potential of EU PIL, and of any incidental harmonisation of domestic civil procedure laws that this may involve. Member State legal systems still need to be able to deal with *any* private international law case that may arise; not merely with those that obligingly fall within the material or temporal scope of a given EU (or other international) provision. Accordingly, the harmonisation of PIL and civil procedure laws by EU Regulation (or by the Hague Convention) must continue to tolerate and accommodate aspects of the domestic laws and procedures concerning cases that fall outside the given harmonisation provision.

B. Disadvantages of the Existing Approach

The approach to harmonisation set out above is not without problems: the Brussels I case law shows that even amongst the original six Member States, it was not necessarily simple to identify and to correct residual domestic procedural peculiarities that might adversely interact with the actual operation of the Brussels Convention.[20] A further issue arising from the minimalist approach is the possibility for legal systems to drift away from the correct application of Convention provisions and towards interpretations that perhaps are unduly influenced by domestic principles and procedural possibilities that, but for the existence of the Convention, would have been available to the domestic court or to one (or both) of the parties.[21] In some circumstances a reference to the CJEU may suffice to correct the drift and to clarify the uniform application of the measure. If, however, there is no prospect of a reference to the CJEU, and assuming that the courts in the relevant Member State cannot be convinced that their corrective intervention in the operation of existing civil procedure rules is mandated by their duties in relation to Article 4(3) Treaty on European Union (TEU), Article 19(1) TEU, or via Article 47 European Union Charter of Fundamental Rights (EUCFR), then a 'legislative' intervention by the EU is currently the only feasible corrective option. For example, previously some courts took the view that they were entitled to raise Brussels Convention exceptions to recognition and enforcement on an own motion basis during an *exequatur* application:[22] this error was neutralised in the course of converting the

---

[20] There are many early cases that illustrate the point, a non-exhaustive selection can include: Case 42/76 *de Wolf v Cox BV* [1976] ECR 1759; Case 43/77 *Industrial Diamond Supplies v Riva* [1977] ECR 2175; Case 15/78 *Société Générale Alsacienne de Banque SA v Koestler* [1978] ECR 1971; Case 166/80 *Klomps v Michel* [1981] ECR 1593 and Case 27/81 *Etablisments Rohr Société Anonyme v Ossberger* [1981] ECR 2431.

[21] See the findings of national reports discussed in part III below, also consider attempts by English courts to employ anti-suit injunctions inside the Brussels I Regime: Case C-159/02 *Turner v Grovit* [2004] ECR I-3565 and Case C-185/07 *Allianz v West Tankers* [2009] ECR I-663.

[22] See the Commission's Explanatory Memorandum COM(1999) 348 final at 21.

Brussels Convention into the Brussels I Regulation by changing the *exequatur* procedure. It should however be noted that such opportunities for corrective interventions may not often be available, or may not be politically feasible.[23]

Identifying and correcting procedural problems is of course more difficult if the problem arises from the interaction of two different, and otherwise individually compliant, sets of civil procedure rules: in this situation it may be that each Member State successfully complies with the requirements of the relevant EU PIL but does so in a way that only causes problems for the individual who would uphold rights or remedies from Member State 'A' in Member State 'B'. At this point we are entering the realm of an emerging European Union form of adaptation or assimilation (*Anpassung/Angleichung*) that is increasingly found in EU PIL legislation as an official means for the court or authorities in Member State 'B' to avoid unnecessary prejudice to the right-holder from Member State 'A'.[24] It is not yet clear how often this European form of adaptation will be applied in practice, nor what effects it will produce in the civil procedure laws of the Member States involved. Further, it remains to be seen what principles and developmental possibilities the CJEU can discover and extract from 'adaptation' when encountering this concept on a preliminary reference.

III. Is There a Compelling Political or Legal Case for Further Harmonisation of Procedural Rules by the EU?

In its 2010 Action Plan the EU suggested that by 2013 there should be a Green Paper concerning the improvement of consistency of the civil procedure in EU legislation and that by the end of 2014 there should be a 'Legislative proposal aimed at improving the consistency of existing Union legislation in the field of civil procedure law'; in a sense therefore the EU has already given a positive indication in 2010 that it tended to favour a general harmonisation of its own laws to improve their internal consistency in relation to procedural law.[25] With respect, this ambitious and widely drawn task (extending across *all* EU legislation containing or affecting civil procedure) was impractical in the time available: the 2010 Action Plan ended in 2014 without the official publication of either a Green Paper or a legislative proposal by the European Commission.[26] Since 2014, a somewhat less ambitious and more sensibly focussed approach to the issue of improving the consistency of the

---

[23] The difficulty is acute if the error is very particular to a given Member State which sees no error, eg the UK in the aftermath of *Re Harrods (Buenos Aires) Ltd (No 2)* [1992] Ch 72 (discussed below in part V) as exemplified by *Continental Bank NA v Aeakos Compania Naviera SA* [1994] 1 WLR 588; or the persistent refusal of the Greek courts to recognise 'disproportionate' foreign costs orders, see http://conflictoflaws.net/2013/excessive-english-costs-orders-and-greek-public-policy/.

[24] See Art 54 of the Brussels Ia Reg and also draft Recital 35 and draft Art 33 of the Commission proposal for a recast Brussels IIa Reg COM(2016) 411/2.

[25] See Action Plan Implementing the Stockholm Programme COM (2010) 171 final, April 20 2010 p 23. For the new approach to action plans see http://europa.eu/rapid/press-release_IP-14-233_en.htm.

[26] A Costs of Non-Europe report was however commissioned by the European Parliament and may be found at N Bozeat, 'Annex. The perspective of having a European Code of Private International Law', 2013, CoNE 3/2013, available at www.europarl.europa.eu/RegData/etudes/etudes/join/2013/504468/IPOL-JOIN_ET(2013)504468(ANN01)_EN.pdf.

civil procedure in EU legislation appears to have been favoured.[27] The current position, as set out in the new-style Action Plan, reflects a preference for a narrower and more research led[28] approach to enhancing consistency in civil procedure law associated with specific issues and sectors of EU legislation including its PIL.[29]

All the evidence indicates that the EU's legislators continue to believe that there is a strong case for further procedural harmonisation at the EU level. The question for this study remains whether there is a compelling case for further specific harmonisation of EU PIL and civil procedure? The answer to this question depends upon what is meant and understood by 'further harmonisation'. If it is understood to refer to a continuation of the EU's standard approach to PIL harmonisation (ie sectional legislative interventions in the domestic PIL of the Member States, supplemented with necessary adjustments to civil procedure rules and gradual improvement negotiated during periodic recasting exercises) the answer, it is submitted, is an uncontroversial 'yes'. Such an approach continues the existing and fully justified harmonising policy designed to replace and to improve national PIL rules and civil procedures that presently have the unintended effect of obstructing EU citizens and businesses as they attempt to live, work and trade within the EU across internal Member State borders.

If, however, 'further harmonisation' is understood to mean something more than the traditional incremental approach, it becomes necessary to consider what this additional aspect might be and how, if at all, it could or should be accommodated, at a reasonable 'resource cost', into the existing system of EU PIL. One possibility mooted by various distinguished scholars is for the EU to engage in an additional codification of principles and procedural rights concerning EU PIL in the form of a Rome 0 and/or a Brussels 0 Regulation.[30]

---

[27] See the study commissioned by the European Parliament presented in February 2015 at a Workshop under the general heading of 'Cross-border activities in the EU—Making life easier for citizens', w http://www.europarl.europa.eu/RegData/etudes/STUD/2015/510003/IPOL_STU(2015)510003_EN.pdf.

[28] This research and policy is now linked to more objective indicators such as the information provided by the EU Justice Scoreboard, see A Dori, 'The EU Justice Scoreboard—Judicial Evaluation as a new Governance Tool' MPILux Working Paper 2 (2015) available from www.mpi.lu/research/working-paper-series/.

[29] In late 2015 the European Commission asked the Max Planck Institute (Luxembourg) to head a study into two aspects of civil procedure: 1) mutual trust and free circulation of judgments, and 2) enforcement of consumer rights derived from EU law. This project is ongoing, see www.mpi.lu/european-commission-study-on-the-impact-of-national-civil-procedure/. See also M Tulibacka, M Sanz and R Blomeyer, Research paper on common minimum standards of civil procedure, European Added Value Assessment, PE 581.385 , https://polcms.secure.europarl.europa.eu/cmsdata/upload/c4f718ce-2e7a-445e-b211-65c8f427791b/EPRS_CIVIL_PROCEDURE.pdf and R Mańko, In Depth Analysis: Europeanisation of civil procedure: Towards common minimum standards? June 2015 PE 559.499, http://www.europarl.europa.eu/RegData/etudes/IDAN/2015/559499/EPRS_IDA(2015)559499_EN.pdf.

[30] The distinction between a Rome 0 Reg and a Brussels 0 Reg turns on whether the proponent wishes to include jurisdiction plus recognition and enforcement in their mooted Reg: in some legal systems (eg German) there is a distinction between the rules concerning applicable law determination (mostly found in the EGBGB—Introductory Code to the Civil Code) and the rules concerning jurisdiction plus recognition and enforcement of foreign judgments (mostly found in the ZPO—Civil Procedure Code and related enactments). The academic literature on the 0 Regulation idea is considerable, for an introduction: see G Rühl and J von Hein, 'Towards a European Code on Private International Law?' (2015) 79(4) *Rabels Zeitschrift* 701 and sources cited at fns 11–15; S Leible and M Müller, 'A General Part for European Private International Law: The Idea of a "Rome 0 Regulation' (2012–13) XIV *Yearbook of Private International Law* 137; and the review article by Elena Rodriguez Pineau, (2013) 9(3) *Journal of Private International Law* 535.

A. A Codification or Introductory Provision for EU PIL via a 0 Regulation?

The gradual and varied development of EU PIL Regulations has led to certain idiosyncrasies and discontinuities between closely related concepts and procedures that one might expect to be identical. Thus the authentic instruments associated with the Brussels I regime cannot be 'recognised' and are only 'enforceable'.[31] The authentic instruments falling under the Brussels IIa regime (including the Maintenance Regulation) are not only to be 'enforced' but must also be 'recognised'.[32] The authentic instruments that fall under the Succession Regulation can be 'enforced' but cannot be 'recognised', they must however in normal cases be 'accepted'.[33] In the more everyday context of the enforcement of civil and commercial judgments, the enforcement procedure of the 2004 European Enforcement Order does not correspond with the enforcement procedure under either the 2001 Brussels I Regulation or the later 2012 Brussels Ia Regulation.[34] The EU PIL relevant to divorce, maintenance, separation and responsibilities of parents to children is scattered across three different Regulations and is afflicted with differing procedures (sometimes, for reasons associated with the failure of certain Member States to take up a given Hague Protocol, differing within the same Regulation)[35] and also with quite variable take up rates amongst the Member States attributable to the use of Enhanced Cooperation procedures.[36] Given such anomalies and other discontinuities across the individual instruments of EU PIL, a basic EU codification of the PIL concepts and procedures contained in these EU Regulations can be understood to offer the tantalising possibility of harmonising a range of concepts and procedures across the EU's PIL Regulations to promote legal certainty amongst the existing EU provisions and to, eventually, simplify the creation of new PIL provisions.[37]

---

[31] Art 58 of the Brussels Ia Reg, Art 57 of the Brussels I Reg and Art 50 of the Brussels Convention of 1968.

[32] Respectively Art 46 of the Brussels IIa Reg and Art 48 of Council Reg (EC) No 4/2009 of 18 December 2008 on jurisdiction, applicable law, recognition and enforcement of decisions and cooperation in matters relating to maintenance obligations, [2009] OJ L7/1 (the Maintenance Reg).

[33] Arts 59 and 60 of Reg (EU) No 650/2012 of the European Parliament and of the Council of 4 July 2012 on jurisdiction, applicable law, recognition and enforcement of decisions and acceptance and enforcement of authentic instruments in matters of succession and on the creation of a European Certificate of Succession, [2012] OJ L201/107 (the Succession Reg).

[34] Reg (EC) No 805/2004 of the European Parliament and of the Council of 21 April 2004 creating a European Enforcement Order for uncontested claims, [2004] OJ L143/15. Amended by Reg (EC) No 1869/2005 [2005] OJ L300.

[35] See the different enforcement procedures (one with and one without an *exequatur* stage) that had to be provided for the EU's Maintenance Reg.

[36] See Council Reg (EU) No 1259/2010 of 20 December 2010 implementing enhanced cooperation in the area of the law applicable to divorce and legal separation, [2010] OJ L343/10 (Rome III).

[37] Proposals for a 0 Reg often refer to the German EGBGB, if not as a model then possibly as an illustration of aspects of their proposal. With respect the EGBGB seems a double-edged and cautionary exemplar of a measure suggested to resolve differences and to clarify concepts. The original EGBGB came into force with the BGB it 'introduced' in January 1900; its original principles frequently required imaginative judicial interpretation and in 1986 and in 1999 it was reformed to reflect a more multilateral ethos. The most common model for a 0 Reg is the Swiss PIL Code of 1987, T Kadner Graziano, 'Codifying European Union Private International Law: The Swiss Private International Law Act a model for a Comprehensive EU Private International Law Regulation' (2015) 11(3) *Journal of Private International Law* 585. For discussion in English of the EGBGB see P Hay, 'From Rule-Orientation to "Approach" in German Conflicts Law The Effect of the 1986 and 1999 Codifications' (1999) 47(4) *American Journal of Comparative Law* 633 and F Rigaux, 'Codification of Private International Law:

Whatever the aesthetic and academic attractions of enhancing consistency of concepts and procedures within EU PIL via 0 Regulations, the reality is that any such Regulation must be designed subject to certain restrictions. First, it is necessary to know what to include in the Regulation: this is not only complicated by differing ideas and attitudes concerning the composition of the subject of PIL across the EU's Member States, but also by the uneven take-up of EU PIL Regulations by the Member States.[38] A general codification of basic PIL principles and procedural rights that is differently applicable in different Member States (or only applies to some areas of EU PIL) appears to be a somewhat contradictory sort of harmonising proposition. A second issue is that any 0 Regulation would have to be capable of co-existing with, rather than hampering, the ongoing legislative efforts to develop new EU PIL Regulations: discussions over a given sectoral PIL issue pertaining to the creation of a new Regulation might be adversely affected if the parties involved in these discussions appreciated that the meaning of the issue under debate was shifting because of parallel discussions concerning one or more PIL concepts in relation to a proposed 0 Regulation. A 0 Regulation would also have to be compatible with the periodic recasting of the terms of existing PIL Regulations. A third issue is that creating a 0 Regulation must not hamper the external international activities of the EU in relation to either negotiation at the Hague Conference, or in relation to arrangements with EEA States. A fourth issue is that agreeing to a 0 Regulation has certain implications for the Member States; not only are there *immediate* questions of sovereignty transfer associated with allowing the EU to authoritatively determine the shape and nature of PIL in a directly applicable Regulation, but there are also significant issues concerning the *consequential* competence of the Member States to thereafter engage in international negotiations on those issues.[39] Finally, as a 0 Regulation will be intended to harmonise across diverse EU Regulations that themselves were created according to (and under) different EU legal competencies, significant complications may be involved in finding a single legal base for a 0 Regulation.[40]

Pros and Cons' (2000) 60(4) *Louisiana Law Review* 1321, http://digitalcommons.law.lsu.edu/lalrev/vol60/iss4/20; M Martinek, 'The Seven Pillars of Wisdom in Private International Law—The German and the Swiss Experience with the Codification of Conflicts Law Rules' (2001) *Chinese Yearbook of Private International Law and Comparative Law* 15, available from http://archiv.jura.uni-saarland.de/projekte/Bibliothek/text.php?id=221.

[38] Consider the position of the UK, Ireland and Denmark and Art 81 of the TFEU: the first two Member States must opt in to be included in the EU's PIL Regs (see Arts 2 and 4 of Protocol 21 TFEU), Denmark however *cannot* so opt in (see Art 1 of Protocol 22 TFEU): accordingly, all are outside the EU Succession Reg. The controversial Rome III Reg (above n 36) that sets out the applicable law for divorce and legal separation, presently applies in only 16 Member States (it will apply to Estonia from February 2018). Regs concerning Matrimonial Property and Property of civil partners are also covered by Enhanced Cooperation (see above n 6) among 17 Member States. Other examples of Regs with patchy domestic coverage (according to the European E-justice portal) include, EU Order for Payment Reg (Reg (EC) No 1896/2006 of the European Parliament and of the Council of 12 December 2006 creating a European order for payment procedure, [2006] OJ L399/1); EU Small claims procedure (Reg (EC) No 861/2007 of the European Parliament and of the Council of 11 July 2007 establishing a European small claims procedure [2007] OJ L199/1. See E Guinchard, 'L'Europe, la procédure civile et le créancier: l'injonction de payer européenne et la procédure européenne de règlement des petits litiges' (2008) 61(1) *Revue trimestrielle de droit commercial et de droit économique* 3ff.

[39] This was one reason why certain Member States were unwilling to see arbitration incorporated into the Brussels Ia Regulation during the relevant recasting process. See P Beaumont and P McEleavy, *Antons' Private International Law* 3rd edn (London, SULI, 2011) 220. On external competence of the EU on PIL generally see P Franzina (ed), *The External Dimension of EU Private International Law After Opinion 1/13* (Mortsel, Intersentia, 2017).

[40] See Rühl and von Hein, above n 30, at 732 discussing the general legislative procedure in Art 81(1) and 2(c) TFEU and contrasting this with the special procedure for family law matters provided by Art 81(3) TFEU. See this and other complications highlighted by von Hein in ch 2 above.

It is accordingly suggested that though there seems to be a clear political and legal case for the continued gradual harmonisation and improvement of EU PIL (and other associated procedural rules) the suggestion that this may be achieved via a 0 Regulation codification of EU PIL is premature. Though the 0 Regulation idea is intriguing, especially to academic lawyers associated with the practice or revision of existing EU PIL, it seems plain that there are other important but barely touched areas of national PIL law and civil procedure law that would also benefit from EU sectoral intervention and that could bring more immediate benefits to EU citizens. With respect to those who have argued for a 0 Regulation, this does not yet seem so necessary as to justify the diversion of EU resources away from other simpler and more pressing harmonisation or recasting opportunities.

IV. What Then Should be Harmonised?

The suggested method of harmonisation and reform advocated by this chapter is essentially, despite certain refinements that will be detailed and explored in part V, a fairly conservative continuation of existing EU approaches and procedures. The question of what should be harmonised can however also include questioning the future role of the EU institutions in harmonisation activities. It is suggested that the EU, and in particular the European Commission, needs to fully appreciate and to reconsider the nature of its responsibility towards the improvement of EU PIL and associated civil procedure laws. Lest the last comment be misunderstood as an unfair criticism, rather than the genuine suggestion for improvement that is intended, it is necessary to explain it.

The EU and its institutions have made a huge and positive contribution to PIL and civil procedures in all 28 Member States and, to a lesser extent, also in the EEA. This contribution is not merely an ongoing academic and legal marvel, but is also of immense practical significance to the citizens of the EU who, mostly, remain utterly unaware of the opportunities and savings in time and money that are facilitated by the EU's harmonised PIL and its associated procedural laws. The question of whether the EU (or its constituent institutions) is currently demonstrating a proper appreciation of its responsibility towards EU PIL is asked because the EU, or aspects thereof, do not always appear to those outside the institutions to appreciate that part of its role concerning EU PIL is to *curate* that body of law. To employ a gardening metaphor, a successful gardener does not just add new plants to his garden, he also has to prune, cut back and even sometimes dig-out those plants. Without a proper strategy for such planting, pruning or cutting back, the garden, the plants and even the gardener will each eventually suffer. At what point will the constituent institutions of the EU identify a clear and transparent strategy for the general and specific curation (including 'pruning, cutting back and digging out') of its own PIL laws?

In one sense the abovementioned calls for one or more PIL 0 Regulations can be connected with the issue of promoting some such abstract review of EU PIL by EU institutions and Member States, leading to an equivalent rationalisation of the law. It is however suggested that it may be simpler and more effective to attempt to bring about such curation and rationalisation by establishing a forum with an open agenda intended to foster a more open-minded engagement and approach to EU PIL issues between the Member States and the institutions of the EU: in effect to borrow aspects of the ideas underpinning the Hague

Conference on Private International Law, but to adapt them for informal intra-EU use to complement the existing EU recasting procedure and to aim to facilitate the curation of EU PIL by identifying what needs cutting back, digging out (etc). It may currently seem counterintuitive to those involved in the EU institutions that they could potentially improve matters for the EU citizen by working informally with the Member States to consider the effective 'suspension' or 'deletion' of aspects of an EU PIL Regulation, but for some PIL Regulations (if not immediately for those that form the subject of this study) this may well be true.[41] If the penetration of EU PIL into Member State legal systems is to be deepened, something of this sort will eventually be required. The cultivation of an open minded and transparent approach to the reform of EU PIL and its associated procedures also has the advantage of allowing important work to facilitate procedural even-handedness between the litigants and participants involved in the legal process at issue. This is always the most difficult and *ongoing* challenge facing any curator of procedural law. It is comparatively easy to find ways to assist only the claimant (or only the defendant). It is much more difficult to balance the interests of each party (and of other 'interested parties') with the interests of justice as considered across 28 Member States in which any resulting judgments are thereafter likely to be automatically enforceable.[42]

A further point for EU institutions to consider, and in favour of the suggestion above, is that as PIL is a difficult and technical legal subject its subtleties may be overlooked or partially misunderstood by supra-national law reformers guided by the formulators of broad and conceptual reform policies such as those necessarily employed in many other areas of EU law reform. Those who then point out difficulties or unintended consequences of proposals, or even of existing EU PIL, may not be being perverse in raising or defending an issue seen by the formulators of reform policy as a mere technical obstacle: it may be that the reform plan has proceeded from an erroneous or partial assumption that requires correction. Demonstrating an open mind concerning this possibility in the course of an ongoing and transparent discussion of EU PIL would not only behove all of the EU's reformers but would also go a long way to achieving the abovementioned, and highly desirable, *ongoing* curation of EU PIL at minimal cost. The unhappy alternative is wasteful of scarce resources, dissipates mutual goodwill and risks the promulgation and the preservation of sub-optimal laws.[43]

---

[41] An obvious candidate for 'suspension' / 'deletion' is (EC) Reg 805/2004. The continuing utility of an *exequatur*-less European Enforcement Order for civil and commercial claims is open to doubt given: a) the abolition of *exequatur* by Reg 1215/2012; b) the variable rate of use of Reg 805/2004; and, c) the demonstrable confusion caused by the interaction of the 2004 Reg with the Brussels I Regime (see Case C-508/12 *Vapenik v Thurner* EU:C:2013:790; OLG Köln 21/11/2014; and, Cour de cassation, civile, Chambre civile 2, 6 janvier 2012, 10-23.518 plus *Lothschutz v Vogel* [2014] EWHC 473 (QB) in which the French courts and the English courts reached opposite conclusions. The Commission withdrew Reg 805/2004 from consideration by the Member States in the wake of the Brussels I recasting exercise: anecdotally this is attributed either to pique or to a Commission refusal to abandon its preferred view of the role of courts in the Member State of origin. The role, if any, of an externally prepared study for the Commission concerning the EEO (Evaluation of the European Enforcement Order (RAND Europe, 2012)) that it is apparently not willing to publish is unclear. The Commission's actions appear to have prevented a simple harmonisation of the enforcement procedures across EU Regs concerning civil and commercial claims.

[42] For example, consider the questions of procedural 'fairness' arising from the 'reversal' of the 'expected' role of claimant and defendant (or judgment creditor and debtor) in the context of an application for a negative declaration, see Case C-133/11 *Folien Fischer AG and Fofitec AG v Ritrama SpA* EU:C:2012:664.

[43] The long-running disagreement concerning the optimal location and nature of any public policy challenge against recognition or enforcement in the context of the recasting of the Brussels I Reg is a good example of what occurs when the Commission, and others, irrationally treat necessary emergency provisions that are clearly under

A. Areas for Further Harmonisation Suggested by our National Reports

The evidence provided by the national reports indicates that the EU PIL contained in the Regulations under consideration is, broadly speaking, functioning as intended in so far as it concerns issues of procedure. It also indicates that the lawyers and courts in each Member State appear to wish to, and usually do, manage to apply the law and procedure associated with EU PIL Regulations in an effective manner. That said, the national reports also indicate a range of recurring problems associated with the procedural application of the relevant PIL Regulations.

Two issues commonly highlighted by national reports were: first, the interaction of rapidly burgeoning EU PIL Regulations, which led to an almost universal request for increased provision of additional training for judges and lawyers;[44] and second, the need to improve the access of courts and lawyers to accurate and useful information concerning the nature and particularly the *meaning* of foreign law, foreign civil procedure and its associated case law.[45] Each general point indicates the welcome fact that legal professionals wish to perform their allotted legal functions properly, but additionally indicates the less comfortable truth that to do so can be difficult. This difficulty, which it is suggested has a systemic aspect, can be particularly acute in the very delay sensitive context of cross-border 'family law' cases that may awkwardly straddle differently organised EU PIL Regulations, and also involve global provisions such as Hague Conventions (or Protocols). This difficulty has inclined some, notably the European Commission, to suggest that for 'family law' cases these complex PIL issues might usefully be concentrated in specialised courts.[46] If the Commission's sensible proposal concerning such concentration, as presently set out in the draft Recast Brussels IIa Regulation, should be adopted generally, this would appear to attempt to answer *one* of the specific concerns noted by many national reports.[47]

A number of the national reports raised issues that, it is suggested, are relatively benign variations on the well-known tendency for courts and lawyers to incline towards familiar

the proper control of the judiciary as general obstacles to progress: for detail, see J Fitchen 440–42 in A Dickinson and E Lein, *The Brussels I Regulation Recast* (Oxford, Oxford University Press, 2015) and M Requejo Isidro, 'On the Abolition of *Exequatur*' in Hess, Bergström and Storskrubb, above n 2.

[44] In the context of 'family law' matters there was also a general wish that such training should include the potential for EU Regs to interact with other 'global' private international law provisions. Concerning judicial training in general see however, 'Building trust in EU-wide justice—a new dimension to European judicial training' http://ec.europa.eu/justice/events/judicial-training-2015/background_en.htm.

[45] This issue was particularly noted by the Belgian report (ch 6 below) to pose problems in relation to the judicial assessment of the formal validity of foreign choice of court agreements. Generally, the European Judicial Network appeared somewhat underused. The Austrian report (ch 11 below) made positive reference to the assistance provided by the ebook-*Civil Law European Judicial Cooperation* available from www.consilium.europa.eu/en/documents-publications/publications/.

[46] See the proposed recast Brussels IIa Reg, 11–13 and its draft Recital 26 and draft Art 22: Proposal for a Council Regulation on jurisdiction, the recognition and enforcement of decisions in matrimonial matters and the matters of parental responsibility, and on international child abduction (recast) Brussels, 30.6.2016 COM(2016) 411 final, http://ec.europa.eu/justice/civil/files/family-matters/brussels2_regulation_en.pdf.

[47] The other main 'family law' issue concerned a perceived lack of coordination between the provisions of the different EU Regs dealing with 'family law' matters and also of disjunctions when EU law provisions might interact with global private international law provisions such as the Hague Maintenance Convention of 2007, the Hague Child Abduction Convention of 1980 and the Hague Child Protection Convention of 1996.

domestic concepts and procedures, rather than to rigidly apply PIL principles (whether European or domestic). Before the examples of this tendency are briefly considered, it may be useful to momentarily reflect upon the feasibility of attempting its eradication, and also to consider the resources required for any such project: two alternative corrective suggestions, drawn from lateral thought, are offered in part four of this chapter. First however, the 'homeward trend' issues raised by the national reports are briefly considered.

The national reports indicate that Member State courts sometimes struggle to properly interpret and construe aspects of EU PIL Regulations. They may be reluctant, for reasons associated with domestic approaches to interpretation, to accord interpretative relevance to matters other than the Articles contained in the Regulation. Thus, while some Member States do routinely consider Recitals in interpreting EU PIL Regulations, in other Member States with differing approaches to interpretation this is *not* the case.[48] A similar point was made in the German report concerning the difficulty of persuading German courts to allow the legislative history of a given EU PIL Regulation to be used in interpretative arguments.

It was also noted that national courts sometimes persist in characterising issues or concepts from EU PIL Regulations that appear to require autonomous characterisations, in accordance with more familiar domestic principles and concepts. This trend does not appear to reflect any considered desire to not apply EU PIL correctly,[49] but mostly reflects an understandable judicial desire to act 'judicially', ie by resolving the instant dispute in a fair and cost effective manner. For what frequently appear to be similar reasons, numerous national reports indicated that courts are often reluctant to make preliminary references to the CJEU because, though this is accepted as the 'correct' procedure, it would raise the costs of litigating and delay justice: it is tempting for national judges to hold that a given matter is *acte clair* to avoid a preliminary reference to the CJEU.[50]

Similar 'homewards' issues of expediency and judicial function are also amongst those involved in the exceptionally difficult context of questions concerning proof of foreign law in national courts by the application of EU PIL Regulations concerning the applicable law.[51]

---

[48] The German (see ch 7 below) and Spanish reports (see ch 9 below) each made it plain that Recitals were not routinely considered.

[49] Such application can also be difficult if a reference leads the CJEU to deduce an autonomous concept that does not 'fit' the domestic use of the concept: eg the difficulties associated with the domestic German or Czech contractual conceptions of *culpa in contrahendo* following Case C-334/00 *Tacconi v HWS* [2002] ECR I-7357 (paras 25–26) in which a non-contractual characterisation was adopted under Art 5 of Brussels I. See BGH, 31 May 2011—VI ZR 154/10. The Czech report (see ch 15 below) also notes domestic difficulties arising from the CJEU's use of the 'foreign' (ie non civil law) concept of the guardian *ad litem* in Case C-327/10 *Hypoteční banka v Lindner* [2011] ECR I-11543 paras 51–52.

[50] See the Polish report (ch 10 below) at fn 11 and 12 for a very surprising instance in which the Polish Supreme Court decided that it itself would provide an answer to a preliminary reference request (Supreme Court 7 October 2011, II CSK 51/11), 2 years later the CJEU answered (to similar effect it would appear) in C-147/12 *ÖFAB, Östergötlands Fastigheter AB v Frank Koot and Evergreen Investments BV*, EU:C:2013:490.

[51] The issue has been addressed by a comparative study commissioned to comply with the Rome II Reg Art 30 see 'The application of foreign law in civil matters in the EU member states and its perspectives for the future: JLS/2009/JCIV/PR/0005/E4' (2011) available at www.econbiz.de/Search/Results?lookfor=%22Schweizerisches+Institut+f%C3%BCr+Rechtsvergleichung%2C+Lausanne%22&type=Institution and has been considered by many academics, including M Illmer, 'Neutrality Matters—Some Thoughts about the Rome Regulations and the So-called Dichotomy of Substance and Procedure in European Private International Law' (2009) 28 *Civil Justice Quarterly* 237, 259; M Jänterä-Jareborg, 'Foreign Law In National Courts: A Comparative Perspective' (2003) 304 *Recueil Des Cours* 193; R Fentiman, *Foreign Law in English Courts: Pleading Proof and Foreign Law* (Oxford, Oxford University Press, 1998) ch 9; and T Hartley, 'Pleading and Proof of Foreign Law: The Major Legal Systems Compared' (1996) 45(2) *International and Comparative Law Quarterly* 271.

Reasons of space prevent detailed examination of this complex question, but it can be noted that across a significant number of the national reports for various reasons of procedure,[52] familiarity, simplicity, speed and cost it was not uncommon for domestic law to be routinely applied by default by a court, rather than for it to formally determine the applicable law via the provisions of the relevant EU Regulation.[53] Though it might have been expected that there would be no such tendency in the legal systems in which there is an *ex officio* obligation on the judge to determine the applicable law, the evidence provided by the national reports (in accordance with earlier academic literature on this issue) does not support this simplistic expectation: instead it seems that there are not only varying practical meanings of an *ex officio* obligation to determine the applicable law,[54] but also a widespread and pragmatic judicial propensity to 'discover' or 'accept' that the failure of the parties to raise the issue of applicable law indicates that they have opted for the domestic law by default and hence obviated any need for the court to seek to apply the EU Regulation to determine the identity of the substantive law.[55]

It is respectfully suggested that this finding concerning the determination of the applicable law *when the issue is not disputed* should give no cause for immediate concern. As long as the EU's Regulations continue to be used correctly[56] when there *is* an applicable law dispute, and if otherwise the consent of all parties is explicitly or implicitly required before the court will pragmatically apply domestic substantive law by default, the injury to the EU's applicable law provisions by such judicial pragmatism appears slight.[57]

Though it may seem counter-intuitive to tolerate any alternative determination of the applicable law, and indeed there is a case for further investigation of this issue, it must be emphasised that the underlying issues are varied and complex: requiring deep consideration

---

[52] For example, in the three UK legal systems a party must plead any foreign law that is to be applied by the court. Should *all* parties intentionally (or accidentally) omit to plead a foreign law, the court will apply its own substantive law to the dispute.

[53] See, inter alia, the national reports from Belgium, Bulgaria, Cyprus, Greece, Poland, the Netherlands, Hungary, Great Britain, Spain and Sweden (see chs 6, 12, 14, 10, 25, 19, 5, 9 and 30 below).

[54] Contrasting approaches to the *ex officio* obligation of the judge concerning the applicable law are noted in the Swedish and German Reports (chs 30 and 7 below). In Sweden the *ex officio* obligation is easily judicially understood, in the absence of objections from the parties, to indicate that the parties have elected to apply Swedish law, hence obviating a need for further enquiry on this point; in the German report a strong *theoretical* approach is described, albeit with expert advice normally provided to the court by external authorities such as the Max Planck Institute (Hamburg).

[55] Consider the differing *ex officio* judicial approaches disclosed by the German, Swedish and Belgian reports (see chs 7, 30 and 6 below) (respectively, 'strict', 'pragmatic' and, 'sometimes independently extemporised'). See also Hartley, above n 51, concerning the *practical* responses of various courts, including German ones, that sometimes infer from silence a mutual agreement to apply domestic law.

[56] Serious concerns on this point in relation to Rome I and Rome II are evident in the Greek report (ch 18 below) and concerning Rome I to a lesser extent in the Hungarian report (ch 19 below). Equally, the uncertainty of Latvian courts to the correct approach to the proof of law—as revealed by the Latvian report (see ch 21 below)—should be addressed.

[57] Though the question of the prevention of abusive or improper choices of an applicable law by the parties should not often arise in the context of litigation in any forum selected by the operation of the jurisdictional provisions of EU PIL, it is conceivable that a choice of another applicable law might require legislative or judicial intervention on that basis. Art 6(4) of the Rome II Reg attempts to prevent such eventualities by restricting party autonomy—this approach however relies on a 'strong' *ex officio* approach to the applicable law and is hence ineffective to prevent an alternative application of the substantive law of the forum in the UK, Ireland, Cyprus (or other EU Member States with a different approach) if the parties agree not to raise the issue and the court allows this: see J Fitchen, 'Choice of Law in International Claims based on Restrictions of Competition' (2009) 5(2) *Journal of Private International Law* 337 at 344ff.

of proof of law, party autonomy, applicable law provisions, jurisdictional provisions and the combined interaction of each with domestic civil procedure rules across all Member State legal systems. This task is formidable and seemingly promises little by way of general practical improvement compared to the status quo, the national reports do not make a compelling case for a *general* reform of proof of foreign law via EU PIL Regulations but could be read to indicate that further research into this area, and also particularly targeted[58] educational efforts, would be useful.

A more specific issue concerning applicable law that is discernible from a number of the national reports,[59] and is capable of a comparatively simple improvement, concerns the temporal application of the Rome II Regulation. From unarguable evidence in the national reports it seems that the temporal application of Rome II has caused difficulties prior to and even after the ruling of the CJEU in C-412/10 *Homawoo*.[60] The view that the temporal application of the Regulation will be cured by the passage of time may correctly be advanced, but arguably underestimates the potential for injustice if torts characterised by long latency periods, such as those concerning product liability or restrictions of competition, are considered.[61]

In concluding this subsection, it is interesting to note areas and issues that *did not* emerge from the national reports as requiring or deserving further harmonisation. In particular, there was little indication from the national reports that matters such as the external dimension of the Brussels Ia Regulation, the applicable law of insurance contracts, the applicable law concerning the assignment or subrogation of contractual obligations, or the exclusion of defamation from the Rome II Regulation, were of any general concern. This observation is not intended to diminish existing cases for reform, but to indicate the difference between the concrete concerns of practice and the more abstract concerns of theory. Ideally, of course, theory and practice should both inform the identification of further areas of EU PIL meriting harmonisation.

V. How Should this Harmonisation be Effected?

The most necessary point to note at this juncture is that the formal options available to effect reform are legally restricted by the competences provided by the TEU and Treaty on the Functioning of the European Union (TFEU). This requires an approach to harmonisation focussing on what is possible. The continuity approach to further harmonisation or recasting set out above and guided by the suggested forum to be established between the institutions and the Member States reflects this reality. The reforms suggested below are

---

[58] In particular, see the report on Greece (ch 18 below) which discloses a range of 'Peculiars'.

[59] See the reports of inter alios, Czech Republic, Greece, Portugal, Italy, Netherlands, Belgium and Slovenia (chs 15, 18, 26, 8, 25, 6 and 29 below).

[60] See Art 32 of Rome II which was explained to create a date of general application of 11 January 2009 distinguished from the date of entry into force provided by Art 31 of the Regul and Art 297 TFEU of 20 August 2007 see Case C-412/10 *Homawoo v GMF Assurances SA*. EU:C:2011:747. Two problematic cases are noted at n 96 of the Portuguese report (ch 26 below).

[61] The absence of consolidating or transitional provisions for such torts is also unfortunate as it may lead to claimants needing to pay *twice* to determine the applicable law(s) for *one* tort, eg under the Rome II Reg from 11 January 2009 and also under whatever domestic provision applied prior to that date.

intentionally as modest and economical of resources as possible. In each case the aim is to allow an effective use of existing EU resources to facilitate the rational and targeted development and curation of EU PIL Regulations and procedures.

A. Suggested Additional Reforms

The first suggestion is intended to maximise the existing curation and reform potential offered by the preliminary reference procedure by adjusting it, as it concerns EU PIL Regulations, to once again allow official parties other than the existing competent courts to make or, especially, to act to *maintain* a reference to the CJEU concerning the proper interpretation of an EU PIL provision. At the moment the preliminary reference procedure is subject to judicial attitudes and the vagaries of a given private dispute. If a reference is not made, or is made but then the parties settle, the CJEU is deprived of the reference and EU PIL is deprived of a decision. The fragility of the current preliminary reference procedure is evident as even in the event that the reference has progressed past the delivery of the opinion by the Advocate General, a settlement still automatically terminates the reference.[62]

Arguably the most spectacular example of the unfortunate effect of settlement in a PIL case occurred in C-314/92 *Ladenimor SA v Intercomfinaz SA*.[63] Here an important reference from the UK's House of Lords, arising in connection with what was then an appeal from the decision of the Court of Appeal in *Re Harrods (Buenos Aires) Ltd No 2*,[64] was withdrawn because the parties settled the case before the CJEU could deliver its decision. The preliminary reference had asked for guidance on up to six main questions concerning the relationship of the Brussels Convention to concepts of national procedural law. In particular, whether the Brussels Convention applied at all to a case concerning allegedly oppressive conduct by the defendant majority shareholders of a company that, though formed in 1913 with its registered office in England, appeared, if considered in relation to the newly adopted English concept of *forum non conveniens*, to have no other relevant connections to the UK (or to the EU).[65] The Court of Appeal in *Re Harrods* had disapproved of earlier English case law[66] that favoured the application of the Brussels Convention and had controversially held that it did not apply to this litigation; approving instead the use of

---

[62] See Case C-175/06 *Tedesco v Tomasoni* EU:C:2007:451. The reference application was withdrawn after the opinion of AG Kokott was delivered but before the CJEU could issue its ruling.

[63] The application for a preliminary ruling was lodged on 22 July 1992 and recorded in the Official Journal ([1992] OJ C219/4 which also lists the six substantive questions asked by the House of Lords) under Case C-314/92 *Ladenimor SA v Intercomfinaz SA*: this application was removed from the court register by an order dated 21.02.94 (see [1994] OJ C103/9 and the Curia web-site http://curia.europa.eu/juris/liste.jsf?language=en&num=C-314/92). In *Owens Bank Ltd v Fulvio Bracco and Bracco Industria Chimica SpA* [1994] ECR I-117 AG Lenz had referred (in para 16 of his Opinion) to the Decision of the ECJ in 'Ladenimor' as 'pending': it does not however appear that the AG in *Ladenimor* (AG Damon) had published his Opinion by the time at which the settlement of the action in the UK caused the application for a preliminary reference to be withdrawn.

[64] *Re Harrods (Buenos Aires) Ltd No 2* [1992] Ch 72. See T Hartley, 'The Brussels Convention and Forum Non Conveniens' (1992) 17(6) *European Law Review* 553 and G Hogan, 'The Brussels Convention, Forum Non Conveniens and the Connecting Factors Problem' (1995) 20(5) *European Law Review* 471.

[65] See the opinion of Lord Goff in *Spiliada Maritime Corp v Cansulex Ltd* [1987] AC 460 at 466ff.

[66] It had earlier been held (in *S & W Berisford Plc v New Hampshire Insurance Co* [1990] 2 QB 631 and *Arkwright Mutual Insurance Co v Bryanston Insurance Co Ltd* [1990] 2 QB 649) that if the dispute was within the scope of the Brussels Convention, only Convention rules could be applied to EU domiciled defendants and hence attempts to declare England not to be *forum conveniens* in relation to such defendants could not proceed.

domestic private international law, including the English *forum non conveniens* doctrine, to refuse jurisdiction despite the litigation plainly disclosing a civil and commercial dispute involving a defendant with an unarguable UK domicile.

The aborted reference in *Ladenimor* thus concerned a range of legal issues of considerable importance to the future development of PIL in both the EU and in the UK: the failure of the preliminary reference meant that many years would pass during which important issues raised by that reference were unresolved. It was not until *Owusu v Jackson* was decided by the CJEU in 2005, following a 2002 preliminary reference from the English Court of Appeal, that the European Court was presented with an opportunity to make absolutely plain that the Court of Appeal in *Re Harrods* had been wrong on the applicability of the Brussels Convention.[67] The correction of this error[68] took nearly a decade during which English courts, other than the House of Lords, and including the Court of Appeal itself, were technically obliged to follow the *Re Harrods* precedent. The wider implications resulting from the withdrawal of the preliminary reference in *Ladenimor* are matters that, for reasons of space, must remain unexplored; it may however be wondered what effect an earlier clarification by the CJEU of the true relationship between the Brussels Convention and the domestic procedural possibilities offered by Member State legal systems might have had on the development of the Brussels I jurisprudence concerning matters such as mutual trust, jurisdiction agreements and the incompatibility of judicial antisuit injunctions with proceedings under the Brussels I regime.[69]

That it is suggested to again allow a wider range of parties to make a preliminary reference to the CJEU indicates that some such possibility existed previously: save for the novel suggestion of introducing a possibility of maintaining an existing reference (despite the collapse of the litigation) this was indeed once the case.[70] The 1971 Protocol concerning the interpretation of the Brussels Convention by the Court of Justice allowed 'competent authorities' in Member States to make preliminary references to resolve conflicts of interpretation concerning the Brussels Convention arising either from CJEU decisions or from decisions on the Convention *made in other Member States*.[71] An essentially identical

---

[67] Case C–281/02 *Owusu v Jackson* [2005] ECR I-1383.

[68] It is not suggested that what is here called an error went unnoticed in the academic literature in the UK or elsewhere, see the discussion, with further references and attributions, provided in A Layton and H Mercer, *European Civil Practice* 2nd edn (London, Sweet & Maxwell, 2004) at paras 13.023–13.027; H Gaudemet-Tallon, 'Le "forum non conveniens", une menace pour la convention de Bruxelles? (A propos de trois arrêts anglais récents)' (1991) 80 *Revue critique de droit international privé* 491; R Fentiman, 'Jurisdiction, Discretion and the Brussels Convention' (1993) 26(1) *Cornell International Law Journal* 59–99; J Harris, 'The Brussels I Regulation and the Re-Emergence of the English Common Law' (2008) 8(4) *The European Legal Forum* 181 at 183ff; also see a note on the matter by E Jayme, 'Grundfragen zum Anwendungsbereich des EuGVÜ' (1992) *IPRax* 357 ff; and generally, P Huber, 'Forum non conveniens und EuGVÜ' (1993) 12 *Recht der internationalen Wirtschaft* 977ff.

[69] Consider for example Case C-116/02 *Gasser v MISAT* [2003] ECR I-14693; Case C-159/02 *Turner v Grovit* [2004] ECR I-3565; Case C-185/07 *Allianz v West Tankers* [2009] ECR I-663 and Case C-536/13 *Gazprom v Lietuvos Respublika* EU:C:2015:316.

[70] The possibility of such references from the Member States ended when the Conventions, which had needed Protocols on interpretation, were replaced with Regs that had no such need. No particular institutional hostility to the alternative reference procedures in the 1971 Protocol is obvious from the Commission proposal to reform the Brussels Convention, however its lack of use may have contributed to an impression of obsolescence.

[71] See Art 4(1) of the 1971 Protocol concerning the interpretation by the Court of Justice of the convention of 27 September 1968 on jurisdiction and the enforcement of judgments in civil and commercial matters [1975] OJ L204/28 and http://curia.europa.eu/common/recdoc/convention/en/c-textes/brux03-idx.htm. The author is grateful to Alexander Layton QC for alerting him to this provision and also for the information that, to the best of his knowledge, it was never used.

provision and procedure was provided by the first Protocol concerning the interpretation of the Rome Convention of 1980.[72] As far as the author has been able to discover, neither of these alternative reference procedures was ever used. The reasons for this lack of use are unclear. It may be that the need for the clarifications offered by the Protocols[73] seemed less pressing when the EU was composed of fewer Member States and when its private international law, as then contained in conventions, was first emerging.[74] It may also be relevant that both alternative reference procedures expressly prevented the levying or recovery of any costs or expenses: put bluntly, the Member State that used these provisions would have had to pay to perfect the theory of EU PIL for the benefit of all. Such altruism may have been less attractive to Governments than merely trusting that the grounds for refusal of recognition or enforcement (or concerning the applicable law) as provided by the Conventions would adequately protect their Member State from practical problems.

If the current preliminary reference procedure concerning EU PIL Regulations was to be reformed, eg by a new Regulation, to again allow an alternative reference procedure to the Member States, but also to introduce the possibility of *maintaining* useful preliminary references, this could provide a quick and low cost way to identify, clarify and resolve problematic issues concerning EU PIL at both the EU level *and* at the Member State level.[75] If such a reform included the possibility for worthwhile references to survive settlement or discontinuation this would answer some of the undoubted vulnerabilities of the existing preliminary reference procedure discussed above, while offering the potential to augment (and indeed to inform) the statelier procession involved in the periodic review of EU PIL Regulations with an advisory opinion from the CJEU. Such a reform of the reference procedure also offers a potential to be employed in a more focussed fashion to address specific local 'peculiars' of procedure or perspective that may continue to quietly obstruct the uniform implementation of EU PIL in certain Member States.[76] It is tentatively suggested that the Member States and the European Commission should be entitled to maintain or commence preliminary references concerning the interpretation of an EU PIL Regulation: it is further suggested that costs and expenses should be capable of being awarded from central EU funds, or to be allocated among the participants, by the CJEU.[77]

The second reform suggestion concerns the abovementioned establishment of an open agenda intra-EU curation forum for representatives of the Member States and of the EU institutions in which interrelationships between aspects of EU PIL instruments could be identified and strategic advice could be offered to enhance recasting across different instruments while also identifying areas of obsolescence. As the proposed forum is, inter alia, intended to assist the strategic operation of the existing recasting procedure, it might be

---

[72] Art 3 of the First Protocol on the interpretation of the 1980 Convention by the Court of Justice (consolidated version) / 1980 Rome Convention [1998] OJ C27/47–51.

[73] Which, significantly, did *not* include the ability for a Member State or other authority to apply to 'take over' an existing reference such as that in C-314/92 *Ladenimor* when the reference was discontinued by settlement.

[74] Neither of the EC Regs that replaced the Brussels or Rome Conventions included an equivalent provision allowing the Member States to make preliminary references.

[75] It is suggested that costs might be kept lower if the 'new' reference procedure should be initiated and proceed in writing to a nominated Advocate General for an initial and paper based evaluation of its merit.

[76] For an example not involving a novel interpretation of the law by the English courts, see the long-standing reluctance of the Greek courts to enforce foreign costs judgments that they deem to be excessive when judged against Greek standards (above n 23).

[77] Possibly to reflect the utility or otherwise of the matter referred.

necessary to revisit aspects of that procedure (and the 2001 interinstitutional agreement on which it is currently based)[78] to allow for the proposed more transparent curation of EU PIL and also for further modifications to reflect the suggested strategic role of the proposed forum in the course of recasting procedures. Furthermore, as the forum suggestion is intended to promote democratic legitimacy and transparency in the mutual curation and further strategic development of EU PIL, it should be accompanied by an obligation on the European Commission, and other relevant EU institutional parties, to make public the outcome of any study or report it has commissioned (or carried out itself) concerning an EU PIL Regulation; if the institution disagrees with any part of any such report its reasons for disagreement can be appended to that report.[79]

VI. Conclusion

This chapter has considered the considerable difficulties of attempting to reform and optimise the civil procedure laws deriving from the EU's PIL Regulations. Low level problems of interpretation across the legal systems of 28 Member States attributable to differing legal cultures, and differing approaches to legal systematisation, currently coexist with high level problems for the EU institutions that must administer a top-down reform and recasting process that can appear deficient in both strategy and aim because it lacks a transparent process for aspects of its curation.

The first of the two novel suggestions for reform offered by this chapter aims to address the low level problem by reforming the preliminary reference procedure to allow the Member States a general ability to independently lodge references concerning the interpretation of *any* EU PIL instrument with the CJEU (as was previously possible under specific Protocols concerning the interpretation of both the Brussels Convention and the 1980 Rome Convention) but to supplement this possibility with the entirely novel possibility of allowing a Member State or the European Commission to *maintain* a preliminary reference that would otherwise be lost to EU jurisprudence by the settlement or discontinuation of the underlying legal dispute.

The second of the two novel suggestions offered by this chapter targets the high level problems by proposing the establishment of an open agenda intra-EU curation forum for representatives of the Member States and of the EU institutions to identify and consider the interrelationship of existing EU PIL instruments and to offer strategic advice to enhance the curation and recasting of different instruments by identifying areas requiring coverage or areas of obsolescence.

Though new and original, each reform suggestion is deliberately modest: such 'modest' suggestions not only have the potential to address a number of the isolated procedural

---

[78] See http://ec.europa.eu/dgs/legal_service/recasting_en.htm and Interinstitutional Agreement of 28 November 2001 on a more structured use of the recasting technique for legal acts [2002] OJ C77/1 at http://eur-lex.europa.eu/legal-content/EN/ALL/?uri=CELEX:32002Q0328.

[79] See above n 41, concerning the as yet unpublished 2012 report on the EEO Reg. If the reason for withholding publication was Commission dissatisfaction, it seems unlikely that this was with the authors as they have subsequently been employed on other projects for the Commission.

problems of EU PIL noted in the national reports generated by this study, but also, and more importantly, to offer a relatively simple and comparatively economic means of swiftly addressing the more general problems currently facing EU PIL and its procedural hetero-geneity. These general problems have recently sparked interest in bold plans to create one or more 0 Regulations concerning PIL, and have even managed to re-invigorate, albeit in a different form, the equally ambitious and long-standing suggestion that specialist courts of one form or another should be constituted for matters involving EU PIL. Though each reform proposal is worth further investigation (particularly the compelling suggestion of 'concentrating' the special situations presented by 'family law' cases in special courts),[80] it is suggested that comparable final outcomes might be achieved more simply, more cheaply, and more quickly by implementing the two more modest suggestions mentioned above. In any case, an open, informed and genuinely intra-EU debate on the nature and constituents of the intended contribution of existing and planned EU PIL Regulations to 'the overriding objective' of procedural civil justice in the EU is long overdue.[81]

---

[80] See comment on pp 11–13 and draft Recital 26 plus draft Art 22 in the Commission's proposed Brussels IIa Reg Recast, above n 46.

[81] On the meaning of the term 'overriding objective' in the reform of English civil procedure in this context see www.justice.gov.uk/courts/procedure-rules/civil/rules/part01.

Part II

Cross-border Litigation Pattern—Empirical Data and Analysis

5

Great Britain

PAUL BEAUMONT, MIHAIL DANOV,
KATARINA TRIMMINGS AND BURCU YÜKSEL

I. Introduction

This chapter is an analysis of some of the issues that can be learned from the British case law on the EU private international law (PIL) instruments covered by the EUPILLAR project (Brussels I and IIa, Rome I and II, and Maintenance Regulations) and of the findings from the qualitative interviews conducted in relation to the operation of those instruments in the two legal systems comprising Great Britain. The study is not comprehensive on the UK due to not taking account of the operation of the EUPILLAR instruments in Northern Ireland.

II. England and Wales

A. Introduction

Datasets have been compiled for the civil and commercial and family PIL cases on the EUPILLAR Regulations before the English and Welsh courts for the period from 1 March 2002 up to 2015.[1] The case law datasets in England and Wales were compiled by conducting searches in electronic databases. Although the free database of the British and Irish Legal Information Institute was used, Westlaw UK was systematically used because it contained more information about the appeal history, making it easier to take account of any related judgments. The databases were searched by entering the relevant Regulation number (eg 44/2001, 2201/2003), and then identifying the PIL cases, in which the EU legislative instrument was considered. This resulted in 354 cases, involving on some occasions more than one judgment; 427 judgments rendered in these cases have now been summarised on the project web site.[2] It should be noted that the last search was done in the summer of 2015, so that the datasets include only a small proportion of the cases in 2015.[3]

---

[1] See more about the research methodology in ch 1. See also M Danov and P Beaumont, 'Measuring the Effectiveness of the EU Civil Justice Framework: Theoretical and Methodological Challenges' (2015–16) XVII *Yearbook of Private International Law* 151, <www.abdn.ac.uk/law/documents/CPIL_Working_Paper_No_2016_2.pdf.

[2] www.abdn.ac.uk/law/research/eupillar-database-559.php.

[3] An interesting competition law judgment (rendered in November 2015) was added as well.

Although the datasets are indicative of the volume of cases in England and Wales, such quantitative data has its limits.[4] First, it is impossible to identify all judgments rendered in cross-border cases—many are not reported or accessible through electronic databases. This makes any quantitative data not entirely reliable. Hence, the need to do interviews with legal practitioners. Second, in some cross-border cases, issues of jurisdiction and choice-of-law are not argued by the parties and therefore judges may not necessarily refer to the relevant PIL instruments in their judgments.[5] Third, it is well established that many cases settle before trial (or even before proceedings are issued) in England and Wales.[6] Nonetheless, the analysis of the case law datasets reveals the number of references to the Court of Justice of the European Union (CJEU) and the number of references requested by a party to a case and/or considered by the court; and the use by the national courts of the Recitals to the Regulations and the CJEU's case law to find the correct interpretation of the Regulations. This data provides us with useful indicators about the effectiveness of the EU PIL framework and its uniform interpretation in particular. That said, deriving all the quantitative data from the identified PIL judgments, which are numerous and occasionally very long in England and Wales, is neither a straightforward undertaking nor a precise science. Therefore, there was a need for qualitative data to be gathered as well.

Moreover, considering only the cases in which PIL issues were raised by the parties (and as a result were discussed by the English courts) strongly suggests that such analyses will be predominantly based on contentious EU PIL cases that are actually litigated.[7] Hence, there was a need to turn to the views of legal practitioners, in particular to find out how the EU PIL framework is shaping litigants' strategies on settlements. It is well established that '[some] cases settle for no better reason than that the claimant is tired of waiting, or does not have the energy to pursue the claim any further. This may arise because of deliberate tactics adopted by the parties.'[8] Due to the specific nature of cross-border disputes, abusive litigation tactics devised under the EU PIL framework could be attributable to the ineffectiveness of the EU institutional framework.[9]

Central to the process of conducting qualitative interviews with legal practitioners was drawing a sampling framework[10] which was to be used when randomly selecting interview participants in England and Wales. To this end, the names of the actively practising barristers as well as the names of the current judges from the High Court and Court of Appeal were drawn from the judgments rendered in the EU PIL cases, as identified for the dataset. Any duplicates were eliminated. However, there were two issues to be addressed. First, the lists of the barristers appeared to include predominantly barristers from London and some other big cities. Second, the names of the solicitors which were drawn from the PIL cases

---

[4] Danov and Beaumont, above n 1.

[5] eg, *Emerald Supplies Ltd & Others v British Airways and Air Canada & Others* [2014] EWHC 3513 (Ch).

[6] H Genn, *Judging Civil Justice* (Cambridge, Cambridge University Press, 2010) 21.

[7] H Genn, 'Preliminary Analysis of Costs Data', *Review of Civil Litigation Costs*, Seminar 26 June 2009, www. ucl.ac.uk/laws/judicial-institute/events/Jackson_Costs_Review_Preliminary_Analysis_of_Costs_Data_.pdf.

[8] The Right Honourable the Lord Woolf, *Access to Justice—Final Report to the Lord Chancellor on the Civil Justice System in England and Wales* (HMSO, 1996) 107.

[9] See more in ch 40 below.

[10] A Wilmot, 'Designing sampling strategies for qualitative social research: with particular reference to the Office for National Statistics' qualitative respondent register' (2005), Paper on qualitative sampling strategies presented to QUEST 2005, Office of National Statistics, www.ons.gov.uk/ons/guide-method/method-quality/general-methodology/data-collection-methodology/reports-and-publications/index.html?format=print.

were far too few. This was due to the fact that most of the reported EU PIL cases specify the names of the law firms rather than the names of the individual solicitors. The list with names of solicitors was drawn to include the names of the leading individuals listed on the Legal 500 and Chambers and Partners. The solicitors' lists aimed to represent both London lawyers and those working elsewhere in England and Wales by adding names of solicitors from regional law firms and branches of large law firms. After any duplicates were eliminated, over 1700 names of legal practitioners (including judges) were identified. The potential interview respondents were randomly selected from each category, and invited to take part in the study. In addition, judges from the UK Supreme Court were invited to take part in the interviews. 20 interviews, involving all the 21 legal practitioners who accepted our invites, were conducted in England and Wales. Although the majority of respondents were from London, it was very helpful to be able to meet some legal practitioners from outside London.

B. Cross-border Civil and Commercial Disputes

The civil and commercial law datasets include 187 PIL cases (and an even greater number of judgments at different stages of the proceedings). A significant number of disputes before the English courts were contractual in nature. In particular, our dataset includes 100 cases (ie 53.5 per cent of the cases) which were concerned with matters relating to contract. There were also 56 cross-border non-contractual disputes which amounted to approximately 30 per cent of the cases in our civil and commercial law dataset. Some 17 cases (ie 9.2 per cent), involved contractual and non-contractual claims which sometimes raised difficult jurisdictional issues.[11] The deduction that the English courts and legal practitioners are predominantly dealing with cross-border disputes in matters relating to contract was further strengthened by the research interview data.

Although only a financial remedy was sought in 62 cases (ie 33 per cent of the cases), a financial remedy in combination with another remedy was sought in 135 cases (ie 72 per cent of all the civil and commercial cases identified). The least sought remedy was the injunctive one which was requested on its own only in five cases. That said, injunctive relief was sought along with another remedy in 27 cases. Declaratory relief was sought in 30 cases, amounting to approximately 16 per cent of the cases in civil and commercial matters. Nonetheless, the research interview data indicates that even when declaratory relief is sought, the declaratory remedy will have a monetary value for the parties, confirming that a financial remedy and its value are affecting the parties' decision whether/where to sue.

The proposition that the value of the claims impacts the litigants' decision whether/where to sue becomes even more obvious when one looks at the value of the claims which are being brought in England. Although the data is missing in over 50 per cent of the reported decisions as to value of the claims in England, it seems that the value of the claims was over €1 million in 37 per cent. Furthermore, the value of the claims was less than €0.5 million in fewer than 10 per cent of the PIL cases in England and Wales. In spite of the missing data, it is a relatively safe assumption that the value of the claims was significantly

---

[11] eg *The Bank of Tokyo-Mitsubishi Ltd and Another v Baskan Gida Sanayi Ve Pazariama as and Others* [2004] EWHC 945; *Mazur Media Ltd and another v Mazur Media GmbH and others* [2004] EWHC 1566; *ET Plus SA and Others v Welter and Others* [2005] EWHC 2115 (Comm).

above €1 million in cross-border EU competition law cases initially, and it was significantly less than €0.5 million in many of the personal injury cases. The deduction that there are predominantly high value claims in England appears to be confirmed by the qualitative interview data which indicates that the lowest value of claim is rarely less than €0.5 million in London, with claims of €50,000 being occasionally seen in the regional firms/offices. Therefore, the data appear to suggest that there may not be effective remedies for many of the claimants whose harm is valued at less than €50,000. Of course, this may be due to the high litigation costs in England and Wales which adversely affects access to effective remedies for litigants with small claims in cross-border cases.[12] The deduction that there may not be effective remedies for certain types of claimants in England and Wales could be further strengthened by noting that the claims are being brought by commercial companies in 147 cases which amounts to 76.5 per cent of the civil and commercial cases. There are weaker parties in approximately 10 per cent of the cases. The weaker parties include insurance policy holders (suing foreign insurance companies for accidents which occurred abroad) and occasionally employees, but no consumers.

England and Wales attracts high-value civil and commercial disputes brought by commercial companies. London is a dispute resolution centre fully benefitting from the current EU model of administration of justice, which provides parties with a free choice where to litigate most civil and commercial disputes.

Although the data about the residence of the claimant was missing in approximately 13 per cent of the cases, the claimant was based in England and Wales in 76 cases which amounted to 40.6 per cent of the civil and commercial cases in the dataset. The fact that many of the claimants preferred to sue in their home jurisdiction is evidence that there are advantages to be gained from suing at the place of their residence. This was clearly indicated during the interviews, and it is particularly the case for small and medium-sized enterprises (SMEs). Although one could say that the data might suggest that the SMEs are less mobile in so far as they prefer to sue in their home jurisdiction, it does not necessarily mean that all the claimants, who sue in the courts at their residence, are not mobile (or non-selective). For example, there were some big and sophisticated multinational groups of companies, having their subsidiaries in England and engaging in jurisdictional battles with a view to having their dispute before the English courts.[13] The fact that the claimants in many of the cross-border cases are selective and mobile could be further strengthened by noting that the claimants in over 30 per cent of the cases in the dataset were residing across the globe, but they nonetheless decided to bring their claims in England and Wales. Moreover, there were multiple claimants from different jurisdictions on 25 occasions (ie 13.4 per cent of the cases in our dataset). This point could be strengthened by pointing out that over 1800 Zambian nationals initiated proceedings against an English domiciled parent company under Article 4 of the Brussels I (Recast) Regulation. In this case, the claims—which were brought together by specialised law firms acting for multiple claimants—were for damages

---

[12] Lord Justice Jackson, 'Fixed Costs—The Time Has Come'—*IPA Annual Lecture*—28 January 2016, www.judiciary.gov.uk/wp-content/uploads/2016/01/fixedcostslecture-1.pdf.
[13] eg *JP Morgan Chase Bank NA v Berliner Verkehrsbetriebe (BVG) Antsalt des Öffentlichen Rechts* [2009] EWHC 1627 (Comm), *JP Morgan Chase Bank NA v Berliner Verkehrsbetriebe (BVG)* [2010] EWCA Civ 390; *McGraw-Hill International (UK) Limited v Deutsche Apotheker—und Arztebank EG, Uniqa Alternative Investments GMBH, Uniqa Capital Markets GMBH, Stichting Ratings Redress, The Royal Bank of Scotland N.V.* [2014] EWHC 2436 (Comm).

caused by environmental pollution in Zambia.[14] Therefore, England is often a venue of choice for many claimants from across the globe. This is certainly something which could be deduced from the interviews with the legal practitioners from London, whose client base is predominantly corporations bringing or defending high value claims.

Furthermore, a recent study, commissioned by the UK Ministry of Justice and undertaken by the British Institute of International and Comparative Law (BIICL), has considered the factors which influence litigants' decisions to issue proceedings in England.[15] Some of the important factors, which were identified in the BIICL report included: the experience of the judges, remedies, procedural rules, impartiality, market practice, English language, experience of lawyers, speed and enforceability of judgments.[16] Although English choice-of-court and choice-of-law agreements were identified as the second most important factor, one could argue that the contracting parties would probably not have included such agreements if it were not for the experience of judges.[17] The EUPILLAR research shows that choice-of-court agreements were considered an important basis of jurisdiction in over 25 per cent of the cases in the English and Welsh civil and commercial dataset.

Another indication that claimants are strategic, when deciding where to litigate, could be deduced from the fact that multiple defendants were sued in England under Article 8(1) (ex Article 6(1)) of Brussels Ia in nearly 12 per cent of the cases. The interview data suggest that the claimants (especially sophisticated claimants) are indeed selective, considering the following factors: potential recovery (getting a result); forcing a settlement; experience of judges; procedure; speed; and cost recovery. The data support the view that access to an effective remedy in cross-border cases depends on allocating jurisdiction before a court that is able to deal with cross-border disputes, applying the correct applicable law(s).[18]

Therefore, a number of commercial companies with high-value claims appear to be suing in England and Wales (despite the high litigation costs), hoping to force a settlement. As previously submitted,[19] there is empirical work undertaken in the United States which demonstrates that 'forum does affect outcome'.[20] Bearing in mind the diverse nature of the EU, the availability of effective remedies (and the speed with which a remedy is awarded) may well be dependent on where the parties litigate. The project on Cross-Border EU Competition Law Actions[21] showed that the place where the parties litigate is carefully selected taking account of the applicable procedural laws. The fact that a specific feature of the

---

[14] *Dominic Liswaniso Lungowe & Others v Vedanta Resources Plc and Konkola Copper Mines Plc* [2016] EWHC 975 (TCC).

[15] E Lein, R McCorquodale, L McNamara, H Kupelyants and J del Rio, *Factors Influencing International Litigants' Decisions to Bring Commercial Claims to the London Based Courts* (Ministry of Justice Analytical Series, 2015).

[16] ibid 15.

[17] See more in ch 1 above.

[18] See more: Danov and Beaumont, above n 1.

[19] ibid.

[20] KM Clermont and T Eisenberg, 'Do Case Outcomes Really Reveal Anything about the Legal System? Win Rates and Removal Jurisdiction' (1997–98) 83 *Cornell Law Review* 581, 607. See also KM Clermont, 'Jurisdictional Salvation and the Hague Treaty' (1999–2000) 85 *Cornell Law Review* 89, 108–09; WE O'Brian Jr , 'The Hague Convention on Jurisdiction and Judgments: The Way Forward' (2003) 66 *Modern Law Review* 491, 497.

[21] M Danov, F Becker and P Beaumont (eds), *Cross-Border EU Competition Law Actions* (Oxford, Hart Publishing, 2013).

civil justice system in England and Wales is that many cases settle before trial[22] may offer an explanation as to why claimants prefer to sue there. This might be seen as yet another indication that potential effective access to an appropriate legal remedy is shaping the litigants' strategies, affecting in particular the parties' decision whether/where to sue. That said, an analysis of the litigants' strategies may expose the weaknesses of the current model of administration of justice in the EU.

i. Jurisdictional Challenges

The parties' disagreement as to the place where their dispute should be heard was determined on 157 occasions which amounts to 84.4 per cent of the cases in the civil and commercial law dataset. If claimants are suing in England and Wales because they believe that this is a place where the effective remedies would be readily available, then the defendant may strategically challenge the jurisdiction and cause delay. Are jurisdictional challenges tactical?

A support for the notion that many of the jurisdictional challenges may be tactical could be derived from a view expressed by Lord Justice Collins, in the highly cited *Kolden* case.[23] In this case, the learned judge dismissed the jurisdictional challenge, 'and express[ed] the hope that the parties (having wasted some £400,000 on this sterile exercise) [were to] turn their attention to dealing with the substance of their dispute.'[24] Some further support for the tactical nature of many of the jurisdictional challenges could be deduced from the fact that the merits of the case were dealt with only in 18 civil and commercial cases in the dataset which amounts to 10 per cent but of course the dataset will only record merits judgments where they are combined with a private international law issue governed by one of the relevant EU PIL Regulations. In 125 cases (66.8 per cent of the cases in the dataset), the English and Welsh court dealt with the jurisdictional issue only. Both jurisdiction and choice-of-law issues were considered (without addressing the merits of the dispute) in 22 cases (11.8 per cent of the cases).[25] The deduction that many disputes about jurisdiction may be strategic finds some support in the research interviews which further indicate that jurisdictional challenges may be among the most common tools deployed by the defendants, aiming to wear down the claimant. The high number of jurisdiction challenges may be reflecting the way the current Brussels I framework shapes the litigants' strategies, affecting the settlement levels which might be significantly discounted in some cases where the defendants are exploiting the ambiguities of the legislative framework, in order to cause delay. The qualitative interview data[26] overwhelmingly demonstrate that jurisdictional

---

[22] H Genn, *Judging Civil Justice* (Cambridge, Cambridge University Press, 2010) 21. See the Civil Justice quarterly statistics, www.gov.uk/government/collections/civil-justice-statistics-quarterly. See more: ch 40.

[23] *Kolden Holdings Ltd v Rodette Commerce Ltd and another* [2008] EWCA Civ 10.

[24] ibid [96].

[25] Of the remaining cases there were six judgments where only a choice-of-law issue was addressed; two judgments in relation to provisional measures; three judgments addressing jurisdiction as well as the recognition and enforcement of judgments; and the remainder were about the recognition and enforcement of judgments.

[26] EUPILLAR—England and Wales—Interview Transcripts No 1, 3, 7, 11, 12, 17, 18 which were 7 out of 8 commercial law legal practitioners interviewed in England and Wales. The difficulties in dealing with jurisdictional challenges were also pointed out by one commercial judge from England and Wales—EUPILLAR—England and Wales—Interview Transcript No 19.

challenges are one of the most common delaying tactics which impact on settlements,[27] particularly where the claimant has a strong (or a relatively strong) claim.[28]

That said, it should be noted that the defendants' jurisdictional challenges were wholly or partly upheld in 50 cases thus over 30 per cent of the challenges succeeded. The high number of successful jurisdictional challenges may indicate that what is being said about defendants being tactical may also be valid for claimants. The potential for tactical manoeuvring by either party in more than one jurisdiction is indicated by an interviewee: 'even though I might conclude that ultimately England is going to have jurisdiction, it does not mean that I will not keep fighting the argument for a year somewhere else for tactical reasons …'.[29]

On the basis of the relatively high success rate of jurisdictional challenges, it may be argued that the English judiciary does not appear to be biased in interpreting Brussels I in a way which allows English courts to assume jurisdiction in cases where they do not have jurisdiction. However, some of the interview respondents do suggest that judges might occasionally assume jurisdiction in cases where they should not have done so. Nonetheless, the overwhelming majority of the interview respondents as well as the case law data strongly suggest that the English judges do it by applying the relevant jurisdiction rules as well as by duly engaging with the relevant case law of the CJEU. Even if it occasionally might appear that English courts assumed jurisdiction or refused to exercise a discretionary stay with a view to dispensing justice, the English courts will not do so unless they established that they had jurisdiction under Brussels I. For example, in *British Airways v SEPLA*,[30] the English courts did not assume jurisdiction because it was held that the parties' dispute was not within the scope of Brussels I. In this case, the claimants were suing two defendants under Article 6(1) (now Article 8(1)). The first defendant, SEPLA, was a syndicate which was representing Spanish pilots. The second defendant, IFALPA, was the Federation of Air Line Pilots Associations which was domiciled in England on 16 November 2012 when the proceedings were initiated in London. The claimants sought damages and declaratory and injunctive relief, arguing that the pilots' strike was in conflict with Articles 49 and 56 TFEU.[31] The defendants challenged the jurisdiction of the English courts, submitting that the dispute was not within the scope of Brussels I. The English High Court upheld the jurisdiction challenge. Mr Justice Field held:

> In my judgement, [the] contention that the claimants' claims are not 'civil and commercial' matters is well founded. The prohibitions on restrictions on the freedoms of establishment and the provision of services within the EU expressed in arts 49 and 56 TFEU import treaty obligations laid upon the Member States, with the result in my view that the enforcement of those obligations is not a civil or commercial matter but one involving the application of public law. True it is that trade unions have been held to be subject to the obligation to maintain the fundamental freedoms enshrined in the EC predecessors to arts 49 and 56, but this in my opinion is because for this purpose they are to be deemed to be emanations of the state.[32]

---

[27] See chs 35 and 40.
[28] See ch 35.
[29] EUPILLAR—England and Wales—Interview Transcript No 7.
[30] *British Airways plc & Anor v Sindicato Espanol de Pilotos de Lineas Aereas & Anor* [2013] EWHC 1657 (Comm).
[31] ibid [1].
[32] ibid [35].

In spite of the fact that the claimants did not appeal, the decision posed interesting questions about the scope of Brussels I because the issue was decided somewhat differently in the *Viking Line*[33] case. In *British Airways* Mr Justice Field noted that the Finnish Seamen's Union ('FSU') had 'withdr[awn] its jurisdictional challenge'.[34] However, in *Viking Line*, Mrs Justice Gloster held that:

> In the present case, jurisdiction as against the ITF [International Transport Workers' Federation] is based on its domicile in England. If this Court were to decline to exercise jurisdiction in this case on comity grounds, the effect would be to defeat the Claimant's claim to jurisdiction not only against the FSU, which is domiciled in Finland, but also against the ITF.[35]

The *Viking Line* case reached the CJEU on an important question of EU law.[36] That said, there still appears to be a level of uncertainty as to the scope of Brussels I in this context. This is largely due to the fact that various national judges may interpret the rules differently, without always making a preliminary reference to the CJEU on the issue of jurisdiction.

The latter point may be strengthened further by briefly considering the judgment of the English High Court in *Canyon Offshore*.[37] In this case, the claimant was a Scottish company, Canyon, which might be seen as an indication that the claimants might be selective, even when they have a choice between courts located in the same Member State. The defendant was a Dutch company, GDF. The sum of money was due under a contract concluded between Canyon and another Dutch company, Cecon. Cecon had sub-contracted to Canyon some of the work which it had to carry out for GDF. The project agreement between Cecon and GDF contained a Dutch jurisdiction clause. The sub-contract contained an arbitration clause. After Cecon fell behind with the payment to Canyon which was due under the sub-contract, GDF offered to pay Canyon directly. Based on this commitment, Canyon's claim was brought against GDF in England. The value of the claim was approximately £3.4 million. The defendant challenged the jurisdiction of the English court. The jurisdictional challenge was dismissed by HHJ Mackie QC, holding that:

> 53 ... I conclude that a normally well informed defendant would be reasonably able to foresee that, apart from at his domicile, he might be sued in either of the places where payment was required to be made under the alleged contract. At the time of assuming the payment obligation, the essence of what he was required to do under the alleged contract, he could readily have discovered that payment was due in Scotland or England. ... On balance, however, I conclude that art.5 gave Canyon a choice between Scotland and England.

> 54 I do not pretend that the issues raised by this aspect of the application are straightforward or based on principles that have been established beyond doubt. Mr Russell suggested that the Court might consider a reference to the European Court under CPR68. I do not consider that it would be appropriate for me to take that step. The Court of Appeal can of course take that step if it thinks

---

[33] *Viking Line ABP v The International Transport Workers' Federation, The Finnish Seamen's Union* [2005] EWHC 1222 (Comm).

[34] *British Airways plc & Anor v Sindicato Espanol de Pilotos de Lineas Aereas & Anor* [2013] EWHC 1657 (Comm) [38].

[35] *Viking Line ABP v The International Transport Workers' Federation, The Finnish Seamen's Union* [2005] EWHC 1222 (Comm) [72].

[36] Case C-438/05, *The International Transport Workers' Federation and The Finnish Seamen's Union* [2007] ECR I-10779.

[37] *Canyon Offshore Ltd v GDF Suez E&P Nederland BV* [2014] EWHC 3810 (Comm).

it necessary. I will however give permission to appeal, at least on the European law aspects of this application.[38]

The English High Court's judgment was rendered on 27 November 2014. More than one year later—on 7 January 2016—the Court of Appeal dismissed the appeal. The judgment is yet to be reported, but no preliminary reference to the CJEU was considered necessary. The case clearly shows how selective the claimants may be as well as demonstrating how the remaining level of ambiguity may be exploited by defendants who wish to delay the resolution of the dispute by raising preliminary issues. It is a relatively safe assumption that, had there been a preliminary reference to the CJEU, a further delay of 12 to 18 months would have been incurred. This level of delay could have an impact on the parties' access to remedies and any settlement negotiations as well as on national judges' willingness to make a preliminary reference to the CJEU.

ii. Parallel Proceedings

The level of complexity and uncertainty increases in high value commercial disputes where the parties start jurisdictional battles involving parallel proceedings in different jurisdictions. The point could be illustrated well by looking at the litigants' strategies in *JP Morgan v BVG*.[39] In this case, the claimants were global providers of banking and financial services. The defendant was a German public institution. The dispute arose out of a swap agreement which contained an English jurisdiction clause. As part of it, the claimants were entitled to protection against the credit risk of 150 companies. JP Morgan commenced proceedings in England, bringing a claim for approximately $112 million. Although the English court was the first seised for the purposes of Brussels I, parallel proceedings were initiated in Germany. BVG challenged the jurisdiction of the English court, submitting that the swap agreement was invalid as it was ultra vires. Mr Justice Teare dismissed the jurisdictional challenge, holding that 'the proceedings … are not principally concerned with the issue of ultra vires and that the issue of ultra vires, viewed in its context, is not one which the policy underlying art 22(2) requires to be decided by the German courts.'[40] The UK Supreme Court made a preliminary reference to the CJEU.[41] After the UK Supreme Court received a copy of the judgment in Case C-144/10, *Berliner Verkehrsbetriebe (BVG), Anstalt des öffentlichen Rechts v JP Morgan Chase Bank NA*, the UK Supreme Court informed the CJEU that 'it did not wish to maintain the reference.'[42] That said, it should be noted that, in this case, the dispute on the preliminary jurisdictional issues lasted for approximately 30 months. This example clearly demonstrates how the current institutional framework may be exploited by the defendants, causing higher costs and delay. The issues reappeared

---

[38] ibid [53 and 54]. Judge Mackie had taken the bold step of concluding that the CJEU's decision in *Besix* no longer applied to Art 5(1)(a) Brussels I cases because of the move away from the requirement of a single place of performance in the CJEU case law on Art 5(1)(b), see paras 49–52, but he did not refer the case to the CJEU even though one party requested a reference. For analyses of the CJEU case law on Art 5(1) (Art 7(1) of the Recast) see chs 33 and 36 below.

[39] *JP Morgan Chase Bank NA v Berliner Verkehrsbetriebe (BVG) Antsalt des Offentlichen Rechts* [2009] EWHC 1627 (Comm) aff'd *JP Morgan Chase Bank NA v Berliner Verkehrsbetriebe (BVG)* [2010] EWCA Civ 390.

[40] *JP Morgan Chase Bank NA v Berliner Verkehrsbetriebe (BVG) Antsalt des Offentlichen Rechts* [2009] EWHC 1627 [53].

[41] C-54/11, *JPMorgan Chase Bank and J.P. Morgan Securities*, 5 July 2011.

[42] ibid [2].

in *Depfa Bank v Provincia di Pisa*[43] and *UBS v Kommunale Wasserwecke Leipzig*[44] where the English courts dismissed the jurisdictional challenges.

The way the 'court first seised' rule is shaping the litigants' strategies may be further illustrated by the pre-emptive strike which was initiated in *McGraw-Hill International (UK) Limited v Deutsche Apotheker and others*.[45] The claimant, S&P, was a global rating service provider, having an English branch. The first four defendants were non-UK based investors. In England, the claimant was seeking a non-liability declaration in the proceedings against these defendants. The claim against the fifth defendant, ABN Amro, was somewhat conditional. If S&P were held liable to the non-UK based investors, then ABN Amro were liable in respect of the same damage which S&P were liable for. Although the English proceedings were initiated on 23 March 2013, the claim form was not served till November 2013. There were parallel proceedings, which were initiated in Amsterdam. ABN Amro challenged the jurisdiction of the English court. It was held that the English court did not have jurisdiction under either Article 5(3) or 6(2) of Brussels I but did so under Article 5(5). Therefore, the English High Court dismissed the defendant's challenge to the jurisdiction, and the parallel proceedings in the Netherlands had to be stayed.

The interview respondents reaffirm the importance of the court-first-seised rule, outlining occasionally how it could be used to drag the parties before Member States' courts which are notoriously slow and delay the resolution of the dispute. The interview data suggest that this can have a big effect on the parties' access to remedies with one interview respondent noting that this might even lead to a claimant giving up on a claim because of the level of uncertainty and delay in some jurisdictions.[46]

iii. Service

The court-first-seised rule is often linked to the question of service. These aspects were thoroughly considered by the English High Court in *Debt Collection London v SK Slavia Praha*.[47] The dispute arose out of a loan agreement for the sum of £2,877,670. The agreement was governed by English law. The defendant was a football club from the Czech Republic. Repayment was demanded by the claimant in the English proceedings. Proceedings were first initiated in the Czech Republic by the defendant in the English proceedings. Although the Czech proceedings were first initiated, the fee required was not paid by the football club. As a result, the claim form was not served on the claimant in the English proceedings. On 12 June 2009, the claim form in the English proceedings was issued. On 4 August, the English proceedings were served on the defendant. The defendant challenged the jurisdiction of the English courts, and requested a stay under Article 27 of Brussels I. On 3 November the High Court dismissed the defendant's application, holding that the English court was first

---

[43] *Depfa Bank plc v Provincia di Pisa* [2010] EWHC 1148 (Comm).

[44] *UBS AG, London Branch & Anor v Kommunale Wasserwecke Leipzig GmbH* [2010] EWHC 2566 (Comm). See also: R Fentiman, 'Disarming the ultra vires Torpedo' (2011) 70 *Cambridge Law Journal* 513.

[45] *McGraw-Hill International (UK) Limited v Deutsche Apotheker—und Arztebank EG, Uniqa Alternative Investments GMBH, Uniqa Capital Markets GMBH, Stichting Ratings Redress, The Royal Bank of Scotland NV* [2014] EWHC 2436 (Comm).

[46] EUPILLAR—England and Wales—Interview Transcript No 15.

[47] *Debt Collection London Ltd & Anor v SK Slavia Praha-Fotbal AS* [2009] EWHC 2726 (QB).

seised. On 4 November 2010, the Court of Appeal dismissed the appeal on the jurisdictional point. Lord Justice Mummery held that 'non-payment of the fee was a failure to take a step required for effecting service'.[48] The key date for determining whether the proviso applied was held to be the date on which the competing proceedings, in this case the English proceedings, were seised under Article 30 of Brussels I.[49] In this case that date was 12 June 2009 and on that date the plaintiff in the Czech proceedings had failed to take the steps necessary to serve the defendant because it had not paid the Czech court fee and therefore on that date the proviso applied. This is a controversial but tenable interpretation of the proviso in Article 30(1) that the 'plaintiff has not subsequently failed to take the steps he was required to take to have service effected on the defendant' but because the issue of the interpretation of the Article 30 proviso was not referred to the CJEU some uncertainty remains as to its correct interpretation.[50] In this case the Czech claimant in the Czech proceedings had not 'failed' completely to take the steps necessary to have service effected on the defendant but rather had delayed the process of serving the defendant by not paying the Czech court fee, even though it could have done so, before the English court had been seised and the English proceedings had been served on it. Lloyd LJ tried to interpret Article 30 of Brussels I carefully by taking account of the *travaux préparatoires*, in particular the Commission's explanatory memorandum in its Proposal for Brussels I stating that the proviso in the first part of Article 30 requires the plaintiff to take 'all the requisite steps to have it served on the defendant'.[51]

The issues regarding service may also crop up, in the context of judgments given in default of appearance, at the stage of recognition and enforcement proceedings. For example, in *Reeve & Others v Plummer*,[52] an appeal was made against an order, registering a Belgian judgment which was rendered in default of appearance. The order was affirmed against two of the judgment debtors, Mr Allany and Mr Thomas. However, the order was set aside against Mr Reeve because he had appealed against the Belgian judgment. Mrs Justice Simler held:

> 30 … Although I accept fully that service was effected in accordance with Belgian law, because it was served by providing a copy to the Belgian public prosecutor in circumstances that applied in this case and therefore service was duly effected, the originating summons did not in fact come to the attention of any of the appellants at any time before the hearing on 25 March 2013, through no fault of theirs. None of them was able, therefore, as a matter of substance, to arrange for his defence based on such service and in advance of that hearing.

> 31 That, however, is not the end of the matter because, as I have described, art.34(2) provides that the judgment shall not be recognised if the defendant was not properly, for the purposes of art.34,

---

[48] *Debt Collection London Ltd & Anor v SK Slavia Praha-Fotbal AS* [2010] EWCA Civ 1250 [27].

[49] ibid [46] per Lloyd LJ and less clearly Burnton LJ [59]. Mummery LJ is even less clear as to when one must determine if the proviso is applicable because he refers to both the date on which the competing court, in this case the English court, is first seised and the date on which the English court's proceedings were served on the defendant in those proceedings, see [27].

[50] A point acknowledged by Burnton LJ ibid at [54]: 'I do not think that Article 30 of the Judgments Regulation, with its reference to the vague and undefined term "failure", and which requires a court to investigate and to determine the procedural law of another jurisdiction, achieves the clarity and simplicity of application that might have been hoped.'

[51] ibid [42].

[52] *Reeve & Others v Plummer* [2014] EWHC 4695 (QB).

served 'unless the defendant failed to commence proceedings to challenge the judgment when it was possible for him to do so'.[53]

Therefore, the question whether the service is effected in accordance with the requirements of fair trial may be subject to heated debates at different stages of cross-border proceedings. Some of the interview respondents do suggest that avoiding service may be an important tactical device which may cause delay. A more effective way of serving the process and in particular the introduction of electronic service might be considered with a view to defeating defendants' abusive litigation tactics.[54]

iv. Applicable Law Issues under the Rome I and Rome II Regulations

As already noted,[55] an effective remedy in a cross-border case may often be dependent on the national judges' ability to identify and apply the same law irrespective of where the parties litigate.[56] Although claimants' selectiveness in deciding where to litigate and defendants' jurisdictional challenges appear to dominate the litigants' strategies, this is not to say that the choice of law is not important. The point was captured well by Mrs Justice Gloster:

> The reason why it appears that Endesa is keen to establish the jurisdiction of the Spanish courts is that it thereby seeks to apply Spanish law to the substantive dispute between itself and NNC. Endesa's position is that, if Spanish law applies, then NNC, as owner of the Vessel, will be unable to raise any defence based on the concept of 'due diligence' under the Hague-Visby Rules, because under the Spanish Commercial Code, there is absolute liability imposed on a carrier for cargo, except for Acts of God and force majeure. I was not addressed as to the merits of this contention, but it forms the basis for this fierce jurisdictional dispute.[57]

That said, the case law indicates that the governing law was not considered in approximately 42 per cent of the cases in the civil and commercial law dataset. Moreover, in some 18 per cent of the cases, the choice of law issue was considered, but not debated by the parties because, for example, there was a governing law clause. The research interview data helpfully suggests that this might be explained by the fact that the governing law could well be pre-determined in many cross-border contractual disputes. Another important finding, which may be deduced from the qualitative research interviews, is that the parties would only invest time and resources to argue the applicable law if it would make a material difference to the resolution of the dispute.[58] This might well explain why the parties disagreed on the question which law should apply to the merits of the dispute only in 36 cases which amounted to approximately 20 per cent of the cases, included in the civil and commercial law dataset.[59]

Furthermore, in 30 other cases (approximately 16 per cent of the dataset), the applicable law was considered by the court with a view to establishing (or not establishing) jurisdiction.

---

[53] ibid [30–31].
[54] EUPILLAR—England and Wales—Interview Transcripts No 12, 13 and 15. See also: Report on the application of Reg (EC) No 1393/2007 COM(2013) 858 final, 5.
[55] Danov and Beaumont, above n 1.
[56] Recital 6 to Rome I and Rome II.
[57] *National Navigation Co v Endesa Generacion SA* [2009] EWHC 196 (Comm).
[58] EUPILLAR—England and Wales—Interview Transcript No 18.
[59] There were a few other cases where parties agreed as to the applicable law.

Under English common law, a judge may exercise its discretion to permit a service of claim form out of the jurisdiction, if a party makes a good arguable case that the contract is governed by English law.[60] This is a lesser standard of proof, which means that the applicable law issue is not fully decided.[61] The point may be illustrated by the parties' pleadings in *SSL v TTK*.[62] The claimant was an English company. The defendant was an Indian company. The dispute arose out of a contract for supply of condoms which were manufactured by the defendant in India. The claimant sought to establish jurisdiction in England, arguing that there was a valid English law and jurisdiction clause. However, the claimant failed to demonstrate that such a clause was incorporated. The English court concluded that the laws of India were applicable to the merits of the dispute.[63] As a result, India was the appropriate court for the trial to take place.

In spite of the fact that the research interviews appear to indicate that there is a level of satisfaction among legal practitioners with Rome I and Rome II and the scope of the applicable law in both instruments, there appears to be a higher level of uncertainty with regard to applicable law in cross-border non-contractual disputes. In particular, there have been choice-of-law disputes with regard to: traffic accidents with an international element,[64] product liability,[65] intellectual property,[66] competition law,[67] and unjust enrichment.[68] The problem may be exacerbated because, due to the fact that the current EU court system is somewhat slow (taking on average 15 months to respond to a preliminary reference request), the judges and parties are often reluctant to make preliminary references to the CJEU. In *Lady Christine Brownlie v Four Seasons Holdings*,[69] Lady Justice Arden stated:

> A further question is whether this court should exercise its discretion to make a reference to the CJEU for a preliminary ruling on the interpretation of Rome II. Questions which might properly be referred include the question whether the presumption that English law is the same as foreign law would apply, and where relevant damage occurred in respect of the claims. ... I do not entertain sufficient doubt about the question whether the presumption that foreign law is the same as English law applies to justify a reference on that question. The other questions are clearly not acte clair in the light of the number of decisions which have reached a different conclusion from my own (see paragraph 74 above). Even so, I do not consider it would be right to make a reference. Such an order would involve considerable delay and commit the parties irreversibly to that route without a clear result at this time to this appeal. Neither party was in favour of this court making a reference: ... I have concluded that it would be inappropriate for this court in this case to make any reference to the CJEU.[70]

---

[60] Practice Direction 6B, https://www.justice.gov.uk/courts/procedure-rules/civil/rules/part06/pd_part06b.

[61] MP Fons, 'Commercial Choice of Law in Context: Looking Beyond Rome' (2015) 78 *Modern Law Review* 241.

[62] *SSL International plc and another v TTK LIG Ltd and others* [2011] EWCA Civ 1170.

[63] ibid [81–82].

[64] eg *Lady Christine Brownlie (Widow and Executrix of the Estate of Professor Sir Ian Brownlie CBE QC) v Four Seasons Holdings Incorporated* [2014] EWHC 273 QB; *Winrow v Hemphill* [2014] EWHC 3164 (QB); *Bianco v Bennett* [2015] EWHC 626 (QB); *Tiffany Moreno v The Motor Insurers' Bureau* [2015] EWHC 1002 (QB).

[65] *Allen and other v Depuy International Ltd* [2014] EWHC 753 (QB).

[66] *Actavis UK Ltd and others v Eli Lilly and Co* [2014] EWHC 1511 (Pat).

[67] *DSG Retail Ltd, Dixons Retail Plc & others v Mastercard Inc & others* [2015] EWHC 3673 (Ch).

[68] *Banque Cantonale De Genève v Polevent Limited, Victor Azria, Enoi SpA* [2015] EWHC 1968 (Comm).

[69] *Lady Christine Brownlie v Four Seasons Holdings Incorporated* [2015] EWCA Civ 665.

[70] ibid [92].

The current institutional framework is not fully geared to ensuring consistent application of the private international law instruments, and this inevitably reflects on the parties' access to remedies in cross-border cases. Although parties to cross-border commercial disputes often prefer to settle out-of-court, the settlement levels may well be affected by an imperfect institutional architecture.[71] Litigants' strategies (including abusive litigation strategies) expose the weaknesses of the current model.

C. Cross-border Family Law Disputes

Mr Justice Munby has recently noted that '[t]he English family justice system is now part of a much wider system of international family justice exemplified by such instruments as the various Hague Conventions and, in the purely European context, by BIIR.'[72] In spite of the fact that not all of the judgments are reported (and not all the cross-border disputes have a connection with other EU countries), the family law dataset includes 167 PIL cases in family law matters (involving occasionally more than one judgment). This reiterates that an effective remedy may often be necessary for private parties in cross-border cases. This poses the following questions: What is the litigation pattern in family law disputes? How does the EU legal landscape affect the litigants' strategies and available remedies in cross-border family law proceedings? How does the litigation pattern in cross-border family law disputes compare to the one in civil and commercial law disputes with an international element?

Before looking at the question how the legislative framework is shaping the litigants' strategies in cross-border family disputes, it should be noted that the data show that the overwhelming majority of the remedies sought are in respect of children (eg care and custody; return of a child; contact order). The highest number of cases in the dataset are in relation to parental responsibility proceedings (75 cases—over 45 per cent of the cases in the family law dataset). Although there are only 41 cases (nearly 25 per cent of the cases in the dataset) which are in respect of child abduction, the interview data indicates that these are the majority of the international family cases before the High Court of England and Wales. Divorce and/or maintenance has arisen only in 29 cases which amounts to approximately 17 per cent of the cases in this dataset. There were identified only 13 reported cases (less than eight per cent) which are primarily concerned with the recognition and enforcement of foreign judgments in England and Wales. In addition, there are a number of cases, where the proceedings between the parties is a complete mixture of some (or even all) of the above.

One may be surprised by the relatively small number of divorce proceedings. However, the interview data suggest that most of the divorce proceedings, in which the parties seek financial remedies, eventually settle. There is one litigation pattern, which characterises cross-border family law disputes, involving children, and another litigation pattern in cross-border family law cases where financial remedies are sought. This is reflected in the

---

[71] See more in ch 35 and 40 of this book.
[72] *In the Matter of E (A Child)* [2014] EWHC 6 (Fam) [17].

specialisms of our interview respondents which show that only judges see all the types of family cases.

i. Litigants' Strategies: Remedies in Cross-border Disputes Involving Children

The disputes involving children appear to involve very committed parties who want a quick remedy. In England, these cases are likely to be heard by very experienced judges, who would also aim to resolve the disputes quickly, taking into account the best interests of the child in parental responsibility and access cases in line with Brussels IIa. The endeavour of the English courts to be compliant with the requirement, imposed by Brussels IIa to hear child abduction cases within 6 weeks, has been clearly acknowledged by the judiciary. Lord Justice Wall noted:

> 85 It is … with a sense of both shock and dismay that I find the chronology in the instant case revealing that the proceedings under the Hague Convention which were launched by the mother on 23 September 2005 were not heard by McFarlane J until 13 February 2006, his judgment being given promptly on 15 February 2006 after overnight reflection following the end of the two day hearing on 14 February. …
>
> 88 As a judge of the Family Division for eleven years, I am acutely conscious of the pressures on the judiciary and on those with responsibilities for listing. Article 11(3) of Brussels II Revised, however, does not admit of debate. It simply must be implemented.[73]

A similar point was made by Lord Justice Thorpe:

> One thing that is clear to me is that the obligation to hear the child must not override the obligation in the same Article 11 to conclude the proceedings within six weeks of issue. It must be implicit in the juxtaposition of the two obligations that the obligation to hear the child will be fulfilled within the six-week duration of the litigation, particularly since in the majority of member states the judge hears a child directly at the final hearing. But to ensure that there is no repetition of the unfortunate development in the present case, it seems to me necessary that in future the question of how and when the court will hear the child, in discharge of its obligations under Article 11(2), must be considered at the first directions appointment and any subsequent direction appointment to ensure that that central ingredient of the case is never out of the spotlight.[74]

The case law and interview data suggest that the English courts have made significant progress in complying with the Brussels IIa Regulation. The habitual residence of the child is an important connecting factor, ensuring that the court having jurisdiction is well placed to provide an effective remedy in cross-border parental responsibility proceedings and child abduction cases. The level of complexity and need for cooperation in these cases was noted by the President of the Family Division *In the Matter of E*.[75] In this case, the care proceedings initiated by a Local Authority were in respect of a child, E. The child was born in England in 2001 and continued to live there. Both parents were Slovakian nationals. As a result, the Slovakian Central Authority got involved. The case received significant media attention in Slovakia. Sir James Munby held that the English court had jurisdiction, refusing

---

[73] *Joelle Vigreux v Patrick Jacques Robert Michel, Pierre-Mathieu Bernard Rene Michel* [2006] EWCA Civ 630.
[74] *In the Matter of F (a Child)* [2007] EWCA Civ 468 [24].
[75] *In the Matter of E (A Child)* [2014] EWHC 6 (Fam).

to transfer the proceedings to Slovakia and approving the local authority's care plan. He gave the following guidance:

> 35 It is highly desirable, and from now on good practice will require, that in any care or other public law case with a European dimension the court should set out quite explicitly, both in its judgment and in its order:
>
> i)   the basis upon which, in accordance with the relevant provisions of [Brussels IIa], it is, as the case may be, either accepting or rejecting jurisdiction;
> ii)   the basis upon which, in accordance with Article 15, it either has or, as the case may be, has not decided to exercise its powers under Article 15.
>
> 36 … Judges must be astute to raise these points even if they have been overlooked by the parties. And where Article 17 applies it is the responsibility of the judge to ensure that the appropriate declaration is made.[76]

The collected data from England and Wales reaffirms the important role of Article 17 and Article 15. But, do all national courts comply with Article 17? The fact that there must be consistent application of the jurisdictional rules across the EU for Brussels IIa was noted during the research interviews, reiterating the need for training for national judges. The issues with the way the current regime may be applied/misapplied in some Member States were exposed in *Re: S (A Child)*.[77] The proceedings concerned a child born in October 2009. The mother was from Croatia, and the father was from Greece. The parties met and married in England. There were a number of proceedings between the parties in both Greece and England. The child was abducted by the father in January 2014, and stayed in Greece. In spite of the fact that the child was habitually resident in the UK, the Greek court, ignoring Article 17 of Brussels IIa, wrongfully assumed jurisdiction. Following an application for a return order which was made by the mother in March 2014, the child was returned to England in August 2014. In October 2014, Mr Justice Wood made an order, determining the living arrangements for the child, and noted:

> 82 It proved very easy for the paternal family to mislead the Greek court as to its jurisdiction, as they appear to have done; and also as to the habitual residence of the child. It took months to rectify this. Even then, having decided that the habitual residence of S was England before the wrongful retention by the father, they did not declare that they had no jurisdiction as is required by Article 17 of the Regulation, nor did they accept that they had no powers, taking account of Articles 8 and 10 of the Regulation, to make more than interim measures pursuant to Article 20 of it.[78]

English family law judges promote a truly EU family justice arena through their practice in applying Article 15. In this context, the English court has made transfer requests in 16 cases, which is over 20 per cent of the parental responsibility proceedings in the dataset. The English court assumed jurisdiction, refusing to make a transfer request in slightly less than 20 per cent of parental responsibility cases in our dataset. The provision was considered in eight other cases, which clearly indicates the important role this provision may have in ensuring that the case is to be heard and determined by an appropriate court. The English

---

[76] ibid [35–36].
[77] *Re: S (A Child)* [2014] EWHC 4643 (Fam).
[78] ibid [82].

courts will have to take account of the guidance given by the CJEU on Article 15 in a recent case.[79]

Finally, it is also an important factor that litigation funding appears to be generally provided in cases involving children. However, there are cases where legal aid may not be available—especially for the abducting parent in child abduction cases. The point was captured well by Lord Justice Thorpe who stated:

> In the court below the judge decided the issue in favour of the unrepresented defendant. However in this court the appellant has the advantage of a specialist solicitor, who has been approved for inclusion on the Central Authorities panel, he has a specialist junior in Mr Khan and he has a specialist leader in Mr Scott-Manderson. Against that array of highly skilled expertise the mother has no guide, only a … skilful and sympathetic interpreter. She made her submission to us with great dignity and with brevity. It may well be that even if she had had Mr Scott-Manderson to put her case he would not have been able to say any more than she said for herself. However those who take these difficult decisions as to how public money should be spent in family law cases should ask themselves whether they have got the balance right in giving so much to the left behind parent, without any investigation of means or merit, and in withdrawing public funding for the defendant, on the ground that she may have an interest in a property in another jurisdiction, that may have value but which could not possibly be utilised to provide immediate funding for urgent litigation.[80]

Hence, there might be an issue of injustice in cases where the litigants are appearing in person.[81] The point about the funding aspects of cases involving children was reiterated by legal practitioners during the research interviews. It is a very good aspect of the international family justice system in England and Wales that these cases are normally dealt with by very experienced, specialised judges and it is good that this example is being followed by the Commission's Proposal for the Recast of Brussels IIa in relation to child abduction cases. However, it is also important for the issue of litigation funding (and legal aid in particular) for cross-border family cases to be considered beyond the context of child maintenance where it is already guaranteed due to the Maintenance Regulation following the Hague Maintenance Convention 2007.[82]

ii. Financial Remedies in Cross-border Matrimonial Disputes

As already noted,[83] due to the fact that an English and Welsh court will normally not apply foreign law(s) in cross-border family law disputes, England is a venue of choice for high value matrimonial disputes. There is a very persuasive view that 'the Brussels 2 regulation … encourages forum shopping, inasmuch as it does not contain, in relation to a suit for divorce, a provision to transfer the suit ….'[84] In spite of the fact that there are not many

---

[79] Case C-428/15, *Child and Family Agency v JD* EU:C:2016:819 requested by the Supreme Court of Ireland.

[80] *In the Matter of K* [2010] EWCA Civ 1546 [50].

[81] EUPILLAR—England and Wales—Interview Transcript No 13.

[82] For an argument to this effect see P Beaumont, L Walker and J Holliday, 'Conflicts of EU Courts on Child Abduction: The Reality of Article 11(6)–(8) Brussels IIa Proceedings across the EU' (2016) 12 *Journal of Private International Law* 211, 251–53. On maintenance see P Beaumont, 'International Family Law in Europe—The Maintenance Project, the Hague Conference and the EC: A Triumph of Reverse Subsidiarity' (2009) 73 *Rabels Zeitschrift für ausländisches und internationales Privatrecht* 509.

[83] Danov and Beaumont, above n 1.

[84] Mr Justice Mostyn in *CC v NC* [2014] EWHC 703 (Fam) [14].

reported cases about the financial remedies in cross-border divorce proceedings, the interview data clearly confirms that wealthy couples are indeed selective about where to seek financial remedies. In particular, the overwhelming view of the interview respondents is that England, where the courts apply English law, is a very attractive jurisdiction for financially weaker parties.

There is a strong case that the court-first-seised rule appears to dominate the litigants' strategies under the current Brussels IIa regime for adults. The qualitative interview data indicate that there is a high level of tactical manoeuvring with a view to securing a more beneficial financial remedy in high value matrimonial disputes, with one legal practitioner noting that:

> We have 400,000 French, living in London at the moment; many of whom are wealthy. They can get divorced either in Paris or in London. In Paris, the marriage contract is binding—no assets are divided. In England, the marriage contract is not binding and is not recognised. So, especially, if … the husband has many millions of pounds, the wife may get … three million, five million, ten million pounds more in London than in Paris. It's very, very stark—the difference.[85]

This example illustrates how the financial remedy drives the litigants' tactics which were spectacularly exposed in the jurisdiction battle that evolved in the *S v S* case.[86] In this case, the proceedings were between a husband and wife who were both French nationals. The parties were married in France in 1997 before moving to England in 2000. The matrimonial home appeared to be in London. In June 2010, the parties separated, with the husband relocating to live in a rented flat in West London. On 30 March 2011, the husband issued judicial separation proceedings in France. Following a conciliation hearing in November 2011, the case progressed onto adversarial mode on 15 December 2011, when the French court issued a declaration that it had jurisdiction under Brussels IIa. That said, 'the law in France stipulates that after 30 months a judicial separation suit which has not been disposed of will lapse. The date and time for such lapsing was midnight on Monday 16th June 2014.'[87] Since the husband remained passive till 8:20 am on 17 June 2014, the wife issued divorce proceedings on 13th June 2014 in England. The husband challenged the English court's jurisdiction, relying on Article 19 of Brussels IIa. He argued that, on 13 June 2014, when the wife issued the divorce proceedings in England, the jurisdiction of the French court had been established. This posed the question whether the English court was first or second seised within the meaning of Brussels IIa. A reference was made to the CJEU to clarify the meaning of 'established' for the purposes of Article 19 of Brussels IIa. On 6 October 2015, the CJEU held that the English court was first seised, stating that:

> 40. A petition for judicial separation had already been filed with the family court of the tribunal de grande instance de Nanterre when the United Kingdom court was seised, on 13 June 2014, of divorce proceedings, giving rise to a situation of *lis pendens* until midnight on 16 June 2014. Once that date had passed, that is to say, at 00.00 on 17 June, since the proceedings before the French court first seised had lapsed as a result of the expiry of the provisions of the nonconciliation order made by that court, only the United Kingdom court seised on 13 June 2014 remained seised of a dispute falling within one of the areas referred to in Article 19(1) of Regulation No 2201/2003. The commencement on 17 June 2014 of divorce proceedings before a French court was subsequent to

---

[85] EUPILLAR—England and Wales—Interview Transcript 16.
[86] *S v S* [2014] EWHC 3613 (Fam).
[87] ibid [13].

the commencement of the proceedings brought before that United Kingdom court. Taking into account the chronological rules laid down by that regulation, it must be held that the effect of that sequence of events is that, subject to its being lawfully seised under the rules in Article 16 of Regulation No 2201/2003, the United Kingdom court became the court first seised.[88]

The case not only demonstrates the effect of the financial remedy on the parties' behaviour, but it also shows what the weaknesses are for the current EU PIL regime (which shapes the litigants' tactics). Indeed, Mr Justice Mostyn identified a case for reform by stating:

> 17 This is a sorry tale of manoeuvring in the face of the seemingly inflexible jurisdiction rules in relation to divorces which are contained in Brussels II Revised. It is a remarkable and regrettable fact that Brussels II Revised contains within Article 15 a procedure which allows a court which has jurisdiction to transfer the case in question to another court within the European Union if it is better placed to hear it, but that power is available only in relation to children's cases. There is no comparable provision within Brussels II Revised which allows a court to transfer a divorce to the courts of another member state on the basis that the courts of that latter member state would be best placed to hear the case. … one can see that in relation to divorce cases the anomalous situation arises that there are no powers … to achieve a transfer to a court which is better placed to hear the case or otherwise is a more convenient forum. It is in the face of this iron inflexibility that the parties in divorce cases engage in such extensive, expensive and futile manoeuvres as have been demonstrated in this case.[89]

Given the importance of the court-first-seised rule, an interesting observation is that five legal practitioners,[90] specialising in cross-border matrimonial disputes, highlighted that there is a risk at the moment that different Member States' courts might tend to interpret the instruments in a way which allows them to establish jurisdiction and apply their own national law. Interestingly, two of them felt that the issue did exist in England and Wales (where judges might be trying to provide a just result for the financially weaker party),[91] but two thought that this was an issue for some of the other Member States.[92] On this basis, one could suggest that this should be an issue for the EU legislator to consider in the course of the ongoing revision of Brussels IIa.

The interview data also suggest that the flip side of the financially weaker party's strategic decision to sue in England is that the other party will be dragged into a jurisdiction where s/he does not want to be. This means that there may often be fierce jurisdictional battles, occasionally involving parallel proceedings, adversely affecting the settlement negotiations. Therefore, in stark contrast with the litigation pattern in cross-border cases involving children, the cases where the financial remedies are to be considered may make parties very tactical, raising preliminary issues and delaying significantly the resolution of the dispute.

The litigants' strategies may well inflate the litigation costs, which is why a number of English judges have noted the high litigation costs in their judgments.[93] In this context, Mr Justice Peter Jackson made the following remark:

> Persistent failure to reach agreement has generated an absurd level of legal costs. I directed the parties to provide schedules of expenditure to date. The wife's costs now amount to £425,000, of which

---

[88] Case C-489/14 *A v B* EU:C:2015:654 [40]. See further ch 41 below, 724–26.
[89] *S v S* [2014] EWHC 3613 (Fam) [17].
[90] EUPILLAR—England and Wales—Interview Transcripts No 6, 8, 9, 16 and 20.
[91] EUPILLAR—England and Wales—Interview Transcripts No 8 and 20.
[92] EUPILLAR—England and Wales—Interview Transcripts No 6 and 16.
[93] eg *JKN v JCN* [2010] EWHC 843 (Fam) [7]; *W Husband v W Wife* [2010] EWHC 1843 (Fam) [4–5].

£114,000 remains unpaid. The husband's costs amount to £500,000, of which £63,000 remains unpaid. The overall bill to the family, now standing at £925,000, will no doubt top £1 million if next month's hearing about the children goes ahead. It should be recalled that this level of expense has been incurred without a basis of jurisdiction having been established, or a page being filed in relation to the ultimate financial orders that will be required.[94]

On this basis, there is a case for reforming the jurisdictional rules or the court-first-seised rule at the EU level. Furthermore, 'special substantive rules for multistate problems',[95] which allow English judges to take account of foreign laws in the family law area might be considered in the UK.

D. Institutional Architecture

As Beaumont and Danov have already noted,[96] devising an appropriate institutional architecture for the interpretation and application of PIL legislative instruments is central to the effective functioning of the EU civil justice system. The point has been reiterated by Hess who has recently noted that 'it is dangerous to regard procedures in isolation, without looking at the institutional framework in which [the relevant] norms are implemented.'[97] This poses the question how effectively the current institutional framework functions in England and Wales.

Lawyers and judges in this jurisdiction have gained significant experience in dealing with complex cross-border disputes. An important indicator, regarding the consistent application of the EU PIL framework, concerns the extent to which English judges are relying on the recitals and CJEU case law. The civil and commercial law dataset shows that, in approximately 80 per cent of the cases (on 150 occasions), the English judges referred to the CJEU case law. Moreover, in 28.3 per cent of the cases in that dataset, the judges also thoroughly engaged with the relevant recitals. Therefore, there is a strong case that the English judges apply and interpret the EU PIL instruments purposively.[98] This was clearly reflected in the qualitative interview data, with one interview respondent noting that 'the general aim of a British court in interpreting regulations is to look at their overall scheme, and to try and make sense of the particular words in the light of that overall scheme.'[99] That said, this does not necessarily mean that the English judges have not 'reached conclusions which have subsequently on a reference been held to be non-compliant with EU law.'[100] For example, before *Owusu*[101] was decided by the CJEU, the English courts had held the opinion that

---

[94] *V v V* [2011] EWHC 1190 (Fam) [62].

[95] AT von Mehren, 'Special Substantive Rules for Multistate Problems: Their role and significance in contemporary choice of law methodology' (1974–75) 88 *Harvard Law Review* 347.

[96] P Beaumont and M Danov, 'The EU Civil Justice Framework and Private Law: "Integration through [Private International] Law"' (2015) 22 *Maastricht Journal of European and Comparative Law* 706–31.

[97] B Hess, 'Harmonized Rules and Minimum Standards in the European Law of Civil Procedure—In-Depth Analysis' PE 556.971 EN, http://www.europarl.europa.eu/RegData/etudes/IDAN/2016/556971/IPOL_IDA(2016)556971_EN.pdf, 11.

[98] EUPILLAR—England and Wales—Interview Transcripts No 4 and 19.

[99] EUPILLAR—England and Wales—Interview Transcript No 19.

[100] ibid.

[101] Case C-281/02, *Andrew Owusu v NB Jackson, trading as 'Villa Holidays Bal-Inn Villas' and Others* [2005] ECR I-1383, EU:C:2005:120.

Brussels I had not precluded the use of the *forum non conveniens* test in a case involving a conflict of jurisdiction between the English courts having jurisdiction under Brussels I and the courts of a non-EU Member State.[102] Although there are cases where the English judges might have misapplied/misinterpreted the relevant EU PIL instruments,[103] these are few and far between.

Whilst a reference to the CJEU may be an appropriate remedy in a case where the interpretation is at issue, the qualitative interview data shows that a real problem is that such a preliminary reference 'does come with a heavy price tag in terms of doing justice speedily. [I]f you make a reference, it is about 18 months, or maybe longer now, which is a very long time to essentially suspend proceedings between the parties to get an answer on that.'[104] This may make English judges and parties reluctant to make references to the CJEU.[105] In a very high proportion of the cases in our civil and commercial law dataset (approximately 88 per cent) no preliminary reference was considered; in only 4.8 per cent (nine) of the cases was a preliminary reference made, and, in seven per cent of the cases a reference was considered (either by the parties or the court) but no such reference was made to the CJEU.

The lack of an effective and efficient support for national judges to consistently apply the EU PIL instruments may reduce the effectiveness of the EU PIL instruments. This would be very much so in cases where the litigators start exploiting the ambiguities of the EU PIL instrument in order to gain a negotiating advantage for their clients in cross-border civil and commercial cases.[106]

In spite of the fact that some common law scholars have heavily criticised some of the CJEU judgments interpreting the Brussels I regime,[107] the English judges do not overtly

---

[102] *Travelers Casualty and Surety Company of Europe Limited and Others v Sun Life Assurance Company of Canada* [2004] EWHC 1704 (Comm). Although the judge's interpretation of Brussels I was wrong, the judge (after applying the *forum non conveniens* test) held that it was more appropriate for a trial to take place in England (rather than Canada).

[103] eg *Tiffany Moreno v The Motor Insurers' Bureau* [2015] EWHC 1002 (QB) [82] identifies an interpretation error which was made in *Jacobs v MIB* [2010] EWCA Civ 1208.

[104] EUPILLAR—England and Wales—Interview Transcript No 4.

[105] For example the House of Lords did not consider the issue of a reference to the CJEU when confronted with what was then a novel point of interpretation of Art 5(1)(b) of Brussels I in *Scottish & Newcastle International v Othon Ghalanos* [2008] UKHL 11 perhaps because the parties were agreed (see para 4) that the issue was governed by English law as a matter of the interpretation of where under the contract was the place of delivery of the goods. Lord Bingham did not take the time to show that a proper interpretation of Art 5(1)(b) requires a reference to where 'under the contract' the goods were delivered or should have been delivered and instead wrongly relied on the parties' reliance on *Tessili v Dunlop* as a good interpretation of Art 5(1)(b) when in fact it only applies to Art 5(1)(a), see para 4. However, Lord Bingham's short judgment is not concurred in by any of the other Law Lords and it is Lord Mance's judgment that is the majority judgment (concurred in by Lords Neuberger and Brown) and he does notice that Art 5(1)(b) has created a notion of the place of delivery of the goods being the place where the obligation which characterises a contract for the sale of goods is to be performed (see para 51) but he does not clearly explain why Art 5(1)(b) requires him to determine where 'under the contract' the goods were [to be] delivered. Having decided that the contract was FOB it should have been enough to say that the place of delivery of goods under an FOB contract is the place of shipment, in this case Liverpool, and therefore the English and Welsh courts have jurisdiction. Otherwise it would seem that a reference to the CJEU would have been necessary to resolve the correct interpretation of Art 5(1)(b). For more on the interpretation of Art 5(1)(b) (7(1)(b) of Brussels Ia) see chs 33 and 36 below.

[106] See more in chs 35 and 40 below.

[107] For example T Hartley, 'The European Union and the Systematic Dismantling of the Common Law of Conflict of Laws' (2005) 54 *International and Comparative Law Quarterly* 813–28; A Briggs, 'The Impact of Recent Judgments of the European Court on English Procedural Law and Practice', http://papers.ssrn.com/sol3/papers.cfm?abstract_id=899689#PaperDownload.

rebel against the CJEU's interpretations. The point was recently made in *Dominic Liswaniso Lungowe & Others v Vedanta Resources Plc and Konkola Copper Mines Plc*[108] where Mr Justice Coulson held:

> 65. In my judgment, there is no basis on which this court could stay the claim against [a UK domiciled defendant] on *forum non conveniens* grounds. I am bound to reach that conclusion by *Owusu*. ...
>
> ... the mere fact that the reasoning in *Owusu* might be said to be capable of sustained criticism does not make the decision any the less binding on me. The result in *Owusu*, and the fact that it has been followed in domestic decisions which are also binding on me ... mean that I am bound to follow it.[109]

Likewise, the English family law judges have endeavoured to provide for a consistent and uniform application of Brussels IIa. A good example is the Court of Appeal's judgment in *Re T*.[110] In this case, the English High Court issued a transfer request, holding that the requirements of Article 15 of Brussels IIa were satisfied.[111] However, Mr Justice Mostyn[112]—when setting out the relevant principles for the transfer of proceedings under Brussels IIa—relied on an English High Court's judgment which specified that '[a]uthority for ... four [out of five relevant] principles derives from *Spiliada*.'[113] Although it was held that the outcome about the transfer of proceedings in this case was consistent with Brussels IIa, the Court of Appeal condemned the approach adopted to the interpretation of Article 15. Lord Justice Thorpe held that:

> The construction of article 15 must be uniform throughout the courts of the member states. It cannot be dominated by a domestic law approach in cases brought under the domestic jurisdiction, whether it be statutory or inherent. The context of the issue before Wilson J and the law that he was applying are radically different to the determination of article 15, which was hardly in being when he was sitting in the domestic case.[114]

The family law dataset shows that, in approximately 29 per cent of the cases (on 48 occasions), the CJEU case law was expressly taken into account. Moreover, in 21 per cent of the cases in that dataset, the relevant PIL instrument's recitals were referred to. The lower proportion of cross-border family cases (than civil and commercial law cases) where the judges engage with the CJEU case law and/or the PIL instruments' recitals may be explained by two reasons which were identified in the qualitative interview data. First, '[t]he number of times that one encounters the need to [refer to the recitals] is very low, because most of the cases

---

[108] *Dominic Liswaniso Lungowe & Others v Vedanta Resources Plc and Konkola Copper Mines Plc* [2016] EWHC 975 (TCC).

[109] ibid [65 and 71].

[110] *Re T (A Child) (Care Proceedings: Request to Assume Jurisdiction)* [2013] EWCA Civ 895.

[111] *The Local Authority v The Mother, The Father, The Child (a minor by his Children's Guardian), The Central Authority of the Republic of Slovakia* [2013] EWHC 521 (Fam).

[112] ibid [16–17].

[113] *M v M (Stay of Proceedings: Return of Children)* [2005] EWHC 1159 (Fam) [6]. See also *Spiliada Maritime Corp v Cansulex Ltd* [1987] AC 460, the leading case on *forum non conveniens* in England and Wales in which the doctrine was adopted into English and Welsh law from Scots law, see A Arzandeh, 'The Origins of the Scottish *Forum Non Conveniens* Doctrine' (2017) 13 *Journal of Private International Law* 130.

[114] *Re T (A Child) (Care Proceedings: Request to Assume Jurisdiction)* [2013] EWCA Civ 895 [19].

are on the beaten path.'[115] Second, the judges may have a high number of cases which they will have to hastily deal with. As one interview respondent noted:

> I think we can impart far greater knowledge and understanding into these cases than the time actually is available to deal with them. The vast majority of these cases: you have to deal with them very quickly; and you have to do justice. And if you have litigants in person or if you have 10 cases in your list, you get through it as quickly as you can; you try to be fair. But I'm afraid you're not looking at the intention of the EU legislature; you are doing your best to come to the right decision in the interests of the children, if there are children; in the interests of applying the Convention, if it's child abduction; and you don't really think about the bigger picture.[116]

The foregoing aspects of the cross-border family law proceedings could explain why there were very few cases in which the English court made (or considered making) a reference to the CJEU. In particular, there were identified only three reference requests which were made by the English and Welsh courts to the CJEU.[117] On two other occasions, making a reference request was considered, without being made to the CJEU.[118] The issue was discussed with the interviewed family law judges from England and Wales, they confirmed that the parties—'very, very unusually'[119]—would request the court to make such a reference to the CJEU.

Another consequence of the high number of cross-border cases is that lawyers do specialise in providing certain types of cross-border litigation services, developing advanced knowledge and understanding of every nuance of the PIL framework in their area of expertise. This knowledge might make them well placed to exploit any of the existing ambiguities/uncertainties of the different aspects of the current PIL framework to the benefit of their clients.

The ambiguities may be significant if the EU PIL instruments are inappropriately drafted with all the difficult issues (which had to be negotiated), featuring in the recitals. This might affect the ability of the judges to interpret the Regulations,[120] allowing for strategic parties to embark on preliminary disputes about how the EU PIL rules should be interpreted. An analysis of the litigants' strategies nicely exposes the weaknesses of the current system. Tactical manoeuvrings may delay the resolution of the dispute, adversely affecting the availability of effective remedies in cross-border cases. The interviews do suggest that the problem may not be with the rules as such. It may well be that the litigants' strategies may be the more difficult (and indeed dynamic) aspect to deal with under the current system. In particular, there may be a significant delay in cases where tactical claims are initiated before an appropriate forum as well as in cases where tactical jurisdictional challenges are raised.

---

[115] EUPILLAR—England and Wales—Interview Transcript No 14.

[116] EUPILLAR—England and Wales—Interview Transcript No 13.

[117] *Barbara Mercredi v Richard Chaffe* [2011] EWCA Civ 272—Case C-497/10 PPU, *Mercredi v Chaffe*, EU:C:2010:829; *PB (mother) v SE (father)* [2013] EWHC 647 (Fam)—Case 436/13, *E v B*, EU:C:2014:2246; and *S v S* [2014] EWHC 3613 (Fam)—Case C-489/14 *A v B* EU:C:2015:654.

[118] *In re I (A Child) (Contact Application: Jurisdiction) (Centre for Family Law and Practice and another intervening)* [2009] UKSC 10; *Wai Foon TAN v Weng Kean* [2014] EWCA Civ 251.

[119] EUPILLAR—England and Wales—Interview Transcript No 14. See also EUPILLAR—England and Wales—Interview Transcript No 13.

[120] EUPILLAR—England and Wales—Interview Transcript No 19.

In the light of the majority for leaving the EU in the referendum in June 2016 it is unwise to suggest any specific reforms of the application of EU PIL in England and Wales. It will be some time before it will emerge which if any aspects of the five EU PIL Regulations will remain part of the law of England and Wales but it is clear that the UK Government will not accept any continuing jurisdiction of the CJEU to rule on English and Welsh cases after Brexit is completed. The EU institutional architecture could be improved by specialist PIL judges in the CJEU able to offer a quicker and more reliable service on interpretation of EU PIL and the EU legislature could help the CJEU and national judges to accurately interpret EU PIL Regulations by reinstating official explanatory reports on their interpretation.

III. Scotland

A. Introduction

Although a part of the UK since 1707, Scotland has its own legal system and court structure as guaranteed by the Treaty and Act of Union 1707. Scotland is regarded as a mixed legal system having been influenced by both English common law and continental civil law.[121]

In Scotland, the majority of civil law cases are dealt with in the country's Sheriff Courts which are located throughout Scotland. The Court of Session is Scotland's highest civil court which deals with all forms of civil cases. It always sits in Edinburgh and is divided into the Outer House which hears the cases as a first instance court and the Inner House which hears the cases from both the Outer House and Sheriff Courts as an appeal court. The judgments of the Inner House may be appealed against to the UK Supreme Court but only a small number of cases are heard by that Court.[122]

This report is based on data gathered from the case law of the courts of Scotland on the Brussels I, Rome I, Rome II, Brussels IIa and Maintenance Regulations between March 2002 and December 2015 and from the interviews conducted in Scotland and London as part of the Project.

The data on case law derives from 13 cases decided by the Scottish courts.[123] Eight of them are family law cases dealt with under Brussels IIa and Brussels I whereas five of them are civil and commercial cases under Brussels I. The search results were subject to a first-step analysis in order to select the cases which raise a point in the context of the five EU Regulations that are examined in the Project. Following this analysis, the selected cases were subject to the second-step analysis for the purposes of this Report and the EUPILLAR Database. There are no reported Scottish cases on the Rome I, Rome II and Maintenance Regulations yet and therefore those parts of the Report are based primarily on the interview data. The case law has been identified through various public and private databases

---

[121] On this issue, see generally K Zweigert and H Kötz (translated by T Weir), *Introduction to Comparative Law* 3rd edn (Oxford, Clarendon Press, 1998) 201–04; E Attwooll, 'Scotland: A Multi-Dimensional Jigsaw' in E Örücü, E Attwooll and S Coyle (eds), *Studies in Legal Systems: Mixed and Mixing* (Alphen aan den Rijn, Kluwer Law, 1996) 17–34.

[122] For this information on the courts structure in Scotland, see www.scotland-judiciary.org.uk/16/0/Court-Structure.

[123] All cases are available in the EUPILLAR Database at https://w3.abdn.ac.uk/clsm/eupillar/#/home.

and law reports. The data on interviews derive from 13 interviews conducted with judges from the UK Supreme Court,[124] Court of Session[125] and Sheriff Courts,[126] and with legal practitioners[127] in Scotland. The interviewees were randomly selected from a long list of potential interviewees which was prepared on the basis of the interviewees' expertise and experience in the field of EU PIL and, in particular, in the application of the Regulations that are examined in the Project.

The case law and interview data indicate that the majority of disputes with a cross-border element in Scotland concern family law matters, particularly child abduction, and that cross-border contractual disputes take the second place.[128] In the field of tort/delict, the interview data indicate that personal injury claims are increasing.[129]

B. Cross-border Civil and Commercial Disputes

The case law data indicate that decided cross-border cases in civil and commercial matters are very rare in Scotland. Indeed, the Scottish dataset includes only five cross-border civil and commercial cases that have been reported, all on Brussels I. The interviews conducted with judges also affirm that cross-border cases in civil and commercial matters are very rare in Scotland.[130] The types of proceedings are quite diverse, but mostly contractual in a broad sense.

On the other hand, the interviews conducted with legal practitioners indicate that there is a demand for cross-border legal advice in Scotland. Legal entities are more likely to seek 'cross-border' advice as they are generally able to identify the matter as involving a cross-border element and consider the implications, whereas when private individuals and consumers seek advice they do not necessarily seek 'cross-border' advice as they are generally not quite aware whether their claim is 'cross-border'.[131]

In the field of contract law, the demand for cross-border advice is particularly high in the oil and gas industry.[132] The oil and gas industry has been playing a major role in the Scottish economy since the discovery of North Sea oil in 1966 and at present Scotland is the largest producer of oil and the second largest of gas in the EU.[133] The advice is sought mostly by large international companies and by some SMEs.[134] In the oil and gas industry, the parties tend to settle or negotiate rather than go to court because they do not want

---

[124] EUPILLAR_Scotland 1.

[125] EUPILLAR_Scotland 2, EUPILLAR_Scotland 3 and EUPILLAR_Scotland 4.

[126] EUPILLAR_Scotland 7, EUPILLAR_Scotland 9 and EUPILLAR_Scotland 13.

[127] EUPILLAR_Scotland 5, EUPILLAR_Scotland 6, EUPILLAR_Scotland 8, EUPILLAR_Scotland 10, EUPILLAR_Scotland 11 and EUPILLAR_Scotland 12.

[128] EUPILLAR_Scotland 1, EUPILLAR_Scotland 2, EUPILLAR_Scotland 3, EUPILLAR_Scotland 4.

[129] EUPILLAR_Scotland 4.

[130] EUPILLAR_Scotland 9, EUPILLAR_Scotland 13. In many contexts family law matters are included within civil and commercial matters, eg in the Hague and EU instruments on taking of evidence and service of documents, but in the EUPILLAR research family law is treated as a separate category partly because under Art 81 TFEU, the legal basis for the EU PIL Regulations, 'measures concerning family law' have to be adopted by unanimity by the Council under the special legislative procedure whereas all other PIL measures are adopted by qualified majority in the Council and majority in the European Parliament under the ordinary legislative procedure.

[131] EUPILLAR_Scotland 12.

[132] EUPILLAR_Scotland 8.

[133] www.snh.gov.uk/land-and-sea/managing-coasts-and-sea/oil-and-gas/.

[134] EUPILLAR_Scotland 8.

to tarnish business relationships, and if they do go to court it is rarely the Scottish courts because the parties typically select English law and the exclusive jurisdiction of the courts of England and Wales in their contracts.[135] This empirical data also indicate that, in general, party autonomy provided for in Brussels I, Rome I and in the legislation in the UK, which applies a modified version of the former and an unchanged version of the latter to intra-UK cases, works well.

The interview data indicate that in the field of tort/delict, there is a reasonable level of demand for cross-border legal advice in personal injury cases. Although some of the demand is for intra-UK cases, there is also demand for cross-border legal advice in cases involving accidents in other EU Member States such as Spain, Romania, Greece and Poland.[136] A legal practitioner stated that their Foreign and Travel Law Department had about 700 to 800 cases at the time of the interview[137] which is quite high. The legal advice is sought from Scots who are injured abroad, foreign nationals who are injured in Scotland, and foreign nationals who are injured abroad but are residing in Scotland.[138] The insurance companies from the EU Member States are often represented by a law firm in Scotland.[139] The interview data indicate that personal injury disputes nearly always settle and only very few of them ever go to a final court hearing.[140]

i. Jurisdictional and Procedural Issues under the Brussels I Regulation[141]

a. Matters Related to the Scope of Application

The Scottish dataset includes one case where a question of the scope of application of Brussels I arose in a divorce action in relation to the enforceability of a decree for payment.[142] This case addressed the distinction between matters of maintenance and matrimonial property. In this case, the Court of Session granted a decree of payment of £1 million but attributed 50 per cent of it to maintenance as this term was used in Brussels I, in order to enable the pursuer to enforce that sum in other EU Member States under Brussels I. An order in respect of maintenance was then within the scope of the Brussels I Regulation with a special rule of jurisdiction under Article 5(2) whereas an order in respect of rights in property arising out of a matrimonial relationship was excluded from the scope of the Regulation by Article 1(2)(a). This is a very practical solution that the Court of Session found before the Maintenance Regulation entered into force and before maintenance was excluded from the scope of Brussels I by Article 1(2)(e) of the Recast. The case may provide guidance for other courts in the EU today as to what is enforceable as maintenance under the Maintenance Regulation in relation to a Scottish judgment on the financial consequences of a divorce.

---

[135] For settlement and alternative dispute resolution in civil and commercial disputes in Scotland, see s III. iv and v below respectively.

[136] EUPILLAR_Scotland 10.

[137] EUPILLAR_Scotland 11.

[138] EUPILLAR_Scotland 10, EUPILLAR_Scotland 11.

[139] EUPILLAR_Scotland 10.

[140] EUPILLAR_Scotland 10, EUPILLAR_Scotland 11.

[141] On this issue, see also P Beaumont and P McEleavy, *Anton's Private International Law* 3rd edn (Edinburgh, SULI, 2011) chs 8 and 9; EB Crawford and JM Carruthers, *International Private Law: A Scots Perspective* 4th edn (Edinburgh, W Green, 2015) chs 7 and 9.

[142] *B v D (also known as AB v CD)*, Court of Session (Outer House), [2006] CSOH 200 (Lord Brodie).

b. Matters Related to Jurisdiction

The Scottish dataset includes two cases where the courts dealt with special jurisdiction rules under Article 5 of Brussels I and both cases represent good practice of the Regulation by the Scottish courts. In *Oceanfix International Ltd v AGIP Kazakhstan North Caspian Operating Co NV*,[143] where the pursuer sued for performance of a contractual monetary obligation and where the defender alleged the plea of *forum non conveniens* in favour of Kazakhstan courts without disputing Aberdeen Sheriff Court's jurisdiction to hear the case, Sheriff Tierney exercised jurisdiction under Article 5(1)(a) on the basis that Aberdeen was the place of payment under the contract and therefore the place of performance of the obligation in question (alternatively under Article 24). In *B v D also known as AB v CD*,[144] where the pursuer raised an action of divorce seeking a capital sum before the Court of Session, Lord Brodie found that the application for financial provision in this action was ancillary to proceedings concerning the status of a person, it had been brought in a court which, according to its own law, had jurisdiction to entertain those proceedings and the relevant jurisdiction had nothing to do with the nationality of the parties and therefore exercised jurisdiction under Article 5(2) of Brussels I.

The case law and interview data indicate that many parties benefit from party autonomy in contractual obligations and that, in general, prorogation of jurisdiction under Article 23 of Brussels I works well. It is difficult to dispute the jurisdiction against a clear and well-drafted exclusive choice-of-court clause.[145] An exclusive choice-of-court clause also helps to reduce the risk that the Member States' courts will seek to interpret the PIL instruments in a way which allows them to establish jurisdiction.[146] The questions of how extensively it is used and of which jurisdiction is chosen seem to depend on the type of contract in question. Cross-border litigation risk is considered to be a factor in the forum selection process.[147] The length of the court proceedings in a particular country is also another factor in the forum selection process, in the sense that the parties occasionally try to avoid selecting jurisdictions having an unfortunate reputation for long court proceedings.[148] Italy was given as an example in interviews.[149]

The Scottish dataset includes two cases where the courts dealt with prorogation of jurisdiction under Article 23 of Brussels I. They are *Dr Bettina Breitenbücher v Cornelia Wittke*,[150] where the pursuer sued for an order for contractual performance before the Court of Session, and *Rolf Barkmann GmbH v Innova House Ltd*[151] which had come before the Sheriff Court in the debate on the defenders' first plea-in-law that challenged the jurisdiction of the Court. In both cases, the Scottish courts' jurisdiction was challenged by relying on Article 23 of Brussels I on the ground that the courts of Germany had exclusive jurisdiction. In the

---

[143] *Oceanfix International Ltd v AGIP Kazakhstan North Caspian Operating Co NV*, Sheriff Court (Grampian, Highland and Islands) (Aberdeen), 2009 GWD 17-266 (Sheriff J K Tierney).

[144] Court of Session (Outer House), 22 December 2006, [2006] CSOH 200 (Lord Brodie).

[145] EUPILLAR_Scotland 8.

[146] EUPILLAR_Scotland 8.

[147] EUPILLAR_Scotland 8, EUPILLAR_Scotland 12.

[148] EUPILLAR_Scotland 8, EUPILLAR_Scotland 12.

[149] EUPILLAR_Scotland 8, EUPILLAR_Scotland 12.

[150] Court of Session (Outer House) [2008] CSOH 145 (Lord Brodie).

[151] Sheriff Court (Grampian, Highland and Islands) (Inverness) 2008 GWD 33-490 (Sheriff D Pyle).

former case, the Court of Session exercised jurisdiction under Article 2 of Brussels I[152] whereas in the latter case the Sheriff Court did not exercise jurisdiction, subject to a hearing on the facts because the German courts had exclusive jurisdiction under Article 23.[153]

Parallel proceedings in civil and commercial matters seem to be very rare in Scotland. Most of the interviewees stated that they had not personally come across parallel proceedings at all.[154] One interviewee stated that it is very rare in personal injury cases.[155] The Scottish dataset includes one case where the court dealt with *lis pendens*-related actions under Articles 27 and 28 of Brussels I and it was in relation to contractual obligations. In *Jacobs & Turner Ltd v Celsius Sarl*,[156] decided by Lord Reed, the pursuer sought declaratory relief and an order for performance and the defenders maintained that the Scottish court should decline jurisdiction and dismiss the action, or in any event, sist the proceedings in accordance with Article 27 or 28 of Brussels I. There were also ongoing French proceedings initiated by Celsius in France. Lord Reed gave a practical interpretation of the notion of the same cause of action by considering the aims of Brussels I and the case law of the CJEU, and concluded that if both sets of proceedings, involving the same parties started in France and Scotland, were to continue, they could give rise to mutually exclusive legal consequences. The judge therefore declined jurisdiction under Article 27 of Brussels I in favour of the French courts and dismissed the action.

The Scottish dataset does not include any cases that involved multiple claimants. The interview data indicate that although it is possible in multi-party agreements in the field of contract,[157] this type of case is not seen in Scotland.[158] In personal injury, although it is much more common for individuals to be injured, there are multiple claimants in cases of road accidents or food poisoning.[159]

c. Matters Related to Recognition and Enforcement

There is no reported Scottish case on the recognition and enforcement of judgments under Brussels I. The interview data indicate that the recognition and enforcement of judicial decisions from other EU Member States in Scotland works well in practice.[160]

The case law data indicate that, in reaching their decisions, Scottish courts endeavour to take account of the practical and legal aspects of the outcome of their judgments under the EU PIL framework by considering in their analysis the capability of their judgments to be recognised and enforced in other Member States under Brussels I, if necessary.

---

[152] The Court examined the meaning and the effect of the jurisdiction clause under the law of Germany as it was the law governing the contract. It held that the parties had not prorogated the exclusive jurisdiction of the Stuttgart courts and that the Court of Session had jurisdiction over the defender by virtue of her Scottish domicile. For a criticism of the judgment, see the summary available on the EUPILLAR database.

[153] On these cases, see also N Shiels, 'European Law in Scotland: EU Council Regulation 44/2001' (2009) *Scots Law Times* 33.

[154] EUPILLAR_Scotland 9, EUPILLAR_Scotland 10.

[155] EUPILLAR_Scotland 11.

[156] Court of Session (Outer House) [2007] CSOH 76 (Lord Reed).

[157] EUPILLAR_Scotland 8.

[158] EUPILLAR_Scotland 9, EUPILLAR_Scotland 10, EUPILLAR_Scotland 12.

[159] EUPILLAR_Scotland 11.

[160] EUPILLAR_Scotland 9, EUPILLAR_Scotland 11, EUPILLAR_Scotland 12.

Wylie v Omniasig SA,[161] *Jacobs & Turner Ltd v Celsius Sarl*[162] and *B v D*[163] can be mentioned as examples.

The interview data indicate that public policy is not often an issue when dealing with recognition and enforcement of judgments[164] and that where it is raised by one of the parties the judges understand very well the exceptional nature of public policy and its extent.[165] However, problems with service can be a major issue.[166]

d. Matters Related to Relations with other Instruments

The interview data indicate that there are certain difficulties arising from interactions between Brussels I and the relevant international instruments, particularly the Convention on the Contract for the International Carriage of Goods by Road ('CMR') and the Convention for the Unification of Certain Rules for International Carriage by Air ('Montreal Convention').[167] The CJEU's interpretations in respect of the relationship between Brussels I and these international conventions are not helpful and indeed are themselves criticised for raising the tension when one considers the approach to the interpretation of international treaties under public international law under the Vienna Convention on the Law of Treaties.[168]

e. Conclusion

The interview data indicate that in general Brussels I has not caused much difficulty in practice since it has been generally understood and lawyers have become familiar with both Brussels I and leading authorities on it.[169] In addition, further improvements have been done to Brussels I by the Recast.[170]

The Scottish case law analysis on Brussels I reveals one example where the Court of Session exercised jurisdiction without determining its international jurisdiction under Brussels I. In *Wylie v Omniasig SA*,[171] a personal injury action brought directly against an insurance company, the court exercised jurisdiction without discussing and determining it under Brussels I in spite of finding Brussels I applicable to the case.

The issue of characterisation (classification) is a problem that was pointed out in the interviews.[172] It was stated that there is a lack of clarity between legal concepts, such as 'contract' or 'tort/delict', dealt with under the Regulations and due to this, there is a concern that their interpretation may differ from one jurisdiction to another, based on their national meanings and understanding in each jurisdiction, rather than the terms being interpreted

---

[161] Court of Session (Outer House) [2012] CSOH 128 (Lord Pentland).
[162] Above n 156.
[163] Above n 144.
[164] EUPILLAR_Scotland 11, EUPILLAR_Scotland 12.
[165] EUPILLAR_Scotland 12.
[166] EUPILLAR_Scotland 11, EUPILLAR_Scotland 12.
[167] EUPILLAR_Scotland 1.
[168] EUPILLAR_Scotland 1.
[169] EUPILLAR_Scotland 11, EUPILLAR_Scotland 12.
[170] EUPILLAR_Scotland 12.
[171] Above n 161.
[172] EUPILLAR_Scotland 2, EUPILLAR_Scotland 4, EUPILLAR_Scotland 12.

autonomously within the EU.[173] There is also a tension arising from the interaction between Brussels I and the relevant international instruments. If correct interpretations are given by the CJEU, this should help to clarify the dividing lines between the categories and concepts under Brussels I and to reduce confusion on its relationship with other international instruments. In general, there is support for better training in PIL for judges and lawyers.

On the other hand, in Scotland, the case law and the interviews[174] do not show any clear evidence of the courts favouring their own jurisdiction in deciding on their international jurisdiction. *Jacobs & Turner Ltd v Celsius Sarl*[175] on *lis pendens*-related actions, *Oceanfix International Ltd v AGIP Kazakhstan North Caspian Operating Co NV*[176] on contract jurisdiction and *Rolf Barkmann GmbH v Innova House Ltd*[177] on prorogation of jurisdiction represent examples of best practice that include good analyses of Brussels I.

ii. Applicable Law Issues under the Rome I and Rome II Regulations[178]

The interview data indicates that the applicable law is one of the factors that affect the strategy of a person once a cross-border action is brought against him and, at that stage, tactically a very careful consideration is given to the most advantageous applicable law for the client.[179] Claimants, particularly more sophisticated claimants,[180] consider which law would govern the merits of the dispute before deciding on the Member State in which to bring the action[181] provided that they are properly advised.[182] It was underlined in the interviews that there is a significant lack of knowledge about Rome II in this area of practice in personal injury cases 'because firms are either ignorant of what the law is, or they are out of date'.[183]

a. Rome I

The Scottish interview data indicate that parties benefit widely from party autonomy in contractual obligations and that freedom of choice under Article 3 of Rome I works well. The questions of how extensively it is used and which law is chosen seem to depend on the type of contract in question.

In rare situations, splitting the applicable law (*dépeçage*), which is allowed under Article 3(1) of Rome I, is seen in multiparty oil and gas contracts to which State oil and gas companies are parties. It was explained by an interviewee that where the State oil and gas companies are reluctant for their transactions to be subject to a foreign law, the solution is sometimes to specify in the contract that any disputes between international oil companies, which are usually considered as the real commercial parties in these contracts, are governed

---

[173] EUPILLAR_Scotland 2.
[174] EUPILLAR_Scotland 12.
[175] Above n 156.
[176] Above n 143.
[177] Above n 151.
[178] On this issue, see also Beaumont and McEleavy, above n 141, chs 10 and 14; Crawford and Carruthers, above n 141, chs 15 and 16.
[179] EUPILLAR_Scotland 10.
[180] EUPILLAR_Scotland 12
[181] EUPILLAR_Scotland 8 and EUPILLAR_Scotland 10.
[182] EUPILLAR_Scotland 11.
[183] EUPILLAR_Scotland 11.

by English law, and that any dispute between the international oil companies and the State oil and gas company are governed by the law of that State oil and gas company.[184]

In Scotland, foreign law is treated as a matter of fact requiring the evidence to be tendered by the parties. The judges face further difficulties in getting an agreement of both parties to accept one expert to express the opinion on the law,[185] misunderstanding or being misinformed about what the foreign law is[186] and, in cases where there are competing expert views about a foreign law, adjudicating between these views.[187] The issue of characterisation is also a problem.[188]

The interview data indicate that the Scottish courts do not favour their own law and they apply the law that they identified according to the relevant choice of law rule, whether it is foreign or not.[189]

b. Rome II

The Scottish interview data indicate that the applicable law is often an issue that is disputed in cross-border personal injury cases.[190] According to two interviewees, in general, the rules in Rome II help to make finding the applicable law easier than it used to be.[191] However, another interviewee stressed that the Rome II rules do not help to make it easier in personal injury cases and asserted that there is general agreement among the personal injury lawyers from different jurisdictions in Europe that the standard of drafting in Rome II is not clear enough.[192] Providing evidence as to the local law and the provisions of Article 4 also seem to pose difficulties.[193]

Rome II does not apply to evidence and procedure under Article 1(3) of Rome II, without prejudice to Article 21 on formal validity and Article 22 on burden of proof. Thus, the matters in relation to evidence and procedure in non-contractual obligations have not been harmonised. The interview data indicate that it is not very clear in personal injury cases whether evidence as to the local law and customs regarding the existence of liability or fault is to be provided, but as a general rule, an opinion from a lawyer in the country where the injury took place is received.[194] A legal practitioner also stated that, due to the necessity of obtaining foreign legal advice, 'Rome II has created financial pressures for individual consumers' and 'that has added greatly to the cost of pursuing this type of claim'.[195]

The Scottish interview data indicate that the general rule under Article 4 of Rome II, ie the law of the country in which the damage occurs, is found foreseeable in personal injury cases since it is the country where the person got injured.[196] A legal practitioner stated that the issue where the damage occurred in fatal cases had caused extreme difficulties in

---

[184] EUPILLAR_Scotland 8.
[185] EUPILLAR_Scotland 9.
[186] EUPILLAR_Scotland 2, EUPILLAR_Scotland 1.
[187] EUPILLAR_Scotland 4.
[188] EUPILLAR_Scotland 12.
[189] EUPILLAR_Scotland 10, EUPILLAR_Scotland 12.
[190] EUPILLAR_Scotland 10.
[191] EUPILLAR_Scotland 10, EUPILLAR_Scotland 12.
[192] EUPILLAR_Scotland 11.
[193] EUPILLAR_Scotland 10, EUPILLAR_Scotland 11.
[194] EUPILLAR_Scotland 10.
[195] EUPILLAR_Scotland 11.
[196] EUPILLAR_Scotland 10.

Scotland, because Scotland has particularly high damages in fatal cases which created pressure to try to have Scots law applied to the claim.[197] However, it was added that this has been settled by the decision of the CJEU in Case C-350/14 *Florin Lazar v Allianz SpA*[198] in which the CJEU found that the damage occurs where the injury occurs, not where the relatives suffer their grief and bereavement.[199] It was acknowledged by the interviewee that there are cases where the *Florin Lazar* interpretation of the CJEU will benefit one side rather than the other, but the interpretation is a more consistent and predictable approach than basing it on where the relatives happen to live.[200]

However, certain problems are still faced as regards Article 4(2) and (3). It was stated in the interviews that Article 4(2) is a major problem in personal injury cases where there is more than one defendant and only one of them is habitually resident in the same country as the claimant.[201] Although in many cases that is the case, Article 4(2) is not clear on this issue.[202] It was underlined by the interviewee that this is a very live issue subject to different arguments in legal practice but the answer still remains uncertain as there has not been a case dealing with this issue yet. As regards Article 4(3), it was stated that the exception clause, ie the manifestly closer connection, is not straightforward to apply and difficult to interpret without any guidance on what that means and it therefore leaves an element of uncertainty.[203]

Under Article 15(c) of Rome II, the law applicable to non-contractual obligations also governs the assessment of damage and the remedy claimed. The interview data indicate that this provision on the scope of the applicable law makes the assessment of damage in personal injury cases easier than it used to be before Rome II, although certain difficulties remain in identifying the applicable law due to the exception clause.[204]

The interview data indicate that Rome II may not work well in personal injury disputes and there are serious problems in practice that cause major delays and expense.[205] The issue of characterisation remains a problem.[206]

The interview data indicate that in Scottish practice there is no favouritism towards Scots law being the applicable law. The law that is identified according to the relevant choice of law rule is applied whether it is foreign or not.[207]

Revising Rome II can be offered as a solution in order to remove the areas of ambiguity and answer the needs of practice, particularly in personal injury disputes, but it is not clear how Article 4 could be improved legislatively. Some ambiguity is inevitable in the 'common habitual residence' criteria because of the ambiguity inherent in the concept of habitual residence for natural persons. In addition some flexibility is required by having an escape clause in Article 4(3) permitting the departure from the law of the place of damage or the law of the common habitual residence of the parties in exceptional cases. The circumstances

---

[197] EUPILLAR_Scotland 11.
[198] EU:C:2015:802. See the EUPILLAR CJEU database and the analysis of that case in ch 33 below at 582–3.
[199] EUPILLAR_Scotland 11.
[200] EUPILLAR_Scotland 11.
[201] EUPILLAR_Scotland 11.
[202] EUPILLAR_Scotland 11.
[203] EUPILLAR_Scotland 10, EUPILLAR_Scotland 11.
[204] EUPILLAR_Scotland 10.
[205] EUPILLAR_Scotland 10, EUPILLAR_Scotland 11.
[206] EUPILLAR_Scotland 10, EUPILLAR_Scotland 11.
[207] EUPILLAR_Scotland 10, EUPILLAR_Scotland 12.

in which such an escape clause might be required cannot be exhaustively listed by the legislature and therefore the matter has to be left to the wisdom of judges guided by academic analysis. The preliminary rulings of the CJEU on Rome II in C-350/14 *Florin Lazar v Allianz SpA*[208] and C-412/10 *Deo Antoine Homawoo v GMF Assurances SA*[209] have clarified some of the ambiguities and offered the right solutions for some of the legal issues that commonly arise in practice. It is to be hoped that as the CJEU has the opportunity to rule on Article 4(2) and (3) of Rome II, it will on a case by case basis gradually set clearer parameters for national judges in interpreting these provisions.

iii. Practice/Process

a. Scottish National Courts' Practice in Interpreting the Regulations/Process Issues

The case-law and interview data indicate that in general, the Scottish courts do well in interpreting the EU PIL Regulations in the fields of both civil and commercial law and family law. They try to ascertain the intention of the EU legislature by various means such as examining the recitals, the explanatory reports, preparatory documents and texts other than in English where relevant. The legislative history is not generally among these interpretation tools.[210] The Scottish judges very rarely look at cases from other EU jurisdictions.[211] They also endeavour to follow and apply the jurisprudence of the CJEU and cite its case-law. As regards Brussels I, one of the most obvious examples of that approach is seen in *Jacobs & Turner Ltd v Celsius Sarl*[212] dealt with in the Court of Session. This approach is applied and followed also at the Sheriff Court level, eg *Oceanfix International Ltd v AGIP Kazakhstan North Caspian Operating Co NV*[213] and *Rolf Barkmann GmbH v Innova House Ltd*.[214]

Despite this endeavour, the judges interviewed have individually indicated that they still find it difficult to interpret the EU PIL Regulations, compared to UK legislation.[215] It was expressed that identifying the correct forum and the correct governing law and issues such as comity, public policy and cultural differences, particularly in relation to family law, can be difficult.[216]

On the other hand, the Scottish judges very rarely consider making a preliminary reference to the CJEU and they have not done so in any of the cases in the dataset.[217] The general tendency of the Scottish judges is to endeavour to solve the disputes by themselves.[218] However, if they see a real point in the case that requires a preliminary ruling, they take the parties' view on making a reference to the CJEU. As regards Brussels I, *Oceanfix International Ltd v AGIP Kazakhstan North Caspian Operating Co NV*[219] and *Rolf Barkmann*

---

[208] Above n 198.
[209] [2011] ECR I-11603. See the EUPILLAR CJEU database and ch 33 below at 581.
[210] EUPILLAR_Scotland 1.
[211] EUPILLAR_Scotland 3.
[212] Above n 156.
[213] Above n 143.
[214] Above n 151.
[215] EUPILLAR_Scotland 3, EUPILLAR_Scotland 4, EUPILLAR_Scotland 9.
[216] EUPILLAR_Scotland 1.
[217] EUPILLAR_Scotland 3, EUPILLAR_Scotland 4, EUPILLAR_Scotland 9.
[218] ibid.
[219] Above n 143.

GmbH v Innova House Ltd[220] are two examples of this approach and, interestingly, both from the Sheriff Courts.[221]

b. Cost and Length of Litigation

The interview data indicate that, in general, cross-border litigation is perceived as being expensive[222] and that the application of substantive rules of foreign law increases the litigation costs because there is a need for a foreign law expert and for having to translate the documents for the expert and the court.[223] A legal practitioner stated that, in personal injury cases, the minimum level of claim that they might accept could be as low as £1,500 and that a value lower than that would be considered too low to make it economically viable.[224]

There is a lack of sufficiently precise case law data on the length of proceedings in civil and commercial cases, but the interview data indicate that disputes about jurisdiction, which tend to be dealt with as a preliminary issue in the UK, and disputes about the applicable law are among the factors on which the length of court proceedings depends in cross-border cases.[225]

It was suggested by the interviewees that the cost and length of litigation would be reduced by the following measures: networks of specialist lawyers,[226] more proactive and rigorous case management,[227] embracing the technological advances in communicating and consulting with people electronically over distances,[228] and registered and officially approved legal experts on foreign law who would be instructed jointly by the parties to deliver an opinion on the foreign law.[229]

iv. Settlement

The interview data indicate that in civil and commercial disputes settlement appears to be preferred over litigation.[230] In the field of contract law, the reasons to settle include: to avoid relationship damage, the small value of the claim, the litigation costs and delay and sometimes the strength of the claimant's claim.[231] In the field of tort and particularly in personal injury, the reasons to settle include: the strength of the claimant's claim, the litigation costs and the strength of the expert report of one party compared to that of the other party.[232]

---

[220] Above n 151.
[221] EUPILLAR_Scotland 3 shows that if a judge indicates that he will refer a case to the CJEU, the parties may settle to avoid the costs and delay associated with a reference.
[222] EUPILLAR_Scotland 8, EUPILLAR_Scotland 9, EUPILLAR_Scotland 10, EUPILLAR_Scotland 11.
[223] EUPILLAR_Scotland 9, EUPILLAR_Scotland 10, EUPILLAR_Scotland 11, EUPILLAR_Scotland 12.
[224] EUPILLAR_Scotland 11.
[225] EUPILLAR_Scotland 10, EUPILLAR_Scotland 11.
[226] EUPILLAR_Scotland 4.
[227] EUPILLAR_Scotland 4, EUPILLAR_Scotland 9.
[228] EUPILLAR_Scotland 12.
[229] EUPILLAR_Scotland 10.
[230] EUPILLAR_Scotland 4, EUPILLAR_Scotland 8.EUPILLAR_Scotland 9, EUPILLAR_Scotland 10, EUPILLAR_Scotland 11. EUPILLAR_Scotland 12.
[231] EUPILLAR_Scotland 8, EUPILLAR_Scotland 12.
[232] EUPILLAR_Scotland 10, EUPILLAR_Scotland 11.

The uncertainty in Rome II was stated as a factor that affects the settlement negotiations in the personal injury disputes under the current legislative framework.[233]

For private individuals, funding seems to be quite a big factor in decisions whether or not to settle whereas for legal entities, in addition to economic factors, reputational damage and confidentiality are also important and do affect their decisions.[234]

v. Alternative Dispute Resolution (ADR)

In Scotland, ADR is used as a means of resolving contractual cross-border disputes to some extent, in particular between the parties in an ongoing relationship and in the industries where a certain degree of expertise is required in resolving the disputes, such as oil and gas.[235]

As far as mediation is concerned, a Sheriff pointed out in the interview that a judge who takes control at a very early stage to identify the issues, drives the case forward and also encourages the parties to sort out things that really ought to be sorted out, can be more effective than mediators in that role.[236]

ADR is not used for cross-border personal injury disputes and it is believed that it does not work in personal injury.[237] As regards consumers, specific protections built in the current system by recognising them as a weaker party are found helpful and whether ADR or online dispute resolution (ODR) could be a better solution for them is considered to be dependent on the circumstances of individuals and the type of ADR or ODR in question.[238]

vi. Remedies

In the field of contract, the case law and interview data[239] indicate that the primary remedy sought in cross-border cases is usually financial. Cross-border contractual cases seeking declaratory or injunctive relief are very rare[240] even where the contract in question explicitly made such a remedy available.[241]

In the field of tort, particularly in personal injury cases, the interview data indicate that the primary remedy sought is always financial, and cross-border cases seeking declaratory or injunctive relief are not seen at all.[242]

vii. Conclusion

In order to overcome some of the difficulties concerning expert witnesses addressed above, the Scottish courts should have the power to insist on a court appointed single expert witness on foreign law rather than having to allow each party to have its own expert.[243]

---

[233] EUPILLAR_Scotland 11.
[234] EUPILLAR_Scotland 12.
[235] EUPILLAR_Scotland 8.
[236] EUPILLAR_Scotland 9.
[237] EUPILLAR_Scotland 11.
[238] EUPILLAR_Scotland 12.
[239] EUPILLAR_Scotland 8, EUPILLAR_Scotland 12.
[240] EUPILLAR_Scotland 8, EUPILLAR_Scotland 9, EUPILLAR_Scotland 12.
[241] EUPILLAR_Scotland 8.
[242] EUPILLAR_Scotland 10, EUPILLAR_Scotland 11.
[243] EUPILLAR, Scotland 1.

C. Cross-border Family Law Disputes

The case law data indicates that cross-border family law cases are fairly rare in Scotland. The dataset includes eight cross-border cases concerning family law matters with other EU Member States. Of these, seven were dealt with under Brussels IIa while one of them was dealt with under Brussels I before the entry into force of the Maintenance Regulation. The types of proceedings are mostly child abduction. There are as yet no reported Scottish cases on the Maintenance Regulation.

The interviews conducted with judges also affirm that intra-EU family law cases are fairly rare in Scotland.[244] A Court of Session judge explained in the interview that:[245]

— Child abduction is almost always cross-border and the Court of Session has about 10 of those per annum.
— Cross-border issues crop up frequently in divorce cases and the Court of Session has about 50 divorce cases raised each year and about a quarter to a third of those have cross-border problems, but not always with EU Member States.
— Parental responsibilities and maintenance do not crop up very often in the Court of Session. They would be more likely to crop up in the Sheriff Court and they are quite common in family cases in general.
— The Court of Session has a reasonable number of relocation cases and again those often raise cross-border issues, although most of those are again not with other EU Member States, and the judge was aware of only one relocation case with another EU Member State.

The interviews conducted with legal practitioners indicate that there is a demand for cross-border legal advice in Scotland sought by foreign nationals and by domiciled Scottish expats.[246] Non-local claimants, ie claimants not habitually resident in Scotland, come up increasingly regularly.[247] However, most of the demand is for intra-UK family law issues and some for the issues involving Scotland and third countries.[248]

The interview data also indicate that cross-border family law disputes almost always settle, which is mostly because of the cost and uncertainty but also because in most financial provision on divorce cases there will be a spectrum in terms of the award which leaves a significant, but not enormous, range in which to settle.[249]

i. Jurisdictional and Procedural Issues under the Brussels IIa Regulation[250]

a. Matters Related to the Scope of Application

The Scottish dataset includes one case where the question of the scope of application of Brussels IIa arose in parental responsibility proceedings. In *Application in respect of*

---

[244] EUPILLAR_Scotland 7.
[245] EUPILLAR_Scotland 3.
[246] EUPILLAR_Scotland 5, EUPILLAR_Scotland 6.
[247] EUPILLAR_Scotland 7.
[248] EUPILLAR_Scotland 5, EUPILLAR_Scotland 6.
[249] EUPILLAR_Scotland 5.
[250] On this issue, see also Beaumont and McEleavy, above n 141, chs 16 and 17; Crawford and Carruthers, above n 141, chs 12 and 14; AB Wilkinson and KM Norrie, *The Law Relating to Parent and Child in Scotland* (Edinburgh, W Green, 2013) chs 10 and 11.

A and B,[251] Sheriff Scott was satisfied that the Regulation covered placement of the child in a foster family under Article 1(2) and the reference to a 'court' under Article 2(1) covered all authorities with jurisdiction in the matters falling within the scope of the Regulation. This was a correct interpretation of the scope of application of Brussels IIa.[252]

b. Matters Related to Jurisdiction

The Scottish dataset includes one case where the issue was divorce jurisdiction under Article 3 of Brussels IIa. In *Williamson v Williamson*,[253] which was upheld by the Sheriff Principal, the divorce proceedings were initiated by the husband, who spent roughly equal times in Scotland and Spain, before the Sheriff Court in Kirkcaldy, relying on Article 3(1)(a) (final indent) of Brussels IIa. The wife contended that the Scottish courts did not have jurisdiction to hear the case as both parties had been resident and domiciled in Spain, and that she intended to raise divorce proceedings in Spain. The Sheriff examined the three conditions laid down in the provision and found in favour of the husband on all three conditions by relying on the definition of 'habitual residence' as being the person's 'centre of interests' as referred to by Alegria Borras in the Explanatory Report to the Brussels II Draft Convention, in Case C-452/93P *Pedro Magdalena Fernández v Commission of the European Communities*[254] and by the English High Court in *L-K v K (No 2)*.[255] The Sheriff was influenced in his interpretation of 'residence for 40 days in the sheriffdom' rule in section 8(2)(b)(i) of the Domicile and Matrimonial Proceedings Act 1973 by giving the word 'residence' an interpretation consistent with that found in Brussels IIa.

The interview data indicate that where the outcome is financial, it does matter where an applicant brings a cross-border claim since the outcome could be different in different jurisdictions.[256] Enforceability is also a very important factor.[257] The length of the court proceedings in a particular country is seen as an important factor in the forum selection process while the main factor is the final outcome particularly if it is financial.[258] Italy was given as an example in one of the interviews where significant delays do occur (eg a divorce can be held up for 10 years).[259]

The Scottish dataset does not include any case on prorogation of jurisdiction under Article 12 of Brussels IIa. The interview data indicate that, in the absence of any clear case law, there might be particular interpretation problems as to when the provision applies.[260]

The Scottish dataset includes one case where the issue was the transfer of jurisdiction under Article 15 of Brussels IIa.[261] In this case, a request was made by a German court to

---

[251] Sheriff Court (Lothian and Borders) (Haddington) [2014] Fam LR 137, [2014] GWD 38-698 (Sheriff JM Scott, QC).

[252] See the CJEU decision in Case C-435/06 *C* [2007] ECR I-10141 discussed in ch 41 below.

[253] Sheriff Court (Tayside, Central and Fife) (Kirkcaldy) [2009] Fam LR 44, [2009] GWD 14-220, [2009] ScotSC 18 (Sheriff AG McCulloch).

[254] *Pedro Magdalena Fernández v Commission of the European Communities* [1994] ECR I-04295.

[255] *L-K v K (No 2)* [2007] EWHC 3202.

[256] EUPILLAR_Scotland 5, EUPILLAR_Scotland 6.

[257] EUPILLAR_Scotland 5.

[258] EUPILLAR_Scotland 6.

[259] EUPILLAR_Scotland 5.

[260] EUPILLAR_Scotland 7. See also Conflicts of EU Courts on Child Abduction, Country Reports May 2016 at 214 by P Beaumont, L Walker and J Holliday available at www.abdn.ac.uk/law/research/conflicts-of-eu-courts-on-child-abduction-417.php.

[261] *Application in respect of A and B* (Lothian and Borders) (Haddington) [2014] Fam LR 137, [2014] GWD 38-698 (Sheriff J M Scott, QC).

the Sheriff Court for the transfer of jurisdiction over proceedings in respect of two children who had been brought to Scotland by their mother and who were made subject to interim compulsory supervision orders pursuant to which they were placed in foster care. The Sheriff accepted the transfer and exercised jurisdiction under the Regulation recognising that it was in the best interests of the children to do so. In *ERG (AP) Petitioner, also known as G v G*[262] and in *C v C*,[263] although the Scottish courts discussed transfer of jurisdiction under Article 15 in relation to child abduction, it was refused in the latter case and found inoperable in the former.

c. Matters Related to Recognition and Enforcement

There is no reported Scottish case deciding on recognition and enforcement of judgments under Brussels IIa but some obiter remarks have been made which are noted at sub-section d below. The interview data indicate that there are recognition and enforcement cases coming from other EU Member States, although it is not as many as intra-UK cases and cases coming from outside the EU, and that it seems to work well.[264] However, there are problems if the issue concerns children.

Problems with service is the most common ground for refusal that is raised when dealing with recognition and enforcement of judgments,[265] because it is not fully known what constitutes service in different jurisdictions.[266]

The interview data indicate that there seems to be a widespread problem in Scotland and in other EU jurisdictions with certificates for enforcement, in particular that they are rarely filled out or not filled out properly.[267]

d. Child Abduction

The Scottish dataset includes five cases on child abduction dealt with in the Court of Session.[268] The other EU Member States in question were France, Spain, Poland and Latvia.

---

[262] Court of Session (Outer House) [2011] CSOH 126 (Lord Stewart).
[263] Court of Session (Inner House, Extra Division), [2008] CSIH 34.
[264] EUPILLAR_Scotland 3.
[265] EUPILLAR_Scotland 5, EUPILLAR_Scotland 6.
[266] EUPILLAR_Scotland 6.
[267] EUPILLAR_Scotland 6.
[268] *HIB Petitioner, known also as B Petitioner* Court of Session (Outer House) [2013] CSOH 187 (Lady Wise)—Art 12 of the Hague Convention settled in the new environment exception (also a combination of Art 13(2) for one child and Art 13(1)(b) for the other if returned without their older sibling; *A Petitioner* Court of Session (Outer House) [2011] CSOH 215, 2012 SLT 370 (Lord Glennie)—Art 13(2) of the Hague Convention; *IGR (AP) Petitioner* Court of Session (Outer House) [2011] CSOH 208 (Lord Brodie)—Art 12 of the Hague Convention settled in the new environment exception; *ERG (AP) Petitioner, also known as G v G* Court of Session (Outer House) [2011] CSOH 126, 2012 SLT 2 (Lord Stewart)—not a wrongful retention of the child; *C v C* Court of Session (Inner House, Extra Division) [2008] CSIH 34, 2008 SC 571. There are some other intra-EU child abduction cases where Brussels IIa was mentioned by the Scottish court but it was not relevant to the decision, see *WT Petitioner* [2007] CSOH 72 (Lord Malcolm), paras 3 and 6, ordering the return of a child to Poland and *AR v RN* [2015] UKSC 35, [2016] AC 76, in which the UK Supreme Court referred to Brussels IIa at para 11 but refused to return the children to France because in its view they were already habitually resident in Scotland at the time of the alleged wrongful retention (4 months after lawfully leaving France with their mother for a planned 12 months stay in Scotland). There is one case where Brussels IIa was not mentioned in the decision but it was not necessary to do so in routinely ordering the return of two children from Scotland to the Netherlands under the Hague Convention, see *H v C* [2006] CSOH 115 (Lord Uist).

In general, the Regulation was applied in these cases in a straightforward way. A return order was granted in only one[269] of the five cases. The average length of the proceedings was 12.2 weeks which is slightly above the timescale proposed in Brussels IIa but is nonetheless highly creditable.

Three cases have been detected where Brussels IIa was not referred to in the judgment although the case fell clearly within the scope of the Regulation as they involved two EU Member States and Brussels IIa may have been relevant to the decision. In *T Petitioner*,[270] the question was whether the child's father had 'custody rights' in relation to his child, after his Polish divorce from the child's mother, for the purposes of Articles 3 and 5 of the Hague Convention. Lady Paton decided that he did have 'custody rights' for the purposes of the Hague Convention without considering the potential relevance of Brussels IIa, in particular Article 2(9) and (11), to this issue. The failure to refer to Brussels IIa probably did not affect the outcome of the case and in due course the child was returned to Poland.[271] In *BJZ Petitioner*,[272] Lady Smith decided by reference only to the Hague Convention that the Dutch Youth Welfare Organisation did not have 'custody rights' under that Convention in order to seek the return of a child from Scotland to The Netherlands but it is possible that a different conclusion could have been reached had she been referred to Brussels IIa, in particular Article 2(9) and (11). In *DR Petitioner*,[273] which concerned an 11 year and five months old girl who was habitually resident in Belgium and who failed to return from a holiday visit to her mother who lived in Scotland, Lord Kinclaven did not make any reference to Brussels IIa and relied solely on the 1980 Hague Child Abduction Convention. In this case, the result would probably not have been different if Brussels IIa had been applied because he ordered the return of the child to Belgium but it would have been better in this case concerning a vulnerable child had he taken proper account of Article 11(2) and (4) of Brussels IIa before ordering the return.

The dataset does not include any cases considering the second chance procedure of Article 11(6)–(8) of Brussels IIa, however, the interview data indicate that it does not function satisfactorily and tends to leave children in a prolonged state of uncertainty.[274]

The Scottish dataset includes cases where the Scottish courts took account of recognition and enforcement issues under Brussels IIa in reaching their decision in child abduction cases. In *A Petitioner*,[275] as regards a Spanish interim order entitling the father to have the children reside with him until the final resolution of the custody proceedings, Lord Glennie noted that the Spanish court had failed to give consideration to Article 11(2) of Brussels IIa and did not seek the views of the children. He remarked that this pointed towards non-recognition of the Spanish judgment in terms of Article 23(b) of Brussels IIa. In *ERG (AP) Petitioner, also known as G v G*,[276] as regards a Latvian interim residence order providing for the child's residence with her mother in Scotland until the final resolution of the custody proceedings, Lord Stewart assessed, inter alia, that to order the return of the child in these

---

[269] *C v C*, ibid.
[270] *T Petitioner* [2007] CSOH 43 (Lady Paton).
[271] See *WT Petitioner* [2007] CSOH 72.
[272] *BJZ Petitioner* [2009] CSOH 136 (Lady Smith).
[273] Court of Session (Outer House), [2011] CSOH 83 (Lord Kinclaven).
[274] EUPILLAR_Scotland 7. See generally on this issue Beaumont, Walker and Holliday, above n 82, 260.
[275] Court of Session (Outer House) [2011] CSOH 215 (Lord Glennie).
[276] Court of Session (Outer House) [2011] CSOH 126 (Lord Stewart).

circumstances may be to deny recognition to the judgment of a Member State court, contrary to Article 21 of Brussels IIa. He refused the return application of the father.

e. Cooperation between Central Authorities in Matters of Parental Responsibility

The interview data indicate that Scotland has a very good Central Authority and this is helpful in the enforcement of judicial decisions from other EU Member States in Scotland.[277]

f. Relations with other Instruments

The interview data indicate that certain difficulties arise from the interactions between Brussels IIa and the relevant international instruments, particularly the 1980 Hague Child Abduction Convention and the 1996 Hague Children's Convention. It was explained that the fact that Brussels IIa exists alongside these two conventions and also that the CJEU has been developing its jurisprudence without much regard to the jurisprudence of non-EU Member States that are party to these conventions, eg Australia, gives rise to difficulties and a degree of confusion.[278] This leads to having different approaches in interpreting the same convention depending on whether the case falls within the scope of Brussels IIa or not.[279]

g. Conclusion

One of the problems is that a cross-border element may not be picked up[280] which would result in Brussels IIa not being taken into account.[281]

The case law and interview data indicate that there are also some practical problems with certain provisions of Brussels IIa. First, 'the second chance procedure' of Article 11(6)–(8) of Brussels IIa in child abduction cases does not function satisfactorily as it results in children being left in a state of prolonged uncertainty.[282] Second, the procedural rules relating to the possibility of the children's hearing declining jurisdiction, considering a request for a transfer under Article 15, or making a request for transfer are unclear which is not in the best interests of children.[283] Third, the issue of when a court is deemed to be seised under Article 16 of Brussels IIa is not particularly clear and has caused interpretation difficulties.[284] Brussels IIa is currently under review so it is hoped that some practical problems with certain provisions of Brussels IIa, eg Articles 11(6)–(8), 15 and 16, will be solved by the EU legislature in the Brussels IIa Recast.[285]

---

[277] EUPILLAR_Scotland 5.

[278] EUPILLAR_Scotland 1.

[279] EUPILLAR_Scotland 1, EUPILLAR_Scotland 5.

[280] EUPILLAR_Scotland 7.

[281] Court of Session (Outer House), [2011] CSOH 83 (Lord Kinclaven).

[282] EUPILLAR_Scotland 3, EUPILLAR_Scotland 5, EUPILLAR_Scotland 6, EUPILLAR_Scotland 7.

[283] *Application in respect of A and B* (Lothian and Borders) (Haddington) [2014] Fam. LR. 137, [2014] G.W.D. 38-698 (Sheriff J M Scott, QC).

[284] EUPILLAR_Scotland 5, EUPILLAR_Scotland 6, EUPILLAR_Scotland 7. Some guidance has now been given by Case C-489/14 *A v B* EU:C:2015:654 noted in the EUPILLAR CJEU database and in ch 41 below at 724–6.

[285] See P Beaumont, L Walker and J Holliday, 'Parental Responsibility and International Child Abduction in the Proposed Recast of Brussels IIa Regulation and the Effect of Brexit on Future Child Abduction Proceedings' (2016) *International Family Law* 307–18 and Beaumont, Walker and Holliday, above n 82 at 260.

Application in respect of A and B,[286] on transfer of jurisdiction under Article 15 of Brussels IIa that included a good analysis of the material scope of Brussels IIa and its rules, and *HIB Petitioner, known also as B Petitioner*[287] on child abduction, that gave appropriate weight to Article 11(4) of Brussels IIa, represent examples of best practice. The case law and interview data indicate that the Scottish courts do not favour their own jurisdiction in deciding on their international jurisdiction.[288]

However, there is support for better training on PIL for judges and lawyers, for dissemination and sharing information between the EU Member States,[289] and for education.[290]

ii. Jurisdictional and Procedural Issues and Applicable Law under the Maintenance Regulation[291]

The Scottish experience on the Maintenance Regulation is very limited. There is one particular issue that was raised in the interviews regarding the recognition, enforceability and actual enforcement of decisions. Problems may occur for the enforcement of Scottish maintenance decisions in other EU Member States due to the fact that the UK is not bound by the 2007 Hague Protocol.[292]

iii. Practice/Process

a. Scotland's National Courts' Practice in Interpreting the Regulations

As regards Brussels IIa, *Application in respect of A and B*[293] is an example of a good approach. However, the Scottish case law data are not sufficient to reach a general conclusion on how the Scottish courts interpret Brussels IIa since most of the Scottish family law cases are on child abduction and, in general, Brussels IIa was applied in these cases in a straightforward way.

b. Cost and Length of Litigation in Cross-border Family Law Disputes

The interview data indicate that, in general, cross-border litigation is perceived as being expensive, but there is a possibility of receiving legal aid.[294]

Most of the family law cases are dealt with in a period of six weeks to six months and in child abduction cases, the average is 12.2 weeks. The interview data indicates that jurisdictional disputes,[295] getting evidence from another jurisdiction,[296] uncertainty as to

---

[286] *Application in respect of A and B* (Lothian and Borders) (Haddington) [2014] Fam. LR. 137, [2014] G.W.D. 38-698 (Sheriff J M Scott, QC).
[287] Court of Session (Outer House) [2011] CSOH 187 (Lady Wise).
[288] EUPILLAR_Scotland 6.
[289] EUPILLAR_Scotland 6.
[290] EUPILLAR_Scotland 5.
[291] On this issue, see also Beaumont and McEleavy, above n 141, ch 19; Crawford and Carruthers, above n 141, ch 13; Wilkinson and Norrie, above n 250, ch 13.
[292] EUPILLAR_Scotland 5, EUPILLAR_Scotland 7.
[293] Sheriff Court (Lothian and Borders) (Haddington) 2014 Fam LR 137; 2014 GWD 38-698.
[294] EUPILLAR_Scotland 5, EUPILLAR_Scotland 6, EUPILLAR_Scotland 7.
[295] EUPILLAR_Scotland 6, EUPILLAR_Scotland 7.
[296] EUPILLAR_Scotland 6.

the interpretation of the Regulations,[297] and the unharmonised procedural rules of EU Member States occasionally cause delay.[298]

iv. Settlement

The interview data indicate that most cross-border family law disputes do settle and that it is done on a balance of risk by taking account of the laws of relevant countries, the cost of continuing the case, an assessment of the relative strengths and weaknesses on both sides, and the risk of losing the litigation.[299] The disputes generally settle after proceedings have been initiated.[300] Some do settle at an earlier stage before the court proceedings have been initiated, and those are often difficult cases.[301]

v. Alternative Dispute Resolution

The interview data indicate that it is appropriate for the parties to use alternative methods for dispute resolution in cross-border family disputes, particularly in relation to children, and that mediation is used in these disputes.[302] All interviewees stated that the use of ADR as a means to resolve cross border family law disputes should be promoted further at EU level.[303] A recent decision of Lord Stewart in a Hague Child Abduction case between Australia and Scotland to include evidence arising from a post-abduction mediation as relevant in the proof of acquiescence as a ground for non-return of an abducted child is highly controversial and should be considered by a higher court.[304] Though it must be acknowledged that on the facts of the case Lord Stewart concluded that the father had acquiesced in the abduction of his child 'even if the mediation evidence were to have been excluded'.[305]

Arbitration is seen as another alternative method for resolving cross-border family disputes although it has not been used widely yet.[306] However, it is acknowledged that the *lis pendens* provisions of the EU PIL Regulations are not helpful in this respect.[307]

---

[297] EUPILLAR_Scotland 5.

[298] EUPILLAR_Scotland 3, EUPILLAR_Scotland 5. There is one case which took more than 60 months to resolve, ie *B v D (also known as AB v CD)* Court of Session (Outer House), [2006] CSOH 200, partially because of a lengthy sist in order to allow the pursuer to apply for legal aid. The history of the delay is recounted by the Court at pp 54–55 of the case report.

[299] EUPILLAR_Scotland 6, EUPILLAR_Scotland 7.

[300] EUPILLAR_Scotland 5, EUPILLAR_Scotland 6.

[301] EUPILLAR_Scotland 5.

[302] EUPILLAR_Scotland 6, EUPILLAR_Scotland 7.

[303] EUPILLAR_Scotland 5, EUPILLAR_Scotland 6, EUPILLAR_Scotland 7.

[304] *FJM, Re Orders Under The Child Abduction and Custody Act 1985 and Answers for CGM* [2015] CSOH 130, 2015 SLT 682. See the concerns expressed by the interviewee in EUPILLAR_Scotland 6 that this may deter people from using mediation or being free and frank about trying to reach a solution in mediation if their views will be used against them as constituting acquiescence in the abduction. However, Lord Stewart decided that the Civil Evidence (Family Mediation)(Scotland) Act 1995 does not apply to mediations after a child abduction [17]–[21] and therefore the evidence that emerged from the mediation was admissible. He said that if the mediation were a 'cross-border mediation' in terms of Dir 2008/52/EC the mediators cannot be compelled to give evidence in terms of the Cross-Border Mediation (Scotland) Regs 2011.

[305] ibid [22].

[306] EUPILLAR_Scotland 7.

[307] EUPILLAR_Scotland 7.

vi. *Conclusion on the Effectiveness of the Current EU PIL Framework*

The case law and interview data indicate that the current EU PIL framework in family law functions effectively overall although there are particular issues to be revised and to be improved especially in Brussels IIa.

As regards the applicable law in family matters, the traditional approach in Scotland is to apply Scots law and thus applicable law is neither considered as an issue nor often disputed.[308] One interviewee criticised that approach and stated that the Scottish courts need to confront that.[309]

D. Conclusion

This empirical study indicates that, overall, the EU PIL framework in civil, commercial and family law functions effectively although there are particular issues that need to be further improved particularly in Rome II and Brussels IIa. The EU Regulations have brought more certainty and predictability to civil, commercial and family law disputes. The tests used and the rules provided for in the Regulations seem clearer than they used to be. The main problem appears to be applying these tests and rules in practice which is not always easy.

Regarding the harmonisation of procedural rules at the EU level, all interviewees expressed that it is too difficult to achieve this, or not possible, or even unrealistic. The interview data indicate that the unharmonised procedural rules do not often create significant difficulties.

The referendum on the UK's membership of the EU (Brexit) took place on 23 June 2016. While Scotland voted in favour of the UK staying in the EU (62:38 per cent), the overall national result in the UK was to leave the EU (52:48 per cent).[310] However, this empirical study on the Scottish experience is still of significant importance for PIL in the UK and the EU, particularly on the following points concerning the best ways to enhance the effectiveness of the application of the Regulations:

— More education of the legal profession and better judicial training on PIL. According to the information gathered from the Judicial Institute for Scotland:

> The Judicial Institute delivers training on a wide range of topics, to the breadth of the judiciary in Scotland. This ranges from induction training when members of the judiciary are first appointed, to courses on specific topics of law such as Housing or Road Traffic, and courses of more general application when carrying out the judicial role, including those on dealing with Party Litigant and Lay Representatives, and on Judgment Writing. Included within these courses there are sessions which have dealt with cross-border cases, particularly in terms of family law and dealing with children. Recent courses on these areas include 'Residence and Contact Cases' and 'Family Law and Mediation'. Consideration of cross-border issues in a broader sense has been given in specific courses on European Law, and on Immigration cases. There is not an individual course which looks at the topic of Private International Law and the conflict of laws, but this is instead

---

[308] EUPILLAR_Scotland 6, EUPILLAR_Scotland 7.
[309] EUPILLAR_Scotland 5.
[310] See www.electoralcommission.org.uk/find-information-by-subject/elections-and-referendums/past-elections-and-referendums/eu-referendum.

something which may arise in courses throughout the curriculum. In addition to the provision of training courses, the Judicial Institute also hosts an online suite of resources, accessible by all members of the judiciary. Within these are documents addressing and drawing attention to issues of a cross-border nature. These include 'Brief Notes' highlighting recent developments— for example around the Brussels Regulation—briefing papers on topics including family law, and other documents of various purposes.

— Therefore, there is still a need for specific training on PIL after Brexit for the judiciary. There might be a funding concern here based on the low volume of cross-border cases in Scotland. On this point, there is scope for cooperation in the UK to offer courses on PIL to all judges.

— Constructive and open dialogue and informal contact between judges in order to learn more about the other Member States' approaches on the issues and to get reliable information, particularly on the content of foreign law.

— Good lawyers that will help judges. There is support for better training for lawyers in private international law.[311] Although it is valid for all jurisdictions, there is the peculiarity in the UK due to the different role of the judiciary that relies upon the lawyers to plead the law and to present the facts. In addition, lawyers have to plead that a foreign law is applicable to the case and lead evidence of foreign law otherwise a judge can only apply Scots law. Therefore, all Scots lawyers need to be trained in PIL when studying for their law degree, not just advocates, and continuing professional development needs to have more PIL training. At present only advocates in Scotland have to pass an exam in private international law before they can become an advocate. So solicitors and judges who were solicitors may have no training in private international law. In a post-Brexit landscape it would make a lot of sense to make private international law compulsory for solicitors in place of EU law.

— At the highest levels (eg between the Inner House of the Court of Session, UK Supreme Court and Court of Justice of the European Union) better dialogue between and shared training of the judges and Advocates General on PIL issues.

— Being able to access and read the cases decided in the courts of the EU Member States. It is hoped that the EUPILLAR Database will be one of the main sources to meet this need. This may well continue to be relevant in the longer term if any aspects of EU PIL are retained in Scotland after Brexit (eg Rome I and II could be retained in Scotland, even in the unlikely event of not being retained in the rest of the UK, as they do not require reciprocal application with our EU partners).[312]

IV. Conclusion

There is a significant contrast between the findings in relation to England and Wales and Scotland. The former is a major centre for international litigation and has a very significant

---

[311] EUPILLAR_Scotland 1, EUPILLAR_Scotland 2.
[312] See *Scotland's Place in Europe* (Scottish Government, 2016) available at www.gov.scot/Resource/ 0051/00512073.pdf. The Scottish Parliament already has competence to legislate on private international law for Scotland and it could choose to mirror EU PIL Regulations after Brexit.

practice in relation to the EU PIL instruments (327 cases on the EUPILLAR database) whereas the latter is not and has a practice that is much smaller than England and Wales even when allowing for the population differential (13 cases on our database). So Scotland had four per cent of the number of decided cases that there were in England and Wales whereas the Scottish population is over nine per cent of that of England and Wales.[313] Both jurisdictions apply the EUPILLAR instruments well and in both systems many cases settle before a judgment is given. England and Wales has a very small practice (12 cases were referred out of 327) and Scotland has no practice (none referred out of 13) in terms of asking guidance from the CJEU on the EUPILLAR instruments. Therefore, in this regard, Brexit will make little difference even if there is agreement with the EU to continue to apply these instruments or either or both of these jurisdictions unilaterally retain any of these instruments (Rome I and II) or the parts of the instruments (eg the parts of Brussels I, Brussels IIa and the Maintenance Regulation) that do not require reciprocity. The right to refer cases to the CJEU will clearly not survive Brexit as the UK Prime Minister has already made this a red line issue in the Article 50 TEU negotiations. However if the UK Parliament or the Scottish Parliament were to retain Rome I and II after Brexit the judges could hardly be prevented from taking cognisance of the case law of the CJEU on those instruments even if they could not refer cases to the CJEU and were no longer bound by the CJEU's rulings. In the area covered by Brussels I it is impossible to predict what will happen after Brexit but our findings suggest that the UK and Scottish Parliaments should take the opportunity to move away from a rigid system based on the court first seised. Instead we should reinstate for our dealings with the EU and EEA States the power to decline jurisdiction on the basis of *forum non conveniens* which is currently retained in both jurisdictions for intra-UK conflicts and conflicts with defenders from outside the EU/EEA. As is well known *forum non conveniens* is the most significant contribution Scotland has made to private international law.[314] The court first seised rule is also objectionable in relation to divorce proceedings under Brussels IIa and it will help to reduce the magnet effect of high financial provision after divorce for women in England and Wales if the English courts could return to the practice of being able to decline jurisdiction on the basis of *forum non conveniens*. Sadly there seems to be no prospect of any flexibility being introduced for divorce proceedings in the current revision of Brussels IIa even though a transfer provision could and should have been proposed by the Commission. In relation to child law the Hague Conventions of 1980, 1996 and 2007 offer a legal framework that is arguably at least as good as that provided by Brussels IIa and the Maintenance Regulation and have the undoubted advantage of creating greater simplicity by having one less legal regime for UK legal practitioners, lay litigants and judges to learn.[315]

---

[313] The UK Census in 2011 records the population of England at 53.01 million, Scotland at 5.295 million and Wales at 3.063 million.

[314] See Beaumont and McEleavy, above n 141, at 359–67 and Arzandeh, above n 113.

[315] See P Beaumont, "Private International Law in the UK after Brexit: comparing Hague Treaty Law with EU Regulations" Centre for Private International Law Working Paper No 2017/2 available at www.abdn.ac.uk/law/research/working-papers-455.php (the printed version is forthcoming in the *Child and Family Law Quarterly*).

As noted earlier the principal lessons from the Great Britain practice for the EU institutional architecture are that specialist PIL judges in the CJEU would be able to offer a quicker and more reliable service on interpretation of EU PIL; the EU legislature could help the CJEU and national judges to accurately interpret EU PIL Regulations by reinstating official explanatory reports on their interpretation; more education of the legal professions and better judicial training on PIL in each of the Member States and in the CJEU; and at least at the highest levels (eg between the CJEU and the highest appellate courts in the Member States) better dialogue between and shared training of the Judges and Advocates General on PIL issues.

6

Belgium

THALIA KRUGER AND ELINE ULRIX[*]

I. Introduction

The Belgian Courts are divided in 13 districts, of which six are Flemish, six French and one German. Each district has a civil court of first instance and separate family,[1] commercial and employment courts.[2] The courts have seats in several places in each district. There are five courts of appeal: Antwerp and Ghent (Flemish), Brussels (Flemish and French), Liège and Mons (French).[3]

The report is based on a case law analysis of and interviews with professionals.[4] The focus is mainly on published case law.[5] Unfortunately a large proportion of Belgian case law is unpublished as there is no systematic publication policy. Therefore, we have also asked our interview respondents whether they had additional cases. Altogether 367 cases were included in the research. We conducted 22 interviews with legal practitioners and judges.[6]

In section II of this report we will present our research findings with regard to cross-border civil and commercial disputes, considering the way Brussels I, Ia and Rome I and II are applied in Belgium. It is not possible in this chapter to discuss all 279 cases in this domain. As the majority (261) concerned Brussels I, this will be the main focus. Section III is devoted to family matters (Brussels IIa and Maintenance). 83 cases concern

---

[*] The authors are grateful to the participants of a workshop which was held on 12 February 2015 in Antwerp.

[1] The separate family courts were only introduced in September 2014. Therefore family cases prior to this date emanate from the civil law courts.

[2] Note that we limit our account in this report to the civil courts.

[3] For more information, see the website of the federal Ministry of Justice: http://justice.belgium.be/fr/ordre_judiciaire/cours_et_tribunaux.

[4] There is a vast amount of legal literature on the instruments, but they were not the focus of this study. See among others B Allemeersch and T Kruger (eds), *Handboek Europees Burgerlijk Procesrecht* (Mortsel, Intersentia, 2015); S Francq, 'La refonte du Règlement Bruxelles I—Champ d'application et compétence' (2013) 119 *Revue de droit commercial belge* 307; E Guinchard (ed), *Le nouveau règlement Bruxelles I bis* (Brussels, Bruylant, 2014); R Jafferali, 'Le règlement Bruxelles I dans la jurisprudence des cours suprêmes (2010-2012)—Allemagne, Belgique, France, Pays-Bas et Royaume-Uni' (2013) 119 *Revue de droit commercial belge* 357; A-M Rouchaud-Joët 'Le nouveau règlement 'Bruxelles I': refonte des règles sur la compétence judiciaire, la reconnaissance et l'exécution des décisions en matière civile et commerciale' (2014) *Journal de droit européen* 2.

[5] On the databases Jura, Juridat, Justel and Stradalex.

[6] There were six interviews with judges and nine with practitioners in the domain of civil and commercial matters and four with judges and three with practitioners in the domain of family law. Most of the interviews were with individuals although some were group discussions. All participants have signed a consent form and their answers were used anonymously.

Brussels IIa and 11 concern Maintenance. In this part the main focus will therefore be on Brussels IIa. Each part first discusses the approaches by lawyers, then the interpretation of specific provisions and last the challenges that judges face when dealing with EU Private International Law.

II. Civil and Commercial Matters

A. Lawyers' Approaches

Interview respondents said that cross-border litigation is more expensive due to legal fees and translation costs. Lawyer's fees are based on an hourly rate. Court fees and the costs that the losing party have to pay to the winning party (by way of indemnity for legal representation) are fixed. This fixed amount of costs remains the same for cross-border cases. However, lawyers can request a higher indemnity on the basis of the complexity of the case. Making such arrangements depends on the judge's discretion.[7]

The interviews suggest that responses to high litigation costs vary. Lawyers tend to first try to negotiate. However, these attempts might be thwarted by the *lis pendens* rule, which gives preference to the court first seised and therefore can induce a rush to the court.[8] One interviewee recounted:

> Generally speaking, we try to negotiate. Only when the negotiations fail, we go to court or to arbitration. There are exceptions. In some instances, we skip the negotiation stage and 'attack' immediately. This is the case, for example, when we want to fix the 'court first seised' in light of the lis pendens provisions. [Cross-border litigation risks] can strain the negotiations. For a Belgian company, it is not the same to be sued in Brussels or in Berlin. Things can escalate more quickly, because the parties have more to lose. On the other hand, they will be more cautious. Proceedings will cost more, and they can take a long time. If parties are aware of the risks they may also try harder to find a negotiated solution.[9]

Factors that lead to settlement include the strength of parties' claims, interim decisions, remarks by the court at the hearing, the passing of time, the length of the proceedings, delaying tactics, a change of management or of legal counsel, the prospect of working together in future, a cost-benefit analysis, the complexity of the case, the uncertainty of the outcome, the disposition of the lawyers, the difficulties with actual enforcement, the rules on international jurisdiction, encouragement by the court to settle.

Mediation is not very popular. Arbitration is a more popular choice, but not in all circumstances. Interviewees recounted reasons to choose arbitration, including the neutrality and specialisation of the arbitrator, confidentiality, efficiency, speed, procedures in English, non-national procedural rules for arbitration, forms of evidence, absence of appeal and ease of enforcement. However, the costs remain a disincentive for some parties. There is some indication that arbitration is more popular between Belgian parties and parties from

---

[7] Art 1022 Code of Civil Procedure.
[8] See more: ch 40 below.
[9] EUPILLAR—Belgium—Interview Transcript B3.

outside the EU. One interviewee noted that: 'Within the European [judicial] area, there is no real need for arbitration, the [EU Private International Law] instruments are useful.'[10] However, when dealing with parties from America or South-East Asia, arbitration provides more protection against legal cultures that are perceived to be very different. The data suggest that escalating the conflict to such a point that proceedings are brought in different jurisdictions leading to the applicability of the *lis pendens* rule is rare.

B. Interpretation of the EU Instruments

i. Characterisation

Characterising the issues before finding the appropriate bases for jurisdiction or conflict-of-law rules has proven a challenge. Belgian courts too often rely on national legal categories rather than considering the autonomous categories which Court of Justice of the European Union (CJEU) case law have laid down. A good example is the interpretation of 'matters relating to contract', specifically in relation to quasi-contracts. The Court of Appeal of Liège was faced with a question of the recovery of undue payments. It turned to Belgian legal writings, rather than seeking an autonomous definition. The Court concluded that a quasi-contract is neither a matter related to contracts nor a matter related to tort and therefore refrained from applying Article 5. This is contrary to the CJEU's more recent judgment in *Profit Investment*.[11] In this case the situation was similar, namely undue payments closely connected to a contract. Of course the Court of Appeal could not have known this future case law, but it could have either posed the question or sought an autonomous interpretation. In any event, according to *Kalfelis*[12] it seems that the Court could not reasonably have come to the conclusion that this is neither contract nor tort (in its broad meaning). In an earlier case the Commercial Court of Hasselt characterised a quasi-contract as a matter related to tort.[13]

Another example that shows that Belgian courts rely on national law when interpreting Brussels I, relates to 'matters relating to tort'. The Mons Court of Appeal qualified the appellant's claim for frivolous and vexatious legal proceedings as a 'matter relating to tort' within the meaning of Article 5(3) because the claim was based on an extra-contractual legal basis under national law.[14] The Court did not consider the autonomous characterisation of the claim. The parties had reached a settlement agreement during previous proceedings which was meant to put an end to all disputes between the parties, so that the appellant's claim had to be assessed in light of that settlement. According to *Brogsitter* civil liability claims which are made in tort under national law, must nonetheless be considered as concerning 'matters relating to a contract' within the meaning of Article 5(1)(a) Brussels I, where the

---

[10] EUPILLAR—Belgium—Interview Transcript B12.

[11] C-366/13 *Profit Investment SIM*, EU:C:2016:282.

[12] C-189/87 *Kalfelis*, EU:C:1988:459.

[13] Hasselt Commercial Court, 12 October 2005, *Elan languages v Venema*, unpublished (cited by P Vanhelmont in (2010) 36 *Limburgs rechtsleven* 50).

[14] Court of Appeal, Mons, 8 May 2014 (2015) 108–09 *Droit de la Consommation* 157, with case note by E Ulrix; Court of Appeal, Brussels, 3 March 2009 (2009) *Jaarboek Handelspraktijken & Mededinging* 374. The basis in national law was Art 1382 of the Civil Code.

conduct complained of may be considered a breach of the terms of the contract, which may be established by taking into account the purpose of the contract.[15]

ii. Contracts (Article 5(1))

The internal logic of Article 5(1) poses difficulties. Belgian courts sometimes apply the general rule of subparagraph (a) instead of the specific rules in subparagraph (b) with regard to sales and services.[16] The so-called '*contrat d'entreprise/aannemingsovereenkomst*' also causes confusion.[17] This is a contract often used in construction, according to which the contractor agrees to carry out the construction work for a specified price. The contractor often also delivers the goods used for the work. Belgian courts avoid defining these contracts as either sale or service contracts and apply subparagraph (a), either implicitly[18] or expressly.[19] A commercial law judge in an interview identified this as one of the main gaps in the current EU Private International Law framework, not only regarding jurisdiction but also regarding the applicable law.[20]

There appeared to be some confusion about whether Article 5(1)(b) referred to the factual or legal place of delivery for sales contracts. The Court of Cassation finally took a view on this issue in 2008. It found that 'the Community legislator opted for a place that can be easily and factually determined, a place that is not dependent on clauses agreed upon by the parties, namely the place where the goods were in fact delivered or had to be delivered'.[21] The Court of Cassation was correct to rule out the application of the conflict-of-laws method, but it went too far when it decided that the agreement between the parties is never relevant.[22] The CJEU decided otherwise in *Car Trim* in 2010.[23] It is an interesting research finding that, thereafter, the Antwerp Court of Appeal adopted the CJEU position in *Car Trim*,[24] but the Commercial Court of Kortrijk still referred to the Court of Cassation.[25]

There was a level of uncertainty with regard to the interpretation of the place of the provision of service under Article 5(1)(b). Belgian courts had experienced difficulties to determine the place of provision of intellectual (and therefore immaterial) services, such as

---

[15] C-548/12 *Brogsitter*, EU:C:2014:148.

[16] eg the Justice of the Peace Brussels used the general rule in a case concerning unpaid legal fees, but this judgment was corrected by the Court of First Instance of Brussels, 24 June 2014 (2014) 133 *Journal des Tribunaux* 792. Other examples of erroneous application: Court of Appeal of Antwerp, 7 May 2008 (2008) 34 *Limburgs rechtsleven* 296 (sale); Commercial Court Brussels 16 August 2005 (2007–08) 71 *Rechtskundig Weekblad* 1460 (services); Commercial Court Brussels, 28 November 2005 (2006–07) 70 *Rechtskundig Weekblad* 969 (sale); Justice of the Peace Maaseik, 29 February 2008 (2008) 34 *Limburgs rechtsleven* 346 (sale); Justice of the Peace Genk, 12 November 2011 (2011–12) 75 *Rechtskundig Weekblad* 1312 (accountancy services).

[17] The problem is not entirely solved by C-381/08, *Car Trim GmbH v KeySafety Systems Srl*, EU:C:2010:90. That case concerned goods to be made according to specifications by the buyer. A *contrat d'entreprise* is more mixed between a service and sales contract.

[18] Justice of the Peace Genk, 22 November 2011 (2011–12) 75 *Rechtskundig Weekblad* 1312.

[19] Commercial Court Hasselt, 11 February 2004, unpublished (AR 03/4286).

[20] EUPILLAR—Belgium—Interview Transcript B5.

[21] Cass 5 December 2008 (2009) 8 (4) *Tijdschrift@ipr.be* 35; *Pasicrisie* 2008 (12) 2854; (2009–10) 73 *Rechtskundig Weekblad* 408, with case note by H Storme (own translation).

[22] Some lower courts followed the Court of Cassation's judgment, eg Commercial Court Kortrijk, 12 February 2009 (2009–10) 73 *Rechtskundig Weekblad* 847; Commercial Court Hasselt, 23 November 2009 (2010) 36 *Limburgs rechtsleven* with case note by P Vanhelmont.

[23] C-381/08 Car Trim GmbH v KeySafety Systems Srl, EU:C:2010:90.

[24] Court of Appeal Antwerp, 12 September 2011 (2013) *Rechtspraak Antwerpen, Brussel, Gent* 1243.

[25] Commercial Court Kortrijk, 10 July 2013 (2014) 30 *Tijdschrift voor Gentse en West-Vlaamse Rechtspraak* 35.

design. In various cases the courts decided that such services were provided at the seat or the office of the designer—as opposed to the place where the product of the designs would be delivered or constructed.[26]

Article 5(1)(a) also posed difficult questions of interpretation. Under this provision, courts should still apply the old case law of the CJEU (the *Tessili* method) which requires the place of performance to be determined in accordance with the law applicable to the contract. However, our research findings show that the Belgian courts do not always follow this method. The Belgian courts sometimes decide that the place of payment under Article 5(1)(a) is at the debtor's place of residence (in line with Belgian law),[27] without examining whether Belgian law is in fact applicable to the claim. For instance, the Brussels Court of Appeal stated that the defendant's obligation to pay (arising from an acknowledgment of debt) must be performed at the defendant's place of residence.[28] The Court thereby avoided the issue of determining the law applicable to the acknowledgment of debt. The interview data have indicated that the task can be very complex.[29] The complexity of the task, but also the fact that courts do not perform it correctly, impacts on the predictability of the jurisdictional rules.

The *Tessili* method furthermore causes difficulty in cases where there are primary and subsidiary obligations. Two cases before the Court of Appeal of Ghent illustrate the problem.[30] Both cases concerned the obligation to give a reasonable notice period in case of termination of an exclusive distribution agreement. When such obligation was not respected, the subsidiary obligation of payment is triggered. The Court found that the obligation under the distribution agreement had to be performed in Belgium and therefore the Belgian courts had jurisdiction. As payment is only a subsidiary obligation, the Court did not consider the place of payment relevant.

iii. Place of Damage

The Belgian courts seem to eagerly assume jurisdiction on the ground that Belgium is the place of damage, both in the online and offline contexts. Before the CJEU's *Pinckney*[31] judgment was rendered, the practice in Belgium varied. Some courts considered the mere accessibility of a website sufficient to conclude that the tort (infringement of copyright) was committed in Belgium.[32] Other courts have considered it necessary for an extra requirement to be satisfied, and have based their finding on the CJEU's *Pammer* judgment[33] (which dealt with consumer contracts and not tort).[34]

---

[26] Court of Appeal Brussels, 27 September 2012 (2013) 107 *Droit des Affairs* 330, with case note by M-C Janssens and S Van de Mosselaer; Commercial Court Namur, 26 June 2013 (2014) 109 *Droit des Affairs* 137.

[27] Pursuant to Art 1247 of the Civil Code.

[28] Court of Appeal Brussels, 1 March 2013, unpublished (RG 09 AR 2111). For a similar reasoning, although obiter, see the judgment of the Court of Appeal of Liège of 13 December 2012, (2014) 120 *Revue de Droit Commercial Belge* 91, with case note by A Hansebout; (2013) 12 (1) *Tijdschrift@ipr.be* 61.

[29] EUPILLAR—Belgium—Interview Transcript B3.

[30] Court of Appeal Ghent 2 May 2005 (2006) 5 (4) *Tijdschrift@ipr.be* 64; Court of Appeal Ghent 5 November 2007 (2008) 7 *Nieuw Juridisch Weekblad* 500.

[31] C-170/12 *Pinckney*, EU:C:2013:635.

[32] Court of Appeal Brussels, 27 September 2012 (2013) 107 *Droit des Affairs* 330, with case note by M-C Janssens and S Van de Mosselaer.

[33] Joined cases C-585/08, *Pammer* and C-144/09, *Hotel Alpenhof*, EU:C:2010:740.

[34] President Commercial Court Brussels, 28 June 2013, (2013) *Revue de droit intellectuel—L'ingénieur-conseil* 573 (trademark infringement through the online sale of goods).

In 2009, the Belgian consumer organisation *Test Aankoop/Test Achats* initiated proceedings before the Commercial Court of Namur against the airline easyJet to terminate the use of certain clauses in its general terms and conditions in violation of consumer legislation.[35] This was considered a tort matter, as there was no contract between the consumer organisation and the airline company. In this case, the Court assumed jurisdiction because it was held that the harmful event occurred in Belgium. The Court considered that easyJet had an office in Brussels and that it offered its services to consumers in Belgium through its website. The Court also considered the coherence of jurisdiction in such tort matters and in consumer contract cases.

In a case before the court of first instance of Leuven a company, Serverscheck, sued Google to stop suggesting the names of illegal copies of its software in Google Toolbar.[36] The court found that it had jurisdiction, since Serverscheck suffered damage in Belgium. The alleged unfair trade practices originate abroad, but end in Belgium, where the damage—the loss of clients—occurs or may occur. While this solution is in line with the CJEU case law, it is noteworthy that the court used language based on the sphere of applicability of Belgian legislation on unfair trade practices, rather than the CJEU language.

This trend of accepting that damage occurred in Belgium is also visible in case law applying Rome II. In *Test-Aankoop v easyJet*[37] a consumer organisation sued easyJet for violations of consumer legislation in its general terms and conditions. On the basis of Article 6 of Rome II the court found that Belgian law applied as the competitive relations or the collective interests of consumers were affected in Belgium.

Two copyright infringement cases brought before the Brussels Court of Appeal dealt with a similar issue of various applicable laws. In the first case, several associations defending the rights of authors, journalists and scholars sued Google Inc to stop the use of their articles for the 'Google News' service.[38] In the second case, a Belgian author's sketches were used in Belgium and Luxembourg, infringing his copyright.[39] The intended audience was situated in Belgium. In both cases, the Brussels Court of Appeal first considered the Berne Convention, which contains a similar rule to Article 8 of Rome II, with only a slight difference in wording. Article 5(2) of the Berne Convention states that 'the extent of protection, as well as the means of redress afforded to the author to protect his rights, shall be governed exclusively by the laws of the country *where* protection is claimed', while Article 8 of Rome II refers to 'the country *for which* protection is claimed.' Neither rule provided a satisfactory answer for 'complex infringement' cases such as the present ones, where the cause of the infringement (the injection of data in a server in the US; the broadcasting of

---

[35] Commercial Court Namur, 10 March 2010 (2011) 92-93 *Droit de la Consommation* (92–93) 46 (with case note by T Kruger). This case was appealed, but the appellant did not contest the finding by the commercial court on jurisdiction and the Court of Appeal therefore did not discuss this issue: Court of Appeal Liège, 23 April 2013 (2014) 105 *Droit de la Consommation* 68 (with case note by T Kruger and R Steennot).

[36] President Court of First Instance Leuven, 1 March 2007 (2007) 12 *Droits intellectuels* 188; (2007) *Jaarboek Handelspraktijken en Mededinging* 772; President Commercial Court Leuven, 2 December 2010, (2011) 16 *Droits intellectuels* 21; (2011) *Rechtspraak Antwerpen Brussel Gent* 1097.

[37] Commercial Court Namur, 10 March 2010 (2011) 92-93 *Droit de la Consommation* 46, with case note by T Kruger.

[38] Court of Appeal Brussels, 5 May 2011, *Auteurs et média* 2012 (2–3) 202; (2011) *Revue de droit intellectuel—L'ingénieur-conseil* 56; (2011) 16 *Droits intellectuels* 265 with case note by F Petillon; (2011) *Jaarboek Marktpraktijken* 896; (2011) 44 *Revue du Droit des Technologies de l'Information* 35, with case note by A De Francquen.

[39] Court of Appeal Brussels, 3 October 2013 (2014) 126 *Revue de jurisprudence de Liège, Mons et Bruxelles* 446; (2014) *Jaarboek Marktpraktijken* 29.

television sketches in Luxembourg) and the damage (the dissemination of data in Belgium; the reception by the intended Belgian audience) were situated in different places. Therefore the Court used the general rule of Article 4. In the first case, the Court decided that the case was more closely connected with Belgium in accordance with Article 4(3). In the second case, the Court applied the law of the country in which the damage occurred, also Belgium, in accordance with Article 4(1).

In another case the same Court found that the targeted market was the Benelux. Therefore Belgian law applied and the Benelux Convention on Intellectual property as integral part of it.[40]

Thus, both with respect to jurisdiction and applicable law, a homeward trend is visible: Belgian courts take the case and apply Belgian law. In doing so, they do not transgress the interpretations given by the Court of Justice of the EU, although they do not always explicitly refer to this case law nor use the Court of Justice's wording.

iv. Jurisdiction in Matters Relating to Insurance

Regarding insurance contracts, the main issue seems to be the question of who exactly qualifies as 'the policyholder, the insured or a beneficiary', and therefore who can benefit from the protective provisions of the Regulation.[41] The Belgian courts have given this phrase a broad interpretation.

The Liège Court of Appeal ruled that solicitors are the beneficiaries of legal costs insurance and may therefore sue the insurer at the place where the law firm is established.[42] Also a person attempting to get information about the life insurance policy of his deceased mother from a bank in Luxembourg was considered to fall within this category of protected persons.[43] The plaintiff sued in Belgium, but the bank claimed that he was still a third party to the insurance policy and did not qualify as either policyholder, insured or beneficiary. The Court of Appeal of Brussels found that as heir to his mother's estate, the plaintiff has the same rights as the deceased, whether as policy holder or insured, unless the policy does not allow such transfer of rights.

v. Choice-of-court Agreements

The dataset contains many Belgian cases in which the validity of choice-of-court agreements is raised. The Belgian courts seem to struggle with the correct interpretation of the three alternatives provided by Brussels I: choice-of-court agreements can either be in writing, or conform with a practice between the parties, or be in line with a usage in the branch of trade in which the parties are active.[44]

First, the distinction between the requirements of writing and a practice between the parties is not always clear. The Court of Appeal of Antwerp has ruled that a choice-of-court clause contained in the general terms and conditions was valid only if it was the result of an oral agreement that came within the framework of a continuing trade relationship between

---

[40] Court of Appeal Brussels, 31 January 2011, (2011) *Jaarboek Marktpraktijken* 640, with case note by C Gommers.
[41] Art 9(1)(b) Brussels I; Art 11(1)(b) Brussels Ia.
[42] Court of Appeal Liège 4 June 2012, (2014) 126 *Revue de jurisprudence de Liège, Mons et Bruxelles* 875.
[43] Court of Appeal Brussels, 14 September 2010 (2011) 130 *Journal des tribunaux* 74.
[44] Art 23(1) of Brussels I; Art 25(1) of Brussels Ia.

the parties.[45] This argument is based on old CJEU case law, based on an old version of the provision, which was worded differently.[46]

Second, Belgian courts generally accept the validity of choice-of-court agreements on the reverse side of the contract if the contract contains a reference to these general terms and conditions.[47] However, there are two judgments in which the courts added a requirement. The courts found that it was insufficient if the first (signed) page of the order confirmation referred only to the general terms and conditions on the reverse; an explicit reference to *the choice of court clause included therein* was required.[48]

Third, the issue of choice-of-court agreements on the reverse side of the invoice has solicited much discussion in case law. Judges have identified this as one of the main issues they struggle with in relation to the formal validity requirements of choice-of-court clauses. When assessing the validity of choice-of-court clauses based on a practice between the parties, Belgian courts usually examine the following cumulative conditions: (i) Is there a sufficiently long and regular trade relationship between the parties and (ii) Did this relationship exist prior to the transaction underlying the dispute?[49] The parties should have used *the same* general terms and conditions throughout their trade relations. It is however not simple to determine how many invoices would amount to a sufficiently long trade relation. Judges consider the intensity of the relationship, the nature of the contracts, the prior negotiations, whether the contract was concluded over a distance or whether the parties met, whether the dispute is linked to the prior trade relations, etc.

Fourth, Belgian courts sometimes *presume* that the party accepted the general terms and conditions of its adversary if he or she never objected to them. Courts take this argument from Belgian commercial law[50] instead of applying the CJEU case law. One interviewee elaborated on this issue, noting that the approach by Belgian courts differs from that of the German *Bundesgerichtshof*.[51]

A fifth problematic area is the language of the choice-of-court agreement. This is not relevant for the determination of the formal validity.[52] However, courts verify whether the recipient could understand the general terms and conditions. In this regard, there has been an evolution in the case law over the course of the years. Initially, some judges rejected the choice-of-court clause (or the general terms and conditions in general) if they were not

---

[45] Court of Appeal Antwerp 30 March 2009 (2012-13) 76 *Rechtskundig Weekblad* 107; Court of Appeal Antwerp 15 April 2013 (2013) 39 *Limburgs rechtsleven* 215, with case note by H Van Gompel.

[46] 25/76 *Galeries Segoura v Société Rahim Bonakdaria*, EU:C:1976:178. During the first workshop Mr Vanhelmont noted that this particular chamber of the Court of Appeal of Antwerp has since changed its approach.

[47] eg Commercial Court Hasselt, 11 December 2002, unpublished (AR 02/03167); Commercial Court Tournai, 11 September 2012 (2013) 119 *Revue de droit commercial Belge* 457. This is a correct application of 24/76, *Estasis Salotti di Colzani Aimo e Gianmario Colzani v RÜWA Polstereimaschinen GmbH*, EU:C:1976:177.

[48] Commercial Court Hasselt, 11 May 2005, unpublished (AR 4187/04); Court of Appeal 14 October 2013 (2014) 40 *Limburgs rechtsleven* 65, with case note by P Vanhelmont.

[49] Court of Appeal Ghent, 1 February 2012 (2013) *Rechtspraak Antwerpen Brussel Gent* 1129, with case note by P Delzandre; (2012-13) 76 *Rechtskundig Weekblad* 24; (2012) 11 (3) *Tijdschrift@ipr.be* 36; Court of Appeal Ghent 29 February 2012, unpublished (2011/AR/1312); Court of Appeal Antwerp, 19 November 2012 (2013) *Rechtspraak Antwerpen Brussel Gent* 1250, with case note by C Clijmans.

[50] Art 25 of the Commercial Code provides that a sales contract can be proved by an accepted invoice. The absence of protest against an invoice amounts to the acceptance of its content, including the general terms and conditions printed on the back of the invoice.

[51] EUPILLAR—Belgium—Interview Transcript B3.

[52] 150/80, *Elefanten Shuh GmbH v Jacqmain*, EU:C:1981:148.

drawn up in the language of the recipient. Now the courts take a more factual approach: they examine not only which languages are spoken by the recipient, but also the language used by the parties in their communications with each other, and if their trade demands that they have a basic knowledge of a 'lingua franca' such as English—all this to determine whether the recipient was able or ought to have been able to understand the choice-of-court clause. Interviewed judges have indicated that this is a difficult matter to decide on.[53]

vi. Recognition and Enforcement

The dataset contains only a few judgments on recognition and enforcement. It appears both from this data and from the interviews that declarations of enforceability are rarely appealed and the grounds for refusing recognition and enforcement are rarely used.

The ground for refusal most often invoked by the parties, as a sort of 'garbage can', is the public policy exception.[54] However, courts rarely accept this ground for refusal. In line with the approach by the Court of Justice of the EU, the Court of Cassation has found that a violation of EU law (in this case Article 17(2) of the Evidence Regulation) was no ground to refuse the recognition of a German judgment.[55] A difference in insurance law (between France and Belgium) does not amount to public policy.[56] Neither does the principle of adversarial proceedings.[57] The Court of Cassation did not accept the averred 'colossal' legal fees in the United Kingdom and refusal by the High Court of representation by a Belgian lawyer as justifying the use of the public policy exception.[58] A foreign civil judgment dating from before the criminal proceedings were introduced can be enforced despite the fact that this would be contrary to Belgian domestic procedural law.[59]

The second ground for refusal is the fact that there was no timely service.[60] In order for this ground of refusal to succeed, the party contesting enforceability must show that he or she used the opportunity of appeal in the state of the original judgment. This requirement causes difficulty. In the only published case in which this ground for refusal was raised, the party contesting enforcement averred that he had been unable to file an appeal against the English judgment within the deadline of 15 days.[61] He argued that the tardiness of the appeal was due to trouble with his legal counsel. The Brussels Court of First Instance deemed this reason insufficient. The delay was due to negligence, since the appellant could have undertaken steps to find another lawyer in the UK. One of the interviewed judges indicated that it is difficult for judges to examine the foreign procedural law and understand whether the defendant was in fact notified in time to safeguard his rights of defence.[62]

---

[53] EUPILLAR—Belgium—Interview Transcript B4, B5 and B14.

[54] Art 34(1) Brussels I; Art 24(1)(a) Brussels Ia.

[55] Court of Cassation 29 April 2010, *Pasicrisie* 2010 (4) 1327.

[56] Court of First Instance Tournai, 28 November 2009 (2010) 129 *Journal des tribunaux* 456.

[57] Court of First Instance Brussels, 13 October 2004 (2005) 19 *Revue générale de droit civil Belge* 125.

[58] Court of Cassation, 24 February 2012 (2012) *Tijdschrift voor Vreemdelingenrecht* 318. The Court found that 'the appellant did not exercise any legal remedy against the decision, and does not show that, in the light of all the circumstances, the available remedies were doomed to failure, regardless of whether those remedies pertain to a request for legal aid or the merits of the case.'

[59] This principle is enshrined in Art 4(1) of the Preliminary Title of the Belgian Code of Criminal Procedure.

[60] Art 34(2) Brussels I; Art 45(1)(b) Brussels Ia.

[61] Court of First Instance Brussels, 13 October 2004 (2005) 19 *Revue générale de droit civil Belge* 125.

[62] EUPILLAR—Belgium—Interview Transcript B8.

Enforcement generally goes well and *exequatur* proceedings are swift, as confirmed by one of the interviewees.[63] Also after the abolishment of *exequatur* enforcement proceedings are going well. However, getting the certificates from foreign courts can be time-consuming and difficult.

On the basis that the declaration of enforceability carries with it the power to proceed to protective measures,[64] the Brussels enforcement judge has ruled that an attachment after a declaration of enforceability had been obtained does not have to fulfil the requirements of Belgian law, such as prior approval by the enforcement judge, since it is governed directly by EU law.[65]

vii. Matters Related to Relations with Other Instruments

The relation between Brussels I and the CMR Convention came up in several cases.[66] In one judgment the court found that the CMR Convention was not applicable because the framework agreement concluded between the parties did not determine the mode of transport.[67]

In a case on a choice-of-court clause, the Court of Cassation found that Belgian law applied to the formal validity of the clause, as the CMR Convention does not provide for any specific requirements.[68] The result was that the court upheld a forum choice taken up in the general conditions on the invoice, on the basis of Article 25 of the Belgian Commercial Code. Such a result would not have been possible if Brussels I were applicable.[69] The Court thus clearly distinguished the law under Brussels I and the CMR Convention.

C. Judges' Challenges

i. Judges' Approaches in General

The general tendency is that Belgian courts are respectful of CJEU case law and apply it when they can. It does happen that the courts overlook the latest developments in the case law.[70] This was confirmed by several respondents in their interviews.[71] It has to do with the following factors: (lack) of training for judges and the lack of the time they can spend on a judgment. Furthermore, the interpretation of the Regulations can be influenced by Belgian law.

---

[63] EUPILLAR—Belgium—Interview Transcript B18.

[64] Art 47(2) Brussels I.

[65] Court of First Instance Brussels (Enforcement Judge) 21 March 2011 (2012) *Ius & Actores* 183; (2011) 118 *Revue de jurisprudence de Liège, Mons et Bruxelles* (36) 1774.

[66] Commercial Court Hasselt, 8 October 2003, unpublished (AR 03/2749); Court of Cassation 29 April 2004, *Arresten van het Hof van Cassatie* 2004 (4) 748; *Pasicrisie* 2004 (5–6) 736; (2005) 4 (3) *Tijdschrift@ipr.be* 23, with case note by T Kruger; Commercial Court Hasselt, 24 November 2004, unpublished (AR 04/4119); Commercial Court Kortrijk, 15 December 2005, unpublished (3233/2005).

[67] Commercial Court Antwerp, 21 December 2007 (2008) *Rechtspraak Antwerpen Brussel Gent* 294; (2007) 6 (4) *Tijdschrift@ipr.be* 2007 (4) 52.

[68] Court of Cassation 29 April 2004, *Arresten van het Hof van Cassatie* 2004 (4) 748; *Pasicrisie* 2004 (5–6) 736; (2005) 4 (3) *Tijdschrift@ipr.be* 23, with case note by T Kruger.

[69] See the discussion about choice-of-court agreements above.

[70] eg Court of Cassation, 29 November 2012, (2013) 51 *Revue du Droit des Technologies de l'Information* 52, with case note by JP Moiny (2013) *Rechtspraak Antwerpen Brussel Gent* 1281, with case by F Debussere; Commercial Court Mons 8 May 2014 (2015) 108-109 *Droit de la Consommation* 157, with case note by E Ulrix.

[71] EUPILLAR—Belgium—Interview Transcript B5, B8 and B12.

One interviewed judge pointed out a fear that judges may miss new developments in the case law of the CJEU, or a change in legislation, because they rely on documentation that they have built up over the years, but they do not have time to verify this information each time.[72]

Aside from the respect for the case law, Belgian judges are reluctant to themselves refer questions for preliminary ruling to the CJEU.[73] One practitioner attributed this to the Belgian (and French) legal culture: 'The Belgian courts are more used to a centralised system of authority where the content of the law is more affirmed than debated and where the court's reasoning is less detailed than eg in Germany or in the UK.'[74] The judges also worry that a request for a preliminary ruling would delay the case too much.

ii. Delays in Proceedings

It seems that the length of the litigation depends more on the national procedural system in general, and does not vary between national and cross-border cases. Because of the judicial backlog of cases, in some courts it simply takes more time to get a hearing date than in others. In some courts, it can take up to a year (or even longer) to obtain a date for the first hearing.[75] What does take longer, is when the court lacks jurisdiction, and the parties have to start again somewhere else.

Delays are furthermore caused by the lack of knowledge of and familiarity with the Regulations among practitioners. Lawyers have an important role to play, especially in correctly pleading the cases before judges. The lawyers that we interviewed were all specialised in private international law, but from the interviews it appears that that is definitely not the case for all lawyers in general. Translation also causes delays.

iii. Assessing Jurisdiction

If the defendant does not appear at the introductory hearing, many judges examine their jurisdiction of their own motion,[76] as required by Brussels I,[77] even when just one of the

---

[72] EUPILLAR—Belgium—Interview Transcript B4.

[73] Examples of cases where a preliminary question would have been helpful: Court of Appeal Antwerp, 20 March 2007 (2007) *Jaarboek Kredietrecht* 161, with case note by C Verdure; Court of Appeal Liège, 13 December 2012, (2014) 120 *Revue du droit commercial Belge* 91, with case note by A Hansebout; (2013) 12 (1) *Tijdschrift@ipr. be* 61. Of course, under the EC Treaties in the Amsterdam and Nice versions, only the highest courts could refer preliminary questions. It is only since the entry into force of the Treaty on the Functioning of the EU (Lisbon version) on 1 December 2009 that Art 267 enabled all courts to pose questions.

[74] EUPILLAR—Belgium—Interview Transcript B3.

[75] One interviewee said: 'Last week, a case was initiated [in May 2015] and the first pleadings, only on the issue of jurisdiction, are set for January 2016. One month later we should know whether the court withholds jurisdiction. Only then will we be able to move on to the merits.'

[76] Among others: Commercial Court Hasselt, 15 February 2002, unpublished (AR 02/1132); Commercial Court Hasselt (2003) 109 *Revue du droit commercial Belge* 352, with case note by T Kruger; (2004-05) 68 *Rechtskundig Weekblad* 833; Commercial Court Kortrijk, 6 November 2013, unpublished (AR 03888/03); Commercial Court Hasselt, 5 January 2005, unpublished (AR 04/5068); Commercial Court Hasselt, 17 May 2006, unpublished (AR 06/1484); Justice of the Peace Brussels 14 November 2006 (2007) 114 *Revue de Jurisprudence de Liège, Mons et Bruxelles* 842; Commercial Court Hasselt, 22 October 2008 (2009-10) 73 *Rechtskundig Weekblad* 933; Commercial Court Kortrijk, 12 February 2009 (2009-10) 73 *Rechtskundig Weekblad* 847; Court of Appeal Antwerp 19 November 2012 (2013) *Rechtspraak Antwerpen Brussel Gent* 1250, with case note by C Clijmans; Commercial Court Kortrijk 10 July 2013 (2014) 30 *Tijdschrift voor Gentse en West-Vlaamse Rechtspraak* 35.

[77] Art 26(1) Brussel I; Art 28(1) Brussels Ia.

parties among multiple defendants fails to enter an appearance and the other defendants do not raise any objections.[78]

The database contains a relatively large number of decisions involving parties who fail to enter an appearance. When asked about the possible reasons for this, most interviewees were left puzzled. Interview respondents suggest that they would never advise clients not to appear.[79] A judge said that courts sometimes receive letters from parties.[80] If these are in the official language of the court, they tend to accept them. If not, this is more difficult in the light of Belgian language laws. However, this ad hoc approach might, in our view, infringe the right to a fair trial as guaranteed by Article 6 of the European Convention on Human Rights and Art. 47 of the EU Charter of Fundamental Rights.

iv. Finding Foreign Law

One of the greatest challenges in cross-border proceedings is finding foreign law. This is problematic both for lawyers and judges. For lawyers it is expensive and hard to find a foreign expert they can trust. They sometimes use it as a strategy, but often try to avoid foreign law or do not raise the issue.

Under Belgian law, finding foreign law is the obligation of the judge.[81] Judges may ask the parties' lawyers for assistance, but the judges carry the ultimate responsibility. This is a difficult and unpopular task. One judge commented:

> Personally, I haven't yet called upon the contact points of the European Judicial Network. What I have done, even though I strictly speaking probably am not allowed to do so, is to reopen the debates and ask the parties to give more information and adopt a position on the laws of [a state in the USA], because I was unable to find any information. In another case I had to apply the notion of acquisitive prescription under [an EU Member State] law. I based my decision entirely on the [the EU Member State's] Civil Code, but I don't know if that corresponds to the way it is applied by the ... courts [in this EU Member State].[82]

Another judge admitted that judges could be tempted to apply Belgian law and would not necessarily raise the issue of the applicable law when the parties had not done so.[83] Judges sometimes ask at the hearing, of their own motion, whether the parties agree to the application of Belgian law.[84] When they draw the parties' attention to the issue, the parties sometimes ask for more time to make submissions on the issue, or they accept the application of Belgian law on the spot.

The homeward trend seems greater for applicable law than for jurisdiction: Member State judges are more inclined to interpret EU instruments in a way which allows them to apply their own law than to take jurisdiction, according to several interviewees.[85]

---

[78] Commercial Court Turnhout, 12 March 2009 (2010) 116 *Revue du droit commercial Belge* 86 (third party proceedings); Court of First Instance Brussels, 17 June 2014 (2015) 88 *Revue générale des assurances et des responsabilités* 15144.

[79] EUPILLAR—Belgium—Interview Transcript B3.

[80] EUPILLAR—Belgium—Interview Transcript B4. This is particularly the case with parties from The Netherlands.

[81] Art 15 Belgian Code on Private International Law.

[82] EUPILLAR—Belgium—Interview Transcript B8.

[83] EUPILLAR—Belgium—Interview Transcript B4.

[84] ibid.

[85] EUPILLAR—Belgium—Interview Transcripts B4, B5, B8 and B18.

One interviewee noted: 'I have the feeling that, where the applicable law is concerned, Belgian courts more willingly apply Belgian law—and if they apply foreign law, they risk giving it a Belgian twist. They tend to jump to conclusions.'[86] Other respondents disagree and say that the Belgian courts apply foreign law quite often.[87] In the case law the trend of preferring to apply Belgian law is not very clear,[88] except in matters of tort, as explained above.

III. Family Law Matters

A. Lawyers' Approaches

In family law cases, the specific circumstances of the case are of paramount importance when interpreting the Regulations. Collecting the facts, access to reliable information, has been identified as a problem.

Forum shopping is much more rife in family cases than in commercial cases. This is especially so in divorce cases. There are various reasons for *forum shopping*. First, it seems that applicants prefer to sue before the courts of the Member State where they are habitually resident. This might be for reasons of convenience and confidence. Second, different courts will apply different laws and parties thus shop for the best substantive outcome. Third, costs are an important consideration.

Costs are also a reason for parties not to initiate or to desist litigation. One interviewee noted:

> The biggest issue is the cost, the steps you have to take, the documents you have to provide, and the cost of it all. Many people abandon a case because they make a cost-benefit analysis and they realise that to retrieve an amount X in maintenance contributions, it would cost them X EUR that they would have to invest without being sure that they will recover their claim. There is a problem of access to justice for financial reasons … It happens that people initiate proceedings for the sake of principle, when there is no financial gain to be had, but these are people who have the means.[89]

The availability of a large selection of fora can deter early settlement. Lawyers consider it more prudent to quickly institute legal proceedings in order to establish jurisdiction. Thereafter, they are prepared to negotiate. One interviewee observed that matters often settle only at the appeal stage.[90] This shows that the jurisdiction rules might encourage a rush to the court rather than seeking an amicable solution.

The interview data indicate that mediation is important and that court proceedings are expensive. However, an interview respondent forewarned that mediation can be used in bad faith, to prolong a factual situation or parties can manipulate the process by presenting a skewed version of the facts.[91]

---

[86] EUPILLAR—Belgium—Interview Transcript B18.
[87] EUPILLAR—Belgium—Interview Transcripts B3 and B10.
[88] This might be due to the approach by the EU legislator to align jurisdiction and applicable law as much as possible so that the issue does not come up that often.
[89] EUPILLAR—Belgium—Interview Transcript B2.
[90] EUPILLAR—Belgium—Interview Transcript B6.
[91] EUPILLAR—Belgium—Interview Transcript B2.

Mediation and amicable settlements are encouraged in Belgium. The new law institut-ing the Family Courts has introduced the mandatory personal appearance of the parties. The goal is to draw the parties' attention to the advantages of mediation and offer them an opportunity to settle the case before taking it any further. Such mediation is conducted in a special chamber of the family court. However, the judges in these chambers often face the problem of jurisdiction: they would prefer to deal with all related issues (divorce, parental responsibility, matrimonial property and maintenance), but each is regulated by a different instrument and it is not always possible to concentrate jurisdiction. Moreover, the parties have little scope to make jurisdiction agreements.

One of the interviewed practitioners mentioned collaborative law as a successful alterna-tive dispute resolution (ADR) method:

> I believe in collaborative law, even more so than in mediation. It relies on the idea that you and the opposing counsel act in all transparency and that you work together to achieve a solution for the parties. You sign a charter of mutual trust, but you also preserve the confidentiality. Achieving that would empty the courts.[92]

B. Interpretation of the EU Instruments

i. *Scope of Brussels IIa*

The courts do not always apply Brussels IIa, but sometimes revert immediately to Article 42 of the PIL Code in divorce proceedings,[93] and to Article 43 in marriage annulment cases.[94] In marriage annulment cases, the courts often,[95] but not always,[96] examine their interna-tional jurisdiction.

There is some debate on the definition of 'marriage'.[97] The Belgian courts tend to apply Brussels IIa to divorce proceedings between spouses of the same sex.[98] They do this as a matter of logic: if same-sex marriages are recognised, same-sex divorce is treated like any other divorce.[99]

---

[92] EUPILLAR—Belgium—Interview Transcript B2.

[93] Court of First Instance of Ghent 27 October 2009 (2010) *Tijdschrift voor familierecht* 35, with case note by J De Meyer; Court of First Instance of Arlon, 12 December 2008 (2009) *Revue trimestrielle de droit familial* 733, with case note by M Fallon.

[94] Court of First Instance Ghent, 4 February 2010, unpublished (AR 06/2987/A); Court of First Instance Ghent, 4 February 2010, unpublished (AR 04/4159/A); Court of First Instance Leuven, 2 February 2009, unpublished (AR 08/1473/A). See J Verhellen in Allemeersch and Kruger, above n 4, 67 fn 30.

[95] In marriage annulment cases: Court of Appeal Ghent, 22 May 2008 (2008) 7 (4) *Tijdschrift@ipr.be* 66; Court of Appeal Brussels, 9 February 2012 (2012) *Revue trimestrielle de droit familial* 618; Court of Appeal Brussels, 25 April 2013 (2013) *Revue trimestrielle de droit familial* 935; Court of First Instance Ghent, 15 January 2015 (2015) 14 (1) *Tijdschrift@ipr.be* 122; Court of Appeal 11 June 2015 (2015) 14 (2) *Tijdschrift@ipr.be* 100.

[96] Court of Appeal Brussels, 19 March 2012 (2012) *Revue trimestrielle de droit familial* 639; Court of Appeal Brussels, 5 January 2012 (2012) *Revue trimestrielle de droit familial* 613.

[97] See discussion by Verhellen, above n 94, 61–64.

[98] Court of First Instance Arlon, 20 November 2009 (2012) *Revue trimestrielle de droit familial* 696, with a case note by C Henricot; Court of First Instance Brussels, 19 June 2013 (2013) 12 (4) *Tijdschrift@ipr.be* 70, with a case note by P Wautelet.

[99] This became clear during the first Belgian national workshop.

The Belgian courts generally find that an application by spouses for separate residences does not fall within the scope of Brussels IIa.[100]

Belgian courts recognise that measures taken to protect the child as part of a youth assistance or child protection programme fall within the scope of the Regulation.[101] The Regulation has furthermore been applied to a '*kafala*' case[102] and an application made by a grandmother for rights of access to her grandchild.[103]

ii. Jurisdiction in Divorce Cases

As noted above, parties most often choose to institute proceedings at the place of their habitual residence. This has resulted in a number of cases where the habitual residence was disputed. Courts have taken various factors into account to establish a habitual residence.[104] These include a fiscal domicile, an intention to return, a letter by the employer, registration in the population register, a lease for the primary residence, credit card purchases, a statement by the landlord, the birth of a child, a statement by a medical centre, a one-month subscription for public transport; an application made for a residence permit; and a request made to the local CPAS (public welfare service) for financial assistance to pay for an urgent hospital case.[105]

As set out above, Belgian courts consider that same-sex divorce falls within the scope of Brussels IIa. This has led to practical difficulties. According to Brussels IIa, a court in a Member State may not base its jurisdiction on national law if another court in the EU has jurisdiction on the basis of the Regulation.[106] Belgian courts have been confronted with the situation in which the EU court that has jurisdiction is one that would not pronounce a divorce between parties of the same sex. Belgian courts have then, contrary to the letter of the Regulation, but in search for a practical solution, turned to the national *forum*

---

[100] President Court of First Instance Brussels, unpublished (05/1410/C); President Court of First Instance Brussels, 31 January 2007, unpublished, (06/1904/C); President Court of First Instance Brussels, 30 May 2007 (2008) 115 *Revue de Jurisprudence de Liège, Mons et Bruxelles* 845, with case note by P Wautelet; Court of First Instance Brussels, 21 November 2007 (2008) *Actualités du droit de la famille* 10; Court of First Instance Liège (2011) 118 *Revue de Jurisprudence de Liège, Mons et Bruxelles* 61, with case note by P Wautelet; (2009) *Revue trimestrielle de droit familial* 888; Court of Appeal Brussels, 21 June 2012 (2013) *Revue trimestrielle de droit familial* 263, with case note by C Henricot.

[101] Court of Appeal Ghent 5 September 2005, *Tijdschrift@ipr.be* 2005 (3) 26; (2005) *Echtscheidingsjournaal* 183, with case note by S Roeland; (2005-06) 69 *Rechtskundig Weekblad* 432; (2006) 7 *Tijdschrift voor Jeugd en Kinderrechten* 24, with case note by I Verdonck; (2006) *Tijdschrift voor Vreemdelingenrecht* 163, with case note by T Kruger; Court of Appeal Mons, 5 March 2007 (2008) *Revue trimestrielle de droit familial* 166, with case note by M Fallon; Court of Cassation, 9 May 2007 (2007) 6 (2) *Tijdschrift@ipr.be* 39; Court of Cassation 21 November 2007, *Pasicrisie* 2007 (11) 2084; (2008) 7 (1) *Tijdschrift@ipr.be* 78.

[102] Court of Appeal Brussels 28 November 2006 (2008) *Revue trimestrielle de droit familial* 90.

[103] Court of Appeal Brussels (Youth Chamber) 4 April 2007 (2007) 126 *Journal des tribunaux* 623; (2008) *Revue trimestrielle de droit familial* 508, with case note by C Henricot.

[104] Habitual residence is also used and defined in Art 4 §2 of the Belgian Code on Private International Law, and courts thus have experience to fall back on.

[105] Court of Appeal Brussels, 30 April 2009 (2011) *Revue trimestrielle de droit familial* 50, with case note by M Fallon; Court of First Instance Brussels, 2 February 2011 (2011) *Actualités du droit de la famille* 96; Court of Appeal Brussels, 17 November 2011 (2012) *Actualités du droit de la famille* 38; Court of Appeal Brussels 25 June 2013 (2013) 12 (3) *Tijdschrift@ipr.be* 59.

[106] Art 7 Brussels IIa; C-68/07, *Sundelind Lopez v Lopez Lizazo*, EU:C:2007:740.

necessitatis.[107] In this way they ensured a divorce forum for the same-sex couples who were not able to get a divorce elsewhere in the EU.[108]

iii. Jurisdiction in Cases of Parental Responsibility

Before the CJEU ruling in *A*,[109] the Belgian courts already defined the habitual residence of the child as 'the place where the child has the centre of its affective, familial, educational and social ties.'[110] The habitual residence of the child is independent from the parents' habitual residence.[111] However, parents do have the power to decide where their child will reside. Two criteria were deemed especially relevant: the intention of the parties and the duration of the stay.[112] Other factors include the place where the child lives, the place where he undertakes school or nursery school and extra-curricular activities, registration in the population register, the language the child speaks.[113] In the case of a one year old infant, the Brussels Court of Appeal found that the mother who often went back and forth between Brussels and London, only returned to Brussels for medical and administrative affairs, and that the life of the couple was based in London.[114] The evidence submitted to the court by the father of the child included the geolocation of phone calls made by the mother, witness statements made by the nanny, driver and other staff, and images of the security cameras of the building in London that showed the mother arriving and leaving. She did rent an apartment in Belgium, with her husband's approval, but the parents never established the marital residence there. She only stayed there for professional reasons, doctor appointments and to visit the maternal grandparents, which was deemed insufficient to establish the habitual residence of the child.

The President of the Court of First Instance of Huy ruled that it is possible that children live and are habitually resident in two countries at the same time.[115] Although the children were enrolled in the Belgian population register, the parents wanted a dual education for them so that they lived in Germany during the week and in Belgium on weekends.

---

[107] Art 11 of the Belgian Code on Private International Law.

[108] Court of First Instance Brussels, 2 December 2011 (2012) *Revue trimestrielle de droit familial* 359, with case note by C Henricot; Court of First Instance Brussels, 9 December 2011 (2012) *Revue trimestrielle de droit familial* 364, with case note by C Henricot; Court of First Instance Arlon, 20 November 2009 (2012) *Revue trimestrielle de droit familial* 696, with case note by C Henricot; Court of First Instance Brussels, 19 June 2013, (2013) 12 (4) *Tijdschrift@ipr.be* 70, with case note by P Wautelet.

[109] C-523/07, *A*, EU:C:2009:225.

[110] eg Court of Appeal Liège, 13 May 2003 (2004) *Revue trimestrielle de droit familial*, 392 (application of the old Brussels II Reg); President Court of First Instance Huy, 10 July 2007 (2008) 151 *Revue du droit des étrangers* 706.

[111] President Court of First Instance Huy, 10 July 2007 (2008) 151 *Revue du droit des étrangers* 706.

[112] Court of Appeal Brussels, 5 May 2009 (2011) *Revue trimestrielle de droit familial* 707 (rendered shortly after the CJEU judgment in C-523/07 *A*, EU:C:2009:225, but the court did not refer to it); Court of Appeal Brussels 4 April 2007 (2007) 126 *Journal des tribunaux* 623; (2008) *Revue trimestrielle de droit familial* 508, with case note by C Henricot.

[113] Court of Appeal Liège 29 June 2010 (2011) *Actualités du droit de la famille* 94; Court of Appeal Ghent, 6 November 2008 (2010) 9 (1) *Tijdschrift@ipr.be* 83; Court of Appeal Brussels (Youth Chamber), 15 May 2012, (3013) *Revue trimestrielle de droit familial* 608; Court of Appeal Antwerp, 15 April 2014 (2014) 13 (3) *Tijdschrift@ipr.be* 165.

[114] Court of Appeal Brussels, 21 June 2012 (2013) *Revue trimestrielle de droit familial* 263, with case note by C Henricot.

[115] President Court of First Instance Huy, 10 July 2007 (2008) 151 *Revue du droit des étrangers* 706.

Belgian courts have used the possibility to transfer jurisdiction[116] in a few cases, also at appeal level. In some cases the Belgian court transferred out[117] and in other cases requested a transfer to Belgium.[118] In all cases where transfer was accepted, this was because the child's habitual residence had changed in the course of the proceedings. In one case the Brussels Court of Appeal refused to transfer the case because it considered that a further delay would not be in the best interests of the child.[119] In another case this court found that a request for transfer of jurisdiction cannot be used to legitimise child abduction.[120]

In an interview a judge mentioned practical problems with the application of the provision on transfer:

> Article 15 Brussels IIa is also a very particular provision and the Regulation doesn't offer much guidance on how to deal with this [in practice]. Again, it suffices to be a little creative. Most civil-law judges are used to being told exactly what to do in the statutes, and if that's not the case, they prefer not to do anything.[121]

iv. Child Abduction

Belgian courts have ruled that the acquiescence in child abduction, which can change the jurisdiction to the place of the child's new habitual residence, cannot just be alleged but must be proved.[122] This can be done by emails between the parties or by documents that a parent signed with respect to schooling.[123] If the father agrees to the removal under certain conditions, such as that he would be allowed to see his children, and these conditions are never met by the mother, his acquiescence is not established.[124]

The second chance procedure has not been used often in Belgium. In order to have access to the second chance procedure, the ground on which a foreign decision is based must be examined. This can be tricky. Some non-return orders are simultaneously based on various grounds.[125] A court can opt for a cascade method to motivate their decisions by enumerating every possible ground for refusal, or their decisions can be short and scantly motivated. Then it becomes difficult to interpret the decision.

---

[116] Art 15 Brussels IIa.

[117] Court of Appeal Antwerp, 15 June 2011, unpublished (2010/JR/297); Court of Appeal Antwerp, 23 December 2011, unpublished (2011/JR/171).

[118] Court of Appeal Brussels 21 June 2012 (2013) *Revue trimestrielle de droit familial* 263, with case note by C Henricot.

[119] Court of Appeal Brussels 27 June 2011 (2012) *Revue trimestrielle de droit familial* 653.

[120] Court of Appeal Brussels, 25 October 2012 (2013) *Revue trimestrielle de droit familial* 617, with case note by C Henricot.

[121] EUPILLAR—Belgium—Interview Transcript B11.

[122] Court of Appeal Brussels, 28 November 2006 (2008) *Revue trimestrielle de droit familial* 203, with case note by M Fallon; President Court of First Instance Brussels, 17 November 2011 (2011) *Actualités du droit de la famille* 222.

[123] Court of Appeal Brussels 5 May 2009 (2011) *Revue trimestrielle de droit familial* 707.

[124] Court of Appeal Mons, 5 March 2007 (2008) *Revue trimestrielle de droit familial* 166, with case note by M Fallon.

[125] eg Arts 3, 12 and 13 Hague Child Abduction Convention. See eg Court of Appeal Brussels 17 June 2010 (2010) *Actualités du droit de la famille* 191; (2010) *Revue trimestrielle de droit familial* 1207, with case note by M Fallon.

Under the Belgian law of civil procedure, there is no right to appeal against a non-return order given if the child was abducted from another EU Member State.[126]

v. Recognition and Enforcement

It happens that the court issues a certificate without hearing the children. In two decisions handed down in 2007, the President of the Brussels Court of First Instance considered it unnecessary to hear the children because the decision was limited in scope, since the Court merely enacted an agreement reached by the parents on the custody schedule during the summer holidays.[127] In another case, the President of the Brussels court did not hear the children due to the urgency of the situation.[128] He expressed the view that the Regulation should have provided for an exception to hearing the child in urgent cases.[129]

The Ghent Court of Appeal did not hear the children because they did not have the necessary discernment, at the age of 10[130] and five.[131] The Court added that under Belgian law, there is no obligation to hear the children.

C. Judges' Challenges

Lack of sufficient resources poses a huge burden for judges. They realise the importance of training, but do not get compensated in their workload for following training. Underfunding of the judiciary is a great problem in Belgium. One judge recounted: 'Recently, I wanted to send an information bundle to the abducting grand-parents of a child in Croatia, but DHL refused to take the parcel because the Justice Department hadn't paid its bills of late.'[132]

Access to foreign legislation is also identified as a problem. However, judges often manage to surmount this. An example is a court using a judgment of the French Court of Cassation in its interpretation.[133]

Time constraints linked to workload and administrative burdens are problematic. It is very hard for judges to keep to the six-week time limit in abduction cases.

Delaying tactics used by the parties seem to be more the result of Belgian procedural rules than of the jurisdiction and applicable law rules in EU instruments. The application of foreign law can cause an increase in lengths and costs. Moreover the lack of knowledge of the applicable [PIL] instruments increases the length of cross-border procedures: 'If people don't know what to do, they sit around and wait and time is lost.'[134]

---

[126] Art 1322*sexies* Code of civil procedure; Court of Cassation 7 June 2013 (2013) *Rechtspraak Antwerpen Brussel Gent* 1269.

[127] President Court of First Instance Brussels, 6 February 2007, unpublished (05/16/C) and 30 May 2007 (2008) 115 *Jurisprudence de Liège, Mons et Bruxelles* 845, with case note by P Wautelet.

[128] President Court of First Instance Brussels, 19 December 2006, unpublished (06/475/C) and 13 February 2007, (2007) *Revue trimestrielle de droit familial* 792.

[129] Referring to Art 41.

[130] Court of Appeal Ghent, 10 December 2009 (2010) 9 (1) *Tijdschrift@ipr.be* 64.

[131] Court of Appeal Ghent, 6 November 2008, (2010) 9 (1)*Tijdschrift@ipr.be* 83.

[132] EUPILLAR—Belgium—Interview Transcript B6.

[133] Court of Appeal Brussels 17 November 2011 (2012) *Actualités du droit de la famille* 38.

[134] EUPILLAR—Belgium—Interview Transcript B6.

Cultural differences pose particular challenges to courts: they may lead the parties to be less trusting of judgments.

There is a homeward trend with respect to jurisdiction and applicable law. As one judge stated: 'As a judge, you are wired/conditioned to administer justice, not to decline jurisdiction! You don't want to leave the parties without a solution.'[135]

Belgian judges, however, take a practical approach. Where parties do not raise private international law issues, courts address them.[136] Judges use the available tools to concentrate or join cases on parental responsibility and maintenance.[137] They seek solutions in order to provide parties with a forum.

IV. Conclusion

The first set of conclusions relates to lawyers and their litigation strategies. Not many Belgian lawyers are specialised in international cases. When they are faced with an international case, many try to turn to Belgian courts and have Belgian law applied. Belgian courts are also popular due to the flexibility of the judges. Mediation is not very popular in commercial cases. In family cases, a recent restructuring of the court system should enhance the use of mediation. However, concentrating all elements of an international family dispute is difficult.

Under the second set of conclusions Belgian courts' interpretations of the EU instruments are considered. Belgian courts generally follow the case law of the CJEU, although it may take some time for this to trickle down. Judges seem more aware of Court of Cassation case law than of CJEU case law. There is a newsletter to alert judges of CJEU case law, but their workload might not always enable them to follow this closely (see below). Delays in case flows are not necessarily caused by EU legislation, but by a number of surrounding factors such as translations, lack of knowledge of foreign law and unclear interaction between national and EU law. Judges are flexible in their approaches and attempt to find solutions to build bridges between national and EU law. However, some legislative guidance (ie adaptation of national procedures to better fit the EU instruments) would be helpful. It should be noted here that a bill is pending to amend the Code on Private International Law in order to incorporate Rome I, II and III, as well as the Maintenance and Succession Regulations, so improvement is in sight. An additional complexity is the existence of international (worldwide) instruments alongside the national and EU instruments. This multi-layered framework causes confusion and mistakes.

The third set of conclusions focus on judges. They are willing to follow the training that is offered, but their workload often makes this impossible. Judges should be compensated in their workload for following training. Training should be given in a mixed context so that judges are confronted with other cultures. Also, they should be trained about cultural

---

[135] EUPILLAR—Belgium—Interview Transcript B11.
[136] eg Court of Appeal Ghent, 27 May 2010 (2010) 9 (3) *Tijdschrift@ipr.be* 62.
[137] Court of Appeal Brussels, 25 June 2013 (2013) 12 (3) *Tijdschrift@ipr.be* 59.

sensitivity. There is a need for resources to allow judges time to do research. Moreover, judges need more staff and courts need proper libraries. Additionally, the building of networks is essential. So too is the building of databases supplying information on foreign law and case law. Many such initiatives already exist. However, judges lack the time and resources to make proper use of them. The issue of resources is the most important problem for the Belgian judiciary.

7

Germany

JAN VON HEIN AND HANNAH DITTMERS

I. Introduction

Germany belongs to the civil law family.[1] Although, generally speaking, a binding force of precedent (stare decisis) does not exist,[2] decisions of superior courts have persuasive effect and are taken into account by lower courts, practitioners and scholars. Court proceedings with a claim having a value of more than 5,000 Euros will usually come before the Regional Court (Landgericht, 'LG') as first instance whereas proceedings concerning a lower value have to be initiated before the Local Court (Amtsgericht, 'AG'). There is an important exception for applications for refusing the recognition and enforcement of foreign judgments under Articles 45(4) and 47(1) of the Brussels I Recast and they are to be brought before the Regional Court regardless of the value of the claim (§1115(1) of the Code of Civil Procedure, 'ZPO').[3]

Private international law ('PIL') rules have mandatory application and a German court has to determine the content of foreign law *ex officio* (see below II.C.i.b). In 2013, 10,255 claimants from other Member States brought their disputes before the local courts in Germany (0.9 per cent) and in 2014, there were 33,027 first instance court judgments involving foreign parties.[4] German states have frequently established specialised chambers in courts for PIL disputes which leads to a more efficient adjudication in dealing with them.[5]

This Report is based on a quantitative and qualitative analysis conducted by the German branch of the EUPILLAR Project. The quantitative analysis rests on German cases uploaded to the EUPILLAR Database. The Database includes 314 cases on Brussels I, 69 cases on Rome I, 42 cases on Rome II, 95 cases on Brussels IIa, 15 cases on the Hague Maintenance Protocol, and 29 cases on the Maintenance Regulation from Germany.

---

[1] *cf* P de Cruz, *Comparative Law in a Changing World* 3rd edn (Abingdon, Taylor & Francis, 2007) 45 ff.

[2] See in more detail F Maultzsch, *Streitentscheidung und Normbildung durch den Zivilprozess* (Tubingen, Mohr Siebeck, 2010) 30–33.

[3] Code of Civil Procedure, 5 December 2005 (Federal Law Gazette I p 3202; 2006 I p 431; 2007 I p 1781), last amended by Art 1 of the Act dated 10 October 2013 (Federal Law Gazette I p 3786).

[4] B Hess, 'From common rules to best practices in European Civil Procedure', presentation given at a conference at the Erasmus-University, Rotterdam (Netherlands), 25 February 2016.

[5] G Rühl and J von Hein, 'Towards a European Code on PIL' (2015) 79 *Rabels Zeitschrift für ausländisches und internationales Privatrecht* (RabelsZ) 701, 747 ff.

The qualitative analysis is based on 20 interviews conducted with judges (from the Federal Court of Justice (BGH), various Courts of Appeal (Oberlandesgericht, 'OLG'), a LG and an AG), lawyers and notaries in different states of Germany. The interviews involved 29 participants.

II. Germany's Experience on Cross-border Civil and Commercial Disputes

A. Jurisdictional and Procedural Issues under the Brussels I Regulation

i. Matters Related to Scope of Application

While some German courts initially applied Brussels I to an action against the managing director of an insolvent company for wrongful trading,[6] the Court of Justice of the European Union (CJEU)—after requests for preliminary rulings by the BGH[7] and the LG Darmstadt[8]—has now settled the matter in favour of the application of the Insolvency Regulation to both jurisdiction and choice of law matters.[9]

There are several decisions on debt restructuring measures concerning bonds issued by Greece.[10] The BGH has recently decided that a unilaterally enacted haircut including private creditors constitutes an act '*iure imperii*'; thus, the German courts are not allowed to hear suits against Greece in such cases.[11] The BGH did not refer this matter to the CJEU because it concerned a public international law question in general and not a specific question of interpreting Brussels I.[12]

In general, the provisions related to the scope of Brussels I correspond to the needs of legal practitioners.

ii. Matters Related to Jurisdiction

There are a few problems regarding jurisdiction matters, but they regularly occur.

a. Article 5 of Brussels I

Regarding Article 5 of Brussels I, the main problems are the classification of claims, the determination of the place of performance and the localisation of the place where the harmful event occurred.

The courts struggle to characterise certain claims with regard to 'matters relating to a contract' and the 'provision of services'. These are payment claims between communities

---

[6] eg OLG Karlsruhe NJW-RR 2010, 714.
[7] BGH NJW 2016, 2660.
[8] LG Darmstadt NZI 2013, 712; Case C-295/13 *H v HK*, EU:C:2014:2410.
[9] Case C-295/13 ibid; Case C-594/14 *Kornhaas*, EU:C:2015:806.
[10] eg BGH NJW 2016, 1659; OLG Schleswig ZIP 2015, 1253; OLG Oldenburg ZIP 2016, 1243.
[11] BGH NJW 2016, 1659, paras 11 ff.
[12] ibid, para 13.

of apartment owners,[13] the granting of loans,[14] the gratuitous provision of services[15] and the activity of a commercial agent.[16] The characterisation of *culpa in contrahendo* under Article 5(1) or (3) of Brussels I is still problematic. The BGH has repeatedly tried to distinguish cases from the CJEU's *Tacconi* decision[17] when the parties did not break-off the negotiations and ultimately reached an agreement.[18]

The determination of the place of performance is difficult in mixed contracts containing both purchase and service elements.[19] Insofar, the courts refer to the contract's main performance.[20]

Regarding the localisation of the place where the harmful event occurred under Article 5(3), there are mainly two problems. The first problem concerns the violation of personality rights by publications on the web. According to the autonomous German rules on jurisdiction (§ 32 of the ZPO) and choice of law (Article 40(1) of the EGBGB),[21] the plaintiff's habitual residence in Germany as such is not sufficient so as to establish jurisdiction and apply German substantive law.[22] With regard to Brussels I, however, the BGH duly follows the CJEU's controversial *eDate* decision.[23]

The second problem concerns the localisation of the place of damage in purely economic loss.[24] In the *Kronhofer* case,[25] the CJEU decided that the term 'place where the harmful event occurred' under Article 5(3) of Brussels I does not refer to the place where the claimant is domiciled by reason only of the fact that he has suffered financial damage there.[26] The BGH, however, emphasised that this decision only refers to a case in which the harmful act was committed *after* the money in question had been transferred to another state.[27] However, if the scheme developed by the alleged tortfeasor was from the outset aimed at inflicting damage on the victim, the place where the bank account was held from which the investor transferred the money had to be characterised as the place of damage.[28] The BGH deliberately refrained from referring the case to the CJEU because it regarded its own interpretation as an *acte clair*.[29] This assumption seemed rather bold.[30] Nevertheless, at least as regards claims for prospectus liability, the CJEU largely settled the matter in the same way

---

[13] See eg LG Frankfurt NJW-RR 2014, 907.

[14] See eg BGH NJW 2012, 1817.

[15] OLG Saarbrücken NJOZ 2011, 1867; *cf* now Case C-9/12 *Corman Collins*, EU:C:2013:860.

[16] See eg OLG Koblenz NJW-RR 2009, 502; OLG Düsseldorf NJW-RR 2008, 223.

[17] Case C-334/00 *Tacconi* [2002] ECR I-7357.

[18] Eg BGH NJW 2011, 2809.

[19] See eg OLGR Köln 2007, 705.

[20] See also R Geimer in R Zöller (ed), *Zivilprozessrecht* 31st edn (Cologne, Otto Schmidt, 2016) Art 7 Brussels Ia para 20.

[21] Introductory Act to the Civil Code, 21 September 1994 (Federal Law Gazette I p 2494; 1997 I p 1061), last amended by Art 55 of the Act dated 8 July 2016 (Federal Law Gazette I p 1594).

[22] BGH NJW 2011, 2059, para 14.

[23] Joined Cases C-509/09 and C-161/10 *eDate* [2011] ECR I-10269; see the follow-up decision of BGH NJW 2012, 2197.

[24] For a comprehensive survey, see M Lehmann, 'Where Does Financial Loss Occur?' (2011) 7 *Journal of Private International Law* 527 with further references.

[25] Case C-168/02, *Kronhofer* [2004] ECR I-6009.

[26] ibid, para 21.

[27] BGH BeckRS 2010, 23912, para 29; BGH BeckRS 2010, 23911, para 31; BGH NJW-RR 2011, 551, para 31.

[28] BGH BeckRS 2010, 23912, para 30; BGH BeckRS 2010, 23911, para 32.

[29] BGH BeckRS 2010, 23912, para 33; BGH BeckRS 2010, 23911, para 35; BGH NJW-RR 2011, 551, para 36.

[30] Opinion of AG Jääskinen in Case C-228/11 *Melzer v MF Global UK*, EU:C:2012:766, paras 31 ff.

that the German courts dealt with the issue,[31] although the CJEU has recently taken a more restrictive approach.[32]

b. Article 23 of Brussels I

The scope of Article 23 Brussels I poses some problems. For example, the question of agency for the conclusion of jurisdiction clauses is not governed by the Regulation (eg the legal consequences and the curing of defective agency agreements).[33] Regarding the formal validity of choice-of-court clauses, there are questions on the exact placement of the clause in the contract document: the OLG Koblenz nullified a jurisdiction clause which was written below the signature field reasoning that the claimant could not reasonably take cognisance of the clause.[34] Jurisdiction clauses presented in standard terms and conditions are permitted but must be explicitly referred to in the main contract and in the same language as used for the main contract.[35]

c. Jurisdiction in Favour of Weaker Parties

The CJEU's *Odenbreit* decision regarding Articles 9 and 11(2) of Brussels I[36] has been frequently criticised for leading the dispute to be heard at a forum that does not coincide with the forum whose law is applicable as the *lex loci damni* under Article 4(1) of Rome II. This divergence creates a need for obtaining expensive expert opinions on foreign law[37] although traffic accident cases frequently give rise to claims of a rather low value.[38] The *Odenbreit* ruling also threw up a number of follow-up questions which have all been decided by the German courts without a further request for a preliminary ruling: (1) is the *Odenbreit* ruling only valid for natural persons or can it be applicable as regards legal entities?[39] (2) Do claims asserted by an assignee fall within the provision's scope?[40] (3) Is it a case of *lis alibi pendens* if the German plaintiff is sued abroad by the insured party?[41] (4) May the injured party be drawn into the proceedings by invoking Article 6(1) of Brussels I?[42] and (5) Is the *Odenbreit* ruling also to be observed within the context of the Lugano Convention, although the pertinent directive on motor insurance is not applicable in the non-EU Lugano contracting States such as Switzerland?[43]

---

[31] Case C-375/13 *Kolassa*, EU:C:2015:37, para 55.

[32] Case C-12/15 *Universal Music International v Michael Tétreault Schilling*, EU:C:2016:449.

[33] BGH NJW 2015, 2584.

[34] See eg OLG Koblenz BeckRS 2013, 16570; see also Geimer in Zöller, n 20 above, Art 25 Brussels Ia para 22.

[35] OLG Hamm IPRax 2006, 290.

[36] Case C-463/06 *Odenbreit* [2007] ECR I-11321.

[37] See s II.C.i.b below.

[38] See in particular E Jayme, 'Der Klägergerichtsstand für Direktklagen am Wohnsitz des Geschädigten (Art 11 Abs 2 i.V.m. Art 9 EuGVO): Ein Danaergeschenk des EuGH für die Opfer von Verkehrsunfällen' in H Kronke and K Thorn (eds), *Grenzen überwinden—Prinzipien bewahren: Festschrift für Bernd von Hoffmann zum 70. Geburtstag* (Bielefeld, Gieseking, 2011) 656, 658.

[39] See eg OLG Frankfurt a.M. NJW-RR 2014, 1339 which found that the ruling is applicable as regards the legal entities.

[40] See eg KG VersR 2014, 1020; OLG Dresden VersR 2015, 382; OLG Koblenz IPRax 2014, 537 (answering in the negative).

[41] See BGHZ 196, 180, answering in the negative.

[42] BGH NJW 2015, 2429, answering in the negative.

[43] *cf* BGHZ 195, 166; Federal Court of Switzerland, 4A_531/2011, 2 May 2012 = BGE 138 III 386, 392; both answering in the affirmative.

The main issue regarding Article 15 is directing professional activities by using websites.[44] The CJEU has defined the term in its judgments of *Pammer/Alpenhof*,[45] *Mühlleitner*[46] and *Emrek*.[47] The latter two decisions originated from German preliminary ruling requests.[48] Before the *Emrek* decision, the German courts had consistently looked for a causal link between the directed activity and the subsequent conclusion of a contract.[49]

Further interpretation problems occur regarding Articles 18 and 19 Brussels I, in particular the so-called *base rule* which is found in the first sentence of Article 8(2) of Rome I and Article 21(1)(b)(i) of the Brussels I (Recast) ('from where') and inspired by the CJEU's earlier case law on the Brussels Convention.[50] The implications of the base rule for mobile employees have become clearer in light of the CJEU's case law on the Rome Convention.[51] For instance, it seems possible to construe the rule in a broader way encompassing a 'hub' used by major airlines, eg Frankfurt, as far as the German Lufthansa is considered.[52]

d. Article 22 of Brussels I

The BGH applied the guidelines established by the CJEU in *Centros*[53] while interpreting the second sentence of Article 22(2) of Brussels I and held that the company's seat has to be determined according to the theory of incorporation.[54]

e. Other Problem Areas

The abuse of the rules in Brussels I has been discussed in the context of the well-known 'Italian torpedo cases',[55] but after the introduction of Article 31(2) of Brussels I (Recast), this problem is now deemed to be solved.[56]

iii. Matters Related to Recognition and Enforcement

The recognition and enforcement of decisions, in particular the now abolished declaration of their enforceability, work fairly well in German legal practice. The declaration of enforceability under Brussels I was rather rarely appealed against by parties.[57]

---

[44] See eg LG Saarbrücken BeckRS 2014, 07804; BGH NJW 2009, 298.

[45] Joined Cases C-585/08 and C-144/09 *Pammer/Alpenhof* [2010] ECR I-12527.

[46] Case C-190/11 *Mühlleitner v Yusufi*, EU:C:2012:542.

[47] Case C-218/12 *Emrek v Sabranovic*, EU:C:2013:666.

[48] LG Saarbrücken BeckRS 2014, 04378; BGH NJW-RR 2012, 436.

[49] See the BGH's order for a preliminary reference, BGH NJW-RR 2012, 436.

[50] Case C-125/92 *Mulox v Hendrick Geels* [1993] ECR I-4075 and Case C-383/95 *Rutten v Cross Medical* [1997] ECR I-57.

[51] Case C-384/10 *Voogsgeerd v Navimer* [2011] ECR I-13275; Case C-29/10 *Koelzsch v État du Grand-Duché de Luxembourg* [2011] ECR I-1595.

[52] BAG NZA 2013, 925.

[53] Case C-212/97 *Centros* [1999] ECR I-1459.

[54] BGHZ 190, 242.

[55] See J Kropholler and J von Hein, *Europäisches Zivilprozessrecht* 9th edn (Frankfurt am Main, Verlag Recht und Wirtschaft, 2011) Art 27 Brussels I, fn 10 ff with further references.

[56] See FG Alférez in A Dickinson and E Lein (eds), *The Brussels I Regulation Recast* (Oxford, Oxford University Press, 2015) Art 31 para 11.49.

[57] B Hess, T Pfeiffer and P Schlosser, Heidelberg Report (Study JLS/C4/2005/03), para 506.

The courts have discussed particular forms of decisions from other Member States, eg a Belgian decision on solely procedural aspects (recognised as being a judgment),[58] a Scheme of Arrangement (recognition refused),[59] and a *decreto ingiuntivo* (partly recognised),[60] as to whether they constitute a 'judgment' within the meaning of Brussels I. Regarding arbitral awards, the BGH changed the approach it had followed in its case law on 'merger awards' prior to 2009[61] and has been holding that such decisions cannot be declared enforceable as they are excluded from the scope of the Brussels I Recast by Article 1(2)(d).

The parties mostly rely on Article 34 (1) and (2) of Brussels I as reasons for the refusal of recognition or enforcement of judgments. However, the appeals are seldom successful.[62] In particular, the German courts had to deal with a Polish provision which stated that if no representative authorised to accept service is appointed, judicial documents addressed to that party shall be placed in the case file and shall be deemed to have been effectively served.[63] After the CJEU[64] had held that a court is bound to apply the EU Service Regulation[65] rather than having recourse to fictitious modes of service, the BGH reconsidered its previous case law and now takes the view that notional service of documents violates the fundamental right to a fair hearing.[66]

Another assertion that used to be raised in exequatur proceedings consisted in claiming that the first court's decision had actually already been complied with, because for example the claimed sum had already been paid to the claimant. The German courts had traditionally accepted such a defence at least if compliance could be readily proven by the debtor.[67] However, Article 45(1) of Brussels I was interpreted by the CJEU in a literal way, due to the use of 'only' therein, blocking any recourse to domestic law during exequatur proceedings.[68] After *Prism*, the German courts changed their course as well.[69] Although Recital 30 to Brussels I (Recast) states that enforcement may be challenged 'in the same procedure' by the debtor in the state of enforcement if he has already paid the sum demanded from him, it remains highly controversial whether the application for refusal of enforcement and a domestic action may be joined.[70]

---

[58] LG Düsseldorf BeckRS 2009, 26584.

[59] OLG Celle ZIP 2009, 1968.

[60] OLG Celle NJW-RR 2007, 718; OLG Zweibrücken BeckRS 2005, 11545.

[61] BGH NJW 2009, 2826.

[62] *cf* the Heidelberg Report, n 57 above, paras 546 (concerning public policy), 548 and 559; G Hohloch, 'Zur Bedeutung des Ordre public-Arguments im Vollstreckbarkeitsverfahren' in D Baetge, J von Hein and M von Hinden, *Die richtige Ordnung, Festschrift für Jan Kropholler zum 70. Geburtstag* (Tubingen, Siebeck, 2008) 809, 817.

[63] BGH NJW 2016, 160 paras 11–21.

[64] Case C-325/11 *Alder v Orlowska*, EU:C:2012:824.

[65] Reg (EC) No 1393/2007 of the European Parliament and of the Council of 13 November 2007 on the service in the Member States of judicial and extrajudicial documents in civil or commercial matters (service of documents), and repealing Council Reg (EC) No 1348/2000.

[66] BGH NJW 2016, 160 paras 11–21.

[67] BGHZ 171, 310, 320 paras 24 ff see for further references Kropholler and von Hein, n 55 above, Art 45 para 6 in fn 8.

[68] Case C-139/10 *Prism Investments v Van der Meer* [2011] ECR I-9511.

[69] OLG Stuttgart BeckRS 2013, 21135; OLG Düsseldorf BeckRS 2015, 16982.

[70] *cf* B Ulrici, 'Anerkennung und Vollstreckung nach Brüssel Ia' (2016) 71 *JuristenZeitung* 127, 135 ff.

iv. Matters Related to Relations with Other Instruments

The BGH held that if a decision had already been certified as a European Enforcement Order, the declaration of enforceability cannot be obtained under Brussels I.[71]

v. Conclusion

a. Problem Areas

There are difficulties that frequently occur in relation to Article 5 of Brussels I. Regarding consumer contracts, most problems concern the question whether a professional's activity was directed towards the state where the consumer is habitually resident. Due to the coherent interpretation of legal terms, the application of Brussels I on employment disputes benefit from the legal certainty already provided by the CJEU's case law on the Rome Convention.

b. Best Practice and Possible Solutions

The problems that arise in applying Articles 5(1) and 15 of Brussels I are primarily rooted in the current structure of the provisions: first, the questionable bifurcation between a *lex causae* (letter a) and an autonomous (letter b) approach to determining the place of performance, and second, the very vague notion of 'directed activity' for consumer contracts. Although German courts in most cases apply the CJEU's case law correctly and request preliminary references rather frequently, those problems could most effectively be solved by a further reform at the EU level that would extend the autonomous approach to determining the place of performance to all contracts and that would give more precise content to the concept of 'direction' in consumer cases.[72]

B. Applicable Law Issues under the Rome I and Rome II Regulations

i. Rome I

According to the legal practitioners interviewed,[73] the Rome I Regulation, particularly its Article 3, is applied without major difficulties.[74] Rome I seems to be applied more often in business-to-business ('B2B') cases compared to business-to-consumer ('B2C') cases. Within the period of time which is addressed by the EUPILLAR Project, there are 36 published decisions of the German courts solely including professionals,[75] whereas consumers were involved in 24 decisions[76] and three decisions concerned consumer associations.[77]

---

[71] BGH NJW-RR 2010, 571.
[72] For more practical measures of reform, see the recommendations in section IV below.
[73] EUPILLAR Germany—Civil and Commercial Law—Lawyers No 6–9.
[74] On the application of this rule, see eg OLG Saarbrücken BeckRS 2015, 12044.
[75] See eg OLG Köln GRUR-RR 2016, 156; BGH NJW 2015, 2584.
[76] See eg BGHZ 203, 68; LG Moenchengladbach BeckRS 2015, 17169.
[77] eg BGH NJW 2010, 1958.

a. Matters Related to the Uniform Rules

The requirements for a tacit choice of law under Article 3 have been frequently dealt with by the courts.[78] At the German EUPILLAR conference, the impression was voiced that the lower German courts tend to assume that there is a tacit choice of law rather than to apply the escape clause in Article 4(3) or the default rule in Article 4(4) of Rome I in order to circumvent the regular connecting factors.[79] However, the case law of the BGH is very clear in this regard and it does not support an overly generous assessment of a tacit choice of law.[80]

The German courts have applied mandatory rules favouring the consumer (such as the ones for the need for transparency and for the prohibition against surprising clauses) pursuant to Articles 3(5) and 10(1) in conjunction with Article 6(2) of Rome I while dealing with choice of law clauses contained in standard terms and conditions underlying B2C-contracts.[81] This approach has recently been confirmed by the CJEU in *VKI/Amazon*.[82] In employment disputes, the German courts have held that even an invalid forum selection clause under Article 21 of Brussels I could be one of the factors to be taken into account in determining whether a tacit choice of law has been clearly demonstrated.[83] The German Federal Labour Court ('BAG') noted that, unless explicitly otherwise agreed upon, a discrepancy between the choice of law and the choice of court cannot be assumed as to be the parties' will. This interpretation is open to doubt and the question should at least to be referred to the CJEU.[84]

There was a recent preliminary reference concerning Article 9(3) of Rome I[85] that had been requested by the BAG.[86] The Court asked if the rule generally prohibits the application of mandatory rules of third states (ie those states whose law is neither applicable to the contract nor in force at the place of performance) or if such rules may be taken into consideration in the state whose law applies to the contract.

According to the BGH, set-off is to be examined under the UN sales law pursuant to Article 7(2) of the United Nations Convention on Contracts for the International Sale of Goods ('CISG') if the mutual claims are based on the same contract governed by the Convention and not under the applicable law designated by Article 17 of Rome I.[87] As the relationship between the two regimes in matters of set-off is not entirely clear, one could consider to request a preliminary ruling on the issue.[88]

---

[78] See eg OLG Köln TranspR 2015, 288.

[79] D Solomon, 'Die Rom I-Verordnung in der deutschen ordentlichen Gerichtsbarkeit' (2016) 115 *ZVglRWiss* 586, 596 ff.

[80] *cf* BGH NJW-RR 2005, 206 (deciding on the absence of a tacit choice of Swiss law and applying the escape clause in order to determine the law governing a contract concerning the assignment of claims secured by mortgages relating to immoveable property in Switzerland).

[81] BGH IPRax 2013, 557.

[82] Case C-191/15 *VKI/Amazon*, EU:C:2016:612.

[83] BAG IPRax 2015, 342 para 36.

[84] J von Hein in T Rauscher (ed), *Europäisches Zivilprozess- und Kollisionsrecht* 4th edn (Cologne, Otto Schmidt, 2016) Art 8 Rome I para 24.

[85] Case C-135/15 *Nikiforidis*, EU:C:2016:774.

[86] BAG RiW 2015, 313.

[87] BGHZ 202, 258.

[88] See von Hein, n 84 above, Art 17 Rome I para 8.

b. Conclusion: Problems, Best Practice, Possible Solutions

Rome I is generally regarded as an appropriate instrument by legal practitioners in Germany.

ii. Rome II

Rome II has mainly been applied to cases concerning traffic accidents[89] and unfair competition.[90] A considerable number of cases concern the use of general terms and conditions towards consumers.[91] The high number of cases involving traffic accidents reflects the aftermath of the CJEU's *Odenbreit* decision.[92] Apart from general questions related to the determination and application of foreign law,[93] such cases throw up intricate problems of drawing the line between the aspects of substance and of procedure. One example is prima facie evidence deduced from a typical pattern of events where, for instance, a driver colliding with another car in front must prove his lack of negligence.[94] Another example is provided by rules on the estimation of damages which are difficult to calculate precisely (eg § 287 of the ZPO).[95] Considerations of expeditious proceedings strongly argue in favour of a procedural characterisation.[96]

C. Practice/Process

i. Germany's National Courts' Practice in Interpreting the Regulations/Procedural Issues

a. Matters of Interpretation and Procedural Issues Regarding Brussels I

In spite of the free movement of judgments ensured by Brussels I, the possibilities of enforcing a title in the chosen jurisdiction is still an important consideration when the decision between various fora is made. Yet, the option to choose between different jurisdictions may also have a negative impact on cross-border disputes because it provides ample possibilities of 'forum shopping'. Although the progressive unification of the EU choice-of-law rules has largely reduced differences in domestic PIL,[97] variations in procedural law remain which may influence parties' choices in this regard. Moreover, legal counsel may anticipate that the opposite side is going to initiate proceedings before a certain court and respond to this by filing an action more quickly before their preferred court in order to ensure this court's jurisdiction over any potential litigation.

---

[89] eg AG Geldern NJW 2011, 686; LG Düsseldorf BeckRS 2012, 17333.
[90] See W Wurmnest, 'Die Rom II-VO in der deutschen Rechtspraxis' (2016) 115 *ZVglRWiss* 624; see eg OLG Hamm MMR 2011, 523.
[91] See eg BGHZ 182, 24; BGH NJW 2010, 1958.
[92] See s II.A.ii.c above.
[93] See s II.C.i.b below.
[94] AG Geldern NJW 2011, 686; LG Saarbrücken NJW 2015, 2823.
[95] LG Saarbrücken NJW-RR 2012, 885.
[96] See R Schaub in H Pruetting, G Wegen and G Weinreich (eds), *BGB Kommentar* 11th edn (Munich, Luchterhand, 2016) Art 15 Rome II para 4.
[97] *cf* Recitals 6 to Rome I and II.

b. Interpretation Matters and Procedural Issues Regarding the General Perception of
   Cross-border Disputes under the Current Legislative Framework

German courts generally do try to interpret notions such as 'contract' or 'tort' in a manner
detached from domestic perceptions.[98] The Regulations' recitals and the legislative history
are factors rather reluctantly taken into account by judges; in this regard, the CJEU's indif-
ference to the Recitals of Rome I and II in *Emrek*[99] and *Kainz*[100] will probably not be very
helpful.

The courts regularly cite the CJEU's case law. Other national courts' judgments are considerably less frequently taken into account. Preliminary references are still mostly requested
by supreme courts, in particular the BGH, although the abolition of ex-Article 68 of the EC
Treaty[101] has significantly increased the number of preliminary references made by lower
courts. From January 2002 to May 2016, there were 25 preliminary references made by
German courts concerning the five Regulations being subject to the EUPILLAR Project, and
12 of them were lodged by supreme courts. Most of the preliminary references concerned
Brussels I or the Brussels Convention (21 cases). Rome I, Rome II and Brussels IIa were
each subject to one preliminary question, whereas the Maintenance Regulation induced
the courts to make two references. In 40 decisions, German courts denied the necessity of a
preliminary reference to the CJEU by stating an *acte clair*.

According to the settled case law of the BGH, judges must apply conflict-of-law rules
ex officio.[102] Therefore, it is not necessary for the parties to plead the application of foreign
law.[103] If the German PIL rules lead to the application of a foreign law, judges have to
determine the content of the foreign law *ex officio*.[104] In legal practice, the courts usually
demand an expert opinion on the content of the foreign law. Eligible expert witnesses
may be, for example, the research fellows of the Max Planck Institute for Comparative
and International Private Law (MPI) in Hamburg or the professors of comparative law at
the German universities. The London Convention on Information about Foreign Law of
7 June 1968[105] is of minor importance because the information obtained through this
channel is of a rather abstract nature.[106] In addition, information regarding foreign law
may also be obtained via the European Judicial Network in civil and commercial matters.
The Federal Office of Justice (*Bundesjustizamt*, 'BFJ') in Bonn, an administrative authority
subordinate to the Federal Ministry of Justice, has been designated as the central point of
contact in this regard.[107]

---

[98] See s II.A.ii.a above.
[99] n 47 above.
[100] Case C-45/13 *Kainz*, EU:C:2014:7.
[101] Consolidated Version of the Treaty Establishing the European Community, [2006] OJ C321E/37.
[102] See, eg BGH NJW 1993, 2305; BGHZ 177, 237.
[103] BGH NJW 1993, 2305.
[104] See BGH NJW 1980, 2022; BGHZ 118, 151.
[105] Federal Law Gazette 1974 II 938.
[106] For an in-depth analysis of the London Convention, see D Schellack, *Selbstermittlung oder ausländische
Auskunft unter dem europäischen Rechtsauskunftsübereinkommen* (Berlin, Duncker & Humblot, 1998).
[107] Further information in German is available at Bundesamt für Justiz, 'Bundeskontaktstelle im Europäischen Justiziellen Netz für Zivil- und Handelssachen' www.bundesjustizamt.de/DE/Themen/Gerichte_Behoerden/
EJNZH/Start/Ueberblick.html?nn=3449864.

According to the settled case law of the BGH, foreign law as such cannot be subject to judicial review by the highest German court in civil matters.[108] In contrast, the BAG grants such a review based on the German Labour Court Act (*Arbeitsgerichtsgesetz*, ArbGG).[109] If a lower court has failed in its procedural duty to apply German PIL rules (including EU PIL rules) *ex officio*, however, such a violation is fully amenable to review even before the BGH.[110]

ii. Cost and Length of Litigation in Cross-border Civil and Commercial Disputes

Disputes with foreign elements frequently pose difficult challenges to national courts, because judges usually do not possess an in-depth knowledge of foreign laws and the lower courts' libraries are often not sufficiently equipped with pertinent literature.[111] Further aspects consist in general problems of service and translations. Concerning the application of foreign substantive law, expert opinions are very costly and time-consuming. In order to alleviate such concerns, the German Council for PIL (Deutscher Rat für IPR), already decades ago, proposed a legislative reform designed to concentrate jurisdiction at the local level, ie venue, for international cases in specialised courts.[112] This recommendation has been adopted in family matters,[113] but so far not with regard to international commercial matters. It is envisaged *de lege ferenda* to introduce special chambers for international commercial matters, using English as the language of proceedings.[114]

iii. Settlement in Cross-border Civil and Commercial Disputes

The number of settlements in international cases is almost as high as in domestic cases. Several practical problems particularly occurring in international cases lead to an increase of the litigation's cost and duration. Parties often experience these difficulties as an incentive to reach amicable settlements. Particular difficulties may occur in the area of EU intellectual property rights. In the *Coty* case,[115] the plaintiff could neither invoke Article 5(3) nor Article 6(1) of Brussels I because the particular defendant domiciling in the state of the court seised had already agreed to an out-of-court settlement.[116] In such scenarios, lawyers must, in the interest of a consolidation of proceedings, advise their clients rather *not* to settle with the 'anchor' defendant.

iv. Alternative Dispute Resolution for Cross-border Civil and Commercial Disputes

Alternative dispute resolution ('ADR') is an area that is generally appreciated and frequently asked for by clients. Therefore, particular ADR instruments, such as mediation, are

---

[108] See BGHZ 198, 14.
[109] BAGE 27, 99 ff; BAG IPRax 2015, 342 para 59.
[110] On this duty, see s II.C.i.b above.
[111] See eg G Kegel and K Schurig, *Internationales Privatrecht* 9th edn (Munich, CH Beck, 2004) § 15 II; J Kropholler, *Internationales Privatrecht* 6th edn (Tubingen, Mohr Siebeck, 2006) § 59 II 1.
[112] Deutscher Rat für IPR, 'Zweite Denkschrift zur Verbesserung der deutschen Zivilrechtsprechung in internationalen Sachen v. 27.4.1982' 46 (1982) *Rabels Zeitschrift* 743–45.
[113] On maintenance, see s III.B.ii; on the protection of children and adults, see s III.A.vi.b below.
[114] BT-Drucks. 18/1287; BT-Drucks. 17/2163.
[115] Case C-360/12 *Coty v First Note Perfumes*, EU:C:2014:1318.
[116] *cf* Opinion of AG Jääskinen in Case C-360/12 ibid, EU:C:2013:764, para 63.

well-practised in Germany and that is why the German practitioners tend to be sceptical towards new kinds of alternative methods. Nevertheless, the EU's recent efforts to increase the use of methods of alternative and online dispute resolution by enacting the Consumer ADR Directive[117] and the ODR Regulation[118] are watched with great interest.[119] Germany has recently transposed the ADR Directive into domestic law.[120]

v. Remedies in Cross-border Civil and Commercial Disputes

Most cross-border disputes concern claims for financial relief. Depending on the field of law, declaratory as well as injunctive reliefs can occur, too. This is the case primarily in intellectual property law.

vi. Conclusion

While the practice of applying EU PIL in Germany can be regarded as functioning comparatively well in general, it still poses typical difficulties inherent in cross-border litigation, particularly as regards the cost and length of proceedings. ADR mechanisms are not considered as urgently necessary by practitioners but their use in international disputes is, generally speaking, welcomed by practitioners.

D. Preliminary Remarks on Effectiveness of the Current EU PIL Framework in Civil and Commercial Law

The provisions of EU PIL are considered as relatively predictable. The principal challenge of their application consists in the principle of autonomous interpretation. The effectiveness of pursuing cross-border claims is mainly influenced by practical difficulties inherent in any cross-border litigation. A better information and continuous legal education of judges and lawyers on the relevant instruments and their content is considered desirable; a field which is already marked by a high degree of activity both at the European and the German level.[121] The effectiveness of EU PIL is further influenced by the general question of how national judges should apply harmonised PIL rules, particularly if the applicability of foreign substantive law should be examined *ex officio*. It has been argued that an *ex officio* application of EU PIL is necessary in order to ensure an '*effet utile*' of the harmonisation of

---

[117] Dir of the European Parliament and of the Council on Alternative Dispute Resolution for consumer disputes and amending Reg (EC) No 2006/2004 and Dir 2009/22/EC, [2013] OJ L165/65.

[118] Reg of the European Parliament and of the Council on online dispute resolution for consumer disputes and amending Reg (EC) No 2006/2004 and Dir 2009/22/EC, [2013] OJ L165/1.

[119] For a comprehensive assessment, *cf* G Rühl, 'Alternative and Online Dispute Resolution for Cross-Border Consumer Contracts: a Critical Evaluation of the European Legislature's Recent Efforts to Boost Competitiveness and Growth in the Internal Market' (2015) 38 *Journal of Consumer Policy* 431–56, with further references.

[120] Federal Law Gazette 2016 I No 9, 25 February 2016.

[121] Apart from the established courses offered by the Deutsche Richterakademie (Academy of German Judges), the Academy of European Law and the European Judicial Training Network, the programme European Civil Procedure for Lawyers which is funded by the Commission should be mentioned, www.europeancivilprocedurefor-lawyers.eu, accessed on 22 September 2016.

conflict-of-law rules.[122] In 2011, an international working group of academics promulgated the so-called 'Madrid Principles' in which they also recommended the *ex officio* application of PIL.[123] A clarification of this point either by the CJEU or by the EU legislature would be desirable.[124]

III. Germany's Experience in Cross-border Family Law Disputes

Cross-border litigation in family matters is fraught with several factual problems and some intricate legal issues. Clear deficits were detected with regard to the service of actions and other documents, language issues and difficulties in communicating with other Member States' courts, particularly in the context of *lis alibi pendens* under Article 19 of Brussels IIa. As is the case with cross-border commercial law disputes, the most problematic issues occur regarding the determination and application of foreign substantive law. Cultural differences in general are a source of problems. The enactment of a Regulation concerning matrimonial property is highly welcomed.[125]

A. Jurisdictional and Procedural Issues under the Brussels IIa Regulation

i. *Matters Related to the Scope of Application*

The scope of application of Brussels IIa poses problems regarding its interaction with other instruments, especially with the Hague Convention on the Protection of Children,[126] which is superseded by the Regulation's provisions on jurisdiction but which provides the conflicts rules on parental responsibility that are lacking in Brussels IIa.[127]

Another problem is the absence of a provision governing preliminary questions.[128] The lack of an autonomous definition of who is considered as a child for the purposes of Brussels IIa gives rise to legal uncertainty which could be remedied easily by transplanting the threshold of 18 years already used in the Hague Conventions on the Protection

---

[122] See HJ Sonnenberger, 'Randbemerkungen zum Allgemeinen Teil eines europäisierten IPR' in Baetge, von Hein and von Hinden, n 62 above, 227, 245.

[123] No IV of the Madrid Principles, see C Esplugues Mota, 'Application of Foreign Law—Harmonisation of Private International Law in Europe and Application of Foreign Law: "The Madrid Principles" of 2010' (2011) 13 *Yearbook of Private International Law* 273, 297.

[124] See CA Monzonís, 'The Urgent Need for Harmonisation of the Application of Foreign Laws by National Authorities in Europe' 3 (2013) *International Journal of Procedural Law* 104 ff; C Esplugues, 'The Long Road Towards a Common Rule on the Application of Foreign Law by Judicial Authorities in Europe' (2010) 15 *Zeitschrift für Zivilprozess International* 201 ff.

[125] *cf* Reg (EU) 2016/1103 of 24 June 2016 implementing enhanced cooperation in the area of jurisdiction, applicable law and the recognition and enforcement of decisions in matters of matrimonial property regimes [2016] OJ L183/1.

[126] On the relation between these instruments see eg OLG Saarbrücken BeckRS 2016, 07949; OLG Karlsruhe NJW-RR 2015, 1415.

[127] See s III.A.v below.

[128] EUPILLAR Germany—Family Law—Judge No 7.

of Children and Adults.[129] Furthermore, it has been suggested that the Regulation should contain a provision on jurisdiction agreements for matrimonial matters, particularly given that Article 5 of the Rome III Regulation now allows for the exercise of party autonomy in selecting the law applicable to a divorce. In addition, a rule providing a *forum neces-sitatis*, as it is already the case in the Maintenance Regulation,[130] may be helpful in some cases. Finally, a clause governing jurisdiction based on a tacit submission of the defendant is deemed necessary.

ii. Matters Related to Jurisdiction

Difficulties of interpretation under Brussels IIa have arisen mainly regarding divorce matters[131] and cases of parental responsibility.[132] Concerns have been voiced that the possibility of parallel heads of jurisdiction might have a negative effect, namely the 'race to the courthouse'.[133] However, especially lawyers regarded the variety of possibilities to be very useful since it leaves them ample room for tactical considerations.[134]

a. Divorce, Legal Separation and Marriage Annulment

Divorce is very frequently addressed in the lawyers' practice in international family law. One case regarding Article 3 of Brussels IIa dealt with the establishment of a *forum neces-sitatis* because the institution of divorce was not known in the applicable Maltese law at the time when the petition for divorce was filed.[135] The analogous application of Article 3 of Brussels IIa was acknowledged concerning an isolated maintenance settlement in cases of a legally binding and completed divorce proceeding.[136] Finally, the rules in Articles 6 and 7 of Brussels IIa are very difficult to understand for practitioners.[137]

b. Parental Responsibility

1. Child Abduction and Return of the Child

The German courts have, led by the consistent case law of the Federal Constitutional Court, for two decades advocated a restrictive reading of the special public policy clause concerning the welfare of the child under Article 13(1)(b) of the Hague Child Abduction Convention.[138]

---

[129] *cf* T Rauscher in Rauscher, n 84 above, Art 1 Brussels IIa para 24; U Spellenberg in D Henrich (ed), *J von Staudingers Kommentar zum Bürgerlichen Gesetzbuch, IPR, Internationales Verfahrensrecht in Ehesachen 1* (Berlin, Sellier-de Gruyter, 2015) Art 1 Brussels IIa para 54.

[130] See s III.B.ii below.

[131] See eg OLG Zweibrücken NJW-RR 2015, 1157.

[132] See eg OLG Karlsruhe BeckRS 2015, 16544.

[133] See s II.C.i.a above.

[134] EUPILLAR Germany—Family Law—Lawyer No 1.

[135] BGH NJW-RR 2013, 641.

[136] OLG Karlsruhe FamRZ 2010, 147; critical towards this interpretation see V Gärtner, 'Internationale Zustän-digkeit deutscher Gerichte bei isoliertem Versorgungsausgleichsverfahren' (2010) 30 *IPRax* 520, 520–22 and P Gottwald, 'Anmerkung zum Beschluss des OLG Karlsruhe v. 17.8.2009 (Intern. Zuständigkeit für isoliertes Versorgungsausgleichsverfahren)' (2010) 57 *Zeitschrift für das gesamte Familienrecht* (FamRZ) 148.

[137] A Schulz, 'Das europäische IPR und IZVR in familienrechtlichen Angelegenheiten', presentation given at the EUPILLAR Workshop on 'Cross-Border Litigation in Europe', Albert-Ludwigs-Universität Freiburg, 20 March 2015.

[138] See eg OLG Hamburg BeckRS 2009, 12550.

2. Access

Regarding Article 9 of Brussels IIa, it was held that the initiation of an amendment procedure—concerning the modification of the right of access—in accordance with Article 16 of Brussels IIa is decisive for keeping the three-month period under this provision.[139] It has also been pointed out that the courts could tend to assume their jurisdiction more easily over another jurisdiction if, for example, that other jurisdiction is considered to attach less importance to the hearing of the child or if one jurisdiction regards the actual possibilities of enforcement in another country being less effective.[140]

3. Other Issues Related to Parental Responsibility

The hearing in proceedings on parental responsibility can cause delays and an increase of costs if it has to be done in person and the parties have to travel from other countries. It should be noted, however, that a court 'must … use all means available to it …, including, when appropriate, those provided for by Regulation No 1206/2001.'[141]

iii. Matters Related to Recognition and Enforcement

Although the principle of an autonomous interpretation is valid in this regard as well, practitioners voiced concerns that the terms 'recognition' and 'enforcement' may be interpreted in a very different manner by the courts of different Member States. The application for a declaration of enforceability of an enforceable decision within the meaning of Article 28 of Brussels IIa was denied in a case where a Polish court had ordered that a child should stay with his or her mother during the proceedings, whereas this led to the father having to give the child back to its mother in accordance with the Hague Convention on the Protection of Children.[142] The court did not consider this to be a decision concerning the return of the child pursuant to Article 40(1)(b) of Brussels IIa. Generally, aspects of public policy and the principle of a fair hearing are often claimed by parties as defences against recognition and enforcement, but these arguments frequently turn out as mere protective assertions.

The courts should be sensitised to issuing the certificate by using the standard form mentioned in Articles 39 and 41 of Brussels IIa in a timely manner. It has been pointed out that the courts still hesitate to use these provisions.

iv. Cooperation between Central Authorities in Matters of Parental Responsibility

In cases of child abduction, the BFJ acts as a procedural representative before the specialised family courts. The BFJ also provides that children are placed in foster care in cross-border procedures in accordance with Article 56 of Brussels IIa.

v. Relations with Other Instruments

The parallel existence of Regulations, state treaties and national law often complicates the application of law due to an unclear systematic relationship of the respective laws and

---

[139] OLG München FamRZ 2011, 1887.
[140] EUPILLAR Germany—Family Law—Lawyer No 3.
[141] Case C-491/10 *Aguirre Zaraga v Pelz* [2010] ECR I-14247, para 67.
[142] OLG München FamRZ 2015, 777.

therefore is sometimes found confusing. The interaction between Brussels IIa on the one hand and the Hague Maintenance Protocol and the Maintenance Regulation on the other hand is regarded as being in need of harmonisation. The need for a provision governing the distinction of Brussels IIa from the applicability of the Hague Convention on the International Protection of Adults has been identified by the practitioners interviewed. The relationship of Brussels IIa with international treaties, particularly the Hague Protection of Children Convention, is considered to be unclear as well on a number of points. On the whole, the current fragmentation of legal sources can lead to substantial legal uncertainties and delays in proceedings.

vi. Conclusion

a. Problem Areas

One problem is the plurality of legal sources. Besides, some provisions are highly difficult to apply and to understand, especially Articles 6, 7 and 16 Brussels IIa, which were discussed most frequently in the interviews with practitioners.

b. Best Practice and Possible Solutions

The European Commission has set up a group of experts on the revision of Brussels IIa.[143] In general, cross-border family law disputes can be addressed best by offering training not only for family law judges, but also for youth welfare offices and other persons regularly involved in such matters. Moreover, specialised chambers and experienced judges ensure the best possible extent of legal certainty. In order to clarify the existing legal sources in international family law, it was proposed to develop a form serving as a checklist which briefly names relevant instruments and their particular scope of application. A form could also be useful for the question of the time when a court is seised. It has been pointed out that the clarification of this issue would save costs in disputes. A hierarchical ranking of heads of jurisdiction could limit the possibilities of 'forum shopping'. A concentration of venue is currently in force for international adoption cases,[144] with respect to the protection of children[145] and of adults.[146]

---

[143] Policy Area: Justice and Home Affairs, Lead DG: JUST—DG Justice and Consumers; The group shall assist the Commission with the revision of Council Reg (EC) 2201/2003 concerning the jurisdiction and the recognition and enforcement of judgments in matrimonial matters and the matters of parental responsibility, repealing Reg (EC) No 1347/2000; members of this group are among others Prof Paul Beaumont, Prof Dr Anatol Dutta, Prof Dr Agnieszka Frackowiak-Adamska, and Prof Dr Thalia Kruger.

[144] See § 187(4) FamFG in conjunction with § 5(1) 1st sentence and § 5(2) of the German Act on the Effects of Adoption (*Adoptionswirkungsgesetz*, ADWirkG).

[145] See § 12 of the German International Family Law Procedure Act (*Internationales Familienrechtsverfahrensgesetz*, IntFamRVG).

[146] See § 6(1) No 1 of the German Protection of Adults Convention Implementation Act (*Erwachsenenschutzübereinkommens-Ausführungsgesetz*, ErwSÜAG).

B. Jurisdiction and Procedural Issues and Applicable Law Under the Maintenance Regulation

i. *Matters Related to the Scope of Application*

There are already a sizeable number of decisions on the Maintenance Regulation and the Hague Protocol,[147] in particular on intertemporal aspects.[148] However, so far, only a few of them have posed substantial difficulties that would have warranted a reference to the CJEU. An exception is the concentration of local jurisdiction in maintenance matters.[149]

A classic problem of characterisation lies in the proper demarcation between questions of matrimonial property and maintenance law.[150] The BGH had to deal with this matter in a decision of 2009 that concerned a so-called 'clean break' under English law by which one of the spouses was awarded a lump sum.[151] The BGH followed the CJEU's decision in *van den Boogard*.[152] In another case, the BGH followed the CJEU's *de Cavel* decision on the characterisation of *prestations compensatoires* under French law as maintenance claims.[153]

The courts have noted that, contrary to Brussels I, the Maintenance Regulation claims universal application regardless of the defendant's domicile.[154] In addition, the question as to whether the Hague Maintenance Protocol or the Hague Convention of 1973 on the Law Applicable to Maintenance Regulations is applicable in relation to Switzerland has given rise to discussion.[155] However, as German law was applicable according to both maintenance regimes, the BGH omitted to decide upon this issue.

Generally speaking, practitioners consider the application of the Maintenance Regulation and the Protocol as rather unproblematic. This could be because important concepts of international maintenance law have already been clarified by the CJEU's previous case law on Article 5(2) of Brussels I and also on its provisions on recognition and enforcement.[156] Moreover, Germany was a party to the Hague Convention on the Law Applicable to Maintenance Obligations of 1973, the precursor to the Hague Protocol of 2007. Thus, the provisions that have not been substantially amended, eg the tacit submission provision,[157] continue to be interpreted in the same manner. Nevertheless, there are important changes both in the Regulation and the Protocol which merit a reconsidering of questions that

---

[147] In the period of time the EUPILLAR project addresses, there were 40 published decisions of German courts where the Hague Protocol and/or the Maintenance Regulation were applied.

[148] eg BGH NJW 2013, 2662; OLG Nürnberg IPRax 2016, 278.

[149] See s. III.B.ii below.

[150] See in more detail M Torga, 'Drawing a Demarcating Line between Spousal Maintenance Obligations and Matrimonial Property in the Context of the New Instruments of European Union PIL' in P Beaumont et al (eds), *The Recovery of Maintenance in the EU and Worldwide* (Oxford, Hart Publishing, 2014) 425; L Walker, *Maintenance and Child Support in Private International Law* (Oxford, Hart Publishing, 2015) 40.

[151] BGH FamRZ 2010, 365; for a more detailed analysis in English, see Torga, ibid, 438 f.

[152] Case C-220/95 *Van den Boogard v Laumen* [1997] ECR I-1147.

[153] BGH NJW 2013, 2597.

[154] OLG Koblenz NJW-RR 2015, 201.

[155] BGH NJW 2013, 2662.

[156] Case C-220/95 *Van den Boogard v Laumen* [1997] ECR I-1147; Case C-143/78 *De Cavel* [1979] ECR 1055; Case C-145/86 *Hoffmann v Krieg* [1988] ECR 645.

[157] See s III.B.ii below.

seemed to be already settled, such as the availability of the jurisdiction at the creditor's habitual residence to public authorities.[158]

ii. Matters Related to Jurisdiction

It is doubtful whether a concentration of local jurisdiction is permissible in cases where an overriding EU Regulation, such as the Maintenance Regulation, governs not only international jurisdiction, but also venue.[159] The CJEU stressed that:

> [C]entralisation of jurisdiction … promotes the development of specific expertise, of such a kind as to improve the effectiveness of recovery of maintenance claims, while ensuring the proper administration of justice and serving the interests of the parties to the dispute.[160]

However, it declined to endow the Member States with unlimited discretion in this regard. It rather decided that:

> Article 3(b) of Regulation No 4/2009 must be interpreted as precluding national legislation … which establishes a centralisation of judicial jurisdiction in matters relating to cross-border maintenance obligations in favour of a first instance court which has jurisdiction for the seat of the appeal court, except where that rule helps to achieve the objective of a proper administration of justice and protects the interests of maintenance creditors while promoting the effective recovery of such claims, which is, however, a matter for the referring courts to verify.[161]

Concentration of international cases would constitute a major step forward that would allow national judges to gain specific knowledge in the application of EU PIL.[162] Yet, the question whether such a concentration is compatible with EU law should not be left to the discretion of Member States' courts.[163] Instead, the EU legislature should consider modifying the EU Regulations accordingly.[164]

The relationship between the Maintenance Regulation and Brussels IIa can be problematic, because ancillary jurisdiction for maintenance claims (such as post-marital maintenance among spouses, child maintenance, etc) is handled differently in various Member States. The problem whether ancillary jurisdiction for child maintenance claims after a divorce is vested in the court having jurisdiction in divorce matters pursuant to Article 3(c) of the Maintenance Regulation (in conjunction with Brussels IIa) or whether such matters should be dealt with by the court having jurisdiction to rule on the question of parental responsibility (Article 3(d) of the Maintenance Regulation) has now been settled by the CJEU in favour of the latter interpretation.[165]

A classic problem of international maintenance law is whether the jurisdiction of the courts in a Member State where the creditor is habitually resident is also available to public

---

[158] See ibid.
[159] See on § 28(1) 1st sentence AUG the request for a preliminary reference by the AG Karlsruhe FamRZ 2014, 1310.
[160] Cases C-400/13 and C-408/13 *Sanders and Huber*, EU:C:2014:2461, para 45.
[161] ibid, para 47.
[162] Rühl and von Hein, n 5 above, 748 and 750.
[163] ibid, 748.
[164] ibid.
[165] Case C-184/14 *A v B*, EU:C:2015:479.

authorities with regard to their claims for reimbursement.[166] While the CJEU denied jurisdiction under Article 5(2) of Brussels I in such scenarios by arguing that the jurisdiction favouring maintenance creditors should be interpreted restrictively,[167] the question remains controversial under Article 3 of the Maintenance Regulation which, at least formally, places the habitual residence of the debtor (subparagraph (a)) and that of the creditor (subparagraph (b)) on an equal footing.[168] Invoking the latter argument, the AG Stuttgart accepted that a public authority could rely on Article 3(b) of the Maintenance Regulation as well.[169] It has been pointed out, however, that in this case, the public body had reassigned the claims to the original creditor; thus, the underlying facts may be distinguished from *Blijdenstein*.[170] On the determination of habitual residence under Article 3 of the Maintenance Regulation, the CJEU's case law on Brussels IIa is followed.[171]

So far, there seems to be no case law involving jurisdiction clauses under Article 4 of the Maintenance Regulation. There are, however, some cases on tacit submission which follow the principle of autonomous interpretation established by the CJEU regarding Article 24 Brussels I.[172]

The Maintenance Regulation's rules on subsidiary jurisdiction in Article 6 and the *forum necessitatis* in Article 7 have been invoked occasionally. The BGH applied the *forum necessitatis* in a case in which a modification of a German title for maintenance could not be obtained from the US courts (the plaintiff's habitual residence) because American procedural law was governed by the principle of 'continuing exclusive jurisdiction' of the court of origin.[173]

Modification rather frequently gives rise to legal problems. Under Article 8(1) of the Maintenance Regulation, a limit is imposed on proceedings for modification of a title on maintenance claims in other Member States while the creditor remains habitually resident in the State in which the decision was given. From this provision, it is usually inferred a contrario that the court of origin remains competent to modify its original decision provided that the creditor keeps his habitual residence in this State.[174] Nevertheless, a clearer provision on the modification of foreign or national titles was considered desirable by practitioners.

iii. Matters Related to Applicable Law

The issue of incidental questions gives rise to legal uncertainty. Under autonomous German PIL rules, the principle of an independent connection of preliminary questions prevails, and this method (ie applying the choice-of-law rules of the *lex fori*) has also been followed by the BGH in a case concerning EU choice-of-law rules, in particular

---

[166] See D Martiny, 'Jurisdiction, Recognition and Enforcement in Cases of Reimbursement Claims by Public Bodies' in Beaumont et al, n 150 above 485, 490 f.
[167] Case C-433/01 *Blijdenstein* [2004] ECR I-981.
[168] Martiny, n 165 above, 491, with further references.
[169] AG Stuttgart NJW-RR 2014, 70.
[170] Gottwald, n 136 above, 149.
[171] OLG Koblenz NJW-RR 2015, 1482.
[172] ibid.
[173] BGH BeckRS 2015, 18936.
[174] BGH BGHZ 203, 372, para 14.

those contained in the Insolvency Regulation.[175] Regarding maintenance obligations, however, many courts and writers have preferred a dependent connection of incidental questions which means that the question of paternity as a preliminary question of a maintenance obligation should be answered by the law designated by the PIL rules of the legal order applicable to the maintenance claim. This approach has been adopted by the OLG Frankfurt with regard to the Hague Protocol as well.[176]

Another uncertainty exists regarding Article 3, in conjunction with Article 5, of the Hague Maintenance Protocol. The wording of Article 5 is rather broad which leads to problems in legal consulting because the lawyers cannot foresee in which way the courts will interpret the provision, especially the term 'if one of the parties objects' therein. Likewise, until when the objection must have been raised in the proceedings may give rise to doubts. The BGH has accepted that the objection may exceptionally be raised before the highest court for the first time if the lower court committed severe procedural errors in determining the applicable law.[177]

In addition to jurisdiction,[178] the issue of modification may give rise to difficulties also in terms of choice of law.[179]

iv. Matters Related to Recognition, Enforceability and Actual Enforcement of Decisions

Generally speaking, the recognition of decisions, the declaration of enforceability and the enforcement of cross-border maintenance claims functions well before the German courts and enforcement authorities. The CJEU's ruling in *Prism*, which excluded the defence of compliance with the title from *exequatur* proceedings,[180] had an impact on maintenance law as well.[181] Nevertheless, a modification of the foreign judgment in the state of origin may cause the original title to lose its formal enforceability, which impedes an execution in the requested Member State.[182]

Insofar as public policy is still available as a defence under Article 24(a) of the Maintenance Regulation, the courts follow the case law established on Article 34(1) of Brussels I.[183]

v. Cooperation between Central Authorities

The central authorities work closely together regarding the enforcement of maintenance claims in foreign countries. A rather unnecessary complication of proceedings results from the fact that the BFJ must be represented by an external lawyer if it appeals a judgment on

---

[175] BGH NJW-RR 2015, 302, para 12 (on Art 4(2)(m) of the Insolvency Reg).
[176] OLG Frankfurt NJW-RR 2012, 1477.
[177] BGH NJW 2013, 2662.
[178] See s III.B.ii above.
[179] BGH BGHZ 203, 372.
[180] See s II.A.iii above.
[181] BGH NJW 2016, 248.
[182] ibid.
[183] BGHZ 182, 188; see I Viarengo, 'The Enforcement of Maintenance Decisions in the EU: *Requiem* for Public Policy?' in Beaumont et al, n 150 above, 476.

maintenance claims.[184] In addition, the conversion of currencies may constitute an obstacle to a successful enforcement.

vi. Conclusion

a. Problem Areas

The relation between the Maintenance Regulation as well as the Hague Maintenance Protocol should to be clarified regarding Brussels IIa and also the PIL rules on matrimonial property. The applicability of the Maintenance Protocol towards third states is an issue which is not assessed uniformly in German legal practice and academic literature. Particular provisions pose specific problems, especially Article 9 of the Maintenance Regulation which concerns the time when a court is deemed to be seised. In general, the problems of application can often be dealt with in an appropriate way.

b. Best Practice and Possible Solutions

The proposed solutions regarding Brussels IIa Regulation in terms of clarification, trainings, specialisation and professional exchange are also valid regarding cross-border maintenance disputes.

C. Practice/Process

i. Germany's National Courts' Practice in Interpreting the Regulations

The provisions regarding EU international family law are considered to be interpreted without major difficulties. The more the practitioners engage with the interpretation of the regulations, the more effectively the instruments will be applied. The practitioners regularly consider the contributions of academic literature, notably in commentaries. The sources enlightening the process of legislation, for example in the *Bonomi* report regarding the Maintenance Regulation, are also being taken into consideration.

ii. Cost and Length of Litigation in Cross-border Family Law Disputes

The cost and length of litigation in international family law disputes increase due to the determination of foreign substantive law. The duration of the child abduction procedure becomes a critical point if a second procedure according to Article 11(6) to (8) Brussels IIa is initiated and in such cases a long period of time elapses between the abduction of the child and an enforceable decision.

iii. Settlement in Cross-border Family Law Disputes

In general, settlements are a favoured option especially due to the fact that some lawyers are not familiar with the litigation of cross-border family law disputes. However, settlement

---

[184] OLG München FamRZ 2015, 1520.

procedures sometimes seem to be protracted intentionally in order to establish a party's habitual residence. In international family law cases, reaching a settlement between the parties is perceived to be slightly more difficult. One reason could be that this area is more closely connected to cultural aspects.

iv. Alternative Dispute Resolution for Cross-border Family Law Disputes

In Germany, parties are encouraged to settle in several different stages of the dispute. Lawyers, public or private institutions, mediators and family judges try to ensure that an amicable settlement is reached. Therefore, further European solutions on this topic are not considered as urgently necessary. The Central Authorities support the solution of an amicable settlement through a mediation procedure.

v. Remedies in Cross-border Family Law Disputes

Regarding the remedies in cross-border family law disputes, there are generally no substantive differences to the situation in civil and commercial matters. However, practitioners also pointed out that less affluent parties engage in cross-border disputes more frequently (particularly on maintenance claims). A conjunction between the current legislative framework and the litigants' tactics exists regarding the decisiveness of the habitual residence: settlement negotiations as well as ADR procedures are liable to be (ab-)used in order to establish a preferred habitual residence. The abolition of *exequatur* for countries being bound by the Hague Protocol in Article 17 of the Maintenance Regulation is considered to contribute to the effective recovery of maintenance claims, although the elimination of public policy gives rise to concerns in this regard.

vi. Conclusion

On the whole, the application of the Brussels IIa and Maintenance Regulations and the Maintenance Protocol functions well. There are minor difficulties which primarily need further routine in cross-border family law disputes. The cost and length of the proceedings are substantially influenced by the issue of determination and application of foreign substantive law. Parties tend to settle to the same extent as they do in national cases; however, settlement procedures gain specific importance regarding the establishment of a habitual residence. ADR mechanisms are welcome but not primarily necessary.

D. Preliminary Remarks on Effectiveness of the Current EU PIL Framework in Cross-border Family Law

Cross-border litigation in family law disputes is generally supported effectively by the EU legislative framework. However, there are some problematic practical issues.[185] From a legal point of view, unclear systematics, delimitations between instruments and interpretations of particular provisions can constitute losses in effectivity.

---

[185] See ss III.A.vi.a, III.B.vi.a above.

IV. Conclusion

The 'Europe of law and justice' according to the Stockholm Programme is generally adequately supported by the EU PIL framework. The overview of cross-border litigation in Germany has demonstrated several problem areas in civil and commercial matters on the one hand and in family matters on the other. The growing number of instruments on EU PIL challenges German legal practitioners at different levels. Issues which complicate handling cross-border disputes can be classified into legal and rather practical problems. Both types of problems affect the parties typically involved in the dispute: national judges, litigants, legal counsels and authorities. For an autonomous interpretation, it is necessary to enhance the exchange on issues of interpretation between courts of different Member States. Specialised chambers in national courts could be another way to better promote legal certainty in applying EU PIL.[186] It has been shown that courts mostly address issues very effectively by referring to the CJEU's case law. A higher degree of specialisation within the CJEU may be helpful as well.[187] Cross-border disputes are more costly because of language problems, service of documents to other Member States and the need for expert opinions. These factual circumstances influence the whole process. The ascertainment and application of foreign substantive law should be facilitated by providing reliable and easily accessible sources of foreign laws. Apart from that, it seems advisable to expand the European Judicial Training Network and the Academy of European Law in order to properly educate and train judges.[188]

---

[186] *cf* Rühl and von Hein, n 5 above, 746 f.
[187] *cf* ibid.
[188] *cf* ibid, 750.

8

Italy

STEFANIA BARIATTI, ILARIA VIARENGO, FRANCESCA C VILLATA,
SARA BERNASCONI AND FILIPPO MARCHETTI[1]

I. Introduction

A. Brief Remarks on the Italian Legal System

In Italy, private international law issues are governed by international and EU PIL rules and, residually, by Law No 218 of 31 May 1995 'Reform of the Italian Private International Law system'. Two provisions of this Law are worth mentioning. On the one hand, Article 3(2) on jurisdiction of Italian courts refers to Sections 2, 3 and 4 of the 1968 Brussels Convention as subsequently amended, thus unilaterally extending the Convention's scope of application to cases where the defendant is not domiciled in a Member State.[2] Second, Article 14 prescribes the *ex officio* assessment of the applicable law, thereby requiring courts to make recourse to foreign law (where applicable).

As to the court system, civil (as opposed to criminal) proceedings are dealt with by 140 Tribunali (Tribunals, 'Trib') as courts of first instance and 26 Corti di Appello (Courts of Appeal, 'App') as courts of second instance. The Corte Suprema di Cassazione (Court of Cassation, 'Cass') is the court of last resort which ensures the correct interpretation of law by lower and appellate courts, and resolves disputes concerning jurisdiction and the internal distribution of competence. In particular, Article 41 of the Italian Code of Civil Procedure ('CPC')—according to which up until the point of the decision on the merits, each party may ask the seised court to request from the Plenary Session of the Supreme Court a preliminary ruling on internal jurisdiction to hear the case—applies also to the issue of international jurisdiction.

---

[1] This Report was drafted under the supervision of Prof Dr Stefania Bariatti. Ss I, II.C–D, s III, paras A.i.b, ii.b, iii.a.3, iii.b, iv, ss III.C–D, and IV should be attributed to Dr Sara Bernasconi; s II.A to Prof Dr Francesca C Villata; s II.B to Dr Filippo Marchetti; s III, paras A.i.a, ii.a, iii.a.1–2, v and s III.B to Prof Dr Ilaria Viarengo; para III.A.vi is to be jointly attributed to Prof Dr Ilaria Viarengo and Dr Sara Bernasconi.

[2] It is a debated issue in Italian legal literature and case law whether the reference made by Art 3(2) of Law No 218/1995 to the 1968 Brussels Convention 'and its subsequent amendments' is to be interpreted as including also Reg (EC) no 44/2001 or should be limited to amendments to the Convention itself. As to case law, see Cass, Sezioni Unite (plenary, hereinafter 'su'), 20 February 2013 No 4211, (2013) *Rivista di diritto internazionale privato e processuale* (hereinafter '*RDIPP*') 482. *cf* Cass, su, 21 October 2009 No 22239, (2010) *RDIPP* 481.

The Tribunali per i minorenni (Juvenile Courts) have competence to hear certain issues in civil cases concerning minors. Although no other specialised court exist, some courts of first instance sitting in major cities (eg Rome, Milan), due to their own internal organisation, are equipped with specialised divisions in charge of particular types of proceedings, such as those on family or employment matters, while competences over proceedings involving company matters, unfair commercial practices, competition law, intellectual and industrial property rights and cross-border public work, supply or service contracts involving companies (together with *class actions*) have been recently concentrated by statute in 22 Tribunali and Corti di Appello.[3] Furthermore, cases involving foreign companies (ie companies having their seat abroad) must be brought before one of 11 designated Tribunali.[4]

B. Research Methodology

This Report is based on the analysis of a) Italian case law applying or making reference to the EU PIL rules included in the research project, b) 15 interviews conducted with judges and practitioners dealing with cross-border disputes, and c) the outcomes of two national workshops held in Milan on 6 February 2015 and 26 May 2016, respectively, with the active participation of academics, judges, practitioners and civil servants involved in the daily application of EU PIL instruments. In relation to point a), more than 450 decisions applying or simply making reference to the EU PIL rules were collected. Public and private databases as well as specialised law journals were searched through. Unfortunately, this is not the whole picture: many decisions, especially those from lower courts, remain unknown, as Italy is not equipped with a general repository that would provide prompt access to case-law. With regard to point b), the interviews involved four lawyers and three judges specialised in family matters and five lawyers and three judges specialised in civil and commercial matters, who sit in different Italian cities.

II. Italy's Experience on Cross-border Civil and Commercial Disputes

A. Jurisdictional and Procedural Issues under the Brussels I Regulation

As to jurisdiction, recognition and enforcement of judgments in civil and commercial matters the Italian research team collected 283 Italian decisions concerning the 1968 Brussels Convention, and Regulations (EC) No 44/2001 ('Brussels I') and (EU) No 1215/2012 ('Brussels Ia').[5]

---

[3] See Art 2 of Law Decree No 1 of 24 January 2012 converted into Law No 27 of 24 March 2012, and Legislative Decree No 168 of 27 June 2003.

[4] Specialised sections are currently in place in Bari, Bolzano, Cagliari, Catania, Genova, Milano, Napoli, Roma, Torino, Trento, Venezia: see Art 10 of Law Decree No 145 of 23 December 2013, converted into Law No 9 of 21 February 2014.

[5] References throughout this Report are made to the Arts of the Brussels I Reg, unless otherwise specified.

i. Matters Related to the Scope of Application

As to the scope of application, Italian courts proved in general well attuned to the Regulation and to the Brussels system as a whole, in relation to both the international element triggering the application of the system itself and the notion of 'civil and commercial matters' together with the definition of the matters excluded from its scope. For instance, with regard to the international element, the Corte di Appello di Genova properly applied the broad notion developed by the Court of Justice in *Owusu* and *Hypoteční banka*[6] by holding the Brussels I Regulation applicable in a dispute between two Italian citizens arising from a road accident that had occurred in Romania, a non-EU Member State at the time.[7] Italian courts have, so far, complied with the Court of Justice of the European Union (CJEU) case law also in relation to the matters excluded from the scope of application of the Brussels I Regulation under Article 1(2), such as the 'status or legal capacity of natural persons, rights in property arising out of a matrimonial relationship, wills and succession'[8] and 'bankruptcy, proceedings relating to the winding-up of insolvent companies or other legal persons, judicial arrangements, compositions and analogous proceedings'[9] or 'social security'.[10]

However, there are some exceptions, mainly due to the difficulty for national judges to abandon domestic legal categories (belonging to both substantive law and private international law) in favour of the autonomous notions of EU PIL. For instance, the Corte di Cassazione held that the Brussels I Regulation did not apply in a dispute between two Italian companies in the presence of a choice-of-court agreement in favour of a Chinese court.[11] The same Court has drawn the line between the notion of 'civil and commercial matters' and 'disputes that result from the exercise of public powers by one of the parties to the case'[12] on the basis of the national provisions distributing jurisdiction between administrative tribunals and ordinary courts.[13]

ii. Matters Related to Jurisdiction

a. Elements to be Considered

As to the elements to be taken into consideration by a court when determining its jurisdiction, Italian courts have followed the guidelines given by the CJEU in its case law[14] and

---

[6] Case C-281/02 *Owusu* [2005] ECR I-1383; C-327/10 *Hypoteční banka* [2011] ECR I-11543.

[7] App Genova, 15 May 2015, (2016) *RDIPP* 564.

[8] Cass, su, ordinanza (order, hereinafter 'ord') 10 December 2013 No 27495, (2014) *RDIPP* 983; ord 12 July 2011 No 15323, (2012) *RDIPP* 441; and ord 23 July 2013 No 17863, (2014) *RDIPP* 633.

[9] See Cass, su, ord 14 April 2008 No 9745, (2008) *RDIPP* 1094, and ord 27 March 2009 No 7428, (2009) *RDIPP* 950; Trib Bari 27 January 2004, (2004) *RDIPP* 1386; Trib Milano, 25 March 2010, *JurisData*; all in line with Case 133/78 *Henri Gourdain* [1979] ECR 733; Case C-111/08 *SCT Industri AB i likvidation v Alpenblume AB* [2009] ECR I-5655; and Case C-157/13 *Nickel & Goeldner Spedition GmbH v «Kintra» UAB* EU:C:2014:2145.

[10] Cass, 7 May 2015 No 9210, in line with Case C-271/00, *Gemeente Steenbergen v Luc Baten* [2002] ECR I-10489.

[11] Cass, 14 February 2011 No 3568, (2011) *RDIPP* 766.

[12] Case 29-76 *LTU Lufttransportunternehmen GmbH & Co KG v Eurocontrol* [1976] ECR 1541 paras 3–4, also confirmed in Cases 814/79 *The Netherlands v Reinhold Rüffer* [1980] ECR 3807, para 8; C-167/00 *Verein für Konsumenteninformation v Karl Heinz Henkel* [2002] ECR I-8111 para 26; C-271/00, *Gemeente Steenbergen v Luc Baten* [2002] ECR I-10489 para 30; C-266/01, *Préservatrice foncière TIARD SA v Staat der Nederlanden* [2003] ECR I-4867, para 22; C-172/91, *Volker Sonntag v Hans Waidmann et al* [1991] ECR I-1993, para 20; and Case C-292/05 *Eirini Lechouritou et al* [2007] ECR I-01519.

[13] See Cass, su, ord 8 July 2015 No 14188, and Cass, su, ord 23 October 2014 No 22554, (2015) *RDIPP* 995.

[14] Case C-375/13 *Harald Kolassa* EU:C:2015:37, para 60; case C-365/88 *Hagen* [1990] ECR I-1845, para 19 s; and Case C-387/12, *Hi Hotel HCF SARL* EU:C:2014:215.

further specified the parameters for assessing jurisdiction. The Corte di Cassazione has stated that jurisdiction has to be assessed on the grounds of the plaintiff's pleas as set out in his claim, and namely with respect to the cause of action, ie the legally protected subjective situation in question as identified with regard to the facts alleged and the legal relationship which they represent.[15] Should any subordinate claim be brought before the seised court, jurisdiction has to be ascertained on the basis of the main claim,[16] even if jurisdiction is grounded on a choice-of-court agreement.[17]

b. General Jurisdiction (Article 2)

Only 14 judgments have considered general jurisdiction under Article 2, sometimes to affirm the jurisdiction of Italian courts, sometimes to underline the alternative character of a special head of jurisdiction applied to the case at issue. This may be due to two facts: on the one hand, the courts do not mention Article 2 when no objections are raised; on the other hand, it is possible that jurisdiction has been affirmed over defendants domiciled in Italy on the ground of Article 3(1) of Law No 218/1995, without considering the scope of application of the Brussels I Regulation.

c. Special Heads of Jurisdiction (Article 5)

Notwithstanding the debate among legal scholars as to the possible double function of special heads of jurisdiction under Article 5 as criteria for determining both jurisdiction and venue, Italian courts have so far followed the approach of the CJEU in *Color Drack*,[18] despite some contradictory signals given by the CJEU itself.[19]

An overview of the case law on Article 5 shows that Italian courts have faithfully followed the evolution of the CJEU case law, sometimes even anticipating it. For example, the Tribunale di Rovereto interpreted the 'place of delivery' relevant under Article 5(1)(b) first indent as the place where the goods are actually made available to the consignee,[20] in line with the later CJEU judgment in the *Car Trim* case.[21] Similarly, the Corte di Appello di Catanzaro stated that an action for liability against directors of a German company brought by Italian claimants was covered by Article 5(3), and that the harmful event took place in Italy, where the economic transaction had to be carried out and the statutory seat of the company which suffered the alleged damages was located,[22] in line with the later *ÖFAB* case.[23]

---

[15] Cass, su, ord 14 July 2014 No 16065, (2015) *RDIPP* 623; Cass 21 October 2009 No 22239, (2010) *RDIPP* 481; su, ord 21 March 2006 No 6217, (2007) *RDIPP* 177. As to possible abuses see Trib Trapani, 9 June 2010, *JurisData*. Previously, even though implicitly, see Cass, su, ord 27 February 2008 No 5091, (2008) *RDIPP* 1090, and ord 21 March 2006 No 6217 cit.

[16] Cass, su, ord 27 February 2012 No 2926, (2012) *RDIPP* 941.

[17] Cass, su, 20 February 2007 No 3841, (2008) *RDIPP* 160.

[18] Cass, su, ord 11 December 2012 No 22731, (2013) *RDIPP* 459, and also Trib Genova, 21 April 2009 No 1631, *JurisData*.

[19] See, recently, Joint cases C-400/13 and C-408/13 *Sanders v Verhaegen* and *Huber v Huber* para 30, EU:C:2014:2461; in the same vein see also Case C-125/92 *Mulox IBC Ltd v Hendrick Geels* para 25 EU:C:1993:306; Case C-440/97 *GIE Groupe Concorde et al* para 31 EU:C:1999:456.

[20] Trib Rovereto, 2 September 2004, (2005) *RDIPP* 162.

[21] Case C-381/08 *Car Trim GmbH* [2010] ECR I-1255.

[22] App Catanzaro, 22 March 2010, (2011) *Banca borsa e titoli di credito* 216.

[23] Case C-147/12, *ÖFAB, Östergötlands Fastigheter AB v Frank Koot and Evergreen Investments BV* EU:C:2013:490.

1. Contractual Matters

Following the path traced by the CJEU, Italian courts have dealt with characterisation issues in relation to the notion of 'contractual matters', including the distinction between the cases falling within Article 5(1)[24] and non-contractual matters covered by Article 5(3),[25] whilst also detaching the correct interpretation from traditional categories of domestic law, for instance in relation to actions concerning pre-contractual liability[26] read in light of *Fonderie Officine Meccaniche Tacconi*.[27]

Article 5(1)(b) first indent has been held applicable to: a contract for the supply of a plurality of goods to be manufactured;[28] a contract granting an exclusive sale licence;[29] a contract whereby an Italian company shall supply to a French company a vehicle for the cleaning of refuse containers as well as two other systems for the cleaning of refuse containers to be installed in frames manufactured by third parties and made available to the Italian company by the said French company.[30]

With regard to the place of delivery relating to any obligation deriving from the contract at issue,[31] Italian case law has always referred to a fact-based[32] autonomous notion[33] referring to the final place of delivery, ie where the goods are physically (as opposed to legally) delivered to the buyer.[34] For this purpose, any unequivocal reference made in the contract[35] must be considered by the seised court,[36] while any reference to the substantive

[24] Art 5(1) has been applied in a number of cases such as: Cass, su, 27 May 2015 No 10878; Trib Roma, 14 February 2011, (2011) *RDIPP* 1088; and Cass, ord 17 July 2008 No 19603, (2009) *RDIPP* 442. For a case where, on the contrary, its application was excluded see Trib Roma, 7 February 2014, (2014) *Le società* 973.

[25] Art 5(3) has been, for instance, applied by App Catanzaro, 22 March 2010, (2011) *Banca borsa titoli di credito* 216; Cass, su, ord 19 May 2009 No 11532, (2010) *RDIPP* 128; Cass., su, ord 10 June 2013 No 14508, (2014) *RDIPP* 413; Trib Milano, 8 May 2009, (2011) *RDIPP* 405; and Cass, su, 27 November 2015 No 24245, *Italgiureweb*.

[26] Cass, su, ord 11 September 2003 No 13390, (2004) *RDIPP* 1008; and Cass, su, ord 10 July 2003 No 10896, (2004) *RDIPP* 674.

[27] Case C-334/00, *Fonderie Officine Meccaniche Tacconi SpA v Heinrich Wagner Sinto Maschinenfabrik GmbH (HWS)*, [2002] ECR I-7357.

[28] Cass, su, ord 2 May 2012 No 6640, (2013) *RDIPP* 169.

[29] Trib Milano, 17 December 2010, *Pluris*.

[30] Trib Padova, 16 November 2010, (2011) *RDIPP* 469.

[31] Case C-386/05, *Color Drack GmbH*, [2007] ECR I-03699; Trib Modena, 9 April 2013, (2014) *RDIPP* 384; Trib Forlì, 22 January 2013, (2014) *RDIPP* 172; Trib Arezzo, 3 July 2006, *JurisData*; Trib Padova, 10 February 2006, (2006) *Giurisprudenza di merito* (hereinafter '*Giur Merito*') 1408.

[32] Cass, su, ord 14 November 2014 No 24279, in *Italgiureweb*; Trib Ivrea, 1 July 2014, in *Pluris*; Trib Reggio Emilia, seat of Modena, 30 April 2014, *Pluris*; Trib Novara, 6 June 2011, (2013) *RDIPP* 171; Trib Trapani, 9 June 2010 cit.

[33] Trib Rovereto, 24 August 2006, (2007) *RDIPP* 741; 2 September 2004 cit.

[34] *Car Trim* n 21 above; Case C-87/10 *Electrosteel Europe SA v Edil Centro SpA* [2011] ECR I-4987; Cass, su, 19 June 2014 No 13941, *De Jure*; Trib Forlì, 22 January 2013, (2014) *RDIPP* 72; Cass, su, ord 2 May 2012 No 6640 cit; Trib Como, seat of Erba, 22 February 2011, (2011) *RDIPP* 787; Trib Lecco, 15 April 2010, (2010) *RDIPP* 221; Cass, su, 5 October 2009 No 21191, (2010) *RDIPP* 150; 30 July 2007, No 16801, *Pluris*; Trib Rovereto, 24 August 2006 cit; Trib Como, 23 March 2006, in *JurisData*; Trib Modena, 15 June 2005 No 1192, *JurisData*; Trib Verona, 22 February 2005, (2007) *RDIPP* 367; Trib Brescia, 28 December 2004, (2005) 3–4 *Int'l Lis* 131; and Trib Rovereto, 2 September 2004 cit.

[35] Trib Piacenza, 14 May 2013, (2014) *RDIPP* 408; Trib Padova, 3 May 2012, (2014) *RDIPP* 362; and Trib Ferrara, 29 January 2004, (2005) *Giur merito* 1556.

[36] Cass, su, 27 November 2015 No 24244, *Pluris*; and ord 6 July 2005 No 14208, (2006) *RDIPP* 447. As to possible references to Incoterms see (in the light of *Electrosteel* n 34 above) Trib Padova, 3 May 2012 cit; Trib Novara, 6 June 2011 cit; Cass, su, ord 20 June 2007 No 14299 e No 14300, (2008) *RDIPP* 511; and ord 6 July 2005 No 14208 cit.

law applicable to the case,[37] be it the national law determined through the conflict-of-laws rules or an international rule,[38] must be rejected.[39]

On the other hand, Article 5(1)(b) second indent has been applied by Italian courts to a dispute for the payment of the price for the organisation of a show taking place in Italy;[40] a consultancy contract to be performed in Italy on the basis of the agreement between the parties;[41] a negative declaratory action lodged by an Italian principal company against a French agent company for the credit claimed by the latter as commissions, severance pay and contractual damages;[42] an action for breach of the obligation to pay the price under two working orders;[43] an action for the payment of the price due for the transport of goods;[44] and a claim for the payment of various sums due under an agency agreement.[45]

Article 5(1)(a) has been rarely applied, given its residual role.[46]

2. Non-contractual Matters

As far as non-contractual matters are concerned, Italian courts have stated that actions for restitution of sums paid but not due (*azione di ripetizione dell'indebito*)[47] and actions for unjust enrichment[48] did not fall within either Article 5(1) or (3), as *ex lege* obligations, to which only Article 2 of the Regulation applies. The recent *Profit Investment* judgment[49] (referred to the CJEU by the Corte di Cassazione)[50] will necessarily lead to a *revirement* of such case law.

As to the determination of the place where the harmful event occurred, Italian case law appears well attuned to the principle of ubiquity established by the CJEU case law in *Bier c Mines de Potasse d'Alsace*.[51]

---

[37] *Car Trim* n 21 above; *Electrosteel* ibid; and Cass, su, ord 21 January 2014 No 1134, (2015) *RDIPP* 143.

[38] Cass, su, 26 February 2016 No 3802, *Italgiureweb*; *contra*, stating the need or possibility to refer to Art 31 of the 1980 Vienna Convention, Cass, su, ord 20 June 2007 No 14300, (2008) *RDIPP* 511; ord 20 June 2007 No 14299 and No 14300 cit; ord 14 June 2007 No 13891, (2008) *RDIPP* 505; ord 14 May 2007 No 10941, (2008) *RDIPP* 221; ord 27 September 2006, No 20887, (2007) *RDIPP* 739; and Trib Padova, seat of Este, 10 January 2006, (2007) *RDIPP* 147.

[39] *Car Trim* n 21 above; *Electrosteel* n 34 above; and Cass, su, ord 21 January 2014 No 1134, (2015) *RDIPP* 143.

[40] Cass, su, 12 October 2015 No 20412, *Italgiureweb*.

[41] Cass, su, ord 18 September 2014 No 19675, (2015) *RDIPP* 653. See also Cass, su, ord 27 February 2012 No 2926 cit, which held Art 5(1) second indent applicable to a consultancy and arranging agreement, even though an exclusive choice-of court agreement prevailed in the case at issue.

[42] Trib Milano, 18 July 2013, (2014) *RDIPP* 629.

[43] Cass, su, ord 1 February 2010 No 2224 cit.

[44] Trib Cuneo, 27 February 2008, (2008) *Giur Merito* 2855.

[45] Cass, su, ord 19 December 2007 No 26746, (2008) *RDIPP* 795.

[46] Trib Padova, 2 May 2014, *Pluris*.

[47] *cf* Cass, su, ord 27 March 2009 No 7428, (2009) *RDIPP* 950; and Trib Bergamo, 21 January 2002, (2003) *RDIPP* 451.

[48] Cass, su, 29 May 2008 No 14201, *De Jure*, on unjust enrichment.

[49] Case C-366/13, *Profit Investment SIM SpA v Stefano Ossi et al* EU:C:2016:282.

[50] Cass, su, 25 June 2013 No 15874, *Italgiureweb*.

[51] Case 21/76, *Handelskwekerij G J Bier BV v Mines de potasse d'Alsace SA*, [1976] ECR 1735. For an application of the *locus acti* criterion see Cass, su, ord 14 July 2014 No 16065 cit; Trib Torino, 10 March 2009, (2010) *RDIPP* 496; Cass, su, 10 September 2013 No 20700, (2014) *RDIPP* 647; and Cass, su, ord 27 February 2012 No 2926 cit. The *locus damni* criterion has been applied, for instance, in the following cases: Cass, su, ord 18 September 2014 No 19675 cit; and Trib Roma, 7 February 2014 cit. Previously, in the same vein see Cass, su, ord 22 May 2012 No 8076, (2013) *RDIPP* 431; and 5 July 2011 No 14654, (2012) *RDIPP* 432.

3. Article 5(4)–(6)

Very few decisions concern the remaining special heads of jurisdiction under Article 5.[52] In particular, Article 5(5) has been used as a further argument to support the declaration of the lack of jurisdiction of Italian courts (in favour of the German courts) in the already mentioned case of the claim for damages suffered by an Italian claimant as a result of the unlawful use of its trademark by a German company, being it a dispute arising out of the operations of a branch, agency or other establishment.[53] The provision has also been mentioned in the proceedings brought by an Italian company against an Austrian bank for the enforcement of a first demand guarantee, in relation to which the seised court stated that the fact that the Austrian bank opened, after the proceedings had been commenced, a subsidiary in Italy, had no relevance for the purpose of determining jurisdiction in so far as there was no link between the object of the dispute at issue and such subsidiary.[54]

d. Article 6

No particular problems have emerged from Italian case law on the special heads of jurisdiction for closely connected claims with multiple defendants (Article 6(1))[55] or on counterclaims (Article 6(3)).[56]

With regard to jurisdiction for third party proceedings, after a period when Italian courts had adopted a very restrictive view on Article 6(2) as covering only the so called *garanzia propria* (typical guarantee),[57] they are now following a broader view according to which the distinction between typical or atypical guarantee is irrelevant to the application of Article 6(2).[58]

e. Protective Jurisdiction: Insurance Contracts, Consumer Contracts and Individual Contracts of Employment

So far few judgments have concerned the special rules on jurisdiction in matters relating to insurance and to consumer contracts.[59] With regard to the latter, and concerning two actions brought in Italy against credit institutions seeking the annulment of purchase orders of Argentinean bonds, the Corte di Cassazione qualified the bank account and deposit contracts concluded between the parties as consumer contracts under Section 4 and affirmed

---

[52] On Art 5(4) see Cass, su, ord 11 February 2003 No 2060, (2003) *RDIPP* 547. On Art 5(6) see Trib Napoli sez spec imprese, 2 July 2014, *Pluris*, and Cass, su, ord 20 June 2014 No 14041, (2015) *RDIPP* 409.

[53] Trib Reggio Emilia, seat of Modena, 30 April 2014 cit.

[54] Cass, su, ord 11 December 2012 No 22731 cit.

[55] Cass, su, ord 18 September 2014 No 19675 cit; Cass, su, ord 14 July 2014 No 16065 cit; and Cass, su, ord 2 December 2013 No 26937, (2014) *RDIPP* 978. For a similar case see also Cass, su, ord 27 February 2012 No 2926 cit.

[56] Cass, su, ord 13 December 2005 No 27403, (2006) *RDIPP* 1059 ss (applying the corresponding provision of the 1968 Brussels Convention).

[57] Cass, su, 15 March 2007 No 5978, (2008) *RDIPP* 173; Cass, 28 March 2006 No 7040, (2007) *RDIPP* 391; 28 Cass, 28 October 2005 No 20998, (2006) *RDIPP* 785; as well as Cass, 7 August 2001 No 10891, (2002) *RDIPP* 753, where connection, under Art 6(2) of the 1968 Brussels Convention, was excluded because the warranty action was based on a freight forwarding contract, whereas the main claim for damages was based on a contract of carriage.

[58] Cass, su, 28 May 2012 No 8404, (2014) *RDIPP* 369, with regard to the 1968 Brussels Convention; 12 March 2009, No 5965, (2009) *RDIPP* 941.

[59] Cass, 18 May 2015 No 10124, *Italgiureweb*; App Milano, 4 December 2007, (2008) *RDIPP* 1076, with reference to Art 12(1) of the 1968 Brussels Convention; and Cass, su, ord 2 April 2007 No 8095, (2008) *RDIPP* 826.

Italian jurisdiction declaring that the prorogation clauses in favour of foreign courts included therein were unenforceable under Articles 16 and 17 of the Brussels I Regulation.[60]

With regard to individual contracts of employment, mirroring *Mahamdia*,[61] Italian courts have affirmed jurisdiction over actions brought against the Italian Ministry of Foreign Affairs by Italian employees who had been hired by Italian embassies or consulates abroad, holding the prorogation clauses contained in the employment contract invalid under Article 21 of the Regulation. The invalidity was due to the fact that the agreement on jurisdiction had been entered into before the dispute arose and created an obligation upon the employee to lodge his claim before a court other than the one provided under the Regulation.[62]

Last, and interestingly, it can be noted that Italian courts, confronted with the determination of the place where the employee habitually carries out his work, relevant under Article 19(2)(a) as a further forum available to the worker,[63] have specified that, if the employee carries out his activities in more than one State, reference shall be made to the place where he organises and plans his working time.[64]

f. Exclusive Jurisdiction

As to exclusive grounds of jurisdiction, the Corte di Cassazione has recently given its decision on jurisdiction in the *Weber v Weber* case[65] in conformity with the principles established by the CJEU on 3 April 2014.[66]

g. Prorogation of Jurisdiction

The majority of cases concern the formal requirements set forth by Article 23. This is so mostly because the practice of commercial relations and the scope of such provisions are limited to formal aspects of the agreement.

As to the scope of a choice-of-court agreement in the case of connected contracts, Italian courts have held the connection irrelevant for the purposes of determining jurisdiction, ruling out the possible extension of the effects of the choice-of-court clause contained in one contract to the others.[67]

Italian courts have always been, conveniently, very cautious in interpreting the content of a choice-of-court agreement, paying particular attention to its wording and context.[68]

---

[60] Cass, su, 18 May 2015 No 10088, *JurisData*; and Cass, su, ord 20 February 2013 No 4211 cit.

[61] Case C-154/11, *Ahmed Mahamdia v République algérienne démocratique et populaire* EU:C:2012:491.

[62] Trib Roma, 9 July 2014, (2015) *RDIPP* 620; Cass, su, 13 April 2012 No 5872, (2013) *RDIPP* 745; and 28 December 2011 No 29093, *JurisData*; 2 December 2011 No 25761, (2013) *RDIPP* 123.

[63] Cass, su, ord 13 December 2007 No 26089, (2009) *RDIPP* 108; and Trib Milano, 4 August 2005, (2006) *RDIPP* 759.

[64] App Venezia, 26 April 2005, (2006) *RDIPP* 746.

[65] Cass, su, 27 November 2015 No 24246.

[66] Case C-438/12, *Weber v Weber* EU:C:2014:212.

[67] Cass, su, 14 June 2007 No 13894; Cass, su, ord 1 February 2010 No 2224 cit; and Cass, su, ord 27 February 2012 No 2926 cit. For a similar case see also Cass, su, ord 18 September 2014 No 19675 cit.

[68] Trib Roma, 14 February 2011 cit. Particular attention to the wording of the clause emerges also in Trib Cremona, 15 November 2014.

h. Coordination of Proceedings

1. *Lis Pendens*

Generally, judgments given by Italian courts concerning *lis pendens*[69] appear to be in line with the CJEU case law on Article 27, particularly with the principles expressed in *Tatry* and *Nipponkoa Insurance* as to negative declaratory actions.[70] However, from the perspective of the relationship between the CJEU and national case law, two cases must be mentioned.

First, the Tribunale di Padova held that if the Italian court ascertained that it had been seised prior to the foreign court (French, in the case at issue) pursuant to Article 30 of the Regulation, it was not required to stay the proceedings and could proceed to verify its jurisdiction, it being irrelevant that the foreign court had provisionally declined jurisdiction and declared that Italian courts were competent to hear the claim.[71]

Second, an old decision by the Corte di Cassazione dealt with relations between civil and criminal proceedings and ruled against *lis pendens* under the Brussels regime between a civil action brought in Italy in criminal proceedings against defendants resident in Italy and two actions (one being between the same parties and involving the same cause of action and the other being a related action) that had been previously brought before civil courts in another Member State.[72]

2. Related Actions

So far, Article 28 of the Brussels I Regulation has often been invoked together with Article 27 but rarely applied alone.[73]

iii. Matters Related to Recognition and Enforcement

First, it is to be noted that Italian courts have adopted a broad notion of 'judgments' under Chapter III, as covering any decision given by a court or tribunal of a Member State, whatever its name or nature, including a judgment affirming jurisdiction in a case of international *lis pendens*.[74]

Furthermore, drawing from *Gothaer* and *Hoffmann*,[75] the Corte di Cassazione held that Articles 32 and 33 of Brussels I governed the recognition of a foreign decision by making an implied reference to the provisions of the Member State of origin. Thus, the court of the requested State shall not define the scope of the *res judicata* effects according to its own law.[76]

Second, as to the procedure for recognition and enforcement, Italian courts have specified some aspects not provided for by the Brussels I Regulation itself. These include: the

---

[69] Cass, su, ord 8 June 2011 No 12411, (2012) *RDIPP* 420; Cass, su, ord 19 May 2009 No 11532 cit; and Cass, 8 November 2008 No 27389, (2009) *RDIPP* 457.

[70] Case C-406/92, *Tatry* [1994] ECR I-5439; Case C-452/12, *Nipponkoa Insurance* EU:C:2013:858.

[71] Trib Padova, 16 November 2010, (2011) *RDIPP* 469.

[72] Cass, su, 7 March 2005 No 4807, (2006) *RDIPP* 164.

[73] Trib Padova, 15 October 2014 cit. For another example see Cass, su, ord 8 April 2011 No 8034, (2011) *RDIPP* 1103.

[74] Cass, su, ord 8 February 2002 No 5127, (2002) *RDIPP* 708.

[75] Case 145/86, *Horst Ludwig Martin Hoffmann v Adelheid Krieg*, [1988] ECR 645.

[76] Cass, 16 May 2014 No 10853, (2015) *RDIPP* 440. The same broad notion was applied to the recognition of an order to pay costs for an indeterminate amount, which had been issued at the end of English proceedings: Cass, su, 1 July 2009 No 15386, (2010) *RDIPP* 447.

(protective) nature of the stay of proceedings which might be granted, under Article 37, by the court of the requested State, if an ordinary appeal against the judgment has been lodged;[77] how the requirement set forth by Article 42 of the Regulation should be fulfilled in case one of the parties against whom enforcement was sought was not timely served with the judgment;[78] the day on which the time-limit for the opposition against the *exequatur*, pursuant to Articles 43(5) and 42(2), begins to run in case the party against whom recognition is sought was not legally informed of the judgment;[79] and the time when the requirement of enforceability prescribed under Article 49 must be satisfied with regard to the *exequatur* in Italy of an *astreinte* given by a Belgian court pursuant to Article 1385-bis, paragraph 1 of the Belgian *Code judiciaire*.[80] Case law has also focused on certain aspects pertaining to the rules of civil procedure relevant to the application of the Brussels I Regulation, such as the kind of act needed to commence the appeal against the *exequatur* under Article 43,[81] or the distribution of jurisdiction for issuing provisional measures pursuant to Article 47.[82]

Third, as to the grounds of non-recognition, so far very few cases have dealt with Article 34. Moreover, at least two of the interviewees noted that, as far as their experience was concerned, such grounds had mostly been invoked speciously with the purpose of delaying the execution of foreign judgments.

Fourth, Italian courts have adopted a restrictive interpretation of the public policy clause under Article 34(1).[83] In the well-known *Gambazzi* case, the Corte di Appello di Milano ruled out any possible contrast with public policy and, consequently, declared enforceable in Italy the judgments issued by an English court against a defendant who had been excluded from the proceedings due to him acting in contempt of court, as no violation of fundamental rights had occurred.[84]

Finally, only a couple of judgments have dealt with the other grounds of non-recognition.[85]

iv. Conclusion

a. Problem Areas

Apart from some minor difficulties concerning characterisation in relation to the scope of application of the Brussels I Regulation, actual enforcement of judgments still represents one of the major areas of concern.

---

[77] Cass, 24 November 2015 No 23974, *Italgiureweb*.

[78] Cass, 15 April 2015 No 7613, *Pluris*.

[79] Cass, su, 13 March 2014 No 5924, (2015) *RDIPP* 146.

[80] Cass, 15 April 2015 No 7613 cit.

[81] Cass, 12 January 2010 No 253, (2010) *RDIPP* 488; and Cass, 3 July 2012 No 13555, *Pluris*.

[82] App Torino, 23 February 2009, (2010) *Giur merito* 3071. On the requirements to be complied with for issuing provisional measures under Art 47 of the Brussels I Reg see: App Cagliari, 8 July 2009, (2010) *Diritto marittimo* 117; App L'Aquila, ord 23 February 2012, (2012) *RDIPP* 744.

[83] App Milano, 11 February 2006, (2007) *RDIPP* 1062, applying the Brussels Convention in line with the CJEU decisions in Case C-619/10, *Trade Agency Ltd v Seramico Investments Ltd* EU:C:2012:531 and Case C-302/13, *fly-LAL-Lithuanian Airlines AS v Starptautiskā lidosta Rīga VAS, Air Baltic Corporation AS* EU:C:2014:2319; Cass, 24 November 2015 No 23974, *Pluris*; and Cass, 15 April 2015 No 7613 cit.

[84] App Milano, 24 November 2010, (2011) *RDIPP* 105.

[85] Cass 16 July 2014 No 16272, (2015) *RDIPP* 629; and App Milano, 26 April 2010, (2010) *RDIPP* 764.

b. Best Practice

Italian courts have proven to be well aware of the need for autonomous interpretation of EU PIL rules in a number of cases.

c. Possible Solutions

All interviewees agreed that more training on EU PIL instruments and the CJEU case law, both for judges and lawyers, would help raise awareness and knowledge.

B. Applicable Law Issues under the Rome I and Rome II Regulations

i. Rome I

The Italian case law concerning Regulation (EC) No 593/2008 ('Rome I') is currently poor in numbers. This may be due to a combination of the lengthy Italian civil proceedings and the unsystematic publication of lower-court decisions in databases. The research team collected three judgments in which the Regulation had been applied or mentioned. In two of those cases, the Corte di Cassazione simply made reference to the Regulation.

a. Matters Related to the Scope of Application

In a dispute concerning the effects of insolvency proceedings on commercial contracts, the Corte di Cassazione dismissed the appeal of a contracting party who claimed a wrongful application of Regulation (EC) No 1346/2000 on insolvency proceedings by lower courts, stating that the 'genetic and functional' aspects of contractual relationships were regulated by Rome I only outside of insolvency proceedings.[86]

b. Matters Related to the Uniform Rules

In a case concerning a donation from a Panamanian company to an Italian resident, the Tribunale di Bologna applied Panamanian law as the law of the country where the party required to effect the characteristic performance of the contract had his habitual residence pursuant to Article 4(2).[87]

c. Conclusion

1. Problem Areas

First, awareness and knowledge of EU conflict-of-laws rules should be increased.

Second, the definition of the material scope of application of Rome I, especially in relation to the excluded matters (such as insolvency) may prove problematic.

Last, the acquisition of the foreign applicable law is an area of relevant concern.

---

[86] Cass, 4 June 2012 No 8931.
[87] Trib Bologna, 9 November 2015.

2. Possible Solutions

All interviewees agreed that they would significantly benefit from more training on EU PIL rules.

As to finding the content of applicable law, they also suggested that websites with foreign laws and foreign case law could be of help. Even though judges are under the obligation to determine the applicable law *ex officio*, cooperation by the parties would be welcomed as well.

ii. Rome II

Italian case law concerning Regulation (EC) No 864/2007 ('Rome II') is currently poor in numbers. As in Rome I, this is probably due to a combination of the lengthy Italian civil proceedings and the unsystematic publication of lower-court decisions in databases. 14 judgments were collected.

a. Matters Related to the Scope of Application

In addition to the temporal scope of the Regulation,[88] the material scope has also caused some uncertainties (see below section II.B.ii.c).

b. Matters Related to Torts/Delicts

So far, four judgments have applied or made reference to the provisions of Chapter II of the Rome II Regulation. In three of these judgments, the court focused on the general rule under Article 4 in relation to disputes arising from road accidents.[89] In one decision, the Tribunale di Bologna ruled that the law of the place of damage—Romanian law in that case—applied regardless of the fact that the habitual residence of the defendant was located in Italy, or that the car was registered and insured in Italy, as these elements did not prove a closer connection with Italy.[90]

With regard to the determination of the damages to be granted to the victim of a road accident that occurred in Hungary, one court decided in favour of the application of Italian law, it being the law of the place where the damage occurred due to the fact that Italy was the country where the victim would suffer the consequences of the damage as interpreted in the light of Recitals 17 and 33 of the Regulation.[91]

Finally, with regard to the infringement of intellectual property rights, a court plainly applied Italian law as it is the law of the place for which protection was claimed.[92]

c. Matters Related to Unjust Enrichment, *Negotiorum Gestio* and *Culpa in Contrahendo*

No case law has so far addressed the matters of *negotiorum gestio* and *culpa in contrahendo*. One decision addressed the matter of the payment of amounts wrongly received, which are expressly included in the scope of application of the rule on unjust enrichment

---

[88] Cass, 18 May 2015 No 10124; Trib Trieste, 11 July 2013; and Cass, No 11680/2014.
[89] Trib Trieste, ord 11 July 2013, (2013) *RDIPP* 796. Here the issue was the law applicable to an interim relief. See below, para e of this section.
[90] Trib Bologna, 17 March 2015.
[91] Trib Modena, 4 December 2015.
[92] Trib Bologna sez spec proprietà intellettuale, 8 July 2010.

(Article 10). In a case for the restitution of a significant amount of money which had been wrongly given by a Panamanian company to an Italian resident, the Tribunal ruled in favour of the application of Italian substantive law, it being the law of the place where the bank transfer was received by the defendant, allegedly pursuant to Article 61 of Italian Law No 218/1995 on Private international law.[93] The Court added that 'even considering the issue of the payment of amounts wrongly received as a tort as defined under Article 2 of the Rome II Regulation …' Italian law would apply.[94]

d. Matters Related to Other Provisions

A surprisingly high number of judgments concerning disputes lacking any international element made reference to Recital 32 of Rome II in matters relating to punitive damages. Such damages have been held unconstitutional by several judgments of the Corte di Cassazione.[95] However, in five purely national cases in which the Regulation was not applicable, lower courts made reference to Recital 32 of said Regulation in order to support the thesis of both a favourable (four cases)[96] or negative (one case)[97] approach of the European Union legal system towards punitive damages.

e. Conclusion

1. Problem Areas

The most problematic aspect of the Rome II Regulation is the imprecisely formulated temporal scope of application. Concerns arise also in relation to the material scope of application, with a particular regard to those matters which qualify as non-contractual matters under the Regulation but not under Italian law.

2. Possible Solutions

See under Rome I, section II.B.i.c.2 above.

C. Practice/Process

i. *Italian National Courts' Practice in Interpreting the Regulations/Process Issues*

An overall overview of the collected cases shows that Italian courts are usually compliant with the CJEU case law, but are cautious in referring questions for a preliminary ruling to the CJEU, despite the parties' requests. The courts often refer to the Corte di Cassazione precedents, which are not binding under Italian law. Reference to recitals is sometimes made to support the court's interpretation.

---

[93] The conflict-of-laws rule under Art 61 of law No 218/1995 actually provides for the application of the law of the place where the fact which gave rise to the wrongful reception took place, and not that of the place where the amount was received. This issue, which only concerns the interpretation of the Italian Private international law legislation, will not be analysed in depth here.

[94] Trib Bologna, 9 November 2015.

[95] See ex multis Cass, 19 January 2007 No 1183.

[96] Trib Milano, 29 August 2012; Trib Milano, 25 March 2011; Trib Milano, 4 March 2011; Trib Rovigo, 7 December 2010.

[97] App Roma, 21 September 2011.

The overall impression of the current system of preliminary references to the CJEU under Article 267 Treaty on the Functioning of the European Union (TFEU) is positive, although some interviewees think that the procedure should be faster and less formal. According to the interviewees, communication and coordination between judges of different Member States would help reduce the risk of divergent interpretation. The introduction of a preliminary ruling on jurisdiction at the EU level has also been suggested.

ii. Cost and Length of Litigation in Cross-border Civil and Commercial Disputes

The Italian interviewees unanimously recognised that the cross-border element increases litigation costs (even though not dramatically in relation to complex cases) due to the need for foreign experts' opinions, specialised legal advice and translation. Interviewees, both lawyers and judges, also confirmed that the proceedings are longer, especially due to the need to apply foreign law. Sometimes, delaying tactics or the need for a preliminary ruling on jurisdiction by the Supreme Court also affect the length of cross-border disputes.

iii. Settlement in Cross-border Civil and Commercial Disputes

Settlement is possible in Italy. According to the interviewees, it mostly occurs after proceedings have been commenced. Settlement depends also on the strength of the claimant's claim, although other external factors may have an influence: for example predictability of solutions, clarity of case law, other existing commercial relations between the parties, time necessary to obtain an enforceable judgment, and enforcement procedure in the country where enforcement will be sought.

iv. Alternative Dispute Resolution for Cross-border Civil and Commercial Disputes

Interviewees deem ADR to be a useful tool, when it comes to very complex and specialised cases. However, they also recognise that Italian courts of first instance sitting in bigger cities, such as Rome or Milan, are now structured in divisions that allow for a deeper specialisation of judges (eg in cases involving companies and intellectual property), with increased competence and reliability.

ADR is deemed to be useful particularly for consumers and small claims. Arbitration is a strong alternative to litigation for disputes between companies, because of wider powers of arbitrators in terms of fact-finding tools, specialisation, and available time and resources to be spent on disputed issues.

Compulsory ADR (as a pre-condition for court proceedings) is considered to be a rather undesirable option.

D. Preliminary Remarks on Effectiveness of the Current EU PIL Framework in Civil and Commercial Matters

The current EU PIL framework seems fairly effective notwithstanding some weaknesses, such as the lack of a common procedure for enforcement of foreign judgments and the absence of coordination between rules on *lis pendens* and choice-of-court agreements, the latter though having already been addressed by the Brussels Ia Regulation.

Limited knowledge and awareness of EU PIL rules by judges, lawyers, court clerks, public officials and other practitioners involved in their daily application, as well as the lack of coordination between judges of different Member States, impair the effectiveness of the EU PIL rules in civil and commercial matters.

III. Italian Experience on Cross-border Family Law Disputes

A. Jurisdictional and Procedural Issues under the Brussels IIa Regulation

The Italian research team collected 117 Italian decisions concerning Regulation (EC) No 2201/2003.

i. *Matters Related to the Scope of Application*

a. Matrimonial Matters

According to Recital 8, the Brussels IIa Regulation should apply only to the dissolution of matrimonial ties and should not deal with issues such as the grounds for divorce. However, Italian courts apply the Regulation also when they are required to adjudicate on a legal separation on fault grounds, thus declaring which of the spouses the separation is to be attributed to, in consideration of his/her behaviour as being contrary to the duties deriving from marriage. In substantive Italian law such a request (*richiesta di addebito*), pursuant to Article 151(2) of the Civil Code, is considered to be so closely related to the application for separation that it cannot be decided separately.[98] In order to extend Italian jurisdiction to the *richiesta di addebito*, curiously a court of first instance even applied Article 5(3) of the Brussels I Regulation, as the court of the place where the harmful event occurred.[99]

b. Parental Responsibility

As to the Regulation substantive scope of application, so far Italian courts have proved very familiar with the notions of 'parental responsibility',[100] 'rights of custody',[101] 'rights of access'[102] and 'wrongful removal or retention',[103] and, more generally, with all the definitions set forth by Article 2 of Brussels IIa. Indeed, as emerged also from the qualitative interviews, Italian judges welcome the existence of the legal notions contained in Article 2(7), (9), (10) and (11), which they usually mention in their decisions.

---

[98] See Cass 30 July 1999 No 8272; Cass 29 March 2005 No 6625; Cass 20 March 2008 No 7450; Trib Milano 12 April 2013; Trib Roma 20 February 2013; Trib Milano 23 July 2012; and Trib Belluno, 30 December 2011, (2012) *RDIPP* 452.

[99] Trib Tivoli 6 April 2011.

[100] See, among others, Juvenile Court of Milan, decreto (decree, hereinafter 'decr') 5 February 2010, (2012) *RDIPP* 140; and Trib Palmi, 28 January 2013, (2014) *RDIPP* 371.

[101] *cf* Juvenile Court of Milano, decr 16 January 2011, (2011) *RDIPP* 484.

[102] Referred to, among others, by Trib Belluno 23 December 2014; and Juvenile Court of Milano, decr 5 February 2010 cit.

[103] See eg Juvenile Court of Milano, decr 16 January 2011 cit. Most of the rules governing child abduction in the Brussels IIa come (unchanged) from the 1980 Hague Convention on civil aspects of international child abduction and this is true also with regard to the relevant definitions.

The application of the rules on parental responsibility usually follows a careful (positive) assessment of the applicability of the jurisdiction rules in matrimonial matters.[104] However, in two cases Italian courts declined jurisdiction, pursuant to Article 8, in matters of parental responsibility over children habitually resident in Switzerland[105] and in a couple of other cases they ruled out the application of the Regulation to parental responsibility claims concerning children habitually resident in Italy but third-state nationals.[106]

ii. Matters Related to Jurisdiction

a. Divorce, Legal Separation and Marriage Annulment

Absent a well-established CJEU case law specifically concerning matrimonial matters, the definition of habitual residence with regard to matrimonial matters is still an open issue. Italian lower courts tend to give to the notion of habitual residence a broad interpretation, whereas the Corte di Cassazione has tried to follow the CJEU guidelines, interpreting it as 'the place where the person has established, on a fixed basis, his permanent habitual centre of interests and where he/she carries out most of his/her personal and eventually professional life'.[107]

However, the intention of the person has a subsidiary and not essential role. The lower courts often base the determination of the habitual residence on the evaluation of documents such as the certificate of residence, the stay permit and the income tax return, without any further examination of the factual circumstances.[108]

Divergences have emerged on whether the reference in Article 3(1)(a) Brussels IIa to an applicant having 'resided' in a country for a year (or six months) prior to the petition meant 'habitual residence' or simply 'residence'.[109]

The use of nationality as a ground of jurisdiction in the case of dual/multiple nationality has also given rise to some doubts. Case law is scarce,[110] but seems to follow the interpretation according to which national provisions, such as Article 19 of the Law No 218/1995, should be disregarded and the common nationality should prevail in order to grant equal treatment in all the Member States.[111] In most cases, both spouses are non-EU Member State nationals and the Italian jurisdiction is founded on habitual residence.[112]

---

[104] See eg Trib Belluno, 6 March 2009, (2011) *RDIPP* 140; and Trib Milano, ord 10 July 2012, (2013) *Giur merito* 194.

[105] Trib Milano, ord 16 April 2014, (2015) *RDIPP* 162; and Trib Milano 10 July 2012 cit, implicitly confirming the non-applicability of the Regulation to children who are not habitually resident in a Member State. See also Cass, su, 2 August 2011 No 16864, (2012) *RDIPP* 684.

[106] Trib Treviso, 4 November 2015, case (a) and (b).

[107] Cass, su, 17 February 2010 No 3680, (2010) *RDIPP* 750; and Cass, su, 25 June 2010 No 15328, (2011) *RDIPP* 435. Although no judgment interpreting the notion of habitual residence of adults has been given by the CJEU yet, case law on children's habitual residence may offer some guidance: cf below n 114.

[108] See Trib Roma, 20 February 2013; Trib Roma, 9 January 2013; Trib Belluno, 30 December 2011 cit; and Trib Trento, 28 April 2011, *Pluris*. However, for an example of examination of the factual circumstances, see Trib Tivoli 6 April 2011, (2011) *RDIPP* 1097.

[109] Trib Pordenone, 14 October 2014, (2014) *RDIPP* 1011.

[110] See eg Trib Milano, 11 May 2012, *Pluris*.

[111] S Bariatti, 'Multiple Nationals and EU Private International Law—Many Questions and Some Tentative Answers' [2011] *Yearbook of Private International Law* 1.

[112] Trib Mantova, 19 January 2016; Trib Roma, 27 January 2015, *Pluris*; Trib Belluno, 30 December 2011 cit; Trib Belluno, 6 March 2009 cit; and Trib Trento, 28 April 2011 cit.

As to *lis pendens* in matrimonial matters, an issue concerns the so-called 'false *lis pendens*' between legal separation and divorce proceedings. Since under Italian law legal separation is the first step in a two-tier procedure for divorce, it is rather common that an application for separation is lodged first in Italy, whereas an application for divorce is lodged afterwards in another Member State.[113]

b. Parental Responsibility

The notion of the child's habitual residence is key to the whole system of rules on jurisdiction in matters of parental responsibility. Italian case law has followed the guidelines provided by the CJEU.[114] Notably, according to the Corte di Cassazione, the child's habitual residence is the place where, de facto, by virtue of a regular and stable presence, the child lives his/her daily life and has the centre of his/her relations, not only with his/her parents.[115] Lower courts have also proven very familiar with such an approach, despite the fact that they seldom make explicit reference to the CJEU case law.[116]

Italian courts appear to be very careful in examining the factual circumstances of the case, excluding any relevance of the subjective element, that is the intention (especially that of the parents) to settle in a certain place, particularly with regard to very young children or babies.[117] The assessment is usually made on documents submitted by the parties, statements made in the proceedings, as well as findings of foreign courts (particularly in cases concerning child abduction). Among the elements taken into consideration there are: the habitual residence of the parents/the parent the child lives with, documents of the national health system, the place where the child attends school and has friends and/or relatives, fiscal documents, car insurance documents, etc. No relevance is given to the parents' or the child's citizenship alone.[118] Where the habitual residence is 'fragmented', according to the Tribunale di Milano, it is necessary to look for the main habitual residence, deriving it from a combination of quantitative and qualitative links with a certain country.[119]

As to the prorogation of jurisdiction in matters of parental responsibility, pursuant to Article 12(1), Italian case law has focused on the condition set forth by Article 12(1)(b), which requires the spouses to accept the prorogation of the jurisdiction of the court competent under Article 3 on matrimonial matters also over parental responsibility matters. In this regard, acceptance has been excluded in case of non-appearance of the defendant.[120]

Italian courts have proved equally prepared to handle Article 15. In all the examined cases concerning case transfer, Italian courts were the courts of the habitual residence of the child/children involved in the proceedings. Well aware of the exceptional nature of such

---

[113] See Trib Milano, 1 June 2012, (2013) *RDIPP* 753; App Perugia, 10 March 2011, (2012) *RDIPP* 153; and Trib Milano, 8 April 2011, (2011) *RDIPP* 1112.

[114] Case C-523/07 *A* [2009] ECR I-2805; and Case C-497/10 PPU *Mercredi v Chaffe* [2010] ECR I-14309.

[115] Cass, su, ord 17 February 2010 No 3680; su, 13 February 2012 No 1984; su, 18 September 2014 No 19664; 11 January 2006 No 397 (referring to a 'generally stable presence').

[116] Trib Belluno, 23 December 2014 cit; Trib Milano, ord 16 April 2014 cit; Trib Milano, 24 March 2014, *Pluris*; Trib Palmi, 28 January 2013 cit; Trib Belluno, 30 December 2011 cit; and Trib Varese, decr 4 October 2010, (2011) *RDIPP* 743.

[117] Juvenile Court of Milano, decr 5 February 2010, as well as Cass 2 February 2005 No 2093 in relation to the 1980 Hague Convention. For a case concerning a newborn see Cass, su, 13 February 2012 No 1984 cit.

[118] Trib Roma, decr 5 November 2013, (2014) *RDIPP* 674.

[119] Trib Milano, ord 16 April 2014 cit.

[120] Trib Belluno, 30 December 2011 cit.

mechanism, after a careful examination of all the factual circumstances of the case at issue, Italian courts rejected in two cases the request to transfer the case,[121] while two other cases were transferred to the authorities of the State of the new residence of the child/children.[122]

With regard to dependent actions, the Tribunale di Varese specified that in cases of *lis pendens* or related actions, although the court second seised shall decline jurisdiction, it may take provisional measures in the best interest of the child who is present in the territory of the State pursuant to Article 20 of the Regulation.[123]

When it comes to provisional, including protective, measures, Italian case law, in line with the CJEU case law,[124] has adopted a strict interpretation of the requirements laid down by Article 20 of the Brussels IIa Regulation.[125] As to the limits of jurisdiction under Article 20, in line with *Detiček*, the Juvenile Court of Milan has recalled that Article 20 did not allow the courts of a Member State (Italy in the case at issue) to take a provisional and urgent measure in matters of parental responsibility aimed at granting to one of the parents the custody of the child who is in the territory of the said State, if the courts of another Member State, which have jurisdiction to hear the substance of the dispute on custody rights, have already issued a decision that provisionally grants the custody of the child to the other parent, and the said decision has been declared enforceable in the territory of the first Member State. However, when the practical means for the exercise of the rights of access have not been exhaustively regulated by the decision issued by the judicial authorities of the Member State having jurisdiction as to the substance of the matter, it is for the Italian probate courts (giudice tutelare) to determine such measures, provided that the essential principles laid down by the said decision are complied with.[126]

1. Child Abduction

The complex system governing child abduction has given rise to various issues. First, faithful to the criterion of proximity, in case of wrongful removal or retention of the child, the courts of the Member State of the child's habitual residence immediately before the abduction shall retain, under Article 10 of the Regulation, their jurisdiction on custody matters,[127] while jurisdiction to order the return of the child is to be determined under the 1980 Hague Convention. Hence, the Corte di Cassazione stated that no infringement of Articles 10 and 11 of Brussels IIa occurred in the case where the Italian court seised by the father in relation to parental responsibility over his daughter (who was habitually resident in Italy before her mother took her to Poland without his consent) took no decision on the return on the child, as the competence over return issues in cases of child abduction involving EU Member States lies with the Central Authority of the State where the child is after the wrongful removal.[128]

---

[121] App Firenze, 15 January 2014, (2014) *RDIPP* 170; and Trib Milano, 11 February 2014, (2015) *RDIPP* 379.

[122] Trib Vercelli, 18 December 2014. For a similar case see also Trib Arezzo, ord 15 March 2011, (2012) *RDIPP* 171.

[123] Trib Varese, decr 4 October 2010 cit.

[124] Case C-403/09 PPU, *Detiček v Sgueglia* [2009] ECR I-12193, and Case C-523/07, A n 114 above.

[125] Trib Milano, decr 16 July 2014 cit; Juvenile Court of Milano, decr 16 January 2011 cit; Trib Vercelli, decr 23 July 2014 cit; and Cass, 16 October 2009 No 22003, (2010) *RDIPP* 463.

[126] Juvenile Court of Milano, decr 5 February 2010 cit.

[127] Juvenile Court of Milano, decr 5 February 2010 cit; and App Bologna, 26 April 2012, *Pluris*.

[128] Cass, 12 May 2015 No 9632.

Second, as to the notion of child abduction, Italian courts seem to be well attuned to Article 2(11) which defines the term 'wrongful removal or retention'.

As to *lit.* a), Italian courts have specified that breaches of rights of custody are not protected by the 1980 Hague Convention[129] and that the existence of custody rights must be assessed in the light of the law of the place where the child was habitually resident before the removal/transfer.[130] Hence, the removal of a child by the parent having the care of her/his person is never wrongful, since the notion of 'rights of custody' includes the right of the parent having the care of the child to determine the child's place of residence,[131] even when he/she is entitled to those rights on the basis of an interlocutory judgment given *inaudita altera parte*.[132]

As to *lit.* b), the Italian Corte di Cassazione properly stated that the assessment of the actual exercise of the rights of custody shall be done *in concreto* on the basis of the circumstances of the case and not of the legal regime governing it.[133] Hence, even in the case of joint rights of custody, the seised court shall verify not only whether the removal of the child across borders was arbitrarily carried out by one parent but also whether it i) prejudices the actual possibility of the other parent to look after the child and satisfy (also financially) in a regular and permanent way the child's fundamental needs, and at the same time ii) prevents the child from benefitting from a regular contact with that parent.[134]

Third, with regard to the most frequently invoked ground for refusing to return a child, ie Article 13(b) of the 1980 Hague Convention, Italian courts have specified that the assessment required under this provision covers only truly grave risks and does not entail any comparative consideration about the best possible solution for the child.[135]

Last, as far as the very sensitive issue of the hearing of the child is concerned, Italian case law has evolved by leaps and bounds. It is a well-established principle now, also in light of the obligations arising from both national and international provisions,[136] that the child shall be heard in any proceedings concerning him/her, as the hearing constitutes a part of the child's right to participate in those proceedings and the formal moment for listening to his/her opinion and needs.[137] As a consequence, even if the hearing is not strictly required in return proceedings, it is generally deemed appropriate—as specifically contemplated by Article 11(2) of Brussels IIa—in order to evaluate the possible objection of the child to his return pursuant to Article 13(2) of the 1980 Hague Convention, unless this appears inappropriate having regard to the age or degree of maturity of the child or, all the more, if it

---

[129] Cass, 4 April 2007 No 8481, even though with regard to a non-intra EU case.

[130] Cass, 7 January 2011 No 277, (2011) *RDIPP* 763; Juvenile Court of Bari, decr 12 January 2011, (2011) *RDIPP* 1113.

[131] Cass, su, 21 October 2009 No 22238, (2010) *RDIPP* 747; on the same issue see also Cass, 4 April 2007 No 8481 cit.

[132] Cass 4 April 2007 No 8481 cit.

[133] Cass, 26 March 2015 No 6139. In the same vein see also Cass, 7 January 2011 No 277 cit, which rejected a father's application for the return of his child on the ground that at the time of the child's removal the father was not exercising his rights of custody, holding the reasons for such non-exercise to be irrelevant.

[134] Cass, 19 May 2010 No 12293, (2012) *RDIPP* 225.

[135] Cass, ord 5 October 2011 No 20365. For further examples of cases where Art 13(b) was invoked see Cass, 25 September 2001 No 11999; 19 August 2015 No 16904; and Juvenile Court of Milano, decr 30 April 2010 cit.

[136] Reference is to be made to Art 315-bis of the Italian Civil Code which was introduced by Law No 219 of 10 December 2012 in order to comply with the obligations arising from Art 12 of the 1989 UN Convention on the rights of the child as well as Arts 3 and 6 of the 1996 European Convention on the exercise of children's rights.

[137] Cass, 22 July 2014 No 16648. See also Cass, su, 21 October 2009 No 22238 cit.

would cause harm to the child. In this respect, the Corte di Cassazione has set the general benchmark of 12 years old.[138]

Some uncertainties still remain as to the value of the child's statements in relation to the order for return. The Corte di Cassazione has recently held that the opinion of a child with a sufficient and adequate degree of maturity opposing the return must necessarily be taken into consideration, thus implicitly recognising the value of the child's views as an autonomous ground for refusing his/her return.[139] This principle is to be confronted, though, with the case law of the European Court of Human Rights.[140]

2. Other Issues Related to Parental Responsibility

With regard to the prohibition to review the jurisdiction of the court of origin set forth by Article 24, the Tribunale di Vercelli denied recognition to a judgment on parental responsibility given by the Romanian court that had been seised in relation to the divorce of the spouses, stating that that court could not legitimately take provisional measures in matters of parental responsibility over the couple's child under either Article 8, since the child was habitually resident in Italy, or Article 20, since the child was not present in Romania.[141]

iii. *Matters Related to Recognition and Enforcement*

a. Certificate Concerning Judgments in Matrimonial Matters and Certificate Concerning Judgments on Parental Responsibility

1. Grounds for Non-recognition of Judgments in Matrimonial Matters

It is generally accepted that there is no violation of public policy, under Article 22(a), if the foreign divorce was obtained without a previous period of separation,[142] or without regulating the connected matters, such as parental responsibility, maintenance or matrimonial property.[143] However, such recognition does not preclude the adoption of economic measures (eg *assegno divorzile* under Article 5 of Law No 898 of 1 December 1970) in separate Italian proceedings.[144]

The only reported case where the public policy exception was successfully raised concerned procedural public policy and involved a Spanish divorce judgment, in which the documents which instituted the proceedings had been served on the respondent according to the rules applicable for proceedings in default of appearance, although the applicant knew that the respondent was resident in Italy. The court held that this violated Article 22(a) of the Regulation. The fact that the respondent did not lodge an appeal against the judgment could not be deemed as an unequivocal acceptance of the divorce according to Article 22(b).[145]

---

[138] Cass, su, 18 September 2014 No 19664.
[139] Cass, 5 March 2014 No 5237, referring to proceedings pursuant to Art 7 of Law No 64/1994 on the ratification of the 1980 Hague Convention.
[140] *Blaga v Romania* App No 54443/10 ECLI:CE:ECHR:2014:0701JUD005444310.
[141] Trib Vercelli, decr 23 July 2014 cit.
[142] Cass, 25 July 2006 No 16978; and App Perugia, 10 March 2011, (2012) *RDIPP* 153.
[143] Trib Belluno, 5 November 2010, (2011) *RDIPP* 756.
[144] Cass, 1 February 2016 No 1863.
[145] App Perugia, 10 March 2011.

With regard to foreign divorce by mutual consent issued by a notary, no cases have been reported regarding the Brussels IIa Regulation.[146]

As to Article 22(c), there is no irreconcilability between a separation judgment given in Italy and a subsequent divorce judgment given in another Member State, since separation may be considered a preliminary issue to divorce and, consequently, there would be no conflict with a subsequent divorce judgment, as pointed out by the Italian Supreme Court in 2009.[147]

2. Certificate Concerning Judgments in Matrimonial Matters

No practical difficulties either with regard to the use of certificates (Articles 39, 41 and 42) or relating to the automatic updating of civil status documents (Article 21) have arisen after an ad hoc ministerial memorandum had stated that registration in civil status records should not be considered as enforcement. No special procedure is therefore required to update civil status records.[148]

3. Recognition and Enforcement of Judgments in Matters of Parental Responsibility

Very few judgments concern recognition and enforcement of judgments in matters of parental responsibility. A decision of the Corte di Cassazione dealing with the recognition of a German judgment on the legal separation of spouses with ancillary orders relating to their children must be recalled in two different respects. First, the Supreme Court stated that ancillary orders relating to children should be considered final and no longer subject to appeal under German law even when such judgment had been appealed to the German Constitutional Court for a violation of fundamental rights, thus being enforceable in Italy under Article 28(1) of Brussels IIa. Second, for the purpose of Article 23(e) of the Regulation, the German final decision on legal separation, including the abovementioned ancillary orders, could not be compared to, and therefore could not be regarded as irreconcilable with an Italian non-final judgment on legal separation and with the provisional measures issued in the relevant separation proceedings pending in Italy.[149]

b. Return of the Child

The Corte di Appello di Milano held that, pursuant to Article 42(1) Brussels IIa, a judgment given by a French court ordering the return of a child to Italy was automatically recognised and enforceable on the basis of an out-of-court agreement between the natural parents of the child without the need for a declaration of enforceability, if the judgment had been certified in the Member State of origin.[150]

---

[146] Some cases involved third states: App Ancona 7 March 2009; Cass, 26 September 2011 No 19602; Trib Milano, 24 June 2013. On this issue, see also the Circular (*Circolare*) of the Ministry of Internal Affairs No 18 of 12 July 2011.

[147] Cass, 16 October 2009 No 22093, (2010) *RDIPP* 463.

[148] Ministry of Justice, Letter 7 January 1997 prot no 1/50/FG/29. More recently see the ministerial memoranda (*Circolari ministeriali*) of the Ministry of Internal Affairs No 24 of 23 June 2006 and No 56 of 22 October 2007, available at www.interno.gov.it.

[149] Cass, 16 October 2009 No 22093 cit.

[150] App Milano, decr 19 August 2006, (2007) *RDIPP* 739.

iv. Cooperation between Central Authorities in Matters of Parental Responsibility

In one reported case the seised court ordered that its judgment be transmitted to the Central Authority under Articles 54 and 55 Brussels IIa.[151]

v. Relationship with Other Instruments

Some difficulties have arisen as to the relationship with instruments concerning maintenance obligations. Notably, on the one hand, certain characterisation issues emerged in Italian case law with regard to the material scope of application of the Regulation (EC) No 4/2009 and the Hague Maintenance Protocol of 2007. On the other hand, the Court of Justice has recently given a preliminary ruling on the interplay between the Brussels IIa Regulation and the Maintenance Regulation,[152] upon a request from the Corte di Appello di Milano.[153]

vi. Conclusion

This analysis has shown that Italian courts are in most cases fairly well attuned to the Brussels IIa Regulation.

a. Problem Areas

Actually, the plurality of concurrent grounds of jurisdiction provided for by the Regulation does not facilitate the coincidence between jurisdiction and applicable law, in particular, when jurisdiction is based on the common nationality of the parties according to Article 3(1)(b) of Brussels IIa and the spouses are habitually resident abroad. Very often, there is a great difficulty in assessing the content of foreign law.

Another area of major concern regards the fragmentation of the EU legislation in family matters.

Moreover, the lack of a European consensus on the notion of habitual residence raises some issues. In this respect, it is disputed in particular, whether the reference in Article 3(1)(a) Brussels IIa to an applicant having 'resided' in a country for a year (or six months if he/she is a national of the Member State in question) prior to the petition requires 'habitual residence' or simply 'residence'. Not surprisingly, in the national practice some divergences emerged. In this respect, the recent reform of Italian divorce law, which cut down the three year period of legal separation previously required in Italy as a condition for a divorce application, will probably reduce the number of so called 'divorce tourists', ie couples of Italian nationals habitually resident in Italy seeking to establish their residence abroad in order to apply for divorce there and bypass such a mandatory requirement.[154]

With regard to parental responsibility, difficulties in handling the complex system created by the combination of the 1980 Hague Convention and the Brussels IIa Regulation emerged as an area of further concern.

---

[151] App Milano, decr 19 August 2006 cit.

[152] Case C-184/14, *A v B* EU:C:2015:479.

[153] On characterisation issues and issues concerning the interplay between regulations see below respectively ss III.B.i. and III.B.ii.

[154] For an example see *Rapisarda v Collandon* (irregular divorces) [2014] EWFC 35.

Moreover, as underlined also by one of the interviewees, actual enforcement of judgments on parental responsibility is very difficult, given the lack of specific procedural rules both in the Regulation and in domestic law. Enforcement of maintenance judgments proves equally difficult.

Communication between judges in child abduction cases is non-existent or very difficult.

At last, the qualitative interviews highlighted the need to increase knowledge and understanding of the EU Regulations in order to enhance their effectiveness. In particular, it is not easy for a judge to cope with the coordination of all these instruments. Therefore, training for judges on cross-border issues should be improved.

b. Best Practice

Italian courts tend either not to keep jurisdiction over children habitually resident abroad or to apply the law of the forum, in relation to both divorce and parental responsibility, despite the difficulties arising from the fragmentation of family matters in the EU PIL Regulations.

B. Jurisdictional and Procedural Issues and Applicable Law under the Maintenance Regulation

i. *Matters Related to the Scope of Application*

Some difficulties as to the material scope of application of the Maintenance Regulation and the 2007 Hague Maintenance Protocol emerged due to the fact that, under Italian substantive law, the concept of maintenance obligation is narrower than the autonomous notion used in EU PIL instruments. Despite some exceptions,[155] most courts have understood well the need to abandon national legal categories,[156] no matter how similar the Italian term *mantenimento* sounds as compared to the one used in the Maintenance Regulation,[157] and refer to the broad and autonomous notion elaborated by the CJEU in relation to Article 5(2) of the 1968 Brussels Convention,[158] including what in Italian substantive law is known as *mantenimento* (maintenance allowances),[159] *alimenti* (alimony), as well as *assegno divorzile* (divorce contribution).

Some doubts have arisen also in relation to the issue of the assignment of the matrimonial home, which seems to be included in the broad notion relevant under the Regulation, despite a contrary opinion.[160]

---

[155] See Trib Roma, 27 January 2015, where the court held the Regulation to be applicable only in relation to the claim for *mantenimento* (maintenance allowances) brought by a Peruvian wife against her husband but not with regard to the claim for *alimenti* (alimony) towards the child's couple.

[156] Cass, 24 July 2003 No 1152, (2004) *RDIPP* 678.

[157] Trib Milano, 1 June 2012; and Trib Belluno 30 December 2011 cit.

[158] Case C-220/95 *van den Boogard v Laumen* [1997] ECR I-1147.

[159] Cass, su, 1 October 2009 No 21053, (2010) *RDIPP* 462; as to lower courts see App Roma, 25 July 2007; Trib Belluno, 30 December 2011 cit; Trib Milano, 11 June 2012, *Pluris*; Trib Milano, 14 February 2013; Trib Milano, 16 February 2013; Trib Milano, 23 July 2012, *Pluris*; Trib Roma, 5 November 2013 cit; Trib Belluno, 12 November 2013, (2014) *RDIPP* 973; Trib Belluno, 23 December 2014 cit.

[160] The Trib Belluno, 30 December 2011 cit applied national PIL rules to determine the law applicable to this issue.

ii. Matters Related to Jurisdiction

As to jurisdiction under Article 3(a) and (b), Italian courts have properly applied the Regulation also to determine jurisdiction over cases concerning citizens of third states, for instance Moroccans, provided that, on the basis of a factual assessment, at the moment of the claim the parties (or at least one of them) are habitually resident in an EU Member State.[161]

As to jurisdiction over ancillary maintenance claims, the Corte di Cassazione has requested a preliminary ruling on the interplay between Brussels IIa and the Maintenance Regulation.[162] The case originated from a judgment of the Tribunale di Milano which had assumed jurisdiction over the legal separation of an Italian couple and maintenance for the benefit of the wife, respectively under Articles 3(b) of Brussels IIa and 3(1)(a) and (c) of the Maintenance Regulation, while it had declined jurisdiction, under Article 3(1)(d) of the Maintenance Regulation, over the maintenance claim in favour of the children, resident in England.[163]

The CJEU has stated that, in the light of the best interests of the child, the court with jurisdiction to entertain proceedings concerning parental responsibility, as defined in Article 2(7) of Brussels IIa, was in the best position to evaluate *in concreto* the issues involved in the application for child maintenance.[164] Consequently, where two courts are seised of proceedings, one concerning the separation or dissolution of the marital bond between married parents of minor children and the other involving parental responsibility over those children, an application for maintenance in respect to those children may be regarded as ancillary only to the proceedings in matters of parental responsibility. Following this judgment, the Corte di Cassazione held that Article 3(d) of the Maintenance Regulation did not confer jurisdiction upon Italian courts over the claim for maintenance obligations towards the couple's children.[165]

Furthermore, as to prorogation of jurisdiction the Tribunale di Belluno affirmed its jurisdiction, pursuant to Article 5 of the Maintenance Regulation, as the defendant entered an appearance without contesting jurisdiction, thus tacitly prorogating Italian jurisdiction. In a more recent decision, the same Tribunal noted that Article 5 constituted an alternative forum since its application is not subordinated to the absence of the grounds of jurisdiction provided for by Articles 3 and 4.[166]

With regard to *lis pendens*, Italian courts have held that jurisdiction was to be assessed on the court's own motion, pursuant to Article 10 of the Regulation,[167] referring to the moment when the claims were filed before the court, with facts and actions taken subsequently by the parties being irrelevant for the purpose of establishing jurisdiction.[168]

---

[161] Trib Belluno, 23 December 2014 cit (holding irrelevant the citizenship of the parties). See also Trib Belluno, 12 November 2013 cit; and Trib Roma, 27 January 2015 cit.
[162] Cass, 7 April 2014 No 8049.
[163] Trib Milano, ord 16 November 2012, *Pluris*.
[164] *A v B* n 152 above.
[165] Cass, su, ord 5 February 2016 No 2276.
[166] Trib Belluno, 23 December 2014 cit.
[167] ibid.
[168] Trib Milano, 16 April 2014 cit.

iii. Matters Related to Applicable Law

So far, no particular problems have arisen in relation to the determination of the law applicable to maintenance obligations.[169] Italian courts do not seem to be eager to apply the law of the forum. Rather, they sometimes appear doubtful with regard to the conflict-of-laws rules applicable to the case at issue. For instance, recently the Tribunale di Roma applied national conflict-of-laws rules, ie Article 45 of the Law No 218/1995, to determine the law applicable to the maintenance obligations towards a couple's child, at the same time applying the Maintenance Regulation and the 2007 Hague Protocol to determine the law applicable to the maintenance obligations between the spouses.[170]

In one particular case, the universal application of the rules of the Protocol led the Tribunale di Milano to properly apply Swiss law.[171]

In many cases the joint application of the Maintenance Regulation and the 2007 Hague Protocol led to the welcome coincidence between forum and ius.[172]

iv. Matters Related to Recognition, Enforceability and Actual Enforcement of Decisions

No case law was found on this issue, although, from the qualitative interviews, a general scepticism as to the effectiveness of the regime on recognition and enforcement of decisions concerning maintenance obligations emerged.

v. Conclusion

So far, Italian courts have proven fairly attuned to the Maintenance Regulation, save for some uncertainties about its material scope of application. However, it appears questionable that sometimes issues relating to maintenance are qualified as de facto issues so that jurisdiction over them is automatically derived from jurisdiction on matrimonial matters determined under Article 3 of Brussels IIa, irrespective of the Maintenance Regulation, thus leading to the automatic application of the Italian law as lex fori.[173]

Again, from both the case law on the Maintenance Regulation and the qualitative interviews conducted within the research project, the fragmentation of the EU legislation in family matters emerged as an area of major concern. Matrimonial matters, maintenance obligations, assignment of the matrimonial home, parental responsibility and so on are all intertwined claims but covered by different regulations which not rarely lead to the jurisdiction of the courts of different States. Such risk has further increased after the CJEU judgment of 16 July 2015.[174]

---

[169] See eg Trib Treviso, 17 July 2014, *Pluris*; Trib Roma, decr 5 November 2013 cit.
[170] Trib Roma, 27 January 2015 cit.
[171] Trib Milano, ord 16 April 2014 cit.
[172] See for instance Trib Belluno, 23 December 2014 cit.
[173] Trib Milano, 16 February 2013 cit; Trib Milano, 14 February 2013 cit; Trib Milano, 23 July 2012, *Pluris*; Trib Milano, 11 June 2012 cit.
[174] *A v B* n 152 above.

Last, qualitative interviews also mentioned the need for a wider and deeper knowledge of EU PIL instruments in family matters by both judges and lawyers in order to avoid mistakes, for instance, as to characterisation issues.

C. Practice/Process

i. *Italy's National Courts' Practice in Interpreting the Regulations*

Even though one interviewee expressed appreciation for the EU PIL instruments, some difficulties in interpreting and applying the Regulations have emerged from Italian case law. The two main reasons are the differences between national substantive law and EU PIL autonomous notions on the one hand, and the need to coordinate a fragmented EU PIL framework in relation to a single case on the other hand.

In order to solve the interpretation issues, the interviewed judges take into consideration primarily EU PIL rules and recitals. Sometimes, writings by legal scholars and official reports on the application of EU PIL instruments are used too. One judge added that he usually cites CJEU case law in his judgments in order to facilitate their circulation in the Member States where recognition or enforcement of his decisions could be sought. On one occasion, a referral for a preliminary ruling was also made.[175] This mechanism is generally appreciated by judges; however, it is rarely requested by lawyers and even more rarely granted by judges.

No trend to interpret EU PIL rules so as to keep jurisdiction or apply Italian law emerged.

More (direct) communication and coordination between courts of different Member State has also been suggested as a method to reduce divergences.

Last, the interviews revealed that, besides interpretation issues, many problems concerning the daily application of EU PIL rules arise also from the lack of knowledge/awareness by lawyers, judges, court clerks and public officials.

ii. *Cost and Length of Litigation in Cross-border Family Law Disputes*

All interviewees recognised that cross-border family law disputes are more expensive than domestic ones, particularly because of lawyers' fees and translation costs. Costs involved in child abduction cases are incredibly high. This affects the parties' behaviour.

The length of litigation is affected as well, especially by the issue of determining the contents of the applicable foreign law and possible problems concerning service abroad. The need for a preliminary ruling under Article 267 TFEU and difficulties to obtain documents/evidence from abroad may also affect the length of proceedings.

iii. *Settlement in Cross-border Family Law Disputes*

Parties in cross-border family law disputes rarely settle and rarely do it before proceedings have commenced. They usually run to establish jurisdiction in their favourite country and only after that they consider settlement. Even though settlement as such is not allowed by

---

[175] *A v B* n 152 above.

Italian substantive law in family matters (except for certain issues), judges tend to suggest that parties' agreed solutions be adopted within court proceedings.

Lawyers also play a role in the achievement of a 'settlement', both before proceedings are commenced (by negotiating on behalf of their clients) and afterwards.

The achievement of agreed solutions is not directly related to the strength of the claimant's claim, as the dividing line between what is right and what is wrong in family matters is often blurred.

iv. Alternative Dispute Resolution for Cross-border Family Law Disputes

Although there is no ADR culture in family matters in Italy, practice reveals an emerging trend in favour of mechanisms and techniques alternative to litigation, such as collaborative law, family mediation or *negoziazione assistita* (assisted negotiations), recently introduced in Italy.[176] However, much depends on the lawyer's training, knowledge and approach. One of the interviewed judges expressed the view that ADR should even be imposed by law as a condition to commence proceedings in family matters.

Under Italian substantive law, family matters are traditionally governed by provisions which the parties cannot derogate from. Inalienable rights (eg personal status) might constitute an obstacle to ADR and other techniques. Furthermore, the need for an enforceable decision which can circulate freely throughout the EU might discourage their use.

D. Preliminary Remarks on Effectiveness of the Current EU PIL Framework in Cross-border Family Law

The fragmentation of EU PIL rules in family matters increases confusion among judges and lawyers and adds complexity to cross-border family law disputes. This is undesirable from the point of view of the effectiveness of the system. Sometimes, though, the same undesirable effect originates from the application of a single instrument: this is the case of Articles 3(1)(b) and 8 Brussels IIa.

As to child abduction, the multi-layered system (1980 Hague Convention as modified by Brussels IIa) is highly complex to handle. Some sensitive issues such as the hearing of the child and compliance with time limits set forth by Article 11 of Brussels IIa result in a certain degree of uncertainty.

Moreover, practical difficulties in the actual enforcement of return orders and other decisions on parental responsibility affect the effectiveness of the current framework.

IV. Conclusion

Both the analysis of Italian case law and qualitative interviews conducted in Italy showed that the current EU PIL framework in civil and commercial matters was fairly effective, despite some weaknesses. Characterisation issues had arisen in a number of cases, but they

---

[176] Law Decree No 132 of 12 September 2014, converted into Law No 162 of 10 November 2014.

were mostly resolved following or even anticipating the solutions adopted by the CJEU. Furthermore, on several occasions, rules of national civil procedure were applied to safeguard the *effet utile* of the EU PIL regulations. Nevertheless, actual enforcement of judgments represents one of the major shortcomings of the system.

As to cross-border family law, the current EU PIL framework is less satisfactory, generally speaking, because of the drawbacks arising from its fragmentation and, more particularly, because of the enforcement issues and the high complexity of the system applicable to child abduction cases.

In relation to both areas, fostering training for all those involved in the actual application of EU PIL rules (judges, lawyers, court clerks and public officials), and the creation of databases containing reliable information on foreign substantive laws and case law appear to be essential in order to raise the effectiveness of judicial cooperation.

9

Spain

CARMEN OTERO GARCÍA-CASTRILLÓN

I. Introduction[*]

Spain's legal system is anchored in the 1978 Constitution (SC)[1] establishing a social, democratic and subject to the rule of law State (article 1.1 SC). Though a unique and indissoluble State (article 2 SC), Spain is administratively structured in 17 self-governing Communities—*Comunidades Autónomas*—enjoying a wide margin of legislative, administrative and executive power (articles 147–148 SC). From the private international law (PIL) perspective it is relevant to note that the country is a multi-unit State. However, the judicial administration system is unique for the whole country (articles 117 and 149.1.5 SP), the Spanish central power has the exclusive competence to negotiate and sign international treaties (articles 93 and 149.1.3 SC)[2] and the national legislative authority is also the only one that can regulate on PIL issues—including internal conflict of laws—(article 149.1.8 SC).

Beyond the possibility of appealing to the Constitutional Court in cases of alleged breach of fundamental rights (*recurso de amparo*, article 53.2 SC), the Spanish judicial system has three instances. For civil and commercial law cases these instances are, first, the first instance courts—*juzgados de primera instancia*—or Labour courts—*Juzgados de lo social*—for labour litigation; second, the 60 Provincial Audiences (Civil Law Cambers)—*Audiencias Provinciales*—or the 17 Superior Courts of Justice of the Autonomous Communities (civil and labour chambers)—*Tribunales Superiores de Justicia de las Comunidades Autónomas*—and, finally, the Supreme Court (First Chamber —civil and Fourth Chamber—labour).

---

[*] The methodology used to analyse the data contained in this report is at the same time quantitative and qualitative. The quantitative presentation of the data is based on the application of descriptive statistical rules. In this sense, data are presented under the form of regular accounting and of percentages. Spanish authorities and courts' decisions have been counted each time that one of the analysed Regulations was mentioned (whether finally applied or not). The decisions that included references to two or more instruments are, therefore, taken into account in the analysis of each of the Regulations. As to the length of each of the proceedings, the time for the appeals has been counted. Tables were made for this report (own source).

[1] English text: www.congreso.es/portal/page/portal/Congreso/Congreso/Hist_Normas/Norm/const_espa_texto_ingles_0.pdf.

[2] Treaties and other International Agreements Law—*Ley 25/2014, de 27 de noviembre, de Tratados y otros Acuerdos Internacionales BOE* n° 288, 28 November. www.boe.es/boe/dias/2014/11/28/pdfs/BOE-A-2014-12326.pdf.

In the first instance level there are a number of courts (62 in 31 venues) that specialise in commercial claims—*juzgados de lo mercantil.* No other specialisation can be found within the private law judicial framework despite the fact that some of the first instance courts are signified as family courts and, obviously, family law cases are assigned to them. A breakdown of the court's system can be found in the following table.

Table 1: Scheme Of The Spanish Civil Courts' System

NATIONAL LEVEL	SUPREME COURT—(*Appeals—Third Instance*)	
	First Chamber (Civil)—Fourth Chamber (Labour)	
	NATIONAL AUDIENCE (*Appeals—Second Instance*)	
	Fourth Chamber (Labour)	
AUTONOMOUS COMMUNITIES LEVEL	SUPERIOR COURTS OF JUSTICE OF THE AUTONOMOUS COMMUNITIES (*Appeals—Second or Third Instance*)	
	First Chambers (Civil & Criminal)—Third Chambers (Labour)	
PROVINCIAL LEVEL	PROVINCIAL AUDIENCES (*Appeals—Second Instance*)	
	Civil sections	
	Commercial Courts (First Instance)	Labour Courts (First Instance)
LOCAL LEVEL	First instance courts	

The Spanish Courts' work in civil and commercial litigation is implemented by judges and Justice Attorneys—*Letrados de la Administración de Justicia* (previously known as Judicial Secretaries). Judges are governed by the General Council for the Judiciary—*Consejo General del Poder Judicial* (CGPJ)—whilst Judicial Secretaries are dependent on the General Secretary for Justice Administration (Ministry of Justice). Their respective functions and the access to each of these professions are regulated in the Judicial Power Organization Act 6/1985 of 1 July, as amended.[3] The selection process guarantees, in an objective and transparent manner, equality of access for all citizens that meet the necessary conditions, possess the necessary abilities, and have the required professional competence and aptitude for exercising the functions. Admittance is granted after passing an open competition and a selection course encompassing practical and theoretical training.

In order to litigate before Spanish Courts, it is generally required to be assisted by a representative *ad litem—procurador*—and defended by a lawyer.[4]

For the purpose of international judicial cooperation, the Spanish Ministry of Justice relies on the State Justice Secretariat (Ministry of Justice), whose Directorate General on International Juridical Cooperation is structured in two sections: the Sub-Directorate for International Legal Cooperation and the Sub-Directorate for EU and International Justice related matters.[5]

---

[3] Arts 330ff, 440ff. Ley Orgánica 6/1985, de 1 de julio, del Poder Judicial, BOE nº 157, 2 July 1985. Consolidated text in www.boe.es/buscar/act.php?id=BOE-A-1985-12666.

[4] Arts 542 and 543 Ley Orgánica 6/1985, n 3.

[5] www.mjusticia.gob.es/cs/Satellite/Portal/es/ministerio/organigrama/secretaria-estado-justicia/direccion-general-cooperacion#id_1215328711694.

For the judiciary, at EU level, it is interesting to note the assisting role played by the European Judicial Atlas.[6] The Spanish Judicial Network of International Judicial Cooperation (REJUE),[7] the Network of Experts in European Union Law (REDUE)[8] and the Spanish Network of Judicial Secretaries for International Cooperation (RESEJ)[9] provide assistance to judges and to Justice Attorneys respectively. Although not expressly organised for this purpose, universities could be of help in this regard.

From 2002 to 2015, cross-border litigation in Spain increased in civil and commercial matters. Family law cases outnumber the other civil and commercial ones perhaps due to the amount of migration to and from Spain. Therefore, the application of EU PIL instruments in Spain has been developed to the extent that they are used as a normative reference and an interpretation tool even when they are not applicable.

Comprising civil and commercial as well as family matters, a study prepared by the Spanish Network of Judicial Secretaries for International Cooperation concluded that in the period 2008–2013, the number of cases of recognition and enforcement of judgments under Brussels I, Brussels IIa and the Maintenance Regulations (in EUPILLAR Project), and the Regulation on the European enforcement order for uncontested claims, rose (281 in 2008 and 959 in 2009) up to a peak in 2012 (1644) and has estabilised since then (964 in 2013).[10]

II. Spain's Experience in Non-family Cross-border Civil and Commercial Disputes

The application of EU PIL instruments in Spain has risen as a result of the increased number of international operations. From 2002 to 2015 a total of 320 cases applied the Brussels I Regulation (BIR), 31 cases referred to the Rome I Regulation (RIR) and 15 to Rome II (RIIR).

Generally claimants are Spanish residents that wish to establish Spanish courts' jurisdiction against foreign companies and non-residents claiming debts against residents (the European order for payment has been used quite a lot but it is not included in this this project). Foreign companies, particularly big ones with subsidiaries, offices or clients in the country frequently ask Spanish lawyers for advice and legal opinions. The advice to foreign firms is usually provided through the mediation of foreign lawyers or law firms (in parallel, Spanish law firms mediate to gain information about foreign legal systems for their Spanish clients).

---

[6] https://e-justice.europa.eu/content_european_judicial_atlas_in_civil_matters-321-en.do?init=true.

[7] Red Judicial Española de Cooperación Judicial Internacional: REJUE comprises 62 highly specialised Magistrates in the subject. The International Relations Service of the General Council of the Judiciary coordinates the Network.

[8] Red de Expertos en Derecho de la UE assists Spanish courts in the application of EU Law and in submitting preliminary questions to the Court of Justice of the European Union (CJEU).

[9] Red de Secretarios Judiciales en cooperación jurídica internacional, www.mjusticia.gob.es/cs/Satellite/Portal/es/areas-tematicas/area-internacional/participacion-ministerio/espanola-secretarios.

[10] Estudio del flujo del Auxilio Judicial Internacional y de los instrumentos de reconocimiento mutuo; 2008–2013. Generously provided by Grupo de Pilotaje RESEJ.

Most legal disputes relate to contracts. In one of the interviewed lawyers' words: 'The typology is varied but, basically, we deal with contractual claims related to sales, distribution contracts and company operations in general'. There are only a few cross-border consumer contract cases since their value is not considered enough to initiate a judicial procedure. Non-contractual disputes frequently relate to traffic accidents. Recognition and enforcement of foreign court's decisions and preventive measures related to procedures opened before foreign jurisdictions are also in the Spanish lawyers' agendas.

However, interviewed judges do not find many international civil and commercial cases in their courts. When they do, they have mostly a contractual character (sales). Recognition and enforcement of Member States' courts decisions, the European payment order procedure and, to a lesser extent, successions (not in the project) are in their portfolios. Provisional measures are rarely sought. The difficulties that judges find in trans-border cases relate to the lack of knowledge of the applicable instruments, both on the lawyers' side (demands are not correctly formulated) and their own.

A. Jurisdictional and Procedural Issues under the Brussels I Regulation

i. Matters Related to the Scope of Application

There are no particular problems in this regard. However, some of the interviewed lawyers raised doubts on the definition of cross-border cases ('would a claim be considered a cross-border case if it is based on a contract between two companies established in Spain that have obligations to be executed in a different country?').

ii. Matters Related to Jurisdiction

According to the interviewed lawyers, parties in the major civil and commercial international litigation cases usually resort to arbitration on the basis of the clauses inserted in their contracts. Even when this is not the case, arbitration is sometimes preferred to courts for time saving purposes (in second instance, a process can take up to two years). In this regard, the short deadlines of Spanish procedural rules and the perceived absence of specialisation of the First Instance Spanish Courts (not so much in the Commercial Courts), also contribute to incline the balance in favour of arbitration or, simply, to prefer a foreign jurisdiction ('a case in Spain is much cheaper than in the UK but parties' autonomous will is more easily respected there').

Choice-of-court agreements are frequent (and intensively negotiated on the basis of parties' trust in the forum—they tend to prefer their own—taking into account costs, particularly the experts' reports, and duration of the proceedings—risks of delays—as well as the applicable law) and Spanish Courts are pointed at in different opportunities. The choice-of-court clauses do not usually present problems except when included in adhesion contracts, particularly for consumers, for which international litigation is not that frequent due to their low economic value (in addition, EU consumer contract law is considered 'too complicated to be regularly followed').

The interviewed judges have faced few cases of choice-of-court agreements and tend to think that the Regulation permits the claimant to choose the jurisdiction that he/she considers beneficial for his interests. Anyhow, they are aware of the fact that 'the Judges need to take into consideration the possible frauds' or 'abuses' regarding consumer or financial cases.

Beyond the cases of choice-of-court agreements, the jurisdiction criteria of the BIR provides adequate and predictable jurisdiction options that, according to the interviewed lawyers, are not often used due to the frequent existence of choice-of-court agreements. In their view, questioning the jurisdiction becomes mostly a dilatory strategy.

Spanish practice deeply respects the existence of choice-of-courts agreements and, when they do not exist, Spanish Courts are not eager to assume jurisdiction in international cases since these are more complicated and they have already more than enough work. From the lawyers and judges' perspective, no nationalist bias is observed in Spanish Courts' decisions. Nevertheless, one judge has also argued that Spanish Courts do not usually discuss their jurisdiction once it has been claimed by one of the parties and, therefore, this attitude favours its establishment. This, however, does not mean that the Regulation jurisdiction rules do not offer a margin of manoeuvre that both, judges and lawyers, believe can be used to establish the jurisdiction of each of the parties' most convenient court and, to this end, jurisdiction rules can be used abusively for dilatory strategies.

According to lawyers, the *lis pendens* and related actions rules in the BIR clearly stimulate a race to the court in order to be the first to present an action. Therefore, a prospective defendant will not wait to have a claim presented against him but will move as fast as possible to his preferred court taking the position of claimant. However, in their experience *lis pendens* cases are not common, whilst related actions cases are a bit more frequent. Recorded data support this impression.[11] In the lawyers' experience, it is not strange to find cases with a plurality of claimants (eg in construction projects) as well as with a plurality of defendants. However, the recorded data show a relatively small number of plurality of defendants' cases.[12] The interviewed judges have occasionally dealt with a case with a plurality of claimants but they usually deal with individual claims.

Overall, the BIR's jurisdictional rules are perceived by lawyers and judges as very reasonable and predictable. They do not perceive any lacuna and would not know any problems that they feel the need to point out.

iii. Matters Related to Recognition and Enforcement

Recognition and Enforcement under the Brussels I system does not seem to pose special difficulties in Spain. Member States' decisions are usually recognised and enforced within two or three months, usually without defendants raising opposition and, when they do, judges are not inclined to accept them unless strongly founded. Moreover, 'Interpretations introduced by the Spanish jurisprudence have clarified those internal aspects not detailed in the Regulation'. However, in some cases lawyers detect a lack of knowledge of EU PIL instruments in First Instance Courts. In addition, when the recognition is by the notaries or

---

[11] *Lis pendens* cases: Madrid Superior Court of Justice (TSJ de Madrid), Judgments no 286/2015, 14 September and no 820/2007, 17 December; Tarragona Provincial Audience (AP Tarragona) Judgment no 94/2012, 5 March. Related action cases: Castilla-La Mancha Superior Court of Justice (TSJ de Castilla-La Mancha), Judgment no 1428, 27 September; Barcelona Provincial Audience (AP Barcelona), Judgments no 467/2009, 14 October and no 427, 16 December; Castellón Provicial Audience (AP Castellón) Judgment no 152/2012, 17 September.

[12] A Coruña Superior Court of Justice (TSJ A Coruña), Judgment no 3012/2014, 27 May, and Alicante Provincial Audience (AP Alicante) Judgment no 32/2014, 13 February.

the Registrar of immovable property it is not uncommon to have doubts since national law institutions do not always correspond to European or foreign law ones (creditors in a public law document are not the creditors any more since they sell their credit through a foreign private document). The interviewed judges are satisfied with the working of the system.

Some lawyers observed that, being subject to parties' hearing in origin, the recognition of provisional measures is complicated. In addition, compliance with this requirement provides the opposing party with the time and the opportunity to adopt measures that will materially impede its execution. It is suggested that provisional measures should be recognisable even when the party was not heard. Otherwise, in order to be sure that the party will not have time to take steps that would allow him to avoid its implementation, it becomes necessary to ask for the provisional measure directly in the execution forum. Data shows that only in two cases the Spanish Courts have adopted preventive measures without having jurisdiction to resolve the issue.[13] It is argued that this kind of split in the court actions is not natural. It is strange, and more complex for the lawyers, to claim the provisional measure in a court different from the one where the substance of the case is being resolved. Anyhow, data shows that Spanish courts have recognised some provisional measures adopted by Member States' courts[14] and that the adoption of provisional measures is frequent in the framework of recognition and enforcement.[15]

Particularly in this regard, judges point to the fact that many aspects of the BIR (Ibis) need to be defined by national law. In Spain, Law 29/2015 on International Cooperation in Civil and Commercial Matters, 30th July, in force from 20 August, has incorporated rules for the implementation of the recognition and enforcement procedure under the Regulation.[16]

iv. Matters Related to Relations with Other Instruments

There are no particular problems in the relation between Brussels I system and other legal instruments. Its implementation has been made in conjunction with other instruments in 23.43 per cent of the cases (75): three cases under the RIR (four per cent), one under Rome II (1.33 per cent), 70 under Brussels IIa (93.33 per cent) and one case under the Maintenance Regulation (1.33 per cent).

v. Conclusion

The BIR system is considered adequate and its application in Spain is not particularly problematic. The difficulties are related to the knowledge of the Regulation itself and to the understanding and interpretation of its concepts. Although the preliminary rulings procedure is easy and there is enough information about it (except for deadlines) Spanish courts have not resorted to the Court of Justice of the European Union (CJEU) on the BIR. Insisting on education and specialisation of lawyers and judges are the most plausible solutions. Along this line, availability of Reports accompanying the Regulation with guiding interpreting criteria and a case law data base would be of help.

---

[13] Barcelona Commercial Court (JM de Barcelona) Writ no /2008, 11 November; Extremadura Superior Court (TSJ Extremadura) Writ no 5/2010, 8 November.

[14] Cádiz Provincial Audience (AP Cádiz) Judgment no 25/2005, 15 September (Maintenance).

[15] ie: Barcelona Provincial Audience (AP Barcelona) Judgment no 15 /2012, 25 January.

[16] Ley 29/2015, de 30 de julio, de cooperación jurídica internacional en materia civil, BOE no 182, 31st July. www.boe.es/diario_boe/txt.php?id=BOE-A-2015-8564.

Some lawyers consider the absence of harmonisation of certain procedural rules such as the time limits and documents to be presented a problem. As to provisional measures, it is suggested that they should be recognised even when the party was not heard since, if the measure was accorded *audita altera parte*, this party would have the time to act in order to impede its enforcement.

As to best practices and possible ways for improvement, reducing the length of time taken to plead jurisdictional issues and for judges to decide upon them would help (ie impose page limits for some written submissions and encourage mediation). Lawyers recall the help provided by forms to ease and speed the processes. The use of new technologies can also assist time- and cost-wise though security of communications would have to be enhanced and guaranteed. This entails a major investment in technologies and in technology training. Anyhow, reducing litigation costs is not always satisfactory since it may affect the quality of justice. The focus should be on the proportionality between costs and the amount of the claim.

B. Applicable Law Issues under the Rome I and Rome II Regulations

i. Rome I

From 2010 to 2015, the RIR has been raised in 31 cases (including one where the Rome Convention was applicable)[17] presented before Spanish courts and Public Registries (Civil and Property) decisions. Its definition of imperative rules was taken as a reference in a court's case dealing with the inscription in the Spanish registry of children born under a surrogate maternity contract[18] while in other cases it is included as a general reference to the normative landscape in the contractual field.

The Regulation has been equally used in cases where the litigants were companies and when they were individuals. Claimants were individuals in 22 cases and companies in nine cases. However, in most cases the defendant was a company (18), followed by a public institution (nine) and, finally, another individual (three). A significant number of cases concerned employment.[19] Consumer contracts,[20] contract resolution,[21] debts or compensatory damages claims are much less frequent.

CJEU case law was only cited in three cases, all of them in second instance court's decisions, to illustrate the concepts of non-contractual liability, labour and consumers' contracts. There was no reference for preliminary ruling to the CJEU.

Applicable law clauses are very frequent in international contracts. They are intensively negotiated on the basis of parties' trust in a particular law (that's why they tend to prefer their own). This way, any dispute on the applicable law can be avoided (parties are very cautious in this regard and do not use the applicable law issue as a dilatory strategy). For the rest of the choice-of-law criteria, Rome I is not seen as a 'model for clarity' and the predictability of this Regulation, as well as that of Rome II, tends to be seen as linked to the resolution of the jurisdiction issue.

---

[17] Madrid Provincial Audience (AP Madrid) Judgment no 39/2014, 3 March.
[18] Valencia Provincial Audience (AP Valencia) Judgment no 286/2011, 23 November.
[19] ie Bilbao Social Court Provincial (JS Bilbao) Judgment no 294/2014, 29 September.
[20] ie Navarra Provincial Audience (AP Navarra) Judgment no 161/2014, 30 June.
[21] León Provincial Audience (AP León) Judgment no 373/2013, 25 September.

When the applicable law issue is not clear, Spanish courts tend to favour the application of forum law. Forum law is well known to them and this avoids the inconvenience of proving foreign law and then interpreting and applying it. According to Spanish law, it is the parties' obligation to prove the content of foreign law. Apart from exceptional circumstances, the judges' intervention in this area is optional.[22]

Under these circumstances, the proof is the main problem for the application of foreign law in Spanish courts. First, most local lawyers find it complex to get hold of the appropriate legal experts in foreign law. Second, these foreign expert opinions are often to be translated. Third, it is obvious that the need of foreign experts entails additional costs in money and time. However, some of the consulted lawyers do not consider that this work excessively prolongs the procedure or raises the costs significantly. On their part, if they wish or are asked to do so, courts need to resort to international judicial cooperation to get information about the applicable foreign law and judges find it difficult to adequately interpret the foreign law and to place it in the proper context. The interviewed judges have not really faced problems in this regard since the applicable law is not generally an issue and, if it is, it does not seem to be hard to determine.

a. Matters Related to the Scope of Application

The only doubt had to do with the characterisation of contractual and non-contractual obligations.

b. Matters Related to the Other Provisions

Lawyers have pointed to the special link between the jurisdiction and the choice-of-law rules and the convenience of resolving the disputes applying forum law. However, in the great majority of cases (29 out of 31) the Regulation is used on its own, without a reference to any other PIL instrument. There is no case of a combined application with the RIIR and only one where it is applied together with the BIR.[23]

c. Conclusion

Despite being considered difficult to read, there are no major problems with RIR beyond the desire for more clear direct solutions in the absence of parties' choice-of-law agreements. Drafting appropriate choice-of-law clauses is considered the best practice in the area.

ii. Rome II

From 2010 until 2015, out of a total of 15 cases, the RIIR has been at issue in situations where the claimants were companies (seven) and individuals (five). The defendant was in the majority of the cases a company (10), in a few an individual (four) and only in one case

---

[22] Foreign law is to be proven by the parties. Courts' intervention in this realm is optional. Arts 281 and 282, Law 7/2000, 7 January, on Civil Procedure -*Ley de Enjuiciamiento Civil*- BOE nº 7, 8 January, and art 33, Law 29/2015, note 16.

[23] Málaga Provincial Audience (TSJ Málaga) Judgment no 777/2015, 14 May.

a public institution. The Regulation was not applicable in one case due to it falling outside its temporal scope.[24]

CJEU case law was cited only in one second instance court's decision. The issue was related to the concept of non-contractual liability. There was no reference for a preliminary ruling to the CJEU.

Most cases dealt with traffic accidents,[25] four were referred to unfair competition situations,[26] one to trademarks. In most of them, the Spanish law was applied due to the regular application of conflict's rules or to the lack of proof of foreign law.[27] Foreign law was applied in few opportunities.[28]

a. Matters Related to the Other Provisions

In the great majority of cases (14), the Regulation is applied on its own without a reference to any other PIL instrument. There is no case of a combined application with the Rome I or BIRs.

b. Conclusion

Beyond its scarcity there is nothing to remark on the RIIR's application in Spain. Difficulties may be related to the proof of foreign law when applicable.

C. Practice/Process

Spanish lawyers consulted agree that the absence of EU common procedural rules is a handicap for applying EU PIL instruments: 'the more harmonized EU procedural laws are, the easier it would be to apply them'. However, whilst they all see this as a very hard and almost impossible goal due to the differing Member States' legal traditions, only some consider this to be a fundamental issue.

Interviewed judges agree on the convenience of certain procedural harmonisation as much as on the difficulties that this endeavour entails. In this regard it is argued that 'it is complex to arbitrate substantive rules setting aside procedural law'. One of them sees no need in harmonising. Others consider that this harmonisation is already taking place without a formal articulation, particularly at the principles' level. What is clearly needed is

---

[24] Madrid Commercial Court no 33 (JM Madrid), Judgment no 2/2014, 9 January (Mexican law was applied).

[25] ie Vizcaya Provincial Audience (AP Vizcaya), Judgment no 306/2013, 13 December; (AP Vigo) Senntence no 293/2014, 16 May; Cáceres Provincial Aucience (AP Cáceres), Judgment 93/2013, 10 April.

[26] Barcelona Provincial Audience (AP Barcelona), Judgments no 228/2014, 26 June and no 209/2014, 11 June, Madrid Commercial Court (JM Madrid) 5 June 2013; and Madrid Provincial Audience (AP Madrid), Judgment no 117/2011, 12 September (concept of non-contractual liability only).

[27] Vigo Provincial Audience (AP Vigo) Judgment no 293/2014, 16 May.

[28] Pontevedra Provincial Audience (AP Pontevedra), Judgments no 469/2012, 6 November and no 522/2012, 13 December; Tuy First Instance Court (JPI Tuy), Judgments of 26 March 2012 and 17 October (Portuguese law; traffic accidents); Madrid Commercial Court no 33 (JM Madrid), Judgment no 2/2014, 9 January (Mexican law, trademarks); and Barcelona Provincial Audience (AP Barcelona) Judgment no 554/2010, 28 October (Belgian law, traffic accident).

that national procedural rules completing the Regulations' prescriptions are adapted to the purposes of these instruments[29] as Law 29/2015[30] has done for BIbisR.

i. Spanish Court Practice in Interpreting the Regulations/Process Issues

The difficulties that judges find in trans-border cases relate to the insufficient knowledge of the instruments both on the lawyers' side (demands are not correctly formulated) and on their own. On the judges' side, the interpretation of Regulations cannot be done in the same way as national law and they argue it is not always easy to find the appropriate applicable jurisprudence. In addition, the low ratio of trans-border cases does not make the study of the EU PIL norms a priority for them. In this regard, it is important to note that PIL subjects were—and still are—not very relevant in the professional preparation of Spanish judges.

Some judges find no problem in interpreting EU Regulations whilst others consider it difficult. The difficulties relate to the terminology and the concepts used in the EU instruments, without forgetting their translations into the different languages. Recitals are said to be taken into consideration for interpretation purposes always (nevertheless in BIR only 6.79 per cent of the cases expressly mention them and in the Rome Regulations only two cases include references to RIR recitals) and CJEU jurisprudence tends to be cited to sustain a decision (28.15 per cent of the BIR cases cited CJEU jurisprudence; 56.32 per cent in second instance and 43.67 per cent in third instance court's decisions, and none in first instance; therefore, in 71.84 per cent of cases CJEU jurisprudence was not expressly cited; as to the Rome Regulations, only one decision included a reference to the CJEU jurisprudence). The European Judicial Atlas in Civil Matters (European E-Justice Portal) is considered a very useful tool. Preliminary questions are considered a good instrument to help uniform interpretation.

In contrast with the mentioned interpretation difficulties, no preliminary question has been referred by Spanish courts on the analysed Regulations, be it on their own motion or responding to a party's petition. It is not frequent that Spanish lawyers feel the need to ask for interpretation to the CJEU. Courts have committed errors but overall the application of the Regulations is acceptable though further explanations and education in EU PIL instruments is felt necessary to improve their application since judges and lawyers are still naturally anchored to their own national law.

It is interesting to note that there are cases where the EU Regulations (Brussels I) are not applicable and, nevertheless, the Spanish courts resort to CJEU jurisprudence in order to provide support for their interpretation, for example, of the national jurisdiction rules.[31]

ii. Cost and Length of Litigation in Cross-border Civil and Commercial Disputes

Cross-border litigation is more expensive if only due to the need to afford the necessary language translations. In addition, when foreign experts and witnesses are needed, their

---

[29] Under the Reg on European order for payment procedure, first instance courts are competent but, in case of opposition, the Reg establishes turning to the contradictory procedure. In cases of debts under labour law the first instance court would have to send the case to the social court.

[30] See n 16.

[31] ie Barcelona Provincial Audience (AP Barcelona) Writ no 32/2015, 12 March.

services and travel costs have to be added to the bill. Nevertheless Spanish jurisdiction is not too expensive and the extra costs of cross-border litigation prevent a claim only when its economic value is not worth it. Beyond the consideration of costs, the risks of obtaining an unsatisfactory judgment and the length of the proceedings are also considered before deciding to initiate a process before the Spanish courts.

The length of the procedures where the BIR was argued in shown in Table 2 below.

Table 2:

Length of the procedures (weeks(w) / months(m))	Percentage of cases
0–6w	0.97
6w–6m	13.26
6–12m	36.89
12–24m	28.80
24–36m	9.06
36–48m	4.53
48–60m	2.58
More than 60m	0.32
Not recorded	3.55

From these cases, 8.41 per cent of the court decisions were not appealed and 77.02 per cent were appealed only once to the corresponding second instance. The 14.56 per cent of the court decisions were appealed twice, to the second and, then, to the third instances.

The duration of the procedures involving the RIR are displayed in Table 3 below.

Table 3:

Length of the procedures (weeks(w) / months(m))	Percentage of cases
0–6w	3.22
6w–6m	29.03
6–12m	29.03
12–24m	19.35
24–36m	3.22
More than 60m	3.22
Not recorded	12.90

In more than half of the cases (19) the first court's decisions were appealed. Second instance decisions were taken to the Supreme Court less frequently (four out of 31 cases).

Under the RIIR the length of the procedures is shown in Table 4 below.

Table 4:

Length of the procedures (weeks(w) / months(m))	Percentage of cases
6w–6m	20
6–12m	13.3
12–24m	33.3
24–36m	6.6
36–48m	6.6
Not recorded	20

In most cases (11) the first court's decisions were appealed. Second instance decisions (four cases) were not taken to the Supreme Court.

iii. Settlement in Cross-border Civil and Commercial Disputes

In one of the interviewed lawyers' words: 'in Spain the settlement culture is scarce'. Although on certain occasions parties' lawyers try to promote agreements before initiating court proceedings and the threat of the claim can be used as a negotiation tool, it is more common to settle once the process is already initiated. When this happens, it is mostly at an advanced point of the procedure, particularly when parties consider that they may lose the case or that it will not be economically convenient to continue due to the procedure's expenses and the uncertainty of its final result. However, overall, once the judicial procedure has started, it is extremely unusual that parties settle their disputes.

iv. Alternative Dispute Resolution for Cross-border Civil and Commercial Disputes

Presently mediation is not a truly material option in Spanish experience. Though cheaper and more efficient than a court or arbitration hearing 'there is no mediation culture in Spain' yet.

Mediation is perceived as a good alternative, particularly in consumer cases, due to lack of proportionality between litigation costs and the claims' amounts. Moreover, in this field the regulatory situation is perceived as very confusing and the EU consumer contract law is considered too complicated to be followed. Mediation could offer a good solution for these conflicts whilst online arbitration—though receiving some support if cheap and easily accessible—is not unanimously accepted. Anyhow, mediation results are still under scrutiny and in certain cases (banks and preferential actions) it is not easy for parties to reach an agreement. In addition, it is perceived that the available information on mediation is not sufficient.

Arbitration is a clear alternative for cross-border commercial litigation. Spanish arbitral institutions are not usually chosen. There is a clear preference for foreign arbitration.

v. *Remedies in Cross-border Civil and Commercial Disputes*

The economic value of the claims presented under the BIR is shown in Table 5 below.

Table 5:

Amounts of the claims (euro)	Percentage of cases
Not recorded	91.58
Less than 1000	4.20
1001–10,000	0.64
10,001–50,000	0.97
50,001–200,000	1.61
200,001–500,000	0.32
500,001–1 million	0.64

Under RIR the amounts were as shown in Table 6.

Table 6:

Amounts of the claims (euro)	Percentage of cases
Not recorded	74.19
1,001–10,000	9.67
10,001–50,000	3.22
50,001–200,000	6.45
200,001–500,000	6.45

Under the RIIR the amounts were as displayed in Table 7.

Table 7:

Amounts of the claims (euro)	Percentage of cases
Not recorded	53.3
Less than 1,000	6.6
1,001–10,000	13.3
10,001–50,000	20
50,001–200,000	6.6

For a big law firm, it is difficult to determine the lowest value of a cross-border civil and commercial claim. The interviewed lawyers pointed out that the minimum value of the claim would be between 20,000 and 500,000 euros.

vi. Conclusion

Spanish experience on cross-border civil and commercial disputes shows a perceived impression that the 'courts are not sufficiently specialized to deal well with trans-border cases'. The reasons lie, beyond the rapid evolution of EU legislation, in the way people join the judicial professions, in the exceptional character of cross-border litigation, and in their heavy workload. Lawyer's expertise does also need furtherance. However, there is a clear perception of a progressive improvement of the Spanish courts' knowledge and use of EU PIL.

D. Preliminary Remarks on Effectiveness of the Current EU PIL Framework in Non-family Civil and Commercial Law

Spanish experience seems to show that current EU PIL is effective. This does not exclude room for improvement. On the contrary, a need for more information, education and training, both for lawyers and for judges and Judicial Attorneys, is needed. In addition, a better adaptation of Spanish procedural rules to BIR I (Ibis) is also missed. Moreover, the proof of foreign law still poses difficulties.

III. Spain's Experience in Cross-border Family Law Disputes

From 2002 to 2015 family law disputes have entailed a large proportion of the international litigation before Spanish courts. In the framework of Brussels IIa Regulation (BIIaR), 295 cases dealt with matrimonial crises, parental responsibility—including child abduction—and maintenance obligations. Maintenance obligations were at issue under BIR (36 out of the 320 BIR registered cases) and, once it came into force, under the Maintenance Regulation (32). The most common cases are divorces and associated parental responsibility and maintenance obligations. Child abduction cases are much less frequent (18/295).

The interviewed lawyers agree on the fact that the demand for legal advice for family cross-border cases has been rising in the last years. It is nationals as much as foreigners demanding it. Due to the characteristics of Spanish immigration, many of the foreigners are of Latin-American and eastern European origin. In some cases, family litigation is related to gender violence cases; ie once the condemned party returns to his country (to avoid imprisonment) the maintenance case arises. Nevertheless, Spanish lawyers do not usually have cross-border cases in their portfolios.

Cases may reach the lawyers as child abduction and, then, derive to a divorce, custody and maintenance claim. They may also arise as a divorce case and derive towards a custody and maintenance claim, or start from the custody and derive towards a maintenance and even child abduction case. These issues usually appear connected.

It is important to recall that in the Spanish judicial system there is no special family jurisdiction. Some of the first instance courts are signified as family courts and, obviously, these cases are assigned to them. Nowadays, 'the number of judges dealing with Family cases is approximately two hundred'. Family court judges are general civil judges and, in the development of their professional career, they do not necessarily remain in these courts. In a judge's words: 'for many judges this is a passing destination'. The more or less experience a judge has in dealing with family issues has a clear influence on the way cases are handled.

A. Jurisdictional and Procedural Issues under the Brussels IIa Regulation

i. Matters Related to Jurisdiction

In 192 out of the 295 cases where the BIIaR was alleged jurisdiction was an issue (65.08 per cent). Spanish courts ended up assuming jurisdiction in 72.91 per cent of the cases (140) and rejecting it in the remaining 27.085 per cent (52 cases).

Courts do not tend to interpret the rules to favour their own jurisdiction. Lawyers perceive that this tendency existed but it is becoming less common. The opposite tendency is perceived since courts prefer avoiding cross-border cases. This is also the view of some of the judges. Anyhow, lawyers are conscious that it is their task to provide the necessary basis to establish the jurisdiction of the court where they present their claim or, on the contrary, its absence—when in the interests of the defendants. In this regard, one judge argues that it is the parties who present the claim and judges 'do not favour one *forum* or another'.

In the lawyers view, the place where the claim is presented is absolutely decisive for the possible results: 'it is fundamental'. There is a natural tendency for a claimant to present the demand in his/her own country considering, among others, language and cultural reasons together with the perception that it could work in his/her favour. When choosing the court, the claimant is taking into consideration not only the procedural issues (as how easy or difficult it could be to notify the defendant) or the costs and duration of the process but, most importantly, the resulting applicable law; in other words, the law that would be more protective of his/her material interests. In this regard, the options offered by the Regulations are useful—particularly for litigants with economic resources—in facilitating forum shopping. In addition, the Regulations' *lis pendens* rule stimulates a 'race to the court' ('the race is feral'). The claimant can, nevertheless, delay the 'race to the court' depending on his/her factual situation: 'when his/her economic situation is good enough and he/she has the custody of the children, waiting and negotiating may be an option'; 'when the economic situation of one of the parties is awful, the demand is presented wherever it is possible'. In this respect, some lawyers' experience shows that the existence of the demand does not always impede the negotiation but can work as a catalyst.

A lawyer argued that in order to avoid forum shopping it would be advisable to switch the present BIIaR alternative forum system towards a hierarchical one. Along this line, a judge points out that the number of jurisdiction options offered by the Regulation may be excessive. However, most of the judges have exceptionally found *lis pendens* cases.[32] Interviewed lawyers have exceptionally dealt with parallel proceedings and do not see it as sensible to create *lis pendens* situations by presenting claims before different jurisdictions once the case has been initiated in one. As they see it, it is not habitual that this kind of dilatory

---

[32] ie Judgment of Madrid Provincial Audience (SAP Madrid), 3 March 2006; Barcelona Provincial Audience (AP Barcelona) Judgment no 161/2015, 20 May; Supreme Court (TS) Judgment no 717/2015, 16 December.

strategy could work for the interest of their clients. One judge points to the fact that the law applicable to divorce and separation is now resolved in many EU countries according to the same rules reduces the risk of finding parallel proceedings.

a. Divorce, Legal Separation and Marriage Annulment

Differences between national legal systems in matrimonial crisis (particularly in parties' economic rights) can be huge and definitively influences the way that the jurisdiction issue is faced by lawyers.

On the judges' view, the application of Regulation 1259/2010 of 20 December 2010 implementing enhanced cooperation in the area of the law applicable to divorce and legal separation (Rome III),[33] has helped very much to resolve the applicable law problem in this area. It is seen as a clear instrument. Anyhow, the applicable law is hardly presented as an issue in cross-border cases where applying Spanish law is the rule. Out of 45 cases where the applicable law was at stake, 26 resulted in the application of Spanish law (57.7 per cent) and 17 of foreign law (37.77 per cent). Judges highlight the difficulties of proving foreign law[34] and, when it is successfully proven, of its interpretation. These cases require a lot of extra time (letters rogatory, appearances) not to mention the additional costs of the procedure. Lawyers add that the 'proof of foreign law is madness'. From this perspective, it is possible to conceive that it can be used as a dilatory strategy.

b. Parental Responsibility

1. Child Abduction

Eighteen out of the 295 cases referring to the BIIaR were child abduction cases.

As to Article 11(6)–(8) BIIaR, judges recognise that this procedure is only used exceptionally and very few cases have been recorded.[35] Nevertheless judges acknowledge that it could be useful when there is a change in the circumstances. On their part, not all the lawyers are aware of it. The ones who are think that it could be useful though one of them does not agree with its existence.

2. Other Issues Related to Parental Responsibility

Overall, the normative situation is considered adequate and no special lacunae are observed despite the fact that 'legal rules can never cover everything'. The entry into force of the 1996 Hague Convention of 19 October 1996 on Jurisdiction, Applicable Law, Recognition, Enforcement and Co-operation in Respect of Parental Responsibility and Measures for the Protection of Children is perceived as an improvement in the Spanish legal system.

As to the 'best interests of the child' one lawyer stated that its interpretation in connection with the proximity principle is not correct since it is important to know about the environment of the non-resident parent. In his view, the 'proximity' criteria and the child's residence leads to nationalistic resolutions which, in most cases, favour the mother's interests.

---

[33] OJ L 343, 29.12.2010.

[34] See n 13.

[35] Granada Provincial Audience (AP Granada), Writ 16 June 2006 (Art 11(6)); Madrid Provincial Audience (AP Madrid), Writ 3 July 2007 (Art 11(8)). See Spanish Report, Aberdeen Centre for PIL www.abdn.ac.uk/law/documents/Conflicts_of_EU_Courts_on_Child_Abduction_Country_Reports_25_May_(Final).pdf.

Another lawyer points to the fact that it is not sufficiently looked upon, that it should be given more importance and more attention should be paid to the minors themselves (hearing the child). Spanish lawyers detect interpretative problems within Spain itself; ie as to the 'best interest of the child', in Valencia it is understood as comprising shared custody whilst that is not the case in the rest of the country. Along this line, another lawyer stresses the convenience of having the divorce and the parent responsibility cases pleaded together.

Judges point to the relative nature of this concept: 'The wide margin of the jurisdiction criteria will always create a dysfunction; for example, when parents are Spanish residents and the child resides with the grandparents in another Member State. The Regulation does not clarify whether the parents are exercising their parental responsibility'. Following Supreme Court doctrine, judges are inclined to understand that the best interests of the child leads to the place where he/she actually stands.

ii. Matters Related to Recognition and Enforcement

In the implementation of the BIIaR 23.72 per cent of the cases dealt with the recognition and enforcement of Member States' courts decisions (70 of 295). In most of them the response was positive (77.14 per cent; 54 of 70 cases). Whilst the majority of these positive cases was only related with the application of this instrument, there were cases where BIR (68.51 per cent—37 of 54 cases) and the Maintenance Regulation (1.85 per cent—one of 54 cases) and other international instruments (1.85 per cent—one in 54 cases) were also involved. The Brussels system principles have also been used to sustain a decision when the Regulations were not applicable.[36]

The percentage of recognition and enforcement rejection was 22.85 per cent (16 of 70 cases). BIIaR was the only instrument leading to the rejection in most cases (87.5 per cent—14 of 16 cases), but the BIR (6.25 per cent—one of 70) and other international sources as the Brussels and Lugano Conventions (12.5 per cent—two of 16 cases) are also mentioned. When other international instruments are the relevant international sources to accept or reject the recognition and enforcement of courts' decisions, reference to the BIIaR is made to support and sustain the legal reasoning of the court and the interpretation of the source at issue.

Lawyers have no difficulty with the recognition and enforcement of Member States' decisions. Judges also think that the system is working well, be it at the courts' or at the Civil Registry level. Public policy or irreconcilable decisions have not been an issue. There may be problems with service (but, overall, they are not taking too long) and with the respect of the minors' and interested parties' rights to a hearing in the foreign jurisdictions.

a. Return of the Child

Out of 18 child abduction cases, a return was ordered in 10 decisions (55.55 per cent) and in six it was rejected (33.33 per cent). In two cases the Spanish courts had no jurisdiction over the claim (11.11 per cent).

---

[36] ie Supreme Court Judgment (STS), 24 October 2007 relied on BIR and BIIaR understanding of default.

b. Relations with Other Instruments

BIIaR was applied in conjunction with other instruments in 29.83 per cent of the cases (88 of 295): with the BIR (81.39 per cent—70 of 88) or the Maintenance Regulation (21.59 per cent—19 of 88) due to the connection of matrimonial crisis and parental responsibility with maintenance obligations. In addition, the 2007 Hague Protocol on the law applicable to maintenance obligations is a source in a small percentage of the cases 3.40 per cent (3 of 88). There is also a reference to the Hague Convention of 25 October 1980 on the Civil Aspects of International Child Abduction.[37]

One of the interviewed lawyers pointed to the difficulty that the interdependency between the Regulations adds to their respective interpretations. 'It would be advisable to have uniform criteria for jurisdiction and applicable law'.[38] Nevertheless, simultaneous application of BIIaR and the Maintenance Regulation does not seem to present any problem for Spanish Judges.

iii. Conclusion

The multiple jurisdiction options under BIIaR are sometimes perceived negatively. To minimise jurisdiction disputes, reducing the optionality provided by BIIaR has been suggested. The habitual residence is proposed as the basic criteria. The courts' best practices are associated with the use of the Guides and the information tools provided by the Council for the Judiciary (CGPJ).[39]

B. Jurisdictional and Procedural Issues and Applicable Law Under the Maintenance Regulation

From 2002 to 2015 Spanish judgments on maintenance obligations based on Article 5(2) of the BIR consists in 36 cases (out of the 309 BIR cases, hence, 11.65 per cent). From 18 June 2011 up to December 2015, 32 Spanish court decisions refer to the Maintenance Regulation. In two of them the Regulation was not applicable for temporal reasons. There is one case where the reference to the Maintenance Regulation is found in combination with the BIR.

Only in one case was the litigant a public institution (3.22 per cent); therefore, in 96 per cent of the cases the litigants were private parties.

96.87 per cent of the cases were centred in maintenance whilst 88.75 per cent (22 cases) were related to divorce and 43.75 per cent (14) to parental responsibility. Despite these percentages, it is interesting to note that in 53.12 per cent of the cases (17) the Maintenance Regulation was applied in combination with BIIaR.

---

[37] Tenerife provincial Audience (AP Tenerife), Writ no 175/2006 18 September.
[38] Divorce and UK resident's children maintenance: Spanish court competent to decide on the divorce would not be entitled to establish the maintenance.
[39] See n 41.

i. *Matters Related to Applicable Law*

The 2007 Hague Protocol has been applied together with the Maintenance Regulation in 21 out of 32 cases (65 per cent). In most cases, forum law was applied (90.90 per cent—30 of 33) whilst the use of foreign law was marginal (15.15 per cent—five of 33).[40] Judges and lawyers point to the fact that, in general terms, the applicable law issue in family law litigation is very much unknown.

Nevertheless, specialised lawyers always evaluate the applicable law issue before deciding where to litigate maintenance cases. Once the jurisdiction has been established, they do not usually find conflicts on the applicable law since forum law is usually applicable. If foreign law is to be applied, the procedure costs inevitably rise due, basically, to the proof of its content and the documents' translation. From this perspective, the applicable law issue could be used as a procedural strategy; be it to avoid the application of foreign law (eluding extra costs and speed the resolution of the case) or to have it applied (delaying the process or trying to force a settlement).

ii. *Matters Related to Recognition, Enforceability and Actual Enforcement of Decisions*

6.25 per cent of the cases were in the field of recognition and enforcement (two of 32). They presented no problem. Both decisions were given by France, a Member State bound by the 2007 Hague Protocol.

iii. *Conclusion*

Costs of maintenance procedures are too high (3,000 euros approximately) for the amount that is usually claimed (300 euros per month approximately). There are difficulties associated with finding the person obliged to pay maintenance when he/she moves to a different country. There are circumstances in which effecting the payments is extremely difficult or impossible. The creation of a fund that would guarantee creditors the payment of a minimum amount may be a solution.

C. Practice/Process

i. *Spanish National Courts' Practice in Interpreting the Regulations*

Both lawyers and judges perceive that interpreting the Regulations is not always easy. They also agree generally on the absence of specialised knowledge of the EU PIL rules and on the 'need of training among judges in international issues related to Family and minors matters', 'judges know that the Regulations exist, but they are not fully aware of their content' and they 'tend to apply their own legal criteria and jurisprudence'. Both of them also

---

[40] Figures explanation: child and mother maintenance were decided in the same case applying national and foreign law respectively. Since there are two maintenance situations, this case is counted twice and included in the two categories: forum/foreign law application.

perceive a normative dispersion that, in the judges' opinion, makes it particularly difficult for practitioners. In this regard, instead of lacunae, a judge feels that there is an EU 'regulatory excess' while others feel that the new norms are sufficient to cover divorce.

When interpreting the Regulations judges say to take 'everything' into consideration. Beyond their recitals and the CJEU jurisprudence, they also resort to Guides of Good Practices and certain resources that the Council for the Judiciary (CGPJ) offers, such as the *Prontuario de Auxilio Judicial Internacional*.[41] In addition, the Spanish Judicial Network of International Judicial Cooperation (REJUE) Contact Points respond to the judges' questions. However, express citation of BIIaR's recitals for interpretative purposes is low (4.06 per cent—12/295 cases). Decisions on the Maintenance Regulation do not include references to recitals. Reference to the CJEU jurisprudence on the BIIaR was made in 11.86 per cent of the cases (35 of 295), mostly (88.57 per cent) in the third instance judgments (32 of 35). First (2.85 per cent—one of 35) and second instance (8.57 per cent, three of 35) courts barely resort to the CJEU jurisprudence. Overall, the result is that in 88.13 per cent of the cases, Spanish courts have not expressly referred to the CJEU case law. As for the Maintenance Regulation, only in one case (out of 32; 3.12 per cent) a second instance court relied on CJEU case law to interpret the 'habitual residence' concept.[42]

Parties have asked Spanish courts to present preliminary questions before the CJEU. Under the BIIaR, this has happened in four cases (1.35 per cent) and the court has always rejected the request. The courts have not presented these questions on their own motion either. One of the interviewed judges mentioned that parties may ask the court to present a preliminary question before the CJEU as a delaying strategy. Anyhow, the procedure before the CJEU is not perceived as complicated and the REJUE offers assistance to Spanish judges willing to use it.

Two of the interviewed lawyers asked the Spanish courts to present a preliminary question once and they felt their experience was not satisfactory on the basis, on the one hand, of the attitude of the Spanish court and, on the other hand, of the delay that it entails in the final resolution of the case. In their regard, the preliminary questions procedure before the CJEU, even when working well, is considered 'very slow'.

As to the absence of EU procedural harmonisation, interviewed judges think that this can be a source of problems. They refer to the situations where it is not clear for them whether decisions from Member States' courts are definitive or have cautionary character. On the Spanish side 'initial measures'—*medidas previas*—have been interpreted by the CJEU as preventive measures when, in our system, they do not have this character. Therefore, it is argued that some procedural harmonisation would be beneficial. Lawyers are divided on this issue. Whilst half of them consider procedural harmonisation absence a clear obstacle for the functioning of the system and would support it, the other half does not give it so much relevance and think it is unnecessary.

ii. Cost and Length of Litigation in Cross-border Family Law Disputes

Lawyers estimate that the costs of the cross-border family law proceedings may double that of a national case. It could be between 7,000 and 8,000 euros approximately in the first year.

---

[41] www.poderjudicial.es/portal/site/cgpj/menuitem.87fc234e64fd592b3305d5a7dc432ea0/?vgnextoid=99556e c8f727f210VgnVCM1000006f48ac0aRCRD&vgnextlocale=en&vgnextfmt=default&lang_choosen=e.

[42] Barcelona Provincial Audience (AP Barcelona) judgment no 58/2015, 20 February.

An average could be around 3,000 euros for the lawyer—the corresponding BAR (*Colegio de Abogados*) establishes a reference tariff scheme and the remaining costs are for the representative *ad litem*, documents, translations and the trips to attend the trial. When there is an appeal, the costs rise and, obviously, its resolution takes longer (two or three years). In the judges' perspective the costs of a cross-border procedure is perceived as high particularly when it is necessary to serve or obtain evidence abroad.

The length of the procedures can be seen in the following tables 8 and 9.

Table 8:

BIIaR	
Length of the procedures (weeks (w)/months (m))	Percentage of cases
Not recorded	5.76
0–6w	0.33
6w–6m	15.25
6–12m	37.96
12–24m	31.18
24–36m	5.08
36–48m	2.71
48–60m	1.35
More than 60m	0.33

There is a high level of appeals to second instance courts (81.69 per cent—241 of 295). Third instance courts have been called to review 39 decisions (13.22 per cent). Only in 15 cases the first instance decision was not contested (5.08 per cent).

Table 9:

Maintenance Regulation	
Length of the procedures (weeks (w)/months (m))	Percentage of cases
6w–6m	3.12
6–12m	34.37
12–24m	46.87
24–36m	15.62

All the cases were appealed to the second instance courts (96.87 per cent) and one of them reached the third instance (3.12 per cent).

In the practitioners' view, the length of a cross-border family law procedure depends 'essentially on the courts'. The judges argue that time for service (or obtaining evidence abroad) also has an influence. Overall, if the case relates to Spanish residents the length of the procedure is 'identical to internal cases' but, when it is necessary to serve someone or obtain evidence abroad, the procedure is delayed. In any case, compliance with the procedural deadlines is not always easy due to the lack of means.

iii. Settlement in Cross-border Family Law Disputes

Lawyers agree that negotiations are desirable and they always advise their clients to take it into consideration. Clients do not always welcome this initiative. Depending on the circumstances, parties prefer resorting to courts directly. Several factors influence this decision particularly the economic situation of the parties and, when there are children, their age. In the last cases, the practical difficulties of implementing an adequate visitation regime (associated with trip costs and school holidays) also leads to a court contest since 'both parties want to have everything'.

Negotiations take place when the process is taking too long but they can also be used as a dilatory strategy. Some parties settle before the trial to avoid their children having to give testimony, some others to avoid costs and/or the time of the proceedings, others due to the pressure from the other party or to the legal uncertainty. Sometimes parties reach an agreement just before the hearings. On other occasions, parties present their agreement to the court during the proceedings. A judge does not perceive differences in this regard between cross-border and purely internal cases. Practitioners as much as judges see no clear pattern for negotiated solutions. This result depends on the particular case and parties' circumstances. Negotiations exist before and during the proceeding.

iv. Alternative Dispute Resolution for Cross-border Family Law Disputes

Interviewed lawyers are divided on this issue. Most of them consider that arbitration could be used in family cross-border matters but it is not sufficiently implemented. Others support mediation as the best option but, though sometimes used, it does not always lead to positive results. Judges perceive that in first instance courts' resort to mediation is becoming more frequent though there are divergent opinions about its success. They also point to the fact that many times they are not aware of the procedure that has to be followed to turn to mediation or that, resorting to mediation, for example in child abduction cases, makes it difficult for them to comply with the procedural deadlines. Additionally, they often find themselves implementing 'a conciliatory role' during the trial. By the stage of the second instance courts resorting to mediation is very difficult.

v. Remedies in Cross-border Family Law Disputes

The amount of the claims are shown in table 10.

Table 10:

BIIaR	
Amounts of the claims (euro)	**Percentage of cases**
Not recorded	90.84
Less than 1,000	8.47
1,001–10,000	0.67

(continued)

Table 10: *(Continued)*

Maintenance Regulation	
Amounts of the claims (euro)	Percentage of cases
Not recorded	59.37
Less than 1,000	37.50
1,001–10,000	3.12

vi. Conclusion

There is a long sustained claim among different Spanish judicial organisations in favour of establishing a special family jurisdiction that would allow the desired specialisation of Courts. The present system, with family courts integrated in the regular civil jurisdiction, does not stimulate judges to remain in these courts and specialise in this field of law.

Regarding the difficulties that the application of the EU family PIL instruments entail judges point to their huge workload which, combined with the relative proportion of cross-border cases, makes it difficult for them to find the time to study. In addition, the procedural deadlines are very short and they need to respond quickly. Lawyers also feel the pressure of short procedural deadlines.

In a large number of cases different Regulations are to be applied simultaneously. In one lawyer's view, resorting to a single Regulation instead of to the existing three (BIIaR, Maintenance and RIIIR) would be a great help. Particularly, the use of the same concepts and criteria in all the instruments is felt as a need. Summarised in a lawyer's words, there is a need to 'elaborate a more uniform and accessible rules' system'. One judge also points to this situation stating that 'the normative dispersion complicates the resolution of the cases'. Though references to the CJEU can solve interpretative problems, Spanish judges have not used them and they delay cases' resolution. A jurisprudence data base and courses and training with judges from different nationalities would help enormously.

D. Preliminary Remarks on Effectiveness of the Current EU PIL Framework in Family Law

In general terms, both lawyers and judges find EU family PIL Regulations' rules sufficient and appropriate. However, in their view, the application of the rules is not fully satisfactory due to the non-sufficient knowledge. It would be necessary to reinforce public information ('TV shows in prime time'), promote courses for judges and legal attorneys and generalise the use of the Guides[43] that should be regularly updated. In addition, the role played by REJUE and the REDUE could be reinforced. 'When the judge and the parties know the EU PIL, everything works much better'.

---

[43] See n 41.

The normative fragmentation united to the absence of clear, coherent and uniform reading of common concepts are felt as major handicaps by the legal operators. Therefore, there is a generally perceived need for more precise concepts in the Regulations, such as 'habitual residence', 'best interests of the child' or 'grave risk' of harm, whose interpretation can be very diverse. Other procedural issues, such as deadlines, service (particularly when it is difficult to locate the addressee) or the proof of foreign law can also bring difficulties. Hence, to ease the application of the Regulations, a better adaptation of internal procedural rules and, particularly, adequate deadlines are needed.

It is suggested that the risk of divergent interpretation of the Regulations between Member States could be reduced through a jurisprudence database helping to identify which norms are applicable and how. In addition, in order to facilitate access to the normative sources and avoid its dispersion as well as to guarantee that family law Regulations work under the same concepts and criteria, it is suggested that family PIL Regulation could be concentrated in a single instrument.

It is argued that the Spanish judicial system could create a specialised family law jurisdiction beyond the general civil one. In addition, the creation of a specialised court in each city or province that centralises the resolution of cross-border family law cases has been suggested.

Sociologically, many of the cross-border family law cases affect people with limited economic resources. The procedures' costs could be reduced if new technologies were used (ie video-conference) and, it has been suggested, translations could be made *ex officio*. In this regard, a judge also pointed to the improvement of the legal aid system—*justicia gratuita*. Other aspects that have also been considered are easing the mechanisms to locate the defendants and debtors abroad and creating a European fund to cover a minimum payment of the maintenance obligations in non-compliance cases. Finally, it is perceived that the development of alternative dispute settlement mechanisms should be further explored and implemented.

IV. Conclusion

The Spanish experience on the application of BIR, BIIaR, RIR, RIIR and the Maintenance Regulation rests in a large number of cases (mostly in the jurisdiction and recognition areas) and it is overall positive. The EU PIL framework is perceived as an effective system to deal with cross-border litigation and even when they are not applicable, Spanish courts use these norms as much as CJEU jurisprudence as reference and interpretative tools. A need to adapt the internal procedural rules is pointed out.

Beyond the existence of successes and errors, there is a perception of a progressive improvement of Spanish courts on the knowledge and use of the EU PIL instruments. However, there is still an important need to improve its expertise by courts and lawyers. The perception that 'courts are not sufficiently specialised to deal with trans-border cases' is due to the rapid evolution of the EU legislation in the Spanish system to join the judicial professions, in the exceptional character of cross-border litigation, and in their heavy workload.

10

Poland

AGNIESZKA FRĄCKOWIAK-ADAMSKA, AGNIESZKA GUZEWICZ
AND ŁUKASZ PETELSKI

I. Introduction

A. Overview of Polish Legal System

In Poland, cross-border proceedings are handled based on legal instruments contained in various legislative acts. These include both national and EU acts of law. National laws apply in matters not regulated by EU legislation. The most important of these are:

— Act of 4 February 2011 on Private International Law,[1] in force from the 16 May 2011, which covers rules on applicable law in nearly all private law relationships (except from those stemming from bills of exchange and cheques).
— Act of 17 November 1964 the Code of Civil Procedure[2] which regulates jurisdiction, recognition and enforceability of judgments in Part IV (Articles 1097 to 115312) entitled 'International civil proceedings'.

B. Methodology of the Research

This report is the result of a research study involving an analysis of case law and interviews with judges and legal practitioners. The researchers analysed around 200 judgments issued by common courts[3] and the Supreme Court[4] (however, of these around 80 were limited to a reference to the rulings without elaborating on the relevant legislation). Altogether, 128 court decisions were analysed. The split according to the relevant EU regulation was as follows:

— Civil and commercial law:
— Brussels I Regulation—58;

---

[1] Journal of Laws 2011, No 80, item 432. English text: http://pil.mateuszpilich.edh.pl/New_Polish_PIL.pdf.
[2] Journal of Laws 1964, No 43, item 296, as amended.
[3] Common courts include: district courts, regional courts and courts of appeal—see Art 1 of Act of 27 July 2001—Law on Common Courts Organisation, Journal of Laws 2001, No 98, item 1070.
[4] See http://network-presidents.eu/page/poland-0.

— Rome I Regulation—18;
— Rome II Regulation—5;
— Family law:
    — Brussels IIa Regulation—31; and
    — Maintenance Regulation—16.

In Poland, even though hearings are public and judgments are announced publicly,[5] judges have no obligation to make their judgments available online. This hinders access to the case law. The scope of the electronic publication of the judgments is determined by the president of the given court on a case-by-case basis, and there is no common framework for case law repositories.[6]

Fourteen interviews were carried out as part of the project: 10 in civil and commercial cases (seven with law practitioners and three with judges) and four in family cases (two with law practitioners and two with judges).

II. Poland's Experience in Cross-border Civil and Commercial Disputes

A. Jurisdictional and Procedural Issues Under the Brussels I Regulation[7]

i. Matters Related to the Scope of Application

In several cases, the proceedings attempted to establish the jurisdiction of Polish courts in matters where the application of the Brussels I Regulation is excluded.[8] There were also ungrounded attempts to exclude the application of the Regulation.[9]

ii. Matters Related to Jurisdiction

The majority of problems are caused by the interpretation and application of Article 5(1) of the Brussels I Regulation. It had frequently gone unnoticed by parties as well as courts of lower instances, but was appropriately remedied by the Supreme Court, that the notion of

---

[5] Art 45 Constitution of the Republic of Poland of 2 April 1997.

[6] Krzysztof Kapelczak and Michał Pieróg, 'Internetowa publikacja orzeczeń sądowych—zagadnienia wybrane' (2015) 1 *Prawo Mediów Elektronicznych* 21.

[7] For Polish writings on Brussels I see for example: Paweł Grzegorczyk, Karol Weitz, *Europejskie prawo procesowe cywilne i kolizyjne* (Vienna, Lexis Nexis, 2012), and on Brussels I bis: Jacek Gołaczyński (ed), *Jurysdykcja, uznawanie orzeczeń sądowych oraz ich wykonywanie w sprawach cywilnych i handlowych. Rozporządzenie Parlamentu Europejskiego i Rady (UE) nr 1215/2012. Komentarz* (Warszawa, Beck, 2015).

[8] Supreme Court, 9 April 2008, V CSK 419/07—case regarding the enforceability of judgments issued as a result of the hearing of claims put forward by former spouses arising from an agreement regulating the repayment of debt incurred prior to the dissolution of the marriage.

[9] Supreme Court, 13 April 2011, V CSK 506/10—case in which the insolvency administrator demanded the repayment of debt comprising part of the bankruptcy estate, arising from agreements entered into by the company subject to prior bankruptcy proceedings.

'contract' contained in Article 5(1)(a) should be interpreted autonomously,[10] whereas the notion of 'the place of performance of the obligation'[11] should be interpreted considering the provisions of substantive civil law relevant to the legal relationship that exists between the parties to the contract.[12]

Furthermore, the courts tend to classify the claims arising from a company's founding act in a manner which lacks consistency. By and large, as it appears to be in line with the case law of the Court of Justice of the European Union ('CJEU' or 'Court of Justice'),[13] the Polish case law generally accepts that claims arising from a company's founding act should be treated as contractual claims.[14] On one occasion, however, the Supreme Court adopted a different stance on this issue.[15] In particular, in its decision of 2011 it stated that Article 5(1) of the Brussels I Regulation indicated that the provision applied solely to contractual obligations.[16] The Supreme Court went on to emphasise that a commercial company's founding act, and the legal relationship it established, was not characterised by the afore-mentioned features. The above conclusion was drawn by the Supreme Court from the fact that it is not legitimate to state that a company is the debtor of its shareholders and the shareholders are the company's creditors, or the other way round. In the abovementioned ruling, the Supreme Court decided that a company was an entity where its shareholders were entitled to remedies 'similar to property rights', ie ownership rights, and the company's founding act was not a contractual obligation but was rather more similar to a property-law agreement.

The interpretation of Article 5(3) of the Brussels I Regulation also raises certain doubts. The case law of the Supreme Court applies primarily the autonomous interpretation of the notion of 'delict' and 'quasi-delict' as well as the interpretation of the 'place where the harmful event occurred or may occur.'[17]

Another problem which has come up in the case law is related to the situation where after the completion of the fact-finding procedure it is revealed that no tort has been commit-ted. In such a situation the parties sometimes argue that, since no tort was committed in the case, Article 5(3) should not be applicable. The Court of Appeal in Wrocław, however, decided that at the stage of examination of jurisdiction, usually at the beginning of the proceedings, the court should decide whether the claim is based on tort or not. However, the above does not refer to a determination of whether 'a tort, delict or quasi-delict' actually occurred.[18]

---

[10] Supreme Court, 5 April 2007, II CSK 260/06.

[11] Save for the exception of a contract for the sale of goods or the provision of services referred to in Art 5(1)(b).

[12] Supreme Court, 22 November 2013, III CSK 13/13; Supreme Court, 27 June 2014, CSK 715/13; and Supreme Court, 29 June 2010, III CSK 255/09.

[13] Case 34/82 *Martin Peters Bauunternehmung GmbH v Zuid Nederlandse Aannemers Verening* [1983] ECR 987.

[14] Court of Appeal in Białystok, 14 July 2011, I ACa 246/11; and Supreme Court, 5 September 2012, IV CSK 589/11.

[15] Supreme Court, 26 January 2011, IV CSK 284/10. As in Poland judgments are not considered to be prec-edents in the strict sense of the word, both attitudes are valid. It is up to the lower courts to decide which one to follow.

[16] ie contracts giving rise to an obligation and clearly identifying the debtor and the creditor, as well as the time, manner and place of performance of the obligation.

[17] Supreme Court, 7 October 2011, II CSK 51/11.

[18] Court of Appeal in Wrocław, 2 September 2011, I ACa 830/11.

The Brussels I Regulation, in Sections 3, 4 and 5, provides for different grounds of jurisdiction in different types of cases. Examples of problems in this respect include:

— Problems associated with the interpretation of Article 11(2) regarding the admissibility of a direct claim against an insurer;[19] and
— Mistaken interpretation by courts of lower instances, remedied by the Supreme Court, of the notion of 'the place where the employee habitually carries out his work or ... the last place where he did so' (Article 19(2)) in cases of a temporary delegation of an employee to work on the territory of a different Member State.[20]

It frequently happens that the parties do not recognise the need for a strict interpretation of some of the provisions of EU regulations, for example Article 22 of the Brussels I Regulation. Nevertheless, the obligation of a strict interpretation of this provision has correctly been identified by Polish courts which decided that neither cases whose subject matter was an earnest money for the purchase of real estate[21] nor cases referring to real estate solely in the context of contractual payment dates[22] might be qualified as cases concerning rights in rem in immovable property. In its decision of 26 January 2011, the Supreme Court stated that Article 22(2) should not apply in cases for the determination of suspension of voting rights stemming from the possession of shares in a company.

Article 24 of the Brussels I Regulation allows a court to gain jurisdiction in cases where the defendant entered an appearance. However, the above does not apply in the situation where the appearance was entered to contest the jurisdiction. The present research indicates that problems may arise in the case where the defendant raises objections against the jurisdiction and, at the same time, objections of a substantive nature. It was decided that in such a situation no engagement in a dispute pursuant to Article 24 took place.[23]

The vast majority of the legal practitioners who were interviewed stated that there was a visible tendency among Polish judges to interpret EU regulations in such a way as to grant jurisdiction to the courts of another Member State. Both legal practitioners and judges believe that the rules of jurisdiction in the Brussels I Regulation are highly predictable (as stated in Recital 11), and there are no gaps in the area of jurisdiction in civil and commercial matters within the EU private international law framework.

iii. Matters Related to Recognition and Enforcement

The present research[24] indicates that in Poland parties excessively often claim a contradiction of the judgment with the public policy. However, it needs to be emphasised that the

---

[19] Court of Appeal in Katowice, 6 March 2012, I ACz 186/12; and Court of Appeal in Poznań, 28 August 2014, I ACz 1066/14.
[20] Supreme Court, 30 October 2012, II PK 77/12.
[21] Court of Appeal in Katowice, 20 November 2009, I ACa 400/09.
[22] Court of Appeal in Poznań, 27 September 2012, I ACz 1589/12.
[23] Court of Appeal in Białystok, 14 July 2011, I ACa 246/11; Court of Appeal in Szczecin, 30 November 2012, I ACz 813/12; and Supreme Court, 5 April 2007, II CSK 260/06.
[24] For same conclusions see Paweł Grzegorczyk, 'Stosowanie rozporządzenia Rady (WE) nr 44/2001 w sprawach dotyczących uznawania i wykonywania orzeczeń sądów państw obcych na tle polskiej praktyki sądowej' (2016) 10 *Europejski Przegląd Sądowy* 18–26.

courts interpret the provision of Article 34(1) of the Brussels I Regulation correctly.[25] In particular, the courts tend to establish that the use of the public policy clause constitutes an exception to the general rule and thus this provision may not be interpreted broadly.[26]

The problem of recognition of decisions regarding the costs of the proceedings poses certain difficulties in situations where such a decision constitutes a separate judgment existing aside of the substantive judgment issued in the case, and it is necessary to evaluate the existence of the grounds for non-recognition provided for in Article 34. Polish courts claim that such an evaluation does not apply to decisions regarding costs, and it is the substantive ruling that should be analysed in this respect.[27]

A common problem associated with the application of Article 34 is the determination of the person who should bear the burden of proof in establishing the grounds for the refusal of enforcement of a judgment. The prevailing opinion is that the obligations in this respect, subject to the applicant's obligation to present documents referred to in Article 53 of the Brussels I Regulation, are borne by the defendant in the proceedings for *exequatur*. The only exception to this rule is found in Article 34(2), meaning that the applicant who raises an objection that the document instituting the proceedings was not served upon him in sufficient time and in such a way as to enable him to arrange for his defence, should refer to factual circumstances and present evidence to prove this objection.[28]

For a judgment given in a Member State to be declared enforceable in another Member State, the judgment is to be still enforceable, at the time of issuing the declaration, in the Member State where it was given. Otherwise, if the judgment is no longer enforceable in the Member State of origin, the court should dismiss the request for the declaration of enforceability of the judgment.[29]

The Brussels I Regulation does not contain any provisions regarding the capacity to be sued in the context of an application for the declaration of enforceability of a judgment issued against joint and several debtors. The Supreme Court has decided that the capacity to be sued shall be given to the parties who are jointly and severally liable.[30] An exception to this rule is allowed in the situation where the application for the recognition is made in relation to a part of the judgment, and this part does not relate to all the parties or participants to the proceedings.[31]

The Supreme Court has further stated that an applicant must lodge a single application for the declaration of enforceability of a judgment issued against all the debtors referred to therein in the event the performance is indivisible.[32] However, in the event the awarded performance is divisible, the applicant may, at his own discretion, file an application against

---

[25] Disputes relating to the conditions for a refusal to recognise a judgment were tackled in a number of cases, eg Supreme Court, 21 March 2007, I CSK 434/06; Court of Appeal in Białystok, 21 December 2007, I ACa 543/07; Supreme Court, 9 December 2010, IV CSK 224/10; and Supreme Court of 7 November 2008, IV CSK 256/08.

[26] Supreme Court, 13 April 2011, V CSK 335/10.

[27] Supreme Court, 27 November 2008, IV CSK 73/08 (Art 34(2)); and Court of Appeal in Katowice, 2 January 2013, V ACz 223/12 (Art 34(1)).

[28] Supreme Court, 13 April 2011, V CSK 335/10; and Supreme Court, 27 November 2008; IV CSK 74/08.

[29] Court of Appeal in Szczecin, 17 January 2013, I ACz 407/12.

[30] Supreme Court, 20 December 2012, I CSK 397/12.

[31] ibid and Supreme Court, 18 January 2007, I CSK 330/06.

[32] Supreme Court, 21 March 2007, I CSK 434/06.

only one of the debtors, some of the debtors or all of the debtors against whom the judgment was declared to be enforceable.[33]

The issue of allowing third parties with a legal interest in the decision to join the proceedings (indirect intervention) raises certain doubts as well. The Supreme Court has decided that the purpose of EU legislation was to simplify the proceedings for granting *exequatur* in the State where the judgment was to be executed, and to this end the legislator created proceedings which constitute an autonomous and closed system of legal remedies.[34] Consequently, the admissibility of filing remedies by the interested third parties against a first instance court's judgment confirming enforceability is excluded even if these third parties would be entitled to claim such a remedy in the state of enforcement.[35]

Doubts have arisen also in relation to the form of the hearing during which the court intends to declare a judgment enforceable. Considering the provision of Article 41 of the Brussels I Regulation (second sentence), it seems that the EU legislator has introduced a two-instance model of considering applications with the first instance being limited to a formal examination of the application and an 'automatic' declaration of enforceability without analysing the substantive legal issues. Because at this stage a debtor is not able to make any submissions on the application at all, it must be assumed that it is inadmissible for the court of first instance to summon a hearing.[36]

The provisions of the Brussels I Regulation indicate clearly which documents should be presented by a party seeking the recognition of a judgment or a declaration of enforceability. The question arises as to whether the court may demand that the applicant presents other documents which are not specified in the provisions of the Regulation. The Supreme Court, in its ruling of 27 November 2008, decided that the court considering an application had to bear in mind that it was necessary to determine if the case fell within the scope of application of the Regulation. If the evidence gathered in the case is not sufficient to evaluate the nature of the case, the court is entitled to demand that the person who is the beneficiary of the proceedings presents additional information in writing or orally.[37]

iv. Conclusion

a. Problem Areas

First, both the parties' representatives and the lower courts have a tendency to interpret EU regulations from the perspective of national law. Consequently, the notions adopted by the EU legislator are interpreted from the perspective of the institutions of the Polish legal system. The parties' representatives and the judges sometimes ignore the fact that certain notions should be interpreted autonomously (eg the notion of 'contract' or 'the place of performance of an obligation' referred to under Article 5(1)(b) of the Brussels I Regulation). Furthermore, it also happens that EU institutions are 'fitted' to the Polish legal regime which adversely affects the effectiveness of EU provisions. An analysis of available case law has revealed also situations when courts issue judgments based on national law rather

---

[33] ibid.
[34] ibid.
[35] ibid.
[36] Supreme Court, 14 December 2006, I CSK 262/06.
[37] Supreme Court, 27 November 2008, IV CSK 74/08.

than EU provisions if the wording of the EU law and the relevant domestic legislation is similar.

Second, the interviews conducted by the researchers indicate that courts interpret EU regulations in such a way as to be able to determine that jurisdiction should be given to the courts of a different Member State. That way judges are able to pass on cases of a cross-border nature, which are considerably more complex than cases with no foreign element.

The problems associated with the interpretation of EU regulations may arise from the lack of knowledge of the case law of the CJEU. The analysis conducted by the researchers revealed that CJEU rulings were quoted in only 38 per cent of the judgments (in the cases relating to the Rome I Regulation the figure was even lower, at 28 per cent).

Another problem is the reluctance of the common courts to ask preliminary questions to the Court of Justice of the European Union. Until the end of December 2015, the common courts had asked only 23 such questions. The Supreme Court asked 13 questions. Six questions were related to cross-border cases, out of which two concerned Regulations within the scope of the present research.[38] The limited number of questions is a result of not only the attitude of courts, but also the fact that the parties (the parties' representatives) very rarely seek such questions to be asked. The present research indicates that in only four per cent of the cases the parties' representatives (or the parties themselves) made a request for reference for a preliminary ruling of the CJEU.

There are also situations when Polish courts themselves decide in cases which should be the subject matter of a question directed to the CJEU. For example, in a case that was pending before the Supreme Court, a party lodged a motion for a question to be asked to the Court of Justice in order to determine whether Article 5(3) of the Brussels I Regulation applied in matters related to the liability of a limited company's directors with respect to this company's outstanding obligations. The Supreme Court decided to answer the question independently and decided that Article 5(3) was applicable.[39] The issue was addressed nearly two years later by the Court of Justice of the European Union in the *ÖFAB* case.[40] Although the ruling of the CJEU was very similar to the above Supreme Court decision, it needs to be emphasised that the Supreme Court resolved the issue in question on its own rather than by asking a preliminary question.

Finally, problems connected with the interpretation of EU regulations may also be the consequence of an inaccurate examination and omission of the contents of the recitals. The analysis conducted by the researchers indicated that in only four per cent of the judgments the courts referred to the intent of the EU legislator as expressed in the recitals.

b. Possible Solutions

The problems associated with the application of the Brussels I Regulation are caused primarily by the erroneous interpretation of the provisions of the Regulation, which arises from the lack of knowledge of the case law of the CJEU. In order to minimise this problem,

---

[38] One related to Brussels I: Case C-70/15 *Emmanuel Lebek v Janusz Domino*, judgment of the CJEU was adopted on 7 July 2016, nyr, another one to Brussels II a: Case C-294/15 *Edyta Mikołajczyk v Marie Louise Czarnecka, Stefan Czarnecki*, opinion of Advocate General Melchior Wathelet was adopted on 26 May 2016, ECLI:EU:C:2016:367.

[39] Supreme Court, 7 October 2011, II CSK 51/11.

[40] Case C-147/12 *ÖFAB Östergötlands Fastigheter AB v Frank Koot and Evergreen Investments BV* EU:C:2013:490.

it is recommended to significantly increase the number of training sessions for judges. This solution was proposed also by the majority of respondents participating in the study.

B. Applicable Law Issues Under the Rome I and Rome II Regulations[41]

i. *Rome I*

a. Matters Related to the Scope of Application

Article 1 of Rome I specifies the scope of application of the Regulation. In spite of a seemingly clear specification of cases in which the Regulation is applicable, this provision may give rise to a level of doubt. One example is cases associated with bankruptcy proceedings, such as cases concerning the exclusion of specific movable property from the bankruptcy estate. In one of the cases subject to the study a party quoted the provisions of the Rome I Regulation when claiming the invalidity of a contract for the transfer of ownership in a movable property to a person who had been declared bankrupt. However, the court correctly stated that in the case in question it was the provisions of the Council Regulation (EC) number 1346/2000 on insolvency proceedings[42] that should have been applied, as they constituted the *legis specialis*.[43]

Problems associated with the scope of application arise also in the case of the Rome II Regulation. The specific nature of the case often requires a determination of whether it is the particular provisions of the Rome I Regulation or the Rome II Regulation that should be applied. It turns out that the qualification of a claim as arising from a tort does not automatically necessitate the applicability of the connecting factors provided for under the Rome II Regulation. It is necessary to emphasise at this point that the Rome II Regulation provides for an exception to the general rule stipulated in Article 4(1) in the form of a corrective rule based on the close connection clause (Article 4(3)). It is difficult to determine a close connection with another State which may potentially pose problems.[44]

b. Matters Related to the Uniform Rules

In Article 3 of the Rome I Regulation the EU legislator adopted a general rule, according to which a contract is subject to the applicable law selected by the parties. The fact that parties to a contract choose the governing law is not usually a problem in the Polish legal practice. The parties often specify the law which their contractual relationship is to be governed by in the relevant agreement itself. Therefore, in the opinion of most legal practitioners interviewed in the study, the problem of applicable law is not a frequent reason for misunderstanding between the parties.

However, problems do arise in the situation where the parties choose the applicable law for instance by means of a clause in the agreement stipulating the need to refer to a specific

---

[41] See for example: M Czepelak, *Międzynarodowe prawo zobowiązań Unii Europejskiej* (Vienna, LexisNexis, 2012) or Maria-Anna Zachariasiewicz, 'Uwagi na temat wybranych orzeczeń sądów polskich z zakresu rozporządzenia nr 593/2008 o prawie właściwym dla zobowiązań umownych (Rzym I)' (2016) *Europejski Przegląd Sądowy* 10, 27–35.

[42] Reg No 1346/2000 of 29 May 2000 on insolvency proceedings [2000] OJ L 160 1–18.

[43] Circuit Court in Rzeszów, 17 June 2014, VI Ga 120/14.

[44] Court of Appeal in Szczecin, 29 May 2014, I ACa 212/14.

law with respect to a part of the contract. The above leads to a situation where the particular elements of the legal relationship will be subject to different legal regimes. In one case, the parties included the Institute Frozen Food Clauses (applied on the grounds of common law) in their agreement. This led to a situation where the agreement was governed by two legal systems—the Polish law (selected implicitly by the parties by way of reference to Polish statutes in the end notes) and the English law (within the scope indicated in the clause).[45]

The possibility of choosing the applicable law for particular parts of the contract is an extremely useful solution for the parties. It may be used by the parties in order to avoid certain mandatory provisions (ius cogens), which are not favourable to them. One example is the choice of foreign law (other than Polish) for the part of the legal relationship relating to liquidated damages. Pursuant to Polish civil law, a debtor may demand a reduction in liquidated damages in the event that the amount of the damages is grossly excessive (Article 484(2) of the Civil Code).[46] In an interview conducted as a part of the study it was revealed that the choice of a foreign law restricted to provisions related to liquidated damages may secure the person entitled to receive such liquidated damages against the reduction of their amount by the court (reduction of damages).

Pursuant to Article 4(3) of the Rome I Regulation, where it is clear from all the circumstances of the case that the contract is manifestly more closely connected with a country other than that indicated in paragraphs 1 or 2 of Article 4, the law of that other country shall apply. The aforementioned provision contains certain vague notions ('it is clear' that the contract is 'manifestly more closely' connected), which raise numerous doubts regarding their interpretation. The closer connection clause is also a source of doubt in relation to the Rome II Regulation.[47]

Case law analysis indicates that, commendably, Polish courts correctly apply Article 5 of the Rome I Regulation which regulates the applicable law in relation to contracts of carriage.[48] Nevertheless, Article 6 of the Rome I Regulation which deals with the applicable law regarding consumer contracts is more problematic. The Regulation enables the parties to choose the applicable law in line with the general rule contained in Article 3. The interpretation of Article 6 was the subject matter of a judgment of the Supreme Court.[49] The Court held that while it was true that Article 6(2) and (3) of the Rome I Regulation enabled the parties to a consumer contract to choose a different legal system to govern the contract between them, this provision did not allow the inclusion of a clause stipulating the choice of a foreign law in the general terms of the contract. This is because the choice of the law applicable to the agreement (in the light of Article 3) must be based on the actual intent of the parties, and thus must be the result of individual arrangements between them.[50]

The applicable law for individual employment contracts is dealt with by Article 8 of the Rome I Regulation. It should be emphasised that in Poland this provision is quoted frequently by the parties for the purpose of determination of applicable law for social insurance issues. The courts, however, agree that the legal relationship which is the source

---

[45] Court of Appeal in Szczecin, 29 September 2014, I ACa 455/14.
[46] Civil Code of 24 April 1964, Journal of Laws of 2016 item 380.
[47] Court of Appeal in Szczecin, 29 May 2014, I ACa 212/14.
[48] Circuit Court in Szczecin, 12 February 2015, VIII Ga 416/14; and Court of Appeal in Rzeszów, 7 November 2013, I ACa 332/13.
[49] Supreme Court, 17 September 2014, I CSK 555/13.
[50] ibid.

of social insurance entitlement and the social insurance relationship itself are two distinct legal relationships which may be subject to the legal systems of different Member States.[51]

c. Conclusion

1. Problem Areas

Giving Priority to Polish Law

The work carried out by the researchers indicates that judges often give priority to the law of the forum, ie the Polish law. This was the opinion of the majority of the law practitioners and judges participating in the interviews. This is mainly because of the lack of knowledge of foreign legal systems and the difficulties associated with determining the contents of foreign law.

Problems with Determining the Applicable Law

In order to determine the contents of the foreign law, Polish judges have to turn to the Ministry of Justice. This solution is time-consuming and often proves ineffective. The advantage is that the provisions of foreign law (along with their translation into Polish) are filed with the documents of the case, which enables the parties to familiarise themselves with the contents of the foreign law.

Lack of Obligation to Inform Parties of the Intention to Apply Foreign Law

Both judges and legal practitioners emphasised the fact that, according to the Polish civil procedure, the judge is not obliged to inform the parties that he intends to apply the law of another country.[52] Such a solution would no doubt boost the effectiveness of the provisions of the Rome I and Rome II Regulations. It would enable the parties to undertake steps to protect their interests. Furthermore, if the parties were informed of the intention of the judge to apply the law of another Member State, they would most certainly provide the judge with various types of information on this legal system (case law, academic publications) which could facilitate the resolution of the case.

High Costs of Cross-border Proceedings

The application of foreign law increases the costs of the proceedings both at the preliminary stage and during the main proceedings. The increase in costs at the preliminary stage is a result of, among others, the fact that the parties' representatives commission opinions regarding the contents of the foreign law, the corresponding legal doctrine and available case-law or seek to provide judges with certified translations of foreign legal acts. The costs of the proceedings can be adversely affected by, among others, the appointment of an expert in the area of foreign law.

---

[51] Court of Appeal in Gdańsk, 11 May 2015, III AUa 155/14; Court of Appeal in Warsaw, 18 February 2014 III AUa 2923/12; Circuit Court in Olsztyn, 25 September 2013, IV U 3152/12; and Supreme Court, 6 June 2013, II UK 333/12.

[52] As opposed to eg German law. See para 139 of Zivilprozessordnung of 5 December 2005 (BGBl. I S 3202; 2006 I S 431; 2007 I S 1781), and judgment of Bundesgerichtshof, 19 December 1975, I ZR 99/74.

Incomplete Nature of the Regulations

The work carried out by the researchers indicates that, overall, there are no significant gaps in the provisions of the Rome I and Rome II Regulations. This is due to the fact that both regulations contain a general rule allowing the determination of the applicable law. However, it is argued that it would be useful if Rome I contained detailed provisions specifying the applicable law in corporate cases. In the case of a share transfer agreement there is no correlation with the registered office of the given company. This means that, for example, in the case of a German shareholder who is a German citizen, selling shares in a Polish company to a Polish citizen on the territory of Poland, the applicable law is the German law since there is no other choice provided.

2. Possible Solutions

In order to increase the effectiveness of the provisions of the Rome I and Rome II Regulations, it would seem desirable to introduce additional solutions enabling faster and more effective determination of the contents of foreign law. In order to facilitate access to the contents of foreign law, it is argued that each Member State should possess a list of experts who could be contacted regarding the contents of the foreign provisions and their interpretation, case law and opinions contained in the legal literature. Another possible solution would be to appoint judges in each Member State (eg one judge for each region of appeal) who would be responsible for providing judges from other Member States with information regarding the case law and the doctrine in the given case. Facilitating the system of exchange of information would surely make it easier for courts to issue rulings based on foreign law.

Finally, it is to be emphasised that an alignment of the applicable law with jurisdiction would also be a favourable solution. Courts know their own legal system best and issuing judgments based on national legislation would be the most favourable solution from the legal (knowledge of the legal provisions, case law and doctrine) as well as technical (speed of resolving cases) perspective, and would ensure the highest quality of the outcome of the legal proceedings.

C. Practice/Process

As regards civil and commercial cases, the work carried out by the researchers indicates that there is a growing need for legal advice in cross-border disputes. Legal advice regarding cross-border cases is sought in principle by legal entities (with registered offices in Poland or abroad). Natural persons (including consumers) do not usually seek legal advice. The vast majority of cross-border disputes arise from contracts. Disputes arising from non-contractual obligations are much less frequent. The parties most frequently pursue monetary claims. In principle, the value of the object of the dispute in cross-border cases is usually very high. Class-action lawsuits in cross-border cases are extremely rare. None of the law practitioners participating in the study ever worked on such a case.

i. *Poland's National Courts' Practice in Interpreting the Regulations/Process Issues*

The present research has revealed that the provisions of EU regulations are interpreted in such a way so as to enable the determination that the given Polish court does not have jurisdiction. Where the court determines that it has jurisdiction over the given case, it will frequently interpret EU Regulations in such a way so as to be able to apply Polish law. In the event of establishing Polish jurisdiction, the courts very often apply (and refer to in their writs) the Polish rules of civil procedure.

ii. Cost and Length of Litigation in Cross-border Civil and Commercial Disputes

a. General Provisions Regarding Costs of Proceedings in Cross-border Cases

The principles applicable to the costs of the proceedings are laid down in the 2005 Act on Court Fees in Civil Cases.[53] The Act does not contain any specific provisions for cross-border cases. In cases involving non-property rights and certain cases involving property rights, a fixed fee is charged at the amount specified in the Act, which is independent of the value of the object of the given dispute.[54] In cases involving property rights a proportional fee is charged at five per cent of the value of the object of the dispute. However, the fee may not be lower than PLN 30 or higher than PLN 100000.[55] The limitation of the amount of the fee makes the pursuit of claims of a high value before Polish courts very favourable.

b. Costs of the Proceedings and Applications for Security

In Poland, it is extremely popular (including in commercial cases of a cross-border nature) to file applications for a so called 'security'. Pursuant to Articles 730–730(1) of the Polish Code of Civil Procedure, security may be requested in every civil case heard by the court or arbitration court.

Filing a request for security allows the parties to obtain preliminary information as to whether their claims are grounded. The plaintiff is obliged to substantiate his claim already at the stage of the proceedings for security. Dismissal of the application for security may suggest that the claim will (at the stage of the main proceedings) probably not be sustained. Therefore, it is a very practical possibility from the economic point of view.[56]

The cross-border element influences the duration of the proceedings. The determination of the applicable law is not, in principle, a very time-consuming activity. However, the duration of the proceedings is extended due to the need to determine the content of foreign law, case law of foreign courts and the foreign doctrine. Duration of the proceedings in cross-border cases is also influenced by difficulties in delivering notifications and the need to have the delivered documents translated.

iii. Settlement in Cross-border Civil and Commercial Disputes

The provisions of the Polish Code of Civil Procedure do not provide for any specific rules on the conclusion of settlement agreements in cross-border cases. The limitations

---

[53] Act on Court Fees in Civil Cases of 28 July 2005, Journal of Laws 2005, No 167, item 198.
[54] ibid, art 12.
[55] ibid, art 13.
[56] A request for security is subject to a court fee of PLN 100 (equal to around EUR 23) pursuant to the Act on Court Fees in Civil Proceedings, art 69(1). On the other hand, the court fee payable for filing a statement of claim amounts to, in principle, 5 per cent of the value of the object of the dispute, capped at PLN 100000 (equal to around EUR 23300).

introduced by the Polish legislator therefore apply to all kinds of disputes. A settlement agreement may be concluded as a result of mediation or conciliatory proceedings.

The present research indicates that the conclusion of a settlement agreement most frequently takes place at an earlier stage before going to the court.

Among the various factors that influence the conclusion of a settlement agreement, the following may be listed: (i) the intent to continue cooperation between the parties, (ii) accruing costs of the proceedings, (iii) the duration of the proceedings, (iv) the unpredictability of the outcome, and (v) the nationality of the parties (Poles rarely tend to seek a settlement).

It is believed that the willingness to settle would be greater if the judge was obliged to inform the parties of the planned outcome of the case.[57] The parties, in anticipation of the future ruling, would be more inclined to negotiate.

D. Preliminary Remarks on Effectiveness of the Current EU PIL Framework in Civil and Commercial Law

Where civil and commercial cases are concerned, the effectiveness of the EU PIL regulations is rather high. A tendency has been observed that the higher instance the court engaged in the given case is, the more effective it proves in the application of EU law.

The courts of lower instances have a tendency to interpret the regulations from the perspective of national law, and the notions adopted by the EU legislator are interpreted from the perspective of the institutions of the Polish legal system. However, this approach is normally corrected by higher instance courts. The courts favour the application of Polish law. It does not often happen that a court refers to the judgments of the Court of Justice. Not many of the judgments of the Polish courts are published.

The Polish Supreme Court handles the application of EU regulations quite well (it often quotes judgments of the Court of Justice), although it tends to independently interpret the regulations even in situations where it would seem more appropriate to seek a preliminary ruling from the CJEU.

III. Poland's Experience on Cross-border Family Law Disputes

A. Jurisdictional and Procedural Issues Under the Brussels IIa Regulation[58]

i. Matters Related to the Scope of Application

Available case law has raised the question whether the Brussels IIa Regulation applies to contact between grandparents and grandchildren. The court of first instance rejected the

---

[57] As is eg in German law. See para 139 of Zivilprozessordnung of 5 December 2005 (BGBl. I S 3202; 2006 I S 431; 2007 I S 1781), and judgment of Bundesgerichtshof, 19 December 1975, I ZR 99/74.

[58] See for example Piotr Mostowik, *Władza rodzicielska i opieka nad dzieckiem w prawie prywatnym międzynarodowym* (Kraków, JAK, 2014).

application of a Polish grandmother for contact with her minor grandson habitually resident in England, on the grounds of Article 8 of the Regulation. The court of second instance set aside the above mentioned decision, indicating in one sentence that the Regulation applied to contact between parents and their children but not to contact between grandparents and their grandchildren.[59] This issue, however, is not entirely clear, although the Guide to Good practice suggests the applicability of the Regulation in such circumstances.[60]

Another problem is related to the question whether the declaration of enforceability on the grounds of the Brussels IIa Regulation covers also those decisions which are subject to an appeal. A court of the first instance erroneously applied the provisions of the Polish Civil Procedure Code and required the plaintiff to apply for a declaration of enforceability of a French ruling issued in a parental responsibility case to present a proof that that judgment was in force. The court of appeal decided that the issue was not governed by the provisions of the Civil Procedure Code, but solely by the provisions of the Brussels IIa Regulation, which indicated that decisions subject to an appeal were also entitled to be recognised and declared enforceable.[61]

ii. Matters Related to Jurisdiction

Most of the problems of jurisdiction arise from the fact that some (especially first instance) courts interpret the provisions of the Brussels IIa Regulation from the perspective of Article 58 of the Polish Family and Guardianship Code, which stipulates that the court hearing the case for divorce is obliged to decide on the parental responsibility over the minor child of both parents. It happens that the court incorrectly decides that, since it is not entitled to rule on matters of parental responsibility (because the child is habitually resident outside Poland), it refuses to hear the case for divorce.[62] The court also interprets the 'superior interests of the child' condition stipulated in Article 12(1) of the Regulation in the light of Article 58 of the Family and Guardianship Code (see below in this section).

Serious difficulties are posed by Article 12 of Brussels IIa Regulation. First, the courts treat the parties' choice differently. The problem arises mostly in the situation where the spouses, being Polish citizens, and their children, reside abroad, and the spouses intend to obtain a divorce and a decision on parental responsibility pursuant to Article 12(1) in Poland. At least three different approaches have been observed here:

— The court accepts the choice of the parties without analysing the conditions for the application of Article 12[63] and exercises its jurisdiction;

---

[59] Circuit Court in Bydgoszcz, 14 September 2011, X Cz 155/11.

[60] The Practical Guide for the Application of Brussels II Regulation, 2005 (Polish version), http://ec.europa.eu/civiljustice/publications/docs/guide_new_brussels_ii_pl.pdf states that 'the right to maintain contact with a child may be granted to a parent with whom the child does not reside or other family members, for instance grandparents …' 33.

[61] Court of Appeal in Kraków, 19 November 2012, I ACz 1719/12.

[62] The matter has been duly remedied by the court of second instance—Court of Appeal in Kraków, 11 January 2016, I A Cz 2406/15.

[63] Court of Appeal in Kraków, 1 April 2015, I Acz 542/15.

— The court accepts the choice of the parties without analysing the conditions for the application, but prefers to transfer the case to another Member State—the State of the habitual residence of the child, pursuant to Article 15;[64]

— The court analyses the 'superior interests of the child': here three different approaches can be identified. In particular, the court decides that the superior interests of the child:

— require that disputes over parental responsibility should be handled by the court with jurisdiction over the place of habitual residence of the child;[65]

— require (as stated also in Article 58 of the Family and Guardianship Code) that it will be beneficial for the parties' child if the issue of parental responsibility is resolved by a local court in line with the Polish law and the local customs and culture to which the parties to the proceedings belong;[66]

— require that the court makes determinations relating to the situation of the child and the nature and strength of his/her connection with the parents' country of origin and consider *in casu* if it is in fact beneficial for the child that the case is resolved by a Polish court, taking account especially of the material situation of the child in the country of their habitual residence.[67]

Furthermore, there is a clear discrepancy in case law regarding the question of definition of 'the time the court is seised' in relation to the defendant for the purpose of Article 12 of the Brussels IIa Regulation. Some courts[68] have held that Article 12(1)(b), relating to the moment of acceptance of jurisdiction, should not be understood in the same way as defined in Article 16(1)(a) of the Regulation. Instead, the moment of acceptance of jurisdiction is the earliest possible point in time at which the parties could possibly accept the jurisdiction. Inasmuch as the application was not filed jointly, the aforementioned point in time for the plaintiff is the moment of submission of the petition, and for the defendant it is the moment of submission of the defence. Another court[69] stated, referring to the case law of the CJEU, that the clear wording of Article 12(1)(b) in connection with Article 16(1)(a) indicated that it was crucial that the parties to the divorce proceedings agreed on the jurisdiction at the latest upon filing the document instituting the proceedings in the court of their choice.

Furthermore, a problem has arisen as to whether the decision to request a transfer of the case to a court in another Member State pursuant to Article 15(1)(b) was subject to a complaint procedure. The Supreme Court analysed this issue on the grounds of Polish procedural law and responded negatively.[70] Nevertheless, on a different occasion the court of second instance was willing to consider such a complaint without analysing its admissibility.[71]

---

[64] Circuit Court in Kielce, 2 October 2014, I C 1586/10.
[65] Circuit Court in Kielce 24 April 2015, IC 130/15.
[66] Court of Appeal in Kraków, 12 August 2015, I Acz 1298/15.
[67] Court of Appeal in Kraków, 8 July 2015, I ACz 1217/15.
[68] Court of Appeal in Katowice, 15 May 2009, V Acz 252/09.
[69] Court of Appeal in Białystok, 28 January 2016, I ACa 835/15.
[70] Supreme Court, 9 December 2010, III CZP 99/10.
[71] Court of Appeal in Kraków, 1 April 2015, I Acz 542/15.

It also happens that the court of first instance makes an erroneous interpretation of the Regulation or applies Polish provisions instead of the provisions of the Regulation, which is subsequently noticed by the court of second instance which makes a correct, or even exemplary, interpretation of the Regulation whilst referring to the case law of the Court of Justice.[72]

iii. Matters Related to Recognition and Enforcement

a. Certificate Concerning Judgments in Matrimonial Matters and Certificate Concerning Judgments on Parental Responsibility

The courts of first instance tend to apply the provisions of the Polish Civil Procedure Code and the requirements contained therein as regards the declaration of enforceability of judgments, which is usually corrected by courts of second instance.[73]

The Supreme Court also decided that Article 23(e) of the Brussels IIa Regulation required that in order to dismiss the application, a judgment submitted for the recognition or declaration of enforceability must be contradictory to another, later judgment regarding parental responsibility of such a wording that makes the two judgments in question impossible to reconcile. Such a judgment does not include a judgment dismissing an application for the return of a child issued on the grounds of Article 13(b) of the Hague Convention on the Civil Aspects of International Child Abduction.[74]

b. Return of the Child

The Supreme Court has dealt with the question whether it was admissible to deny enforceability of a judgment referred to in Article 11(8) and Article 42.[75] The Supreme Court analysed the relevant provisions of the Regulation as well as the objective and nature of the procedure provided for in Article 11(8) as an exception to the rule, and answered negatively.

Finally, there were two cases in which Polish courts were asked to enforce a judgment issued by a court of another Member State in the circumstances specified in Article 11(8). In both cases, the enforcement proceedings are pending and the rulings have not been effectively enforced to date.[76]

iv. Conclusion

a. Problem Areas

The main problem hindering a comprehensive analysis of the case law of Polish courts regarding the Brussels IIa Regulation is the lack of publication of judgments in electronic

---

[72] Court of Appeal in Kraków, 15 January 2013, I ACz 2057/12 (stay of proceedings pursuant to art 19, and the application for injunctive relief); and Court of Appeal in Wrocław, 28 February 2014, I ACz 248/14 (interpretation of art 19).

[73] eg Court of Appeal in Kraków, 19 November 2012, I ACz 1719/12, providing that the declaration of enforceability pursuant to Brussels IIa covers also decisions which are subject to an appeal.

[74] Supreme Court, 24 August 2011, IV CSK 566/10.

[75] Since Art 42(1) provides only that it is not possible to deny the recognition of such a judgment. Supreme Court, 17 September 2014, I CSK 426/14.

[76] A Belgian judgment (pending since 2012) and a French judgment (pending since 2013). The enforcement proceedings are conducted by the District Court in Wałbrzych under file no V Nsm 777/12 and the District Court for Warsaw—Śródmieście in Warsaw in case no III Nsm 276/13 respectively.

databases. Indeed, it is only the judgments of the Supreme Court and the Court of Appeal in Kraków, Wrocław and Białystok, and rarely other courts' decisions that are made publicly available.

Furthermore, there is no specialisation in the judicial profession, meaning that a cross-border case may be referred to any judge. This means that, in practice, a judge may be assigned such a case only once in several years, while appropriate handling of cross-border cases requires advanced expertise and up-to-date knowledge of the case law of the Court of Justice.

b. Possible Solutions

According to the researchers, it seems that there is a need for a comprehensive publication of court decisions. Also, judicial specialisation in cross-border family cases would be a good solution. However, in order to prevent the problem of parties' access to the court, such cases should be heard by several courts rather than only one, located in Warsaw.

The inclusion of references to relevant EU instruments in the Civil Procedure Code, similar to those found in the 2011 Act on Private International Law, would raise judges' awareness of the situations in which EU law should be applied.

B. Jurisdictional and Procedural Issues and Applicable Law Under the Maintenance Regulation[77]

i. Matters Related to the Scope of Application

There are no particular difficulties associated with the scope of application of the Maintenance Regulation. In one case the court of second instance decided that the first instance court should first consider if the case called for the application of the provisions of the Regulation and the Hague Protocol, and only then decide if the provisions of the Brussels I Regulation were applicable.[78]

ii. Matters Related to Jurisdiction

The most serious doubts are associated with general provisions on jurisdiction and also with jurisdiction based on the appearance of the defendant in court (Articles 3 and 5).

Available judgments provide examples of premature determination of the lack of jurisdiction by first instance courts, resulting in the rejection of the maintenance claim. Courts of second instance have emphasised the incorrectness of such decisions.[79]

Sometimes, difficulties in the examination of jurisdiction are associated with the incorrect determination of the place of habitual residence of the defendant or creditor, which tends to be understood as the place of residence or address of permanent residence. On the other hand, commendably, the awareness of the EU mechanism of interpretation is increasing in Polish courts and the courts are beginning to use the autonomous interpretation

---

[77] See for example Anna Juryk, *Alimenty w prawie prywatnym międzynarodowym* (Vienna, LexisNexis, 2011).
[78] Court of Appeal in Wrocław, 31 January 2012, I ACz 137/12.
[79] Circuit Court in Gliwice, 11 March 2014, III Cz 417/13; Circuit Court in Kraków, 10 January 2014, XI 1Cz 574/13; and Circuit Court in Bydgoszcz, 11 July 2013, X Cz 134/14.

when determining the notion of a child's habitual residence, which leads to understanding the place of habitual residence as the place where the child has his/her centre of interests.[80]

Alarmingly, decisions based on Polish legislation instead of relevant EU legal provisions are not an exception. In one case, the court of first instance correctly decided that it did not have jurisdiction, however, erroneously adopted a legal justification based not on the provisions of the Regulation but rather on Polish procedural law. This irregularity was noticed by the court of second instance which highlighted the priority of EU law and its direct effect, and added that the provisions of the Regulation contained a closed system of jurisdiction.[81]

It is also worth noting that in the available case law, an interesting phenomenon was studied regarding the possibility for a court to hear a case for the award or increase of maintenance along with a counter claim for the decrease of maintenance. The Regulation does not offer an answer to this question. It was not questioned at the first instance, however, the court of second instance decided that the rationale of the legislator who intended to avoid splitting maintenance cases related to the same legal relationship between courts of different Member States was in line with the plaintiff's decision to bring the counter claim before the Polish court.[82]

iii. Matters Related to Applicable Law

Pursuant to Article 15 of the Maintenance Regulation, Polish courts determine the applicable law based on the provisions of the Hague Protocol.[83] However, in a case for the increase of maintenance which involved a defendant resident in Denmark, the court considered Polish law as the applicable law, based on the provisions of the 1973 Hague Convention on the Law Applicable to Maintenance Obligations.[84] It also needs to be emphasised that in another case, which concerned a claim for the increase of maintenance, the court of first instance did not examine the problem of jurisdiction and determination of applicable law at all, which was then highlighted by the court of second instance.[85]

The interviews conducted indicate that the parties, and sometimes even their representatives, are unaware that foreign law may be applicable to their case. For example, a plaintiff residing in Sweden was surprised to learn that due to the Hague Protocol, Swedish law, which did not provide for a maintenance obligation between former spouses, was applicable to her case. As for the Hague Protocol, practical problems arise in relation to the UK which is not a party thereto, although it is subject to the Maintenance Regulation. It was noted by one interviewee that due to the large-scale emigration of Poles to the UK, there are numerous cases of this type which have given rise to considerable practical difficulties.

---

[80] District Court in Kłodzko, 12 February 2013, III RC 771/12.
[81] Circuit Court in Bydgoszcz, 14 July 2013, X Cz 119/14.
[82] Circuit Court in Olsztyn, 27 May 2015, VI RCa 40/15.
[83] District Court in Trzebnica, 21 May 2014, VII RC 171/13 regarding an increase in maintenance and decision of the Court of Appeal in Poznań, 21 May 2014, I ACz 610/14 regarding injunctive relief with respect to maintenance claims.
[84] District Court in Wrocław, 23 May 2013, III RC 589/12.
[85] Circuit Court in Bydgoszcz, 3 April 2014, X Ca 14/14.

iv. Matters Related to Recognition, Enforceability and Actual Enforcement of Decisions

The following problems have arisen in relation to the recognition, enforceability and actual enforcement of maintenance decisions: 1) Determination of applicable law for the purpose of the establishment of the period of limitation of claims on account of the loss of enforceability of the judgment issued by a German court;[86] 2) analysis of the conditions for refusal to declare the enforceability of a judgment issued by a German court, provided for under Article 24(b) of the Maintenance Regulation;[87] and 3) existence of an obstacle preventing the determination of enforceability of a French judgment on the ground of the failure to deliver the document instituting the proceedings.[88]

There are also certain practical problems associated with the recognition and enforcement of foreign judgments. Sometimes procedural writs are returned several times with similar, or even identical inquiries, which delays the proceedings. It also happens that authorities in the foreign state do not respond to requests and there are no effective means to force them to cooperate.

v. Cooperation between Central Authorities

The judges have emphasised the need for a practical exchange of information and experience through direct contact between the Central Authorities of various Member States in order to learn about the procedures for awarding and enforcing maintenance obligations in other countries. This will help to tackle the limitations associated with a mere analysis of the wording of foreign law.

vi. Conclusion

a. Problem Areas

In the Polish legal system judgments issued in maintenance cases are usually not published at all, which makes access to them difficult. The decision on the publication of a judgment is usually made by the presiding or the reporting judge.

Available case law shows the lack of references to the recitals of the relevant EU instruments, judgments of the Court of Justice, and foreign legal literature. This is unfortunate not least as the conducted interviews indicate that Recitals 9 and 11[89] to the Maintenance Regulation are particularly useful, for example, when the court seeks to justify a rejection of the claim.

b. Best Practice

Cross-border cases are perceived as more complex than domestic cases. Therefore, an informal institution of the judge specialising in maintenance cross-border cases has gradually appeared in Poland, with such a judge being appointed in each court division, although

---

[86] Circuit Court in Gliwice, 11 February 2014, III Ca 1545/13.
[87] Court of Appeal in Rzeszów, 5 July 2013, I ACz 442/13.
[88] Court of Appeal in Rzeszów, 24 August 2012, I ACz 477/12.
[89] Both indicating the privileged position of the maintenance creditor.

with no entitlement to additional remuneration. Such judges participate in the training organised by the National School of Judiciary and Public Prosecution, however, the availability of such training is limited.

c. Possible Solutions

Judges would benefit from regular training sessions, conferences and workshops during which they could work on case studies in small groups. Furthermore, meetings and other forms of contact with judges from other EU countries would prove valuable for the mutual exchange of experience regarding the practical aspects of functioning of a different legal system. Also, there are no practical guides or materials available in Polish which would support the work of the judges in cross-border cases.

The judges who were interviewed for the project also advocated the introduction of a compulsory legal representation or at least the obligation to appoint an attorney for notifications in every cross-border case.

C. Practice/Process

i. *Poland's National Courts' Practice in Interpreting the Regulations*

Due to the lack of harmonised procedural rules, each Member State uses its own procedural system, and practical problems arise in the area of the exchange of letters and notifications,[90] the seising of the court,[91] the appearance of the parties and the participation of legal representatives in the proceedings. The cooperation with the authorities of some Member States tends to lead to effective enforcement of maintenance obligations (eg Germany), while with regards to other States, difficulties in contacting the authorities lead to lower effectiveness (eg Italy and Spain). The contact forms which were introduced[92] aimed to simplify the cooperation between the authorities of different States, but in practice, the main problem is the lack of binding time frames for the particular activities (eg provision of information), or the lack of consequences in the event of an infringement of an existing deadline, in particular in relation to Annex 5 to the Maintenance Regulation. It is due to the aforementioned reasons that the measures provided for in the Maintenance Regulation are considered insufficient for the effective enforcement of maintenance obligations.

ii. *Cost and Length of Litigation in Cross-border Family Law Disputes*

The application of foreign law to cases relating to maintenance obligations delays the proceedings because the contents of the relevant foreign legislation must be obtained from the Ministry of Justice, which takes a long time and furthermore the text is often provided without a Polish translation, which must be commissioned separately.

---

[90] The delivery of the first writ tends to take an extremely long time.
[91] In some states it is the moment of the receipt of the claim, while in others it is the moment of effective delivery thereof.
[92] Annexes I–IX to the Maintenance Regulation.

D. Preliminary Remarks on Effectiveness of the Current EU PIL Framework in Cross-border Family Law

The underlying problem for researchers in family law cases is the lack of availability of the judgments issued in cross-border cases. It is possible that the real reason behind the reluctance of the courts of lower instances to publish their judgments is that they are not very proficient in the application of EU instruments. This is in particular due to the complexity of EU regulations and the multitude of sources of law. Another problem is the lack of formal specialisation of judges in cross-border cases. Although specialisation exists informally in some courts, it is not a comprehensive solution to the problem.

To sum up, commendably, EU law was applied correctly in most of the available judgments of the Courts of Appeal. However, the frequency of references to CJEU judgments is fairly low.

11

Austria

FLORIAN HEINDLER AND BEA VERSCHRAEGEN

I. Introduction

Austria's legal system has its origin in the development of statehood during the era of enlightened absolutism in the eighteenth century. The Austrian civil code was enacted in 1812 and the current organisation of the courts and civil procedure rules dates back to the nineteenth century.

II. Austria's Experience in Cross-border Non-family Civil and Commercial Disputes

Due to the large number of cases handled by the Austrian courts that apply Brussels I, Rome I and Rome II, a selection of cases has had to be made. This selection was based on either quantitative[1] or qualitative[2] criteria.

A. Jurisdictional and Procedural Issues Under the Brussels I Regulation

The Brussels I recast has been considered by Austrian doctrine[3] and judges. In a few cases the Austrian Supreme Court (SCt) had to point out that the Brussels I recast applied and reformulated the reference to Brussels I (2001) made either by the parties or by another court.

---

[1] eg where similar problems emerged in numerous cases, or where issues affected or will affect a large number of companies and citizens.

[2] eg where issues address a fundamental social issue or place a particular burden on the company or citizen concerned.

[3] cf D Czernich, G Kodek and P Mayr (eds), *Europäisches Gerichtsstands- und Vollstreckungsrecht* 4th edn (Vienna, Lexisnexis, 2015); T Domej, 'Die neue Brüssel Ia-Verordnung: Änderungen im Zuständigkeitsbereich' in B König and P Mayr (eds), *Europäisches Zivilverfahrensrecht in Österreich IV Die Brüssel Ia Verordnung und weitere Reformen* (Vienna, Manz, 2015); B Köllensperger, 'Die neue Brüssel Ia-Verordnung: Änderungen bei Anerkennung und Vollstreckung' in König and Mayr, ibid.

i. Matters Related to the Scope of Application

The first issue concerns the limitation of the scope of application with regard to the exercise of State authority (*acta iure imperii*). Numerous cases[4] have been brought before Austrian courts in connection with the legal measures undertaken by the Greek government in order to restructure Greek state bonds.[5] Austrian bondholders filed claims before Austrian courts relying on jurisdiction in accordance with Article 5(3) Brussels I (Article 7(2) Brussels I recast).[6] The Hellenic Republic (defendant) argued that the claim of the Austrian bondholders had arisen in connection with the exercise of State authority. The SCt reached its decision before the joined cases *Fahnenbrock v Hellenic Republic* had been decided by the Court of Justice of the European Union (CJEU).[7] The SCt has generally come to the same conclusion as the CJEU,[8] but it has not pointed out the necessity of autonomous interpretation of *acta iure imperii*, instead referring to the terms and principles of public international law.

The second issue concerns the limitation of the scope of application with regard to 'rights in property arising out of a matrimonial relationship'. Recently, in a case dealing with compensation for a private investigator to learn about a spouse's adultery (in a legal system that incorporates fault in the concept of divorce) two lower instance court decisions have been set aside by the SCt which has ultimately affirmed the nexus of specific expenditures and matrimonial measures.[9]

ii. Matters Relating to Jurisdiction

Prorogation of jurisdiction is often disputed, in particular, whether subsequent prorogation of jurisdiction has happened,[10] under which circumstances prorogation of jurisdiction might happen in general terms and conditions,[11] and whether a jurisdiction clause may be an unfair term unless individually agreed upon.[12]

A case decided by the SCt concerning a bus driver working for an Austrian company in the city of Linz but domiciled in the Czech Republic (most likely during his parental leave) illustrated the difficulties employers face bringing proceedings for approval of the dismissal before the courts of the Member State in which the employee is domiciled.[13] In the said case, Czech Republic courts require translation of documents and would have to familiarise themselves with Austrian labour regulations.

The SCt has sent a request to the CJEU for a preliminary ruling, including the question as to whether credit agreements constitute the provision of a service under Article 7(1)(b) Brussels I recast.[14]

---

[4] OGH RdW 2016, 332; OGH JBl 2016, 47; OGH RdW 2014, 529.
[5] *cf* the similar facts of the cases: Joined Cases C-226/13, C-245/13, C-247/13 and C-578/13 *Fahnenbrock v Hellenic Republic*, EU:C:2015:383.
cf s II.A.ii of this chapter.
[6] *cf* s II.A.ii of this chapter.
[7] *cf Fahnenbrock* supra n 5.
[8] OGH RdW 2014, 529.
[9] OGH Zak 2016, 91.
[10] *cf* OGH Zak 2015, 79.
[11] *cf* OGH RdW 2015, 237.
[12] *cf* Case C-191/15 *Verein für Konsumenteninformation v Amazon EU Sàrl*, EU:C:2016:388 Opinion of AG Saugmandsgaard.
[13] See Art 22(1) of the Brussels I recast and OGH ecolex 2015, 892.
[14] OGH 31 March 2016 no 1 Ob 31/16i.

iii. Matters Related to Recognition and Enforcement

The SCt has deemed that service of documents must be in line with common EU standards but need not adhere to the details of Austrian law on service of documents.[15]

Furthermore, the study has shown that litigants face difficulties when they are required to enforce a claim under Brussels I if the defendant has become insolvent. In accordance with Austrian civil procedural law, claims against an insolvent legal entity may be registered by a court in a claims' registration list (*Anmeldeverzeichnis*) if they are not appealed by the insolvency manager. Claims that have been approved and entered into the claims' registration list are directly enforceable in Austria in accordance with Article 1 of the Act on the Enforcement of Judgments 1896 (*Exekutionsordnung*). However, Austrian courts refuse to provide a confirmation according to Annex V Brussels I (2001) stating that the entry is not a judgment and that claims brought against an insolvent legal entity are excluded by Article 1 from Brussels I.[16] Consequently, any Austrian creditors wishing to enforce a claim already approved by the Austrian insolvency manager of the debtor have to initiate new proceedings abroad.

iv. Conclusion

A coherent strategy of sending requests for preliminary rulings to the CJEU cannot be observed.

Alignment of forum and ius is vital for effective cross-border litigation. Thus further attempts should be undertaken to facilitate a principle of alignment of forum and ius in particular in employment contracts.

Decisions could pay more attention to the effectiveness of the outcome for litigants and costs for EU Member States' courts and depart from a formalistic interpretation of the Regulations, eg in the case of providing a certificate for entries in the Austrian claims' registration list.

B. Applicable Law Issues Under the Rome I and Rome II Regulations

Both Regulations have been properly applied instead of the former Austrian Law on Private International Law, which itself has been partly repealed in accordance with the grandfathering rules of the Rome I and Rome II Regulations.[17]

i. Rome I

a. Matters Related to the Scope of Application

In relation to the scope of application of Rome I, the SCt recently referred the matter of a cross-border merger transaction to the CJEU for a preliminary ruling.[18] The CJEU ruled that the law applicable to the interpretation of a loan contract, to how those obligations are

---

[15] OGH ecolex 2015, 391.
[16] Higher Regional Court of Innsbruck 19 December 2013 no 1 R 226/13i.
[17] SCt on grandfathering rules *cf* OGH IPRax 2014, 358.
[18] OGH RdW 2014, 709.

extinguished and to the performance of the obligations following a cross-border merger by acquisition of the debtor, is the law which was applicable to the contract before the merger, whereas the law applicable to provisions governing the protection of creditors is that which is applicable to the merger.[19]

b. Matters Related to the Uniform Rules

The validity of a choice of the applicable law by the parties was regularly discussed in the judgments, in particular whether a subsequent choice of law had been made[20] and whether the applicable law may be agreed in general terms or by mutual consent, eg by using stipulations that correspond with Austrian non-mandatory law (affirmative SCt).[21]

c. Matters Related to Other Provisions

In relation to the nullity of an obligation under Italian procurement law, the SCt set aside a decision by the Higher Regional Court Graz, which had applied Italian procurement law as an internationally mandatory rule.[22] The judgment outlined the difficulties faced by the SCt in establishing whether Italian procurement law in the particular case may be regarded as an internationally mandatory rule.

d. Conclusion

The study of cases regarding the law applicable to contractual obligations in Austria has revealed complexities in dealing with cross-border mergers that presumably can be found in other types of cross-border reorganisation transactions as well.[23] Public policy and internationally mandatory rules are an indispensable component of private international law (PIL) regulations. However, in practice the interpretation of public policy and the definition of foreign and domestic internationally mandatory rules are complex and make judgments less predictable.[24]

ii. Rome II

a. Matters Related to the Scope of Application

Austrian courts have recently dealt with the question as to whether an action for an injunction in consumers' interests under Directive 2009/22/EC concerns a contractual or a non-contractual obligation.[25] In the SCt decision number 2 Ob 204/14k dated 9 April 2015, the SCt made a request to the CJEU for a preliminary ruling. AG Saugmandsgaard followed

---

[19] Case C-483/14 *KA Finanz AG v Sparkassen Versicherung AG Vienna Insurance Group*, EU:C:2016:205.

[20] OGH 11 August 2015 no 4 Ob 225/14p: one party claimed that Austrian data protection law is applicable, the other party was silent.

[21] *cf* OGH ecolex 2015, 322; OGH 24 March 2015 no 8 Ob 98/14s (Rome Convention).

[22] OGH ecolex 2012, 384; Higher Regional Court Graz 16 March 2012 no 5 R 126/10d.

[23] *cf* G Eckert, *Internationales Gesellschaftsrecht: Das internationale Privatrecht grenzüberschreitend tätiger Gesellschaften* (Vienna, Manz, 2010) 775 ff.

[24] J Schacherreiter, 'Eingriffsnormen in der Rom I-VO zwischen Parteiautonomie und gesellschaftsrechtlichen Steuerungsinteressen' in B Verschraegen (ed), *Rechtswahl: Grenzen und Chancen* (Vienna, Jan Sramek, 2010).

[25] *cf* OGH 21 May 2015 no 1 Ob 67/15g; OGH RdW 2015, 361.

the assumption made by the SCt (with reference to the German Bundesgerichtshof Xa ZR 19/08) and supported the opinion that an action for an injunction in the consumers' interests may fall under Article 6(1) of Rome I, as it includes the use of unfair terms that are likely to affect the collective interests of consumers.[26] The CJEU accepted this argument.[27]

b. Matters Related to Torts/Delicts

The SCt was concerned with the question as to whether the judgment of a Dutch court on the litigant's entitlement ensuing from Benelux trademarks on the use of certain vodka brands could bind the Austrian courts in relation to the issue of the statute of limitations.[28] The SCt concluded in respect of CJEU case law[29] that the objective limitations for the binding effect of the Dutch judgment may be determined in accordance with Dutch substantive law.

Various issues were raised in the SCt decision number 4 Ob 147/14t dated 18 November 2014.[30] Litigants brought a claim seeking an order that a competitor ought to stop issuing statements referring to payment of climate neutrality compensation. Austrian courts referred to Article 6(1) of Rome II,[31] which states that the law applied shall be the law of the State where competitive relations are, or are likely to be, affected. Seeking an order in particular for the UK, the SCt observed that the UK had implemented Directives 2006/114/EC and 2005/29/EC in all its territorial units, including Scotland, whereas claims based on civil law were governed by the law of the respective territorial unit in accordance with Article 25 of Rome II (mentioning England and Scotland). In addition, the SCt concluded that a right to bring proceedings may be qualified either as procedural or as a substantive legal issue. The SCt was concerned that Rome II is not decisive on that point. Since the SCt has been able to set aside the decision of the Higher Regional Court Linz, instructing the court of first instance to commission a legal opinion,[32] it has abstained from making a request to the CJEU for a preliminary ruling on the interpretation of Article 15 of Rome II.

C. Practice/Process

i. *Austria's National Courts' Practice in Interpreting the Regulations/Process Issues*

Only the SCt judgments are generally published. Decisions by other Austrian courts in civil and commercial matters are only selectively published. On the basis of a key word search, 475 decisions by the SCt refer to Brussels I, 43 decisions refer to Rome I, and 43 decisions refer to Rome II.[33]

---

[26] Case C-191/15 *Verein für Konsumenteninformation v Amazon EU Sàrl*, EU:C:2016:388 Opinion of AG Saugmandsgaard.

[27] ibid.

[28] OGH 11 August 2015 no 4 Ob 30/15p.

[29] Reference was made to Case 145/86 *Horst Ludwig Martin Hoffman v Adelheid Kriegl*, [1988] ECR 645 and to Case C-456/11 *Gothaer Allgemeine Versicherung AG et al vs Samskip GmbH*, EU:C:2012:719.

[30] OGH GRUR Int 2015, 481.

[31] *cf* Higher Regional Court Linz 19 May 2014 no 6 R 85/14h.

[32] The SCt instructed the court to establish whether under English/Scots law the litigant would have an enforceable right against the defendant not being awarded within the sole discretion of a national agency.

[33] As of 2 July 2016.

Austrian courts regularly request preliminary rulings from the CJEU. By 1 January 2016, Austrian civil courts had requested a preliminary ruling from the CJEU a total of 218 times.[34] Between 20 June 2012 and 24 November 2015, 23 requests for preliminary rulings had been made by the Austrian civil courts, of which 12 were initiated by the SCt and 11 by lower-instance courts.

ii. Settlement in Cross-border Civil and Commercial Disputes

Austria still charges a settlement fee for out-of-court settlements at the rate of two per cent of the value of the settlement agreement,[35] which constitutes an obstacle to out-of-court settlements,[36] but once a claim is brought, settlement is relatively common in civil and commercial disputes.

D. Preliminary Remarks on Effectiveness of the Current EU PIL Framework in Civil and Commercial Law

In its judgments, the SCt takes CJEU judgments into account along with doctrine, as long as this is published in the German language. Obstacles to effectiveness result from a less than pragmatic approach adopted by the SCt coupled with a very selective method of making requests to the CJEU for preliminary rulings. Even though a request for a preliminary ruling prolongs the proceedings in the referred case, systematic development of the EU PIL framework in civil and commercial law by way of creating a coherent pattern of CJEU decisions would make cross-border litigation more efficient as well as more predictable.

III. Austria's Experience on Cross-border Family Law Disputes

A. Jurisdictional and Procedural Issues Under the Brussels IIa Regulation

Under Austrian law the court is deemed to be seised when a claim is brought before the court, eg a parent requests custody and this claim is then served upon the other parent, the procedure is deemed to have started on the day the parent filed the request.[37]

Many decisions of the SCt have dealt with the lack of jurisdiction in the sense of Article 17 of Brussels IIa. The SCt has consistently held that the question whether a court has jurisdiction must be examined *ex officio* at any time during the proceeding. The court may, therefore, reject the case *a limine*.[38]

---

[34] Austrian Ministry of Justice 4 January 2016 no BMJ-EU15116/0014-EU/2015.
[35] Reduced to one per cent of the settlement's value if a claim has been brought and court fees are due.
[36] *cf* Art 33 Fees and Duties Act 1957 (*Gebührengesetz*).
[37] See OGH 19 December 2005 no 8 Ob 120/05p.
[38] See inter alia OGH 11 September 2008 no 7 Ob 155/08g.

i. Matters Related to Jurisdiction

a. Divorce, Legal Separation and Marriage Annulment

In conformity with Brussels IIa the courts have held that the court second seised shall stay its proceedings—provided it basically has jurisdiction—until the court first seised has rendered a final decision on its jurisdiction. The court second seised has no discretion in this respect.[39]

b. Parental Responsibility

1. Child Abduction

A recent case dealt with the interplay of the Hague Child Abduction Convention (1980 Convention), the Hague Child Protection Convention (1996 Convention), the Brussels IIa Regulation and domestic law regarding jurisdiction.[40] The boy, a German national, the legitimate child of a German national married in Austria to a national from Paraguay, was abducted by his mother from Austria to Paraguay. The return of the child under the 1980 Convention was declined by the Paraguayan court because the convention was not yet in force in relation to Austria. The father then applied for sole custody, whereas the mother claimed that the Austrian courts lacked jurisdiction in accordance with Article 110 of the Austrian law on jurisdiction 1895 (*Jurisdiktionsnorm* 1895). The court of appeal affirmed jurisdiction on the basis of Article 7 of the 1996 Convention. The SCt took the view that the child had his habitual residence in Austria before he was taken to Paraguay but by the time the father applied for sole custody, the child was already habitually residing in Paraguay, taking into consideration that the legality of the stay is not relevant[41] and the duration of the residence exceeded six months.[42] Hence, neither Article 8 of Brussels IIa nor Article 5 of the 1996 Convention applied. Under Article 7(2)(a) of the 1996 Convention the child was wrongfully removed to Paraguay. Basically, the authorities of the Contracting State in which the child was habitually resident immediately before the removal keep their jurisdiction until the child has acquired a habitual residence in another State (Article 7(1) of the 1996 Convention), which correlates to Article 10 of Brussels IIa. But the requirements of Article 7(1)(b) of the 1996 Convention were not complied with, therefore Austrian jurisdiction was denied for the custody proceedings.

The case paradigmatically demonstrates the complexity of the interplay of various international and EU instruments and the burden it places on the courts to act swiftly.

If a child is wrongfully removed, the requested State shall decide that it lacks jurisdiction under Article 8 of Brussels IIa.[43]

---

[39] *cf* OGH 9 September 2002 no 188/02a to name one example.
[40] See OGH 28 August 2014 no 6 Ob 116/14y.
[41] *cf* OGH 19 December 2012 no 6 Ob 217/12y.
[42] The six months' period is only an indication for the establishment of habitual residence. Other factors (eg home, personal or other links to the country) need to be taken into consideration as well. See EFSlg 79.089 Higher Regional Court Vienna 19 September 1995 no 43 Nc 22/95, EFSlg 101.617 Higher Regional Court Vienna 1 January 2002 no 42 Nc 16/02a.
[43] See OGH 15 May 2012 no 2 Ob 288/11k.

2. Other Issues Relating to Parental Responsibility

The term 'parental responsibility' (Article 2(7) of Brussels IIa) is a uniform notion, therefore, any differentiation according to specific aspects of such responsibility under domestic law is not relevant.[44] The same applies to eg 'rights of custody' (Article 2(9) of Brussels IIa). Austrian courts follow the CJEU case law.[45]

ii. Matters Related to Recognition and Enforcement

a. Certificate Concerning Judgments in Matrimonial Matters and Certificate Concerning Judgments on Parental Responsibility

In the absence of consent between the parties a court can issue a formal certificate on parental custody and contact rights under Article 107 of the Austrian law on non-contentious proceedings 2003 (*Außerstreitgesetz* 2003).[46]

b. Return of the Child

In conformity with the CJEU case law[47] the SCt has decided that a request for return of a child is different from an action on parental custody.[48]

iii. Cooperation between Central Authorities in Matters of Parental Responsibility

The Austrian Central Authority (CA) has close links with the relevant EU institutions and with the Permanent Bureau of the Hague Conference. It is eager to work in line with the law and to proceed quickly. In addition, the CA makes sure that judges throughout Austria are well informed on current developments and the proper functioning of the law.

iv. Relations with Other Instruments

Brussels IIa provides for stricter rules regarding child abduction than the 1980 Convention.[49] The purpose of Brussels IIa to limit child abduction is welcome but the lack of parallelism with the 1980 Convention is most unfortunate and has led to proceedings before the European Court of Human Rights (ECtHR) and putting at risk the efficiency of the 1980 Convention.[50]

---

[44] See OGH 26 February 2015 no 8 Ob 14/15i; Case C-523/07 *A* ECLI:EU:C:2009:225, Case C-436/13 *E* ECLI:EU:C:2014:2246, Case C-376/14 PPU *C* ECLI:EU:C:2014:2268.

[45] Case C-400/10 PPU *McB* ECLI:EU:C:2010:582.

[46] *cf* OGH 13 July 2010 no 4 Ob 82/10b.

[47] Case C-376/14 PPU *C* above n 44.

[48] OGH 26 February 2015 no 8 Ob 14/15i.

[49] Higher Regional Court Vienna 42 R 229/06x EFSlg 114.674.

[50] The decision rendered by the ECtHR 8 January 2009 *Neulinger v Switzerland* INCADAT HC/E/ 1001 was not generally approved by lawyers and Austrian cases following *Neulinger* have been awaited with great interest. eg ECtHR 15 January 2015 *Povse v Austria* INCADAT HC/E/ 1205. In *MA v Austria* appl no 4097 15 January 2015 the ECtHR reiterated that the positive obligations under Art 8 ECHR must be interpreted in the light of the Hague Abduction Convention (with further references). The entanglement of both instruments seems to cause uncertainty. Indeed, to some extent requests for return of a child are made under the Hague Abduction Convention in combination with Brussels IIa, see Fucik, *Statistische Auswertung aller Kindesentführungsverfahren mit Österreichbezug. Rückgabeanträge nach dem HKÜ von 1.1.2011 bis 1.7.2015*, iFamZ 2015, 307, whom we wish to thank for the statistical data on abduction cases.

v. Conclusion

a. Problem Areas

Brussels IIa provides no special clause on jurisdiction regarding stateless persons and refugees. It seems wise to treat them like nationals of the forum, ie to confirm jurisdiction in matters relating to divorce, legal separation or marriage annulment when the stateless person or the refugee has his or her habitual residence in the territory (Article 3(1)(a) of Brussels IIa).

b. Best Practice

The e-book *Civil Law European Judicial Cooperation* contributes to the understanding of judicial cooperation in Europe. Together with the e-training on EU law, these tools are certainly extremely important. The regular updates of information on eg Article 68 of Brussels IIa are a further step in this direction. They are published in the Official Journal and consulted by Austrian practitioners.

B. Jurisdictional and Procedural Issues and Applicable Law Under the Maintenance Regulation

i. Matters Related to Jurisdiction

The SCt held that if a child has been living more than one year with the custodial parent in the country of residence and also attends school there, it is reasonable to assume that the child is habitually residing in that country. The SCt repeated that a habitual residence can be established in another country even where the child was wrongfully removed from the country of origin.[51]

The Austrian SCt dealt with the question whether mother and child are the 'same parties' in two proceedings within the meaning of Article 12 of the Maintenance Regulation.[52] It made a request for a preliminary ruling, which was withdrawn a year later and the case was deleted from the list.[53]

ii. Matters Related to Recognition, Enforceability and Actual Enforcement of Decisions

Referring to the CJEU decision regarding the interpretation of Brussels I,[54] the SCt[55] denied the possibility to raise substantive objections under the Maintenance Regulation.

---

[51] OGH 29 August 2013 no 1 Ob 136/13a.
[52] OGH 6 June 2013 no 6 Ob 240/12f.
[53] Case C-442/13 *Nagy* ECLI:EU:C:2014:2038. In one set of proceedings the child made a claim against the father for past and current child support, in divorce proceedings the father sought a determination of his maintenance obligation relating to that child and of support upon divorce due to the mother.
[54] Case C-139/10 *Prism Investments* ECLI:EU:C:2011:653.
[55] OGH 29 October 2013 no 3 Ob 149/13b.

A series of decisions relate to the characterisation of titles to support in the sense of the 2007 Hague Protocol.

The SCt decided that provisional support in the sense of Article 382(1)(8)(a) Act on the Enforcement of Judgments 1896 (*Exekutionsordnung*) is not a title to support as such, but rather a procedural tool to claim a substantive title to support. Therefore, provisional support under the Austrian law on enforcement of judgments is not support in the sense of the Hague Protocol.[56]

Some claims for support are characterised under domestic law as claims under succession law. This applies to the duty of a parent to support his/her children when the parent passes away. This prevailing opinion implies that the duty expires upon the death of the parent and a new duty to support may arise for the heirs (Article 233 of the Austrian Civil Code, ABGB). This means that no duty of an heir can exist, if the estate has no value. Thus without assets no heir can be held responsible to pay child support. The question is, however, whether such characterisation is accurate under the Hague Protocol.[57] The function of support is to cover the needs of the dependent in proportion to the living standard of the deceased.[58] Strictly speaking, such a title is support in the sense of the Hague Protocol. However, the Protocol requires that the maintenance obligation arises from a family relationship (Article 1). The heir need not necessarily be a family member, yet he/she may be liable to pay support. As the ground for the support is the family relationship between the parent and the child and because the Hague Protocol demands a wide scope of application, such maintenance obligations should be characterised as falling within the scope of application of the Protocol. How Austrian courts are to deal with the scope of application of the Hague Protocol on the one hand and of the Succession Regulation (Article 1(2)(2)) on the other remains to be seen.

It seems that there is no decision yet made by an Austrian court as to whether questions relating to the status of a person should be dealt with independently of or in accordance with the law applicable to the maintenance claim.

iii. Cooperation between Central Authorities

The cooperation of the Austrian CA with other CAs seems to function well.

iv. Conclusion

a. Problem Areas

Some cases concerned the application of the Protocol *ratione temporis*.[59] Maintenance claimed under the Protocol can include maintenance for the past.

---

[56] See OGH 25 March 2014 no 10 Ob 7/14y; OGH 22 December 2011 no 1 Ob 235/11g.

[57] A similar problem arises regarding the claim for support under Arts 94 and 796 Austrian Civil Code, if his/her spouse (or registered partner) passes away. A further example is the claim of a survivor who was entitled to maintenance from the deceased who was killed in an accident caused by a third party. Under domestic law the third party may be held liable to pay maintenance, but whether such an obligation can be characterised as maintenance stemming from a family relationship has not yet been decided by a national court. The same is true for claims based on unjust enrichment or damages filed by the putative father against the true father or against the child and/or the mother.

[58] See OGH 6 December 2000 no 7 Ob 290/00y.

[59] OGH 4 June 2014 no 7 Ob 83/14b.

b. Best Practice

Austrian practitioners are extremely well and regularly trained by experts on cross-border maintenance.

c. Possible Solutions

The coordination on the EU level of jurisdictional and conflict rules regarding maintenance on the one hand and the availability of social support, such as advance child support, is highly desirable (at least within the EU).

C. Practice/Process

i. *Austria's National Courts' Practice in Interpreting the Regulations*

The practice of the Austrian courts in interpreting the Brussels IIa and Maintenance Regulations is good.

ii. *Cost and Length of Litigation in Cross-border Family Law Disputes*

Controversial family law disputes may take years. At the end of the day, parties with an average income and more debts/liabilities than assets may have nothing left but enormous lawyer's fees and procedural costs to cover.

   Most courts order the parties to seek mediation. Yet, difficult cases may involve a mediation which takes six months or longer. As mediators are not allowed to provide legal counselling, the parties still need to be properly informed and counselled. A variety of institutions, courts included, offer basic information and counselling free of any costs, but this is often insufficient in cross-border cases. Hence, most parties face the costs for mediation and the costs for legal counselling and representation before the court.

   Most parties are well aware that lapse of time may be an extremely strategic tool to their advantage or disadvantage. Generally, one can observe that time is used and misused as a weapon to discourage the other party and/or to establish social integration, which is an aspect of habitual residence.

iii. *Settlement in Cross-border Family Law Disputes*

Courts are highly motivated to have the family law dispute settled. First of all, because that eases the entire process, second, because the parties get involved in reaching a consensual result. In most cases, this has a de-escalating effect and decreases the costs of the procedure.

   Yet, where parties are represented by a lawyer, there is a tendency to prolong the proceedings by filing numerous briefs and seeking multiple remedies thereby escalating the dispute and the costs of the proceedings.

iv. *Alternative Dispute Resolution for Cross-border Family Law Disputes*

Most courts order alternative dispute resolution. Depending on the joint income of the parties, such disputes may be subsidised by the State. In this respect, cross-border cases have become quite common. Only mediators enrolled in the list administered by the Federal Ministry of Justice are accredited mediators, and accredited mediators enrolled in the list of the Federal Ministry of Family and Youth Affairs are allowed to act as co-mediators. Both need a different core competence (eg business, architecture, environment, education, medicine, politics, law, psychology, psychotherapy and counsellor). Cross-border mediations involve at least two languages. Every oral and written communication is to be translated and few mediators have the necessary skills and the time required for such mediations. The additional work is not paid and the mediators' team receives EUR 220 per hour including VAT. The result is that few mediators are willing to assume such a burden although the number of cross-border mediations is increasing. Hence, parties with a migration background with little or no income and with poor knowledge of German might not receive a good service.

D. Preliminary Remarks on Effectiveness of the Current EU PIL Framework in Cross-border Family Law

Enhanced cooperation has partly made cross-border work easier, partly, however, more difficult. The SCt only deals with questions of law and the applicable law is considered under Austrian law as a question of law, not as a question of fact.

12

Bulgaria

TEODORA TSENOVA AND ANTON PETROV*

I. Introduction

Bulgaria is a civil law jurisdiction and has been a member of the EU since 1 January 2007. The first codification of private international law in Bulgaria came into force just two years earlier—on 21 May 2005—with the adoption of the Code of Private International Law ('CPIL'). The CPIL currently applies with regard to matters which are not dealt with by the relevant EU regulations. With this in mind, the purpose of this report is to indicate how the EU PIL framework is applied in Bulgaria, with a focus on Brussels I, Brussels IIa, Rome I and II, and the Maintenance Regulation. On the basis of an analysis of the relevant case law, it is also evaluated whether there is a need for further training for national judges and lawyers, so that they could be able to more effectively deal with cross-border civil and commercial cases.

All Bulgarian courts are empowered and obliged to implement the EU PIL regulations. The administration of justice in cross-border civil and commercial cases comprises three court instances. The first instance court would be either a district or provincial court, depending on the subject matter of the dispute. Provincial courts also act as second instance appellate courts against the decisions of the district courts, whereas appeals against first instance decisions of provincial courts are dealt with by the courts of appeal. The highest court for civil and commercial disputes in Bulgaria is the Supreme Court of Cassation ('SCC').

The question whether a Bulgarian court has jurisdiction over a civil or commercial dispute with an international element is determined by the first instance court seised either *ex officio*[1] or after a jurisdictional challenge is raised by the defendant.[2] The court's ruling, upholding the defendant's jurisdictional challenge and dismissing the case due to lack of competence may be appealed.[3] However, an appeal against a court's decision to assume

---

* The views and opinions expressed in this report are those of the authors and do not necessarily reflect those of the institutions to which they are affiliated or the official policy or position of any Bulgarian law enforcement agency.

[1] Art 15(1) of the Civil Procedure Code ('CPC').
[2] Art 15(2) CPC.
[3] Arts 15(2) and 274(1) CPC.

jurisdiction, dismissing a defendant's jurisdictional challenge, may not be made before the closure of the first instance court proceedings. For this reason, private appeals against negative rulings on jurisdiction reach the appellate stage and are resolved much faster. The actual procedural delays depend on the average workload of the competent courts which could vary. However, these delays are not peculiar to the way EU PIL rules are applied by the individual judges, but are rather inherent to the organisation and management of the Bulgarian judicial system.

There is no official statistical data about the number of cases with an international element brought before the Bulgarian courts, nor on the number of cases in which one or another of the EU regulations, subject to this report, has been applied. Although a significant number of court decisions were reviewed for the purposes of this report[4] (over 200 with respect to the Brussels I Regulation and over 300 with respect to the Brussels IIa Regulation), it is highly likely that there are some other relevant judgments which were not identified. The main source of information used for the purpose of this report is the website legalacts.justice.bg, which is a web-based platform maintained by the Supreme Judicial Council where various judicial acts of the Bulgarian courts are published. The second source relied upon is the SCC website (www.vks.bg), where its own decisions are published.

II. Brussels I

The Bulgarian courts are increasingly familiar with the Brussels I Regulation which they rely upon when assuming jurisdiction in cross-border cases. Although the number of the relevant PIL cases was small in the first years following the accession of Bulgaria to the EU, there has been, since 2011, a gradual increase in the number of decisions in which the courts relied on Brussels I with a view to establishing jurisdiction in cross-border disputes. Another positive development is that the Bulgarian courts tend to be engaging on more occasions with the relevant case law of the Court of Justice of the European Union ('CJEU'). That said, at the time of writing, the Bulgarian courts have made only one reference for a preliminary ruling on the interpretation of Brussels I. The request was made by the Sofia City Court, asking the CJEU to interpret the scope of Article 22(1) of Brussels I. It was not clear whether Article 22(1) applies with regard to non-contentious proceedings, initiated by a national of a Member State who had been declared to lack full legal capacity, seeking authorisation to sell an immovable property located in another Member State. The CJEU held that this type of proceedings was not within the scope of Article 22(1).[5]

Our research findings indicate that most of the judgments appear to be in conformity with the rules of Brussels I. Among the publicly available decisions there are many cases with an international element where the courts have applied the general jurisdiction rule under Article 2.[6] The Bulgarian judges have also dealt with cross-border cases concerning

---

[4] The relevant decisions have been identified through keyword search in the below mentioned sources.
[5] C-386/12, *Siegfried János Schneider*, EU:C:2013:633.
[6] E.g. Decision of 11.11.2011, Vratsa Provincial Court, commercial case 36/2011; Decision 39 of 01.02.2010, Plovdiv Provincial Court, 11 panel, commercial case 436/2009.

the special jurisdiction rules of Article 5, such as disputes related to contract (for sale of goods[7] and provision of services[8]), disputes related to delicts,[9] disputes arising out of operations with a branch or another establishment.[10]

In most of the cases the defendants did not challenge the jurisdiction of the Bulgarian courts, but on several occasions challenges were raised and successfully upheld.[11] There was one unsuccessful jurisdictional challenge in a case concerning restitution claims in relation to an invalid contract, where a Bulgarian company sued a British company in Bulgaria under Article 5(1) of Brussels I. The defendant challenged the jurisdiction of the Bulgarian court and the first instance court upheld the challenge. The judge took the view that, due to the invalidity of the contract, there was no contractual relationship between the parties and Article 5(1) could not be invoked.[12] The claimant's appeal was allowed by the Varna Court of Appeal, holding that the first instance court had to assume jurisdiction under Article 5(1). It was held that the concept 'matters relating to a contract' was broad enough to cover a claim for restitution of sum of money under a contract which was invalidated.[13] This judgment is in line with the Brussels I regime, considering that the CJEU recently held 'that actions seeking the annulment of a contract and the restitution of sums paid but not due on the basis of that contract constitute "matters relating to a contract"'.[14] Based on this judgment and the previous CJEU case law on the interpretation of 'matters relating to a contract', as well as other related cases,[15] it follows that underlying criterion to assess whether an unjust enrichment case falls under Article 5(1) is whether the claim is related to (results from) a contractual relation, irrespective of whether such a contractual relation was annulled.

There are also judgments in cross-border disputes related to individual employment contracts. In these cases, the Bulgarian courts considered choice of law aspects,[16] assuming jurisdiction as the court of the place where the employee habitually carries out his work.[17] In the single judgment identified in relation to a consumer contract, the jurisdiction of the Bulgarian courts was based on the domicile of the consumer.[18]

There were several non-contractual disputes arising out of traffic accidents[19] and, on one occasion, there was a tortious claim.[20] In all these cases, the defendants were not locally

---

[7] Decision 151 of 4.12.2014, Pazardzhik Provincial Court, commercial case 125/2013.

[8] Ruling of 21.03.2016, Sofia City Court, 2 panel, private civil case 562/16; Ruling 2287, Plovdiv Provincial Court, 8 panel, private civil case 1713/2014.

[9] Ruling 495 of 2012, SCC, 1 civil panel, private civil case 456/2012; Ruling 886 of 9.11.2011, SCC, 2 commercial panel, private commercial case 130/2011; Ruling.39 of 24.01.2015, Peshtera District Court, civil case 750/2008; Ruling 328/13.05.2015, Pazardzhik Provincial Court, 2 panel, private civil case 430/ 2015.

[10] Decision of 04.03.2009, Sofia City Court, VI—5 panel, civil case of 2007.

[11] Ruling 2287 of Plovdiv Provincial Court, 8 panel, private civil case 1713/2014.

[12] Ruling 5382 of 19.11.2012, Varna Provincial Court, commercial case 1184/2012.

[13] Ruling of 13.03.2013, Varna Appellate Court, commercial case 96/ 2013.

[14] Case C-366/13, *Profit Investment Sim SpA* EU:C:2016:282, [58].

[15] Case C-102/15, *Gazdasági Versenyhivatal v Siemens Aktiengesellschaft Österreich*, EU:C:2016:607.

[16] Decision 111 of 15.05.2015, SCC, 3 panel, civil case 4455/2014.

[17] ibid; Ruling 357 of 1.06.2015, SCC, 4 civil panel, private civil case 1082/2015.

[18] Ruling 305 of 10.05.2014, Pazardzhik Provincial Court, 4 panel, civil case.269/2014.

[19] Ruling 495 of 2012, SCC, 1 civil panel, private civil case 456/2012; Ruling 886 of 9.11.2011, SCC, 2 commercial panel, private commercial case 130/2011.

[20] Ruling.39 of 24.01.2015, Peshtera District Court, civil case 750/2008.

domiciled and the harmful event occurred abroad, so that the Bulgarian courts had no jurisdiction. In another case, arising out of a traffic accident which occurred in Germany and caused the death of the son of the claimant, the Bulgarian court, engaging with the relevant CJEU case law, assumed jurisdiction on grounds of Article 11 (2) in relation to Article 9 (1) (b) of Brussels I.[21]

There was one high value insurance dispute where a *lis pendens* objection was raised. The claim concerned a marine insurance policy for a yacht, which was damaged in an incident that occurred in 2008 near Italy. The claimant was a Bulgarian company and the insurer was a German company. The Bulgarian court assumed jurisdiction under Article 9(1) of Brussels I. The defendant challenged the jurisdiction of the Bulgarian court. After the judges carefully analysed the available information about the cases pending before the Italian courts, the defendant's jurisdictional challenge was dismissed.[22] The dispute subsequently reached the SCC on substantive law points. The Bulgarian highest court remitted the case to the Bourgas Court of Appeal, in order for the judges to take a view on the merits.[23] This indicates how complex and time-consuming some cross-border disputes could be which might have an impact on the parties' effective access to remedies in cross-border cases.

The following issues are identified with respect to the way in which Brussels I is applied by the Bulgarian courts. First, there are some cases with an international element, where the courts took a decision on the merits, without examining the question of international jurisdiction.[24] Since none of the defendants involved seemed to raise the issue on international jurisdiction either, one could assume that the defendants submitted to the jurisdiction of the Bulgarian courts by entering an appearance. Nevertheless, this is still an issue because, under the applicable Bulgarian rules, the courts were supposed to check their jurisdiction *ex officio*.

Second, in a few court decisions dating back primarily from the first years of application of Brussels I in Bulgaria, the courts wrongfully relied on the CPIL in determining its jurisdiction.[25] There were also cases where the CPIL and Brussels I were simultaneously referenced. This could be regarded as an indication that some of the Bulgarian judges have insufficient experience in dealing with cross-border cases. The deduction that further training is needed may be further sustained by noting there are isolated cases where the courts prematurely applied Regulation 1215/2012 (rather than Regulation 44/2001).[26]

Third, when applying Article 59, the courts correctly conclude that the domicile of an individual should be determined in accordance with Bulgarian law. Since the national legislation does not contain a definition of the concept of 'domicile', the courts usually apply the definition of habitual residence from the CPIL. However, considering the differences

---

[21] Decision of 11.05.2015, Sofia City Court, 1 panel, civil case 5189/2013.

[22] Decision 23 of 23.04.2014, Bourgas Court of Appeal, commercial case 50/2014.

[23] Decision 115 of 15.08.2016, SCC, 2 panel, commercial case 3428/2014.

[24] Decision 571 of 28.03.2016, Sofia City Court, commercial case 2382/2012; Decision 54 of 12.02.2015, Bourgas Provincial Court, commercial case 81/2013; Decision 5364 of 18.10.2011, Sofia City Court, civil case 8891/2011; Decision of 24.10.2013 of Sofia District Court, civil case 19467/2012.

[25] Decision 7830 of 16.11.2015, Sofia City Court, civil case. 10390/2013.

[26] Ruling 3335 of 03.07.2015, Plovdiv Provincial Court, 10 panel, private civil case 1763/2015.

in both categories, this approach should not be supported.[27] There is a strong case for a legislative intervention or an interpretative decision of SCC in the light of the fact that the legal practice of the different Bulgarian courts is not consistent. Some of the courts take into account the permanent address; the current address of the individual is considered as a dominant factor by other judges; and both types of administrative registration have been considered in some other cases.[28] There are also cases where the court has analysed the domicile of an individual by taking into account factual criteria, without making references to the formally registered current or permanent address.[29] The level of variation in the local practice leads to a lack of predictability about the conclusion which a court could reach on this matter that is so important for assuming jurisdiction under the EU PIL framework.[30]

A few isolated cases have been identified in which the first instance court wrongly examined the grounds for refusal of the recognition of a foreign judgment under Article 34.[31] That said, it should be noted that this was more of an issue in the judgments rendered in the first years of the Brussels I's application. Indeed, in all cases where the first instance courts had refused to recognise a judgment on the ground of Article 34, their decisions were reversed by the appellate courts.[32]

III. Applicable Law—Rome I and Rome II

Publicly available decisions of Bulgarian courts in which Rome I and Rome II have been interpreted and applied are limited in number.

A. Rome I

In cross-border contractual disputes, the vast majority of available cases relate to international sale of goods, where the parties to the agreement had their place of business in contracting states to the Convention on Contracts for the International Sale of Goods ('CISG') and had not excluded expressly its application.[33] In addition, there appear to be many decisions where the courts correctly recognised the application of the law chosen by the parties in an employment contract;[34] applied the rules of Article 4 regarding contract for sale of

---

[27] See more in T Tsenova, 'Commentary of Art 59 of Brussels I' in N Natov et al (eds), *The Brussels I Regulation, Commentary* (Sofia, Ciela Norma AD, 2012) 566.

[28] Decision 587 of Pazardzhik Provincial Court on commercial case 577 of 2015; Ruling of 01.10.2014 of Varna Destruct Court, private civil case 2178 / 2014.

[29] Ruling 839 of 14.04.2016, Plovdiv Provincial Court, 7 panel, private civil case 458/2016.

[30] Recital 11 of Brussels I and Recital 15 of Brussels Ia.

[31] Decision of 24.10.2013, Sofia City Court, VI-I panel, commercial case 4624/2013; Order 256 of 17.07.2012, Vidin Provincial Court, private civil case 336/2012; Decision 2429 of 08.12.2015, Sofia Court of Appeal, 10 panel, civil case 2215/2015.

[32] Decision 325 of 07.01.2016, SCC, 4 civil panel, civil case 3166/2015.

[33] Decision 151 of 4.12.2014, Pazardzhik Provincial Court, commercial case 125/2013; Decision 571 of 28.03.2016, Sofia City Court, commercial case 2382/2012; Decision 644 of 11.04.2016, Sofia City Court, commercial case 8529/2013; Decision 1003 of 21.12.2015, Varna Provincial Court, commercial case 1537/2015; Decision 1693 of 24.04.2013, Plovdiv District Court, civil case. 8664/2011.

[34] Decision 618 of 5.05.2016, Ruse District Court, civil case. 5002/2015.

goods[35] and services;[36] applied Article 5 (2) regarding contracts for carriage of passengers,[37] or Article 7 in relation to insurance contracts.[38]

In a decision related to a distribution agreement the court ruled that the choice-of-law specified in the general terms of the supplier, which were provided to the distributor only with the invoice, was not valid. This decision was supported by the reasoning that the requirement to familiarise the other party with existing general terms before contract execution, as required by German law (chosen to govern the relations under the same general terms), was not satisfied.[39] Therefore, the court dealt with the case in accordance with the law determined under the rules of Article 4(1) (f) of Rome I, which happened to be Bulgarian law.

It is an interesting observation that, in most of the reviewed cases, the courts apply Bulgarian law and only in a few of the available decisions the courts have applied a foreign law. The main problems identified with respect to the application of Rome I by the Bulgarian courts can be summarised as follows. First, there are cases where the question of applicable law has not been analysed at all, resulting in application of Bulgarian substantive law.[40] Second, in a few court decisions instead of applying Rome I, the courts apply the CPIL.[41] Although the outcome in respect to the applicable law would have been the same irrespective of the statutory base, this is yet another indication that the national judges need further training in identifying the correct legal grounds. Third, a case was identified where the court applied Bulgarian employment law irrespective of the choice-of-law made by the parties. This was done on the basis that Bulgaria was the place where the employee carried out their work habitually and the relevant rules provided specific protection.[42]

B. Rome II

All of the reviewed cases relate to indemnification claims resulting from traffic accidents. In this respect the courts have examined a variety of disputes, among which are claims for compensation against the National Bureau of the Bulgarian Motor-vehicle Insurers,[43] reimbursement claims against the tortfeasor by the insurer,[44] reimbursement claims of the insurer of the injured party against the insurer of the tortfeasor,[45] claims for damages by the injured party against the insurer of the tortfeasor.[46] In most of the available decisions the Bulgarian courts correctly apply the rules of Article 4 (1) of Rome II, referring inter alia to the case law of the CJEU, including where this leads to application of a foreign law.

---

[35] Decision 1341 of 24.07.2013, Sofia City Court, commercial case 3150/2011.
[36] Decision 373 of 27.12.2013, Varna Court of Appeal, commercial case 592/2013.
[37] Decision of 24.10.2013, Sofia District Court, civil case 19467/2012.
[38] Decision 5364 of 18.10.2011, Sofia City Court, civil case 8891/2011.
[39] Decision 117 of 19.01.2015, Sofia Court of Appeal, commercial case 4721/2013.
[40] Decision of 09.02.2015 of Varna Provincial Court, V panel, civil case 238082014; Decision of 04.03.2009, Sofia City Court, VI—5 panel, commercial case of 2007.
[41] Decision 159 of 10.12.2015, Shumen Provincial Court, commercial case 643/2014; Decision 52 of 04.02.2016, Plovdiv Provincial Court, commercial case 582/2013.
[42] Decision 111 of 15.05.2015, SCC, 3 civil panel, civil case 4455/2014.
[43] Decision 110 of 10.03.2014, Kystendil District Court, civil case 835/2013.
[44] Decision 16198 of 11.08.2014, Sofia City Court, civil case 14722/2013.
[45] Decision of 08.04.2016, Sofia City Court, commercial case 1314/2015.
[46] Decision 7830 of 16.11.2015, Sofia City Court, civil case 10390/2013.

The main problem identified is that some Bulgarian judges appear to misunderstand the distinction between direct and indirect damages, which has led to Bulgarian law being regarded as applicable in cases where it should not have been applied in conflict with the objective to have the same law applicable irrespective of where the parties litigate.[47] In particular, there are some cases where the courts wrongly concluded that the Bulgarian law, being the law of the place of habitual residence of the injured party, is applicable to the merits of a cross-border dispute because this was the place where the injured party suffered moral damages.[48]

IV. Cross-border Family Law Disputes

A. Brussels IIa

The vast majority of Bulgarian court practice on the relevant EU regulations relate to matrimonial matters and matters of parental responsibility. The Bulgarian courts correctly interpret and apply the criteria under Article 3 as alternative grounds for international jurisdiction in matrimonial matters.[49] Most often, it is the common nationality of both spouses (ie Article 3 (2)) that is used as a ground for assuming jurisdiction.[50] When applying the habitual residence criterion, the courts conduct full analysis of the relevant facts to determine the state of habitual residence.[51]

With respect to matters of parental responsibilities the most common ground to assume jurisdiction is Article 8, ie the habitual residence of the child. The courts determine this factor by analysing the facts relevant to residence, but the level of detail applied differs to a considerable extent—ranging from comprehensive examination[52] to a formal discussion on current and permanent address.[53] Bulgarian courts often rely on Article 12 as a ground for jurisdiction in parental responsibility cases.[54] They generally apply correctly Article 10 and Article 11 and the relation between Brussels IIa and the 1980 Hague Convention.[55]

---

[47] Recital 6 of Rome II.

[48] Decision 16350 of 15.08.2014, Sofia City Court, civil case 8076/2012; Decision of 01.10.2015, Sofia City Court, civil case 8115/2012.

[49] Ruling 715 of 20.12.2010, SCC, 4 civil panel, private civil case 645/2010; Ruling 7559 of 04.05.2012, Sofia City Court, private civil case 2512/2012; Ruling 605 of 19.02.2013, Blagoevgrad Provincial Court, civil case 47/2013; Ruling 937 of 15.12.2014, SCC, 4 civil panel, private civil case 4035/2014.

[50] Decision of 24.07.2015 of Varna District Court, 10 panel, civil case 13892/2014; Ruling 763 of 08.12.2015, Pazardzhik Provincial Court, ll panel, private civil case 906/2015.

[51] Ruling 605 of 19.02.2013 of Blagoevgrad Provincial Court on civil case 47/2013; Ruling No 7559 of 04.05.2012 of Sofia City Court, Civil Chamber on private civil case No 2512/2012.

[52] Ruling of 14.12.2015, Dimitrovgrad District Court, civil case 1628/2015; Decision 231 of 19.11.2015, SCC, 3 civil panel, civil case 181/2015; Decision of 29.07.2015, Targovishte Provincial Court, civil case 151/2015.

[53] Decision 271 of 13.01.2014, Sofia City Court, 2 matrimonial panel, civil case 13131/2013; Ruling 21 of 12.01.2010, SCC, 4 civil panel, private civil case 733/2009.

[54] Ruling 3448 of 13.07.2015, Plovdiv Provincial Court, 1 panel, private civil case 1910/2015; Ruling 744 of 18.11.2013, SCC, 4 civil panel, private civil case 4818/2013; Ruling 763 of 08.12.2015, Pazardzhik Provincial Court, 1 panel, private civil case 06/015; Ruling 38 of 25.01.2011, SCC, 3 civil panel, private civil case 647/2010.

[55] Decision 764 of 05.02.2013, Sofia City Court, 5 matrimonial panel, civil case 15247/2012; Decision 4808 of 24.06.2013, Sofia City Court, 5 matrimonial panel, civil case 5233/2013.

Only one reference for preliminary ruling on the application of Brussels IIa has been made by the Bulgarian courts. It was sent by the SCC asking the CJEU to interpret whether a request for a court order replacing the consent of one of the parents for issuance of an international travel document of the child (absent the consent of that parent) falls under the scope of the regulation. With its judgment on case C-215/15[56] the CJEU confirmed that such proceedings fall in the scope of Brussels IIa.

Although Brussels IIa is correctly applied, there are still isolated cases of mixing the application of Brussels I, Brussels IIa and the CPIL, mainly in recognition and enforcement cases.[57] The main problems identified with respect to the application of Brussels IIa can be summarised as follows.

First, some courts rely on formal criteria when applying Article 3, like permanent address, nationality, current address. The same issue is identified in relation to Article 8, where many courts rely heavily on criteria like presence of the child in the country, habitual residence of the parents who are taking care of the child, current address of the child.

Second, when applying Article 12, some courts do not investigate the interests of the child at all and consider sufficient the acceptance of jurisdiction by both parents.[58] In several decisions the fact that the court had jurisdiction with respect to the matrimonial matter on grounds of Article 3 was regarded as sufficient to substantiate jurisdiction over matters of parental responsibility, without analysis of the requirements under Article 12.[59] There are also decisions where the court simply declares that it has jurisdiction under Article 12 in light of the superior interest of the child, without any analysis or justification of this conclusion.[60]

B. Maintenance Regulation

There are just a few publicly available cases where the courts refer to and apply the Maintenance Regulation. The most common ground used by the Bulgarian courts is the ancillary jurisdiction under Article 3(1)(d), namely pursuant to their jurisdiction on a parental responsibility claim, filed together with a maintenance claim.[61] There are also cases where the international jurisdiction is based on the habitual residence of the defendant (Article 3 (1) (a)).[62] In several cases for maintenance modification the Maintenance Regulation was also correctly referred to and applied.[63]

The reviewed cases do not reveal material concerns regarding the application of Article 15 and determination of the applicable law. Most of the available recognition

---

[56] C-215/14, *Gogova v Iliev*, EU:C:2015:710.

[57] Order of 22.10.2013, Pleven Provincial Court on civil case 1071/2013.

[58] Ruling 402 of 28.06. 2011, SCC, 4 civil panel, private civil case 289/2011; Ruling 763 of 08.12.2015, Pazardzhik Provincial Court, 1 panel, private civil case 906/015.

[59] Ruling 38 of 25.01. 2011, SCC, 3 civil panel, private civil case 647/2010.

[60] Decision of 24.07.2015, Varna District Court, 10 panel, civil case 13892/2014; Ruling 937 of 15.12. 2014, SCC, 4 civil panel, private civil case 4035/2014.

[61] Ruling 3841 of 10.09.2015, Plovdiv Provincial Court, 10 civil panel, private civil case 2269/2015; Ruling 3711 of 13.08.2015, Plovdiv Provincial Court, 10 civil panel, private civil case 2162/2015.

[62] Decision 778 of 28.05.2015, Pleven District Court, 12 panel, civil case 912/2015.

[63] Ruling 720 of 3.10.2014, SCC, 4 civil panel, private civil case 4451/2014; Decision 301 of 7.10.2013, SCC, 4 civil panel, civil case 2578/2013.

and enforcement cases are in compliance with the Maintenance Regulation[64] and it can be concluded that the Bulgarian courts predominantly apply Article 75 correctly.[65] The main problem identified is that, occasionally, there is no examination of whether the court has international jurisdiction. For example, a Bulgarian national files a claim for amendment of awarded maintenance against a Bulgarian national, and irrespective of the fact that both parties habitually reside in another Member State, the Bulgarian court assumes jurisdiction.[66]

V. Conclusion

The research findings from the survey of national case law indicate that that the main problems with application of the EU PIL regulations in Bulgaria are predominantly due to insufficient experience. Indeed, the most significant problem observed is non-application, or more precisely, the lack of examination of the questions of international jurisdiction and/or applicable law even where the facts of the case indicate presence of an international element.

Considering that the issues of PIL can be faced by judges in all courts throughout the country with rising frequency, the main problem with the judicial practice in Bulgaria is how to achieve adequate quality of decision-making in the cross-border context, whereas delays from jurisdictional challenges seem less relevant (due to local procedural specifics). The authors believe that an efficient (both in terms of cost and quality) manner of handling the problems arising out of the insufficient experience of the Bulgarian judges to deal with cross-border disputes would entail:

1. More training in PIL issues—there should be specialised seminars for all judges at least once every year, covering the newest trends in national and CJEU case law.
2. More possibilities for judges to interact and exchange experience at national level, considering an online best practices archive or similar electronic tools.
3. More opportunities for theoretical expertise and case law exchange between judges within the EU—a possible way to achieve this is an integrated information-sharing platform.

---

[64] Decision 32 of 20.02.2015, SCC, 3 civil panel, civil case 2699/2014.
[65] Ruling 404 of 3.02.2015, Varna Provincial Court, private civil case 99/2015; Order 1554 of 10.07.2013, Pazardzhik Provincial Court, civil case 538/2013; Order 6845 of 2.07.2013, Varna Provincial Court, private civil case 1997/2013.
[66] Decision 323 of 21.05.2012, Yambol Provincial Court, civil case 4259/2011.

13

Croatia

IVANA KUNDA

I. Introduction

Croatia acceded to the European Union on 1 July 2013.[1] Since then the courts have been obliged to apply the EU Regulations, but before that and where still no EU instrument is applicable, the Private International Law Act (the PIL Act) is applied.[2]

From the methodological point of view, this report is based primarily on searches in the incomplete, publically available databases in Croatia. In addition, the author was kindly permitted by the President of the Municipal Court in Rijeka to access their database '*e-spis*'. This was done in relation to cases brought before the Municipal Court in Rijeka in 2015 and the first half of 2016 (by 8 July).[3] The court decisions found as a result of the online and internal court database searching and browsing are for the purpose of this report complemented by decisions which the author has become aware of.[4] Unfortunately, the case law relevant for this report is not analysed in Croatian scholarship, the publications in the respective areas date prior to or immediately after the accession,[5] with a few notable exceptions related to family law.[6]

The focus of this report is on Brussels I. Croatian case law in the field of family law is being collected and analysed under two ongoing research projects.[7]

---

[1] See Treaty concerning the accession of the Republic of Croatia to the European Union, [2012] OJ L122/10.

[2] *Zakon o rješavanju sukoba zakona s propisima drugih zemalja u određenim odnosima*, Službeni list SFRJ 43/1982 and 72/1982, Narodne novine 53/1991 and 88/2001. For a brief note on the Croatian PIL system see D Babić, 'International Private Law' in T Josipović (ed), *Introduction to the Law of Croatia* (Alphen aan den Rijn, Kluwer, 2014) ch 15, 439–54.

[3] The total number of the P category cases was 7625 in 2015 and 1561 in 2016 (by 8 July), while the total number of the P Ob category cases was 1000 in 2015 and 241 in 2016 (by 8 July).

[4] These decisions are cited in the footnotes without any reference as to the source, and the copies thereof are held with the author.

[5] eg V Tomljenović and I Kunda (eds), *The Brussels I Regulation: Challenges for Croatian Judiciary*, (Rijeka, Pravni fakultet u Rijeci, 2012); J Garšić (ed), *Europsko građansko procesno pravo—izabrane teme*, (Zagreb, Narodne novine, 2013); N Bodiroga-Vukobrat et al, *Europsko obiteljsko pravo* (Zagreb, Narodne novine, 2013); I Kunda (ed), *Family and children: European expectations and national reality* (Rijeka, Pravni fakultet u Rijeci/HUPP, 2014); B Ljubanović et al, *Procesno—pravni aspekti prava EU* (Rijeka, Pravni fakultet Sveučilišta Josipa Jurja Strossmayera u Osijeku, 2016).

[6] eg T Hoško, 'Child Abduction in Croatia: Before and After the European Union Legislation' in M Župan (ed), *Private international Law and the jurisprudence of European Courts—Family at focus* (Osijek, Pravni fakultet u Osijeku, 2015) 159–84.

[7] See eg EU Judiciary Training on Brussels IIa Regulation: From South to East (JUST/2014/JTRA/AG/EJTR/6854) brussels2family.eu, and Planning the future of cross-border families: a path through coordination—EUFam's (JUST/2014/JCOO/AG/CIVI 4000007729) www.eufams.unimi.it/project/.

II. Issues Under the Brussels I Regulation

A. Matters Related to the Scope of Application

There is usually no problem in terms of *application in time*,[8] and where the lower court disregards that, the higher court corrects it.[9] However, a few cases show some confusion about the applicable instruments and their relationship, such as in the case in which the Municipal Court in Čakovec deciding in the first instance correctly applied the Brussels I Regulation, while the County Court in Varaždin deciding on appeal confirmed this part of the decision but in its reasons confusingly also cited the Croatian PIL Act.[10] In a recognition and enforcement case related to temporal scope of application, the County Court in Zagreb rightly distinguished between two decrees by a German court concerning the costs of the proceedings and subjected the one rendered on 16 January 2013 to the 1967 bilateral Convention on legal assistance in civil, family and criminal matters, and the other rendered on 13 December 2013 to the Brussels I Regulation, citing the Court of Justice of the European Union (CJEU) case law.[11]

The matter of *personal scope of application* was dealt with in a case related to the infringement of intellectual property rights brought before the Commercial Court in Zagreb in 2015.[12] The holder of Croatian national trademarks and the then Community (now European Union) trademarks, a USA based company, filed a lawsuit against a company with its address in Ukraine who was named as receiver of the allegedly infringing goods. The goods were intended for Hungary but were detained by the Croatian customs authorities while in transit in Croatia. The first instance court decided that it had no jurisdiction as the Brussels I Regulation did not apply because the defendant's domicile was not in the European Union and the matter was not covered by the exclusive jurisdiction in Article 22.[13]

In another case, the Commercial Court in Split stated that because the plaintiff is a legal person having its seat in Algeria, a non-Member State, the Brussels I Regulation does not apply.[14] Yet, in the next sentence the Court, anticipating possible problems with this

---

[8] See in relation to the proceedings regarding the merits, eg *Visoki trgovački sud Republike Hrvatske*, 17. Pž-9201/13-4, decree of 25.5.2015 (confirming *Trgovački sud u Zadru*, P-213/12, decree of 2.8.2013), accessible at www.iusinfo.hr. See in relation to the proceedings regarding the recognition and enforcement, eg *Visoki trgovački sud Republike Hrvatske*, 62. Pž-7439/13-3, decree of 24.9.2015 (annulling for reasons other than temporal scope of application: *Trgovački sud u Bjelovaru*, R1-32/12-14, decree of 28.2.2013).

[9] See eg *Visoki trgovački sud Republike Hrvatske*, 64. Pž-7109/14-3, decree of 1.4.2015 (annulling *Trgovački sud u Zagrebu, Stalna služba u Karlovcu*, P-3476/13, decree of 8.7.2014).

[10] *Županijski sud u Varaždinu*, Gž-1708/15-2, decree of 3.7.2015 (partially confirming and partially annulling *Općinski sud u Čakovcu*, P-125/14-28, decree of 17.2.2015), accessible at www.iusinfo.hr.

[11] *Županijski sud u Zagrebu*, Gž-804/2015-2, decree of 23.2.2015 (confirming *Općinski građanski sud u Zagrebu*, R1-484/2014, decree of 25.7.2014 and R1-484/2014-6 supplementing decree of 15-9-2014). The Court cited the CJEU case C-514/10 *Wolf Naturprodukte GmbH v SEWAR spol s ro*, EU:C:2012:367.

[12] *Visoki trgovački sud Republike Hrvatske*, 73. Pž-6741/15-3, decree of 12.10.2015 (annulling *Trgovački sud u Zagrebu*, P-2071/15, decree of 31.8.2015).

[13] Deciding on the appeal, the High Commercial Court pointed out that the documents in the file concerning the plaintiff indicate that the plaintiff was incorporated under Dutch law. Although the plaintiff's domicile is irrelevant under Brussels I, it is relevant in the context of the application of the EU Trademark Regulation. As per the High Commercial Court the plaintiff's domicile is to be ascertained under Art 94 of the EU Trademark Regulation in conjunction with Art 60 of the Brussels I Regulation, which the first instance court failed to do.

[14] *Trgovački sud u Splitu*, 16 P-622/14, decree of 24.7.2015.

position, reasoned: 'In case the higher court does not share the same opinion as this court, it is added ...', this part of the reasoning explaining that jurisdiction cannot be established even under the Brussels I Regulation.

In relation to the *material scope of application*, there has been a request for a preliminary ruling addressed to the CJEU from the Municipal Court in Pula[15] asking a question on the applicability of the Brussels I Regulation Recast in case of default of payment for parking. The public/private law nature of this obligation is doubtful because the company providing the parking service is founded and owned by the local authority (the City of Pula) and the terms and conditions under which the service is provided are defined in the acts (rules, decisions, orders) rendered by this authority rather than the company management. On the other hand, in the pre-EU context the Constitutional Court of the Republic of Croatia ruled in favour of the private contractual relationship. In its 2008 judgment the Constitutional Court stated that despite the fact that the rules on the parking service are prescribed by the local authority, they are to be characterised as terms and conditions within the meaning of the Obligations Act[16] which, if properly notified, become part of the standard service contract concluded by adhesion.[17] It is to be seen whether the same characterisation will result before the CJEU following the principle of autonomous interpretation. The other question asked of the CJEU is whether the Brussels I Regulation Recast applies to notaries in Croatia who have important competences in the enforcement procedure under Croatian national law. However, under Article 3 of the Recast such inclusions within the term 'court' are provided for Hungarian notaries and the Swedish Enforcement Authority.

B. Matters Related to Jurisdiction

The usual pattern in cases which concern a *right in rem in an immovable* located in Croatia, is that court has jurisdiction pursuant to Article 22(1) of the Brussels I Regulation, however, this issue is often neither invoked by the parties nor mentioned in the reasons of the judgment.[18] The situation was the same before accession to the European Union, because the jurisdiction issue was in principle never discussed.[19] However, the situation seems to

---

[15] Case C-551/15: Request for a preliminary ruling from the *Općinski sud u Puli-Pola* (Croatia) lodged on 23 October 2015—*Pula Parking doo v Sven Kalus Tederahn*.

[16] The Obligations Act is the equivalent to the civil code and features as the *lex generalis* for all civil obligations in the Republic of Croatia. *Zakon o obveznim odnosima*, Narodne novine 35/2005, 41/2008, 125/2011 and 78/2015.

[17] *Ustavni sud Republike Hrvatske*, U-II-355/2007, decree of 10.12.2008, available at www.usud.hr/hr/praksa-ustavnog-suda.

[18] eg *Visoki trgovački sud Republike Hrvatske*, VI Pž-1074/05-4, decree of 19.6.2006 (confirming *Trgovački sud u Rijeci*, XVI-P-1283/2003-18, decree of 10.1.2005); *Općinski sud u Rijeci, Stalna služba u Opatiji*, 82-P-378/2016-11, judgment of 29.4.2016; *Općinski sud u Rijeci, Stalna služba u Krku*, P-7502-2015-2, judgment of 14.1.2016; *Općinski sud u Rijeci*, P-7484/2015-12, judgment of 3.6.2016; *Općinski sud u Rijeci*, P-2386/14, judgment of 30.7.2015; *Općinski sud u Rijeci, Stalna služba u Opatiji*, 81 P-4196/2015, judgment of 29.12.2015; *Općinski sud u Rijeci, Stalna služba u Malom Lošinju*, P-3915/15, judgment of 14.5.2015; *Općinski sud u Rijeci, Stalna služba u Malom Lošinju*, P-3645/15, judgment of 7.10.2015; *Općinski sud u Rijeci, Stalna služba u Crikvenici*, P-970/2015, judgment of 3.7.2015 (in this case, the claims against the defendant were for handing over the possession of a wrongfully detained part of the plaintiffs' land, tearing down the wall wrongfully built on the plaintiffs' land and rebuilding the traditional wall previously existing on the plaintiffs' land, and in default of the defendant, the plaintiffs are permitted to do that at the cost of the defendant).

[19] *Visoki trgovački sud Republike Hrvatske*, 70. Pž-9506/13-4, decree of 16.3.2016 (confirming *Trgovački sud u Osijeku*, P-774/12-52, decree of 8.3.2013); *Visoki trgovački sud Republike Hrvatske*, 91. Pž-7564/10-3, decree of 2.4.2014 (annulling for reasons other than jurisdiction *Trgovački sud u Zagrebu*, P-926/07, decree of 31.5.2010).

be slowly changing. Thus, in the above cited case before the County Court in Varaždin, the claim in contract (to declare null and void a loan contract containing an agreement on securing the claim by means of a mortgage) was combined with the claim to invalidate the entry in the Land Register based on that contract and agreement and to erase the entry so that the previous legal situation be restored. The Court characterised the latter issue as the right *in rem* within the meaning of Article 22(1) as a question of 'mortgage and ownership' registered to the names of the defendants.[20] Although one might be inclined to interpret the issue so to fall under Article 22(3),[21] it is also important to note that the entry in the register is a constituent element for obtaining a right *in rem* under Croatian law just as the invalidity and consequential erasing of the entry is a constituent element of losing that right, for instance where it is established that a contract on the sale of an immovable is null and void.[22] In Croatian practice, the entry in the Land Registry is simply a way of phrasing the claim, which in fact concerns the dispute related to entitlement to the right or interest in the immovable, and not at all mistaken entry or the like.[23]

The Commercial Court in Split[24] heard a case brought by a company domiciled in Algeria against two companies domiciled in Croatia and a company domiciled in England. The English party as seller and Algerian party as buyer concluded the contract for sale of iron rods, produced by one of the Croatian defendants and forwarded by the other. The problem was that the buyer did not receive the rods due to the arrest of the ship, but the seller received payment because the terms of the documentary letter of credit were satisfied. The Algerian company claimed that the damage, mostly in the amount paid by the bank to the seller, was caused to them because of the fraudulently continued loading regardless of the arrest only to satisfy the terms of the letter of credit. Regarding the jurisdiction under Article 5(1)(b) of the Brussels I Regulation, the Court held that Croatia is not the *forum solutionis* because goods were to be delivered to the buyer in Algeria. Likewise, the English party cannot be joined as co-defendant to two defendants having domiciles in Croatia because the claims are not sufficiently closely connected given that the claim against the Croatian defendants is based on non-contractual liability and the claim against the English defendant is based on contractual liability. This part of the reasoning appears convincing. However, the main justification should not have been the contractual and non-contractual nature of the claims as the Court appears to erroneously put forward,[25] but rather the detail that the claims against the Croatian companies were based on different facts in comparison to the one against the English defendant. While the claim against Croatian companies

---

[20] Above n 15.

[21] See eg B Audit, *Droit international privé* (Paris, Economica, 2000) 466; L de Lima Pinheiro, in U Magnus and P Mankowski (eds), *Brussels Ibis Regulation* (Cologne, Otto Schmidt, 2016) 574–75.

[22] The latter was the matter for decision in the case before the *Općinski sud u Rijeci, Stalna služba u Opatiji*, judgment of 16.7.2015. The Court failed to consider the issue of jurisdiction.

[23] See eg *Općinski sud u Rijeci, Stalna služba u Opatiji*, 82-P-4244/2015-12, judgment of 27.4.2016. The plaintiff claimed there was a mistaken entry in the Land Register and asked the registry court to correct it. The defendant disagreed. Hence, the registry court instructed the plaintiff to solve the dispute before the municipal court. In the proceedings before the municipal court, the registration is simply the way to phrase the issue, while the essential issue at dispute is whether the plaintiff is the owner.

[24] Above n 19.

[25] CJEU clearly stated that the fact that claims have different legal basis does not preclude application of Art 6(1) of the Brussels I Reg. CJEU case C-98/06 *Freeport plc v Olle Arnoldsson*, EU:C:2007:595. See also CJEU case C-645/11 *Land Berlin v Ellen Mirjam Sapir*, EU:C:2013:228.

concerned allegedly fraudulent issuing of EUR.1 certificate concerning the origin of the rods, the claim against the English seller was based on fraudulent loading continued which was subsequent to the arrest and omission to inform the buyer of the arrest. Therefore, the judge should have considered whether and to what extent the English seller was implicated in the fraudulent issuing of EUR.1 certificate as well as whether the defendants conspired to commit the alleged fraud. On this basis, one could argue that, as might be inferred from the judgment, the Court could have assumed jurisdiction under Art 6(1) of the Brussels I Regulation for the respective part of the clam against the English defendant. The Court failed to make this distinction which shows well how complex cross-border tortious claims against multiple defendants may be.

As regards prorogation, the High Commercial Court emphasised that the prorogation agreement is valid if in writing, regardless of where it is entered into. The Court further explained that the nature and connection between two loan contracts from 2002 and 2011 is not such that the later contract is auxiliary to the former and that hence the prorogation clause in the former cannot extend to the later. The validity of the prorogation agreement might be questionable from the point of view of the defendant's allegation that the plaintiff did not exist since it was registered as a company only in 2004. Finally, the High Commercial Court emphasised that the claims did not only relate to contractual matters, but to erasing the mortgage from the Croatian Land Registry which the court rightfully characterised under Article 22 of the Brussels I Regulation as a matter of exclusive jurisdiction. The Court added that, under Article 6, a person may be sued before the *forum rei sitae* (for immovable) if the contractual claim is related to an *in rem* claim.

C. Matters Related to Recognition and Enforcement

In the abovementioned case concerning the recognition and enforcement of two German decisions on costs of the proceedings, the County Court in Zagreb had the opportunity to discuss the public policy defence.[26] The respondent claimed that the decisions on the cost of the proceedings were a sequel to the 2012 decisions on merits whereby the same German court rejected her claim based on the law on extra-marital partners according to which children born out of wedlock before 1 July 1949, as she was, do not have the right to inheritance. She invoked Article 14 of the Constitution of the Republic of Croatia[27] and Article 14 of the European Convention on Human Rights (ECHR). The County Court in Zagreb held that because the decision on costs was decided as a separate matter of economic interest, independent form the merits of the litigation, there was no violation of public policy. Whatever the position regarding the Croatian public policy in the case at hand, this argument is not convincing. It would entail that, regardless of the fact that the decision on the merits violates the public policy, the costs resulting from the proceedings in which such violation occurred should be nevertheless enforced in the requested country. This is not coherent in the light of the nature and role of the costs of proceedings in both Croatian (and German) law. They can hardly be called independent from the merits, as in principle they depend on

---

[26] Above n 16.
[27] *Ustav Republike Hrvatske*, Narodne novine 85/2010 (codified version) and 5/2014.

the claim value and success of a party in the legal dispute.[28] As a rule, the costs are decided on together with the merits, only the calculation is sometimes made in a separate document for efficiency purposes (as in the case at hand). It seems unlikely that in a reverse, more common situation, in which a decision contains the part on the merits and the part on the costs, and where the former is considered contrary to the requested country's public policy, the latter would still be recognisable and enforceable there.

III. Croatian National Courts' Practice in Interpreting the Regulations

Croatian judges seem to be struggling with basic problems, such as scope of application. In at least one case,[29] a court relied on a CJEU judgment in interpreting the law. In another case, scholarship had clearly been relied on without explicit citation.

IV. Cost and Length of Litigation in Cross-border Civil and Commercial Disputes

There is no data on length of the proceedings specific to cross-border litigation. The systematic data concerning the length of proceedings in Croatia has been collected since the beginning of 2016 based on the criteria established by the European Commission for the Efficiency of Justice (CEPEJ).[30] The Croatian legal system does not appear to be particularly attractive to litigants except perhaps to those practising delaying strategies or wanting slow but inexpensive justice.

In general, the cost of the proceedings consist of several factors: the court fees, lawyer's fees and other costs, such as the expert witness costs. The court fees are generally very low and thus contribute to a high-litigation culture in Croatia.[31] Despite no mention of private

---

[28] See Art 154 of the Civil Procedure Act (*Zakon o parničnom postupku*, Službeni list SFRJ 4/1977, 36/1977, 36/1980, 6/1980, 69/1982, 43/1982, 58/1984, 74/1987, 57/1989, 20/1990, 27/1990 and 35/1991, Narodne novine 53/1991, 91/1992, 112/1999, 129/2000, 88/2001, 117/2003, 88/2005, 2/2007, 96/2008, 84/2008, 123/2008, 57/2011, 25/2013 and 89/2014) which provides that the losing party has to pay the other party's costs. In the case of a partially lost case, either the losing party pays for the proportionate amount of the other party's costs or each party bears its own costs. Likewise, under Ss 91–92 of the Code of Civil Procedure (*Zivilprozessordnung*, In der Fassung der Bekanntmachung vom 05.12.2005 (BGBl I S 3202, ber 2006 S 431, 2007 S 1781), zuletzt geändert durch Gesetz vom 05.07.2016 (BGBl I S 1578)) the principle is that the prevailing party has the right to be reimbursed for the recognised costs and in a case of partial success this applies proportionately.

[29] The other case is the case citing Case C-90/97 *Robin Swaddling v Adjudication Officer*, EU:C:1999:96, in the family law context: *Županijski sud Dubrovniku*, Gž.1366/14 of 15 October 2014, www.iusinfo.hr.

[30] *Pokazatelji učinkovitosti za 2016.*, available at the official website of the Ministry of Justice of the Republic of Croatia https://pravosudje.gov.hr/pravosudni-sustav-11207/sudovi/pokazatelji-ucinkovitosti/1207.

[31] *Zakon o sudskim pristojbama*, Narodne novine 74/1995, 57/1996, 137/2002, 125/2011, 112/2012, 157/2013 and 110/2015. The court fee is paid for each activity (statement of claim, judgment/decree, appeal etc). The calculation is made based on the claim value. For instance, for the statement of claim initiating the litigation the minimal court fee is HRK100 payable for claims up to HRK3.000 in value, while the maximum court fee is HRK5.000 for any claim exceeding HRK15.000. Since 2011, the court fee for the appeal is double the fee for the statement of claim, in order to discourage what in Croatia is a regular practice—to appeal. It is interesting to note that the court fee for decree on recognition and enforcement is only HRK100 and on appeal is only HRK160.

international law in this context, it is possible to request a double fee in a cross-border case, the decision depending on the complexity of a particular case.[32] Contingency fees are limited to 30 per cent of the award.[33] When a Croatian lawyer provides legal advice and representation to a party abroad, the costs are calculated under the law of that country.[34]

V. Settlement and Alternative Dispute Resolution for Cross-border Civil and Commercial Disputes

Settlement rates are not very high in Croatia. Judges, some of which are now also educated for conciliation, regularly suggest to the parties to attempt conciliation and temporarily stay the proceedings for that purpose. The conversation with municipal court judges in Rijeka on 12 July 2016, revealed that the majority of the parties to whom they suggested mediation prefer judge-mediators (other than the one that is deciding their case) to other mediators because the court-assisted mediation is free of charge unlike the one before other entities providing mediation services.

Arbitration, on the other hand, is not so common before the Permanent Court of Arbitration attached to the Croatian Chamber of Commerce,[35] and there is no data about the frequency of arbitration clauses in cross-border contracts. Despite the fact that a considerable number of arbitral cases remain hidden from the public eyes, the number of recognitions and enforcements of foreign arbitral awards in Croatia might provide some indication as to (non-)popularity of arbitration among Croatian parties in their cross-border transactions. The recent study concerning the operation of the 1958 New York Convention in Croatia, mentions only a small number of cases.[36]

VI. Conclusion

Courts are experiencing some confusion regarding the applicable instruments (EU or Croatian).[37] On the other hand, there seems to be a fair understanding of the provisions

---

[32] No 37 of the Tariff.

[33] No 39 of the Tariff.

[34] No 40 of the Tariff.

[35] In the past quarter of a century, there have been around 50 arbitration disputes.

[36] The study explains that there are indications about the number of cases most likely being small, while the study covers only some of them due to their unavailability through existing databases or inefficient search engines. V Butorac Malnar, 'Interpretation and application of the New York Convention in Croatia' in GA Bermann (ed), *Recognition and Enforcement of Foreign Arbitral Awards—Application of The New York Convention by National Courts* (New York, Springer, 2017).

[37] Similar situations exist in a few family law cases. A case in point is divorce between two Croatian nationals, with their domiciles registered in Croatia and, as may be concluded from the scarce data in the second instance decision, probably had their habitual residences in Germany. To resolve the divorce claim dated 27 May 2014, the Municipal Court in Koprivnica invoked the Croatian PIL Act regarding jurisdiction and the Rome III Reg regarding the applicable law. The County Court in Varaždin correctly stated that Croatia is not participating in the Rome III Reg and that the jurisdiction is subject to the provisions of the Brussels IIa Reg (although superfluously trying to explain that the jurisdiction would also be existing under the national provisions). *Županijski sud u Varaždinu*, Gž Ob-36/15-2, decree of 17.2.2016 (confirming *Općinski sud u Koprivnici*, 9P-527/14-17, judgment and decree of 20.3.2015), accessible at www.iusinfo.hr.

on exclusive and special jurisdiction and choice of court agreements in Brussels I, owed partially to comparable notions in the Croatian private international law. As a rule, in cases which fail to address the jurisdictional issue (usually the rights *in rem*), the Croatian courts have competence. However, one court erred in not applying its own public policy in the recognition proceedings. As a final note, the vast majority of errors made at first instance are effectively corrected at second instance. In Croatia a large proportion of decisions are appealed. A dissatisfied party may also ask for a review before the Supreme Court of the Republic of Croatia. As a final resort, the Constitutional Court of the Republic of Croatia may act upon a complaint where, as a result of the erroneous application of the rules on jurisdiction and/or applicable law, the party's constitutional freedoms or fundamental rights have been violated.[38]

---

[38] See eg *Ustavni sud Republike Hrvatske*, U-III-1162/2001, decision of 5.12.2001.

14

Cyprus

NIKITAS E HATZIMIHAIL[*]

I. Introduction

Cyprus has been an independent country since 1960 and a European Union (EU) Member State since 2004. Its legal system is increasingly described as *mixed*.[1] Unlike classic mixed jurisdictions, in Cyprus, the 'core' of the legal system (namely obligations, commercial and company law, testate succession, criminal law and procedural law of all sorts) follows the English common law tradition: colonial-era legislative 'codifications' of the common law constitute the starting point in all these fields. English-trained lawyers continue to dominate the legal elite and it took over 30 years after independence for the official language (Greek) to supplant English as the language of legal practice. Common law constitutes the residual law for private and criminal law matters (but English legislative reform of the common law, since 1960, is to be disregarded). Only family law and administrative law constitute civilian enclaves, and even in these areas English notions are encroaching. On the other hand, things have been gradually changing. The demographic explosion of the Cyprus bar and the creeping awareness of the potential of European private law to provide legal solutions are posing a challenge for the system's English pillars.[2] At the same time, the recent innovations in English international civil litigation are gradually making their way in Cyprus's commercial practice.

Today, Cyprus is an internationalised economy, with a noticeable presence in asset management and especially corporate and fiduciary services. Whereas there is some truth to the stereotype of Cyprus providing a basis for assets, companies and trusts for non-residents, it must be noted that now a significant proportion of its residents come from both former Soviet republics and Eastern and Central European EU Member States. Most of these individuals are workers, who tend to raise family law and simple civil claims, but there is also a noticeable number of Russian and Ukrainian business people and their families.

Prior to EU accession, Cyprus private international law (PIL) was ironically the only subject not addressed by comprehensive domestic legislation, in the colonial era or after

---

[*] Thanks and acknowledgements, for illuminating conversations and information, to Pavlos Neofytou Kourtellos, Laris Vrahimis, Michael Chatzipanagiotis, George Serghides and especially Kyriakos Kyriakides.

[1] S Symeonides, 'The Mixed Legal System of the Republic of Cyprus' (2003) 78 *Tulane Law Review* 441; N Hatzimihail, 'Cyprus as a Mixed Legal System' (2013) 6 *Journal of Civil Law Studies* 37.

[2] N Hatzimihail, 'On Law, Legal Elites and the Legal Profession in a (Biggish) Small State: Cyprus' in P Butler and C Morris (eds), *Small States in a Legal World* (New York, Springer, 2017), 213–244.

independence. The orientation towards English conflict of laws was almost complete, with judicial authorities mostly provided by English case law, a role acknowledged to the principal English reference works and Dicey and Morris constituting the leading authority in PIL matters. Cyprus courts have traditionally applied Cyprus law in cases before them. Cases coming before Cyprus courts traditionally had a strong connection with the forum, even after the explosive development of the past few decades. Tools such as *forum non conveniens* became especially popular, both as a means of disposing of certain kinds of cases and as a guiding light of jurisdictional thinking. The principal non-EU legislative reform concerned the promulgation of the Foreign Court Judgments (Recognition, Registration and Enforcement According to Convention) Law 2000, which applies to judgments, awards or even enforceable decisions by 'bodies' of countries with which Cyprus has mutual-enforcement agreements (now including EU instruments).[3]

Cyprus has a two-instance judicial system. At the trial level, District Courts are courts of general jurisdiction: all civil cases are adjudicated by a single judge. In 1990, Family Courts were established and have gradually acquired jurisdiction over most types of family-law cases. Tribunals also have jurisdiction for certain types of employment and rent-control disputes. All appeals are judged by the 13 justices of the Supreme Court of Cyprus (in three-member panels for civil and criminal cases). The Supreme Court also acts as constitutional court, administrative appellate court; it has trial-level jurisdiction, in single bench, over prerogative writs and admiralty cases and until 2016, when a first instance Administrative Court was created, it filled that role as well. The Supreme Court cases are published in official reports, as well as in the open-access legal information site CyLaw.

II. Cyprus's Experience on Cross-border Civil and Commercial Disputes

A. Jurisdictional and Procedural Issues Under the Brussels I Regulation

The vast majority of cases concern the Brussels I Regulation (with references to the Brussels I Recast having recently begun). This includes 18 appellate decisions (as well as 25 decisions on writ applications) by the Supreme Court and over 200 trial court decisions; however, many of the appellate—and most trial-level—cases involve casual references or present little doctrinal interest. In some other cases, the real issues are connected with the European Enforcement Order and the Service Regulation.[4]

This is natural, given both the Regulation's scope and long life, and the procedural orientation of Cyprus's civil and commercial litigation. Awareness of the Regulation within the legal profession was also prompted by the *Orams* case:[5] in 2006, enforcement of a 2004–2005 Cyprus judgment against an English couple that claimed to have acquired ownership over land in northern Cyprus (under military occupation of Turkey with application of the EU

---

[3] L 121(I)/2000 [2000] EE I(I), 3420.
[4] See below 277–278.
[5] C-420/07, EU:C:2009:271.

acquis suspended pending solution to the Cyprus problem) was sought in England under Brussels I and was eventually granted after a European Court of Justice (ECJ) decision.

i. Matters Related to the Scope of Application

Questions concerning the Regulation's scope of application tend to come up, occasionally, in the course of efforts to avail litigants of its tools. A typical example can be seen in the effort of a Russian resident to obtain interim orders regarding the allegedly sizeable Cyprus-located assets controlled by her husband, also a Russian resident. The claimant's counsel invoked Brussels I to establish jurisdiction over the several Cypriot companies allegedly controlled by the co-defendant. The Limassol District Court held that, being a marital-property case, it fell outside the Regulation's scope of application. It declined jurisdiction by invoking the *forum non conveniens* doctrine.[6]

In an action filed prior to Cyprus accession to the EU and the Regulation's coming into force in Cyprus, the Supreme Court held that the Regulation was to apply to the enforcement of an English judgment which became final in 2006.[7]

ii. Matters Related to Jurisdiction

a. Jurisdiction Over Contract Claims

Most Brussels I cases concern contractual disputes, primarily regarding commercial transactions. Many Cyprus-related international contracts include jurisdiction clauses and the strong forum policy in favour of jurisdictional agreements is confirmed by the courts in the application of Brussels I.[8]

Some of these cases involve jurisdiction disputes under Article 5(1) of Brussels I. The Supreme Court has endorsed the principle that the place of the 'principal obligation' has jurisdiction under Article 5(1).[9] Forum jurisdiction was consequently upheld over a dispute involving a distribution agreement with effect in Cyprus.[10] However, in November 2013, the Nicosia District Court asserted jurisdiction over a contractual dispute where Ireland, the domicile of the defendant, was the place of the goods' delivery, on the ground that the obligation to be performed in the actual case concerned the payment, in Cyprus, of the remainder.[11] In December 2013, another Supreme Court panel addressed a very similar case and held that Article 5(1)(b) has pre-empted that jurisdictional rule and therefore the Cyprus courts had no jurisdiction over another Irish defendant.[12] In May 2014, a senior Supreme Court Justice declined to issue a writ of prohibition in the first case.[13]

---

[6] *Potavina v Potavin* (Limassol DCt 27.10.2014).
[7] *Ironhold Estates Ltd v Travelworld Vacation Ltd* [2010] 1 CLR 452.
[8] See eg *Hampton Advisory Group SA v Bost AD* [2012] 1 CLR 549; *Digimed Communications Ltd v Nera ASA* [2010] 1 CLR 625.
[9] See eg *Hampton Advisory Group SA v Bost AD* [2012] 1 CLR 549.
[10] *Friesland Hellas AEBE v Clappas Trading House Ltd* [2011] 1 CLR 1200.
[11] *G Kallis (Manufacturers) Ltd v Dunnes Stores* (Nicosia DCt, 25.10.2013).
[12] *Loughrans Stores Ltd v DP Agroproducts Ltd*, SCt, 23.12.2013.
[13] *Re Dunnes Stores* (SCt, Civ pet, 29.5.2014).

b. Jurisdiction Over Consumer Contracts

Consumer jurisdiction is being increasingly invoked, usually as a defence against jurisdiction, mostly without success, even by individuals clearly engaged in business.[14] The more interesting cases concern litigation between Cyprus banks and foreigner purchasers of land—or guarantors of like contracts entered into by companies registered in Cyprus.[15] Many of these contracts also contained unilateral jurisdiction clauses. Looming over these cases is the apparent involvement of broker or financial consultants active in the place of the buyers' domicile, who may have worked closely with people and entities in Cyprus in ways conceivably falling within the scope of Article 15(1)(c). On their side, banks have argued, repeatedly but ultimately unsuccessfully, that mortgages fall under Article 22.1. Courts are having a harder time with the argument that such real-estate purchases were made for investment purposes and thus fall outside the scope of consumer jurisdiction: recently, the Paphos District Court (home to many of these cases) held otherwise, staying proceedings against UK residents.[16]

c. Jurisdiction Over Tort Claims

There is little case law, on the contrary, regarding jurisdiction for tort. In a recent case concerning the breach of a Memorandum of Understanding, it was held that since the co-defendant Channel Islands partnership was not party to the agreement itself, as opposed to its officers and agents, jurisdiction against it could only be grounded on Article 5(3) with Cyprus not being the place where the harmful event occurred.[17]

d. Provisional Measures—Interim Relief

Cyprus is a regular forum for interim relief applications. The courts have been following in this field, at a smaller pace and with occasional reluctance, the modern developments in English commercial litigation. Endorsement, by the full bench of the Supreme Court in 2007 of the worldwide effect of Mareva orders, overturning previous case law, was a milestone in that regard,[18] but most of the action takes place in the Nicosia and Limassol District Courts. The limits that EU instruments may be placing on such procedural tools are still being explored, as the principal cases have involved third-country or Cypriot nationals/residents; at the same time, the consolidation and expansion of the European judicial space

---

[14] *Polykarpou v TUI Poland SpZoO* [2011] 1 CLR 1808.

[15] These latter cases are covered by the Court of Justice of the European Union (CJEU) ruling in *Česká spořitelna v Feichter* C-419/11, EU:C:2013:165. In the far more numerous instances, of an individual mortgagee, the Cypriot seller company (usually real-estate developers) signed as guarantors and were named as co-defendants. See eg *Alpha Bank Cyprus Ltd v McNally* (Larnaca DCt 21.7.2016);

[16] *Alpha Bank Cyprus Ltd v Bell* (Paphos DCt, 30.8.2016); same in Alpha Bank Cyprus v Wright (Paphos DCt, 16.9.2016).

[17] See eg *Directo Capital Investments Ltd v Global Finance* (SCt, 18.7.2016).

[18] *Seamark Consultancy Services Ltd v Lasala* [2007] 1 CLR 162. For a discussion of the Supreme Court's evolving case law, and changing attitudes toward English procedural innovations, see N Hatzimihail, 'Reconstructing Mixity: Sources of Law and Legal Method in Cyprus' in V Palmer et al (eds), *Mixed Legal Systems, East and West* (Farnham, Ashgate, 2015) 75, 94–96.

is increasing the potential of Cyprus as a venue for obtaining judgments enforceable in other Member States.[19]

An interesting case under Article 31 of Brussels I involved the application for a freezing order by a German shipyard against a Cypriot ship management and a Dutch holding company, in the context of court proceedings in Germany. After noting that Article 31 enabled the Cyprus courts to exercise auxiliary jurisdiction and that the Reichert requirement of 'a real link between the subject matter of the measures sought and the territorial jurisdiction' of the forum was met, Psara-Miltiadou PDC found that the applicants had violated the duty of disclosure and dismissed their application.[20]

iii. Matters Related to Recognition and Enforcement

Enforcement litigation is a staple of Cyprus commercial practice and raising procedural hurdles is quite a common tool for practitioners and judges alike. Ex parte proceedings were a common feature of early-stage Cypriot civil litigation even prior to EU accession and empirical evidence would suggest that Brussels I has been relatively successful in providing a simplified procedural regime for enforcement formalities.[21] In the words of Michaelidou J, the Regulation's 'spirit and letter', as reflected in Article 41, aims to enable the applicant to have the judgment recognised as soon as possible, which is a goal served by the ex parte nature of the first stage of the process.[22] On the other hand, writ requests are still not uncommon, even if most are denied, and mistakes can be and are made at the enforcement stage. For example, in 2012 the Supreme Court reversed a trial court's judgment and set aside an enforcement decree that failed to state explicitly the time limit within which the judgment debtor could move to set aside the decree.[23]

The case law has stressed that the applicant for enforcement does not need to prove that the judgment debtor has assets in the Member State where enforcement is sought.[24] In another case, Demetriadou SDJ dismissed an application made by an interested party other than the judgment debtor (allegedly bona fide purchasers of imported cars blocked at the Customs office as a result of the enforcement proceedings) to intervene in enforcement proceedings of an English County Court judgment on the basis of Article 33(2) of Brussels I.[25]

iv. Matters Related to Relations with Other Instruments

Brussels I has been invoked in proceedings involving the European Enforcement Order.[26] In the case of foreign purchasers of land in Cyprus who financed their purchase by mortgage

---

[19] For example, the failed application in *Potavina*, n 6 above, states as co-defendants one Russian resident and eight Cypriot, one Russian, one Panamanian and three BVI companies.

[20] *Turbo-Technik Reparatur Werft GmbH & Co KG v Passat Shipmanagement Ltd* (Limassol DCt, 17.11.2009).

[21] *Ironhold Estates Ltd, T/A Henipa Hotel v Travelworld Vacation Ltd* [2010] 1 CLR 452.

[22] *In re Valenora Co Ltd* (SCt, Civ pet, 16.7.2013); endorsed, among other, in *JSC BTA Bank v Ablyazov* (Nicosia DCt, 24.7.2015).

[23] *Kyratzis v Christo & Co* [2012] 1 CLR 2804.

[24] *JSC BTA Bank v Ablyazov* (Nicosia DCt, 6.12.2014).

[25] *BMW Financial Services (GB) Ltd v White Horse Financial Services Europe Ltd* (Larnaca DCt, 5.11.2009).

[26] See notably *Polykarpou v TUI Poland SpZoO* (2011) 1 CLR 1808.

loans issued by local banks, validity of service effected under the Service Regulation was the main legal point.[27]

v. Conclusion

Cyprus has at present a two-tier regime for international civil litigation cases. Cases falling within the territorial scope of the Regulation are handled under EU PIL. At the same time, the English common law constitutes a residual system of jurisdiction and enforcement for the other cases. In the long-term, that system runs the risk of falling behind in attention, unable to keep track even of reforms in English civil litigation.

B. Applicable Law Issues Under the Rome I and Rome II Regulations

Contrary to jurisdiction and enforcement, there is little reference in the Cyprus case law regarding Rome I and Rome II. They have been referred to in five trial-instance decisions: two of them merely cited European case law as authority on other points and the other three, which primarily addressed procedural issues, involved contracts with a foreign choice-of-law clause. Even though there is little analysis, the Cypriot forum's policy of upholding choice-of-law clauses is clearly affirmed.[28] One of the cases examined the possible application of Rome II alongside Rome I. It involved a commercial agency agreement providing for arbitration and designating the foreign principal's law as applicable to the agreement. The principal sought ex parte injunctions from a Cyprus court, relying on the applicability of Cyprus law as *lex loci damni*, but the Larnaca District Court dismissed the application on the ground that the foreign law was applicable to the contract.[29]

Practical and procedural considerations may explain this astonishing lack of cases concerning applicable law issues. A key reason may well be that Rome I applies only to contracts concluded after 17 December 2009, and it is still relatively early for such contracts to produce disputes triggering final judgments. However, this can only be a partial explanation and does not account regarding Rome II. A more pertinent reason may be that Cyprus treats foreign law as *factum*; thus it is up to counsel to allege the applicability of foreign law and provide evidence as to the content of the foreign law in question. Traditionally, counsels have been very reluctant to explore the possibility that foreign law might be applicable. In fact, the few exceptions where foreign law was applied tend to concern cases with a choice-of-law clause.

C. Practice/Process

Civil litigation in Cyprus is modelled after English civil procedure prior to the Lord Woolf reforms. Civil practice, with the partial exception of big commercial cases, is not devoid

---

[27] See *Alpha Bank (Cyprus) Ltd v Si Senh Dau*, SCt 13.9. 2013 and 12.4.2016, leading to the only Cypriot preliminary reference on a PIL matter: C-519/13, EU:C:2015:603.

[28] *Taramidis v Abercrombie & Kent Ltd* (Nicosia DCt, 29.5.2015).

[29] *Geniki Tachydromiki Ellados (Cyprus) Ltd v Nan Global Ltd*, interim judgment (Larnaca DCt, 22.12. 2015).

of procedural formalism. As a result, much effort by counsels (and judges) is spent on avoiding errors in formalities. For example, in a 2014 enforcement case under Brussels I, applicants stated as the basis of their claim, not just the Regulation, all potentially pertinent Cypriot statutory law and Civil Procedure Rules and the inherent powers of the Court, but also CJEU cases and 'the Regulations (sic) of Natural Justice.'[30]

The Foreign Court Judgments (Recognition, Registration and Enforcement According to Convention) Law 2000[31] constitutes the cornerstone of enforcement proceedings. Enforcement of judgments not covered by the scope of EU or international instruments is effected by an action on the foreign judgment.

Civil litigation in Cyprus usually takes less time than in many other countries. The existence of only one trial instance certainly helps. However, proceedings at trial level may take up to five or six years. This creates an incentive to settle and it also accounts for the increased importance of interim relief remedies in domestic as well as in international disputes.

Settlement is a key component of the dispute resolution system, but alternative dispute resolution (ADR) is a new field in Cyprus, with the exception of arbitration. Active regimes of domestic arbitration operate in the building and the banking retail sectors. Regarding international arbitration, Cyprus is the seat of many companies who are parties to arbitration proceedings, as well as a venue for interim relief and award enforcement proceedings. Mediation is available for civil and commercial disputes[32] and training programmes have been in operation for the past few years, but it is still too early for it to have any actual impact on the settlement of disputes and there is no evidence of international mediation.

D. Preliminary Remarks on Effectiveness of the Current EU PIL Framework in Civil and Commercial Law

After more than 10 years of application in Cyprus, it can be said that Brussels I has made substantial inroads into the legal profession and practice. It would appear that the initial trepidation of courts and practitioners has given over to a willingness to explore jurisdictional issues, even if obvious errors are not uncommon. Cypriot appellate authorities are finally available and can guide lower courts. The tendency to look into European authorities has also increased. Without denying the transformative effect that Brussels I has had on the Cyprus legal system (especially when considered alongside its sibling instruments such as the Regulation on European enforcement order for uncontested claims[33] and the Service Regulation) a lot of work remains towards educating courts and the bar.

Things are much more sobering regarding Rome I and II, whose lack of recorded impact is astonishing—until one considers that it can often take up to five years for a judgment to be rendered in a dispute. Be that as it may, a proper evaluation of the impact of especially Rome I would necessitate empirical research into contract practice, pending cases and disputes settled prior to the issuance of judgments.

---

[30] *JSC BTA Bank*, n 24 above.
[31] L 121(I)/2000, n. 3 above.
[32] Certain Issues of Mediation in Civil Disputes Law 2012 (L 121(I)/2012) [2012] EE I(I), 4365.
[33] [2004] OJ L143/15.

III. Cyprus's Experience on Cross-border Family Law Disputes

Even though the Cyprus judicial system is in principle and by tradition a unitary one, family justice is generally administered by separate Family Courts, operating as courts of special jurisdiction at the trial level and being subject to appellate review by a technically distinct instance constituted by a panel of rotating Supreme Court justices (the Appellate Family Court). In contrast to procedural and conflicts law, substantive family law is strongly influenced by Greek family law. Cyprus has also been unusually active in Hague Conference activities on family law, especially child abduction. The Ministry of Justice and Public Order is acting as the Central Authority for both Hague and EU instruments. On the other hand, for a variety of reasons (namely: the way in which jurisdiction over family disputes developed; the preference for domicile, and now habitual residence, as opposed to nationality as connecting factor; and the mentality of both judges and practitioners), family litigation in Cyprus has been very strongly connected to the lex fori and Cyprus did not opt into Rome III.

A. Jurisdictional and Procedural Issues Under the Brussels IIa Regulation

i. Matters Related to the Scope of Application

One case concerns the Regulation's temporal scope where it was found that a judgment made final in Greece prior to the Regulation's coming into force would be respected without considering whether the Regulations' provisions on jurisdiction might have enabled the jurisdiction of the Cyprus courts.[34]

ii. Matters Related to Jurisdiction

There is no reported case law regarding jurisdictional issues over divorce or marriage annulment. Applications for divorce must conform—in the very least, appear to conform—to the residency requirements of Article 3. Jurisdictional objections have been raised in a few cases that were withdrawn before judgment could be rendered.

Things are different regarding parental responsibility, where one parent and especially the child are located abroad. The tensions involved have led to appeals to the Supreme Court, which is not that usual for family cases. The Court has affirmed the Family Courts' reluctance to hear child custody claims in a case where children have their habitual residence in another Member State.[35] In another case, reference was made to the children's 'particular relationship' with the Member State.[36]

---

[34] *Zenonos v Zisaki* [2009] 1 CLR 661.
[35] *Indjirdjian v Downing* [2010] 1 CLR 1217.
[36] *Zenonos v Zisaki* [2009] 1 CLR 661.

iii. Matters Related to Recognition and Enforcement

Reported cases raising recognition and enforcement issues under the Regulation also tend to involve parental responsibility—both child custody and abduction/return cases. Cyprus courts appear to be respectful of the judgments of their foreign brethren.

An example of child custody concerns a Slovakian judgment granting divorce and regulating child custody, as well as maintenance issues (under Brussels I). The judgment was enforced, replacing the prior Cypriot judgment on pre-divorce arrangements as to child custody and maintenance.[37]

As to abduction cases, the Supreme Court has stressed the need to defer to the 'primary goal' of the 1980 Hague Child Abduction Convention, defined as the return of the child, in declining to stay enforcement,[38] and this reasoning has been adopted by trial courts regarding Brussels IIa.[39] There are also cases where the request for return was granted, with the trial court characterising the children's relocation in Cyprus as a tactical move by the respondent.[40]

iv. Cooperation between Central Authorities in Matters of Parental Responsibility

The Central Authority for Cyprus has not evidently had problems in communicating with, and showing the expected courtesy, to the Central Authorities of other Member States in matters of parental responsibility. The Central Authority appears to have been primarily drawing on its experience with the Hague Conventions.

v. Relations with Other Instruments

The Hague Child Abduction Convention still appears to be given priority over the Regulation. In child abduction cases involving requests from the EU Member States, both the Convention and the Regulation are named as legal basis of the action/request and are invoked in the judgment. This is due primarily to the extensive experience of both central authority and the liaison government lawyers with the Hague Convention and the Hague Conference practices, that has been carried over to judges and even part of the family bar.

vi. Conclusion

Application of Brussels IIa in Cyprus tends to involve primarily matters of parental responsibility, in which courts, government and practitioners are inclined to draw from their experience with the Hague Conventions, notably the Abduction Convention.

B. Jurisdictional and Procedural Issues and Applicable Law Under the Maintenance Regulation

The only decisions presently available concerning the Maintenance Regulation involve requests for enforcement of Member State judgments awarding maintenance support.

---

[37] *Jurinyi v Tiourioumkina* (Larnaca FamCt, 13.9. 2011).
[38] *Christofil v Minister of Justice* [2010] 1 CLR 655.
[39] *Minister of Justice v Ioannou* (Larnaca FamCt, 19.3.2013).
[40] *Minister of Justice v Naijjar Cox* (Larnaca FamCt, 5.1.2016).

Application of the Regulation in this regard builds on the substantial experience of both Family Courts and the Ministry of Justice and Public Order (the designated Central Authority) with cooperation between central authorities. Remarkably, both decisions raise questions—they also help illustrate the ambivalent mentality of the Cypriot judiciary.

On the one hand, there is procedural formalism. In 2013, a senior family judge dismissed the application for enforcement of a Polish judgment against a Polish national residing in Cyprus.[41] The application was filed by the Cypriot Central Authority which then forwarded to the Polish Central Authority the request, along with the necessary documentation under the Regulation and the completed Application Form of the Regulation's Annex VI. Karatzis PFC held that such form could not trigger the jurisdiction of any Cyprus court and that the Regulation did not alter the existing procedural rules for recognition/enforcement of judgments in Cyprus; therefore any application had to be filed in accordance with the usual procedure for submitting such applications made under any international convention or instrument under L 121(I)/2000. Regardless of whether one agrees with the result, this was one of the rare cases in which the judge actually did his own research, instead of primarily relying upon counsel.

On the other hand, comity and proclaimed deference to the spirit of the EU Regulation led the Paphos Family Court to enforce a Lithuanian default judgment, as forwarded via the central-authority channel, against the Cypriot father who had objected to the enforcement on the ground of not having been duly served: the Regulation's preamble and provisions are quoted at length, as if they would preempt such an objection.[42]

C. Practice/Process

Cyprus family litigation follows a system of separating divorce or annulment proceedings, parental responsibility proceedings, marital property proceedings, and proceedings on the matrimonial home. As a result, even though there is no process for a consensual divorce sanctioned by a court decree, divorce proceedings themselves are rarely truly confrontational. It takes up to a year for most divorces, an average of two years for child custody and maintenance proceedings and anything between two and six years for marital-property litigation.

ADR has not been officially introduced in family law. A bill on family mediation has been pending for years in the House of Representatives and is expected to be soon passed into law.

D. Preliminary Remarks on Effectiveness of the Current EU PIL Framework in Cross-border Family Law

The demographic changes in Cyprus have led to a certain degree of internationalisation in family litigation, which is expected to increase further. Though timid by other Member

---

[41] *In Re Tomaszewski* (Limassol FamCt, 7.2.2013).
[42] *Re Fylaktou* (Paphos FamCt, 30.3. 2014).

State standards, the transformation is remarkable considering that even a quarter-century ago, family litigation was a matter for religious institutions.

Divorce litigation does not appear to raise many jurisdictional concerns. That is not surprising given the compartmentalisation of litigation following the dissolution of marriage into separate proceedings. Things are expected to be different once an EU regime on marital property (pecuniary relations between spouses) comes into play and that should lead to issues regarding jurisdiction, interim relief and enforcement, as well as applicable law.

The two areas that have so far produced case law are parental responsibility and the Maintenance Regulation. In the former, case law has built on the existing experience with cooperation between central authorities and judges' networks. Specialisation and the training of key individuals appear to have helped. In the latter area, the recorded examples are disappointing. The involvement of central authorities that has ushered in may have led, early on, to embarrassing procedural incidents. However, it is expected that familiarisation in practice with the Maintenance Regulation, perhaps with the help of some training initiatives, will set things on a proper course.

IV. Conclusion

The process of integrating EU PIL into Cypriot civil and commercial litigation is still underway and, in fact, in its early stages. The process will inevitably necessitate a transformation of certain aspects of the domestic legal culture. Developments regarding PIL are quite similar to the general attitude towards the potential of EU law as a tool before the domestic courts: it takes time—and someone who has both awareness of the potential of EU law and the incentive to use it. So the challenge is to make such knowledge more accessible to as much of the legal profession as possible by training or by showing them that this can win a case.

Growing awareness among lawyers and judges must be translated into deeper understanding of the instruments, their norms and underlying policies—and stronger acquaintance with pertinent authorities. Many of the earlier—and odder—decisions refer to EU PIL rather superficially (quotations of Regulation provisions, though of educative value, do not necessarily constitute a useful authority!), or refer to no authorities.[43] Even in some appellate cases (including the one that made a preliminary reference to the ECJ)[44] we see references only to English case law.[45] Recent case law provides examples of better understanding by counsel and judge alike.[46] But we are still, at best, in the end of the beginning.

---

[43] *BMW Financial Services*, n 25 above.
[44] *Alpha Bank*, n 27 above.
[45] *Hampton Advisory Group*, n 8 above, citing, as to the place of principal obligation, *Union Transport Plc v Continental Lines SA* [1992] 1 WLR 15. C-302/02 *Owusu v Jackson* is also cited as [2005] QB 801.
[46] *JSC BTA Bank*, n 24 above.

15

Czech Republic

MONIKA PAUKNEROVÁ, MARTA ZAVADILOVÁ AND JIŘÍ GRYGAR*

I. Introduction

The Czech Private International Law Act (PIL Act)[1] expressly anticipates the priority of promulgated international treaties and directly applicable provisions of European Union law over its provisions (Section 2 PIL Act).

The structure, style and formulation of EU Regulations results from compromises reached by EU Member States. Czech courts can sometimes project their specific perception into the interpretation of unified legal rules.

Unification is far from simple. Each State is guarding its own legal culture and is prepared to make concessions in favour of the common solution only if it can gain some benefit for itself—for example, a smoother course of international disputes, quicker process of service and evidence taking, the possibility to recognise and enforce judgments abroad, etc. Unification is the art of compromise and States know that the benefit of unified legislation consists in increased legal certainty in cross-border relations. Agreeing uniform legislation, often at the cost of making concessions, is one thing; however, uniform application and interpretation of that legislation is another thing. Uniform interpretation within the EU is created by the case law of the Court of Justice of the EU (CJEU). Eg in Czech law pre-contractual liability may be characterised as contractual with respect to the fact that in the Civil Code it is included in the general provisions regulating contract (Sections 1728–1730 Civil Code),[2] however, the relevant particular provisions of the Civil Code lead either to contractual liability (Section 2913 Civil Code), or to non-contractual liability (Section 2910 Civil Code).[3] In EU law, the Rome II Regulation clearly classifies pre-contractual liability as a non-contractual obligation.[4] Similarly, the CJEU defines a pre-contractual obligation as

---

* The authors would like to thank the anonymous peer reviewer for very helpful comments on an earlier version of this chapter.

[1] Act No 91/2012 Sb, PIL Act.

[2] See Ss 1728–1730 Civil Code, Act No 89/1912 Sb.

[3] The Civil Code *culpa in contrahendo* provisions are modelled after Arts 6–8 of the European Contract Code (Code Européen des Contrats). The point on contractual or non-contractual understanding of *culpa in contrahendo* in Czech law is still debatable: rather, the reason for the inclusion of pre-contractual liability in the introductory part of the Civil Code dealing with contracts may have been that the pre-contractual liability is closely connected with the negotiation of a contract and precedes its conclusion.

[4] See Art 12 Rome II—*culpa in contrahendo* which is defined in para 1 as a non-contractual obligation arising out of dealings prior to the conclusion of a contract.

a civil delict (see *Tacconi*).[5] Sometimes the courts utilise national elements or specific legal institutions in their decision-making; for example, in *Lindner* a guardian *ad litem* was used even though it is unknown to many foreign procedural codes.[6]

Unification, or at least harmonisation, of the interpretation of EU legislation would undoubtedly contribute to the achievement of legal certainty.

The Supreme Court of the Czech Republic and other appellate courts participate in the unification of case law in these areas; they present quite a few decisions relating to these Regulations on their websites.[7]

Legal assistance is provided by the International Civil Department of the Ministry of Justice and the Internal Judicial Network for cooperation in civil and commercial matters, a platform for judges and others involved in cross-border cases.

II. Czech Experience in Non-family Cross-border Civil and Commercial Disputes

A. Jurisdictional and Procedural Issues Under the Brussels I Regulation

i. Matters Related to Jurisdiction

The Czech courts often deal with jurisdiction in relation to consumer contracts. A typical case is when a foreign national stays for a short time in the Czech Republic and concludes there a consumer contract giving his or her temporary address in the Czech Republic (which cannot usually be considered as a domicile, eg a workers' hostel). Later the consumer leaves the country. The courts often appoint an *ex officio* representative (guardian *ad litem*) for the absent consumer and continue the procedure, see the preliminary ruling of the CJEU in the *Lindner* case.[8] Nevertheless, it remains unclear how the investigation of the place of the defendant's residence in other EU countries should be done. The CJEU has, unfortunately, said only '*what*' should be done, but not '*how*'. Czech courts do not have appropriate tools to carry out investigations in other EU Member States. The Czech Supreme Court has given some guidance in decision Number 33 Cdo 123/2012 where it noted that the courts should investigate in all available databases (eg approaching the municipal authority in the last known residence of the defendant, the prison service, the employment agency or social security authorities), or use the tools of international judicial cooperation.[9] The investigation may create a significant extension of the overall length of the proceedings.

---

[5] Case C-334/00 *Tacconi* [2002] ECR I-17357 para 21.

[6] Case C-327/10 *Hypoteční banka v Lindner* [2011] ECR I-11543 see paras 51–52. For details see M Pauknerová, 'Defendants with Unknown Address' in P Lindskoug, U Maunsbach, G Millqvist, P Samuelsson, H-H Vogel (eds), *Essays in Honour of Michael Bogdan* (Lund, Juristförlaget i Lund, 2013) 411.

[7] Supreme Court of the Czech Republic—number of published cases: Brussels I—44; Brussels IIa—7; Maintenance Reg—2; Rome I—1; and Rome II—1. Upper and regional courts: Brussels I—19; Brussels IIa—10; Maintenance Reg—1; and no cases published on the Rome I and II Regs.

[8] Above n 5.

[9] Decision of the Supreme Court No 33 Cdo 123/2012 od 27.3.2013.

The Supreme Court had earlier decided that the inapplicability of the Brussels I Regulation where a defendant has an unknown residence does not exclude the jurisdiction of the Czech courts.[10] According to Article 16(2) of Brussels I the courts of the Member State in whose territory the defendant had his last known domicile (*address stated in the contract*) have jurisdiction.[11] There is a recent Czech Supreme Court decision confirming this reasoning on jurisdiction of Czech courts with respect to a citizen of a third country.[12]

The place of performance in sale of goods contracts[13] is the place where the goods should be delivered according to the contract, otherwise the place where the goods were physically handed over or should have been handed over to the buyer.[14]

The Supreme Court examined[15] the question whether there is a sufficiently clear determination of the court under Article 23(1) of Brussels I, if the parties agreed to the jurisdiction of the '*general court of the manufacturer*'. The Supreme Court concluded that, since choice-of-court agreements are excluded from the scope of the Rome I Regulation,[16] it is necessary to proceed by the conflict-of-law rules of the *lex fori*. The Czech PIL Act was applied, but it does not explicitly regulate the question of the law applicable to choice-of-court agreements. Doctrine was followed according to which the choice-of-court agreement is a contract with procedural effects and as a procedural matter is governed by the *lex fori*.

The term '*general court of the manufacturer*' should therefore be interpreted according to the *lex fori*, ie according to Czech law. Under the Czech Civil Procedure Code, the '*general court of a legal entity*' is the court, where the legal entity is seated, thus the general court of the manufacturer is the court where the manufacturer has its seat. By selection of the territorial jurisdiction in the Czech Republic participants also established the international jurisdiction of the Czech courts. The choice-of-court agreement therefore clearly conferred jurisdiction on the Czech courts under Article 23(1) of Brussels I. Under the Brussels I Recast the substantive validity of the choice-of-court agreement is determined by the law of the Member State of the chosen court, which in this case would be Czech law.

The tendency of courts to annul the entire contract, if it contained provisions contrary to the requirements of consumer protection, was corrected on the basis of the CJEU decision in the *Pereničc* case.[17] It was declared that a consumer contract is valid when, disregarding the abusive provisions contained therein, it otherwise meets the requirements of a consumer contract.[18]

An interesting decision of the Supreme Court deals on the place of performance of the obligation to pay the price for a share in a private limited company (under Article 5(1)(a) of the Brussels I Regulation) concluding that the place of performance is the seat of the seller.[19]

---

[10] Decision of the Supreme Court No 33 Cdo 2485/2008 of 26.5.2011.
[11] Decision of the Supreme Court No 32 Cdo 5208/2009 of 30.11.2011.
[12] Decision of the Supreme Court No 30 Nd 25/2014 of 2.6.2014.
[13] Art 7(1)(b) of the Brussels I Reg recast.
[14] Decision of the Supreme Court No 23 Cdo 3689/2011 of 29.11.2011.
[15] Decision of the Supreme Court No 30 Cdo 2626/2014 of 17.12.2014. Now Art 25 of the recast.
[16] Art 1(2)(e) of the Rome I Reg.
[17] Case C-453/10 *Pereničc* EU:C:2012:144.
[18] Decision of the Supreme Court No 33 Cdo 4601/2008 of 16.9.2010 and decision of the Constitutional Court No Pl ÚS 1/10 of 9.2.2011.
[19] Decision of the Supreme Court No 29 Cdo 2842/2013 of 30.9.2015. This decision touches on Rome I issues.

ii. Matters Related to Recognition and Enforcement

Under Article 66 of Brussels I, the Regulation applies only to legal proceedings instituted and to documents formally drawn up or registered as authentic instruments after its entry into force, but it was unclear whether it means the entry into force in the State of origin or in the State of recognition and enforcement. The Supreme Court concluded that a decision may be recognised under Brussels I only if at the time the judgment was issued both States, ie the State of origin and the State in which recognition and enforcement is sought, were applying unified jurisdictional rules.[20] The same interpretation was given by the CJEU.[21]

B. Applicable Law Issues Under the Rome I and Rome II Regulations

i. Rome I

a. Matters Related to the Scope of Application

The application of the Rome I Regulation is very rare and therefore it seems that Czech courts do not apply this Regulation as often as they should. They wrongly apply the Czech Private International Law Act instead. The Supreme Court has noted[22] that Brussels I and Rome I complement each other in terms of interpretation—and so a violation of an obligation within the meaning of the Rome I Regulation may also incur liability to pay a contractual penalty[23] if a contractual penalty was agreed as a result of a breach of terms of the contract, specifically in cases of late payments. A claim for a contractual penalty is therefore a claim related to the contract.[24] In the already cited Supreme Court's decision Number 29 Cdo 2842/2013 concerning a share purchase agreement, the Supreme Court, apart from jurisdictional questions, was also dealing with choice-of-law issues. It concluded that the Rome Convention was not applicable to share purchase agreements because of the corporate law exclusion in Article 1(2)(e). This conclusion should apply also to the Rome I Regulation, as it contains the very same exclusion. The Supreme Court applied the provisions of the old Czech Act on Private International Law dealing with contractual issues.[25]

b. Matters Related to the Uniform Rules

The Supreme Court pointed out that the Rome I Regulation distinguishes (in the absence of choice of applicable law) between contracts whose subject is a right *in rem* in immovable property (among other things the transfer of ownership of immovable property) and contracts for the sale of goods.[26]

---

[20] Decision of the Supreme Court No 31 Cdo 2325/2008 of 14.7.2010.
[21] Case C-514/10 *Wolf Naturprodukte GmbH* EU:C:2012:367.
[22] Decision of the Supreme Court No 30 Cdo 1941/2015 of 14.1.2016.
[23] See M Pauknerová, *Evropské mezinárodní právo soukromé* (*European Private International Law*, in Czech) 2nd edn (Prague, CH Beck, 2013) 175; AJ Bělohlávek, *Římská úmluva a Nařízení Řím I: komentář v širších souvislostech evropského a mezinárodního práva soukromého* (*Rome Convention and Rome I Regulation in broader connections of European and Private International Law*, in Czech) Vol 2 (CH Beck, 2009) 1497.
[24] Art 12 of Rome I and Art 5(1)(b) of Brussels I.
[25] Sec 10, Act No 97/1963 Sb, on Private International Law and the Rules of Procedure Relating thereto.
[26] Decision of the Supreme Court No 33 Cdo 2905/2011 of 29.3.2012. See Art 4(1) of Rome I.

ii. Rome II

a. Matters Related to Unjust Enrichment, *Negotiorum Gestio* and *Culpa in Contrahendo*

In the public database of the Supreme Court decisions there are only two decisions regarding the Rome II Regulation: regarding unjust enrichment and punitive damages.

The Supreme Court stated that the courts of lower instance referred to the incorrect law[27] because the law applicable to non-contractual obligations was governed by a directly applicable Regulation of the European Union—namely the Rome II Regulation and this Regulation applied to events giving rise to damage which occurred after 11 January 2009.[28] Under Article 2(1) of Rome II a non-contractual obligation includes a relationship constituted by an unjust enrichment. Under Article 10(2) of Rome II as the claimant's residence and the headquarters of the other party to the dispute were located in the Czech Republic, the Supreme Court concluded that the obligation in this case was subject to Czech law as the law of the common habitual residence of the parties.[29]

The Supreme Court concluded that the recognition of a foreign decision granting punitive damages is not automatically a breach of public policy even though Czech law does not allow for punitive damages in private law cases. Recognition of judgments granting punitive damages may be refused on the basis of public policy if the amount of punitive damages is manifestly disproportionate to the harm it was intended to compensate. In such a case a conflict with the Czech Charter of Fundamental Rights and Freedoms would arise, as it constitutes a disproportionate interference with the right to own property.[30] Only after carefully considering human rights and proportionality criteria can the court decide what limits, if any, are imposed on the recognition and enforcement of the damages award on the ground of public policy.[31]

C. Practice/Process

i. Czech National Courts' Practice in Interpreting the Regulations/Process Issues

The procedure which the Czech courts must follow when they have international jurisdiction was succinctly described by the Supreme Court, as follows:

> If the court finds the presence of an international element in the proceedings, it is required to deal with the question, under which law must the legal relationship be assessed. Characterisation of the relationship from the perspective of private international law (ie whether or not it is a relationship with an international element) and, if so, the subsequent identification of the applicable law, the content and the method of its application must precede the factual and legal assessment of the case.[32]

---

[27] Act No 97/1963 Sb, on international and procedural private law, in force until 31.12.2013.
[28] Arts 31 and 32 of Rome II.
[29] Decision of the Supreme Court No 28 Cdo 3204/2014 of 25.11.2014.
[30] Art 4(4) and Art 11(1) of the Charter.
[31] Decision of the Supreme Court No 30 Cdo 3157/2013 of 22.8.2014.
[32] Decision of the Supreme Court No 33 Cdo 2377/2012 of 28.11.2013.

ii. Cost and Length of Litigation in Cross-border Civil and Commercial Disputes

Proceedings in these types of cases do not bring any increased costs compared to similar cases without a cross-border element (apart from the costs associated with proof of foreign law). The length of proceedings relating to the application of EU PIL Regulations is not tracked statistically. It can be stated that it generally tends to be higher only in cases of difficulties with service of documents to a foreign State, or in connection with the establishment of foreign law. Last but not least, sometimes it is the case that a judge tries to avoid or postpone deciding a case with cross-border implications, as he finds questions of private international law too complex.

iii. Alternative Dispute Resolution for Cross-border Civil and Commercial Disputes

In these types of cases the Act on Mediation is applicable in the same way as in purely national disputes.[33] The court may order the parties to meet with a mediator for three hours and to interrupt the proceedings for up to three months.

III. Czech Experience on Cross-border Family Law Disputes

A. Jurisdictional and Procedural Issues Under the Brussels IIa Regulation

i. Matters Related to Jurisdiction

a. Divorce, Legal Separation and Marriage Annulment

Czech courts do not have many problems with the jurisdictional rules in divorce proceedings. A court applied the Regulation *per analogiam legis* for the dissolution of a registered partnership stating that, although registered partnerships were not within the scope of the Regulation, it was feasible to apply it in the particular case *per analogiam*, because the national law did not provide any jurisdictional norm for such partnerships.[34]

Specific issues might arise due to inconsistency between Czech law and the law of another State in divorce cases. Under Czech law, custody and maintenance of the children of the spouses must be judicially resolved before a divorce is granted. In cases where the child is not habitually resident in the Czech Republic, the Czech courts might have jurisdiction for divorce, but not for the custody proceedings. If the law of the habitual residence of the child does not provide a custody procedure specifically for custody after the divorce (but without divorce), it might hinder obtaining the divorce decision in the Czech Republic.

---

[33] Mediation Act No 202/2012 Sb.
[34] Decision of the District Court of Rokycany No 6 C 59/2011 of 20.9.2011. The judgment reflects the national law before the entry into force of the new Private International Law Act, ie before 1 January 2014.

b. Parental Responsibility

1. Child Abduction

The number of parental child abductions increases every year in the Czech Republic. In 2000 the Czech Central Authority dealt with eight incoming and six outgoing cases, in 2015 there were 28 and 42.[35] The most frequent places are other EU Member States (particularly Slovakia, United Kingdom, Germany, Austria, Italy and Spain).

A key player in this area is the Central Authority—The Office for International Legal Protection of Children (hereinafter 'Office') which not only receives and transmits return applications but acts as a mediator. The Office is often successful in reaching amicable arrangements without the cases going to court.[36] The Office provides assistance to applicants but does not represent them or children in return proceedings. Access to free legal aid in return proceedings is the weakest point of the Czech system of assistance provided to the applicants.[37]

The jurisdiction for return proceedings is centralised at the Municipal Court in Brno (first instance) and the Regional Court in Brno (second instance). Review before the Supreme Court is not permitted in return proceedings. Some cases, however, have been heard by the Constitutional Court. The correct use of protective measures in child abduction cases is not clear.[38] The proper functioning of the supplementary rules (Article 11) presumes close communication between courts and Central Authorities and mutual respect for their procedural steps, however, many problems occur in practice. The major obstacle is the dilatoriness or even unwillingness to cooperate by authorities in some Member States. Another obstacle to proper functioning of Article 11 arises from differences in national laws. The understanding of one court, about what measures are sufficient to protect the child in terms of Article 11(4) of Brussels IIa, might not necessarily meet the understanding of courts and legal orders in another Member State. It might be very difficult for the judge who decides on return to know whether a condition for safe return will be enforced in the State where the child is returned.

The current system of special rules for abduction in the Regulation needs revision by strengthening Central Authorities, not only as intermediaries in the judicial proceedings, but also as those who can persuade the parents to find an amicable solution.

2. Other Issues Related to Parental Responsibility

One of the most common problems is jurisdiction where the child's property is in the Czech Republic but not the child. A typical example is where the child is an heir in succession. This child lives abroad and the only connection with the Czech Republic is the

---

[35] The statistics provided by the Central Authority include cases where the Central Authority is involved. Other cases, where return applications are submitted to a court directly, are not registered.

[36] The statistics show that at least one quarter of the cases end with agreement between the parents before or even during judicial return proceedings. Since 2010 a return order has had to be enforced only in three cases.

[37] In the past, the applicants were represented by the Office but it was criticised for being seen to compromise its independence. Unfortunately, there is still no system for obtaining specialised lawyers who would provide free legal aid. Free legal aid can be provided in 'intra-Union' cases on the basis of the Legal Aid Directive 2003/8/EC [2003] OJ L26/41.

[38] Unfortunately, the CJEU case law has not brought sufficient clarity in this regard (eg Case C-210/10 PPU *Povse v Alpago* [2010] ECR I-6673).

succession. If the child acts in the succession, eg he or she refuses the inheritance, he or she has to be represented by guardian *ad litem*, who has to be appointed by a court and then the court approves the relevant legal act of the guardian in the name of the child. The CJEU confirmed that the appointment of a guardian and consent of the court to the legal act in the name of the child fell under the scope of the Regulation, therefore the courts in the Member State of the habitual residence of the child were competent.[39] This result, however, creates lots of problems in judicial practice. Even if the law of the habitual residence of the child provides for similar rules, it might be difficult to establish a person or an institution as a proper guardian for property interests in a foreign country. Under certain circumstances, the jurisdiction might be established under Article 12(3) of Brussels IIa in the State where the property is located,[40] otherwise, the general jurisdiction remains the only possibility.

There are uncertainties in the application of Article 12. The requirement of a 'connection' between an application for divorce and an application for custody is problematic, as it is not possible to combine both in one procedure in the Czech Republic. The courts however interpret 'connection' to encompass applications that are in two separate procedures, if one of them (custody after divorce) is a substantive condition for the other (divorce). Other difficulties with the application of Article 12, especially the scope of paragraph 3 and the form of 'unequivocal manner' of acceptance of the jurisdiction,[41] have been partially explained by the CJEU.[42]

Certain problems arise also with the transfer of jurisdiction under Article 15. All of the cases observed by the rapporteurs occurred in the context of parental child abduction. It was not the Regulation itself that was unclear, but the lack of sufficient national implementation. It is not clear how 'formal' the process of transfer has to be, what the proper form of decision of the court on transfer has to be and whether the decision can be appealed. The change of international jurisdiction might significantly affect the procedural rights of the parties. The communication between courts involved in the transfer is not always smooth. Due to the language barrier the Central Authorities and liaison judges are usually involved. In one case the requesting Czech court waited seven months for the answer of the requested foreign court.

In some cases, where the child was abducted, courts dealt with concurrent proceedings in another Member State, where *lis pendens* (Article 19(2)) should be applied. Frequently, the abducting parent immediately after moving with the child to another State, applies in that State for sole custody. The left-behind parent reacts usually with some delay and applies for custody before a competent court in the State of habitual residence of the child. It happens that the first seised court, although not internationally competent, does not declare its non-competence immediately, but waits for the result of the return procedure, which seldom is finished in six weeks (in one case 22 months). In these cases, the court of the State where the child was abducted to, often issues a preliminary order on custody for the abducting parent till the final decision on return. If the return proceedings last much more than six weeks, the preliminary order becomes in fact a decision on the merits, despite the lack of

---

[39] Case C-404/14 *Matoušková* ECLI:EU:C:2015:653. See also decision of the Supreme Court No 30 Nd 201/2013 of 11.11.2015.

[40] C-404/14 *Matoušková* ibid, para 37.

[41] Judgment of the Supreme Court No 30 Cdo 1994/2013 dated 27.1.2015.

[42] Case C-656/13 *L* ECLI:EU:C:2014:2364; *Matoušková*, above n 32; Case C-215/15 *Gogova* ECLI:EU:C:2015:710.

jurisdiction. The Supreme Court decided that a procedure initiated in one Member State only on grounds of Article 20 (provisional measures) could not lead to *lis pendens* under Article 19(2).[43]

ii. Matters Related to Recognition and Enforcement

In child abduction cases, problems were encountered with recognition and enforcement of orders securing the return of the child under Article 11(4). A Czech mother abducted the child to the Czech Republic from Greece and a Czech appellate court ordered the return of the child to Greece with some conditions and safeguards, including the right of the mother to stay with the child after the return. These safeguards, however, were not respected by the Greek authorities and immediately after the return (at the airport), the child was removed from the mother.[44]

iii. Cooperation between Central Authorities in Matters of Parental Responsibility

The experience of the Czech Central Authority shows that the level of services provided differs significantly in the Member States. In some Member States difficulties repeatedly arise in child abduction cases, eg long delays in answering requests and unwillingness to connect with other national authorities or to convey some information. The relationship between the Regulation and the Evidence Regulation is not always clear.

iv. Relationship with Other Instruments

The relationship between the Regulation and bilateral treaties on legal assistance with third States which had been concluded before the Czech Republic joined the EU can be problematic. The Regulation does not provide a norm for this relationship. It is necessary to apply the primary Union law (Article 351 TFEU). These bilateral treaties have a broad scope of application including family law matters. The jurisdictional norms in these treaties might result in the same solution as the Regulation, however in some cases they differ.

v. Conclusion

We can conclude that the Regulation is known and in most cases properly applied by Czech courts and the Central Authority. The current work on revision of the Regulation in response to the Commission's Proposal for a recast of Brussels IIa provides an opportunity to improve the current system.[45] The principle of mutual trust should be supported by revision of the supplementary provisions to the 1980 Hague Child Abduction Convention (Articles 10, 11 and 42) and by strengthening the role of Central Authorities and their duties. Multiplicity of procedures and decisions in child abduction cases should be avoided.

---

[43] Decision of the Supreme Court No 30 Cdo 2554/2013 of 26.2.2014.

[44] One of the authors has a copy of the Czech return order but sadly it is not published.

[45] 'Proposal for a Council Regulation on jurisdiction, the recognition and enforcement of decisions in matrimonial matters and the matters of parental responsibility, and on international child abduction (recast)' COM(2016) 411/2 http://ec.europa.eu/justice/civil/files/family-matters/brussels2_regulation_en.pdf.

The question whether we need the override return procedure in Article 11 within the EU is in the air. If it is too early to exclude it, it must be at least properly revised.[46]

B. Jurisdictional and Procedural Issues and Applicable Law Under the Maintenance Regulation

When observing the practice of the Czech courts the Maintenance Regulation is applied without serious obstacles. The Supreme Court has not yet dealt with the interpretation of the Regulation as a principal question. Under Czech law the decision on parental responsibility (custody) is connected with the decision on a maintenance obligation toward the child in one procedure. In two cases, the Supreme Court indicated that the international jurisdiction should be based primarily on the Brussels IIa Regulation and that the jurisdiction based on the Maintenance Regulation in the Czech Republic could not include the jurisdiction for parental responsibility.[47]

The Central Authority under the Maintenance Regulation is the Office for International Legal Protection of Children (the same authority as under the Brussels IIa Regulation). The total amount of enforced maintenance is increasing every year.[48] The most frequent 'partners' are Germany, Italy, United Kingdom, Slovakia, Austria and Poland.

IV. Conclusion

The number of preliminary questions to the CJEU is relatively low and about half are asked by the supreme courts. On the other hand, there has been a handful of interesting preliminary references to the CJEU from Czech courts dealing with private international law issues, apart from *Lindner* also, eg, C-111/09 (*Bilas*, Article 24 Brussels I), or C-419/11 (*Feichter*, promissory notes falling under Article 5(1)(a) Brussels I).

Public access to case law in cases with an EU law element is only to the small number of decisions of the Supreme Court. Decisions of lower courts are not publicly accessible. The Supreme Court conducts analyses of the decisions of lower courts and for decisions issued from 2004 to 2011 the most frequently applied Regulations are Brussels I (50 per cent) and Brussels IIa (15 per cent).

---

[46] See Commission Staff Working Document Impact Assessment on the recast of Brussels IIa SWD(2016) 207 final.

[47] Judgments of the Supreme Court No 21 Cdo 4909/2014 dated 19.3.2015 and 21 Cdo 3572/2015 dated 4.11.2015.

[48] Maintenance from abroad: 2013—19 046 000 CZK, 2014—30 005 000 CZK, 2015—23 709 000 CZK; maintenance to abroad: 2013—10 452 000 CZK, 2014—13 144 000 CZK, 2015—15 311 000 CZK.

16

Finland

GUSTAF MÖLLER

I. Introduction

Legislative texts represent the primary source of direction and guidance to Finnish Courts. For elaboration and clarification of legislative provisions or for guidance when no statute is directly addressed to the question presented, the lawyer and later the judge or arbitrator, will turn to reported judicial decisions, to the commentaries of legal scholars, and to *travaux préparatoires*.

The general court hierarchy consists of (1) the district courts, (2) the intermediate courts of appeals, and (3) the Supreme Court. Cases decided by the intermediate courts of appeal may be appealed further to the Supreme Court only if the Supreme Court grants leave to appeal.

Anyone who is dissatisfied with an administrative decision by a governmental or municipal agency pertaining to his or her rights or obligations, may challenge the lawfulness of the decision before an administrative court. The Supreme Administrative Court is the court of last resort in administrative cases. The majority of the categories of cases handled by the Supreme Administrative Court are not subject to the requirement of leave to appeal. As a rule, therefore, the parties have a right to appeal, and the Supreme Administrative Court issues a decision on the merits.

In this report I have with some exceptions reviewed only those cases that are published in the database or elsewhere. Almost all those cases are reviewed in this report. Only such published cases that I have deemed can be of no or little interest in this context, eg cases in which the Brussels I Regulation has only been mentioned in passing or in which the real issue is whether an international convention, ie the Convention on the Contract for the International Carriage of Goods by Road (CMR), (Geneva, 19 May 1956), applies, are not dealt with in this report. Neither have I reviewed unpublished cases from the intermediate courts of appeal that are only mentioned in the database but have not been published anywhere.

II. Finland's Experience on Cross-border Civil and Commercial Disputes

A. Jurisdictional and Procedural Issues Under the Brussels I Regulation

i. Matters Related to the Scope of Application

Matters related to the scope of application of the Brussels I Regulation have in light of the published or reported cases not given rise to any major problems in practice. However, in a case concerning the enforcement of a penalty to be paid to the other parent, imposed by a decision given by a Belgian Court in order to ensure compliance with the rights of access, the question arose whether the Brussels I Regulation or the Brussels IIa Regulation was applicable.[1]

After having referred the question to the Court of Justice of the European Union (CJEU) for a preliminary ruling and the CJEU having answered the question,[2] the Supreme Court concluded in its judgment of 24 March 2016 that the application related to the enforcement of a penalty payment intended to ensure compliance with the rights of access granted to the applicant in a Belgian judgment and was thus an ancillary measure in a matter concerning parental responsibility, which falls within the scope of the Brussels IIa Regulation. From the judgment of the CJEU it could also be seen that recovery of a penalty payment forms part of the same scheme of enforcement as the judgment concerning the rights of access that the penalty safeguards and the latter must therefore be declared enforceable in accordance with the rules laid down by the Brussels IIa Regulation.

ii. Matters Related to Jurisdiction

The question how to interpret the rules on jurisdiction in the Brussels I Regulation has in some cases arisen in Finnish courts.

In one case the question arose whether an action for the termination of co-ownership in undivided shares of immovable property in Spain by way of sale by an appointed agent falls within the category of proceedings, which have as their object rights *in rem* in immovable property within the meaning of Article 22(1) of the Brussels I Regulation so that the courts of the Member State in which the property is situated would have exclusive jurisdiction under that provision.[3]

After having referred the question to the CJEU for a preliminary ruling and receiving an affirmative answer,[4] the Supreme Court stated in its decision of 21 March 2016 that according to Article 22(1) of the Brussels I Regulation the courts of the Member State in which the property is situated have exclusive jurisdiction in proceedings which have as their object rights *in rem* in immovable property. Thus the Spanish courts had exclusive jurisdiction and accordingly the action had to be dismissed as inadmissible.

---

[1] KKO 2016:23.
[2] Case C-4/14 *Bohez* EU:C:2015:563.
[3] KKO 2016:21.
[4] Case C-605/14 *Komu and others* EU:C:2015:833.

In another case before the Supreme Court the question was whether an agreement conferring jurisdiction on Finnish Courts included in an insurance contract between the policyholder and the insurer was binding on an insured habitually resident in another Member State.[5]

In this case no question was referred to the CJEU for a preliminary ruling. The Supreme Court held in its decision of 4 February 2014 that the insurer and the policyholder could not under Article 13(3) of the Brussels I Regulation (44/2001) agree with binding effect for the insured that the insurer may bring proceedings in a matter relating to the insurance contract against the insured in another state than in the Member State in which the insured was domiciled when the proceedings were instituted.

Moreover, the Supreme Court stated that one could conclude from the CJEU's judgment in *Société financière et industrielle du Peloux*[6] that a jurisdiction clause in an insurance contract between an insurer and a policyholder could be binding on the insured, if the insured had explicitly accepted the clause. A jurisdiction clause shall be in accordance with Article 23 of the Brussels I Regulation. However, in this case it had not even been alleged that the insured had agreed that a specific court shall have jurisdiction in such a way as provided for in Article 23 of the Brussels I Regulation. Neither the insured's position as CEO of the policyholder nor the fact that he had received compensation under the insurance contract could be regarded as such circumstances because of which the insured could be held to have explicitly accepted the jurisdiction clause.

In a case, which is currently pending before the Supreme Court, the question is whether Article 6(2) of the Brussels I Regulation shall be interpreted as covering an action on a warranty or guarantee or another equivalent claim closely linked to the original action, which is brought by a third party, as permitted by the national law, against one of the parties with a view to its being heard in the same proceedings. The problem seems at least partially to have been due to discrepancies in the various language versions of the Brussels I Regulation.

The Supreme Court referred the question for a preliminary ruling to the CJEU which ruled[7] that Article 6(2) of the Brussels I Regulation (44/2001) must be interpreted to the effect that its scope includes an action brought by a third party, in accordance with national law, against the defendant in the original proceedings, and closely linked to those original proceedings, seeking reimbursement of compensation paid by that third party to the applicant in those original proceedings, provided that the action was not instituted solely with the object of removing that defendant from the jurisdiction of the court which would be competent in the case.

The Supreme Court has given its decision on 12 September 2016 and found in accordance with the ruling of the CJEU that the District Court had jurisdiction.[8]

In a case concerning the infringement of designs finally decided by the Helsinki Court of Appeal, the question was to what extent the Finnish courts had jurisdiction in disputes relating to the infringement of designs registered in Finland, Italy and France.[9]

---

[5] KKO 2014:3.
[6] Case C-112/03 [2005] ECR I-3707.
[7] Case C-521/14 *SOVAG* EU:C:2016:41.
[8] KKO 2016:59.
[9] Case S 05/1495.

In that case the Helsinki Court of Appeal confirmed in its decision of 16 November 2005 the Helsinki District Court's decision of 31 March 2005 concerning the jurisdictional issues. The Helsinki District Court held in its decision that actions concerning infringements of various national designs are not so closely connected that it was desirable to hear and determine them together to avoid the risk of irreconcilable judgments resulting from separate proceedings. Thus the Helsinki District Court found that it had no jurisdiction to hear and determine the actions brought in so far as they were based on infringement of designs registered in France and Italy. However, between the actions, which were based on infringement of designs registered in Finland, there was a close connection within the meaning of Article 6(1) of the Brussels I Regulation. Consequently the Helsinki City Court had jurisdiction to hear and determine those actions.

In a decision of 19 October 2012 the Helsinki Court of Appeal noted that the district court had not taken a stand on the issue whether a jurisdiction clause included in an Air Charter Agreement complied with the formal requirements of Article 23 of the Brussels I Regulation.[10] The case was remanded to the district court.

iii. Matters Related to Recognition and Enforcement

The Helsinki Court of Appeal held in its decision of 12 October 2012 that neither under the Brussels I Regulation nor under national law was it possible to grant a negative declaratory judgment, according to which a judgment given in another Member State cannot be enforced in Finland.[11]

In a case finally decided by the Vaasa Court of Appeal the question was if recognition of a judgment given by an Estonian court shall be refused on the ground that the recognition would be manifestly contrary to public policy (*ordre public*) in Finland, since the respondent had not had an opportunity to present his defence. Moreover, the question was whether the summons to the court's oral hearing was a document equivalent to a document instituting the proceedings and whether recognition shall be refused since the respondent had not been invited to the oral hearings of the Estonian court.[12] In its decision of 1 October 2015 the Vaasa Court of Appeal answered the questions in the negative and confirmed the district court's judgment declaring the judgment enforceable.

iv. Matters Related to Relations with Other Instruments

The only matter related to relations with other instruments is the one mentioned above under section II.A.i.

v. Conclusions

In particular the district courts, but also the intermediate courts of appeal, have not until quite recently had much experience of private international law matters. However, due to the published decisions of the Supreme Court and courses arranged by various authorities and organisations judges in the lower courts are now more familiar with EU private

---

[10] Case S 11/2486.
[11] Case S 12/1870.
[12] Case S14/1041.

international law issues. The district courts and the intermediate courts of appeal seem, in the light of published or reported cases, not so far to have submitted any requests for a preliminary ruling to the CJEU. This has had the consequence that cases that could, if such a request had been made, have been finally decided in the first or the second instance, have been dealt with in all three instances.

B. Applicable Law Issues Under the Rome I and Rome II Regulation

i. *Rome I*

a. Matters Related to the Scope of Application

The only reported case, in which an applicable law issue under the Rome I Regulation has arisen, related to the question whether the Rome Convention or the Rome I Regulation was applicable. In that case Vaasa Court of Appeal noted that the Rome I Regulation applied to contracts concluded after 17 December 2009.[13] Thus the Rome Convention and not the Rome Regulation applied to a contract of carriage concluded before that date.

ii. *Rome II*

There is no published or reported case in which the Rome II Regulation has been applied. The only published or reported case in which the Rome II Regulation has been referred to is the Supreme Court's decision of 5 July 2010.[14] In that case a Finn had in 2005, ie before the date the Rome II Regulation became applicable, killed another Finn in Estonia. The victim's closest relatives instituted civil proceedings against the perpetrator in Finland, where he served his sentence, and claimed damages for mental suffering (emotional distress).

The Supreme Court noted that before the Rome II Regulation became applicable the principal rule in Finnish private international law had been that the law of the place where the damage occurred shall apply. Since the connections to Finland in this case were not so strong that the case because of them would have a manifestly closer connection to Finland than Estonia, Estonian law was deemed to be applicable in this case.

III. Finland's Experience on Cross-border Family Law Disputes

A. Jurisdictional and Procedural Issues Under the Brussels IIa Regulation

i. *Matters Related to the Scope of Application*

In a case decided by the Supreme Administrative Court the questions were: 1) whether the Brussels IIa Regulation applied to the enforcement of a public law decision in connection

---

[13] Case S13/912.
[14] KKO 2010:51.

with child welfare, relating to the immediate taking into care of a child and its placement in a foster family outside the home, taken as a single decision, in its entirety, 2) if the answer to the first question was in the affirmative, whether it was possible given that the Brussels IIa Regulation takes no account of the legislation harmonised by the Nordic Council on the recognition and enforcement of public law decisions on placement, but solely of a corresponding private law convention, nevertheless to apply this harmonised legislation based on the direct recognition and enforcement of administrative decisions as a form of cooperation between administrative authorities to the taking into care of a child.[15]

After having referred those questions to the CJEU for a preliminary ruling and the CJEU having answered question one in the affirmative and question two in the negative,[16] the Supreme Administrative Court in its decision of 30 January 2008 noted that the CJEU had by its judgment of 27 November 2007 decided the questions referred for a preliminary ruling and that according to that judgment Article 1(1) of the Brussels IIa Regulation is to be interpreted to the effect that a single decision ordering a child to be taken into care and placed outside its original home in a foster family is covered by the term 'civil matters' for the purposes of that provision, where that decision was adopted in the context of public law rules relating to child protection. Moreover, the Supreme Administrative Court noted that according to the judgment of the CJEU the Brussels IIa Regulation must be interpreted as meaning that harmonised national legislation on the recognition and enforcement of administrative decisions on the taking into care and placement of persons, adopted in the context of Nordic cooperation, may not be applied to a decision to take a child into care that falls within the scope of that Regulation.

ii. *Matters Related to Jurisdiction*

a. Divorce, Legal Separation and Marriage Annulment

There are only two reported divorce cases in which a jurisdictional or procedural issue under the Brussels IIa Regulation has arisen. One of these cases was finally decided by the Helsinki Court of Appeal on 8 June 2012.[17] The facts can be summarised as follows.

The applicant, who was a Finnish citizen, and the other party, who was a Swedish citizen, lived in Cyprus. Both spouses had their domicile in Helsinki. Since none of the parties was habitually resident in Finland and since only one of the spouses was a Finnish citizen, Finnish courts did not have jurisdiction. The fact that the applicant worked in a Finnish Embassy was not held relevant.

The other case was finally decided by the Helsinki Court of Appeal on 9 April 2014.[18] The Finnish courts had jurisdiction under Article 3(1) of the Brussels IIa Regulation since both spouses were habitually resident in Finland although they were Zambian citizens.

---

[15] KHO 2008:4.
[16] Case C-435/06 *C* [2007] ECR I-10141.
[17] Case S12/750.
[18] Case S 13/3265.

b. Parental Responsibility

1. Child Abduction

The question where a child is habitually resident has come up in some child abduction cases both before the Brussels IIa Regulation came into force and thereafter.

In the Supreme Court's decision of 17 November 2008 the question was whether a child was abducted from Scotland to Finland.[19]

The Supreme Court stated at the outset that, since the case was related to the United Kingdom, not only the Hague Convention on the Civil Aspects of International Child Abduction, but also the Brussels IIa Regulation was applicable. Further, the Supreme Court observed that that the concept 'habitual residence' was not defined in either of those instruments. However, it was established that 'habitual residence' in the Conventions, drawn up by the Hague Conference on Private International Law, means the place or the country where a person de facto lives and where he/she has his central environment. Also in the Brussels IIa Regulation. the concept 'habitual residence' had the same meaning. When determining where a person has his or her habitual residence one takes into account above all such circumstances that can be objectively ascertained, for example the duration and continuity of residence, social ties and other similar circumstances relating to a person or his/her profession and which show the factual connection to the State where the party is staying. The Supreme Court further stated that it has been stated in case law concerning the aforementioned Hague Convention that a settled intention to stay or not to stay in a country may be of some importance even though this circumstance is of less importance than the other aforementioned circumstances. As to a little child who is not yet able to independently decide the purpose of its stay, the habitual residence of the custodian, family ties and other social ties are relevant. Finally the Supreme Court stated that the concept 'habitual residence' must, in any event, be interpreted in conformity with the aims of the Convention and the Regulation, which was to protect a child from the harmful effects of its removal from a well-known and stable environment to a foreign State by a person who has joint custody over the child.

The Supreme Court held that the children were habitually resident in Finland and rejected the father's application that the children had to be returned to Scotland. Two judges dissented and held that the children were habitually resident in Scotland and that the children had to be returned to Scotland.

The question of where a child was habitually resident again came before the Supreme Court in a child abduction case from Estonia to Finland.[20]

The Supreme Court held in its decision of 18 June 2015 that it was not shown that the child's stay in Estonia was intended to be of a permanent nature. Taking into account the relatively short stay no such firm social environment in Estonia had been established for the child such that Estonia would instead of Finland have become its habitual residence. Thus the Supreme Court held that the child was in December 2014 habitually resident in Finland. On these grounds the father's application for the return of the child was rejected.

---

[19] KKO 2008:98.
[20] KKO 2015:44.

2. Other Issues Related to Parental Responsibility

In a case decided by the Supreme Administrative Court on 30 June 2009 the question was how the concept 'habitual residence' in Article 8(1) of the Brussels IIa regulation, like the associated Article 13(1), was to be interpreted in Union law, bearing in mind in particular the situation in which a child has a permanent residence in one Member State but is staying in another Member State, carrying on a peripatetic life there.[21]

After having referred the question to the CJEU for a preliminary ruling and the CJEU had answered the question,[22] the Supreme Administrative Court taking into account all the facts presented in the case held that the family lived in both countries alternately. Thus it was necessary to evaluate whether the children had more ties to Finland or Sweden. Based on the evidence presented in the case the children's identity and their social and cultural ties were closer to Finland than to Sweden and they could not on the basis of their social and cultural connections be regarded to have become integrated in Sweden to such an extent that their habitual residence for the purposes of Article 8(1) would be in Sweden. Moreover, the Supreme Administrative Court held that the fact that the children needed psychiatric treatment had to be taken into account.

On these grounds the Supreme Administrative Court held that the children were habitually resident in Finland.

iii. *Matters Related to Recognition and Enforcement*

a. Rights of Access

In the aforementioned decision of the Supreme Court of 24 March 2016 the Supreme Court held, after receiving an answer to the question from the CJEU,[23] that a penalty payment to be paid to the other parent, imposed by a decision given by a Belgian court in order to ensure compliance of a judgment on rights of access, could be declared enforceable in Finland in accordance with the provisions on recognition and enforcement in the Brussels IIa Regulation, if the amount of the payment had been finally determined by the courts of the Member State of origin.[24] However, in the same decision the Supreme Court noted that a foreign judgment which orders a periodic penalty payment is enforceable in the Member State in which enforcement is sought *only* if the amount has been finally determined by the courts of the Member State of origin. Since this had not been done the application was dismissed as inadmissible.

b. Return of the Child

The Supreme Court's decision of 27 October 2009 was about the question whether a 15 year old child, who objected to being returned, had attained an age and a degree of maturity at which it was appropriate to take account of the child's views.[25]

The Supreme Court noted that the child had come from Estonia to Finland voluntarily, when the child was 14 years old and no dispute concerning the custody of the child was

---

[21] KHO 2009:68.
[22] Case C-523/07 *A* [2009] ECR I-2805.
[23] See above n 2.
[24] KKO 2016:23.
[25] KKO 2009:85.

pending. No such dispute had even later become pending. Moreover, it had to be taken into account that the Hague Convention on the Civil Aspects of International Child Abduction ceases to apply when the child attains the age of 16 years. In the case at hand the child was 15 years old. Under the Hague Convention it was possible to give considerable weight to the views expressed by a child who has attained that age. When a 15 year old child objects to be returned it was therefore, taking also into account the purpose of the Hague Convention, reasonable to assume that the child shall not be returned.

On these grounds the Supreme Court decided that the child should not be returned.

iv. Relations with Other Instruments

Finland and Sweden have under Article 59 of the Brussels IIa Regulation declared that the Convention of 6 February 1931 between Denmark, Finland, Iceland, Norway and Sweden comprising international private law provisions on marriage, adoption and guardianship, hereinafter the Nordic Convention, together with the Final Protocol thereto, will apply, in place of the rules of the Brussels IIa Regulation.

The Nordic Convention's relation to the Brussels IIa Regulation was dealt with in the Supreme Court's decision of 30 June 2008.[26]

The Supreme Court noted that only such judgments that fall under Article 8 of the Nordic Convention were judgments relating to rights of access within the meaning of Article 22 of the Nordic Convention. Only access rights granted in a judgment relating to legal separation or divorce fall under Article 8 of the Nordic Convention. In this case the father who had been granted access rights had sought enforcement of a judgment, which had been given in proceedings, which had been instituted after the divorce. Thus the Nordic Convention did not apply.

v. Conclusion

The Brussels IIa Regulation caused in the beginning some problems in the lower courts since cases requiring the application of private international law have until recently been quite rare. Today thanks to the precedents from the Supreme Court and education the Brussels IIa Regulation does not seem to cause any significant difficulties for judges and for such advocates that have become specialised in family law matters with an international element. Most difficulties seem to relate to the question where a child shall be deemed to be habitually resident.

B. Jurisdictional and Procedural Issues and Applicable Law Under the Maintenance Regulation

There are no published or reported cases related to the application of the Maintenance Regulation. However, there are some unreported cases on recognition and enforcement of maintenance decisions coming from EU Member States bound by the Hague Protocol on Applicable Law.

---

[26] KKO 2008:80.

In a case decided by the Helsinki Court of Appeal the father lodged an appeal and requested that the decision of a district court by which a Dutch decision relating to maintenance had been declared enforceable be set aside.[27] He argued that payment of maintenance to a person of age (until the child reaches the age of 21) was unreasonable and contrary to the public policy of Finland. In its decision of 20 April 2012 the Helsinki Court of Appeal rejected the appeal on the ground that the fact, that the provisions relating to maintenance applied by the Dutch Court differed from Finnish provisions relating to maintenance, does not mean that the decision would be contrary to public policy.

In a decision of the Helsinki Court of Appeal of 5 June 2013 an appeal against a decision of a district court by which an Estonian decision relating to maintenance had been declared enforceable was rejected on the ground that under Article 42 of the Maintenance Regulation a decision given in a Member State may under no circumstances be reviewed as to its substance in the Member State in which recognition, enforceability or enforcement is sought.[28]

In a decision of the Helsinki Court of Appeal of 18 July 2013 an appeal against a decision of a district court, by which an Estonian decision relating to maintenance had been declared enforceable, was rejected on the ground that under Article 34(1) of the Maintenance Regulation the court with which an appeal is lodged shall refuse or revoke a declaration of enforceability only on one of the grounds specified in Article 24. The applicant had not shown any such ground.[29]

IV. Conclusion

It can be concluded that the Brussels I and Brussels IIa Regulations nowadays work relatively well in Finland. However, in order to save time and costs the district courts and in particular the intermediate courts of appeal should be encouraged to submit requests for preliminary rulings to the CJEU, whenever a problem of interpretation arises which has not yet been solved by a judgment of the CJEU.

---

[27] Case S 11/3192.
[28] Case S 13/681.
[29] Case S 13/1315.

17

France

HORATIA MUIR WATT, SABINE CORNELOUP, LAURENCE USUNIER,
DIDIER BODEN, JEREMY HEYMANN AND DAVID SINDRES*

I. Introduction

French courts do not seem to have any major difficulty in adapting to the EUPILLAR Regulations. This is hardly surprising, since the structure, methods and concepts used are largely familiar.

II. France's Experience on Cross-border Civil and Commercial Disputes

A. Jurisdictional and Procedural Issues Under the Brussels I Regulation

i. Matters Related to the Scope of Application

The Cour de cassation considered on several occasions that the jurisdiction of a French Labour Court (Conseil de prud'hommes) should be determined by application of Article 19 of the Regulation in cases where the matter at stake was referring to the terms and conditions of an employment contract, even if an E 101 certificate (now A1 certificate) had been issued in the first place.[1] Thus, even though this certificate is strongly connected to 'social security' matters, this raises no obstacle to the application of the Brussels I Regulation in cases where employment contracts are central to the dispute.

Similarly, the Cour de cassation has held that the non-application of the Regulation to 'the status or legal capacity of natural persons' (or 'rights in property arising out of a matrimonial relationship')[2] could not preclude the application of the said Regulation to disputes where the recognition and enforcement of another Member State's judgment is sought, as long as the part of the judgment that has to be recognised or enforced is not related to such a matter.[3]

* Thanks for the input from the anonymous referees. Due to editorial constraints, the current version of this Report must be considered as an abridged one.

[1] Cass soc, 10 June 2015, no 13-27.799 to no 13-28.853; Cass soc, 29 September 2014, no 13-15.802.

[2] Cass civ 1, 5 November 2014, no 13-19.812.

[3] Cass civ 1, 3 December 2014, no 13-22.672—financial penalties.

Recently, the Cour de cassation had also to compare the scope of application of both the Insolvency Regulation and the Brussels I Regulation to determine whether wage claims fell within the scope of the latter or the former. It held in favour of the application of the latter.[4]

ii. Matters Related to Jurisdiction

a. Article 2/4 (Brussels I/Brussels Ia)

Case law regarding Article 2 of the Brussels I Regulation (now Article 4 of the Brussels I Recast Regulation) remains rare in France, which tends to show that this provision does not give rise to many difficulties. The Cour de cassation considered that the only relevant date to ascertain the domicile of the defendant was the one at which the claim was filed[5] and affirmed the binding character of this Article for the defendant.[6]

b. Article 5(1)/7(1) (Brussels I/Brussels Ia)

French case law relating to Article 5(1) of the Brussels I Regulation (now Article 7(1) of the Brussels I Recast Regulation) is very abundant. Many rulings relate to the definition of contractual matters. French courts tend to apply Article 5(1) to claims based upon the voidness of the contract.[7]

Besides, the Cour de cassation has considered on several occasions that the action whereby the recipient of a promise of gains sought to constrain the author of the promise to abide by his commitment fell within the scope of Article 5(1).[8]

On the contrary, claims arising from the wrongful termination of a contract have been analysed as matters relating to torts on the—debateable—ground that the French substantive rule governing this issue—Article L 442-6 I 5° of the Commercial code—belongs to tort law.[9] However, this latter stance seems to have been condemned by the Court of Justice of the European Union (CJEU) in its recent *Granarolo* ruling of 14 July 2016,[10] which decides that claims deriving from Article L 442-6 I 5° shall be characterised as contractual in cases where a contract, at least tacitly, had been concluded between the parties before the termination of their relationship occurred.

There are also many decisions from the Cour de cassation, rendered both prior and after the *Car Trim*[11] and *Falco*[12] cases, which define the contours of sales of goods and of provisions of services. The Cour de cassation thus considered as a provision of service an agreement pursuant to which one party was supposed to conceive, build and deliver advertising materials.[13] It is also worth underlining that, following the *Corman-Collins*

---

[4] Cass soc, 28 October 2015, no 14-21.319.

[5] Cass civ 1, 31 May 2005, no 03-11.732.

[6] Cass ch mixte, 11 March 2005, *Société Codéviandes* (two rulings), no 02-41.371 and no 02-41.372; see also Cass civ 1, 17 January 2006, no 02-12.745.

[7] See Toulouse Court of Appeal, 25 November 2003, no 03/02022; and before, Cass civ 1, 25 January 1983, no 81-16.415; Cass civ 1, 27 June 2000, no 98-15.979 and no 98-10.359.

[8] Cass civ 1, 7 May 2010, no 09-14.324; Cass civ 1, 23 February 2011 (five rulings), no 09-71.791, no 09-71.796, no 09-71.768, no 09-71.794, and no 09-70.884; Cass civ 1, 4 May 2011, no 10-13.696.

[9] Cass com, 15 September 2009, no 07-10.493; Cass com, 18 January 2011, no 10-11.885; Cass com, 13 December 2011, no 11-12.024.

[10] Case C-196/15.

[11] Case C-381/08 [2010] ECR I-1255.

[12] Case C-533/07 [2009] ECR I-3327.

[13] Cass civ 1, 27 March 2007, no 06-14.402; and also Cass civ 1, 14 November 2007, no 06-21.372.

ruling,[14] the Cour de cassation modified its stance regarding distribution agreements: while it used to consider those agreements as neither sales of goods, nor provisions of services,[15] it now accepts they constitute provisions of services referred to in Article 5(1)(b).[16]

In cases where a service is prepared and conceived in one Member State, to be delivered in another Member State, the Cour de cassation tends to localise the provision of service in the place of delivery for the purpose of Article 5(1)(b).[17]

c. Article 5(3)/7(2) (Brussels I/Brussels Ia)

Generally speaking, the case law relating to Article 5(3) of the Brussels I Regulation (now Article 7(2) of the Brussels I Recast Regulation) is not raising many difficulties.

One could however observe that two specific matters have created—and for one of them still creates—some hesitation, raising a certain amount of questionings.

The first series of matters was related to the determination of a relevant criterion to determine the jurisdiction of French Courts in disputes giving rise to cyber-torts. The legal question at stake was referring to the choice of a relevant criterion to apply: targeting or accessibility? The First Civil Chamber of the Cour de cassation held in favour of the accessibility criterion,[18] whereas the Commercial Chamber of the same Cour de cassation decided to apply the targeting criterion.[19] Now that the CJEU clearly considered, in different cases, that the accessibility criterion is the relevant one and with a special link given to the localisation of the centre of the interests of the victim of a violation of the rights of the personality,[20] the opposition that divided the two above-cited Chambers of the Cour de cassation is likely to disappear.

The second series of matters is still related to the interpretation of domestic liability rules applying to the termination of an established business relationship.[21] The legal question at stake is to determine whether such a provision can be classified—or not—in the category of matters relating to tort. The Commercial Chamber of the Cour de cassation considers that it is, but such an assertion can be—and is—questioned. The French courts will have to apply a very recent CJEU ruling classifying an action for damages founded on an abrupt termination of a long-standing business relationship as an issue of contract if a tacit contractual relationship existed between the parties.[22]

d. Article 22/24 (Brussels I/Brussels Ia)

The Paris Court of Appeal has decided that the validity of a patent is an arbitrable issue when invalidity is raised as a defence in a contractual claim about a licence agreement.[23]

---

[14] Case C-9/12 EU:C:2013:860.

[15] Cass civ 1, 23 January 2007, no 05-12.166—Cass civ 1, 5 March 2008, no 06-21.949—Cass civ 1, 9 July 2008, no 07-17.295.

[16] Cass civ 1, 19 November 2014, no 13-13.405.

[17] Cass civ 1, 27 March 2007; Cass civ 1, 14 November 2007, cited supra; Cass civ 3, 12 September 2012, no 09-71.189.

[18] Cass civ 1, 9 December 2003, no 01-03.225.

[19] Cass com, 9 March 2010, no 08-16.752.

[20] Cases C-509/09 and C-161/10 *eDate and Martinez* [2011] ECR I-10269; Case C-170/12 *Pinckney* EU:C:2013:635; Case C-441/13 *Hejduk* EU:C:2015:28.

[21] Art L 442-6, I 5° of the French Commercial Code—See also below, Art 1 of the Rome II Reg.

[22] Case C-196/15, *Granarolo* EU:C:2016:559—question referred by the Paris Court of Appeal.

[23] CA Paris, 28 February 2008, *Rev arb* 2008. 712, note T Azzi.

The compatibility of this ruling with the *GAT* case[24] and the current drafting of Article 24(4) is doubtful.

e. Article 23/25 (Brussels I/Brussels Ia)

French courts have been confronted with a number of difficulties in applying EU rules to jurisdiction agreements.

Concerning the scope of application of Article 25 of the Recast Regulation, French case law illustrates the uncertainty generated by the silence of this provision about the requirement of internationality. In a case decided in 2005, the Cour de cassation ruled that Article 17 of the Brussels Convention applied only to international disputes, but it adopted a confusing definition of the concept of internationality, holding that a sub-contract of construction was not international because, but for the German seat of one of the contracting companies, the transaction was entirely connected to France and the intention of the parties was to treat the situation as domestic.[25]

Concerning the substantive validity of jurisdiction agreements, 'assymmetric' agreements (imposing one of the parties to sue in the elected forum, while the other party reserves himself the right to sue in any other competent court) have raised specific difficulties. Unlike other Member States' courts, French courts are reluctant to enforce this type of agreement. The Cour de cassation denied enforcement to such agreements, first for 'potestativity' (ie the unenforceability of a contractual promise made subject to a condition precedent left to the discretion of the promisor)[26] and subsequently for lack of predictability.[27] More recently, the Cour de cassation accepted to enforce an asymmetric clause, but only because the clause provided for a limited number of alternative fora for the party that was not bound to sue in the elected court.[28] This case law reveals that French courts have problems dealing, not only with asymmetric, but also with non-exclusive jurisdiction agreements. In all these cases, it is also questionable that French courts assessed the substantive validity of the agreement under the French *lex fori* (eg by referring to the French concept of potestativity), without inquiring first about its applicability to the agreement.

On the contrary, French courts enforce agreements providing both parties an option between litigation in the elected court and arbitration,[29] even though it is not settled that the CJEU would uphold such agreements.

Other difficulties might arise in the future regarding the substantive validity of jurisdiction agreements. The first one is related to the fact that Article 25(1) now provides for a choice-of-law rule under which the substantive validity of a jurisdiction agreement is governed by the law of the country of the elected court. Recital 20 makes it clear that this reference to the law of the country of the elected court includes its choice-of-law rules. Each time the elected court is a French court, this rule is likely to create uncertainty, since French choice-of-law rules on this issue are very unclear. Few cases have dealt with the problem of the law governing the substantive validity of jurisdiction clauses and they

---

[24] Case C-4/03 [2006] ECR I-6509.
[25] Cass civ 1, 4 October 2005, no 02-12.959.
[26] Cass civ 1, 26 September 2012, no 11-26.022.
[27] Cass civ 1, 25 March 2015, no 13-27.264.
[28] Cass civ 1, 7 October 2015, no 14-16.898.
[29] Cass civ 1, 12 June 2013, no 12-22.656.

are contradictory.[30] The second difficulty is related to the recent reform of French contract law. New Article 1171 of the French Civil Code protects all contracting parties from unfair terms, even in commercial transactions, where the terms of the contract were drafted by one of the parties instead of being freely negotiated between the parties. Since it is well established that, in consumer contracts, a jurisdiction agreement might be an unfair term,[31] French courts will certainly have to clarify whether jurisdiction agreements stipulated in 'B2B' contracts might also be characterised as unfair terms.

Another issue is that of the effects of jurisdiction agreements on third parties. Outside the two specific situations settled by the CJEU in *Tilly Russ*,[32] for transportation contracts and *Refcomp*,[33] for 'chains of contracts' cases, French courts extend jurisdiction agreements to third parties in a wide number of situations, eg where the agreement is part of the 'economy of the transaction',[34] where two agreements are so closely related that they form a unique transaction (where one contract was entered into between two companies and the other contract was entered into between one of the companies and the director of the other company),[35] or because of the implicit assent of the defendant to the clause.[36] The compatibility of this case law with EU law is unclear.

f. Article 31/35 (Brussels I/Brussels Ia)

Since the ruling of the CJEU in *St Paul Dairy*,[37] it is unclear whether the power of French courts to help the parties collect evidence '*in futurum*', in order to secure evidence for a potential future trial, can be exercised under Article 35 of the Recast.[38]

iii. *Matters Related to Recognition and Enforcement*

The Cour de cassation considered that the irreconcilability between an arbitral award and a judgment from another Member State could not preclude the *exequatur* of the latter inasmuch as arbitration is not included in the realm of the Lugano Convention.[39]

It also accepted, in the *Stolzenberg* case,[40] that a Mareva injunction issuing a freezing order was a provisional measure in civil matters which could benefit from the simplified mechanism of recognition and enforcement.

French courts have adopted a restrictive view of the public policy exception to the recognition and enforcement of foreign judgments. In the abovementioned *Stolzenberg* case, the Cour de cassation considered that a freezing order known in English law as a Mareva injunction was not contrary to public policy.[41] It has also recognised and enforced

---

[30] CA Paris, 10 October 1990, *Revue critique droit international privé* 1991. 605, note H Gaudemet-Tallon, and Cass civ 1, 3 December 1991, no 90-10.078.

[31] Cases C-240/98 to C-244/98, *Océano Grupo Editorial SA* [2000] ECR I-4941.

[32] Case 71/83 [1984] ECR 2417.

[33] Case C-543/10 EU:C:2013:62.

[34] Cass civ 1, 13 February 2013, no 11-27.967, in a case of subrogation.

[35] Cass civ 1, 23 March 2011, no 09-72.312.

[36] Cass com, 4 March 2014, no 13-15.846.

[37] Case C-104/03 [2005] ECR I-3481.

[38] Cass civ 1, 11 December 2001, no 00-18.547 and Cass civ 1, 4 May 2011, no 10-13.712.

[39] Cass civ 1, 4 July 2007, no 05-14.918.

[40] Cass civ 1, 30 June 2004 no 01-03.248 and 01-15.452.

[41] ibid.

foreign judgments which provided no justification for their rulings, insofar as the court required to recognise and enforce these judgments had been provided with documents that could be regarded as equivalent to a justification.[42]

In cases where a judgment is given in default of appearance, French courts exert a rigorous control on whether the defendant was served with the document instituting the proceedings or with an equivalent document in sufficient time and in such a way as to enable him to arrange for his defence. For instance, the Cour de cassation ruled that the mere fact that a registered letter with acknowledgment of receipt had been sent to a French defendant was not sufficient proof since there was no evidence he had indeed received the letter.[43]

Concerning the condition of absence of irreconcilability of judgments, the Cour de cassation refused to enforce a Greek ruling on the merits, on the ground that it was irreconcilable with a previous interim measure issued in France.[44]

iv. Matters Related to Relations with Other Instruments

The Cour de cassation decided that a matter was within the scope of the 1952 Brussels Convention for the unification of certain rules relating to civil jurisdiction in matters of collision rather than the scope of the Brussels I Regulation[45] and that the Geneva Convention on Contracts for the International Carriage of Goods by Road (known as the CMR Convention) prevailed over the Regulation.[46]

B. Applicable Law Issues Under the Rome I and Rome II Regulations

i. Rome I

a. Scope of Application (Article 1)

Must the words 'situations involving a conflict of laws' be taken seriously, and if so, how must they be interpreted? A party to a contract alleged that this contract 'was completely carried out in France'. The Cour de cassation decided that a Court of Appeal, 'having found that the contract presented an international character, was therefore right to have applied the regulation'.[47]

b. Party Autonomy (Article 3)

The cases of implicit choice-of-the-law of the contract are very rare in France. The cases of *dépeçage* are even rarer. The two rarities meet in a decision of the Social Chamber of the Cour de cassation, which judged that

> having noted that the employer had initiated the procedure of lay-off of Mr X ... according to the
> rules of French law and had determined the rights of the discharged employee by application of

---

[42] See for instance, Cass civ 1, 17 January 2006, no 03-14.483; Cass civ 1, 20 September 2006, no 04-11.653; Cass civ 1, 28 September 2006, no 04-90.031; Cass civ 1, 22 October 2008, no 06-15.577.

[43] Cass civ 1, 12 April 2012, no 10-23.023.

[44] Cass civ 1, 20 June 2006, no 03-14.553.

[45] Cass com, 16 September 2014, no 13-13.880.

[46] Cass com, 11 October 2011, no 10-25.813—Art 31 of the CMR Convention.

[47] Cass civ 1, 1 March 2016, no 14-22.608.

that same law, which the employee had accepted by demanding that same application, the Court of Appeal could, by these sufficient reasons, decide that it unquestionably resulted from the circumstances of the case that the parties to the contract had chosen to subject the termination of their contract to the rules of the French law, regardless of the fact that the contract was theoretically governed by the German law as the law of the place where the employee habitually carried out his work.[48]

c. Overriding Mandatory Provisions (Article 9)

Can a State's legal provisions be characterised as overriding mandatory provisions when they relate to questions specifically provided for by Articles of the Regulation (for example Article 6 on the law applicable to consumer contracts, or Article 11 on the law applicable to formal validity)? The Cour de cassation twice gave generally positive answers.[49]

French courts characterise parsimoniously norms of the *lex fori* as overriding mandatory provisions. Such a characterisation was refused even when the provisions in question were regarded by many commentators as very important for the political, social or economic organisation of the country:

(a) Article L 132-8 of the French Commercial Code conferring to the road carrier an action in payment of its services against the sender and the consignee as legal guarantors of the payment of the carriage;[50]

(b) Articles L 341-2 and L 341-3 of the French Consumer Code, requiring the signature of the natural person who guarantees a payment to a professional creditor to be preceded by a handwritten mention to ensure a better protection of the guarantor;[51]

(c) Articles L 134-1 *et seq.* of the French Commercial Code, implementing the Council Directive 86/653/EEC of 18 December 1986 on the coordination of the laws of the Member States relating to self-employed commercial agents.[52]

Some commentators wonder whether this last judgment is really compatible with the *Ingmar GB* and *Unamar* judgments of the CJEU.[53]

The same refusal to characterise as overriding mandatory provisions Articles L 134-1 *et seq.* of the French Commercial Code was previously expressed in another case that fell within the scope of application of the implementing law but not in the scope of application of the Directive.[54]

By contrast, the following French legal rules were applied as overriding mandatory provisions:

(a) Article L 132-1 of the French Consumer Code, implementing Council Directive 93/13/EEC of 5 April 1993 on unfair terms in consumer contracts.[55]

---

[48] Cass soc, 4 December 2012, no 11-22.166.
[49] Consumer contract: Cass civ 1, 23 May 2006, no 03-15.637; Formal validity: Cass com, 14 January 2004, no 00-17.978.
[50] Cass com, 13 July 2010, no 10-12.154.
[51] Cass civ 1, 16 September 2015, no 14-10.373.
[52] Cass com, 5 January 2016, no 14-10.628.
[53] Case C-381/98 [2000] ECR I-9305; Case C-184/12 EU:C:2013:663.
[54] Cass civ 1, 21 October 2015, no 14-20.924.
[55] Cass civ 2, 7 April 2016, no 15-13.775, loan of money with a choice of the Swiss law.

(b) The provisions of 31 December 1975 Act on subcontracting, insofar as they protect the subcontractor, as regards the modernisation of a building situated in France.[56]

Finally, with regard to foreign laws, French courts applied the law of Ghana prohibiting the importation of meat from France as an overriding mandatory provision.[57] Consequently, the Court of Appeal of Poitiers declared null and void a contract of carriage of meat from France intended for import into Ghana (29 November 2011). Whether the judges directly applied the law of Ghana or took it into consideration when applying the French *lex contractus* (Article 1133 of the Civil Code on the nullity of contracts contrary to *ordre public* and morality)[58] was not explicitly stated, but Article 9 of the Regulation is usually understood in France as providing a direct application of the overriding mandatory provisions. It is thus almost certain that it is the reasoning the French judges had in mind in this case.

ii. Rome II

The Cour de cassation decided that according to Article 28 of the Rome II Regulation, the Hague Convention of 1971 on the Law Applicable to Traffic Accidents takes precedence over the Regulation, as the Convention has not been concluded exclusively between Member States, even if the dispute involves only EU Member States.[59]

III. French Experience on Cross-border Family Law Disputes

A. Jurisdictional and Procedural Issues Under the Brussels IIa Regulation

i. Matters Related to the Scope of Application

a. Divorce, Legal Separation and Marriage Annulment

Several cases indicate recurring difficulties in relation to the proper scope of the Regulation in respect of common national jurisdictional rules including the 'jurisdictional privilege' by reason of French nationality.[60] It is accepted however that it may apply even when all the parties are foreign.[61]

The Regulation seems to have been applied without difficulty to issues of nullity of marriage.[62]

---

[56] Cass ch mixte, 30 November 2007, no 06-14.006; Cass civ 3, 25 February 2009, no 07-20.096.
[57] Cass com, 16 March 2010, no 08-21.511.
[58] On 1st October 2016, when the Ordinance no 2016-131 of 10 February 2016 on the reform of contract law came into force, former article 1133 of the civil Code was replaced by new Article 1162.
[59] Cass civ 1, 30 April 2014, no 13-11.932.
[60] Cass civ 1, 25 March 2015, no 13-26.131.
[61] Cass civ 1, 12 December 2006, no 05- 16.705.
[62] Cass civ 1, 28 November 2007, no 06-16.443.

ii. Matters Related to Jurisdiction

a. Divorce, Legal Separation and Marriage Annulment

Courts have sometimes wrongfully attempted to reintroduce a hierarchy between the various criteria, as in French common law.[63]

While double nationality has always been a sensitive issue, the case-law post-*Hadadi* seems to be well settled.[64]

The determination of residence remains problematic, since the diversity of definitions under EU law in different contexts is clearly confusing.[65]

b. Parental Responsibility and Child Abduction

It has been held that the unambiguous consent of both parents was necessary to prorogate jurisdiction when Article 12(1) of the Regulation applies.

The definition of common custody has proved to be tricky in the past[66] as has the assertion of the rights of the father in determining the child's residence,[67] and so has the status of new-borns. Post-*Mercredi*, the problem has arisen as to what happens when the mother has moved with the child.[68]

The bulk of litigation concerns the risk for the child under Article 13 of the Hague Child Abduction Convention. Much of it involves the judicial assessment of the adequacy of protective measures in the state of origin, under Article 11(4) of Brussels IIa.[69]

The courts in the State of refuge may be reluctant to accept that its emergency jurisdiction ceases when the court of the State of origin decides on the protection of the child, paving the way for its immediate return.[70]

c. Lis Pendens

The variety of applicable regimes has created confusion, particularly where there are two sets of parallel proceedings, one in divorce and the other for maintenance.[71]

Moreover, since Article 19 of the Brussels IIa Regulation does not require that the two courts seised actually have jurisdiction, there is a risk of strategic conduct which has led to specific difficulties in relation to the chronology of seising. When two claims have been registered on the same day, and one party can prove the time of the registration, the burden of proof of prior seising lies on the other.[72]

When a judgment from a third state fulfils the conditions of French common private international law (PIL), it will be recognised even if the French proceedings were commenced before the foreign proceedings.[73]

---

[63] Cass civ 1, 24 September 2008, no 07-20.248.
[64] Cass civ 1, 17 February 2010, no 07-11.648.
[65] Cass civ 1, 12 January 2011, no 09-71.540.
[66] Cass civ 1, 14 December 2005, no 05-12.934.
[67] Cass civ 1, 24 June 2015, no 14-14.909. See also Cass civ 1, 5 March 2014, no 12-24.780.
[68] Cass civ 1, 26 October 2011, no 10-19.905. See also Cass civ 1, 13 May 2015, no 15-10.872.
[69] For example, see Cass civ 1, 20 October 2010, no 08-21.161.
[70] Cass civ 1, 8 July 2010, no 09-66.406.
[71] Cass civ 1, 12 December 2006, no 04-15.099.
[72] Cass civ 1, 11 June 2008, no 06-20.042.
[73] Cass civ 1, 30 September 2009, no 08-18.769. See also Cass civ 1, 9 September 2015, no 14-18.869.

iii. Relations with Other Instruments

Certain cases tend to refer to the Hague Convention alone.[74]

In a case of the common nationality of the spouses, the French courts have asserted jurisdiction on the basis of Article 3(b) when the claimant is suing for maintenance under Article 5(2) of the Lugano Convention.[75]

B. Jurisdictional and Procedural Issues and Applicable Law Under the Maintenance Regulation

i. Matters Related to Applicable Law

It has been held that a French judge had to ascertain in the individual case whether the application of a foreign law, under which the spouse renounced in advance the right to a compensatory allowance, might be contrary—or not—to French public policy.[76]

Party choice-of-law has been effective in cases of maintenance agreements.[77]

---

[74] Cass civ 1, 26 October 2011, no 10-19.905.
[75] Cass civ 1, 25 March 2015, no 13-26.131.
[76] Cass civ 1, 8 July 2015, no 14-17.880.
[77] Cass civ 1, 11 March 2009, no 08-13.431—Under Art 7 of the 2007 Hague Protocol.

18

Greece

ASPASIA ARCHONTAKI AND PAATA SIMSIVE

I. Introduction

The Greek private international law ('PIL') rules had been codified in the Civil Act of 1856 which was then replaced by the Greek Civil Code ('GCC') in 1946.[1] The Greek Code of Civil Procedure ('GCCP'), adopted in 1967, also embodies a number of PIL rules on international jurisdiction, and recognition and enforcement of foreign judgments. The current PIL of Greece is largely shaped by international conventions and EU regulations, and supplemented by the relevant national laws.

II. Greece's Experience on Cross-border Civil and Commercial Disputes

A. Jurisdictional and Procedural Issues under the Brussels I Regulation

i. Matters Related to the Scope of Application

The reported cases from first instance courts ('FICs'), Courts of Appeal ('CoA') and the Supreme Court ('SC') do not show any particular difficulties on the scope of application of Brussels I.[2]

ii. Matters Related to Jurisdiction

The Greek courts have struggled with jurisdiction relating to insurance. They have declined jurisdiction over insurance claims submitted against insurance brokers under Article 9 on the ground that the provision applies only to claims against the insurer.[3] In case of multiple

---

[1] S Vrellis, *Private International Law in Greece* (Alphen aan den Rijn, Kluwer Law International BV, 2011) 29.

[2] See eg, Patras FIC (interim measures) Case No 25-9/2014, Conseil d'Etat (CE) Case No 1026/2004, SC Case No 1857/2007, Rhodes FIC Case No 165/2006, Ioannina CoA Case No 133/2006.

[3] Thessaloniki CoA Case No 546/2006. See also SC Case No 1882/2014; SC Case No 419/2014; SC Case No 442/2013; SC Case No 37/2012.

fora loci delicti, the Greek SC admitted that the claimant has the option to choose to sue among the countries where the damage occurred.[4]

iii. Matters Related to Recognition and Enforcement

Article 39(2) of Brussels I and Article 905(1) of the GCCP provide different solutions on the local jurisdiction of the courts as regards enforcement and the former prevails over the latter.[5]

Foreign creditors living abroad and willing to enforce a foreign judgment in Greece have to appoint a guardian *ad litem*.[6] Although the declaration is made before the Secretariat of Athens FIC,[7] the Greek courts have accepted appointments made by notary deeds or consular powers of attorney as valid.[8] The SC has adopted even a more liberal approach by stating that an attorney appointed in accordance with Article 96 of the GCCP can also be deemed as guardian *ad litem*.[9]

The legal remedy provided in Article 43 of the Regulation is, without exception, the only means available to challenge the decision on *exequatur*.[10] Both the Greek and English versions of the Regulation describe the legal remedy in Article 43 as an 'appeal' which, according to Annex 3, shall be lodged with the CoA. However, this is misleading because it is a fundamental rule in Greek civil practice that an 'appeal' is lodged with the secretariat of the court that rendered the decision (in this case the FIC, not the CoA). Consequently, actions lodged with the secretariat of the FIC have been dismissed due to improper submission. The Greek courts have found the word 'appeal' in Article 43 'unfortunate'.[11] In Greek law, a judicial decision on *exequatur* is not classified as 'judgment' but a 'judicial order'.[12] As a result, the CoA assumes the function of the FIC and therefore the word 'appeal' should be understood as 'first instance suit'. The distinction is crucial and has serious practical outcomes since, in the Greek judicial system, an 'appeal' is lodged with no service to the defendant[13] whereas a 'first instance suit' is to be lodged within one month of service.[14]

iv. Matters Related to Relations with Other Instruments

The Greek courts[15] have accepted that Articles 5 and 6 of the Convention on the Recovery Abroad of Maintenance[16] are to be interpreted as supplementary to Brussels I. Thus, it is

---

[4] SC Case No 295/2000.

[5] Thessaloniki CoA Case No 1694/2011. For the relevant analysis see A Anthimos, 'Exequatur Proceedings According to the Brussels I Regulation in Greece' (2014) *Revue Hellénique de Droit International* 1007.

[6] Arts 142 and 143 of the GCCP. According to Thessaloniki CoA Case No 267/1999 and East Crete CoA 139/2014, failure to make that appointment is not sufficient to reject the recognition of the judgment. *cf* Thessaloniki FIC Case No 511/1994.

[7] Art 142(1) of the GCCP.

[8] Thessaloniki FIC Case No 24084/2007.

[9] SC Case No 608/2008.

[10] Thessaloniki FIC Case No 13066/2008 rejecting third party proceedings.

[11] See SC Case No 1028/2009, SC Case No 608/2008, SC Case No 1024/2001.

[12] SC Case No 1028/2009, Thessaloniki CoA 267/1999.

[13] Art 491(1) of the GCCP.

[14] Art 43(2) and Annex III of Brussels I.

[15] Athens FIC Case No 6028/2010.

[16] The Convention was ratified by the Greek Legislative Decree No 4421/1964.

possible for a claimant to ask for the transmission of a judicial decision to the competent authority in another Member State ('MS') by requesting its recognition and enforcement under Article 32 et seq of Brussels I.

v. Conclusion

a. Problem Areas

The wording of Article 43 of the Regulation misleads practitioners about the procedure to follow for the enforcement of foreign judgments in Greece.

b. Best Practice

In principle, the Greek courts apply and interpret Brussels I correctly. Where necessary, they take a purposive approach and apply some national procedural rules to cases by analogy in order to overcome practical difficulties posed by the wording of the Regulation.[17]

c. Possible Solutions

A minor revision is still needed in Article 43 of Brussels I as the problem was not addressed in the Brussels I Recast[18] because either the EU legislator was unaware of the problem or the Greek courts had already found a workable solution.

B. Applicable Law Issues Under the Rome I and Rome II Regulations

i. Rome I

a. Matters Related to the Scope of Application

The Greek courts have, in a limited number of cases, applied Rome I to non-contractual obligations[19] or to contractual obligations involving no international element.[20]

There are cases where the Greek courts, contrary to Article 28, have applied Rome I to contracts concluded before 17 December 2009[21] and in some of them they have applied the Rome Convention[22] and Rome I together.[23]

b. Matters Related to the Uniform Rules

The Greek courts ignore the structure of Article 4. They interpret the connecting factors provided in Article 4 as alternatives among which they can choose freely to determine

---

[17] For instance, they apply Art 585 of the GCCP by analogy in cases where the application of Art 43 of Brussels I poses a problem, see, eg Patras CoA Case No 628/2006.

[18] Reg (EU) No 1215/2012 of the European Parliament and of the Council of 12 December 2012 on jurisdiction and the recognition and enforcement of judgments in civil and commercial matters (recast), [2012] OJ L351/1.

[19] Piraeus FIC Case No 4068/2013.

[20] Piraeus FIC Case No 3086/2011.

[21] Athens FIC Case No 158/2012, Athens CoA Case No 4467/2010.

[22] 1980 Rome Convention on the law applicable to contractual obligations, [1980] OJ L266/1.

[23] Piraeus CoA Case No 223/2013, Piraeus CoA Case No 428/2013, Drama FIC Case No 11/2011, Piraeus CoA Case No 428/2009, Piraeus CoA Case No 738/2008.

the law of the country with which the contract is most closely connected.[24] They use the default rule in Article 4(4) as a general clause encompassing all the connecting factors provided in Article 4(1) and (2) by seeing them as mere indications of the possible national laws with which the contract could be most closely connected.

c. Matters Related to Other Provisions

Pursuant to Article 25, the Greek courts apply the relevant international conventions ratified by Greece before the adoption of Rome I.[25]

As regards public policy of forum under Article 21, it is well-established case law that foreign applicable law may not be refused merely on the fact that 'the applicable law is unknown to Greece or it is contrary to overriding mandatory rules'.[26]

d. Conclusion

1. Problem Areas

The courts misinterpret Article 4 of Rome I, which jeopardises the uniform application, and occasionally struggle with determining its temporal and material scope of application.

2. Best Practice

The Greek courts' broad interpretation of Article 21 represents best practice.

3. Possible Solutions

Workshops and seminars should be organised for judges, lawyers and legal practitioners with a view to clarifying the scope of application and structure of Rome I.

ii. Rome II

a. Matters Related to the Scope of Application

One of the problems that the Greek courts have faced is whether or not Rome II applies to all types of obligations *ex lege*. The Greek SC has recently ruled that Rome II does not cover all types of *ex lege* obligations.[27] The problem arises from the fact that the Greek text of Rome II uses 'adikopraksia' under Article 4, however unlike 'faits dommageables', used in the French text, 'adikopraksia' is considered to be too restrictive to cover all types of *ex lege* obligations and it covers only tort.[28] Due to the absence of a clear provision on the issue, the Greek courts applied by analogy Article 4(1) of the Rome Convention and Article 25(b) of the GCC, according to which in contractual obligations 'applicable is the law that befits the contract taking account of all the specific circumstances'.

---

[24] Piraeus FIC Case No 5261/2013, Volos MMC Case No 199/2013, Rodopi FIC 199/2013.
[25] See Kavala FIC Case No 440/2011 where the Court applied the Hague-Visby Rules of 25.8.1924, as amended by the Brussels Protocols 23.2.1968 and 26.12.1979.
[26] Athens CoA Case No 4467/2010.
[27] Piraeus FIC Case No 3075/2012.
[28] Professor Tsouca underlines that the Regulation neither covers nor excludes non-contractual obligations derived from law, see eg, Ch Tsouca, 'Note on the Judgement of Piraeus FIC No 3075/2012' Savigny—Private International Law Blog, January 2014.

Contrary to Article 31, the Greek courts have applied Rome II, in a number of cases, to the disputes arising before the entry into force of the Regulation.[29]

b. Matters Related to Torts/Delicts

The Greek courts do not respect the structure of Rome II in determining the applicable law. There are cases where the courts applied the rules provided in Articles 4 to 9 even though there was a choice-of-law agreement pursuant to Article 14, in order to justify the parties' choice.[30] In some cases, they applied several connecting factors provided in Article 4(1), (2) and (3) altogether[31] in order to strengthen their position to apply Greek law.

In a few cases, the Greek courts applied the general rule in Article 4 instead of the special rules provided for particular types of torts in Articles 5 to 9.[32]

c. Matters Related to the Common Rules

The Greek courts' approach on overriding mandatory provisions is rather limited.[33] The provisions of the Laws of 551/1915[34] and 762/1978[35] are regarded by the Greek courts as overriding mandatory rules. The courts apply Greek law to determine the notion of 'family' of a person sustaining damage, even if the person does not have a Greek citizenship.[36]

In dealing with matters related to burden of proof under Article 22 of the Regulation, the Greek courts are obliged by Article 337 of the GCCP to take account of and apply foreign applicable law *ex officio* and without to be proved by the parties. The judge is free to find the content of the foreign applicable law by any means under Article 337 GCCP.

d. Matters Related to Other Provisions

As regards public policy of forum under Article 26, the Greek courts have found that foreign applicable law may not be refused merely on the fact that 'the applicable law is unknown to Greece or it is contrary to overriding mandatory rules'.[37]

e. Conclusion

1. Problem Areas

The Greek courts occasionally do not follow the structure of Rome II and of its rules.

---

[29] Chania FIC Case No 123/2012, Piraeus CoA Case No 12/2011.

[30] Piraeus FIC Case No 5261/2013.

[31] ibid.

[32] Athens FIC Case No 4658/2012.

[33] E Liaskos, 'Article 16 Overriding Mandatory Provisions' in A Bolos (ed), *Private International Law for Non-contractual Obligations* (Athens, P N Sakkoulas, 2014) 487.

[34] Under this Law, persons working in the navy or, in case of their death, their relatives are entitled to claim compensation for damages arising from workplace accidents, see, eg Piraeus CoA Case No 220/2010.

[35] The Law defines the responsibility of a foreign delegate in seafarer disputes, see Piraeus CoA Case No 546/2010.

[36] SC Case No 525/2010.

[37] Athens CoA No 4467/2010.

2. Best Practice

The Greek courts have applied Rome II to unjust enrichment, *negotiorum gestion* and *culpa in contrahendo* in a satisfactory manner[38] and adopted a broad interpretation of Article 17 to cover rules of safety and conduct to prevent accidents.

3. Possible Solutions

The issue of *ex lege* non-contractual obligations needs to be addressed in the revision of Rome II. The Regulation should be mainstreamed through the conduct of seminars.

C. Practice/Process

i. *Greece's National Courts' Practice in Interpreting the Regulations/Process Issues*

Where the Regulations and national law have similar provisions, the Greek courts rely on national provisions unless they are inconsistent with the Regulations.[39]

ii. *Cost and Length of Litigation in Cross-border Civil and Commercial Disputes*

The length of litigation depends on the location of a court hearing the case and it is longer in the courts of the main cities, such as Athens, Piraeus and Thessaloniki. A civil action filed in 2016 in Athens would be heard in 2022. Average time for the court to render its decision would be two years. This is because of the heavy workload of the courts, strikes in judiciary, and the weak Alternative Dispute Resolution ('ADR') tradition. Due to long delays, provisional orders and interim measures are sought very often. The hearing of the provisional order is set within two days from the filing of the petition and the order is issued on either the same or the following day. Interim measures should be filed within 30 days after the decision on provisional order was made and issued at the latest within 30 days.[40]

For ordinary procedures, the plaintiff will have to pay for a court stamp which is approximately 0.8 per cent of the value of the subject matter of the dispute. The cost of the procedure including attorney's fee is awarded to be paid by the defeated party. In case of partial victory and partial defeat of the litigants, the court sets off the costs.[41]

The Law Number 3226/2004 contains special provisions for the residents of other EU countries requesting legal aid in civil and commercial matters. Article 10 of this Law provides for a number of financial aids including the costs related to interpreters, translations and travel. The Greek Ministry of Justice is the competent authority to file such a request.

iii. *Settlement in Cross-border Civil and Commercial Disputes*

Article 293 of the GCCP sets out the general legislative framework for the judicial and extrajudicial settlement of disputes. The judicial settlement takes place in the form of a

---

[38] Patra FIC Case No 244/2015, Larissa CoA Case No 348/2015, Piraeus CoA Case No 4238/2013, Volos FIC Case No 199/2013.
[39] For the relevant examples concerning local jurisdiction of the courts, see s II.iii above.
[40] K Papadiamantis, 'Greece' in R Clark (ed), *The Dispute Resolution Review* (London, Law Business Research Ltd, 2013) 306.
[41] ibid, 302.

statement before a court, judge representative or public notary and results in *ipso jure* termination of the dispute. On the other hand, the extrajudicial settlement does not terminate the dispute, but it establishes the basis for objecting to the admissibility of the action before a court. If the party is successful in his objection, the court is bound to set the operative part of its judgment in accordance with the settlement agreement. If the agreement is concluded after a FIC rendered its decision, parties can raise it before the CoA.

iv. Alternative Dispute Resolution for Cross-border Civil and Commercial Disputes

Despite the fact that the court litigation is very lengthy, it is still the first preference of parties for dispute resolution. However, with the adoption of a number of instruments, more disputes have been referred to ADR.

Mediation was established by the Law Number 3898/2010 and judicial mediation was established by the Law Number 4055/2011 for further enhancement of ADR in civil matters. Judicial mediators are appointed in every FIC and have the authority to take a more proactive role by offering non-binding settlement proposals than mediators who, as a matter of principle, would refrain from offering such proposals.

International arbitration is governed by the Law Number 2735/1999 based on the UNCITRAL Model Law. Cross-border civil and commercial disputes as well as certain categories of public law disputes, such as tax related matters,[42] may be subject to arbitration. There are only limited grounds for the annulment of arbitral awards.[43]

Labour disputes can be referred to ADR including conciliation, mediation and arbitration.[44]

v. Remedies in Cross-border Civil and Commercial Disputes

The Greek courts accept to issue provisional measures ordering a protective attachment of debtor's property deemed to be insecure.[45] They issue provisional measures even in relation to high technological complexities. In a recent case involving claims of breach of intellectual property rights, the court ordered technological measures to block all websites that accommodated the illegal trade of the product.[46]

The Greek courts have awarded non-pecuniary remedies[47] and remedies for moral harm[48] in cross-border civil and commercial disputes.

---

[42] The arbitrability of tax related matters has been well accepted by the Greek courts, see especially CE Case No 1793/1991.

[43] According to Art 898 of the GCCP, the CoA is the competent court to request the annulment of arbitral awards.

[44] See, eg the Greek Laws No 1876/1990, No 3899/2010, No 4046/2012 and the Act of the Ministerial Council 6/2012.

[45] In a case, in making the decision for provisional measures and ordering the protective attachment, the court also considered that plaintiff's request for recognition and enforcement of Welsh courts' judgments in Greece was pending before another court, Athens FIC Case No 7924/2009. Similarly, the Greek courts ordered the protective attachment of all property, movable and immovable, as a provisional measure, see, eg Piraeus FIC Case No 3086/2011.

[46] Athens FIC Case No 4658/2012.

[47] The Athens multi-member court ordered the restitution of the copies of invoices to the claimant, see, eg Athens FIC Case No 1568/2011.

[48] See, eg Dodecanese CoA Case No 220/2013, where the court awarded compensation for moral harm in a dispute involving a criminal defamation through a publication pressed in the United Kingdom.

vi. Conclusion

The length of litigation is a significant problem in Greece. ADR offers parties time and cost efficient access to justice, compared to the court litigation.

D. Preliminary Remarks on Effectiveness of the Current EU PIL Framework in Civil and Commercial Law

Although there are certain matters that need to be revised, the current legislative framework of EU PIL in civil and commercial law is, in general, considered effective. However, its efficiency is undermined by the ineffective administration of justice in Greece. The legislation enacted in the past few years showed significant progress on the administration of justice, but practice indicates that the problems are inherited in the system.

III. Greece's Experience on Cross-border Family Law Disputes

A. Jurisdictional and Procedural Issues Under the Brussels IIa Regulation

i. Matters Related to the Scope of Application

Greece is the only Member State where Islamic law (Sharia) is applicable to family issues between Greek Muslim citizens living in the region of Thrace. The proceedings before the mufti are merely religious and the decisions are binding. However, they are excluded from the scope of application of Brussels IIa which may lead to unequal results for this group of EU citizens.

In a joint action on parental responsibility and maintenance obligations, the Greek courts extend the material scope of application of Brussels IIa to maintenance obligations.[49]

ii. Matters Related to Jurisdiction

a. Divorce, Legal Separation and Marriage Annulment

The European legislator uses the word 'or' to indicate that the grounds provided in Article 3(1)(a) are established alternatively. However, it does not use 'or' between Article 3(1)(a) and Article 3(1)(b). Therefore, the Greek courts, by following a strict textual interpretation of Article 3, cumulatively apply one of the grounds of habitual residence and the common nationality of the spouses in determining their jurisdiction.[50] Furthermore, they on their own motion decline jurisdiction where one of the two nationalities of the wife is common with the nationality of the husband.[51]

---

[49] Grevena FIC Case No 96/2013, Athens FIC Case No 2995/2010.
[50] Thessaloniki FIC Case No 1226/2014.
[51] Athens CoA Case No 2712/2011.

Legal separation is not recognised in Greek law and divorce is the only possibility to resolve matrimonial disputes.[52]

b. Parental Responsibility

1. Child Abduction

In the majority of the cases, the Greek courts have assumed jurisdiction on the ground that Greece was the country where the child was wrongfully removed to or retained in under the 1980 Hague Child Abduction Convention[53] and relied on only the Convention without making any reference to Article 11 of Brussels IIa.[54] As a result, the child's right to be heard has been ignored in numerous cases.[55]

In a limited number of child abduction cases, the Greek courts have decided also on the rights of custody and access by ignoring the fact that the return of a child should be decided separately and autonomously.[56]

2. Access

Based on Article 9, the Greek courts have held that a child might acquire a habitual residence on the very first day of its lawful move.[57]

3. Other Issues Related to Parental Responsibility

The Greek courts have stressed that the right to parental responsibility includes choosing the minor's residence in another Member State and that a restriction on this issue would be contrary to the European principle of free movement.[58]

iii. Matters Related to Recognition and Enforcement

a. Certificate Concerning Judgments in Matrimonial Matters and Certificate Concerning Judgments on Parental Responsibility

In the Greek version of Article 33, the term 'prosfigi' is used to refer to administrative procedures. This leads to serious interpretation difficulties because the Greek courts consider that the decision on a declaration of enforceability of a judgment is not a court decision, but an administrative order.[59]

---

[52] E Vassilakakis and V Kourtis, 'The Impact and Application of the Brussels II Regulation in Greece' in K Boele-Woelki and CG Bilfuss (eds), *Brussels II bis: Its Impact and Application in the Member States* (Mortsel, Intersentia, 2007) 138; K Fountedaki, *Oi ypotheseis gonikis merimnas sto neo Kanonismo 2201/2003* (Athens, Sakkoulas, 2004) 132.

[53] Therefore, there are not many cases on Art 10 of Brussels IIa.

[54] Thessaloniki CoA Case No 1467/2012, Athens FIC Case No 2393/2015. See also, Agrinio FIC Case No 340/2009, Athens CoA Case No 8468/2007 where the courts referred to Art 11 but did not apply it.

[55] Thessaloniki FIC Case No 9457/2012, Athens CoA Case No 8468/2007. See also, Ch Apalagaki, 'Oi rythmiseis tou Kanonismou 2201/2003 gia tin apagogi paidion' (2005) *Armenopoulos* 1015, 1018.

[56] Piraeus FIC Case No 6827/2012; cf Thessaloniki FIC Case No 9457/2012, Thessaloniki CoA Case No 1467/2012.

[57] Athens FIC Case No 713/2015, Thessaloniki FIC Case No 13063/2015, Thessaloniki FIC Case No 22101/2011, Kavala FIC Case No 24/2009.

[58] Kavala FIC Case No 24/2009.

[59] Athens CoA Case No 589/2008. On the consequences of this distinction, see s II.A.iii above. See also, E Cioupsidou, 'Zitimata ton Kanonismon 2201/2003 kai 1347/2000 sxetika me ti diethi dikaiodosia kai anagnorisi apofaseon stis gamikes diafores' (2005) *Elliniki Dikaiosini* 653, 654.

b. Rights of Access and Return of the Child

The reported cases do not indicate any particular difficulty concerning these matters.

iv. Relations with Other Instruments

Although Brussels IIa prevails over the 1996 Hague Convention on Protection of Children[60] in relation to the matters of jurisdiction, recognition and enforcement, the Greek courts apply Brussels IIa and the 1996 Hague Convention together to decide on their jurisdiction.[61]

v. Conclusion

a. Problem Areas

The exclusion of the proceedings before the mufti from the scope of application of Brussels IIa, the relationship between Brussels IIa and other international instruments, the interpretation of the legal remedies provided in Article 33 due to the wording of the provision and the ambiguity in some provisions of the Regulation, eg on dual nationality, pose problems.

b. Best Practice

In interpreting the notion of parental responsibility, the Greek courts always take account of the EU principles.

c. Possible Solutions

In some cases, the margin of discretion given to the Member State in interpreting Brussels IIa jeopardises the principle of legal security. The ambiguity in certain provisions, eg Articles 3(1) and 9, should be removed to guarantee the uniform application of the Regulation.

Seminars and workshops for judges, attorneys and legal practitioners should also be organised to mainstream the Regulation.

B. Jurisdictional and Procedural Issues and Applicable Law Under the Maintenance Regulation

i. Matters Related to the Scope of Application

Until 2015, it was not clear whether the Maintenance Regulation applies to same-sex marriages or partnerships, since such institutions were not recognised in Greece.[62] With the extension of civil unions to same-sex couples in 2015,[63] same-sex relationships are now

---

[60] The Convention was ratified by the Greek Law No 4020/2011.
[61] Athens FIC Case No 713/2015, Thessaloniki FIC Case No 13063/2015.
[62] A Douga and V Koumpli, 'On the Regulation on maintenance obligations in Greece' (2014) *Revue Hellenique de Droit International* 931, 950.
[63] Law 4356/2015, Opinion of the Legal Council of the Hellenic State 432/2006.

characterised as family relationships in Greece falling under the scope of the application of the Regulation.

ii. Matters Related to Jurisdiction

The reported cases do not indicate any particular difficulty concerning these matters.

iii. Matters Related to Applicable Law

The Greek courts have made a few references to the Maintenance Regulation in determining the law applicable to maintenance obligations. They continue to apply the old provisions of the GCC,[64] holding that such obligations are primarily governed by the law of the common nationality of the spouses or the law of the common nationality of the child and its parents.[65]

iv. Matters Related to Recognition, Enforceability and Actual Enforcement of Decisions

By virtue of Article 75(2)(a) of the Maintenance Regulation, the Greek courts have only been indirectly concerned with the recognition, enforceability and enforcement of decisions given in a Member State not bound by the 2007 Hague Protocol. However, in almost all cases,[66] the courts reviewed the substance of decisions and breached Article 42 of the Regulation. Contrary to Article 75(2) of the Regulation, the courts, while applying Section 2 of Chapter IV, simply ignored Section 3 of Chapter IV.

By considering the rationale of Article 30 of the Regulation, the Greek courts decided that the party against whom enforcement is sought shall not be summoned.[67]

v. Conclusion

a. Problem Areas

It is common practice for the Greek courts to continue to rely on the reasoning of previous decisions decided before the Maintenance Regulation and therefore the Regulation is misapplied by the courts. Moreover, the Greek courts often do not apply the Maintenance Regulation in deciding the law applicable to maintenance obligations and determine the applicable law according to the GCC.

---

[64] See eg, Athens FIC Case No 2097/2015, Athens FIC Case No 12028/2014. The courts have referred to the provisions of the Regulation only in few cases, see eg Athens FIC Case No 67/2016.

[65] Arts 14, 18, 19 and 20 of the GCC provide for three more connecting factors, ie (i) the latest habitual residence of the spouses or (ii) the country to which the spouses were most closely connected or (iii) the nationality of the child. However, it is the law of the common nationality generally applied to maintenance obligations.

[66] Rhodes FIC Case No 98/2014, Rhodes FIC Case No 72/2014, Alexandoupoli FIC Case No 97/2015, Thessaloniki FIC Case No18373/2014.

[67] ibid.

b. Best Practice

As regards matters related to jurisdiction, the Greek courts have applied the Regulation in a satisfactory manner. The characterisation of same-sex relationships as family relationships falling under the scope of the application of the Regulation is an advancement.

c. Possible Solutions

The Maintenance Regulation should be mainstreamed to judges, attorneys and legal practitioners through seminars and workshops in order to raise the awareness in relation to the Regulation and to ensure its correct application.

C. Practice/Process

i. *Greece's National Courts' Practice in Interpreting the Regulations*

The Greek courts follow either a liberal or a very strict textual approach in interpreting the Regulations. There is no consistency in this regard. Generally, they interpret the Regulations in a way which allows them to establish jurisdiction and apply Greek law.

ii. *Cost and Length of Litigation in Cross-border Family Law Disputes*

In addition to the information provided above,[68] in maintenance claims, according to Article 173(4) of the GCCP, the debtor spouse has to pay in advance the expenses and fees[69] of the plaintiff/creditor spouse.

In family law cases, a decision is rendered, on average, within one year starting from the filing of the action. In child abduction cases, it is even up to six months. The procedure may be considerably shorter in case of uncontested divorces due to the abolition of the second hearing taking place six months after first one.

iii. *Settlement in Cross-border Family Law Disputes*

Cross-border family law and civil and commercial law disputes are subject to the same legal framework. However, settlement agreements on maintenance issues are scarce in Greece, possibly because of the obligatory nature of most of the maintenance provisions especially in relation to child maintenance.[70]

In family law disputes, by virtue of Article 602 of the GCCP, the Greek courts have discretion to attempt to reconcile the spouses or to postpone giving the ruling up to three months.

iv. *Alternative Dispute Resolution for Cross-border Family Law Disputes*

Under the Greek Law Number 3898/2010 implementing the Directive 2008/52,[71] mediation in cross-border family law disputes may be initiated by the parties, the Central Authority,

---

[68] See s II.C.ii above.
[69] This is up to 300 euros.
[70] Douga and Koumpli, n 62 above, 959.
[71] Dir 2008/52/EC of the European Parliament and of the Council of 21 May 2008 on certain aspects of mediation in civil and commercial matters, [2008] OJ L136/3.

the Ministry of Justice or the consulate. It only covers the issues of parental responsibility and maintenance obligations. Divorce is excluded from its scope since a court's decision is mandatory.

v. Remedies in Cross-border Family Law Disputes

It is possible to seek damages for moral harm and permanent injunctions in a divorce case[72] and maintenance case, however there is no reported case where these remedies are awarded.

vi. Conclusion

Parties prefer court litigation to an extra-judicial settlement or a settlement through ADR. National legislation allows courts to reconcile parties and to set off the proceedings costs in favour of the creditor.

D. Preliminary Remarks on Effectiveness of the Current EU PIL Framework in Cross-border Family Law

The effectiveness of the current legislative framework is undermined mainly by some terminological inconsistencies (eg Article 33 of Brussels IIa) and the non-regulation of eg dual nationality and the religious proceedings before the mufti. The Maintenance Regulation is not known to many practitioners and its incorrect application or non-application jeopardises the current EU PIL framework in cross-border family law.

IV. Conclusion

With the exception of the Maintenance Regulation, the application of the EU Regulations in Greece is overall very good. The Greek courts are willing to offer solutions in line with the Regulations and to interpret and apply the Regulations in a way to ensure predictability and legal certainty. Nevertheless, there are still areas that need further reform both on the Regulations and on the Greek courts' practices and approaches.

---

[72] Art 592(2) of the GCCP.

19

Hungary

CSONGOR ISTVÁN NAGY

I. Introduction

EU private international law (PIL) instruments are regularly applied by the Hungarian judiciary. Hungarian courts have been fairly active in terms of referring PIL cases to the Court of Justice of the European Union (CJEU),[1] contributing to the development of EU conflict of laws.

My research produced a good number of cases where EU PIL rules were applied. The precise numbers are: 29 cases concerning the Brussels I Regulation; 22 cases in relation to the Brussels IIa Regulation; 26 cases applying the Rome I Regulation; nine cases where the Rome II Regulation was considered; the Maintenance Regulation was considered on three occasions.[2] The aim of this chapter is to evaluate the work of the Hungarian courts in these cases.

II. Cross-border Civil and Commercial Disputes

As already noted, the survey of the publicly available judgments produced 29 Hungarian cases where a reference was made to the Brussels I Regulation. In approximately half of the cases (17 matters), no substantive issues of interpretation emerged.[3] That said, there were

---

[1] See eg C-527/10 *Erste/BCL* EU:C:2012:417; C-519/12 *Hochtief* EU:C:2013:674; Case C-210/06 *Cartesio* EU:C:2008:723; C-378/10 *VALE* EU:C:2012:440; C-102/15 *Gazdasági Versenyhivatal v Siemens* EU:C:2016:60.

[2] It has to be noted that while all Hungarian judgments are publicly available, court orders are not published, except they are selected by one of the judicial collections. The court adopts an order when it does not decide in the merits of the case, for instance, in case it terminates the proceedings on procedural grounds. These court orders may apply EU private international law instruments, in particular if the court established that it has no jurisdiction. Accordingly, the number of cases applying the Brussels I and the Brussels IIa Reg may be greater.

[3] Case *Gf.IX.30.384/2009* (Supreme Court), reported as BH+ 2010.5.224; Case *Pfv.II.21.290/2007* (Supreme Court), reported as EH 2008.1700; Case *Pfv.II.22.073/2009* (Supreme Court), reported as EH 2010.2141 and BH+ 2013.1.33; Case *Gf.30372/2012/7* (High Court of Appeal of Debrecen); Case *G.40057/2012/118* (Court of Appeal of Debrecen); Case *G.40685/2012/38* (Court of Appeal of Budapest); Case *G.41053/2008/89* (Court of Appeal of Budapest); Case *P.20648/2011/40* (Court of Appeal of Budapest); Case *Gf.20087/2009/7* (High Court of Appeal of Győr); Case *Gf.20424/2009/2* (High Court of Appeal of Győr); Case *Pf.20112/2014/9* (High Court of Appeal of Győr), appealed from Case *P.20052/2012/79* (Court of Appeal of Győr); Case *Pf.20136/2008/8* (High Court of Appeal of Szeged); Case *P.20406/2011/71* (Court of Appeal of Szeged); Case *P.21860/2007/89* (Court of Appeal of Zalaegerszeg); Case *Pf.21124/2014/5* (Court of Appeal of Zalaegerszeg); Case *G.20203/2012/100* (Court of Appeal of Szolnok; Case *10.Gf.40.417/2011/12* (High Court of Appeal of Budapest), reported as ÍH 2012.82.

a number of jurisdictional challenges which resulted in heated debates about jurisdiction. Two of the Hungarian cases culminated in preliminary rulings (in Case C-519/12 *Hochtief*[4] and in Case C-102/15 *Gazdasági Versenyhivatal v Siemens*).[5]

A. Jurisdictional and Procedural Issues under the Brussels I Regulation

The scope of Brussels I was subject to a major jurisdictional dispute in Case C-102/15 *Gazdasági Versenyhivatal v Siemens*. In Hungarian competition procedure, condemned undertakings have to pay the fine even if they attack it before the court. If the court's final judgment quashes, in full or in part, the fine, it has to be refunded with interest. This happened in this case. However, the Hungarian Competition Office (HCO), after refunding, attacked the final judgment before the Supreme Court with an extraordinary appeal and the latter reinstated the fine. Siemens paid back the fine but, failing specific statutory rule, refused to refund the interest. The HCO claimed back the interest on the basis of civil law's rules on unjust enrichment. The CJEU established that the HCO claim was not civil or commercial in nature, hence, the Brussels I was not applicable.

In Case *Gfv.IX.30.186/2010*, reported as EH 2010.2237, the Supreme Court applied the Brussels I Regulation to an administrative authority's termination of a sponsorship contract, as the authority did not act in its capacity as a public authority.

There were a number of cross-border contractual disputes where the issue of jurisdiction has been disputed. In Case *Gfv.IX.30.187/2011*, reported as EH 2011.2416 and BH+ 2013.1.33,[6] the Supreme Court interpreted Articles 7(1) and 7(2) of the Brussels I Regulation in the context of pre-contracts (*culpa in contrahendo*). The Court established that as the contract to be executed on the basis of the pre-contract was to be concluded in Hungary ('the place of performance of the contract would have been determined in Hungary'), Hungarian courts had jurisdiction under Article 7(1). That is, in case of pre-contracts, the place of the conclusion of the contract is to be regarded as the place of performance under Article 7(1). The court also referred to Article 7(2) of the Brussels I Regulation. In this regards, the damages were defined partially as the expenses and partially as the loss of profits. The court noted that the loss of profits occurred in Hungary, as did a part of the expenses, hence, the place of the damages also established the jurisdiction of Hungarian courts.

The parties got involved in another jurisdictional battle in Case *Gf.20003/2015/10* (High Court of Appeal of Győr).[7] This was a contractual dispute concerning the transfer of shares in limited liability companies. The defendants were domiciled in Luxembourg and the Channel Islands. The court assumed jurisdiction over the non-EU based defendant according to the Hungarian rules. It should be noted that according to Hungarian law, business shares are not negotiable instruments (contrary to shares is stock corporations). The court conceived the agreement as a sales contract and defined the place where the goods were to be delivered as the country where the acquisition of the business shares was to be registered.

---

⁴ Case *Gf.40560/2011/6* (High Court of Appeal of Budapest).
⁵ Above n 1.
⁶ Appealed from Case *G.41503/2006/41503* (Court of Appeal of Budapest).
⁷ Appealed from Case *G.20348/2013/83* (High Court of Appeal of Győr).

As the transfer of the shares in a company seated in Hungary has to be registered in Hungary, the place of performance was Hungary and Hungarian courts had jurisdiction under Article 7(1) of the Brussels I Regulation.

In Case *Gf.30410/2013/3* (High Court of Appeal of Szeged),[8] the defendant wanted to set off its claim for compensation for legal costs it was awarded in a procedure in the Czech Republic against the same plaintiff concerning the same subject-matter. The Hungarian court recognised the Czech decision on legal costs. The plaintiff argued that the Hungarian court had no jurisdiction over the set-off. The High Court of Appeal of Szeged established its jurisdiction on the basis of Article 8(3) of the Brussels I Regulation.

In Case *Gf.20062/2015/8*, the High Court of Appeal of Győr interpreted the concept of consumer contract. It assumed jurisdiction holding that, in the context of a choice-of-court agreement included into the creditor's standard terms, a loan contract does not qualify as a consumer contract, if its purpose is to build structures on the plots owned by the debtor and its family, including an apartment complex of 18 apartments and a restaurant. The definition of consumer contracts was dealt with by the Court of Appeal of Szeged in Case *P.21044/2015/16*. It held that the contract could not be regarded as being concluded outside the debtor's trade or profession, if the agreement fell partially outside the economic and professional activity.

In Case *Gf.I.30.343/2013*, reported as ÍH 2014.58, the High Court of Appeal of Szeged held that domain name registration is covered by Article 22(4) of the Brussels I Regulation. The Court considered that the registration of a domain name is similar to trademarks and as Article 24(4) of the Brussels I Regulation refers to 'proceedings concerned with the registration or validity of patents, trademarks, designs, or other similar rights required to be deposited or registered', Hungarian courts have exclusive jurisdiction over domain names registered in Hungary.

In Case *Gf.VII.30.228/2013/4* (Supreme Court),[9] the parties entered into a distribution contract which contained a German choice-of-court clause. A subsequent dispute between the parties was settled via a memorandum. The Supreme Court held that the choice-of-court agreement covering the distribution contract did not extend to the memorandum, as the latter was not simply the consequentiality of the distribution contract but created a new contractual obligation (the supplier promised to buy the products it sold before). Accordingly, the Hungarian court assumed jurisdiction as the place of performance was in Hungary.

Hungarian courts, under Hungarian PIL rules, had the tendency of taking a restrictive approach as to choice-of-court agreements. It is hoped that Hungarian courts will not follow this approach as to the Brussels I Regulation, although the statutory language of the two instruments is similar.

There appears to be only one published case in relation to the recognition and enforcement of foreign judgments.[10] In Case *P.20071/2014/11*, the Court of Appeal of the Budapest Region dealt with Article 45(1)(b) of the Brussels I Regulation. In this case, the Court held

---

[8] Appealed from Case *G.40009/2013/15* (Court of Appeal of Gyula).

[9] Appealed from Case *14.Gf.40.512/2012/2* (High Court of Appeal of Budapest), appealed from Case *8.G.40.554/2010/34* (Court of Appeal of Budapest), tried on remand as Case *G.42072/2014/17* (Court of Appeal of Budapest).

[10] It has to be noted that there are other unreported decisions concerning recognition and enforcement. These cases largely remain unreported because they normally get closed with a court order rather than a judgment.

that in the recognition stage it may be examined only whether the service of the document occurred 'in sufficient time and in such a way' that it did not impair the defendant's right of defence. In case of an error of service, the primary question is whether the error was grave enough to deprive the defendant of the possibility to defend himself. In this case, the Court answered the question in the negative.

All in all, the Brussels I Regulation has been applied in numerous cases and Hungarian courts seem to have tackled the problem of the application of the Brussels I Regulation properly. Some of the matters raised questions of interpretation not fully settled in the CJEU's jurisprudence (eg set-off, place of performance of pre-contracts, place of delivery in case of transfer of shares in limited liability companies) and courts seem to have handled them plausibly.

The jurisdictional rules of Hungarian PIL were brought in line with Brussels I (or more precisely with the Lugano Convention). The advantage of this was that Hungarian courts have become increasingly familiar with the Brussels rules long before accession. A drawback of this might be (though this is more a risk than a fact) that courts might apply the case law developed as to Hungarian jurisdictional rules also to the Brussels I Regulation.

B. Applicable Law Issues Under the Rome I and Rome II Regulations

i. Rome I

The survey of the publicly available judgments produced 26 Hungarian cases where a reference was made to the Rome I Regulation. In the overwhelming majority of these cases, no substantive issues of interpretation emerged: in 10 cases the court established that the Rome I Regulation was not applicable *ratione temporis*,[11] while in 12 other cases the interpretation of the Regulation was clear.[12]

---

[11] Case *Pf.20271/2014/3* (High Court of Appeal of Budapest), appealed from Case *P.20648/2011/40* (Court of Appeal of Budapest); Case *G.40110/2013/45* (Court of Appeal of Zalaegerszegi); Case *Pf.639898/2014/5* (Court of Appeal of Budapest), appealed from Case *P.20986/2014/12* (Court of the II and III District of Budapest); Case *Gf.40100/2013/8* (High Court of Appeal of Budapest); Case *Pf.20267/2013/3* (High Court of Appeal of Győr); Case *B.12/2012/144* (Court of Appeal of the Region of Budapest); Case *G.20348/2013/83* (Court of Appeal of Győr); Case *G.40138/2010/64* (Court of Appeal of the Budapest Region); Case *Gf.30372/2012/7* (High Court of Appeal of Debrecen); Case *P.22877/2012/10* (Court of Appeal of Budapest).

[12] Case *Gf.40333/2015/5* (High Court of Appeal of Budapest), appealed from Case *G.42072/2014/17* (Court of Appeal of Budapest) (the court applied the law of the seller, which was Hungarian law); Case *Pf.20074/2011/5* (High Court of Appeal of Győr), also reported as Case ÍH 2012.66 (an Austrian lawyer claimed attorney's fee from his client; the court applied Austrian law as the law of the service provider); Case *Gf.20013/2015/4* (High Court of Appeal of Győr), appealed from Case *G.40031/2014/8* (Veszprém Court of Appeal) (as to a contract for the carriage of goods, the court applied the law of the habitual residence of the person providing the service); Case *Pf.20095/2015/5* (High Court of Appeal of Budapest) (the case contains references to the Rome I Reg but the court in fact applied the 1980 Rome Convention to a consumer contract and found that Hungarian law was applicable); Case *Pf.20168/2013/5* (High Court of Appeal of Győr), appeal from Case *P.20197/2012/33* (Court of Appeal of Győr) (mere reference to the Rome I Reg); Case *Gf.30587/2013/4* (High Court of Appeal of Debrecen), appealed from Case *G.40186/2011/34* (Court of Appeal of Debrecen) (the law applicable to the assignment was not to be established because the assigned claim was rejected); Case *Gf.40117/2013/7* (High Court of Appeal of Budapest) (the case concerned a contract of carriage and Hungarian law was applicable due to Art 5(1) of the Rome I Reg; the court also applied the COTIF-CÍM, promulgated in Hungary by Law-Decree 2 of 1986); Case *G.40864/2008/169* (Budapest Court of Appeal); Case *G.40685/2012/38* (Court of Appeal of Budapest) (the parties chose the applicable law.); Case *Pf.20234/2014/2* (Court of Appeal of Kaposvár) (absent party choice, the court

In Case *G.20348/2013/83*, the Rome I Regulation was not applicable *ratione temporis*. However, the Court of Appeal of Győr, as obiter dicta, indicated that the Rome I Regulation would not apply anyway: one of the contracting parties was Austrian but the other one was from the Cayman Islands. It seems that the Court misconceived the scope of the Rome I Regulation as applying only to EU matters. This stance appears to be flawed, since the Rome I Regulation has universal application and is applicable irrespective of whether the case has an EU element or not (Article 2 of the Rome I Regulation).

In *Case Gf.40321/2014/9*,[13] the parties stipulated the application of the Hungarian Civil Code. The High Court of Appeal of Budapest considered this to be an implicit choice of Hungarian law.

On the other hand, in Case *Gf.40051/2014/8*,[14] the High Court of Appeal of Pécs, when examining whether the parties chose German law, found the references to the German Civil Code (BGB) insufficient, because the contract also referred to the Hungarian Civil Code.

The parties were Hungarian companies (seated and registered in Hungary) and entered into a construction contract, which used the 'Vergabe- und Vertragsordnung für Bauleistungen' (VOB), a German standard contract worked out for construction projects. The VOB contains references to German law. The High Court of Appeal of Pécs held that that the references of the VOB to the provisions of the German Civil Code (BGB) were not sufficient to establish the choice of German law, as the contract contained references also to certain sources of Hungarian law.

In Case *Pf.20370/2013/6*, the High Court of Appeal of Pécs apparently misconceived party autonomy and ignored the parties' agreement on the applicable law without any detailed analysis. It found in the context of the Rome I Regulation that the choice of Austrian law was invalid because it went counter to the general principle that the law of the country has to be applied to which the case is most closely connected.

In Case *Gf.20062/2015/8*, the 1980 Rome Convention was applied but the High Court of Appeal of Győr referred also to the Rome I Regulation when interpreting the Convention, specifically as to the concept of mandatory norms. Austrian law was applicable to the case. Contrary to the defendants' allegations, the Court established that the Hungarian rules on the coming into existence, form, validity, substantive elements, rights and obligations, their performance and the termination of the legal relationship did not meet the requirements of Article 9(1) of the Rome I Regulation. Furthermore, the Court also held that the application of the mandatory rules is warranted chiefly in cases where the parties choose the law of a state the fact pattern has no connection to. This condition was not met either, since the fact pattern, through the plaintiff and its business activity, was connected to Austria.

It can be concluded that the Hungarian courts have encountered the Rome I Regulation in numerous cases and applied it without substantive issues. There are still some problems, however. As noted above, the Rome I Regulation was not applied in a case with a significant non-EU element; in a case the court suggested that the parties may choose only a law that is connected to the matter.

---

applied Hungarian law with reference to Art 4(1)(c) of the Rome I Reg); Case Gf.40496/2012/5 (High Court of Appeal of Budapest), appealed from Case G.40313/2011/27 (Court of Appeal of the Budapest Region) (the Court applied the law of the seller's habitual residence, which was Slovak law); Case *Gf.30147/2013/5* (High Court of Appeal of Szeged) (the law of the seller's habitual residence was applied, which was Hungarian law).

[13] Appealed from Case *G.40368/2012/52* (Court of Appeal of Budapest).
[14] Appealed from Case *G.40161/2013/47* (Court of Appeal of Zalaegerszeg).

ii. Rome II Regulation

Only nine Hungarian cases applying the Rome II Regulation were identified. In one of the cases the court established that the Rome II Regulation was not applicable *ratione temporis*.[15] There were no significant issues concerning the interpretation of the Regulation in four of the other cases.[16]

Issues of characterisation and scope emerged in cases involving traffic accidents. The courts have considered the law applicable to delictual liability as extending to the rules on compulsory motor vehicle liability insurance. This approach will have to be rectified in cases where the law governing the insurance contract is different from the one which applies to the non-contractual obligation.

In Case *Pfv.20852/2014/6*,[17] both the tortfeasor and the victim were Hungarian citizens and the accident happened in Hungary. However, the Supreme Court examined the question of applicable law because the car owned by the plaintiff was registered in Germany. The Supreme Court held that Hungarian law was applicable to the claim and, as part of that, also applied Act LXII of 2009 on mandatory motor vehicle liability insurance. Although, in this case, no substantive difference was made, the Court's interpretation appears to have been less than accurate in so far as the terms of the mandatory motor vehicle insurance were treated as delictual in nature. This may be regarded as an error of characterisation. The Rome II Regulation does not apply to contractual obligations (the relationship between the tortfeasor and the insurance company it has a contract with). This could be an issue, if the wrongdoer's car had been stationed in another Member State and he had had a contract with a foreign insurance company. A similar problem emerged in Case *Pf.641647/2013/4*, where the Court of Appeal of Budapest applied Hungarian law (as the place of the accident) and the Hungarian rules on mandatory motor vehicle liability insurance. Consequently, the issues of characterisation emerged in matters involving traffic accidents (distinction between the tort and the motor vehicle liability insurance). Hungarian courts have treated these issues in a rather summary manner. That said, this could be explained by the fact that the characterisation appeared to have no impact on the final outcome of the case.

In addition, it should be pointed out that the Hungarian courts have been very permissive as to party autonomy. An interesting judgment was rendered in Case *P.21013/2011/49*, where the parties requested the application of Hungarian law. The Court of Appeal of Győr did consider this as a choice-of-law agreement within the meaning of Article 14(1) of the Rome II Regulation. This also happened in Case *Pf.631007/2014/3*.[18] An interesting feature of this case was that the parties chose Hungarian law in the second instance proceedings. The Court of Appeal in Budapest considered this as a valid choice. It is a peculiar case because the court of first instance mistakenly applied Hungarian law. The court of second instance identified the misinterpretation of Rome II, but accepted the parties' agreement on the application of Hungarian law.[19]

---

[15] Case *Gf.40013/2015/15* (High Court of Appeal of Pécs).
[16] Case *Pf.20095/2015/5* (High Court of Appeal of Budapest); Case *Gf.40117/2013/7* (High Court of Appeal of Budapest); Case *Pf.20174/2011/10* (High Court of Appeal of Győr); Case *G.40057/2012/118* (Court of Appeal of Debrecen).
[17] Appealed from Case *Pf.640701/2013/4* (Court of Appeal of Budapest).
[18] Appealed from Case *P.89765/2012/31* (Central District Court of Pest).
[19] See more: CI Nagy, *Private International Law in Hungary* (Leiden, Kluwer, 2012) 76–77, para 158.

III. Cross-border Family Law Disputes

There were 22 Hungarian cases considering the Brussels IIa Regulation. On 10 occasions, no substantive issues of interpretation emerged.[20]

Under Hungarian law, a significant part of family law issues related to children, including the exercise of access rights, are handled by the Guardianship and Child Protection Office ('gyámhivatal'). In Case *Pfv.II.20.622/2009*, reported as BH 2009.10.298 and EH 2009.1961, the Supreme Court held that the Guardianship and Child Protection Office is to be regarded as a 'court' for the purposes of the Brussels IIa Regulation.

Hungarian courts have been reluctant to apply the Brussels IIa Regulation to matters having a significant non-EU element. In particular, in Case *Pfv.II.21.847/2014*, reported as BH+ 2016.1.26, the Supreme Court held that the Brussels IIa Regulation did not apply to a matter with a significant non-EU element. In this case, the wife was a Hungarian national. The husband was a French citizen. The wife requested the court to dissolve their marriage concluded in Paris, seeking custody over their child (a French-Hungarian dual citizen) born in Tokyo, and maintenance. Prior divorce proceedings had been issued by the husband in Bora Bora (French Polynesia), where the parties appeared to reside at the time the procedure was launched. The Supreme Court refused to apply the Brussels IIa Regulation's jurisdictional rules, because French Polynesia did not come under the Regulation's scope of application. This appears to be not entirely consistent with Article 6 of the Brussels IIa Regulation, which provides that a spouse who is habitually resident or a national of a Member State can be sued only in accordance with the Regulation's jurisdictional rules ('may be sued in another Member State only in accordance with Articles 3, 4 and 5').

In the Hungarian judicial practice, habitual residence, as one of the central concepts of the Brussels IIa Regulation's jurisdictional rules, is treated as a fact-intensive issue and is analysed on a case-by-case basis. Courts interpret this concept uniformly in the various legal instruments (Brussels IIa Regulation, Hague conventions and domestic law). As to the child's habitual residence, courts do not attribute primary relevance to the length of the stay but, instead, take into consideration the parents' decision and common will.[21] In Case *Pfv.II.20.123/2015*, reported as BH+ 2015.11.465, the Supreme Court established that if the parties move with the child to another country for a long period of time, though without the intention to settle, and sell their movables in Hungary and rent out their real estate for an indefinite duration, the child's habitual residence changes. In Case *Pfv.II.20.910/2011*, reported as EH 2011.2318, the Supreme Court held that the child's place of habitual residence does not move to Hungary, if the parents consider their employment here as provisional and maintain their habitual residence in the other country.

In Case *Pfv.II.21.710/2013*, reported as BH+ 2014.8.352, the Supreme Court examined the requirements of a choice-of-court agreement embedded in Article 12(3) of the

---

[20] Case *Pfv.II.21.129/2011* (Supreme Court), reported as BH 2013.1.19; Case *Pfv.II.21.677/2011* (Supreme Court), reported as BH 2012.6.154; Case *Pfv.II.21.339/2011* (Supreme Court), reported as BH 2012.9.224 and EH 2011.2411; Case *Pfv.20798/2009/7* (Supreme Court); Case *P.102782/2012/55* (Central District Court of Pest); Case *P.20568/2007/16* (District Court of Zalaegerszeg); Case *P.20521/2014/31* (Court of Appeal of Székesfehérvár); Case *Bf.836/2008/6* (Court of Appeal of Nyíregyháza); Case *Pf.20218/2013/8* (High Court of Appeal of Debrecen); Case *Pfv.II.22.065/2012* (Supreme Court), reported as BH 2013.10.271.

[21] See Case reported as BH 2014/180.

Brussels IIa Regulation. It noted that during the first instance procedure (where the court rejected the parties' motion) the child's interests would have been best served if the first instance court had tried the case and decided on the placement of the child. This would have worked well because at that time all interested parties had been staying in Hungary. The court of first instance misinterpreted Article 12(3) of the Brussels IIa Regulation, mistakenly declining jurisdiction and terminating the proceedings. However, due to the change of circumstances, this flawed decision could not be rectified.

In Case *Pfv.II.20.622/2009*, reported as BH 2009.10.298 and EH 2009.1961, the Supreme Court interpreted Article 9(1) of the Brussels IIa Regulation in an idiosyncratic manner. Article 9(1) provides that if the child moves lawfully to another Member State, the courts of the previous habitual residence retain jurisdiction 'during a three-month period *following the move* for the purpose of modifying a judgment on access rights issued in that Member State before the child moved',[22] provided the holder of access rights remains in this country. In contrast, as obiter dicta, the Supreme Court indicated that, in a case where the Hungarian court authorised the child's move from Hungary to Italy (ie the change of the habitual residence), the three-month period starts running from the date of the judgment authorising the move.

Article 11(2) of the Brussels IIa Regulation requires the court to ensure 'that the child is given the opportunity to be heard during the proceedings unless this appears inappropriate having regard to his or her age or degree of maturity.' The Supreme Court has consistently held that the court does not have to hear the child via a psychologist but may hear him directly and assess whether the child's declaration should be taken into consideration having regard to his age and degree of maturity.[23]

In Case *Pfv.II.20.769/2013*, reported as BH 2013.12.344, the Supreme Court dismissed the plaintiff's submission, and refused to assume jurisdiction based on appearance, because the defendant consistently challenged the jurisdiction of Hungarian courts. In Case *Pfv.II.22.073/2009*, reported as EH 2010.2141, the Supreme Court established that the defendant implicitly submitted to the jurisdiction of Hungarian courts by making submissions on the merits of the case. The defendant's prior request for a transfer of the case to another Hungarian court was regarded as an indication that the defendant accepted, tacitly but unequivocally, the jurisdiction of Hungarian courts. Indeed, the question of venue transfer within Hungary could be considered only if Hungarian courts had jurisdiction under Brussels IIa. The defendant also submitted to the jurisdiction of Hungarian courts by declaring that he was willing to enter into a settlement in accordance with the psychologist's opinion, provided it was not obviously flawed or abusive. The Supreme Court considered that the foregoing two declarations implied that the defendant submitted to the jurisdiction of Hungarian courts which also served the best interests of the child.

Hungarian courts do diligently recognise and enforce foreign judgments. In Case *Pfv.II.21.380/2010*, reported as BH 2011.6.167, the Supreme Court established that the recognition and enforcement of a judgment rendered in another Member State cannot be refused on the ground that enforcement is pending in respect of the Hungarian court's judgment concerning the child's abduction.

---

[22] Emphasis added.
[23] Case *Pfv.21601/2009/5* (Supreme Court), reported as BH 2010.5.123; Case *Pfv.II.20.461/2013* (Supreme Court), reported as BH 2014.3.80; Case *Pfv.II.20.461/2013* (Supreme Court), reported as BH 2014.3.80.

In Case *Pfv.II.21.068/2013*, reported as BH 2014.8.248, the Supreme Court held that the recognition and enforcement of a judgment rendered in another Member State cannot be refused, if an opportunity to hear the child was offered, but could not materialise because the party concerned obstructed this. In this case the Belgian court established that, despite the fact that the date of the hearing was carefully selected, the child did not attend the hearing, with a medical certificate being presented two weeks thereafter. The Supreme Court held that it was at the Belgian court's discretion to reschedule the hearing or render a final judgment.

In Case *Pfv.II.21.068/2013*, reported as BH 2014.8.248, the Supreme Court held that it is obviously not counter to Hungarian public policy to recognise a foreign judgment, if the foreign procedural rules are different from the Hungarian ones. The public policy exception cannot be invoked merely because the foreign procedure and decision is irreconcilable with the domestic mandatory rules.

In Case *Pfv.II.21.594/2014*, reported as BH+ 2015.5.211, the defendant requested the Hungarian court to reject the recognition and enforcement of an Italian judgment because he could not present his case. However, the Supreme Court established that he had the possibility to take part in the procedure. It was held that the requirement that the document instituting the procedure had to be served in sufficient time and in an appropriate way implied that the defendant had to have a real chance to appear in person and/or to hire a local attorney. The refusal of recognition and enforcement is an exceptional rule, which can be used only if the defendant is not afforded sufficient time to organise.

All in all, it can be established that, despite some errors, Hungarian courts have been coping well with the application of the Brussels IIa Regulation both as to jurisdiction and recognition and enforcement. That said, it should be noted that the reported cases on the application of the Maintenance Regulation are very rare. My survey produced only cases where the Regulation was mentioned, with no substantive analyses being made.[24]

IV. Conclusion

Hungarian experience with EU law instruments suggests that the treatment of cases involving the application of EU PIL differs in no way from other PIL matters (not covered by EU PIL) in terms of costs, length of litigation and remedies, and that the current EU PIL framework in civil and commercial matters is sufficiently effective. Evidently, in comparison to purely domestic matters, international elements entail an added level of complexity, which may inflate costs and affect the length of proceedings, especially if foreign law applies, given that judges are obviously more comfortable with applying Hungarian law. All in all, the existing shortcomings may be obviated via effective training and exchange of experience among national courts.

---

[24] Law Unification Decision 2/2013 of 9 May 2013 on the sequence of satisfaction of claims from the moneys coming in from the enforcement procedure; Case *Pf.635995/2014/7* (Court of Appeal of Budapest), appealed from Case *P.102782/2012/55* (Central District Court of Pest); Case *Pf.20218/2013/8* (High Court of Appeal of Debrecen).

20

Ireland

MAEBH HARDING

I. Introduction

Ireland is a small democratic republic.[1] The 1937 Constitution[2] provides the framework of the legal system and guarantees fundamental rights for citizens. The Constitution was amended by referendum to allow Ireland to join the European Communities in 1972.[3] Article 29.4.3⁰ authorised the state to agree amendments to European Union ('EU') founding treaties without referendum, but only where such amendments did not alter the essential scope or objectives of the European Communities.[4] Fresh referendums were considered necessary to ratify the Single European Act,[5] the Maastricht Treaty,[6] and the Amsterdam Treaty.[7] Two consecutive referendums were required to ratify both the Nice Treaty[8] and the Lisbon Treaty[9] when the Irish people rejected the proposals on first consideration.

Ireland has negotiated a protocol to opt in to EU measures relating to judicial cooperation in civil law cases[10] and has taken part in Brussels I,[11] Brussels II,[12] Brussels IIa,[13] Brussels I Recast,[14] Rome I[15] and Rome II.[16]

Generally, *lex fori* is applied by the courts in family cases regardless of the origins of the parties.[17] Ireland is not part of enhanced cooperation in relation to applicable law in

---

[1] Population 4.76 million, 2016 Census, www.census.ie.

[2] Bunreacht na hÉireann.

[3] ibid, Art 29.4.3⁰ as inserted by the Third Amendment of the Constitution Act 1972.

[4] *Crotty v An Taoiseach* [1987] IR 713, 767.

[5] Tenth Amendment of the Constitution Act 1987.

[6] Eleventh Amendment of the Constitution Act 1992.

[7] Eighteenth Amendment of the Constitution Act 1998.

[8] Twenty-fourth Amendment of the Constitution Bill 2001(rejected) and Twenty-sixth Amendment of the Constitution Act 2002.

[9] Twenty-eighth Amendment of the Constitution Bill, 2008 (rejected) and Twenty-eighth Amendment of the Constitution Act 2009.

[10] Protocol No 4 1997 annexed by the Treaty of Amsterdam to the EC Treaty. This protocol is maintained by Protocol No 1 annexed to the Treaty of Lisbon [2007] C306/165.

[11] Recital 20.

[12] Recital 24.

[13] Recital 30.

[14] Recital 40.

[15] Recital 44.

[16] Recital 39.

[17] M Ní Shúilleabhain, 'Marriage, Divorce and Stagnation In The Irish Conflict Of Laws' (2014) 52 *The Irish Jurist* 68–89; see also W Binchy, *Irish Conflict of Laws* (Oxford, Butterworths, 1988) Chs 10–11.

divorce and legal separation[18] or in relation to property regimes associated with marriage[19] and registered partnership.[20] However, Ireland is part of the Maintenance Regulation[21] including its applicable law provisions and is bound by the Hague Protocol 2007.[22]

The lowest level of the Irish court system is the District Court which has limited civil jurisdiction to hear claims up to €15,000.[23] The Circuit Court hears civil cases up to the value of €75,000.[24] Larger civil claims start in the High Court. The Commercial Court division of the High Court was established in 2004[25] and hears disputes between commercial bodies where the value of the claim is at least €1 million.

In family matters, the District Court and Circuit Court have concurrent jurisdiction. Cases involving international and more complex matters are generally instituted in the High Court. However, applications to place a child into care are made in District Court.[26]

Appeals from the High Court and Circuit Court are heard by the Court of Appeal since its establishment in 2014,[27] and only issues of appeal that raise issues of major public importance are heard by the court of final appeal; the Supreme Court.

The overall numbers of reported and unreported judgments dealing with the EU private international law ('PIL') framework were small. Four cases addressed issues relating to Rome I and Rome II, 39 cases raised issues relating to Brussels I and 91 cases involved issues relating to Brussels IIa.[28]

II. Ireland's Experience on Cross-border Civil and Commercial Disputes

A. Jurisdictional and Procedural Issues Under the Brussels I Regulation

i. Matters Related to Jurisdiction

In *Nicole Hassett*[29] an issue relating to the scope of Article 22(2) was referred to the Court of Justice of the EU ('CJEU'). Two Irish Health Boards sought an indemnity from individual

---

[18] Council Reg (EU) No 1259/2010, [2010] OJ L343/10.
[19] Council Reg (EU) No 2016/1103, [2016] OJ L183/1.
[20] Council Reg (EU) No 2016/1104, [2016] OJ L183/30.
[21] Council Reg (EC) No 4/2009 of 18 December 2008 on jurisdiction, applicable law, recognition and enforcement of decisions and cooperation in matters relating to maintenance obligations, [2009] OJ L7/1, Recital (46).
[22] 2009/941/EC: Council Decision of 30 November 2009 on the conclusion by the European Community of the Hague Protocol of 23 November 2007 on the Law Applicable to Maintenance Obligations, [2009] OJ L 331/17.
[23] Courts and Civil Law (Miscellaneous Provisions) Act 2013, Part 3.
[24] ibid.
[25] Rules of the Superior Courts Order 63A.
[26] Child Care Act 1991, s28.
[27] Court of Appeal Act 2014, following changes to Art 34 of the Constitution (and the adoption of the Thirty-third Amendment of the Constitution (Court of Appeal) Act 2013).
[28] Numbers of cases found on Irish legal databases on 1 June 2016. This chapter also contains updates on this case law since that time.
[29] Case C-372/07 *Nicole Hassett v South Eastern Health Board and Cheryl Doherty v North Western Health Board* [2008] ECR I-07403.

doctors following a settlement for serious personal injuries. The doctors were joined to the actions for damages as third parties. They, in turn, sought a contribution from their professional organisation (MDU) and when MDU refused to grant the request they applied to have MDU joined as an additional third party. MDU objected, claiming that jurisdiction to question the validity of the decision of its Board of Management was the exclusive competence of the English courts, because the company had its seat in England. The Irish High Court rejected MDU's objection and, on appeal, the Supreme Court stayed proceedings and referred the matter. The CJEU found that the issue did not fall within the scope of Article 22(2). MDU's decision was challenged as breaking the contractual obligations between a member and the association. It is not sufficient for a legal action to involve a decision made by an organ of a company to trigger Article 22(2) as otherwise, actions brought against a company would nearly always come within the jurisdiction of the company's seat. This would undermine the general deference in the Regulation for the defendant's domicile.

The interpretation of the scope of exclusive jurisdiction clauses has occupied the courts. In *Bio-medical Research Ltd v Delatex*,[30] the Supreme Court emphasised that such clauses should be strictly construed to ensure that a true consensus between the parties exists. An exclusive jurisdiction clause relating to 'all matters in dispute hereunder' in a sale of goods contract was not considered to apply to a dispute over distribution rights. However, both the context of the claim and the precise wording of the clause are equally important. In *Leo Laboratories Ltd v Crompton BV*,[31] the courts emphasised the need for a common sense approach to the context of such a clause. Here an exclusive jurisdiction clause relating to matters 'arising out of or on account of a contract' deprived the Irish court of jurisdiction because the defendant's claim in tort could not be considered independently of the contractual relationship between the parties. In *Bushell Interiors v Leicht Küchen AG*,[32] Hogan J found that a clause in a contract for supply of goods referring to disputes arising 'directly or indirectly' from the contract was worded in such a way as to apply to issues relating to a distributor agreement.

A number of cases have raised questions of jurisdiction involving the use of websites directed at the UK rather than websites specifically directed at the smaller Irish market. In *Coleman v MGN Ltd*,[33] the failure of a plaintiff to prove that anyone in Ireland had accessed a defamatory article about him, available online, was fatal to his defamation claim. In *Harkin v Towpik*,[34] a website operating in sterling with a UK domain name, while readily accessible by an Irish client base, was not considered to be directed to the Irish market within the meaning of Article 15(1). Whereas in *McDonald v AZ Sint Elisabeth Hospital*[35] a similar website which had an Irish phone number and a consultation centre in Dublin was considered so directed.

Whether the courts should stay proceedings where a third country's courts are first seised was addressed in *Goshawk v Life Receivables Ireland Ltd*.[36] Proceedings had been ongoing

---

[30] [2000] 4 IR 307.
[31] [2005] IESC 31.
[32] [2015] IECA 211.
[33] [2012] IESC 20.
[34] [2013] IEHC 351.
[35] [2014] IEHC 88.
[36] [2009] IESC 7.

in Georgia, USA when the plaintiff commenced proceedings for negative declarations in Ireland. The defendant was an Irish registered company. An application to stay proceedings in Ireland was refused on the basis that the courts were obliged to deal with the case under Brussels I. The High Court held that the common law doctrine of *lis alibi pendens*, being an aspect of *forum non conveniens*, was unlikely to have survived the ruling in *Owusu*.[37] Reflexive effect of Brussels I was not accepted because non-Member States were not bound by the terms of the Regulation. The Supreme Court held that the issue was not an *acte clair* and that it was necessary to refer the question to the CJEU, but the case settled before the reference. The decision has been criticised as allowing the use of Member State courts for 'foiling' foreign litigation.[38]

The issue of *forum non conveniens* was again addressed in *Meylut Abama v Gama Construction (Ireland)*[39] where the Irish courts had jurisdiction under Article 18. The defendants argued that because the plaintiff had served them with an incorrect form stating that the action was a common law action, the proceedings could be set aside on the basis of common law principles. This argument was not upheld by the High Court, the Regulation applied and a stay based on *forum non conveniens* was simply not possible following *Owusu*.

In *Websense IT Ltd v Itway Spa*,[40] an exclusive jurisdiction clause gave the Irish courts jurisdiction. However, prior proceedings had been commenced in Italy. The Irish proceedings were stayed pending rejection of jurisdiction by the Italian courts. However the Supreme Court drew attention to the impracticality of the Regulation rules and suggested that a review was highly desirable.[41]

In *Ryanair Ltd v Unister GmbH*,[42] it was suggested that the court should be slow to make procedural orders while handling a jurisdictional challenge as by doing so they may be trespassing on what will ultimately be the proper jurisdiction of another Member State court.

ii. Conclusion

Although the courts have followed the letter of the Regulation and refused stays where the court is seised in an effort to undermine ongoing litigation in non-EU states, it is clear that the older common law remedies are perceived to have provided more flexibility.

The tactic of seising other Member States' courts for negative declaratory relief in defiance of an exclusive jurisdiction clause is now addressed by Brussels I Recast, but it may still cause delay as following *Ryanair*,[43] the Irish courts will be slow to make procedural orders while jurisdiction is in dispute.

---

[37] Case C-281/02 *Owusu v Jackson trading as Villa Holidays Bal-Inn Villas and others* [2005] ECR I-1383.
[38] D Kenny, 'Goshawk Dedicated Ltd v Life Receivable Ireland Ltd—Jurisdiction, *Lis Alibi Pendens* and problematic use of the Brussels Regime' (2009) 12 *Trinity College Law Review* 5.
[39] [2015] IECA 179.
[40] [2014] IESC 5.
[41] ibid [51].
[42] [2013] IESC 14.
[43] ibid.

B. Applicable Law Issues Under the Rome I and Rome II Regulations

There is very little litigation in relation to Rome I and Rome II.

In *SPV Sam Dragon v GE Transportation Finance (Ireland) Limited*,[44] a claim for damages arising from the failure to remove a charge from the Korean shipping register was dismissed. The court found that although damage had occurred in number of different countries, the more connected country was Korea under Article 4 of Rome II.[45] No obligation to de-register the charge existed under Korean law. The court added weight to its decision by pointing out that no obligation to de-register the charge existed under Belgian law either and also investigated obligations under maritime custom and practice.

In *Peter Kelly v Groupama*[46] the court found that the French methodology for assessing damages for personal injury had to be adhered to under Rome II but characterised non-obligated steps as matters of practice which could be governed by *lex fori*. Thus the court had regard to Irish levels of compensation as well as the French Book of Quantum. Moreover, the court held that French law left room for judicial discretion as to the final amount. The court awarded nearly double the damages suggested by the French book of quantum. It is difficult to conclude from this one case whether the court was awarding Irish damages in disguise, but it is certainly an area to watch.

C. Preliminary Remarks on Effectiveness of the Current EU PIL Framework in Civil and Commercial Law

Ireland encounters problems in relation to the uncertainty of the EU regime in cases involving litigation in non-Member States. It is too early to tell if the applicable law rules of Rome I and Rome II are causing problems.

III. Ireland's Experience on Cross-border Family Law Disputes

A. Jurisdictional and Procedural Issues Under the Brussels IIa Regulation

i. Matters Related to the Scope of Application

In *Health Service v SC and AC*,[47] an order to place a child in a secure unit in England was found to be within the material scope of Brussels IIa as a civil order relating to the exercise of parental responsibility, even though the order deprived the child of her liberty. The CJEU

---

[44] [2012] IEHC 240.
[45] *Dumez France v Hessishche Landesbank* [1990] ECR 1-49, *Marinari v Lloyds Bank plc* [1995] ECR 1-2719, and *Hillside (New Media) Ltd v Bjarte Baasland & Others* [2010] EWHC 3336 (Comm).
[46] [2012] IEHC 177.
[47] Case C-92/12 PPU *Health Service Executive v SC and AC*.

drew a distinction between situations in which secure accommodation is ordered for the protection of a child and where it is ordered to punish a child for a criminal offence.[48] The ruling gives certainty to the practice of sending extremely vulnerable children abroad for specialist therapeutic care rather than relying on unsuitable alternatives in Ireland.[49] The need for such orders to be declared enforceable in the other Member State before being enforced there is an important safeguard for the rights of children.

ii. Matters Related to Jurisdiction

a. Divorce, Legal Separation and Marriage Annulment

The Irish Constitution allows divorce only where there has been four years' separation out of the previous five, the breakdown is irreconcilable and proper financial provision has been made.[50] The constitutionality of Brussels II[51] and Brussels IIa was challenged in *YNR v MN*[52] because foreign divorces were given effect in Ireland in contravention of the constitutional restrictions. This argument was rejected, because Brussels II had been properly adopted as part of Irish law.

Some issues have arisen in relation to divorce decrees from other jurisdictions that predate the coming into force of Brussels II. For example, in *DT v FL*,[53] a Dutch divorce decree from 1994 was not recognised in Ireland because it predated the Regulation and the Irish courts exercised jurisdiction over fresh judicial separation proceedings.

The Irish courts have found that jurisdiction under Article 3 of Brussels IIa is mandatory and that *forum non conveniens* did not survive the Regulation, at least in relation to decisions about marital status in *O'K v A*.[54] The 'centre of interest' test laid down by the English courts in *Marinos v Marinos*[55] was also adopted in this case.

The steps needed to seise a court under Article 16(1)(a) of Brussels IIa became an issue in *MH v MH*.[56] The husband sued for judicial separation in Ireland and the wife sued for divorce in England. The husband lodged an initiating document on 7 September 2015 at 2.30pm and a summons was issued simultaneously. The wife's divorce petition was received at 10.30am on 7 September 2015 by the divorce processing centre in England and was issued on 11 September 2015. The court held that the time of 'lodging' under Article 16(1)(a) should be interpreted as the time of receipt rather than the time of issue. This meant that the Irish courts were second seised and Irish proceedings were stayed. This decision, relying in part on comments from the CJEU,[57] is contrary to the previous understanding of

---

[48] ibid [65]–[66].

[49] *DG v Ireland* (2002) 35 EHRR 33.

[50] Art 41.3. 2°.

[51] Council Reg (EC) No 1347/2000 of 29 May 2000 on jurisdiction and the recognition and enforcement of judgments in matrimonial matters and in matters of parental responsibility for children of both spouses, [2001] OJ L160/19.

[52] [2005] IEHC 335.

[53] [2006] IEHC 98.

[54] [2008] IEHC 243.

[55] [2007] EWHC 2047 (Fam).

[56] [2015] IEHC 771.

[57] Case T-310/12 *Yuanping Changyuan Chemicals Co. Ltd v Council*, ECLI:EU:T:2015:295, [84].

the English courts. The CJEU has since confirmed the decision.[58] Clark[59] and Hodson,[60] lawyers for the husband in the case, argue that the decision has significant implications for practice. Not all courts allow out of hours delivery or time stamp receipt. Online delivery will soon be available in some Member States which will again cause differences in treatment.

b. Parental Responsibility

Where the Irish court has declared no jurisdiction under Article 17 or transferred jurisdiction under Article 15, difficulties have arisen in ensuring that practical steps are taken to further the best interests of the child.

In *Re KJ*,[61] the child, habitually resident in Scotland, was in interim care in Ireland. The High Court declared no jurisdiction under Article 17 but made orders giving the Child and Family Agency authority to place the child into the care of Dundee City Council. The jurisdiction for making such orders was unclear. The Court of Appeal held that Article 20 does not grant jurisdiction to make freestanding practical orders for return.[62] This was affirmed by the Supreme Court.[63] O'Donnell J clarified the appropriate steps to be taken in such a case. The District Court should have established that its jurisdiction was limited to provisional and protective orders under Article 20 and made an order to secure the child's position while awaiting action from the Scottish Court. O'Donnell J distinguished between this case, where the Scottish Court had given no indication as to whether return was in the best interests of the child, and *CFA v RD*,[64] where the English courts had actively sought assistance in returning a child who had been placed in the care of Birmingham City Council. O'Donnell J emphasised that it was up to the Scottish Court to decide if return was in the best interests of the child or whether an Article 15 transfer was appropriate. If no action was taken by the Scottish courts the Irish courts could take substantive measures, if and when the child became habitually resident in Ireland.[65]

In *CFA v JD*,[66] the CJEU confirmed that Article 15 transfers are still possible in public law cases after a conflicting view was taken by AG Wathelet. The CJEU emphasised the exceptionality of such a transfer within the scheme of the Regulation.[67] The court requesting transfer must rebut the strong presumption in favour of the court of the child's habitual residence by considering whether the transfer will provide 'genuine and specific added value'[68] to the decision. The transferring court may take into account the rules of procedure

---

[58] Case C-173/16 *MH v MH*, EU:C:2016:542.
[59] S Clark, 'The Race to Court under EU Brussels II: A New Approach?': www.familylawweek.co.uk/site.aspx?i=ed158074.
[60] D Hodson, 'Priority of Proceedings under EU Brussels II: An Irish High Court Decision may Mean All Change after 15 Years of Practice': www.familylaw.co.uk/news_and_comment/priority-of-proceedings-under-eu-brussels-ii-an-irish-high-court-decision-may-mean-all-change-after-15-years-of-practice#.VysgjfkrKUl.
[61] [2015] IECA 86.
[62] ibid [68].
[63] *Child and Family Agency v CJ and Anor* [2016] IESC 51, [24].
[64] [2014] IESC 47.
[65] n 63 above, [25].
[66] Case C-428/15 *Child and Family Agency v JD*, EU:C:2016:819, [33] and [36].
[67] ibid [47] and [48].
[68] ibid [57].

in the other Member State, such as capacity for hearing evidence, but not different rules of substantive law.[69]

Transferring jurisdiction in public law cases raises a danger that action may not be taken by foreign authorities and the Irish courts then lack jurisdiction to take further action. Presumably this is what the CJEU means by the need for the transferring court to be satisfied that transfer will not be detrimental to the child's situation.[70] In *HSE v MA & SS*,[71] the Irish court drew attention to the practical need for the HSE to drive along transfer requests by seeking directions in England and Wales.

Better information sharing and co-operation between national public authorities would render the court of the child's habitual residence better placed to make decisions in public law cases. This could allow placement with extended family in another country to be monitored with the co-operation of the foreign authority without the need to transfer jurisdiction to the foreign courts.

1. Child Abduction

In *R v R*,[72] the court confirmed that a full welfare assessment on the merits is not required to safeguard the best interests of the child in abduction cases[73] following the comments of the European Court of Human Rights Grand Chamber in *X v Latvia*.[74]

Irish courts have determined that a child can change habitual residence without the consent of both parents with parental authority, but the fact that there are two holders of parental authority is factually relevant to determining a child's habitual residence. In *DE v EB*,[75] the Court of Appeal made a distinction between cases where the moving parent had sole rights to determine where the child should live at the time of removal and cases in which those rights were shared with another parent. The court noted that the CJEU ruling in *Mercredi*[76] applied to the former case where the appropriate emphasis is the centre of interests of the child by reference to integration. However in the second scenario, the moving parent cannot be certain that the move is permanent and this uncertainty must be weighed against other matters of fact which might demonstrate a degree of integration.[77] To ignore the uncertainty would undermine the concept of wrongful retention.

iii. Matters Related to Recognition and Enforcement

In *McN v JR*,[78] the mother applicant had difficulties understanding the implications of a return order in relation to access and therefore identifying the appropriate venue to approach in order to modify access arrangements. An order for the children to be returned to their father in Ireland had been enforced by the Irish courts. The order included a

---

[69] ibid.
[70] n 66 above, [58].
[71] *HSE v MA & SS* [2013] IEHC 239; *HSE v MW & GL* [2013] IEHC 280; *HSE v LG & JJ* [2013] IEHC 297 which were all determined by Birmingham J.
[72] [2015] IECA 265.
[73] *JJ v L McL* [2013] IEHC 549.
[74] Application No 27853/09.
[75] [2015] IECA 104. See also *C v M* [2015] IESC 12; Case C-376/14 PPU, *C v M*, ECLI:EU:C:2014:2268.
[76] Case C-497/10 PPU, *Barbara Mercredi v Richard Chaffe* [2010] ECR I-14309.
[77] n 75 above, [31].
[78] [2015] IEHC 70.

record that the father was content for specific contact to happen, and was subject to undertakings by the mother to return the children after contact, but no substantive provision was made for the mother to have contact. The mother applied to the Irish courts to vary access and was directed to the local District Court to apply for new orders. She also applied to the English courts but was referred back to the Irish District Court. She eventually began enforcement proceedings against the father for failure to comply with the original order, but as there were no operative provisions in relation to access to enforce she was eventually directed to bring fresh proceedings in the local District Court after considerable delay and expense.

a. Certificate Concerning Judgments in Matrimonial Matters and Certificate Concerning Judgments on Parental Responsibility

The civil registrar refused to recognise a Lithuanian divorce given in default of appearance under Article 22(b) of Brussels IIa[79] and did not authorise the husband to marry again. The wife's place of residence was unknown and the Lithuanian courts had served process by public announcement. On judicial review the decision of the registrar was upheld. The court held that the onus is on the people getting married to show that foreign divorces were properly obtained and capable of being recognised in the state.

In private child law cases an order for return is often sought even where there is an extant order relating to custody that could be directly enforced.[80] The interactions between the different processes of establishing custody rights, enforcement, return and substantive orders following an order of non-return do not seem to be well understood by litigants and cause delays.

For example, in *AO'K v MK*,[81] a sole custody order for the mother was made by the Irish courts. Shortly afterward the child was taken to Poland and the Polish courts issued non-return orders. The mother then sought an order under Article 11(7) of Brussels IIa and an order to enforce the original custody order. After a full welfare-based hearing, an order for return was made and certified under Article 42.[82]

In many cases, an order for non-return is determinative of the substantive issue and no submissions are made following transmission of documents.[83] In *EE v O'Donnell*,[84] the process of sending documents relating to a Swedish order of non-return from the High Court to the Circuit Court itself caused confusion as the father incorrectly believed that he had commenced new proceedings at High Court level.[85]

b. Return of the Child

The Irish courts have considered the different defences to wrongful removal. In *SR v MMR*,[86] the Supreme Court reiterated that the onus is on the person asserting consent to

---

[79] *Chaudhry v An tArd Cháraitheoir* [2015] IEHC 522.
[80] *RK v IG* [2010] IEHC 424.
[81] [2011] IEHC 82.
[82] *AO'K v MK (No 2)* [2011] IEHC 360; see also *MF v VN* [2015] IEHC 538.
[83] eg *MP v GO'S* [2013] IEHC 419; *CD v DS* [2013] IEHC 114.
[84] [2013] IEHC 418.
[85] ibid [15].
[86] [2006] IESC 7.

show that it was real, positive and unequivocal. In *R v R*,[87] the court also drew attention to the importance of whether the parent had received legal advice when giving 'consent'.

Grave risk is a difficult test to satisfy[88] and undertakings are commonly used to obviate risk.[89] Article 20 defences based on the child's constitutional right to remain part of a marital family where involuntary adoption in a foreign country is proposed have not been upheld.[90] Indeed in *HSE v MW*,[91] a transfer of jurisdiction case, the availability of adoption in England was a reason why transfer was in the best interests of the child.

Orders for return have been set aside on the basis that the child has not been given the opportunity to be heard.[92] There is a general working practice that it is inappropriate to hear a child under 6[93] and a child's objection is not determinative particularly where the child's fears can be appropriately managed.[94] Return has been refused on the basis of the wishes of older children.[95]

iv. Relations with Other Instruments

In *GT v KAO*,[96] a father's application for custody rights in Ireland was adjourned pending the hearing of his application for return of the children by the English courts. English return proceedings were then adjourned pending a decision from Ireland on whether or not the retention was wrongful. The delay hearing the custody rights issues could have been fatal to this application and demonstrates confusion as to how the mechanisms for return affect the determination of substantive issues.

v. Conclusion

Getting a child back to the country with jurisdiction after a transfer of jurisdiction or a declaration of no jurisdiction is problematic. Where the foreign court has made an order for return and issued a certificate relating to the judgment this is more straightforward,[97] but where this is not done there are limits to what the Irish court can do other than encourage the child protection authorities to get involved in 'jollying along' foreign proceedings.

In private law cases the interaction between substantive proceedings, orders for return and enforcement of existing child custody orders is not well understood. This leads to multiplication of legal proceedings and delays for the parents involved.

---

[87] [2015] IECA 265.
[88] *A Bu v J Be* [2010] IESC 39; *PN v TD* [2008] IEHC 51.
[89] *DE v EB* [2015] IEHC 180.
[90] *Nottinghamshire County Council v KB and KB* [2011] IESC 48.
[91] [2013] IEHC 280.
[92] *SR v SR* [2007] IEHC 423; *MN v RN* [2008] IEHC 382.
[93] *A Bu v J Be* [2010] IESC 38; *N v N* [2008] IEHC 382.
[94] *SR v SR*, n 92 above. See also *UA v UTN* [2011] IESC 39.
[95] *G v R* [2012] IEHC 16 where the child was 13.
[96] [2007] IESC 55. See also *Foyle Health Trust v EC* [2006] IEHC 448; *DZ v KD* [2008] IEHC 176.
[97] *Coventry City Council v MS* [2010] IEHC 303.

B. Jurisdictional and Procedural Issues and Applicable Law Under the Maintenance Regulation

There are no reported cases on the Maintenance Regulation.

C. Practice/Process

i. Ireland's National Courts' Practice in Interpreting the Regulations

The prevalence of Article 15 transfer requests in public law cases suggests a willingness to offload child protection cases to potentially better equipped public authorities rather than continuing in co-operation with foreign authorities. It is important that where the Irish courts have jurisdiction, they do not abdicate responsibility for family law decisions to a foreign court merely because the foreign family law system seems better equipped. Brussels IIa should not be used to sidestep inadequacies in the Irish family law system which might otherwise be highlighted and made the subject of domestic reform.

D. Preliminary Remarks on Effectiveness of the Current EU PIL Framework in Cross-border Family Law

Relinquishing of jurisdiction by the Irish courts in Articles 15 and 17 cases has caused practical difficulties in returning children to the country of jurisdiction and ensuring that meaningful action is taken.

Moreover the interaction between the multiple instruments in family law cases causes complications for litigants.

IV. Conclusion

In commercial cases Irish courts have deferred to the force of EU regulations over common law principles, albeit somewhat reluctantly. Changes made by Brussels I Recast may be enough to address concerns about the impracticality of the Regulation.

Litigants in family law cases encounter delay and confusion caused by the multiplicity of international instruments touching on their case and also because national orders are not necessarily drafted with international enforcement in mind. Holistic advice on how to resolve the underlying dispute and a more pragmatic approach to court procedure in such cases is needed.

21

Latvia

IRĒNA KUCINA

I. Introduction

Meeting the accession criteria, Latvia harmonised its legislative acts with the *acquis communautaire* and joined the European Union ('EU') in 2004. Latvia belongs to the continental (Romano-Germanic) law systems.

In Latvia, there is no national private international law ('PIL') or implementing law concerning the Brussels I, Rome I, Rome II, Brussels IIa and Maintenance Regulations. However the Civil Procedural Law[1] is supplemented with two chapters on child abduction. In recent years, there are more and more judgments which can be regarded as the best practice of the Latvian courts on the application of Brussels I. Especially the judgments of the Supreme Court include a broad analysis and reasoning and also references to the interpretation of the Court of Justice of the European Union ('CJEU').

Rome I and Rome II have not been frequently applied in the Latvian courts and the relevant judgments do not include an extensive analysis and reasoning. The references to the CJEU's interpretation are still lacking.

Brussels IIa has been frequently applied in the Latvian courts. The Latvian judges have a considerable experience on the application of Brussels IIa and they are well trained by the Latvian and foreign experts on the subject. Since 1 March 2015, child abduction cases are concentrated only in one first instance court with a possibility of being subject to an appeal. Latvia has a three level court system, the so called 'clear' three-level court system: district (city) courts—first instance; regional courts—second instance; and the Supreme Court—third instance.[2] However there are several exceptions when access to justice is granted in two or seldom in one instance, like it is done with child abduction cases. Beside the so-called 'general courts' there are established orphan's courts. In accordance with the Law on Orphan's Courts,[3] an orphan's court is a guardianship and trusteeship institution established by a municipality or city local government.

---

[1] Ch 74 on 'Return of a Child to the State, which is his or her Place of Residence'; Ch 77 on 'Cases Regarding the Wrongful Removal of Children across Borders to a Foreign State or Detention in a Foreign State'; and Ch 77 on 'Cases Regarding the Wrongful Removal of Children across Borders to Latvia or Detention in Latvia' of the Civil Procedure Law, Latvijas Vēstnesis, No 326/330 (1387/1391).

[2] The Law on Judicial Power, Ziņotājs, No 1.

[3] Latvijas Vēstnesis, No 107 (3475).

The application of the Maintenance Regulation by the Latvian courts is poor. There is no extensive analysis and reasoning in the judgments and the Regulation is sometimes misapplied.

The post of the Adviser on EU Law issues was established in the Supreme Court in 2013.[4]

II. Latvia's Experience on Cross-border Civil and Commercial Disputes

A. Jurisdictional and Procedural Issues Under the Brussels I Regulation

i. Matters Related to the Scope of Application

In 2013, the Latvian Supreme Court made a preliminary ruling request to the CJEU and asked some questions including on the interpretation of Article 1 of Brussels I.[5] The case, ie C-302/13 *flyLAL-Lithuanian Airlines AS v Starptautiskā lidosta Rīga VAS and Air Baltic Corporation AS*,[6] concerned recognition and enforcement in Latvia of a Lithuanian court judgment ordering provisional measures or protective measures. FlyLAL (a Lithuanian company) sought compensation for damages it alleged it suffered because the Latvian national airways company and national airport, in its view, abused its dominant position in the flights' market by concluding an anti-competitive agreement between themselves. The Latvian national airways company and national airport concluded this agreement in accordance with a Latvian Regulation from the Cabinet of Ministers adopted according to public law (*acta iure imperii*). The CJEU ruled that an action seeking legal redress for damage resulting from alleged infringements of EU competition law comes within the notion of 'civil and commercial matters' under Article 1(1) of Brussels I and, therefore, falls within the scope of the Regulation.

ii. Matters Related to Jurisdiction

The jurisdiction rules in Articles 2, 5(a) and (b), and 23 of Brussels I have been fairly frequently applied in the Latvian courts. Other jurisdiction rules, except the ones in Articles 5(5) and 7, have been rarely applied or not applied at all. Jurisdiction is not an issue usually disputed in Latvia.

Nevertheless, the Latvian Supreme Court's preliminary ruling request in Case C-302/13 *flyLAL-Lithuanian Airlines*[7] concerned also the interpretation of Article 22(2) of Brussels I. The CJEU ruled that the action in question was not covered by Article 22(2) because the subject matter of the substance of the dispute concerned a compensation claim, not the validity of the decisions of the organs of companies.

---

[4] http://at.gov.lv/en/about-the-supreme-court/structure/the-division-of-case-law/.
[5] Supreme Court, 15 May 2013.
[6] EU:C:2014:2319.
[7] ibid.

iii. Matters Related to Recognition and Enforcement

Certain amendments were made in the Latvian Civil Procedure Law to align the national procedure for recognition with the procedure of recognition/declaration of enforceability provided in Brussels I and to introduce Brussels I's recognition procedure into the Latvian Civil Procedure Law. According to the Latvian Civil Procedure Law, the decision in the first instance court on a declaration of enforceability of a foreign judgment shall be taken within 10 days from the initiation of the case.

The question of non-recognition of judgments from other Member States has been raised often in Latvia. There are two significant cases on the issue. The first case is *Avotiņš v Latvia* decided by the European Court of Human Rights (ECtHR) on 23 May 2016.[8] In 2004, a Cypriot court ex parte examined a case brought by a Cypriot company against a Latvian national and decided that the Latvian national had to repay to the Cypriot company a debt of USD 100,000. The Cypriot company sought recognition and enforcement of the Cypriot judgment in Latvia under Brussels I. The defendant raised an objection that he had not been duly informed about the proceedings in the Cypriot court because he had been unable to receive the summons sent twice to the address which he had indicated in the notarial debt deed with the Cypriot company. The Latvian Supreme Court granted recognition and enforcement of the Cypriot judgment according to Brussels I on the ground that the defendant had been given an opportunity to appeal against the Cypriot judgment. The defendant submitted an application against Latvia before the ECtHR. The ECtHR noted that Cypriot law afforded the applicant, after he had learned of the existence of the judgment, a perfectly realistic opportunity of appealing despite the length of time that had elapsed since the judgment had been given. It found that the Latvian Supreme Court had sufficiently taken account of the applicant's rights and that there had been no violation of Article 6(1) of the European Convention on Human Rights.

The second case is C-302/13 *flyLAL-Lithuanian Airlines*[9] concerning, inter alia, the interpretation of Article 34(1) of Brussels I. The CJEU ruled that the mere invocation of serious economic consequences does not constitute an infringement of public policy of the Member State in which recognition is sought, which would permit the refusal of recognition and enforcement in that Member State under Article 34(1).

iv. Conclusion

On matters related to jurisdiction, judgments usually do not include extensive argumentation and reasoning and references to the CJEU case law are usually still lacking at the level of first instance or regional courts. Provisions concerning recognition and enforcement are applied better by Latvian courts and judgments usually include good argumentation and reasoning as well as references to the CJEU case law, particularly at the Supreme Court level.

---

[8] Application no 17502/07, [2016] ECHR 440.
[9] n 6 above. These two CJEU cases and another case referred from Latvia, Case C-619/10 *Trade Agency* EU:C:2012:531 that relates to public policy and default judgments, are discussed by Beaumont and Yüksel in ch 33 below.

B. Applicable Law Issues Under the Rome I and Rome II Regulations

Rome I and Rome II have not been frequently applied in the Latvian courts. Until 18 April 2016, there were only 17 published decisions and judgments in which the courts mentioned Rome II and there are 49 published decisions and judgments in which the courts referred to Rome I. The judgments do not usually include extensive argumentation and reasoning. The references to the CJEU case law are still lacking but to be fair there is not much of that yet.[10]

As provided in Chapter 80 on 'Application of Foreign Laws to Trying of Civil Cases' of the Civil Procedure Law the party who raises the application of foreign law shall submit to the court the text of the foreign law with a certified translation into the official language. Where the submitted content is not clear to the court, it, *ex officio* or upon the request of one of the parties, may seek information under a bilateral or multilateral treaty, where applicable, and where not applicable through the Ministry of Justice of Latvia. In Latvia there is no established non-governmental body responsible for providing the text of foreign law. The European Convention of 7 June 1968 on Information on Foreign Law and bilateral treaties concerning access to information on the content of foreign law are applied very rarely due to the fact that in practice foreign law is infrequently applied. There is still no good practice and common understanding between lawyers on the application of foreign law. There are major differences among opinions as to whether the application of foreign law is a matter of fact or of law. Some lawyers still consider that the judge has to apply and clarify the content of foreign law whereas others argue that the parties are obliged to prove the application of foreign law. As regards the application of Rome I and Rome II, in the majority of cases, judges do not intervene in the parties' position on the application of foreign law since in civil proceedings the adversarial principle still exists. So, if one of the parties in its application or during a court hearing raises the application of foreign law and the other party does not object to it, that law will apply. In 2015, the Latvian Supreme Court delivered a judgment which involves very extensive reasoning and analysis of the relationship between Rome II and the Hague Convention on the Law Applicable to Traffic Accidents.[11] The facts of the case were as follows: SIA UGO AUTO (the lessee) and SIA Swedbank Līzings (the lessor) concluded in Latvia a leasing agreement concerning a semitrailer SCHMITZ SCS 24L. The semitrailer then was subleased by SIA UGO AUTO to SIA ALFA BALTIK. However, the semitrailer was damaged in a traffic accident in Lithuania caused by a drunk driver of a VW JETTA, who crashed into a Renault Laguna, which later crashed into the semitrailer. The VW JETTA was insured by ERGO Lietuva which in Latvia was represented by AAS ERGO Latvija. SIA UGO AUTO submitted a claim against AAS ERGO Latvija in a Latvian court seeking damages. The claim was based on Latvian law, namely Articles 18 and 31 of Compulsory Civil Liability Insurance of Owners of Motor Vehicles Law[12] and Article 12 of the Road Traffic Law.[13] The main issues were which court had jurisdiction and whether Latvian or Lithuanian law was applicable. The first instance court and the Court of Appeal found that the Latvian courts had jurisdiction and that Latvian law was applicable because the defendant had not fulfilled the procedural duty under Article 654 of the Civil Procedure Law to submit to the court the translated text of the applicable Lithuanian law and had not

---

[10] See Beaumont and Yüksel, ibid.
[11] Supreme Court, 1 July 2015.
[12] Latvijas Vēstnesis, 65 (3013).
[13] Latvijas Vēstnesis, 274/276 (989/991).

specified which legislation under Lithuanian law should be applied. Therefore, the courts considered that the defendant with its actions chose the application of Latvian substantive law by relying on Article 14 of Rome II. However the Supreme Court dismissed the Court of Appeal's decision on the ground that the applicable law had not been properly determined and the application of the Hague Convention on the Law Applicable to Traffic Accidents instead of Rome II had not been discussed. Considering Recital 36 and Article 28 of Rome II, the Hague Convention should have been applied to the case and the Court of Appeal interpreted Article 14 of Rome II. The fact that the defendant did not submit to the court the relevant translation of Lithuanian law cannot be perceived as an agreement on the application of Latvian law.

The Supreme Court gave another very notable judgment in a case where the question of application of foreign law was raised.[14] The case concerned a car owned by A, insured by SAS ERGO Lietuva and stolen in Lithuania. B had bought the car in the Lithuanian market and upon his attempt to register the car in Latvia a criminal investigation was started and it was determined that B was an acquirer in good faith. B sold the car to C who then re-sold it to D. Later on, the Latvian insurance company, which had paid compensation to A for the stolen car, brought a claim in the Latvian courts against B, C and D with third persons State Police and AS GE Money for the recognition of property rights and payment of damages. The claim was based on Latvian civil law. The first instance court had rejected the claim but the Court of Appeal partially accepted it and decided that D should return the car to the plaintiff. The claims against B and C were refused. The Court of Appeal declared that SAS ERGO Lietuva had to be recognised as the owner of the car because it had paid compensation to A in accordance with the terms of the insurance contract. The Supreme Court dismissed the Court of Appeal's decision because the claim arose out of tort and the existence of rights to bring an action in a court should be determined in accordance with Article 19 of Rome II regardless of whether or not the defendant had fulfilled the procedural duty under Article 654 of the Civil Procedure Law. It found that according to Article 5.4 of the Civil Procedure Law and Article 18 of the Law on Judicial Power, the court has a duty in certain cases to apply foreign law on its own initiative. It decided that the ownership of the car should be determined under Lithuanian law.

III. Latvia's Experience on Cross-border Family Law Disputes

A. Jurisdictional and Procedural Issues Under the Brussels IIa Regulation

i. *Matters Related to Jurisdiction*

a. Divorce, Legal Separation and Marriage Annulment

The provisions of the Family Law Part (mainly articles 69, 70, 74 and 77) of the Civil Law of the Republic of Latvia[15] and Part P of the Notariate Law[16] provide a complete list of

---

[14] Supreme Court, 17 December 2015.
[15] Valdības Vēstnesis, No 41.
[16] Latvijas Vēstnesis, No 48.

situations when a marriage can be dissolved. In Latvia, only a court or a notary is eligible to dissolve the marriage. Divorce by a notary could be obtained only in cases where spouses have agreed thereon and (1) if they do not have a joint minor child and joint property; or (2) where they have a joint minor child or joint property, if they have entered into a written agreement regarding custody of the joint minor child, rights of access, child's means of support and division of the joint property.[17] The court shall dissolve the marriage if the application of one or both spouses is received.

In matters regarding dissolution or annulment of a marriage, settlement by the parties shall be permitted only in disputes related to family legal relationships (Section 238, paragraph 1). Discontinuation of an action regarding dissolution of a marriage or termination of a court proceeding regarding dissolution of marriage is not an impediment to the adjudication of the remaining claims on the merits.[18]

'Legal separation', 'registered partnership' and 'same-sex marriage' do not exist under Latvian law. Accordingly, there are no provisions for divorce or annulment of same-sex marriages or registered partnerships and it is not possible to recognise and enforce judgments given in another Member State in respect of such marriages and partnerships.

b. Parental Responsibility

Parental responsibility proceedings in Latvia are dealt with by the general courts or by the Orphan's Court (the so-called custodial court). The general courts deal only with custody, access rights, place of residence and maintenance. The Orphan's Court deals with issues concerning child protection, such as suspension of the custody rights, establishment of out-of-family care, and appointment of the guardian. Proceedings before the Orphan's Court, according to national law, are administrative proceedings even though in other Member States such matters are dealt with as civil matters. Therefore, in Latvia, there is a two-level approach in dealing with parental responsibility matters, inter alia, in cross-border cases.

There are several situations when the Orphan's Court reported cases where the custody rights of the minor had been suspended from his parents and the guardianship of the child had been established, and after the establishment of the guardianship, the guardian moved to another Member State together with a ward where they continued to live for several years. Having reviewed the case after a year, the Orphan's Court clarified that the reasons for the suspension of the child's custody rights still apply. The Orphan's Court decided to submit the claim statements to the Latvian Court regarding the removal of custody rights from the parents, however the court refused to accept such claim statements, indicating that, according to the first part of Article 244 of the Civil Procedure Law, an action for matters arising from custody and access rights shall be brought in a court according to the place of residence of the child. Additionally, the court found that at the time the court was seised the child's habitual place of residence was in another Member State.[19]

This problem is due to the courts' misinterpreting Article 8 of Brussels IIa by concentrating on the time when the general court is seised and disregarding the earlier time when the case about the parental responsibility was first initiated at the Orphan's Court. The further

---

[17] The Notariate Law, mainly Arts 325–39.
[18] Art 241 of the Civil Procedure Law.
[19] Jūrmala Court, 1 June 2012; Valka District Court, 28 May 2012—the emphasis added by the author.

actions of the Orphan's Court by submitting the claim statements to the general courts regarding the removal of custody rights from the parents is just a further review of the specific case involving the same child and the same parents. As a result it is not clear what further actions the Orphan's Court should take: (1) Should the Orphan's Court contact the competent court in the other Member State with a request to assume jurisdiction in accordance with Article 15 of the Regulation, or (2) should the Orphan's Court submit the relevant claim statement to the court in the other Member State with the help of the solicitor/ lawyer practising in that Member State regarding the removal of the custody rights from the parents; or (3) should the Orphan's Court proceed to close the case file without any legal resolutions as the Latvian Orphan's Court/ the courts no longer have jurisdiction? At the EU level, a broader interpretation of the wording of Article 8 of the Regulation can be considered and, for example, Article 8 can be understood as 'the *courts or administrative authorities* of a Member State *shall have jurisdiction* in matters of parental responsibility over a child who is habitually resident in that Member State at the time the court *or administrative authority* is seised'. At national level, it is worth using different soft law instruments, such as guides to good practice, and offering general training to judges on the Regulation in order to help them to understand that the time and place (institution) are not to be distinguished when the statement of claim within one particular family case is brought for consideration. It is also worth mentioning that in several Member States there is no such legal term as 'removal of custody rights'.

1. Child Abduction

As regards Article 11 of Brussels IIa, the Latvian courts request the Orphan's Court to report on the child's opinion in return proceedings. The Orphan's Court, taking the child's age and maturity into account, uses appropriate measures to hear the child's opinion, ie either they hear the child themselves or they use the report of a psychologist/psychiatrist who heard the child.

Upon the receipt of an application for the return of a child to his or her place of residence, a judge shall give a decision not later than the next day on acceptance of the statement of claim and initiation of a matter.

Matters regarding child abduction to Latvia or retention in Latvia if the place of residence of the child is in another state shall be adjudicated in a court sitting within 15 days after the initiation of the matter.[20] An ancillary complaint may be submitted in respect of the first instance court decision within 10 days. A regional court (the second and final instance court in child abduction matters) shall adjudicate an ancillary complaint within 15 days after the initiation of the appeal proceedings.[21] Therefore, the relevant legislation ensures that the six week rule is met. However in practice, due to exceptional circumstances (mainly because of the defence based on Article 13(1)(b) of the 1980 Hague Convention) the timescale in the Regulation and in national law, in the majority of cases, is exceeded.

As regards Article 11(4) Brussels IIa, in several cases, the Latvian courts fail to establish that adequate arrangements have been made to secure the protection of the child after his or her return.[22] In their judgments, the courts state that adequate arrangements to secure

---

[20] Art 644[19] para 1 of the Civil Procedure Law.
[21] Art 644[21] para 1 of the Civil Procedure Law.
[22] Riga City Vidzeme Suburb's Court, 2 July 2012; Riga City Vidzeme Suburb's Court, 28 December 2012.

the child after his or her return cannot be made by definition. The reason is mainly that the abductor mother announces that she is not willing to return with the child and based on psychological reports the courts establish that the child cannot be separated from his or her abductor mother otherwise it will expose the child to physical or psychological harm or otherwise place the child in an intolerable situation. Consequently the courts do not even request information on protection measures from the Member State where the child habitually lived before the wrongful removal or retention.

According to national law it is not mandatory for the person who requested the return of the child to attend the court hearings in person. In all cases the applicant is represented either only by a lawyer assigned by the Central Authority (free of charge since Latvia did not make a reservation on this) or the applicant is heard in person if he or she wishes to attend the hearing.

There are no cases where the Latvian Court was seised with the application in accordance with Article 11(7–8) of Brussels IIa. However, in respect of Article 11(6), if the Latvian court has issued an order on non-return pursuant to Article 13 of the 1980 Hague Convention, the court immediately, through the Latvian Central Authority, transmits a copy of the court order and of the relevant documents, in particular a transcript of the hearings, to the court having jurisdiction or the Central Authority in the Member State where the child was habitually resident immediately before the wrongful removal or retention. From the experience of the Latvian institutions, courts in some Member States consider proceedings under Article 11(6)–(8) as a review of the non-return judgments of the Latvian courts, not as proceedings concerning the parental responsibility for the child as a result of which it may or may not request the return of the child.

ii. *Matters Related to Recognition and Enforcement*

Practical difficulties have been faced with regard to Article 21(3), in particular, in understanding the term 'any interested party'. There are many situations where a court of another Member State grants custodial rights of the Latvian child to a guardian or to a competent institution in that Member State (eg the UK and Ireland). Consequently, the guardian or the institution is entitled to perform all actions on behalf of the child, such as managing the acquisition of citizenship for the child and submitting an application to issue the child's identity documents. There were situations when the Citizenship and Migration Office of Latvia, in order to proceed with the child's citizenship or passport matters, requested to obtain the relevant judgment of the Latvian court on the recognition of the judgment given by the court in another Member State in relation to the child's custodial rights. After the intervention of the Latvian Central Authority it was further explained that 'any interested party' refers to a party who took part in the proceedings which resulted in the relevant judgment being given.

a. Return of the Child

The relevant rules applicable to the enforcement of a return order issued by a court of the Member State to which the child was abducted under Article 11(3), and of a certified return order issued by the court of origin under Article 11(8), are prescribed in Chapter 74 of the Civil Procedure Law[3] on 'Return of a Child to the State, which is his or her Place of

Residence'. It is a relatively new chapter effective from 1 October 2011. There are only two cases, one with Georgia[23] and the other with Lithuania[24] where these rules were applied.

iii. *Cooperation between Central Authorities in Matters of Parental Responsibility*

Child placement under Article 56 of Brussels IIa in Latvia includes a child's placement not only in an institution or in a foster family, but also in guardianship (usually with the relatives of the child) which is the most common form of child placement in Latvia. In other EU Member States, such placement is considered as a form of placement with relatives (ie kinship care or placement) and/or with friends which does not fall within the scope of Article 56.

B. Maintenance Regulation and the 2007 Hague Protocol

Some amendments were made in the Latvian Civil Procedure Law in order to facilitate the procedures provided for in Articles 19–20 of the Maintenance Regulation. It is provided in Article 4 of the Maintenance Guarantee Fund Law[25] that the Administration of Maintenance Guarantee Fund shall perform the functions of the Central Authority of Latvia on the application of the Maintenance Regulation. The Administration of the Maintenance Guarantee Fund shall, upon necessity without special authorisation, represent foreign persons in court and other governmental and municipal authorities, provided that the persons are entitled to receipt of legal aid according to the Maintenance Regulation. The Regulation of the Cabinet of the Ministers of the Republic of Latvia No 571 on 'Procedure by which the Administration of the Maintenance Guarantee Fund exercises functions of the Central Authority in cross border maintenance matters' was adopted on 19 July 2011 in order to provide appropriate exercise of functions of the Central Authorities of the Maintenance Regulation.

Decisions given in a Member State not bound by the 2007 Hague Protocol shall be decided in the first instance court and declared enforceable or not enforceable within 10 days from the initiation of the case. Amendments in the Latvian Civil Procedure Law were made in order to ensure the time limit (according to Article 32 of the Maintenance Regulation) in which an appeal against the declaration of enforceability shall be lodged, to align the national procedure for recognition with the procedure of recognition/declaration of enforceability provided in the Maintenance Regulation and to introduce the Maintenance recognition procedure into the Latvian Civil Procedure Law.

The declaration of enforceability was sought in three reported cases and two of them came through the Central Authorities. In one of these cases, the declaration of enforceability was denied because the decision was given in a Member State bound by the 2007 Hague Protocol and thus it was directly enforceable.

The Latvian Central Authority transmitted 145 applications in 2014 and 239 applications in 2013 for the recognition and declaration of enforceability or for the enforcement

---

[23] Riga District Court, 9 December 2013; Riga Regional Court, 27 January 2014.
[24] Riga City Zemgale Suburb's Court, 3 October 2014; Riga Regional Court, 5 November 2014.
[25] Latvijas Vēstnesis, No 101 (3049).

of a Latvian judgment in the requested Member State; and 45 applications in 2014 and 403 applications in 2013 were made for locating the debtor.[26] The number of the received applications is not that high. However, there are some issues as regards the cooperation with other Central Authorities. The tasks of Central Authorities provided in the Maintenance Regulation are not understood in a common way and there are delays in the execution of requests, difficulties with the translation of documents, and different types of requirements to submit evidence in order to prove that the request comes from the Central Authority before executing it.

There are six reported cases on the Maintenance Regulation in which the applications in the Latvian court were submitted through the Latvian Central Authority.

Analysis shows that the Maintenance Regulation is poorly applied by the Latvian courts. The judgments of the courts do not include extensive argumentation and reasoning and sometimes they are wrong. The Latvian courts referred to articles concerning jurisdiction in 17 decisions or judgments and in most of them jurisdiction was established. The courts have not dealt with the provisions on the applicable law yet. There is no Supreme Court decision on the Maintenance Regulation which could give guidance to the lower courts, possibly because the maintenance decisions are quite rarely appealed against.

IV. Conclusion

There are still some specific areas of EU PIL which should be developed in Latvia not only in court practice, but also by legislative bodies. There is still some lack of knowledge on the application of some of the EU Regulations. As regards jurisdiction and recognition and enforcement issues, non-recognition grounds are applied by the first instance courts inappropriately, cross-border maintenance proceedings are decided without any specific analysis of the Maintenance Regulation rules, and the scope of application of the EU Regulations is mostly not analysed. At the EU level, the cooperation between Central Authorities on the application of the Maintenance Regulation should be strengthened by providing a common understanding of tasks of Central Authorities between Member States.

The Latvian courts have good experience as regards the application of Brussels I and Brussels IIa.

More training is still needed for judges, advocates and lawyers. However, there is no single recipe for good application of the EU Regulations because they cover a lot of different issues and in some cases very specific knowledge is required. Sometimes the specialisation of judges and specialised courts or jurisdictions could be required at national level. Judicial reforms depend on national law policy makers but in some cases recommendations of international organisations can be very helpful.

---

[26] www.ugf.gov.lv/lat/aktualitates.

22

Lithuania

KRISTINA PRANEVIČIENĖ

I. Introduction

Lithuania is a civil law country. Its legal system is based on the principles laid down in the Lithuanian Constitution[1] and the Constitutional Court monitors the compliance with these principles. Courts of general competence (Supreme Court, Court of Appeal, five regional courts and 49 district (local) courts) deal with civil and criminal cases. Specialised administrative courts (Supreme Administrative Court and five regional administrative courts) deal with administrative cases.

When Lithuania became a Member State of the European Union (EU) on 1 May 2004, the country had already had a broad experience in dealing with the so-called 'European cross-border cases' involving an EU Member State. On 13 July 2004, a Constitutional Act was adopted by the Lithuanian Parliament.[2] The increase in the number of intra-EU disputes due to the high level of immigration and also the rapid development of international business have resulted in the EU regulations being applied frequently by the Lithuanian courts. Lots of judicial training courses have been provided and funded by the EU institutions and national authorities in the last 12 years. In order to ensure the proper implementation of the EU legislation on civil procedure, the Law on the Implementation of the EU and International Acts regulating Civil Procedure[3] was adopted on 13 November 2008 and was last amended on 15 May 2014.[4] The legal doctrine in the field of EU law has also developed very rapidly and efficiently.[5]

---

[1] *Official Gazette*, 1992, No 33-1014.

[2] It provides that 'European Union Law is an integral part of the legal system of the Republic of Lithuania. If it comes from the Treaties under which the European Union is based, the legal norms of the European Union are applied directly, and in case of conflict they prevail over the laws and other legal acts of the Republic of Lithuania.' No IX-2343, *Official Gazette*, 2004, No 111-4123.

[3] No X-1809, *Official Gazette*, 2008, No 137-5366.

[4] No XI-890, *TAR*, 2014, No 2014-05780.

[5] For the leading literature, see eg V Nekrošius, *European Civil Procedure Law* (Vilnius, Justitia, 2009); V Vėbraitė, *Study Material Introduction to European Civil Procedure* (Vilnius, Vilniaus Universiteto Leidykla, 2014); V Mikelėnas, *Introduction to Private International Law* (Vilnius, Justitia, 2001); V Mizaras, *Rome II Regulation and Lithuanian International Private Law* in Private Law: *Past, Present and Future: Liber Amicorum Valentinas Mikelėnas* (Vilnius, Justitia, 2008) 203–29; I Vėgėlė, *European Union Law* (Registrų Centras, 2011).

II. Lithuania's Experience on Cross-border Civil Disputes and Civil Procedure Governing the Commercial Disputes

A. Jurisdictional and Procedural Issues Under the Brussels I Regulation

i. Matters Related to the Scope of Application

The Lithuanian courts have not struggled with the material scope of application of Brussels I under Article 1. The courts emphasise that the Regulation applies in all civil and commercial matters according to Article 1(1). For instance, it was decided that a case for the award of the debts fell into the category of civil cases and, therefore, the Regulation was found applicable to the qualification and the authorisation of the Polish court order to be enforced under the rules of Brussels I.[6]

The Supreme Court dealt with a case concerning the relationship between Brussels I and the Insolvency Regulation.[7] By relying on the criteria laid down in the jurisprudence of the Court of Justice of the EU (CJEU), it ruled that the Insolvency Regulation was not applicable where the bankruptcy administrator made a request unrelated to the bankruptcy case because such an application did not fall within the exclusion of Article 1(2)(b) of Brussels I. The application of the bankruptcy administrator was regarded as a civil dispute falling under the general jurisdiction rule of Brussels I (under the official statutory seat of the company).

ii. Matters Related to Jurisdiction

The Supreme Court dealt with a case concerning Articles 9(1)(b) and 11(2) of Brussels I[8] by thoroughly analysing the judgment of the CJEU in case C-463/06.[9] The Supreme Court held that in a traffic accident, which took place in a Member State, a victim had a right to bring a direct action against an insurer established in another EU Member State before the court of his permanent residence (for legal entities, it is that of permanent establishment) for damages he suffered. Even though the first instance court and the Court of Appeal had refused to accept the claim, the Supreme Court reversed that decision and stressed that a compensation claim for damages suffered in an accident was a 'civil' and commercial 'matter' falling within the scope of Brussels I under Article 1(1) and that the jurisdiction therefore was to be determined according to its rules.[10]

The Supreme Court dealt with the jurisdiction rules in matters relating to a contract in a case concerning a claim for financial obligations.[11] The defendant, a company registered in Denmark, claimed that the Lithuanian courts did not have jurisdiction under Brussels I. The first instance court found that the claimant brought an action against the defendant for the payment for goods delivered to the defendant after the opening of bankruptcy proceedings. It ruled that the action was derived directly from the insolvency proceedings

---

[6]   *Zorka BIS Sp Z o o w Pszczynie v 'LAS FREIGHT'*, Court of Appeal, 17 September 2015.
[7]   *Accuratus v SIA Aquabaltia Group Latvia*, Supreme Court, 30 January 2014.
[8]   *Transtira v 'AXA Insurance UK Plc'*, Supreme Court, 3 July 2015.
[9]   Case C-463/06, *FBTO Schadeverzekeringen NV v. Jack Odenbreit* [2007] ECR I-11321, paras 25–30.
[10]   *Transtira v 'AXA Insurance UK Plc'*, Supreme Court, 3 July 2015.
[11]   *MCTL International v A/S SPANVALL*, Supreme Court, 3 February 2016.

to which Brussels I does not apply. It found that the Insolvency Regulation[12] was not applicable either because Denmark did not participate in this Regulation; therefore, it applied the national legislation. The Court of Appeal upheld the decision but also stated that as the claimant brought a requirement not closely related to the bankruptcy case, the first instance court wrongly relied on Article 1(2)(b) of Brussels I. Article 5(1)(a) of Brussels I (now Article 7(1)(a) of Brussels Ia) is a special alternative jurisdiction rule giving the claimant an opportunity to choose to sue in the courts for the place of performance. In the present case, the claimant was registered in Lithuania and it sought to meet its monetary requirement. The place of performance of the obligations arising from the contract was in Lithuania and therefore the claimant brought the action, under Article 5(1)(a) of Brussels I, before the Lithuanian courts. After analysing the Brussels I rules and citing the jurisprudence of the CJEU, the Supreme Court decided that Article 5(1) of Brussels I points out an obligation as the main criteria and the contract characterised by the delivery obligation was deemed to be a 'sales' contract under the first indent of Article 5(1)(b).[13] The Supreme Court emphasised that this special rule of jurisdiction regarding contractual obligations establishes the place of delivery as an autonomous separate criterion which is to be applied to all claims arising from the same 'sales' contract, not only to those arising from the delivery obligation.[14] Therefore, it held that the court having jurisdiction shall be determined in accordance with the first indent of Article 5(1)(b) and that a person with a domicile in a Member State may be sued in matters relating to a sales contract in the Member State in which the goods were or should have been delivered.

iii. Matters Related to Recognition and Enforcement

The Lithuanian courts have generally dealt with the issues related to recognition and enforcement of judgments from other Member States without facing any particular problems.

A complicated situation arose in the *Gazprom* case in which the Supreme Court referred to the CJEU[15] to ask whether recognition and enforcement of an arbitral award classified as an anti-suit injunction may be refused on the ground that the exercise by a Lithuanian court of the power to rule on its jurisdiction would be restricted after such recognition and enforcement.[16] The CJEU stated that Brussels I does not preclude a Member State's court from recognising and enforcing, or from refusing to recognise and enforce, an arbitral award prohibiting a party from bringing certain claims before a court of that Member State, since it does not govern the recognition and enforcement, in a Member State, of an arbitral award issued by an arbitral tribunal in another Member State. As a result, the Supreme Court did not apply Brussels I and decided the recognition and enforcement of an arbitral award under the national rules of civil procedure.[17] The Advocate General ('AG') Wathelet emphasised in his opinion that:

> [A]s regards breach of an arbitration agreement, the response of the Brussels I Regulation (recast) is to exclude arbitration completely from its scope, with the consequence that the verification, as

---

[12] [2015] OJ L141.

[13] Case C-533/07 *Falco Privatstiftung and Rabitsch v Gisela Weller-Lindhorst* [2009] ECR I-03327, para 54; case C-381/08 *Car Trim GmbH v KeySafety Systems Srl* [2010] ECR I-01255, para 32.

[14] Case C-386/05 *Color Drack GmbH v Lexx International Vertriend GmbH* [2007] ECR I-03699, para 26.

[15] *Gazprom*, Supreme Court, 23 October 2015.

[16] Case C-536/13 '*Gazprom*' OAO v Republic of Lithuania.

[17] *Gazprom*, Supreme Court, 23 October 2015.

an incidental question, of the validity of that agreement does not fall within its scope, and to refer the parties to arbitration. … An anti-suit injunction is therefore the only effective remedy available to an arbitral tribunal in order to rule in favour of the party who considers that the arbitration agreement has been breached by the other contracting party."[18]

Even though the CJEU did not take the opportunity to accept such a broad interpretation, the outcome of the national case was in favour of arbitration.

iv. Conclusion

a. Problem Areas

The Lithuanian case law analysis indicates that the main problem is Brussels I and arbitration. Recital 12 to Brussels Ia which clearly defines the relationship between the judicial proceedings and arbitration could help the courts in dealing with cases related to arbitration.

b. Best Practice

The Lithuanian courts are not reluctant to make preliminary references to the CJEU. Where the jurisprudence of the CJEU is clear and well-established, they apply Brussels I without any difficulty and also cite the CJEU case law in their judgments.

B. Applicable Law Issues Under the Rome I and Rome II Regulations

i. Rome I

a. Matters Related to the Scope of Application

The temporal scope of application of Rome I was questioned in a case concerning a commission contract related to a purchase-sale contract for horses which had been signed in Germany and terminated by the defendant.[19] The claimant argued that Rome I was to be applied to the case, whereas the defendant alleged that Rome I was not applicable because the subject matter of the dispute, ie the legality of the purchase-sale contract, did not fall within the scope of Rome I. The Supreme Court emphasised that Rome I applies to contracts concluded after 17 December 2009 and since the contracts in question were concluded in 2008, it found Rome I not applicable to the case.

The Court of Appeal found Rome I inapplicable on the same ground in a case concerning a dispute related to a loan agreement concluded in 2005.[20]

b. Matters Related to the Uniform Rules

A case between two parties from different EU Member States was heard by the Vilnius Regional Court. The claimant (an insurance company) asked the Court to apply subrogation rules and to award against the defendant (a Swedish company) damages and the

---

[18] Opinion of AG Wathelet in Case C-536/13 'Gazprom' OAO v Republic of Lithuania. For a discussion of the CJEU decision in *Gazprom* see ch 33 below.
[19] *AD v AJ, D-C S*, Supreme Court, 25 May 2015.
[20] *ZP, JP v LG, IG*, Court of Appeal, 17 September 2015.

annual interest which arose when the claimant had been compensated under the insurance agreement.[21] The damage arose because the defendant under a contract delivered the third party, ie the Vilnius Poultry, 20,315 newborn chickens contaminated with salmonella. Vilnius Poultry suffered huge financial loss due to this and it was compensated by the insurance company. The Court applied the escape clause in Article 4(3) of Rome I and found that the applicable law was Lithuanian law. According to the Court, although the contracting parties were in different countries, the contract was more closely connected with Lithuania because goods had been delivered to Lithuania, the causal event giving rise to the damage was in Lithuania, and subrogation was held in Lithuania. It is open to criticism that the Court did not discuss the applicability of the rules provided in Article 4(1) or (2) and gave its judgment by only relying on Article 4(3) without giving a clear explanation as to why it decided to apply the escape clause therein.

In dealing with cases under Article 8 concerning individual employment contracts, the Lithuanian courts have cited the relevant case law of the CJEU on the Rome Convention. In a case dealt with in the Panevėžys Regional Court, where the parties had agreed to settle their disputes in Latvia under Latvian law according to the employment contract, in interpreting Article 8(1) of Rome I, the Court considered the case law of the CJEU on Article 6(1) of the Rome Convention.[22] Given that the purpose of Article 6 was to improve areas where one contracting party's interest is different from the other party's interests, and to ensure the adequate protection for the socially and economically weaker party in contractual relations,[23] the Court found that the Lithuanian Labour Law mandatorily regulates the legal aspects of the employment relations and provides a greater security for workers, and that therefore it should be applied to the dispute.[24]

c. Conclusion

The Lithuanian courts do well in interpreting the temporal scope of Rome I. The case law shows that where relevant the Lithuanian courts consider the CJEU's interpretation on the Rome Convention while dealing with Rome I cases. However, the courts should bear in mind that when applying the escape clauses (eg Article 4(3) of Rome I) instead of the general rules (eg Article 4(1) or (2) of Rome I), the judgment has to explain clearly why the court has decided to do so.

ii. Rome II

a. Matters Related to the Scope of Application

Although there is a very limited case law on Rome II, the cases show that the Lithuanian courts struggle to apply Rome II and to decide whether the cases fall within the scope of Rome I or Rome II. The Supreme Court made a preliminary reference to the CJEU concerning the law applicable to actions for indemnity between two insurance companies, ie Gjensidige Baltic and PZU Lithuania, following a road traffic accident which

---

[21] *Ergo Insurance SE v Blenta*, Vilnius Regional Court, 21 October 2014.

[22] Case C-384/10 *Jan Voogsgeerd v Navimer SA* [2011] ECR I-13275; case C-64/12 *Anton Schlecker v Melitta Josefa Boedeker* EU:C:2013:551.

[23] Case C-29/10 *Heiko Koelzsch v État du Grand-Duché de Luxembourg* [2011] ECR I-01595.

[24] *EJ v RAB 'AUTO KADA'*, Panevėžys Regional Court, 23 February 2016.

occurred in Germany.[25] A vehicle coupled with a trailer damaged a property belonging to a third person. The vehicle was insured against civil liability with a Lithuanian subsidiary of Gjensidige Baltic and the trailer was insured against civil liability with PZU Lithuania. Following the claim filed in Germany, Gjensidige Baltic paid compensation and brought an action for indemnity against PZU Lietuva to recover half of the amount paid pursuant to German law which, according to Gjensidige Baltic, was the applicable law under Articles 3 and 8 of the 1971 Hague Convention on the law applicable to traffic accidents as the law of the country where the accident occurred. The Vilnius district court upheld the claim and decided that, in accordance with Article 4(1) of Rome II, German law applied to the non-contractual obligation arising from the event giving rise to the damage and that under German law, liability on account of the damage resulting from a road traffic accident caused by a vehicle coupled with a trailer must be shared. The Vilnius regional court heard the appeal and dismissed the claim on the ground that the issues relating to the civil liability should be solved on the basis of the compulsory insurance contract, and that Rome II was not applicable. The court found that the defendant's obligation derived from the compulsory insurance contract and Lithuanian law was applicable to this contract under Rome I. The court dismissed the claim under Lithuanian law (Civil Code of the Republic of Lithuania[26] and the Law on Compulsory Insurance Against Civil Liability in Respect of the Use of Motor Vehicles).[27,28] On appeal, the Supreme Court was in doubt which Regulation (ie Rome I or Rome II) was applicable to the case and requested a preliminary ruling. The CJEU clarified that the law applicable to an action for indemnity between the insurer of a tractor unit, which has compensated the victims of an accident caused by the driver of that vehicle, against the insurer of the trailer coupled to it at the time of that accident, is to be determined in accordance with Article 7 of Rome I if the rules of liability in tort, delict and quasi-delict applicable to that accident by virtue of Article 4 et seq of Rome II provide for an apportionment of the obligation to compensate for the damage.[29]

b. Conclusion

The Lithuanian courts sometimes struggle to make a distinction between the scope of application of Rome I and Rome II. However, the CJEU has clarified the relationship between these two instruments which will be helpful in dealing with similar situations in the future.

C. Practice/Process

i. *Cost and Length of Litigation in Cross-border Civil and Commercial Disputes*

The decided cases show that cross-border litigation is lengthy in Lithuania. For instance, in the case of *AD v AJ, D-C S*,[30] it took more than two and a half years for the courts to reach a decision at the appeal stage.

---

[25] *Gjensidige Baltic v PZU Lietuva*, Supreme Court, 8 October 2014.
[26] *Official Gazette*, No 74-2262, 2000.
[27] *Official Gazette*, No 56-1977, 2001.
[28] *Gjensidige Baltic v PZU Lietuva*, Vilnius Regional Court, 8 November 2013.
[29] Joined Cases C-359/14 and C-475/14 *'Ergo Insurance' SE v 'If P&C Insurance' AS and 'Gjensidige Baltic' AAS v 'PZU Lietuva' UAB DK*, EU:C:2016:40 at para 2 of the ruling.
[30] n 19 above.

When the proceedings involve a preliminary reference to the CJEU, they take much longer. For example, in the case *Gjensidige Baltic v PZU Lithuania*, the appeal proceedings took 10 months; the cassation proceedings until the preliminary reference request took almost a year; and the preliminary ruling was given in 15 months. Thus the proceedings in this case took about three years.

ii. Alternative Dispute Resolution for Cross-border Civil and Commercial Disputes

Alternative dispute resolution (ADR) is not widely used for cross-border civil and commercial disputes in Lithuania. Arbitration still remains one of the most popular means of ADR. Mediation is also used. On 15 July 2008, the Lithuanian Parliament adopted the Civil Dispute Conciliation and Intermediation Law,[31] which is now under review to be replaced by a Mediation Law. The Government encourages parties to use mediation actively in domestic civil disputes.

D. Preliminary Remarks on Effectiveness of the Current EU Private International Law (PIL) Framework in Civil and Commercial Law

The Regulations in civil and commercial matters are well applied by the Lithuanian courts. The parties are also aware of the Regulations and rely on them. However, the courts sometimes find it difficult to apply Rome II, in particular, when an issue is related to both contract and delict. The jurisprudence of the CJEU is very helpful in such situations.

III. Lithuania's Experience on Cross-border Family Law Disputes

A. Jurisdictional and Procedural Issues Under the Brussels IIa Regulation

i. Matters Related to the Scope of Application

The recent case law concerning the scope of application of Brussels IIa reflects the problems concerning the application of Brussels IIa and the Maintenance Regulation in the same case. In a recent case, the Panevėžys Regional Court upheld a decision of the first instance court which did not exercise jurisdiction in a parental responsibility case in connection with the child maintenance issue.[32] The father declared that he would move from Lithuania to Ireland where he got a permanent job. The habitual residence of his son was also in Ireland. As the mother's habitual residence was in Lithuania, the father applied to the

---

[31] *Official Gazette*, No 87-3462, 2008.
[32] *JŠ v DŠ*, Panevėžys Regional Court, 18 February 2016.

Lithuanian court to ask to establish the habitual residence of his son with him and to award maintenance for his son. The first issue was covered by Brussels IIa while the second one was covered by the Maintenance Regulation. The Court stated that:

> [J]urisdiction to deal with cases related to maintenance obligations in Member States shall lie with the court which, according to its own law, has jurisdiction to entertain proceedings concerning parental responsibility if the matter relating to maintenance is ancillary to those proceedings, unless that jurisdiction is based solely on the nationality of one of the parties. Since the applicant seeks from the court not only to order maintenance, but also to determine the minor's residence with him, he acknowledged that the case is related to parental responsibility, and jurisdiction issues are dealt with in accordance with the provisions of Brussels IIa. Since the applicant's and the child's habitual residence is not Lithuania, but Ireland, the courts of Lithuania do not exercise jurisdiction, but the Irish courts do (Article 8 of Brussels IIa).[33]

That interpretation leads to the conclusion that a claimant is placed in a less favourable position than if he had only asked the Court to award the child maintenance under Article 3(a) of the Maintenance Regulation.

ii. Matters Related to Jurisdiction

a. Divorce, Legal Separation and Marriage Annulment

The Lithuanian courts are sometimes requested to decide on both the divorce and parental responsibility issues while the child is resident in another EU Member State. In cases where jurisdiction can be established only for divorce but not for the parental responsibility issues (which should be determined by the courts of the habitual residence of a child), the courts often refuse to deal with the entire case. The courts do not appreciate the prorogation option in Article 12 and they do not take advantage of it.[34] Prorogation allows a court, which has jurisdiction to hear divorce but not parental responsibility, to deal with both questions together. Prorogation is an exception provided in Article 12 to the general rule of jurisdiction in Article 8. Prorogation is not just limited to exercising jurisdiction for divorce and parental responsibility, it is rather a common exception to the rule that can be applied to other cases meeting the legislative criteria. The existence of prorogation conditions however does not limit the application of the general jurisdiction rules and the general jurisdiction and the prorogation jurisdiction can exist parallel to each other.[35]

In divorce proceedings, usually several related requests (eg divorce, establishment of the habitual residence of the child, child maintenance and division of the assets) are brought altogether before one court. The Supreme Court has emphasised that in such cases the court has to first distinguish these requests, then to define the concrete international (foreign) element for each of them and to separately determine the applicable law for each of them.[36]

---

[33] ibid.

[34] *Review for the application of the International and European Union law as addressing the issue of jurisdiction in family matters*, Supreme Court, 2015, 43, Case law no AC-43-1, 632-713.

[35] ibid; Ulrich Magnus et al, *Brussels IIbis Regulation* (Munich, Sellier European Law Publishers, 2012) 148.

[36] n 34 above.

b. Parental Responsibility

1. Child Abduction

As the child abduction cases within the EU are dealt in accordance with Brussels IIa and the 1980 Hague Convention on the Civil Aspects of International Child Abduction (1980 Hague Convention), these cases are usually very complex and they demand very specific skills for the lawyers dealing with them.

The pure non-return situation can be envisaged in a case which originated from the application of an Albanian citizen father, who applied to the court asking to issue judicial authorisation for the return of his child to the child's country of origin and the country of habitual residence, ie the United Kingdom of Great Britain and Northern Ireland.[37] He indicated that the mother took the child to Lithuania without his consent. Since the child was born in the UK, both parents had parental obligations imposed by law in the UK under which the child's removal or retention without the consent of the other parent was a violation of that parent's custody rights and unlawful under Article 3 of the 1980 Hague Convention and Article 2(11) of Brussels IIa. The Court of Appeal held that although under the rules of the 1980 Hague Convention the applicant's claim could be satisfied, ordering the child's return would be potentially detrimental to the young child's welfare and could cause damage to the child's best interests. The Court continued that under Article 13 of the 1980 Hague Convention, there are cases when the requested court is not obliged to return the child. The Court assessed that the applicant sought to take revenge on the mother and did not really want to look after a child. The father's use of violence against the members of the family especially in the face of a minor child was absolutely intolerable and posed a direct threat to the interests of the child. Therefore, in accordance with Article 13(1)(b) of the 1980 Hague Convention, the Court decided that there was a substantial risk if the child had been returned to the country of origin and transferred to the temporary care of his father and that the return would have exposed the child to physical or psychological harm or otherwise placed the child in an intolerable situation. Accordingly, the Court refused to order the return of the child.

2. Access

The Panevėžys Regional Court dealt with a case in which the Lithuanian nationals, mother and child, were resident in Germany and the father requested the rights of access to the minor child. Considering both the mother and the child were habitually resident in Germany, the Court did not exercise jurisdiction to hear the case.[38]

3. Other Issues Related to Parental Responsibility

In a case before the Kaunas District Court, the grandparents (Lithuanian nationals, living in Lithuania) asked the court to issue a communication order between them and the minor grandchild living in the UK with his parents (Lithuanian nationals).[39] By considering the habitual residence of the child as the main criterion to establish jurisdiction, it upheld the

---

[37] *SM v DVM*, Court of Appeal, 31 January 2013.
[38] *DA v IS*, Panevėžys Regional Court, 22 August 2013.
[39] *RP and DP v SD and ŽD*, Kaunas Regional Court, 16 June 2014.

first instance court's decision which had decided that the competent courts to hear the case were the relevant courts in the UK according to Article 8(1) of Brussels IIa.

iii. *Matters Related to Recognition and Enforcement*

a. Certificate Concerning Judgments in Matrimonial Matters and Certificate Concerning Judgments on Parental Responsibility

The Lithuanian Supreme Court made a preliminary reference to the CJEU in *Rinau*.[40] The mother was Lithuanian and the father was German, and they were both, with their minor child, habitually resident in Germany. While the divorce case was pending in Germany the mother took the child to Lithuania. The German courts awarded temporary custody to the father. The father claimed that the child had been abducted and requested the return of the child to Germany, but the Lithuanian courts refused the request. The German courts gave a final decision in the divorce case awarding custody to the father and issued a certificate under Article 42 of Brussels IIa. The mother asked the Lithuanian courts not to recognise the part of the German judgment regarding custody and the return of the child. The CJEU ruled that the later decision of the German court regarding the return overruled the Lithuanian court's decision; that suspension, change or even the annulment of the initial decision not to return was an internal procedure of the state and had no effect on the subsequent German court's decision overruling the decision of the country where the child was abducted to and that issuing the certificate under Article 42 was essential because there was no possibility to apply for non-recognition or appeal.[41] Therefore, the child had to be returned.

b. Return of the Child

In a case dealt with in the Court of Appeal, the mother had brought her one year old daughter to Lithuania from the child's habitual residence in Italy and the father initiated the return proceedings in Lithuania and also applied to the Italian courts which appointed him as an exclusive guardian of the child. The father requested the recognition and enforcement of the Italian order in Lithuania. The Court of Appeal decided that the Italian order was inconsistent with the best interests of the child and it violated the Lithuanian public policy and thus refused the recognition and enforcement on this basis.[42] It can be questioned whether such argumentation is compatible with the principle of mutual trust.

iv. *Conclusion*

It poses a problem where the Lithuanian courts refuse to decide on divorce matters if there is a parental responsibility issue to be solved in another jurisdiction. This sometimes results in the Lithuanian nationals who want to divorce but are living abroad with their children not getting divorced in Lithuania, because under Lithuanian law the parental responsibility issues must be settled in the divorce case and divorce cannot be granted before this is done.

---

[40] *IR v MR*, Supreme Court, 25 August 2008.
[41] Case C-195/08 PPU *Rinau* [2008] I-05271.
[42] *FS v NJ*, Court of Appeal, 16 March 2015.

B. Jurisdictional and Procedural Issues and Applicable Law Under the Maintenance Regulation

i. Matters Related to Recognition, Enforceability and Actual Enforcement of Decisions

a. Decisions given in a Member State bound by the 2007 Hague Protocol

Lithuania is bound by the 2007 Hague Protocol (Protocol). When the Lithuanian courts deal with cases in which the decision is given in a Member State bound by the Protocol, they clearly emphasise that there is no special procedure requiring recognition and enforcement of the decision and there is no possibility to oppose its recognition. Moreover, under Article 17(2) of the Maintenance Regulation, a decision rendered in a Member State bound by the Protocol which is enforceable in that State shall be enforceable in another Member State without the need for a declaration of enforceability. The Lithuanian courts clarify that an applicant or his/her representative can produce a decision for the execution to the bailiff (Article 650(1) of the Code of Civil Procedure of the Republic of Lithuania[43] (CCP)). The applicant must also comply with the conditions of authenticity of the copy of a foreign decision, or the extract of the decision of the court of origin which should be prepared under the form annexed to the Maintenance Regulation and translated into the Lithuanian language. A document proving the amount of any arrears is sometimes required to be enclosed. All documents must be submitted to the bailiff (Articles 584.1(5), 587.9, 590 of the CCP, Article 20 of the Maintenance Regulation).[44]

The Supreme Court dealt with an issue, sought by a Lithuanian mother habitually residing with her child in Germany, concerning the recognition and enforcement of a German court judgment which established the paternity and awarded the child maintenance to be paid by the father (Lithuanian national, habitually resident in Lithuania). As the EU Regulations leave the paternity questions out of their scope of application, the paternity part of the German decision was recognised and enforced under the national rules of civil procedure whereas the maintenance part was recognised and declared enforceable under the Maintenance Regulation (Articles 23 and 26).[45] Since Germany is bound by the Hague Protocol, in future cases the courts should apply Section I of Chapter IV of the Maintenance Regulation (Articles 17–22) which would make the declaration of enforceability unnecessary.

IV. Conclusion

The effectiveness of the current EU PIL framework in Lithuania is rather good. The courts usually apply the EU Regulations well.

In civil and commercial matters, the main problems concern the interpretation of Rome II. In complicated cases, the courts do not avoid making preliminary references to the CJEU and the jurisprudence of the CJEU is always helpful.

---

[43] *Official Gazette*, 2002, No 36-1340.
[44] *AL*, Court of Appeal, 7 June 2013.
[45] *IČ v AZ*, Supreme Court, 29 May 2015.

In family law matters, there are more difficult problems. The child return proceedings under Brussels IIa and the Hague Convention are always very complicated. As Brussels IIa clearly establishes that the final word in the return proceedings belongs to the court of the habitual residence of a child when the Hague return is refused on Article 13 grounds, the courts should always take into account this legal norm and refuse a return on Article 13 grounds only in exceptional cases. This should help to improve the effectiveness of the EU PIL framework in family matters and ensure the principle of mutual trust between the Member States.

More training and education for judges and other legal practitioners on EU PIL is recommended.

23

Luxembourg

CÉLINE CAMARA

I. Introduction

Luxembourg is a trilingual,[1] civil law country. The legal system is a dual one divided into two branches, ie the judicial one on the one hand, and the administrative one on the other hand. The civil court system is divided into three levels. There are three magistrate courts (justices de paix), two district courts (Tribunaux d'arrondissement) and the Superior Court of Justice that is composed of both the Court of Appeal and the Supreme Court (Cour de cassation). There is neither a systematic publication of decisions nor a publically accessible repository of case law in Luxembourg. This report is primarily based on case law collected through the District Court of Luxembourg[2] and on interviews conducted at the same court.

II. Luxembourg's Experience on Cross-border Civil and Commercial Disputes

A. Jurisdictional and Procedural Issues Under the Brussels I Regulation

The majority of cases on the Brussels I Regulation are related to jurisdiction matters, in particular challenges of jurisdiction.

i. Matters Related to the Scope of Application

There are two main problems stemming from the case law analysis regarding the scope of application of Brussels I, ie the interplay between the jurisdiction rules of Brussels I and of domestic law,[3] and the difficult delineation between the scopes of Brussels I and the Insolvency Regulation.[4]

---

[1] French, German and Luxembourgish are the three official languages.

[2] The following analysis is based on a total of 150 decisions: 51 cases on Brussels I, 20 cases on Rome I, 19 cases on Rome II, 60 cases on Brussels IIa, and 10 cases on the Maintenance Reg.

[3] Tribunal Luxembourg, 26 February 2014, no 155204; Cour d'appel Luxembourg, 21 January 2015, No 38554.

[4] Council Reg (EC) No 1346/2000 of 29 May 2000 on insolvency proceedings, [2000] OJ L160/1. See eg Cour d'appel Luxembourg, 27 June 2007, No 31943; Cour d'appel Luxembourg, 5 July 2012, No 38262; Cour d'appel Luxembourg, 27 November 2013, No 38262.

Regarding the first issue, first instance courts appear to struggle to draw a line between cross-border European Union (EU) cases and non-EU cases with an international element. For instance, the Court of Appeal overruled a judgment where the first instance court exercised jurisdiction pursuant to an exorbitant jurisdiction rule based on nationality under Article 14 of the Luxembourg Civil Code[5] and thereby failed to apply Brussels I.[6] This practical difficulty illustrates the complexity of the coexistence of two regimes on jurisdiction. It also impacts the length of proceedings by resulting in lengthy litigation over the proper place of litigation[7] before the national courts start dealing with the merits of the case.

Regarding the second issue, the decisions related to the interplay between Brussels I and the Insolvency Regulation shed light on the influence of national law when the courts have to decide whether a matter is covered by one of these EU Regulations or by national law. This illustrates the risk of 'nationalising' uniform law which also jeopardises the uniform application of the rules of Brussels I. The Court of Appeal explicitly refers to the Court of Justice of the EU (CJEU) case law in order to highlight the necessity to use an autonomous interpretation, especially in defining the material scope of application of Brussels I.[8]

ii. Matters Related to Jurisdiction

The vast majority of the Brussels I cases concern Article 5 and show that the national courts have difficulties in applying this provision. Notably, the first instance courts tend to apply Article 5(1)(a) instead of Article 5(1)(b) and as a result they wrongfully decline jurisdiction in particular in cases involving contracts for provision of services. One of the main examples of this misapplication lies in one of the few Supreme Court decisions.[9] In this case, the claimant was a lawyer who brought an action against a person he counselled (ie the defendant in the case at stake) to request the payment of his lawyers' fees. The defendant was domiciled in France. The magistrate court declined jurisdiction by arguing that where a request for payment is made by a creditor domiciled in Luxembourg against a debtor domiciled in France, the place of performance of the obligation would be France since a request for payment is regarded to be a transferable debt according to Luxembourgish law. The decision was then upheld by the District court. The Supreme Court overruled the decision and held that the first instance court violated Article 5 of Brussels I by ruling that it had no jurisdiction under Article 5(1)(a) because Article 5(1)(b) was applicable in this case since the contract at hand was a contract for the provision of services.

Regarding the protective rules, the case law analysis reveals that there is a tendency for litigants to rely on Article 15 of Brussels I in order to contest jurisdiction of the Luxembourgish courts and particularly where there is a jurisdiction clause in favour of another State in the consumer contract. In most of these cases, the litigants have been

---

[5] Code civil en vigueur dans le Grand-Duché de Luxembourg. This provision has substantially the same wording as the more known French exorbitant jurisdiction rule in Art 14 of the French Civil Code.

[6] Cour d'appel Luxembourg, 27 June 2007, No 31943.

[7] A Briggs, 'Forum non satis: Spiliada and an inconvenient truth' (2011) 3 *Lloyd's Maritime and Commercial Law Quarterly* 329.

[8] See the judgments Cour d'appel Luxembourg, 21 January 2015, No 38554 and Tribunal Luxembourg, 26 February 2014, No 155204 referring to Case C-133/78 *Gourdain v Nadler* [1979] ECR 73.

[9] Cass 15 April 2010, No 21/10, Registre 2741.

unsuccessful.[10] The courts, by didactically applying the conditions in Article 15, conclude that the contract in question is not falling into the scope of Article 15. At least once however, a litigant successfully raised the *ratione loci* lack of jurisdiction of the French courts by arguing that the jurisdiction clause granting jurisdiction to the French court was not valid pursuant to Article 17.[11]

The decisions concerning the protective rules for employment contracts shed light on the difficult interplay between the jurisdiction rules of Brussels I and the domestic jurisdiction rules. Most of these cases concern abusive dismissal. In several cases, employees domiciled in Luxembourg argued that the Luxembourg courts had jurisdiction under Article 20(1) of Brussels I although the cases were purely internal situations to which national rules on jurisdiction should have been applied.[12] The employees also tend to appeal against first instance decisions on the ground that the first instance court did not follow the hierarchy of norms and it applied the national rules on jurisdiction instead of Article 20 of Brussels I.[13] This appeal argument illustrates a common confusion regarding the distinction between jurisdiction and venue. In confirming the first instance decisions, the appeal court clearly draws a line between the application of the Brussels I Regulation to decide whether the Luxembourg courts have jurisdiction, and once it is decided that they have jurisdiction, the application of domestic rules to determine which court in Luxembourg will hear the case as the venue.

iii. Matters Related to Recognition and Enforcement

The States involved in matters related to recognition and enforcement are mainly neighbouring countries of Belgium, Germany and France.

Most of the decisions concerning recognition are limited to a mere reference to Article 33 of Brussels I. Some cases illustrate how litigants try to contest recognition on the (subsequently repealed) ground that the required court did not verify the competence of the court of origin.[14]

Regarding enforcement proceedings, most of the cases concern an appeal against an application for a declaration of enforceability under Article 43. In a vast majority of these cases, the appeal has been rejected.[15] It appears that the use of Article 43 is the last resort to buy time before the actual enforcement of the decision. Two main difficulties should be highlighted. One of them is that in a considerable number of decisions, the litigants have referred to the Brussels Convention instead of Brussels I.[16] Second, the non-conformity with the domestic requirements as to the procedure for a declaration of enforceability under Article 40(1) of Brussels I has resulted in the inadmissibility of the application for a

---

[10] Tribunal Luxembourg, 1 December 2009, No 112.601; Tribunal Luxembourg, 21 June 2013, No 146.829; JP Luxembourg, No 3851/12.

[11] Tribunal Diekirch, 20 November 2013, No 17937.

[12] Cour d'appel Luxembourg, 27 November 2013, No 38262.

[13] JP Esch/Alzette, 16 December 2011, No 2851/2011; Cour d'appel Luxembourg, 15 January 2012, No 40320; Cour d'appel Luxembourg, 27 November 2013, No 36672; Cour d'appel Luxembourg, 15 January 2015, No 40307.

[14] Cour d'appel Luxembourg, 26 February 2009, No 32134.

[15] Cour d'appel Luxembourg, 28 June 2007, No 31700; Cour d'appel Luxembourg, 12 July 2007, No 31294; Cour d'appel Luxembourg, 3 June 2009, No 33120; Cour d'appel Luxembourg, 3 March 2011, No 3552.

[16] Cour d'appel Luxembourg, 12 July 2007, No 31294; Cour d'appel Luxembourg, 13 September 2009, No 31813.

declaration of enforceability in several cases.[17] In a decision dated 8 January 2009, the Court of Appeal overruled the decision of the District Court on the ground that the *exequatur* application did not comply with Luxembourgish law.[18] A lawyer from an EU Member State practising under the original title of his home-country must work in conjunction with a lawyer certified in Luxembourg in order to apply for an *exequatur* procedure.[19] This issue is partially resolved by Brussels Ia which provides that an authorised representative is not required for a party to seek enforcement.[20]

iv. Conclusion

Regarding the scope of application of the EU and national rules on jurisdiction, both litigants and courts seem to have difficulties. The wrong application of Article 5 of Brussels I results in litigation over where to litigate and also lengthier proceedings.

The recognition and enforcement of other Member States' decisions is very effective in Luxembourg. Nonetheless, lawyers tend to refer to the wrong instruments or to use the wrong certificates.

B. Applicable Law Issues Under the Rome I and Rome II Regulations

i. Rome I

a. Matters Related to the Scope of Application

The main issue as to the scope of application is that the litigants rely on the Rome Convention[21] instead of the Rome I Regulation.[22]

b. Matters Related to the Uniform Rules

Most of the decisions on Rome I concern Articles 3 and 4. In several cases, the courts have had to clarify the scope of Articles 3 and 4 on the one hand and of Article 14 on the other hand.[23] As is the case in jurisdiction matters, litigants tend to rely on protective rules related to consumer contracts under Article 6. In several decisions, the court ruled that the contract does not fall within the scope of Article 6.[24]

---

[17] Cour d'appel Luxembourg, 8 January 2009, No 31963; Cour d'appel Luxembourg, 12 March 2009, No 32529.

[18] Cour d'appel Luxembourg, 8 January 2009, No 31963. In another case, the District Court had issued a declaration of enforceability but it was later declared inadmissible pursuant to the appeal of the other party: Cour d'appel Luxembourg, 12 March 2009, No 32529.

[19] Dir 98/5/EC of the European Parliament and of the Council of 16 February 1998 to facilitate practice of the profession of lawyer on a permanent basis in a Member State other than that in which the qualification was obtained, [1998] OJ L077/36, Art 5(4).

[20] Reg (EU) No 1215/2012 of the European Parliament and of the Council of 12 December 2012 on jurisdiction and the recognition and enforcement of judgments in civil and commercial matters (recast), [2012] OJ L351/1.

[21] Convention on the law applicable to contractual obligations (consolidated version), [1980] OJ C27/36.

[22] Tribunal Luxembourg, 29 January 2013, No 143992; Tribunal Luxembourg, 10 April 2013, No 145626.

[23] Tribunal Luxembourg, 16 November 2011, No 117 885; Cour d'appel Luxembourg, 8 January 2015, No 40561.

[24] Tribunal Luxembourg, 21 June 2013, No 146.829.

ii. *Rome II*

Both litigants and first instance courts tend to not make any reference to Rome II on the applicable law. On several occasions, in accordance with Article 28(1) of Rome II, the District Court applied the 1971 Hague Convention on the Law Applicable to Traffic Accidents[25] in disputes concerning road accidents.[26] Luxembourg courts refer to the French case law in order to clarify the prevalence of the 1971 Hague Convention over Rome II.

C. Practice/Process

Despite the limited number of cases due to the size of the country, the possibility to refer to the French case law represents a real asset to ensure a rather uniform application of the rules.[27] Most of the decisions, especially from higher courts, refer to the EU Regulations in a very didactic way.

Regarding recognition and enforcement of foreign decisions, the proceedings are mainly centralised in the District Court of Luxembourg. This concentration ensures predictability and efficiency as judges and clerks are very familiar with the procedures and the EU Regulations. According to an empirical study related to *exequatur* in Luxembourg, between 2008 and 2009, out of 338 applications for a declaration of enforceability, 100 per cent of the decisions were declared enforceable[28] which is a great illustration of the successful application of Brussels I.

Regarding the applicable law, the courts mainly face cases where the applicable foreign law is of one of the neighbouring countries. Given the trilingualism of Luxembourg, the application of these laws is not problematic. The courts have access to all legislation and doctrine of the neighbouring countries. The London Convention[29] is rarely used.

III. Luxembourg's Experience on Cross-border Family Law Disputes

A. Jurisdictional and Procedural Issues Under the Brussels IIa Regulation

i. *Matters Related to the Scope of Application*

The temporal scope of application of Brussels IIa has raised some issues in Luxembourg. In a divorce case, on the question whether the Brussels II Regulation[30] or the Brussels IIa

---

[25] The Court relied on the French case law: Cass Civ 1ère, 30 April 2014, No 13-11932.

[26] Cour d'appel Luxembourg, 13 October 2010, No 32124; Tribunal Luxembourg, 12 June 2015, No 126/15; Tribunal Luxembourg, 15 November 2011, No 137249.

[27] The Luxembourgish courts very often refer to the French Cour de cassation case law.

[28] G Cuniberti and M Muller, 'Une étude empirique sur la pratique de l'exequatur dans la Grande Région' (2013) 140 *Journal du droit international (Clunet)* 1. It is to be noted that the scope of the study is wider than the Brussels I Reg. Only 82 per cent of the decisions are on Brussels I.

[29] European Convention on Information on Foreign Law, London, 7/6/1968, European Treaty Series—No 62.

[30] Council Reg (EC) No 1347/2000 of 29 May 2000 on jurisdiction and the recognition and enforcement of judgments in matrimonial matters and in matters of parental responsibility for children of both spouses, [2000] OJ L160/19.

Regulation was to be applied to the case. The court clarified that, according to Article 72 of Brussels IIa, Brussels IIa applies to actions instituted from 1 March 2005 and since the petition for divorce had been filed in 2004, the court found that Brussels II was still applicable to the case.[31]

A decision dated 5 June 2013[32] raised the question of the material scope of application of Brussels IIa. The case concerned filiation and the claimant relied on Brussels IIa in order to establish the paternity of the alleged father living in France. The Public Prosecutor raised that the Luxembourg courts did not have jurisdiction under Brussels IIa. The court found that since filiation matters were not covered by Brussels IIa, domestic jurisdiction rules should be applied and accordingly it declined jurisdiction pursuant to the domestic rules.

On the question whether the delegation of parental responsibility falls within the scope of the Regulation, it has been affirmed by the courts that that issue is covered by the Regulation.[33]

ii. Matters Related to Jurisdiction

a. Divorce, Legal Separation and Marriage Annulment

The complex delineation between Articles 3, 6 and 7 is problematic. Where the defendant is neither an EU national nor residing in the EU, the Luxembourg courts seem to follow a reasoning which appears not to be in line with the CJEU's interpretation in C-68/07 *Sundelind*.[34] In some cases where the defendant was a third State national, the courts applied the domestic jurisdiction rules on the ground that the third State involved was not a party to Brussels IIa.[35] This reasoning of the Luxembourg courts, solely based on the fact that the third State at stake is not bound by Brussels IIa, results in a misapplication of Article 7 and a potential violation of the exclusivity of the EU grounds.

b. Parental Responsibility

1. Child Abduction

The procedural rules in Article 11 of Brussels IIa and their interplay with Article 13(1)(b) of the Hague Convention on the Civil Aspects of International Child Abduction are addressed in several decisions.[36] The courts have clarified that the prompt return mechanism set out in Article 11 of Brussels IIa only applies in cases where children have been unlawfully retained/removed in terms of Article 3 of the Hague Convention. Pursuant to Article 3 of the Hague Convention, two conditions must be fulfilled for the removal or the retention to be considered unlawful, ie the abduction should first be in breach of custody rights, and second the custody rights at hand should be actually exercised at the time of the abduction.

---

[31] Tribunal Luxembourg, 19 April 2007, No 89525.

[32] Tribunal Luxembourg, 5 June 2013, No 139035.

[33] Tribunal Luxembourg, 2 May 2013, No 141177; Tribunal Luxembourg 9 May 2012, No 141737; Tribunal Luxembourg, 11 December 2013, No 102847.

[34] Case C-68/07 *Kerstin Sundelind Lopez v Miguel Enrique Lopez Lizazo* [2007] ECR I-10403.

[35] Tribunal Luxembourg, 13 December 2007, No 109956; Tribunal Luxembourg, 29 January 2009, No 112357.

[36] Tribunal Luxembourg, 12 October 2010, No 132742; Tribunal Luxembourg, 20 October 2010, Nos 133067 et 133042; Tribunal Luxembourg, 15 June 2012, No 145238; Tribunal Luxembourg, 10 July 2012, No 144473; Tribunal Luxembourg, 19 December 2012, No 149284.

2. Other Issues Related to Parental Responsibility

The principle of *perpetuatio fori* is particularly used in situations where several relocations have occurred. The Luxembourg courts have, on multiple occasions, referred to the difference between Article 8 and the exceptions set by Articles 9 and 10.[37]

There are numerous decisions concerning prorogation in Article 12 of Brussels IIa. It appears that the litigants tend to rely on Article 12 while not fulfilling the strict conditions therein, especially the condition of an express agreement between parties.[38]

c. Common Provisions

The scope of Article 20 raises some issues regarding the application of the *lis pendens* rule under Article 19. The courts have indicated, on several occasions, that a claim on the merits and a claim for provisional measures do not qualify as a *lis pendens* situation pursuant to Article 19.[39]

Another issue is related to the scope of such provisional measures. The Luxembourg courts constantly rule that they can only grant provisional measures relating to persons or assets located in Luxembourg, or otherwise they have to decline jurisdiction. The recurrence of such extraterritorial claims sheds light on a practical problem which might be strongly linked to the peculiar geographical situation of Luxembourg. Besides, it appears that parties tend to consider that the general grounds of jurisdiction in Article 3 are also relevant to determine which court has jurisdiction to grant provisional measures. Article 20 seems to be neglected by the litigants.

iii. Matters Related to Recognition and Enforcement

a. Certificate Concerning Judgments in Matrimonial Matters and Certificate Concerning Judgments on Parental Responsibility

The Luxembourg first instance court stated that an interim order shall cease to apply when the court having jurisdiction over the substance of the matter rendered its decision.[40] The issue of translation of the decisions rendered in another language has been raised in some cases[41] but the Luxembourg first instance court did not take these decisions into consideration because they were not translated. Although the use of standard forms is supposed to facilitate the free movement of judgments, it appears that parties have some difficulties in understanding the use of such certificates.

---

[37] Cour d'appel Luxembourg, 9 February 2012, No 36528; Tribunal Luxembourg, 7 November 2012, No 138922; Cour d'appel Luxembourg, 28 November 2012, No 38813.

[38] Tribunal Luxembourg, 2 February 2012, No 124602; Tribunal Luxembourg, 12 July 2012, No 112401; Tribunal Luxembourg, 13 December 2012, Nos 1337378 et 134058.

[39] Tribunal Luxembourg, 13 July 2007, No 108656; Tribunal Luxembourg, 4 March 2008, No 112405; Tribunal Luxembourg, 28 December 2009, No 124923; Tribunal Luxembourg, 14 July 2010, Nos 127555 et 12957. Tribunal Luxembourg, 29 July 2011, No 137433; Tribunal Luxembourg, 15 November 2011, No 120194; Tribunal Luxembourg, 18 June 2013, No 153519.

[40] Tribunal Luxembourg, 8 January 2008, No 104237.

[41] Tribunal Luxembourg, 29 January 2009, No 97323.

b. Rights of Access

The use of the fast-track procedure seems to have raised some difficulties.[42] The courts have used the wording of Article 21(1) to state that the French decision was automatically recognised. The Court of Appeal emphasised that in order to be enforced in Luxembourg, the decision must be declared enforceable. This statement contradicts the letter of Brussels IIa. Indeed, according to Articles 40 and 41, judgments on rights of access can be enforced without a declaration of enforceability.[43] It is regrettable that the Court did not expand on this point by clarifying that the traditional *exequatur* procedure coexists along with this new optional fast track procedure. It is up to the parties to choose between both procedures.

iv. *Relations with Other Instruments*

The practical difficulties seem to arise in relation to two main instruments, ie the Brussels I Regulation and the Maintenance Regulation.[44]

Parties tend to assume that the court having jurisdiction over matrimonial matters also has jurisdiction over maintenance obligations. The Luxembourg courts have stated that there is a fragmentation of jurisdiction.[45] The delineation of the scope of application seems also problematic in relation to recognition and enforcement matters. The multiplicity of EU instruments in the field of family matters poses difficulties. The fragmentation makes the proceedings more complex for the parties, practitioners and courts.

v. *Conclusion*

The application of residual grounds of jurisdiction seems to be problematic in matrimonial matters. The Luxembourg courts do not follow the approach set by the CJEU in *Sundelind*.[46] Therefore, there might be cases where Luxembourg courts apply domestic grounds of jurisdiction whereas in fact the Brussels IIa grounds are relevant. Article 7 should be replaced by some common residual grounds of jurisdiction like it has been done in some recent Regulations (the Maintenance and Succession Regulations)[47] in order to avoid this difficulty.

The application of Article 20 has raised a lot of difficulties. The clarification of its scope and the harmonisation of a rule regardless of the *lex fori* would be welcome.[48]

---

[42] Cour d'appel de la jeunesse Luxembourg, 26 March 2007, No 31882.

[43] The Brussels IIa Reg thereby abolished *exequatur* for judgments on access rights and the return of abducted children.

[44] Tribunal Luxembourg, 4 October 2007, No 109259; Tribunal Luxembourg, 17 June 2008, Nos 11341 and 113949; Cour d'appel Luxembourg, 30 April 2009, No 32999; Cour d'appel Luxembourg, 11 March 2010, No 34352; Tribunal Luxembourg, 10 January 2013, No 141449; Tribunal Luxembourg, 20 June 2013, No 139144; Cour d'appel Luxembourg, 2 April 2014, No 39643.

[45] Cass, 30 January 2014, No 7/14—Registre 3282; Tribunal Luxembourg, 10 July 2015, No 1949/2015.

[46] n 36 above.

[47] Reg (EU) No 650/2012 of the European Parliament and of the Council of 4 July 2012 on jurisdiction, applicable law, recognition and enforcement of decisions and acceptance and enforcement of authentic instruments in matters of succession and on the creation of a European Certificate of Succession, [2012] OJ L201/107.

[48] Proposal for a council Reg on jurisdiction, the recognition and enforcement of decisions in matrimonial matters and the matters of parental responsibility and on international child abduction (recast), COM(2016) 411 final, Art 12.

The use of the possibility to transfer a case in parental responsibility matters pursuant to Article 15 has been used in a very limited number of cases.

The provisions on recognition and enforcement have been applied less frequently than those on jurisdiction. It appears that the parties do not know which instrument they should rely on (Brussels I or Brussels IIa). Grounds of non-recognition seem to have been mainly used for dilatory purposes. The fast track procedure, which is optional and available for access rights and return orders, is neither promoted nor mentioned by the Luxembourg courts. The complete abolition of *exequatur*, as proposed by the EU Commission,[49] would solve this problem.

The rules on the applicable law contained in other instruments should be inserted in Brussels IIa in order to have a comprehensive instrument.

B. Jurisdictional and Procedural Issues and Applicable Law Under the Maintenance Regulation

There are just a few cases related to the Maintenance Regulation, probably partially due to the relatively recent entry into force of the Regulation. Most of the decisions are default judgments.

i. Matters Related to the Scope of Application

The main problem is related to the temporal scope. There are incorrect references to the Brussels I Regulation's declaration of enforceability while the decision is—pursuant to the Maintenance Regulation—directly enforceable.[50] Besides, litigants refer to the abolition of *exequatur* while, according to the *ratione temporis*, the Brussels I Regulation applies to that matter.[51]

ii. Matters Related to Jurisdiction

In a decision dated 9 January 2014,[52] the Magistrate Court assumed jurisdiction under Article (3)(b) and rendered a default judgment ruling that the default defendant (whose former habitual residence only could be localised) had to provide for child support. One of the main difficulties appears to be related to the default defendant and the difficulty to localise his habitual residence. However the multiplicity of fora available, especially the one relying on the habitual residence of the creditor– can mitigate this problem. When it comes to the enforcement of these decisions, one might nonetheless wonder how efficient it is in practice.

A decision dated 26 February 2014[53] illustrates the didactic application of the territoriality principle to assume jurisdiction in order to take provisional measures. The decision concerns the scope of application of Article 14 and whether a measure that was

---

[49] ibid, Art 30.
[50] JP Luxembourg, 31 January 2012, Rep no 284/2012; JP Esch/Alzette, 14 August 2015, Rep no 2029/2015.
[51] JP Esch/Alzette, 8 July 2014, Rep no 1850/2014.
[52] JP Luxembourg, 9 January 2014, Rep Fiscal/14.
[53] Tribunal Luxembourg, 26 February 2014, No 158786.

considered, according to national law, a provisional measure could be characterised as such for the purpose of Article 14. The courts made some reference to the Luxembourg civil procedure rules regarding the measure at stake and also to Luxembourgish doctrine.

iii. Matters Related to Applicable Law

Two decisions that are precisely related to the question of applicable law have been identified. In the first one, the court determined to apply the Hague Protocol since both Romania and Luxembourg are bound by it.[54] The second decision[55] stressed the practical and complex articulation of the instruments for the litigants (and their counsel). It also reflects the fragmentation of the rules and the lack of coordination between the different fields covered by the EU private international rules on family matters.

iv. Matters Related to Recognition, Enforceability and Actual Enforcement of Decisions

A decision rendered on 8 January 2014 concerns enforcement of a decision given in a Member State bound by the 2007 Hague Protocol.[56] A Romanian divorce order was issued in April 2008 and it included an award for child support payable by the father (defendant). The mother requested this judgment to be enforced in Luxembourg where the child's habitual residence was located. The court clarified the fact that both Romania and Luxembourg are bound by the Protocol before referring to Article 685-3 of the Civil Code of Procedure[57] that implements Article 17 of the Maintenance Regulation.

A decision dated 31 January 2012 illustrates the application of Article 17 of the Maintenance Regulation.[58] In another decision,[59] there was severe confusion as to the scopes of application (both material and temporal). The judge had to clarify the need for an *exequatur* procedure as the decision to be enforced was rendered in May 2007 and therefore subject to a declaration of enforceability. The court referred the claimant to the court of origin in order to obtain a declaration of enforceability of the original French decision.

In a decision of 14 August 2015,[60] the Justice of the Peace of Esch-sur-Alzette, referring to Articles 17 and 75 of the Maintenance Regulation, clarified that the French decision at stake should be enforced without any declaration of enforceability.[61]

---

[54] JP Luxembourg, 9 January 2014, Rep/14.

[55] Tribunal Luxembourg, 22 May 2014, No 107/2014.

[56] JP Luxembourg, 8 January 2014, Rep fiscal/14.

[57] '[L]es décisions rendues dans un Etat membre lié par le protocole de La Haye sur la loi applicable aux obligations alimentaire … sont reconnues au Luxembourg sans qu'il soit nécessaire de recourir à aucune procédure et sans qu'il soit possible de s'opposer à la reconnaissance.'

[58] JP Esch/Alzette, 31 January 2012, Rep no 284/2012.

[59] JP Esch/Alzette, 8 July 2014, Rep no 1850/2014.

[60] JP Esch/Alzette, 14 August 2015, Rep no 2029/2015.

[61] It is a didactic decision referring to the Luxembourgish doctrine and mentioning that the role of the Justice of the Peace is not to examine the decision as to its substance.

C. Practice/Process

i. Luxembourg National Courts' Practice in Interpreting the Regulations

In addition to the explanations given above in section II.C, in the field of family law, the paramount importance of the best interests of the child is a common theme in both interviews and case law.

D. Preliminary Remarks on Effectiveness of the Current EU PIL Framework in Cross-border Family Law

The fragmentation of the rules in different instruments is particularly problematic. Most of the judgments encompass several issues (divorce, parental responsibility and maintenance obligations) which result in great practical difficulties at the time of enforcement. Some judges have had to contact lawyers or parties in order to clarify which part of the judgment needed to be declared enforceable. Lawyers do not master the different instruments and they often refer to the wrong instrument. Courts also have particular difficulties with filling up Maintenance obligation certificates which are regarded as the most complex of all the EU Regulations' forms.

IV. Conclusion

From a Luxembourgish perspective, the Regulations appear to be effective overall. National courts very often rely on French case law and doctrine. Therefore, despite the limited case law, the practice of the Luxembourg courts is not isolated. In addition, national courts tend to refer to CJEU case law and the fact that the CJEU is next door seems to particularly raise the awareness of domestic judges. Decisions—especially from the Court of Appeal and the Supreme Court—are very didactic with regards to EU PIL application. The rules on recognition and enforcement are particularly effective given the specialisation of the courts.

From the practitioner perspective, there are two main hurdles to the effectiveness of the Regulations. Firstly, the fragmentation of rules—especially in family matters—has raised some difficulties. More training and a more comprehensive compilation of EU PIL rules would be helpful. Second, in order to enhance the effectiveness of the Regulations, a systematic publication of case law would be welcome. The absence of a public repository of case law limits the awareness of the stakeholders and has been particularly problematic for lawyers.

24

Malta

ANTOINE G CREMONA, CLEMENT MIFSUD-BONNICI AND CALVIN CALLEJA

I. Introduction

Malta joined the European Union ('EU') in 2004. Prior to the transposition of the *acquis communautaire*, statutory rules on private international law ('PIL') were scarce. The Code of Organisation and Civil Procedure ('COCP') did contain detailed rules on jurisdiction[1] and there were some miscellaneous conflict-of-laws rules in the Civil Code on succession and matrimonial property.[2] Maltese courts tend to refer to the common law of England and Wales (not based on statute) in case of gaps (*lacunae*) in Maltese private international law. This is due to the fact that Malta was a British colony up to 1964. This had a tremendous impact on the Maltese legal system, which may be defined as a mixed legal system. This is relevant to our debate from two perspectives. First, Malta adopted an adversarial procedural system (which may have implications on whether rules of EU Regulations may be raised *ex officio* by judges and/or on how foreign law is treated). Second, Malta borrowed conflict-of-laws rules from the common law.

Since Malta did not have a very strong tradition of PIL, the coming into force of the EU PIL Regulations posed a challenge for Maltese judges, lawyers and notaries alike. This was particularly important in view of the growth in service-based industries (eg financial services and gaming) and strengthening of traditional sectors (ship and aircraft registration) which have prevalent cross-border implications. Although some mistakes were made along the way, one should note that even the initial cases on the Brussels I Regulation[3] demonstrated that there is a level of familiarity with the Regulation. This was due to the receptiveness of judges and practitioners to the new changes, but also a degree of collegiality and cooperation between all stakeholders involved to make sure everyone gets up to speed with this new body of rules. With this in mind, one should note that Malta's experience with the EU PIL instruments has been positive.[4]

---

[1] Ch 12 of the Laws of Malta.

[2] Ch 16 of the Laws of Malta.

[3] Council Reg 44/2001 on jurisdiction and the recognition and enforcement of judgments in civil and commercial matters (Brussels I) [2001] OJ L12/1.

[4] It is perhaps worth noting that EU PIL instruments provide a degree of clarity and certainty in a system that lacked rigid rules on private international law. It also provided a statutory basis for the development of the discipline in a jurisdiction that was unused to having to rely on judge-made law.

II. Malta's Experience on Cross-border Civil and Commercial Disputes

A. Jurisdictional and Procedural Issues Under the Brussels I Regulation

i. *Matters Related to the Scope of Application*

Judgments which specifically concern the applicability of the Brussels I Regulation and the Brussels Ia Regulation[5] (together 'Brussels I regime') are limited in number. This is largely owing to a clear-cut distinction at law whereby the legislator sets out a hierarchy of laws in Article 742 of the COCP.[6] The Maltese Courts have had few occasions on which a decision had to be reached as to the application of local or EU law on jurisdictional rules. The clear wording of the law has allowed both regimes to operate independently of one another, even though EU PIL instruments are supreme.[7] In *Maltrad (Holdings) Limited v Coll*, the direct effect of the Brussels regime in Malta was affirmed.[8] More importantly, the Court stated that that regime prevails over any domestic law with which it may be in conflict. In this case, the Court of Appeal[9] went further and overturned the judgment of the First Hall, Civil Court.[10] The first instance court had assumed jurisdiction on the basis of a choice-of-law clause in favour of Maltese law which was not a valid basis for jurisdiction under the Brussels regime. In this context, the Court of Appeal held that there was no prorogation of jurisdiction on the basis of this clause.[11]

That said, in *Muiris Seasmus Mahon v GOAGT Limited et*,[12] the Industrial Tribunal confused the notions of jurisdiction and competence by broadening the scope of application of national law, that is, the Employment and Industrial Relations Act.[13] It simply stated that it was competent to hear all cases whereby an allegation of unfair dismissal had been made without reference to the Brussels I regime, even though the employee was domiciled in Ireland and the employer had branches in Malta (that is the respondents).[14] Neither did the

---

[5] Reg 1215/2012 on jurisdiction and the recognition and enforcement of judgments in civil and commercial matters (recast) [2012] OJ L351/1.

[6] Ch 12 of the Laws of Malta, Art 742(6): 'Where provision is made under any other law, or, in any regulation of the European Union making provision different from that contained in this article, the provisions of this article shall not apply with regard to the matters covered by such other provision and shall only apply to matters to which such other provision does not apply.'

[7] See *LR Composizioni Profumati Srl v Ocean Group Limited*, First Hall Civil Court (11 May 2015). cp *Diego Righi v Emerald Shipping Limited*, Industrial Tribunal (10 May 2011).

[8] Court of Appeal (27 March 2015).

[9] Court of Appeal (27 March 2015).

[10] First Hall Civil Court (10 June 2014).

[11] Interestingly, the applicant also claimed that there was jurisdiction on the basis of s II of Brussels Ia. The Court pointed out that the agreement had not fixed the 'place of performance' of the obligation assumed by the respondent to repay the money lent to him (this was a loan agreement). It also went on to state that there was nothing to intimately link the loan with the Maltese Islands and invoke the jurisdiction of the latter. It was disappointing that the Court of Appeal referred to the Civil Code to determine where the place of performance of the contractual obligation was located. This appears to run contrary to the principle of autonomous interpretation fundamental to EU PIL instruments.

[12] Industrial Tribunal (8 May 2015).

[13] Ch 452 of the Laws of Malta.

[14] The application of Maltese law as against the Brussels I Reg would not have altered the outcome of the decision.

Tribunal take cognisance of the place where the employee habitually carried out his work, which is a possible basis for jurisdiction as per Article 21(1)(b) of Brussels Ia.

An example of the earlier cases, which canvasses some of the difficult issues presented before the Maltese courts, is *GIE Pari Mutuel Urbain v Bell Med Ltd et*.[15] In this case, it was noted that the question whether a dispute fell within the ambit of the Brussels regime was separate and distinct from the issue of jurisdiction of the foreign court. Since the question whether the dispute between the parties is within the scope of the Brussels regime was not addressed by the French court, there was nothing to prevent the Maltese Court of Appeal from taking a view on the matter. In delivering a final judgment[16] the Court of Appeal held that the appellant company had exercised public law powers to protect a monopoly, noting that its primary objective was the regulation of French public policy with regard to horse-racing betting. Since it had not acted in the private law sphere to regulate civil or commercial business between private persons, the Court of Appeal refused recognition and enforcement of the French judgment on account of being outside the scope of application of the Brussels I regime. Likewise and more recently, in *Giovanni Sidoti v European Insurance Group Limited*,[17] the Court of Appeal held that the enforcement of an arbitral award was expressly excluded by Article 1(2)(d) of Brussels Ia.

ii. Matters Related to Jurisdiction

Generally, the Maltese Courts correctly apply the Brussels I Regime. There are a number of jurisdictional disputes, showing a high degree of sensitivity in cases where jurisdiction agreements were invoked in commercial transactions.

The Maltese courts assumed jurisdiction under Article 2 in *DeBono noe v No Stop Technology Ltd*.[18] In this case, the defendant was domiciled in Malta. He challenged the court's jurisdiction by submitting that a distribution agreement, between the parties, contained a jurisdictional agreement. The jurisdictional challenge was dismissed because the court established that the choice-of-court agreement was never clearly and conclusively accepted by the claimant.[19] It was held that a mere reference by one of the parties in an invoice to the 'terms and conditions', which include a choice-of-court agreement, was not sufficient to satisfy the requirements of Article 23.

PWA Co Limited v Luisa Spagnoli SPA[20] is an interesting case where the Maltese Courts sustained a jurisdictional challenge due to an Italian jurisdictional clause. In affirming the application of the jurisdictional clause to the claims raised by the applicant, the Maltese Court referred to *Benincasa* where a similar agreement was considered.[21] It should be noted that, in this case, the Court cited Article 1002 of the Civil Code[22] which states that there shall be no room for interpretation where the terms of an agreement are clear. Albeit erroneous, these references may be considered as superfluous and unremarkable, ultimately having no impact on the outcome of the Court's decision. That said, the reference might

---

[15] Court of Appeal (26 June 2007).
[16] *GIE Pari Mutuel Urbain v Bell Med Ltd et*, Court of Appeal (28 September 2007).
[17] Court of Appeal (11 March 2016).
[18] First Hall Civil Court (30 June 2011).
[19] See also Case 24/76 *Estasis Salotti v Rüwa* [1976] ECR 1831.
[20] First Hall Civil Court (12 April 2013).
[21] Case C-269/95 *Benincasa v DentalkitSrl* [1997] ECR I-3767.
[22] Ch 16 of the Laws of Malta.

also be an indication that legal traditions/heritages may impact on the interpretation of EU PIL instruments.

iii. Matters Related to Recognition and Enforcement

Proceedings relating to the recognition and enforcement of judgments from the courts of other EU Member States in Malta are efficient and unproblematic. This is largely due to a dedicated team of judges that deal with such matters on a regular basis. The Courts are quick to recognise and enforce foreign judgments, provided that the Brussels I regime requirements are met.

The recognition and enforcement of judgments would be denied only in cases where the conditions for refusal of recognition and enforcement are very clearly met. For example, in *Elf Aquitaine v Guelfi*,[23] the Court of Appeal dismissed the judgment-debtor's submission that the enforcement of the French judgment would manifestly violate public policy because, under Maltese law, civil proceedings are independent from criminal proceedings. It was held that, with reference to *Bamberski*,[24] the principle that civil and criminal proceedings are kept distinct is not fundamental.

Public policy was also unsuccessfully invoked as a defence against the recognition and enforcement of an Italian judgment in *Cartiera Lucchese Spa v Climaco Group Limited*.[25] The Maltese court dismissed the judgment-debtor's argument that the Italian Tribunal's summary proceedings breached the right to a fair hearing on two counts—the insufficiency of time given to the respondent to prepare his defence and the failure to notify the respondent with the acts pertaining to the proceedings brought against it. It was held that the summary proceedings do not necessarily deprive the respondent of the opportunity to present its case, as long as it was notified and allowed to prepare its defence, both in sufficient time.

That said, a recent judgment delivered by the First Hall Civil Court reveals a rather glaring misapplication of Brussels Ia. In *De Marco Noe Vs Randazzo Lidia et*,[26] the presiding judge declared as enforceable in Malta a *Tribunale di Palermo* judgment regarding insolvency of a company. Admittedly, the judgment was delivered a mere three months following the coming into force of Brussels Ia. However, the exclusion of insolvency proceedings[27] from civil and commercial matters under Article 1(2) was the same under its predecessor, that is, the Brussels I Regulation. Curiously enough, the respondent did not invoke the inapplicability of the Brussels I regime either. It remains to be seen whether such a defence will be raised at appeal stage.

iv. Matters Related to Relations with Other Instruments

One area where there appears to be a level of confusion is the relationship between the Brussels I Regime and a prior bilateral agreement, which Malta had struck up with the United Kingdom to facilitate enforcement of judgments. This bilateral agreement was made

---

[23] Court of Appeal (13 May 2008).
[24] Case C-7/98 *Dieter Krombach v André Bamberski* [2000] ECR I-1935, para 37.
[25] Court of Appeal (12 February 2016).
[26] First Hall Civil Court (26 April 2016).
[27] Insolvency proceedings form the subject matter of Reg (EU) 2015/848 of the European Parliament and of the Council on insolvency proceedings (recast) [2015] OJ L141/19.

a part of Maltese law in a statutory act of parliament by the name of the British Judgments (Reciprocal Enforcement) Act.[28] This bilateral agreement has been superseded by the Brussels I Regime, see Article 69 of Brussels Ia, but may take effect again after Brexit occurs.

In *Catalyst Managerial Services v Libya-Africa Investment Portfolio*,[29] by virtue of a judgment given by the High Court of Justice of England and Wales, Queen Bench's Division, the applicant company was acknowledged as a creditor of the respondent for a total sum of $15,422,924.00. By using the Brussels I Regulation as a basis for enforcement, the Court correctly deprived the respondent company of wider defences available to it under the British Judgments (Reciprocal Enforcement) Act, which adopted a different procedure for the enforcement of judgments stemming from the courts in the UK.

B. Rome I and Rome II

Maltese judgments which have been delivered on the Rome I Regulation[30] and Rome II Regulation[31] are scarce, but it is known from preliminary judgments on the Brussels I regime and from our professional experience that there are a number of pending cases waiting to be decided on these two Regulations.

There is one judgment of the First Hall Civil Court which contemplated the Rome I Regulation. In *DeBono noe v No Stop Technology Limited*, which was already briefly discussed above, the claimant sought the payment of €79,141.68 for products sold and consigned to the defendant.[32] The defendant had been registered in Italy, but re-domiciled in Malta in 2010. On the other hand, the claimant was a company registered in Hong Kong with an agent in Germany. The Court confirmed that the Rome I Regulation applied as the 'supreme law' in this case. An earlier preliminary judgment delivered by the same Court declared that there was no distributorship agreement between the parties and that therefore there was no choice-of-law agreement. The First Hall Civil Court opted for a combined reading of Article 4(1)(a) and Article 19(2) of the Rome I Regulation to select the law where the seller has his habitual residence, namely, the location of a branch. Owing to a number of factors, namely the responsibility bestowed on the German agency for the execution of the sales, the carrying out of the sale by that agency, the payment of price to the same agency in a German bank account and the German VAT number of that agency, it was held that the applicable law was German law.

A judgment delivered by the Industrial Tribunal in the earlier *Diego Righi v Emerald Shipping Limited*[33] attempted to clarify the Maltese position on the governing of contractual obligations prior to the coming into effect and the application of the Rome I Regulation. Indeed, both parties argued in favour of the application of the Rome Convention on Contractual Obligations (Ratification) Act. However it is worth noting that, owing to the imminent coming into force of the Rome I Regulation, the Minister responsible

---

[28] Ch 52 of the Laws of Malta.
[29] First Hall Civil Court (12 January 2016).
[30] Reg 593/2008 on the law applicable to contractual obligations (Rome I) [2008] OJ L177/6.
[31] Reg 864/2007 on the law applicable to non-contractual obligations (Rome II) [2007] OJ L199/40.
[32] First Hall Civil Court (3 April 2012).
[33] Industrial Tribunal (10 May 2011).

never issued the legal notice required at law for the said Act to come into force.[34] The decision of the Industrial Tribunal was therefore incorrect since it affirmed the applicability of the Rome Convention on Contractual Obligations (Ratification) Act. However, the application of conflict-of-laws rules based on common law rules (which were applicable at the time) by the Maltese Courts would have led to the same result, that is, that Swiss law was applicable to the case.

In *Pol-Euro Shipping Lines Plc SA v Zejt Marine Services Limited*, the Rome II Regulation was extensively and accurately applied, providing a thorough evaluation of the local interpretation of its provisions, particularly Article 4.[35] Briefly, the facts of the case are as follows: two vessels collided in the port of Sousse, Tunisia. The owner of one of the vessels was a Polish company (the applicant), while the owner of the second vessel was a Maltese company (the respondent). However, at the time of the collision, the Polish-owned vessel had been leased out to a Maltese company. The Court held that the place where the collision occurred and where the damage was suffered was the same. These factual circumstances fall directly within the ambit of Article 4(1) of the Regulation. Therefore, the applicable law should be the place where the damage occurred irrespective of the country where the event which gave rise to the damage occurred. It should be noted that the Court rejected the argument that the general applicability of Article 4(1) could be derogated from by the flag which a ship carries. In fact, Article 4(1) does not distinguish between a physical or moral person or a vessel. The Court referred to academic literature[36] to confirm that the applicable law should not be identified by looking at the law of the flag of the vessel. Therefore, Article 4(1) was deemed to be the applicable provision, as a result of which Tunisian law was the law applicable to the case. The Court went on to dismiss the applicant's invocation of the exception contained in Article 4(2), ie common habitual residence. It was held that, since one of the parties was not resident in Malta, the Article 4(2) exception could not be applied in this case. The Court also turned down the applicants' argument that Article 4(3) should prevail over Article 4(1), holding that there was one connecting factor, namely the location of the ship's owner in Poland, which did not point towards Malta.

III. Malta's Experience on Cross-border Family Law Disputes

A. Jurisdictional and Procedural Issues Under the Brussels IIa Regulation

An increase in free movement of citizens of the European Union led to a climb in the numbers of personal relationships between foreigners and Maltese nationals which made

---

[34] Ch 482 of the Laws of Malta.

[35] First Hall Civil Court (12 December 2013).

[36] Liz Heffernan, 'Rome II: Implications for Irish Tort Litigation' in John Ahern and William Binchy (eds), *The Rome II Regulation on the Law Applicable to Non-Contractual Obligations: a New International Litigation Regime* (Leiden, Martinus Nijhoff Publishers, 2009); J Fawcett, J Carruthers and P North (eds), *Cheshire, North and Fawcett, Private International Law* 14th edn (Oxford, Oxford University Press, 2008).

recourse to this Regulation necessary. The Maltese Courts appear to be well-versed in issues relating to the applicability of the Brussels IIa Regulation. This may be attributed to the fact that Malta has specialised and dedicated courts on family disputes.

i. Matters Related to Jurisdiction

a. Divorce, Legal Separation and Marriage Annulment

Above all, it should be noted that there are not many cases raising questions about the scope of application of Brussels IIa. In *ABC v DE*,[37] the applicant sought to establish jurisdiction under Article 3 of the Regulation. The respondent's jurisdictional challenge was dismissed. The Court held that a brief period of absence, for whatever reason, does not prevent the acquisition of habitual residence. The concept of habitual residence, it said, is determined by the intent and the actual fact of establishing a home in a particular country. The Court went on to declare that it was endowed with jurisdiction from the moment the applicant filed the letter of mediation on 12 February 2015.

Mediation was a determining factor in *AB v CB*,[38] where the respondent raised a plea on the basis of the Brussels I regime. However, the Court pointed out that whereas the Brussels I regime governs civil and commercial matters, the Brussels IIa Regulation deals with, 'separation and other marital proceedings'. As a result, Article 7 of the Brussels I regime did not cater for family law proceedings, which are excluded from the remit of the Regulation. In this case, the Maltese court assumed jurisdiction under Article 3 of Brussels IIa insofar as divorce and other related issues were concerned. The Court established that the applicant had been a resident of Malta for the preceding five years and was still a resident of the same. The Court further refused the respondent's request for a stay of proceedings under Article 19 of the Brussels IIa Regulation. Although divorce proceedings were filed in the United Kingdom two days prior to the institution of equivalent proceedings in Malta, the Court came to the conclusion that the Maltese Courts were first seised with jurisdiction to hear the case. Its rationale was based on the fact that,

> under Maltese Law, separation proceedings have to start by filing a letter in the registry to start the mediation process, which will precede contentious separation proceedings in court if an agreement is not reached between both parties within a fixed time period. After the end of mediation proceedings and where an agreement has not been reached between both parties, either party may file a law suit for marital separation, if the law suit is not filed, then separation proceedings are deemed to have been abandoned. However, if a law suit is filed within the specified time period as per regulation 7 of LN397/2003, then the separation process is considered to be an ongoing one.

Thus, one cannot institute separation proceedings without having first made an attempt at mediation. Article 16 creates two alternative rules for when a court is deemed to be seised and national courts have to determine which of those rules apply for their system and then interpret how those rules are to be applied in relation to that system.

---

[37] Civil Court (Family Section) (30 June 2015).
[38] Civil Court (Family Section) (31 May 2016).

b. Parental Responsibility

1. Child Abduction

In *Director of Department for Social Welfare Standards v Sharon Rose Roche*,[39] the Court of Appeal examined the earlier judgment given by the superior courts in Gozo.[40] This earlier judgment turned down the request to order the child's return to England on the basis of Article 11(4) of the Brussels IIa Regulation. The justification for its decision lies in the fact that the 'adequate arrangements' required by the foregoing Article were not in place to guarantee the protection of the child upon his return. It was held that the concept of habitual residence should be interpreted autonomously with reference to the situation prior to the child's abduction. Were this to be otherwise, the spectrum of varying definitions could result in different national courts claiming jurisdiction or in reluctance to claim jurisdiction in the first place. Consequently, the Court concluded that the habitual residence of the child is a fact to be determined according to the situation as it existed prior to his abduction from the United Kingdom in this case. It was further held that the rationale of Article 10 is to prevent a change in jurisdiction in the case of an abduction. Apart from this, the Court of Appeal in its previous judgment considered the issue of acquiescence of the father for the child to remain in Gozo and came to the conclusion that there had been no consent or acquiescence on behalf of the father.

ii. Matters Related to Recognition and Enforcement

a. Rights of Access

The Court of Appeal has displayed a particularly strict adherence to the Brussels IIa Regulation and the resulting jurisprudence of the Court of Justice of the European Union (CJEU). By way of example, in *Direttur tad-Dipartiment għal Standards fil-Ħarsien Soċjali v Lara Maria Merlevede nee' Borg St. John*,[41] the Maltese Court cited *Zarraga v Pelz*[42] wherein the CJEU offered an explanation of Article 40 of the Brussels IIa Regulation. The CJEU stated that a judgment enforceable in terms of Article 40 of the Regulation and which would have led to the issuing of the certificate in the Member State of origin (as occurred in the Maltese case), is recognised and enforced automatically in another Member State without there being the possibility of opposing its recognition.

The Court dismissed the appellant's argument that the procedure listed in Article 41(2) of the Brussels IIa Regulation had not been followed in its entirety because the child had not been heard. The Court stated that the Regulation does permit the issuing of the certificate even if the minor is not heard, provided that this omission results from the inappropriateness of such hearing in view of the child's tender age. This is what happened in this case, and thus the issuing of the certificate did not suffer from any irregularity. Moreover, the Court also stressed that it is not necessary for the provisions regarding access to be contained in a judgment given ad hoc specifically to address the issue of rights of access. There is nothing

---

[39] Court of Appeal (17 May 2016).

[40] There are other child abduction cases under Maltese law but this recent judgment was selected for discussion by way of illustration.

[41] Court of Appeal (31 January 2014).

[42] Case C-491/10 PPU *Zarraga v Pelz* [2010] ECR I-14247.

in the Regulation in question which prevents the enforcement of part, and not the whole, of a foreign judgment ie that part which considers and contains a decision regarding access to minors.

b. Return of the Child

In *Direttur għal Standards fil-Ħarsien Soċjali v Mario Attard*,[43] the Court applied Article 42(1) of the Regulation. The judgment of the English High Court of Justice, Family Division was duly certified in the form laid down in Annex IV of the Regulation. Thus, the Court of Appeal enforced the judgment, ordering the return of the minor.

iii. Cooperation between Central Authorities in Matters of Parental Responsibility

An examination of various judgments reveals a tendency between national Central Authorities to cooperate in order to identify the location of the minor child, and ultimately request its return. As was the case in *Direttur tad-Dipartiment għal Standards fil-Ħarsien Soċjali v Anita Maria Horry nee Montebello*,[44] this standard request is often made under the auspices of the Hague Convention on the Civil Aspects of International Child Abduction, specifically Article 7 of the same. This bears testimony to the intimate relationship between the latter Convention and the Brussels IIa Regulation.[45] Such request is also frequently accompanied and followed by a statement in acknowledgement of the fact that the Maltese Central Authority has been authorised to act on behalf of one of the parents.[46]

However, that is not the extent of their cooperation. In *Direttur tad-Dipartiment għal Standards fil-Ħarsien Soċjali v A B C nee DE*,[47] the French Central Authority corresponded with the Director of Department for Social Welfare Standards ie the Maltese Central Authority. It requested the latter to cooperate and take the measures necessary in order to induce and improve the application of the Brussels IIa Regulation, with the ultimate aim of implementing the decision of the French Court as per Articles 54 and 55(b) of the Regulation.

In delivering judgment, the Maltese Court also ordered a copy of the mother's plane tickets (purchased by the father) to be sent to the French Central Authority, with the latter being bound to reciprocate.

iv. Relations with Other Instruments

As has already been alluded to, the closest relationship which the Brussels IIa Regulation has, is with the Hague Child Abduction Convention. Indeed, one may speak of an emerging trend among Maltese courts to treat the two as inseparable in intra-EU child abduction cases—where one is invoked, the other follows. This of course is understandable in view of the similarity in the matters regulated by either as well as the textual references to

---

[43] Court of Appeal (15 December 2006).
[44] Court of Appeal (3 December 2010).
[45] Council Reg (EC) No 2201/2003 concerning jurisdiction and the recognition of judgments in matrimonial matters and the matters of parental responsibility.
[46] *Direttur tad-Dipartiment għal Standards fil-Ħarsien Soċjali v Michael Caruana*, Court of Appeal (3 August 2012).
[47] Civil Court (Family Section) (8 August 2013).

the Convention contained in the Regulation. However, this element of interrelatedness has developed into a habit to cite the two instruments interchangeably as providing the basis on which judgment will be delivered, but then refraining from providing any further explanation. In fact, in *Direttur tad-Dipartiment għal Standards fil-Ħarsien Soċjali v Anita Maria Horry nee Montebello*,[48] the Court largely based its decision on Article 13 of the Hague Convention. Although the Regulation was acknowledged as the point of departure, there is no other mention of it in the judgment. This may be due to the fact that the Brussels IIa Regulation expressly refers to Article 13 of the Convention.

IV. Conclusion

As is clearly evident from our findings illustrated above, the Maltese judiciary appears to be confident in the application of the EU PIL instruments and applies them correctly in the majority of cases. Even where we spotted mistakes, it was generally the case that it was corrected at appeal or otherwise did not make a difference to the outcome. It would be equally a mistake to fail to acknowledge that judgments do not always paint a clear picture of the facts of the case and there might be circumstances not known to the reader which may have affected the judgment of the judge in question.

That being said, legal practitioners in Malta feel fairly comfortable with making submissions on the basis of the EU PIL instruments, but also confident that a Maltese judge will understand those submissions and apply the relevant rules correctly. It is still to be seen whether the same experience will be felt with respect to the Maintenance Regulation but we do not see any reason why that should not be the case.

---

[48] Court of Appeal (3 December 2010).

25

The Netherlands

AUKJE VAN HOEK, IAN SUMNER AND CATHALIJNE VAN DER PLAS

I. Introduction

Due to a particularity in the Dutch law on dismissal, the courts handle a lot of cases on termination of employment contracts, often at the request of the employer. These also include cross-border cases.[1] Consumers rarely use the court system, as the Netherlands has a well-developed system of consumer complaints boards.[2] The city of Rotterdam is well known for its maritime practice, whereas the city of Amsterdam is an important financial centre and operates as a centre for foreign companies which establish a holding company in the Netherlands for tax purposes. These economic characteristics are reflected in the case load of the courts. The largely international practice of the (maritime division of the) Rotterdam court led to the introduction—by way of experiment—of an option to litigate in English before the Rotterdam court.[3] The Amsterdam court will in future be supplemented by an English language 'Netherlands commercial court'.[4]

Judgments of all Dutch courts may be published on the website of the judiciary (rechtspraak.nl). This website contains approximately one per cent of all judgments. The selection is based on presumed relevance.[5] For the purpose of the discussion on Brussels I, we used case law on rechtspraak.nl and/or the database of NIPR (the Dutch repository for private international law) from 1 August 2010 onwards. Within that set we focused on judgments of the Supreme Court and on judgments of the appellate courts which were commented upon in literature (case notes). As the Rome I and Rome II Regulations have not produced extensive case law yet, a more comprehensive coverage is applied there. The part on family law is based on case law and on the experience of the author as an expert adviser in the field.

---

[1] Until recently the relevant legal provision was deemed to be an overriding mandatory provision which was to be applied whenever the termination affected the Dutch labour market.

[2] MJ Ter Voert, CM Klein Haarhuis, *Geschilbeslechtingsdelta 2014* (WODC report) 14: In approx five per cent of legal problems experienced by citizens some type of mediation takes place, four per cent of problems lead to court procedures and 11 per cent to some type of extra-judicial settlement. www.wodc.nl/onderzoeksdatabase/2406-geschilbeslechtingsdelta-2014.aspx.

[3] www.rechtspraak.nl/Organisatie-en-contact/Organisatie/Rechtbanken/Rechtbank-Rotterdam/Nieuws/Paginas/Pilot-Engelstalig-procederen-in-handelszaken.aspx.

[4] www.rechtspraak.nl/SiteCollectionDocuments/20150120-Plan-Netherlands-Commercial-Court.pdf.

[5] All supreme court cases except obviously unfounded appeals and/or standard summary dismissals; most judgments of lower courts sitting in bench, all cases pertaining to the Lugano Convention and the Hague Child Abduction Convention 1980. Website www.rechtspraak.nl/Uitspraken-en-nieuws/Uitspraken/Paginas/Selectiecriteria.aspx.

II. The Netherlands Experience in Cross-border Civil and Commercial Disputes

A. Jurisdictional and Procedural Issues Under the Brussels I Regulation

i. Matters Related to the Scope of Application

A specific Dutch problem with regard to the scope of application of Brussels I relates to the position of the Dutch Collective Settlement Act (WCAM)—a procedure for making settlements applicable to all potential claimants.[6] Other decisions given in the past five years relate to the demarcation vis-à-vis the Insolvency regulation,[7] arbitration[8] and the public domain.[9] Furthermore, we found a decision on the question whether the competence to order a provisional examination of a witness falls within the scope of application of Brussels I (a qualified yes).[10]

ii. Matters Related to Jurisdiction

Preliminary rulings have been requested (and not yet been rendered) with regard to Articles 5(3)[11] and 22(4)[12] of Brussels I. Noteworthy is the decision in which the rationale of *Solvay/Honeywell* on the relation between Article 31 and 22(4) Brussels I serves as a basis for the conclusion that Article 22(4) Brussels I does not preclude a court's competence on the basis of Articles 2 or 6(1) Brussels I to order a provisional cross-border prohibition against infringement, if the defendants in the preliminary relief proceedings argue by way of defence that the patent invoked is invalid.[13]

We note uncertainty as to the application of Article 22(2) Brussels I to the Dutch proceedings on the forced sale of shares ('*geschillenregeling*'). Although in literature and in some case law it is argued that the Dutch courts should be exclusively competent with regard to such requests of forced sales of shares if it concerns the shares of a Dutch entity,[14] the restrictive interpretation of Article 22(2) Brussels I seems to prevent such an approach.

In Dutch legal practice companies are advised to include forum selection clauses not only in the general conditions but also to mention the presence of a forum selection clause in the reference to those general conditions. This advice is based on a not fully consistent court practice which seems to be more strict with regard to Article 23 Brussels I than—and therefore not in accordance with—Court of Justice of the European Union (CJEU) case law.[15]

---

[6] NL:GHAMS:2010:BO3908.
[7] NL:GHSHE:2013:CA2317.
[8] NL:HR:2010:BN8533.
[9] NL:HR:2014:2816; HR2012:BX7456; NL:GHARL:2015:6649.
[10] NL:HR:2010:BN8533.
[11] NL:HR:2015:36.
[12] NL:RBDHA:2015:5716.
[13] NL:GHDHA:2014:1727.
[14] NL:RBOBR:2013:CA2363.
[15] C-322/14 *Majdoub v CarsOnTheWeb* EU:C:2015:334.

Finally, it seems that most case law on Brussels I results from intellectual property (IP) disputes. Maybe this accounts for the dominance of Article 5(3) and the lack of annotated cases on Article 5(1).

iii. Matters Related to Recognition and Enforcement

The *Hoge Raad* ruled that Brussels I applies to the recognition and enforcement of the civil part of a Belgian criminal judgment,[16] as well as to the recognition and enforcement of a decision of a German court that contains an order to pay a fine in order to ensure compliance with a judgment given in a civil and commercial matter.[17]

The public policy exception in Article 34(1) of Brussels I does not preclude the recognition and enforcement of a German *Anerkennntnisurteil* that lacks grounds; it depends on the context in which a court decision has been rendered to what extent such decision must provide grounds. In another group of decisions it was ruled that the Dutch court has to check whether the German decision conflicts with Article 22(1) Brussels I, despite the fact that the defendant failed to appeal against the German decision accepting jurisdiction.

B. Applicable Law Issues Under the Rome I and Rome II Regulations

i. Rome I

Cross-border cases are only a small minority of cases.[18]

a. Matters Related to the Scope of Application

Many cross-border cases fall under the application of a uniform law treaty, such as CMR (Road Transport), CNMI (Inland Waterways) and CISG (International Sales of Goods). In those cases the Rome I Regulation may be referred to for issues not covered by the treaties. When issues arise as to the scope of application, these mainly pertain to the application of the uniform law treaties, rather than the scope of Rome I. Some issues as to the scope of Rome I do however arise as to the property law aspects of voluntary assignment and with regard to the material validity of forum choices and arbitration clauses. Though the latter topics are outside the scope of application of the Regulation, based on a provision of Dutch law the provisions of Rome I are applied to these cases as well.[19]

b. Matters Related to the Uniform Rules

The case law contains a mix of topics, including distribution contracts, personal sureties, medical treatment, employment, real estate projects, transport and sales. We found no instances of the application of Article 6.

---

[16] NL:HR:2014:2816.

[17] HR:2012:BX7456 following on from Case C-406/09 *Realchemie Nederland* EU:C:2011:668.

[18] A search for civil cases on '593/2008' in the case law database produced 173 hits. In most cases however, the Rome I Reg was mentioned as not being applicable *ratione tempori*. NIPR gave 85 hits.

[19] Art 10:154 BW (Dutch civil code).

A recurring topic is the question whether a contract was entered into and/or whether it contains a valid choice-of-law—the latter often as part of the question whether there is agreement on the application of general conditions. Based on Article 10 the courts will apply the putatively chosen law to this latter question.

The annotated cases deal almost exclusively with employment contracts,[20] with the single exception of a case on personal surety.

c. The Application of Overriding Mandatory Provisions

Overriding mandatory provisions are pleaded mainly in the area of international employment as well. But the application of overriding mandatory provisions is also pleaded with regard to gambling (one case).

d. Matters Related to Other Provisions

The Netherlands is a contracting party to the Hague Agency Convention. Based on Article 25 of Rome I, this Convention is routinely given precedence over Rome I, also in cases involving Member States which are not a party to the Convention. This reduces decisional harmony within the EU, but is not a point of serious debate in the Netherlands.

ii. Rome II

a. Matters Related to the Scope of Application

137 cases were found citing Rome II—most of which are on closer inspection not covered by Rome II *ratione tempori*. One case involved a parking fine related to non-authorised parking in Antwerp (Belgium). Surprisingly enough, the court excluded the claim from the application of Brussels I for not being civil and commercial, but applied Rome II to the issue of applicable law.[21]

Of the 137 cases 29 dealt with intellectual property rights. Most of these are straightforward tort cases, but some are linked to the putative termination of a licence agreement. The second largest group deals with liability of officers and shareholders vis-à-vis third parties (19 cases). In those cases, a distinction has to be made between the law applying to the legal entity as such, insolvency law and tort law. The Netherlands being the navigable delta of two major European rivers, it comes as no surprise to find (riverine and maritime) collisions in third place. But as 'tort' is an open category in Dutch law, the set contains a myriad of claims based on all kind of 'wrong doings'. Quite a large group is based on liability for use of procedural rights: conservation measures which turn out later to be unsupported by a substantive claim, execution of a non-final judgment which is overturned in appeals, filing of a noxious claim, wilful reliance on a no longer valid foreign judgment etc. Also issues with regard to property rights pop up under the guise of tort claims: selling a picture

---

[20] In two prominent cases in which the foreign employer pleaded a closer connection to the common country or origin, this claim was rejected by the court. In a reverse situation (Dutch employer, Dutch worker), in a non-annotated case, the plea was followed by the court.

[21] NL:RBMNE:2014:5455.

without permission of the owner, refusing to hand-over stolen property etc. In some cases the delimitation with the Rome I Regulation is problematic. Parties to a (putative) contract may rely on tort or *negotiorum gestio* as a subsidiary base for their claim. Voidance of the contract may lead to claims for restitution, which under Dutch law may classify as being based on unjust enrichment. In these cases, the classification under Dutch substantive law seems to be used for private international law purposes as well, without the court referring to the European origin of (some of) the concepts. No preliminary questions were referred to the CJEU.[22]

The annotated cases deal with liability of officers and shareholders of companies,[23] and cross-border industrial action.[24]

b. Matters Related to Torts/Delicts

The Dutch practice struggles with the application of the *locus damni* rule. Under the previous (national) rule the place of the damages was only relevant for choice-of-law purposes in case of damage to persons, goods and/or the environment. The extension of the rule to more abstract types of damage—including pure financial loss—is met with criticism. There are also questions as to the application of the mosaic principle in case of scattered damage in non-IP cases. In a case of double application by analogy, the *e-Date* decision of the CJEU was applied to the interpretation of the place of the damage in Rome II with regard to a claim based on wrongful publication on the internet.[25] The problems associated with the *locus damni* rule might explain why, in disputed cases, the courts are quite willing to resort to the closer connection rule in cases of pure financial loss. But the closer connection rule is also used to refer back to the place of the tort rather than the common habitual residence eg in a case of medical malpractice (patient against doctor).

Transnational employment may lead to complex interactions of contractual and non-contractual issues which may undermine the effectiveness of Article 9. An example of—in our view—proper application of Article 9 can be found in ECLI:NL:RBROT:2014:7049, JAR 2014/222 note Franssen.

c. Matters Related to Unjust Enrichment, *Negotiorum Gestio* and *Culpa in Contrahendo*

Dutch lower courts tend to use the classification under domestic law as a starting point for the classification as contractual (Rome I) or non-contractual (Rome II) for choice-of-law purposes.

d. Matters Related to Other Provisions

The Netherlands is a party to the Hague Conventions on traffic accidents and product liability. These are routinely given precedence over Rome II.

---

[22] Compare on this issue in the context of jurisdiction: Case C-366/13, EU:C:2016:282.

[23] NL:GHARL:2015:6649, JOR 2016/89 note Van der Plas; NL:RBAMS:2012:BW3790 (Rome II not applicable *ratione temporis*) JOR 2012/177 note Olden.

[24] RBROT:2014:7049, JAR 2014/222 note Franssen.

[25] NL:HR:2016:1054 (*Dahabshiil*). Compare NL:GHSHE:2015:3904 (*Google USA*).

C. Practice/Process

i. Dutch National Courts' Practice in Interpreting the Regulations/Process Issues

In the Netherlands both the choice-of-law rules and foreign law have to be applied *ex officio*.[26] In a case of 2012 Advocate-General Vlas extended this duty to Article 7 of the Rome Convention: according to him the court has to apply foreign overriding mandatory provisions *ex officio*.[27] In practice, the application of foreign overriding mandatory provisions is extremely rare and doesn't occur unless one of the parties seeks to rely on the provision.

Also the duty to ascertain the content of foreign law *ex officio* is not always abided by—courts may invite the parties to submit pleadings on the content of foreign law,[28] appoint an expert or use Dutch law as a point of reference. These practices—which shift the financial burden of the enquiry to the parties—may be promoted by the fact that since 2010 the costs of seeking information on foreign law through the international legal institute (IJI) in the Hague is no longer fully covered by the ministry of justice but falls within the budget of the courts themselves.

To avoid the costs associated with the application of foreign law, courts may—and in practice regularly do—invite parties to make a choice-of-law in favour of *lex fori*. They also may assume that such a choice has tacitly been made when parties only refer to Dutch law in their submissions and pleadings. This may cause problems if one of the parties has second thoughts and wants to plead the application of foreign law on appeal.[29]

ii. Cost and Length of Litigation in Cross-border Civil and Commercial Disputes

In the plan for a Netherlands commercial court (NCC) the Dutch judiciary is depicted as cost-effective in comparison to the English court system and Dutch lawyers as less expensive than their US and UK counterparts.[30] However, the cost and length of litigation is increasingly becoming a problem in domestic cases as well. After the government raised the courts fees, the use of the court system for debt collection has dropped, evidenced by a sharp decrease of default judgments. There is little information on the extra costs and duration in cross-border cases.[31] According to a well-known IP lawyer, PIL complications do in fact deter claimants in IP cases from demanding extraterritorial injunctions.[32]

---

[26] Art 10:2 BW. RJ Blauwhoff and JMJ Keltjens, 'Rechtsvinding van buitenlands recht: wat wordt er van de rechter verwacht?' [2014] *Trema* 19–24, https://www.iji.nl/media/1010/artikel-trema.pdf.

[27] NL:PHR:2012:BW1254.

[28] See for example *NIPR* 2012-484.

[29] NL:PHR:2012:BV1523.

[30] Anglo-American style procedures would be approx five times as expensive as Dutch procedures.

[31] The plan for the NCC estimates that an international case before the NCC should cost approx. Euro 26.500 per case in court fees (if 50 per cent is settled before judgment) for the court to break even.

[32] www.dickvanengelen.nl/home/ie-ipr/boek-2007-webversie/hfst-v-internationale-rechtshandhaving/3-jurisdictie-grensoverschrijdende-procedures/3-1-grensoverschrijdende-veroordelingen.

iii. Settlement in Cross-border Civil and Commercial Disputes and ADR[33]

There are no special rules for cross-border disputes (in non-family matters—there is a special facility for Child Abduction cases). The plan for the NCC gives an estimate of a 50 per cent settlement rate after the start of the proceedings in first instance in commercial cases.

Consumers from EU countries Norway and Iceland can use the Dutch system of consumer complaint boards for complaints against Dutch providers covered by these boards— they are referred to the European Consumer Centres in their home state for assistance.[34] Specialised commercial ADR exists inter alia in international finance (http://primefinance-disputes.org/).

iv. Remedies in Cross-border Civil and Commercial Disputes

As a rule, Dutch courts do not hesitate to hand down cross-border injunctions.[35] Also non-money claims are regularly asked for and granted in cross-border situations.

III. The Netherlands' Experience in Cross-border Family Law Disputes

A. Jurisdictional and Procedural Issues Under the Brussels IIa Regulation

i. Matters Related to the Scope of Application

The question has arisen whether the concept of 'divorce' in Article 1 Brussels IIa also includes a possible divorce petition of a same-sex couple.[36] According to Dutch case law and literature,[37] this question is answered in the affirmative; same-sex couples are brought within this definition, albeit that with respect to registered partnerships they do not fall within the scope of the Regulation.

The distinction between parentage on the one hand and parental responsibility on the other can lead to complicated situations.[38] In many cases, a father who has been denied the possibility to recognise his child files a petition to the court for substitute permission to recognise the child. This is oftentimes coupled with an ancillary petition for a contact

---

[33] See also Aukje van Hoek and Joris Kocken, 'The Netherlands' in C Esplugues, JL Iglesias, G Palao (eds), *Civil and Commercial Mediation in Europe*, pt I (national mediation rules and procedures) and II (cross-border mediation) (Antwerpen, Intersentia, 2013 and 2014).

[34] https://www.degeschillencommissie.nl/english/.

[35] For an exception see NL:RBLIM:2013:4521. The general stance of the Dutch courts is based on the *Interlas* case of the Supreme Court: see www.dickvanengelen.nl/home/ie-ipr/boek-2007-webversie/hfst-v-internationale-rechtshandhaving/3-jurisdictie-grensoverschrijdende-procedures/3-1-grensoverschrijdende-veroordelingen. Only in clear cut cases under uniform law he would advise to demand an extra-territorial injunction.

[36] See, for example, I Curry-Sumner, *All's well that ends registered?* (Antwerpen etc, Intersentia, 2005) 428–29.

[37] See, for example, M Bogdan, 'Registered partnerships and EC law' in K Boele-Woelki and A Fuchs (eds), *Legal Recognition of Same-sex Couples in Europe* (Antwerpen etc, Intersentia, 2001) 171–77.

[38] See, for example, NL:GHDHA:2013:4924.

arrangement to be set. These two petitions—although highly connected—do not both fall within the substantive scope of the Brussels II-bis Regulation.

The Netherlands applies the rules of Brussels IIa to situations which fall outside of the scope of the Regulation.[39] In highly exceptional circumstances, reference may be made to the *forum necessitatis* provision in Article 9 of the Dutch Code of Civil Procedure.[40]

ii. Matters Related to Jurisdiction

a. Divorce, Legal Separation and Marriage Annulment

The main issue that normally arises is the factual determination of the habitual residence of the parties.[41] As the CJEU has only issued judgments with respect to the definition of the term 'habitual residence' in the context of children, Dutch courts have resorted to applying the same criteria with respect to the determination of the habitual residence of adults.[42]

In a case before the Court of Appeal of The Hague, the Court held that it had jurisdiction on the grounds of Article 9(b) Dutch Code of Civil Procedure (*forum necessitatis*), despite the fact that the Brussels IIa Regulation was applicable.[43] The case concerned a couple resident in Malta. In this case, Malta was the only country according to the Regulation that had jurisdiction to entertain divorce proceedings, but Maltese law (at that time) did not allow for divorce. As a result, the parties were unable to divorce. The Dutch court, applying principles of *favor divortii*, determined that resort had to be made to the *forum necessitatis* provision in Dutch private international law.

With respect to references to nationality in Article 3, it would also appear that the Dutch courts use the *Hadadi* decision to determine that formal possession of the nationality is required regardless of where the reference to nationality is made (ie Article 3(1)(a)(6), 3(1)(b) or Article 6).[44]

b. Parental Responsibility

1. Child Abduction

In the Netherlands, this jurisdiction has been concentrated with one court, namely the District Court of The Hague.[45] All return proceedings are therefore brought before this Court and initiated on the grounds of the Hague Child Abduction Convention. If the abduction is intra-EU, then the extra provisions laid down in Article 11 Brussels IIa will also be applied. If the child has been wrongfully removed to another European Union Member State, then the Dutch court will retain jurisdiction on the grounds of Article 10 Brussels IIa.[46] Article 7 Hague Child Protection Convention 1996 is applied in cases involving an abduction to a non-EU Member State.

---

[39] Art 4(1) Dutch Code of Civil Procedure.
[40] T de Boer and F Ibili (eds), *Nederlands Internationaal Personen- en Familierecht* (Deventer, Kluwer, 2012) 137–38.
[41] NL:GHSHE:2011:BU4882.
[42] Case C-497/10 PPU *Mercredi* EU:C:2010:829 and Case C-523/07 *A* EU:C:2009:225.
[43] Hof Den Haag 21 December 2005, (2006) *NIPR* 101.
[44] de Boer and Ibili, above n 40, 139.
[45] Art 11 Dutch Child Abduction Implementation Act.
[46] NL:GHSHE:2011:BU4882.

2. Access

Article 9 of the Regulation allows for a special rule on the modification of a pre-existing judgment on the rights of access. In practice, this provision is very rarely used and has not provided for any case law at all in Dutch practice. Part of the reason is that the provision itself includes a three-month time frame within which the petition must be filed, but this is from the moment of the lawful move. In this case, the move has taken place with consent, and normally does not lead immediately to a dispute. As a result, the moment at which a dispute arises is normally in practice long after the three-month period has expired. In that case, Article 9 can no longer be used, and instead parties are bound by the main rule contained in Article 8, coupled with the possibility to have proceedings transferred via Article 15.

3. Other Issues Related to Parental Responsibility

Article 8

According to Article 8, the courts of a Member State shall have jurisdiction in matters of parental responsibility over a child who is habitually resident in that Member State at the time the court is seised. This has raised three main issues. First, the determination of habitual residence has caused problems. A mother with sole parental responsibility left the Netherlands and indicated that she was moving to Spain. Instead she moved to Portugal. Two weeks thereafter the father filed for a contact arrangement to be set by a court in Amsterdam, as well as sole parental responsibility (and a subsidiary claim for joint parental responsibility). The question arose whether the Dutch court has jurisdiction in the case. If the habitual residence of the child was deemed to be in the Netherlands, then the Dutch court would have jurisdiction, if not then the Portuguese courts would be deemed to have jurisdiction. The Dutch courts held that although the removal of the child from the Netherlands by the mother was not wrongful, her intention was clear to ensure that the father and the child were denied contact. The permanence of the residence in Portugal was not established, and the centre of the child's life was at the time of filing of the petition still in the Netherlands. As a result, the Dutch courts had jurisdiction to deal with the petition of the father. In the end, the Dutch court awarded the father sole parental responsibility, a decision which then needed to be recognised and enforced in Portugal (see below).

The second issue that causes some difficulty for the Dutch courts, but would not necessarily appear to be a problem with the Brussels IIa Regulation itself, relates to the moment at which the habitual residence needs to be determined. According to Article 8 this should be at the moment that the petition is filed. This therefore precludes references to facts and circumstances that occur after this date. However, it is sometimes the case that the court will take account of facts and circumstances that occur after the date of filing of the petition, especially if an extended period of time has elapsed between the filing of the petition and the date of the hearing.

The third and final issue that relates to this provision is the concept of *perpetuatio fori*. It becomes increasingly difficult to justify that the Dutch courts should retain jurisdiction over a case even after a significant period of time has elapsed since the filing of the initial petition. If the child now lives in another EU Member State, reference has increasingly been made to Article 15 (discussed below).

Article 15

Article 15 has begun to be used by Dutch courts normally only if one of the parties explicitly requests a transfer.

Article 20

The Dutch Supreme Court was asked whether the petition to renew an emergency protection order, supervision order and placement out of the house fell within the scope of Article 20. The Dutch Supreme Court held that although the original judicial decision for a supervision order together with an emergency out-of-house placement fell within the scope of Article 20, and thus these orders could be issued in respect of children who were on holiday in the Netherlands (but who had their habitual residence in England and Wales), but that this provision could not be used with respect to the renewal of such orders as the 'urgent' nature of the petition was no longer present.

iii. Matters Related to Recognition and Enforcement

a. Rights of Access

The question has arisen that if the person who is in possession of an access decision, which satisfies the conditions laid down in Brussels IIa, wishes to enforce the foreign decision, whether the Dutch authorities have any possibility to prevent such contact from taking place, if the circumstances have changed since the foreign access decision was made. The second issue that has arisen is whether the provisions of Section 4, Chapter III apply if the person wishing to have the foreign decision regarding access rights enforced does not have the Article 41 certificate. Is the Article 41 certificate regarded as a pre-requisite to the enforcement of a foreign access decision without the need for a declaration of enforceability? Both of these issues have not yet led to published decisions.

iv. Cooperation between Central Authorities in matters of parental responsibility

There is no real information available on this issue apart from the number of cases on Article 56, Brussels IIa. There have been 28 cases dealt with by the Central Authority, 8 outgoing and 20 incoming. All, except one, were intra-EU cases mainly dealing with the placement of children in Germany.

v. Relations with Other Instruments

Interaction with the Hague Child Protection Convention causes many practical problems.[47]

B. Jurisdictional and Procedural Issues and Applicable Law Under the Maintenance Regulation

i. Matters Related to the Scope of Application

Couples who cohabit do not, according to substantive Dutch law, owe each other a maintenance obligation. If, however, they decide that they wish to support each other if their relationship breaks down, then they are entitled to do so in a contractual maintenance agreement. According to Article 1, it is unclear whether such a maintenance obligation falls

---

[47] See, for example, NL:GHARL:2014:805.

within the scope of the Regulation, as this is not based on family relationship, parentage, marriage and affinity. According to previous Dutch case law, the term 'family relationship' should be understood as meaning based on family law. As a contractual maintenance requirement is based in contract law according to Dutch law, the question arises whether this issue is covered by the Regulation.

ii. Matters Related to Jurisdiction

In some jurisdictions the term 'creditor' refers to the child, whereas in others the term refers to the adult who is caring for the child and thus receiving the child maintenance. This can cause problems. If a mother has a non-EU nationality and lives outside the EU with her child, whereas the Dutch father lives in the Netherlands, if he requests a modification of a previous decision, the Dutch courts would be deemed to have competency if the phrase 'parties' in Article 6 refers to the child and him (assuming that the child also has Dutch nationality through the father), but would not have jurisdiction if the term referred to the mother and father. Despite the uncertainty, no Dutch court has seen the need to refer a case to the CJEU.

iii. Cooperation between Central Authorities

At present the only issue that has arisen is whether the terms of co-operation also apply when the Dutch Central Authority is requested to assist a maintenance creditor living in the Netherlands, when the maintenance debtor files a modification request through the foreign Central Authority. According to the Regulation, it would appear that the Dutch Central Authority is to assist in the making of the application, but the application has already been made. The issue is important because if the Dutch Central Authority is obliged to assist the maintenance debtor in his request for modification, this would create a conflict of interests as the Dutch Central Authority is oftentimes also the procedural representation for the creditor in the initial proceedings.

C. Practice/Process

i. Dutch National Courts' Practice in Interpreting the Regulations

The Netherlands has a practice of referring to cases from the Court of Justice of the European Union in its case law. It is interesting to note that references to the CJEU in the field of family law are oftentimes sent from lower courts whereas references pertaining to Brussels I, and Rome I and II almost exclusively originate from the Dutch Supreme Court. Recently the sheer number of rulings from the CJEU has led to a number of decisions not being applied by Dutch courts.

ii. Settlement in Cross-border Family Law Disputes

Issues have arisen in the context of cross-border abduction cases, dealing with the problem of jurisdiction. The cross-border mediation that has been created and welcomed in the Netherlands is only aimed at reaching a settlement within the context of the abduction proceedings. It is not intended to create a complete package of agreements dealing with ancillary matters of maintenance, the division of care or the property settlement. However, due to the complexity of the family setting, in many cases this is indeed what the parties desire to have arranged, and not simply a decision on whether the child will be returned. In practice the Dutch court will take jurisdiction to homologate an agreement on future residence of the child, parental rights and visiting rights, when the agreed future residence is situated in the Netherlands.[48]

D. Preliminary Remarks on Effectiveness of the Current EU PIL Framework in Cross-border Family Law

One thought for the EU legislature in this field should be to consolidate and better co-ordinate the legislation that is applicable to ensure the effective application of these instruments in practice.

---

[48] Aukje van Hoek, 'Mediation in Cross-Border Family Matters, The Dutch Experience' in Ivana Kunda (ed), *Family and Children; European Expectations and National Reality* (Rijeka, Rijeka Faculty of Law, 2014) 79–85.

26

Portugal

ELSA DIAS OLIVEIRA, JOÃO GOMES DE ALMEIDA, EUGÉNIA
GALVÃO TELES, SUSANA MALTEZ AND RAQUEL CORREIA

I. Introduction

As Portugal is a Civil Law system, codified statutes prevail, although under specific circumstances the Supremo Tribunal de Justiça (STJ) can deliver judgments unifying jurisprudence.[1] Both the STJ and Tribunais de Relação (TR) are appeal courts. Proceedings are usually instituted before first instance courts.

The applicable law is determined and applied *ex officio* whether or not parties prove its content.[2]

The Portuguese database only includes cases decided by appeal courts.

II. Portugal's Experience on Cross-border Civil and Commercial Disputes

A. Jurisdictional and Procedural Issues Under the Brussels I Regulation

i. Matters Related to the Scope of Application

The material scope of the Brussels I Regulation was generally respected in jurisdiction and recognition matters.[3]

ii. Matters Related to Jurisdiction

In sale of goods contracts, the relevant obligation is effective delivery of the goods,[4] particularly their final destination.[5] Incoterms, including Ex Works, were considered to relate only

---

[1] See Arts 688–695 Civil Procedure Code (CPC).

[2] See Art 348 Civil Code (CC).

[3] eg STJ 03-03-2005 Case:04A4283. All cited decisions are available in Portuguese at www.dgsi.pt, unless otherwise stated.

[4] eg STJ 04-07-2013 Case:1816/08.5TBVLG.P1.S2.

[5] eg Tribunal da Relação do Porto (TRP) 05-06-2008 Case:0831114.

to the transfer of the risk, and were thus irrelevant in determining the place of delivery.[6] Yet, the decisions are prior to *Electrosteel*.[7] Some rare decisions still resort to the applicable law to identify the place of delivery of goods.[8]

In a recent case[9] where both parties considered the supply of manufactured window frames to be a provision of services, the STJ characterised it as a sale of goods because the merchandise was delivered at the buyer's domicile, without mentioning the *CarTrim*[10] criteria.

Agency contracts are characterised as provisions of services under Article 5(1)(b),[11] whereas distribution agreements have fallen under Article 5(1)(a),[12] despite the STJ identifying the promotion and distribution of the goods in a given area as the character-istic performance. These decisions preceded *Corman-Collins*.[13] In factoring, the services characterisation is clearly established under Article 5(1)(b) and in international factoring, the characteristic performance of the inter-factors agreement was considered to be that of the importing factor.[14]

Article 5(1)(a) applied in a contract for the televised transmission of football games, as it neither provided for the sale of goods nor provision of services.[15]

In Article 5(3), courts usually interpret the 'place where the harmful event occurred' correctly.[16]

Jurisdiction under Article 6(1) was refused because the Portuguese anchor defendant only joined the proceedings after the claim was lodged.[17]

A Portuguese plaintiff suffered damages working in Andorra for an employer insured by a French company; he sued the French insurer in Portugal. Although he was domiciled in Portugal, the court directed him to Andorra (place of the wrongful damage) or France (domicile of the insurer): Article 9(1)(b) 'beneficiaries' do not include 'injured parties'.[18] When the claim is not based on the insurance contract, the application of Article 9 is also refused.[19]

Article 19(2)(b) was applied where a director worked habitually abroad but was hired in Portugal.[20] In another case, the application of Article 19 was refused because the employee worked in Portugal for less than one month, the only available rule being the employer's domicile in the United Kingdom.[21]

---

[6] eg STJ 23-10-2007 Case:07A3119.
[7] Case C-87/10 *Electrosteel* [2011] ECR I-04987.
[8] eg TRP 05-06-2008 Case:0831114.
[9] STJ 05-04-2016 Case:27630/13.8YIPRT-A.G1.S1.
[10] Case C-381/08 *Car Trim* [2010] ECR I-01255.
[11] STJ 04-08-2010 Case:4632/07.8TBBCL.G1.S1.
[12] eg STJ 29-04-2010 Case: 622/081TVPRT.P1.S1.
[13] Case C-9/12 *Corman-Collins* EU:C:2013:860.
[14] STJ 21-06-2011 Case:985/09.1TVLSB.L1.S1.
[15] STJ 21-05-2009 Case:4986/06.3TVLSB.S1.
[16] eg, STJ 24-10-2007 Case:07S2098.
[17] STJ 27-02-2003 Case:03B102.
[18] STJ 03-03-2005 Case:04A4283.
[19] STJ 25-01-2012 Case:1710/10.0TTPNF.P1.S1.
[20] TRP 16-04-2012 Case:13/10.4TTPRT-A.P1.
[21] TRL 10-09-2014 Case:2641/13.7TTLSB.L1-4.

The severability of jurisdiction clauses is systematically affirmed even though the validity of these clauses is quite frequently challenged.[22]

Article 38 of the Portuguese Agency Act[23] limits any choice-of-law compromising the application of the Portuguese (more favourable) termination rules. It has been unsuccessfully invoked against jurisdiction clauses because a choice of a foreign court is not affected by Article 38.[24]

The relevance of other national requirements, in particular the Portuguese Unfair Contract Terms Act (UCTA)[25] and its Article 19(g) 'serious inconvenience v legitimate interests' test is not definitively settled.

Under the prevailing view, Article 23's 'exclusive and exhaustive nature' rules out all national controls,[26] including those based on the UCTA. Yet, in some decisions, the reasoning makes it difficult to understand if the UCTA is rejected because of Article 23 or simply because no consumer is involved.[27]

More generally, despite affirmations of Article 23's all-encompassing nature, with regular quoting of *Castelletti*[28] and *Elefanten Schuh*,[29] the re-introduction of national rules through the interpretation of Article 23(1)'s 'written form' requirement is discernible in some decisions.[30] The same courts, considering similar facts, apply Article 23(1) and consider that the 'tacit consent' test is fulfilled.[31] Some (rare) decisions even apply the UCTA directly, rejecting jurisdiction clauses printed on the back of invoices.[32]

Very few decisions deal with Article 23(b) or (c) criteria.[33]

Jurisdiction clauses were challenged as Article 23 was deemed inapplicable to non-international cases. Initially courts defended a restrictive concept of internationality, not treating as relevant, inter alia, that one party was a Spanish company's subsidiary and limiting Article 23 to cases with parties domiciled in different countries or contracts concluded and/or performed in a foreign country.[34] More recently, in swap contracts, a more flexible and comprehensive approach was adopted and Article 23 applied. The swaps were entered into between a Portuguese bank, ultimately a subsidiary of a Spanish bank, and

---

[22] eg, STJ 28-02-2008 Case:07B1321, quoting case C-269/95 *Benincasa v Dentalkit* [1997] ECR I-03767.

[23] Decreto-Lei 178/86;amendment: Decreto-Lei 118/93.

[24] Among others, the uniform jurisprudence decision STJ 28-02-2008 Case:07B1321. The point did not integrate the operative part; all subsequent decisions go in the same direction: STJ 27-05-2008 Case:08B278, TRL 14-06-2011 Case:6207/09.8TBOER.L1-7, TRL 01-02-2011 Case:57/10.0TBOER.L1-7.

[25] Decreto-Lei 446/85; last amendment: Decreto-Lei 323/2001.

[26] eg, expressly: STJ 19-11-2015 Case:2864/12.6TBVCD.P1.S1; quoting CJEU case law, namely C-159/97 *Castelletti* [1999] ECR I-01597.

[27] Referring expressly to this ground as one of the reasons to refuse, among others, the UCTA application: STJ 19.11.2015 Case:2864/12.6TVBCD.P1.S1; TRL 19-11-2013 Case:1001/10.6TVLSB.L1-1: considering a company as a consumer; reversed by reason of, *inter alia*, the commercial nature of both parties—STJ 11-02-2015 Case:877/12.7TVLSB.L1-A.S1.

[28] Case C-159/97 *Castelletti* [1999] ECR I-01597.

[29] Case C-150/80 *Elefanten Schuh GmbH v Jacqmain* [1981] ECR 01671

[30] eg STJ 09-07-2014 Case:165595/11.1YIPRT.G2.S1.

[31] eg STJ 11-02-2015 Case:877/12.7TVLSB.L1-A.S1 where the text of the decision refers to the clause being necessarily checked 'by a party exercising reasonable care'.

[32] eg STJ 09-07-2014 Case:165595/11.1YIPRT.G2.S1.

[33] TRL 08-10-2009 Case:47/08.9TNLSB.L1-6: applying the 'international trade usages' criteria to the choice of transporter's courts.

[34] TRP 23-05-2006 Case:0620651.

various Portuguese publicly-owned regional companies. They contained an International Swaps and Derivatives Association clause granting jurisdiction to English courts and a choice-of-law clause for application of English law.[35] Both parties were domiciled in Portugal, where the contract was also concluded and performed.[36] Yet, several international elements were considered as relevant: the international nature of the negotiation process; the existence of underlying contracts with international elements; the ability under the contract to perform the obligations in a foreign country, under a 'Multibranch Party' clause; and the choice of a foreign law,[37] despite Article 3(3) of the Rome Convention's applicability.[38] The courts did not take any position on the application of Article 3(3) to the choice-of-law; they only pointed out that its applicability would not prevent the choice from being 'international'. There are even hints on the 'intrinsic' international nature of swaps and other financial derivatives markets.[39] The STJ did not consider if the jurisdiction clause, in itself, was enough for the situation to be international.[40]

Portuguese courts seem to consider that the relevant point in time to assess the validity of jurisdiction clauses is the moment the proceedings are instituted.[41] Whether the validity of a jurisdiction clause at the time of the contract's conclusion should be upheld despite it being invalid under the new rules remains a disputed issue.[42]

Claims that violation of choice-of-court agreements amounted to procedural abuse have been systematically rejected.[43]

It was decided that choice-of-court does not affect the parties' ability to submit to other courts.[44] Previous submission does not preclude the ability to invoke choice-of-court in subsequent lawsuits: the court considered that submission only covers the subject-matter of the dispute before the court.[45] The relevant moment is the defendant's first answer to the claim ('*contestação*').[46] Despite the Portuguese version of Article 24 referring to the 'sole purpose' of contesting jurisdiction, courts unanimously accept that defendants can contest on the merits without submitting if they contest the jurisdiction at least as soon as the merits.[47]

Courts examine international jurisdiction rules *ex officio*[48] except when jurisdiction clauses[49] are invoked unless they affect exclusive or protective jurisdiction.

---

[35] STJ 26-01-2016 Case:540/14.4TVLSB.S1; STJ 04-02-2016 Case:536/14.6TVBLSB.L1.S1; STJ 11-02-2015 Case:877/12.7TVLSB.L1.A.S1.

[36] STJ 26-01-2016 Case:540/14.4TVLSB.S1.

[37] STJ 04-02-2016 Case:536/14.6TVLSB.L1.S1; STJ 26-01-2016 Case:540/14.4TVLSB.S1; STJ 11-02-2015 Case:877/12.7TVLSB.L1-A.S1.

[38] STJ 04-02-2016 Case:536/14.6TVLSB.L1.S1.

[39] STJ 04-02-2016 Case:536/14.6TVLSB.L1.S1; STJ 11.02.2015, Case:877/12.7TVLSB.L1-A.S1.

[40] As there were enough elements of internationality covered by CJEU case law, namely Case C-478/12 *Maletic* EU:C:2013:735 and Case C-281/02 *Owusu* [2005] ECR I-1383, the request for a referral for a preliminary ruling was refused under Case C-283/81 *CILFIT* [1982] ECR 03415.

[41] STJ 27-05-2008 Case:08B278; the point was however relatively immaterial as the requirements were similar: the conflict was between the application of Art 17 of the Brussels Convention or Art 23 of the Reg.

[42] Referring to the 'legal framework in force when the contract is concluded' as the relevant point in time: STJ 28-02-2008 Case:07B1321.

[43] eg STJ 04-02-2016 Case:536/14.6TVLSB.L1.S1.

[44] STJ 27-05-2008 Case:08B278.

[45] TRP 01-10-2015 Case:588/13.6TVPRT.P1.

[46] TRL 10-09-2014 Case:2641/13.7TTLSB.L1-4.

[47] eg STJ 10-05-2007 Case:07B072.

[48] STJ 03-03-2005 Case:04A4283.

[49] STJ 11-02-2015 Case:877/12.7TVLSB.L1-A.S1.

iii. Matters Related to Recognition and Enforcement

Five main questions were unequivocally addressed:

1. National courts follow an independent interpretation of the term 'judgment', as prescribed in Article 32;[50]
2. Partial declaration of enforceability is feasible, either at the applicant's request[51] or by a court's decision;[52]
3. The exclusion of arbitration applies to judgments by a court of a Member State enforcing an arbitral award;[53]
4. Chapter III applies both to judgments still susceptible of ordinary appeal[54] and decisions vulnerable to other judicial challenges,[55] following the extensive interpretation of Article 46 by the Court of Appeal, in order to stay proceedings not only when an ordinary appeal can be lodged against the judgment but also when it can be modified or reversed if irreversible economic damage is foreseeable;[56]
5. Provisional and protective measures can also be recognised and enforced.[57]

No specific problems arose regarding recognition itself. Difficulties arising from an incidental question of recognition[58] or from a *res judicata* plea blocking further proceedings were correctly resolved.[59] At this stage, the party against whom enforcement was sought could not interfere nor could the judge make a review under Articles 34 or 35.[60]

Irregularities affecting Article 42(2) notifications, namely lack of service or absence of internal law prescribed documents, resulted in several appeals on grounds of public policy. These were usually correctly rejected because those formalities were subsequent to the decision of enforceability itself (the only act under scrutiny). The questions should be raised before the court where application was first submitted, and answered by national procedure rules.[61] Lack of notification invoked before the right court thwarted the enforceability of the judgment, notwithstanding the possibility of a later declaration attributing enforceability after regular notification.[62]

Finally, parties not appealing against an Article 43 enforcement order are precluded, at the enforcement stage, from relying on a valid ground.[63]

Courts recurrently prevent controls not mentioned in Article 34, under the mutual trust between courts and free circulation of judgments principles.[64] A correct articulation with Articles 35 and 36 has prevented control of jurisdiction of the Member State of origin's

---

[50] Tribunal da Relação de Évora (TRE) 14-12-2006 Case:260/06-3.
[51] TRL 8-10-2015 Case:4070/09.8TVLSB.L1-2.
[52] TRL 27-09-2007 Case:5177/2007-2.
[53] TRL 27-09-2007 Case:5177/2007-2, mentioning C-190/89 *Rich* ECR I-03855.
[54] TRP 12-09-2011 Case:7045/10.0TBVNG.P1.
[55] Namely the Italian '*decreto ingiuntivo*'.
[56] Tribunal da Relação de Coimbra (TRC) 20-01-2009 Case:545/07.1TBOBR.C1.
[57] TRL 26-01-2016 Case:736/14.9TVLSB.L1-7. Cf TRL 12-09-2013 Case:7614/12.4TBCSC.L1-6.
[58] TRL 26.01.2016 Case:736/14.9TVLSB.L1-7.
[59] TRL 08-10-2015 Case:4070/09.8TVLSB.L1-2.
[60] STJ 09-07-2015 Case: 134/14.4TBCBC.G1.S1.
[61] TRC 17-03-2015 Case:979/14.5TBFIG.C1; TRL 21-02-2008 Case:373/2008-2.
[62] TRL 16-06-2009 Case:4684/06.8TBOER-A-7.
[63] TRP 21-09-2010 Case:1900/08.5TJVNF-B.P1.
[64] eg STJ 09-07-2015 Case:134/14.4TBCBC.G1.S1.

court[65] and analysis of the applicable law[66] under the public policy heading, conferring the necessary respect to the finding of facts and law made by the court of origin.[67]

Insufficient reasoning is systematically alleged as an infringement of public policy. However, appeal courts have rejected this contention for several reasons: incongruence with the exclusive demand of a copy of the judgment in Article 53; no reference to this in the Article 34 grounds for refusal; lack of reasoning is not considered a ground for refusing recognition in Portuguese internal law;[68] and the STJ states that the foreign judgment should not be reviewed on the merits.[69]

Portuguese case law reveals a restrictive attitude towards the scope of public policy in Brussels I.[70] The STJ differentiated public policy from international public policy and established that scrutiny of the former would inevitably lead to a revision on substance[71] and quotes CJEU case law in favour of this restrictive attitude.[72]

Violations of public policy are sometimes upheld[73] and breaches of Portuguese substantive public policy can be prevented.[74]

Besides that, Article 34(2) has been judiciously applied, following European Union case law courts adopt a functional definition.[75] It is sufficient that the document is served on the defendant in sufficient time and in such a way as to allow him to prepare his defence.[76]

Whenever defendants object on non-notification grounds[77] the judge of enforcement may examine whether the documents instituting the proceedings were properly served.[78] Notwithstanding the information contained in an Article 54 certificate and the French court's pronouncement that all required steps to discover the defendant's address were taken, recognition and enforcement was refused because the court of origin had decided on false factual premises.[79]

The STJ recently relied on CJEU case law[80] to hold that an Article 54 certificate does not have binding legal effect, considering that, under Articles 36 and 45(2), denial of review as to substance is circumscribed to foreign judgments. Consequently, the State of enforcement's power to carry out its own examination of the premises underlying individual provisions and examine conformity with the evidence of the information contained in an Article 34(2) certificate is never excluded.[81]

---

[65] STJ 25-11-2014 Case:1298/13.OTTLSB.L1.S1.

[66] TRP 30-06-2011 Case:158/07.8TBMDB.P1.

[67] STJ 20-06-2013 Case:1939/11.3T2AVR.C1.S1; STJ 11-03-2010 Case:2580/08.3TVLSB.L1.S1.

[68] TRE 14-12-2006 Case:260/06-3; TRL 12-12-2006 Case:5397/2006-7.

[69] eg STJ 20-11-2014 Case:7614/12.4TBCSC.L1.S1.

[70] eg TRL 26-01-2016 Case:736/14.9TVLSB.L1-7.

[71] STJ 20-06-2013 Case:1939/11.3T2AVR.C1.S1.

[72] eg STJ 09-07-2015 Case:134/14.4TBCBC.G1.S1. Most commonly quoted are Case C-7/98 *Krombach* [2000] ECR I-01935; Case C-38/98 *Renault* [2000] ECR I-02973; and Case C-394/07 *Gambazzi* [2009] ECR I-02563.

[73] eg TRL 08-02-2007 Case:3876/2006.

[74] STJ 09-07-2015 Case:134/14.4TBCBC.G1.S1. Cf TRL 15-01-2009 Case:7639/2007-6.

[75] In particular, Case C-283/05 *ASML* [2006] ECR I-12041.

[76] eg TRE 10-01-2013 Case:134/11.6TBCUB.E1 and TRL 21-01-2016 Case:5007/13.STBCSC.L1-6.

[77] Specially based on Case C-619/10 *Trade Agency* EU:C:2012:531.

[78] Tribunal da Relação de Guimarães (TRG) 27-10-2014 Case:134/14.4TBCBC.G1; TRE 10-01-2013 Case:134/11.6TBCUB.E1.

[79] TRL 21-01-2016 Case:5007/13.STBCSC.L1-6.

[80] Case C-619/10 *Trade Agency* EU:C:2012:531.

[81] STJ 09-07-2015 Case:134/14.4TBCBC.G1.S1.

Courts apply Article 34(2) correctly precluding reliance on formal irregularities in the Member State of origin which did not cause injustice to the defendant, including where the defendant failed to commence proceedings in the State of origin to challenge the default judgment if it was effectively possible for him to do so.

iv. Matters Related to Relations with Other Instruments

Delimitations in relation to both the Brussels Convention and the (recast) Brussels I Regulation have been clearly established.[82] Articulation with the European Enforcement Order Regulation has also been made, establishing that no further *exequatur* procedures were necessary.[83] A decision from the Tribunal da Relação de Guimarães (TRG) deals with the application of the European Order for Payment Regulation.[84] The Service Regulation is often interconnected with Article 34(2) of the Brussels I Regulation and the possibility of refusing judgment even when Article 19(2) conditions are met and duly respected.[85] Finally, within its scope, the Maintenance Regulation prevails over the Brussels I Regulation.[86]

v. Conclusion

In insurance, a clearer distinction between Article 9(1)(b) 'beneficiaries' and Article 11 'injured parties' would help, as well as a clarification of the notion 'based in contract'.

Despite being generally upheld, jurisdiction clauses seem to have the paradoxical effect of encouraging litigation instead of preventing it. Even if the prevailing view is that Article 23 requirements are 'exhaustive and exclusive' there are some contradictory decisions that need to be ironed out.[87]

The only new issue concerns the internationality pre-requisite. As seen above, Portuguese courts recently took a very liberal and comprehensive interpretation of the requirement. The consequences of this approach are significant, in particular if one considers the new solutions for choice-of-court agreements in the recast Regulation. A referral to the CJEU has been requested. It should establish if the conditions mentioned above in the context of swaps are sufficient for the contract to be international and Article 23 to apply. The referral also considers the possibility that a jurisdiction clause alone can establish internationality.[88]

A consistent practice was achieved concerning recognition and enforcement. National rules were residually invoked and applied, perhaps because Portugal's former recognition system already favoured formal recognition and was close to the Regulation purposes.

Notwithstanding the restrictive conception of public policy adopted by Portuguese courts, it is routinely alleged by the parties, especially when Article 34(2) is involved or where documents instituting the procedure are alleged to have been improperly served. Courts are therefore compelled to examine the circumstances underlying each notification

---

[82] Respectively TRE 14-12-2006 Case:260/06-3 and TRL 21-01-2016 Case:5007/13.STBCSC.L1-6.

[83] TRE 17-12-2015 Case:572/14.2TBPTG-B-E1.

[84] TRG 10-12-2013 Case:691/11.7TVPRT-A.G1.

[85] TRL 08-02-2007 Case:3876/2006.

[86] TRP 03-06-2013 Case:1707/11.2TBPVZ-A.P1.

[87] The situation of uncertainty is expressly recognised in STJ 11-11-2003 Case:03A3137.

[88] Pending Case C-136/16 *Sociedade Metropolitana de Desenvolvimento*.

whenever someone objects on non-service bases. This approach compromises the Regulation's central purpose of simplification. Yet, it was not eradicated by the CJEU[89] which found that exceptional cases where the right to a fair hearing is breached that are not covered by Article 34(2) can fall under Article 34(1). Either these cases are strictly stated in a clearer way or litigation is bound to increase.

B. Applicable Law Issues Under the Rome I and Rome II Regulations

i. Rome I

Scope rules are generally well applied. Surprisingly, a first instance court decided it lacked jurisdiction based on Rome I but the Tribunal da Relação do Porto (TRP) reversed the decision explaining the difference between jurisdiction and choice-of-law.[90] Due to temporal scope issues almost all appeal decisions still apply the Rome Convention.[91]

In a judgment concerning the sale of a defective crane, the STJ decided that foreign law must be interpreted within the context of the system to which it belongs and in accordance with that system's interpretative rules, which imposes recourse to the dominant case law and doctrine.[92] At stake was a TRP decision that, under a literal interpretation, characterised the time period of Article 1490 of the Spanish Civil Code as *prescrição*, which ceases to run during judicial vacations, while the prevalent view in Spanish case law and doctrine favours characterisation as *caducidad*. The STJ also analysed Portuguese law (country of performance) and Spanish law (*lex causae*) in the context of Article 12(2) of Rome I. It concluded that the solution given in both laws is similar but mentioned solely Portuguese law in its summary.

The Tribunal da Relação de Lisboa (TRL) characterised as a provision of services a contract—termed 'management mandate'—whereby X should 'rent' out to third parties the use of Y's timeshare in an immovable property and pay Y a fixed amount. The court held that the focus of the contract was on the 'service' provided by X, remuneration being the difference between the amount paid and the 'rents' that X actually received. It did not mention Article 4(2).[93]

Cases on employment contracts show a tendency to apply Portuguese law and concerns about compliance of foreign law with Portuguese constitutional provisions on job security (Article 53) and the right of defence (Article 32). Often cases present methodological problems, in particular, regarding the distinction between mandatory rules, overriding mandatory rules and public policy,[94] although a recent STJ decision indicates significant improvement.[95]

---

[89] eg Case C-7/98 *Krombach* [2000] ECR I-01935.

[90] TRP 29-10-2013 Case:153217/12.8YIPRT.P1. Confusion by lawyer:TRG 04-02-2016 Case:571/15.7T8 VRL.G1.

[91] eg STJ 14-01-2016 Case:529/13.0TTOAZ.P1.S1.

[92] STJ 26-02-2015 Case:693/10.0TVPRT.C1.P1.S1.

[93] TRL 19-11-2015 Case:604/12.9TCFUN.L1-6.

[94] eg TRP 02-06-2014 Case:930/08.1TTPRT.P2; TRL 15-12-2011 Case:149/04.0TTCSC.L1-4.

[95] STJ 12-05-2016 Case:2998/14.2TTLSB.L1.S1.

All cases apply the Rome Convention, thus falling outside the remit of this report. However, the main trends may persist under the Regulation since the revision was minimal in this context.

The two published appeal judgments show difficulties with Article 4's requirement of characterising the contract and with distinguishing, under Article 12(2), between applying the law of the place of performance and merely taking it into account, particularly where it is the *lex fori*.

The STJ decision sets a good example by analysing all pertinent Articles of the Regulation, Spanish statutory law, case law and doctrine and stressing the importance of following foreign case law and doctrine in interpreting foreign law.

ii. Rome II

a. Matters Related to the Scope of Application

In general, Articles 31 and 32 were correctly interpreted and the Regulation was only applied to events giving rise to damage after 11 January 2009.[96] *Homawoo*[97] has been correctly quoted by the courts.

In a few cases, the Regulation was applied when proceedings were brought after 11 January 2009 even though the events giving rise to damage occurred before that date.[98]

b. Matters Related to Torts/Delicts

Interpretation of 'direct damage' was usually made according to Recitals 16–17 and CJEU case law.[99] However, in some cases, it was decided that direct damage occurred where the indirect consequences took place, eg, where the plaintiff was when patrimonial loss was suffered.[100]

In a few cases, the courts interpreted the concept of damage according to Portuguese law and Portuguese authors on that law.[101]

c. Matters Related to the Common Rules

In traffic accidents, courts apply the rules of the country where the accident took place, without mentioning Article 17. Only Article 4(1) was wrongly mentioned.[102]

d. Conclusion

The principal problem relates to the interpretation of the concept of 'direct damage'. Nonetheless, courts often applied the Regulation correctly.

---

[96] eg STJ 11-4-2013 Case:186/10.6TBCBT.S2; TRL 29-10-2015 Case:2691/13.3TCLRS.L1-2.
[97] Case C-412/10 *Homawoo* [2011] ECR I-11603.
[98] eg decision reversed by STJ 1-3-2012 Case:186/10.6TBCBT.S1; decision reversed by TRP 31-01-2011 Case:545/10.4TJPRT.P1.
[99] eg STJ 1-4-2014 Case:1061/12.5TVLSB.L1.S1.
[100] eg TRL 28-11-2013 Case:1061/12.5TVLSB.L1-2.
[101] eg TRL 28-11-2013 Case:1061/12.5TVLSB.L1-2; TRG 29-10-2013 Case:225/12.6TBAMR.G1.
[102] See STJ 1-4-2014 Case:1061/12.5TVLSB.L1.S1.

C. Preliminary Remarks on Effectiveness of the Current EU PIL Framework in Civil and Commercial Law

In general, courts apply the Regulations correctly, although occasionally evidencing a certain lack of familiarity with the most recent case law from the CJEU.

In cases of contradictory decisions on Portuguese law, courts can resort to uniform jurisprudence decisions. These decisions can be relevant to the Regulations' application, especially their articulation with national law. Pragmatically, (albeit methodologically incorrect), Portuguese courts are sometimes more influenced by them than by CJEU case law.

The fact that Rome I and Rome II are more recent, their respective temporal scope of application and the duration of proceedings in Portugal[103] probably contributed to the insignificant number of published decisions applying these Regulations.

III. Portugal's Experience of Cross-border Family Law Disputes

A. Jurisdictional and Procedural Issues Under the Brussels IIa Regulation

i. *Matters Related to the Scope of Application*

In one case Brussels IIa was applied to the recognition of a Channel Islands' divorce judgment (wrongly considering it to be issued in the United Kingdom).[104] However, in another case, it was correctly decided that Brussels IIa does not apply to a Channel Islands' divorce judgment (Article 355 Treaty on the Functioning of the European Union (TFEU)).[105]

Portuguese courts do not apply Brussels IIa to the dissolution of registered partnerships, and thus, national rules were applied in a case involving the recognition of a Dutch decision that dissolved a registered partnership.[106]

ii. *Matters Related to Jurisdiction*

a. Divorce, Legal Separation and Marriage Annulment

In matrimonial matters, the Tribunal da Relação de Coimbra (TRC) has ruled that parties must provide the necessary evidence for the judge to apply Article 3 in the pleadings. Otherwise, jurisdiction could only be established taking account of the residence where

---

[103] In 2013, the average length of first instance cases was 39 weeks, p 13 *in* www.dgpj.mj.pt/sections/noticias/os-numeros-da-justica_2/downloadFile/attachedFile_f0/Os_numeros_Justica_2014.pdf?nocache=1450447204.76.

[104] TRL 10-5-2011 Case:1105/10.5TYRLSB1.

[105] TRC 8-5-2012 Case:233/11.4T2OBR.C1.

[106] TRL 3-12-2015 Case:853/14.5YRLSB.L1-2.

the respondent was served. As service occurred in France, it was ruled that the Portuguese courts lacked jurisdiction (Article 17).[107]

b. Parental Responsibility

1. Child Abduction

The concept of 'wrongful removal or retention'[108] has been, for the most part, correctly applied. In one case, the mother removed her child from Poland to Portugal, without the consent of the father and against a Polish provisional decision. The mother instituted proceedings in Portugal. The removal was ruled unlawful, because the father had the right of custody, and the child was habitually resident, before the removal, in Poland. Portuguese courts thus lacked jurisdiction (Article 10).[109]

In another case, the first instance court (incorrectly) decided the removal was not unlawful as it was done by one of the persons who had the right of custody[110] and could, therefore, decide on the child's habitual residence. This decision was reversed on appeal.[111]

STJ has ruled that courts cannot decide on the merits of rights of custody in Hague Child Abduction Convention proceedings to obtain the return of a child.[112]

In the light of the urgent nature of the proceedings instituted in order to obtain the return of a child wrongfully removed or retained under the Hague Child Abduction Convention, it has been ruled that courts may waive evidentiary proceedings requested by the parties if they deem there to be enough evidence to make a decision on the relevant issues under the Convention.[113]

2. Other Issues Related to Parental Responsibility

It has been ruled that appeals of national decisions on parental responsibility do not have suspensory effects.[114] Since the ruling, national law has changed and now states that, in general, the appeal does not have staying effects, but expressly allows a court to make a different decision.[115]

There is ample case law on the concept of the child's habitual residence.[116] Article 12(3) has been applied to assert the Portuguese courts' jurisdiction, for example where the child resided in France for a year, the rule was applied as both the child and parents had Portuguese nationality and the parents accepted the Portuguese courts' jurisdiction.[117]

---

[107] TRC 28-06-2011 Case:255/09.5TBFZZ.C1.

[108] Art 2(11).

[109] TRC 02-05-2013 Case:220/09.2TBCCHA.E1.

[110] Without the consent of the other.

[111] TRL 24-03-2009 Case:2273/07.9TMLSB7.

[112] STJ 24-06-2010 Case:622/07.9TMBRG.G1.S1; STJ 05-11-2009 Case:1735/06.OTMPRT.S1.

[113] TRL 05-06-2012 Case:773/08.2TBLNH.L17; TRC 22-06-2010 Case:786/09.7T2OBRA.C1.

[114] STJ 05-11-2009 Case:1735/06.OTMPRT.S1.

[115] Art 32/4 Lei 141/2015.

[116] Most recently, STJ 28-01-2016 Case:6987/13.6TBALM.L1.S1, citing Case C-497/10 PPU *Mercredi* [2010] ECR I-14309 and Case C-523/07 *A* [2009] ECR I-2805.

[117] TRL 20-01-2009 Case:10097/2008-7.

iii. Matters Related to Recognition and Enforcement

a. Certificate Concerning Judgments in Matrimonial Matters and Certificate Concerning Judgments on Parental Responsibility

In some cases,[118] the party asking for recognition of a judgment in matrimonial matters issued in another Member State institutes proceedings according to the (inapplicable) national rules on the recognition of foreign judgments.

It has been ruled that an appeal against a decision declaring a foreign judgment on parental responsibility enforceable[119] suspends the decision's effects until the matter is decided with *res judicata* effects.[120]

b. Return of the Child

Courts have ruled that automatic recognition and enforcement of decisions on the return of children is only applicable with an Annex IV Brussels IIa certificate. In one case, a child was unlawfully removed from Germany to Portugal by his father. The Portuguese courts issued a decision of non-return, pursuant to Article 13 of the Hague Child Abduction Convention, and duly transmitted the decision to the German courts under Article 11(6) of Brussels IIa. The German court issued a decision under Article 11(8) of Brussels IIa insisting upon the return of the child to Germany. A copy of the decision, accompanied by the certificate of Annex II Brussels IIa, was brought to the Portuguese proceedings by the mother, who requested the immediate enforcement of the decision. TRP refused to apply Article 42 Brussels IIa, as the correct certificate was not presented.[121]

iv. Conclusion

The application of the Regulation to the dissolution of same-sex marriages remains an open question.

The main published case law concerns Article 11. Compliance with the six weeks' deadline appears difficult if all appeals are to be decided within that time frame.

In matters of recognition, the main problem seems to be that the parties (wrongly) institute proceedings according to the (inapplicable) national rules on recognition of foreign judgments.

B. Jurisdictional and Procedural Issues and Applicable Law Under the Maintenance Regulation

Only two published decisions on the Maintenance Regulation were found. In one, a French judgment issued in 2008 was presented as an enforceable order. It ordered the husband to

---

[118] Most recently, TRC 05-05-2015 Case:211/14.1YRCBR.
[119] Art 33.
[120] TRL 27-09-2010 Case:1239/09.9TMLSB-A.L1-1.
[121] TRP 31-03-2011 Case:2254/09.8TMPRT-B.P1.

pay provisional maintenance to his wife and was enforceable in France. It was wrongly ruled as enforceable in Portugal without the need for a declaration of enforceability. Although France is a Member State bound by the 2007 Hague Protocol, the French judgment was issued before the Regulation's date of application. As such, the rules on abolition of *exequatur* should have been inapplicable (Article 75(2)).[122]

In the other, the debtor asked for a reduction of the maintenance obligation. Article 5 of the Hague Protocol was applied by way of Article 15 of the Maintenance Regulation and German law was considered to have a closer connection with the marriage. The solution is debatable: marriage (1980), divorce and maintenance agreement (2000) occurred in Germany, but, according to the proven facts of the case, both debtor and creditor lived in Portugal since before 2000.[123]

C. Preliminary Remarks on Effectiveness of the Current EU PIL Framework in Cross-border Family Law

The decision[124] to use the place of service to establish the respondent's residence and jurisdiction on the basis of Article 3 Brussels IIa appears incorrect mainly because Article 3 uses *habitual residence* and not mere residence to establish jurisdiction. As such, Article 7 should have been used. Its difficult articulation with Article 6 could, however, explain an intent to stay within the jurisdictional bases of Article 3. In a future recast, it would be desirable if none of the jurisdictional bases were left to national law.

An obiter dictum in three TRL decisions states, based on Recital 12, that nationality of the child and parents can be used to determine the court better placed to rule on the best interests of the child. This statement, if construed broadly, is worrying. However, in two cases, the ruling appears sound: in one, nationality was considered in the context of Article 12(3);[125] in another, the child had his habitual residence in Portugal and the mother, without consent, took him to Luxembourg three weeks before the proceedings were initiated in Portugal.[126] In the third case, less so. The Court ruled that the criterion of proximity, interpreted according to Recital 12 of the Regulation, gives jurisdiction to the Portuguese courts. It did so based on the common nationality of the parents and child, the residence of the father in Portugal, the fact that all of them previously lived in Portugal and that— according to the Court—the mother and child only recently lived in England.[127]

Even so, most of the published decisions show that courts are familiar with the current EU PIL Framework in Cross-border Family Law and, in general, apply it correctly.

---

[122] TRP 03-06-2013 Case:1707/11.2TBPVZ-A.P1.
[123] TRC 31-05-2016 Case:582/13.7TMCBR.C1.
[124] Above s III.A.ii.a.
[125] TRL 20-01-2009 Case: 10097/20087.
[126] TRL 27-03-2012 Case:703/11.4TBLNH.L11.
[127] TRL 22-09-2011 Case:1729/10.0TMLSB-B.L1-8.

IV. Conclusion

In general, the Regulations analysed are applied properly by the courts.

Although Private International Law is taught to all students taking Portuguese law degrees, legal disputes on these matters are not very frequent. This may explain why the most recent CJEU judgments are not always quoted, as well as a little unfamiliarity with some aspects of the Regulations. In order to correct mistakes, better continuing training on the Regulations should be given to all legal practitioners and judges.

27

Romania

ILEANA M SMEUREANU, LUCIAN ILIE AND ALEXANDRA EMA DOBRE[1]

I. Introduction

Romania's diplomatic relations with the European Union (the EU) date back to the early 1990s. In 1991, Romania entered into a Trade and Cooperation Agreement with the EU, followed by its application for membership in 1995. After signing the Accession Treaty in 2005, the country joined the EU in 2007. Almost 10 years after accession to the EU, Romanian courts have already made use of many EU instruments including the Brussels I, Brussels IIa, Rome I and Rome II Regulations (the 'Regulations'). These instruments take precedence over national law but do not exist in a vacuum; where relevant, in areas reserved to domestic regulation, they rest on national laws. Among those, the most significant are the New Romanian Civil Code (RCC) and the New Romanian Code of Civil Procedure (RCCP). The RCC and RCCP replaced old codes that dated back to 1865,[2] as part of a general legal reform to align national legislation to the EU and other modern international law instruments. The RCC entered into force in 2011 at the end of a seven year drafting and deliberation process,[3] and declares the supremacy of EU law over its own provisions in its Article 5. The RCPC, and among others regulates private international law relations.[4] RCPC entered into force in early 2013 after a comparably lengthy drafting process.[5]

While the beginnings were slow and sometimes hesitant, Romanian parties and courts appear to make use of EU instruments. Under the current state of law, however, there is no tracking system to account for the number and type of cases in which matters were decided under EU law.[6] That makes it difficult to have an accurate view as to where Romanian courts stand. Based on publicly available information, however, national courts and Romanian

---

[1] This chapter does not constitute legal advice to any person or the representation of any person. The views expressed in this chapter are the authors' alone and should not be associated with or representative of the views of their respective law firms or institution.

[2] The RCC and RCCP were amended several times during the post-communist period.

[3] Law No 71/2011 on the application of the RCC.

[4] Prior to the entry into force of the RCCP, private international law was governed by the now repealed Law No 105/1992.

[5] The RCCP was enacted by Law No 76/2012 concerning the application of Law No 134/2012.

[6] To obtain information, the authors contacted the Romanian Ministry of Justice and the Romanian Cabinet at the European Parliament and learned that a project concerning the establishment of such a database is under consideration.

parties appear to have explored some but not all the areas covered by the Regulations, as described below.

II. Romania's Experience in Cross-border Civil and Commercial Disputes

A. Jurisdictional and Procedural Issues Under Brussels I

In 2003, Romania enacted a law on international judicial assistance in civil and commercial matters[7] to facilitate and taking of evidence through letters rogatory cross-border exchange of judicial and extrajudicial information and contents of foreign law. The same year, Romania acceded to the 1965 Convention on the Service Abroad of Judicial and Extrajudicial Documents in Civil or Commercial Matters.[8] Prior to Romania's accession to the EU, the recognition and enforcement of foreign judgments was governed by bilateral treaties and conventions concluded with other counties, complemented by Law Number 105/1992 on the regulation of private international law relations.[9] After the country joined the EU on 1 January 2007, Romanian courts started applying the Brussels I Regulation to cross-border disputes in civil and commercial matters, but continued to apply the old instruments to pre-existing disputes.[10] Law Number 105/1992 subsisted until 2013, when it was replaced by the more modern private international law provisions of the RCCP, Book VII.

The question of the temporal application of Brussels I to foreign judgments rendered before Romania joined the EU was one of the first issues the Romanian courts had to decide. In October 2006, months before accession, two French judgments issued in 1999 and 2003 respectively were brought for recognition and enforcement before the Bucharest Tribunal. By the time the case was registered with the competent court, Romania had joined the EU and Brussels I enjoyed direct application. In the ensuing legal proceedings, the parties raised the application of this new legal instrument. After a lengthy legal battle at first instance and appeal levels, the Romanian High Court of Cassation and Justice (the HCCJ) held that the matter could not be decided under Brussels I, Article 66, as the foreign proceedings, the ensuing judgments, and the subsequent applications for recognition and enforcement had all occurred before the Regulation came into force.[11] As such, Article 33 calling for recognition 'without any special procedure being required' could not apply. Instead, the matter was to be decided under the old law, i.e. the 1974 Convention for

---

[7] Law No 189/2003, republished in amended and consolidated form by Law No 61/2015.

[8] Law No 124/2003 on Romania's accession to the Convention on the Service Abroad of Judicial and Extrajudicial Documents in Civil or Commercial Matters adopted in the Hague on 15 November 1965.

[9] Arts 165–78. Law No 105/1992 as subsequently amended was repealed by Law No 76/2012 concerning the application of Law No 134/2012 for the application of the RCCP.

[10] In 2012, a recast Brussels I Reg replacing the 2001 Reg was adopted. The recast became effective on 10 January 2015.

[11] HCCJ Decision No 867/2012, 1st Civil Chamber dated 10 February 2012.

Legal Assistance in Civil and Commercial Matters between Romania and France, with all the relevant requirements contained therein.[12]

A similar conclusion was reached by another Romanian court requested in 2006 to enforce a 2004 decision issued by a tribunal in Milan in a dispute between two Romanian corporations. The losing party opposed recognition on the grounds that it had not been properly served or notified of the underlying dispute so that it could participate in the proceedings, and the decision was made in default of appearance. The HCCJ established that Romanian courts had discretion to decide whether the foreign court had respected the subpoena process.[13] Improper service was one of the reasons for refusing enforcement under the applicable Romanian law, which the Court observed, contained language almost identical to Article 34 of Brussels I. At the time of the decision, Brussels I was already in force in Romania, but remained inapplicable to the case at hand because both the foreign decision and the application for recognition and enforcement had been made before the entry into force of the Regulation. Therefore, the HCCJ applied the old law, and having found that the subpoena process had been observed under the 1954 Hague Convention, recognised the foreign decision.

Finally, the HCCJ had the opportunity to apply Brussels I in a *forum non conveniens* dispute between two lower courts in an employment matter. In 2011, a Serbian national initiated legal proceedings against its Romanian employer over payment for work completed in Romania. The HCCJ was called to intervene after the Maramureş Tribunal, the court at the Serbian national's place of employment, declined jurisdiction in favour of the Bucharest Tribunal, and the latter referred the dispute back to the court first seised. The HCCJ found that the dispute fell within the scope of Brussels I, Article 19(1), which provided that 'an employer domiciled in a Member State may be sued in the courts of the Member State where he is domiciled'.[14] As the employer was domiciled in Romania, Romanian courts had jurisdiction over the dispute. Yet, the issue of which particular Romanian court was competent to determine the controversy was left to domestic law, which referred the matter to the court at the claimant's domicile or residence. As those were seemingly located in Serbia, the HCCJ concluded that despite an overall competence of Romanian courts, it was impossible to decide which one could resolve the dispute. Pursuant to Article 155 of Law Number 105/1992, the competent court in such instances was the Bucharest Tribunal.

Romanian courts have also dealt with cross-border disputes between Romanian and Danish parties. In such cases, they recognised the application of Brussels I by virtue of Council Decision 2006/325/EC.[15] Such was the case of a contractual dispute over the acquisition of windmills for electricity production between a Romanian enterprise and a Copenhagen company. After the first deliveries were made, the Romanian party concluded that the windmills did not have the expected characteristics and initiated an action for annulment, claiming restitution of price plus interest before a Romanian court. The court

---

[12] ibid.

[13] HCCJ Decision No 3869/2008, 1st Civil Chamber, dated 11 June 2008.

[14] HCCJ Decision No 5277/2013, 1st Civil Chamber, dated 14 November 2013.

[15] Council Decision of 27 April 2006 concerning the conclusion of the Agreement between the European Community and the Kingdom of Denmark on jurisdiction and the recognition and enforcement of judgments in civil and commercial matters [2006] OJ L120/22.

asserted jurisdiction pursuant to Brussels I, Articles 1(1) and 5(1)(a) read together with Council Decision 2006/325/EC.[16]

Finally, while applying Brussels I, Romanian courts have also had the opportunity to refer questions of interpretation of EU law to the Court of Justice of the European Union (CJEU) for a preliminary ruling. Recently, the HCCJ seised the CJEU with a question concerning the issue of prorogation of jurisdiction in the context of a trademark assignment dispute between a US corporation and two Romanian parties brought before a Romania court.[17] The CJEU decided the question related to the interpretation of Brussels I, Article 24 in March 2016.[18]

B. Applicable Law Issues Under the Rome I and Rome II Regulations

Examples involving the application of Rome I and Rome II are relatively rare. Moreover, Romanian courts do not publish all their decisions, making it impossible to monitor their case law without inside information and access to paid databases.

i. The Rome I Regulation

The Rome I Regulation applies to contractual obligations in civil and commercial matters when both parties are EU nationals. Where contracts are concluded with a party residing in a non-EU Member State, the RCC continues to apply.[19] In any of these instances, Romanian courts show deference to the choice-of-law made by the parties, whenever available. In exceptional cases, the RCCP allows Romanian courts to disregard the parties' choice if that was made to avoid mandatory legal provisions that would have otherwise governed their contract. Additionally, the RCC reserves the following matters to the exclusive application of Romanian law: insolvency of Romanian companies, land and other immovable assets located in Romania, anti-competitive practices affecting a relevant market on the Romanian territory, Romanian registered patents and trademarks, and certain corporate matters.

If no such matters are at stake and no agreement between the parties exists, then the fall-back provisions of Rome I, Article 4, become applicable.

Although examples are sparse, Romanian and other EU courts have had the opportunity to consider this provision in a few contracts involving Romanian parties. One of these cases involved a contract for the purchase of special medical laboratory equipment concluded

---

[16] This example is cited in I Kunda and CM Gonçalves de Melo Marinho, 'Practical Handbook on European Private International Law' (2010) elaborated within the project *Improving the knowledge of new EU regulations of the members of the national Judicial networks in civil and commercial matter in the MS of the EU*, p 76, available at http://old.just.ro/LinkClick.aspx?fileticket=Mx%2BaR1qqfmU%3D&tabid=2285.

[17] HCCJ, preliminary question requested on 5 December 2014.

[18] *Taser International Inc v SC Gate 4 Business SRL and Cristian Mircea Anastasiu* Case C-175/15, EU:C:2016:176.

[19] In this sense, RCC Art 2640(1) provides:

    (1)   The law applicable to contractual obligations is determined according to the European Union law.

    (2)   In matters not covered by European Union law, the provisions of this Code apply to the law applicable to legal relations, unless otherwise provided by international conventions or any other special provisions.

between a Romanian clinic and a Dutch producer.[20] The delivery under the contract was scheduled for 1 February 2010, but the equipment arrived only three weeks later, causing delays and damages on the clinic's side. In the ensuing dispute, the Dutch party argued that any action was time-barred by a contractual provision which provided that any claims could be raised within one year after the disputed event occurred. The Romanian party relied instead on the seller's law (Dutch law), which provided a statute of limitations of five years. At the time of the dispute, Romania was a party to the UN Convention on the Limitation Period in the International Sale of Goods (1974) whereas the Netherlands was not.[21] Thus, where the parties failed to make an explicit choice-of-law, Rome I was to govern the determination of the applicable law. In such a case, the applicable law is that of the country where the seller's habitual residence is located. The Dutch seller, a legal person, had its 'habitual residence' at its place of central administration, the Netherlands. Pursuant to Rome I, Article 12(1)(d), the applicable law extends also to statutes of limitations. Hence, Dutch law governed the issue of statute of limitations.

Another case with a Romanian party concerned the choice-of-law in a distribution contract between a Romanian car producer and a Greek company.[22] The distributor failed to comply with its obligations to sell the minimum number of cars and to pay the fixed monthly amount agreed under the contract for a period of six months. A legal battle before a Greek court followed with the Greek party relying on the precarious economic situation of its country and the corresponding legal theory *rebus sic stantibus* to justify its contractual default. The Romanian party, in turn, contested both the latter's factual and legal arguments. The facts of the dispute revealed no explicit or implicit choice-of-law so Rome I, Article 4(1)(f) applied. The Greek court therefore decided the matter under the law of the distributor's place of central administration, i.e. Greek law.

Yet another case involving a Romanian party involved the application of Rome I, Articles 4(1)(c) and 4(1)(d). The dispute concerned a Romanian tenant and an Italian landlord.[23] The tenant, a Romanian Erasmus student, rented an apartment in Milan for a period shorter than six months and, without his landlord's permission, brought in another tenant. The landlord challenged this additional tenancy and sought legal advice on the law applicable to the tenancy contract. The two parties did not share the same country of habitual residence and the contract did not appear to contain a choice-of-law provision. However, the tenancy had at its core an immovable asset located in Italy—a circumstance that pointed towards the application of Italian law. It appears that a similar conclusion would have resulted also from the application of Rome I, Article 4(3) as the circumstances did not point to any other 'more closely connected' law than Italian law.

A Romanian party was also involved in a contract for carriage of passengers with no explicit choice-of-law provision. A Danish tourist purchased a ticket for a trip from Greece to Romania with a ferryboat operated by a Romanian company. The tourist could not eventually get on board on the predicted day and time because the ferryboat company oversold

---

[20] This example is cited in Kunda and de Melo Marinho, above n 16 at 10–12.

[21] Pursuant to Art 3(1)(b), the 1974 UN Convention applies if the rules of private international law lead to the application of the law of a Contracting State to the sales contract.

[22] This example is cited in Kunda and de Melo Marinho, above n 16 at 12–14.

[23] Ibid at 13–14. The authors have no knowledge whether the issue was amicably resolved between the parties or was deferred to the Italian courts.

its tickets. The tourist thus decided to sue the ferryboat company for his delay and additional expenses before Romanian courts. The general terms and conditions on the ticket pointed however to the application of Bolivian law; this was an invalid choice-of-law for a transaction falling under the incidence of Rome I, Article 5(2). In the absence of a choice-of-law, Article 5(3) pointed to 'the law applicable shall be the law of the country where the passenger has his habitual residence, provided that either the place of departure or the place of destination is situated in that country'. However, the law of the country of the tourist's habitual residence (Denmark) was not the same with either the place of departure (Greece) or that of destination (Romania). In such cases, Article 5(3) provides that the applicable law would be the law of the country where the carrier has his habitual residence. As the carrier's central administration was located in Romania, the court applied Romanian law.

ii. The Rome II Regulation

The Rome II Regulation governs the law applicable to cross-border non-contractual obligations, covering existing obligations or obligations likely to arise from torts as well as obligations resulting from unjust enrichment.[24]

The core provisions of Rome II are designed for cases in which the parties fail to choose a particular law to govern their non-contractual obligations. These provisions include Article 4, the application of which was invoked in a traffic accident case involving a Romanian national and resident injured in Hungary by a car insured by a Slovak insurance company and driven by a Hungarian national and resident.[25] The Romanian party initiated proceedings before the Romanian courts for personal injury and indirect damages against the Slovak insurer. As the parties did not have their habitual residence in the same country, Article 4(2) did not apply. Similarly, no pre-contractual relationship existed between the victim and the insurer to trigger the application of Article 4(3). The case was therefore decided under the general formula of Article 4(1). As the accident (direct damage) occurred in Hungary, the applicable law to determine the liability question and the amount of damages was Hungarian law. The question of whether the victim could bring a claim for compensation directly against the insurer was also decided under Hungarian law as the law applicable to non-contractual obligations and the law applicable to insurance contracts by virtue of Rome I, Articles 7(3) and (4). The final question was what was the applicable law governing the Slovak insurer's redress claim against the Hungarian wrongdoer. The issue of subrogation is set forth in Rome II, Article 19 read together with Rome I, Article 15. Under these provisions, the redress claim was governed by Hungarian law as the law applicable to the insurer's obligation of compensation.

Another case with a Romanian element involved a situation of unjust enrichment under Article 10.[26] A Romanian national erroneously directed a payment order of a conference fee to a natural person instead of the Italian institution that organised the event. The natural person having an account at the same bank as the Italian institution was an Austrian national. The Romanian national relied on a case of unjust enrichment to recover the erroneous payment. The question of the applicable law was resolved under Article 10(3), which

---

[24] Rome II Art 2.
[25] This example is cited in Kunda and de Melo Marinho, above n 16 at 37–38.
[26] Ibid at 44–45.

pointed to the law of the country where the unjust enrichment took place. As the bank account wrongly credited with the conference fee amount was situated in Italy, Italian law therefore applied. Article 10(1) concerning a 'relationship existing between the parties' and Article 10(2) pointing to a situation where the parties 'have their habitual residence in the same country' were found irrelevant as the Romanian and Austrian nationals neither had a pre-existing relationship, nor were they residing in the same country. Finally, the circumstances of the case did not suggest any other manifestly closer connection with another country, so Article 10(4) was also irrelevant.

C. Practice/Process

The usual remedies available under Romanian law are specific performance and, where that is not possible, damages. Compensatory damages can be coupled only with delay damages but not with specific performance. Injunctive relief is also available. The costs of civil court proceedings consist of judicial fees, attorneys' fees and experts' fees. As a general rule, the unsuccessful party must pay the costs. Interest is awarded on the amount claimed, as the case may be, and not on costs.

Concerning out of court resolution of disputes, RCCP, Book VII, Title IV deals with international arbitration, largely following the principles and structure of the 1985 UNCITRAL Model Law on International Commercial Arbitration. Provisions on mediation can be found both in the RCCP and in Law Number 192/2006 on mediation and organisation of the mediator profession. Finally, the RCCP does not regulate negotiations as an alternative dispute resolution (ADR) method. However, courts can request the parties to attempt to reach an amicable settlement at any time during the proceedings and can acknowledge written settlements of pending disputes.

III. Romania's Experience in Cross-border Family Law Disputes

A. Jurisdictional and Procedural Issues Under the Brussels IIa Regulation

The Brussels IIa Regulation[27] governs jurisdiction and the recognition and enforcement of judgments in matrimonial matters and matters of parental responsibility. Romanian courts have developed a rich jurisprudence in the application thereof, reflecting the post-accession reality of intra-EU mobility of Romanian citizens and the dynamics of their family relations. In assessing their jurisdiction, the Romanian courts have the possibility, just like their EU counterparts, to obtain access to further information through several avenues, for example by submitting requests to the Ministry of Justice, International Law and Judicial Cooperation, by contacting the national representatives of the European Judicial Network, or by directly addressing foreign courts.

---

[27] [2003] OJ L338/1.

i. Matters Related to Jurisdiction

A particularity of the Romanian legal system is that notaries public are competent to declare a dissolution of marriage by consent. In such cases, the spouses may agree on all the effects of divorce, including child maintenance. Where an EU element is involved, such procedure falls under the scope of Brussels IIa, Article 2(1), and Article 137(2) of Law Number 36/1965.[28]

Romanian courts have developed a solid body of jurisprudence over the alternative competence of the Member States' national courts pursuant to the criteria in Brussels IIa, Article 3. For example, the HCCJ confirmed the jurisdiction of Romanian courts to hear matters relating to a divorce under Article 3(1)(b), where the marriage was officiated in another Member State but both spouses had Romanian citizenship.[29] In another case, pursuant to Article 3(1)(a), Romanian courts asserted jurisdiction in a divorce claim where the spouses were habitually resident in Romania.[30]

Finally, Romanian courts were also called to interpret Brussels IIa, Article 19 (*lis pendens*) when, prior to the Romanian court being seised with the case, a Spanish court had received a divorce claim from the same plaintiff. Even though the Spanish court only granted interim relief, the Romanian court declined jurisdiction on the grounds that such measures represented a preliminary stage of divorce proceedings under Spanish law, recognising that the Spanish court had already asserted its jurisdiction.[31]

ii. Matters Related to Recognition and Enforcement

The Romanian courts have also dealt with applications for recognition and enforcement of foreign judgments. For example, the Timişoara Court of Appeal held that a prior decision on maintenance made by a Romanian court was not irreconcilable with a court decision in a dispute between the same parties issued in Spain. The applicant sought recognition of a Spanish divorce judgment in Romania, aiming at enforcing the child maintenance obligation contained therein. Relying on Brussels IIa, Article 24(c), the defendant opposed enforcement on the grounds that he was already paying maintenance under a court decision rendered in Romania before the Spanish decision. The Court of Appeal held that the prior judgment of the Romanian court was only a provisional measure under Brussels IIa, Article 14 issued prior to the divorce in Spain. Once the divorce was pronounced, the Spanish court also made a final determination of child maintenance. Recognition of the Spanish judgment was therefore granted.[32]

In another case, the Galaţi Court of Appeal explained the application of Brussels IIa, Article 9 dealing with the competence of courts in case of a lawful move of a child from one Member State to another. The Romanian court held that the applicant should have initiated an action to modify the initial judgment during the three-month period following the

---

[28] Law No 36/1965 on notaries and notarial activity, which provides that 'before checking the territorial jurisdiction, the notary public will check if the law applicable to divorce is the Romanian law'.
[29] HCCJ (1st Civil Chamber) Case No 687, decision dated 27 February 2014.
[30] Galaţi Court of Appeal (1st Civil Chamber), Case No 105, decision dated 21 February 2011.
[31] Ploieşti Court of Appeal (1st Civil Chamber), Case No 2824, decision dated 15 October 2013.
[32] Timişoara Court of Appeal (1st Civil Chamber), Case No 38 dated 3 March 2015.

move of the children to Italy. Once the three month deadline elapsed, the Romanian court no longer had jurisdiction to modify the judgment on access rights.[33]

B. Jurisdictional and Procedural Issues and Applicable Law Under the Maintenance Regulation

Council Regulation Number 4/2009 (the Maintenance Regulation)[34] replaced the provisions applicable to maintenance obligations under Brussels I.

i. Matters Related to Jurisdiction

Jurisdiction over maintenance can be established on the grounds set forth in Articles 3 to 7 of the Maintenance Regulation. Parties may also agree on a choice of the competent court. In an attempt to increase legal certainty, the Romanian Ministry of Justice has published on its website a so-called 'legal map' to assist the parties to determine the court with territorial jurisdiction for the place of residence of either the debtor or the creditor.

ii. Matters Related to Applicable Law

Pursuant to Article 15, the law applicable to maintenance obligations shall be determined in accordance with the 2007 Hague Protocol on the Law Applicable to Maintenance Obligations (the 'Protocol'). Article 3 of the Protocol states that the law governing the dispute is that of the State of the creditor's habitual residence save where the Protocol provides otherwise. This rule is applicable also in Romania, as it is bound by the Protocol through the EU's approval of it, and national courts are bound by it under the RCC Article 2612.

iii. Matters Related to Recognition and Enforcement

The HCCJ was called upon to deal with an application for enforcement of a judgment rendered in 2010 by the District Tribunal of Vienna that established the paternity of a minor and a maintenance obligation. The Romanian Court stated that, under Article 23(1) and (2) of the Maintenance Regulation, a decision made by another Member State that was not bound by the Protocol at that time could only be recognised in other Member States if there were no grounds for refusal. As the judgment in question was not manifestly contrary to Romanian public policy, the HCCJ proceeded to its recognition and enforcement.[35]

iv. Practice/Process

The Romanian Ministry of Justice acts as the Central Authority for the purposes of the Maintenance Regulation. After receiving a specific maintenance request or a request for specific measures, the Ministry of Justice forwards it to the authority or body having the

---

[33] Galaţi Court of Appeal (1st Civil Chamber), Case No 532 dated 2 November 2011.
[34] [2009] OJ L7/1.
[35] HCCJ (2nd Civil Chamber) Case No 1006/2014 dated 13 March 2014.

relevant personal information, to the competent local bar association, to the Chamber of Judicial Enforcement Officers or to the competent court.[36] Importantly, however, the Central Authority neither represents nor assists the creditor in court proceedings.

Under Romanian legislation, applications for the determination or modification of maintenance are exempt from stamp duty. Although legal representation is not mandatory, any interested party may request public legal aid if its income to fund a lawyer is insufficient. Exceptionally, public legal aid is granted independently of the applicant's financial situation where the right to legal aid or free legal aid is provided for by a special law as a protection measure in cases involving minors and persons with disabilities.

IV. Conclusion

Romania's accession to the EU triggered a transformation of judicial cooperation in civil and commercial matters, facilitating interaction through harmonised rules of direct application. In that process, Romanian courts have embarked on an important mission to apply a new body of legislation. Some of their decisions are freely available on the Internet, but a great deal of jurisprudence escapes public knowledge either because the courts do not publish them or because access is restricted by paid subscription. Increased legal certainty for users and accountability of national courts require the creation of public databases of judgments, including but not limited to those applying EU law.

---

[36] European Judicial Network in civil and commercial matters—Romania (https://e-justice.europa.eu/content_maintenance_claims-47-ro-en.do?member=1#toc_1).

28

Slovakia

MIROSLAVA VOZÁRYOVÁ AND KATARÍNA BURDOVÁ

I. Introduction

In the Slovak Republic a difference is made between general courts and a separate court, which is the Constitutional Court of the Slovak Republic. Independent and impartial courts administer general justice. The Slovak Republic has a two-level court system, district courts are competent to try proceedings at first instance and regional courts hear cases as appeal courts. The Supreme Court of the Slovak Republic hears extraordinary remedies. Being the supreme judicial body, the Supreme Court never acts as a first instance court.

The courts decide in civil and criminal matters and also judicial review of decisions by administrative bodies. They decide in panels of judges unless the law provides that a single judge shall decide in the matter.

II. Slovak Experience on Cross-border Civil and Commercial Disputes

In the Slovak Republic, the main legal source of the rules of jurisdiction applicable to cross-border disputes in civil and commercial matters is the Act Number 97/1963 of the Official Journal of the Slovak Republic Collection of Laws on Private International Law and Rules of Procedure related thereto, as amended (the PIL Act). Traditionally, case law is not regarded as a binding source of law by continental legal theory and, in this respect, Slovakia is no exception. Nevertheless, some scholars do attribute to case law of higher courts the effects of 'quasi-precedents'.

A. Jurisdictional and Procedural Issues Under the Brussels Ia Regulation

i. Matters Related to Jurisdiction

The PIL Act supplies rules of jurisdiction for cases not covered by the Brussels Ia Regulation, in particular cases where the defendant has his habitual residence outside of the EU.

ii. Matters Related to Recognition and Enforcement

No official information about the numbers of recognition and enforcement decisions, authentic instruments and judicial settlements carried out by Slovak courts is available but we assume that the relevant titles for recognition and enforcement in Slovakia do mostly come from neighbouring states, and the majority of them from the Czech Republic.

iii. Conclusion

a. Problem Areas

Article 25 deals with the prorogation of jurisdiction that enables the parties to agree on the courts of a Member State that have jurisdiction to settle any disputes which have arisen or which may arise in connection with a particular legal relationship. The substantive validity of the agreement is determined by the law of the chosen Member State. There are no practical problems in the application of this Regulation in Slovakia.

b. Best Practice

As examples of best practice we consider the contact points of the European Judicial Network in civil and commercial matters. National contact points have been created within each district court and the Ministry of Justice distributes information pertinent to the application of the European acquis on a regular basis. The role of the contact point is to advise her/his colleagues on the correct implementation of this and other Regulations. Also, a seminar with practical cases is arranged once a year.

c. Possible Solutions

Due to the recent adoption of the Brussels Ia Regulation, there is a lack of practical experience and public knowledge about the new provisions on jurisdiction of Slovak courts in cross-border disputes within the EU, but this will naturally change as time passes.

B. Applicable Law Issues Under the Rome I and Rome II Regulations

i. Rome I

In general, the Rome I Regulation works well; its practical application is appropriate and sufficient. Based on answers from several courts, there has been very little case law on the Rome I Regulation in our jurisdiction.

a. Matters Related to the Uniform Rules

For individual employment contracts, the Regulation stipulates the principle of the most favourable law. The parties can choose the applicable law according to Article 3. However, the application of the chosen law cannot have the result of depriving the employee of the protection afforded to him by the mandatory rules of the law applicable by default, ie in the absence of choice. That is, theoretically, the autonomy of the parties only works in favour of the weaker party. The comparison is carried out between the content of the law chosen by the parties and the mandatory rules, ie the rules that cannot be derogated from by contract, of the law applicable had the parties not made any choice. In principle, the question of whether the comparison is to be made between individual rules, institutions or the two legal systems as a whole must be solved according to the same criteria developed in relation to the Rome Convention. The question of whether the comparison has to be carried out by the judge *ex officio* or on application of an interested party is determined by the *lex fori*. The law applicable by default is the *lex loci laboris*, namely, the law of the country 'in which' or, 'from which' the employee habitually carries out his work in performance of the contract. The expression 'from which' was not stipulated in the Rome Convention. It has been introduced—following the case law of the Court of Justice of the European Union (CJEU) on Article 19 of the Brussels I Regulation—in order to cover those employees who do not carry out their job in the territory of only one country, but where there is a country which constitutes a sort of 'base of operations'. This is normally the case with employees who work in aircraft. In such cases, the law of the country which serves as a base for the worker is to be considered as the *lex loci laboris*.[1] Furthermore, the new text clarifies that the country where the employee habitually works is not deemed to have changed just because he is temporarily posted to another country or countries. This clarification is also taken from the case law of the CJEU in the context of the Brussels I Regulation.[2]

b. Conclusion

In the context of the aforementioned questions concerning individual employment contracts more precise wording of the relevant provision would be good.

ii. Rome II

In general, the Rome II Regulation works well and its practical application is appropriate and sufficient. Based on the answers from several courts, there has been very little case law on the Rome II Regulation in Slovakia.

a. Matters Related to Torts/Delicts

There are no difficulties in applying the provisions related to torts/delicts. When both provisions are applicable, Article 7 should take precedence over Article 5.

b. Conclusion

Given the lack of practical experience with the Regulation, we do not suggest any major changes. However, it might be helpful to consider changing the criterion *lex loci damni infecti* for class actions for the criterion *lex loci delicti commissi*. It could also be considered

---

[1] Case C- 125/92 *Mulox IBC Ltd v Hendrick Geels* [1993] ECR I-4075; Case C-383/95 *Petrus Wilhelmus Rutten v Cross Medical Ltd.* [1997] ECR I-57; Case C-440/97 *GIE Groupe Concorde and Othes v The Master of the vessel ‚Suhadiwarno Panjan' and Others* [1999] ECR I-6307; Case C-37/00 *Herbert Weber v Universal Ogden Services Ltd.* [2002] ECR I- 2013; Case C-437/00 *Giulia Pugliese v Finmeccanica SpA, Betriebsteil Alenia Aerospazio* [2003] ECR I- 3573.

[2] Francisco Garcimartín Alférez, 'The Rome I Regulation: Much Ado about Nothing?' (2008) *The European Legal Forum* 61–80.

to include non-contractual obligations arising out of violations of privacy and rights relating to the personality in the Rome II Regulation.

C. Practice/Process

i. Slovak National Courts' Practice in Interpreting the Regulations/Process Issues

In general, the evaluation shall be based on official statistics. However, no official databases exist in Slovakia and statistics have been kept only from 1 January 2016. Nevertheless, it is possible to conclude that overall Slovak courts implement the EU Regulations in a proper way.

ii. Cost and Length of Litigation in Cross-border Civil and Commercial Disputes

Court fees are governed by Act Number 71/1992.[3] The amount is fixed or formulated as a percentage, or a combination of the two (depending on the type of the claim). Furthermore, the costs of civil proceedings depend to a great extent on whether an oral hearing will take place in the course of the proceedings. The court also has discretion regarding the choice of evidence and the costs. Therefore, it is difficult to foresee the actual costs before the proceedings.

iii. Settlement in Cross-border Civil and Commercial Disputes

Settlement is governed by the Code of the Civil Dispute Procedure[4] and can be defined as an agreement concluded by the parties before or during the civil dispute procedure which contains the settlement of their rights and obligations.

iv. Alternative Dispute Resolution for Cross-border Civil and Commercial Disputes

There are two basic types of ADR established by Slovakian law: mediation and arbitration. Another type of dispute resolution stipulates the Code of Civil Dispute Procedure, which except for court proceedings establishes also a 'Conciliation proceeding'.[5] The court shall use appropriate methods to exert its educational influence in conciliation proceedings.

v. Conclusion

The Slovak Republic implements these EU Regulations without significant problems.

III. Slovak Experience on Cross-border Family Law Disputes

The conduct of proceedings in matrimonial matters, in matters related to parental responsibility, and in matters of maintenance is regulated in the Slovak Republic by the

---

[3] Act No 71/1992 on Court Fees as amended.
[4] Act No 160/2015 Code of the Civil Dispute Procedure.
[5] ibid, Art 148.

Civil Proceedings Code for Non-Adversarial Proceedings (the CPCNP),[6] which lays down the rules of local jurisdiction of civil courts in proceedings related to these matters.[7] Rules of international jurisdiction for matters not governed by the EU acquis or international treaties are included in the PIL Act.

A. Jurisdictional and Procedural Issues Under the Brussels IIa Regulation

i. Matters Related to the Scope of Application

The Brussels IIa Regulation in Article 1(1) uses the term 'marriage'.[8] This term is defined in Article 41(1) of the Constitution of the Slovak Republic as a unique bond between a man and a woman.

Divorce, separation and annulment of marriage are among the matters falling within the scope of the Brussels IIa Regulation. Slovak law recognises proceedings on divorce, proceedings on declaring a marriage void, and proceedings on declaring a marriage non-existent. The Slovak legal theory currently agrees that all of the proceedings listed above fall within the scope of the Regulation,[9] although there had been some doubts as to whether including the proceedings on declaring a marriage non-existent within the scope of the Regulation was suitable.[10] The reason for this was that in such proceedings persons other than the husband or wife may act as the petitioner, meaning that the jurisdiction criterion related to the petitioner's habitual residence may create an exorbitant jurisdiction.[11]

ii. Matters Related to Jurisdiction

a. Divorce, Legal Separation and Marriage Annulment

Article 3(2) applies the criterion of the common nationality of the husband and wife. The Slovak court can establish its jurisdiction also in respect of persons with dual citizenship in view of Section 33 of the PIL Act, according to which persons with dual citizenship are deemed Slovak citizens if at least one of their citizenships is Slovak.

Since the Slovak Republic does not participate in the enhanced cooperation in the area of the law applicable to divorce,[12] the applicable law is primarily established by the PIL Act, ie the law of the country of common citizenship of the husband and wife at the time of the commencement of the proceedings, and if the husband and wife do not share common citizenship, the *lex fori*.[13]

---

[6] Three new codes apply in the Slovak Republic with effect from 1.07.2016—Act No 160/2015 Civil Proceedings Code for Adversarial Proceedings; Act No 161/2015 Civil Proceedings Code for Non-Adversarial Proceedings; and Act No 162/2015 Administrative Proceedings Code. These have replaced the decades-old Civil Procedure Code.

[7] The CPCNP, s 1.

[8] The Slovak legal order does not recognise the institution of registered partnership for either homosexual or heterosexual couples.

[9] P Lysina, M Ďuriš and M Haťapka, *Medzinárodné právo súkromné* 2nd edn (Bratislava, CH Beck, 2016) 339.

[10] P Lysina, N Štefanková, M Ďuriš and M Števček, *Zákon o medzinárodnom práve súkromnom a procesnom:.Komentár* 1st edn (Bratislava, CH Beck, 2016) 223.

[11] See Case C-294/15 *Mikolajczyk* EU:C:2016:772.

[12] Council Reg (EU) No 1259/2010 of 20 December 2010 implementing enhanced cooperation in the area of the law applicable to divorce and legal separation ([2010] OJ L343/10).

[13] The PIL Act, s 22.

b. Parental Responsibility

1. Child Abduction

Cases of wrongful removal or retention of a child have long been on the rise in Slovakia. If a child is wrongfully removed or retained within the territory of the Slovak republic and an application for the child's return is filed, specialised courts of first and second instance decide in these cases.[14]

2. Access

Courts decide most frequently on the arrangement of access rights reached in the course of divorce proceedings involving proceedings on parental responsibility under Article 12 of the Brussels IIa Regulation. In all other access cases, jurisdiction is based on Article 8 of the Brussels IIa Regulation. The authors are not aware of any cases where a Slovak court has based its jurisdiction on the provisions of Article 9 of the Brussels IIa Regulation.

3. Other Issues Related to Parental Responsibility

In the context of the application of Article 15 of the Brussels IIa Regulation the practice points to delays caused by the failure of the requested court to inform the requesting court about the acceptance of jurisdiction in a timely manner.[15] Another problem may arise during the procedure under Article 15(1)(a) when the requested court is not informed that the case involves a referred jurisdiction as the parties concerned fail to state this fact in their motion for commencing proceedings.[16]

iii. Matters Related to Recognition and Enforcement

The enforcement of decisions on return used to be very problematic in Slovakia. In particular, in the past, problems used to arise from the fact that the same court did not have jurisdiction for both the return and the enforcement proceedings. This led to undesirable situations when, for example, a court rejected the enforcement of a decision on return due to the decision being unenforceable, because the return order did not impose on the abductor a specific obligation to ensure the return of the child or state a time limit for the child's return. Recently new rules for the enforcement of decisions in matters related to parental responsibility, including return orders, have been adopted, drawing on best practices abroad, with the intention to make the enforcement quicker and more effective.

iv. Relations with Other Instruments

In connection with the relationship between the Brussels IIa Regulation and the Hague Convention of 1996[17] (the 1996 Convention) the Slovak academic literature points out in

---

[14] The first instance courts are the District court Košice I, the District court Banská Bystrica and the District court Bratislava I. The appellate courts are the Regional court in Košice, the Regional court in Banská Bystrica and the Regional court in Bratislava.

[15] 'Methodology of the Centre for international protection of children and youth' 28, available on www.cipc.sk.

[16] Miloš Haťapka, 'Answers to questionnaire to Member States concerning application of Brussels IIbis regulation', unpublished internal document.

[17] Convention of 19 October 1996 on Jurisdiction, Applicable Law, Recognition, Enforcement and Co-operation in Respect of Parental Responsibility and Measures for the Protection of Children.

particular the ambiguity in the application of the Regulation in the following case: if a court having jurisdiction in accordance with the Brussels IIa Regulation finds that a court of a third country bound by the 1996 Convention is better placed to deal with the relevant case and the child concerned has its habitual residence in an EU Member State, is it possible to apply Article 8 of the 1996 Convention on the transfer of jurisdiction?[18]

v. Conclusion

As shown above, the provisions on return proceedings are one of the most problematic aspects of the application of the Brussels IIa Regulation. These proceedings place a burden on the courts and encourage courts with jurisdiction under Article 10 not to decide on parental responsibility until proceedings on return are concluded as decisions issued in Member States with jurisdiction under Article 10 prior to the conclusion of the proceedings on return cannot be certified under Article 42 and enforced without the need for proceedings on *exequatur*.

The Slovak legal literature proposes the removal of Article 11 of the Brussels IIa Regulation and the adoption of a mechanism that will ensure a prompt issue of a final decision on parental responsibility by a court having jurisdiction and the prompt recognition and enforcement of this decision in other Member States in the case of an intra-EU child abduction.[19]

B. Jurisdictional and Procedural Issues and Applicable Law Under the Maintenance Regulation

i. Matters Related to the Scope of Application

Although the Maintenance Regulation has a very broad scope of application, it does not unequivocally address its application to the case of a maintenance obligation arising from registered partnerships and marriages between persons of the same sex, which are not recognised by the Slovak legal order.

ii. Matters Related to Jurisdiction

The Slovak version of the Maintenance Regulation was affected by an incorrect translation of Article 3(1)(a) of the Regulation, where the term 'obliged' was used instead of the correct term 'defendant'.[20] However, the available data suggest that the incorrect translation did not cause any problems in the practical application of the Regulation.

The fact that *perpetuatio fori* is not clearly stipulated appears to be more problematic in connection with Article 3(1) (a) and (b). If *perpetuatio fori* was not to be applied under the

---

[18] Elena Júdová, 'Fragmentácia a koherencia európskej úpravy rodinného práva' (2015) *Acta Iuridica Olomucensia*, Volume 10, Issue 2, 73, 84.

[19] Katarína Burdová, 'Medzinárodné únosy detí—čas na vlastný európsky prístup?' [2013] *Bratislavské právnické fórum* 1150–54.

[20] The correction was made by Corrigendum to the Council Reg (EC) No 4/2009 of 18 December 2008 on jurisdiction, applicable law, recognition and enforcement of decisions and cooperation in matters relating to maintenance obligations, [2009] OJ L7/1.

regime of these provisions, this could cause problems in cases where maintenance can only be granted under the applicable law from the day of the filing of the relevant petition.

An academic expert[21] pointed out in connection with Article 3(c) of the Maintenance Regulation that excluding joint jurisdiction in cases where the jurisdiction in the first proceedings is based solely on the nationality of one of the parties concerned may cause problems in the case of maintenance for a minor child of divorcing parents. The court carrying out the proceedings on divorce of a husband and wife who share common nationality could base its jurisdiction in parental responsibility proceedings on Article 12 of the Brussels IIa Regulation, but could not claim jurisdiction in proceedings on child maintenance (since the conditions under Article 3(3) are not met and prorogation of the jurisdiction is excluded under Article 4(3)). The maintenance debtor may use the objection of lack of jurisdiction under Article 5 of the Maintenance Regulation for tactical purposes to postpone the decision in this matter.

But there is also a view[22] that this interpretation of Article 12 Brussels IIa may be seen as questionable, since jurisdiction in parental responsibility in this case is not, stricto sensu, a jurisdiction based on nationality, but rather on prorogation. In view of the recent CJEU jurisprudence, there is not such a strong causal link between the divorce and child maintenance as between parental responsibility and child maintenance.[23]

iii. Matters Related to Recognition, Enforceability and Actual Enforcement of Decisions

The enforcement of decisions is entrusted in the Slovak Republic to the courts' executors (bailiffs) acting under an authorisation granted by the courts. If proceedings on *exequatur* are required prior to enforcing a decision, the provisions of the Maintenance Regulation are applied in connection with the provisions of the PIL Act.

C. Practice/Process

i. Slovak National Courts' Practice in Interpreting the Regulations

The application and interpretation problems referred to above are resolved mainly by decisions of the courts of higher instance and education of judges. Additional problems arise from the fragmentation of the PIL legal framework requiring experience and knowledge of the EU Regulations. The lack of experience and knowledge in this area by judges of the courts of lower instance has become apparent in particular in relation to the following: proceedings on divorce are linked by obligation with proceedings on parental responsibility and the maintenance obligation. In certain cases the Slovak courts correctly based the jurisdiction in divorce on the Brussels IIa Regulation, but automatically (based on national procedural law) linked these proceedings with proceedings on parental responsibility and maintenance obligations without examining whether they indeed can establish jurisdiction

---

[21] Júdová, above n 17, 88.
[22] M Haťapka, unpublished opinion.
[23] See Case C-184/14 *A v B* EU:C:2015:479 discussed in ch 41 below.

in these matters in accordance with Article 12(1) of the Brussels IIa Regulation and the Maintenance Regulation.

ii. Cost and Length of Litigation in Cross-border Family Law Disputes

No data on the duration of proceedings with a foreign element is available. The cost of proceedings in the Slovak Republic includes the court fees, cash expenses of the parties concerned and their representatives, lost income, advance payments for evidence, and remuneration for representation by attorneys. Proceedings in family law matters are in most cases exempt from court fees.

iii. Settlement in Cross-border Family Law Disputes

Courts strive to lead parties involved in proceedings on parental responsibility and maintenance to amicable resolution of disputes, which should result in an agreement reached by the parties concerned. If the relevant court approves an agreement reached by the parties concerned, parents are not allowed to file an appeal against the ruling approving their agreement. While courts strive to encourage amicable resolution in proceedings on divorce, a divorce decree by consent is excluded in this type of proceeding. The amicable resolution of the case by a husband and wife amounts to a withdrawal of the relevant petition for divorce.[24]

iv. Alternative Dispute Resolution for Cross-border Family Law Disputes

Courts may invite parties to proceedings on divorce and proceedings on parental responsibility and maintenance to attempt amicable resolution through mediation.[25] Arbitration is not admissible in family law disputes.

v. Remedies in Cross-border Family Law Disputes

Regular and extraordinary remedies exist pursuant to the CPCNP. No extraordinary remedies may be applied for in relation to decisions issued in proceedings on return of the child. Constitutional challenges may be filed once the remedial measures provided for by the Slovak legal order have been exhausted; these challenges are decided by the Constitutional Court of the Slovak Republic.

D. Preliminary Remarks on Effectiveness of the Current EU PIL Framework in Cross-border Family Law

It is possible to agree[26] that decision-making in family law cases with a foreign element places a great burden on courts in the Member States. Mere navigation through the

---

[24] E Horváth and A Andrášiková, *Civilný mimosporový poriadok—komentár* (Bratislava, Wolters Kluwer, 2016) 142–50.
[25] The CPCNP, paras 96 and 118.
[26] Júdová, above n 17, 94.

numerous legal instruments of various origins and identification of the rules that should be applied in the relevant situation requires significant experience and the situation in family law disputes is even more complicated than in civil and commercial matters where jurisdiction criteria are stipulated in a single Regulation.

In addition, the current EU legal framework assumes in certain cases that the Regulations are known to the physical persons, who are consequently capable of defending their rights (for example in the case of the provisions of Article 5 of the Maintenance Regulation) or are aware of the consequences of their decisions (for example a parent granting a consent to the change of a child's habitual residence 'should' be aware that the change of the habitual residence also results in the change of the applicable law governing the maintenance obligation and affects the jurisdiction of the court).

Therefore, the codification of (at least) the jurisdictional rules relating to family matters in a single instrument would significantly simplify their practical application.[27]

---

[27] ibid.

29

Slovenia

SUZANA KRALJIĆ

I. Introduction

The Republic of Slovenia (RS) is a small country (20,273km^2) with a population of 2.06 million. According to the Constitution of the Republic of Slovenia (CRS),[1] the RS is a democratic republic (Article 1 CRS) governed by the rule of law and a social state (Article 2 CRS). The state's authority is based on the principle of the separation of legislative, executive and judicial powers (Article 3(2) CRS), with a parliamentary system of government. The National Assembly (NA) is the highest legislative authority in the RS (90 members) and has the right to enact laws (Article 80(1) CRS). The Government of the RS is the executive body and the supreme body of the state administration.

All courts in the RS act in accordance with the principles of constitutionality, independence and the rule of law. The unified system of courts consists of courts with general and specialised jurisdiction. Courts with general jurisdiction include 44 district, 11 circuit and four higher courts (HC), and the Supreme Court (SCRS). Specialised courts comprise four labour courts, a social court and the Administrative Court, which provides legal protection in administrative affairs and has the status of a higher court. The Constitutional Court of the Republic of Slovenia (CCRS) is the highest authority with regard to the protection of constitutionality, legality, human rights and basic freedoms, and is separated from the regular judicial system. It is composed of nine judges.

II. Slovenia's Experience on Cross-border Civil and Commercial Disputes

The RS became a full Member State (MS) of the EU on 1 May 2004. Until then, the act regulating the general rules of private international law had been the Private International Law and Procedure Act.[2] With the entry into the EU, the RS became bound by the EU legal

---

[1] Constitution of the Republic of Slovenia (*Ustava Republike Slovenije* (CRS)): Uradni list Republike Slovenije (UL RS) (Official Gazette RS), Nos 33/91-I, with amendments.
[2] Private International Law and Procedure Act (*Zakon o mednarodnem zasebnem pravu in postopku* (PILPA): UL RS, no 56/99.

order, including in cross-border civil and commercial matters. Thus, on 1 May 2004, the following came into effect:

— Council Regulation (EC) Number 44/2001 of 22 December 2000 on jurisdiction and the recognition and enforcement of judgments in civil and commercial matters (Brussels I);[3]
— Council Regulation (EC) Number 2201/2003 of 27 November 2003 concerning jurisdiction and the recognition and enforcement of judgments in matrimonial matters and the matters of parental responsibility, repealing Regulation (EC) Number 1347/2000 (Brussels IIa);[4]

Later, the following three regulations were adopted:

— Regulation (EC) Number 593/2008 of the European Parliament and of the Council of 17 June 2008 on the law applicable to contractual obligations (Rome I);[5]
— Regulation (EC) Number 864/2007 of the European Parliament and of the Council of 11 July 2007 on the law applicable to non-contractual obligations (Rome II);[6]
— Council Regulation (EC) No 4/2009 of 18 December 2008 on jurisdiction, applicable law, recognition and enforcement of decisions and cooperation in matters relating to maintenance obligations (MR).[7]

No special national private international law rules or implementing laws related to the abovementioned five EU Regulations were adopted.

We have detected the following general difficulties or common problems associated with all five EU Regulations:

a)   The rapid accumulation of Regulations and, consequently, many new and often complicated rules related to jurisdiction, applicable law, recognition and enforcement cause problems to judges. Consequently, some judges seek to avoid the use of the Regulations in matters with an international element.[8]
b)   Judges face language problems, related to the lack of linguistic skills on their part, and sometimes to inadequate translations of the Regulations, Conventions and case law;
c)   The RS has a minimalistic approach towards implementing Regulations;[9]
d)   Only a small number of judges have the skills to correctly apply the Regulations. Although the judges' knowledge of the Regulations has improved in the past years, there is still a need for judicial education and training. The judges at Higher Courts and at the Supreme Court are more adept at using the Regulations and the Court of Justice of the European Union (CJEU) case law;
e)   Judges have made it clear that they need more professional literature;

---

[3] [2001] OJ L12/1.
[4] [2003] OJ L338/1.
[5] [2008] OJ L177/6.
[6] [2007] OJ L199/40.
[7] [2009] OJ L7/1.
[8] N Betetto, 'Implementacija procesnih uredb v slovenskem pravu in praksi slovenskih sodišč' (2009) 11 *Pravna praksa* 29.
[9] Betetto, ibid, 31.

f)   Judges face the problems caused by differences in the national legal systems (28 MSs);[10]
g)   Judges, especially in lower courts, have problems to keep up with the developments as to the Regulations and related case law; and
h)   Mediation is rarely used in cross-border matters.

A. Jurisdictional and Procedural Issues Under the Brussels I Regulation

The majority of cases are related to Brussels I, which has the most fruitful and diverse case law of all five Regulations. The RS does not gather case law statistics on cases on the basis of the Regulations. Indeed, the present database is not structured according to the Regulations, which would make access to cases quicker and more convenient.[11]

i. Matters Related to the Scope of Application

Immediately after the accession to the EU, courts encountered problems connected to the temporal element or the question of the inter-temporal effect of Brussels I, as they applied Brussels I to procedures that had started before Slovenia became a member of the EU,[12] or did not apply Brussels I in spite of the fact that they should have applied it in line with the temporal criteria. With time, these uncertainities were resolved.

In some cases, courts have followed the principle of autonomous EU interpretation of the term 'civil and commercial matters'. Accordingly, they held that it was not appropriate to subsume every matter under 'civil and commercial matters'. In particular, it is not possible for Brussels I to be applied to civil law relationships with the presence of a strong public law element (eg liability for actions of the state authority).[13] Such relationships do not belong under Brussels I in spite of the fact that, under Slovenian legislation, such a relationship falls within the civil law procedure. In the same way, following the autonomous EU interpretation, procedures without an element of conflict do not belong among the 'civil and commercial matters' (eg some Slovenian non-contentious procedures, including registration procedures).[14] The SCRS took the clear position that when deciding whether it is a civil matter under Brussels I, the law of the State where recognition shall take place, shall be applied. It is through recognition that a foreign judicial decision is incorporated into the legal order of the State of recognition.[15]

---

[10] For example: the boundary between private and public law varies between Member States; differences between national rules etc.

[11] Slovenian case-law database: www.sodnapraksa.si/.

[12] *VSL I Cpg 242/2009*; 17 June 2009.

[13] SCRS (*Decision CP 21/2008*) refused the appeal, where the appellant argued the exceptions of Art 1 of Brussels I, as there was neither a public law element present in the case nor did it fall within the exceptions of Art 1(2) Brussels I. Also CCRS dealt with the question of *acta iure imperii* (*Up-13/99-24*; 8 March 2001) regarding recognition of reparation for damage done in WWII.

[14] A Galič, 'Mednarodna pristojnost po Uredbi št. 44/2001' (2007) 1 *Pravosodni bilten* 188.

[15] *VSRS Cp 15/2014*; 14 May 2015.

ii. Matters Related to Jurisdiction

With regards to jurisdiction, Slovenian courts have not encountered any particular difficulties. Questions that have arisen were resolved as follows.

a)   *Prorogatio tacita* (Article 24): The court confirmed that a case of tacit prorogation was made out as the defendant had entered an appearance and no other court had exclusive jurisdiction.[16] Therefore, the Slovenian court had jurisdiction.[17]

b)   Jurisdiction in insurance matters (Article 11): The case involved a Slovenian driver involved in a traffic accident in Romania caused by a truck driven by a Turkish citizen. The HC decided that the purpose of the establishment of the national insurance bureau was for the bureau to assume rights and obligations from insurance contracts. It was stated on the website of the defendant that one of his functions was to assume responsibility for handling of requests related to accidents caused by foreign drivers in Romania, as a state bureau. It followed that the defendant had the role of an insurance company in relation to the injured party. The fact that the liability was based on the law and not on an insurance contract did not change this conclusion. Article 11(2) expressly determines that the provisions of Articles 8, 9 and 10 shall apply to claims filed by the injured party directly against the insurance company (ie direct claims that are not based on an insurance contract between the injured party and the insurer).[18]

c)   Jurisdiction in consumer contracts (Article 15): the court held that the question of whether a contract may be defined as a consumer contract was based exclusively on Article 15, and, as such, included contracts on services connected to health treatment abroad.[19]

iii. Matters Related to Recognition and Enforcement

The above mentioned temporal aspect of the application of Brussels I arose in a case where the question of time limitation regarding the application of Brussels I and the MR appeared in connection with enforcement of a maintenance decision. Namely, the court held that in respect of a court decision passed in a MS before the date of the entry into force of the MR, the recognition and enforcement of which was sought in another MS following the entry into force of the MR, Brussels I was to be applied, if this decision fell within the scope of application of Brussels I for the purposes of recognition and enforcement. The court correctly applied Brussels I, but then sought to conduct recognition and enforcement after the MR was already in force. The HC held that the MR had been adopted on 18 December 2008 and entered into force on 1 February 2009 according to its Article 76. In the rejection of the application, the court of first instance incorrectly referred to unchanged Article 75. The correction was published on 10 January 2009 in the EU Official Journal L7.[20]

Under Brussels I, a judgment shall not be recognised, if such recognition is manifestly contrary to public policy in the MS in which recognition is sought (Article 34(1)). Slovenian

---

[16]   *VSK Cpg 108/2013*; 17 October 2013.
[17]   *VSM I Cp 947/2015*; 12 January 2016.
[18]   *VSK Cpg 128/2013*; 30 August 2013.
[19]   *VSM I Cp 1093/2015*; 19 January 2016.
[20]   *VSM III Cp 867/2013*; 2 December 2013.

courts have faced this in several cases and decided that the threshold 'contrary to public policy' would be met only if the result of the recognition would be simply unsustainable. Mere opposition to national rules is not sufficient to justify that the judgment of a MS of the EU would be in conflict with the public policy of the State of recognition.[21] Further, the court was of the opinion that the right to be heard was a fundamental right which must be granted to the defendant in the court and which was elevated to the constitutional level in most MSs of the EU and was also a part of the international public order.[22]

The application of Brussels I revealed that the *exequatur* was an obstacle to the free circulation of judgments, entailed unnecessary costs and delays for the parties, and discouraged companies and citizens from seeking recognition and enforcement. Therefore, under Brussels Ia, a judgment given in a MS, which is enforceable in that MS, will be enforceable in another MS without any declaration of enforceability being required (Article 39). It seems that while Brussels Ia has closed some gaps, it opened a lot of new ones (eg it has not removed the grounds to challenge a foreign judgment, but only transfered the battle from the grounds for refusal of recognition to the stage of enforcement).[23]

B. Applicable Law Issues Under the Rome I and Rome II Regulations

i. Rome I

Apart from the above mentioned common problems, judges have not experienced any specific problems related to the application of Rome I.

a. Matters Related to the Scope of Application

In one case the HC handled the question of temporal application of Rome I. It established that Rome I did not apply to the credit contract in question but the Rome Convention (RC) was applicable as the credit relationship had been entered into before 17 December 2009, ie before the entry into force of Rome I. The case concerned the question of unlawfulness. By giving consent[24] to direct enforceability of a notarial deed, the creditor enabled the debtor to avoid using the path of litigation. The court stressed that the enforceable title gained in this way would be in contradiction of a mandatory rule of the forum.[25] Slovenian law does not allow interest on interest,[26] and in the case of a consumer contract, due to the public interest in the protection of consumers, a mandatory rule is used by Slovenian courts disregarding the law otherwise applicable to the contract (Article 7(2) of RC). This RC provision led in the present case to the use of mandatory rule provisions regulating the consumer protection in the context of loans, regarding the amount of interest as representing a special mandatory rule due to the public interest in consumer protection.[27]

---

[21] *VSRS Cpg 4/2006*; 13 June 2006.

[22] *VSRS Cpg 6/2014*; 26 February 2014.

[23] V Rijavec, J Sladič and JC Gomes, 'Introductory Chapter' in V Rijavec, T Ivanc and T Keresteš (eds), *Simplification of Debt Collection in the EU* (Alphen aan den Rijn, Wolters Kluwer Law, 2014) 5–6.

[24] Within the framework of party autonomy.

[25] *VSM I Ip 196/2015*; 29 May 2015.

[26] Prohibition of interest on interest is regulated by Art 375 of the Obligations Code (*Obligacijski zakonik*): UL RS, no 97/07–OCV.

[27] *VSM I Ip 196/2015*; 29 May 2015.

b. Matters Related to the Uniform Rules

In the following case we are facing again the problem of Rome I not being applied. The HC established that the defendant had practised law in Austria as a lawyer, where he had his seat. The court concluded that it had to establish first whether to apply Slovenian or Austrian law. However, as the court of first instance did not take a stand regarding applicable law, the HC was unable to evaluate the first instance decision.[28]

c. Conclusion

Due to the small number of Rome I cases it is not possible to make any realistic assessment, except for the already mentioned common problems (for example, judges facing language problems; the lack of high-quality literature; and problems with keeping up with rapid legal developments).

ii. Rome II

Only a few cases in which Rome II had been applied were found. Beside early problems related to the temporal aspect of the application,[29] no specific problems were detected. In one case, the court dealt with the question of the relationship between the Convention of 4 May 1971 on the Law Applicable to Traffic Accidents (HCLATA) and PILPA. The court confirmed that HCLATA had an advantage over PILPA and stressed that Rome II permits the use of HCLATA.[30] There were two cases related to applicable law under Article 8 (Infringement of intellectual property rights),[31] but no problems were detected.

C. Practice/Process

i. Slovenia's National Courts' Practice in Interpreting the Regulations/Process Issues

As already mentioned, the large and rapid stream of Regulations and case law initally caused problems in the intepretation of the Regulations. Nevertheless, judges regularly attend training sessions and, as a result, their knowledge and interpretation of the Regulations has improved. Judges at the SCRS display a good knowledge of the Regulations. Similarly, the knowledge of first instance court judges has improved and this is reflected in the quality of their decisions when interpreting the Regulations.

ii. Cost and Length of Litigation in Cross-border Civil and Commercial Disputes

One of the fundamental objectives of the Regulations is to ensure legal certainty and, thereby, positively affect the costs and the speed of the litigation. However, it is not possible to confirm whether this objective has been achieved in the RS since there are no specific statistics on this topic. The use of Regulations presents a degree of legal uncertainty, which is reflected particularly in the case of the possibility of forum shopping.

---

[28] *VSL I Cp 836/2015;* 29 June 2015.
[29] *Decision II Ips 1001/2007;* 16 December 2010.
[30] *VSL I Cp 1591/2015;* 23 September 2015.
[31] *VSL II Cp 1909/2014-*1 October 2014; and *VSL II Cp 2009/2009–*30 September 2015.

iii. Alternative Dispute Resolution for Cross-border Civil and Commercial Disputes

The field of alternative dispute resolution (ADR) is regulated in the RS by the Act on Alternative Dispute Resolution and Judicial Matters[32] and Out-of-Court Resolution of Consumer Disputes Act,[33] which can be used also in cross-border civil and commercial matters. Despite the fact that ADR is welcome and can contribute significantly towards limiting the length of the litigation and reducing its costs, it is still not much used in cross-border civil and commercial matters. The main reasons for this are the distance between the parties, the complexity of the disputes, and language barriers.

iv. Conclusion

The majority of available decisions relate to Brussels I, due to its long application and broad scope. The teething problems encountered by the judges in the process of the application of the Regulations (eg the temporal aspect) are now over. The CJEU case law is certainly a good guide for Slovenian judges, which is evident in the citations of the cases in Slovenian decisions. Most of the difficulties are related to jurisdiction (Brussels I), while applicable law does not indicate any major problems (Rome I and II).

D. Preliminary Remarks on Effectiveness of the Current EU PIL Framework in Civil and Commercial Law

The adoption of the Regulations is welcome because it has led to the harmonisation of private international law rules within the EU. This should increase legal certainty for the parties and decrease the costs and length of disputes. However, there are still certain areas of concern (eg forum shopping, public policy and differences between national rules). Some problems have been resolved with Brussels Ia (eg *exequatur*).

III. Slovenia's Experience on Cross-border Family Law Disputes

A. Jurisdictional and Procedural Issues Under the Brussels IIa Regulation

i. Matters Related to the Scope of Application

The scope of Brussels IIa is defined in Article 1 of the Regulation. In the RS, the term 'court' implies not only court proceedings, but also administrative proceedings. Therefore, Slovenian administrative proceedings by the Centre for Social Work (CSW) also fall within the scope of Brussels IIa.

---

[32] Act on Alternative Dispute Resolution and Judicial Matters (*Zakon o alternativnem reševanju sodnih sporov* (AADRJM): UL RS, no 97/09; 40/12.

[33] Out-of-Court Resolution of Consumer Disputes Act (*Zakon o izvensodnem reševanju potrošniških sporov*): UL RS, no 81/15.

ii. Matters Related to Jurisdiction

In some cases, problems arose regarding the interpretation of 'habitual residence'. The HC explained that habitual residence was to be considered as the place where a party is resident exclusively due to employment. It is irrelevant that a party has been registered in that place only for a short period of time and that it did not have the intention to remain there permanently. A mere formal declaration of habitual residence or the fact that someone is registered in a State as a temporary or permanent resident is not sufficient for the purposes of Brussels IIa.[34]

a. Parental Responsibility

1. Child Abduction

Prior to 2012, the Central Authority (CA) for the Hague Abduction Convention (HAC) was the Ministry of Interior Affairs. This situation caused numerous problems, mainly because of the lack of specialist knowledge on the part of the Ministry. Therefore, in 2012 this role was transferred to the Ministry of Labour, Family and Social matters (MLFSM). Today, both CAs (HAC and Brussels IIa) are at the same Ministry.

The RS does not have the so-called 'concentrated jurisdiction' for child abduction matters. Instead, jurisdiction is given to 11 district courts. Some of these district courts have judges who are specialised in family law matters. Alarmingly, judges at smaller district courts stated that they had no or very modest practical experience with child abduction cases. Nevertheless, judges with experience emphasised and praised the good cooperation with the Slovenian CA. The concentration of jurisdiction would be useful and also feasible as the RS is a small country and every district can be reached from the capital Ljubljana within two hours (if we proceed on the assumption that the District Court of Ljubljana would have jurisdiction and specialised judges).

Some cases on the return of the child resulted in the rejection of the return application due to a grave risk that the return would expose the child to physical or psychological harm or otherwise place the child in an intolerable situation.[35] Worryingly, the return proceedings were too long and therefore undermined the purpose of Brussels IIa and the HAC.[36]

Problems have occurred also in relation to the court practice regarding the hearing of the child. Since the failure to hear the child could lead to the refusal of recognition of the resulting Slovenian judgment abroad, the RS is working towards the improvement of the child hearing standards.[37]

In the RS, it is still an open question whether non-contentious or enforcement proceedings should be used in securing the actual return of a child following a return order granted

---

[34] *VSM III Cp 1643/2007–27* August 2007; *VSK Cp 431/2008–7* May 2008; *VSL IV Cp 1237/2012–3* May 2012.

[35] *VSM I Ip 623/2010–20* July 2010; *VSL IV Cp 1297/2012–9* May 2012; *VSL IV Cp 1/2015–28* January 2015.

[36] S Kraljić, 'Resna nevarnost kot razlog za zavrnitev vrnitve protipravno odpeljanega ali zadržanega otroka' (2015) 3 *Pravosodni bilten* 59–77; S Kraljić and K Drnovšek, 'Elterliche Internationale Kindesentführung, in M Župan (ed), 'Private International Law in the Jurisprudence of European Courts—family at focus' (Faculty of Law in Osijek, 2015) 185–203.

[37] S Kraljić, '12. člen KOP-pravica otroka do svobodnega izražanja v sodnih in upravnih postopkih' (2016) 1 *Pravosodni bilten* 11–30.

by a Slovenian court. The decsion as to which procedure will be used in a concrete case will depend on the facts of the case and on the decision of the judge.

2. Access

In the case of *Detiček v Sgueglia*[38] a request for a preliminary ruling was made under the urgent procedure, as to whether there was jurisdiction under Article 20 of Brussels IIa. The CJEU vehemently rejected the jurisdiction of the Slovenian court under Article 20. The CJEU stated that the opposite decision would undermine the principles on which Brussels IIa was based. The Court held that for jurisdiction under Article 20, three conditions had to be satisfied.[39] The CJEU criticised that the order would undermine the child's fundamental right under Article 24(3) of the Charter of Fundamental Rights of the EU to maintain a personal relationship with both parents, which can only be restricted if it is justified by another interest of the child that takes priority.[40]

iii. Matters Related to Recognition and Enforcement

One of the reasons for the non-recognition of a decision by a court of a Member State is an obvious violation of the public policy of that MS. RS is a MS of the EU and the Council of Europe and the so-called European public policy is part of Slovenian public policy.[41] The courts of the RS have to reject foreign court decisions, in spite of the fact that they do not violate domestic Slovenian public policy, if they violate European public policy. On the contrary, Slovenian courts may not reject judgments of foreign courts in spite of their opposition to domestic Slovenian public policy, if this rejection would be unacceptable or disproportionate from the European perspective.[42]

iv. Cooperation between Central Authorities in Matters of Parental Responsibility

The CA cooperates efficiently with other governmental agencies, especially the Ministry of Justice (MJ), the Ministry of the Interior and the CSW. Communications are verbal, by mail and electronically. The CA also has a very good working relationship with judges.

v. Conclusion

The Slovenian CA has only one employee. In 2014, the CA handled 13 cases on international child abduction. This means that the only employee dealt with all 13 cases. So, one may talk about understaffing at the Slovenian CA;[43] however, based on the above annual number of cases, the current staffing structure seems sufficient. Nevertheless, a sole employee could pose a problem in the case of absence for example due to illness or attendance at a training

---

[38] Case C-403/09 PPU *Jasna Detiček v Maurizio Sgueglia* EU:C:2009:810.

[39] ibid para 39.

[40] ibid para 59.

[41] J Kramberger Škerl, 'Javni red pri priznanju in izvršitvi tujih sodnih odločb' (2005) 65 *Zbornik znanstvenih razprav* 267–73.

[42] *VSRS II Ips 462/2009*; 28 January 2010.

[43] The problem related to understaffing is also visible in the Slovenian HCCH Country Profile, which, due to lack of personnel, has not been updated since 2012. See www.hcch.net/en/publications-and-studies/details4/?pid=5416&dtid=42.

session. In case the number of cases rises, the duties will increase and it will be necessary to increase the number of employees at the CA accordingly.

Problems are related also to the child's right to be heard (especially in return proceedings). That is at the discretion of the judge, who makes the decision to hear the child on the basis of the child's age and capability to understand the meaning and consequences of his/her opinion.

a. Possible Solutions

It would be more appropriate for the CA to be under the auspices of the MJ since the CA exercises the powers conferred by Brussels IIa and HAC that fall under the MJ. The formation of common minimum standards concerning the hearing of the child could contribute to the extension of safeguards for children. In the EU, there are 28 MSs which differ in their court systems, child law regulations (substantive and procedural) and approaches to hearing children. Therefore, the common minimum standards could lead to a higher level of uniform rules which could provide the MS and parties with more predictability and legal security, and could increase the effectiveness of return orders.

B. Jurisdictional and Procedural Issues and Applicable Law Under the Maintenance Regulation

The MR is also represented by very little case law, however, there is a visible, although slow, tendency towards an increase.

i. Matters Related to the Scope of Application, Applicable Law or to the Recognition, Enforceability and Actual Enforcement of Decisions

No specific problems related to the scope of application, applicable law or to the recognition, enforceability and actual enforcement of decisions have been identified.

ii. Matters Related to Jurisdiction

The Slovenian court dealt with the question of jurisdiction in a case involving the Slovenian Maintenance Fund (SMF), under Brussels I that had determined jurisdiction in matters of maintenance prior to the MR. The case is mentioned here as, had it been dealt with under the MR, the decision would have been the same. In this case, the Slovenian Court encountered the problem of the distinction between the term 'maintenance matter' and 'other civil matters'. The child's habitual residence was in the RS, and the father's domicile was in Russia. The father did not pay maintenance and his maintenance debt amounted to 2,800 Euros. The court rejected jurisdiction under Article 5(2) of Brussels I as the plaintiff was not the child but the SMF, which was the creditor in relation to the father. The right of the SMF was based on the decision of the maintenance replacement made by the SMF, and not on the relationship between the child and the father. The Court held that it was not a litigation over maintenance because the SMF did not pay maintenance but rather a maintenance replacement. Therefore, this was a pure money claim acquired by the cession.

Based on this, neither Brussels I nor the MR was applicable. Therefore, Slovenian PILPA was applicable and the general jurisdictional provision (*actor sequitur forum rei*) was used. Consequently, Russian courts had jurisdiction.[44]

iii. Conclusion

The frequency of the application of the MR is slowly increasing, and it is expected that more cases will bring more open questions in the future.

C. Practice/Process

i. Slovenia's National Courts' Practice in Interpreting the Regulations

In addition to the aforementioned common critical points related to all five Regulations, the Slovenian courts encountered problems in the application of Brussels IIa regarding the interpretation of habitual residence, the temporal criteria and the hearing of the child, due to divergent national approaches in this respect.

ii. Alternative Dispute Resolution for Cross-border Family Law Disputes

The AADRJM imposes on the courts of first and second instance the obligation to enable the parties in family and other civil matters to use ADR. Mediation is available at all stages, but court-connected mediation is available only during the court proceedings and the judge must take care whether the case is suitable for mediation. The ADR, especially mediation, should have an impact on the costs and length of litigation. Mediation is particularly welcome in international child abduction cases. No concrete information is available regarding the numbers of cross-border family law disputes where mediation was used—successfully or unsuccessfully.

D. Preliminary Remarks on Effectiveness of the Current EU PIL Framework in Cross-border Family Law

In spite of the fact that the RS has been a MS of the EU for 12 years, the presence and visibility of the use of the Regulations is still at a low level. Due to this, we estimate that this field is still under-researched and in urgent need of additional research. Regarding the actual court decisions, it is obvious that certain judgments (IV Cp 1792/2007) can only be understood as a consequence of a lack of knowledge. Judges who are interested in this field are in search of additional education in the RS (eg in relation to the hearing of the child, jurisdiction and child abduction) and abroad.

---

[44] *VSM I Cp 328/2007*; 13 February 2007.

IV. Conclusion

The early issues that followed the entry of the RS into the EU (eg the lack of understanding of the difference between material and procedural law) have been resolved but time has brought new problems. Judges experience difficulties due to the difference between the national legal regime and the EU Regulations as the latter frequently differ from national legislation. The gathering of relevant statistical data should be considered; it would be welcomed by judges as well as other stakeholders such as insurance companies and law faculties.

30

Sweden

MICHAEL BOGDAN AND ULF MAUNSBACH

I. Introduction

The Swedish legal system is generally considered to belong to the Nordic sub-family of 'continental' legal systems. The Nordic systems are often considered to be more practical and pragmatically orientated and less conceptualistic than German and French law; they lack comprehensive private law codifications similar to the German *Bürgerliches Gesetzbuch* or the French *Code civil*; and they are not influenced by Roman law to the same degree as French and German law. Most materials about Swedish law are available in the Swedish language only and are thus rarely accessible to non-Nordic jurists.[1]

Sweden is a member of the European Union (EU), having joined its predecessor, the European Communities, on 1 January 1995. The directly applicable EU Private International Law (PIL) statutes, among them the Rome I,[2] Rome II,[3] Brussels Ia,[4] Brussels IIa,[5] and the Maintenance Regulations[6] constitute parts of Swedish private international law and they have done so since the day each of them became applicable. However, the amount of Swedish case law and Swedish legal writing on them is very limited, mainly due to the fact that Sweden is a relatively small jurisdiction in terms of population, resulting in a limited number of disputes. Another possible factor is that Swedes are not particularly litigious and that many—probably most—commercial disputes are either settled or decided by arbitrators rather than by courts of law.

It is also important to mention that in the Swedish legal system, judicial decisions of higher courts are not considered to constitute binding precedents, even though they have

---

[1] A summary presentation in English of the Swedish legal system, written by leading Swedish experts in their respective legal fields, is M Bogdan (ed), *Swedish Legal System* (Stockholm, Norstedts Juridik, 2010).

[2] Reg 593/2008 of 17 June 2008 on the law applicable to contractual obligations, [2008] OJ L177/6.

[3] Reg 864/2007 of 11 July 2007 on the law applicable to non-contractual obligations, [2007] OJ L199/40.

[4] Reg 1215/2012 of 12 December 2012 on jurisdiction and the recognition and enforcement of judgments in civil and commercial matters (recast), [2012] OJ L351/1, and its predecessor: Reg 44/2001 of 22 December 2000 on jurisdiction and the recognition and enforcement of judgments in civil and commercial matters, [2001] OJ L12/1 ('Brussels I').

[5] Reg 2201/2003 of 27 November 2003 concerning jurisdiction and the recognition and enforcement of judgments in matrimonial matters and the matters of parental responsibility, repealing Reg 1347/2000, [2003] OJ L338/1.

[6] Reg 4/2009 of 18 December 2008 on jurisdiction, applicable law, recognition and enforcement of decisions and cooperation in matters relating to maintenance obligations, [2009] OJ L7/1.

considerable persuasive authority. The general Swedish court of last resort in matters covered by the five Regulations mentioned above is the Swedish Supreme Court, whose decisions are published in yearly volumes of *Nytt Juridiskt Arkiv* (NJA). Not all of its judgments are reported in full though, as those considered less interesting are merely presented summarily as 'notices'. Decisions of the Swedish courts of first instance remain generally unpublished and unknown, whereas a small selection of judgments rendered by the courts of appeal is published in the yearly volumes of *Rättsfall från hovrätterna* (RH). Private international law issues arise sometimes even in the centralised Labour Court, whose decisions are normally published in the yearly volumes of *Arbetsdomstolens domar* (AD). Sweden also has a system of administrative courts, which may occasionally have to deal with the Brussels IIa Regulation, for example if the family status of a person is to be recorded in the official population register or is relevant for the purposes of immigration or welfare benefits.[7]

When interpreting directly applicable EU law, Swedish courts lack one auxiliary source of law that has traditionally been considered very important in Sweden, namely the *travaux préparatoires*, in particular the Government Bills submitted to the Parliament in connection with the Government's legislative proposals. Their function is in respect of EU Regulations to some extent fulfilled by the recitals, but these are much less detailed than the *travaux préparatoires* that Swedish judges have been used to. At the same time, Swedish courts seem to be rather reluctant to refer questions regarding interpretation of EU law to the Court of Justice of the European Union (CJEU) for preliminary rulings.

As mentioned above, Swedish legal writing regarding the five Regulations is relatively meagre. There are, of course, some articles published in Swedish legal periodicals and the Regulations are presented, in a relatively concise manner, in the standard Swedish textbook on private international law.[8] Only two out of the five above-mentioned Regulations have been analysed and commented on in proper monographs written by Swedish authors, namely the Brussels I Regulation of 2000[9] and the Rome II Regulation.[10]

It should also be kept in mind that Sweden is a party to the European Convention for the Protection of Human Rights and Fundamental Freedoms of 1950 and that pursuant to Chapter 2, Section 19 of the Swedish Constitution (*Regeringsformen*) this Convention has a semi-constitutional status and is directly applicable in Swedish courts. Experience of other countries shows that in some situations conflicts may arise between Sweden's obligations under EU law and those under the Convention.[11] It is not quite clear which of the two instruments should prevail in such cases.

---

[7] More detailed general information about the Swedish judicial system can be found on www.domstol.se/Funktioner/English/.

[8] See M Bogdan, *Svensk Internationell Privat- och Processrätt* 8th edn (Stockholm, Norstedts Juridik AB, 2014) 8. cf also M Bogdan, *Concise Introduction to EU Private International Law* 3rd edn (Groningen, Europa Law Publishing, 2016).

[9] See L Pålsson, *Bryssel I-förordningen jämte Bryssel- och Luganokonventionerna* (Stockholm, Norstedts Juridik, 2008). This commentary is to a large extent still useful for the interpretation of some parts of the Brussels Ia Reg.

[10] See M Hellner, *Rom II-förordningen* (Stockholm, Norstedts Juridik, 2014).

[11] See, for example, the judgments of the European Court of Human Rights in the cases of *Šneersone and Kampanella v Italy* A no 14737 (2009) and *Povse v Austria* A no 3890 (2011), both dealing with cross-border child abductions.

II. Sweden's Experience on Cross-border Civil and Commercial Disputes

A. Jurisdictional and Procedural Issues Under the Brussels I Regulation

i. Introductory Remark

So far, the Brussels Ia Regulation has not given rise to any published Swedish court decisions. However, there are almost 40 published cases dealing with its predecessors, ie the 1968 Brussels Convention[12] and the Brussels I Regulation,[13] as well as with its 'sisters', the Lugano Conventions of 1988 and 2007. Most of these cases are not of particular interest, but some of them may be relevant for the understanding of identically worded provisions of the Brussels Ia Regulation. Most of the cases concern jurisdiction whereas only a few deal with recognition and enforcement of judgments.

Space constraints make it impossible to present this case law in a meaningful manner within the framework of this short chapter. We have therefore decided to limit ourselves to mentioning a couple of cases illustrating the interrelationship between Swedish law and the Regulation.

ii. Matters Related to Jurisdiction

In several decisions involving the Brussels I jurisdictional rules, the Supreme Court relied on the so-called 'assertion doctrine' (*påståendedoktrinen*) of Swedish procedural law.[14] According to this doctrine, whenever a certain disputed fact is relevant both for jurisdiction and for the substance of the dispute, the assertion by the plaintiff that the fact exists is accepted as correct for the purposes of jurisdiction, unless the assertion is manifestly incorrect. The main purpose of the doctrine is to avoid having to check the existence of the same fact twice, first for the purpose of jurisdiction and, if jurisdiction is found to exist, once again when dealing with the substance of the dispute. For example, if the plaintiff brings an action relating to tort, claiming that according to Article 7(2) of the Brussels Ia Regulation Swedish jurisdiction can be based on the respondent having caused damage in Sweden, whereas the respondent denies the existence of any such damage, the court will in principle assume jurisdiction and leave the issue of the damage to be resolved within the framework of the examination of the merits of the case. An important consequence of this approach under Swedish procedural law is that if the court dismisses the action on the merits, the decision will have the effect of *res judicata* and prevent the plaintiff from

---

[12] See the Convention of 22 September 1968 on jurisdiction and the enforcement of judgments in civil and commercial matters, [1998] OJ C27/3. The Convention applied in Sweden as from 1 January 1999 until its rules were replaced by those of the Brussels I Reg.

[13] See Reg 44/2001 of 22 December 2000 on jurisdiction and the recognition and enforcement of judgments in civil and commercial matters, [2001] OJ L12/1.

[14] See eg NJA 2005, 586, NJA 2007, 1000 and NJA 2012, 483.

starting new proceedings in another Member State, whereas a dismissal on the ground of the lack of Swedish jurisdiction would not have such effect. A recent CJEU judgment somewhat restricts the possibilities of Swedish courts to use the assertion doctrine in the context of jurisdiction under the Brussels Ia Regulation, as it stipulates the obligation to assess all available evidence, including the arguments put forward by the defendant, without requiring a comprehensive taking of evidence.[15]

A case illustrating that in some situations Swedish procedural law must be adapted to the Brussels rules was decided by the Supreme Court in a matter concerning a provisional protective measure granted to a Luxembourg plaintiff.[16] After the respondent objected to the jurisdiction of Swedish courts and claimed that Luxembourg courts had exclusive jurisdiction due to a prorogation agreement between the parties, the plaintiff withdrew his claim. According to Swedish procedural law, this should lead to an immediate cancelling of the provisional measure. Nevertheless, the Supreme Court, without any clear support in the Swedish Code of Judicial Procedure (1942:5, as amended), decided that the provisional measure would remain in force and accorded the plaintiff one month to initiate proceedings in a competent court in Luxembourg.

iii. Matters Related to Recognition and Enforcement

Pursuant to the principle that procedural matters not governed by the Regulation are governed by the *lex fori* (Swedish law), the Supreme Court has decided, with reference to Article 40(1) and 55(2) of the Brussels I Regulation of 2000, that it is for the party applying for a declaration of enforceability to bear the costs of translation of the documents into Swedish, irrespective of the fact that the costs of translation would be higher than the amount the applicant was entitled to under the judgment in question, so that the enforcement would be meaningless.[17] This decision is relevant not only for the enforcement of older judgments subject to the Brussels I Regulation, but also for the application of Article 37(2) of the Brussels Ia Regulation.

The Supreme Court has also held that in accordance with Swedish procedural law, the judgment debtor is not obliged to compensate the judgment creditor for costs connected with the first stage of the proceedings for a declaration of enforceability, ie the stage where pursuant to Article 41 of the Brussels I Regulation the judgment debtor is not entitled to make any submissions on the application.[18]

iv. Conclusion

A general conclusion regarding the application of the Brussels/Lugano rules in Swedish courts is that there are no serious problems. Swedish courts have become accustomed to them and they are generally applied in accordance with the interpretative guidance provided by the CJEU.

---

[15] See Case C-12/15 *Universal Music v Schilling* EU:C:2016:449.
[16] See NJA 2006, 364.
[17] See NJA 2011, 345.
[18] See eg NJA 2009, 632.

There are no available statistics in Sweden that would make it possible to draw conclusions regarding cross-border cases as to costs and the length of litigation.

B. Applicable Law Issues under the Rome I and Rome II Regulations

i. Introductory Remark

According to the opinion traditionally prevailing in Swedish legal writing, applicable foreign law is to be applied upon the court's own initiative (*ex officio*), including in business-to-business disputes that are of such a nature that they could be settled. Nevertheless, Swedish courts sometimes tend to interpret the silence of the parties regarding the issue of applicable law as meaning that the parties agree on the application of Swedish law.[19] However, the number of cases from Swedish courts in this area is very small, which makes it problematic to draw reliable conclusions.

A factor that may contribute to the lack of court cases is the fact that Sweden is a popular place for carrying out arbitration proceedings that deal with international commercial disputes. As arbitral awards are usually confidential and unpublished, and as an incorrect application of conflict rules by arbitrators cannot in principle be subject to appeal to Swedish courts of law, it is not known to what extent the Rome I and Rome II Regulations are applied by arbitrators. Furthermore, the arbitrators used in international commercial arbitration taking place in Sweden are frequently foreign jurists and their practice does not necessarily reflect the views prevailing in Sweden.

ii. Rome I

There are no published cases. There are some published decisions of the Supreme Court and of the Labour Court where the Regulation's predecessor, the Rome Convention of 1980,[20] was or should have been applied, but they are of no particular interest. In most of them, the parties agreed on the application of Swedish law.[21] In one case, the Labour Court seems to have mistakenly disregarded Articles 3(4) and 8(1) of the Convention (corresponding to Articles 3(5) and 10(1) of the Rome I Regulation) by not applying the law chosen by the parties to the validity of the choice-of-law clause itself.[22]

iii. Rome II

There appears to be only one published decision applying the Rome II Regulation, namely a provisional judgment of the Labour Court concerning the law applicable to

---

[19] See, eg NJA 1977, 92.
[20] See the Convention on the law applicable to contractual obligations, opened for signature in Rome on 19 June 1980 (80/934/EEC).
[21] See, eg, NJA 2008, 24, AD 2009 No 39, AD 2009 No 76, AD 2015 No 70.
[22] See AD 2007 No 2.

the legality of an industrial action in the absence of a collective agreement between the parties.[23] Article 9 of the Regulation stipulates that the law applicable to a non-contractual obligation in respect of the liability of workers, employees and their organisations for damages caused by an industrial action is the law of the country where that action is to be or has been taken. This gave rise to the question of whether Article 9 covers also the issue of the legality per se of the industrial action, or merely the consequences of its unlawfulness, ie the issues of liability. Recital 28 of the Regulation states clearly that Article 9 is without prejudice to the conditions relating to the exercise of industrial action, but the Labour Court decided to avoid this question and expressed the view that due to the circumstances *in casu*, the legality would be governed by the same law (Swedish law) regardless of whether Article 9 applied or not. The value of this decision as precedent is thus very small, especially as it was provisional and thus was not based on an in-depth legal analysis.

iv. Conclusion

Due to the scarcity of published judicial decisions, it is not possible to draw any far-reaching conclusions about the functioning of the Rome I and Rome II Regulations in Sweden. In some cases, even though the outcome was consistent with the Regulations, it is not certain whether they were consciously applied by the court, as they were not explicitly referred to.

A general observation is that Swedish courts and parties to disputes within Sweden tend to accept or even prefer Swedish law and that Swedish courts tend to interpret silence of the parties as an acceptance of *lex fori*. Consequently, a general recommendation to parties who seek foreign law to be applied would be to plead it, rather than to expect the court to apply foreign law on its own initiative.

C. Preliminary Remarks on Effectiveness of the Current EU PIL Framework in Civil and Commercial Law

As already indicated, due to the scarcity of case law, it is difficult to make a substantial and statistically reliable assessment regarding the effectiveness in Sweden of the current EU PIL framework in civil and commercial law. However, it can be said that Swedish courts are reluctant to send preliminary questions to the CJEU, but at the same time they respect the existing CJEU case law.

Regarding costs and length of litigation we cannot, as stated, draw any specific conclusions, but it is obvious that cross-border disputes are generally more complex than the domestic ones, which leads to higher costs in terms of both costs and time.

It is to be added that mediation is becoming important in Sweden, even though arbitration is still the leading alternative to traditional court proceedings.

---

[23] See AD 2011 No 95.

III. Sweden's Experience on Cross-border Family Law Disputes

A. Jurisdictional and Procedural Issues Under the Brussels IIa Regulation

i. Matters Related to Jurisdiction

a. Child Abduction

Almost all of the published decisions regarding the Brussels IIa Regulation deal with parental responsibility, especially cross-border child abductions.[24]

In one Supreme Court case,[25] a father domiciled in the Czech Republic applied for the return of children who had been retained in Sweden by the mother without the father's consent. The Court held that at the time of the move the children had their habitual residence in the Czech Republic and that the retention had been wrongful under the Regulation and the 1980 Hague Convention, but the return order was refused because in the meantime the mother had obtained a Czech court's provisional permission to stay in Sweden together with the children.

Two published decisions of appellate courts deal with Article 13(1)(b) of the 1980 Hague Convention on the Civil Aspects of International Child Abduction, permitting to refuse to return an abducted child if there is a grave risk that the return would expose the child to physical or psychological harm or otherwise place the child in an intolerable situation. Article 11 of the Brussels IIa Regulation can be said to incorporate the Convention into EU law, albeit with some additions. Thus, Article 11(4) of the Regulation provides that the refusal on the basis of Article 13(1)(b) of the Convention is not permitted if it is established that adequate arrangements have been made to secure the protection of the child after its return. In one appellate decision,[26] the court declared that Article 13(1)(b) of the Convention (or rather the Swedish Act 1989:14 implementing the Convention) has to be interpreted restrictively and decided that the abducted child be returned to Finland because the risk of harm was not sufficiently proved, in spite of the fact that a Finnish court had issued a protective order forbidding the violent father from contacting the mother (there were also circumstances indicating that the mother had been advised to move with the child to Sweden by the Finnish social welfare authorities, which even covered the costs of the move). An opposite approach was taken in another appellate decision,[27] where the return to Italy of a child wrongfully moved to Sweden by its mother was refused because of the alleged undiagnosed health problems of the child, in spite of a guarantee from the competent Italian authorities that the child would receive proper care in Italy. The court

---

[24] But see NJA 2008, 71, where the Supreme Court, after having obtained a preliminary ruling from the CJEU in the matter of *Sundelind Lopez v Lopez Lizazo* (Case C-68/07 *Sundelin Lopez v Lopez Lizazo* EU:C:2007:740), held that it had no jurisdiction in the divorce case.

[25] See NJA 2012, 269.

[26] See RH 2006 No 60.

[27] See RH 2014 No 5.

interpreted Article 11(4) of the Brussels IIa Regulation as to cover only cases where the refusal had to do with a harmful environment rather than with the child's health. Such restrictive interpretation of Article 11(4) is, to say the least, highly controversial.

b. Other Issues Related to Parental Responsibility

In a decision rendered in 2006,[28] the Supreme Administrative Court applied Swedish law when examining Swedish jurisdiction to protect a child by placing it in a foster family or an institution. The relevant Swedish provisions are in Sweden deemed to belong to the area of public (welfare) law. A subsequent CJEU judgment, concerning the same family but initiated by a request submitted by a Finnish court, shows that the Supreme Administrative Court had erred by not applying the Brussels IIa Regulation, because the CJEU, using autonomous interpretation, considered the issue to be a 'civil matter'.[29]

In 2011, the Swedish Supreme Court had to decide whether Swedish courts had jurisdiction in a case where the father sued for the custody of a child who was in the sole custody of the mother, who had moved from Sweden to Indonesia, taking the child with her.[30] This was not a child abduction case, because the mother, in her capacity as the sole custodian, was under Swedish law entitled to decide where the child would live. Pursuant to Article 8 of the Brussels IIa Regulation, the courts of a Member State have jurisdiction in custody matters over a child who is habitually resident there at the time the court is seised. When examining the habitual residence of the child, the Supreme Court referred to the case law of the CJEU and concluded that despite the short time since the move to Indonesia, the child could not be considered to have its habitual residence in Sweden any longer. As no other Member State had jurisdiction under the Regulation, the residual jurisdiction of Swedish courts under Article 14 depended on autonomous Swedish jurisdictional rules, but as these rules were found to correspond to those of the Regulation, the father's action was dismissed. An interesting aspect of this decision is that it confirms that the application of the Brussels IIa Regulation does not presuppose any connection between the case and an EU Member State other than that of the forum.[31]

B. Jurisdictional and Procedural Issues and Applicable Law Under the Maintenance Regulation

There are no published cases. There is some case law, dating from the time before the enactment of the Maintenance Regulation, concerning the recognition and enforcement of maintenance judgments pursuant to the Lugano Convention, but these decisions are not relevant any more for the interpretation of the Regulation.[32] In one case, a Polish default

---

[28] See RÅ 2006 ref 36.
[29] See Case C-523/07 *Re A* EU:C:2009:257.
[30] See NJA 2011, 499.
[31] Cf the CJEU judgment in the case of *Owusu v Jackson*, (Case C-281/02 *Owusu v Jackson* EU:C:2005:120) concerning the scope of the Brussels Convention of 1968.
[32] See eg NJA 2001, 911; RH 2004 No 35.

judgment regarding maintenance was refused enforceability by the Swedish Supreme Court pursuant to Article 34(2) of the Brussels I Regulation because the defendant in the Polish proceedings had not been served with the document instituting the proceedings and therefore had not been able to arrange for his defence.[33]

C. Preliminary Remarks on Effectiveness of the Current EU PIL Framework in Cross-border Family Law

Our preliminary remarks as to the effectiveness of the current EU PIL framework in cross-border family law to a large extent coincide with our observations above as to the effectiveness of the framework in civil and commercial law, except that arbitration does not play an important role in family law.

IV. Conclusion

Our first concluding comment is to underline once more the fact that there is a very limited number of Swedish cases. Furthermore, although an eager recipient of new technology in general, Sweden remains a developing country as regards systematic electronic publication of case law. It is therefore difficult to find relevant statistical data, even regarding the few cases that have actually been decided. In addition, some information (eg the costs) is usually deleted even from the published judgments.

One observation is that Swedish courts seem to follow obediently the CJEU case law in close relation to the wording of the judgments. Another observation is that there is a slight trend to favour *lex fori* as regards applicable law. This, however, is a problem related to human nature and it can hardly be totally eliminated.

As to the need for reform we have no particular suggestions. This might seem like an excessively careful conclusion, but it indicates that there are no serious problems regarding the application of EU private international law in Sweden. One reform in this field has actually just taken place. Until recently, the Svea Court of Appeal in Stockholm had a monopoly with regard to almost all *exequatur* proceedings regarding foreign judgments. Due to amendments that entered into force on 10 January 2015, this responsibility was moved to a number of district courts, but this procedural reform is not expected to entail any substantive changes in practice.

---

[33] See NJA 2012 N 20.

31

Promoting Efficient Litigation?

STEPHEN DNES[1]

I. Introduction

The EU's approach to streamlining jurisdiction implies at least a degree of approval for an increased role for litigation. This is a point requiring careful management from a wider social perspective, because although the enforcement of a rule can bring significant efficiency benefits, there is always the risk that the significant resources employed in litigation might not, in fact, give rise to net social benefit. The aim of this chapter is to consider the state of play with the reforms in light of whether a wider social benefit is, in fact, being achieved. In doing so, it expressly adopts the rule-utilitarian framework of using an efficiency benchmark on an economic approach, and while it is acknowledged that there can be theoretical limitations to any utilitarian approach, it is hoped that the insights gained from the application of the framework demonstrate its own utility in this case.[2]

In brief outline, the main question from an economic perspective is whether an activity is socially beneficial, meaning that society enjoys a positive *net* benefit from the activity. To take a straightforward example, the enforcement of a tort law duty of care is highly likely to promote social welfare, because the rule that compensation must flow where *unreasonable* risks have been taken is likely to promote cost-effective prevention measures. In Judge Calabresi's famous phrase, the 'least cost avoider' is encouraged to take the steps needed to avoid the accident,[3] but only those that are efficient, as discussed below with reference to the famous *Carroll Towing* case.[4] The main idea is that the costs of enforcing the rule are

---

[1] The author thanks participants at the EUPILLAR conference held at the London School of Economics in May 2016 for their helpful contributions. The usual disclaimer applies.

[2] Well-known limitations turn especially on the scope for 'utility monsters' whose utility is derived from decreases in others' utility (ie envious preferences) but whose gain is greater than the other party's loss, hence increasing social welfare overall. However, cases like that of the utility monster are rather stylised, and seem unlikely to emerge in reality. A better assessment of the use of utilitarian approaches perhaps lies in practical aspects, including whether they are useful in gaining insight into the operation of rules, and especially on whether statistical analysis suggests that the causal effects posited by some writers exist to a satisfactory level of statistical robustness.

[3] See especially G Calabresi, *The Costs of Accidents: A Legal and Economic Analysis* (New Haven CT, Yale University Press, 1970). The literature applying Judge Calabresi's insights is very broad and is reviewed in G Dari-Mattiacci and N Garoupa, 'Least-Cost Avoidance: The Tragedy of Common Safety' (2009) 25(1) *Journal of Law, Economics and Organization* 235–61.

[4] *United States v Carroll Towing Co* 159 F.2d 169 (2d Cir 1947). For a detailed and more formal treatment, see also RA Posner, 'An Economic Approach to Legal Procedure and Judicial Administration' (1973) 2(2) *Journal of Legal Studies* 399, 402.

below the economic benefit from having the rule: in this case, fewer accidents result from the cost-effective prior care encouraged by the rule.

A significant question in the decision to expand the role for litigation is whether the increased litigation is net beneficial, or perhaps net harmful, and the question is a challenging one because of the scope for some litigation to be helpful, and some harmful. This chapter will attempt to evaluate aspects of the emerging litigation pattern from this wider social perspective. First, however, a detailed analysis of two questions is required: (1) The definition of net socially beneficial litigation, and (2) with this definition in place, whether efficiency turns separately on the procedural rules in place or whether it is simply derived from it. Following this theoretical analysis, it goes on to a third question, (3) considering the emerging litigation pattern and how this fits into the wider question of social benefit.

II. Welfare Analysis of Litigation

A. The Promotion of Efficient Practices

The foundational idea in any economic analysis of law is that the incentive properties of laws should be considered with a view to their wider social impact.[5] Many laws significantly impact incentive structures, and, especially in a commercial context, are often designed to remedy incentive properties that would themselves be less than optimal. A core example is the role of the law of contract in promoting long-term investment. Other devices might exist to encourage long-term investment in commercial interactions but it is doubtful that they would be as efficient as having a general legal rule of enforcement.[6]

As above, tort law provides another core example of the role the law can play in promoting cost-effective care. The *Carroll Towing* case is especially instructive and bears close analysis, in line with its foundational status as the focus of significant analysis by economic analysts of law. The case provides the general rule on negligence in many (but not all) US jurisdictions, and is analogous in role to *Donoghue v Stevenson* in English negligence law.[7] In similar vein to Lord Atkin's well-known 'neighbourhood principle' by which duties of care are owed on the basis of a range of factors defining sufficient neighbourhood between claimant and defendant, notably proximity, Judge Learned Hand outlined a probabilistic approach to defining the scope of a duty of care. In a statement that has echoed through law school classrooms ever since, Judge Hand said:

> The owner's duty, as in other similar situations, to provide against resulting injuries is a function of three variables: (1) The probability that she will break away; (2) the gravity of the resulting injury,

---

[5] The canonical work on the economic analysis of law is Judge Posner's Treatise *Economic Analysis of Law* (first published 1977, 9th edn, Alphen aan den Rijn, Aspen, 2014). Many other works have followed, but Posner's remains the sole Treatise on the subject.

[6] The legal system is of course not the only element in protecting a relationship-specific investment; other examples include signalling mechanisms, eg opulent banking premises emphasising liquidity and stability, and reputational investments designed to encourage repeat business, thereby lowering transaction costs. However, it is doubtful that these mechanisms alone would suffice to encourage the optimal level of investment, compared with the added value brought by the law in enforcing the contract in question.

[7] *Donoghue v Stevenson* [1932] UKHL 100.

if she does; (3) the burden of adequate precautions. Possibly it serves to bring this notion into relief to state it in algebraic terms: if the probability be called P; the injury, L; and the burden, B; liability depends upon whether B is less than L multiplied by P: ie, whether $B < PL$.[8]

One can debate how far the resulting 'calculus of negligence' can be applied consistently in practical cases, but the underlying idea is highly compelling from the perspective of social welfare. First, one estimates the scope of a burden that would have prevented the accident in question. Then, one estimates the size of the loss, adjusted for the probability that it might take place. In this way, where applied correctly, a rational actor would take steps to prevent accidents where doing so is cost effective. Significant debate can be had over how far this approach is in practice optimal, and the scope of a negligence rule to leave some losses uncompensated (absent other intervention, eg government compensation for losses caused by truly exceptional risks) may give disquiet. Yet the core point for our analysis could not be clearer: the application of the calculus, at least in most cases, will result in the promotion of cost effective care. Whatever methodological debate might be had, one is safe in saying that in the core case the application of the rule leads to incentives towards taking steps that are net beneficial considering their costs and benefits. Therefore, expanding this type of litigation seems likely to promote welfare, at least where its benefits are net positive and the resources involved in doing so are relatively modest.

It is important to note here that a very substantial gain can be had from broadening the scope of such a rule, eg through the removal of arguably arbitrary impediments such as jurisdictional bars, not least because the existence of a well-known rule, if efficient, is likely to encourage efficient practices in its shadow. Applying *Carroll Towing* as an example, it is likely that cost-effective care is expanded by the existence of the rule and that the costs involved in litigation will be substantially outweighed by negotiation taking place in the shadow of the rule.

In this calculus, it is helpful to distinguish public and social costs, which can significantly diverge. Private litigation costs are those borne by the party bringing the litigation, eg legal fees. These will often be internalised by the litigation process: whether or not they are shifted from one party to another, it is doubtful that they would have a significant impact beyond those who are party to the litigation. By contrast, many of the wider costs and benefits of litigation are social in character, meaning that they fall on society at large.[9]

The divergence between the social and private costs of litigation can pose significant issues in encouraging efficient litigation, and might be an important point for reforms to litigation procedures to address. There is scope for the transaction costs associated with class actions having scope to overwhelm the private benefit from the cases, despite potentially significant social benefits, especially where strategic incentives arise to withhold information and so to drive divergence between private and social costs, as posited by game theoretic analysis.[10] For this reason, public enforcement was often the starting point for

---

[8] *Carroll Towing*, above n 4, 173.

[9] See eg TJ Micheli, *Economics of the Law, Torts, Contracts, Property, Litigation* (Oxford, Oxford University Press, 1997) Ch 9. The point was developed very extensively in literature on the economics of litigation in the 1980s: See L Kaplow, 'Private Versus Social Costs in Bringing Suit' (1986) 15(2) *Journal of Legal Studies* 371–86; See also S Shavell, 'The Social Versus the Private Incentive to Bring Suit in a Costly Legal System' (1982) 11 *Journal of Legal Studies* 333. See more in A Dnes, *The Economics of Law: Property, Contracts and Obligations* 2nd edn (Mason, South-western College Publishing, 2004) ch 8.

[10] IPL P'ng 'Strategic Behavior in Suit, Settlement, and Trial' (1983) 14(2) *Bell Journal of Economics* 539–50.

such cases, and the move to a greater role for private litigation will need to take careful account of the divergence between private and social costs in these cases.

In the contemporary context, at least on the assumption that rules applied by EU law are welfare-enhancing, there may be substantial gains from the expansion of jurisdiction under a more consolidated jurisdictional position, if there is relatively low level of enforcement of the rules at present. For example, EU competition law forbids a number of economically harmful activities, eg 'hardcore' price-fixing cartels.[11] Environmental and product design rules might be thought to have a similarly helpful impact, if enforced. Yet the enforcement appears to be partial: cartels remain widespread, consumer rights laid out in legislation remain unclaimed, and many government offices do not always comply with the letter of the applicable EU law.[12] To the extent that there is benefit from enforcing the rules, it is possible that the Commission's moves to ease the jurisdictional hurdles faced by cases could result in a very substantial wider social benefit, eg if cartels become less common, if consumer rights are honoured, and if greater transparency in administration results.

B. Scope for Inefficient Litigation

On the other side of the ledger, there is always scope for litigation to be net harmful. This could occur where costs are excessively high and benefits from cases rather small. Although in principle such cases should settle, the incentive to settle will depend on surrounding procedural rules.[13] And even so, settlement tactics can be complex and can sometimes amount to a shake-down of innocent companies: especially where litigation *risk* is significant, a company might rationally settle even an utterly baseless claim rather than incur expense in litigating the matter. In these cases, increasing the scope to litigate might diminish social welfare, and great care might be needed to avoid expanding access to fora in which the social benefit from litigation is less clear.

Perhaps the most important point to note here is that a more detailed analysis is required than simply assuming that increasing compensation is *always* beneficial.[14] In this, it is notable that the EU Commission has firmly adopted a compensatory aim in its approach, at least to competition law damages claims: an area where the Commission has been particularly vocal and where its analysis is particularly clear. In fairness, it is likely, as noted above, that the current level of cartel deterrence is sub-optimal and that increased enforcement is likely to be socially beneficial. Nevertheless, if compensation alone is the focus, rather than the *net benefit* of compensation, there would seem to be a risk that the net benefit could

---

[11] Art 101 TFEU forbids agreements with anti-competitive 'object or effect', including a price-fixing cartel. See also Commission Reg (EU) No 330/2010 of 20 April 2010 on the application of Art 101(3) of the Treaty on the Functioning of the European Union to categories of vertical agreements and concerted practices (analysis of 'hardcore' restrictions denying the benefit of the Reg under Art 4).

[12] See especially M Danov, F Becker and P Beaumont (eds), *Cross-Border EU Competition Law Actions* (Oxford, Hart Publishing, 2012) ch 1, suggesting a significant enforcement gap.

[13] See B Kobashi and J Parker 'Civil Procedure', entry 7000 in the *International Encyclopaedia of Law & Economics* (New York, Springer, 2017) for an overview of the literature on the incentive properties of cost-shifting rules.

[14] See S Dnes, 'An Economic Approach to Remedies in Private Competition Claims' in Danov, Becker and Beaumont, above n 12 (analysis of the EU Commission's policy on compensation v deterrence in competition law cases).

sometimes be negative if the compensation aim is pursued relentlessly without regard to the net costs and benefits of the attendant litigation thereby encouraged. If no other message is drawn from the economists' points about net welfare enhancement in this context, it is perhaps that care is needed to keep an eye on the net litigation costs and to ensure that reforms, especially if applied at the EU level, contain elements encouraging good litigation practice, eg cost management and cost shifting aspects, that are designed not only to provide redress but also to do so in a net socially beneficial way. By keeping both objectives firmly in mind, there may be scope to ensure that the litigation currently being encouraged takes place in the best possible way, and that an exclusive focus on a compensation objective does not cloud the wider picture in which compensation and its notable benefits are not the only factor in the relevant calculus. Indeed, one powerful tension in the moves to harmonise jurisdiction lies in the question of whether it is better to apply a single, unified approach, or whether a degree of competition between jurisdictions is more desirable.[15]

C. Efficiency Analysis of Procedure versus Substance

An important qualification to the above argument lies in the independent importance of procedural aspects of litigation, distinct from the substantive rules that they enforce. Since both procedure and substance are factors of the same function—here, net utility from litigation—there is always scope to argue that the procedural aspects are not relevant to the extent that issues could, at least in theory, always be resolved solely with reference to the underlying substantive rules. For example, if all EU Member States applied the same calculus of negligence rule and this were *already* acting efficiently, it is unclear what benefit would exist in harmonising the jurisdiction or other procedural aspects provided that efficient redress is available in each individual case. Some savings might conceivably exist in consolidating claims, but it is doubtful that this efficiency would dominate, or at least be particularly noticeable, in situations where the underlying rule is already welfare-enhancing.

In short, it is possible to argue that attention should lie on the substantive rule, rather than the procedure by which it is enforced. It is doubtful, however, that procedural matters can be neglected in this way. One way to see this clearly is to ask the question the other way round, that is, to ask whether *procedure* can ever dominate *substance*, rather than to ask whether substance is *capable of* dominating procedure. The answer here is clear: at least in some jurisdictions, the underlying rule can be completely dominated by the procedural elements under which the rule is enforced. For instance, antitrust litigators in the United States describe the practice alluded to above under which plaintiff firms bring cases in the knowledge that a risk-averse defendant might wish to settle for a small fraction of the total claim, rather than run a risk of a much larger claim being awarded at trial.[16] Although great care is needed not to allow this well-known abuse to dominate thinking to the extent that it displaces the examples of welfare-enhancing settlement—the social gains from which could conceivably dominate social loss from the abusive awards—it is clear that looking solely

---

[15] See Danov, Becker and Beaumont, above n 12, ch 1.

[16] See R Preston McAfee, 'Strategic Abuse of the Antitrust Laws' (2005) 2 *Journal of Strategic Management Education* 1 (describing strategic abuses of the law).

to the substantive rule is mistaken. A common-sense test of the same point can be seen in the EU by considering how some jurisdictions display considerably greater enforcement of the same underlying rules, eg the differential scope to bring a follow-on claim for damages under a public enforcement decision at the EU level, the scope to do so varying very considerably from jurisdiction to jurisdiction.

For all of the importance of procedure that the above analysis suggests, it would still be a mistake to discount any welfare-enhancing role from differentiation between jurisdictions. National practices might have arisen from different social contexts, in which some differentiation in approach might simply be efficient. For example, the availability of treble damages under US antitrust law is a major factor in the abusive litigation strategy by which plaintiff firms extract rent-seeking settlements. Yet this difference may reflect the greater role of litigation in sanctioning firms, in the absence of nationalisation of monopoly industries. Therefore, tolerating a degree of rent-seeking activity at the plaintiff bar might be more sensible than it would be in other jurisdictions where other approaches, such as nationalisation of monopoly assets, were applied to the same underlying problem.[17]

At the purely procedural level, differences can also arise because of different court systems and different business practices yielding a spread of efficient practice geared to each location and set of practices. Great care might be needed in addressing any perceived enforcement gap, to ensure that any such differences are properly accounted for and that the reasons driving them are properly investigated, to avoid the situation arising where a harmonised rule maps poorly onto what might be a sensible practice at the national level. In short, care is needed to see that a net efficiency analysis is also applied to procedural aspects, at least if looking to what the appropriate aim of harmonisation methods ought to be. Here, the reticence in piercing the veil of national procedure in all but the most limited circumstances might be put under greater scrutiny, with a view to considering the net benefit of the rules.[18]

In conclusion, then, it seems that procedural aspects will also be highly relevant to the underlying question of net social benefit from litigation, and that a careful—if ambitious—analysis might begin to consider means by which to distinguish efficient and inefficient procedural aspects, to enable wider social benefit from a reduction in a perceived enforcement gap to occur. These factors would then need to be considered alongside the net social benefit from the substantive rule itself.

---

[17] A significant contrast exists between American and European responses to market power, especially in network industries that lend themselves to the accretion of market power: compare, eg, the use of very strict regulation of AT and T, rather than erstwhile public ownership as in the case of BT, and the continuing ownership fragmentation of the US power grid, in contrast with the monopoly position of National Grid in the UK. These are but two examples of differences in industrial context that might sensibly drive differentiation in the applicable law, especially on the market power point. See more in P Camasasca and R van der Bergh, *European Competition Law and Economics: A Comparative Perspective* (London, Sweet & Maxwell, 2001) (providing comparative analysis of EU and US approaches to market power regulation).

[18] A rare example of an exception to the usual deference lies in the competition law damages directive, Dir 2014/104/EU of the European Parliament and of the Council of 26 November 2014 on certain rules governing actions for damages under national law for infringements of the competition law provisions of the Member States and of the European Union (providing inter alia for substantive procedural harmonisation of a baseline level of provision of documents to litigants) analysed by J Fitchen in ch 39 below.

III. Analysis of the Litigation Pattern

If one conclusion stands out particularly clearly from the above economic analysis, it is that policy makers and legislators should pay at least some attention to the net social effects of changes to jurisdictional rules, and that a single objective or a relatively narrow set of objectives should not be allowed to predominate over the overall welfare effect of a set of rules. With this in mind, it is possible to turn to the emergent pattern of application disclosed in the national reports, to see how harmonisation measures are being applied when viewed from this economic perspective.

Before doing so, it is helpful to consider whether the social costs and benefits (ie efficiency) analysis above might vary depending on the type of legal system in question. A significant body of literature exists that contrasts many aspects of litigation procedure, with a view to whether they achieve economic efficiency. In this context, the EUPILLAR project is of particular interest because it spans common law and civil law jurisdictions, allowing for detailed practical insight into whether there is a substantive difference between inquisitorial and adversarial processes in terms of the discernible litigation pattern.[19] Indeed, the relative roles of judges in the different systems feeds into a well-known debate about the relative efficiency of inquisitorial and adversarial systems.[20]

A. Application of EU Regulations

Perhaps the most important threshold question is whether there is at least some degree of comfort in applying the EU legislation: absent a reasonable degree of comfort on this point, it is doubtful that any serious attempt at harmonisation would be anything but costly and counterproductive. Happily, there appears to be a reasonable level of comfort in applying the rules: the Maltese report, in particular, notes a high level of comfort with the rules, albeit that, as with many other jurisdictions, there is perhaps something of a learning curve in dealing with them.[21] However, no report suggested that these difficulties are anything other than a normal learning curve, and so one can expect the issues with unfamiliarity to be ironed out with the passage of time.

B. Cost of Analysis of Foreign Law

If there is a major bar to cross-border enforcement, then, it lies not in the reception of the rules but rather in the cost of analysing foreign law. This point was flagged numerous times

---

[19] F Parisi, 'Rent-seeking Through Litigation: Adversarial and Inquisitorial Systems Compared' (2002) 22 *International Review of Law and Economics* 193–216.

[20] See G Tullock, 'Defending the Napoleonic Code over the Common Law' (1988) 2(1) *Research in Law and Policy Studies* 3–27. cf R A Posner, 'Comment: Responding to Gordon Tullock' (1988) 2(1) *Research in Law and Policy Studies* 29.

[21] Ch 24.

in many reports; for example, the Belgian report singles out the high cost of determining foreign law and the high cost of using experts for this purpose:

> One of the greatest challenges in cross-border proceedings, is finding foreign law. This is problematic both for lawyers and judges. For lawyers it is expensive and hard to find a foreign expert they can trust. They sometimes use it as a strategy, but often try to avoid foreign law or do not raise the issue.[22]

This cost aspect in turn suggests that there might be an enduring barrier to cross-border enforcement on cost grounds, suggesting that there may be sub-optimal enforcement of the law, at least on the assumption outlined above that the substantive rule is efficient.

Subject to the widespread observation that costs could be high in estimating foreign law, some reports noted an uptick in cross-border enforcement following the abolition of the *exequatur*, fitting Posner's hypothesis that doctrines of judicial notice can increase litigation efficiency, as well as lowering litigation costs.[23] For instance, the Slovenian report notes that increased enforcement seems to have followed this change.[24] The strong suggestion here is that there is an enduring barrier to cross-border enforcement, and again on the assumption that there is an enforcement gap, moves such as the abolition of the *exequatur* seem to have contributed to closing the gap.

C. Arbitration or Harmonisation?

From an economic perspective, a particularly interesting aspect of the reports lies in the line between arbitration and litigation. Specifically, a burning question lies in whether there is scope for mandatory jurisdiction to undermine arbitral awards, which may be more efficient in the circumstances. Here, it is important to emphasise the point from the Swedish report that suggests that in Sweden arbitration currently dominates litigation and that there is a significant international arbitration practice that sits above the use of courts: 'Many—probably most—commercial disputes are either settled or decided by arbitrators rather than by courts of law.'[25]

Although not necessarily a complete answer, because of the arguable need for a fall back jurisdiction even in the case of arbitration, there is perhaps quite a notable contrast between the use of arbitration and the use of litigation for commercial disputes. In short, if the choice is being made not to litigate but instead to arbitrate in certain jurisdictions in the EU, this might strongly suggest that care is needed not to upset these arbitration dynamics because of the potential to undermine what is, in fact, the practical route by which redress is achieved. In other words, there may be a need to ensure that if litigation is encouraged, it does not come at net cost if a price is paid in some way by apparently thriving cross-border arbitrations.

---

[22] Ch 6.

[23] Posner, above n 4, 435.

[24] Ch 29 ('With the application of Brussels I in past years, it also became evident, that the *exequatur* is an obstacle to the free circulation of judgments, entails unnecessary costs and delays for parties, and discourages companies and citizens.').

[25] Ch 30.

In this context, the experience in England and Wales, with very sophisticated claimants shouldering large cost burdens, is perhaps especially instructive. As with the Swedish experience on arbitration, there is scope to argue that sophisticated claimants, at least, are already quite well-served: their position might be distinguished from smaller claimants who are less likely to benefit from arbitration proceedings, and might find costs in the English High Court prohibitive.[26] One possible conclusion from this pattern of very widespread arbitration and very expensive litigation for some of the most sophisticated claims might suggest that future reforms could be addressed most profitably at the cases *not* within this well-served constituency. Perhaps most helpful would be a means of enforcement for diffuse and dispersed claims that do not fit into this arbitration/expensive litigation category and are perhaps underserved at present.

Indeed, the English experience is of particular note in relation to the debate on adversarial proceedings: given the choice, parties seem happy to shoulder the higher costs of English litigation. As they have at least a degree of control over these costs in adversarial proceedings, this perhaps suggests that the potential efficiencies from inquisitorial proceedings identified by Tullock are not being seen, or at least, that litigants are not demanding them.[27] Of course, any such conclusion is necessarily tentative, because it could be that the high costs of litigation are a barrier to entry for claimants, who may be risk averse and have latent demand for a cheaper system. That said, there seems little trend towards the cross-border use of inquisitorial regimes on cost grounds, even when choice exists, pointing away from the suggestion that inquisitorial systems save costs: it might well be the case, as Posner suggests, that freeing up resources in litigation does not reduce net litigation spend, but rather directs resources to investment in other areas of litigation.[28]

D. Settlement Dynamics

Settlement dynamics also stand out when reading the reports from an economic perspective. Care is needed here because of the scope for settlement to represent efficient, but also inefficient, practices, as outlined above. It is never clear, in the abstract, whether a settlement is net beneficial or net harmful, without further analysis. However, one interesting point made in the German report is that the author perceives no particular difference in the attractiveness of settlement as between national and international cases.[29] This is surprising, because in the abstract one would expect the costs and difficulty of a cross-border claim to deter settlement, diminishing the potential net benefit from 'good' settlements whose incentive properties are welfare-enhancing.

This suggests that there may be scope to encourage efficient settlement of international cases, the scope to do so being perhaps greater than one would assume from first principles. Of particular note here is the scope to bring competitive pressure to litigation

---

[26] Ch 5 ('A number of commercial companies with high-value claims appear to be suing in England (despite the high litigation costs), hoping to force a settlement.').
[27] Tullock, above n 20.
[28] Posner, above n 4.
[29] Ch 7.

proceedings, diminishing settlement costs. For example, the Austrian report notes a two per cent tax on settlements, which seems likely to deter settlement at the margin for no obvious social welfare gain; in fact, the tax may discourage efficient settlement.[30] With the greatest respect, it is perhaps measures such as these—which would strike some economists as at least potentially protectionist in character—where consumer redress would be well-served by increasing the scope to bring claims that circumvent national protectionist measures. Happily, there is evidence in the Austrian report that, as in so many places, the litigation pattern is slowly but surely emerging with greater strength, paving the way for increased redress for consumers.

IV. Conclusion

This chapter has attempted to place the litigation pattern disclosed in the national reports into wider context, from an economic perspective that seeks to maximise wider social welfare. In doing so, it has recounted some of the best-known cases and analyses of writers and judges adopting such a perspective, pointing to an important role for considering the wider costs and benefits of litigation, rather than simply the adoption of relatively simplistic or limited sets of objectives, eg assertions relating to compensation without further analysis of the social costs and benefits of such awards. The analysis suggests a powerful role for the estimation of social costs and benefits from litigation in terms of procedure as well as substance, suggesting that, from an economic perspective at least, there may be scope to consider beginning to assess jurisdictional reforms for the substantive and procedural efficiency gains they yield—and sometimes, that they do not yield. In other words, increasingly broad jurisdictional harmonisation might yet come to require a substantive analysis of the efficiency properties of that harmonisation.

Applying this approach to the specifics of the national reports, the chapter found that most jurisdictions are slowly moving towards more litigation, although costs of foreign experts remain a significant barrier to litigation in many cases. Perhaps most interestingly, evidence appears to exist that well-funded commercial litigants *already* have access to redress from arbitration proceedings, and for the rare cases where these are inadequate, do not seem to be deterred from the use of one of the most expensive jurisdictions. In other words, a spontaneous order seems to have emerged in which redress is successfully obtained for many commercial parties and care may be needed not to disturb this presumptively-efficient spontaneous order.

If there is a need for reform, then, it perhaps lies in smaller claims, where the appetite for redress seems to be limited by cost factors that could helpfully be addressed through measures to consolidate claims across jurisdictions, allowing for the greatest possible redress. If this is targeted at the most socially harmful activities, there may be significant scope to increase net social welfare from harmonised rules designed to promote claims, provided

---

[30] Ch 11 ('Austria still charges a settlement fee for out-of-court settlement at the rate of two per cent of the value of the settlement agreement, which constitutes an obstacle to out-of-court settlement but once a claim is brought, settlement is relatively common in civil and commercial disputes.').

that these are carefully designed to address only those cases where net benefit seems particularly likely, and not speculative. Such a mechanism might sit alongside other currently-functioning aspects of the regime—notably, the redress that appears to be available to larger commercial parties—complementing the existing regime and thus running less risk of displacing a well-functioning redress system in a way that might *not* be socially beneficial. As a final, and perhaps rather ambitious conclusion, there may be scope to increase competition between jurisdictions in those cases where existing litigation systems have socially harmful or protectionist elements, increasing redress for consumers.

Whether the political appetite for this ambitious harmonisation exists is an important question, but at least from an economic perspective there appears to be a strong case that the experience with the abolition of the *exequatur* could be but the first step towards a more meaningfully integrated redress system for smaller claims. At the very least, the social costs that might have been associated with that change appear not to have materialised, suggesting that there is scope for further effort to close an enforcement gap that may exist for socially beneficial cases not currently being brought.

32

Data Analysis: Important Issues to be Considered in a Cross-border Context

MIHAIL DANOV

I. Introduction

As explained elsewhere,[1] the EU model of administration of justice in cross-border private law disputes is based on private international law (PIL) instruments which primarily aim to provide effective remedies for litigants in cross-border cases. The success of this model is dependent on Member States judges' ability to swiftly and consistently apply the relevant PIL instruments, allocating jurisdiction and specifying applicable laws in cases with an international element. There is a real risk that different national judges, who share different legal traditions and heritages, inconsistently apply the PIL rules.

The problems are exacerbated by the current institutional architecture which, if not suited to supporting national judges, may hamper the effectiveness of the EU PIL framework. Although there is a possibility for national judges to make a preliminary reference to the Court of Justice of the European Union (CJEU), the CJEU ruling will only provide guidance as to the interpretation of the PIL rules which must still be applied by the national judges. Moreover, the time it takes for the CJEU to deliver its preliminary ruling on PIL issues in all but the cases dealt with under the urgent preliminary ruling procedure ('PPU') causes very significant delay, reducing the value of the remedy for the claimant and working against the EU policy-makers' objective to provide for an effective remedy in cross-border cases.

An analysis of the empirical data, collected within the EUPILLAR framework, indicates how the remedies—sought by parties—impact their decisions whether/where to sue. Since the EU legal landscape can shape the litigants' strategies which may in turn impact on the settlement dynamics, the parties' tactics can expose the weaknesses of the current regime, adversely affecting the available remedies in cross-border cases. In other words, an analysis of the way the current EU legal landscape shapes the litigants' strategies in different types of cross-border cases indicates which aspects of the current institutional framework need to be revised in order to provide effective remedies for litigants in cross-border cases.

---

[1] M Danov and P Beaumont, 'Measuring the Effectiveness of the EU Civil Justice Framework: Theoretical and Methodological Challenges' (2015/2016) *Yearbook of Private International Law* 151–80.

II. Remedies Impact Parties' Decisions Whether/Where to Sue

In a UK context, Genn led a research study,[2] which aimed to 'establish the frequency with which members of the public are faced with problems for which a legal remedy exists ("justiciable problems")',[3] considering how people resolve such problems and the result/ remedies they can obtain. In a United States context, Miller and Sarrat[4] have considered 'the availability and kind of *institutionalization of remedy systems*'[5] which is defined by them as 'the extent to which there are well known, regularized, readily available mechanisms, techniques, or procedures for dealing with a problem.'[6] Hartnell[7] discussed some central aspects of the EU civil justice institutionalisation, making a case that '[f]urther research is needed before the European Union's civil justice project can be evaluated.'[8]

The EUPILLAR research project aims to assess the effectiveness of the current EU PIL regime that is the foundation of the EU civil justice framework which primarily aims to provide effective remedies for private parties in disputes with an international element.[9] Measuring the effectiveness of the EU PIL framework presupposes an analysis of the question whether there are effective remedies for parties in cross-border private cases. The response to this question is important because the main objective of the EU is to 'maintain ... and develop ... an area of freedom, security and justice'.[10] Central to achieving this objective is for the Member States' courts to apply the PIL Regulations consistently, providing access to effective remedies for private parties in cross-border cases.[11] Brussels Ia, 'respects fundamental rights and observes ... the right to an effective remedy guaranteed in Article 47 of the Charter'[12] which clearly states that '[e]veryone whose rights and freedoms guaranteed by the law of the Union are violated has the right to an effective remedy before a tribunal ...' But, how to define 'effective remedy' for the purposes of assessing the effectiveness of the current institutional framework? What are the main features of an effective remedy in cross-border cases?

The 'right to an effective remedy' is a fundamental human right[13] which is derived from Article 13 of the European Convention on Human Rights (ECHR). It should be noted that, in the light of Article 13 ECHR, the Committee of Ministers has adopted a *Guide to Good*

---

[2] H Genn, *Paths to Justice: What People Do and Think about Going to Law* (Oxford, Hart Publishing, 1999).
[3] ibid 5.
[4] RE Miller and A Sarrat, 'Grievances, Claims and Disputes: Assessing the Adversary Culture' (1980–81) *Law and Society Review* 525.
[5] ibid 563—the emphasis is in the original.
[6] Ibid.
[7] HE Hartnell, 'EUstitia: Institutionalizing Justices in the European Union' (2002–03) 23 *Northwestern Journal of International Law and Business* 65.
[8] ibid 138.
[9] Danov and Beaumont, above n 1.
[10] Recital 3 to Brussels Ia; Recital 1 to the Maintenance Reg; Recital 1 to Brussels IIa; and Recital 1 to Rome I.
[11] See more in Ch 1 above.
[12] Recital 38 to Brussels Ia.
[13] Charter of Fundamental Rights of the European Union.

Practice in respect of Domestic Remedies.[14] The guide specifies the 'general characteristics of an effective remedy'[15] by putting forward the following definition:

A remedy is only effective if it is available and sufficient. It must be sufficiently certain not only in theory but also in practice,[16] and must be effective in practice as well as in law,[17] having regard to the individual circumstances of the case. Its effectiveness does not, however, depend on the certainty of a favourable outcome for the applicant.[18]

In the EU context, Van Gerven[19]—making inter alia reference to Article 13 ECHR— has drawn a 'distinction between right and remedy and in that connection between "constitutive" and "executive" remedial rules.'[20] The 'constitutive' element was considered to be related to the substantive law establishing the right which should be protected. The 'executive' component was defined as covering such aspects as: standing to sue; extent and scope of liability, including heads of damages; burden and standard of proof; and limitation periods.[21] However, Van Gerven's distinction—which was made in the context of 'enforcement of [EU] law, in relation to claims brought by private parties before national courts'[22]—is somewhat blurred. It fails to make a distinction between the claimant's *entitlement to a remedy* which would depend on the applicable law in cross-border cases, on the one hand, and *access to remedies* which is subject to the set of procedural rules applicable at the place where the parties litigate as well as subject to enforceability of a local judgment abroad. Even if one considers EU law enforcement only, then access to an effective remedy should be dependent on establishing jurisdiction before an appropriate Member State court.[23] Once jurisdiction has been assumed, a private party should be entitled to an effective remedy because there is a breach of EU law rules which form part of the Member State's legal order. In other words, the claimant's entitlement would still be dependent on the scope of applicable national law, which determines the right to compensation. Moreover, it is only fair to note that, after Van Gerven's piece had been published, the EU legal landscape was modified. It is now well established that:

The law applicable to non-contractual obligations under [the Rome II] Regulation shall govern in particular:

(a) the basis and extent of liability, including the determination of persons who may be held liable for acts performed by them;

---

[14] Directorate General Human Rights and Rule of Law Council of Europe, *Guide to Good Practice in respect of Domestic Remedies* < www.echr.coe.int/Documents/Pub_coe_domestics_remedies_ENG.pdf > accessed 13 January 2017, adopted by the Committee of Ministers on 18 September 2013.

[15] ibid 11–13.

[16] 'See *McFarlane v Ireland*, App No 31333/06, 10 September 2010, paragraph 114; *Riccardi Pizzati v Italy*, App No 62361/00, Grand Chamber judgment of 29 March 2006, paragraph 38.' (cited in the original). ibid 12.

[17] 'See *El-Masri v "the former Yugoslav Republic of Macedonia"*, App No 39630/09, 13 December 2012, paragraph 255; *Kudła v Poland*, App No 30210/96, judgment of 26 October 2000, paragraph 152.' (cited in the original). ibid 12.

[18] See *Guide to Good Practice in respect of Domestic Remedies* (above n 14) 12. In the original a reference is given at the end of our quote to *Kudła v Poland*, ibid, at para 157.

[19] W Van Gerven, 'Of Rights, Remedies and Procedures' (2000) 37(3) *Common Market Law Review* 501, 526.

[20] ibid 526.

[21] ibid 525.

[22] ibid 501.

[23] *Viking Line ABP v The International Transport Workers' Federation, The Finnish Seamen's Union* [2005] EWHC 1222 (Comm); *British Airways plc & Anor v Sindicato Espanol de Pilotos de Lineas Aereas & Anor* [2013] EWHC 1657 (Comm).

(b) the grounds for exemption from liability, any limitation of liability and any division of liability;

(c) the existence, the nature and the assessment of damage or the remedy claimed;

(d) within the limits of powers conferred on the court by its procedural law, the measures which a court may take to prevent or terminate injury or damage or to ensure the provision of compensation;

(e) the question whether a right to claim damages or a remedy may be transferred, including by inheritance;

(f) persons entitled to compensation for damage sustained personally;

(g) liability for the acts of another person;

(h) the manner in which an obligation may be extinguished and rules of prescription and limitation, including rules relating to the commencement, interruption and suspension of a period of prescription or limitation.[24]

Therefore, different Member States' laws may be used to determine whether a claimant is entitled to a remedy as well as to ascertain the available remedy. For example, if an illegal cartel (in conflict with Article 101 Treaty on the Functioning of the European Union (TFEU)) had caused harm to consumers and businesses across the EU, then different Member States' laws would need to be applied by a national judge when assessing damages (ie claimants' remedy) in a cross-border context.[25] The important role, which Member States' laws are to play in this context, was recently acknowledged by Directive 2014/104/EU on antitrust damages actions, harmonising Member States' substantive laws (eg limitation periods and the availability of a passing on defence). In spite of the level of harmonisation, a recent comparative study, led by Monti,[26] looked at the way interest is being calculated across the EU. His research findings highlight 'some notable variations across the jurisdictions, which raise doubts about the capacity of some legal systems to afford full compensation.'[27] This indicates that the claimant's *entitlement to remedy* would vary, depending on which law would be applicable.

Furthermore, the fact that Directive 2014/104/EU[28] aims to harmonise certain procedural rules (eg disclosure of evidence) is also an acknowledgment that the *access to remedies* may be often dependent on the applicable set of procedure rules which is, in line with Article 1(3) of Rome II, to be pre-determined by the place where the parties litigate. The English High Court[29] and Court of Appeal[30] have noted that, due to different sets of rules of procedure, evidence and costs, the remedies awarded by the different Member States' courts may be different even in cases where the relevant substantive laws and principles

---

[24] Art 15 of Rome II.

[25] M Danov, *Jurisdiction and Judgments in Relation to EU Competition Law Claims* (Oxford, Hart Publishing, 2010). See also Ch 39 below by J Fitchen.

[26] G Monti, 'EU law and interest on damages for infringements of competition law—A comparative report' (2016) EUI Working Paper LAW 2016/11, http://cadmus.eui.eu/bitstream/handle/1814/40464/LAW_2016_11.pdf ?sequence=3&isAllowed=y.

[27] ibid [76].

[28] On certain rules governing actions for damages under national law for infringements of the competition law provisions of the Member States and of the European Union [2014] OJ L349/1 (discussed by Fitchen, ch 39 below). This Directive was to be implemented into the national laws of the Member States by 27 December 2016, see Art 21.

[29] *Steven John Kilfoy Wall v Mutuelle De Poitiers Assurance* [2013] EWHC 53 (QB).

[30] *Steven John Kilfoy Wall v Mutuelle De Poitiers Assurance* [2014] EWCA Civ 138.

are the same. Hence, for the purposes of assessing the effectiveness of the current private international law framework, one should make a distinction between *entitlement to remedy* (which is to be determined by the governing law/s) and *access to remedy* (which is dependent on establishing jurisdiction before an appropriate court whose judges are able to swiftly apply the relevant PIL instruments, dispensing justice in cross-border cases). What is an effective remedy would depend on the facts of the case. Although damages (ie monetary remedies) would be often sought and awarded in cross-border commercial cases, a return of a child would be an effective remedy in child abduction cases, for example.

The access to an available remedy may often be dependent on where the parties bring their cross-border case which is why the claimants may be very selective. An interesting case, which demonstrates that the available remedies would be at the heart of the forum selection process, is *Re NEF Telecom Co BV*.[31] In this case, there was an application seeking a court sanction for arrangements with creditors under section 899 of the Companies Act. The application was made by a Dutch company and a Bulgarian company. The scheme creditors were both UK domiciled and non-UK domiciled. The jurisdiction of the English court was challenged by a senior creditor, Mr Toth. The issues of jurisdiction were important because none of the companies involved were incorporated in England. Although there was a preliminary issue as to the application of the Brussels I regime in such a case, the English High court assumed jurisdiction, without addressing the scope of Brussels I. In this context, Mr Justice Vos, as he then was, held:

42 … if the Judgments Regulation applies—which I do not decide—it is quite clear that art 23 would be applicable so as to give the English court jurisdiction.

43 … if the Judgments Regulation applies because some of the creditors are to be regarded as defendants to the applications for sanction then, where one of those defendants is domiciled in the United Kingdom, that gives the court jurisdiction under art 6. … therefore there is no doubt, if the Judgments Regulation applies, that jurisdiction could be established.

44 As regards art 4, which Briggs J thought to be a good argument, that too would be applicable here, if the argument is correct. …

45 My conclusion is quite clear. Whichever way one looks at the legal position under the Companies Act and under the Judgments Regulation, jurisdiction can be established.[32]

The importance for the parties' arrangements with the creditors to be sanctioned by the court under section 899 of the Companies Act (being an available remedy) can be demonstrated by a series of reported decisions rendered in cases[33] with an international element, posing very interesting questions as to the scope of the Brussels I regime.

The fact that access to available remedies, which may vary in the different jurisdictions, appeared to be among the factors informing the claimant's suing decision was also apparent in *Simpson v Intralinks*.[34] In this case, the claimant, Ms Simpson, lived and worked in Germany. The defendant was an English company that employed the claimant. The claims against the employer were for sexual discrimination and equal pay. The employer challenged

---

[31] *Re NEF Telecom Co BV* [2012] EWHC 2944 (Ch).
[32] ibid [42–45].
[33] *In re Rodenstock* [2011] EWHC 1104 (Ch); *Primacom Holding GmbH v A Group of the Senior Lenders & Credit Agricole* [2011] EWHC 3746 (Ch); *Re APCOA Parking (UK) Ltd* [2014] EWHC 1867 (Ch).
[34] *Simpson v Intralinks* [2012] IL Pr 34.

the jurisdiction of the English court, submitting that the employment contract included a German law and jurisdiction clause. On this basis, the employment judge upheld the jurisdictional challenge, taking the view that the English courts had no jurisdiction. The decision of the Employment Judge was reversed by the UK's Employment Appeal Tribunal, holding that the claimant was entitled to bring the claim in England under Article 19 of Brussels I. The claimant's entitlement to a remedy in this case was largely dependent on the application of English law to the merits of the dispute. The claimant argued that English law was to have a mandatory character. Mr Justice Langstaff sustained the claimant's submission, holding that:

> The effect of the Rome Convention, which is applicable because proof of contract is a necessary step in the claim, is that German law is the applicable law. However, art 7(2) provides that nothing in the Convention is to restrict the application of mandatory rules of the law of the forum. The effect of art 7(2) is thus that the provisions of s. 6 of the Sex Discrimination Act and s 1 of the Equal Pay Act (which are such mandatory rules) are applicable notwithstanding that the applicable law generally is German.[35]

Another example which illustrates how the access to an available and effective remedy impacts parties' decisions where to sue was *James Petter v EMC*.[36] In this case, the claimant was employed by the English subsidiary of an American company, EMC. He was holding the post of Global Director which put him in a position to make a contribution to the success of the company. This entitled the claimant to benefit from a Stock Plan which awarded him certain common stock. His contract contained a restrictive covenant as well as a choice-of-court agreement. Mr Petter resigned from his post, giving notice on 15 January 2015. He intended to take up employment with a competitor of his employer. On 27 February 2015, EMC started proceeding in the courts of Massachusetts, invoking the exclusive jurisdiction clause. EMC sought a declaration to rescind the most recent award of stock granted to Mr Petter. On 13 March 2015, Mr Petter started proceedings in England, seeking a declaration that he did not act in breach of contract as well as declarations that the restrictive covenant and the restrictive terms of the Stock Plan were unenforceable. Mr Petter went further, seeking an anti-suit injunction against EMC. EMC challenged the jurisdiction of the English court. The English High Court dismissed the jurisdictional challenge, establishing jurisdiction under Section V of Brussels Ia. However, it refused to award the requested anti-suit injunction. Both parties appealed. The Court of Appeal upheld that the English courts had jurisdiction. It also allowed Mr Petter's appeal, awarding an anti-suit injunction as an effective remedy which was intended to enforce EU public policy, protecting the weaker party to an employment contract from being sued outside the EU on the basis of a choice of court agreement.

Therefore, the probability to obtain an available and effective remedy may well be the most important consideration which affects the claimant's decision whether/where to sue in cross-border cases. This patently demonstrates that, as already noted,[37] there is a triangular relationship between the allocation of jurisdiction and identification of applicable law, on the one hand, and the parties' access to an available and effective remedy, on the other hand. That said, once a claim had been initiated by the claimant, then an important

---

[35] ibid 54.
[36] *James Petter v EMC Europe Limited and EMC Corporation* [2015] EWHC 1498 (QB); [2015] EWCA Civ 828.
[37] Danov and Beaumont, above n 1.

question would be how the current EU legal landscape would affect the litigants' tactics in cross-border cases.

III. The EU Legal Landscape Shapes the Litigants' Strategies

In domestic disputes, commentators[38] have suggested that the litigant's decision whether to litigate (or settle) is based on a remedy-cost analysis. Some important considerations are: claimant's estimation about his/her entitlement to a legal remedy (including its value); the probability of obtaining a remedy; litigation costs (including the possibility of obtaining third party litigation funding); and settlement costs. That said, Johnson[39] has submitted that:

> [I]t is impossible to analyze litigation decisions without taking into account the factors influencing lawyers' decisions. Most litigation decisions are made, or substantially influenced, by lawyers. Therefore, even within the constraints of the economic maximization postulate, a model that fails to consider lawyer motivations is inadequate.[40]

There would be even more factors affecting the decision of litigators and litigants whether to litigate or settle in cross-border cases. In particular, it is well established that there might often be more than one set of lawyers from different countries which means that the litigation costs will be inflated even further.[41] The level of complexity and litigation expenses could be higher because, for example, parties' evidence may need to be collected in different jurisdictions. Furthermore, issues about the applicable law (and evidence of foreign law/s) would have to be considered along with the ability of national judges to apply foreign law/s and dispense justice in cross-border cases. With this in mind, the current EU legislative framework, which has been adopted under Article 81 TFEU,[42] would have to be carefully considered when parties to private disputes with an international element devise their litigation strategies. On the one hand, under the current EU model of administration of justice in cross-border cases, the parties (and potential claimants) may often have a choice where to litigate.[43] On the other hand, there might be prolonged jurisdictional challenges and parallel proceedings. This sort of 'litigation about litigation'[44] would bring even more uncertainty, inflating the ligation costs further and putting a strain on the litigants' financial resources, which could ultimately have a bearing on the remedies/settlement.[45] An analysis of the way in which the current EU legal landscape is shaping the litigants' strategies would expose the weaknesses of the current regime, indicating what areas require further improvements.

---

[38] RA Posner, *Economic Analysis of Law* 8th edn (Alphen aan den Rijn, WoltersKluwer, 2011) 761–67. See also RA Posner, 'An Economic Approach to Legal Procedure and Judicial Administration' (1973) 2(2) *Journal of Legal Studies* 399; WA Landes and RA Posner, 'Adjudication as a Private Good' (1979) 8(2) *Journal of Legal Studies* 235.

[39] E Johnson Jr , 'Lawyers' choice: A Theoretical Appraisal of Litigation Investment Decisions' (1980–81) *Law and Society Review* 567.

[40] ibid 568.

[41] EUPILLAR—England and Wales—Interview Transcript No 20.

[42] Danov and Beaumont, above n 1.

[43] eg Arts 4, 7(1), 7(2), 8(1) and 25 of Brussels Ia.

[44] AF Lowenfeld, 'Introduction: The Elements of Procedure: Are they Separately Portable?' (1997) 45(4) *American Journal of Comparative Law* 649, 651.

[45] See s IV below. Considered further in Chs 34, 39 and 40 below.

The EU legal landscape in civil and commercial matters is dominated by the EU PIL rules, which promote a level of judicial cooperation between the EU Member States' courts, with a view to ensuring that there are effective remedies for litigants in cross-border cases.[46] The EU model of administration of justice in cross-border private law disputes has progressed through harmonisation of EU PIL rules. Even if one had favoured 'Europeanization of civil procedures',[47] it would be difficult to deny that:

> The policy [of judicial cooperation] is based on the principle of mutual recognition, and grounded in the European law enforcement system which is largely decentralized. The process of harmonization appears to be proceeding with great caution. It is rather contemplated to be a process of gradual change, starting with encouraging mutual trust, cooperation and exchange of information among the national judicial authorities. The EU is in the stage of judicial cooperation rather than procedural unification.[48]

It is well established that a degree of unification would not be possible under the current 'European judicial architecture'[49] which only provides for preliminary references to assist national judges with the interpretation (rather than the application) of the EU PIL rules. Therefore, even on occasions where the procedural rules which allocate jurisdiction were—for example—unified in a Regulation which is directly applicable across the EU, it is a relatively safe prediction that no unification would materialise in practice unless the procedural rules in question were 'uniformly administered'.[50]

Should the current EU landscape change by having even more harmonisation at EU level? An EU funded project[51] is nearing completion at the Max Planck Institute, Luxembourg.[52] The study is conducted on the basis of two main assumptions which were clearly specified in the tender specifications.[53] First, it appears to be assumed that 'the existing divergences in national procedural rules hinder the realisation of the objective of a free circulation of judgments, in particular by undermining mutual trust between the justice systems of the Member States.'[54] That said, the EUPILLAR project data appears to suggest that, despite the fact that there were problems in some cases, 'the scale of the ... problems',[55] which were identified in *Krombach*[56] and *Gambazzi*,[57] should not be overstated with regard to cross-border civil and commercial law matters under the Brussels I regime. For example, in England and Wales, it is not only that many cases settle before trial (ie a very small proportion of the cases would go all the way to a final judgment on the merits as opposed to

---

[46] Danov and Beaumont, above n 1; P Beaumont and M Danov, 'The EU Civil Justice Framework and Private Law: "Integration through [Private International] Law"' (2015) 22 *Maastricht Journal of European and Comparative Law* 706–31.

[47] M Tulibacka, 'Europeanization of Civil Procedures: In Search of a Coherent Approach' (2009) 46(5) *Common Market Law Review* 1527.

[48] ibid 1540.

[49] C Timmermans, 'The European Union's Judicial System' (2004) 41(2) *Common Market Law Review* 393, 403.

[50] A T von Mehren, 'Choice of Law and the Problem of Justice' (1977) 41 *Law and Contemporary Problems* 27, 32.

[51] http://ted.europa.eu/udl?uri=TED:NOTICE:188196-2015:TEXT:EN:HTML&tabId=.

[52] Max Planck Institute, *Press Release* 24 November 2015, www.mpi-ierpl.lu/fileadmin/mpi/medien/news/2015/12/24/Press_release_Max_Planck_Institute_Luxembourg_20151124.pdf.

[53] See Tender Specifications Attached to the Invitation to Tender, JUST/2014/RCON/PR/CIVI/0082.

[54] ibid 16.

[55] ibid 8.

[56] Case C-7/98 *Krombach*, EU:C:2000:164.

[57] Case C-394/07 *Gambazzi*, EU:C:2009:219.

a judgment on a PIL issue), but also the recognising court would make sure that there is a high threshold for refusing to recognise and enforce foreign judgments.[58] Notwithstanding, different considerations might be relevant for the recognition and enforcement of judgments in family law matters.[59] Under Brussels IIa, which was adopted well after the 1968 Brussels Convention, the English courts—as an interviewee, an English and Welsh family law judge, put it—may not have 'yet arrived at the critical mass that allows for an optimal way of dealing with this.'[60] Some specific issues may arise as the right of a child to be heard may occasionally be an issue at the stage of recognition and enforcement. In a recent case, Lord Justice Ryder held:

> [F]or reasons of comity or mutual respect, there is a high threshold to the identification of a fundamental principle. There should be no tendency in the enforcement process under [Brussels IIa] to fail to recognise and hence enforce orders made by Member States. To the extent that there are different approaches to how a child is to be heard both domestically and among Member States this court and indeed any court of enforcement should be astute to identify the principle and not just one of the procedural options that may or may not be available in any particular Member State.
>
> … the rule of law in England and Wales includes the right of the child to participate in the process that is about him or her. That is the fundamental principle that is reflected in our legislation, our rules and practice directions and our jurisprudence.[61]

Is there a case for further harmonisation in this context in the light of Article 24 of the Charter of Fundamental Rights?[62] Or is there actually a need for consistent application of the rules which are already in place? Another problem, which appears to be common, concerns the enforcement of foreign judgments specifying the relevant contact arrangements. Due to the fact that circumstances may subsequently change, contact orders may pose particularly difficult questions at the recognition and enforcement stage.[63] The issues were nicely summarised by one of our interview respondents, an English and Welsh family law judge, as follows: 'I will do my absolute utmost to enforce [the contact order]. But inevitably, the circumstances will have changed. … [A]nd you always have to change it in some way.'[64]

Moreover, the location of the child may change, affecting the national court's competence to order the return of the child. The level of complexity and the weaknesses of the current EU PIL framework were exposed in *Re C*.[65] In this case, the proceedings were concerned with a child, born in 2003. The parties were British citizens who had married in England in January 2005. They lived together in Belgium, where they separated in 2010 or 2011. Following their divorce in Belgium, the mother and the child came to live in England in March 2011. In October 2011, the father made an application for a summary return of the

---

[58] EUPILLAR—England and Wales—Interview Transcript No 7, considered further in Ch 40 below. See also *Reeve & Others v Plummer* [2014] EWHC 4695 (QB) and *Ioanna Christofi v National Bank of Greece (Cyprus) Ltd* [2015] EWHC 986 (QB).

[59] eg *MD v CT* [2014] EWHC 871 (Fam).

[60] EUPILLAR—England and Wales—Interview Transcript No 14.

[61] *In the Matter of D (A Child) (International Recognition)* [2016] EWCA Civ 12 [42 and 44].

[62] The Commission is proposing to strengthen the right of the child to be heard in its Proposal for a Recast of Brussels IIa, COM(2016) 411 final, esp pp 4 and 15.

[63] *S (Brussels II (Revised): Enforcement of Contact Order), Re* [2008] 2 FLR 1358.

[64] EUPILLAR—England and Wales—Interview Transcript No 13.

[65] *Re C* [2012] EWHC 907 (Fam).

child to Belgium. On the ground of Article 13(1)(a) of the Hague Convention on Child Abduction, the father's application for the return of the child to Belgium was dismissed by Mr Justice Hedley. On 31 January 2012, the father initiated proceedings in Belgium, seeking the return of the child to Belgium on the ground of Article 11(7) and (8) of Brussels IIa. On 14 March 2012, the Belgian court ordered the return of the child to Belgium. The English court refused to enforce the Belgian order in England. In this context, Mr Justice Moylan held:

> [G]iven that this court has had jurisdiction since at least 25th November 2011, pursuant to Article 8(1), or alternatively since at least 8th December 2011, pursuant to Article 12(3), and given that the child is located here and the subject of continuing proceedings directed towards determining what orders should be made in accordance with the child's best interests, I have declined to enforce the order of the Belgian court.[66]

Should these problems be addressed by further harmonisation of national procedural rules? Or should the EU PIL framework be revised by amending/abolishing 'the second chance procedure' of Article 11(6)–(8) of Brussels IIa?[67] There is a strong case that any harmonisation of national procedural laws, without considering the way the current PIL framework is functioning in the light of the current institutional framework, would be premature and cost ineffective in so far as considerable efforts and resources may be spent to satisfy an insignificant concern. This would be particularly so if there are a number of more pressing issues which directly and/or indirectly impair litigants' effective access to remedies in cross-border cases.

The second assumption, which the Max Planck's evaluation study is based on, is that to a certain 'extent national procedural laws and practices [may not] ensure the procedural protection of EU consumer rights.'[68] The issues about 'access to legal remedies'[69] for injured parties with small claims is not new in the academic literature. The EU institutional framework would be important in this context because it is well established that '[m]any familiar procedural devices appear to be designed, in part at least, to reduce the expense of litigation.'[70] In the United States context, Posner has made the following observations:

> [T]he use of the class action as a means of achieving economies of scale in litigation by pooling a large number of similar claims ... The effect of such pooling is to lower the litigation-expense threshold. Suppose that there are 100 identical claims, each having an expected value if litigated of $10, and the minimum cost of each plaintiff's litigating his claim would be $50. The claims will not be brought separately. Since they are identical, presumably much of the work of the lawyers in the 100 cases, had they been brought, would have been duplicative. This implies that if the cases could be merged together into one case, the cost of litigation would be less than 100 times the threshold cost for each case, probably much less.[71]

That said, any procedural reform with regard to enforcement at national level of EU consumer protection laws should carefully consider the implications of the relevant

---

[66] ibid [92].

[67] See P Beaumont, L Walker and J Holliday, 'Conflicts of EU Courts on Child Abduction: The Reality of Article 11(6)–(8) Brussels IIa Proceedings Across the EU' (2016) 12(2) *Journal of Private International Law* 211–60.

[68] See Tender Specifications Attached to the Invitation to Tender, JUST/2014/RCON/PR/CIVI/0082, p 16.

[69] Posner (1973), above n 38 at 438.

[70] Posner, ibid at 435.

[71] ibid 439–40.

EU institutional framework. For example, as already noted,[72] it is well established that there are no effective remedies for consumers who have suffered harm resulting from EU competition law infringements.[73] How to address this issue? What is the main problem which needs to be addressed? Is it to do with national procedural laws?[74] Is it do with the inefficient enforcement regime, which involves public enforcement proceedings (a decision of a regulator and lengthy appeals before the General Court and the Court of Justice of the European Union) and private (occasionally parallel and related) proceedings before national courts?[75] Is it to do with the problem about the inability of the current PIL instruments to effectively co-ordinate cross-border EU competition law actions, involving multiple injured parties and multiple infringers from across the EU?[76] If each of these aspects is part of the problem, then harmonising certain national procedural rules may be a less than effective and efficient way of dealing with far more complex problems.

Moreover, the 2015 EU Justice Scoreboard[77] strongly suggests that some Member States' courts would be more effective and efficient than others in providing remedies in cross-border cases. It is not only that some judges would be more experienced as some Member States appear to be attracting more cross-border cases, but also the training and qualification of the judges across the EU varies enormously. Some judicial systems may not be in a position to attract qualified people to join the bench. After relying on empirical studies, Posner[78] has noted that:

> In a system in which competitive promotion is the key to obtaining increased income, prestige, and job satisfaction, as in the civil judiciaries,[79] it is difficult to attract highly qualified applicants unless the criteria for promotion are objective.[80]

Recruiting well qualified candidates may be even more of an issue in Member States where there are '[s]erious allegations of corruption and trading of influence in the judiciary'.[81] The level of variation of the judges' qualification and experience across the EU may be yet another aspect, indicating that the institutional architecture may need to be revamped, in order to provide effective remedies, whilst dealing with abusive litigation tactics and reducing litigation expenses. The diversity across the EU, which is driven by the different

---

[72] See Ch 1 above.

[73] M Danov and S Dnes, 'Cross-Border EU Competition Litigation: New Evidence from England and Wales' in M Danov, F Becker and P Beaumont (eds), *Cross-Border EU Competition Law Actions* (Oxford, Hart Publishing, 2013) 33–60; M Danov, D Fairgrieve and G Howells, 'Collective Redress Antitrust Proceedings: How to Close the Enforcement gap and provide redress for consumers' in ibid at 253–82.

[74] Dir 2014/104/EU, above n 29; Schedule 8 to the UK Consumer Rights Act 2015.

[75] M Danov and F Becker, 'Governance Aspects of Cross-Border EU Competition Law Actions: Theoretical and Practical Challenges' (2014) 10(3) *Journal of Private International Law* 359–401; M Danov, 'Cross-Border Aspects of EU Competition Law Enforcement: A Comprehensive Reform Needed?' in V Tomljenovic, N Bodiroga-Vukobrat, V Butorac Malnar and I Kunda (eds), *EU Competition and State Aid Rules: Public and Private Enforcement* (forthcoming 2017).

[76] M Danov, *Jurisdiction and Judgments in Relation to EU Competition Law Claims* (Oxford, Hart Publishing, 2010); Danov, Becker and Beaumont (eds), above n 73.

[77] COM(2015) 116 final.

[78] Posner, *Economic Analysis of Law*, above n 38, 709.

[79] MR Schneider, 'Judicial Career Incentives and Court Performance: An Empirical Study of the German Labour Courts of Appeal' (2005) 20(2) *European Journal of Law and Economics* 127 cited by Posner, ibid.

[80] Posner, *Economic Analysis of Law*, above n 38, 709.

[81] Report from the Commission to the European Parliament and the Council on Progress in Bulgaria under Co-operation and Verification mechanism COM(2016) 40 final, p 40.

social and legal heritages, indicates that there could be inconsistencies in the application of any harmonised (or even unified) rule across the EU. In other words, there is a real risk for any harmonised/unified PIL rule to be inconsistently applied by the different judges across the EU.

Therefore, the central question must be how to make the current system work more effectively. It is beyond doubt that dealing more effectively with any jurisdictional challenges would be central to devising an effective regime.[82] Indeed, any jurisdictional challenge is a source of delay which makes 'the expected value of litigating to the plaintiff shrink more rapidly than the expected cost of litigating to the defendant.'[83] A level of delay, which is caused by jurisdictional challenges, will generate legal uncertainty, undermining the authority of the court seised and deflating the claimants' expectations about the outcome of the cross-border litigation which would reduce the value of that litigation before a court whose jurisdiction could not be swiftly established. With this in mind, uncertainty about the jurisdiction of the court seised to deal with a cross-border private case must be distinguished from '[u]ncertainty about probable outcomes'.[84] Therefore, tactical jurisdictional challenges, which generate excessive delay, may have an impact on the claimant's decision to issue proceedings as well as on his/her decision to continue with the issued proceedings in cross-border cases.

The problems would be exacerbated, if the PIL framework does not effectively 'minimise the possibility of concurrent proceedings'[85] in different Member States, creating a real risk for irreconcilable judgments to be rendered. The point was captured by Mr Justice Teare who stated:

> 28. I accept that it is unsatisfactory that both the English and (so far) the Italian courts have decided, in circumstances where Pisa has exercised its powers of self-redress, that it is within their respective jurisdictions to determine the validity of the Swaps. That situation is unsatisfactory because it gives rise to the risk of irreconcilable judgments in two member states. If the English court gives judgment on the Banks' claims on the Swaps in favour of the Banks and if the Italian Supreme Court (following a determination by the court appointed expert in favour of Pisa) upholds the decision of the Consiglio di Stato it can be envisaged that there will or may be difficulties in enforcing the English court's judgment in Italy. In those circumstances it is understandable that the Banks have sought to find a solution to this unsatisfactory situation before the parties incur the costs of a trial on the merits of the claims on the Swaps in the English court.

> 29. However, I have come to the conclusion that a solution to that unsatisfactory situation cannot properly be found in a reference by the English court to the ECJ.[86]

How to avoid parallel proceedings more effectively? The current EU PIL framework inevitably shapes the litigants' strategies. The qualitative interview data demonstrate that, given the level of delay incurred in some jurisdictions, the court-first-seised rule can create incentives for both bona fide claimants and non-bona fide claimants to quickly issue proceedings. On the one hand, bona fide claimants may well be selective in suing before the courts which will quickly deal with the cases. On the other hand, non-bona fide claimants may issue

---

[82] See Ch 5 above.
[83] Posner, 'An Economic Approach', above n 38, 420.
[84] ibid, 430 and 450.
[85] Recital 21 to Brussels Ia.
[86] *DEPFA Bank plc & Anor v Provincia di Pisa* [2012] EWHC 687 (Comm) [28–29].

claims before courts which are notoriously slow in providing effective remedies for litigants in cross-border cases, benefiting from both the ineffectiveness of the EU PIL framework and the inefficiencies of some of the national judicial systems.

The tactical nature of the litigants' behaviour in a recent cross-border case, involving parallel proceedings, was condemned by Mr Justice Birss, stating:

> 39 … To describe what has happened in this case as mere lateness is unreal. In this case the court has already given judgment both on infringement and on the validity of the CTMs [Community Trade Marks] in issue on the points which were in issue at trial. In my judgment for this point to be raised at this stage in these proceedings is wholly unprecedented and is certainly 'rare and exceptional'.
>
> …
>
> 41 Whatever the parties' respective motives were or are, since the policy behind these articles is to avoid irreconcilable judgments or at least the risk of irreconcilable judgments, the policy is wholly defeated if the point is only taken after a judgment in the court second seised has been given. That is what has happened in this case.[87]

This may pose real difficulties for litigants in cross-border cases. Although the model of enhanced judicial cooperation in the administration of justice through EU PIL instruments has no alternative in a diverse Union, the model may need to be carefully reviewed to effectively deal with jurisdictional challenges and parallel proceedings in cross-border cases. In this context, it would be important to consider how the litigants' strategies—shaped by the current PIL framework—affect the available remedies and settlement negotiations in cross-border cases.[88]

IV. The Litigants' Strategies Affect the Available Remedies: Some Issues to be Considered

It was already noted above[89] that there is a case that the probability for the parties to obtain a desired legal remedy[90] in cross-border cases is among the most important considerations affecting their decisions whether/where to sue. On this basis, one may well argue that a low probability (or an excessive delay) of obtaining a remedy would result in a claimant giving up on a claim or accepting a significantly discounted compensation.[91] In cross-border cases, the parties may devise different litigation tactics depending on the remedy sought by the claimant and depending on the strength (or indeed the relative strength) of the claimant's claim.

It should be noted that the collected data in England and Wales[92] appear to suggest that there is a tendency for the parties to delay the resolution of disputes when financial

---

[87] *Hearst Holdings Inc v AVELA Inc* [2014] EWHC 1553 (Ch) [39 and 41].
[88] See Chs 35 and 40 below.
[89] See above s II.
[90] H Genn, 'Understanding Civil Justice' (1997) 50(1) *Current Legal Problems* 155, 173.
[91] See Chs 5 and 40.
[92] See Ch 5 above.

remedies are being sought (and the claimant has a relatively strong claim), but the litigants would be less prone to use delaying tactics in disputes which involve children. Equally, judges would tend to resolve cross-border cases, involving children, as quickly as possible. This may explain why, for example, the proceedings in PIL family cases before the English courts—a significant majority of which involve children—last for approximately 255 days (the data is missing for 38 cases, approximately 30 per cent of the cases), calculated from the day when the claim form was issued until the last available judgment on the PIL aspect was rendered.[93] On most occasions, the family law judges will also deal with the merits of the case. An entirely different litigation pattern appears to characterise the PIL civil and commercial cases before the English and Welsh courts, which last for approximately 415 days (the data is missing on 40 occasions, approximately 21per cent of the cases). The tactical nature of the jurisdictional challenges in these cases becomes apparent when considering that the merits of the cases along with the PIL issue were dealt with in 18 civil and commercial cases.[94] Indeed, in the majority of the PIL civil and commercial cases, the court dealt with the PIL issue only.[95] This is a clear indication that, assuming that there is a relatively strong claim, a level of tactical manoeuvring would be much more common in cases where the available remedy has a monetary value. Equally, parties to some high value cross-border matrimonial proceedings may be strategically driven. This was captured by Mr Justice Holman, when making the following remarks:

> 4 The reason why the issue arises is patently one of tactical manoeuvring by each of these parties in which, as I have been told today, they have now jointly invested around £120,000 to £130,000 in legal fees. As such, a divorce in either England or Sweden would be just as effective and just as appropriate as a means of dissolving their marriage. But each patently shares a common belief (whether correct or not) that the wife would receive greater financial provision if the divorce is here than if it is in Sweden.

> 5 The husband, who works for a bank, has produced a schedule of assets which asserts or admits that the overall wealth of these parties is just under £9 million, of which just over £800,000 is joint and the remainder in his sole name. So, quite considerably more or less for the wife may be at stake. Although both parties are each patently engaged in tactical manoeuvring, it is permissible to do so and each is perfectly entitled to seek to take advantage of the legal position as it now is in the events which have happened.[96]

This quotation illustrates well that any tactical manoeuvring will have an impact on the costs as well as on financial remedies, causing delay. That said, the diverse nature of the Union makes any analysis of the collected data extremely difficult. In the light of the different problems which litigants and national judges face in relying on the PIL framework across the EU, it will be particularly difficult for the EU policy-makers to decide on how to improve the effectiveness of the current EU PIL framework.

On the one hand, some Member States[97] have become dominant in attracting high value cross-border commercial and matrimonial disputes. The lawyers in these jurisdictions have acquired advance knowledge and tactical skills which allow them to exploit the weaknesses

---

[93] Considering the family law dataset which is discussed in Ch 5 above.
[94] See more in Ch 5 above.
[95] ibid, considering the civil and commercial law dataset which is discussed there.
[96] *W Husband v W Wife* [2010] EWHC 1843 (Fam) [4–5].
[97] eg Ch 5 above.

of the current PIL regime to the benefits of their clients. On the other hand, the judges and lawyers in other Member States[98] appear to be inexperienced and barely familiar with the PIL instruments and their implications. With this in mind, an analysis of the litigation strategies conceived under the current EU PIL framework allows the author to identify the major issues, which need to be considered further, as potentially undermining the parties' effective access to remedies in cross-border cases.

A. Access to Remedies—Lack of Experience of Judges and Legal Practitioners in some EU Member States: An Issue

Some particular issues, which could impair the effectiveness of the current EU PIL framework, may be identified by looking at the legal practice in some of the new Member States, where the judges and lawyers have less experience in dealing with cross-border cases. As already noted, even if a claimant has a strong (or relatively strong) claim, his/her effective access to remedies could be impaired by badly devised strategies which (mis)led him/her to issue proceedings before the wrong court and embark on jurisdictional battles which would be subsequently lost.[99] The parties' access to remedies could be hampered if a Member State court wrongfully assumed jurisdiction misapplying EU PIL.[100]

Moreover, poorly devised litigant's strategies and the lack of experience of the national judges could have a significant impact on the claimants' access to remedies, even if a claim had been issued before a court which had jurisdiction under the Brussels regime. This could be illustrated by a relatively recent Bulgarian case,[101] which was initiated by a Bulgarian citizen in Bulgaria. The claimant was suing for damages caused by a road traffic accident which occurred on 20 May 2011 in Germany. As a result of the accident, the claimant's son—who had been working in Germany—died. The accident was caused by a drunk driver. There were criminal proceedings in Germany, establishing the driver's liability. The damages caused to the claimant had to be assessed by the Bulgarian courts. But poorly devised litigation strategies meant that there were to be two sets of proceedings.

In the first set of proceedings, the claimant was suing the driver before the Provincial Court in Pernik, Bulgaria. Since it seems the defendant was domiciled in Germany[102] and did not appear in person (and was not represented), it was surprising that the Bulgarian court did not consider whether it had jurisdiction under Brussels I. The lack of any reasoning on this issue in the judgment flies in the face of Article 26(1) of Brussels I which states:

> Where a defendant domiciled in one Member State is sued in a court of another Member State and does not enter an appearance, the court shall declare of its own motion that it has no jurisdiction unless its jurisdiction is derived from the provisions of this Regulation.

---

[98] eg Ch 12 above.

[99] Ch 40.

[100] *Re: S (A Child)* [2014] EWHC 4643 (Fam) discussed in Ch 5 above.

[101] Decision 248 of 24.04.2014, Provincial Court of Pernik, case No 427/2013. The author is thankful to Anton Petrov and Teodora Tsenova who cited Decision 3122 of 11.05.2015 of Sofia City Court, Civil Division, 1st panel, case No 5189/2013 in Ch 12 above. This helped the author to identify the case.

[102] The issue of the domicile was not addressed at all. However, it is stated that the defendant is from town G, G. It is assumed by the author that the second 'G' stands for Germany. See Decision 248 of 24.04.2014, Provincial Court of Pernik, case No 427/2013.

The lack of appropriate reasoning in this context is certainly problematic. Similarly, despite the fact that Rome II should have been applied, in order to determine the applicable law, the Bulgarian court completely ignored Article 4(1) of Rome II. If the Bulgarian court had applied Rome II, then German law would have to be applied as the accident occurred in Germany. Moreover, the Commission's proposal for Rome II leaves no doubt that 'the designated law governs the question whether an action can be brought by a victim's heir to obtain compensation for damage sustained by the victim.'[103] Instead of engaging with any of the Rome II provisions, on 24 March 2014 the Bulgarian judge applied Bulgarian law, awarding compensation of approximately €50,000.

One may reasonably assume that, after the claimant's lawyers had probably realised that the tortfeasor did not have enough money to pay the awarded compensation, a second set of proceedings was issued against the driver's German domiciled insurer. The second claim arising out of the same accident was subsequently brought before the Sofia City Court.[104] In these proceedings, the Bulgarian court exercised jurisdiction under Articles 9(1)(b) and 11(2) of Brussels I. It was held that the insurer should pay the compensation. Although the claimant (in reliance on Bulgarian law) sought a higher level of compensation in the second claim, the Sofia City Court stated that it could not review the assessment of damages made by the Pernik Regional court. Interestingly, Rome II was not considered at all by the parties and/or judges in this case. This example shows that the way the EU PIL instruments are applied (or not applied) by national judges can affect the parties' *entitlement to remedy* as well as their *access to remedies* in cross-border cases.

B. Access to Remedies—Reasoning and Persuasiveness of Member States' Court Judgments Applying EU PIL: An Issue

Another problem, which reflects the existing level of diversity in the EU, concerns the way a judgment's reasoning is being drawn, when the relevant PIL instruments are applied in cross-border cases, by the various EU Member States' judges. The need for the court's ruling on its own jurisdiction to be substantiated is important for the effective administration of justice in cross-border cases as well as for the judgment's persuasiveness.

The issue can be illustrated by another Bulgarian case[105] which involved a jurisdictional dispute. In this case, the proceedings were initiated by a Bulgarian company, Prim 41 Ltd. The defendant was a UK company, Access Ltd. The cause of action was for unjust enrichment. The claimant sought the restitution of a sum of money paid under a contract which was no longer valid between the parties. The claimant argued that the Bulgarian court was competent to hear and determine the dispute under Article 5(1) of Brussels I. The defendant challenged the jurisdiction of the Bulgarian court, noting that the claim had to be brought before the UK courts, where the defendant was domiciled. The Varna Regional Court upheld the defendant's jurisdictional challenge. It was held that, due

---

[103] The European Commission's Proposal for a Regulation of the European Parliament and the Council on the Law Applicable to Non-Contractual Obligations ('Rome II') COM(2003) 427 final, p 24.

[104] Decision 3122 of 11.05.2015 of Sofia City Court, Civil Division, 1st panel, case No 5189/2013 which is discussed further in Ch 12 above.

[105] Ruling of 13.03.2013 of Varna Appellate Court, Commercial Chamber on commercial case No 96/2013. The judgment is discussed in Ch 12. The author is grateful to Tsenova and Petrov for identifying this case.

to the lack of a contractual relationship, the Bulgarian court had no jurisdiction under Article 5(1) to hear and determine the restitutionary claim.[106]

However, the court of the first instance's judgment was reversed by the Varna Appellate Court. The second instance court held that the Bulgarian court was competent because the concept of 'matters relating to a contract' under Article 5(1) was broad enough to cover a claim for restitution of money which was paid under a contract which was no longer valid between the parties. In spite of the existing level of uncertainty about the scope of the concept 'matters relating to a contract' and claims for restitution of money under a contract which was no longer binding between the parties, the whole judgment of the Varna Appellate Court dealing inter alia with this complex issue amounted to approximately 450 words in total. Such a model of administration of justice in cross-border cases flies in the face of 'the obligation of the administration to give reasons for its decisions.'[107]

The reasoning (or rather the lack of reasoning) of the Bulgarian court judgment is a real issue which may undermine the effectiveness of the institutional framework. The issue of jurisdiction was only very briefly addressed. This approach makes it, for example, very difficult even to say why the parties were not bound by any contractual relationship. Was the contract void *ab initio*? Or was the contract terminated? These are important questions which appeared to have been overlooked. The Varna Appellate Court's judgment does not appear to be entirely consistent with the Brussels I regime.[108] The difficult issues about the claims for restitution of money and the scope of 'matters relating to contract' were subsequently considered by the CJEU in *Profit Investment Sim SpA*.[109] In this case, the CJEU held that if a claim for nullity of a contract is brought together with a closely linked claim for restitution of money, then the court seised has jurisdiction to hear both claims under Article 5(1). It should be noted that the CJEU decision finds support in the academic literature. In particular, it has been submitted that '[i]t would be strictly unadvisable to split jurisdiction between courts, one determining whether the contract is void and the other dealing with the consequential remedies.'[110] Mankowski strengthened his argument by making a reference to Article 12(1)(e) of Rome I which states that the 'law applicable to a contract … shall govern … the consequences of nullity of contract.'[111] However, this would not be a valid argument, if there was no claim 'seeking the annulment of a contract'[112] and both parties agreed that the contract was not valid. The Bulgarian court neither addressed these issues head on nor considered making a preliminary reference to the CJEU.[113]

There is a strong case for this type of problem to be addressed at EU level. A good example of the impact, which could be made by a well-reasoned judgment, is the decision rendered by the UK House of Lords (as it then was) on the application of Article 5 to claims for restitution of a sum of money paid under a contract which was void *ab initio*.[114] In this case, the original contract was an interest rate swap agreement between Kleinwort Benson and

---

[106] Ruling No 5382 of 19.11.2012, Varna Regional Court, case No 1184/2012.

[107] Art 41(2)(c) of the EU Charter of Fundamental Rights.

[108] A different view is expressed by Tsenova and Petrov in Ch 12 above.

[109] Case C-366/13 *Profit Investment Sim SpA* EU:C:2016:282.

[110] P Mankowski, 'Article 5' in U Magnus and P Mankowski, *Brussels I Regulation* (Munich, Sellier, 2012) 88, 132.

[111] ibid 131–32.

[112] ibid [58]. See also ibid [17].

[113] *Kleinwort Benson v Glasgow City Council* [1999] 1 AC 153 (HL).

[114] ibid. Compare Mankowski, above n 110.

Glasgow City Council. The contract was invalidated as being *ultra vires*. Kleinwort Benson was suing in England under Article 5(1) for the restitution of money paid under the contract. A majority of the UK House of Lords held that a claim for restitution of money paid under a contract, which was void *ab initio*, does not fall within Article 5(1) of Brussels I. The latter provision would only be relevant if the claim was based on a particular contractual obligation.[115] The judgment, which was rendered on 30 October 1997, was so well reasoned that it was considered highly persuasive beyond the UK borders. AG Wahl in giving his recent opinion in *Gazdasági Versenyhivatal v Siemens Aktiengesellschaft Österreich*[116] stated that:

> [I]t is legitimate to infer from the omission made in Article 5(3) of claims based on restitution that this is precisely due to the absence of any close connecting factor consistently linking such claims to any jurisdiction other than the defendant's domicile.[117]

AG Wahl went on to state '[o]n this point I concur with the judgment of Lord Goff in Kleinwort Benson …'[118] That said, the judgment of the CJEU exposes another problem with the effectiveness of the current EU civil justice framework. In *Gazdasági Versenyhivatal*, it took about 15 months for the CJEU to state that the dispute was not within the scope of the Regulation.[119] The slowness of the CJEU to provide preliminary rulings and the inexperience of some of the EU Member States may cumulatively impair the litigants' access to effective remedies in cross-border cases.

Even if one could argue that the lack of experience of some of the EU national judges and the inadequate reasoning of the judgments in some jurisdictions should be dealt with by providing more training for them, then a case for more comprehensive reform may be made by considering the way the EU PIL is functioning in some of the leading EU jurisdictions. An entirely different type of issue is displayed in the more sophisticated jurisdictions where judges and lawyers have developed advanced skills in dealing with cross-border disputes.

C. Access to Remedies—Litigants' Exploiting the Weakness of the EU PIL: An Issue about the Institutional Architecture and Rigid Rules

There are some aspects of the EU PIL framework which are not functioning effectively and this can be exploited by a party in order to delay the resolution of the dispute.[120] This will adversely affect the other party's expectations about the outcome of the litigation which is likely to affect the amount at which the parties agree to settle.[121]

Given the fact that a significant number of jurisdictional challenges are raised across the EU, lawyers in the leading jurisdictions—which have consistently been attracting high value and highly complex cases—have developed some advanced knowledge and understanding

---

[115] *Kleinwort Benson v Glasgow City Council* [1999] 1 AC 153 (HL) 167 (Lord Goff).
[116] Case C-102/15 *Gazdasági Versenyhivatal v Siemens Aktiengesellschaft Österreich*—Opinion of AG Wahl, EU:C:2016:225.
[117] Ibid [69].
[118] ibid [69], fn 46.
[119] Case C-102/15 *Gazdasági Versenyhivatal v Siemens Aktiengesellschaft Österreich* EU:C:2016:607.
[120] See more in Chs 5 and 35.
[121] See more in Chs 35 and 40.

about the nuances of the relevant PIL provisions and case law.[122] This puts them in a good position to advise on cross-border litigation strategies. In particular, the legal practitioners in some jurisdictions allow their clients to gain negotiating advantages by devising strategies which exploit the weaknesses of the current EU civil justice system. Heated debates about the nuances of PIL instruments (and lengthy jurisdictional challenges in particular) mean that the lawyers on both sides have to spend more time to provide adequate legal advice to parties in cross-border cases. Disputes on preliminary PIL issues mean that the parties have to spend longer in court, making it increasingly difficult for judges to take a view on the interpretation of the PIL instruments in a cross-border context.[123] As already noted above, this will increase the litigation costs for the parties. More importantly, any legal uncertainty about the authority of a court to hear and determine a dispute with an international element generates a delay, deflating parties' expectations about the outcome of the case and impacting on the settlement negotiations.[124]

Moreover, it is not only the problem of jurisdictional challenges which needs to be addressed at EU level, but also the issue of parallel proceedings which needs to be looked at. Parallel proceedings increase both the litigation costs and the level of uncertainty due to the fact that potentially irreconcilable judgments may be rendered. Given the importance of the court-first-seised rule and the level of variation in the way the national legal systems are functioning, tactical claims may be initiated before the courts in jurisdictions which are notoriously slow in dealing with civil and commercial disputes. As one interview respondent noted, there is a case for:

> [H]aving more uniformity within the EU court structures, so that you don't get bogged down, as you would do in Greece and in Italy; and you're giving people a great litigation tactic on a plate there; to start proceedings knowing that it will take 10 years, and if you appeal, it's 20; and we just don't see the end of it.[125]

The extent of the problem is identified in the Greek national report which states that '[a] civil action filed in 2016 in Athens would be heard in 2022 an average time for the court to render its decision would be two years.'[126] Therefore, litigation tactics not only inflate the litigation costs by exploiting the high level of complexity in disputes with an international element,[127] but they also impair litigants' access to effective remedies in cross-border cases. The problem is not new, the Commission tried to address the issue with the court-first-seised rule by proposing that:

> [T]he court first seised shall establish its jurisdiction within six months except where exceptional circumstances make this impossible. Upon request by any other court seised of the dispute, the court first seised shall inform that court of the date on which it was seised and of whether it has established jurisdiction over the dispute or, failing that, of the estimated time for establishing jurisdiction.[128]

---

[122] See Ch 35 below.
[123] See Ch 5 above.
[124] See Ch 40 below.
[125] EUPILLAR—England and Wales—Interview Transcript No 12.
[126] See Ch 18 above.
[127] See Recital 22 to the Brussels Ia Reg. See also Case C-116/02 *Erich Gasser GmbH v MISAT Srl*, EU:C:2003:657.
[128] Art 29(2) of the Commission Proposal for the Brussels I Recast COM(2010) 748 final.

One way for the litigants to manage this type of cross-border litigation risk is to include a choice-of-court agreement along with the same country's law chosen as applicable to the merits of the dispute. This is something which is being further encouraged by the Brussels I (Recast) Regulation which is intended to inter alia 'enhance the effectiveness of exclusive choice-of-court agreements'.[129] Needless to say, this type of strategy may not work in cases where the parties could not reach a choice-of-court agreement. Therefore, one should consider whether a solution modelled on Article 15 of Brussels IIa could work for those cases.

The national reports do suggest that the litigants across the EU have shown their ability to exploit the ambiguities that are generated by the current EU PIL instruments.[130] It is a real issue that the current regime does not provide the necessary flexibility for judges to defeat abusive litigation tactics, providing effective remedies for litigants in cross-border cases. This is an important issue which must be addressed with a view to creating a well-functioning EU civil justice system. As one interview respondent from England and Wales put it:

> [Judges should be] entitled to assume in general terms that measures like these regulations are intended to lead, both as regards jurisdiction and as regards governing law, to a generally sensible result. However, because they adopt bright line approaches, there may be some cases where the perfect result is not achieved in the interest of certainty. Nonetheless, one assumes that generally the result is intended to be sensible. For example that the litigation won't be scissored up into 50 separate sets of litigation each assigned to a different country. One assumes that generally there will be a possibility of dealing with coherent issues in a coherent fashion.[131]

This is an important aspect of the institutional architecture which needs to be addressed by the policy-makers as a priority.

Another particularly important issue in this context is to consider how to involve consumers in a cross-border collective redress action in mass harm situations. The importance for providing effective remedies for consumers in such cases will be illustrated by the MasterCard litigation before the UK Competition Appeal Tribunal (CAT). It is worth noting that, despite an 80 per cent discount, the court awarded nearly £70 million to a UK chain of supermarkets.[132] Most recently, a multi-billion collective redress claim action was initiated on behalf of 46 million UK consumers, on an opt-out basis, for over £14 billion. A litigation funder will finance the litigation with the sum of up to £40 million.[133] This is indeed a significant development, but it is a real issue that, given the MasterCard business activities, the current PIL framework does not provide for a real pan-EEA collective redress action.[134] If this is not addressed, then there will not be effective remedies for a significant number of injured parties across the EU.

---

[129] See Recital 22 to the Brussels Ia Reg.

[130] See more in Ch 35 below.

[131] EUPILLAR—England and Wales—Interview Transcript No 19.

[132] *Sainsbury's Supermarkets Ltd v MasterCard Incorporated & others* [2016] CAT 11.

[133] Quinn Emmanuel—Firm News, 'MasterCard Facing Claim of up to £14 Billion Damages from UK Consumers in Landmark Collective Action' < www.quinnemanuel.com/the-firm/news-events/firm-news-mastercard-facing-claim-of-up-to-14-billion-damages-from-uk-consumers-in-landmark-collective-action/.

[134] See Ch 39 below.

V. Conclusion

The collected data and national reports demonstrate that the parties' desire to obtain a remedy (achieve a desirable result) has a major impact on the decisions of litigants on where to sue, shaping their litigation tactics in cross-border cases. Given the triangular relationship between the available remedy in cross-border cases and the place of litigation (ie the issue of jurisdiction) and applicable law, the legal landscape in relation to private international law has a pivotal role to play in this context. An analysis of the foregoing national reports indicate that, depending on where the litigation takes place, the parties may face different types of problems in disputes with an international element. More specifically, the parties' effective access to remedies may be impaired by the ineffectiveness of the current EU PIL framework, deficiencies of national judicial systems and/or the insufficient experience of some national judges and litigators to deal with cross-border cases.

The EU PIL framework appears to shape the litigants' strategies which need to be carefully considered when measuring the effectiveness of EU PIL. An examination of the way in which EU PIL shapes the litigants' strategies in the leading jurisdictions has helped us to identify the weakness of the institutional architecture in relation to the EU PIL framework. A case for an institutional reform can be made because strategic litigants can design litigation tactics, utilising the EU PIL Regulations, with a view to impairing the effective access to remedies of their opponents in disputes with an international element.[135] It is important to consider what the effect of parties' tactical manoeuvring is on the litigants' decision to continue with the litigation as well as on any settlement dynamics and ultimately parties' effective access to remedies in disputes with an international element.[136] This analysis should allow us to identify which aspects of the current institutional architecture need to be revised in order to facilitate private parties' access to effective remedies in cross-border cases.

---

[135] See Ch 35 below.
[136] See Ch 40 below.

Part III

Litigating Cross-border Civil and Commercial Disputes—A Europe of Law and Justice

33

Cross-border Civil and Commercial Disputes Before the Court of Justice of the European Union

PAUL BEAUMONT AND BURCU YÜKSEL

I. Introduction

In the European Union (EU), private international law (PIL) aspects of civil and commercial matters are regulated by the Brussels Ia Regulation—which replaced the Brussels I Regulation—on jurisdiction and the recognition and enforcement of judgments, the Rome I Regulation on the law applicable to contractual obligations and the Rome II Regulation on the law applicable to non-contractual obligations.[1] Between 1 March 2002, ie the date of entry into force of Brussels I, and 31 December 2015, the Court of Justice of the EU (CJEU) rendered 78 relevant judgments[2] in the preliminary ruling requests concerning Brussels I (74 judgments), Rome I (one judgment) and Rome II (three judgments).

This chapter examines in detail these judgments rendered by the CJEU on the Brussels I, Rome I and Rome II Regulations in order to assess to what extent the CJEU has dealt appropriately with the harmonised PIL rules provided for cross-border civil and commercial matters in the EU. Where necessary, this analysis on the CJEU case law dataset will be supplemented by empirical evidence gathered from 16 interviews[3] conducted with the officials of the Commission,[4] the Council,[5] the European Parliament[6] and with members of the CJEU.[7]

---

[1] In this context, the authors are using the term 'civil and commercial matters' to encompass the Brussels I, Rome I and Rome II Regs and to exclude the 'family law matters' covered by Brussels IIa and the Maintenance Reg. The authors are aware that 'civil and commercial' encompasses family law matters in the context of the Hague and EU instruments on Service of Documents and Taking of Evidence and that until Brussels Ia maintenance issues were included in the Brussels Convention and Brussels I Reg.

[2] English summaries of all judgments are available on the EUPILLAR Database at www.w3.abdn.ac.uk/clsm/eupillar/#/home.

[3] The interviewees were selected from a long list of potential interviewees. This list was prepared on the basis of the interviewees' expertise and experience in the field of EU PIL and, in particular, in the application of the regulations that are examined in the EUPILLAR Project, namely the Brussels I, Rome I, Rome II, Brussels IIa and Maintenance Regs.

[4] EUPILLAR_EU 1, EUPILLAR_EU 8, EUPILLAR_EU 9, EUPILLAR_EU 12.

[5] EUPILLAR_EU 2, EUPILLAR_EU 10, EUPILLAR_EU 11, EUPILLAR_EU 12, EUPILLAR_EU 13, EUPILLAR_EU 14, EUPILLAR_EU 16.

[6] EUPILLAR_EU 15.

[7] EUPILLAR_EU 3, EUPILLAR_EU 4, EUPILLAR_EU 5, EUPILLAR_EU 6, EUPILLAR_EU 7. For a detailed analysis that builds on empirical data gathered from these interviews, see B Yüksel, Ch 3 on 'An Analysis of the Effectiveness of the EU Institutions in Making and Interpreting EU Private International Law Regulations'.

II. Interpretation of the Rules on Jurisdiction and the Recognition and Enforcement of Judgments in Civil and Commercial Matters under the Brussels I Regulation

A. Matters Related to the Scope of Application (Article 1)

i. 'Civil and Commercial Matters' (Article 1(1))

Under Article 1(1) of Brussels I, the scope of application of Brussels I is limited to 'civil and commercial matters' and not extended, in particular, to revenue, customs or administrative matters, which have been preserved in Article 1(1) of Brussels Ia. The CJEU has interpreted the concept of 'civil and commercial matters' within the meaning of Article 1(1) in six cases. Overall, the CJEU has done well in ensuring the autonomous interpretation of the concept free from national law, however when the issue in question involves penal measures, as will be seen below, the CJEU needs to be more principled in its interpretation.

C-420/07 *Meletis Apostolides v David Charles Orams and Linda Elizabeth Orams*[8] was referred to the CJEU in English proceedings between Mr Apostolides (a Cypriot national) and the Orams (a British couple), regarding the recognition and enforcement, in the UK under Brussels I, of two Cypriot court judgments given in an action brought against the Orams by Mr Apostolides concerning immovable property in the northern area where the Cyprus Government does not have effective control. The CJEU interpreted various provisions of Brussels I in this case,[9] and one of them was Article 1. The CJEU was asked, inter alia, whether the suspension of the application of the *acquis communautaire* in the northern area, provided for by Article 1(1) of Protocol No 10,[10] precludes the application of Brussels I to the Cypriot court judgments concerning the land in the northern area. The CJEU assessed that that fact does not nullify the obligation to apply Brussels I in the Cyprus Government-controlled area where the Cypriot judgment had been given and that it does not mean that Brussels I must thereby be applied in the northern area (by analogy, paragraph 31 of C-281/02 *Owusu*).[11] The CJEU also found that the case concerns 'civil and commercial matters' under Article 1(1) considering the object of the action and its being between individuals.

In C-406/09 *Realchemie Nederland BV v Bayer CropScience AG*,[12] concerning the enforcement in the Netherlands of fine payment orders given in respect of an alleged patent infringement by the German courts pursuant to the German Civil Code (ZPO) to be paid to the German State, the CJEU interpreted whether the orders fell within the scope of Brussels I under Article 1. The CJEU examined the question by taking account of Recital 19

---

[8] [2009] ECR I-03571 (Grand Chamber) ('Apostolides').

[9] See also s II.D.i.b.1 below.

[10] [2003] OJ L236/955.

[11] C-281/02 *Andrew Owusu v N B Jackson, trading as 'Villa Holidays Bal-Inn Villas' and Others* [2005] ECR I-01383 (Grand Chamber) ('Owusu').

[12] [2011] ECR I-09773 (Grand Chamber) ('Realchemie Nederland').

and its case law on the Brussels Convention.[13] It affirmed C-420/07 *Apostolides* that Brussels I's scope, limited to 'civil and commercial matters', is determined essentially according to the factors characterising the nature of the legal relationships between the parties to the action or the subject matter of the action. As regards interim measures, the CJEU affirmed 143/78 *Cavel*[14] and C-391/95 *Van Uden*[15] that their inclusion in scope is determined not by their own nature but by the nature of the rights that they serve to protect. It observed that even though the fine at issue is punitive and having a penal nature under the ZPO, the dispute is between two private persons concerning an allegation of patent infringement and the action intends to protect private rights and does not involve the exercise of public powers by one of the parties to the dispute. It found that the legal relationship between Bayer and Realchimie must be classified as 'a private law relationship' and is covered by the concept of 'civil and commercial matters' in Brussels I. It stated that although the fine imposed must be paid to the German State, the fine is not recovered by the private party or on its behalf, and the actual recovery is made by the German judicial authorities, those specific aspects of the German enforcement procedure cannot be regarded as decisive as regards the nature of the right to enforcement. The CJEU explained that the nature of that right depends on the nature of the subjective right, for infringement of which enforcement was ordered, ie Bayer's right to exploit exclusively the invention protected by its patent. The CJEU did not agree with AG Mengozzi[16] and it held that Brussels I applies to the recognition and enforcement of a decision of a court or tribunal that contains an order to pay a fine in order to ensure compliance with a judgment given in a civil and commercial matter.

This case is subject to criticism on a few points. As regards the length of the proceedings, it took the CJEU too long to decide (ie two years). As regards the interpretation on the merits of the case, the Grand Chamber gave a broader definition of civil and commercial matters than AG Mengozzi. This leaves the question remaining whether it is really appropriate to allow private parties to enforce foreign orders which will be paid to a foreign State rather than a private party and whether this is not a classical 'penal law' provision which should not fall within the scope of the EU PIL regime. AG Mengozzi pointed out that only focusing on the subject matter of the main proceedings to determine what constitutes a civil or commercial matter can lead to absurd results, such as a term of imprisonment imposed on someone who does not comply with a financial order in a civil case becomes enforceable as a civil or commercial matter.[17] This cogent point was not dealt with by the CJEU in its reasoning. AG Mengozzi was surely right to say that the public law elements of the fine were enough to take it outside the scope of Brussels I[18] in particular because the fine was paid to the State and not to the private party. This distinction gains support also from the Schlosser Report.[19] The CJEU needs to be more principled and only include what are

---

[13] Convention of 27 September 1968 on jurisdiction and the enforcement of judgments in civil and commercial matters, [1998] OJ C27/1.

[14] 143/78 *Jacques de Cavel v Louise de Cavel* [1979] ECR 01055 ('Cavel').

[15] C-391/95 *Van Uden Maritime BV, trading as Van Uden Africa Line v Kommanditgesellschaft in Firma Deco-Line and Another* [1998] ECR I-07091 ('Van Uden').

[16] See the AG's Opinion, EU:C:2011:209.

[17] See ibid para 49.

[18] See ibid paras 60–72.

[19] See para 29 of the Report by Prof P Schlosser on the 1978 Accession Convention on jurisdiction and the enforcement of judgments in civil and commercial matters, [1979] OJ C59/71 ('Schlosser Report') 84.

genuinely civil matters within the scope of Brussels I, not penal measures like imprisonment or fines, regardless of the nature of the main proceedings in the action.

In C-645/11 *Land Berlin v Ellen Mirjam Sapir and Others*,[20] the interpretation of Articles 1(1) and 6(1)[21] was referred to the CJEU in German proceedings between the Land Berlin and 11 persons concerning the repayment of an amount overpaid in error following an administrative procedure designed to provide compensation in respect of the loss of real property during persecution under the Nazi regime. The Land Berlin, which also acted on behalf of the Federal Republic of Germany, had unintentionally made the overpayment and so it sought to recover from the defendants on the basis of unjust enrichment and a tortious act. The issue at question was whether the action concerned a 'civil and commercial matter'. Citing C-420/07 *Apostolides* and C-154/11 *Mahamdia*,[22] the CJEU reaffirmed that although certain actions between a public authority and a person governed by private law may come within the scope of Brussels I, it is otherwise where the public authority is acting in the exercise of its public powers. By examining the basis and the detailed rules governing the bringing of the action, it found that the action in relation to the right to compensation fell into 'civil and commercial matters'.

C-49/12 *The Commissioners for Her Majesty's Revenue & Customs v Sunico ApS and Others*[23] was referred to the CJEU in Danish proceedings between HMRC (the tax authority of the UK) and Sunico and others (companies established in Denmark and private persons residing there) concerning the procedure to determine the validity of an attachment order made at the request of HMRC in respect of assets belonging to the defendants in Denmark. HMRC brought court proceedings in the UK and Denmark to claim damages resulting from an alleged value added tax (VAT) carousel type fraud. The main issue was whether this action whereby a public authority of one Member State claims, from natural and legal persons resident in another Member State, damages in respect of loss caused by a conspiracy to commit VAT fraud in the first Member State was a civil and commercial matter under Article 1(1) of Brussels I. Reaffirming its interpretation in Case C-645/11 *Sapir and others*, the CJEU stated that although certain actions between a public authority and a person governed by private law may come within the scope of Brussels I, it is otherwise where the public authority is acting in the exercise of its public powers. By agreeing with AG Kokott,[24] the CJEU asserted that, in the context of the present legal relationship, HMRC did not exercise any exceptional powers by comparison with the rules applicable to relationships between persons governed by private law and it observed that HMRC's claim against the defendants in the UK was not based on public law involving the exercise of powers of a public authority, but on English tort law. It accordingly held that, in principle, the action was a civil and commercial matter covered by Brussels I. However, it also stated that it was for the referring court to ascertain whether the request for information which HMRC addressed to the Danish authorities affects the nature of the legal relationship between HMRC and the defendants and whether HMRC was in the same position as a person governed by private law in its action against the defendants sued in the UK.

---

[20] EU:C:2013 (Third Chamber) ('Sapir and others').

[21] See also s II.C.i.b below.

[22] C-154/11 *Ahmed Mahamdia v People's Democratic Republic of Algeria* EU:C:2012:491 (Grand Chamber) ('Mahamdia').

[23] EU:C:2013:545 (Third Chamber) ('Sunico and Others').

[24] See the AG's Opinion, EU:C:2013:231.

In its judgment, the CJEU followed a purposive and contextual interpretation of the Denmark-EC parallel agreement on the application of Brussels I[25] by relying on its preamble. It clarified that any Danish court or tribunal can refer questions on the interpretation of Brussels I to the CJEU. A literal interpretation of the agreement would have restricted references to only courts or tribunals against whose decision in the particular case there is no judicial remedy. However, this can only be understood by reading AG Kokott's Opinion[26] as the CJEU does not deal with the wording of Article 6(1) which is indeed the key provision in the parallel agreement on the jurisdiction of the CJEU.[27] On the merits of the case, the CJEU wisely gave a wide interpretation to 'civil and commercial matters' to cover a tort case where a public authority is not exercising any exceptional powers in the action. By implication it is clear that having the potentially unlimited resources of the State is not an 'exceptional power'.

C-302/13 *flyLAL-Lithuanian Airlines AS v Starptautiskā lidosta Rīga VAS and Air Baltic Corporation AS*,[28] on the interpretation of Articles 1, 22(2),[29] 34(1)[30] and 35(1) of Brussels I, was referred to the CJEU in Latvian proceedings between flyLAL (a Lithuanian airline in liquidation) and two Latvian companies, concerning a request for recognition and enforcement of a Lithuanian court order for provisional/protective measures in Latvia. The Latvian State owned at least a majority shareholding in each of the co-defendants. Thus, the CJEU was asked whether an action seeking legal redress for damage resulting from alleged infringements of EU competition law is a 'civil and commercial matter' covered by Brussels I. The CJEU referred to its settled case law on Brussels I and the Brussels Convention on the interpretation of 'civil and commercial matters', Recital 7 to Brussels I, and Article 5(3) and (4) and it found that the action relates to tort, delict or quasi-delict, is civil and commercial in nature and covered by Brussels I. The CJEU noted that the exercise of public powers by one of the parties to the case excludes it from civil and commercial matters. However, it found no exercise of public powers. The crucial issue in determining whether this was a civil and commercial matter was that none of the parties to the case were 'exercising public powers' in relation to the matters being litigated. The action was 'not against conduct or procedures which involve an exercise of public powers by one of the parties to the case, but against acts carried out by individuals'.[31] As AG Kokott pointed out: '[t]he applicability of Brussels I is to be assessed in accordance with the same criteria as the Court has developed in relation to the economic activity test in the sphere of competition law.'[32] This was effectively followed by the Third Chamber.[33]

In C-523/14 *Aannemingsbedrijf Aertssen NV and Aertssen Terrassements SA v VSB Machineverhuur BV and Others*,[34] the CJEU interpreted Articles 1, 27 and 30 in the course of proceedings between the Aertssen companies (incorporated under Belgian law), and

[25] [2005] OJ L299/62.
[26] See paras 30–36 of the AG's Opinion.
[27] See paras 27–28 of the judgment.
[28] EU:C:2014:2319 (Third Chamber) ('flyLAL-Lithuanian Airlines').
[29] See also s II.C.v.b below.
[30] See also s II.D.i.b.1 below.
[31] See para 37 of the judgment.
[32] See para 38 of the AG's Opinion, EU:C:2014:2046.
[33] See para 33 of the judgment.
[34] EU:C:2015:722 (Third Chamber)('Aertssen'). See also s II.C.viii below.

two companies (incorporated under Netherlands law) and Mr van Sommeren concerning an allegation of fraudulent conduct against the defendants. As regards Article 1, citing C-172/91 *Sonntag*,[35] the CJEU observed that, while the complaint's aim was to set in motion a criminal prosecution and while the investigation undertaken by the Belgian court was criminal in nature, the fact remained that its purpose was also to resolve a dispute between private persons concerning compensation for harm which one of those persons considered it had suffered as a result of the fraudulent conduct of others. The CJEU found that the legal relationship between the parties is 'a private law relationship' covered by the 'concept of civil and commercial matters' in Brussels I (by analogy C-406/09 *Realchemie Nederland*, paragraph 41). Citing 120/79 *Cavel*, it also noted that it is apparent from Article 5(4) that Brussels I's scope extends to an action seeking compensation which is ancillary to criminal proceedings, which, since they pertain to criminal matters, are otherwise excluded from it. It held that the action is covered by Article 1(1).

It is important to note that although in this case the Third Chamber cited C-406/09 *Realchemie Nederland* in paragraph 32 of the judgment, it was careful this time to restrict the scope of Brussels I to the civil aspect of the criminal proceedings, in particular 'in so far as its object is to obtain monetary compensation for harm allegedly suffered by the complainant'.[36] This means that the compensatory civil matters fall within the scope of Brussels I but the main criminal proceedings and any non-compensatory aspects of the proceedings do not. In C-406/09 *Realchemie Nederland*, much to the concern of AG Mengozzi, the CJEU decided there that where the main proceedings were civil and commercial all ancillary matters were in principle (even those that are penal where the penalty is not used to compensate the victim) within the scope of Brussels I.

ii. Excluded Matters (Article 1(2))

Under Article 1(2) of Brussels I and Ia, certain matters are excluded from the scope of application. Among these excluded matters, the status or legal capacity of natural persons, proceedings relating to the winding-up of insolvent companies or other legal persons, and arbitration have been interpreted by the CJEU in 10 cases. The interpretation given by the CJEU as regards the status or legal capacity of natural persons (one case) and bankruptcy, proceedings relating to the winding-up of insolvent companies or other legal persons (seven cases) are wise and do not indicate any particular problems whereas its interpretation as regards arbitration (two cases) is contentious.

a. Status or Legal Capacity of Natural Persons (Article 1(2)(a))

In C-386/12 *Siegfried János Schneider*,[37] referred to the CJEU in Bulgarian non-contentious proceedings brought by Mr Schneider (a Hungarian national placed under guardianship pursuant to Hungarian legislation) for authorisation to sell his share of a property situated in Bulgaria, the CJEU was asked to interpret the applicability of the exclusive jurisdiction

---

[35] C-172/91 *Volker Sonntag v Hans Waidmann, Elisabeth Waidmann and Stefan Waidmann* [1993] ECR I-01963 ('Sonntag').
[36] See para 36 of the judgment.
[37] EU:C:2013:633 (Third Chamber)('Schneider'). See also s II.C.v.a below.

rule in Article 22(1) to non-contentious proceedings. The CJEU firstly stressed that Brussels I applies in 'civil and commercial matters', but not to 'the status or legal capacity of natural persons' under Article 1. The CJEU cited its case law on Article 16(1)(a) of the Brussels Convention which it found also applicable in construing Article 22(1) of Brussels I according to Recital 19. The CJEU particularly cited C-115/88 *Reichert and Kockler*[38] and C-343/04 *ČEZ*[39] where it found, under Article 16(1)(a) of the Convention, that:

> the exclusive jurisdiction of the courts of the Contracting State in which the property is situated does not encompass all actions concerning rights *in rem* in immovable property, but only those which both come within the scope of the convention and are actions which seek to determine the extent, content, ownership or possession of immovable property or the existence of other rights *in rem* therein and to provide the holders of those rights with protection for the powers which attach to their interest.

The CJEU accordingly observed that the sole aim of the main proceedings was to determine whether it is in the interests of Mr Schneider, who lacks full legal capacity, to dispose of his immovable property and that his rights *in rem* as owner of that property were not being called in question. The CJEU found that this question did not fall within the scope of Brussels I because it was directly linked to the legal capacity of the natural person under Article 1(2)(a). The CJEU also referred to the Jenard Report[40] which supported this way of interpretation.

This was a straightforward case in which the CJEU gave a correct interpretation in a reasonably short period of time, ie 13 months, without an AG's Opinion. It is wise for the CJEU to give a restrictive interpretation to the scope of Brussels I in relation to the 'status or legal capacity of natural persons' and to give a broad interpretation to that exclusion in line with the Jenard Report on the original Brussels Convention where the exclusion comes from.[41]

b. Bankruptcy and Insolvency (Article 1(2)(b))

Quite a lot of cases before the CJEU have concerned the dividing line between the Brussels I Regulation and the Insolvency Regulation.[42] As will be individually assessed below, the CJEU has given wise and helpful interpretations in these cases by emphasising that the Insolvency Regulation should not be given a broad scope and that the legal basis of the action is the crucial factor.

C-111/08 *SCT Industri AB i likvidation v Alpenblume AB*[43] was referred to the CJEU in proceedings between two Swedish companies, SCT and Alpenblume, concerning an action to recover ownership of shares which had been held in an Austrian company by SCT and which were sold to Alpenblume. That action was brought following an Austrian court judgment which declared Alpenblume's acquisition of those shares to be invalid. The CJEU

---

[38] C-115/88 *Mario P A Reichert and others v Dresdner Bank* [1990] ECR I-00027 (Fifth Chamber) ('Reichert and Kockler').

[39] C-343/04 *Land Oberösterreich v ČEZ as* [2006] ECR I-04557 (First Chamber) ('ČEZ').

[40] P Jenard, Report on the Brussels Convention, [1979] OJ C59/1.

[41] For Art 22, see also s II.C.v below.

[42] Council Reg (EC) No 1346/2000 of 29 May 2000 on insolvency proceedings, [2000] OJ L160/1, ('Insolvency Reg').

[43] [2009] ECR I-05655 (First Chamber) ('SCT Industri').

was asked whether a decision by which a court of another Member State held a transfer of shares effected in the context of insolvency proceedings to be invalid, on the ground that the liquidator who had made the transfer lacked the power to dispose of assets situated in that Member State, fell under the exception in Article 1(2)(b) of Brussels I. The CJEU firstly noted that the Insolvency Regulation was not applicable to this case since the insolvency proceedings had been opened before the entry into force of the Insolvency Regulation. The CJEU cited its relevant case law on the Brussels Convention, particularly 133/78 *Gourdain*,[44] where it had held that an action is related to bankruptcy if it derives directly from the bankruptcy and is closely linked to proceedings for realising the assets or judicial supervision, otherwise it falls within the scope of the Brussels Convention. In interpreting the exception, it also took account of the Jenard Report. It observed that Article 1(2)(b) of Brussels I has the same exception and therefore the position is the same. It then examined whether there was a close link between the court action and the insolvency proceedings. It found that that link was particularly close in the present case for the following two main reasons: 1) the transfer at issue in the main proceedings and the action for restitution of title to which it gave rise, were the direct and indissociable consequence of the exercise by the liquidator—an individual who intervened only after the insolvency proceedings had been opened—of a power which he derived specifically from the provisions of national law governing that type of proceedings; and 2) the ground on which the Austrian court had held invalid the transfer of the shares related, specifically and exclusively, to the extent of the powers of that liquidator in insolvency proceedings and, in particular, his power to dispose of the assets situated in Austria. The CJEU thus found the exception in Article 1(2)(b) applicable. The judgment was given in 15 months, without an AG's Opinion.

C-292/08 *German Graphics Graphische Maschinen GmbH v Alice van der Schee*[45] was referred to the CJEU in Dutch proceedings regarding the enforcement of a German court order in the Netherlands. The first question was whether, before being able to declare that a judgment should be recognised for the purposes of Article 25(2) of the Insolvency Regulation on the basis of Brussels I, the referring court must determine whether the judgment is within the scope of Brussels I. The CJEU considered Article 25 of the Insolvency Regulation dealing with the recognition and enforceability of judgments other than those directly concerning the opening of insolvency proceedings. It observed that among those judgments, there are some judgments coming within the scope of neither the Insolvency Regulation nor Brussels I. Based on the wording of Article 25(2) of the Insolvency Regulation, it found that the application of Brussels I to a judgment under that provision is subject to the condition that the judgment falls within the material scope of Brussels I. Thus, the CJEU held that the national court must determine whether the judgment is within the material scope of Brussels I before it declares that the judgment, not within the scope of the Insolvency Regulation, should be recognised in accordance with Brussels I. The other questions referred to the CJEU concerned whether the action brought by the seller against the purchaser based on the reservation of title clause is excluded from the scope of Brussels I under Article 1(2)(b). Considering Recitals 2, 7 and 15 to Brussels I, the CJEU observed that the legislature's intention in setting out a broad definition of the concept of

44 133/78 *Henri Gourdain v Franz Nadler* [1979] ECR 00733 ('Gourdain').
45 [2009] ECR I-08421 (First Chamber) ('German Graphics').

'civil and commercial matters' in Article 1(1) was to broaden the scope of the article, which is also supported by Recital 6 to the Insolvency Regulation. It consequently stated that the scope of application of the Insolvency Regulation should not be broadly interpreted. The CJEU took account of its relevant case law on the Brussels Convention. It affirmed 133/78 *Gourdain* that an action is related to bankruptcy if it derives directly from the bankruptcy and is closely linked to proceedings for realising the assets or judicial supervision, and also affirmed C-339/07 *Seagon*[46] that an action with such characteristics does not fall within the scope of the Brussels Convention. It observed that, in the present case, that link was neither sufficiently direct nor sufficiently close to exclude the application of Brussels I because the action concerning that reservation of title clause constituted an independent claim, as it was not based on the law of the insolvency proceedings and required neither the opening of such proceedings nor the involvement of a liquidator. It found that the mere fact that the liquidator was a party to the proceedings was not sufficient to classify the German proceedings as proceedings deriving directly from the insolvency and being closely linked to proceedings for realising assets. It held that the claim brought in Germany did not fall outside the scope of application of Brussels I. The CJEU dealt with this straightforward case reasonably quickly, in 14 months, without an AG's Opinion.

In C-213/10 *F-Tex SIA v Lietuvos-Anglijos UAB 'Jadecloud-Vilma'*,[47] the CJEU interpreted whether the assignee of the liquidator's claim against a third party is covered by the Insolvency Regulation or Brussels I. The case was referred to the CJEU in Lithuanian proceedings between F-Tex (with its registered office in Latvia) and Jadecloud (with its registered office in Lithuania), concerning the return of a sum which was paid to Jadecloud by NPLC (with its registered office in Germany) when NPLC was insolvent. The CJEU addressed and defined the scope of the two Regulations. As regards the exclusion in Article 1(2)(b) of Brussels I, after citing 133/78 *Gourdain* and considering the Jenard and Schlosser Reports and also Recital 7 to Brussels I, it found that Article 1(2)(b) of Brussels I excludes from its scope only actions which derive directly from insolvency proceedings and are closely connected with them. Then, it examined whether the action in question had a direct link with the insolvency of the debtor and was closely connected with the insolvency proceedings. It is to be noted that the CJEU distinguished the present case from C-339/07 *Seagon* where it had held in connection with an action by which the applicant, in his capacity as liquidator, requested, by way of an action to set a transaction aside by virtue of the debtor's insolvency, the repayment of a sum paid by the latter, that such an action was covered by Article 3(1) of the Insolvency Regulation. Unlike in C-339/07 *Seagon*, the applicant in this case was not acting as a liquidator, ie a body responsible for insolvency proceedings, but as the assignee of a right. The CJEU observed that once the right is acquired by the assignee, the exercise by the assignee of that right is not closely connected with the insolvency proceedings. It therefore concluded that the action in the main proceedings was not closely connected with the insolvency proceedings. Consequently, without the need to rule on the existence of any direct link between that action and the insolvency of the debtor, it found that action was not covered by Article 3(1) of the Insolvency Regulation and, symmetrically, that it did not concern bankruptcy or winding-up under Article 1(2)(b) of Brussels I. It accordingly found

---

[46] C-339/07 *Christopher Seagon v Deko Marty Belgium NV* [2009] ECR I-00767 (First Chamber) ('Seagon').
[47] EU:C:2012:215 (First Chamber) ('F-Tex').

that the action was covered by Brussels I under Article 1(1). The judgment was given in 23 months and without an AG's Opinion.

In this case, the assignee of the liquidator's claim against a third party was not bringing a claim which was 'closely connected' to the insolvency proceedings. This was so because the assignee was acting for itself rather than to increase the assets of the insolvent company, the applicable law governing the insolvency proceedings made no link with the assignee's claim which could be brought after those proceedings were closed, and unlike in C-111/08 *SCT Industri*, neither the validity of the liquidator's assignment nor the power of the liquidator to make the assignment was in issue. Therefore, it was wise for the CJEU to decide in the *F-Tex* case that the action was within the scope of Brussels I rather than the Insolvency Regulation.

C-147/12 *ÖFAB, Östergötlands Fastigheter AB v Frank Koot and Evergreen Investments BV*,[48] on the interpretation of Articles 1(2)(b), 5(1) and 5(3), was referred to the CJEU in Swedish proceedings between ÖFAB (established in Sweden), and Mr Koot (residing in the Netherlands) and Evergreen Investments (established in the Netherlands) concerning the refusal by the latter to meet the debts of Copperhill (a limited company established in Sweden). The CJEU noted that the actions in question did not constitute insolvency proceedings and did not concern the exclusive prerogative of the liquidator to be exercised in the interests of the general body of creditors, but of rights which ÖFAB was free to exercise in its own interests. It accordingly found that they fell within the scope of Brussels I. This was a useful interpretation by the CJEU reaffirming the narrow scope of the insolvency exception in Article 1(2)(b). The judgment was given in 15 months and without an AG's Opinion.

C-157/13 *Nickel & Goeldner Spedition GmbH v 'Kintra' UAB*,[49] on the interpretation of Articles 1(2)(b) and 71(1), was referred to the CJEU in the Lithuanian proceedings between Nickel & Goeldner (a company incorporated under German law and having its registered office in Germany) and Kintra (a company incorporated under Lithuanian law and having its registered office in Lithuania that had been placed in liquidation), in relation to the payment of a sum for services comprising the international carriage of goods. One of the questions that the CJEU dealt with was whether the action fell within the scope of the Insolvency Regulation or Brussels I. The CJEU referred to its case law that relies on the preparatory documents of the Brussels Convention, and the relevant recitals to the Brussels I and Insolvency Regulations regarding their scope of application and held that the legislature's intention on their scope was that the concept of civil and commercial matters under Brussels I should be interpreted broadly while the scope of application of the Insolvency Regulation should not. The CJEU also noted that its decisive criterion is whether the right or the obligation which respects the basis of the action finds its source in the common rules of civil and commercial law or in the derogating rules specific to insolvency proceedings. The CJEU held that the action at issue did not have a direct link with the insolvency proceedings opened in relation to the applicant since it was an action for the payment of a debt arising out of the provision of services in implementation of a contract for carriage and the fact that it was taken by the insolvency administrator did not substantially amend its nature. The CJEU decided that the action came under the concept of civil and commercial matters in Brussels I. The judgment was given in 17 months and without an AG's Opinion.

---

[48] EU:C:2013:490 (Fifth Chamber) ('ÖFAB'). See also s II.C.i.a.3 below.
[49] EU:C:2014:2145 (First Chamber) ('Kintra'). See also s II.F.i above.

C-649/13 *Comité d'entreprise de Nortel Networks SA and Others v Cosme Rogeau liquidator of Nortel Networks SA and Cosme Rogeau liquidator of Nortel Networks SA v Alan Robert Bloom and Others*,[50] a preliminary ruling on the Insolvency Regulation, concerned also the interpretation of Article 1(2)(b) of Brussels I. It was referred to the CJEU in in the context of (i) an action brought by comité d'entreprise de Nortel Networks SA (NNSA) (the works council of NNSA) and others against Mr Rogeau, acting as court-appointed liquidator in the secondary insolvency proceedings opened in France in respect of NNSA ('the secondary proceedings'), seeking, inter alia, the making of a severance payment, and (ii) an action brought by Mr Rogeau, acting as court-appointed liquidator in the secondary proceedings, seeking that the joint administrators in the main insolvency proceedings opened in the United Kingdom in respect of NNSA ('the main proceedings'), be joined as third parties. Although the first part of the question referred to the CJEU solely related to the allocation of international jurisdiction between the court hearing the main proceedings (ie the English High Court) and the court hearing the secondary proceedings (ie the referring court) under the Insolvency Regulation, the CJEU first examined whether the referring court's jurisdiction was governed by the Insolvency Regulation or by Brussels I. The CJEU noted that the disputes before the referring court fell within the context of the application of a large number of agreements concluded by or between the parties before it. It observed that the jurisdiction to rule on the dispute concerning the interpretation of one or more of those agreements may be governed by Brussels I, even though the dispute was between the liquidators in two sets of insolvency proceedings, one main and the other secondary, each of which falls within the Insolvency Regulation. After reaffirming its approach on the issue and noting that it was for the referring court to assess the content of the agreements in question, it found that the rights or obligations on which the actions before the referring court were founded derive directly from insolvency proceedings, were closely connected with them and had their source in Articles 3(2) and 27 of the Insolvency Regulation, so that that Regulation was applicable.

It is interesting to note that, in *Nortel*, the CJEU raised the issue of the possible applicability of Brussels I for it to be discussed at the oral hearing in this case even though it had not been raised by the referring court or by those who submitted written observations (including the Commission and the French and UK Governments).[51] Having raised the issue the CJEU, guided by AG Mengozzi,[52] held that on the evidence presented to it the legal basis of the claims before the French court was insolvency law.[53] The CJEU's decision in *Nortel* is a useful summary of the approach of the CJEU on the dividing line between the Brussels I Regulation and the Insolvency Regulation that the crucial factor is whether the right or the obligation which forms the basis of the action has its source in the ordinary rules of civil and commercial law or in derogating rules specific to insolvency proceedings.

c. Arbitration (Article 1(2)(d))

The CJEU has interpreted the relationship between arbitration and Brussels I in two cases. Particularly C-185/07 *Allianz SpA, formerly Riunione Adriatica di Sicurtà SpA, Generali*

---

[50] EU:C:2015:384 (First Chamber) ('Nortel').
[51] See para 22 of the AG's Opinion, EU:C:2015:44.
[52] See paras 23–29 of the judgment.
[53] See ibid paras 25–30.

Assicurazioni Generali SpA v West Tankers Inc,[54] which was the first preliminary ruling on the issue, received huge criticism and that led to a reinforcing of the exclusion of arbitration from the scope of Brussels Ia in Recital 12 and Article 73(3) by giving precedence to the New York Convention.[55]

In *West Tankers*, referred to the CJEU in English proceedings, the CJEU was asked whether it is consistent with Brussels I for a court of a Member State to make an order to restrain a person from commencing or continuing proceedings in another Member State on the ground that such proceedings are in breach of an arbitration agreement. The Grand Chamber, agreeing with AG Kokott,[56] found that if the main subject matter of the proceedings in the court first seised, ie a claim for damages before the Italian courts in this case, comes within the scope of Brussels I, a preliminary issue concerning the applicability of an arbitration agreement, including in particular its validity, also comes within its scope. This finding was supported by paragraph 35 of the Evrigenis and Kerameus Report on the Greek accession to the Brussels Convention.[57] It followed that the objection of lack of jurisdiction raised by West Tankers before the Italian courts on the basis of the existence of an arbitration agreement, including the question of the validity of that agreement, came within the scope of Brussels I and that it was therefore exclusively for the Italian courts to rule on that objection and on its own jurisdiction, pursuant to Articles 1(2)(d) and 5(3). Accordingly, on the basis of the CJEU's analysis, the use of an anti-suit injunction to prevent a court of a Member State, which normally had jurisdiction to resolve a dispute under Article 5(3), from ruling, in accordance with Article 1(2)(d), on the very applicability of Brussels I to the dispute brought before it necessarily amounted to stripping that court of the power to rule on its own jurisdiction. Such an anti-suit injunction also ran counter to the trust which the Member States accord to one another's legal systems and judicial institutions and on which the system of jurisdiction under Brussels I is based (see, to that effect, C-159/02 *Turner v Grovit*,[58] paragraph 24).

This highly controversial decision of the CJEU, given in 22 months, was in line with AG Kokott's Opinion which unfortunately did not cite any academic literature on such an important and controversial issue as the relationship between Brussels I and arbitration. The CJEU's reliance on the subject matter of the main issue in the proceedings being within the scope of Brussels I to bring the incidental question on the validity of an arbitration agreement into the scope of Brussels I has the potential to undermine the efficacy of arbitration agreements in Europe. The danger of the *West Tankers* ruling is that it makes it too easy for a commercial party to try to evade an arbitration agreement that it has entered into by choosing to begin substantive litigation in a court in the EU that is relatively slow or relatively hostile to arbitration agreements.

C-536/13 *'Gazprom' OAO v Lietuvos Respublika*[59] gave the CJEU the opportunity to review its controversial judgment in *West Tankers*. The case was referred to the CJEU in a Lithuanian appeal brought by Gazprom, established in Russia, against the refusal to

---

[54] [2009] ECR I-00663 (Grand Chamber) ('West Tankers').

[55] Convention on the Recognition and Enforcement of Foreign Arbitral Awards (New York, 1958) ('New York Convention').

[56] See paras 53 and 54 of the AG's Opinion, EU:C:2008:466.

[57] [1986] OJ C298/1.

[58] [2004] ECR I-03565 (Full Court).

[59] EU:C:2015:316 (Grand Chamber) ('Gazprom').

recognise and enforce an arbitral award in Lithuania. The Grand Chamber examined whether recognition and enforcement of the arbitral award classified as an anti-suit injunction may be refused on the ground that the exercise by a Lithuanian court of the power to rule on its jurisdiction would be restricted after such recognition and enforcement. After noting that arbitration is excluded from the scope of Brussels I, the CJEU referred to its judgment in *West Tankers* and pointed out how these two preliminary rulings differed from each other. The CJEU observed that there was no question of an infringement of the principle of mutual trust as the order had been made by an arbitral tribunal, not by a court of a Member State. It also added that the New York Convention does not relate to a 'particular matter' within the meaning of Article 71(1) of Brussels I since that article governs only the relations between Brussels I and conventions dealing with particular matters within the scope of Brussels I. The CJEU held that Brussels I does not preclude a Member State's court from recognising and enforcing, or from refusing to recognise and enforce, an arbitral award prohibiting a party from bringing certain claims before a court of that Member State, since it does not govern the recognition and enforcement, in a Member State, of an arbitral award issued by an arbitral tribunal in another Member State. This judgment was not in line with the Opinion of AG Wathelet[60] who tried to re-open the issue of intra-EU anti-suit injunctions given by courts to uphold arbitration agreements. The CJEU did not take up that issue, confining itself to allowing anti-suit injunctions made by arbitral tribunals.[61]

The relationship between litigation and arbitration under Brussels I is now clearer after the changes made to Brussels I in Brussels Ia[62] and the AG's Opinion and CJEU judgment in *Gazprom* that anti-suit injunctions granted by arbitral bodies are compatible with Brussels I and the decisions on the validity or invalidity of an arbitration agreement cannot be recognised and enforced under Brussels I. However, the interview data indicates that there is still some scope for different interpretations since some interviewees have the view that the problems arising from the relationship between litigation and arbitration have not been entirely solved yet in Brussels Ia[63] as Recital 12 only clarifies the situation to some extent.[64] One interviewee suggested that neither the New York Convention nor Brussels Ia deals with the situation where there is a conflict between an arbitral award and a court judgment, and that there is a need to regulate the issue by inserting a provision into Brussels Ia.[65] However, the natural construction of Recital 12 and Article 73(2) of Brussels Ia seems to be that in the event of a conflict between a court judgment capable of recognition and enforcement under Brussels Ia and an arbitral award enforceable under the New York Convention the latter will prevail.[66] This interpretation suggests that where litigants try to evade their arbitration agreement by choosing to begin substantive litigation in a court in the EU that

---

[60] See the AG's Opinion, EU:C:2014:2414.

[61] See also CP Ojiegbe, 'From *West Tankers* to *Gazprom*: anti-suit injunctions, arbitral anti-suit orders and the Brussels I Recast' (2015) 11 *Journal of Private International Law* 267.

[62] See Recital 12 and Art 73(2) of Brussels Ia.

[63] EUPILLAR_EU 14.

[64] EUPILLAR_EU 13.

[65] EUPILLAR_EU 13. One problem with this suggestion is the risk of transferring some exclusive external competence from Member States to the EU in relation to arbitration, see CP Ojiegbe, *The Interface Between International Commercial Arbitration and the EU Judgments Regulation* (University of Aberdeen, PhD thesis, 2017).

[66] See P Beaumont and M Danov, 'The EU Civil Justice Framework and Private Law Integration through (Private International) Law' (2015) 22 *Maastricht Journal of European and Comparative Law* 706, 728–29.

is relatively slow or hostile to arbitration agreements, there is nothing to prevent the other party to the arbitration agreement going to arbitration and asking the arbitral body to issue an anti-suit injunction. The decision on the incidental question does not circulate in the EU under Brussels Ia and therefore the arbitration tribunal and the courts of the seat of the arbitration will be free to decide that the arbitration agreement is valid and engage in a race to judgment on the substance with the court that decided the arbitration agreement was invalid.

B. General Provisions (Articles 2–4) (Articles 4-6 of Brussels Ia)

The general provisions on jurisdiction are set out under Articles 2 to 4 of Brussels I. The CJEU has interpreted Articles 2 and 4, which correspond to Articles 4 and 6 of Brussels Ia respectively, in two cases.

C-9/12 *Corman-Collins SA v La Maison du Whisky SA*,[67] on the interpretation of Articles 2 and 5(1)(a) and (b) of Brussels I, was referred to the CJEU in Belgian proceedings between Corman-Collins (established in Belgium) and La Maison du Whisky (established in France) regarding a claim for compensation due to the termination of a distribution agreement between them. On the question whether Brussels I precludes the application of a Belgian jurisdiction rule conferring jurisdiction over proceedings relating to the termination of an exclusive distribution agreement, the answer of the CJEU was obvious that if a case presenting an international element falls within the scope of Brussels I and if the defendant is domiciled in a Member State, Brussels I rules must be applied and prevail over national rules of jurisdiction.

C-292/10 *G v Cornelius de Visser*,[68] on the interpretation of Articles 4(1), 5(3), 26 and 34(2) of Brussels I, was referred to the CJEU in German proceedings between Ms G and Mr de Visser concerning an action for liability arising from the uploading onto an internet site of photographs in which she appears partly naked. Although there were many factors indicating that the defendant was in the EU, that was not absolutely certain, so the CJEU was asked whether Article 4(1) of Brussels I precludes the application of Article 5(3). In C-327/10 *Hypoteční banka*,[69] the CJEU already had interpreted the jurisdiction rules in Article 16 in situations when a consumer's domicile is unknown and this case gave the opportunity to the same five judges in the First Chamber to extend their analysis also to non-consumer defendants. Citing paragraph 42 of C-327/10 *Hypoteční banka*, the CJEU stated that the expression 'is not domiciled in a Member State', used in Article 4(1) means that application of the national rules rather than the uniform rules of jurisdiction is possible only if the court seised of the case holds firm evidence to support the conclusion that the defendant, a citizen of the EU not domiciled in the Member State of that court, is in fact domiciled outside the EU. It observed that in the absence of such firm evidence, the international jurisdiction of a court of a Member State is established under Brussels I when the conditions for application of the jurisdiction rules laid down therein are met. The CJEU

---

[67] EU:C:2013:860 (First Chamber) ('Corman-Collins'). See also s II.C.i.a.1 below.

[68] EU:C:2012:142 (First Chamber) ('G'). See also s II.C.i.a.2 and s II.C.vii below.

[69] C-327/10 *Hypoteční banka as v Udo Mike Lindner* [2011] ECR I-11543 (First Chamber). For the analysis on this case, see s II.C.iii.b below.

stated that this analysis is also valid as to Article 5(3). It accordingly found that Article 4(1) of Brussels I does not preclude the application of Article 5(3) to an action for liability arising from the operation of an internet site against a defendant who is probably an EU citizen but whose whereabouts are unknown if the court seised of the case does not have firm evidence to support the conclusion that the defendant is in fact domiciled outside the EU. It took too long, ie 21 months, for the CJEU to give its judgment particularly when it is considered that the judgment was given without an AG's Opinion.

C. Matters Related to Jurisdiction (Articles 2–31) (Articles 4-35 of Brussels Ia)

i. Special Jurisdiction (Articles 5–6) (Articles 7 and 8 of Brussels Ia)

The special jurisdiction rules are set out under Articles 5 and 6 of Brussels I, which corresponds to Articles 7 and 8 of Brussels Ia. Most of these cases concern the jurisdiction rules under Article 5 of Brussels I.

a. Jurisdiction Rules Under Article 5 (Article 7 of Brussels Ia)

The CJEU has dealt with a number of preliminary ruling requests concerning Article 5 of Brussels I which indicates that characterisation is a significant issue on which the national courts need guidance. As will be individually assessed below, some of the CJEU interpretations are controversial.

1. Matters Relating to a Contract (Article 5(1)) (Article 7(1) Brussels Ia)

The CJEU has interpreted the meaning of 'place of performance' where the goods or the services are delivered in different places. In the absence of a clear use of party autonomy to determine the issue in the contract, it is not always clear what the principal place of delivery of goods or the main place of provision of services is. The absence of clarity is resolved by applying different approaches in different cases.

In C-386/05 *Color Drack GmbH v Lexx International Vertriebs GmbH*,[70] the CJEU interpreted the first indent of Article 5(1)(b) where the goods were delivered in different places within a single Member State. The Fourth Chamber noted that Article 5(1)(b) establishes the place of delivery as the autonomous linking factor to apply to all claims founded on one and the same contract for the sale of goods rather than merely to the claims founded on the obligation of delivery itself. It decided that the first indent of Article 5(1)(b), determining both international and local jurisdiction, seeks to unify the rules of conflict of jurisdiction and, accordingly, to designate the court having jurisdiction directly, without reference to the domestic rules of the Member States. It continued that where there are several places of delivery of the goods, 'place of performance' must be understood, for the purposes of application of Article 5(1)(b), as the place with the closest linking factor between the contract and the court having jurisdiction. In such a case, the closest linking factor will, as a general rule, be at the place of the principal delivery, which must be determined on the basis of

---

[70] [2007] ECR I-3699 (First Chamber) ('Color Drack').

economic criteria. To that end, it stated that it is for the national court seised to determine whether it has jurisdiction in the light of the evidence submitted to it. If it is not possible to determine the principal place of delivery, each of the places of delivery has a sufficiently close link of proximity to the material elements of the dispute and, accordingly, a significant link as regards jurisdiction. In such a case, the plaintiff may sue the defendant in the court for the place of delivery of its choice on the basis of the first indent of Article 5(1)(b). However the CJEU was careful to confine its ruling to cases where all the places of delivery were in the same Member State as in this case, because then the ruling does not create an unforeseeable country for the defendant to be sued in.

The CJEU in *Color Drack* interfered in what are best left to be dealt with as internal matters for Member States by trying to determine which courts within a Member State have jurisdiction as being the 'place' within that Member State where the goods were delivered or should have been delivered and further by trying to lay down detailed rules as to what happens when there is more than one place of delivery in the same Member State. AG Bot would wisely have left a significant measure of procedural autonomy to be determined by national law.[71]

Whilst in *Color Drack* there was no divergence from C-256/00 *Besix*[72] on Article 5(1) of the Brussels Convention by allowing Article 5(1)(b) to apply where there are multiple places of performance, because in international terms there was only one place of performance (ie Austria), the judgment in *Color Drack* has led the CJEU to depart from *Besix* for Article 5(1)(b) in subsequent cases where the places of performance were in different Member States even though AG Bot had warned against this in his Opinion in *Color Drack* because the objective of foreseeability would be lost.[73] The first example of this was seen in C-204/08 *Rehder*[74] where the CJEU interpreted 'the place of performance' in Article 5(1)(b) in German proceedings concerning a compensation claim under Regulation 261/2004 regarding air passenger rights[75] due to a flight cancellation from Germany to Lithuania. The CJEU noted that the case raised the question of the applicability of Article 33 of the Montreal Convention[76] in determining jurisdiction. Citing C-344/04 *IATA*,[77] it observed that the right relied on under Regulation 261/2004 is a passenger's right to a standardised and lump-sum payment following the cancellation of a flight and it is independent of compensation for damage under Article 19 of the Montreal Convention. Since the right relied on in the present case was introduced under Regulation 261/2004 alone, it found that the claim must be examined under Brussels I. It then observed that the interpretation given in C-386/05 *Color Drack*, in the case of sale of goods where there are several places of delivery within a single Member State, should apply to the provision

---

[71] See para 128 of the AG's Opinion, EU:C:2007:105.

[72] C-256/00 *Besix SA v Wasserreinigungsbau Alfred Kretzschmar GmbH & Co KG (WABAG) and Planungs- und Forschungsgesellschaft Dipl Ing W Kretzschmar GmbH & KG (Plafog)* [2002] ECR I-01699 ('Besix').

[73] See fn 30 of the AG's Opinion.

[74] C-204/08 *Peter Rehder v Air Baltic Corporation* [2009] ECR I-06073 (Fourth Chamber) ('Rehder').

[75] Reg (EC) No 261/2004 of the European Parliament and of the Council of 11 February 2004 establishing common rules on compensation and assistance to passengers in the event of denied boarding and of cancellation or long delay of flights, and repealing Reg (EEC) No 295/91, [2004] OJ L 46/1.

[76] Convention for the Unification of Certain Rules for International Carriage by Air.

[77] C-344/04 *The Queen, on the application of International Air Transport Association and European Low Fares Airline Association v Department for Transport* [2006] ECR I-00403 (Grand Chamber).

of services in more than one Member State. It stated that a differentiated approach would contradict with proximity and predictability. As regards the place where the main provision of services is to be carried out, it found that the place of the registered office or the principal place of establishment of the airline, the place where the contract for air transport is concluded, the place where the ticket is issued and places where the aircraft may stop over do not have the necessary close link to the contract. It stated that only 'places of departure and arrival' have a direct link to the services and those words must be understood as agreed in the carriage contract made with one airline which is the operating carrier. It thus held that a person claiming compensation on the basis of Regulation 261/2004 may sue, as a matter of his choice, the defendant in the court in whose jurisdiction one of those places may be found under the second indent of Article 5(1)(b) of Brussels I. It added that the applicant retains the option to sue before the courts of the defendant's domicile under Article 2(1) which in the present case was, pursuant to Article 60(1), the court within the jurisdictional district of which the air carrier has its registered office, central administration or principal place of business. The judgment was given in 13 months and without an AG's Opinion.

At first glance, it can be said that if Article 5(1)(b) is the applicable provision, it is reasonable for the CJEU in *Rehder* to give a passenger who is a party to an air transport contract with one airline the right to sue in either the place of departure or the place of arrival of the aircraft under Article 5(1)(b). However, it would have been more consistent with the wording of Article 5(1) of Brussels I to find that there is not a single characteristic place of provision of services in an air passenger contract and therefore Article 5(1)(b) does not apply and thus by virtue of Article 5(1)(c) the test in Article 5(1)(a) applies. If Article 5(1)(a) had been applied to this case, then it is arguable that the place where Air Baltic would have been obliged to perform the obligation in question (ie to pay compensation to Mr Rehder for his cancelled flight) would either be where Mr Rehder lived or had his personal bank account (both probably in Germany). Therefore the application of Article 5(1)(a) would probably have also led to the German courts having jurisdiction without the need to distort the meaning of that Article.

It is to be highlighted that there are some problems with the judgment in *Rehder*. Two questions need particular attention in this respect: 1) should the air transport carrier be able to sue the passenger at either the place of departure or place of arrival for a negative declaration?; and 2) what are the implications for other types of contracts for the provision of services or delivery of goods where services are provided or goods are delivered in more than one Member State? Uncertainty is created for many of these contracts because it is not clear which court or courts have jurisdiction under Article 5(1)(b).

In C-19/09 *Wood Floor*, the CJEU interpreted the special jurisdiction rule for provision of services contracts in Article 5(1)(b) in the context of a compensation claim for the termination of a commercial agency contract performed in several Member States. Regarding the applicability of the second indent of Article 5(1)(b) where services are provided in several Member States, the CJEU affirmed C-386/05 *Color Drack* and C-204/08 *Rehder* and held that the second indent of Article 5(1)(b) is applicable in the case in which services are provided in several Member States. Regarding the criteria according to which the place of performance of the obligation is to be determined in the case of a commercial agency contract, it observed that the characteristic performer is the commercial agent and therefore, the 'place of performance' is, in principle, the place of the main provision of services by the agent. As regards the criteria according to which the place of the main provision of services must be determined, the CJEU stated that it has to be identified on the basis of that contract, failing that it is to be determined on the basis of the place of actual performance, ie the place where the agent has in fact for the most part carried out his activities in the performance of the contract, provided that the provision of services in that place is not contrary to the parties' intentions as it appears from the provisions of the contract. If that place cannot be determined on this basis either, AG Trstenjak[78] suggested that it is the place where the commercial agent has its registered office. But, sadly, the CJEU did not agree with the AG and stated that it is where that agent is domiciled on the ground that it can always be identified with certainty, is predictable, and has a link of proximity with the dispute. The registered office is at least clear whereas the domicile of a commercial agent is not clear as the place where he or she lives (and is domiciled as a natural person) may not be the same as the place where the commercial agent as a business has its principal place of business, registered office or central administration (all possible domiciles of a non-natural person under Brussels I and all could be in different Member States). The CJEU dealt with the case in about 14 months.

The CJEU created a default rule, the domicile of the commercial agent, in *Wood Floor* that constitutes a *forum actoris*. The rule cannot be derived from the text of Article 5(1)(b) or its negotiating history. A much more natural interpretation of Article 5(1) is to only apply Article 5(1)(b) where there is a single State that is the place of the provision of services based on the agreement of the parties in the contract or failing that based on the facts of the case. If no such single State emerges as the place of provision of the services, then it is necessary to apply Article 5(1)(a) and focus on the place of performance of the obligation in question in the dispute. The intention of the Union legislature was to provide for the easy cases in Article 5(1)(b) not to force the difficult/complex cases into an artificial home in Article 5(1)(b) based on a connecting factor created by judicial creativity. AG Trstenjak was incorrect to suggest that all contracts for the provisions of services must be shoehorned into Article 5(1)(b), unless performance of the services was not in an EU Member State.[79] She acknowledged that the solution she and ultimately the CJEU came up with of focusing on the commercial agent's habitual residence or domicile was creative and not in line with the text.[80]

As seen in these cases, the meaning of 'place of performance' where the goods or the services are delivered or provided in different places leads to uncertainties in the absence of a clear use of party autonomy to determine the issue in the contract. In its interpretation, the CJEU has resolved this by sometimes giving the claimant a completely free choice (eg C-386/05 *Color Drack*) or a more limited choice (eg C-204/08 *Rehder*) and by sometimes inventing a single place as the default rule (eg C-19/09 *Wood Floor Solutions*). The decision to allow multiple places of performance to have jurisdiction under Article 5(1)(b) was a major departure from the CJEU's decision in C-256/00 *Besix*, despite the warning from AG Bot in C-386/05 *Color Drack* not to do so, as seen above. Therefore, the decision

---

[78] See the AG's Opinion, EU:C:2010:6.

[79] See ibid para 86.

[80] See ibid para 93. For a clear critique of the case, see P Beaumont and P McEleavy, *Anton's Private International Law* 3rd edn (Edinburgh, SULI, 2011) 304–06.

whether or not to apply *Besix* to Article 5(1)(b) cases should only have been taken by a Grand Chamber with the help of an AG's Opinion not by a Chamber without the help of an AG's Opinion.

In C-533/07 *Falco Privatstiftung and Thomas Rabitsch v Gisela Weller-Lindhorst*,[81] the CJEU interpreted the 'provision of services' in Austrian proceedings concerning the performance of a contract pursuant to which the claimants licensed the defendant to market, in Austria, Germany and Switzerland, video recordings of a concert and the marketing of audio recordings of the same concert without any contractual basis. The first question was whether the contract in question was a contract for the provision of services under Article 5(1)(b). After noting that the wording of the provision does not answer this question, the CJEU examined the question in the light of the origins, objectives and scheme of Brussels I, and also took account of the objectives of Recitals 2 and 11. The CJEU observed that the general jurisdiction rule in Article 2 is complemented, in Article 5(1), by a special jurisdiction rule in matters relating to a contract on the basis of proximity, ie the existence of a close link between the contract and the court called upon to hear and determine the case. Agreeing with AG Trstenjak,[82] it stated that the owner of an intellectual property right does not perform any service in granting a right to use that property and undertakes merely to permit the licensee to exploit that right freely. The CJEU took the view that it was immaterial whether the licensee of an intellectual property right holder is obliged to use the intellectual property right licensed. It underlined that the broad logic and scheme of the jurisdiction rules in Brussels I require a narrow interpretation of the special jurisdiction rules, including the rule in Article 5(1). It also considered the definition of the concept of 'services' in the Community directives on VAT. Agreeing with the AG, it stated that that definition is a negative definition which is, by its very nature, necessarily broad and thus it did not interpret the concept in Article 5(1)(b) in the light of the definition given in the Community directives on VAT. It also observed that extending the scope of application of the second indent of Article 5(1)(b) would amount to circumventing the intention of the Community legislature in that respect and would have a negative impact on the effectiveness of Article 5(1)(c) and (a). Thus, it found that a contract under which the owner of an intellectual property right grants its contractual partner the right to use that right in return for remuneration is not a contract for the provision of services under Article 5(1)(b). The other question was whether, in order to determine jurisdiction under Article 5(1)(a), reference must still be made to the principles which result from the CJEU case law relating to Article 5(1) of the Brussels Convention. The CJEU observed that those provisions are identical. Considering Recital 19 and also the continuity of the Convention and the consistency between the two instruments, the CJEU gave an affirmative answer.

Falco was an excellent AG's Opinion and judgment of the CJEU showing full respect for the legislature. In her Opinion AG Trstenjak gave an excellent account of the submissions of the parties and interveners, the academic writings on Article 5(1) of Brussels I, the legislative background and the case law on Article 5(1) of the Brussels Convention. She and the CJEU wisely did not include intellectual property licensing agreements into the category of services contracts preferring the intention of the legislature (not to give an 'extended'

---

[81] [2009] ECR I-03327 (Fourth Chamber) ('Falco').
[82] See the AG's Opinion, EU:C:2009:34.

interpretation of services in this context)[83] to that expressed by the Commission in its intervention in the case.

AG Trstenjak began her Opinion in dramatic style saying that: 'Almost no other provision of Community law has been the subject at the time of its adoption, of such intense negotiations'.[84] Later she described the negotiations on Article 5(1) as 'very long and complex' and for further details on the negotiations and the options that were examined for the wording of Article 5(1) of Brussels I she, in footnote 108, referred to 'Beaumont, PR, 'The Brussels Convention Becomes a Regulation: Implications for Legal Basis, External Competence and Contract Jurisdiction', in Fawcett, J (ed), *Reform and Development of Private International Law. Essays in Honour of Sir Peter North*, Oxford University Press, New York, 2002, p 15 et seq; Kohler, C, 'Revision des Brüsseler und Luganer Übereinkommens', in Gottwald, P (ed), *Revision des EuGVÜ—Neues Schiedsverfahrensrecht*, Gieseking-Verlag, Bielefeld, 2000, p 12 et seq'.[85] It is clear that AG Trstenjak was not entirely happy with the compromise text arrived at on Article 5(1), but putting her personal opinions to one side she wisely gave an interpretation of that provision that was consistent with the negotiating history. As she stated in her Opinion, the definition of 'services' in Article 5(1)(b) is not to be as broad as the definition in primary EU law, the legislature deliberately kept room for the old Brussels Convention case law on Article 5(1) to still apply to cases falling within Article 5(1)(a) and there is no need to try too hard to squeeze cases into Article 5(1)(b).[86] The CJEU also wisely closely followed the advice of the AG and did not give too extensive an interpretation to services or too broad an interpretation of the scope of Article 5(1)(b). The CJEU wanted to respect the will of the legislature, which is apparent particularly in paragraphs 41 to 43 of its judgment.

In C-381/08 *Car Trim GmbH v KeySafety Systems Srl*,[87] the CJEU interpreted the division between sale of goods and provision of services, and the concept of the place of delivery in the context of the contractual obligations of the parties in relation to the supply of components for the manufacture of airbag systems. The first question concerned how 'contracts for the sale of goods' are to be distinguished from 'contracts for the provision of services', under Article 5(1)(b), in the case of contracts for the supply of goods to be produced or manufactured, where the customer has specified certain requirements with regard to the provision, fabrication and delivery of the components to be produced. The CJEU observed that Article 5(1)(b) is silent as to both the definition of the two types of contract and the distinguishing features of those two types of contract in the context of a sale of goods which at the same time involves the provision of services. Citing C-533/07 *Falco*, it noted that for the purposes of determining the court with jurisdiction, Article 5(1)(b) identifies as a connecting factor the obligation which characterises the contract in question.

---

[83] See ibid para 63.
[84] See ibid para 1.
[85] The latter source is from a highly respected German private international lawyer who was involved in the Brussels/Lugano Convention negotiations from 1997–99 as an observer for the CJEU as a very senior member of its staff. Only the former source, as a member of the UK delegation, was present throughout the negotiations on the revision of the Brussels/Lugano Convention in 1997–99 and the affirmation of the Art 5(1) text that had been agreed in those negotiations by the Council Working Party on the Brussels I Reg.
[86] See ibid paras 94–99 of the AG's Opinion. The correct historical interpretation of Art 5(1) arrived at by reference to the works by Beaumont and Kohler cited therein.
[87] [2010] ECR I-01255 (Fourth Chamber) ('Car Trim').

It then examined the characteristic obligation of the contracts at issue considering the definitions in Directive 1999/44,[88] CISG[89] and the UN Convention on the Limitation Period in the International Sale of Goods as an indication. It found that the fact that the goods to be delivered are to be manufactured or produced beforehand does not alter the classification of the contract at issue as a sales contract. It recalled that it had reached the same conclusion regarding public procurement contracts in C-300/07 *Hans & Christophorus Oymanns*.[90] It also took into consideration that KeySafety did not provide Car Trim any raw materials. It thus found that the contract must be classified as a 'sale of goods' under Article 5(1)(b). As regards the second question, citing C-386/05 *Color Drack*, it affirmed that the rule in Article 5(1)(b) establishes the place of delivery as the autonomous linking factor to apply to all claims founded on one and the same contract for the sale of goods rather than merely to the claims founded on the obligation of delivery itself, but it also noted that Brussels I is silent as to the definition of 'delivery' and 'place of delivery'. Considering predictability and proximity, it held that the place of delivery must be determined on the basis of the provisions of the contract; if this is impossible without reference to the substantive law governing the contract, that place is the place where the physical transfer of the goods took place, as a result of which the purchaser obtained, or should have obtained, actual power of disposal over those goods at the final destination of the sales transaction.

Unfortunately, AG Mazák's Opinion in *Car Trim* is very poor.[91] It is an example of where it would be better to have a specialist AG dealing with PIL issues. The Opinion gives no references to academic writings, gives no guidance on how to differentiate between a sale of goods and provision of services contract and fails to acknowledge the existence of party autonomy under Article 5(1)(b) even for determining the place of delivery of the goods far less for agreeing another place of performance, eg place of payment, relevant for determining jurisdiction under Article 5(1)(b). On the other hand, the CJEU's judgment in *Car Trim* is good on the division between sale of goods and provision of services contracts, on the acknowledgment of the role of party autonomy in determining the place of delivery of the goods,[92] and the creation of a default rule for the place of delivery of the goods in sales contracts.[93]

In C-87/10 *Electrosteel Europe SA v Edil Centro SpA*,[94] referred to the CJEU in Italian proceedings between Electrosteel (established in France), and Edil Centro (established in Italy) concerning the performance of a sale of goods contract between them, the CJEU interpreted the 'place of delivery' under Article 5(1) in the context of contracts using Incoterms. Before deciding *Electrosteel*, the CJEU gave its preliminary ruling in C-381/08 *Car Trim*. The CJEU observed that that interpretation can be transposed to the present case. Then, it examined

---

[88] Dir 1999/44/EC of the European Parliament and of the Council of 25 May 1999 on certain aspects of the sale of consumer goods and associated guarantees [1999] OJ L 171/12.

[89] United Nations Convention on Contracts for the International Sale of Goods (Vienna, 1980) (CISG).

[90] C-300/07 *Hans & Christophorus Oymanns GbR, Orthopädie Schuhtechnik v AOK Rheinland/Hamburg* [2009] ECR I-04779 (Fourth Chamber).

[91] See the AG's Opinion,EU:C:2009:577.

[92] However, there is no discussion of whether this goes further to allow the selection of a different place of performance although to be fair that was not relevant in this case.

[93] However, the reference to 'final' destination has been questioned by AG Kokott in a later case, ie C-87/10 *Electrosteel*, showing the value of in-depth analysis by an AG, EU:C:2011:116.

[94] [2011] ECR I-04987 (Third Chamber) ('Electrosteel').

how the words 'under the contract' are to be interpreted and to what extent it is possible to take into consideration terms and clauses in the contract which do not identify directly and explicitly the place of delivery. By an analogy with Article 23, it observed that the EU legislature wished consideration to be taken of commercial usage in interpreting the Brussels I provisions, in particular, Article 5(1)(b). It also acknowledged the usages' important role in international trade especially if they are collected, explained and published by recognised professional organisations and widely followed in practice by traders, such as International Chamber of Commerce (ICC)'s Incoterms. It found that in order to determine the place of delivery, the referring court must take them into account in so far as they enable that place to be clearly identified. It then examined whether they merely lay down the conditions relating to the allocation of the risks connected to the carriage of the goods or the division of costs between the contracting parties, or whether they also identify the place of delivery of the goods. As regards Incoterms, it agreed with AG Kokott[95] that an 'Ex Works' clause entails not only the application of rules on 'Transfer of risks', and 'Division of costs', but also, and separately, the application of rules on 'Delivery' and 'Taking delivery'. It held that in distance selling, the place of delivery must be determined on the basis of the provisions of that contract under the first indent of Article 5(1)(b) and that in verifying whether that place is determined 'under the contract', the national court must take account of all the relevant terms and clauses of that contract which are capable of clearly identifying that place, including terms and clauses which are generally recognised and applied through the usages of international trade or commerce, such as Incoterms. It added that if it is impossible to determine that place on that basis, without referring to the substantive law applicable to the contract, that place is the place where the physical transfer of the goods took place, as a result of which the purchaser obtained, or should have obtained, actual power of disposal over those goods at the final destination of the sales transaction.

The CJEU in C-87/10 *Electrosteel* wisely accepted the use of Incoterms in commercial contracts as an easy and common means whereby the parties can agree the place of delivery of the goods and interpreted Article 5(1)(b) of Brussels I as respecting such party autonomy. AG Kokott helpfully explained Incoterms at paragraphs 7–10 of her Opinion. It is unfortunate that the Third Chamber gives a completely unnecessary and irrelevant obiter opinion in paragraph 24 potentially limiting party autonomy in the choice of the place of delivery of the goods if it is neither the country of origin nor the country of destination of the goods. AG Kokott helpfully highlighted the remaining open question of whether the parties can agree under Article 5(1)(b) to a place of performance other than the place of delivery of the goods or the place of provision of services.[96] In order to respect the intentions of the EU legislature and the text of the Regulation, the CJEU should permit the choice of a different place of performance by the parties to the contract. This is so because the phrase 'unless otherwise agreed' was inserted into the compromise text of Article 5(1)(b) at the end of the negotiations on the revision of the Brussels and Lugano Conventions in 1999 in addition to the phrase 'under the contract' which was already in the text. Therefore the text itself and the drafters' intentions clearly indicate that parties must have autonomy to determine the place of performance and not just the place of delivery of the goods or the place of

---

[95] See the AG's Opinion, EU:C:2011:116.
[96] See paras 34–35 of the AG's Opinion.

provision of services.[97] AG Kokott also wisely suggested that in cases where the parties have not defined the place of delivery of the goods in their contract that place, for the purposes of Article 5(1)(b), should be the place where the physical transfer of the goods to the purchaser took place. She suggested dropping the CJEU's additional, confusing requirement in *Car Trim* of 'at the final destination of the sales transaction'. However, the Third Chamber just repeated these words without any explanation.

C-419/11 *Česká spořitelna, as v Gerald Feichter*,[98] on the interpretation of Articles 5(1)(a) and 15(1), was referred to the CJEU in Czech proceedings between Česká spořitelna (having its registered office in the Czech Republic) and Mr Feichter (domiciled in Austria) concerning an unpaid promissory note issued by the Feichter company (with its registered office in the Czech Republic) and signed on behalf of the Feichter company by its managing director, Mr Feichter. He also signed it, as an individual, on its face, marking it 'per aval'. The referring court was uncertain as to whether its jurisdiction must be determined under the rules relating to consumer contracts under Article 15 or under Article 5(1)(a). The CJEU observed that Article 5(1)(a) presupposes the establishment of a legal obligation freely consented to by one person towards another and on which the claimant's action is based. Agreeing with AG Sharpston,[99] it found that the relationship is a matter relating to contract because the aval giver, by signing the promissory note on its face under the indication 'per aval', voluntarily consented to act as the guarantor of the obligations of the maker of that promissory note. It also stated that since the place of performance of the obligation is expressly indicated on the promissory note, the referring court is required, in so far as the applicable law permits that choice as to place of performance of the obligation, to take into account that place in order to determine its jurisdiction under Article 5(1)(a).

In C-419/11 *Česká spořitelna*, the CJEU continued to apply its case law on Article 5(1) of the Brussels Convention to the interpretation of Article 5(1)(a) of Brussels I. The CJEU showed sensitivity to the fact that it cannot impose a complete solution as to when the parties can choose the place of performance of the obligation in question under Article 5(1)(a). The place of performance of the obligation in question is determined by the law governing that obligation according to the conflict rules of the court before which the proceedings have been brought. Therefore, it is for the forum's PIL rules to determine the law governing the obligation in question and for that law to determine how much party autonomy is permitted in choosing the place of performance. However, the CJEU placed an upper limit on the amount of party autonomy which is permitted in this context by not permitting the choice of a place of performance which has 'no real connection with the reality of the contractual relationship'.[100] This restriction seems rather odd given that Article 23 (Article 25 of Brussels Ia) imposes no such restrictions on party autonomy in choosing a court and the wording of Article 5(1)(b) implies that the parties can determine anywhere as the relevant place of performance for the obligation in question for matters covered by that para by the use of the phrase 'unless otherwise agreed'.

---

[97] See P Beaumont, 'The Brussels Convention Becomes a Regulation: Implications for Legal Basis, External Competence, and Contract Jurisdiction' in J Fawcett (ed), *Reform and Development of Private International Law: Essays in Honour of Sir Peter North* (Oxford, Oxford University Press, 2002) 9, 20.

[98] EU:C:2013:165 (First Chamber) ('Česká spořitelna'). See s II.C.iii.a above.

[99] See the AG's Opinion, EU:C:2012:586.

[100] See para 56 of the judgment.

In C-9/12 *Corman-Collins*, one of the questions that the CJEU dealt with was whether distribution agreements are covered by Article 5(1)(a) or (b). Agreeing with AG Jääskinen,[101] the CJEU stated that regardless of the diversity in commercial practice, distribution agreements take the form of a framework agreement, and the grantor undertakes to sell to the distributor, which it has chosen for that purpose, the goods to be ordered by the distributor in order to satisfy the requirements of its clients, while the distributor undertakes to purchase from the grantor the goods he needs. Citing C-19/09 *Wood Floor*, it reaffirmed that the special jurisdiction rules provided for the contracts for the sale of goods and the provision of services in Article 5(1)(b) have the same origin, pursue the same objectives (ie unifying of the jurisdiction rules and predictability) and occupy the same place in the scheme established by Brussels I. Then, it analysed whether a distribution agreement falls into one of those two categories of contracts. Citing C-381/08 *Car Trim*, it recalled that a contract which has as its characteristic obligation the supply of a good will be classified as a 'sale of goods'. It observed that this classification may be applied to a long-term commercial relationship between two economic operators, where that relationship is limited to successive agreements, each having the object of the delivery and collection of goods, but it underlined that it does not correspond to the general scheme of a typical distribution agreement characterised by a framework agreement with the aim of undertaking for supply and provision concluded for the future by two economic operators, including specific contractual provisions regarding the distribution by the distributor of goods sold by the grantor. Citing C-533/07 *Falco*, the CJEU reaffirmed that the concept of 'services' requires at least that the party who provides the service carries out a particular activity in return for remuneration and considering the typical obligations that a distribution agreement contains it held that a distribution agreement may be classified as a contract for the supply of services under the second indent of Article 5(1)(b).

This case is subject to criticism on a few points. As regards the length of the proceedings, it took the CJEU too long (ie more than 22 months) to decide. As regards the interpretation on the merits of the case, *Corman-Collins* is a controversial decision because distribution contracts are a kind of complex contract that many of the negotiators, of the Brussels/Lugano Revision in the late 1990s that reached the substantive agreement on the text of Article 5(1) which was later adopted into the Brussels I Regulation, expected to be governed by Article 5(1)(a) rather than 5(1)(b).[102] In a typical distribution contract, both parties have significant obligations to perform and it seems very artificial to designate one of the parties as the service provider. Whereas applying Article 5(1)(a) to distribution contracts creates a greater likelihood that the dispute will have a close connection with the court hearing it, because it is the place of performance of the particular obligation in dispute rather than the somewhat arbitrarily determined place where the services are held to be provided for the contract as a whole under Article 5(1)(b). The CJEU in *Corman-Collins* states that the place where the 'services were provided' in a distribution contract is where the distributor distributes the grantor's products. If the dispute is about the grantor's duties under the contract not being fulfilled then the place where the distributor distributes the grantor's products may have no connection with the issues in dispute.

---

[101] See the AG's Opinion, EU:C:2013:273.
[102] See eg Beaumont, above n 97, 15–21.

It is quite shocking that such an important and innovative decision on the classification of distribution contracts in *Corman-Collins* was taken by a Chamber of three judges. AG Jääskinen placed some weight on Recital 17 of Rome I in his Opinion classifying distribution contracts as contracts for services but even he acknowledged that Rome I created a special rule in Article 4 for this type of contract rather than keeping them under the 'services' contracts rule.[103] However, the CJEU did not refer to Rome I perhaps because of a sensible reluctance to interpret Brussels I through an instrument adopted after it and perhaps because they were conscious of the fact that the rule in Article 4 of Rome I has an escape clause which the rule in Article 5(1)(b) of Brussels I does not.

C-469/12 *Krejci Lager & Umschlagbetriebs GmbH v Olbrich Transport und Logistik GmbH*[104] was referred to the CJEU in Austrian proceedings between Krejci Lager (a company established in Vienna under Austrian law) and Olbrich Transport (a company established in Germany under German law) where the former sought payment of the storage fee of EUR 325 from the latter for goods stored on one of its sites located in Vienna under the storage contract between them. The referring court, the court of last instance for this claim as its value was less than EUR 5 000, felt compelled to ask a question to the CJEU to interpret the applicability of Article 5(1) in this case. The CJEU considered that the reply to this question may be clearly deduced from existing case law or admits of no reasonable doubt and thus it decided to rule by reasoned order under Article 99 of its Rules of Procedure. Citing its decisions in C-204/08 *Rehder* and C-19/09 *Wood Floor Solutions*, the CJEU reaffirmed that the second indent of Article 5(1)(b) gives an autonomous definition of the place of performance of the obligations arising from contracts for the provision of services in order to reinforce the objectives of unifying the rules of jurisdiction and ensuring predictability. The CJEU found that the contract in question concerned the storage of goods and it clearly constituted a 'provision of services' on the following grounds: the predominant element of a storage contract is that 'the warehousekeeper undertakes to store the goods concerned on behalf of the other party to the contract' and this 'entails a specific activity, consisting, at the least, of the reception of goods, their storage in a safe place and their return to the other party to the contract in an appropriate state'. The CJEU observed that the contract in question did not concern the rental of premises, but the storage of goods and thus it constituted a contract for the 'provision of services' under Article 5(1)(b). The CJEU also noted that jurisdiction relating to the contracts for rental of premises is governed by the exclusive jurisdiction rule in the matter of tenancies of immovable property under Article 22(1).

In requesting this preliminary reference in *Krejci Lager*, the Austrian court considered that the answer to the question of interpretation of EU law was not so obvious that no room was left for reasonable doubt. However, this was indeed a straightforward case concerning a claim with a very low value. The case was dealt with by the CJEU, without an AG's Opinion, in less than 13 months. The CJEU essentially told the Austrian court that even though it was a court of last instance for this type of low value claim it could have decided the case without referring it to the CJEU as the reply to the question 'may be clearly deduced from existing case-law or admits of no reasonable doubt' under Article 99 of the CJEU Rules

---

[103] See the AG's Opinion, para 58.
[104] EU:C:2013:788 (Tenth Chamber) ('Krejci Lager').

of Procedure.[105] The reason was that on any possible factual finding the referring court had jurisdiction under Brussels I, either under Article 5(1)(b) or under Article 22(1), and therefore it did not need to determine which of these was correct in order to establish jurisdiction. The case is a clear example that if the CJEU is to have sufficient time to interpret novel and difficult questions of interpretation national courts should avoid wasting time and costs by referring straightforward cases to the CJEU that they can decide themselves.

2. Matters Relating to Tort, Delict or Quasi-delict (Article 5(3)) (Article 7(2) of Brussels Ia)

The CJEU has interpreted jurisdiction in matters relating to tort, delict or quasi-delict under Article 5(3) in a number of cases.

In C-189/08 *Zuid-Chemie BV v Philippo's Mineralenfabriek NV/SA*,[106] the CJEU interpreted the 'place where the harmful event occurred' in Article 5(3) as regards Dutch proceedings concerning the delivery by Philippo's to Zuid-Chemie of a contaminated product used for the manufacture of fertiliser. In its examination, the CJEU took account of its relevant case-law on the Brussels Convention. Citing 21/76 *Bier*,[107] C-167/00 *Henkel*,[108] C-18/02 *DFDSTorline*,[109] and C-168/02 *Kronhofer*,[110] it reaffirmed that the 'place where the harmful event occurred' in Article 5(3) covers both the place where the damage occurred and the place of the event giving rise to it, so that the defendant may be sued, at the option of the claimant, in the courts for either of those places. It observed that, in the present case, the parties agreed that Belgium was the place of the event giving rise to the damage, but they disagreed as regards the place where the damage occurred. Referring to its settled case law, the CJEU reaffirmed that the place where the damage occurred is the place where the event which may give rise to liability in tort, delict, quasi-delict resulted in damage. Citing 21/76 *Bier* and C-68/93 *Shevill*,[111] it stated that the 'place where the damage occurred' is the place where the event which gave rise to the damage produces its harmful effects, ie the place where the damage caused by the defective product actually manifests itself in this case. It observed that the place where the damage occurred was Zuid-Chemie's factory in the Netherlands where the defective product was processed into fertiliser and caused the substantial damage to that fertiliser. Thus, it held that the words 'place where the harmful event occurred' designate the place where the initial damage occurred as a result of the normal use of the product for the purpose for which it was intended.[112] This was a straightforward case dealt with by the CJEU in 14 months without an AG's Opinion.

---

[105] See para 18 of the order.

[106] [2009] ECR I-06917 (First Chamber) ('Zuid-Chemie').

[107] 21/76 *Handelskwekerij G. J. Bier BV v Mines de potasse d'Alsace SA* [1976] ECR 01735 ('Bier').

[108] C-167/00 *Verein für Konsumenteninformation v Karl Heinz Henkel* [2002] ECR I-08111 (Sixth Chamber).

[109] C-18/02 *Danmarks Rederiforening, acting on behalf of DFDS Torline A/S v LO Landsorganisationen i Sverige, acting on behalf of SEKO Sjöfolk Facket för Service och Kommunikation* [2004] ECR I-01417 (Sixth Chamber) ('DFDS Torline').

[110] C-168/02 *Rudolf Kronhofer v Marianne Maier and Others* [2004] ECR I-06009 ('Kronhofer').

[111] C-68/93 *Fiona Shevill, Ixora Trading Inc., Chequepoint SARL and Chequepoint International Ltd v Presse Alliance SA* [1995] ECR I-00415 ('Shevill').

[112] In the light of this answer, there was no need to answer the second question concerning whether jurisdiction can be founded in the place of damage if the loss is purely financial because that was a hypothetical question in this case given the physical damage.

The joined cases C-509/09 and C-161/10 *eDate Advertising GmbH v X* and C-161/10 *Olivier Martinez and Robert Martinez v MGN Limited*[113] produced another controversial judgment of the CJEU where it interpreted Article 5(3) regarding online infringements of personality rights. The joint case was referred to the CJEU in two sets of proceedings, between X (domiciled in Germany) and eDate Advertising (established in Austria), and Olivier and Robert Martinez (a French actor and his father) and MGN (a company governed by English law), concerning the civil liability regarding information and photographs published on the internet. The CJEU took account of its relevant case law on the Brussels Convention, in particular C-68/93 *Shevill*. It already found in *Shevill* that in the case of defamation by means of a newspaper article distributed in several Contracting States that the term covered both 'the place where the damage occurred' and 'the place of the event giving rise to it'. Therefore, it decided in *Shevill* that an action for damages against the publisher may be brought either before 'the courts of the Contracting State of the place where the publisher of the defamatory publication is established', or before 'the courts of each Contracting State in which the publication was distributed where the victim claims to have suffered injury to his reputation'. It also held in *Shevill* that the former had jurisdiction to award damages for all of the harm caused by the defamation whereas the latter had jurisdiction to rule solely in respect of the harm caused in the State of the court seised. Agreeing with AG Cruz Villalón,[114] the CJEU found those considerations applicable to other media and means of communication infringing personality rights. However, it distinguished the placing online of content on a website from the regional distribution of media since the former content may be consulted instantly by an unlimited number of internet users throughout the world. It acknowledged that the internet reduces the usefulness of the criterion relating to distribution and decided that the victim may bring an action against the publisher, in respect of all the damage caused, either before 'the courts of the Member State in which the publisher of that content is established' or before 'the courts of the Member State in which the centre of [the alleged victim's] interests is based'. This interpretation constitutes a radical departure from *Shevill* which has created a *forum actoris* and also judicial law-making with no support from the Brussels I's preparatory work or from the Recitals. The plaintiff can now sue for all damage in his centre of interests which is usually his habitual residence.

AG Cruz Villalón, in the joined cases C-509/09 and C-161/10 *eDate Advertising*, was aware of the 'balancing' exercise required when dealing with online infringements of rights of the personality recognising the importance of the conflicting right of freedom of expression,[115] but this seems much more lacking in the CJEU judgment. The CJEU created an entirely new rule in favour of alleged victims of online personality right torts which is a clear *forum actoris* that may limit freedom of expression in many places by allowing the habitual residence of the claimant to have jurisdiction to adjudicate on all the damage caused globally by the tort. The AG was aware of the need for technological neutrality in the rules in Brussels I,[116] but the CJEU failed to deliver this by retaining *Shevill* for offline defamation cases. The AG's technologically neutral 'centre of gravity' of the tort dispute[117]

---

[113] [2011] ECR I-10269 (Grand Chamber) ('eDate Advertising').
[114] See the AG's Opinion, EU:C:2011:192.
[115] See ibid para 3.
[116] See ibid para 53.
[117] See ibid paras 55–67.

is preferable to the CJEU's special treatment of victims in online personality torts but is not entirely convincing. The best solution would have been for the CJEU to stick with the *Shevill* solution for online as well as offline personality rights torts and leave it to the legislature to make any changes.

In C-292/10 *G* which was analysed above,[118] the CJEU decided that Article 4(1) of Brussels I does not preclude the application of Article 5(3) to an action for liability arising from the operation of an internet site against a defendant who is probably an EU citizen but whose whereabouts are unknown if the court seised of the case does not have firm evidence to support the conclusion that the defendant is in fact domiciled outside the EU. The First Chamber's interpretation that the special rule of jurisdiction in Article 5(3) of Brussels I (Article 7(2) of Brussels Ia) applies whenever there is a lack of firm evidence to support the conclusion that the defendant is in fact domiciled outside the EU shows its determination to maximise the scope of application of EU law. The makers of Brussels I, following those of the Brussels Convention, probably intended that national law should apply to determine jurisdiction whenever it cannot be proven that the defendant is domiciled in the EU, unless one of the special rules is applicable that does not require the defendant to be domiciled in the EU, eg the exclusive jurisdictions. Indeed the authors of Brussels Ia fought off attempts by the Commission to eliminate the national law rules showing their commitment to the retention of national law rules of jurisdiction in relation to non-EU domiciliaries (except in the case of the protective jurisdictions for consumers and employees). It is very surprising that a Chamber of the CJEU felt so bold as to be able to make the law and in doing so to make it very difficult for Member States to reverse the judgment unless it is opened up by a Commission Proposal in a subsequent revision of Brussels Ia.

In C-523/10 *Wintersteiger AG v Products 4U Sondermaschinenbau GmbH*,[119] the CJEU interpreted Article 5(3) regarding infringements of intellectual property rights. This case was referred to the CJEU in Austrian proceedings between Wintersteiger (established in Austria) and Products 4U (established in Germany) concerning Wintersteiger's application to prevent Products 4U from using an Austrian trade mark 'Wintersteiger' as a keyword on the website of a paid referencing service provider. The referring court asked the CJEU under what conditions the advertising by use of the Austrian trade mark on a website operating under a country-specific top-level domain '.de' may confer jurisdiction on the Austrian courts under Article 5(3) to hear an action for an injunction against the use of an Austrian trade mark. Citing joined cases C-509/09 and C-161/10 *eDate Advertising*, the CJEU reaffirmed that 'place where the harmful event occurred or may occur' in Article 5(3) covers both the place where the damage occurred and the place of the event giving rise to it, so that the defendant may be sued, at the option of the applicant, in the courts for either of those places. As regards the place where the damage occurred, the CJEU stated that it had already held in C-189/08 *Zuid-Chemie* that it is the place where the event which may give rise to liability in tort, delict or quasi-delict resulted in damage. It then made a distinction between infringement of personality rights and intellectual property rights. Considering the principle of territoriality and its interpretation in joined cases C-236/08 to C-238/08 *Google*

---

[118] See s II.B above.
[119] EU:C:2012:220 (First Chamber) ('Wintersteiger').

France[120] and C-324/09 *L'Oréal*,[121] it found that the courts of the Member State in which the trade mark is registered have jurisdiction. As regards the place of the event giving rise to the harmful event, it noted that the territorial limitation of the protection of a national mark does not exclude the jurisdiction of courts other than the courts of the Member State in which that trade mark is registered. It thus found that the action may be brought before either the courts of the Member State in which the trade mark is registered or the courts of the Member State of the place of establishment of the advertiser.

The First Chamber, in C-523/10 *Wintersteiger*, following AG Cruz Villalón,[122] correctly resisted the temptation to extend the judgment in joined cases C-509/09 and C-161/10 *e-Date Advertising* beyond personality rights' torts. So the place of damage was not equated with the claimant's centre of interests. However, it did give a very broad interpretation to the place of damage for alleged trade mark infringements as effectively being the place where the trademark is registered. The reasoning of the CJEU seems to be a bit more restricted than this by referring to the existence of an advert on the internet that might breach the foreign trade mark, albeit with a top level domain name different from the country of registration of the trade mark. This is not a real restriction because the CJEU does not even require that the internet site is accessible in the country where the trademark is registered or that it be in the language of that country (even though both these things were the case in *Wintersteiger*). It is not clear why the CJEU gave such a broad interpretation to the place of damage. It never explains what the nature of the damage is or even could be in this type of case. Surely damage only takes place if the goods that are in breach of the trademark actually end up in the country of registration given the territorial nature of the trademark. By essentially assuming that the place of registration is the place of damage without demonstrating what damage took place or could have taken place there the CJEU is also creating a claimant-friendly jurisdiction for intellectual property infringements. The CJEU's repeated assertions that the special jurisdictions in Article 5 (Article 7 of Brussels Ia) are exceptions to the defendant's domicile in Article 2 (Article 4 of Brussels Ia) which should be interpreted restrictively therefore ring rather hollow.

In C-133/11 *Folien Fischer AG, Fofitec AG v Ritrama SpA*,[123] the CJEU interpreted for the first time whether an action for a negative declaration falls within the scope of Article 5(3). The case was referred to the CJEU in German proceedings between Folien Fischer (established in Switzerland) and Fofitec (part of the Folien Fischer group of companies having its registered office in Switzerland), and Ritrama (established in Italy) concerning the application submitted by the claimants for a negative declaration, relating to the absence of liability in tort/delict in competition matters. The CJEU was asked whether the jurisdiction in Article 5(3) also exists regarding an action for a negative declaration in which a potential injuring party asserts that the party potentially injured by a particular situation has no

---

[120] Joined cases C-236/08 to C-238/08 *Google France SARL and Google Inc. v Louis Vuitton Malletier SA (C-236/08), Google France SARL v Viaticum SA and Luteciel SARL (C-237/08) and Google France SARL v Centre national de recherche en relations humaines (CNRRH) SARL and Others (C-238/08)* [2010] ECR I-02417 (Grand Chamber) ('Google France').

[121] C-324/09 *L'Oréal SA and Others v eBay International AG and Others* [2011] ECR I-06011 (Grand Chamber) ('L'Oréal').

[122] See the AG's Opinion, EU:C:2012:90.

[123] EU:C:2012:664 (First Chamber) ('Folien Fischer').

claim in tort or delict. The CJEU considered the wording and aim of Article 5(3). It noted that an action for a negative declaration arises from the fact that the claimant was seeking to establish that the pre-conditions for liability, as a result of which the defendant would have a right of redress, were not satisfied. The CJEU agreed with AG Jääskinen[124] that such an action entailed a reversal of the normal roles in matters relating to tort or delict, since the claimant was the party against whom a claim based on a tort or delict might be made, while the defendant was the party whom that tort or delict may have adversely affected. However, it stated that that reversal of roles did not exclude that action from Article 5(3)'s scope. By citing C-292/10 *G* and C-523/10 *Wintersteiger*, it affirmed that Article 5(3)'s aims of ensuring that the court with jurisdiction is foreseeable and preserving legal certainty are not connected either to the allocation of the respective roles of claimant and defendant or to the protection of either. The First Chamber decided that Article 5(3)'s aim is not protecting the weaker party and found that Article 5(3) is not contingent upon the potential victim initiating proceedings. Relating to *lis pendens*, it made a distinction between the applicant's interest in an action for a negative declaration and in proceedings seeking to have the defendant held liable for causing loss and ordered to pay damages. It affirmed C-406/92 *Tatry*[125] that an action seeking to have the defendant held liable for causing loss and ordered to pay damages has the same cause of action as an action brought by that defendant seeking a declaration that he is not liable for that loss. The CJEU did not follow the opinion of the AG and held that an action for a negative declaration seeking to establish the absence of liability in tort, delict or quasi-delict falls within the scope of Article 5(3).

Until the CJEU's decision in *Folien Fischer*, the question whether an action for a negative declaration falls within the scope of Article 5(3) of Brussels I had already split national courts.[126] It seems that a majority of national courts and the AG did not think that Article 5(3) applies to such actions. The First Chamber's judgment seems to be a correct reading of the text and of the history of the negotiations leading up to Brussels I. The issue of negative declarations was controversial during the negotiations on the revision of the Brussels and Lugano Conventions (1997–99) but no effort was made to outlaw them for tort jurisdiction even though they had already been allowed by the CJEU for the purposes of establishing *lis pendens* in C-406/92 *Tatry*. Nonetheless, it would have been wise for the CJEU to have dealt with the case in a Grand Chamber.

It is to be noted that the signals from the CJEU on how to interpret Article 5(3) are not entirely consistent. The decision of a Grand Chamber to allow a victim of a personality rights' tort to be able to sue in their centre of interests (usually their habitual residence) in the joined cases C-509/09 and C-161/10 *eDate Advertising* in the year before this decision in *Folien Fischer* seems to indicate that the victim of at least some torts is a weaker party who needs to be allowed to sue in their own forum like an employee, consumer or insured person. On the other hand, the First Chamber does not try to reconcile its decision with *eDate Advertising*, perhaps mindful that a negative declaration designed to deal with all the issues arising from a personality rights tort will have to be launched in the victim's centre of interests and therefore that particular weaker party is protected from the possible

---

[124] See the AG's Opinion, EU:C:2012:226.
[125] C-406/92 *The owners of the cargo lately laden on board the ship 'Tatry' v the owners of the ship 'Maciej Rataj'* [1994] ECR I-05439 ('Tatry').
[126] See para 38 of the AG's Opinion.

harmful effects of allowing negative declarations under Article 5(3). However, it is suggested in this chapter that the EU legislature should commission a study carefully considering all the possible permutations for negative declarations in tort cases as well as the use in practice of tort negative declarations before the next revision of Brussels I to see if it does create an unacceptable risk of torpedo actions[127] leading to an effective denial of justice in certain slow jurisdictions.

In C-228/11 *Melzer v MF Global UK Ltd*,[128] the CJEU interpreted the application of Article 5(3) to co-perpetrators established in different Member States. The case was referred to the CJEU in German proceedings between Mr Melzer (domiciled in Berlin, Germany) and MF Global (a brokerage company established in the UK) concerning a claim for damages in relation to trading in stock market futures. Initially, Mr Melzer was solicited as a client by telephone and his file was managed by WWH (a company established in Düsseldorf, Germany) which then opened an account for him with MF Global. The CJEU first noted that despite the contractual nature of the relationship between Mr Melzer and MF Global, the action was based solely on tort. After reaffirming the principles it established in its case law on Article 5(3), by agreeing with AG Jääskinen,[129] the CJEU stated that the question was not the identification of the place where the damage occurred. It was rather the interpretation of the concept of 'the place of the event giving rise to the damage' in a situation where only one of the presumed perpetrators of an alleged harmful act was sued before a court within whose jurisdiction it had not acted. The CJEU observed that in that situation the connecting factor based on the defendant's acts is absent and Article 5(3), in accordance with the objectives and general scheme thereof, precludes the event giving rise to the damage from being regarded as taking place within the jurisdiction of that court. By interpreting the special jurisdiction rule in Article 5(3) restrictively as an exception to Article 2(1), the CJEU refused to extend the application of Article 5(3) to co-perpetrators. It, by considering Recital 2, stated that the use of national legal concepts in Brussels I would give rise to different outcomes among the Member States and therefore it did not find 'the reciprocal attribution to the place where the event occurred' permitted. It also considered in its judgment that the attribution of jurisdiction to hear disputes against persons who have not acted within the jurisdiction of the court seised remains possible under Article 6(1) of Brussels I, if the conditions laid down therein, in particular the existence of a connecting factor, are fulfilled. This type of case involving more than one defendant domiciled in different Member States can be dealt with under Article 8(1) of Brussels Ia. It would not be fair to extend the jurisdiction jeopardy of defendants to the place of acting of their alleged co-tortfeasors under Article 7(2). Of course defendants do face jurisdictional jeopardy under Article 7(2) of Brussels Ia in any Member State where their allegedly tortious actions have caused damage even if such damage is not foreseeable. AG Jääskinen made a wise plea in his Opinion, to the CJEU not to 'surreptitiously rewrite' what was then Article 5(3) of Brussels I (now Article 7(2) of Brussels Ia).[130] He argued that an overbroad interpretation of Article 5(3) undermines the 'central mechanism' of the Regulation—the *actor sequitur forum rei*

---

[127] Raised by the AG at para 70 of the Opinion.
[128] EU:C:2013:305 (First Chamber) ('Melzer').
[129] See the AG's Opinion, EU:C:2012:766.
[130] See ibid para 66.

principle. Certainly this judgment is a healthy counterbalance to the CJEU's excessively broad interpretation of the place of damage jurisdiction in internet personality rights torts under Article 5(3) in the joined cases C-509/09 and C-161/10 *eDate Advertising*. However, it took too long for the CJEU to reach a judgment in this case (ie two years).

C-170/12 *Peter Pinckney v KDG Mediatech AG*[131] was referred to the CJEU in French proceedings between Mr Pinckney (a French resident) and KDG Mediatech AG (a company established in Austria) concerning a claim for damages resulting from the alleged infringement of Pinckney's copyright. After dealing with an inadmissibility claim and finding the questions admissible in contrast to AG Jääskinen,[132] the CJEU started its analysis on substance. The CJEU reaffirmed the principles on Article 5(3) established in C-228/11 *Melzer*. However, it recognised that, unlike *Melzer*, this case did not concern the possibility to sue one of the presumed perpetrators of the alleged damage before the court seised on the basis that it was the place of the event giving rise to the damage. The question was whether that court had jurisdiction on the ground that it was the court for the place where the alleged damage occurred. The CJEU cited its judgments in the joined cases C-509/09 and C-161/10 *eDate Advertising* and C-523/10 *Wintersteiger* where it had interpreted Article 5(3) as regards infringements committed via the internet and produced their effects in numerous places, and distinguished between infringements of personality rights and infringements of intellectual and industrial property rights in identifying the place where damage allegedly caused via the internet occurred. It observed that copyright is subject to the principle of territoriality, but since copyrights must be automatically protected in all Member States by Directive 2001/29,[133] they may be infringed in each Member State under the applicable substantive law. Accordingly, it found that as regards the alleged infringement of a copyright, jurisdiction to hear an action in tort, delict or quasi-delict is already established in Article 5(3) in favour of the court seised if the Member State in which that court is situated protects the copyrights relied on by the plaintiff and that the harmful event alleged may occur within the jurisdiction of the court seised. It stated that the likelihood of a harmful event arises from the possibility of obtaining a reproduction of the work from an internet site accessible within the jurisdiction of the court seised. But, it continued that that court has jurisdiction only to determine the damage caused in the Member State within which it is situated. This interpretation meant that the criteria of mere accessibility of a foreign website can be the basis of jurisdiction in Article 5(3).

In *Pinckney*, AG Jääskinen argued for the import into Article 5(3) internet tort cases of the criteria of 'directing activities' in Article 15(1)(c) on consumer contracts. Therefore the mere 'accessibility' of the internet site in the jurisdiction would not be enough but rather the 'activity of the website' would have to be aimed at the relevant jurisdiction.[134] The CJEU rejected this approach at paragraph 42 of its judgment pointing out that this concept is in the text of Article 15(1)(c) and not in the text of Article 5(3). It is a matter for the legislature to decide whether to reform Article 5(3). Given the territorial nature of copyright it seems reasonable to enable a claimant to sue for damages in each jurisdiction in the EU where a

---

[131] EU:C:2013:635 (Fourth Chamber) ('Pinckney').

[132] See the AG's Opinion, EU:C:2013:400.

[133] Dir 2001/29/EC of the European Parliament and of the Council of 22 May 2001 on the harmonisation of certain aspects of copyright and related rights in the information society. [2001] OJ L167/10.

[134] See paras 67–68 of the AG' Opinion.

breach of copyright may occur. Nothing in this case suggests that the UK companies marketing the CD would not sell it wherever an internet buyer in the EU reading the internet site sought to purchase the CD. Of course this last point is a factual matter for a national court to consider when deciding whether or not 'harm' may occur in their jurisdiction.

C-360/12 *Coty Germany GmbH v First Note Perfumes NV*[135] was referred to the CJEU in German proceedings between Coty Germany (a perfumes and cosmetic products producer and distributor established in Germany), and First Note Perfumes (a perfume wholesaler established in Belgium), concerning an alleged infringement of a Community trade mark and of German law against unfair competition. The CJEU was asked to interpret whether, in the event of an allegation of unlawful comparative advertising or unfair imitation of a sign protected by a Community trade mark, prohibited by the law against unfair competition of the Member State in which the court seised is situated, Article 5(3) attributes jurisdiction to hear an action for damages based on the national law against one of the presumed perpetrators who is established in another Member State and is alleged to have committed the infringement in that State. The CJEU first noted that, under Article 14(2) of the Community Trade Mark Regulation,[136] actions concerning a Community trade mark may be brought under the law of Member States relating in particular to civil liability and unfair competition. Thus, it observed that the jurisdiction to hear such actions is not governed by that Regulation but by Brussels I. The CJEU then reaffirmed the principles on Article 5(3) that it had established in C-228/11 *Melzer*. It distinguished between the place where the causal event occurred and the place where the damage occurred. It accordingly recalled that Article 5(3) does not allow jurisdiction to be established, on the basis of the place of the event giving rise to the damage, to hear an action for damages based on the law on combating unfair competition of the Member State in which the court seised is situated against one of the presumed perpetrators of that damage who has not acted within the jurisdiction of the court seised. However, the scope of the question was not limited to the place where the causal event occurred. So, the CJEU went on its analysis with the place where the damage occurred and it reached a different conclusion. Citing C-523/10 *Wintersteiger* and C-170/12 *Pinckney*, it reaffirmed that regarding damage resulting from infringements of an intellectual and commercial property right, the occurrence of damage in a particular Member State is subject to the protection, in that State, of the right in respect of which infringement is alleged. It added that this can also be applied to infringements of unfair competition. It accordingly observed for the present case that an action relating to an infringement of that law may be brought before the German courts, to the extent that the act committed in another Member State caused or may cause damage within the jurisdiction of the court seised. The CJEU held that Article 5(3) allows jurisdiction to be established, on the basis of the place of occurrence of damage, to hear an action for damages based on that national law brought against a person established in another Member State who is alleged to have committed, in that State, an act which caused or may cause damage within the jurisdiction of that court. The judgment was given in 22 months and was in line with the Opinion of AG Jääskinen.[137]

---

[135] EU:C:2014:1318 (Fourth Chamber) ('Coty Germany').
[136] Council Reg (EC) No 40/94 of 20 December 1993 on the Community trade mark, [1994] OJ 1994 L 11/1.
[137] See the AG's Opinion, EU:C:2013:764.

It is to be underlined that the CJEU is now wedded to a very broad construction of the place of damage wing of Article 5(3) of Brussels I by following C-170/12 *Pinckney* in C-360/12 *Coty Germany*. The actions of the Belgian defendant in Belgium 'may' cause damage to the holder of a Community trade mark in Germany by being a breach of German unfair competition law. On the facts of this case that is not an unreasonable conclusion as the Belgian defendant knew it was selling goods to a German business that might try to resell those goods in Germany. However, the lack of a foreseeability clause in Article 5(3) means that a seller of any goods in any country in the EU may have to anticipate being sued in any other country in the EU if the buyer tries to resell those goods in breach of a local unfair competition law that the original seller was unaware of. This is potentially unfair to such sellers.

In C-387/12 *Hi Hotel HCF SARL v Uwe Spoering*,[138] the CJEU interpreted Article 5(3) in the context of copyright infringements. The case was referred to the CJEU in German proceedings between Mr Spoering (a photographer residing in Germany) and Hi Hotel (established in France) concerning a claim for an order to cease an infringement of copyright and for compensation. The CJEU observed that the question in this case was where there are several supposed perpetrators of the damage allegedly caused to rights of copyright protected in the Member State of the court seised (in this case Germany), whether Article 5(3) allows jurisdiction to be established with respect to one of those perpetrators who did not act within the jurisdiction of that court. The CJEU cited its decision in C-228/11 *Melzer* where it held that Article 5(3) does not allow jurisdiction to be established on the basis of the place of the causal event with respect to one of the supposed perpetrators of the damage who has not acted within the jurisdiction of the court seised. But, it continued its analysis because the present question was not limited to establishing jurisdiction on the basis of the causal event of the alleged damage. The CJEU reaffirmed its decision in C-170/12 *Pinckney* and further held that

> Article 5(3) does allow the jurisdiction of that court to be established on the basis of the place where the alleged damage occurs, provided that the damage may occur within the jurisdiction of the court seised. If that is the case, the court has jurisdiction only to rule on the damage caused in the territory of the Member State to which it belongs.

In following *Pinckney* the CJEU has clearly established that in a breach of copyright tort case the place of damage can only rule on the damage caused by the breach of copyright in its own territory. Given the territorial nature of copyright this is not unreasonable. The CJEU applies the mosaic effect approach to the jurisdiction of the place of damage in copyright torts as it first did in relation to defamation in C-68/93 *Shevill*. This is logical given the territorial nature of copyright. The judgment was given in 20 months and without an AG's Opinion.

C-45/13 *Andreas Kainz v Pantherwerke AG*,[139] referred to the CJEU in the Austrian proceedings between Mr Kainz (residing in Austria), and Pantherwerke AG (an undertaking established in Germany) concerned a claim for damages suffered by Mr Kainz on the basis of liability of Pantherwerke for a defective bicycle. The CJEU interpreted Article 5(3) as regards the identification of the place of the event giving rise to the damage in relation to

---

[138] EU:C:2014:215 (Fourth Chamber) ('Hi Hotel').
[139] EU:C:2014:7 (Fourth Chamber) ('Kainz').

liability for defective products. The CJEU first noted that although, under Recital 7 to Rome II, the EU legislature sought to ensure consistency between Brussels I and the substantive scope and provisions of Rome II, it does not mean that the former is to be interpreted in the light of the latter. The CJEU cited *Zuid-Chemie* where it had found with regard to product liability that the place of the event giving rise to the damage is the place where the event which damaged the product itself occurred. It accordingly found that this is, in principle, the place where the product in question was manufactured. The CJEU did not agree with Mr Kainz's argument that the interpretation of special jurisdiction in matters relating to tort, delict or quasi-delict must take into account not only the interests of the proper administration of justice but also those of the person sustaining the damage, thereby enabling him to bring his action before a court of the Member State in which he is domiciled. The CJEU reaffirmed its finding in C-133/11 *Folien Fischer* that Brussels I is specifically not designed to offer the weaker party stronger protection. It also noted that Mr Kainz's argument that the place of the event giving rise to the damage is the place where the product in question was transferred to the end consumer or to the reseller does not guarantee that that consumer will, in all circumstances, be able to bring an action before the courts in the place where he is domiciled since that place may be elsewhere or even in another country.

Kainz was a correct interpretation of Article 5(3) and consistent with the settled case law of the CJEU. The CJEU gave its judgment fairly quickly in this case in about 11.5 months. The CJEU regarded the place of the event giving rise to the damage in product liability cases as having been settled by an earlier case as being the place of manufacture of the product and therefore gave judgment in a three judge Chamber without hearing an Opinion from the AG. It does mean that in cases like this one the forum and the applicable law are not aligned because Article 5(1) of Rome II points towards the application of Austrian law on these facts and the only way German law would be applicable is by the application of the escape clause in Article 5(2). This might point more towards the reform of Article 5 of Rome II than Article 7(2) of Brussels Ia, but it is inevitable that the jurisdiction and the applicable law will not always be aligned given that the claimant has a choice of fora in which to bring an action.

In C-352/13 *Cartel Damage Claims (CDC) Hydrogen Peroxide SA v Akzo Nobel NV and Others*,[140] the CJEU dealt with a private competition law dispute involving a jurisdiction issue. The case was referred to the CJEU in German proceedings between CDC (domiciled in Belgium), and the defendants (domiciled in various Member States), concerning the applicant's action for damages brought by virtue of claims for damages which were directly or indirectly transferred to it by 71 undertakings having allegedly suffered loss as a result of an infringement of Article 81 EC and Article 53 of the Agreement on the European Economic Area of 2 May 1992.[141] The questions referred to the CJEU concerned the interpretation of Articles 5(3), 6(1) and 23 of Brussels I. On the question as regards the applicability of Article 5(3) and the place where the harmful event occurred, unlike AG Jääskinen,[142] the CJEU found Article 5(3) operable in cartel damages actions. The CJEU interpreted in the context of a cartel damages claim that the place where the damage occurred is in each

---

[140] EU:C:2015:335 (Fourth Chamber) ('Cartel Damage Claims'). See also s II.C.i and s II.C.vi,a below.
[141] [1994] OJ L1/3.
[142] See the AG's Opinion, EU:C:2014:2443.

individual victim's registered office. It found that the victim can choose to bring his action for damages against several companies having participated in the infringement under Article 5(3) before the courts of the place in which the cartel was definitively concluded or the place in which one agreement in particular was concluded which is identifiable as the sole causal event giving rise to the loss allegedly suffered, or before the courts of the place where its own registered office is located. Although the CJEU stated that Article 5(3) should be interpreted strictly, the result it reached is rather broad.[143] It took 22 months for the CJEU to give its decision.

In C-375/13 *Harald Kolassa v Barclays Bank plc*,[144] the CJEU interpreted jurisdiction in a prospectus liability claim. The case was referred to the CJEU in Austrian proceedings between Mr Kolassa (domiciled in Austria), and Barclays (established in the UK), regarding an action for damages based on the contractual, pre-contractual, tortious or delictual liability of that bank as a result of the loss in value of a financial investment made by Mr Kolassa through a financial instrument issued by the bank and acquired from a third party. The CJEU was asked several questions concerning the interpretation of Articles 5(1)(a), 5(3) and 15(1) of Brussels I. The CJEU found that a legal obligation freely consented to by Barclays with respect to Mr Kolassa was lacking even if, under the national law applicable, Barclays had certain obligations towards him and therefore it held that jurisdiction may not be invoked under Article 5(1) for the purposes of the action brought against Barclays and based on the bond conditions, breach of the information and control obligations and prospectus liability. The CJEU reiterated that the concept in Article 5(3) covers all actions which seek to establish the liability of a defendant and do not concern matters relating to a contract within the meaning of Article 5(1). The CJEU noted that the mere fact that the applicant has suffered financial consequences does not justify the attribution of jurisdiction to the courts of the applicant's domicile if both the events causing loss and the loss itself occurred in the territory of another Member State, as was the situation in the case giving rise to the judgment in C-168/02 *Kronhofer*. The events giving rise to the damage claimed took place where Barclays had its seat (UK) and the place where the loss occurred was where the investor suffered it. It ruled that the courts where the applicant is domiciled have jurisdiction, on the basis of the place where the loss occurred, particularly when the loss occurred directly in the applicant's bank account held with a bank established within the area of jurisdiction of those courts.

In C-441/13 *Pez Hejduk v EnergieAgentur.NRW GmbH*,[145] the CJEU interpreted the jurisdiction rule in Article 5(3) in cases of copyright infringement via the internet. The case was referred to the CJEU in Austrian proceedings concerning an application for a declaration of an infringement of a right related to copyright as a result of photographs created by Ms Hejduk being made available on the website of EnergieAgentur without her consent. The CJEU noted that although copyright rights must be automatically protected, in particular in accordance with Directive 2001/29,[146] in all Member States, they are subject to the

---

[143] This broad interpretation is supported for policy reasons by J Fitchen, Ch 39 on 'Private Enforcement of Competition Law'.

[144] EU:C:2015:37 (Fourth Chamber) ('Kolassa'). See also s II.C.iii.a below.

[145] EU:C:2015:28 (Fourth Chamber).

[146] Dir 2001/29/EC of the European Parliament and of the Council of 22 May 2001 on the harmonisation of certain aspects of copyright and related rights in the information society, [2001] OJ L167/10.

principle of territoriality and thus capable of being infringed in each Member State in accordance with the applicable substantive law. The CJEU interpreted the causal event giving rise to the alleged damage as being the activation of the process for the technical display of the photographs on the website which took place at the seat of the company in Germany and therefore does not attribute jurisdiction to the court seised. The CJEU then examined whether the court may have jurisdiction on the basis of the place where the alleged damage occurred. The CJEU referred to its case law ruling that Article 5(3) does not require, in particular, that the activity concerned be 'directed to' the Member State in which the court seised is situated, which means that it is irrelevant whether the website in question was directed at Austria. The place of damage is any place where the photographs placed on the website are accessible. Applying the criterion in C-170/12 *Pinckney*, the CJEU held that the courts of each Member State, which is a place of damage in principle, have jurisdiction only to rule on the damage to copyright or rights related to copyright caused in their own Member State. The judgment is not in line with the Opinion of AG Jääskinen.[147] The AG had proposed to the CJEU that only the first limb of Article 5(3) should apply in cases where the breach of copyright or a related right occurs by something appearing on the internet which can be accessed in any Member State. If the AG's proposal had been followed, then the Article 5(3) jurisdiction would often be the same as the defendant's domicile under Article 2 as it was in this case.

3. Characterisation Between Contract and Tort, Delict or Quasi-delict Matters Under Article 5 (Article 7 of Brussels Ia)

National courts have grappled with the dividing line between 'matters relating to contract' under Article 5(1) and 'matters relating to tort, delict or quasi-delict' under Article 5(3). The CJEU has dealt with several cases on the issue of characterisation in determining jurisdiction under Article 5.

In C-147/12 *ÖFAB* as discussed above,[148] the referring court asked some questions to the CJEU also on the interpretation of Article 5(1) and 5(3). The first three questions concerned whether the actions against the defendants relate to tort, delict or quasi-delict covered by Article 5(3) because they allowed Copperhill to continue to carry on business although it had been undercapitalised and forced to go into liquidation. The CJEU noted that the actions did not constitute insolvency proceedings and did not concern the exclusive prerogative of the liquidator to be exercised in the interests of the general body of creditors, but of rights which ÖFAB was free to exercise in its own interests. It accordingly found that they fell within the scope of Brussels I. It then reaffirmed the principles it set in its case law on the Brussels I Regulation and the Brussels Convention as regards the concepts of 'matters relating to contract' and 'matters relating to tort, delict or quasi-delict'. It observed that the actions in the present case seek to compensate the harm resulting from the fact that the companies were unable to obtain full payment from Copperhill for the work they had carried out. It found that the actions were covered by Article 5(3). The CJEU found the fourth question inadmissible due to the lack of the factual and legislative context of the question. The fifth and sixth questions concerned where the harmful event occurred in this case. The CJEU observed that the place where the harmful event occurred must be highly

---

[147] See the AG's Opinion, EU:C:2013:400.
[148] See s II.A.iib above.

predictable for both the applicants and the defendants, and also it must be a particularly close connecting factor between the dispute and the courts of the place where the harmful event occurred. It held that it is the place where the company carried out its business and the financial situation related to those activities were connected to. The last question concerned whether the fact that the claim at issue had been transferred from the original creditor to another had any impact on the determination of jurisdiction under Article 5(3). By considering a tort continues to be closely connected to the place where the harmful event occurred even though the claims at issue have been transferred, it held that this transfer has no such impact. It observed that a contrary answer would make jurisdiction unpredictable. This was a very useful interpretation by the CJEU giving guidance on the place where the harmful event occurred due to the actions of directors and shareholders by considering proximity and ease of taking evidence. It was wise of the CJEU not to answer the fourth question as to whether Article 5(3) covers an action brought by a creditor against a shareholder of a company which has undertaken to pay the latter's debts. The CJEU rightly pointed out that the Swedish court had not supplied it with sufficient factual information about the nature of the 'undertaking' or the legal basis or the subject matter of the action brought against the person who gave the 'undertaking'.

C-548/12 *Marc Brogsitter v Fabrication de Montres Normandes EURL and Karsten Fräßdorf*[149] was referred to the CJEU in German proceedings between Mr Brogsitter (domiciled in Germany), and Fabrication de Montres Normandes EURL (a company established in France) and Mr Fräßdorf (domiciled in Switzerland), concerning claims that Mr Brogsitter claimed to have suffered from conduct of the co-defendants allegedly amounting to unfair competition. The German court was uncertain whether civil liability claims made in tort under German law should not also be considered as concerning 'matters relating to a contract' under Article 5(1) and thus falling within the jurisdiction of the French courts. The CJEU recalled that its case law on the Brussels Convention is also valid for Brussels I as regards the equivalent provisions and cited its judgment in 189/87 *Athanasios Kalfelis v Bankhaus Schröder, Münchmeyer, Hengst and Co and others*[150] where it found that the concept of 'matters relating to tort, delict or quasi-delict' under Article 5(3) covers all actions which seek to establish the liability of a defendant and which do not concern 'matters relating to a contract' under Article 5(1). Citing C-167/00 *Henkel*, the CJEU stated that the nature of civil liability claims is to be determined regardless of their classification under national law. It then observed that although the parties were bound by a contract, the mere fact that one contracting party brings a civil liability claim against the other is not sufficient to consider that claim concerning 'matters relating to a contract' under Article 5(1). However, it also underlined and held that civil liability claims, which are made in tort under national law, must be considered as concerning 'matters relating to a contract' under Article 5(1) where the conduct complained of may be considered a breach of contract, which is for the referring court to determine by taking into account the purpose of the contract. That will a priori be the case where the interpretation of the contract which links the defendant to the applicant is indispensable to establish the lawful or unlawful nature of the conduct complained of against the former by the latter. It is to be noted

---

[149] EU:C:2014:148 (Seventh Chamber) ('Brogsitter').
[150] [1988] ECR 05565 (Fifth Chamber) ('Kalfelis').

that it is unhelpful that a key issue of characterisation—the dividing line between tort and contract—is decided by a Chamber of three judges without an AG's Opinion and with no prior decision of the CJEU directly in point. Having said that the focus on whether interpretation of the contract is necessary to establish the unlawful nature of the conduct seems like a good start in this tricky exercise of characterisation but it remains to be seen whether it solves all the problems.

C-47/14 *Holterman Ferho Exploitatie BV and Others v Friedrich Leopold Freiherr Spies von Büllesheim*[151] was referred to the CJEU in Dutch proceedings between a company (established in the Netherlands) and its three subsidiaries (established in Germany under German law), and Mr Spies (a German national domiciled in Germany), as regards his liability as manager of those companies and a claim that he be ordered to pay damages. After answering the question on the applicability of the jurisdiction rules for employment contracts under Articles 18 to 21 of Brussels I, the CJEU examined whether an action brought by a company against its former manager on the basis of an alleged breach of his obligations under company law comes within the concept of matters relating to a contract and if so where it was performed. The CJEU stated that since there was an obligation freely assumed by one party towards another, the action fell within matters relating to a contract. Regarding the place of performance, the CJEU noted that the activity concerned was classified as a provision of services under Article 5(1)(b), and that in the absence of any derogating stipulation in the articles of association of the company, or in any other document, it was for the referring court to determine the place where Spies in fact, for the most part, carried out his activities in the performance of the contract, provided that the provision of services in that place was not contrary to the parties' intentions as indicated by what was agreed. On the applicability of Article 5(3), the CJEU ruled that Article 5(3) applies to all actions which seek to establish the liability of a defendant and do not concern 'matters relating to a contract' within the meaning of Article 5(1) and that the action is a matter relating to tort/delict where the conduct complained of may not be considered to be a breach of the manager's obligations under company law, that being a matter for the referring court to verify. The CJEU also held that it is for the referring court to identify, on the basis of the facts of the case, the closest linking factor between the place of the event giving rise to the damage and the place where the damage occurred. The judgment was in line with the Opinion of AG Cruz Villalón.[152] However, the answer to the question on the applicability of Article 5(3) is strange. It seems to imply that any breach of company law by a manager is a breach of contract rather than a delict but the reason why is not explained by the CJEU and the use of the word 'between' seems to ask the referring court to find the single place that most closely links the place of the event giving rise to the damage and the place where the damage occurred. The CJEU intended that courts determine separately which jurisdiction is most closely linked to the delict as the place of the event giving rise to the damage and which is most closely linked to the delict as the place of damage and allow the claimant to choose to sue in either. In this case the place of the event giving rise to the damage may be the place where Spies carried out his duties as manager of the company and the place of damage is where the damage manifested itself first.

---

[151] EU:C:2015:574 (Third Chamber) ('Holterman'). On this case, see also s II.C.iv below.
[152] See the AG's Opinion, EU:C:2015:309.

b. Co-defendants (Article 6) (Article 8 of Brussels Ia)

C-103/05 *Reisch Montage AG v Kiesel Baumaschinen Handels GmbH*[153] concerned a dispute between the parties in relation to repayment of a debt. The Second Chamber of the CJEU stated that:

> Article 6(1) … may be relied on in the context of an action brought in a Member State against a defendant domiciled in that State and a co-defendant domiciled in another Member State even when that action is regarded under a national provision as inadmissible from the time it is brought in relation to the first defendant. However, the special rule on jurisdiction provided for in Article 6(1) … cannot be interpreted in such a way as to allow a plaintiff to make a claim against a number of defendants for the sole purpose of removing one of them from the jurisdiction of the courts of the Member State in which that defendant is domiciled (see, in relation to the Brussels Convention, Case 189/87 *Kalfelis* [1988] ECR 5565, paras 8 and 9, and *Réunion européenne and Others*, para 47). However, this does not seem to be the case in the main proceedings.

It is unfortunate that the CJEU did not give fuller reasoning for upholding the application of Article 6(1) in this case given that AG Ruiz-Jarabo Colomer, a noted expert on PIL, in his Opinion wanted to disapply the provision because there was no risk of irreconcilable judgments as the proceedings against the anchor defendant had to be ruled as inadmissible at the outset of the proceedings. It is a legitimate concern to avoid Article 6(1) ((Article 8(1) of Brussels Ia) being abused because the case against the anchor defendant is simply a ruse to bring another party into the jurisdiction. In this case it would appear that the claim against the anchor defendant had to be ruled inadmissible, under national law, at the outset of the proceedings. It is not clear therefore why the CJEU took the view that this was not a case where the sole purpose of the action against the first defendant was to remove the second defendant from its domicile in Germany.

In C-98/06 *Freeport plc v Olle Arnoldsson*,[154] the CJEU received two questions concerning the interpretation of Article 6(1) in the context of proceedings in Sweden between Mr Arnoldsson and an English company, Freeport plc ('Freeport'). In answer to the first question the CJEU said:

> where a court's jurisdiction is based on Art 2 of that Regulation, as is the case in the main proceedings, application of Article 6(1) of the Regulation becomes possible if the conditions set out in that provision and referred to in paragraphs 39 and 40 of this judgment are met, without there being any need for the actions brought to have identical legal bases.

The conditions in those paras are: 'it must be ascertained whether, between various claims brought by the same plaintiff against different defendants, there is a connection of such a kind that it is expedient to determine those actions together in order to avoid the risk of irreconcilable judgments resulting from separate proceedings (*Kalfelis*, para 13)'. The Court has had occasion to point out that, 'in order that decisions may be regarded as contradictory, it is not sufficient that there be a divergence in the outcome of the dispute, but that divergence must also arise in the context of the same situation

---

[153] [2006] ECR I-06827 (Second Chamber) ('Reisch Montage').
[154] [2007] ECR I-08319 (Third Chamber) ('Freeport').

of law and fact (*Roche Nederland*,[155] para 26).' In relation to the second question the Court said:

> Article 6(1)... applies where claims brought against different defendants are connected when the proceedings are instituted, that is to say, where it is expedient to hear and determine them together to avoid the risk of irreconcilable judgments resulting from separate proceedings, without there being any further need to establish separately that the claims were not brought with the sole object of ousting the jurisdiction of the courts of the Member State where one of the defendants is domiciled.

The judgment was partially in line with the Opinion of AG Mengozzi[156] and it was delivered in 19 months.

In C-98/06 *Freeport* the Third Chamber abandoned the 'ousting' of jurisdiction of another court where one of the defendants is domiciled concept that the Second Chamber of the CJEU had upheld in C-103/05 *Reisch Montage* (paragraph 32) and which was derived from the CJEU's case law on Article 6(1) of the Brussels Convention. The Third Chamber did so without acknowledging it was departing from precedent and without explaining why it was not following the advice of AG Mengozzi in *Freeport* that the ousting exception should be preserved to protect against fraud relating to the jurisdiction and wrongful intent as to the selection of the court by the claimant. The AG did not think that either of these criteria were met in this case on the evidence presented to him but wanted to see the possibility retained in law. It is not wise for the CJEU to create contradictory decisions between Chambers and to do it without any proper discussion of the policy issues involved. It would be better to avoid very hard to define tests like 'ousting' the jurisdiction of another court and instead focus on whether the objective conditions for the application of Article 6(1) are met—particularly ensuring that the claim against the anchor defendant is a real one and not a scam to drag in the defendants that are not domiciled in that jurisdiction.

In C-462/06 *Glaxosmithkline and Laboratoires Glaxosmithkline v Jean-Pierre Rouard*,[157] the CJEU interpreted the special jurisdiction rule in Article 6(1) in respect of co-defendants as being applicable to the action brought by an employee against two companies established in different Member States which he considers to have been his joint employers. In Brussels I, jurisdiction over individual contracts of employment is the subject of Section 5 of Chapter II. Section 5, which contains Articles 18 to 21 of the Regulation, seeks to ensure that employees are afforded the protection referred to in Recital 13 thereto. It is apparent from the wording of the provisions of Section 5 that they are not only specific but also exhaustive. Thus, it is clear from Article 18(1) of the Regulation, first, that any dispute concerning an individual contract of employment must be brought before a court designated in accordance with the jurisdiction rules laid down in Section 5 and, second, that those jurisdiction rules cannot be amended or supplemented by other rules of jurisdiction laid down in that Regulation unless specific reference is made thereto in Section 5 itself. Article 6(1) of the Regulation does not fall within Section 5 and it is not referred to there, unlike Article 4 and Article 5(5), the application of which is preserved expressly by Article 18(1) thereof.

---

[155] C-539/03 *Roche Nederland BV and Others v Frederick Primus and Milton Goldenberg* [2006] ECR I-06535 ('Roche Nederland').

[156] See the AG's Opinion, EU:C:2007:302.

[157] [2008] ECR I-03965 (First Chamber) ('Glaxosmithkline').

It is therefore clear that a literal interpretation of Section 5 leads to the conclusion that that Section precludes any recourse to Article 6(1). As regards the possibility of interpreting Article 6(1) as meaning that only an employee should be able to rely on that provision, as suggested by AG Poiares Maduro,[158] this would run counter to the wording of the provisions of both Article 6(1) and Section 5. In addition, there would be no reason to restrict the protective logic of such an argument to Article 6(1), alone, and it would be necessary to accept that employees, and they alone, should be able to rely on any rule of special jurisdiction provided for in Brussels I which could serve their individual interests. The transformation by the CJEU of the rules of special jurisdiction, aimed at facilitating sound administration of justice, into rules of unilateral jurisdiction protecting the party deemed to be weaker would go beyond the balance of interests which the Community legislature has established in the law as it currently stands. Therefore, such an interpretation would be difficult to reconcile with the principle of legal certainty, which is one of the objectives of the Regulation and which requires, in particular, that rules of jurisdiction be interpreted in such a way as to be highly predictable, as stated in Recital 11. Brussels I, notwithstanding the objective of protection referred to in Recital 13, does not afford particular protection to an employee in a situation such as Rouard's since, as a claimant before the national courts, there is no rule of jurisdiction available to him that is more favourable than the general rule laid down in Article 2. In those circumstances, the answer to the question referred must be that the rule of special jurisdiction provided for in Article 6(1) of Brussels I cannot be applied to a dispute falling under Section 5 concerning the jurisdiction rules applicable to individual contracts of employment. Article 20(1) of Brussels Ia allows employees to bring proceedings under Article 8(1) (formerly Article 6(1)).

AG Poiares Maduro's conclusion in *Glaxosmithkline* that 'the failure to take account of the case where a number of related claims are brought against a number of defendants in Section 5 must be understood as a lacuna in that text' was probably correct.[159] In applying Article 8(1) of Brussels Ia to cases brought by employees against more than one employer helpful guidance can be found in AG Poiares Maduro's Opinion at paragraph 36.

In C-145/10 *Eva-Maria Painer v Standard VerlagsGmbH and Others*,[160] the CJEU interpreted the applicability of Article 6(1) of Brussels I where the actions brought against different defendants have identical legal bases. The case was referred to the CJEU in proceedings between a freelance photographer and five newspaper publishers (one established in Austria and the rest in Germany) concerning their use of some photographs. Considering Recital 11, the fact that Article 6(1) is a special jurisdiction rule and its interpretation in C-98/06 *Freeport*, the CJEU observed that the provision must be strictly interpreted. The CJEU noted that the answer is not apparent from the wording of Article 6(1). As regards the purpose of Article 6(1), by taking Recitals 12 and 15 into account, the CJEU observed that the rule in Article 6(1) first meets the wish to facilitate the sound administration of justice, to minimise the possibility of concurrent proceedings and thus to avoid irreconcilable outcomes if cases are decided separately. Second, by citing 189/87 *Kalfelis* and C-51/97

---

[158] See the AG's Opinion, EU:C:2008:22.

[159] As a member of the UK delegation in the negotiations on the revision of the Brussels and Lugano Conventions (1997–99) and in the Council Working Party on Brussels I, Paul Beaumont can testify that it was not a deliberately created omission.

[160] [2011] ECR I-12533 (Third Chamber) ('Painer').

Réunion européenne and Others, it stated that that rule cannot however be applied so as to allow an applicant to make a claim against a number of defendants with the sole object of ousting the jurisdiction of the courts of the State where one of those defendants is domiciled. It affirmed its interpretation in *Freeport* that in assessing whether there is a connection between different claims, that is to say a risk of irreconcilable judgments if those claims were determined separately, the identical legal bases of the actions brought is only one relevant factor among others and thus it is not an indispensable requirement for the application of Article 6(1). It thus held that a difference in legal basis between the actions brought against the various defendants, does not, in itself, preclude the application of Article 6(1), provided however that it was foreseeable by the defendants that they might be sued in the Member State where at least one of them is domiciled. It added that is for the referring court to assess, in the light of all the elements of the case, whether there is a risk of irreconcilable judgments if those actions were determined separately. AG Trstenjak[161] proposed some reforms to the CJEU's case law on Article 6(1) but sadly these are not discussed or followed by the Third Chamber.

The CJEU's decision in C-145/10 *Painer* casts very little light on how Article 6(1) of Brussels I (Article 8(1) of Brussels Ia) should be interpreted. The ruling is couched in negative terms and leaves to the national court the difficult task of interpretation without any real guidance. AG Trstenjak, however, had read some critiques of the CJEU's prior case law on Article 6(1)—which is unclear and contradictory—and tried to provide greater clarity on the interpretation of one of the more difficult Articles in Brussels I. She rightly rejected applying the CJEU's case law on Article 34(3) of Brussels I on what constitutes irreconcilable judgments at the recognition and enforcement stage (ie legal consequences that are mutually exclusive) because this would destroy the purpose of Article 6(1) as such mutually exclusive consequences can only arise when the judgments are given between the same parties whereas Article 6(1) envisages the prevention of irreconcilable judgments between one plaintiff and two different defendants.[162] The AG focused on the need for a 'sufficiently close connection' between the anchor claim (the one against the person who is domiciled in the forum where the action is being brought) and the claims against the other defendants. It is the connection with the anchor claim that makes the Article 6(1) jurisdiction foreseeable for all defendants.[163] The AG suggests that there must be a 'single factual situation' and that therefore there must be 'concerted parallel conduct' of the anchor defendant and the other defendants.[164] If this is demonstrated, then the risk of irreconcilable judgments is automatic because there is always an abstract risk in those cases of irreconcilable judgments.[165] On the surface the AG's points are convincing. It is a weakness of the methodology of the CJEU that all the hard work of an AG in suggesting reforms is left hanging with no analysis by the Court. If the Court is not minded to follow an AG's reasoned suggestions it should indicate why in its judgment so that litigants in the future know what the CJEU actually believes about the interpretation of the relevant piece of law—in this case Article 6(1) of Brussels I.

---

[161] See the AG's Opinion, EU:C:2011:239.
[162] See ibid paras 58–66.
[163] See ibid paras 95–99.
[164] See ibid paras 91–94.
[165] See ibid paras 100–02.

C-616/10 *Solvay SA v Honeywell Fluorine Products Europe BV and Others*,[166] on the interpretation of Articles 6(1), 22(4) and 31, was referred to the CJEU in proceedings between Solvay (established in Belgium) and Honeywell Fluorine (established in the Netherlands) and Honeywell Belgium and Honeywell Europe (both established in Belgium), regarding the alleged infringement by various parties of a European patent that Solvay was the proprietor of. On the applicability of Article 6(1), taking account of Recitals 11, 12 and 15, and also citing C-145/10 *Painer*, the CJEU affirmed that the purpose of Article 6(1) is to avoid irreconcilable judgments resulting from separate proceedings and that, as a special jurisdiction rule, it must be strictly interpreted. Referring to C-539/03 *Roche Nederland* and agreeing with AG Cruz Villalón,[167] the CJEU observed that, due to specific features of the present case, the potential divergences in the outcome of the proceedings are likely to arise in the same situation of fact and law. The reason is that each court will have to examine the alleged infringements under different national legislation governing the various national parts of the European patent alleged to have been infringed and it is possible that they will culminate in irreconcilable judgments resulting from separate proceedings. The CJEU found that where two or more companies established in different Member States, in proceedings pending before a court of one of those Member States, are each separately accused of committing an infringement of the same national part of a European patent which is in force in yet another Member State by virtue of their performance of reserved actions with regard to the same product, is capable of leading to 'irreconcilable judgments' resulting from separate proceedings as referred to under Article 6(1). The CJEU further found that it is for the referring court to assess whether such a risk exists, taking into account all the relevant information in the file.

The CJEU distinguished *Solvay* from C-539/03 *Roche Nederland*, which did not allow Article 6(1) of Brussels I to be used in relation to a dispute over a European patent, because in this case defendants from different Member States were being accused of infringing the same national elements of a European patent in the same Member State, rather than in different Member States.[168] The CJEU's distinguishing of *Roche Nederland* in *Solvay* is to be welcomed as making patent litigation involving multiple defendants slightly more efficient.

In C-645/11 *Sapir and Others*,[169] one of the issues that the CJEU dealt with was the application of Article 6(1). There were 11 defendants in this case and six of them who were domiciled in Israel, the UK and Spain challenged the jurisdiction of the German courts. After citing C-98/06 *Freeport* and C-145/10 *Painer*, the CJEU observed that both claims have their origin in a single situation of law and fact, ie the right to compensation, and directed at the same interest, ie the repayment of the erroneously transferred surplus amount. It accordingly found Article 6(1) is applicable where there is a close connection between the claims lodged against several defendants domiciled in other Member States in the case where those defendants rely on rights to additional compensation which it is necessary to determine on a uniform basis. It then examined whether the existence of the domicile of a co-defendant in another Member State is a condition for the application of Article 6(1). It observed that the provision refers expressly to defendants domiciled in the EU and thus in order to sue

---

[166] EU:C:2012:445 (Third Chamber) ('Solvay'). See also s II.C.v.c and s II.C.ix below.
[167] See the AG's Opinion, EU:C:2012:193.
[168] See paras 18–29 of the AG's Opinion.
[169] See s II.A.i above.

a co-defendant before the courts of a Member State under Article 6(1), it is necessary that that person should be domiciled in another Member State. It held that Article 6(1) is not intended to apply to defendants who are not domiciled in another Member State, in the case where they are sued in proceedings brought against several defendants, some of whom are also persons domiciled in the EU. It is a useful judgment in order to clarify the meaning of the close connection in Article 6(1) and to confirm the provision's inapplicability to defendants domiciled outside the EU. The CJEU wisely rejected the extension of Article 6(1) (Article 8(1) of Brussels Ia) to non-EU domiciliaries because that is clearly a matter governed by national law as a result of Article 4(1) (Article 6(1) of Brussels Ia). The CJEU confirmed that a case comes within the scope of Article 6(1) (Article 8(1) of Brussels Ia) where there is a different legal basis for some of the claims (in this case the claim against 10 defendants was for unjust enrichment and the claim against the eleventh defendant was for tort) where all the claims are directed at the same interest (in this case the repayment of the erroneously transferred allegedly surplus payment).

In C-352/13 *Cartel Damage Claims* as discussed above,[170] the defendants were established in various Member States, apart from Evonik Degussa GmbH which had its registered office in Germany. Later on, CDC withdrew its action against Evonik following a settlement with that undertaking. One of the questions that the CJEU dealt with was whether the conditions to establish jurisdiction under Article 6(1) were met even though the applicant had withdrawn its action against the sole co-defendant domiciled in the State of the court seised. The CJEU reaffirmed that in order for judgments to be regarded as irreconcilable it is not sufficient that there be a divergence in the outcome of the dispute, but that divergence must also arise in the context of the same situation of fact and law and that it did in this case since the cartel agreement amounted to a single and continuous infringement. The requirements for holding the defendants liable in tort, jointly and severally are to be determined by the national law of each Member State, not by the Commission decision. National laws may differ on this issue which may lead to irreconcilable judgments, within the meaning of Article 6(1), if actions were brought before the courts of various Member States. It was foreseeable by the defendants, because of the Commission decision, that they might be sued in the Member State where one of them is domiciled. The CJEU found that the applicant's withdrawal of the action against the only German defendant does not affect the application of Article 6(1) unless there is firm evidence to support the conclusion that the parties had colluded to artificially fulfil, or prolong the fulfilment of, that provision's applicability. Simply holding negotiations with a view to concluding an out-of-court settlement does not in itself prove such collusion but concealing the fact that a settlement had been reached before the Article 6(1) proceedings had begun would do so. Although the CJEU stated that Article 6(1) should be interpreted strictly, the result it reached is rather broad.

ii. Jurisdiction in Matters Relating to Insurance (Articles 8–14) (Articles 10–16 of Brussels Ia)

The CJEU has interpreted the jurisdiction rules in matters relating to insurance, which are set out under Articles 8–14 of Brussels I (Articles 10–16 of Brussels Ia), without having much difficulty.

---

[170] See s II.C.i.a.2 above and s II.C.vi.a below.

In C-463/06 *FBTO Schadeverzekeringen NV v Jack Odenbreit*,[171] the CJEU interpreted Articles 9(1)(b) and 11(2) of Brussels I in the context of an action brought in Germany by the injured party directly in a road traffic accident which occurred in the Netherlands against the insurer of the person responsible for that accident. The CJEU examined whether the reference to Article 9(1)(b) in Article 11(2) is to be understood as meaning that the injured party may bring an action directly against the insurer in the courts for the place in a Member State where the injured party is domiciled, provided that such a direct action is permitted and the insurer is domiciled in a Member State. The CJEU noted that Article 9(1)(b) does not merely attribute jurisdiction to the courts for the place where the persons listed therein are domiciled, but, on the contrary, it lays down that the courts for the place where the plaintiff is domiciled have jurisdiction, thereby giving such persons the option of suing the insurer before the courts for the place of their own domicile. Thus, to interpret the reference in Article 11(2) to Article 9(1)(b) as permitting the injured party to bring proceedings only before the courts having jurisdiction under that latter provision, that is to say, the courts for the place of domicile of the policy holder, the insured or the beneficiary, would run counter to the actual wording of Article 11(2). Thus, the role of that reference is to add injured parties to the list of plaintiffs contained in Article 9(1)(b). The application of that rule of jurisdiction to a direct action brought by the injured party cannot depend upon the classification of that injured party as a 'beneficiary' within the meaning of Article 9(1)(b), since the reference to that provision in Article 11(2) thereof allows that rule of jurisdiction to be extended to such disputes without the plaintiff having to belong to one of the categories in Article 9(1)(b). That line of reasoning is also based on teleological interpretation. According to Recital 13, the Regulation aims to guarantee more favourable protection to the weaker party than the general rules of jurisdiction provide for. To deny the injured party the right to bring an action before the courts for the place of his own domicile would deprive him of the same protection as that afforded by Brussels I to other parties regarded as weak in disputes in matters relating to insurance and would thus be contrary to the spirit of the Regulation. Brussels I strengthened such protection as compared with the Brussels Convention. The CJEU ruled that the injured party may bring an action directly against the insurer before the courts for the place in a Member State where that injured party is domiciled, provided that a direct action is permitted and the insurer is domiciled in a Member State. This was a clear-cut case. The CJEU gave its judgment in 13 months and without an AG's Opinion.

C-347/08 *Vorarlberger Gebietskrankenkasse v WGV-Schwäbische Allgemeine Versicherungs AG*[172] was referred to the CJEU regarding an action for recovery by a social security institution established in Austria against an insurer established in Germany. The question was whether the social security institution, statutory assignee of the rights of the directly injured party, may bring an action directly before the courts of its Member State of establishment against the insurer of the person allegedly liable for the accident, established in another Member State under Articles 9(1)(b) and 11(2). The CJEU observed that there are differences between the different language versions of Article 11(2). It stated that the French version refers to the person who directly suffered the damage whereas the German, Spanish,

---

[171] [2007] ECR I-11321 (Second Chamber) ('FBTO').
[172] [2009] ECR I-08661 (Third Chamber) ('Vorarlberger Gebietskrankenkasse').

Czech, Danish, Estonian, Italian, Polish, Slovak and Swedish versions use a term equivalent to 'injured party'. It also cited C-463/06 *FBTO* where it had ruled that the purpose of the reference in Article 11(2) is to add injured parties to the list of plaintiffs contained in Article 9(1)(b), without restricting the category of persons having suffered damage to those suffering it directly. Thus, it found that Article 11(2) refers to the injured party. On the first question, it affirmed *FBTO* that that reference means that the courts for the place where an injured party is domiciled have jurisdiction as regards an action brought directly against the insurer of the person allegedly responsible, provided that such an action is permitted and that the insurer is domiciled in a Member State. With regard to the insurance of the civil liability arising from motor accidents, it considered the relevant provisions of Directives 72/166[173] and 2000/26[174] and found that the injured party has the right to bring an action before the courts of his domicile against the insurer of the person allegedly responsible. It then examined whether a social security institution, acting as statutory assignee of the rights of the person injured in a motor accident, also has that right. It stated that, in order to ensure full effect and an autonomous interpretation of Brussels I, the application given to specific legal forms of substitution provided for by Austrian law cannot have an effect on the interpretation of the Brussels I provisions. It considered that the purpose of the jurisdiction rules in matters of insurance is to protect the weaker party, so their application should not be extended to persons for whom that protection is not justified. Affirming C-77/04 *GIE*,[175] it did not regard the social security institution as an economically weaker party and less experienced legally than a civil liability insurer. Thus, it found that a social security institution, acting as statutory assignee of the rights of the directly injured party in a motor accident, cannot rely on Articles 9(1)(b) and 11(2) in order to bring an action directly before the courts of its Member State of establishment against the insurer of the person allegedly responsible for the accident, where that insurer is established in another Member State.

The CJEU, in C-347/08 *Vorarlberger Gebietskrankenkasse*, wisely restricted the protective jurisdiction provisions on insurance to weaker parties to comply with the clear intention of the Union legislature seen in Recital 13 to Brussels I. The CJEU made a useful *obiter* observation that if an assignee of the rights of the directly injured party can be considered to be a weaker party, eg the heirs of the person injured in the accident, then the assignee will benefit from the protective jurisdiction provisions.[176] The judgment was given in 13 months, without an AG's Opinion.

---

[173] Council Dir 72/166/EEC of 24 April 1972 on the approximation of the laws of Member States relating to insurance against civil liability in respect of the use of motor vehicles, and to the enforcement of the obligation to insure against such liability, [1972] OJ L 103/1.

[174] Dir 2000/26/EC of the European Parliament and of the Council of 16 May 2000 on the approximation of the laws of the Member States relating to insurance against civil liability in respect of the use of motor vehicles and amending Council Dirs 73/239/EEC and 88/357/EEC (OJ 2000 L 181, p 65), as amended by Dir 2005/14/EC of the European Parliament and of the Council of 11 May 2005, [2005] OJ L 149/14.

[175] C-77/04 *Groupement d'intérêt économique (GIE) Réunion européenne and Others v Zurich España and Société pyrénéenne de transit d'automobiles (Soptrans)* [2005] ECR I-04509 (First Chamber) ('GIE').

[176] See para 44 of the judgment.

iii. Jurisdiction over Consumer Contracts (Articles 15–17) (Articles 17–19 of Brussels Ia)

The CJEU has interpreted the jurisdiction rules in consumer contracts, which are set out under Articles 15–17 of Brussels I (Articles 17–19 of Brussels Ia), in a few cases.

a. Article 15 (Article 17 of Brussels Ia)

In C-180/06 *Renate Ilsinger v Martin Dreschers*,[177] the CJEU interpreted Article 15(1)(c) of Brussels I as regards the entitlement of a consumer to whom misleading advertising had been sent to seek payment, in judicial proceedings, of the prize which he has apparently won. The judgment was partially in line with the Opinion of AG Trstenjak.[178] The CJEU held that although the application of Article 13(1) of the Brussels Convention is limited to contracts which give rise to reciprocal and interdependent obligations between the parties (see C-96/00 *Gabriel*,[179] paragraphs 48 to 50, and C-27/02 *Engler*,[180] paragraphs 34 and 36), the scope of Article 15(1)(c) of Brussels I is not limited to such situations. However, it held that Article 15 of Brussels I is applicable only if the legal proceedings concerned relate to a contract which has been 'concluded' between a consumer and a professional. Such conclusion requires the professional to declare itself to be unconditionally willing to pay a prize to that consumer and for the consumer to accept it. It continued that it is for the national court to determine whether that requirement is fulfilled in the dispute before it. In the light of those factors, and in the absence of a substantial difference in drafting between Article 15 of Brussels I and Article 13 of the Brussels Convention as regards the requirement of the conclusion of a contract between the parties, it held that the case law resulting from the judgments in C-96/00 *Gabriel* and C-27/02 *Engler*, relating to the second of those provisions, must be transposed to Article 15. If there is such similarity between a provision of the Brussels Convention and a provision of Brussels I it is necessary to ensure, in accordance with Recital 19 to the latter, continuity in the interpretation of those two instruments thereby ensuring observance of the principle of legal certainty. Article 15(1)(c) cannot apply to legal proceedings such as those at issue in the main proceedings if the professional did not undertake contractually to pay the prize promised to the consumer who requests its payment. In that case, Article 15(1)(c) is applicable to such legal proceedings only on condition that the misleading prize notification was followed by the conclusion of a contract by the consumer with the company evidenced by an order placed with the latter. This case took far too long (37 months) particularly given the fact that it was brought by a weaker party, a consumer, who had to wait for justice for an extraordinary long time in the CJEU.

In joined cases C-585/08 *Peter Pammer v Reederei Karl Schlüter GmbH & Co KG* and C-144/09 *Hotel Alpenhof GesmbH v Oliver Heller*,[181] the CJEU interpreted the concepts of 'package travel' and activity 'directed to' the Member State of the consumer's domicile under Article 15(1)(c) and (3). The joint case was referred to the CJEU in two disputes, between, (i) Pammer (residing in Austria) and Karl Schlüter (established in Germany) concerning

---

[177] [2009] ECR I-03961 (First Chamber) ('Ilsinger').
[178] See the AG's Opinion, EU:C:2008:483.
[179] C-96/00 *Rudolf Gabriel* [2002] ECR I-06367 (Sixth Chamber) ('Gabriel').
[180] C-27/02 *Petra Engler v Janus Versand GmbH* [2005] ECR I-00481 (Second Chamber) ('Engler').
[181] [2010] ECR I-12527 (Grand Chamber) ('Pammer and Hotel Alpenhof').

reimbursement of the cost of a freighter voyage booked through a German intermediary and (ii) Hotel Alpenhof (operating in Austria) and Heller (residing in Germany) concerning his refusal to pay his hotel bill for a stay booked by using an email address obtained on the internet. On the question whether the contract in C-585/08 is a transport contract under Article 15(3), considering that the legislature intended to cover the same types of contracts in Article 15(3) of Brussels I and Article 6(4)(b) of Rome I, the CJEU interpreted the former in the light of the latter which refers to 'package travel'. It found that the service offered by the voyage fulfils the necessary conditions for a 'package' in Article 2(1) of Directive 90/314.[182] It held that the contract concerning a voyage by freighter providing for a combination of travel and accommodation for an inclusive price is a transport contract. On the question concerning criteria under which a trader whose activity is presented on its website or on that of an intermediary can be considered to be 'directing' its activity to the consumer's domicile under Article 15(1)(c) and whether the fact that those sites can be consulted on the internet is sufficient for that activity to be regarded as such, the CJEU ruled that:

> [i]t should be ascertained whether, before the conclusion of any contract with the consumer, it is apparent from those websites and the trader's overall activity that the trader was envisaging doing business with consumers domiciled in one or more Member States, including the Member State of that consumer's domicile, in the sense that it was minded to conclude a contract with them.

> The following matters, the list of which is not exhaustive, are capable of constituting evidence from which it may be concluded that the trader's activity is directed to the Member State of the consumer's domicile, namely the international nature of the activity, mention of itineraries from other Member States for going to the place where the trader is established, use of a language or a currency other than the language or currency generally used in the Member State in which the trader is established with the possibility of making and confirming the reservation in that other language, mention of telephone numbers with an international code, outlay of expenditure on an internet referencing service in order to facilitate access to the trader's site or that of its intermediary by consumers domiciled in other Member States, use of a top-level domain name other than that of the Member State in which the trader is established, and mention of an international clientele composed of customers domiciled in various Member States. It is for the national courts to ascertain whether such evidence exists.

> On the other hand, the mere accessibility of the trader's or the intermediary's website in the Member State in which the consumer is domiciled is insufficient. The same is true of mention of an email address and of other contact details, or of use of a language or a currency which are the language and/or currency generally used in the Member State in which the trader is established.

The Grand Chamber correctly ensured, in *Pammer and Hotel Alpenhof*, that the definition of 'package travel' in Article 6(4)(b) of Rome I coheres with that in Article 15(3) of Brussels I as the legislature favours, in principle, such cohesion of interpretation between Brussels I and Rome I.[183] The CJEU also made a good job of giving guidance to the national courts on how to interpret directing activity under Article 15(1)(c) of Brussels I.

---

[182] Council Dir 90/314/EEC of 13 June 1990 on package travel, package holidays and package tours, [1990] OJ L158/59.
[183] See Recitals 7 and 24 to Rome I.

In C-190/11 *Daniela Mühlleitner v Ahmad Yusufi and Wadat Yusufi*,[184] the CJEU interpreted whether Article 15(1)(c) applies only to distance contracts. It was referred to the CJEU in Austrian proceedings between Ms Mühlleitner (domiciled in Austria) and Mr A Yusufi and Mr W Yusufi concerning the rescission of a sale contract of a motor vehicle, reimbursement of the purchase price, and a claim for damages. Ms Mühlleitner found the car on the internet, went to Germany, signed the contract there and bought the car from the defendants. The CJEU took account of a literal, historical and teleological interpretation of Article 15(1)(c) and gave a negative answer. It firstly stated that the provision does not expressly make its application conditional on the fact that the contracts falling within its scope have been concluded at a distance. It then took account of the explanatory memorandum accompanying the Brussels I Proposal[185] where the Commission considered that

> the fact that the condition in old Article 13 [of the Brussels Convention] that the consumer must have taken the necessary steps in his State has been removed means that Article 15, first paragraph, point (3), [now Article 15(1)(c) of the Brussels I Regulation] applies to contracts concluded in a State other than the consumer's domicile.

It also noted that paragraphs 86 and 87 of joined cases C-585/08 and C-144/09 *Pammer and Hotel Alpenhof* were just the CJEU's rebuttal of arguments made in that case and were not positive statements of legal conditions to be followed in subsequent cases. The CJEU rightly held that Article 15(1)(c) does not require the contract between the consumer and the trader to be concluded at a distance. The judgment was in line with the Opinion of AG Cruz Villalón.[186]

The CJEU gave a literal construction to Article 15(1)(c), in C-190/11 *Mühlleitner*, in not requiring that a consumer contract is concluded at a distance in order to fall within its scope and supported this construction with historical interpretation by referring to the Report of the European Parliament's Legal Affairs Committee explaining why a requirement that a consumer contract be concluded at a distance was not included in the text of Brussels I.[187] The main reason for thinking that a consumer contract has to be concluded at a distance is a misreading of the joint Commission/Council declaration in relation to Article 15 of Brussels I (agreed at the time when Brussels I was adopted and recorded in Recital 24 to Rome I). The declaration gives the conclusion of a distance contract as an example of evidence of a trader directing its activities to the State where the contract was concluded but it is only an example and not a pre-condition.

In C-419/11 *Česká spořitelna*,[188] one of the questions that the CJEU dealt with was the applicability of Article 15 where the company manager gave an aval on behalf of the company. The CJEU stated that Article 15(1) applies if three conditions are met. The first one is a contracting party is to be a consumer acting outside his trade or profession. It cited its case-law on Article 13(1) of the Brussels Convention where it held that the condition refers only to the private final consumer, not engaged in trade or professional activities, and that the special jurisdiction rules for consumer contracts serve to ensure the protection of the

---

[184] EU:C:2012:542 (Fourth Chamber) ('Mühlleitner').
[185] COM(1999) 348 final- CNS 99/0154, [1999] OJ C376E/1.
[186] See the AG's Opinion, EU:C:2012:313.
[187] See para 40 of the judgment.
[188] See s II.C.i.a.1 above.

consumer as the weaker party therefore they should not be extended to persons for whom that protection is not justified. Citing C-464/01 *Gruber*[189] and C-269/95 *Beinincasa*,[190] it reaffirmed that only contracts concluded outside and independently of any trade or professional activity or purpose, 'solely' for the purpose of satisfying an individual's own needs in terms of private consumption, are covered by the special rules to protect the consumer and that such protection is unwarranted in contracts concluded for the purpose of a trade or professional activity. It accordingly found that this condition is not met in the present case because Mr Feichter, as the aval giver, became the guarantor of the obligations of the company of which he is the managing director and in which he has a majority shareholding. Agreeing with AG Sharpston, it observed that he cannot be regarded as acting outside and independently of any trade or professional activity or purpose while he has close professional links with the company, such as its managing director or majority shareholder. The CJEU correctly held that, since Mr Feichter cannot be considered as a consumer in this context, Article 15 is not applicable. AG Sharpston indulged in some interesting speculation suggesting that a natural person guarantor could be a consumer in certain cases, eg the parents of a minor child who takes out a contract for a smartphone should be regarded as consumers when they act as guarantors for their child's contract.[191]

C-218/12 *Lokman Emrek v Vlado Sabranovic*,[192] on the interpretation of Article 15(1)(c), was referred to the CJEU in German proceedings between Mr Emrek (domiciled in Germany) and Mr Sabranovic (operating a business selling second-hand motor vehicles in France, close to the German border) concerning claims under a warranty following the conclusion of a sale contract for a second-hand motor vehicle. Sabranovic had an internet site containing the contact details for his business, including French telephone numbers with the international dialling code and a German mobile telephone number and the main issue was whether Sabranovic's commercial activity was directed to Germany although Emrek had learnt about the business from acquaintances, not from the internet site. The CJEU firstly noted that it had already answered the second question in its previous judgment in C-190/11 *Mühlleitner* that Article 15(1)(c) does not require the contract between the consumer and the trader to be concluded at a distance. The first question was whether Article 15(1)(c) requires the existence of a causal link between the means used to direct the commercial/professional activity to the Member State in which the consumer is domiciled, namely an Internet site, and the conclusion of the contract with that consumer. The CJEU observed that the wording of the provision does not expressly require the existence of such a causal link. It then followed the teleological interpretation and observed that the addition of the unwritten condition concerning the existence of a causal link would be contrary to the aim of the provision, ie protecting consumers as the weaker parties. By agreeing with AG Cruz Villalón,[193] it found that the requirement of prior consultation of the internet site by the consumer could give rise to problems of proof, in particular in cases where the contract was not concluded at a distance through that site, which would tend to dissuade consumers from bringing actions under Articles 15 and 16 of Brussels I and weaken the aim

---

[189] C-464/01 *Johann Gruber v Bay Wa AG* [2005] ECR I-00439 (Second Chamber) ('Gruber').
[190] C-269/95 *Francesco Benincasa v Dentalkit Srl* [1997] ECR I-03767 (Sixth Chamber) ('Benincasa').
[191] See paras 38–39 of the AG's Opinion.
[192] EU:C:2013:666 (Third Chamber) ('Emrek').
[193] See the AG's Opinion, EU:C:2013:494.

of the protection of consumers. However, the CJEU agreed with the AG also on the point that the causal link may constitute strong evidence which may be taken into consideration by the courts when determining whether the activity is in fact directed to the Member State in which the consumer is domiciled. The CJEU recalled that, in C-585/08 and C-144/09 *Pammer and Hotel Alpenhof*, it had established a non-exhaustive list of factors capable of constituting evidence which national courts may use to determine whether the essential condition of commercial activity directed to the Member State of the consumer's domicile is fulfilled, and in C-190/11 *Mühlleitner* added other factors to the non-exhaustive list. It held that Article 15(1)(c) does not require the existence of a causal link between the activities directed at the consumer's place of domicile, and the contract; but the existence of the causal link constitutes evidence of the connection between the contract and such activity.

This interpretation in *Emrek* is a very broad interpretation of Article 15 that allows a consumer to bring an action at his domicile even if he concludes a contract abroad with a trader for reasons other than the seller's directed activity. Traders who advertise their goods and services on a website in a way that suggests they are trying to attract foreign consumers are exposed to the jurisdiction of the domicile of the consumer even when that consumer comes to the trader's premises and buys their goods or services without ever having read the trader's website. Traders' websites may be carefully designed to avoid this by only giving national telephone numbers (without international dialling codes) and by avoiding anything that can be interpreted as an attempt to persuade a consumer from outside the country to buy from them.

In C-375/13 *Kolassa*,[194] one of the questions that the CJEU dealt with was whether the conditions laid down in Article 15(1) were met where a consumer has acquired a bearer bond from a third party professional without a contract having been concluded between that consumer and the issuer of the bond. The CJEU ruled that jurisdiction may not be invoked under Article 15(1) for the purposes of an action brought against the issuer of the bond on the basis of the bond conditions, breach of the information and control obligations and liability for the prospectus.

In C-297/14 *Rüdiger Hobohm v Benedikt Kampik Ltd & Co KG and Others*,[195] the CJEU interpreted Article 15(1)(c), read in conjunction with Article 16(1), in the course of proceedings between Mr Hobohm (domiciled in Germany) and Benedikt Kampik, Mr Kampik and Mar Mediterraneo (established in Spain) concerning the repayment of sums of money made available to Mr Kampik by Mr Hobohm in respect of a sale of an apartment in a tourist complex. In interpreting the directed activity in Article 15(1)(c), citing C-375/13 *Kolassa* and the case law cited therein in paragraph 23, the CJEU reaffirmed that all three conditions of Article 15(1) must be fulfilled in determining jurisdiction. After finding that the first and second conditions were fulfilled, it examined whether the existence of a link between the brokerage contract and the transaction-management contract allows the conclusion that the transaction-management contract comes within the scope of the activity 'directed to' Germany by Mr Kampik and, if so, what the nature of such a link must be. Considering the objectives set out in Recitals 11, 13 and 15, the purpose of consumer protection stated in its relevant Brussels Convention case law, and the necessity to interpret Article 15 strictly

---

[194] See s II.C.i.a.2 above.
[195] (Fourth Chamber) EU:C:2015:844 ('Hobohm').

as being a departure from the general rule in Article 2 and the special contract jurisdiction rule in Article 5(1), it found that Article 15(1)(c) may be applied to a contract such as the transaction-management contract at issue in the main proceedings in so far as it is closely linked to a contract such as the brokerage contract. Regarding the determination of the constituent elements of such a close link, it observed that following the developer's insolvency it was not possible to achieve the economic objective of the brokerage contract, ie the effective enjoyment of the apartment purchased by the Hobohms. It thus found that even though there is no legal interdependence between the brokerage contract and the transaction-management contract, there is an economic link between those two contracts. It held that:

> 'It is for the national court to determine whether the constituent elements of that link are present, in particular whether the parties to both of those contracts are identical in law or in fact, whether the economic objective of those contracts concerning the same specific subject-matter is identical and whether the second contract complements the first contract in that it seeks to make it possible for the economic objective of that first contract to be achieved.

The judgment was partially in line with the Opinion of AG Villalón and it was delivered in 18 months.

The Fourth Chamber in *Hobohm* has developed the law on consumer contract jurisdiction beyond that advised by AG Cruz Villalón. The CJEU is willing to accept that the consumer can sue in his own domicile against a trader domiciled in another Member State when the trader has not directed his activities to the consumer's domicile in relation to that contract when taken in isolation. The CJEU allows such jurisdiction where the contract in issue is 'closely linked' to an earlier contract concluded between the same parties which did arise out of the activities of the trader directed at the country where the consumer is domiciled. The CJEU lays down very restrictive conditions on what the close link has to be in this case[196] but the risk of this kind of judicial development is that these conditions will be relaxed gradually in subsequent cases until all follow on contracts are covered by the consumer contract protective jurisdiction rules. AG Cruz Villalón was not prepared to stretch the law in this way[197] and it is unfortunate that the CJEU did not engage with his Opinion in its ruling. The AG wanted to take an evidentiary approach which still requires that the follow on contract arises out of activity directed to the Member State of the consumer's domicile:

> The second alternative in Article 15(1)(c) of Council Regulation (EC) No 44/2001 of 22 December 2000 on jurisdiction and the recognition and enforcement of judgments in civil and commercial matters, in conjunction with the second alternative in Article 16(1) thereof, must be interpreted as meaning that, in the particular circumstances of the main proceedings, the existence of an earlier contract between the parties, and in respect of which there is a substantive causal link, is capable of constituting evidence that the activity pursued by the professional is 'directed' to the Member State of the consumer's domicile; this must be assessed in the light of all the facts available to the national court.

---

[196] See paras 36 and 37 of the judgment.
[197] See paras 33 and 38.

b. Article 16 (Article 18 of Brussels Ia)

In C-327/10 *Hypoteční banka*, the CJEU interpreted Article 16(2) in situations when a consumer's domicile is unknown. The case was referred to the CJEU in Czech proceedings between a bank (governed by Czech law and established in Prague, Czech Republic), and Mr Lindner (a German national whose address was unknown) seeking to secure payment of a sum regarding a mortgage loan which the bank had granted to him. The first question was whether Brussels I was applicable where one of the parties to the court proceedings is a national of a Member State other than that in which those proceedings are taking place. The CJEU referred to C-281/02 *Owusu* where it held regarding the Brussels Convention that the international nature of a legal relationship may derive from the fact that the situation at issue in the proceedings is such as to raise questions relating to the determination of international jurisdiction. The CJEU stated that the foreign nationality of one of the parties to the proceedings is not taken into account by the jurisdiction rules of Brussels I, but agreed with AG Trstenjak[198] that it may raise questions relating to the determination of the international jurisdiction. Considering legal certainty and the purpose of Brussels I to guarantee the protection of defendants who are domiciled in the EU, it held that Brussels I is applicable to the proceedings in which the defendant is a foreign national and has no known place of domicile in the State of the court seised. The second question was whether Brussels I precludes a national law provision which enables proceedings to be brought against persons whose domicile is unknown. Citing C-18/02 *DFDS Torline*,[199] the CJEU noted that Brussels I does not unify the procedural rules and found that it does not preclude the application of a provision of national procedural law of a Member State which, with a view to avoiding situations of denial of justice, enables proceedings to be brought against, and in the absence of, a person whose domicile is unknown, if the court seised of the matter is satisfied, before giving a ruling in those proceedings, that all investigations required by the principles of diligence and good faith have been undertaken with a view to tracing the defendant. It also interpreted Article 16(2), requiring an action against a consumer to be brought only in the courts of the Member State in which the consumer is domiciled, in respect of consumers whose current domicile is unknown. It found that the courts of the Member State in which the consumer had his last known domicile have jurisdiction under Article 16(2) to deal with proceedings in the case where they have been unable to determine, pursuant to Article 59, the defendant's current domicile and also have no firm evidence allowing them to conclude that the defendant is in fact domiciled outside the EU.

The CJEU gave an innovative judgment, in C-327/10 *Hypoteční banka*, by deciding that when a consumer's domicile is unknown the consumer can be sued at the place of their last known domicile. This judicial law-making is designed to avoid a denial of justice but a safer way of preventing such a denial of justice would be to follow AG Trstenjak's view that not knowing where a consumer is domiciled takes you outside the scope of the harmonised rules of jurisdiction in Brussels I into the scope of the national law rules preserved by Article 4 of Brussels I. The CJEU should leave law-making to the EU and national

---

[198] See the AG's Opinion, EU:C:2011:561.
[199] C-18/02 *Danmarks Rederiforening, acting on behalf of DFDS Torline A/S v LO Landsorganisationen i Sverige, acting on behalf of SEKO Sjöfolk Facket för Service och Kommunikation* [2004] ECR I-01417 (Sixth Chamber) ('DFDS Torline').

legislatures. It seems extraordinary that such overt law-making should be done by a Chamber of the Court. It means that the national legislatures and courts in the EU have lost the competence to deal with these cases by a decision of a Chamber of the CJEU that can only be overturned by a qualified majority in the Council and a majority in the European Parliament if the Commission is willing to make a Proposal to change the rule adopted by the Chamber.

C-478/12 *Armin Maletic and Marianne Maletic v lastminute.com Gmbh and TUI Österreich GmbH,*[200] on the interpretation of Article 16(1), was referred to the CJEU in the Austrian proceedings between Mr and Mrs Maletic (domiciled in Austria), and lastminute.com GmbH (having its registered office in Germany) and TUI Österreich GmbH (having its registered office in Austria), concerning payment of a sum arising from the booking by the Maletics through lastminute.com of a package holiday organised by TUI. The main issue to determine was whether Brussels I was applicable to a contracting partner and whether there was an international element justifying its application. The CJEU analysed the issue in the light of Recitals to Brussels I, and its relevant case law on both Brussels I and the Brussels Convention. By citing C-281/02 *Owusu*, the CJEU reaffirmed that the international character of the legal relationship need not necessarily derive from the involvement, either because of the subject matter of the proceedings or the respective domiciles of the parties, of a number of Contracting States. Thus, it found that Brussels I is applicable *a fortiori* to the case since the international element is present as regards both lastminute.com and TUI. The CJEU further observed that even assuming that the single transaction may be divided into two separate contractual relationships, the contractual relationship with TUI cannot be classified as 'purely' domestic since it was inseparably linked to the other contractual relationship made through the travel agency in another Member State. The CJEU also considered the objectives of protecting the consumer as the weaker party (Recital 13) and of minimising the possibility of concurrent proceedings and accordingly irreconcilable judgments to be given (Recital 15). It observed that pursuing parallel proceedings in Austria for the connected actions against two operators involved in the booking would not be consistent with these objectives. The CJEU thus held that the concept of 'other party to the contract' in Article 16(1) of Brussels I also covers the contracting partner of the operator with which the consumer concluded that contract and which has its registered office in the Member State in which the consumer is domiciled. This was a correct interpretation of Article 16(1) and the CJEU gave its judgment, without an AG's Opinion, fairly quickly in this case in less than 13 months. The claim in this case was EUR 1,201.38 together with interest and costs. It is remarkable that low value claims like *Maletic* can end up being ruled upon by the CJEU. It shows that the legal system in Austria is geared up to make it possible for small claims to be litigated in the normal courts but this is not the case throughout the EU. One has to question whether it is really cost effective and proportionate to involve so much high level judicial manpower over such a long period to resolve small claims.

iv. Jurisdiction Over Individual Contracts of Employment (Articles 18–21) (Articles 20–23 of Brussels Ia)

The CJEU has interpreted the jurisdiction rules on individual employment contracts, which are set out under Articles 18–21 of Brussels I (Articles 20–23 of Brussels Ia), in two cases.

---

[200] EU:C:2013:735 (Eight Chamber) ('Maletic').

C-154/11 *Mahamdia*, on Articles 18(2) and 21, is an important case on State immunity and on the interpretation of the branch, agency or establishment jurisdiction in relation to employment contracts. It was referred to the CJEU in German proceedings between Mr Mahamdia, an employee at the Algerian Embassy in Berlin, and Algeria arising from the employment contract containing a jurisdiction clause giving exclusive jurisdiction to the Algerian courts. Algeria challenged the German courts' jurisdiction by relying on state immunity and the jurisdiction clause in the contract. The CJEU was asked to interpret whether an embassy is an 'establishment' under Article 18(2) and whether Article 21 applies where a jurisdiction agreement, conferring exclusive jurisdiction on a third state's court, was concluded before a dispute arises. The CJEU reaffirmed the two criteria it had established for the concept of 'branch', 'agency' and 'other establishment' in its case law on the Brussels Convention: 1) 'The concept implies a centre of operations which has the appearance of permanency, such as the extension of a parent body. It must have a management and be materially equipped to negotiate business with third parties, so that they do not have to deal directly with the parent body' (paragraph 11 of 139/80 *Blanckaert & Willems*)[201] and 2) 'The dispute must concern acts relating to the management of those entities or commitments entered into by them on behalf of the parent body, if those commitments are to be performed in the State in which the entities are situated' (paragraph 13 of 33/78 *Somafer*).[202] As regards the first one, it observed that an embassy may be equated with a centre of operations which has the appearance of permanency and contributes to the identification and representation of the State from which it emanates. As regards the second one, it observed that a dispute on employment relations has a sufficient link with the functioning of the embassy regarding the management of its staff. Agreeing with AG Mengozzi,[203] it stated that state immunity may be excluded if the legal proceedings relate to acts performed *iure gestionis* not falling within the exercise of public powers. It thus found that as regards contracts of employment concluded by an embassy on behalf of the State, the embassy is an 'establishment' under Article 18(2) where the functions carried out by the employee do not fall within the exercise of public powers. On the second question, the CJEU took account of the wording and purpose of Article 21. It observed that it does not follow either from the wording or from the purpose that a jurisdiction agreement may not confer jurisdiction on the courts of a third State, provided that it does not exclude the jurisdiction conferred by Brussels I. It thus held that a jurisdiction agreement concluded before a dispute arises falls within Article 21(2) in so far as it gives the employee the possibility of bringing proceedings, not only before the courts ordinarily having jurisdiction under the special rules in Articles 18 and 19, but also before other courts, which may include courts outside the EU.

The Grand Chamber, in C-154/11 *Mahamdia*, carefully followed the CJEU's case law on Article 5(5) of the Brussels Convention and employed it to find that an embassy is an establishment for a State. The exact scope of State immunity under customary international law in relation to employment contracts is far from clear.[204] There is a lack of theoretical agreement as to whether one should focus on the functions of the employee (either their

---

[201] 139/80 *Blanckaert & Willems PVBA v Luise Trost* [1981] ECR 819 ('Blanckaert & Willems').
[202] 33/78 *Somafer SA v Saar-Ferngas AG* [1978] ECR 02183 ('Somafer').
[203] See the AG's Opinion, EU:C:2012:309.
[204] See ibid, para 23.

nature or purpose or both) or the nature of the contract or both. AG Mengozzi did not attempt a definitive answer to the problem but rather gave one unexplained proviso to the non-applicability of State immunity: 'provided that the employee's functions were unconnected with the exercise of public powers by the State.' The CJEU went further in trying to give guidance on the limits of State immunity. It wisely (because the issue is unclear and courts should be careful not to act like legislatures by making sweeping pronouncements in a particular case when all the possible scenarios have not been put before them) gives a potentially broader scope to State immunity with a twofold requirement for its exclusion: 'where the court seised finds that the *functions* carried out by the employee do not fall within the *exercise of public powers* or where the *proceedings* are not likely to *interfere with the security interests of the State*.'[205]

In C-47/14 *Holterman*,[206] the CJEU dealt with the connection between a company and its manager who is also a shareholder. The CJEU stated that this connection can be classified as an individual employment contract for the purpose of Article 18(1) if he can be considered as a worker for the purpose of Article 18(2). Following the Jenard-Möller Report on the Lugano Convention,[207] the CJEU affirmed that an employment contract presupposes 'a relationship of subordination of the employee to the employer' and that if his shareholding in the company was such that his 'ability to influence' was 'not negligible', he would not be a worker. It ruled that, where the company sues the person who performed the duties of director and manager of that company in order to establish misconduct on the part of that person in the performance of his duties and to obtain redress from him, Articles 18–21 preclude the application of Article 5(1) and (3) provided that that person, in his capacity as director and manager, for a certain period of time performed services for and under the direction of that company in return for which he received remuneration, that being a matter for the referring court to determine. The judgment was in line with the Opinion of AG Cruz Villalón.[208]

v. *Exclusive Jurisdiction (Article 22) (Article 24 of Brussels Ia)*

The CJEU has interpreted the exclusive jurisdiction rules under Article 22 of Brussels I (Article 24 of Brussels Ia) in a number of cases.

a. Rights *In Rem* in Immovable Property or Tenancies of Immovable Property (Article 22(1))

In C-386/12 *Schneider*,[209] on the applicability of the exclusive jurisdiction rule in Article 22(1) to non-contentious proceedings, the CJEU found that this question does not fall within the scope of Brussels I because it is directly linked to the legal capacity of the natural person under Article 1(2)(a). The CJEU was wise to give a restrictive interpretation to the scope of Article 22(1) of Brussels I by correctly applying Recital 19 and thereby relying on

---

[205] See para 56 of the judgment, emphasis added.
[206] See s II.C.i.a.3 above.
[207] P Jenard and G Möller, Report on the Convention on jurisdiction and the enforcement of judgments in civil and commercial matters done at Lugano on 16 September 1988, [1990] OJ C189/57.
[208] For the AG's Opinion, see EU:C:2015:309.
[209] See s A.ii.a above.

its own case law on Article 16(1) of the Brussels Convention, particularly C-115/88 *Reichert and Kockler* and C-343/04 *ČEZ*. The CJEU also referred to the Jenard Report which supported this way of interpretation.

C-438/12 *Irmengard Weber v Mechthilde Weber*,[210] on the interpretation of Articles 22(1), 27(1) and 28(1), was referred to the CJEU in proceedings between two sisters, co-owners of a property in Munich, in which Ms I Weber sought an order that her sister consent to the entry on the Land Register of Ms I Weber as the owner. In its interpretation, the CJEU considered its case law on the Brussels Convention and on Brussels I and gave particular weight to the Schlosser Report. The CJEU found the action which sought a declaration before the Italian court that a right *in rem* in immovable property situated in Germany has not been validly exercised falls within the category of proceedings which have as their object a right *in rem* in immovable property under Article 22(1). This interpretation by the CJEU which followed the Opinion of AG Jääskinen[211] is consistent with the nature of the exclusive jurisdiction rule.

In C-605/14 *Virpi Komu and Others v Pekka Komu and Jelena Komu*,[212] the CJEU interpreted the applicability of Article 22(1) in the course of Austrian proceedings between the five co-owners (domiciled in Finland) of an immovable property situated in Spain concerning the termination, by way of sale, of the co-ownership in undivided shares of that property. The CJEU, recalling its case law in C-438/12 *Weber* and the case law cited at paragraph 40 therein on Article 16(1)(a) of the Brussels Convention, decided that an independent definition must be given in EU law to the phrase 'in proceedings which have as their object rights in rem in immovable property'. It also recalled, by citing C-343/04 *ČEZ* and the case law cited at paragraphs 26 and 27 therein, that Article 22(1) must not be given an interpretation broader than is required by its objective because it is an exception to the general jurisdiction rules in Article 2(1). Considering the Brussels Convention and the Jenard Report, the CJEU reaffirmed that the essential reason for conferring exclusive jurisdiction on the courts of the *locus rei sitae* is proximity. It also recalled that this exclusive jurisdiction does not encompass all actions concerning rights in rem in immovable property, but only those which seek to determine the extent, content, ownership or possession of immovable property or the existence of other rights in rem therein and to provide the holders of those rights with protection for the powers which attach to their interest. It reaffirmed its settled case law that the difference between a right in rem and a right in personam is that the former, existing in corporeal property, has effect *erga omnes*, whereas the latter can be claimed only against the debtor. The CJEU observed that, in the present case, an action for termination of the co-ownership of immovable property constitutes proceedings which have as their object rights in rem in immovable property falling within the exclusive jurisdiction of the courts of the Member State in which the property is situated. It stated that clearly such an action, designed to bring about the transfer of a right of ownership in immovable property, concerns rights in rem which have effect *erga omnes* and is intended to ensure that the holders of those rights can protect the powers attached to their interest, as supported by the considerations of sound administration of justice underlying Article 22(1). It found that in a case where the rules of substantive applicable law would involve an assessment of

---

[210] EU:C:2014:212 (Third Chamber) ('Weber'). See also s II.C.viii.
[211] See the AG's Opinion, EU:C:2014:43.
[212] EU:C:2015:833 (Seventh Chamber).

whether physical partition of the properties is feasible when terminating the relationship of co-ownership, such an assessment would also be capable of giving rise to checks, by means of expert reports, which the courts of the Member State in which those properties are situated would be best placed to order. Thus, it held that an action for the termination of co-ownership in undivided shares of immovable property by way of sale, by an appointed agent, falls within the category of proceedings 'which have as their object rights *in rem* in immovable property' under Article 22(1). This was a straightforward case dealt with by the CJEU quickly in less than 12 months, without an AG's Opinion.

b. Validity of the Constitution, the Nullity or the Dissolution of Companies or Other
   Legal Persons or Associations (Article 22(2))

In C-372/07 *Hassett and Doherty*,[213] the CJEU interpreted the applicability of Article 22(2) to Irish proceedings in which two doctors claimed an indemnity and/or a contribution from their mutual defence organisation, the MDU, in respect of any sum which—in the context of medical negligence actions brought by Hassett and Doherty against the health boards for which those doctors worked—either doctor might be ordered to pay by way of indemnity to the health boards. The CJEU observed that Article 16 of the Brussels Convention and Article 22 of Brussels I are identical in essence. It cited its relevant case law on the Brussels Convention, in particular 73/77 *Sanders*,[214] C-8/98 *Dansommer*[215] and C-343/04 *ČEZ*, where it had held that Article 16 introduces an exception to the general rule governing the attribution of jurisdiction and therefore it must not be given an interpretation broader than is required by its objective, since its effect is to deprive the parties of the choice of forum which would otherwise be theirs and, in certain cases, it results in the parties being brought before a court which is not that of the domicile of any of them. It also took account of the Jenard Report. It observed, in order for Article 22(2) to apply, it is not sufficient that a legal action involve some link with a decision adopted by an organ of a company (by analogy, in relation to Article 16(1) of the Brussels Convention, C-294/92 *Webb*[216] and C-8/98 *Dansommer*). It stated that otherwise all legal actions brought against a company—whether in matters relating to a contract, tort or delict, or any other matter—would almost always come within the jurisdiction of the courts of the Member State in which the company has it seat and this would thus extend the scope of Article 22(2) beyond its objective. It found that that provision covers only disputes in which a party is challenging the validity of a decision of an organ of a company under the company law applicable or under the provisions governing the functioning of its organs, as laid down in its Articles of Association. In the present case, the doctors did not challenge the fact that the MDU's Board of Management was empowered under that company's Articles of Association to adopt that decision. They challenged only the manner in which that power was exercised. The CJEU found that the disputes did not fall within the scope of Article 22(2). This was a straightforward case. The judgment was given in 14 months and without an AG's Opinion.

---

[213] C-372/07 *Nicole Hassett v South Eastern Health Board and Cheryl Doherty v North Western Health Board* [2008] ECR I-07403 (First Chamber) ('Hassett and Doherty').
[214] 73/77 *Theodorus Engelbertus Sanders v Ronald van der Putte* [1977] ECR 02383 ('Sanders').
[215] C-8/98 *Dansommer A/S v Andreas Götz* [2000] ECR I-00393 (Sixth Chamber) ('Dansommer').
[216] C-294/92 *George Lawrence Webb v Lawrence Desmond Webb* [1994] ECR I-01717 ('Webb').

C-144/10 *Berliner Verkehrsbetriebe (BVG), Anstalt des öffentlichen Rechts v JPMorgan Chase Bank NA, Frankfurt Branch*[217] was referred to the CJEU in proceedings between BVG (a legal person governed by public law whose seat is in Germany) and the Frankfurt Branch of JPM (an American investment bank having its seat in the US) concerning a financial derivative contract. The CJEU interpreted Article 22(2) in the context of 'a review, necessary only as a collateral question, of the effectiveness, under the statutes, of decisions of organs [of a company]' since BVG pleaded that its own decisions were invalid as a collateral or preliminary issue. The CJEU first noted that there is a certain divergence among the various language versions of Article 22(2) and thus it interpreted the provision by taking account of matters other than its wording, in particular the purpose and the general scheme of Brussels I. Considering its interpretation on the Brussels Convention and the Jenard Report, the CJEU stated that Article 22(2) must be interpreted strictly. It observed that a broad interpretation of Article 22(2) would be contrary to Brussels I's purpose in Recital 11, ie the jurisdiction rules are to be highly predictable, and also to the principle of legal certainty. After reaffirming C-372/07 *Hassett and Doherty*, it added that a broad interpretation is not consistent with the specific objective of that provision, which consists simply in centralising jurisdiction to adjudicate upon disputes concerning the existence of a company or the validity of the decisions of its organs, in order to avoid conflicting judgments being given. It thus held that Article 22(2) does not apply to proceedings in which a company pleads that a contract cannot be relied upon against it because a decision of its organs which led to the conclusion of the contract is supposedly invalid on account of infringement of its statutes. The judgment was given fairly quickly in 13 months and without an AG's Opinion.

Berliner, where the CJEU decided that Article 22(2) of Brussels I (Article 24(2) of Brussels Ia), only applies to proceedings whose 'principal subject matter' comprises the validity of the constitution, the nullity or the dissolution of the company, legal person or association, or the validity of the decisions of its organs[218] is an excellent example of historical, contextual and purposive interpretation to resolve a problem caused by conflicting language versions of an EU law provision.[219]

In C-302/13 *flyLAL-Lithuanian Airlines*,[220] one of the questions that the CJEU dealt with was whether the action seeking legal redress for damage resulting from alleged infringements of EU competition law constitutes proceedings having as their object the validity of the decisions of organs of companies under Article 22(2). Referring to paragraph 26 of its judgment in C-372/07 *Hassett and Doherty*, the CJEU found that the action was not covered by Article 22(2) because the subject matter of the substance of the dispute concerned a compensation claim, not the validity of the decisions of the organs of companies.

c. Registration or Validity of Patents, Trademarks, Designs, or other Similar Rights (Article 22(4))

In C-616/10 *Solvay*,[221] concerning proceedings on the alleged infringement by various parties of a European patent, Solvay also lodged an interim claim against the defendants,

---

[217] [2011] ECR I-03961 (Third Chamber) ('Berliner').
[218] Para 44 of the judgment.
[219] Notably the then Judge Lenaerts was the rapporteur.
[220] See also s II.A.i above and s II.D.i.b.1 below.
[221] See s II.C.i.b above and s II.C.ix below.

seeking provisional relief in the form of a cross-border prohibition against infringement until a decision had been made in the main proceedings. The CJEU dealt with whether Article 22(4) precludes the application of Article 31 on provisional, including protective, measures. The CJEU underlined that Articles 22(4) and 31 regulate different situations, they have a distinct field of application and they do not refer to each other. It explained that Article 22(4) concerns the attribution of jurisdiction to rule on the substance in proceedings relating to a clearly defined area whereas Article 31 is designed to apply regardless of any jurisdiction as to the substance. It thus found that Article 31 is independent in scope from Article 22(4), but nonetheless it examined whether the CJEU case law on Article 16(4) of the Brussels Convention leads to a different conclusion. It, in particular, considered C-4/03 *GAT* where it interpreted Article 16(4) of the Brussels Convention widely in order to ensure its effectiveness. It found that the reasons which led it to interpret widely the jurisdiction under Article 22(4) of Brussels I do not require the disapplication of Article 31 in the present case. It accordingly confirmed that Article 22(4) does not preclude the application of Article 31.

The CJEU distinguished C-616/10 *Solvay* from C-4/03 *GAT*, in that a national court that does not have jurisdiction over the substance of a dispute concerning a European patent can grant provisional measures under Article 31 of Brussels I even when the validity of the patent is raised in those proceedings. The rule in C-4/03 *GAT* that the courts of a Member State seised of an infringement action in relation to a European patent must stay their proceedings as soon as the issue of validity of the patent is raised does not apply to proceedings for provisional and protective measures where the court seised is exercising its jurisdiction under Article 31 of Brussels I. At least this is the case where the court seised does not rule on the validity of the patent, but instead will refuse to grant the provisional and protective measure if there is a reasonable, non-negligible possibility that the patent invoked would be declared invalid by the competent court.[222] The CJEU's distinguishing of C-4/03 *GAT* in C-616/10 *Solvay* is to be welcomed as methods of making patent litigation involving multiple defendants slightly more efficient.

vi. Prorogation of Jurisdiction (Articles 23–24) (Articles 25 and 26 of Brussels Ia)

The CJEU has dealt with the prorogation of jurisdiction under Articles 23 and 24 of Brussels I (Articles 25 and 26 of Brussels Ia) in a few cases.

a. Jurisdiction Agreements (Article 23)

In C-543/10 *Refcomp SpA v Axa Corporate Solutions Assurance SA and Others*,[223] the CJEU interpreted whether a jurisdiction clause in a contract can be transmitted to a third party under Article 23. The case was referred to the CJEU in French proceedings between Refcomp (with its registered office in Italy) and Axa Corporate (with its registered office in France), Axa France (established in France), Emerson (with its registered office in France) and Climaveneta (with its registered office in Italy) seeking to establish the liability of Refcomp (the manufacturer) before the French courts. Refcomp relied on a jurisdiction

---

[222] See para 49 of the judgment.
[223] EU:C:2013:62 (First Chamber) ('Refcomp').

clause in favour of the Italian courts contained in the contract between itself and Clima-veneta (the third party sub-buyer). The CJEU noted that the wording of Article 23 does not indicate whether a jurisdiction clause may be transmitted beyond the circle of the parties to a contract, to a third party, but that it clearly indicates that its scope is limited to cases in which the parties have 'agreed' on a court. Considering its case law on Article 17 of the Brussels Convention (in particular C-106/95 *MSG*[224] and C-159/97 *Castelletti*),[225] the CJEU observed that ensuring the real consent of the parties is one of the aims of Article 23(1). It stated that the jurisdiction clause incorporated in a contract may, in principle, produce effects only in the relations between the parties who have given their agreement to the con-clusion of that contract and in order for a third party to rely on the clause it is, in principle, necessary that the third party has given its consent to that effect. It however recognised that the conditions and the forms under which the third party may be regarded as having given his consent may vary in accordance with the nature of the initial contract. It considered its case law where it assessed certain conditions and the forms under which the third party may be regarded as having given his consent as regards statutes of companies (C-214/89 *Powell Duffryn*),[226] maritime transport contracts (71/83 *Tilly Russ*,[227] C-159/97 *Castelletti* and C-387/98 *Coreck Maritime*),[228] and distinguished the present case. Agreeing with AG Jääskinen,[229] the CJEU rightly held that a jurisdiction clause agreed in the contract concluded between the manufacturer of goods and the buyer thereof cannot be relied on against a sub-buyer who, in the course of a succession of contracts transferring ownership concluded between parties established in different Member States, purchased the goods and wishes to bring an action for damages against the manufacturer, unless it is established that that third party has actually consented to that clause under the conditions laid down in Article 23.

As regards the length of the procedure, C-543/10 *Refcomp* is a case where the CJEU took far too long to give a ruling (26 months). As regards the CJEU's interpretation, the decision may be controversial in legal systems based on French law, but is surely correct. A choice-of-court clause in the original contract between the manufacturer and the first buyer should not be binding on subsequent buyers of the goods along a chain from the first buyer, because they do not become parties to the contract between the manufacturer and the first buyer. The exception is where the second or subsequent buyer consents to the jurisdiction clause applying to it (and indeed even that consent will only make the jurisdiction clause applicable between the consenting party and any other party that accepts their acceptance of the jurisdiction clause as consensus in idem is needed).[230]

---

[224] C-106/95 *Mainschiffahrts-Genossenschaft eG (MSG) v Les Gravières Rhénanes SARL* [1997] ECR 00911 (Sixth Chamber) ('MSG').

[225] C-159/97 *Trasporti Castelletti Spedizioni Internazionali SpA v Hugo Trumpy SpA* [1999] ECR I-01597 ('Castelletti').

[226] C-214/89 *Powell Duffryn plc v Wolfgang Petereit* [1992] ECR I-01745 ('Powell Duffryn').

[227] 71/83 *Partenreederei ms Tilly Russ and Ernest Russ v NV Haven- & Vervoerbedrijf Nova and NV Goeminne Hout* [1984] ECR 02417 ('Tilly Russ').

[228] C-387/98 *Coreck Maritime GmbH v Handelsveem BV and Others* [2000] ECR I-09337 (Fifth Chamber) ('Coreck Maritime').

[229] See the AG's Opinion, EU:C:2012:637.

[230] In the light of the later case of C-366/13 *Profit Investment SIM v Ossi and Others* EU:C:2016:282 it seems that the CJEU (see paras 32–36) regards Case 71/83 *Tilly Russ* EU:C:1984:217 and C-214/89 *Powell Duffryn* EU:C:1992:115 as setting the normal rule on when third parties are bound by jurisdiction clauses and *Refcomp* as being an exception.

In C-352/13 *Cartel Damage Claims*,[231] one of the questions that the CJEU dealt with was whether the effects of the jurisdiction agreements contained in contracts for the supply of goods, by the virtue of Article 23, on the court's jurisdiction under Article 5(3) and/or Article 6(1). The CJEU found that the court should regard a jurisdiction clause concluded under Article 23 which abstractly refers to all disputes arising from contractual relationships as not extending to a dispute relating to the tortious liability that one party allegedly incurred as a result of the other's participation in an unlawful cartel. By contrast, a jurisdiction clause contained in a contract for supply of goods will apply to disputes concerning liability incurred as a result of an infringement of competition law if the clause refers to such disputes, even if the effect thereof is a derogation from the special jurisdiction laid down in Article 5(3) and/or Article 6(1).

C-322/14 *Jaouad El Majdoub v CarsOnTheWeb.Deutschland GmbH*,[232] on the interpretation of the formal validity requirements of jurisdiction agreements under Article 23(2) of Brussels I, was referred to the CJEU in German proceedings between a German car dealer and a German company, in relation to his internet purchase of an electric car from the website of the defendant. The general terms and conditions for internet sales transactions contained an agreement conferring jurisdiction on the courts in Leuven, Belgium. The purchaser agreed to the general terms and conditions of sale on the website by clicking on a hyperlink which opens a window, ie 'click-wrapping' and the main issue was whether 'click-wrapping' meets the requirements of Article 23(2) of Brussels I. The CJEU ruled that accepting the general terms and conditions of a contract for sale by 'click-wrapping' concluded by electronic means, which contains a jurisdiction agreement, constitutes a communication by electronic means which provides a durable record of the agreement within the meaning of Article 23(2), where, as in this case, it is possible to print and save the text of those terms and conditions before the conclusion of the contract. This is a correct interpretation of Article 23(2) which the CJEU gave taking full account of a literal, historical and teleological approach. The CJEU referred to the Pocar Report on the Lugano Convention[233] which interprets the same text as that agreed in the original Brussels I Regulation and also to the Commission's Explanatory Memorandum on its proposal for the Brussels I Regulation in 1999.[234] The judgment was given without an AG's Opinion.

b. Tacit Prorogation of Jurisdiction (Article 24)

In C-111/09 *Česká podnikatelská pojišťovna as, Vienna Insurance Group v Michal Bilas*,[235] the CJEU interpreted Article 24 where the special jurisdiction rules in matters relating to insurance (set out in Section 3 of Chapter II of Brussels I) are not complied with and where the defendant enters an appearance without contesting its jurisdiction. The CJEU observed that the second sentence of Article 24 contains a rule which delimits the scope of the general rule provided in the first sentence of Article 24, and consequently it must be regarded as an exception and interpreted restrictively. It stated that the second sentence of Article 24 cannot be understood as enabling the application of the general rule in the first sentence to

---

[231] See s C.i.a.2 and s C.i.b above.
[232] EU:C:2015:334 (Third Chamber) ('CarsOnTheWeb').
[233] Explanatory report by Professor Fausto Pocar, [2009] OJ C319/1.
[234] COM/99/0348 final—CNS 99/0154, [1999] OJ C376E/1.
[235] [2010] ECR I-04545 (Fourth Chamber) ('ČPP Vienna Insurance Group').

be excluded in respect of disputes other than those to which it expressly refers. This interpretation was already given by the CJEU on its case-law relating to Article 18 of the Brussels Convention. Ruling in proceedings where the parties had concluded an agreement on jurisdiction, the CJEU stated in 150/80 *Elefanten Schuh*[236] and 48/84 *Spitzley*[237] that neither the general scheme nor the objectives of the Convention provide grounds for the view that the parties are prevented from submitting their dispute to a court other than that stipulated in the agreement. It accordingly found that since the special jurisdiction rules in matters relating to insurance are not exclusive, the court seised, where those rules are not complied with, must declare itself to have jurisdiction where the defendant enters an appearance and does not contest that court's jurisdiction. It added that Article 35 does not prevent the recognition of the judgment given by that court. It thus held that the court seised, where the rules in Section 3 of Chapter II of Brussels I were not complied with, must declare itself to have jurisdiction under Article 24 where the defendant enters an appearance and does not contest that court's jurisdiction, since entering an appearance in that way amounts to a tacit prorogation of jurisdiction. This was a straightforward case dealt with by the CJEU fairly quickly in 14 months and without an AG's Opinion.

This decision of the CJEU in C-111/09 *ČPP Vienna Insurance Group* is clearly correct. The CJEU rightly stated at paragraph 32 that the Union legislature would have to revise Brussels I if a duty were to be imposed on a court to warn parties covered by the protective jurisdictions (consumers, employees and insured persons, etc) of the risks of contesting the merits without contesting the jurisdiction where the court only has jurisdiction by virtue of Article 24. This change was indeed adopted in Article 26 of Brussels Ia.

In C-144/12 *Goldbet Sportwetten GmbH v Massimo Sperindeo*,[238] the CJEU interpreted whether a statement of opposition, not challenging the jurisdiction, to an order under the European Order for Payment Procedure Regulation,[239] constitutes a tacit prorogation of jurisdiction within the meaning of Article 24 of Brussels I. The CJEU answered in the negative. By agreeing with AG Bot,[240] it observed that the statement of opposition can produce the effects only set out in the European Order for Payment Procedure Regulation (ie that that Regulation does not apply). Even though the statement of opposition does not contain any challenge to jurisdiction and it does contain arguments on the substance of the case this cannot be regarded as constituting the entering of an appearance under Article 24 of Brussels I. The judgment was given in 14 months and this was a correct interpretation of the interrelationship of the European Order for Payment Procedure Regulation and Brussels I and of the effects of opposition statements on jurisdiction. A statement of opposition to a European Order for Payment can never constitute an appearance for the purposes of Article 24 of Brussels I. This is considered to be correct because the statement of opposition has the effect of ending the European Order for Payment Procedure but it can never be a step in the follow on civil proceedings in which jurisdiction must be determined under Brussels I.

---

[236] 150/80 *Elefanten Schuh GmbH v Pierre Jacqmain* [1981] ECR 01671 ('Elefanten Schuh').
[237] 48/84 *Hannelore Spitzley v Sommer Exploitation SA* [1985] ECR 787 ('Spitzley').
[238] EU:C:2013:393 (Third Chamber).
[239] Reg (EC) No 1896/2006 of the European Parliament and of the Council of 12 December 2006 creating a European order for payment procedure, [2006] OJ L 399/1.
[240] See the AG's opinion, EU:C:2013:136.

C-112/13 *A v B and Others*,[241] on the interpretation of Article 24, was referred to the CJEU in Austrian proceedings concerning an action for damages brought against A by B and others claiming that A had abducted their husbands or fathers in Kazakhstan. The CJEU was asked whether the appearance entered by the court-appointed representative amounts to an appearance being entered by the absent defendant, establishing the international jurisdiction of that court, under Article 24. The CJEU noted that the Austrian courts had no jurisdiction to hear the case under Brussels I unless A had entered an appearance before the court seised under Article 24. It also observed that a court-appointed representative under Austrian law has a wide power of representation including the power to enter an appearance for the absent defendant. The CJEU agreed with AG Bot[242] that the tacit prorogation of jurisdiction under Article 24 is based on a deliberate choice made by the parties regarding jurisdiction, which presupposes that the defendant was aware of the proceedings brought against him. It continued that an absent defendant upon whom the document instituting proceedings has not been served and who is unaware of the proceedings against him may not be regarded as having tacitly accepted the jurisdiction of the court seised. It added that, in those circumstances, the absent defendant cannot provide the representative with all the necessary information and also the representative appearance may not be regarded as tacit acceptance, by the defendant, of the court's jurisdiction. The CJEU found that a contrary interpretation would not be consistent with the objectives of Brussels I that the jurisdiction rules should be highly predictable as set out in Recital 11. Citing C-327/10 *Hypoteční banka* and C-292/10 *G*, it added that its interpretation is also supported by the applicant's right to an effective remedy as guaranteed by Article 47 of the Charter of Fundamental Rights of the European Union,[243] which must be implemented in conjunction with respect for the defendant's rights of defence under Brussels I.

In this case, the CJEU rightly distinguished two situations by stating that: the procedural steps taken by the court-appointed representative under Austrian law have the effect under Austrian law that A must be regarded as having entered an appearance before the court seised, but such steps by the representative without the defendant's approval cannot be regarded as amounting to an appearance being entered by that defendant under Article 24 of Brussels I as this would not strike a fair balance between the right to an effective remedy and the rights of the defence. Article 24 is based on the idea of tacit consent to the jurisdiction. Therefore, it is clearly correct that a defendant should only be found to have tacitly consented under Article 24 (Article 26 of Brussels Ia) when appearance is entered by a representative if the defendant has approved of such appearance.

vii. *Examination as to Jurisdiction and Admissibility (Articles 25–26)* (*Articles 27–28 of Brussels Ia*)

There are two cases which raised issues on the examination as to jurisdiction and admissibility which are set out under Articles 25 and 26 of Brussels I (Articles 27 and 28 of Brussels Ia).

---

[241] EU:C:2014:2195 (Fifth Chamber) ('A v B and others').
[242] See the AG's Opinion, EU:C:2014:207.
[243] [2000] OJ C364/1.

In C-292/10 *G*,[244] where there were many factors indicating that the defendant was in the EU but that was not absolutely certain, the CJEU found that Article 26(2) must be understood as requiring a court seised of a matter within the scope of Brussels I not to issue a default judgment unless it is satisfied 'that all investigations required by the principles of diligence and good faith have been undertaken to trace the defendant'.

In C-375/13 *Kolassa*,[245] one of the questions that the CJEU dealt with was whether the national courts, in determining jurisdiction, must conduct a comprehensive taking of evidence or start from the premiss that the facts asserted by the applicant are correct. The CJEU held that it is not necessary to conduct a comprehensive taking of evidence in relation to disputed facts, but it is permissible for the court seised to examine its jurisdiction in the light of all the information available to it, including, where appropriate, the allegations made by the defendant. By its interpretation, the CJEU showed respect for the independence of the national courts in determining their jurisdiction by allowing them to take account of the defendant's allegations when deciding whether or not they have jurisdiction under Brussels I. AG Szpunar had correctly encouraged the CJEU to do so by saying that Article 24 of Brussels I requires defendants to be able to present their arguments against the national court's jurisdiction.[246]

viii. Lis Pendens—*Related Actions (Articles 27–30) (Articles 29–32 of Brussels Ia)*

In C-438/12 *Weber*,[247] one of the questions that the CJEU dealt with was *lis pendens* in cases where the second seised court has exclusive jurisdiction under Article 22(1). The CJEU observed that since the second seised court has exclusive jurisdiction, a judgment given by the first seised court which fails to take account of Article 22(1) cannot be recognised in the State where the immovable property is situated pursuant to Article 35(1). It found that in those circumstances, the second seised court cannot stay its proceedings or decline jurisdiction, and that it must give its ruling on the substance in order to comply with the exclusive jurisdiction rule. The CJEU interpreted Article 27(1) as meaning that before staying its proceedings the second court seised with exclusive jurisdiction is authorised to consider whether any judgment of the first seised court will be recognised in the other Member State. This case also gave the CJEU the opportunity to re-consider its highly controversial interpretation in C-116/02 *Gasser*[248] as regards *lis pendens* in the context of choice-of-court agreements, but AG Jääskinen and the Third Chamber both preferred to distinguish C-438/12 *Weber* from C-116/02 *Gasser* on the basis that there was no equivalent to Article 35(1) of Brussels I applicable at the recognition and enforcement stage for a failure to respect an exclusive choice of court agreement.

C-438/12 *Weber* is a very pragmatic decision by the CJEU reading into Article 27 of Brussels I on *lis pendens* an exception to the rigid first seised rule for exclusive jurisdictions in Article 22 of Brussels I (Article 24 of Brussels Ia) which the CJEU was not willing to read into the *lis pendens* rule in C-116/02 *Gasser* for exclusive choice-of-court agreements in

---

[244] See also s II.B; and s II.C.i.a.2 above.
[245] See also s II.C.i.a.2 and s II.C.iiia above.
[246] See the AG's Opinion, EU:C:2014:2135.
[247] See also s II,v.a above.
[248] C-116/02 *Erich Gasser GmbH v MISAT Srl* [2003] ECR I-14693 ('Gasser').

Article 23 of Brussels I. Although neither the AG nor the Third Chamber say so, this pragmatism may have been inspired by the reversal of *Gasser* on this point by the EU legislature in Article 31(2) of Brussels Ia.

C-1/13 *Cartier parfums—lunettes SAS and Axa Corporate Solutions assurances SA v Ziegler France SA and Others*,[249] on the interpretation of Article 27(2), was referred to the CJEU in the French proceedings between Cartier parfums and its insurance company, and the carrier companies, concerning compensation for damage sustained by the claimants as a result of the theft of goods during their international transport by road from France to the UK. In French proceedings brought by Axa against the defendants seeking their joint and several liability for payment of the amount it had compensated Cartier, Ziegler raised a plea of *lis pendens* under Article 27 of Brussels I since it had already lodged a claim before the High Court in England against Cartier, Saflog and Wright Kerr Tyson Ltd (a company incorporated under English law) in order to determine liability and calculate the damage sustained by Cartier as a result of the theft. The CJEU was asked to interpret the scope of the expression 'jurisdiction of the court first seised is established' under Article 27(2) of Brussels I. The CJEU pointed out that Brussels I does not set out any circumstances regarding this provision and analysed the question by taking the overall scheme and the purpose of the Regulation into account in the light of Recitals to Brussels I, its relevant case law on both Brussels I and the Brussels Convention and also the Jenard Report. The CJEU observed that the system established by Brussels I was devised to avoid prolonging the length of time for which proceedings were stayed by the court second seised, when, in reality, the jurisdiction of the court first seised may no longer be challenged. It also observed that the *lis pendens* rule aims also to avoid negative conflicts of jurisdiction. Thus, the CJEU held that the jurisdiction of the court first seised is established under Article 27(2) of Brussels I where the court second seised does not have exclusive jurisdiction under Brussels I, the court first seised has not declined jurisdiction of its own motion and none of the parties has contested that jurisdiction up to the time at which a position is adopted which is regarded by national procedural law as being the first defence on the substance submitted before that court. This is a wise and pragmatic way of resolving a problem in divergent French academic opinions. The judgment was given in 13 months and without an AG's Opinion.

In C-523/14 *Aertssen*,[250] one of the issues that the CJEU dealt with was the applicability of Article 27(1). In that case, the Aertssen companies lodged in Belgium a complaint concerning allegations of fraud seeking to join to criminal proceedings a civil action against a company (incorporated under Netherlands law) and its subsidiaries including the defendants for the loss they suffered as a result of the fraud. The Aertssen companies also submitted in the Netherlands two civil applications for authorisation to serve an attachment order on VSB and others and the second one was granted subject to the condition of initiating the main proceedings. They accordingly brought in the Netherlands before the referring court a substantive action seeking the liability of the defendants and the provisional payment for their loss. Citing C-406/92 *Tatry* regarding 'the same parties', the CJEU observed that the fact that the parties to the civil action do not have the power to undertake a criminal prosecution cannot alter the fact that those parties are the same parties as the applicants and

---

[249] EU:C:2014:109 (Third Chamber).
[250] See s II.A.i above.

defendants to the action brought before the referring court, in so far as the latter are also referred to in the complaint seeking to join a civil action to proceedings in Belgium. Citing C-39/02 *Mærsk*[251] regarding 'the cause' of action, it observed that in the two parallel sets of proceedings, it is a common feature that the Aertssen companies consider that they suffered harm as a result of fraudulent acts and it is not inconceivable that those proceedings have the same cause. Citing C-111/01 *Gantner*,[252] 144/86 *Gubisch*[253] and C-452/12 *Nipponkoa Insurance*[254] regarding 'the object' of an action, it observed that the Aertssen companies seek compensation for the harm suffered by them. It thus found that, without prejudice to the determination to be made by the referring court all the criteria in Article 27 are satisfied. The CJEU seems determined to interpret Article 27 on *lis pendens* 'broadly'.[255] This is good for avoiding irreconcilable judgments but may mean that civil justice is dependent on how efficient the criminal justice system is in cases like *Aertssen* where the civil proceedings are ancillary to criminal proceedings. Further research is needed into how efficiently civil proceedings are resolved in countries where they are combined with criminal proceedings as envisaged in Article 5(4) of Brussels I (Article 7(3) of Brussels Ia).

In C-523/14 *Aertssen*, the CJEU also dealt with the determination of the time when the magistrate is deemed to be seised under Article 30. The CJEU found that where the complaint need not, under the applicable national law, be served the time which must be chosen for the purposes of holding that magistrate to be seised is the time when that complaint was lodged. This was an uncontroversial decision dealt with timeously by the CJEU.

ix. Provisional, Including Protective, Measures (Article 31) (Article 35 of Brussels Ia)

In C-616/10 *Solvay*, the CJEU found that the exclusive jurisdiction rule in Article 22(4) concerning the registration or validity of patents, trademarks, designs or other similar rights does not preclude the application of Article 31 by other courts.[256]

D. Matters Related to Recognition and Enforcement (Articles 32–56) (Articles 36–51 of Brussels Ia)

The CJEU have interpreted the rules concerning matters related to recognition and enforcement under Articles 32 to 56 of Brussels I in a number of cases. Some of the corresponding provisions in Brussels Ia (Articles 36–51) are significantly different because of the abolition of the declaration of enforceability.[257] As will be assessed individually below, the interpretation of the CJEU in some of these cases raises some concerns.

---

[251] C-39/02 *Mærsk Olie & Gas A/S v Firma M. de Haan en W. de Boer* [2004] ECR I-09657 (Third Chamber) ('Mærsk').

[252] C-111/01 *Gantner Electronic GmbH v Basch Exploitatie Maatschappij BV* [2003] ECR I-04207 ('Gantner').

[253] 144/86 *Gubisch Maschinenfabrik KG v Giulio Palumbo* [1987] ECR 04861 (Sixth Chamber) ('Gubisch').

[254] C-452/12 *Nipponkoa Insurance Co. (Europe) Ltd v Inter-Zuid Transport BV* EU:C:2013:858 (Third Chamber) ('Nipponka Insurance').

[255] See paras 39 and 45 of the judgment.

[256] See s II.C.i.b and s II,C,v,c above.

[257] For a relatively succinct analysis of those differences see P Beaumont and L Walker, 'Recognition and Enforcement of Judgments in Civil and Commercial Matters in the Brussels I Recast and some Lessons from it and the recent Hague Conventions for the Hague Judgments Project' (2015) 11 *Journal of Private International Law* 31

i. Recognition

a. Articles 32 and 33

In C-456/11 *Gothaer Allgemeine Versicherung AG and Others v Samskip GmbH*,[258] the CJEU interpreted Articles 32 and 33 of Brussels I. This case involved four German insurance companies and Krones AG (a German company insured by them), against Samskip (a German subsidiary of Samskip Holding BV, an undertaking founded in Iceland and established in the Netherlands), concerning the delivery by Samskip of a brewing installation to a purchaser, Cerveceria Cuauthemoc Monezum ('the recipient'), a Mexican undertaking. The dispute involved an action for compensation brought before the referring court in Germany by the claimants concerning damage allegedly caused to that installation during transport. The Belgian courts had dismissed as inadmissible similar actions brought before them on the ground that the bill of lading, drawn up when Samskip took delivery of the installation in Belgium, contained an exclusive jurisdiction clause in favour of Icelandic courts. The CJEU was asked whether Article 32 also covers a judgment by which a court of a Member State declines jurisdiction on the basis of a jurisdiction clause, even though that judgment is classified as a 'procedural judgment' by the law of another Member State. In examining these questions, the CJEU considered the wording of Article 32 and the objectives set out in Recitals 2 ('simple' recognition), 6 ('free movement of judgments'), 16 and 17 ('mutual trust') to Brussels I. It observed that a restrictive interpretation of the concept of judgment would give rise to a category of judicial decisions which are not among the exhaustively-listed exceptions set out in Articles 34 and 35 which could not be categorised as 'judgments' for the purposes of Article 32 and which the courts of other Member States would accordingly not be obliged to recognise. It found that such a category of decisions would be incompatible with the system established by Articles 33 to 35. Agreeing with AG Bot,[259] it held that Article 32 also covers a judgment by which the court of a Member State declines jurisdiction on the basis of a jurisdiction clause, irrespective of how that judgment is categorised under the law of another Member State. The other question was whether under Articles 32 and 33 the court before which recognition is sought of a judgment by which a court of another Member State has declined jurisdiction on the basis of a jurisdiction clause is bound by the finding—made in the grounds of a judgment, which has since become final, declaring the action inadmissible—regarding the validity of that clause. Considering the Jenard Report, its interpretation in 145/86 *Hoffmann*,[260] and the concept of *res judicata* under EU law, it found that a judgment by which a court of a Member State has declined jurisdiction on the basis of a jurisdiction clause, on the ground that that clause is valid, binds the courts of the other Member States both as regards that court's decision to decline jurisdiction, contained in the operative part of the judgment, and as regards the finding on the validity of that clause, contained in the *ratio decidendi* which provides the necessary underpinning for that operative part. The CJEU created a uniform definition of

---

at 35–42 and for a much more in-depth analysis see J Fitchen, P Franzina and X Kramer in A Dickinson and E Lein (eds) *Brussels I Recast* (Oxford, Oxford University Press, 2015) 373–539.

[258] EU:C:2012:719 (Third Chamber) ('Gothaer').
[259] See the AG's Opinion, EU:C:2012:554.
[260] 145/86 *Horst Ludwig Martin Hoffmann v Adelheid Krieg* [1988] ECR 00645 ('Hoffman').

res judicata which extends even to judgments given by EU national courts under unharmonised rules of jurisdiction.

The CJEU's conclusion to give an autonomous definition to the *res judicata* effects of judgments given by courts in the EU under Brussels I (even if the judgment relates to unharmonised jurisdiction rules) has proved controversial.[261] It would have been preferable if the EU legislature had decided on an autonomous definition of the effects of judgments rather than the CJEU creating such a definition. It means that judgments in national courts in the EU on cases that are not based on the harmonised rules of jurisdiction in Brussels I but which fall within the scope of Brussels I can have greater effects than they do in the country where the judgment was rendered. This is because the judgment is binding not only as to its operative part but also as to the *ratio decidendi* (the reasons for the decision in the operative part) in other EU Member States. A more modest CJEU concerned to follow the guidance available from the Jenard Report and its earlier case law would have followed the advice of the Austrian and Swiss Governments in *Gothaer*[262] and given the foreign judgment the 'effect' that it enjoys in the State where it was rendered.

b. Article 34

1. Public Policy (Article 34(1)) and Improper Service (Article 34(2))

In C-283/05 *ASML Netherlands BV v Semiconductor Industry Services GmbH (SEMIS)*,[263] the CJEU interpreted whether, under Article 34(2), the condition that it must be 'possible', within the meaning of that provision, to commence proceedings to challenge the default judgment in respect of which enforcement is sought, requires that the judgment should have been duly served on the defendant, or whether it is sufficient that the latter should have become aware of its existence at the stage of the enforcement proceedings in the State in which enforcement is sought. The CJEU decided that only knowledge by the defendant of the contents of the default judgment guarantees, in accordance with the requirements of respect for the rights of defence and the effective exercise of those rights, that it is possible for the defendant, within the meaning of Article 34(2), to commence proceedings to challenge that judgment before the courts of the State in which the judgment was given. That conclusion cannot call into question the effectiveness of the amendments made by Article 34(2) to the equivalent provisions in Article 27(2) of the Brussels Convention. As AG Léger has pointed out, in paragraphs 58 and 60 of his Opinion,[264] Article 34(2) is intended, in particular, to prevent a defendant from waiting for the recognition and enforcement proceedings in the State in which enforcement is sought in order to claim infringement of the rights of defence, when it had been possible for him to defend his rights by bringing proceedings against the judgment concerned in the State in which the judgment was given. Article 34(2) does not mean, however, that the defendant is required to take additional steps going beyond normal diligence in the defence of his rights, such as those consisting in

---

[261] See eg E Torralba-Mendiola and E Rodriguez-Pineau, 'Two's Company, Three's a Crowd: Jurisdiction, Recognition and *Res Judicata* in the European Union' (2014) 10 *Journal of Private International Law* 403.
[262] See para 65 of the AG's Opinion.
[263] [2006] ECR I-12041 (First Chamber) ('ASML').
[264] EU:C:2006:617.

becoming acquainted with the contents of a judgment delivered in another Member State. The judgment was in line with the AG's Opinion and it was delivered in 17 months.

The First Chamber, in *ASML*, clarified that under the Regulation the observance of the 'rights of defence' of a defendant in default of appearance is ensured by a double review. In the original proceedings in the State in which the judgment was given, it follows from the combined application of Article 26(2) of Brussels I and Article 19(1) of the Service Regulation,[265] that the court hearing the case must stay the proceedings so long as it is not shown that the defendant has been able to receive the document which instituted the proceedings or an equivalent document in sufficient time to enable him to arrange for his defence, or that all necessary steps have been taken to this end. If, during recognition and enforcement proceedings in the State in which enforcement is sought, the defendant commences proceedings against a declaration of enforceability issued in the State in which the judgment was given, the court hearing the action may find it necessary to examine the ground for non-recognition or enforcement in relation to default judgments provided for in Article 34(2) of Brussels I.[266] Even though the declaration of enforceability has been abolished by Brussels Ia the system of double review still exists (see Articles 28(2) and 45(1)(b) and 46).

The CJEU, in C-283/05 *ASML*, has read into the Brussels I Regulation a requirement that the defendant is served with the default judgment before that judgment can be enforced in another Member State. The First Chamber did so in order to give further protection to the rights of the defence. AG Léger would have gone further and imposed a duty on the person seeking enforcement of a judgment to inform the defendant of the remedies that are available in the country that granted the default judgment to challenge it.[267] The CJEU did not deal with these suggestions and also did not clarify whether the default judgment has to be translated if it is written in a language that the recipient cannot understand. Recital 32 and Article 43 of Brussels Ia shows that service of the default judgment will always be necessary under Brussels Ia no later than when the certificate provided for under Article 53 of the Regulation is served on the defendant. Brussels Ia also clarifies the right of the person against whom enforcement is sought to ask for a translation of the judgment if it is in a language he does not understand and is not an official language in the place in the State where he is domiciled and the fact that pending receiving such a translation only provisional measures can be taken against him.[268]

In C-420/07 *Apostolides*,[269] the CJEU also interpreted both public policy and improper service grounds. Regarding the public policy ground, the question was whether the fact that a judgment given by the courts of a Member State (in this case Cyprus) concerning land situated in an area of that State over which its Government does not exercise effective control (in this case the northern area) cannot, as a practical matter, be enforced where the land is situated constitutes a ground for refusal of recognition or enforcement under

---

[265] Reg (EC) No 1393/2007 of the European Parliament and of the Council of 13 November 2007 on the service in the Member States of judicial and extrajudicial documents in civil or commercial matters (service of documents), and repealing Council Reg (EC) No 1348/2000 [2007] OJ L324/79.

[266] See also the reference to Arts 26(2) and 34(2) of Brussels I in a decision on the Service Reg by the Grand Chamber in C-443/03 *Leffler* at para 68.

[267] See paras 67–68 of the AG's Opinion.

[268] See Beaumont and Walker, n 257 above, 40–41.

[269] See also s II.A.i above and s II.D.i.c below.

Article 34(1). The CJEU noted that the referring court did not refer to any fundamental principle within the UK legal order which the recognition or enforcement of the judgments in question would be liable to infringe. It observed that in the absence of such a principle, no refusal to recognise the judgments under Article 34(1) would be justified on the ground that they concern the land in the northern area where the Cyprus government does not exercise effective control. It noted that such a fact could be relevant under Article 38(1). But, it found that the judgments are not totally unenforceable in the Member State of origin. It observed that the fact that claimants might encounter difficulties in having judgments enforced in the northern area cannot deprive them of their enforceability and, therefore, does not prevent the courts of the Member State in which enforcement is sought from declaring such judgments enforceable. Regarding the improper service ground, the question was whether the recognition or enforcement of the default judgment may be refused under Article 34(2) by reason of the fact that the defendant was not served with the document instituting the proceedings or with an equivalent document in sufficient time and in such a way as to enable him to arrange for his defence, where he was able to commence proceedings to challenge that judgment before the courts of the Member State of origin. The CJEU observed that Article 34(2) does not necessarily require the document which instituted the proceedings to be duly served, but does require that the rights of the defence are effectively respected. It was common ground that the Orams commenced such proceedings in the Member State of origin to challenge the default judgment, so the CJEU held that Article 34(2) cannot legitimately be relied upon. The judgment was given in 19 months and was in line with the Opinion of AG Kokott.

There are two interesting issues to examine in C-420/07 *Apostolides*.[270] First, the condition in Article 3(1) of Brussels I (Article 39 of Brussels Ia) that a judgment is 'enforceable' in the State of origin does not require that it can be 'enforced' there at all but rather only that it is legally enforceable. In this case, it is very doubtful whether the Orams had any assets in the part of Cyprus that is effectively controlled by the Cypriot Government and therefore it was only enforceable there in law (and in theory) but could not be enforced there. Second, the Commission raised in the case the possibility that enforcing the Cypriot judgment in this case might be contrary to international public policy because of the harm it could do to the chances of resolving the de facto split in Cyprus between the recognised Government in the south and the unrecognised Government in the north. However AG Kokott rejected this submission in this case,[271] partly because it is not clear whether or not the recognition of the Cypriot judgment by the courts in the UK would harm attempts at reconciliation of the two parts of Cyprus. Although the CJEU did not comment on the point, the English Court of Appeal, in deciding the case after receiving the preliminary ruling from the CJEU, also rejected the argument based on international public policy.[272]

C-619/10 *Trade Agency Ltd v Seramico Investments Ltd*[273] was referred to the CJEU in Latvian proceedings concerning the recognition and enforcement in Latvia of a judgment

---

[270] For a careful analysis of this decision and of the follow up decision in the English Court of Appeal, see P Beaumont and E Johnston, 'Can *Exequatur* be Abolished in Brussels I whilst Retaining a Public Policy Defence?' (2010) 6 *Journal of Private International Law* 249, 256–59.

[271] See paras 101–12 of the AG's Opinion.

[272] See Pill LJ in [2010] EWCA Civ 9, paras 58–66 and Lloyd LJ at para 118.

[273] EU:C:2012:531 (First Chamber) ('Trade Agency').

delivered by the UK High Court where the defendant relied on Articles 34(1) and (2). The referring court asked two questions of the CJEU. The first question was where the defendant brings an action against the declaration of enforceability of a judgment accompanied by the certificate, claiming that he has not been served with the document instituting the proceedings, whether the court of the Member State hearing the application for enforcement has to check, under Article 34(2), whether the information in the certificate is consistent with the evidence as regards service on the defendant. The CJEU interpreted Article 34(2) by considering the wording and aim of the provision, and took account of Recitals 16 and 17. Reaffirming C-139/10 *Prism Investments*,[274] it observed that at the first stage of the application in Article 41, the authorities of the Member State in which enforcement is sought must not carry out any assessment of the elements of fact and law of the case decided by the judgment, enforcement of which is sought. However, at the second stage when the declaration of enforceability is served on the defendant, the declaration may be the subject of dispute brought by the defendant under Article 43 based on the grounds set out in Articles 34 and 35. It reaffirmed C-283/05 *ASML* that at that stage the ground in Article 34(2) aims to ensure that the rights of defence of a defendant in default of appearance delivered in the Member State of origin are observed by a double review. Agreeing with AG Kokott,[275] it found that the fact that the foreign judgment is accompanied by the certificate cannot limit the scope of the assessment to be made pursuant to the double control, by the court of the Member State in which enforcement is sought, once it examines the ground in Article 34(2). Thus, the court has to verify that the information in that certificate is consistent with the evidence. The second question was whether a judgment given in default of appearance, which disposes of the substance of the case but which does not contain any assessment of the subject matter or the basis of the action and which is devoid of any argument on the merits thereof, may be refused under Article 34(1) due to the public policy ground that it infringes the right of the defendant to a fair trial under Article 47 of the EU Charter on Fundamental Rights. After confirming the exceptional nature of the public policy ground and citing C-341/04 *Eurofood* and C-394/07 *Gambazzi*, the CJEU agreed with the AG and held that the court may to do so only if it appears to it, after an overall assessment of the proceedings and in the light of all the relevant circumstances, that the judgment in question is a manifest and disproportionate breach of the defendant's right to a fair trial referred to in Article 47(2) of the Charter, on account of the impossibility of bringing an appropriate and effective appeal against it. The CJEU gave its judgment in 20 months.

Under Article 34(2) of Brussels I, unacceptable service in the court of origin is not enough to justify non-recognition and enforcement of the resulting judgment if the defendant had an adequate and timely opportunity to appeal against the judgment in the court of origin. AG Kokott, in C-619/10 *Trade Agency*, was of the view that if under English law the appeal against the default judgment could still be brought in England and Wales after the defendant was served with the default judgment during the recognition and enforcement proceedings in Latvia, then any inadequacies in the original service in the English proceedings do not justify a refusal to recognise and enforce the English judgment under Article 34(2) of

---

[274] C-139/10 *Prism Investments BV v Jaap Anne van der Meer* [2011] ECR I-09511 (Fourth Chamber) ('Prism Investments').
[275] See the AG's Opinion, EU:C:2012:247.

Brussels I. On the public policy defence to recognition and enforcement under Article 34(1) of Brussels I, the First Chamber emphasised that the defendant needs to be able to bring an appeal against the default judgment in the State of origin and therefore that judgment must, in principle, be sufficiently reasoned to make an appeal possible. It acknowledged the advantages of procedural efficiency if courts are able to issue default judgments by relying on the claims of fact and law made by the claimant in his submissions to the court. However, it left the national court to check if the English claim form (giving the claimant's reasons why it believed it was entitled to a remedy) was simply endorsed by the English court in its default judgment and if so, provided the defendant was served with that claim form and the defendant was able to appeal against the default judgment in England, there would be no breach of public policy.

In C-302/13 *flyLAL-Lithuanian Airlines*,[276] one of the questions that the CJEU dealt with was whether the failure to give reasons regarding the determination of the amount of the sums concerned by the provisional/protective measures granted by the judgment or the invocation of serious economic consequences constitute a ground to refuse the judgment's recognition on the basis of public policy under Article 34(1). After referring to its judgment in C-619/10 *Trade Agency*, the CJEU observed that there was no lack of reasoning, the parties had the opportunity to bring an action against the decision in Lithuania and they exercised that option, and thus the basic principles of a fair trial were respected. Regarding the consequences, by agreeing with AG Kokott, that public policy seeks to protect interests expressed through a rule of law, and not purely economic interests, the CJEU found that the mere invocation of serious economic consequences does not constitute an infringement of the public policy of the Member State in which recognition is sought. This was a strict interpretation of the public policy ground consistent with its nature. Both the Third Chamber[277] and AG Kokott[278] wisely left open the question whether public policy could have been invoked to refuse to recognise and enforce a foreign judgment when it not only had the effect of freezing assets but actually required the transfer of assets from one party to another. AG Kokott also wisely referred to 'interests expressed in a rule of law' (to include economic interests that society recognises through a legal provision)[279] rather than the narrower formulation employed by the Third Chamber 'legal interests which are expressed through a rule of law',[280] even though the Third Chamber at this point was purporting to follow the AG's Opinion.

C-681/13 *Diageo Brands BV v Simiramida-04 EOOD*,[281] concerning the public policy ground in Article 34(1), was referred to the CJEU in Dutch proceedings between Diageo Brands BV (which is the proprietor of the trade mark of the whisky brand of Johnny Walker having its registered office in the Netherlands and which places that brand of whisky on the market in Bulgaria through a local exclusive importer) and Simiramida (which is established in Bulgaria and trades in alcoholic beverages) in relation to a claim for damages made by Simiramida for the injury caused to it by a seizure carried out at the request of

---

[276] See s II.A.i and s II.C.v.b above.
[277] See paras 57–58 of the judgment.
[278] See paras 88–89 of the AG's Opinion.
[279] See ibid see para 84.
[280] See para 56 of the judgment.
[281] EU:C:2015:471 (First Chamber).

Diageo of goods which were intended for Simiramida. The allegation was that the Bulgarian court judgment holding the seizure to be unlawful cannot be recognised in the Netherlands on the ground that it is manifestly contrary to public policy in the Netherlands, within the meaning of Article 34(1) of Brussels I, due to the Bulgarian court's manifest misapplication of EU law. The CJEU held that the fact that a judgment given in a Member State is contrary to EU law does not justify that judgment's not being recognised in another Member State on the grounds that it infringes public policy in that State where the error of law relied on does not constitute a manifest breach of a rule of law regarded as essential in the EU legal order and therefore in the legal order of the Member State in which recognition is sought or of a right recognised as being fundamental in those legal orders. The CJEU further held that that is not the case of an error affecting the application of a provision such as Article 5(3) of Directive 89/104/EEC.[282] The CJEU decided that save where specific circumstances make it too difficult or impossible to make use of the legal remedies in the Member State of origin, the individuals concerned must avail themselves of all the legal remedies available in that Member State with a view to preventing a breach of public policy before it occurs. This is particularly so where the alleged breach of public policy stems from an alleged infringement of EU law. The judgment was in line with the Opinion of AG Szpunar.[283]

2. Irreconcilable Judgments Involving the Same Cause of Action and Between the Same Parties (Article 34(4))

In C-157/12 *Salzgitter Mannesmann Handel GmbH v SC Laminorul SA*,[284] the CJEU was asked whether Article 34(4) also covers irreconcilable judgments given by the courts of the same Member State. The case was referred to the CJEU in German proceedings brought between Salzgitter (a company established in Germany) and Laminorul (a company established in Romania) concerning an application for a declaration of enforceability in Germany of a Romanian court judgment which Salzgitter was ordered to pay EUR 188,330 to Laminorul for a delivery of steel products. The CJEU reaffirmed its approach in C-619/10 *Trade Agency* that the provision should be interpreted according to not only its wording but also the system established by Brussels I and its objectives. In its analysis, the CJEU also considered Recitals 15–17. By agreeing with AG Wahl,[285] it observed that the wording of Article 34(4), read in the light of the notion of 'judgment' in Article 32, indicates the non-enforcement ground of the irreconcilability of judgments given in two different States. It added that this interpretation is also supported by the principle of mutual trust. It noted that the list of grounds for non-enforcement is exhaustive and according to its settled case law those grounds must be interpreted strictly and may not therefore be given, an interpretation by analogy pursuant to which judgments given in the same Member State would also be covered. Thus, it held that Article 34(4) does not apply to two irreconcilable judgments given by courts of the same Member State (ie state of origin). It was correct to interpret Article 34(4)'s grounds for refusing recognition and enforcement strictly even in this case because Salzgitter, in answer to a question by AG Wahl at the oral hearing, admitted that it

---

[282] First Council Dir 89/104/EEC of 21 December 1988 to approximate the laws of the Member States relating to trade marks, [1989] OJ L040/1.

[283] See the AG's Opinion, EU:C:2015:137.

[284] EU:C:2013:597 (Fourth Chamber).

[285] See the AG's Opinion, EU:C:2013:322.

had 'ample opportunity to contest the second judgment in Romania'.[286] AG Wahl at paragraph 39 of his opinion pointed out that the grounds for refusal of recognition under the Brussels I Regulation in relation to irreconcilable judgments do not require both judgments to be enforceable, provided that they entail legal consequences that are mutually exclusive.

c. Article 35

In C-420/07 *Apostolides*,[287] one of the questions the CJEU dealt with was whether Article 35(1) authorises the court of a Member State to refuse recognition or enforcement of a judgment given by the courts of another Member State concerning land situated in an area of the latter State over which that State's Government does not exercise effective control. The referring court was unsure whether the fact that the judgment concerns land in the northern area where the Cyprus Government does not exercise effective control may be regarded as an infringement of the jurisdiction rule in Article 22(1) and, therefore, justify a refusal to recognise or enforce the judgment under Article 35(1). The CJEU observed that the *forum rei sitæ* rule in Article 22(1) concerns the international jurisdiction of the Member States' courts and not their domestic jurisdiction. It stated that the fact that the land is in the northern area may possibly have an effect on the domestic jurisdiction of the Cypriot courts, but cannot have any effect for the purposes of Brussels I. It accordingly held that Article 35(1) does not authorise the court of a Member State to refuse recognition or enforcement of a judgment given by the courts of another Member State concerning land situated in an area of the latter State over which its Government does not exercise effective control.

In C-111/09 *ČPP Vienna Insurance Group*,[288] the CJEU addressed the recognition of a judgment under Article 35(1) given by a court declaring itself to have jurisdiction under Article 24 where the special jurisdiction rules in matters relating to insurance are not complied with. The CJEU stated that Article 35 concerns non-recognition of judgments given by a court without jurisdiction and it is therefore not applicable where the judgment is given by a court with jurisdiction. It found that that is true, of a court seised, even though those rules on special jurisdiction are not complied with, before which the defendant enters an appearance and does not contest that court's jurisdiction, because such a court in fact has jurisdiction under Article 24. This interpretation was clearly correct.

ii. Enforcement

a. Appeal the Decision on the Application for a Declaration of Enforceability (Article 43)

In *C-167/08 Draka NK Cables Ltd, AB Sandvik International, VO Sembodja BV and Parc Healthcare International Limited v Omnipol Ltd*,[289] the CJEU interpreted the notion of a 'party' who can appeal the decision on the application for a declaration of enforceability under Article 43(1). It was referred to the CJEU in Belgian proceedings brought by certain creditors of the Central Bank of Iraq (CBI) established in Finland, Sweden, the Netherlands, and Ireland, against another creditor of CBI, Omnipol established in the Czech Republic,

---

[286] See para 44 of the AG's Opinion.
[287] See also s II.A.i; and s II.D.i.b.1 above.
[288] See also s II.C.vi.b above.
[289] [2009] ECR I-03477 (First Chamber) ('Draka').

regarding a Belgian enforcement order authorising the enforcement of a Dutch judgment concerning Omnipol's claims against CBI. The CJEU was asked whether, under Article 43(1), a creditor of a debtor may lodge an appeal against a decision on the request for a declaration of enforceability even if he has not formally appeared as a party in the proceedings in which another creditor of that debtor applied for that declaration of enforceability. The CJEU observed that, in considering the systems of the Brussels Convention and Brussels I, Article 43(1) of Brussels I must be compared with the combined wording of Articles 36 and 40 of the Convention. After that comparison, it found that the change in wording to Article 43(1) of Brussels I had not resulted in a substantive change, and so its interpretation on the Brussels Convention relating to enforcement of decisions was still valid for the corresponding provisions of Brussels I. It cited joined Cases 9/77 and 10/77 *Bavaria Fluggesellschaft and Germanair*[290] and C-432/93 *SISRO*[291] where it had held that the principle of legal certainty and the objectives of the Brussels Convention require a uniform application of the legal concepts and legal classifications. It also cited C-414/92 *Solo Kleinmotoren*[292] and C-260/97 *Unibank*[293] where it had affirmed that the principal objective of the Brussels Convention is providing a simple and rapid enforcement procedure, whilst at the same time giving the party against whom enforcement is sought an opportunity to bring an appeal. Interpreting the enforcement procedure rules strictly, the CJEU already found in 148/84 *Deutsche Genossenschaftsbank*[294] that Article 36 of the Brussels Convention excludes procedures whereby interested third parties may challenge an enforcement order under domestic law. It thus found that the scope of the right conferred by the Belgian Civil Code on the applicants, who could not be placed on the same footing as the debtor, is irrelevant. It also recalled its finding in 148/84 *Deutsche Genossenschaftsbank* that interested third parties may contest execution by means of the procedures available to them under the law of the State in which execution is levied. It considered that the redress procedures available against a declaration of enforceability are expressly made available only to the applicant and the defendant in Recital 18. It ruled that a creditor of a debtor cannot lodge an appeal against a decision on a request for a declaration of enforceability under Article 43(1) of Brussels I if he has not formally appeared as a party in the proceedings in which another creditor of that debtor applied for that declaration of enforceability. This was a straightforward case dealt with by the CJEU quickly in 12 months, without an AG's Opinion.

b. Grounds for Refusal (Article 45)

C-139/10 *Prism Investments*, on the interpretation of Article 45(1), was referred to the CJEU in Dutch proceedings concerning enforcement in the Netherlands of a Belgian court decision ordering payment of a sum of money where Prism Investments maintained that the Belgian judgment had already been complied with in Belgium by means of a financial settlement. After underlining the rationale behind the recognition and enforcement rules expressed in Recitals 16 and 17, the CJEU affirmed C-420/07 *Apostolides* that the grounds

---

[290] [1977] ECR 1517.
[291] [1995] ECR I-2269.
[292] [1994] ECR I-2237.
[293] [1999] ECR I-3715.
[294] [1985] ECR 1981.

for revocation of the declaration of enforceability in Articles 34 and 35 are exhaustive and must be interpreted restrictively. It observed that compliance with the judgment in the Member State of origin is not one of those grounds. Agreeing with AG Kokott,[295] it also noted that the question whether or not the requirements of that financial settlement were fulfilled could require an extensive examination of the facts regarding the claim which would be difficult to reconcile with Brussels I's objectives. It also agreed that compliance with a judicial decision does not deprive that decision of its enforceable nature, or lead to its being given legal effects that it would not have in the Member State of origin, and that recognition concerns the specific characteristics of the judgment in question, without reference to the elements of fact and law in respect of compliance with the obligations arising from it. It held that Article 45 precludes the court with which an appeal is lodged under Article 43 or Article 44 from refusing or revoking a declaration of enforceability of a judgment on a ground other than those set out in Articles 34 and 35, such as compliance with that judgment in the Member State of origin. The CJEU gave a very literalistic interpretation in this case which raises the questions whether it is consistent with the Brussels I's objective to require the court to uphold a declaration of enforceability even though the judgment had been complied with in the Member State of origin and could no longer be enforced there, and whether this serves procedural economy.

The obsession with a literal construction of Article 45(1) of Brussels I is hard to justify given that a literal construction is clearly wrong. A contextual reading of Brussels I reveals that there are other grounds for denying recognition and enforcement that can be raised at the declaration of enforceability stage, eg grounds for non-recognition and enforcement of judgments laid down in a convention on 'particular matters' which is in force between the Member State of origin and the Member State addressed (see Article 71 of Brussels I) and the equivalent provision in relation to EU law 'specific matters' in Article 67 of Brussels I.

It is to be noted that in Brussels Ia the abolition of the declaration of enforceability should lead to the problem in C-139/10 *Prism Investments* disappearing as the EU grounds for refusal of enforcement and other national grounds for refusal of enforcement should be dealt with in the same proceedings.[296]

E. Transitional Provisions (Article 66)

In C-514/10 *Wolf Naturprodukte GmbH v SEWAR spol s ro*,[297] referred to the CJEU in Czech proceedings initiated in 2007 concerning the recognition and enforcement in the Czech Republic of an Austrian judgment delivered in 2003, the CJEU interpreted the temporal scope of Brussels I under Article 66. Given that the Czech Republic acceded to the EU in 2004, the referring court asked the CJEU whether, for the application of Brussels I to the recognition and enforcement of a judgment, it is necessary that Brussels I was in force both in the Member State of origin and in the Member State addressed at the time of delivery of that judgment. The CJEU agreed with AG Cruz Villalón[298] that Brussels I entered into force

---

[295] See the AG's Opinion, EU:C:2011:401.
[296] See Recital 30 to Brussels Ia and the discussion in Beaumont and Walker, above n 257, 34.
[297] EU:C:2012:367 (Third Chamber) ('Wolf Naturprodukte').
[298] See the AG's Opinion, EU:C:2012:54.

on 1 March 2002, in accordance with Article 76, however, in the territory of States which, like the Czech Republic acceded to the EU on 1 May 2004, it entered into force only on that date. The CJEU observed that Article 66(1) or (2) does not specify whether the concept of the 'entry into force' refers to the entry into force of Brussels I in the State of origin, or in the State addressed. In interpreting the concept, the CJEU considered the close link between the rules on jurisdiction and the rules on the recognition and enforcement of judgments in Brussels I, which proposes that only judgments delivered in accordance with the jurisdictional rules of Brussels I will be enforced under it. After considering its judgments in Opinion 1/03 and in 125/79 *Denilauler*[299] and taking account of the Jenard Report, the CJEU observed that the application of the simplified recognition and enforcement rules of Brussels I, which protect the claimant especially by enabling him to obtain the swift, certain and effective enforcement of the judgment delivered in his favour in the Member State of origin, is justified only to the extent that the judgment which is to be recognised or enforced was delivered in accordance with the jurisdiction rules therein. These rules protect the interests of the defendant, in particular by the special jurisdiction rules in Articles 5 to 7. It also observed that Brussels I contains certain mechanisms, eg Article 26(1) and (2), which protect the defendant's rights during the original proceedings in the State of origin, but which apply only if the defendant is domiciled in a Member State. It concluded that, in the light of the history and the scheme and purpose of Article 66, the concept of 'entry into force' must be understood as the date from which Brussels I applies in both the Member States concerned. It held that for the application of Brussels I to the recognition and enforcement of a judgment, it is necessary that at the time of delivery of that judgment Brussels I was in force both in the Member State of origin and in the Member State addressed.

The decision of C-514/10 *Wolf Naturprodukte* is a broadly sensible decision on how the transitional provision in Article 66 of Brussels I should apply to recognition and enforcement of judgments from one EU Member State in another EU Member State that only joined the EU after the original entry into force of Brussels I on 1 March 2002. By requiring that at the time of delivery of the judgment in the State of origin Brussels I must have been in force both in the State of origin and in the State addressed the Court went some way to ensuring that the rights of the defence are protected. However, perhaps AG Cruz Villalón was wise to suggest going further by requiring that, unless the specific requirements of Article 66(2) are satisfied at the time of the judgment, Brussels I already be in force in the State addressed at the time when the proceedings were instituted in the State of origin. This is the only way to guarantee that in the State of origin the Regulation's jurisdiction rules will have been applied by the courts there. If the Regulation's rules of jurisdiction are not applied in the State of origin, there is a risk that the rights of the defence provided by those rules and other provisions in the Regulation will not be guaranteed to the defendant.

F. Matters Related to Relations with Other Instruments (Articles 67–72)

The CJEU has in a number of cases interpreted the relationship between Brussels I and other instruments, particularly the Convention on the Contract for the International

---

[299] 125/79 *Bernard Denilauler tegen SNC Couchet Frères* [1980] ECR 01553 ('Denilauler').

Carriage of Goods by Road (CMR) and the Convention on the Recognition and Enforcement of Foreign Arbitral Awards (New York Convention). The interpretation of the CJEU
in the cases below indicates that the CJEU needs to re-consider its interpretation on this
issue.

i. CMR

C-533/08 *TNT Express Nederland BV v AXA Versicherung AG*[300] was referred to the CJEU in
proceedings between TNT and AXA concerning the enforcement, in the Netherlands, of a
German judgment ordering TNT to pay compensation for the loss of goods in the course
of international carriage by road. The CJEU firstly noted that the dispute between TNT and
AXA falls within the scope of both the CMR and Brussels I, and that its interpretation on
the Brussels Convention should be taken into account. The first and fifth questions were
on the applicability of the rules governing jurisdiction and recognition and enforcement
in the CMR under Article 71 of Brussels I. The CJEU observed that it is apparent from the
wording of Article 71 that the legislature provided for the application of the specialised
Conventions in the event of there being concurrent rules. It recalled that it had already
found in C-406/92 *Tatry* that the rules laid down in specialised Conventions have the effect
of precluding the application of the provisions of the Brussels Convention relating to the
same question. However, the CJEU considered some Recitals and stressed that Article 71
cannot have an effect that conflicts with the principles underlying the legislation of which
it is part. It ruled that the rules governing jurisdiction, recognition and enforcement that
are laid down by a Convention on a particular matter, such as the *lis pendens* rule set out
in Article 31(2) of the CMR, and the rule relating to enforceability set out in Article 31(3)
therein, apply provided that they are highly predictable, facilitate the sound administration
of justice and enable the risk of concurrent proceedings to be minimised and that they
ensure, under conditions at least as favourable as those provided for by the Regulation,
the free movement of judgments in civil and commercial matters and mutual trust in the
administration of justice in the EU (*favor executionis*). The CJEU held that it does not have
jurisdiction to interpret the provisions of the CMR.

It is argued in this chapter that the CJEU is wrong in C-533/08 *TNT Express Nederland*
to think that the objectives stated in some of the Recitals to Brussels I should act as a constraint on the clear will of the Union legislature to defer to specialised Conventions falling within the scope of Article 71 of Brussels I even for purely intra-EU cases. The Court
is wrong because the legislature reinforced the clear wording of Article 71 of Brussels I
with a specific Recital on this issue (ie Recital 25) that reveals the motivation of the Union
legislature and expressly gives supremacy to those Conventions over the Regulation's provisions.[301] Furthermore it is clear from the wording of Article 71(2)(a) that these specialised Conventions are intended to have special weight within the EU because a Contracting
State to such a Convention can apply the rules of jurisdiction contained therein even if the
defendant is domiciled in another EU Member State that is not a party to that Convention.

---

[300] [2010] ECR I-04107 (Grand Chamber) ('TNT Express Nederland').
[301] Recital 25 states that: '*Respect for international commitments* entered into by the Member States means that
this Regulation *should not affect conventions* relating to specific matters to which the Member States are parties.'
Emphasis added.

The issue came before the CJEU also in C-452/12 *Nipponkoa Insurance* in German proceedings between Nipponkoa Insurance (a Dutch company) and Inter-Zuid Transport concerning a payment of compensation for damage suffered in the course of international transport of goods by road. Nipponkoa Insurance and the German Government raised a preliminary point that the referred questions essentially concerned Article 31 of the CMR of which the CJEU did not have jurisdiction to interpret. Citing paragraph 63 of C-533/08 *TNT Express Nederland*, the CJEU acknowledged it had no jurisdiction to interpret Article 31 of the CMR but the referred questions concerned the interpretation of Brussels I so it had jurisdiction. Citing paragraph 54 of C-533/08 *TNT Express Nederland*, the CJEU stated that it had already answered the first question in its case law and reaffirmed that Article 71 of Brussels I precludes the interpretation of the CMR in the EU in a way that leads to results which are less favourable for achieving the sound operation of the internal market than those resulting from the provisions of Brussels I and accordingly the principles of free movement of judgments and mutual trust in the administration of justice are observed. As regards the second question, the CJEU found that Article 71 of Brussels I precludes an interpretation of Article 31(2) of the CMR according to which an action for a negative judgment in a Member State does not have the same cause of action as an action for indemnity between the same parties in another Member State. The CJEU's interpretation encourages forum shopping by carriers in international road transport damages cases to swiftly seek for a negative declaratory judgment in 'carrier friendly' jurisdictions.

The CJEU is rather disingenuous in saying, in C-452/12 *Nipponka Insurance*, that it has no jurisdiction to interpret Article 31 of the CMR and yet to then interpret Article 71 of Brussels I in a way that does not respect Recital 25 to Brussels I.[302] The CJEU is ruling that Article 31 of the CMR cannot be interpreted in a way that is inconsistent with Brussels I. This is blatant judicial activism that is completely unjustified. The EU legislature expressly decided that the jurisdiction provisions and the substantive provisions on recognition and enforcement in the specialist conventions covered by Article 71 of Brussels I (including the CMR) are not to be affected by Brussels I. The case in hand is not a conflicts of jurisdiction case because the negative declaratory judgment had already been awarded in the Netherlands before the German indemnity action was commenced. Therefore the real issue in this case should have been the recognition and enforcement of the Dutch negative declaratory judgment in accordance with the substantive provisions of the CMR rather than the substantive provisions of Brussels I. The CJEU should have seen that the German court was asking the wrong questions and should have given a much more accurate and deferential interpretation of Article 71 of Brussels I respecting the capacity of the specialist conventions falling within that provision (including the CMR) to have their own substantive rules on recognition and enforcement which are not required to be interpreted in the light of the objectives and wording of Brussels I.

In C-157/13 *Kintra*,[303] one of the questions that the CJEU dealt with was also where the dispute falls within the scope of both Brussels I and the CMR, which instrument's rules are to be applied. After stating that it is for the referring court to determine whether the carriage services in question meet the conditions for application of the CMR, the CJEU

---

[302] Recital 25 was cited in para 6 of the judgment but not referred to in the Third Chamber's reasoning.
[303] See also s II.A.ii.b above.

referred to its previous interpretation of Article 71 of Brussels I and noted that the CMR is covered by that provision and therefore has, in principle, the effect of precluding the application of provisions of Brussels I relating to the same question. The CJEU held that where a dispute falls within the scope of both Brussels I and the CMR, according to Article 71(1) of Brussels I, a Member State may apply the jurisdiction rules in Article 31(1) of the CMR.

It is alarming that the CJEU plays a dangerous game with the obligations of the Member States to comply with the specialised Conventions and their entitlement to do so under Article 71 of Brussels I by subjecting it to a rather vague test set out in paragraph 38 of the C-157/13 *Kintra* judgment. In this case, the test was met as the CMR rules of jurisdiction were not very much broader than the equivalent rules in Brussels I but it is argued in this chapter that it is not for the CJEU to make such comparisons as the Member States have given priority to the rules of jurisdiction in specialised conventions by the clear wording of Article 71 of Brussels I and have not modified that clarity in Brussels Ia in the light of earlier CJEU case law. The path embarked upon by the CJEU shows a lack of respect for international law, for the will of the legislative institutions of the EU and for the principle of legal certainty as the application of the jurisdiction rules in specialised conventions is subject to the whim of the CJEU.

ii. New York Convention

The relationship between Brussels I and the New York Convention was addressed by the CJEU in C-536/13 *Gazprom*.[304] The CJEU noted that the New York Convention does not relate to a 'particular matter' within the meaning of Article 71(1) of Brussels I since that article governs only the relations between Brussels I and conventions dealing with particular matters within the scope of Brussels I (see now Recital 12 to and Article 73(2) of Brussels Ia).

III. Interpretation of the Rules on the Law Applicable to Contractual Obligations Under the Rome I Regulation

The CJEU case law dataset of EUPILLAR includes one case on Rome I. C-396/13 *Sähköalojen ammattiliitto ry v Elektrobudowa Spółka Akcyjna*[305] on the relationship between Rome I and Directive 96/71 concerning the posting of workers in the framework of the provision of services[306] was referred to the CJEU in Finnish proceedings in relation to the pay claims arising out of employment relationships. Although the referring court asked for guidance in relation to the law applicable to the assignment of pay claims under Article 14 of Rome I, the First Chamber did not deal with this issue directly. It only decided that the governing law of the standing of the trade union to bring proceedings on behalf of the posted workers before the referring court is Finnish procedural law according to the principle of the *lex fori*.

---

[304] See also s II.A.ii.c above.
[305] EU:C:2015:86 (First Chamber).
[306] [1997] OJ L18/1.

The judgment is not in line with the Opinion of AG Wahl.[307] Indeed, the AG's Opinion is much more interesting in explaining the relationship between the two instruments.[308] The AG took the view that Article 3(1) of Directive 96/71 is a special conflict-of-law rule relating to contractual obligations in relation to particular matters within the meaning of Article 23 of Rome I.[309] Article 3(1) of Directive 96/71 makes the law applicable to certain mandatory rules mentioned in the Directive (including minimum rates of pay) the place where the worker is posted to (in this case Finland) which applies regardless of the fact that the employment contract is governed by the law of another country (in this case Poland). The assignability of these mandatory rule based claims governed by Finnish law is also governed by Finnish law by virtue of Article 14(2) of Rome I.[310] The AG was helped in reaching this conclusion by Recital 23 of Rome I because posted workers are 'weaker parties' who can benefit from special conflict-of-law rules.[311]

IV. Interpretation of the Rules on the Law Applicable to Non-contractual Obligations under the Rome II Regulation

The CJEU case law dataset of EUPILLAR includes three cases on Rome II and as will be individually assessed below, the CJEU has given very helpful interpretations in all of them.

C-412/10 *Deo Antoine Homawoo v GMF Assurances SA*,[312] the first preliminary ruling request that the CJEU received on Rome II, concerned the interpretation of the scope *ratione temporis* of Rome II under its Articles 31 and 32 in combination with Article 297 TFEU.[313] It was referred to the CJEU in English proceedings commenced on 8 January 2009 for personal injury and indirect damages sustained as a result of a road traffic accident which had occurred on 29 August 2007. Agreeing with AG Mengozzi,[314] the Fourth Chamber ruled that on the basis of Articles 31 and 32, Rome II applies only to events giving rise to damage occurring after 11 January 2009 (ie Rome II's date of entry into force pursuant to Article 297 TFEU) except for Article 29. Thus, it is the only time to be considered by the national courts in determining the scope *ratione temporis* of Rome II. The CJEU arrived at this result by interpreting Rome II in the light of its Recitals (6, 13, 14 and 16) and its objective (predictability, legal certainty and uniform application), which was an excellent interpretation.

C-240/14 *Eleonore Prüller-Frey v Norbert Brodnig and Axa Versicherung AG*,[315] on the interpretation of inter alia Article 18 of Rome II and Article 67 of Brussels I, was referred

---

[307] See the AG's Opinion, EU:C:2014:2236.
[308] See ibid, paras 40–57.
[309] See ibid, paras 50–51.
[310] See ibid, paras 56 and 57.
[311] See ibid, para 53.
[312] [2011] ECR I-11603 (Fourth Chamber) ('Homawoo').
[313] Consolidated version of the Treaty on the Functioning of the European Union [2012] OJ C326/47.
[314] See the AG's Opinion, EU:C:2011:546.
[315] EU:C:2015:567 (First Chamber) ('Prüller-Frey').

to the CJEU in Austrian proceedings in relation to compensation for damage sustained as the result of an air accident in Spain. The First Chamber gave a judgment in line with the Opinion of AG Szpunar[316] and ruled that a person who has suffered damage is entitled to bring a direct action against the insurer of the person liable to provide compensation under Article 18 of Rome II, where such an action is provided for by the law applicable to the non-contractual obligation, determined in accordance with Article 4 of Rome II, regardless of the provision made by the law that the parties have chosen as the law applicable to the insurance contract. The question on Brussels I was dependent on the applicability of the 1999 Montreal Convention[317] to the case. Since the CJEU found that the Montreal Convention was not applicable to the case, it decided that there was no need to answer this question.

C-350/14 *Florin Lazar v Allianz SpA*[318] is a very interesting preliminary ruling on Article 4(1) of Rome II referred to the CJEU in Italian proceedings which raised the question whether the damage sustained by the close relatives of a person who died in a road traffic accident constitutes 'damage' or 'an indirect consequence of a tort or delict' under Article 4(1) of Rome II. Agreeing with AG Wahl,[319] the CJEU found that it must be classified as 'indirect consequences' of the accident under Article 4(1) of Rome II. The CJEU gave a correct interpretation in this case that ensures the foreseeability and legal certainty as to the damage suffered by the close relatives of the deceased in personal injury cases. Recitals 16 and 17 to Rome II and the Commission's Proposal for Rome II were helpful tools for the CJEU in reaching this decision. AG Wahl made an important point that it is clear from the *travaux préparatoires* for Rome II that the Council and Commission rejected the European Parliament's attempts to introduce greater flexibility into Rome II for the applicable law in relation to traffic accidents and kept Article 4(1) as the rule in such cases.[320] He also gives the correct interpretation to Recital 33 to Rome II, which was introduced at the insistence of the European Parliament in the conciliation committee, as being no more than a 'request' to the court hearing the case, 'as far as possible' to 'take into account' in 'assessing damage suffered by persons who are not resident in the country where the fatal accident occurred, differences in the standard of living and the expenses actually incurred or borne by those victims in their country of residence.'[321] The applicable law will determine the amount of damages awarded and all that Recital 33 does is request that as far as that applicable law allows the judge should take into account the actual losses of victims in their country of residence and any future losses based on the standard of living there. In a much more obiter comment, AG Wahl hints at a relatively wide interpretation of the escape clause in Article 4(3):

[t]he rule laid down in Article 4(1) of the Rome II Regulation can be disregarded under Article 4(3) of that regulation where it produces unreasonable results, in favour of the law of the country with which the situation in question is manifestly most closely connected. That escape clause makes it possible, for example where the person liable and the person sustaining damage do not have their habitual residence in the same country, to apply the law of the country which is considered to be the centre of gravity of the situation at issue. Such a clause would prove its usefulness if it were

---

[316] See the AG's Opinion, EU:C:2015:325.
[317] Convention for the Unification of Certain Rules for International Carriage by Air.
[318] EU:C:2015:802 (Fourth Chamber) ('Florin Lazar').
[319] See the AG's Opinion, EU:C:2015:586.
[320] ibid para 26.
[321] ibid para 82.

established, for example, that, unlike the situation at issue in the main proceedings, the residence of the immediate victim of the accident, the residence of the person presumed to be responsible or any other circumstance surrounding the occurrence of that accident are outside the country in which the accident occurred and relate to another country.[322]

However, although Article 4(3) can be used to correct injustice in individual cases the focus of the assessment is on establishing whether a particular law has a manifestly closer connection with the tort as a whole, not just those victims concerned with the indirect consequences of the tort, than with the law of the place of damage (Article 4(1)) or the law of the common habitual residence of the person claimed to be liable and the person sustaining damage. Properly applied Article 4(3) will not be resorted to very often. This has the benefit of upholding the legal certainty and predictability of the rules in Article 4(1) and (2) and of helping to keep down the costs of insurance (not least by keeping down the amount of litigation and the costs associated with it).

V. Conclusion

From the entry into force of Brussels I in March 2002 until December 2015, the CJEU interpreted the Brussels I, Rome I and Rome II Regulations in 78 relevant cases. As the analysis in this chapter demonstrates, in this period of time covering 13 years, the approach that the CJEU followed changed from time to time. In some cases, the CJEU followed a literalistic and strict approach whereas in other cases its approach was rather broad or sometimes vague. There are certain issues where the CJEU reviewed its existing interpretation and changed it where necessary when it had the opportunity to do so with new preliminary rulings.

However, in general, it can be concluded that the CJEU has done a reasonably good job. In its judgments the CJEU has referred to travaux préparatoires, recitals to the regulations and the explanatory reports[323] in ascertaining the intention of the EU legislature when interpreting these Regulations.[324] Some judgments are excellent examples of literal, historical, contextual and purposive interpretation to resolve the problem, notably C-533/07 *Falco*, C-87/10 *Electrosteel*, C-190/11 *Mühlleitner*, C-154/11 *Mahamdia*, C-47/14 *Holterman*, C-438/12 *Weber*, C-616/10 *Solvay*, C-322/14 *CarsOnTheWeb*, C-112/13 *A v B and Others* and C-144/10 *Berliner* on Brussels I and C-412/10 *Homawoo* and C-350/14 *Florin Lazar* on Rome II. In the majority of cases, the CJEU's interpretations are helpful. On the other

---

[322] ibid para 81 (footnote omitted).

[323] On the interpretation tools, see also Ch 3 by B Yüksel.

[324] However, some interviewees connected with the legislative institutions of the EU, stated that they have the impression that sometimes the Court first looks and tries to find a result and then it justifies that result with the interpretation tools and cite them so long as they are helpful for this justification: EUPILLAR_EU 10, EUPILLAR_EU 11. Another interviewee stated that, in terms of the interpretation tools, the Court relies on what it needs to rely on in order to get to a result but the reason for which is not always clearly declared: EUPILLAR_EU 14. EUPILLAR_EU 15 is in the same line by stating that 'It is traditional to say they look at the spirit, scheme and context and the wording and all the rest of it and they certainly do. These magic formulae are recited and then the Court may do something completely different in order to reach what it wishes to do.' EUPILLAR_EU 16 is also in the same line.

hand, there are a number of cases where the CJEU has given controversial interpretations with which the present authors do not agree, or do not agree in full, particularly C-406/09 *Realchemie Nederland*, C-185/07 *West Tankers*, C-204/08 *Rehder*, C-103/05 *Reisch Montage*, C-98/06 *Freeport*, C-145/10 *Painer*, C-327/10 *Hypoteční banka*, C-456/11 *Gothaer*, C-386/05 *Color Drack*, C-292/10 *G*, C-297/14 *Hobohm*, C-9/12 *Corman-Collins*, C-19/09 *Wood Floor Solutions*, C-139/10 *Prism Investments*, and joined cases C-509/09 and C-161/10 *e-Date Advertising*. In addition, the cases concerning the relationship between Brussels I and international instruments, particularly CMR, demonstrate that the CJEU needs to re-consider its interpretations in future preliminary references to give more respect to the will of the EU legislature by abiding by the international treaties that Member States are bound by.

The case law analysis indicates that the Court follows the AG's Opinion in a large number of cases and in this sense the Opinions of the AGs are very influential.[325] There are also a number of the cases where the present authors believe that the CJEU reached an incorrect interpretation but it could have been averted or ameliorated by better use of the AG's Opinion including C-145/10 *Painer*, C-87/10 *Electrosteel*, C-406/09 *Realchemie Nederland*, C-386/05 *Color Drack*, the joined cases C-509/09 and C-161/10 *eDate Advertising*, C-103/05 *Reisch Montage*, C-98/06 *Freeport*, C-412/10 *Hobohm* and C-327/10 *Hypoteční banka*, In a number of cases the CJEU's interpretation was acceptable but could have been better with greater use of the AG's Opinion such as C-49/12 *Sunico and others*, C-514/10 *Wolf Naturprodukte* and C-396/13 *Sähköalojen*. The standard of the AG's Opinions in the cases analysed is generally very good and there are only a few cases where more could reasonably be expected from them particularly C-185/07 *West Tankers*, C-381/08 *Car Trim* and C-133/11 *Folien Fischer*. In nearly all the cases where the CJEU decided to dispense with an AG's Opinion this caused no harm but it would have been better had an AG's Opinion been given in C-204/08 *Rehder* and C-548/12 *Brogsitter*.

Usually the CJEU's decisions on the number of judges to hear the cases were appropriate but sometimes cases raising important issues of principle with significant commercial effects were dealt with by too few judges (three in C-9/12 *Corman-Collins* and C-548/12 *Brogsitter* and five in C-133/11 *Folien Fischer*) and likewise in relation to the outer limit of the scope of Brussels I as it impinges on national legislative competence (five in C-292/10 *G* and C-327/10 *Hypoteční banka*).

---

[325] See Ch 3 by B Yüksel.

34

Legal Certainty and Predictability in the EUPILLAR Project's Regulations: An Assessment

CARMEN OTERO GARCÍA-CASTRILLÓN

I. Introduction

The EUPILLAR Project reflects on the development of the European Union (EU) Civil Justice framework through the analysis of the implementation of certain Private International Law (PIL) Regulations by the national courts and the judgments of the Court of Justice of the European Union (CJEU). Both national courts and the CJEU are indispensable agents in the progressive creation of the already considerably evolved area of civil justice. National courts daily administer justice through the application of EU norms playing a crucial institutional role for the EU while the CJEU slowly over time provides a uniform interpretation of these norms. The obviousness of the essential role played by legal certainty in the creation of the EU Civil Justice framework needs no more explanation. It is also self-evident that EU PIL should help increase legal certainty and remove differences in treatment that are a consequence of national laws.[1] This paper aims to assess and reflect on the state of play of legal certainty in the EU concerning the application of the EUPILLAR project's Regulations by the courts in the EU.

II. Right to Justice and the Concepts of Legal Certainty and Predictability in the EU Legal Framework

The objective of creating a civil justice area within the EU is found in the Treaty on the Functioning of the European Union (TFEU)[2] and is an outworking of the EU value of

---

[1] See X Kramer et al, *A European Framework for Private International Law: current gaps and future perspectives*. Legal Affairs, Directorate General for Internal Policies, PE.462.487, 2012, p 75, www.europarl.europa.eu/studies.

[2] In the words of the Treaty on the Functioning of the EU (TFEU), consolidated version [2012] OJ C326, '(T)he Union shall constitute an area of freedom, security and justice with respect for fundamental rights and the different legal systems and traditions of the Member States' Art 67(1)). Regarding judicial cooperation in civil matters see Title V, ch 3 (Art 81).

justice according to the EU Treaty (Article 2) and the EU's commitment to fundamental rights through the EU Treaty (Article 6), the Charter of Fundamental Rights of the European Union (CFREU) (Article 47)[3] and as part of the general principles of EU law the special significance given to the European Convention for the Protection of Human Rights and Fundamental Freedoms (ECHR).[4] According to the jurisprudence of the European Court of Human Rights (ECtHR), legal certainty constitutes one of the fundamental aspects of the rule of law (the legality principle) on which the interpretation of the right to a fair trial has to rely.[5]

The concept of legal certainty is linked with the protection of the parties' legitimate expectations[6] on the basis of the rule of law. Its role in PIL can encompass the preservation or stability of legal situations when confronted with their internationalisation (enabling security or continuity; therefore, material certainty or acceptability of the decisions) though it is generally understood as the predictability of the results when applying legal norms.[7] Predictability is essential for any administration of justice and, therefore, for the creation of a civil justice system within the EU. However, and without abandoning the rule of law, any legal system cannot anticipate and cover every possible legal case. In addition to the eventual lacunas, when applying the norms national courts have to face the difficulties of international situations and the existence of certain ambiguities in their texts together with the constant changes in the needs of society. All this has argued in favour of a predictability dimension centred in a so-called reasonableness principle[8] under which the judges' role is to balance material justice together with parties' expectations.

EU civil judicial cooperation is trying to achieve effective access to justice in cross-border cases.[9] Conceived as part of the rule of law, it is not surprising that legal certainty or predictability are not, as such, expressly mentioned in the EU Treaties. Nevertheless, the Action Plan Implementing the Stockholm Programme mentions predictability when it refers to

---

[3] Consolidated version of the Treaty on European Union; and the Charter of Fundamental Rights of the European Union of 7 December 2000, as adopted at Strasbourg, on 12 December 2007, [2012] OJ C 326.

[4] European Convention for the Protection of Human Rights and Fundamental Freedoms, adopted at Rome, on 4 November 1950, as amended. www.echr.coe.int/Documents/Convention_ENG.pdf. ('Right to a fair trial'). The CJEU has established the 'special significance' as a 'guiding principle' for its case law of the ECHR. See C-4/73 *Nold* [1974] ECR 491 (para 13).

[5] *Beian v Romania* (no 1), no 30658/05, § 39, ECHR 2007-V; *Okyay and Others v Turkey*, no. 36220/97 § 73. ECHR 2005-VII.

[6] ECHR *Unédic v France*, no 20153/04, § 74, 18 December 2008.

[7] See, for example, E Paunio, 'Beyond Predictability—Reflections on Legal Certainty and the Discourse Theory of Law in the EU Legal Order' (2009) 10 *German Law Review* 1469; J Raitio, 'The Principle of Legal Certainty as a General Principle of EU Law' in U Berniz, J Nergelius, C Cadner (eds), *General Principles of EU Law in a Process of Development* (Alphen aan den Rijn, Kluwer, 2008).

[8] A Lowenfeld, *International Litigation and the Quest for Reasonableness* (Oxford, Clarendon Press, 1996) 229–31. Along this line, FA Mann, 'The Doctrine of International Jurisdiction Revisited after Twenty Years' (1984) 186 *Hague Collected Courses* 28–29, points that the 'principle of reasonableness ... appears unobjectionable, so long as it is understood that mere political, economic, commercial or social interests are to be disregarded when it comes to weighting which every test of reasonableness implies ... for arbitrariness is substantially the same as unreasonableness.' O Corten, 'The Notion of "Reasonable" in International Law: Legal Discourse, Reason and Contradictions' (1999) 48(3) *International and Comparative Law Quarterly* 613.

[9] See Art 81 TFEU which also contains the following objectives of particular relevance for this chapter: (c) the compatibility of the rules applicable in the Member States concerning conflict of laws and of jurisdiction and (f) the elimination of obstacles to the proper functioning of civil proceedings, if necessary by promoting the compatibility of the rules on civil procedure applicable in the Member States.

strengthening people's confidence in the EU Civil Judicial area both from the business and the personal-family perspectives.[10]

III. Legal Certainty in EUPILLAR's Project Regulations

Of the Regulations under the EUPILLAR project, only the Rome II Regulation (RIIR) (Recital 14) expressly recognises in general terms that '(T)he requirement of legal certainty and the need to do justice in individual cases are essential elements of an area of justice'.[11] Rome I (RIR)[12] and RIIR (Recital 6 in both) place their focus on the improving 'the predictability of the outcome of litigation' together with the 'certainty as to the law applicable and the free movement of judgments', for which, in the case of these Regulations, the EU needs uniform conflict-of-laws rules regarding contractual and non-contractual obligations.[13]

The Brussels Regulations (concerning jurisdiction and recognition and enforcement of judgments) give much less prominence to legal certainty and predictability in their texts. The Brussels IIa Regulation[14] (BIIaR) does not mention it at all. It only includes one mention to the 'proximity' of the jurisdiction criteria established for matters of parental responsibility (Recital 12).[15] This principle, generally associated with predictability, is absent in the rest of the Regulations. The Brussels I Regulation (BIR/BIaR) refers to predictability only in the context of the jurisdiction rules (Recital 11/Recital 15).[16] Along this line, BIaR has added that legal certainty is ensured with the special jurisdiction grounds since they are founded on the existence of a close connection that guarantees their foreseeability for the defendant (Recital 16).[17] Finally, the Maintenance Regulation mentions legal certainty and predictability as objectives that can be reached by allowing the parties to agree on the

---

[10] The Action Plan Implementing the Stockholm Programme, COM(2010) 171 final, says: 'Union law can facilitate mobility and empower citizens to exercise their free movement rights. For international couples, it can reduce unnecessary stress when they divorce or separate and can *remove the current legal uncertainty for children and their parents in cross-border situations*. It can help eliminate barriers to the recognition of legal acts and lead to the mutual recognition of the effects of civil status documents. When *citizens* drive to another Member State and are unfortunate enough to have an accident, they *need legal certainty* on the limitation periods of insurance claims', p 4; and 'Union law can help by *increasing businesses' need for legal certainty* and at the same time guaranteeing the highest level of consumer protection', p 5 (emphasis added).

[11] Reg 864/2007 [2007] OJ L199.

[12] Reg 593/2008 [2008] OJ L177.

[13] The text of the Recitals says: '[there is a need] in order to improve the predictability of the outcome of litigation, certainty as to the law applicable and the free movement of judgments, for the conflict-of law rules in the Member States to designate the same national law irrespective of the country of the court in which an action is brought.'

[14] Reg 2201/2003 [2003] OJ L338.

[15] Recital 12: 'The grounds of jurisdiction in matters of parental responsibility established in the present Regulation are shaped in the light of the best interests of the child, in particular on the criterion of proximity'.

[16] Reg 44/2001 [2001] OJ L12, superseded by Reg 1215/2012, [2012] OJ L351. 'The rules of jurisdiction should be highly predictable.'

[17] Recital 16: 'The existence of a close connection should ensure legal certainty and avoid the possibility of the defendant being sued in a court of a Member State which he could not reasonably have foreseen'.

competent court (Recital 19).[18] RIIR associates party autonomy as a choice-of-law criteria to the objective of legal certainty (Recital 31).[19]

As to the acknowledgement of the Regulations' contribution to legal certainty, it is important to note that before the adoption of RIIR there was the same choice-of-law rule in many EU Member States for non-contractual obligations—the *lex loci delicti commissi* principle—but it was not interpreted and applied uniformly. The Regulation aimed to reduce the uncertainty by unifying the choice-of-law rules in the field (Recital 15).[20] In other words, the existence of broadly the same national rules could not provide for legal certainty and the implementation of a uniform EU body of rules—including general, specific and escape norms—was meant to provide legal certainty and predictability.

The Brussels Regulations give less general relevance to legal certainty in the Recitals than the Rome Regulations, particularly RIIR, which resort to this principle more actively. Perhaps this can be explained by the fact that the Rome Regulations are subsequent in time and, therefore, more evolved, but then one would expect more references in the Recitals to Brussels Ia. Another possible explanation is the role played by the German Presidency in the Council in finalising RIIR. However, the next sections will reveal that in the CJEU case law, legal certainty and predictability arguments are made in Brussels I cases.

IV. Interpretation, Characterisation and Consistency

One cannot forget that these Regulations are to be applied by national courts as part of the EU civil justice system. In this regard, the general interpretative competence attributed to the CJEU by the preliminary ruling system (Article 267 TFEU) is a basic tool to gradually secure legal certainty and predictability in all EU courts by national courts following the rulings of the CJEU on the interpretation of the Regulations.

It is also clear that, being EU norms, the concepts used by the Regulations, though nurtured from each of the Member States' legal systems, have their own autonomous understanding. The Regulations' Recitals point to this issue[21] and their Articles facilitate definitions. The CJEU has expressly acknowledged that the autonomous concepts of the BIR jurisdiction rules, and particularly their connecting factors, constitute a means to reinforce the legal certainty objective that they pursue.[22] This assertion could be easily endorsed

---

[18] Recital 19: 'In order to increase legal certainty, predictability and the autonomy of the parties, this Regulation should enable the parties to choose the competent court by agreement on the basis of specific connecting factors.'

[19] Recital 31: 'To respect the principle of party autonomy and *to enhance legal certainty the parties should be allowed to make a choice*. This choice should be expressed or *demonstrated with reasonable certainty* by the circumstances of the case.' (emphasis added).

[20] Recital 15: 'The principle of *lex loci delicti commissi* is the basic solution for non-contractual obligations in virtually all the Member States but the practical application of the principle where the component factors of the case are spread over several countries varies. This situation engenders uncertainty as to the law applicable.'

[21] Recitals 11 and 15 (15 BIaR) BIR 'The domicile of a legal person must be defined autonomously so as to make the common rules more transparent and avoid conflicts of jurisdiction', 'the determination of the time when a case is regarded as pending. For the purposes of this Regulation that time should be defined autonomously'. Recitals 11 and 30 RIIR 'Therefore for the purposes of this Regulation non-contractual obligation should be understood as an autonomous concept'; 'Culpa *in contrahendo* for the purposes of this Regulation is an autonomous concept'.

[22] As to BIR see C-533/07, *Falco* [2009] ECR I-3327 (para 26): 'In order *to reinforce the primary objective of legal certainty* which governs the rules of jurisdiction, *that criterion of a link is defined autonomously by Regulation 44/2001 ...*' (emphasis added).

as to the rest of the PIL Regulations. However, it has been noted that, on certain occasions, the autonomous concepts provided by the Regulations are not easily transferable to Member States practice, leading to disruptive case law that prejudices predictability. For instance, there is no definition of 'domicile' in Bulgaria and, when applying BIR (Article 59), courts resort to the habitual residence concept fluctuating between the permanent and the current addresses.[23] It is also relevant noting the difficulties perceived in the use of the habitual residence concept in family litigation under BIIaR—particularly with regard to children— where the CJEU case law shows certain doubts,[24] and under the Maintenance Regulation, where the CJEU in a rather unclear and overly intrusive way attempts to place parameters on the geographical scope of habitual residence within a particular part of a Member State.[25] Interestingly, none of these cases expressly mention legal certainty or predictability.

Like the interpretative criteria established by the Vienna Convention on the Law of Treaties, the CJEU interpretative rules are based on the literal texts, their objective and general scheme, their legislative history, and their context.[26] Following this criteria, as to the EUPILLAR Regulations it is possible to conclude that the Court takes into consideration the proximity of the links to the litigious question and its foreseeability for the parties.

In addition, it is important to recall the fact that the EUPILLAR Regulations are not applied in isolation. On the contrary, it is not unusual that they are applied in combination between themselves, with other EU norms or with international treaties. For legal certainty purposes it is therefore necessary to adopt rules on their relationships and, in case there is no clearly established priority of one over another, to be aware of the need for a consistent interpretation. All EUPILLAR Regulations contain rules setting the relations among different normative instruments—EU[27] and international.[28] However, only the Rome Regulations expressly refer to interpretative consistency in relation to BIR (Recital 7).[29] Nevertheless, the CJEU has only expressly faced this issue regarding RIR. In *Andreas Kainz* the Court established that

[A]lthough it is apparent that the EU legislature sough to ensure the consistency between BIR, on the one hand, and the substantive scope and the provisions of RIR, on the other, that does not mean, however, that the provisions of BIR must for that reason be interpreted in the light of the provisions of RIR. The objective of consistency cannot, in any event, lead to the provisions of BIR being interpreted in a manner which is unconnected to the scheme and objectives pursued by that regulation.[30]

---

[23] See ch 12 above.

[24] Whilst in *Mercredi* (C-497/10 PPU EU:C:2010:829) it provides a balance between facts and custodial parents' intent, in *C v M* (C-376/14 EU:C:2014:2268) it seems to rely mostly on the existence of a provisional court decision. P Beaumont and J Holliday, *Recent Developments on the meaning of 'habitual residence' in Alleged Child Abduction Cases*, Working Paper Aberdeen Centre for Private Internacional Law, 2015/3 www.abdn.ac.uk/law/documents/ Recent_Developments_on_the_Meaning_of_Habitual_Residence_in_Alleged_Child_Abduction_Cases_.pdf.

[25] C-400/13 and C-408/13, *Sanders* and *Huber* EU:C:2014:2461 (para 47) discussed in chs 41 and 44 below.

[26] For a detailed analysis with regard to legal certainty see K Lenaerts and J Gutiérez-Fons, *To Say What the Law of the EU Is: Methods of Interpretation and the European Court of Justice.* EUI Working Papers. AEL 2013/9 AEL_2013_09_DL.pdf.

[27] Arts 67 BIR/BIaR, 68 Maintenance, 23 RIR, 27 RIIR.

[28] Arts 68–71 BIR/BIaR, 59–61 BIIaR, 69 Maintenance, 24–25 RIR, 28 RIIR.

[29] Recital 7: 'The substantive scope and the provisions of this Regulation should be consistent with Regulation 44/2001 and the instruments dealing with the law applicable to contractual / non-contractual obligations.'

[30] It is mentioned in the legal context in, C-45/13, *Andreas Kainz* EU:C:2014:7 (para 8); see also para 20.

Ultimately, the response to the doubts experienced by national courts in the application of EU Regulations is borne by the CJEU through the preliminary rulings proceeding. In one way or another, all the preliminary questions resolve difficulties in order to establish criteria that will improve predictability and certainty in the application of the rules. Consequently, this way the Court contributes to guaranteeing the right to a fair trial for any legal or individual persons subject to them. As to EUPILLAR Regulations and resorting to PIL methodology, it could be said, though it may sound simplistic, that this task fundamentally amounts to the characterisation or classification of their norms.

V. Particular Issues

The following paragraphs will address the CJEU case law where legal certainty and/or predictability have been at issue. Apart from certain cases regarding the Regulations' scope and choice of law issues, some refer to the compatibility of the Regulations' rules with other normative sources, whilst the vast majority cover jurisdiction issues. There is no relevant reference to legal certainty and/or predictability in the recognition and enforcement field.

A. The Regulations' Scope and Characterisation Issues

Determining the scope of the Regulations is essential for legal certainty. Whilst the territorial scope of the Regulations seems to be certain, their substantive and temporal scope is what has generated doubts that required the interpretation of the CJEU. In the first case, much of the Court's work entailed the characterisation of different situations in accordance with the autonomous concepts used by the Regulations.

As to the temporal scope of RIIR, the Court established in *Homawoo* that, following Article 31, the Regulation applies to events giving rise to damage occurring after 11 January 2009 since:

> [S]uch an interpretation is the only one which ensures, ... the full attainment of the Regulation's objectives, that is to say, the predictability of the outcome of litigation, legal certainty as to the law applicable and the uniform application of that regulation in all Member States.[31]

However, it has been reported that the experience of national courts, particularly Italian, shows confusion about the temporal scope of application that affect the predictability of the system.[32] Though the Court has faced questions relating to the temporal scope of BIR/BIaR, its answers have not expressly resorted to predictability or legal certainty arguments. The Court has given a number of preliminary rulings on the Regulations' substantive scope of application that, at the bottom line, entail the autonomous characterisation of the concepts. In particular, this has been the case for, among others, civil and commercial

---

[31] C-412/10, *Homawoo* EU:C:2011:747 (para 34). The referring national court, doubted if the date on which the proceedings seeking compensation for damage were brought or the date on which the applicable law was determined by the court seised have no bearing on determining the scope *ratione temporis* of the Reg.

[32] See ch 8 above.

matters,[33] contractual and non-contractual obligations,[34] maintenance obligations, domicile, parental responsibility and child abduction, etc. Although it has been reported that the doubts about these autonomous concepts and, moreover, the lack of adjustment to national legal systems affect legal certainty and predictability,[35] CJEU jurisprudence barely resorts to these principles in preliminary rulings.

For instance, regarding the material scope of the BIIaR, Advocate General Wathelet based his conclusions in *Mikolajczyk* on the predictability objective of that Regulation. The Court was asked whether matrimonial annulment proceedings initiated after the death of one of the partners were covered by the Regulation. He stated that

> the objective of BIIaR is to offer EU citizens a high level of predictability and legal clarity as to the jurisdiction, recognition and enforcement of national courts' matrimonial decisions with an international character. Excluding from its scope the matrimonial nullity proceedings in case of decease of one of the partners would be against the spirit and the objectives of this Regulation.[36]

As a general issue, some doubts have been raised as to the determination of the situations' internationality. The diversity and complexity of situations with foreign links in modern life has developed in cases where the relevance of the international element is questioned and, therefore, the application of the Regulations. At present there is a case pending before the CJEU regarding BIR.[37] This uncertainty, expressed by some national legal operators,[38] has particular incidence in French courts' experience.[39]

But it is not only the characterisation of the situations covered by the Regulations that has a significant relevance for legal certainty and predictability. The CJEU case law providing definition of concepts used to establish special jurisdiction rules is very significant, especially regarding BIR/BIaR. The Court's jurisprudence declares the existence of a contract when parties have somehow manifested their mutual consent (Article 5(1)/7(1)). In any other case litigation is to be characterised as non-contractual (Article 5(3)/7(2)). In particular, expressly relying on the legal certainty objective of the Regulation through the unification of highly predictable jurisdiction rules, the Court has established that 'an action for damages founded on an abrupt termination of a long standing business relationship is not a matter of tort if a tacit contractual relationship existed between the parties ...'.

---

[33] For example, in C-645/11, *Land Berlin* EU:C:2013:228 (para 38), it is established that the concept 'includes an action for recovery of an amount unduly paid in the case where a public body is required by an authority established by a law providing compensation in respect of acts of persecution carried out by a totalitarian regime to pay to a victim by way of compensation part of the proceeds of the sale of land has as the result of an unintentional error paid to that person the entire sale price and subsequently brings legal proceedings seeking to recover the amount unduly paid'.

[34] See above n 21 and ch 33 above.

[35] See ch 8 above.

[36] AG Opinion 16 May 2016, C-294/15, *Mikolajczyk* EU:C:2016:367 (para 30). The Court decision dated 13 October 2016 EU:C:2016:772 has confirmed this approach (paras 32–33). A third person can initiate those proceedings but Art 3(1)(a) does not apply.

[37] C-136/16, *Sociedade Metropolitana de Desenvolvimiento S.A.* removed from the register on 10 March 2017, EU:C:2017:237. For earlier decisions discussing internationality see C-327/10 *Lindner* [2011] ECR I-11543 and C-292/10 *G* EU:C:2012:142.

[38] See ch 9 above.

[39] The Cour de cassation adopted a confusing definition of the concept of internationality, holding that a sub-contract of construction was not international because, but for the German seat of one of the contracting companies, the transaction was entirely connected to France and the intention of the parties was to treat the situation as domestic. Cass civ 1, 4 October 2005, no 02-12.959. See ch 17 above.

'Demonstration of the existence of this relationship must be based on a body of consistent evidence …' and it is for the national 'referring court to ascertain whether such a body of consistent evidence exists'.[40]

B. Jurisdiction

BIR/BIaR point to the predictability of their jurisdiction links whilst BIIaR only mentions the proximity of the jurisdiction criteria provided for parental responsibility matters and Maintenance makes no reference to this issue. Nevertheless, any legislator designing jurisdiction rules boosts the connecting factors that respond to the predictability principle and, to this end, proximity is a clear input that not only helps from the perspective of the right to justice, but also for the procedural efficiency and economy.

The CJEU has mostly resorted to legal certainty and predictability arguments in the framework of BIR jurisdiction rules. Beyond the cases where the reference to these concepts is limited to recalling Recital 11 within the legal context of its final decision, the case law reflects on this principle regarding the parties' choice of court, the plurality of defendants' situations, the special jurisdiction rules and the *lis pendens* cases.

First, the CJEU has clearly stated that it is apparent from its Recitals 2 and 11 (15 BIaR) that BIR 'seeks to unify the rules of conflicts of jurisdiction in civil and commercial matters by way of rules of jurisdiction which are highly predictable'.[41] Moreover, Recital 11, together with number 12, 'sets out the relationship between the various rules of jurisdiction and their purpose'.[42] It has also stated that, overall, BIR 'pursues an objective of legal certainty' and that this objective 'consists in strengthening the legal protection of persons established in the EU, by enabling the applicant to identify easily the court in which he may sue and the defendant reasonably to foresee before which court he may be sued'.[43] Therefore 'the interpretation of BIR norms is done in order to reinforce the primary objective of legal certainty'.[44]

When interpreting the Brussels Convention, the initial references to the legal certainty principle in the CJEU decisions were not limited to the jurisdiction rules, but were expressed in general terms stating that 'the Court has repeatedly held that the principle of legal certainty is one of the objectives of the Brussels Convention'.[45]

---

[40] C-196/15 *Granarolo Spa* EU:C:2016:559 (paras 26–28). The evidence may include in particular the existence of a long-standing business relationship, good faith between the parties, the regularity of the transactions and their development over time expressed in terms of quantity and value, any agreements as to prices charged and/ or discounts granted and the correspondence exchanged.

[41] *Granarolo*, ibid (para 16); C-175/15, *Taser International Inc* EU:C:2016:176 (para 32); C-381/08, *Car Trim GmbH*, EU:C:2010:90 (para 12); C-533/07 *Falco* [2009] ECR I-3327 (paras 21 and 22), note 22; C-386/05, *Color Drack* [2007] ECR I-3699 (para 19).

[42] *Color Drack*, ibid.

[43] *Falco* above n 22 (paras 21–22); *Color Drack* above n 41 (para 20); *Car Trim GmbH* above n 41 (para 26); *Taser* above n 41 (para 32); C-103/05, *Reisch Montage* EU:C:2006:471 (paras 24–25). As to the Brussels Convention, see Case C-383/95 *Rutten* [1997] ECR I-57 (para 13) and C-295/95 *Farrell* [1997] ECR I-1683 (para 13).

[44] *Car Trim GmbH* above n 41 (para 26).

[45] Case 38/81 *Effer* [1982] ECR 825 (para 6); Case C-26/91 *Handte* [1992] ECR I-3967 (paras 11, 12, 18–19); Case C-129/92 *Owens Bank* [1994] ECR I-117 (para 32); Case C-288/92 *Custom Made Commercial* [1994] ECR I-2913 (para 18); Case C-440/97 *GIE Groupe Concorde and Others* [1999] ECR I-6307 (para 23); and Case C-256/00, *Besix SA*, EU:C:2002:99 (para 24).

Regarding preliminary issues, the Court has established that the predictability objective cannot be attained if the application of jurisdiction rules could vary 'according to whether a preliminary issue, capable of being raised at any time by one of the parties, exists, on the ground that this would alter the nature of the dispute.'[46] Therefore, jurisdiction has to be established on the basis of the initial claim and preliminary issues should be solved by that Court.

i. Defendant's Domicile

There is no doubt about the legal certainty provided by the defendants' domicile forum. Plurality of defendants' cases seised in the Member State where one of them is domiciled (Article 6(1) BIR/8(1) BIaR) do raise predictability concerns. The Court characterises this rule as a special forum that, like other special jurisdiction rules,

> must be interpreted, first, in the light of recital 11 … according to which the rules of jurisdiction must be highly predictable and founded on the principle that jurisdiction is generally based on the defendant's domicile and jurisdiction must always be available on this ground save in a few well-defined situations in which the subject-matter of the litigation or the autonomy of the parties warrants a different linking factor.[47]

Anyhow, for the plurality of defendants' forum to be applied two conditions have to be met.

First, the defendants have to be domiciled in a Member State; otherwise, the rule is not applicable to them. In *CDC*, where the Court had to face the alleged misuse of the plurality of defendants' rule due to the ulterior agreement between the claimant and the defendant domiciled in the chosen forum, there is no reference to legal certainty or predictability beyond the inclusion of Recital 11 in the decision's legal context.[48] Second, the claims have to be so closely connected that there is a risk of irreconcilable judgments resulting from separate proceedings. Whilst in some cases, as in *Land Berlin*—the only one that expressly mentions legal certainty within the legal context—the CJEU rules on the existence of this risk,[49] in others it leaves the national courts to evaluate it.[50]

Legal certainty is also considered, but only in the legal context of the Court's decision, when interpreting the jurisdiction criteria for third party proceedings (Article 6(2)) to conclude that

> it includes an action brought by a third party in accordance with national law against the defendant in the original proceedings and closely linked to those original proceedings … provided that the action was not instituted solely with the object of removing that defendant from the jurisdiction of the court which would be competent in the case.[51]

---

[46] C-144/10, *Berliner Verkehrsbetriebe (BVG)* EU:C:2011:300 (para 35).

[47] C-616/10, *Solvay* EU:C:2012:445 (para 20); C-145/10, *Painer* EU:C:2011:798 (para 75); C-98/06 *Freeport* EU:C:2007:595 (para 36).

[48] C-352/13, *Cartel Damage Claims (CDC) Hydrogen Peroxide SA* EU:C:2015:335.

[49] *Land Berlin* above n 33 (para 48).

[50] C-616/10, *Solvay* above n 47 (para 30). Without mentioning legal certainty, it states that proceedings in different Member States against companies accused of committing a European patent infringement with regard to the same products can lead to 'irreconcilable judgments'.

[51] C-521/14, *Sovag* EU:C:2016:41 (para 47). Action seeking reimbursement of compensation paid by that third party to the applicant in the original proceedings.

In addition to legal certainty and predictability, it seems clear that this approach contributes to procedural efficiency.

ii. Choice of Court

Regarding party autonomy, legal certainty in situations of express and of implied choice of jurisdiction under BIR has received attention from the Court. Article 24, the submission or implied choice rule, applies despite the existence of a previous express agreement on the jurisdiction. In this regard, citing recitals 11 and 12, in *Taser* the CJEU established that 'when there is a choice of court agreement but the claim is presented in the defendant's domicile, if he does not dispute the jurisdiction, it may stem from Article 24'. Moreover the court of the defendant's seat that has been seised is precluded from declaring that it has no jurisdiction *on its own motion*.[52] However, if a defendant domiciled in a Member State other than that of the court seised is not served with the document instituting proceedings, remains absent and the court appoints a representative *in absentia*, the establishment of the international jurisdiction of the court under Article 24 on the basis of the representative's appearance 'cannot be regarded as predictable'. In other words, in the light of Article 47 CFREU, to interpret that a court-appointed representative entering an appearance on behalf of an absent defendant amounts to an appearance being entered by that defendant 'would not be consistent with the objectives of the rules on jurisdiction'.[53]

Regarding express choice-of-jurisdiction, Article 23 'is intended to lay down itself the conditions as to form which jurisdiction clauses must meet, so as to ensure legal certainty and to ensure that the parties have given their consent'.[54] In other words, formal requirements are meant to guarantee the compliance with the substantive requirements; that is, consent and whether the choice-of-court is clear enough; both leading to predictability and legal certainty.[55] Citing Recital 11 (with and without Recital 12) in the Court's decision's legal context and, therefore, implying that the predictability requirement would be satisfied, forum selection clauses of Member States' courts included in contracts' general terms and conditions are to be admitted if certain conditions are met. In *Höszig Kft* the Court has confirmed that the existence of consent to a jurisdiction clause set in a contract's general terms and conditions requires, first, that the text of the contract signed by both parties contains an express reference—which can be controlled by a party applying normal diligence—to the general conditions including the jurisdiction clause, and, second, that those general conditions containing the jurisdiction clause were actually communicated to the other contracting party.[56] In addition, following its well-established jurisprudence,[57] it ruled that the clarity requirement is satisfied by designating the jurisdiction of the courts

---

[52] C-175/15, *Taser International Inc* above n 41 (para 36).

[53] C-112/13, *A*, EU:C:2014:2195 (paras 57 and 61).

[54] C-222/15, *Höszig Kft*. EU:C:2016:525 (para 32). As to the Brussels Convention see C-159/97, *Castelletti* EU:C:1999:142 (para 34).

[55] In Spanish jurisprudence, expressly acknowledging that the formal requirements of jurisdiction clauses are those established in BIR; that internal law cannot take precedence, and stating that those requirements are meant to provide legal certainty and to guarantee parties' consent, see, for example, Decree JM Barcelona no 78/2015, 5 March and the Supreme Court judgment of 27 May 2008.

[56] *Höszig Kft* above n 54 (para 40).

[57] Art 23 does not require that the competent court be determined on the jurisdiction clause wording alone. 'It is sufficient that the clause state the objective factors on the basis of which the parties have agreed to choose a

of a city in a Member State.[58] As to the formal requirements that provide the requested predictability and legal certainty, in *Jaouad El Majdoub*, regarding the communication by electronic means (Article 23(2)), it was established that acceptance of an electronic contract by click wrapping entails that party's consent if the system makes it possible to print and save the text of the terms and conditions of the contract before it is concluded.[59]

On whether jurisdiction clauses agreed in contracts can be relied on against third party sub-contractors, the CJEU initially distinguished between the clauses included in bills of lading for maritime transport and those in other types of contract. Whilst in the first ones the jurisdiction clause incorporated may be relied on against a third party to that contract if it has been adjudged valid between the carrier and the shipper and, by virtue of the relevant national law, on acquiring the bill of lading the third party succeeded to the shipper's rights and obligations;[60] in cases where the clause was inserted in a sales contract, the CJEU established in *Refcomp* that it cannot be used against a third party sub-buyer 'unless it is established that he has actually consented to that clause'. This decision responded to the need to assure the uniformity of the jurisdiction rules since referring to national laws in order to establish whether the clause could be used or not

> would give rise to different outcomes among the Member States liable to compromise the aim of unifying the rules of jurisdiction. ... Such a reference to national law would also be an element of uncertainty incompatible with the concern to ensure the predictability of jurisdiction which is, as stated in recital 11 in the preamble to the Regulation, one of its objectives.[61]

However, leaving aside these arguments about legal certainty, the CJEU reversed in *CDC* by stating that

> [O]nly where a party not privy to the original contract had succeeded to an original contracting party's rights and obligations in accordance with national substantive law as established by the application of the rules of private international law of the court seised of the matter could that third party nevertheless be bound by a jurisdiction clause to which it had not agreed.[62]

This approach—with case-specific requirements—has been recently followed in *Profit Investment*, where the choice-of-court was claimed by a bonds' insurer against the bonds' issuer (jurisdiction clauses inserted in prospectus).[63]

The legal certainty and predictability of BIR's application has raised concerns regarding asymmetric jurisdiction agreements. Asymmetric agreements—those where the parties have different choices and obligations—have received different consideration in a number

---

court or the courts to which they wish to submit their disputes. Those factors, which must be sufficiently precise to enable the court seised to ascertain whether it has jurisdiction, may, where appropriate, be determined by the particular circumstances of the case'. Case C-387/98, *Coreck*, EU:C:2000:606 (para 15).

[58] *Höszig Kft.* above n 54 (paras 43 and 47).

[59] C-322/14, *Jaouad El Majdoub* EU:C:2015:334 (para 40).

[60] 71/83, *Russ* EU:C:1984:217 (para 24); *Castelletti* above n 54 (para 41); C-387/98 *Coreck* above n 57 (paras 23–27).

[61] C-543/10, *Refcomp SpA* EU:C:2013:62 (para 39).

[62] *CDC* above n 48 (para 65).

[63] C-366/13, *Profit Investment Sim* EU:C:2016:282 (paras 33, 34 and 36). The requirements, that are to be verified by the national court, are: (i) validity of the jurisdiction clause in the relationship between the issuer and the financial intermediary, (ii) that the third party, by acquiring those bonds on the secondary market, succeeded to the financial intermediary's rights and obligations attached to those bonds *under the applicable national law*, and (iii) that the third party had the opportunity to acquaint himself with the prospectus containing that clause.

of Member States. Unlike Spanish Courts,[64] French courts are reluctant to enforce this type of agreement on the basis of, first, their 'potestativity' (ie the unenforceability of a contractual promise made subject to a condition precedent left to the discretion of the promisor) and, second, their lack of predictability.[65] When they have admitted them, it was because the clause provided for a limited number of alternative fora for the party that was not bound to sue in the elected court.[66] In Spain, legal certainty and predictability are understood to support the result that favours respect for party autonomy. It seems clear that, for an EU Civil Justice system it is necessary to have a common uniform response. The introduction into BIaR of a choice-of-law rule for substantive validity of a choice-of-court agreement, referring to the law of the chosen court including its private international law rules, leaves open the issue as to whether asymmetry is a question of substantive validity or a question of what constitutes a choice of court agreement falling within Article 25 of the Recast (formerly Article 23 of BIR).

As to parties' choice of non-Member States' courts (*derogation fori*), the effect of legal certainty and predictability considerations may be said to be still unclear. The CJEU has not as yet expressly resolved the issue and Member States' courts have sustained different reactions towards its acceptance in cases where a Member State Court would have jurisdiction according to BIR. In situations where the defendant challenges the Member State's courts' jurisdiction—since following *Taser* a court will not do it *ex officio* except in exclusive jurisdiction cases—in favour of that of a third State, legal certainty and predictability would require a common and autonomous response.

iii. Special and Exclusive Jurisdictions

Turning to the special jurisdiction rules, that is, those founded on the nature of the dispute, the CJEU has established that they must be interpreted restrictively and cannot give rise to an interpretation going beyond the cases expressly envisaged. This is also the case for exclusive jurisdiction criteria since 'a strict interpretation' of Article 22 BIR 'which does not go beyond what is required by the objectives pursued by it is particularly necessary because the jurisdiction rule which it lays down is exclusive'. A broad interpretation 'would be contrary, first, to one of the general aims of the regulation, laid down in recital 11 in its preamble, namely to seek to attain rules of jurisdiction that are highly predictable, and second, to the principle of legal certainty'.[67]

As to contractual disputes, Article 5(1)(b) BIR establishes rules that have the same origin, pursue the same objectives and occupy the same place in the scheme established by that Regulation.[68] The Court acknowledged that Article 5(1)(b) uses as a connecting factor 'the obligation which characterises the contract in question' and therefore, to be characterised as a contract falling within Article 5(1)(b), the characteristic obligation of the contract

---

[64] Madrid Provincial Audience Decree no 147/2013, 18 October 2013 ES:APM:2013:1988A.

[65] Cass 1ère Civ, 26 September 2012, No 11–26.022 (*Rothschild*); Cass 1ère Civ, 25 March 2015 No 13-27.264 (*Crèdit Suisse*), and Cass 1ére Civ, 7 October 2015, no 14–16.898 (*Apple*).

[66] *Conflictus legum*. In all these cases it is also questionable that French Courts assessed the substantive validity of the agreement under French *lex fori*.

[67] *Berliner* above n 46 (paras 32–33).

[68] C-9/12, *Corman-Collins* (para 32); C-19/09, *Wood Floor Solutions* [2010] ECR I-2121 (para 26); *Land Berlin* above n 33 (para 32).

must be the supply of a good or the provision of services.[69] Therefore, it is understood that this link aims towards the objective of predictability for the parties. In addition, the Court states that, to fulfil this objective, that criterion must be defined 'autonomously, in order to reinforce the objectives of unifying of the rules of jurisdiction and predictability', be it for sales or for service contracts.[70] However, with the exception of the *Falco* case,[71] the CJEU seems determined to characterise all contracts within Article 5(1)(b), even those complex contracts like distribution agreements,[72] that in the advance of a decision from the Court it would be very hard to say have a single characteristic obligation of the supply of a good or the provision of services. One therefore has to question the CJEU's commitment to predictability for parties in advance of litigation.

The Court recognises in *ÖFAB* that 'the aim of proximity in the rules of special jurisdiction laid down in Article 5(1) and (3) … based on the existence of a particularly close connecting factor between the dispute and the courts of the place where the harmful event occurred'. When the liability of a member of the board of directors or a shareholder of a company for that company's debts is claimed, the search for proximity precludes 'the determination of the court having jurisdiction being dependent on the nature of the debts of the company concerned' since this could imply 'multiplying the courts with jurisdiction to hear actions calling into question the same improper conduct'. Moreover, such an interpretation 'would not have the degree of predictability required by recital 11 in the preamble' particularly as regards a defendant who is held liable for the debts of another.[73]

As to contracts for which protective fora have been provided, a recent question referred to the CJEU mentions 'the need for predictability and legal certainty which governs the adoption of the rules on jurisdiction and enforcement of judgments in civil and commercial proceedings' in a labour law case. The question raises the interpretation of the place where the employee habitually carries out his work (Articles 19(2)–21(2) BIaR) wondering if it is comparable to that of the 'home base' defined in the Regulation used to determine which social security legislation applies to workers in the European air navigation sector.[74]

Regarding consumer contracts, predictability is referred to as an objective in assessing the requirement of the professional's activity being 'directed to' the Member State of the consumer's domicile.[75] This issue is considered among the more problematic in the application of BIR.[76] The Court has established guiding criteria in this respect that

---

[69] *Corman-Collins*, ibid (paras 34–35); *Car Trim* above n 41 (para 31); *Falco* above n 22 (para 54).

[70] *Corman-Collins SA* ibid (para 32); C-19/9; *Wood Floor Solutions*, above n 68 (para 23); C-469/12, *Krejci Lager & Umschlagbetriebs GmbH* EU:C:2013:788 (para 22); C-204/08, *Rehder*, EU:C:2009:439 (paras 33 and 36); *Car Trim* ibid (para 49); *Color Drack* above n 41 (para 23). Those objectives are the same for Art 5(1)(b) first and second indent 'since the rules of special jurisdiction provided for contracts for the sale of goods and the provision of services have the same origin, pursue the same objectives and occupy the same place in the scheme established by that Regulation'.

[71] *Falco*, above n 22.

[72] *Corman-Collins*, above n 68. See chs 33 and 36.

[73] C-147/12, *ÖFAB, Östergötlands Fastigheter AB*, EU:C:2013:490 (para 41); *Car Trim* above n 41 (para 48); and C-228/11, *Melzer* EU:C:2013:305 (para 26).

[74] C-168/16, *Nogueira, et al C Crewlink Ltd.* Pending; C-169/16, *Moreno Óscar v Ryanair Ltd.* Pending. See below s V.E.

[75] C-297/14, *Rüdiger Hobohm*, EU:C:2015:844 (para 30).

[76] See ch 7 above.

should help to provide legal certainty and predictability[77] and could be said to amount to the characterisation of the requirement. In addition, it has faced a situation where a second contract, associated to the first one, was concluded by a consumer. In this case, 'with regard to the guarantee of predictability' if the professional then proposes to conclude and does conclude another contract, which on its own does not come within the scope of the professional activity directed to the Member State of the consumer's domicile, but which is closely linked to the earlier contract which did come within the scope of that activity, that professional may reasonably expect both contracts to be subject to the same rules of jurisdiction.[78] It is for the national court to determine whether the constituent elements of that link are present.[79]

The special forum provided for non-contractual obligations (Articles 5(3)–7(2) BIaR) leads to the courts where the harmful event occurred or may occur. In *Andreas Kainz*, considering that 'rules governing jurisdiction should be predictable, in so far as both the manufacturer as defendant and the victim as applicant may reasonably foresee that those courts will be in the best position to rule on a case concerning, inter alia, the finding that the product in question is defective', it was established that in claims against the manufacturer 'the place of the event giving rise to the damage (cause) is the place where the product in question was manufactured'.[80] In *Universal Music*, in locating the place of the harmful event through the analysis of the facts of the case, the Court established that the determination of jurisdiction 'satisfies the requirements of predictability and certainty laid down by the Regulation, since the conferral of jurisdiction ... is justified for reasons of the sound administration of justice and the efficacious conduct of the proceedings'.[81]

Regarding personality rights allegedly infringed online, the determination of the place of the harm has led the Court to implement the concept of 'centre of interests' of the prejudiced person that, overall, coincides with his habitual residence. The CJEU believes that this criterion complies with the predictability required by BIR since it 'allows both the applicant easily to identify the court in which he may sue and the defendant reasonably to foresee before which court he may be sued' 'given that the publisher of harmful content is, at the time at which that content is placed online, in a position to know the centres of interests of the persons who are the subject of that content'.[82] This option is open to the claimant in respect to all the damage experienced in parallel with the possibility of resorting to the courts of each Member State where the content placed online is or has been accessible for local damages only.[83] This approach has received some criticism since it creates a *forum actoris* when previously the CJEU and the legislature have taken the view that the governing principle of *actor sequitur forum rei* should be adhered to and the exceptions to it in the special jurisdictions should be interpreted restrictively.

---

[77] C-585/08 and C-144/09, *Pammer* and *Hotel Alpenhof*, EU:C:2010:740 (paras 76–84).

[78] *Hobohm*, above n 75 (para 39).

[79] *Hobohm*, ibid (para 40). The elements are 'in particular whether the parties to both of those contracts are identical in law or in fact, whether the economic objective of those contracts concerning the same specific subject-matter is identical and whether the second contract complements the first contract in that it seeks to make it possible for the economic objective of that first contract to be achieved'.

[80] *Andreas Kainz* above n 30 (para 28).

[81] C-12/15, *Universal Music International Holding BV* EU:C:2016:449 (para 33).

[82] C-509/09 and C-161/10, *e-Date Advertising GmbH* EU:C:2011:685 (para 50); *Falco* above n 22 (para 22).

[83] *e-Date Advertising* ibid (para 52).

C. Procedural Norms

Legal certainty or predictability has not been argued in cases dealing with the control of one Member State's jurisdiction by the courts of another Member State (ie anti-suit injunctions). Famous cases such as *West Tankers, Overseas Union Insurance and Others, Turner* and *Gasser* base the exclusion of any obstruction to a Member State's exercise of its power to decide by itself on its jurisdiction, on the trust which the Member States accord to one another's legal systems and judicial institutions and on which the system of jurisdiction is based, and on the eventual risk of depriving the claimant of the judicial protection to which he is entitled.[84] The CJEU has only expressly resorted to the legal certainty reasoning when facing the *forum non conveniens* doctrine in *Owusu* concluding that, if the court having jurisdiction under the Brussels Convention was allowed to apply it, the legal certainty principle, 'which is the basis of the Convention', would be undermined.[85]

As to procedures pending in different Member States' courts, the Court established that

> it is conducive to the legal certainty sought by the Convention that, in cases of *lis pendens*, it should be determined clearly and precisely which of the two national courts is to establish whether it has jurisdiction under the rules of the Convention.[86]

In the family law area, the CJEU decision in *Aguirre Zárraga*[87] dealt with the hearing of the child in the process leading to the adoption of a return order in the courts of the habitual residence of the child in an abduction case. The intended enforcement of a decision by a Spanish court in Germany under BIIaR was questioned due to the non-hearing of the child in Spain. According to the mutual trust rule established in BIIaR the Court decided in favour of the enforceability in Germany of the Spanish order under the presumption that Member States maintain an equivalent human rights' protection. Although it was not expressly mentioned legal certainty lies at the bottom of this decision. However, this approach, which derives from the BIIaR removal of the public policy exception, has been criticised as giving more weight to legal certainty and mutual trust than to the fundamental rights of the child (Article 24 CFREU) and possibly entailing violations of the ECHR.[88]

D. Applicable Law

There is almost no express reference to predictability and legal certainty in the Court's Rome Regulations' jurisprudence. In particular, as to the choice of law in consumer

---

[84] C-185/07 *West Tankers* EU:C:2009:69 (paras 29–31); Case C-351/89 *Overseas Union Insurance and Others* [1991] ECR I-3317 (para 23); C-116/02 *Gasser* [2003] ECR I-14693 (para 48); C-159/02 *Turner* EU:C:2004:228 (para 24).

[85] C-281/02, *Owusu* [2005] ECR I-1383 (para 41).

[86] *Gasser*, above n 84 (paras 51 and 72).

[87] C-491/10, *Aguirre Zárraga* EU:C:2010:828.

[88] See eg L Walker and P Beaumont, 'Shifting the Balance Achieved by the Abduction Convention: The Contrasting Approaches of the European Court of Human Rights and the European Court of Justice' (2011) 7 *Journal of Private International Law* 231. Anyhow, ECtHR, 30 June 2005, *Bosphorus v Ireland*, no 45036/98, doctrine can mitigate the infringement risk though the presumption of compatibility of EU law with ECHR except 'if, in the circumstances of a particular case, it is considered that the protection of the ECHR was manifestly deficient'. See ECtHR 6 December 2012, *Michaud v France* no 12323/11, and 18 June 2013, *Povse v Austria* no 3890/11. For a more

contracts (Article 14 RIR), in *Verein für Konsumenteninformation* the Court only approaches the concept of predictability by mentioning, in the legal context, the 'reasonable certainty' required by Articles 10 and 14.[89]

E. Consistency and Continuity

Consistency of PIL Regulations with other legal instruments, be they EU norms or international conventions, is essential for legal certainty and predictability purposes. The existence of a plurality of EU PIL Regulations, particularly in family matters, is considered as a source of difficulties that affect legal certainty in a number of Member States.[90] Interpretation consistency between PIL Regulations themselves is particularly relevant for legal certainty since they often resort to the same or similar concepts or connecting factors. Recital 7 of both Rome Regulations expressly require a consistent interpretation as to the relationship with BIR and between themselves. Furthermore, the Court has stated that 'continuity of interpretation is, moreover, consistent with the requirements of legal certainty which dictate that the long standing case law of the court which the community legislature did not intend to alter, should not be called into question'.[91]

Though without expressly relating consistency to legal certainty or predictability, it has called the Court's special attention to the non-contractual forum of BIR (Article 5(3)/7(2) BIaR) due to its differences from Article 4 RIIR. The place of the harm covers the place of the event giving rise to the damage and the first place of damage in BIR whilst it is limited to the latter under RIIR. In *Wintersteiger* after insisting on an autonomous interpretation of the concept 'place of the event giving rise to the damage' and the search for consistency between BIR and 'the substantive scope and the provisions of' RIIR, the Court stated

> that does not mean, however, that the provisions of [BIR] must for that reason be interpreted in the light of the provisions of [RIIR]. The objective of consistency cannot, in any event, lead to the provisions of [BIR] being interpreted in a manner which is unconnected to the scheme and objectives pursued by that regulation.[92]

Therefore, certain inconsistencies may remain to fulfil the objectives of the Regulations. As long as they comply with these objectives, these inconsistencies do not have to prejudice legal certainty and predictability.

In *ERGO Insurance* the Court was asked how to interpret both Rome Regulations and Directive 2009/13/EC in order to determine the law or laws applicable to an action brought by an insurer of a tractor unit, which compensated a victim for all the harm sustained as a result of the accident involving both the tractor vehicle and the trailer coupled to it, against

---

comprehensive analysis of how the rights of the child to be heard in child abduction cases under BIIaR has been and should be handled see P Beaumont, L Walker and J Holliday, 'Conflicts of EU Courts on Child Abduction: the Reality of Article 11(6)-(8) Brussels IIa Proceedings across the EU" (2016) 12 *Journal of Private International Law* 211.

[89] C-191/15, *Verein für Konsumenteninformation* EU:C:2016:612 (paras 8 and 14).
[90] See chs 7, 8 and 9 above.
[91] *Car Trim* above n 41 (para 53).
[92] *Andreas Kainz* above n 30 (para 20).

the insurer of the trailer. The Court, relying on Recital 7 of RIR and RIIR, established that, after acknowledging that Directive 2009/103/EC does not contain any specific conflict-of-laws rule, stated that the Rome Regulations must be interpreted taking into account not only the aim of consistency in their reciprocal application but also in the application of BIR. Hence, the Court's definition of contractual and non-contractual obligations for the Rome Regulations follows what had already been established for BIR.[93]

Legal certainty and predictability is also at stake when it comes to the interaction of EUPILLAR Regulations with specialised international conventions. Furthermore, RIIR allows for the primary application of certain conventions, such as the Hague Convention on the Law applicable to traffic accidents, which is felt by some Member States as a source of uncertainty.[94]

In *TNT Express Nederland*, a case involving the Convention on the Contract for the International Carriage of Goods by Road (CMR), the Court held that even though Article 71 provides for the application of such conventions, they 'cannot compromise the … principles which underlie judicial co-operation in civil and commercial matters in the EU …'. In addition, their application cannot undermine the

> free movement of judgments in civil and commercial matters, predictability as to the courts having jurisdiction and therefore legal certainty for litigants, sound administration of justice, minimisation of the risk of concurrent proceedings, and mutual trust in the administration of justice in the European Union.[95]

This seems to lead to a case by case analysis. Hence, under this line, in *Nickel & Goeldner Spedition GmbH* the Court held that, although Article 5(1)(b) BIR offers the claimant less choice than Article 31(1) CMR, this 'fact is not such as to affect the compatibility of Article 31(1) of the CMR with principles which underlie judicial cooperation in civil and commercial matters in the EU'. The Court accepted that, in certain circumstances, the applicant may have the choice between the courts of the place of departure and those of the place of arrival. It stated that

> such a choice granted to the applicant, apart from respecting the criterion of proximity, also satisfies the requirement of predictability, in so far as it allows the applicant, as well as the defendant, easily to identify the courts before which proceedings may be brought. What is more, it is consistent with the objective of legal certainty, since the applicant's choice is limited to two possible judicial fora within the framework of the second indent of Article 5(1)(b).

To conclude, Article 71 BIR

> must be interpreted as meaning that, in a situation where a dispute falls within the scope of both the regulation and the CMR, a Member State may, in accordance with Article 71(1) of that regulation, apply the rules concerning jurisdiction laid down in Article 31(1) of the CMR.[96]

---

[93] C-359/14 and C-475/14, *ERGO Insurance SE*. EU:C:2016:40 (paras 40–45).

[94] See chs 6 and 9 above.

[95] C-533/08, *TNT Express Nederland BV* EU:C:2010:243 (para 49); C-157/13, *Nickel & Goeldner Spedition GmbH* EU:C:2014:2145 (para 38); C-452/12, *Nipponkoa Insurance Co* EU:C:2013:858 (para 36).

[96] *Nickel & Goeldner Spedition GmbH*, ibid (paras 41–42). See also ch 33 above.

VI. Conclusions

Whilst legal certainty and predictability are marginally mentioned in EUPILLAR Regulations, they are integral parts of the right to justice. The uniform interpretation of the Regulations by the CJEU is essential to comply with these principles by providing clear guidance to national courts and legal operators. Though the Court's express reference to these principles is not frequent, their unmentioned presence in the legal reasoning can often be discerned. The CJEU's interpretative contribution to characterising the concepts in the EUPILLAR Regulations is significant for generating legal certainty after their decisions which may be absent from the texts themselves. However, the CJEU must be careful not to be so keen to create legal certainty for the future that it undermines the will of the legislature or jeopardises the human rights of the people involved in the litigation.

35

Effective Remedies in Cross-border Civil and Commercial Law Disputes: A Case for an Institutional Reform at EU Level

MIHAIL DANOV AND PAUL BEAUMONT

I. Introduction

The EUPILLAR data indicate that the parties' desire to obtain an effective remedy impacts on the parties' decision whether/where to issue proceedings in cross-border cases. Central to the assessment of the effectiveness of the current EU private international law (PIL) regime, which is the foundation of the EU civil justice framework, is providing an answer to the question whether there are effective remedies[1] for private parties in civil and commercial law cases with an international element. This is reflected in the fact that the current PIL framework aims to provide for an optimal level of legal certainty and predictability which appears to be of primary importance to the effective access of parties to remedies in cross-border disputes with an international element within the EU.[2] The analysis of the way the EU PIL framework is functioning is important because the legal landscape in relation to PIL will impact on the litigants' strategies. An ineffective EU PIL regime would not be able to deal with abusive litigation tactics which may impair parties' effective access to remedies.

As a part of the assessment of effectiveness of the EU PIL framework, the authors examine how the current PIL shapes the litigants' strategies. In this context, the main features of the EU civil justice system as well as the role of national judges, applying the PIL instruments, are considered with a view to identifying the aspects which would impair the parties' effective access to remedies in cross-border cases. As already noted,[3] there would be

---

[1] The important issues which need to be considered in this context are identified in Chs 1 and 32. See also: Pt II of this chapter.

[2] Recitals 15 and 16 to the Brussels Ia Reg; Recitals 6, 16 and 39 to the Rome I Reg; Recitals 6, 14, 15 and 31 to the Rome II Reg. Of course legal certainty and predictability have to be balanced with the need to avoid significant injustices in individual cases caused by the rigid application of inflexible rules. The cost of a degree of flexibility in the private international law rules designed to avoid such individual injustice may be a less effective regime as more individual litigation is encouraged.

[3] Ch 32.

diverse sets of problems in the different EU Member States. Although the experience of the judges and litigators to deal with the relevant EU PIL rules[4] could impair effective access to remedies in some jurisdictions, this type of issue could be addressed by providing appropriate training to the national judges. The need for Member States' judges to be trained in applying the PIL instruments appears to be acknowledged by the EU Commission's Justice Programme which has now set action grants to support European judicial training.[5] However, an important research finding is that the litigants' strategies devised under the current EU PIL framework are the more dynamic and difficult aspect which needs to be carefully addressed by the EU policy-makers with a view to devising an effectively functioning EU civil justice system.

A case for a more comprehensive institutional reform may be made, if the EU PIL framework does not allow for national judges to successfully defeat parties' litigation tactics—devised under the relevant EU PIL Regulations—which could impair access to remedies in cross-border cases. With this in mind, it should be noted that an important feature of the EU civil justice model is that it is based on the principle of 'mutual trust in the administration of justice in the Union'.[6] This provides claimants with a certain degree of choice in deciding where to litigate their cross-border disputes.[7] This aspect of the EU PIL framework has promoted the creation of a market for cross-border litigation services, with some lawyers actively specialising in offering this type of legal advice. An analysis of the way the EU PIL framework shapes the litigants' strategies in cross-border cases initiated in the leading (or dominant) jurisdictions may help us to identify the weaknesses of the current regime.

A specific feature of the EU is that the process of administration of justice in cross-border cases varies in the different EU Member States. In some Member States,[8] low court fees may have an effect on a party's decision to issue cross-border court proceedings (which might also be a cultural thing, occasionally). As a result, the judges in these Member States may be dealing with many small cross-border claims. Although this might be regarded as an indication that lower litigation costs could incentivise SMEs and consumers to bring actions, the diverse nature of the Union does suggest that this type of variation will remain. That said, the claimants—bringing their small claims in reliance on a national policy promoting small court fees—will normally sue in their home states, so that they will hardly have any choice to make in this context. In other words, a market for cross-border litigation services would pre-suppose a level of adjudicatory competition[9] which could only thrive with regard to high value disputes with an international element, involving certain claimants who are not afraid to take cross-border litigation risks and meet the relevant costs.

Therefore, some Member States may have a high number of cross-border claims because a national policy (eg small court fees and contingency fees) may be promoting a high level of

---

[4] ibid.

[5] eg JUST-JTRA-EJTR-AG-2016—Action grants to support European judicial training (European Commission, 2016), http://ec.europa.eu/research/participants/portal/desktop/en/opportunities/just/topics/just-jtra-ejtr-ag-2016.html.

[6] Recital 26 to the Brussels Ia Reg.

[7] This is, of course, subject to Art 24 of the Brussels Ia Reg.

[8] eg Austria and Spain.

[9] B Hess, 'Harmonized Rules and Minimum Standards in the European Law of Civil Procedure—In-Depth Analysis' PE 556.971 EN (European Parliament, 2016) < www.europarl.europa.eu/RegData/etudes/IDAN/2016/556971/IPOL_IDA(2016)556971_EN.pdf, 14.

litigiousness, whilst other jurisdictions may be attractive to litigants because their national system of administration of justice is appealing to the parties' needs. The consequences of these developments for the effective functioning of the EU PIL system may be numerous. First, some jurisdictions appear to be consistently attracting more high value cross-border commercial law cases than others. Without pretending to be able to identify all the factors explaining why this is the case, it is a relatively safe assumption that the lawyers and judges in Member States with infrequent cross-border cases may be somewhat less familiar with the application and interpretation of the PIL instruments in complex commercial disputes with an international element.

Second, even though the national reports[10] do indicate that the Member States generally correctly apply the EU PIL regime, the uncertainties/ambiguities about the interpretation/ application of the EU PIL instruments can cause a level of delay. This can hamper the claimants' access to effective remedies in cross-border cases. This would be particularly so for claimants who are less mobile (or have to sue in jurisdictions where for whatever reason lawyers and judges have less experience in applying these rules) as well as for defendants who—on the basis of some of the special jurisdictional rules—are brought into jurisdictions where the judicial systems are not functioning effectively.

Third, one may object to the deduction that the main source of the delay is the way the EU PIL rules are being applied by national judges. This argument may be strengthened by putting forward that a level of delay, which would impair the parties' effective access to remedies, could be the result of deficiencies in the functioning of the relevant national judicial system.[11] Nonetheless, it could be argued that an EU PIL framework which is not adjusted to deal with the deficiencies of the national judicial systems by providing for a transfer of proceedings[12] could be ineffective, encouraging abusive litigation tactics. It should be for the EU policy-makers to devise rules which should facilitate parties' access to effective remedies in cross-border cases. In other words, if there are problems with some of the national judicial systems and there is no flexibility in the EU PIL rules which would allow judges to 'do justice in individual cases',[13] then this makes the EU civil justice framework less than effective.

Fourth, over time the lawyers and judges in the leading (and indeed dominant) jurisdictions in the EU have gained significant experience in dealing with complex cross-border disputes. Some of the law firms can be promoting certain jurisdictions as a venue of choice for the high-value cross-border cases which normally involve highly sophisticated and selective claimants with deep pockets or with another funding scheme in place. Given the high costs of cross-border litigation and the monetary value of the remedies sought in some cross-border cases, it could be easily explained why such high-value cases are becoming increasingly attractive for litigation funders. It appears that the litigation funders are increasingly active in promoting access to justice in respect of appropriate 'meritorious claims',[14] which is yet another indication that the relative strength of the claims would be

---

[10] See Pt II of this book.

[11] eg Greece in Ch 18 above.

[12] Compare Art 15 of Brussels IIa.

[13] Recital 14 to Rome II.

[14] See The Association of Litigation Funders in England and Wales, *Litigation Finance* http://associationof-litigationfunders.com/litigation-finance/. See also N Bernal, 'Litigation Funding Report: Broader Appeal' www.thelawyer.com/issues/6-june-2016/litigation-funding-report-broader-appeal/.

inter alia considered in this context. These developments mean that, as already noted,[15] the lawyers in some jurisdictions have developed advanced knowledge of every nuance of the PIL framework, so that they are well placed to exploit any of the existing ambiguities/ uncertainties of the different aspects of the current PIL framework. In other words, sophisticated parties may devise various delaying strategies under the current regime, raising jurisdictional challenges and/or initiating parallel proceedings. These litigation tactics are normally and primarily aimed to wear down the financial resources of the claimant and impact on the settlement dynamics by raising the level of uncertainty and adversely affecting the claimant's expectations about the outcome in cross-border cases.[16]

The EUPILLAR paradigm is that the way the EU PIL framework shapes the litigation strategies in the jurisdictions where the parties initiated complex cross-border disputes should be carefully considered when making the assessment of the effectiveness of the EU PIL instruments. This would be important because the parties' tactics devised under the current EU PIL would expose the weaknesses of the current regime. As a part of this analysis, whilst taking account of the national reports, the authors primarily consider the litigants' strategies in England and Wales. The adopted approach is justified by the fact that this is one of the leading EU jurisdictions where judges and litigators have specialised in dealing with highly complex cross-border disputes, developing advanced knowledge and understanding about the nuances of the relevant EU PIL Regulations. An analysis of the way the parties' strategies devised under the current EU PIL could impair parties' effective access to remedies in the cutting-edge jurisdictions should indicate what aspects of the current regime need to be reformed.

II. Parties' Strategies: EU Legal Landscape—A Level of Legal Uncertainty—Effective Remedies

The value of the remedy and the level of costs are important in cross-border cases because, as discussed above,[17] the data suggest that the claimant's decision whether/where to issue cross-border proceedings is preceded by a cost-remedy balancing exercise which will factor in how the PIL framework is functioning in the courts having jurisdiction to hear and determine the dispute. The EUPILLAR theory is that any analysis of the question whether the parties have access to effective remedies in cross-border cases needs to take account of the higher litigation costs, which—due to the higher level of complexity—appear to characterise disputes with an international element.[18]

In this section, the possible sources of delay and legal uncertainty, which might defeat the objectives of the EU PIL framework and adversely affect litigants' access to remedies in cross-border cases, will be examined. There are two elements of the right to an effective remedy in cross-border cases which are considered for the purposes of the relevant data

---

[15] See Ch 32 above.
[16] See more in Ch 40 below.
[17] See Ch 32 above.
[18] This could well be deduced by the qualitative data from England and Wales.

analysis. First, parties consider the desired remedies, which (even if declaratory or injunctive in nature) normally have a monetary[19] value in civil and commercial cases with an international element. The claimant's *entitlement* to such a remedy and the scope of the defendant's liability are determined by the governing law/s. In this context, the current EU PIL framework on applicable law/s must be carefully considered.

Second, despite the fact that the same applicable law/s should apply to contractual and non-contractual obligations irrespective of where the parties litigate in the EU,[20] the place of litigation is important in the light of the diverse nature of the Union. It is well established that 'each litigant considers the costs and probable outcomes of further litigation steps and weighs them against economic benefits obtainable without further proceedings'.[21] The jurisdictional rules and the place where the parties litigate will have an impact on the parties' *access* to effective remedies in disputes with an internal element. Any access to a remedy may depend on the relevant procedural rules and costs as well as on the experience of judges to apply the foreign laws and dispense justice in a cross-border case. The effective access to remedies may be restricted by litigants' strategies which cause further delay by exploiting the existing/uncertainties of the current EU PIL regime thereby inflating the litigation costs in cross-border cases. All these features of the EU legal landscape may shape the litigants' strategies under the current PIL framework. In other words, the sophisticated parties may well consider the national judges' ability to deal with cross-border cases along with the various features of national judicial systems, devising litigation tactics under the current EU PIL framework which might impact on their opponents' expectations about the outcome of the litigation.[22]

A. 'Effectiveness of Exclusive Choice-of-court Agreements'[23] under the Brussels I Regime

One of the main objectives of Brussels Ia is 'to enhance the effectiveness of exclusive choice-of-court agreements and to avoid abusive litigation tactics'[24] by providing an exception to the court-first-seised rule. This is now reflected in Article 31(2) of the Regulation which states that:

> [W]here a court of a Member State on which an agreement ... confers exclusive jurisdiction is seised, any court of another Member State shall stay the proceedings until such time as the court seised on the basis of the agreement declares that it has no jurisdiction under the agreement.

The rationale of this amendment which provides for an 'exception to the general *lis pendens* rule [is] to deal satisfactorily with a particular situation in which concurrent proceedings may arise.'[25] This is in line with the doctrine of 'one-stop method of adjudication'[26]

---

[19] See Chs 5 and 7 above.
[20] Recital 6 to Rome I and Rome II.
[21] E Johnson Jr , 'Lawyers' Choice: A Theoretical Appraisal of Litigation Investment Decisions' (1980–81) *Law and Society Review* 567, 567–68.
[22] See more in Ch 40 below. See also: Ch 5 above.
[23] Recital 22 to Brussels Ia.
[24] ibid.
[25] ibid.
[26] *Fili Shipping Co Ltd and others v Premium Nafta Products Ltd and others* [2007] UKHL 40 [27].

which is widely adopted in England and Wales. Although the qualitative interview data from England and Wales[27] suggest that the adopted Brussels Ia rule will work effectively, one should not forget that the modification in question was intended to address a particular problem which was spectacularly exposed in *Erich Gasser*.[28] Bearing in mind that the CJEU judgment was rendered on 9 December 2003 (ie over 11 years before Brussels Ia entered into force), one could say that Article 31(2) serves as an example which demonstrates the slowness of the EU legislative process to fix problems in civil and commercial matters. This level of delay means that, for a number of years, there had been a very effective weapon which could have been used by non-bona fide litigants to defeat a choice-of-court agreement, adversely affecting bona fide parties' access to remedies in the EU.

Moreover, the Brussels Ia amendment is based on the assumption that the parties' business relationships will involve only one transaction (or a series of transactions) with the same choice-of-court agreement between the same parties. The case law does suggest that the effectiveness of choice-of-court agreements and the problem of concurrent proceedings in particular may still be an issue in disputes arising out of a series of transactions, which contain various dispute resolution clauses that may be used with regard to different transactions between the same parties. The potential problems were illustrated in *Deutsche Bank v Sebastian Holdings*.[29] In this case, the claimant, Deutsche Bank, was a global investment bank which was incorporated in Germany, having an office in London. The defendant, Sebastian Holdings, was a company incorporated under the laws of Turks and Caicos Islands. The parties entered into a series of equities trading agreements as well as into a number of foreign-exchange (FX) agreements. The parties' equities trading agreement, EIMA, was the first agreement between the parties, providing the contractual framework for parties' derivative transactions. This agreement contained an English jurisdiction clause. Also there were foreign-exchange agreements between the parties. The foreign-exchange prime brokerage agreement (FXPBA), authorised Sebastian holdings to act as agent on behalf of Deutsche Bank. This agreement included a New York non-exclusive jurisdiction agreement. An agent master agreement (AMA), included an English jurisdiction clause. A few days later, the parties signed a Pledge and Pledgeholder Agreement, which was governed by Swiss law. According to its terms, 'the Pledgee [Deutsche Bank] shall also have the right to bring an action against the Pledgor [Sebastian Holdings] before the competent court at its place of residence or before any other competent court.'[30] There were four other agreements, which were related to the first EIMA. An equities prime brokerage agreement (EPBA) included an exclusive English choice-of-court agreement. Similarly, a listed futures and options agreement (LFOA) and master netting agreement (MNA) both included English jurisdiction agreements. Finally, there was an overseas securities lender's agreement between the parties, setting out 'the terms and conditions upon which the parties would lend and borrow securities to each other,'[31] and all disputes arising under this agreement were to be resolved by arbitration in London.

---

[27] EUPILLAR—England and Wales—Interview Transcript No 19.

[28] Case C-116/02 *Erich Gasser GmbH v MISAT Srl*, EU:C:2003:657.

[29] *Deutsche Bank AG v Sebastian Holdings Inc* [2009] EWHC 2132 (Comm). Compare: *UBS AG and UBS Securities LLC v HSN Nordbank* [2008] EWHC 1529 (Comm) aff'd *UBS AG and UBS Securities LLC v HSN Nordbank* [2009] EWCA Civ 585.

[30] *Deutsche Bank AG v Sebastian Holdings Inc* [2009] EWHC 2132 (Comm) [15].

[31] ibid [22].

After Deutsche Bank demanded a sum of approximately $120 million which was allegedly due under the FXPBA, on 24 November 2008, Sebastian Holdings issued proceedings in New York, seeking a non-liability declaration. On 21 January 2009, Deutsche Bank commenced the proceedings in London, demanding sums in excess of $120 million which was allegedly due under the MNA. Sebastian Holdings challenged the jurisdiction of the English court. The High Court dismissed the challenge, stating that there was no contractual bar for the claim to be brought in England. In December 2009, Mr Justice Burton refused an application for a stay of the English proceedings[32] which meant that the concurrent proceedings were bound to continue. On 20 August 2010, the Court of Appeal affirmed that, due to the existence of the jurisdiction clause and at least one of the parties being domiciled in an EU Member State, the English Court had jurisdiction under the Brussels I regime.[33] The English court decided to give effect to the intention of the parties 'even if this may result in a degree of fragmentation in the resolution of disputes between parties to the series of agreements.'[34] It is a real issue that the way the dispute resolution clauses were drafted meant that there were to be parallel and related proceedings between the same parties.

Moreover, the ineffectiveness of the current regime is exposed by the fact that it took nearly two years for the highly experienced judges to resolve the jurisdictional dispute in this case, with another set of proceedings taking place in another jurisdiction. This example indicates that the way the jurisdiction clauses in the series of related contracts are drafted may turn out to be a source of legal uncertainty, posing difficult questions as to where the parties should litigate. This means a high level of uncertainty and litigation costs which can impair parties' access to remedies in cross-border cases.

Given the importance of choice-of-court agreements for the resolution of cross-border commercial disputes, one should consider why the parties could have included clauses which 'might be said to conflict, as disputes which are related or overlap might arise under different agreements in the series.'[35] One way of explaining this is to adopt Lord Justice Thomas's approach, holding that:

> [T]he clauses do not in fact conflict, as they envisage claims being brought under the different agreements for monies owed under each agreement, even if the defences may overlap. The language of the agreements plainly envisages this and … it is entirely rational for businessmen to agree to this.[36]

Another way of explaining the level of uncertainty generated in cases where there are conflicting dispute resolution agreements may be by suggesting it was all due to careless drafting. Although, since it was intended to give to the respondents some flexibility to draw on their personal practical experience, there were no specifically drafted interview questions about conflicting dispute resolution agreements, the issues were raised by two of the interview respondents in England and Wales. It was noted by one interview respondent[37]

---

[32] *Deutsche Bank AG v Sebastian Holdings Inc* [2009] EWHC 3069 (Comm).
[33] *Sebastian Holdings Inc v Deutsche Bank AG* [2010] EWCA Civ 998.
[34] ibid [50].
[35] ibid [65].
[36] ibid.
[37] EUPILLAR—England and Wales—Interview Transcript No 3.

that conflicting dispute resolution clauses do find their way into an agreement because drafters may occasionally be careless in relying on previously used documents without properly amending them and making sure that the agreement included the jurisdictional clause which the parties had in mind. This may well be a valid explanation, if the conflicting dispute resolution agreements are forming part of the same contract. However, it is difficult to explain why such sophisticated parties as Deutsche Bank[38] and UBS[39] had included conflicting dispute resolution clauses in a series of related agreements with their counterparts.

Yet another way of explaining the existence of dispute resolution clauses selecting different fora, which appear to feature in a series of related agreements between the same parties, is strategic drafting by the parties and their lawyers, hoping to create confusion which they could benefit from, once a dispute has arisen. The point was made by one interview respondent[40] in England and Wales, who noted that dispute resolution clauses selecting different fora in a series of related agreements are quite common. It was noted that the issues may be even more complex if in addition to the various jurisdictional clauses, there is an arbitration clause which is incorporated into another agreement forming part of the same series of transactions between the same parties. The interview respondent in question indicates that, if this had been done deliberately, then one of the parties could have believed that it would gain a negotiating advantage by multiple fora having jurisdiction with regard to different transactions forming part of a series of related contracts. The level of uncertainty generated by this type of drafting by lawyers, which could (or could not) have been done deliberately, inevitably has an impact on the effectiveness (or rather ineffectiveness) of the choice-of-court agreement/s.

The jurisdictional disputes could become even more complex with even less predictable outcomes, if tortious claims and contractual claims arising out of a series of related transactions incorporating various choice-of-court (and/or arbitration) agreements are initiated.[41] More importantly, multiple sets of proceedings—arising out of related agreements between the same parties—initiated in different jurisdictions would have an effect on litigation costs, settlement negotiations and ultimately effective access to remedies for parties in cross-border cases. The incorporation of conflicting jurisdictional clauses in a series of related transactions might have an impact on the level of legal uncertainty and litigation costs, which may be inflated if there are concurrent proceedings. This in turn may have an impact on settlement negotiations and on parties' access to remedies in such cases.[42]

The overall conclusion is that the parties and their lawyers may be very creative when it comes to exploiting the weaknesses of the current EU PIL regime. This is particularly so in high value commercial law disputes. The fact that it took over 11 years for the EU policy-makers to deal with the *Gasser* problem indicates that legislative amendments at EU level may not be sufficient on their own to deal with abusive litigation tactics. A better institutional architecture is also needed to enhance the effectiveness of the EU civil justice

---

[38] ibid.
[39] *UBS AG and UBS Securities LLC v HSN Nordbank* [2008] EWHC 1529 (Comm) aff'd *UBS AG and UBS Securities LLC v HSN Nordbank* [2009] EWCA Civ 585.
[40] EUPILLAR—England and Wales—Interview Transcript No 7.
[41] ibid.
[42] See Ch 40.

system. An appropriate institutional framework would enable Member States' judges to more effectively deal with this type of problem in the EU. The need to do so may be further strengthened by providing other examples which illustrate the way the current PIL framework shapes the litigants' strategies in cross-border cases.

B. Jurisdictional Challenges as Tactical Devices Under the Brussels I Regime

It is well established that one of the major successes of the Brussels I regime is to 'facilitate the free circulation of judgments.'[43] The conclusive statistical evidence strengthening this deduction can be derived from the Heidelberg Report[44] which appears to suggest that the free circulation of foreign judgments in civil and commercial matters is an achievement which the Brussels I regime has fundamentally contributed to.[45]

The EUPILLAR case law data and qualitative interview data reaffirm that this is the situation in the UK,[46] Belgium,[47] Germany,[48] Italy[49] and Spain.[50] Although problems appear to be reported in Poland, a closer look suggests that the problems appear to have been with the lack of experience of Polish courts in applying the Brussels I regime, which have been largely resolved by the Polish Supreme Court.[51] It has restrictively applied the public policy exception laying down detailed rules about the burden of proof, prevalence of EU rules, the default of appearance requirements, and the capacity of joint and several judgment-debtors to be sued for the purposes of enforcement of foreign judgments under Brussels I.[52] The deduction that the recognition and enforcement of foreign judgments creates no significant difficulties in the majority of the EU Member States, however, does not necessarily mean that the all the major objectives of the Brussels I regime are effectively pursued in the EU.

The collected data appear to suggest that there are particularly difficult issues which arise with regard to 'enhanc[ing] access to justice',[53] which is important with a view to enabling litigants to obtain effective remedies in cross-border cases. In particular, the national reports indicate that jurisdictional challenges (and occasionally pre-emptive strikes initiated before the courts of Member States which are notorious for being slow)[54] may be used as a tactical device to cause a level of delay and legal uncertainty under the current EU civil justice system.

---

[43] Recitals 1, 6, 27 and 33 to the Brussels Ia Reg.

[44] B Hess, T Pfeiffer and P Schlosser, *Study JLS/C4/2005/03—Report on the Application of Regulation Brussels I in the Member States* (Heidelberg, 2007) http://ec.europa.eu/civiljustice/news/docs/study_application_brussels_1_en.pdf [52–53].

[45] ibid [52–53]. For an early analysis of whether the abolition of exequatur by the Recast of Brussels I will help the free circulation of judgments see L Timmer, 'Abolition of *Exequatur* under the Brussels I Regulation: Ill Conceived and Premature?' (2013) 9 *Journal of Private International Law* 129.

[46] See Ch 5 above.

[47] See Ch 6 above.

[48] See Ch 7 above.

[49] See Ch 8 above.

[50] See Ch 9 above.

[51] See Ch 10 above.

[52] ibid.

[53] Recital 1 to Brussels Ia.

[54] eg *Cooper Tire and Rubber Co Europe Ltd v Shell Chemicals UK Ltd* [2010] EWCA Civ 864 and *The Alexandros T* [2013] UKSC 70.

Therefore, an analysis of the litigants' strategies in the contentious cross-border cases may be employed in order to identify the weakness of the EU PIL framework. In particular, the overall view appears to be that the jurisdictional rules are good and well thought out but they could be exploited by litigants to gain a tactical advantage. The reality is that the jurisdictional challenges are being raised in each and every EU Member State.[55] This is not surprising. As one interview participant from England and Wales noted, it would be impossible 'to suggest that you can get a perfect system that meant there was never any dispute about jurisdiction'.[56] However, it is important to analyse how effectively the jurisdictional challenges are dealt with by Member States' judges, in order to consider the effect tactical challenges have on costs, remedies and settlements in cross-border cases under the current system. As already noted,[57] in England and Wales, in a significant proportion of the cases in the civil and commercial law dataset the question whether the English and Welsh court has jurisdiction was subject to heated debates between the parties. Although many of these jurisdictional challenges would have been tactical, approximately one third of the defendants' jurisdictional challenges had been wholly or partly upheld in England and Wales. This may well be interpreted as a strong indication that claimants are being tactical too.[58] As submitted in the German report, 'the initiation of proceedings for strategic purposes can affect the opposite party's perception of the entire dispute in a negative way, having an adverse impact on the party's willingness to settle or cooperate.'[59] The point is further reflected in the Spanish report which summarises the qualitative interview data by noting that parties may be strategic when choosing where to litigate.[60]

The strategic nature of the claimant's decision where to sue taken cumulatively with the tactical nature of some of the defendants' jurisdictional challenges mean that the question how these challenges are dealt with is important. The Brussels Ia Regulation is silent on the way in which jurisdictional challenges are to be dealt with across the EU. As a result, there is a level of variation in this respect. For example, in England and Wales, 'a defendant who wishes to [challenge the court's jurisdiction] may apply to the court for an order declaring that it has no such jurisdiction or should not exercise any jurisdiction which it may have.'[61] If a defendant's jurisdictional challenge had been dismissed and the first instance court had assumed jurisdiction, then a permission to appeal on a preliminary issue of jurisdiction (ie before hearing the merits of the case) could be given in England and Wales.[62]

In some other countries,[63] however, if a first instance court had assumed jurisdiction by dismissing a defendant's jurisdictional challenge, then no appeal on the issue of jurisdiction could be made before the court in question had determined the merits of the case, increasing the parties' exposure to costs. Increasing the litigation costs, whilst there is a level of uncertainty as to the seised court's competence to hear and determine the dispute, may be a factor which may be exploited by both parties with a view to gaining a

---

[55] See Pt II of this book.

[56] EUPILLAR—England and Wales—Interview Transcript No 18.

[57] See Ch 5 above.

[58] ibid.

[59] See Ch 7 above.

[60] See Ch 9 above.

[61] Civil Procedure Rules—Part 11—Disputing the Court's Jurisdiction—Rule 11(1)(a) and (b).

[62] Civil Procedure Rules—Part 52—Appeals—Rule 52.3.

[63] See eg Ch 12 above.

negotiating advantage.[64] The need to have the issue of jurisdiction determined as a preliminary issue before the merits of the case had been argued was put forward by one interview respondent[65]—a judge from England and Wales.

The case for a level of harmonisation at EU level in this context could be made in view of the important role of jurisdictional challenges under the Brussels I regime. Indeed, even if the system is functioning very well in facilitating the recognition and enforcement of foreign judgments across the EU, claimants' and defendants' tactical behaviour with regard to establishing/challenging jurisdiction may delay the resolution of cross-border disputes, adversely affecting litigants' settlement negotiations which will have an impact on parties' access to effective remedies in cross-border cases.[66] The point came through clearly in the qualitative interview data presented by the Belgian report, when discussing the length of proceedings, noting that: 'What does take longer, is when the court lacks jurisdiction, and the parties have to start again somewhere else.'[67]

Strategic litigants may well be exploiting the uncertainties/ambiguities of the current EU PIL framework by amplifying the difficulties in cross-border cases. Increasing the level of complexity in cross-border cases does appear to have a negative impact on some Member States' judges' decisions whether to assume jurisdiction. In particular, judges in some Member States might start trying to avoid dealing with the difficult cases. For example, it has been submitted that 'Spanish Courts are not eager to assume jurisdiction in international cases since these are more complicated and they have already more than enough workload.'[68] Similarly, a German interview respondent has noted that 'there might be even a slight tendency [for some German judges] to deny international jurisdiction, given the fact that cross-border cases are perceived as being accompanied with particular difficulties.'[69] This could be a significant issue because some strategic defendants may challenge jurisdiction in some Member States, making it complex for judges and claimants in cross-border cases, wearing down the financial resources of the claimant and deflating his/her expectations about the outcome of the case.

Therefore, jurisdictional battles appear to be a common feature of the current regime in all the Member States. Although the German report states that 'the provisions of Brussels I are appropriate to the needs of legal practitioners in the field of civil and commercial law',[70] one could easily see from the report that jurisdictional disputes are quite common. In particular, the scope of Brussels I has been questioned in Germany, posing interesting questions about its interrelationship with the Insolvency Regulation as well as whether disputes in relation to bonds issued in Greece are covered by the Regulation.[71] Furthermore, the German report indicates that there appear to be even more debatable issues between the parties in cross-border contractual disputes, raising concerns about the application of Articles 5(1) and 23 of Brussels I (now Articles 7(1) and 25 of the Brussels Ia Regulation). Similarly, Article 5(3) (now 7(2) of Brussels Ia) has been the subject of heated

---

[64] See Ch 39 below.
[65] EUPILLAR—England and Wales—Interview Transcript No 19.
[66] See Ch 39 below.
[67] See Ch 6 above.
[68] See Ch 9 above.
[69] See Ch 7 above.
[70] ibid.
[71] ibid.

debates in cross-border tort disputes. Similar problems, resulting in heated debates about jurisdiction, appear to have arisen in Belgium,[72] Italy[73] and Spain.[74]

The problems are exacerbated because the current EU institutional architecture is not suited to swiftly providing support to national judges with regard to the interpretation of the PIL instruments. The current timeline of about 15 months for the CJEU to deliver its rulings on a preliminary issue on jurisdiction does not appear to facilitate parties' access to an effective remedy in cross-border cases. Moreover, as an interviewee from England and Wales noted, following a reference to the CJEU, '[y]ou still have the problem then how you interpret the European Court of Justice's judgments.'[75] This may explain why—in some Member States—the judges, who aim to dispense justice in individual cross-border cases, are reluctant to make a reference to the CJEU on a preliminary PIL issue, seeing it as a measure of last resort.[76] The *CDC*[77] case shows the ineffectiveness of the current institutional architecture. The claims in this case were in relation to cross-border EU competition law infringement for the period from 31 January 1994 to 31 December 2000.[78] The proceedings for damages brought by private party victims were issued in Germany on 16 March 2009. Since the claim against the only German defendant settled, the jurisdiction of the German court under Article 6(1) (Article 8(1) of Brussels Ia) was challenged. A preliminary reference was received by the Court of Justice in June 2013. It took nearly two years for the CJEU to render its judgment in May 2015, which means that some years after the infringement had stopped, the parties ultimately resolved the jurisdictional dispute, establishing jurisdiction in Germany. However, the time which had elapsed could certainly be regarded as an indication that some significant evidential hurdles were yet to be overcome. This may be one of the many reasons why there are very few consumers (if any) who would ever consider bringing a competition law damages claim.[79]

C. The Court-first-seised Rule—Parallel Proceedings

The court-first-seised rule appears to be having a major influence on the litigants' tactics in cross-border cases across the EU.[80] The *Erich Gasser* case, which was already discussed above, clearly demonstrates how a non-bona fide party could deploy abusive litigation tactics, dragging the other party into a jurisdiction where the courts are notoriously slow in resolving disputes (and taking a view on the issue of jurisdiction in particular). This inevitably has an effect on defendants' willingness to continue with cross-border proceedings in such a jurisdiction. The expectations about the outcome could be adversely affected.

---

[72] See Ch 6 above.
[73] See Ch 8 above.
[74] See Ch 9 above.
[75] EUPILLAR—England and Wales—Interview Transcript No 18.
[76] See Chs 5 and 6 above.
[77] Case C-352/13 *Cartel Damage Claims* EU:C:2015:335. Discussed in Ch 33 above.
[78] Case COMP/F/38.620— *Hydrogen Peroxide and perborate*, Commission Decision of 03.05.2006 relating to a proceeding pursuant to Art 81 of the EC Treaty and Art 53 of the EEA Agreement C(2006) 1766 final [351–60].
[79] M Danov, 'Cross-Border Aspects of EU Competition Law Enforcement: A Comprehensive Reform Needed?' in V Tomljenovic, N Bodiroga-Vukobrat, V Butorac Malnar and I Kunda (eds), *EU Competition and State Aid Rules: Public and Private Enforcement* (forthcoming).
[80] See also Ch 40 below.

As a result, the value of litigation could drop for a party faced with the prospect of spending an excessively long period of time litigating a dispute about the court's jurisdiction.

In spite of the fact that the problem with choice-of-court agreements has now been adequately addressed by the Brussels Ia Regulation, the problem will continue to persist for parties who are considering suing under any of the other jurisdictional bases. The effect the court-first-seised rule appears to have on the litigants' strategies is nicely captured by the Spanish report which indicates that pre-emptive strikes occasionally may be initiated by some strategic parties.[81]

In view of this, it may be difficult to explain why there are not so many cases in Spain, involving parallel proceedings. One possible reason might be the chilling effect which the court-first-seised rule may have on the litigants' decisions whether to continue with the proceedings or to accept a settlement offer (albeit a significantly discounted one, perhaps). The point appears to be nicely highlighted in the interviews from England and Wales,[82] with one interview respondent stating:

> [T]he court-first-seised rule has really come to the fore in the last few years. That's a challenge because it can lead to delay or it can lead to injustice; and this fiction that all EU jurisdictions are the same—it costs people money and it deters people from doing business and that's a problem.[83]

As already noted,[84] the interview data from England and Wales suggest that the court-first-seised rule could even lead to a claimant deciding to discontinue the proceedings in the light of the fact that the delay in some jurisdictions may be excessive.[85] Even if one could say that a remedy for all these problems would be to include a choice-of-court agreement, it would be very difficult to do so with regard to cross-border non-contractual disputes which may occasionally affect injured parties in different EU Member States. Therefore, despite the recent revision of the Brussels I regime, the need to reconsider the court-first-seised rule should be on the legislative agenda. There is a tendency by the CJEU to use the court-first-seised rule of Brussels I when it is not relevant and thereby allowing negative declaratory actions to be initiated as a delaying tactic to avoid justice.[86]

D. Applicable Laws

It should be noted that there are less cases in the EUPILLAR database involving choice-of-law than those involving jurisdiction. A judge who was interviewed in England and Wales stated that 'jurisdiction is really important; people mind where their litigation takes place.'[87] In spite of the fact that there might be difficulties for judges to apply foreign laws in

---

[81] See Ch 9 above.
[82] See Ch 5 above.
[83] EUPILLAR—England and Wales—Interview Transcript No 15.
[84] See Ch 5 above.
[85] See Ch 40 below.
[86] See Case C-452/12 *Nipponkoa Insurance Co (Europe) Ltd v Inter-Zuid Transport BV* EU:C:2013:858. The EU legislature should also expressly reverse the tendency of the CJEU to give insufficient respect to the text of Art 71 of Brussels I by not giving full effect to specialist conventions (see Case C-533/08 *TNT Express Nederland* [2010] ECR I-4107 and Case C-157/13 *Nickel & Goeldner Spedition GmbH v "Kintra" UAB* EU:C:2014:2145). See more on these cases in Ch 33 above.
[87] EUPILLAR—England and Wales—Interview Transcript No 19.

some jurisdictions,[88] applying foreign laws in cross-border civil and commercial law cases appears to be not uncommon in England and Wales. Although the application of foreign law/s will increase the litigation costs, the interview data suggest that the costs of application of foreign law should not be overstated. In particular, the English and Welsh judges, faced with a significant number of civil and commercial PIL cases, appear to be confident and experienced in applying foreign laws in disputes with an international element.

The higher number of jurisdictional disputes in comparison to the choice-of-law disputes in many if not all EU Member States may also be partially explained by the fact that it takes two parties to disagree about the applicable laws. In other words, even if a defendant raises another law as being applicable, the claimant would not disagree unless the governing law would make a material difference to the resolution of the dispute. As one legal practitioner from England and Wales put it, a 'claimant will decide whether the dispute about the applicable law is something that is important enough to them to warrant the time delaying consequences of fighting it.'[89] Therefore, it is not that the choice-of-law issues are not important, but the parties' decision whether to argue about the governing law (or to factor the various uncertainties surrounding the identification/application of foreign laws into the settlement negotiations) is strategically driven. In other words, in England and Wales, the parties' decision whether to enter into a dispute about governing law will factor in the benefits which a party will derive from applying one set of laws rather than another compared to the costs of persuading the court that the foreign law is applicable and then of proving the foreign law.

The importance for the national judges to be able to interpret and apply Rome I and Rome II in cross-border disputes is confirmed by the qualitative data from Belgium, Germany, Italy and Spain.[90] These reports suggest that the ability of national judges to identify and apply the foreign laws would be central to dispensing justice, providing effective remedies for parties in cross-border cases. In this context, von Hein has submitted that: '[d]isputes with foreign elements frequently pose difficult challenges to national courts because judges usually do not possess an in-depth knowledge of foreign laws and the lower courts' libraries are often not sufficiently equipped with pertinent literature.'[91]

The difficulties and variations when it comes to application of foreign law will be even greater in the light of the different procedural rules in place. For example, in England and Wales, once a dispute has arisen about the content of the foreign law, then each party will have to prove it, rebutting the presumption that the foreign law is the same as English law. The effect of Article 4(1) of Rome II on this presumption was recently discussed by the English Court of Appeal in *OPO v MLA*[92] where Lady Justice Arden held:

> I do not accept the submission that, even though there is no evidence as to Ruritanian law, the presumption that foreign law is the same as English law does not apply. That is a rule of evidence

---

[88] See Pt II of this book above.

[89] EUPILLAR—England and Wales—Interview Transcript No 18. See also Ch 5 above. The Netherlands national report (Ch 25 above) discusses the tendency of parties not to plead foreign law in order to save costs and how impractical it is to try to force parties and courts to apply foreign law given that someone has to pay for the costs of doing so. The situation in the Netherlands appears to be somewhat similar to the one in Hungary (Ch 19 above).

[90] See Chs 6–9 above.

[91] See Ch 7 above.

[92] *OPO v MLA* [2014] EWCA Civ 1277.

applied by the English courts. As such it is not affected by the Regulation. The choice of law rules laid down by Article 4 apply for the purposes set out in Article 15 of the Regulation, which does not extend to rules of evidence. Article 22 of the Regulation deals with the burden of proof but only in relation to the constituents of the tort in question …[93]

A somewhat different approach is adopted in Germany where the 'court has to determine the content of foreign law *ex officio* and is not restricted by the information provided by the parties to the case.'[94] These variations inevitably have an effect on the litigation costs in the different jurisdictions. This means that the litigants' strategies in complex cross-border cases could be different in the various jurisdictions, indicating that the way the current EU PIL is being implemented and applied by the Member States' courts has an impact on litigants' strategies (ie on a party's decision where to sue).

III. The Level of Legal Uncertainty and Remedies: Cost-shifting—Litigants' Behaviour and Settlements in Cross-border Cases

The current EU landscape appears to be shaping the litigants' strategies in cross-border cases, aiming to gain a negotiating advantage in any settlement negotiations. The level of legal uncertainty may be exploited by the sophisticated claimants quickly issuing proceedings in jurisdictions where settlements could be forced.[95] Equally, the defendants appear to be creative in exploiting the weaknesses of the current PIL regime by raising jurisdictional challenges or even initiating pre-emptive strikes in appropriate cases, with a view to causing legal uncertainty and benefit in the settlement negotiations. The point was clearly put forward by one of the interview respondents from England and Wales:

> What I will say about the EU regulations, especially Brussels, is that the regulations are complex and complicated. And I think that from a practitioner's point of view you are always looking to exploit that complexity. I think there is a way where you can try and harmonise things, but when you get to the interpretation it is going to be very different. …
>
> …
>
> … commercial litigation is going to remain complicated, complex. Because human relationships are complex and people are going to be looking to exploit any gap in the system.[96]

Since the CJEU does not deal appropriately and in a timely fashion when asked to interpret the PIL instruments, there is a real risk for national judges to inconsistently apply the PIL instruments. Although the qualitative data does suggest that the risk is there, the national reports generally show that PIL instruments are interpreted correctly. Moreover, many issues of interpretation have been resolved by the CJEU. That said, the current institutional

---

[93] ibid [108].
[94] See Ch 7 above, discussing Art 293 of the German Code of Civil Procedure (ZPO).
[95] See Ch 40 below.
[96] EUPILLAR—England and Wales—Interview Transcript No 7.

framework is not fully geared to defeating abusive litigation tactics which are primarily aimed to cause a delay by exploiting the ambiguity of the nuances of the interpretation of the PIL provisions in a cross-border context.

The above deduction could be strengthened by taking a closer look at the national reports which do suggest that the cross-border cases may raise difficult issues. Due to a level of legal uncertainty and/or ambiguity as to the interpretation of Brussels I, Rome I and Rome II, there can be delays which adversely affect settlements/remedies in cross-border cases. The level of uncertainty further increases in cases where the parties decide to dispute the law applicable to the merits of their dispute. As already noted,[97] applicable law disputes pose difficult questions about the interpretation of the Rome I and Rome II Regulations as well as about the evidence of the content of foreign law/s. Further issues may arise with regard to trials in disputes with an international element because parties' evidence may be in different jurisdictions and documents may be drafted in different languages, indicating that parties may need to seek advice from lawyers practising in different jurisdictions.

Another closely linked factor, which must be considered with regard to the settlement negotiations, concerns the litigation costs in civil and commercial disputes with an international element. Indeed, the qualitative interview data suggest that the resolution of these disputes will be more costly because the level of complexity is greater in cross-border civil and commercial cases than in domestic ones. This would be very much so in cross-border disputes involving jurisdictional challenges and parallel proceedings which, as discussed above, generate a level of uncertainty, questioning the competence of the court seised and creating a risk of irreconcilable judgments. Indeed, bearing in mind the greater complexity which appears to be a characteristic feature of many cross-border disputes, there will be higher litigation costs for private parties as well as higher 'societal costs'.[98]

The costs for society will be particularly high because the success of the EU PIL instruments, which are set to ensure judicial cooperation in civil and commercial matters, is dependent on the ability of national judges to apply them properly. EU Member States need to invest in the training of national judges to deal with these instruments. Over time a growing number of EU Member States courts' judgments dealing with the relevant PIL issues will be rendered. Lawyers will have to spend more time to fully prepare in order to give excellent advice to parties in cross-border cases. In other words, the greater complexity of the disputes with an international element taken together with the increasing demand for cross-border legal advice suggest that the parties will be devoting more time and money in resolving the disputes. An unintended consequence is that the growing number of judgments from the various EU Member States is likely to generate greater legal uncertainty about the nuances of the relevant provisions. In theory, there is a view that:

> [M]erely adding to the number of cases, statutes, scholarly glosses, and other data of legal prediction does not ensure more certainty in the law. Such increasingly dense 'legal information' can as easily confuse an issue as clarify it, and may also support conflicting resolutions.[99]

---

[97] See Chs 5, 6, 7, 8, 9 and 10 above.

[98] J Bronsteen, 'Some Thoughts About the Economics of Settlement' (2009) 78 *Fordham Law Review* 1129, 1133.

[99] A D'Amato, 'Legal Uncertainty' (2010) Northwestern University School of Law Scholarly Commons—Faculty Working Papers. Paper 108, http://scholarlycommons.law.northwestern.edu/facultyworkingpapers/108, 8.

Although the EUPILLAR study may not have produced enough data to conclusively support this theory, there is evidence that some defendants are prepared to exploit every ambiguity in order to cause a delay, forcing a settlement under terms which the claimant would not otherwise accept. One could argue that increasing the number of EU PIL rules under the current institutional framework, without appropriate attention to the ability of the national judges to consistently and swiftly apply them and without ensuring that the CJEU can help them with a swift and reliable expert interpretation, could lead to greater legal uncertainty and significantly discounted compensation in cross-border cases. This is particularly so because any legislative amendment would take a long time to be negotiated and then it will cause fresh uncertainty upon its entry into force.

The research interviews from England and Wales indicate that the relative strength of the claimant's claim and the cost-shifting rules will have a central role to play with regard to settlements/remedies. On the one hand, if the claim is weak, then the defendant will have incentives to get a judgment on the merits quickly, without employing any delaying strategies. On the other hand, if the claimant has a relatively strong claim, then a defendant may start exploiting the weaknesses of the current PIL regime by (initiating occasionally pre-emptive strikes or) raising jurisdictional challenges and/or disputing the applicable law. This would put a strain on the courts' resources which are necessary to appropriately deal with these cases. As a result, there would be delay and legal uncertainty which inflate the litigation costs and have a bearing on the settlement dynamics and ultimately remedies.

In this context, one should consider the effect of the cost-shifting rules. It is well established that 'under the British system [of cost shifting], there will be a trial if and only if the plaintiff's estimate of the expected judgment exceeds at least the sum of their expected legal costs.'[100] Although the cost-shifting rules are intended to ensure that no claimant will initiate a weak claim, this is not necessarily so in cross-border cases where the court-first-seised rule may encourage parties to bring weak claims before EU Member State courts which are notoriously slow in order to drag the other party there, gaining an advantage in the settlement negotiations. Similar advantages may be gained by defendants who are raising jurisdictional challenges, causing uncertainty as to the competence of the court seised with the dispute. In spite of the fact that the cost-shifting rules are an important feature of forcing settlements, one must factor in the value of the claims:

> [T]he problem for the [defendant] is that a $20 million claim and a $100 million claim probably cost the same in legal costs to defend. So $5m of legal costs in a $20m claim has a greater impact on the [defendant] than $5m costs in a $100m claim. So there is a level where the quantum of costs does impact on the [settlement] decision.[101]

The interplay between the cost-shifting rules, on the one hand, and the available remedies and access to such remedies, on the other hand, may be even more complex if there is uncertainty as to the content of the relevant substantive law/s.[102]

---

[100] S Shavel, 'Suit, Settlement and Trial: A Theoretical Analysis Under Alternative Methods for the Allocation of Legal Cost' (1982) 11 *Journal of Legal Studies* 55, 64. See also M Danov and S Dnes, 'Cross-Border EU Competition Litigation: New Evidence from England and Wales' in M Danov, F Becker and P Beaumont (eds), *Cross-Border EU Competition Law Actions* (Oxford, Hart Publishing, 2013) 33–60.

[101] EUPILLAR—England and Wales—Interview Transcript No 7.

[102] See HSE Graville, 'The Efficiency Implications of Cost Shifting Rules' (1993) 13 *International Review of Law and Economics* 3; CF Beckner III and A Katz, 'The Incentive Effects of Litigation Fee Shifting When Legal Standards Are Uncertain' (1995) 15 *International Review of Law and Economics* 205.

It may be true that when faced with high costs and a level of uncertainty as to the outcome, some claimants may prefer to accept significantly discounted compensation.[103] However, equally it may be a valid proposition that, if there is a high level of uncertainty as to the available remedy, then '[t]here may well be factors the other way which enable the claimant to turn the cross-border aspect of matters to its advantage [so that] some defendants may prefer to settle'[104] in the light of the cost-shifting rules. Particularly difficult issues will arise in cases where a defendant is faced with identical and related claims, arising out of the same cross-border infringement, brought by different claimants in different Member States. A defendant, faced with the high cost of defending those claims,[105] may prefer to settle. That said, in theory 'the possibility of economising on litigation costs by settling can have adverse effects on the legal system when one or both parties use the threat of costly suit as a mechanism for inducing an adversary to submit to a costly settlement.'[106] This flies in the face of the EU policy-makers' objectives to provide for effective remedies for litigants in cross-border cases.

Another adverse consequence of the high litigation costs is the low number of cross-border cases which are initiated by weaker parties and consumers in particular.[107] The difficulties for consumers or consumer organisations[108] in accessing remedies are exposed in the EU Member States[109] where they have been active in bringing such actions. Indeed, a number of jurisdictional challenges have prompted time-consuming preliminary references to the CJEU.[110] The level of delay in the light of the existing level of uncertainty would have impacted on the litigation costs, making it extremely difficult for consumers with low value claims to access effective remedies in cross-border cases. As a result, the Brussels Ia objective 'to ensure the protection of consumers'[111] may not be effectively pursued under the current EU PIL framework. Although this is not entirely a PIL issue, a case for doing something about it in cross-border transactions may be made because the data suggest that the cross-border dimension adds a level of complexity. The lack of effective remedies for consumers is a major concern in mass harm situations with an international element. In such cases, harm would have been caused to consumers across different EU Member States. If there are no effective remedies for consumers in cross-border mass harm situations, then damages of multiple millions or even billions[112] on a yearly basis would remain uncompensated across the Union. Much of what has been submitted with regard to antitrust damages

---

[103] K Binmore, *Fun and Games: A Text on Game Theory* (Lexington MA, Heath and Company, 1992) 193–94; A Farmer and P Pecorino, 'Pretrial Negotiations with Asymmetric Information on Risk Preferences' (1994) 14 *International Review of Law and Economics* 273. See also Danov and Dnes, above n 100.

[104] EUPILLAR—England and Wales—Interview Transcript No 1.

[105] See the discussion about 'nuisance' in Shavel, above n 100, 72; EA Snyder and TE Kauper, 'Misuse of the Antitrust Laws: The Competitor Plaintiff' (1991) 90 *Michigan Law Review* 551; and Danov and Dnes, above n 100.

[106] S Salop and L White, 'Private Antitrust Litigation: An Introduction and Framework' in L White (ed), *Private Antitrust Litigation, New Evidence, New Learning* (Cambridge MA, MIT Press, 1988) 1, 27.

[107] See Chs 5 and 9 above.

[108] *Test Aankoop/Test Achats*—2010-03-10 Tribunal de commerce, Namur—cited in Ch 6 above.

[109] See Chs 6 and 7 above.

[110] Cases C-585/08 and C-144/09 *Pammer/Alpenhof*, EU:C:2010:740; Case C-190/11 *Muhlleitner*, EU:C:2012:542; Case C-218/12 *Emrek*, EU:C:2013:666; and Case C-397/14 *Hobohm*, EU:C:2016:256. See more in Ch 7 and 33 above.

[111] See Recital 14 to the Brussels Ia Reg.

[112] The amount of '€25.7 billion yearly' is the estimate in respect of EU competition law damages—a significant proportion of which, being passed to consumers, would be cross-border in nature. See the Report for the European Commission, Contract DG COMP/2006/A3/012, *Making Antitrust Damages Actions More Effective in*

actions is equally relevant here in so far as 'consumers would be reluctant to bring such actions due to the negligible amount of damages suffered by them in comparison with the high litigation costs.'[113] The litigation funders might have an important role to play in this context, but this would be subject to creating a more effectively functioning EU civil justice system which is a long way off at present.

Therefore, there is a strong case that the litigants' strategies do have an impact not only on settlement dynamics,[114] but also on injured parties' decisions whether to sue at all in cross-border cases.

IV. Concluding Remarks

An analysis of the current EU PIL framework strongly suggests that the EU civil justice system is less than optimally effective in providing remedies for private parties in cross-border civil and commercial law cases. The real issue is that, in spite of the EU objective to provide an optimal level of legal certainty in disputes with an international element, it is difficult for the EU Member States' judges who face various hurdles in applying the relevant EU PIL instruments. The problems are different in the various Member States. In some Member States, there is a level of legal uncertainty as to the interpretation of the relevant PIL instruments because the judges and lawyers there have insufficient experience in applying them. Although one might suggest that this type of problem could be solved by providing more training for national judges, an analysis of the way the current EU PIL is functioning in the dominant jurisdictions where judges and lawyers have a cutting edge experience in applying the relevant PIL instruments indicates that training on its own is not an adequate solution.

In particular, it appears to be clear that the lawyers in the leading jurisdictions have developed some advanced knowledge and understanding about the nuances of the relevant PIL provisions and case law. This puts them in a good position to give advice on litigation strategies allowing litigants to gain negotiating advantages by exploiting the weaknesses of the current EU civil justice system. To this end, a party may legitimately benefit from the court-first-seised rule or cause a level of uncertainty by using it as a delaying tactic. Likewise jurisdictional defences are often entirely legitimate but sometimes are wholly or largely used as a delaying tactic. These litigation tactics have an impact on the settlement negotiations,[115] flying in the face of the EU civil justice framework's objective of providing effective remedies for litigants in cross-border disputes.

An attempt could be made to reduce the level of uncertainty by creating databases, like the EUPILLAR database, which contain summaries of the various national judgments applying the relevant EU PIL. Such databases are a powerful learning tool but they could

---

the EU: Welfare Impact and Potential Scenarios (2007), http://ec.europa.eu/competition/antitrust/actionsdamages/files_white_paper/impact_study.pdf.

[113] M Danov, D Fairgrieve and G Howells, 'Collective Redress Antitrust Proceedings: How to Close the Enforcement gap and provide redress for consumers' in Danov, Becker and Beaumont, above n 100, 254, 269.

[114] See Ch 40 below.

[115] See more in Ch 40 below.

increase the possibilities for the lawyers to exploit the weaknesses of EU PIL by exploiting the ambiguities in the nuances of the judgments rendered by national judges representing different legal traditions. An appropriate solution to deal with the constantly evolving litigants' strategies is to devise an appropriate institutional architecture which enables Member States' judges to provide effective remedies for litigants in cross-border cases. Part of that strategy lies with the EU legislature providing greater clarity as to its intentions in EU PIL by the use of properly approved explanatory reports. The other part of the strategy is to reform the CJEU so that it has greater specialisation of judges, in particular a Chamber of Judges and at least one Advocate General with high level expertise in private international law, and greater capacity to give speedy and well informed preliminary rulings faithfully reflecting the intentions of the EU legislature.

36

Cross-border Contract Litigation in the EU

ZHENG SOPHIA TANG

I. Introduction

European Union conflicts rules are well established in cross-border contracts compared to many other areas. The harmonised conflicts system in contract at the Community level was established by 1980 through the Brussels Convention on jurisdiction and recognition and enforcement of judgments and the Rome Convention on applicable law.[1] The system was later updated and modernised on a number of occasions. The Brussels Convention had been replaced by the Brussels I Regulation in 2001,[2] which was then revised by the Recast Regulation in 2012.[3] The Rome Convention was replaced by the Rome I Regulation in 2008.[4] Regardless of the recent modernisation of the European Union (EU) contractual conflicts system, the Court of Justice of the EU (CJEU) interpretation of relevant rules in the predecessors often continues to be applicable to the current law.[5] There is rich case law concerning interpretation and application of the contractual conflicts system in court practice.

Considering both jurisdiction and choice-of-law rules, the EU conflicts system in contract demonstrates two main objectives: certainty and fairness. Certainty is the major principle for commercial contracts. In such contracts, where the parties are sophisticated commercial players with equal bargaining power, the law is not playing a role to create unnecessary compliance costs to the parties, but to protect the parties' reasonable expectations. It is trusted that the parties should be entitled to handle their own affairs rationally

---

[1] The Convention on jurisdiction and the enforcement of judgments in civil and commercial matters (Brussels Convention) was first adopted in 1968 and amended in 1978 on the accession of Denmark, Ireland and the United Kingdom (UK). The Brussels Convention provides Community jurisdiction rules for civil and commercial matters, including contract. In 1980, the Convention on the law applicable to contractual obligations (Rome Convention) was adopted, which provides the Community choice of law rules for contract. The adoption of the Rome Convention marked the establishment of the Community conflicts system for contractual litigation.

[2] Reg No 44/2001 on jurisdiction and recognition and enforcement of judgments in civil and commercial matters, [2001] OJ L12/1.

[3] Reg (EU) No 1215/2012 on jurisdiction and recognition and enforcement of judgments in civil and commercial matters (recast), [2012] OJ L351/1.

[4] Reg (EC) No 593/2008 on the law applicable to contractual obligation (Rome I), [2008] OJ L177/6.

[5] Case C-167/00 *Henkel* [2002] ECR I-8111, para 49; Case C-111/01 *Gantner Electronic* [2003] ECR I-4207, para 28; Case C-533/07 *Falco Privatstiftung and Rabitsch* [2009] ECR I-3327, paras 50–51.

and any unreasonable legal intervention is undesirable. The law, therefore, should promote efficiency by encouraging the parties to comply with their agreement, or by directing the parties to the country which is naturally predictable by both parties at the time of contracting. The objective of certainty is expressly stated in the recitals of both the Recast Regulation and Rome I.[6]

Fairness is the main principle for special contracts with inequality of bargaining and litigation power, including consumer, employment and insurance contracts. It is believed that in those contracts the stronger party may abuse its power to the disadvantage of the weaker party and the conflicts rules should be tilted in favour of the weaker party to balance the unequal power. The objective of fairness, in terms of weaker party protection, is also demonstrated in the recitals.[7] However, certainty continues to be one of the major concerns. The protection granted to the weak should be appropriate and not cause unnecessary cost to business. Certainty also helps the weaker party's access to justice.

II. Conflicts Rules in Commercial Contracts

A. Party Autonomy

Party autonomy grants the parties the freedom to choose the competent court and the applicable law. Although this principle is now also adopted for non-contractual litigation,[8] it plays a more significant role in contractual litigation. Contract creates a premeditated relationship between the parties, which allows the parties to plan and allocate litigation risk in advance, including negotiating and concluding a jurisdiction and choice of law clause. It could, in principle, provide certainty and predictability.

In practice, however, party autonomy could not prevent all disputes and uncertainty on jurisdiction and applicable law. In particular, the EU conflicts rules provide much flexibility to the parties to designate the chosen forum and law. Furthermore, commercial contracts, in many cases, are entered into very quickly, informally, orally, or they sometimes involve multiple documents of different kinds.[9] The flexible EU law and unconventional means to conclude commercial contracts may generate disputes on party autonomy. It is reasonable to argue that party autonomy could produce certainty in principle, but the specific rules should be carefully thought through to make certainty really happen.

i. Existence of a Choice

Disputes may arise as to the existence of a conflicts clause, for example, whether the conflicts clause contained in a separate document is successfully incorporated in the current

---

[6] Recitals 15 and 16 to the Recast Reg; Recitals 6 and 16 to Rome I.

[7] Recital 18 to the Recast Reg; Recital 23 to Rome I.

[8] Reg (EC) No 864/2007 on the law applicable to non-contractual obligations (Rome II), [2007] OJ L199/40, Art 14.

[9] LF Manning, 'Choice of Law for Commercial Contracts' [1961] *Boston College Law Review* 241, 243.

contract,[10] whether the parties have a consensus on an alleged jurisdiction clause inserted unilaterally by one party,[11] and whether the parties agree on a jurisdiction clause impliedly by following their common business patterns or having mutual understanding of the common practice in the profession.[12] The Recast Regulation does not provide clear rules on determining the existence of a jurisdiction clause. Instead, it provides relatively broad rules on the formality of a jurisdiction clause. A choice-of-court agreement may be formally valid if it is in writing or evidenced in writing, in a form that accords with common practice between the parties or in a form that accords with international usage.[13] The formal requirements are exhaustive. Under the national law of some countries, an agreement may be concluded orally or by conduct; however such an agreement would fall foul of Article 25 if it does not meet one of the conditions therein.[14] Does it mean that Article 25(1) determines not only whether a jurisdiction clause is formally valid but also whether it is actually concluded? It has been suggested by some that if an agreement is concluded in a form in accordance with Article 25, it is deemed enough evidence proving that a choice exists as the purpose of the formal requirement is to ensure the existence of consent.[15] This is particularly true in terms of the latter two conditions in the provision. Common practice and commercial usage are used by some courts to ascertain the existence of consent in the absence of an explicit agreement, and the consent is presumed to exist where the jurisdiction clause is consistent with the common practice between the parties or the international usage.[16] Article 25 thus excludes the application of national law in determining the existence and formal validity of a jurisdiction clause.

However, others disagree.[17] They intend to examine whether a jurisdiction clause is subject to a consensus between the parties first,[18] especially in contracts not concluded in a formal manner, such as the incorporation of a standard form contract in a separate document,[19] subscribing to the company statute by a shareholder,[20] the battle of the form case, and contracts concluded online.[21] Even within courts treating existence and formal validity as separate issues, different approaches are adopted to examine the existence of a clause. The CJEU usually does not apply national law or conflict-of-laws to the issue of existence, but it treats the existence of consensus as a matter of fact and relies on evidence

---

[10] *Chester Hall Precision Engineering Ltd v Service Centres Aero France*, [2014] EWHC 2529 (QB); *Credit Suisse v Societe Generale D'Enterprises* [1997] CLC 168; *Fosby v Ranovito* [2010] 1 Lloyd's Rep 384; *7E Communications Ltd v Vertex Antennentechnick GmBh* [2007] 1 WLR 2175.

[11] Case 24/76 *Estasis Salotti v RUWA* [1976] ECR 1831 and Case C-322/14, *Jaouad El Majdoub v CarsOnThe Web.Deutschland GmbH*, ECLI:EU:C:2015:334.

[12] Case C-106/95 *MSG v Gravieres Rhenanes* [1997] ECR I-911.

[13] Art 25(1).

[14] Case 150/80 *Elefanten Schuh v Pierre Jacqmain* [1981] ECR 1671, para 26. L Merrett, 'Article 23 of the Brussels I Regulation' (2009) 58 *International and Comparative Law Quarterly* 545, 546.

[15] L Collins et al, *Dicey, Morris and Collins: Conflict of Laws* 15th edn (London, Sweet & Maxwell, 2012) paras 12.122–125. *Chester Hall*, above n 10; *Knorr-Bremse v Haldex Brake Products GmbH* [2008] ILPr 26; *Credit Suisse*, above n 10; *Fosby*, above n 10; *7E Communications*, above n 10.

[16] Case C-159/97 *Trasporti Castelletti Spedizioni Internazionali SpA v Hugo Trumpy SpA* [1999] ECR I-1597.

[17] A Briggs, *Agreements on Jurisdiction and Choice of Law* (Oxford, Oxford University Press, 2008) para 7.12.

[18] *Estasis Salotti*, above n 11, para 7. See also *MSG*, above n 12, para 15; *Trasporti Castelletti*, above n 16, para 19.

[19] *Estasis Salotti*, ibid.

[20] Case C-214/89 *Powell Duffryn* [1992] ECR I-1745, paras 16–19 and Case C-543/10, *Refcomp SpA v Axa* EU:C:2013:62.

[21] *Jaouad El Majdoub*, above n 11.

to prove if the parties have entered into an agreement.[22] The most the CJEU has done is, based on the evidence and facts of the case, take the existence of consensus into consideration to interpret if a jurisdiction clause meets the formal requirements in Article 25(1).[23] National courts, on the other hand, may apply national law instead. For example, *Ryanair v Billigfluege.de GMBH*[24] concerned a 'browse-wrap' contract which contained a jurisdiction clause. Before applying the formal requirements under Article 23(1) of Brussels I which corresponds to Article 25(1) of the Recast, the Irish High Court examined whether the party's screen-scraping activity constituted consent to the jurisdiction clause and it applied national law to decide if the jurisdiction agreement was successfully concluded.[25]

This issue has long existed in the Brussels jurisdiction scheme, and it has not been simplified after the Recast Regulation modernised the previous jurisdiction rules. The Recast Regulation has made an important reform by introducing a uniform choice-of-law rule on the substantive validity of jurisdiction clauses.[26] However, the existence and substantive validity of a contract term are two separate issues[27] and it is not clearly suggested that the same choice-of-law shall be applicable in deciding whether a jurisdiction clause has been concluded.

ii. Lis Pendens *and the 'Italian Torpedo'*

One of the most important improvements of the Recast Regulation is the legislative correction of the *Gasser v MISAT*[28] judgment that unreasonably has hampered the effectiveness of a jurisdiction clause and encouraged an 'Italian Torpedo'.[29] According to *Gasser*, a non-chosen court, if seised first, would have priority over a chosen court in a jurisdiction clause in ruling on the validity of such a clause. The Recast Regulation finally reforms the *lis pendens* rule in Article 31 which provides that:

> 2. Without prejudice to Article 26, where a court of a Member State on which an agreement as referred to in Article 25 confers exclusive jurisdiction is seised, any court of another Member State shall stay the proceedings until such time as the court seised on the basis of the agreement declares that it has no jurisdiction under the agreement.

> 3. Where the court designated in the agreement has established jurisdiction in accordance with the agreement, any court of another Member State shall decline jurisdiction in favour of that court.

Pursuant to the new Article 31, a chosen court now has priority over a non-chosen but first seised court. This revision largely improves effectiveness of a choice-of-court clause and provides certainty to the parties. However, what if the chosen court is not seised? In such a

---

[22] Case C-366/13 *Profit Investment Sim SpA v Stefano Ossi*, ECLI:EU:C:2016:282, paras 24–29.

[23] eg *Estasis Salotti*, above n 11.

[24] *Ryanair v Billigfluege.de GMBH* [2010] ILPr 22.

[25] See also *Bols Distilleries BV v Superior Yacht Services Ltd* [2007] 1 WLR 12 and *Africa Express Line Ltd v Socofi SA* [2009] EWHC 3223 (Comm).

[26] Art 25(1).

[27] See, in general, J Beatson, A Burrows, J Cartwright, *Anson's Law of Contract* 13th edn (Oxford, Oxford University Press, 2016) Pts II and IV; M Chen-Wishart, *Contract Law* 5th edn (Oxford, Oxford University Press, 2015) Pts I and III; E McKendrick, *Contract Law* 11th edn (London, Palgrave, 2015) Pts I and III.

[28] Case C-116/02 *Erich Gasser GmbH v MISAT Srl* [2003] ECR I-1469.

[29] T Hartley, 'Choice-of-court Agreements and the New Brussels I Regulation' (2013) 129 *Law Quarterly Review* 309, 309–11.

case, *lis pendens* does not exist. If a non-chosen court is obliged to stay jurisdiction wherever a defendant alleges that a jurisdiction clause exists, it may create an unreasonable barrier to the claimant. It would be particularly unfair if a valid jurisdiction clause indeed does not exist and the claimant is forced to sue in the alleged chosen court. A defendant would have to bring the action in the chosen court before it could apply for a stay under Article 31(2) of the Regulation. If not, the non-chosen court still could take jurisdiction.[30]

This interpretation may encourage a defendant to act quickly in order to prevent being sued in a non-chosen forum. However, what if the defendant brings the action in the chosen court excessively late? Where a defendant believes the non-chosen court has no jurisdiction, it may not submit a defence and it may simply ignore the action. According to the above analysis, the seised court may take jurisdiction and continue the substantive proceedings. The defendant, once being aware of the consequence, may bring the action in the chosen court and challenge jurisdiction at this stage. Would the application for stay be rejected by the reason of delay? The Recast Regulation does not suggest anywhere it could. Rejection is inconsistent with the explicit wording of Article 31(2). However, it is inappropriate to award the defendant the right to challenge jurisdiction of the seised court at any stage of the proceedings, which would cause delay, waste of resources and costs. The EU authority should clarify the procedural requirement for the application for a stay under Article 31(2).

B. Special Jurisdiction

Although the EU party autonomy rules are not free from criticism, they still largely reduce uncertainty and litigation risk in commercial contracts. More difficulty exists in contracts in the absence of choice. In such circumstances, the defendant should either be sued in its domicile,[31] or pursuant to one of the special jurisdiction rules based on the close connection principle or as one of multiple defendants in the domicile of any of the defendants where the actions are closely connected.[32] It is necessary to note that although suing under the general jurisdiction is more straightforward and rarely rejected by courts, the claimant usually wishes to sue the defendant in other countries, which may be the claimant's domicile or the natural forum where evidence is more readily accessible. Therefore, special jurisdiction is relied on more frequently than general jurisdiction in practice.

Special jurisdiction rules in contracts are contained in Article 7(1) of the Recast Regulation which states that:

A person domiciled in a Member State may be sued in another Member State:

(1) (a) in matters relating to a contract, in the courts for the place of performance of the obligation in question;

(b) for the purpose of this provision and unless otherwise agreed, the place of performance of the obligation in question shall be:

— in the case of the sale of goods, the place in a Member State where, under the contract, the goods were delivered or should have been delivered,

---

[30] ibid, 312ff.
[31] Art 4(1) of the Recast Reg.
[32] Arts 7 and 8 of the Recast Reg.

—   in the case of the provision of services, the place in a Member State where, under the contract, the services were provided or should have been provided;

(c) if point (b) does not apply then point (a) applies.

Article 7(1) clearly demonstrates the legislative purpose to improve certainty. Its precedent, Article 5(1) of the Brussels Convention, only contains point (a) of the provision that leaves much doubt on which country is the place of performance of the obligation in question.[33] Article 7(1) simplifies this issue by providing a straightforward rule for the sales and services contracts. However, Article 7(1) (Article 5(1) of the Brussels I Regulation) is not free from criticism. A number of questions continue to present in practice which need further clarification.

i. Place of Performance by Agreement

First, the place of performance could be agreed by the parties. If such an agreement exists, the agreed place would have special jurisdiction under Article 7(1). However, must the agreement be express or could it also be implied? The CJEU might have suggested an affirmative answer. Article 7(1)(b) is clearly worded in a way suggesting the place of delivery and the place where services are provided should be determined 'under the contract'. In other words, all contract terms should be considered to figure out the parties' intention.[34] In *Electrosteel Europe SA v Edil Centro Spa*,[35] the sale of goods contract between the Italian seller and the French buyer contained an 'ex works' clause. Pursuant to Incoterm, this clause means that the carrier took charge of the goods at the seller's premises and delivered them to the buyer's place of business. Referring to then Article 23(1) of the Brussels I Regulation, which accepts implied choice-of-court through international commercial usages, the CJEU believed that there is no reason to preclude international usage from being used in interpreting other provisions of the Regulation.[36] In deciding the place of delivery 'under the contract', the court must take account of all contract terms and international usage, including Incoterms.[37]

ii. Sales Involving Carriage of Goods

It is presumed that the place of delivery and the place where services are provided are easy to determine, which, however, is not true. Taking international sale of goods as an example, the contract usually includes the carriage of goods. The seller would deliver the goods to the carrier, who would transport the goods and deliver them to the buyer. It is questionable whether the place of delivery is the final destination of the goods, which usually is the domicile of the buyer; the place where the seller delivers the goods to the carrier, which usually is the domicile of the seller; or the place where the seller legally discharges its obligation to deliver. Where the parties have expressly agreed on the place of delivery, the chosen place

---

[33] European Commission, 'Proposal for the Brussels I Regulation' COM(1999) 348 final, 14; Case 14/76 *De Bloos* [1976] ECR 1497; and Case 12/76 *Tessili v Dunlop AG* [1976] ECR 1473.
[34] Case C-381/08 *Car Trim* [2010] ECR I-1255, para 56.
[35] Case C-87/10 *Electrosteel Europe SA v Edil Centro Spa* [2011] ECR I-4987.
[36] ibid para 21.
[37] ibid paras 22–26.

should have jurisdiction under Article 7(1)(b).[38] If the parties do not choose the place of delivery, the CJEU stated, in *Car Trim*, that the place of delivery in an international sale of goods involving international carriage, for the purpose of Article 7(1)(b) should be the place 'where physical transfer of the goods took place, as a result of which the purchaser obtained, or should have obtained, actual power of disposal over those goods at the final destination of the sales transaction'.[39] This interpretation distinguishes physical transfer of goods from transfer of risk and transfer of ownership. It is possible that the risk and owner-ship are transferred to the buyer before actual physical delivery. Although the buyer may legally acquire the ownership and power of disposal at a different time and place, only the actual/physical delivery should be considered to determine jurisdiction. This interpreta-tion reflects the objective of certainty and uniformity. The adoption of the factual delivery criterion aims to avoid the application of substantive law or private international law of a Member State. It was stated in the Commission Proposal for the original Brussels I Regula-tion that one of the purposes for reform of the special jurisdiction rules was to 'remedy the shortcomings of applying the rules of private international law' and to adopt a pragmatic approach based on a purely factual criterion.[40]

However, there are two types of factual delivery taking place, ie delivering the goods to the first carrier and delivering the goods to the buyer. The CJEU accepts the second place, stating it is 'the most consistent with the origins, objectives and scheme' of the Regulation. The final destination is highly predictable and has a close proximity with the contract.[41] The goods usually remain in this place after delivery and the operation of the performance of delivery is completed in the final destination.[42] This interpretation is pro-buyer.

iii. Performance in More than One Country

The CJEU has interpreted Article 7(1)(b) in a number of cases where the goods are delivered or services provided in more than one Member State. Instead of limiting the court's jurisdiction to performance within its territory, the principle is adopted to central-ise all the claims arising out of the contract in the principal place of performance.[43] It helps preventing concurrent proceedings on related claims and reducing the litigation cost for the claimant.

The centralisation approach improves certainty and efficiency and, in particular, benefits the claimant. The question is whether it protects the claimant by increasing the litigation risk of the defendant. The CJEU suggests that any place of performance should be predict-able by the defendant. Furthermore, the defendant is also free from the risk of being sued in multiple states, and the efficiency resulting by eliminating concurrent proceedings ben-efits not only the claimant but also the defendant.[44] These arguments are correct assuming that the claimant is willing to bring actions for all the claims even if it is required to sue in

---

[38] See s II.B.i above.

[39] *Car Trim*, above n 34.

[40] The Commission Proposal for a Council Reg (EC) on jurisdiction and the recognition and enforcement of judgments in civil and commercial matters (COM(1999) 348 final), 14; cited in *Car Trim*, ibid, para 52.

[41] *Car Trim*, ibid, para 61.

[42] ibid.

[43] Case C-386/05 *Color Drack GmbH v Lexx International* [2007] ECR I-3699, paras 37–38; Case C-19/09 *Wood Floor v Silva Trade* [2010] ECR 2121.

[44] *Color Drack*, ibid, para 44.

multiple courts. This may not be true in reality. Without the centralisation approach, the claimant would be reluctant to bring multiple actions, especially where the loss in some countries is small. It may prefer to bring one action in the principal place of business only for claims arising out of this country. The court, therefore, does not need to examine the performance in other Member States, which would reduce litigation costs and increase efficiency. This argument, however, is unjustifiable. The localisation approach may force the claimant to give up part of its rights to sue and may lead to efficient breach of contracts by the defendant. Efficiency should not be achieved at the cost of justice.

Jurisdiction should be centralised in the country with the closest link with the contract. According to the CJEU, this country should be the principal place of performance.[45] The principal place of performance is determined by considering contract terms and, in the absence of contract terms, the actual performance.[46] In the sales contract, the principal place of delivery is determined pursuant to economic criteria;[47] in the services contract, where economic criteria cannot be relied on, it depends on the time spent and importance of activities carried out in various Member States.[48] Where the principal place of performance cannot be determined pursuant to the above criteria, inconsistent interpretations exist. According to the CJEU in *Color Drack*, the claimant is free to bring the action in the court of any place of delivery for all the claims where the principal place of delivery cannot be identified.[49] It is also accepted in *Rehder v Air Baltic* that where the services provided in more than one country are indispensible, the claimant could sue in either place of service.[50] However, in *Wood Floor*, which concerns the provision of services by commercial agents in multiple Member States, the CJEU stated that if the place of the main provision of services cannot be determined on the basis of the contract or actual performance, it should be identified by taking account of 'the objectives of predictability and proximity'.[51] In this particular case, the CJEU held the main place of services lies in the agent's domicile, because it is likely the agent will provide substantial services there.[52] It raises a question: if the principal place of performance cannot be determined by economic criteria, must it be identified by considering the objectives of predictability and proximity, or could the claimant directly bring the action in any court of performance? It is necessary to note that *Rehder v Air Baltic* is a dispute between a passenger claimant and an airline defendant, which is excluded from the protective jurisdiction scheme because it is a transport contract. The CJEU's decision that permits the consumer to sue in either place of performance nevertheless brings the same level of protection to the passenger. In *Wood Floor*, on the other hand, the defendant is a commercial agent, which also receives special protection under EU law. The CJEU's decision that limits the claimant's choice of jurisdiction is consistent with the general idea of protection of commercial agents. The two decisions generate a suspicion: given that the CJEU gave different decisions in *Rehder* and *Wood Floor*, does it intend to set up a general principle applicable to all subsequent cases, or is it taking into consideration

---

[45] ibid para 40.
[46] *Wood Floor*, above n 43, para 40.
[47] *Color Drack*, above n 43, para 40.
[48] *Wood Floor*, above n 43, paras 41–42.
[49] *Color Drack*, above n 43, para 42.
[50] Case C-204/08 *Rehder v Air Baltic* [2009] ECR I-6073, para 44.
[51] *Wood Floor*, above n 43, paras 41–42.
[52] ibid.

the nature of the disputes and the power balance between the parties? It is likely that, although without explicitly saying so, the CJEU has taken the weaker party protection into account. This implied intention, however, might bring uncertainty to commercial practitioners in practice.

Furthermore, although the principal place of performance would have the closest link with the contract in most cases, it may not have the closest link with the dispute. If the defendant, for example, breaches the contract only in the Member States, which are not the principal place of delivery, the action against the defendant may have no connections with the principal place at all. It is hard to justify centralising the action for claims relating to performance in other countries than the principal place of business. It is, however, unknown whether the claimant is obliged to either sue in the defendant's domicile, or in the principal place of performance in such circumstances, or whether the claimant could sue the defendant in one of the states of delivery which does have connections with the actual claim.

iv. Classification

Article 7(1) suffers from classification problems. Before applying Article 7(1), it is always necessary to decide, first of all, whether the dispute is 'a matter in relation to a contract', and second, whether the contract is a sale of goods or provision of services contract. As a primary principle, concepts in the EU jurisdiction scheme should not be interpreted according to national law or private international law, but a uniform independent EU meaning.[53] In contrast to sale of goods, which is characterised by supplying goods and transferring ownership of goods, it is more difficult to define services. The CJEU defines services as one of the parties carrying out the particular activity in return for remuneration.[54] This interpretation is broad enough to cover most contracts whose subject matter is labour or professional skills. However, it does not make classification of services easier. It still depends on courts' discretion and should be decided in individual cases. Not all 'particular activities' amount to services. In *Falco Privatstiftung v Gisela Weller-Lindhorst*,[55] the CJEU held that a licensing contract is not a contract for provision of services, because the licensor is not required to perform any 'positive' activity and its obligation under the contract is not to challenge the licensee's use of the intellectual property right.[56] It means that only 'positive' activities can be regarded 'services'.

What if both parties are required to perform 'positive' activities? For example, in publication contracts, the author should submit the manuscripts to the publisher according to conditions in the contract and grant the publishers the (exclusive) copy right. The publisher carries out the activity to produce and distribute the final products. Both parties would carry out some positive activities. Is this type of contract falling within the scope of services? If so, who is the service provider? It is suggested by the CJEU that in complicated contracts involving multiple obligations, classification depends on the characteristic obligation.[57] Again, it may take some brains to decide which obligation, in a complicated

---

[53] eg Case C-89/91 *Shearson Lehman Hutton v TVB* [1993] ECR I-139; Case 33/78 *Somafer SA v Saar-Ferngas AG* [1978] ECR 2183; and Case C 147/12 *ÖFAB* [2013] ECR, para 27.

[54] Case C-533/07 *Falco Privatstiftung and Rabitsch* [2009] ECR I-3327, para 29.

[55] ibid.

[56] ibid, para 31.

[57] *Falco Privatstiftung and Rabitsch*, above n 54, para 54; *Car Trim*, above n 34, paras 31–32.

contract, is the characteristic one. In the publication contract, is it the publisher's obligation to publish or the author's obligation to submit manuscripts and transfer copyrights?

Another complicated contract that needs analysis is a franchise contract. Recital 17 of Rome I suggests that both distribution and franchise contracts are classified as services contracts for the purpose of Article 7(1) of the Recast Regulation. This interpretation does not bind the court and it may over-simplify the problem. A franchise contract also involves the transfer of intellectual property rights: the franchisor allows the franchisee to use its trademark/patent to conduct its business in return for monetary consideration. This has been ruled as a 'negative' obligation and excluded from the scope of services. However, the franchisor also has positive obligations to perform, eg by providing training and other assistance to the franchisee. Could these obligations render the contract a services contract? The answer is not straightforward. The franchisor's obligations include licensing and also training and assistance. However, in some franchise contracts, the main obligation is licensing and other obligations are supplementary. If one can only take the characteristic obligation into consideration, the characteristic obligation in a franchise contract is not much different from a licensing contract. In other franchise contracts involving complicated operation skills and procedure, training and assistance may be equally important. Such franchise contracts might be classified as services.

Questions may also arise as to remuneration. As a general rule remuneration refers to money or other monetary benefits. In *Corman-Collins v La Maison du Whisky*,[58] the CJEU ruled that remuneration should be interpreted more flexibly to include not only monetary payment but also all types of advantages.[59] Therefore, a distribution agreement is classified as a contract for the provision of services in the Recast Regulation. The distributor's activity to distribute the grantor's product is the characteristic service. The distributor receives advantages of exclusivity and relevant assistance from the supplier, which represent economic values and can be counted as remuneration. It is noted that in almost all commercial contracts, both parties would receive advantages of certain economic value, which means that the presence of remuneration usually should not be a question.

C. Default Applicable Law

Uncertainty also exists in Rome I.[60] Article 4 provides harmonised choice-of-law rules for contracts without a choice-of-law agreement. Article 4 of Rome I has departed from Article 4 of the Rome Convention, by adopting fixed connecting factors for eight common types of contracts (the hard and fast rules),[61] by limiting the use of the principle of characteristic performance,[62] and by lifting the threshold of the escape clause (the closest connection principle).[63] The purpose of the reform is to increase certainty and efficiency.

---

[58] Case C-9/12 *Corman-Collins v La Maison du Whisky*, EU:C:2013:860.

[59] ibid, paras 39–40.

[60] This Chapter only deals with Art 4. Art 3 of the Rome I Reg largely follows Art 3 of the Rome Convention which has been studied thoroughly in earlier researches. See, eg J Hill, 'Choice of Law in Contract under the Rome Convention' (2004) 53 *International and Comparative Law Quarterly* 325.

[61] Art 4(1).

[62] Art 4(2).

[63] Art 4(3) and (4).

However, it is hard to argue that Rome I could indeed achieve certainty. Applying the hard-and-fast rule usually will be very straightforward, but it suffers from the difficulty of classification. Questions may arise to distinguish sale of goods from provision of services. The scope of services is also uncertain. If a uniform definition of services shall be provided in the conflicts scheme, the case law on the Brussels I Recast (Brussels I Regulation) shall be applicable in Rome I.

The characteristic performance rule applies to contracts falling out of the scope of Article 4(1). This rule traditionally suffers from uncertainty. It is not always easy to identify the characteristic performer of a contract and in some contracts the characteristic performer simply does not exist, eg both parties' performances are equally complicated and important to the operation of the contract. Unfortunately, these complicated contracts, in which the characteristic performer cannot be easily identified, are generally excluded from the scope of Article 4(1). In other words, Article 4(2) cannot offer much help in practice.

Furthermore, the characteristic performance rule also applies to contracts covered by more than one category in Article 4(1).[64] The purpose of this condition is to apply Article 4(2) to any contracts that cannot be clearly classified as any type in Article 4(1). It is, however, necessary to note that although Article 4(1) of Rome I provides different connecting factors for eight types of contracts, these contracts are not mutually exclusive to each other. For example, sale of goods contracts in Article 4(1)(a) and sale of goods by auction in Article 4(1)(g) are overlapping. Recital 17 also suggests that services contracts in Article 4(1)(b) cover franchise contracts in Article 4(1)(e) and distribution contracts in Article 4(1)(f). The wording of Article 4(2) might indicate that all these contracts that fall in one category in general but specific rules are provided for them given their special characteristics fall within the scope of Article 4(2). These two provisions, therefore, are not perfectly compatible.

Where Article 4(1) and (2) cannot apply, the applicable law is determined by the closest connection principle.[65] This principle may lead to a lot of uncertainty as it completely depends on the discretion of the court by calculating and weighing all the linking factors of a contract. Different courts may put different weight on some factors. In particular, in complicated contracts, multiple connecting factors exist in various countries, leading to greater diversity. In such cases, the uniform choice-of-law rules may not lead to the uniformity and the applicable law continues to depend on which court hears the case. Furthermore, it is not unusual to find that there is no one single country clearly being the centre of gravity. There is no further guidance to designate the applicable law in such cases.

The final difficulty arises out of the escape clause. Even if the governing law may be determined pursuant to Article 4(1) and (2), the court may decide the law of the other country should apply instead if 'it is clear from all the circumstances of the case that the contract is manifestly more closely connected with' another country.[66] It again depends on the court to exercise its decision in determining if there is another country with a manifestly closer connection. The word 'manifestly' suggests the escape clause should not be applied lightly. A mere closer connection would not justify derogation from Article 4(1) and (2). However, it is always easier to explain the principle than applying it in practice. There is no clear-cut line between closer connection and manifestly closer connection.

---

[64] Art 4(2).
[65] Art 4(4).
[66] Art 4(3).

Article 4 of Rome I cannot produce great certainty to the contracting parties. On the other hand, the discretion-oriented principles may open new debatable points and increase litigation costs. Bearing in mind the difficulty of Article 4, sophisticated commercial players may be encouraged to insert choice of law agreements in their contracts to reduce future uncertainty.[67]

III. Contracts with Inequality of Bargaining Power

For contracts with inequality of bargaining power, the EU legislature pays most attention to the need of weak party protection. However, certainty continues to be one of the objectives. Take consumer contracts as an example. Where the business targets a consumer's domicile, the effect of jurisdiction and choice-of-law clauses is largely limited. The consumer should only be sued in the consumer's domicile but can choose to sue the business either in the business' domicile or in the consumer's domicile and the consumer can be protected by the level not lower than mandatory rules in his habitual residence.[68] The test for 'targeting' is well designed to ensure certainty. The protective conflicts rules balance the purposes of weak party protection and certainty.

A. Targeting Test

Is it really easy to decide whether a business has 'targeted' a consumer's domicile or habitual residence? A number of judgments have been rendered by the CJEU interpreting 'targeting' in various circumstances, especially in online contracting. The Recast Regulation and Rome I use broad terms. For example, Article 17(1)(c) of the Recast Regulation provides that a business has targeted consumers' domicile if 'the contract has been concluded with a person who pursues commercial or professional activities in the Member State of the consumer's domicile or, by any means, directs such activities to that Member State or to several States including that Member State'.[69] The exact meaning of the broad term 'direct … to' generated a lot of debates in the past and commentators have proposed a few approaches, such as accessibility,[70] profitability,[71] country-specific-indicia,[72] activity of the website,[73] and ring-fencing,[74] to interpret this concept in online transactions.

---

[67] For more, see Z Tang, 'Law Applicable in the Absence of Choice' (2008) 71 *Modern Law Review* 785.

[68] Art 18 of the Recast Reg.

[69] Art 17(1)(c) of the Recast Reg. See also Rome I, Art 6(1).

[70] VznGr Den Haag, *NIPR* 2005, 168; OGH 9 Nc 110/02; LG Feldkirch 3 R 259/03; European Commission, 'Proposal for a Council Regulation (EC) on jurisdiction and the recognition and enforcement of judgments in civil and commercial matters' ('Commission Proposal'), COM(99)0348 final, [1999] OJ C 376E/1, Recital 13.

[71] A Thünken, 'Multi-State Advertising Over The Internet And The Private International Law Of Unfair Competition' (2002) 51 *International and Comparative Law Quarterly* 909, 935.

[72] German Appellate Court, the judgment of 12/15/2004—U 1855/04.

[73] Amendment 37 from the Parliament in the 'Proposal for a Council Regulation on Jurisdiction and the Recognition and Enforcement of Judgements in Civil and Commercial Matters' ('Parliament Proposal'), A5-0253/2000 COM (1999) 348-C5-0169/1999–1999/0154 (CNS), [2001] OJ C146/94, 97–8.

[74] ibid, Art 37.

In its recent decisions, the CJEU provides a hybrid approach to interpret the meaning of Article 17(1)(c). In the joint judgments for *Pammer v Reederei* and *Hotel Alpenhof GesmbH v Heller*,[75] the CJEU expressly rejected the accessibility approach, ie the business is deemed to have targeted the consumer's home country if it operates a website that is accessible in that country. If the only connection between the business and the consumer's domicile, besides the concluded contract, is the accessibility of the website, this business does not target that country. The CJEU also ruled that some factors are conclusive that the business has targeted the consumer's home state, for example, the business provides an express statement, either on the website or somewhere in the contract or confirmation, that it intends to trade with consumers from certain countries. Most cases fall between the two scenarios and the court should consider all the relevant factors to decide if the business has 'manifested its intention to establish commercial relations' with consumers domiciled in certain countries. Relevant factors include international nature of the activity at issue, the provision of the international code of the business telephone number, using the top-level domain of a particular foreign country, using the neutral top-level domain, providing itineraries guiding travel from other Member States to the business's home to receive services, mentioning the composition of international customers from various Member States, language and currency.

It is important to note that the CJEU judgment is not completely consistent with the previous joint statement made by the Council and the Commission which suggests that the country specific indicia are irrelevant. Country specific indicia is clearly adopted by the CJEU as one of the factors that may indicate the business's intention. The CJEU's approach is an appropriate one because no rigid guidance can work effectively in a cross-border commercial world marked by the frequent adoption of new commercial models and the frequent updating of communication technology. The flexibility, however, may leave uncertainty to the parties and reduce the business's capacity to manage its commercial risk and set up its marketing strategy.

In order to provide sufficient protection to consumers, the CJEU ruled that the only requirement for the objective connection is the 'targeting' test. As far as the business has targeted the consumer's domicile, all consumers in that country could rely on the protective jurisdiction and choice-of-law rules, irrespective of whether the contract that gives rise to the dispute is the direct result of the targeting activity. The protective conflicts rules, thus, apply to both distance contracts and contracts concluded in the business's domicile.[76] In *Emrek v Sabranovic*,[77] a German consumer bought a car in France by placing an order in the French company's premises in person. The French company maintained a website, providing its contact information, including the international code of a telephone number. The CJEU held that the protective conflicts rules must apply and there is no need for a causal link between the targeting activity and the contract. This decision is justifiable in that, first, it is hard to prove whether the particular contract is the result of the targeting activity and, second, once the business has targeted a particular country, the business should have reasonable expectation that it might be subject to the courts of this country. Although these

---

[75] Joined cases C-585/08 and C-144/09 *Pammer v Reederei* and *Hotel Alpenhof GesmbH v Heller* [2010] ECR I-12527.
[76] Case C-190/11 *Mühlleitner v Yusufi*, EU:C:2012:542.
[77] Case C-218/12 *Lokman Emrek v Vlado Sabranovic*, EU:C:2013:666.

reasons are justifiable, the business may lose the chance to manage its commercial risk. For example, it could not predict which transaction, per se, would give rise to the risk of cross-border litigation. It also loses the sense to adjust the price of transactions to reflect the commercial risk. The final result may be that the business would systematically increase the price of its products sold online and offline to cover the potential risk of being sued abroad.

B. Classification

Classification also leads to some uncertainty. In practice, disputes exist as to whether a contract is indeed a 'consumer contract'. There are a lot of contracts falling in the grey area between typical commercial and consumer contracts, such as investment contracts, franchising contracts in which the franchisee is an unprofessional individual and contracts with mixed purposes. There are inconsistent rulings concerning contracts with mixed purposes. In *Gruber v Bay Wa*,[78] the CJEU provides that contracts with mixed purposes are non-consumer contracts, except where the usage for business purposes is 'so little as to be negligible'. In *Ceska Sporitelna AS v Feichter*,[79] the CJEU stated that '[o]nly contracts concluded outside and independently of any trade or professional activity or purpose, solely for the purpose of satisfying an individual's own needs in terms of private consumption' are consumer contracts. It does not allow any leeway to contracts in which the professional purpose exists but is negligible. The interpretation given in *Ceska* improves certainty, but it reduces the number of contracting parties that might enjoy protection as consumers.

C. Efficiency Test

It is necessary to note that some commentators argue, from an economic perspective, that the protective conflicts rules increase transaction costs for businesses that want to enter into a broad internal market. In order to reduce commercial risk, some businesses may decide not to trade in other countries and others may decide to increase the price. The cost of commercial risk, eventually, will be transferred to consumers.[80] This argument presumes that there is a perfect competitive market where the prices could correctly reflect the cross-border litigation risk of transactions. In this market, if the litigation risk is reduced, the business will accordingly reduce the prices, and vice versa. This market, however, does not exist in reality. In other words, without protective conflicts rules, businesses may be happy to unilaterally insert jurisdiction and choice-of-law clauses to reduce commercial risks or even to hamper consumers' ability to sue, without reducing prices and taking all the additional benefits result from the reduction of risk.[81]

One may argue that consumers may enter into contracts rationally by comparing various suppliers. If a business inserts an unfavourable conflicts clause in the contract and does

---

[78] Case C-464/01 *Gruber v Bay Wa* [2005] ECR I-00439.
[79] Case C-409/11 *Česká spořitelna AS v Feichter*, EU:C:2013:165.
[80] G Bone, 'Party Rulemaking' (2012) 90 *Texas Law Review* 1329, 1364; RA Hillman and JJ Rachlinski, 'Standard-Form Contracting in the Electronic Age' (2002) 77 *New York University Law Review* 429, 439.
[81] Bone, ibid, 1365.

not reduce the price, it has put itself in an inferior position in the market because rational consumers would select other suppliers. This argument presumes that, first, consumers are adequately rational and, second, there are no factors other than the conflicts clause that may affect the price. Both presumptions are unrealistic. First, consumers can barely make truly rational choices. Many e-consumers simply enter into contracts without carefully calculating the risk or making any comparison. Although some e-consumers may rely on the comparison website to help make decisions, the website usually only compares the price without any warnings on the potential remedy risk in the future. Furthermore, most consumers would not actually read the business's terms and conditions, and even if they read themm, they would not pay attention to any conflicts clauses. Therefore, it is unrealistic to argue that the business will be obliged to adjust their price to reflect the risk brought about by the conflict-of-laws. Second, even if consumers are rational enough to link the price with the conflicts clause (which is highly unlikely in practice), there are many other factors that affect the price, such as the cost of production, transportation, storage, staffing, management and legal risk. Putting all the relevant factors together, the cost of legal risk only affects the final price very lightly. Within the legal risk, the additional risk associated with cross-border litigation occupies an even smaller proportion.[82] The argument to rely on the market to protect consumers is unrealistic.

It is thus concluded that the EU protective conflicts rules are necessary and they do not cause great inefficiency in economic terms. The legal framework, in general, balances the two objectives of protecting the weaker party and providing commercial certainty. The competent court and applicable law in most cases are easily predictable. However, uncertainty continues to exist in classification between ordinary contracts and consumer contracts and also in the application of the targeting test.

IV. Conclusion

The EU conflicts rules in cross-border contracts have been improved continuously. A lot of previous difficulties that hampered the effective application of the law in practice have been addressed by the later reforms and the CJEU's judgments. All those reforms and interpretations have shown a consistent tendency to improve certainty and predictability for the parties. Certainty is an objective not only in ordinary commercial contracts, but also in contracts with inequality of bargaining power. Although the protective conflicts rules make fairness the most important goal, they also seek to balance fairness and certainty. It is necessary to note that certainty may not necessarily lead to efficiency. The law can only promote commercial efficiency if it allocates risk in the most appropriate and reasonably predictable way. As a result, certainty cannot be achieved by establishing rigid and improper rules. In ordinary commercial contracts, authorities should trust sophisticated commercial participants which are in the best position to allocate their own commercial risk, and provide them with as much autonomy as they can. The law will only be there to assist such autonomy to be exercised in a mutually predictable manner. In the absence of autonomy, certainty is

---

[82] ibid, 1366.

achieved by considering the most reasonable expectations of rational businessmen in this field and the rules should avoid being too rigid. In consumer contracts, certainty should be achieved by appropriate legal intervention, given the existence of inequality of power. It is fair to conclude that the EU conflicts scheme in contractual litigation is generally successful in providing certainty without sacrificing other important values in both commercial and consumer contracts.

However, uncertainty continues to exist, though only on a small number of occasions. Uncertainty is mainly caused by ambiguous and not well thought-through legislative provisions; inconsistent and unclear CJEU interpretation in some cases; and inconsistency between jurisdiction and choice-of-law rules. They are not fundamentally problematic but small weaknesses reduce certainty and efficiency of cross-border transactions. These weaknesses are relatively easy to address by updating the legislation or the CJEU's interpretation. Attention should be paid to the consistency between existing judgments on the same provision and related provisions. Guidance needs to be detailed enough to avoid different implementation and misunderstanding by national courts.

37

Cross-border Non-contractual Disputes: The Legislative Framework and Court Practice

MICHAEL WILDERSPIN[*]

I. Introduction

This chapter analyses the European Union (EU) instruments on international jurisdiction and choice-of-law insofar as they consider cross-border non-contractual disputes and it relates them to the questions whether the institutional architecture is suited to providing an effective remedy, and whether the Court of Justice of the EU (CJEU) deals adequately with private international law issues. As to the question whether national courts properly apply the acquis, some specific examples are included from the national reports.

As regards institutional architecture, the most important Treaty provision designed to ensure correct and uniform application of EU law is Article 267 Treaty on the Functioning of the European Union (TFEU) which establishes the preliminary reference procedure. The infringement procedure (Article 258 TFEU), which can be deployed against Member States which fail to transpose or to apply the acquis, is of little use in the civil law field, where most instruments adopted at EU level are Regulations, which do not require transposition. The preliminary reference procedure has undoubtedly been effective in putting flesh on the bones of the Regulations in this field and in giving guidance to national courts as to how they are to interpret them. In dealing with such references, the Court is primarily concerned to give a workable and clear answer to the national court making the reference but, at the same time, it should also aim to provide a clear and principled interpretation of the relevant provision which will be of use to national courts and practitioners faced with similar cases. In this author's view, some recent judgments in this field have failed to take adequate account of either function, in particular the latter.

Since the preliminary reference procedure is merely an interlocutory step in national proceedings, it will add to the time taken before judgment can be given by the national court. If proceedings before the CJEU take too long, national courts may be deterred from making references (and litigants from requesting them). The Court is thus under pressure to act

[*] Legal Adviser, European Commission. The opinions expressed in this paper are those of the author alone and do not necessarily represent the views of the European Commission.

quickly. In recent years, it has made considerable (and quite successful) efforts to reduce the time taken to process a reference. However, it is not certain that this has always been done without the increased speed having some adverse impact on the quality of judgments.

Finally, there must be some doubt as to whether all judges of the CJEU possess sufficient expertise to deal adequately with the private international law cases with which they have been dealing. Whilst the Court sometimes produces excellent and well-reasoned judgments,[1] recent case law in this field contains numerous examples of judgments that are unworkable,[2] inadequately reasoned,[3] inconsistent with one another[4] or just plain wrong.[5]

II. International Jurisdiction

Broadly speaking, where a defendant is domiciled in a Member State, jurisdiction is governed by the harmonised rules of the Brussels I Recast Regulation[6] (Brussels Ia). The basic rule is that the defendant is to be sued before the courts of the Member State in which he is domiciled,[7] but this rule is supplemented by a number of other heads of jurisdiction.[8]

As regards non-contractual disputes, the most important provisions are Article 7(2) (formerly 5(3) (the *forum delicti*) and Article 8(1) (formerly 6(1)), which, where there is more than one defendant, allows all defendants to be sued before the courts of the EU domicile of one of them, if there is a close connection between the claims. Despite the fact that the interpretation of these provisions had already given rise to difficulty, the opportunity was not taken by the legislature to amend them in 2012.

A. *Forum Delicti*: Article 7(2)

Article 7(2) allows a defendant to be sued in a Member State other than that of his domicile 'in matters relating to tort, delict or quasi-delict, in the courts for the place where the harmful event occurred or may occur'.

i. *Experience before the CJEU*

This provision, along with its predecessors, has been the subject of much litigation before the CJEU. Between 1976[9] and 2004, the Court delivered 11 judgments concerning

---

[1] eg C-412/10 *Homawoo* EU:C:2011:747 and C-191/15 *Verein für Konsumenteninformation v Amazon* EU:C:2016:612.

[2] C-196/15 *Granarolo* EU:C:2016:559.

[3] C-375/13 *Kolassa* EU:C:2015:37.

[4] *cf* eg C-364/93 *Marinari* EU:C:1995:289, C-168/02 *Kronhofer* EU:C:2004:364, *Kolassa* ibid and C-12/15 *Universal Music* EU:C:2016:449.

[5] C-376/14 PPU *C v M* EU:C:2014:2268, where the Court delivered a plainly wrong judgment, despite AG Szpunar having shown the correct path to follow. See J Pirrung, 'EuEheVO und HKÜ: Steine statt Brot' (2015) 3 *IPRax* 207.

[6] Reg 1215/2012 on jurisdiction and the recognition and enforcement of judgments in civil and commercial matters (recast), [2012] OJ L351/1, Arts 4 and 5.

[7] Art 4(1).

[8] Arts 7–26.

[9] Beginning with 21/76 *Bier v Mines de Potasse* EU:C:1976:166.

Article 5(3) of the Brussels Convention. Following a lull of five years, between 2009 and 2016 the Court delivered no fewer than 18 judgments on Article 5(3) of Regulation 44/2001, with a further three pending at the time of writing. This pattern is partly explicable by the fact that under the Brussels Convention references could be made by courts of appeal and supreme courts but under the Brussels I regime until 2009 only supreme courts could make references. Since the entry into force of the Lisbon Treaty, all courts may avail themselves of this possibility. A second reason may be the increasing use of the internet, which has posed a number of challenges to the application of the rules on jurisdiction, in particular Article 7(2).

a. Scope of Article 7(2) and its Relationship with Article 7(1) (the *Forum Contractus*)

In *Kalfelis*,[10] the Court defined the scope of Article 7(2) in negative terms, holding that it 'covers all actions which seek to establish the liability of a defendant and which are not related to a contract'.[11] If taken literally, this would mean that, taken together, Article 7(1) and (2) cover the entire range of civil obligations, with point one covering the cases where there has been a voluntary assumption of liability,[12] and point two covering the remainder, irrespective of how the liability is characterised under national law.[13] In principle it is this approach that the Court has followed, but it has recently been thrown into some disarray by various judgments.

In *Granarolo*,[14] the Court held that liability imposed by a French statutory provision for the abrupt termination of an established business relationship, *in casu* the distribution by one party of the other's products, but without a framework agreement or exclusivity agreement, did *not* fall within the scope of Article 7(2), provided that there existed a 'tacit contractual relationship', which would have to be determined on the basis of the existence of a long-standing business relationship, regularity of the transactions and their quantity and value, prices and discounts and correspondence.[15] With respect, the result is, both in terms of its reasoning and its workability, a prime example of how *not* to write a judgment. The Court ignores the fact that the national court had made it clear that the liability in question was distinct from contractual liability and entirely independent of any remedy for breach of a contract. Liability depended rather on the existence of an 'established business relationship'; furthermore, in the circumstances of the case, the national court had stressed that (unlike the case of *Corman-Collins*)[16] there was no framework contract between the parties. In reaching its conclusion, the CJEU invokes in a rather facile manner the principle that *characterisation* must be carried out autonomously, irrespective of the characterisation under national law,[17] but ignores the fact that it is still necessary to take into account for this purpose the basis of liability and the operation of the rule under national law. Here the liability was imposed independently of any liability for breach of contract; contracts were relevant only in that the parties must at some stage have concluded a number of them.

---

[10] Case 189/87 EU:C:1988:459.
[11] ibid para 16.
[12] C-26/91 *Handte* EU:C:1992:268.
[13] See ch 8 above for some specific examples of how this distinction operates in practice.
[14] Above n 2.
[15] ibid, para 28.
[16] C-9/12 EU:C:2013:860.
[17] *Granarolo*, above n 2, para 19.

The judgment is also unworkable in that it requires the national court to examine in considerable factual detail whether there is 'a tacit contractual relationship' as a precondition to determining whether the situation before it falls within Article 7(1) or 7(2). This is bad enough, in that it is requiring the court to carry out a detailed factual analysis at this preliminary stage, but it is aggravated by the fact that it is not clear precisely what this concept embraces; it seems to be halfway between an 'established business relationship' and a framework contract. Furthermore, there is a partial but not total overlap between the criterion used to determine liability ie 'established business relationship' and those used to determine whether there is a 'tacit contractual relationship', of which the existence of an established business relationship is but one.[18]

The judgment can be contrasted with the well-reasoned Opinion of AG Kokott: at paragraphs 18–23 she correctly identifies the basis of the liability as being the failure to conclude new contracts (as opposed to breaching existing ones), and draws a parallel with the *Tacconi* judgment[19] which holds that the abrupt breaking of contractual negotiations is delictual in nature, before concluding that the liability in question falls under Article 7(2).

Recently the Court has also been confronted with borderline cases in which liability is neither contractual nor based on some act (whether fault based or otherwise) of the defendant.[20] In such cases, since point one cannot be applicable, the Court must decide whether liability falls under point two or whether it falls outside the scope of Article 7 entirely.

In *Austro-Mechana v Amazon*,[21] the Court had to determine whether a provision of Austrian law that authorised individuals to make reproductions of copyright protected material but, at the same time, provided that the persons who placed the recording equipment on the market were obliged to pay fair remuneration, via a copyright collecting society, to the author of the work, fell within the scope of Article 7(2). The straightforward argument that the *Kalfelis* case law and the expression 'quasi-delictual', which clearly encompassed liability other than classic tortious liability flowing from a wrongful act, meant that, taken together, Article 7(1) and (2) cover the whole range of civil obligations, with any liability not being based on a voluntary assumption of liability *ipso facto* falling within the scope of Article 7(2), being implicitly rejected by the Court. However, it ultimately concluded that the liability in issue was covered by Article 7(2), but did so on the basis of very tortuous reasoning.

First, the Court appears (at paragraph 44) to hold that liability under Article 7(2) may arise only if the claimant has suffered damage resulting from a harmful event. In so doing, the Court omits to examine whether 'quasi-delict' contemplates liability not based on a harmful event, and ignores the approach that the Court itself took in *Kalfelis*, which makes no mention of the need for the presence of a harmful event. The consequence of this reasoning, one might assume, would be to exclude the liability in issue in the case itself, which involves neither damage nor a harmful event. However, the Court thereupon proceeded to tie itself in knots, holding that, although that act of copying was specifically authorised

---

[18] ibid para 26.
[19] C-334/00 EU:C:2002:499.
[20] See ch 25 above, according to which the Dutch courts have dealt with a number of such cases but have not found it necessary to make any references for a preliminary ruling; see however C-12/15 *Universal Music* above n 4 and C-47/14 *Holterman Ferho* EU:C:2015:574.
[21] C-572/14 EU:C:2016:286.

both by the national law and the Directive underlying it,[22] the levy payable was to provide 'compensation for the harm suffered by the authors resulting from such unauthorised copy by the latter' (paragraph 43). The latter phrase is incomprehensible in English partly thanks to a translation error: in the authoritative German version, the expression is 'Schaden ..., der durch solche, von ihnen nicht erlaubte, Kopien entsteht', which can properly be translated as 'harm that arises from such copies unauthorised by them (ie the authors)'. Therefore the failure by Amazon to collect the levy and to pass it on to the rights collecting society must, according to the Court, be seen as a harmful event. However, it is wrong to say that the compensation offsets the harm suffered by unauthorised copying, simply because the copying *is* authorised. More accurately, the purpose was to compensate for the loss of the claim for what would, in the absence of the scheme, have been a copyright infringement. The Court then goes on to define the harmful event as failure by Amazon to collect and pass on the levy.[23]

Given the close link between liability for infringing copyrighted material and the system in question, which aimed to ensure equivalent compensation for the authors of protected works, it is difficult not to have some sympathy with the result. However, the reasoning of the Court underlying that result contains so many basic flaws that it is difficult to know where to start. First, the authors suffered no harm; the scheme merely aimed to provide them with compensation for what was no more than notional loss arising from perfectly lawful use. Second, a failure to pay a levy imposed by the law is not of itself a harmful event; holding it to be so implies that any failure to pay money owed to another party is, of itself, tortious.

The main objection to the reasoning in the judgment is that it is both formalistic (by insisting on damage and a harmful event even where the liability is not based on a wrongful act) and flawed (in that it in reality invents both to satisfy this test) that it fails to discharge the Court's function of interpreting the Regulation sufficiently clearly that the judgment enables national courts and practitioners to apply the case law to similar but not identical problems.

The issue of liability to make restitution arising out of amounts unduly received where there is no contract between the parties[24] but, at the same time, no wrongdoing on the defendant's part is one example. Can it be reasonably deduced from *Austro-Mechana* that this falls within Article 7(2)? If one looks at the starting point in *Austro-Mechana*, the answer would appear to be no: in such a case there is no damage and still less a harmful event. On the other hand, the Court's very broad understanding of both of these expressions in the *Austro-Mechana* judgment suggests that they could be stretched to cover this situation.[25] This question arose in *Siemens Österreich*[26] in which the Court, having held that the situation (which had its genesis in the imposition of a fine by a national competition

---

[22] Art 5(2) of Dir 2001/29 allows Member States to make exceptions to the reproduction right provided by the Dir, provided that the rightholders receive fair compensation.

[23] This picks up on an idea put forward by AG Saumandsgaard Oe in his Opinion in the case EU:C:2016:286.

[24] In C-366/13 *Profit Investments* EU:C:2016:282, the Court held that where money has been unduly received under the terms of a *contract* that turns out to be void, the claim for the return of the money unduly paid falls within the scope of Art 7(1).

[25] This was the view of AG Darmon in C-89/91 *Shearson Lehman Hutton* EU:C:1993:15, basing himself on the broad terms used by the Court in *Kalfelis*.

[26] C-102/15 EU:C:2016:607.

authority) was not a civil and commercial matter and thus did not fall within the scope of the Regulation, declined to answer the question on the scope of Article 7(2). The question thus remains unresolved. However, in his Opinion, AG Wahl emphatically concluded that such liability did not fall within the scope of Article 7(2) and rejected the contention of AG Saumandsgaard Oe in *Austro-Mechana* that failure to pay money owed is itself a harmful event; however, that contention must have been accepted by the Court in *Austro-Mechana* since it underlay its conclusion that the liability in issue did fall within the scope of Article 7(2).

A further issue that has given rise to problems is the scope of Article 7(2) where presumptively non-contractual liability arises in the context of a contract between the parties. It can be contended that such a case involves both tortious and contractual elements and that jurisdiction in respect of each head of liability must be determined by using the appropriate provision of Article 7; on the other hand, it can be maintained that the non-contractual liability is so closely linked to the contractual relationship that it is subsumed under Article 7(1). In *Brogsitter*,[27] in which the claimant sued the defendant for both breach of contract and for torts which arose (loosely speaking) in connection with the contract, the Court had an opportunity to resolve this important question. Rather than treating the case as significant, the Court assigned it to a three judge Chamber, dispensed with both a hearing and an AG's Opinion and, instead of giving a clear and workable answer, held that where one contracting party sues the other, Article 7(1) applies only if the conduct is a breach of contract, which will normally be the case 'where the interpretation of the contract … is indispensable to establish the lawful or … unlawful nature of the conduct'.[28]

Although the point is not clear from the judgment, the order for reference made it clear that none of the claims could have arisen had the contract not been concluded. However, the test promulgated by the Court requires more than a mere causal connection between the contract and the acts which, absent the contract, would have been tortious, but instead requires a more precise and casuistic examination of the terms of the contract.[29]

The judgment can be criticised not merely because the test promulgated requires a detailed factual examination of the terms of the contract but also because it is not clear what it actually means. A situation where the claim is tortious in nature but the defendant may have a contractual defence is one example. Where a patent holder sues a licensee for alleged infringement of the patent and the defendant claims that the allegedly infringing act is permitted by the licensing agreement, if one takes the wording of *Brogsitter* literally, this situation would appear to fall within the scope of Article 7(1), since the respective obligations of the parties can be determined only by reference to the contract. However, it is submitted that the Court cannot possibly have intended this result; the nature of the claim (patent infringement) is undoubtedly tortious and the contract is relevant only as a defence.

Having promulgated a strict test in *Brogsitter*, the Court appears to have backtracked in *Holterman Ferho*.[30] In that case, a company sued a person who was both an employee

[27] C-548/12 EU:C:2014:148.

[28] ibid paras 22–26.

[29] C Wendelstein, ‚Wechselzeitige Begrenzung von Vertrags- und Deliktsgerichtsstand im Rahmen des europäischen Zuständigkeitsrechts' (2015) 3 *Zeitschrift für europäisches Privatrecht* 3.

[30] Above n 20.

and director/manager of the company for breach of contract (as an employee) and for breach of his statutory duty under company law as director/manager. The national court asked essentially: i) whether the special protective provisions of the Regulation applicable to employment contracts applied to all actions brought against an employee of a company (Article 21) even to the extent that action is based on his liability as a director; ii) in the negative, whether breach of the duties of a director/manager fell under Article 7(1) or 7(2); and iii) for guidance as to the determination of the 'place of performance' and 'place of the harmful event'.

The *Brogsitter* methodology would suggest that the claim relating to breach of the employment relationship would fall under Article 21 but the statutory claim for breach of duty as a director/manager, determined by company law and thus not dependent on the contract between the parties, would fall under Article 7(2). Alternatively, since the case concerned an employment relationship, it would be possible to hold that the *Brogsitter* approach would undermine the protection offered to the employee by Article 21 and thus subsume all claims arising in connection with the employment relationship, including the breach of statutory duty, under the Article 21 regime.[31]

Instead, the Court adopted a rather woolly intermediate position. Having reformulated (or rather misinterpreted) the first question as asking whether the claim against the defendant as the director/manager of the company fell within Article 21, the Court gave a delphic reply, holding that this depended on the degree of subordination of the director to the company; if it transpired that he had a 'not negligible' influence on the company's board then he was not to be treated as an employee. This reply is inadequate for a number of reasons: it fails to distinguish between the claim for breach of the employment contract and the statutory claim and would appear, by effectively treating the director as not being an employee if he is an influential member of the board, to apply also to the claim for breach of the employment contract. It also requires a detailed factual enquiry by the national court, contrary to the principle that issues of jurisdiction should be resolved summarily without the need for such detailed assessments. On the second question, the Court held that, if the director is to be treated as director rather than employee, the claim against him is nevertheless to be treated as contractual since the relationship could not have come about without the consent of both parties.

A priori this is a defensible view, but is inconsistent with *Brogsitter*: the director's liability was an objective liability imposed by law and the determination of whether it had been breached was not dependent on an interpretation of the individual employment contract. *Brogsitter* would thus suggest that it should have been treated as tortious.[32]

b. The Application of the Rule: Place of Causal Event and Place of Damage

As is well known, at an early stage the Court held that the connecting factor of 'the place where the harmful event occurred' means 'both the place where the damage occurred and the place of the event giving rise to it'.[33] Where damage is caused in more than one Member

---

[31] As did the English Court of Appeal in *Alfa Laval Tumba v Separator Spares International* [2013] All ER 463.

[32] As the English Court of Appeal did in *Base Metal Trading v Shamurin* [2004] EWCA Civ 1316 in the context of determining the applicable law.

[33] *Bier*, above n 9, paras 24 and 25.

State, the courts of that State have jurisdiction only over the harm suffered there, whereas the courts of the Member State of the event giving rise to the damage have jurisdiction in respect of the entire harm.[34]

1. Financial Loss

This rule works perfectly well in the case of physical damage to property or person but runs into difficulty in the case of immaterial damage, as illustrated by *Kronhofer*[35] and its progeny. In that case, a claimant domiciled in Austria sued defendants domiciled in Germany for financial loss. Essentially, the defendants had persuaded the claimant to allow them to engage in speculative transactions on his behalf in London; operationally, he transferred money from his Austrian bank account to a special account in Germany. The claimant sought to sue the defendants in Austria on the basis of Article 7(2), arguing that the loss that he sustained affected the whole of his assets in Austria. Since the national court held that both the causal event and the damage took place in Germany, the Court had little difficulty in holding, in the light of its earlier *Marinari* judgment,[36] that the Austrian courts had no jurisdiction. The decision is undoubtedly correct in the light of the pre-existing case law, and provided an adequate answer to the referring court, but provides no guidance to courts that may be confronted with cases in which the facts are similar but not identical. And in *Kolassa*,[37] the Court departed from *Kronhofer* in a factually very similar case.

In *Kolassa*, the claimant was domiciled in Austria, where he sued a foreign defendant, Barclays Bank, to recover loss incurred from having purchased, through an intermediary, bearer bonds issued by Barclays Bank and sold on to consumers in Austria via an intermediary. At the time of issue of the bonds, Barclays Bank had issued a base prospectus that was distributed, at its request, in Austria.

Since there was no contract between the parties, the Court held that the liability fell within the scope of Article 7(2) (which was not in serious doubt) and, more controversially, that the loss occurred where the applicant was domiciled, 'in particular when the damage occurred directly in the applicant's bank account held with a bank established' in that place.[38]

While the result is not as such unreasonable—Barclays had, after all, distributed the prospectus in Austria—it is nevertheless difficult to reconcile with *Kronhofer* and even harder to pinpoint exactly on what basis the Court was purporting to distinguish that precedent. Was it because the claimant had transferred the money to buy the certificates, thereby incurring loss, directly from his bank account in Austria, whereas in *Kronhofer* the transfers had been made from a specially opened bank account in Germany? The Court hints at this in paragraph 55 of *Kolassa*: it clearly treats this factor as relevant. If it was the Court's intention to treat this factor as *ipso facto* decisive, it would be difficult to think of a worse and more formalistic reason to distinguish *Kronhofer*. In both cases disbursements had been made from the claimant's bank account in Austria, the only difference being that in *Kronhofer* the payments had transited through a bank account in Germany. Was it because in *Kronhofer* the national court had already held that the harmful event and the damage had occurred

---

[34] C-68/93 *Shevill* EU:C:1995:61, para 33.
[35] Above n 4.
[36] ibid.
[37] ibid.
[38] ibid para 55.

in Germany whereas that question was actually asked of the Court in *Kolassa*, thereby justifying a different result on the basis of substantially the same facts? The Court does not mention this possibility. Or was it because the defendant had willingly had the prospectus distributed in Austria? On this latter point, the Court is maddeningly inconsistent: at paragraph 53 it specifically rejects the distribution of the prospectus in Austria as being the harmful event but, at paragraph 56 makes the point that the solution in the case complies with the requirement of foreseeability since the issuer of a certificate who publishes or distributes a prospectus in a Member State should anticipate that persons domiciled in that Member State, might invest in the certificate and suffer loss. If the distribution of the prospectus was a relevant factor, it still seems an inadequate reason to distinguish *Kronhofer*, since in that case the claimant had equally (and far more directly) been approached (or 'targeted') in his own Member State.

In short, *Kolassa* cannot be said to have given much guidance to national courts as to how to apply Article 7(2) to cases of pure financial loss.[39] And, since then, the Court appears to have reverted to a more traditional position. In *Universal Music*[40] it purported to distinguish *Kolassa* on the basis that, in that case, the result was reached 'within the specific context of the case which gave rise to the judgment, a distinctive feature of which was the existence of circumstances contributing to attributing jurisdiction to those courts'[41] but without identifying in any way what those circumstances were. Instead, the Court makes a general reference to the Opinion of AG Szpunar, the AG in both cases. In *Universal Music* he came to the same conclusion as the Court but, at points 44 and 45 of his Opinion, he distinguished *Kolassa* specifically on the grounds of the distribution by the defendant of the prospectus in Austria in that case. This was the factor to which he had attached great weight in his Opinion in *Kolassa* but which the Court had not treated as decisive in its judgment in that case.[42] The reader is thus left totally in the dark as to what those circumstances were.

Intuitively, one can feel sympathy with the result in *Kolassa* but, from the case law as it stands, one can merely draw the very general conclusion that, in order to conclude that financial damage is suffered in the place where the claimant holds his bank account, there must be some further contacts linking the defendant to that place; at the same time it is impossible to know what those contacts might be. In fact, the Court's approach bears a resemblance to a weighing of contacts test, with the judge having a wide margin of discretion to determine what factors should be taken into account. This however is contrary to the basic philosophy of the Regulation, which aims to provide rules of jurisdiction that are 'highly predictable' as the Court never ceases to underline in its standard introductory mantra to any judgment interpreting Brussels I.

---

[39] But see M Lehmann, 'Prospectus Liability and Private International Law: Assessing the Landscape after the CJEU's *Kolassa* Ruling (Case C-375/13)' (2016) 12(2) *Journal of Private International Law* 318.

[40] Above n 4.

[41] ibid para 37.

[42] But see C-352/13 *CDC* EU:C:2015:335, which concerned the place of damage in the case of different companies that suffered damage by reason of a cross-border cartel. Here the Court stated that the place of damage for each claimant is the place in which that claimant's registered office is situated. This enables a concentration of jurisdiction in that place without the need to determine in which national markets the claimant has in fact suffered financial damage. This type of approach is feasible only in the case of a cross-border cartel. There is no reason why it should apply in the case of a breach of purely national competition law, for example if a French company doing business in Germany suffers damage by reason of a cartel that has effects in that country only, the place of damage should be Germany, as opposed to France.

2. Interference with Personality Rights

In *Shevill*,[43] one of the seminal cases on the notion of the place of damage criterion, the Court held that, in the case of an action for libel through a publication in the press, the place of damage was the Member State in which the offending material was distributed, provided that the claimant was known there. If publication occurred in several Member States and the claimant sued in only one of them, the courts of that Member State would have jurisdiction in respect only of the damage caused in that Member State.[44] Latterly, it was debated whether this rule was still appropriate for the internet age. In *eDate and Martinez*,[45] the claimants (domiciled in Germany and France respectively) claimed that their privacy was violated by publications put on the internet by a publisher established in Austria and the UK respectively. At the stage of both the written procedure and the hearing, the focus of the debate was on whether *Shevill* was still good law, the argument against this being that it could have a chilling effect on publication and lead to forum-shopping. However, in the judgment, the Court, developing an idea launched by the AG in his Opinion in the case, decided to develop its interpretation of Article 7(2) so as to invent an entirely new head of jurisdiction, restricted to cases of infringement of personality rights through the internet, whereby the claimant would have the option to bring the action before the courts of the place in which he had his 'centre of interests', which would normally coincide with the place of his habitual residence. Furthermore, this new head of jurisdiction was a free gift to the claimant, it being open to him to sue in every Member State in which the online content was accessible, in respect of the damage caused in the Member State, in accordance with the *Shevill* case law.

The judgment in *eDate and Martinez* is, on several counts, a remarkable exercise in judicial law-making. First, the Court based its judgment on an idea raised for the first time in the AG's Opinion. Thus the interested parties had no opportunity to comment on it either in the written pleadings or at the hearing. Second, the Court created a *forum actoris*, a phenomenon to which it normally is resolutely hostile. Third, by creating a head of jurisdiction that is applicable only in respect of the internet, the Court violated the principle of technological neutrality. Last, and most significantly, the judgment has precisely the chilling effect on publication that the Court had earlier appeared anxious to avoid, in particular in that it creates the *forum actoris* merely as an added option.[46] It thus gives the claimant the best of both worlds—he may sue at home if he wishes but equally may sue in any Member State where the online content is accessible. Furthermore, by having introduced what is effectively a new head of jurisdiction under Article 7(2), the Court has created the risk that national courts do not restrict that basis of jurisdiction to cases of violation of personality right but extends it to tortious acts in general. There is already some empirical evidence of

---

[43] Above n 34.

[44] ibid paras 32 and 33. If the claimant wished to sue in respect of the entire damage, he always had the option of suing in the courts of the Member State of the defendant's domicile (by virtue of Art 4) or in that of the place where the publisher was established (as place of the harmful event under Art 7(2)).

[45] Joined Cases C-509/09 and C-161/10 EU:C:2011:685.

[46] Cf the Opinion of AG Cruz-Villalón in the same case. The AG, rather more than the Court, attempts to grapple with these issues and find a balanced solution; in particular, he argues that if a person is libelled or has his privacy violated online, the forum of the centre of his interests is relatively easily identified and thus foreseeable for both claimant and defendant (paras 55–67). This is true only if the defendant is well-known.

this happening despite the Court's having, in the later *Wintersteiger* judgment,[47] restricted the scope of the judgment to personality rights.[48] Similarly, in at least one case, a national court applied *eDate* to a choice-of-law problem, holding the applicable law to be that of the country of the claimant's habitual residence.[49]

ii. Joining Defendants before the Courts of the Domicile of One of Them: Article 8(1)

Article 8(1) of the Brussels Ia Regulation allows the claimant to sue a defendant domiciled in a Member State other than that of the forum

> where he is one of a number of defendants, in the courts for the place where any one of them is domiciled, provided the claims are so closely connected that it is expedient to hear and determine them together to avoid the risk of irreconcilable judgments resulting from separate proceedings.

The present author has already had the opportunity to subject the Court's case law in this field to a critical analysis, published in 2012.[50] He concluded in essence that: i) the case law was too lax regarding the first condition, ie that proceedings be properly brought against the 'anchor defendant' but far too restrictive as regards the second condition, relating to the risk of irreconcilable judgments; ii) that the original sin lay in the wording of Article 8(1)[51] which placed too much weight on the risk of irreconcilable judgments to the exclusion of any other factors that might make it expedient to determine all the claims against the various defendants in the same forum;[52] and iii) that this fault, attributable in part to the legislature, was compounded by the Court's extremely restrictive interpretation of what were irreconcilable judgments, in particular the requirement that the judgments be not merely divergent but also that they arise in the context of the same situation of fact and law.[53]

Since then, beginning with its judgment in *Painer*,[54] which broadly followed the Opinion of AG Trstenjak who had examined the overwhelmingly negative reaction to the Court's judgment in *Roche Nederland* and subjected that judgment to excoriating criticism,[55] the Court has reviewed its case law and has, in this author's view, set itself on a course which does more justice to the underlying *ratio legis* of Article 8(1) and which strikes a far better balance between the interests of claimant and defendant.

---

[47] C-523/10 EU:C:2012:220. See ch 33 above.

[48] See C-194/16 *Bolagsupplysingen*, pending and a judgment of the Belgian Hof van Cassatie which applied the *eDate* principles to an online betting case (see ch 6 above).

[49] See ch 25 above.

[50] M Wilderspin, 'Jurisdictional Issues: Brussels I Regulation' in J Basedow, S Francq and L Idot (eds) *International Antitrust Litigation* (Oxford, Hart Publishing, 2012) 41.

[51] Which was itself based on the formula that the Court used in its judgment in *Kalfelis* above n 10.

[52] The Jenard Report stated quite simply that 'in order for this rule to be applicable, there must be a connection between the claims, as for example in the case of joint debtors'. This simple statement captures the essence of the rule and it, rather than the statement in *Kalfelis*, which is unnecessarily based on the wording of Art 30(3) (the *forum non conveniens* provision of the Reg).

[53] Wilderspin above n 50; on the case law see in particular the notorious judgment in C-539/03 *Roche Nederland* EU:C:2006:458.

[54] C-145/10 EU:C:2011:798.

[55] Opinion of AG Trstenjak in *Painer*, ibid paras 39–105.

However, rather than treating the danger of irreconcilable judgments as merely one criterion that must be fulfilled in order for it to be expedient to hear the cases together,[56] the Court remains fixated on this as the primary criterion while, however, considerably relaxing its understanding of what irreconcilable judgments may entail.[57]

While the overall result is considerably better, it is in this author's view regrettable that the Court did not have the courage to follow the suggestion of AG Trstenjak and focus more on the overall question of connection between the claims rather than the narrow issue of possible irreconcilability of judgments.

III. Applicable Law

The main instrument in this field is the Rome II Regulation.[58] The judgments of the Court on this regulation are few in number but, in general, the Court has dealt well with the issues arising.

A. Temporal Application

Rome II contains an oversight which is entirely the responsibility of the legislature, in that Article 32 provides that the Regulation applies from 11 January 2009 whereas Article 31 provides that it applies to events giving rise to damage which occur after its 'entry into force'. Since the (largely notional) 'entry into force' occurred on 20 August 2007, a literal interpretation of Articles 31 and 32 would have the effect of bestowing retrospective application on the Regulation by making its uniform rules apply to situations having arisen between 20 August 2007 and 10 January 2009. The issue aroused a great deal of controversy in academic circles and was also of practical importance, particularly in the UK,

---

[56] This was what AG Trstenjak recommended in her Opinion in *Painer*, ibid. See in particular para 102: the condition of the risk of irreconcilable judgments is 'a simple description of the objective of the proviso, but does not have the character of an autonomous condition'.

[57] See in particular C-98/06 *Freeport* EU:C:2007:595; C-145/10 *Painer*, above n 54 (even if the national laws on which the different actions are based are different, this does not prevent the claims being connected provided that it was foreseeable for the defendants that they might be sued in the forum of the anchor defendant); C-616/10 *Solvay* EU:C:2012:445 (in a case with very similar facts to *Roche Nederland*, above n 53, the Court distinguishes that judgment on the basis that, in *Solvay*, the defendants were accused of infringing the same patents, as opposed to individual companies in the same group separately infringing different national parts of a European patent. In reality, it is difficult to know whether the facts really were so different or whether the claimant in *Solvay* had simply spotted a way to escape the constraints of *Roche Nederland*); C-645/11 *Sapir* EU:C:2013:228 (in that case, the claimant had allegedly made overpayments, stemming from the same factual background, to 10 of the 11 defendants and the 11th defendant, a lawyer, was sued on the basis of negligence. The Court held that all the claims were sufficiently closely connected) and C-352/13 *CDC*, above n 42, (a case of private enforcement of competition law where the defendants had already been fined for participation in a cartel which qualified as a single and continuous infringement of Art 101 TFEU: this was as clear a case as could be imagined for the application of Art 8(1). Doubt arose simply because the action against the anchor defendant had been settled before the case came on for trial. Nevertheless, the Court held that this factor did not of itself preclude the application of Art 8(1)).

[58] Reg 864/2007 on the law applicable to non-contractual obligations [2007] OJ L199/40.

where the Regulation has had a considerable impact on the calculation of damages, with the role of the lex fori being much reduced. It is perhaps no surprise that the preliminary reference that gave the Court the opportunity to provide a sensible interpretation of the text of the Regulation came from England.[59] Rather than yielding to the temptation of rigidly insisting on the literal meaning of the words used, the Court, following the Opinion of AG Mengozzi,[60] held that the intention of the legislature was that the Regulation should apply only to events having occurred as from 11 January 2009.[61]

B. Borderline between Rome I and Rome II

The Court has adopted the approach that characterisation at the applicable law stage should mirror that used at the stage of determining jurisdiction; this is entirely in accordance with the will of the legislature, which has regularly made reference to this principle in the recitals in the preamble of both Regulations.[62]

However, the Court has been prepared to depart from a rigid application of this principle where it would lead to anomalous results. For example, in *Verein für Konsumenteninformation v Amazon*[63] the Court was confronted with a question relating to the delimitation between the respective scopes of Rome I and Rome II. The claimant, a consumer protection association, brought an action in Austria, against the defendant, domiciled in Luxembourg, in which it sought, inter alia, to have the court order the defendant to remove certain of the contractual terms in its standard form contracts proposed to Austrian consumers. The Court held, following its judgment in *Henkel*,[64] that the matter was primarily non-contractual,[65] since there was no contractual nexus between claimant and defendant. However, as regards the identification of the national law that was to determine whether the standard contractual terms were unlawful, the Court accepted that this should be the same law as that which would apply in an individual action between a consumer and the defendant company, ie should be determined by reference to Rome I.[66] The Court is to be applauded for making this differentiation and for emphatically rejecting the very unconvincing view of AG Saumandsgaard Oe on this point, who was prepared to accept with equanimity that the law applying to the public interest action could be different from that applying to an individual action, with the attendant risk that a contractual term that

---

[59] C-412/10 *Homawoo* above n 1.

[60] The AG's analysis acknowledged more candidly that the legislature had made a mistake, whereas the Court was more inclined to save the legislature's blushes on this point, see C Brière, 'Champ d'application ratione temporis du Règlement "Rome II"' (2012) 139(2) *Journal du droit international* 693, 702.

[61] Despite the fact that the Court could not have been much clearer, there is still evidence that Italian and Greek courts continue to apply Rome II to events that occurred before its date of application (see chs 8 and 18 above).

[62] Recitals 7 to Rome I and Rome II.

[63] Above n 1.

[64] C-167/00 EU:C:2002:555, in which the Court held that, for jurisdictional purposes, a collective action brought by a consumer protection against a company fell within the scope of Art 7(2) of the Brussels I Reg.

[65] More precisely, the Court held, above n 1, correctly it is submitted, that the matter fell within the scope of Art 6 of Rome II, as a matter relating to unfair competition.

[66] ibid paras 51–58.

might be perfectly legitimate under the law applicable to the contract could be treated as unlawful, and ordered to be removed, in a collective action.[67]

C. Application *Mutatis Mutandis* of Case Law on the Brussels I Regulation

In *Lazar*,[68] the Court had to interpret Article 4(1) of Rome II where relatives of a person who had been killed in a road accident in Italy sued the tortfeasor in Italy for compensation for the harm that they personally had suffered. The question arose as to whether, in respect of the claimants' resident in Romania the place of damage was Italy or Romania. Article 4(1) provides that the applicable law is 'the law of the country in which damage occurs irrespective of the country in which the indirect consequences of that injury occur'.

Conceptually, a case could be made for saying that the relatives' claim was distinct from that of the deceased since they were claiming in their own right (ie to vindicate their own protected interest) rather than merely as heirs of the deceased; conversely, it could be argued that their damage was merely an indirect consequence of the original tort. As regards Article 7(2) of the Brussels I Regulation, the Court had already come down in favour of saying that, where one company (a parent company) suffered financial loss as a result of damage done to a subsidiary, the damage to the parent company occurred in the country in which the damage to the primary victim was sustained.[69] The very explicit distinction drawn between direct and indirect damage in Article 4(1) Rome I was evidently based on the Brussels I case law, to which reference was made in the Commission's explanatory memorandum.[70] It was thus difficult to imagine a clearer case for basing the judgment on the precedents established under the Brussels I Regulation, in particular *Dumez France*. However, in its judgment the Court makes no reference to that case law or to the relevant paragraph in the Commission's explanatory memorandum. Instead, it refers to Recital 17 to Rome II, which specifies that in a case of personal injury, the place of damage is the place where the injury was sustained and concludes peremptorily that the damage suffered by the relatives occurred in the country of the accident.[71] The Court makes no attempt to grapple with the argument that this principle does not necessarily extend to the situation where the damage complained of is not as such the personal injury suffered by the primary victim but is, rather, damage suffered by another person and which merely flows from the initial injury. The Court then buttresses this deduction with a reference to the commentary in the explanatory memorandum on Article 15 of the Regulation, which deals with the scope of the applicable law and which specifies that that law determines, inter alia, 'persons entitled to compensation for damage suffered personally'. To conclude from that provision that the damage suffered by such a person is deemed to have occurred in a particular country is a *non sequitur*.

The Court's methodology is all the more surprising since AG Wahl made a thorough and convincing analysis of the Court's existing case law on Article 7(2) Brussels I to conclude that it could be applied *mutatis mutandis* to Article 4(1) Rome II.

---

[67] Opinion, paras 62–66.
[68] C-350/14 EU:C:2015:802.
[69] C-220/88 *Dumez France* EU:C:1990:8, paras 14–22.
[70] COM(2003) 427 final.
[71] *Lazar*, above n 68, para 25.

Whilst the result is certainly correct, both in terms of discerning the intention of the legislature and in providing a workable solution, the methodology, once again, leaves a lot to be desired and leaves the reader in the dark as to precisely the reasons underlying the judgment.

IV. Overall Conclusion

Whereas with Rome II, it is too early to draw any definite conclusions, as intimated in the introduction, the Court has not always been consistent in its interpretation of either Article 7(2) or Article 8(1) of Brussels I. With Article 7(2), the problem with the case law has not been so much with the result reached in the judgments but rather the inadequate and sometimes inconsistent reasoning. With Article 8(1), the problem has been rather that, having set itself on such a wrong course in *Roche Nederland*, the Court, despite having rowed back very significantly from the position in that case, has not had the courage to overrule it formally.

However, not all problems of interpretation can be laid at the door of the Court, in particular where case law has caused problems but the legislature has not taken its responsibility to amend the legislation. It is noteworthy that in the revision exercise of 2012, the Commission did not propose any amendment to the wording of either of these provisions. It is thus up to the Court itself to resolve these problems of interpretation.

38

Litigating Cross-border Intellectual Property Disputes in the EU Private International Law Framework

PAUL TORREMANS

I. Introduction

We think of intellectual property as a global phenomenon. Rightholders enjoy protection around the globe for their intellectual property. But even when rightholders emphasise that their works are protected globally, eg by the often used phrase that this motion picture or piece of software is protected by the (copyright) laws of the United States and other countries, which one finds on DVDs and sites from which one downloads software, one already gets an indication that the intellectual property reality across borders is a bit more complex. The EU is fully part of this international framework that forms the landscape in which EU private international law rules, dealing with cross-border intellectual property disputes, operate.

It is only fair to note that 'international copyright', 'international patent law' or 'international trade mark law' do not exist as a single global and uniform regime or model law. Let us take copyright as an example. It suffices to read the emblematic Berne Convention 1886. Yes, there are grand principles, but key concepts such as literary and artistic works and originality are not defined. There is, in other words, no harmonised single criterion to decide which works could be copyright works, and which originality criterion they need to meet to effectively qualify for such protection. In addition, there is by no means a standard and complete list of exceptions and limitation to the copyright of the rightholders to guarantee the users' interests, such as the right of access to information. One could develop the same argument for patents and trademarks along the lines of the Paris Convention 1883. But let us not duplicate matters and continue with the copyright example.

That very same Berne Convention does on the positive side contain the principle of national treatment. Its 'international copyright' approach is based on the simple technique of giving foreign authors and creators access to the national copyright systems of the Member States of the Convention by treating them in each Member State as if they were a national of that Member State.[1] In an era where access to such legal protection was governed

---

[1] See eg P Goldstein and PB Hugenholtz, *International Copyright: Principles, Law, and Practice* 2nd edn (Oxford, Oxford University Press, 2010) 91–115.

by the criterion of nationality[2] this was an important step and one that is almost baffling by its sheer simplicity. But national treatment enshrines also the underlying reality into the international copyright regime. That underlying reality is one of a patchwork of national copyright regimes based on the idea of one national copyright act per country, based on common ideas in the area and on the minimum standards that are found in the Convention (ie copyright covers literary and artistic works (whatever that means in detail), protects the author and has limitations and exceptions for the users). International copyright protection is therefore guaranteed on the basis of a patchwork of national copyright regimes and national copyright acts.

This may have worked well in an era where copyright works were exploited on a national basis, ie where authors of literary works had a different publisher in each country and where each publisher roughly covered only the national market.[3] In such a model there is a parallelism between national exploitation of copyright works and national copyright regimes that govern the protection and the use and exploitation of such works. But that model no longer exists. In the online environment (and even in the decades that preceded it, but then on a smaller scale) copyright works are exploited globally. That cross-border exploitation operates at a global scale and the user does not even necessarily know from where in the world he or she downloads the copyright work. And a rightholder expects respect for its rights and remedies, be it damages or permanent injunctions, to operate at a cross-border level. What has not changed is the territorial national character of copyright law. The parallelism between copyright law and copyright exploitation no longer exists. Instead one finds a major inconsistency and a massive source of potential conflict.

Leaving copyright to one side, one may be tempted to argue that the introduction (or future introduction) of single EU-wide intellectual property rights in the patent, trademark and design fields fundamentally changes the picture in the EU. Sure enough, a single right can be helpful, but the legislator has simply added that single right on top of the 28 national rights (and the European patent) that remain in existence and operate in parallel. The loss of complexity is therefore barely perceivable. There is, therefore, plenty of scope for cross-border licensing and cross-border infringement cases in the EU. The EU private international law framework will then be called upon to decide which court will have jurisdiction and which law will apply.[4] The remainder of this chapter will look at how well the framework copes with that challenge.

II. Jurisdiction

In an EU context, one is looking at the application of the Brussels I Regulation[5] to intellectual property cases, as they are after all civil and commercial cases and fall therefore within

---

[2] For a strong defence of an approach based on nationality see eg G Koumantos, 'Sur le droit international privé du droit d'auteur' [1979] *Il Diritto di Autore* 616 and 'Private International Law and the Berne Convention' (1998) *Copyright* 415.

[3] See JJ Fawcett and P Torremans, *Intellectual Property and Private International Law* 2nd edn (Oxford, Oxford University Press, 2011) Ch 12.

[4] See ibid at 671.

[5] Council Reg (EC) No 44/2001 of the European Parliament and of the Council of 22 December 2000 on jurisdiction and the recognition and enforcement of judgments in civil and commercial matters [2001] OJ L12/1

the scope of the Brussels I Regulation. Rather than to try to summarise all the aspects of the Brussels I Regulation that are relevant, let us look at a typical practical scenario that shows the often problematic link between the jurisdiction rules and intellectual property.

The contrast between national intellectual property rights, which are still granted on the basis of the territoriality principle, and which, as a consequence, logically produce on the one hand parallel rights in several countries and on the other hand the international exploitation of such rights, results in a scenario where similar violations, mostly performed by defendants with a mutual relationship between them, give rise to claims based on similar national provisions on intellectual property. In a copyright on the Internet context this could involve the unauthorised use of copyright material on websites operated by national subsidiaries of a multinational company. The ubiquitous nature of the Internet means that there is potentially infringement and damage on a global basis because websites can be accessed from everywhere. Even a scenario in which a single party uploads copyright material in an unauthorised way gives rise to a global infringement issue. More territorial features will be present with regard to the illegal downloading of films or music by an individual user in a certain country. There are, in other words, plenty of copyright infringement scenarios in which one needs to determine the competent court and the scope of its jurisdiction.

A. Article 4

Article 4 of Brussels Ia (Article 2 of Brussels I) allows for a set of proceedings to be initiated against an EU-domiciled defendant in the jurisdiction where he or she is domiciled. There is no reason why this rule cannot be used effectively in cross-border intellectual property cases. It may even be extremely effective if there is a single infringer. A single case in a single court can then deal with the EU-wide infringing activity of such a defendant. The approach may be less suitable if the defendant resides in a Member State that is far away from the Member State in which the rightholder is based, if the alleged infringer does not carry out any allegedly infringing activity in the forum (the court will merely deal then with infringement in other countries and have to apply foreign laws) or if there are multiple defendants. In the latter scenario, Article 4 does not allow the whole matter to be centralised before a single court. Instead, there would be separate sets of related proceedings in each of the Member States in which a defendant is domiciled. If one takes the factual example of the *Painer* case[6] one ends up with a scenario where the identical allegedly infringing use of the picture of Natasha Kampusch, taken by Ms Painer, by German and Austrian newspapers would result in two independent cases, ie Ms Painer would have to bring the case against the German newspapers in Germany and the identical case against the Austrian newspapers in Austria. This places a heavy (financial) burden on the rightholder, especially as Internet cases may often involve more than two jurisdictions. Multiple cases also add to the

---

(here referred to as Brussels I), replaced as of 10th January 2015 by the recast version Reg (EU) No 1215/2012 of the European Parliament and of the Council of 12 December 2012 on jurisdiction and the recognition and enforcement of judgments in civil and commercial matters (recast) [2012] OJ L351/1 (here referred to as Brussels Ia).

6 Case C-145/10 *Eva-Maria Painer v Standard Verlag GmbH* EU:C:2011:798.

workload of the courts and the parties will not understand why, at least potentially, what they see as the same conduct in the same business framework is dealt with differently in the various jurisdictions.

B. Article 7(2)

Article 7(2) Brussels Ia (Article 5(3) of Brussels I) provides for an alternative solution. Jurisdiction is also given to the courts of the place of the harmful event and to the courts of the place of the damage.[7] In a copyright on the Internet situation the easiest example of the place of the harmful event is the place where copyright material is uploaded to the Internet without the authorisation of the rightholder. Damage will occur wherever the material is downloaded or potentially even merely accessed. This rule has a lot of potential in the context of copyright infringement on the Internet. But it can also be applied in cross-border patent and trademark scenarios. The rule provides a good solution if an alleged infringer who resides elsewhere commits an allegedly infringing act in a Member State. The courts of that Member State are then well placed to deal with the (whole) case, because there exists a strong link between the facts of the case and the jurisdiction.[8] Matters are less obvious when it comes to the place of the damage, as in many copyright cases the ubiquitous nature of the Internet means that there is potentially damage, and therefore jurisdiction, everywhere. That then means that the standard scenario involves a multitude of claims submitted country by country, apparently as a logical consequence of the territoriality principle.[9]

Parallel registered rights such as patents and trademarks lead to the same outcome. This has been re-enforced by recent decisions[10] from the Court of Justice of the European Union (CJEU) that stress the factual nature of the examination under Article 7(2) of Brussels Ia. The chain of recent decisions starts with the *Melzer* case.[11] This case did not involve intellectual property at all, but in relation to the first limb of Article 7(2), the CJEU set out the principle that the jurisdiction analysis should be based on a factual examination and should not involve elements of substantive law. That sounded logical and when the Court was given an opportunity to rule on the second limb of Article 7(2) a bit later in the *Pinckney* case[12] one should not be surprised that it applied the same approach to that second limb.

Pinckney was a copyright case, but not really an Internet case. In essence it is about hard copies of CDs delivered by mail order, even if the order could be placed over the Internet. No royalties were paid for these CDs and therefore the Court came to the factual conclusion that since they could be delivered in each Member State there was at least allegedly damage in each Member State and that damage could then form the basis of jurisdiction in each Member State. The CJEU did however restrict that jurisdiction to the local damage in the

---

[7] See P Torremans, 'Jurisdiction for Cross-border Intellectual Property Infringement Cases in Europe' (2016) 53(6) *Common Market Law Review* 1625.

[8] Declarations of non-infringement can lead to bizarre outcomes and so called torpedo effects, see *General Hospital Corp v Asclepion Laser Technologies GmbH*, Italian Supreme Court, 10 June 2013, [2014] IIC 822.

[9] See Fawcett and Torremans, above n 3, Ch 5.

[10] See Case C-228/11 *Melzer v MF Global UK Ltd* EU:C:2013:305; Case C-170/12 *Pinckney v Mediatech* EU:C:2013:635; and Case C-360/12 *Coty Germany v First Note Perfumes NV*, EU:C:2014:1318.

[11] ibid.

[12] Above n 10.

Member State concerned. That brings us back to a purely territorial approach. The problem that arises here is broader than that though. A purely factual approach is unable to take into account that from a copyright perspective this would be less than an appropriate solution in cross-border intellectual property (IP) cases. *Pinckney* was a weird case, as the defendant was not the party selling and delivering the CDs, but the party who had manufactured the CDs on behalf of the absent distributor. The manufacturer had not acted in the jurisdiction where the case was brought and its copyright liability is dubious under any applicable law. But all that is exclusively for the substantive dispute in the CJEU's approach and is not relevant when the jurisdiction of the court is being examined. And the CJEU's approach seems now very much written in stone, as it declined the suggestion of its Advocate General to reconsider when shortly afterwards a trademark case arose.[13]

Whilst it is positive to avoid dealing already with substantive law matters at the jurisdiction stage, as this could give rise to a second mini trial of the same issues, the reality is that the mere factual potential presence of an act leading to damage or damage in the jurisdiction is very easy to demonstrate in IP cases if one disregards the question whether or not the claimant even has a reasonable chance of winning the case on the substance (eg is it at least arguable that the factual act or damage amounts to an infringing act in the jurisdiction in the light of substantive IP law and its territorial nature). Even hopeless cases will therefore pass the jurisdiction stage and this opens the door to harassment of a defendant by suing in multiple Member States, knowing that the defendant may not be able to afford to defend all these cases to the end of all the substantive trials. It is positive though that the CJEU limits these cases to local damage in each jurisdiction. Despite that, copyright infringement cases will necessarily be showing damage in every single Member State if one takes a purely factual approach. Each national court will therefore have jurisdiction for the local damage. That may be suitable in certain cases where the infringement is obvious and it could allow the rightholder to sue in his own court if there is also damage there, avoiding a potentially unaffordable case in a faraway Member State in which the defendant resides, but in cases of less straightforward infringement one can easily harass a potentially weaker defendant and push it into a disadvantageous settlement by bringing cases in multiple jurisdictions. The *Hejduk* case[14] presented such an Internet-based scenario and despite the fact that the Advocate General had suggested a limit to the provision, ie the (local) damage based provision should not apply to cases of ubiquitous infringement, the CJEU stuck to its approach. According to the Court:

> Article 5(3) … must be interpreted as meaning that, in the event of an allegation of infringement of copyright and rights related to copyright guaranteed by the Member State of the court seised, that court has jurisdiction, on the basis of the place where the damage occurred, to hear an action for damages in respect of an infringement of those rights resulting from the placing of protected photographs online on a website accessible in its territorial jurisdiction. That court has jurisdiction only to rule on the damage caused in the Member State within which the court is situated.[15]

The accessibility of a website (based on a server elsewhere) in a Member State containing unauthorised copyright protected photographs was sufficient as a base for jurisdiction.

---

[13] *Coty*, above n 10.
[14] Case C-441/13 *Pez Hejduk v EnergieAgentur* EU:C:2015:28.
[15] ibid at para 39.

Mere access in a Member State will therefore be sufficient. It will need to be seen as factually enough to demonstrate damage in the Member State concerned. This amounts to an incredibly low threshold that leaves matters wide open to abuse.

Let us now leave the law as it stands to one side for a moment. The *Pinckney-Hejduk* approach in combination with the ubiquitous nature of the Internet and the automatic protection granted by copyright may create the option to sue an alleged defendant in places where success in the substantive case is unlikely. This is undesirable and the European Max Planck Group on Conflict of Laws in Intellectual Property (CLIP) group, of which the author is a member, therefore proposed to add a proviso to the jurisdiction rule:

Article 2:202: Infringement

In disputes concerned with infringement of an intellectual property right, a person may be sued in the courts of the State where the alleged infringement occurs or may occur, unless the alleged infringer has not acted in that State to initiate or further the infringement and her/his activity cannot reasonably be seen as having been directed to that State.[16]

At least it gives the uploader the option to clearly restrict its material to a certain number of countries through the use of a certain language or through the use of material that is clearly only of interest to certain communities. There is, however, a delicate balance to be struck and a merely territorial approach is often undesirable in an Internet context, as it may effectively make the right unenforceable if the right holder has to sue on a country by country basis and an effective remedy may not be obtained in cross-border cases. Article 4 may sometimes provide the solution, but this is, eg, not the case if the infringement has no link with the place of residence of the alleged infringer. The CLIP group therefore proposes the following solution to deal with ubiquitous infringement cases in an effective way:

Article 2:203: Extent of jurisdiction over infringement claims

(1) Subject to paragraph 2, a court whose jurisdiction is based on Article 2:202 shall have jurisdiction in respect of infringements that occur or may occur within the territory of the State in which that court is situated.

(2) In disputes concerned with infringement carried out through ubiquitous media such as the Internet, the court whose jurisdiction is based on Article 2:202 shall also have jurisdiction in respect of infringements that occur or may occur within the territory of any other State, provided that the activities giving rise to the infringement have no substantial effect in the State, or any of the States, where the infringer is habitually resident and

(a)   substantial activities in furtherance of the infringement in its entirety have been carried out within the territory of the State in which the court is situated, or

(b)   the harm caused by the infringement in the State where the court is situated is substantial in relation to the infringement in its entirety.[17]

This rule counterbalances the proviso added to the main jurisdiction rule in this area.

---

[16] European Max Planck Group on Conflict of Laws in Intellectual Property, *Conflict of Laws in Intellectual Property: The CLIP Principles and Commentary* (Oxford, Oxford University Press, 2013) 69.
[17] ibid at 85.

C. Article 8(1)

Returning to the approach *de lege lata*, intellectual property has been the object of considerable harmonisation over the years, on the basis of both international treaties and European Union law. Without going into too much detail, it is obvious that the combination of territorial (national) intellectual property rights and their exploitation beyond national boundaries raises questions related to the possible application of Article 8(1) Brussels Ia (Article 6(1) of Brussels I).[18] A *forum connexitatis* offers in fact the possibility to pursue the infringement of what, from a commercial point of view, is often considered as a single right, rather than a bundle of parallel national intellectual property rights. Thus, the copyright infringement performed in a uniform manner, for example by the commercialisation of a copy of the copyright protected poster by related defendants, is pursued as a single case before a single court. Article 8(1) offers therefore an interesting opportunity in a number of intellectual property cases. However, Article 8(1) is principally targeted at defendants residing in different Member States acting with a common agenda,[19] and this is in contrast with the most common scenario of intellectual property rights infringement, which involves both parallel rights and defendants that act (individually) in a parallel fashion, whether or not they act within a group of companies.

One could therefore expect anything but a straightforward case when the Court looked for the first time at the potential application of Article 8(1) of the Brussels Ia Regulation in a case concerning intellectual property rights in *Roche Nederland*.[20] At the very least, one can state that this judgment is controversial.[21] In short, Primus and Goldenberg had filed an application for a European patent; and they had obtained a patent, according to the European Patent Convention, as a bundle of national patents. They claimed that the Roche group had infringed their European patent. In practice the infringement was performed in each country, every time by the local branch of the Roche group, but the case was handled and coordinated by the group's central unit. Therefore, it would have been useful for Primus and Goldenberg to have the whole case treated by a single court. This was also possible because Dutch courts had developed for the purposes of Article 8(1) the so-called 'spider in the web' doctrine.[22] The *Roche* case seemed to be a typical case. The spider's web of patent infringement had been weaved, or at least conceived, by the central unit of the group. The local branches merely carried out this strategy. Why not entrust the coordinated infringement of the European patent to a single court, the court of the spider, whose competence was recognised by Article 8(1)?

Yet, was the existence of a spider at the centre of the web of patent infringement the right starting point? According to the text of Article 8(1) the presence of a spider implies a link between the claims, doubtless a close link. However, this is not what Article 8(1) requires.

---

[18] See Torremans, above n 7.

[19] For example: *Pearce v Ove Arup Partnership Ltd* [2000] Ch 403 and *Chiron Corp v Evans Medical Ltd and Others* [1996] FSR 863.

[20] Case C-539/03 *Roche Nederland BV et al v Frederick Primus and Milton Goldenberg* [2006] ECR I-6535.

[21] Fawcett and Torremans, above n 3, paras 11.05 et seq and A Kur, 'A Farewell to Crossborder Injunctions? The ECJ Decisions GAT v LuK and Roche Nederland v Primus and Goldenberg' (2006) 37 *IIC—International Review of Intellectual Property and Competition Law* 844–55. See also ch 37 above.

[22] Court of Appeal of The Hague, *Expandable Grafts Partnership v Boston Scientific BV* [1999] FSR 352.

It requires that the cases are 'so closely connected that it is expedient to hear and determine them together to avoid the risk of irreconcilable judgments resulting from separate proceedings'. A risk of irreconcilable judgments is the *conditio sine qua non* to apply Article 8(1) which constitutes a derogation from Article 4 and takes away one or more defendants from the forum of their domicile. Different judges can rule differently on a particular case, even if their decision is grounded on the same facts and on the same law. But Article 8(1) does not have the purpose of preventing such divergence. The only risk that needs to be averted is that of contradictory judgments that are incompatible between themselves. This risk exists only if two judges of two countries decide, on each side, on the same factual and legal situation.[23] If we take an example from the field of intellectual property rights, this risk exists if the defendant A, domiciled in X, together with the defendant B, domiciled in Y, manufactures in Z reproductions of an artwork by an author, without the author's authorisation, and puts them on the market. If a judge in country X exerts her jurisdiction on the basis of Article 4 of Brussels Ia over defendant A, and another judge in the country Y does the same in relation to defendant B, both judges would decide the same dispute. In this case there is the risk that the same activity performed together in the country Z by the two parties (and to which the law of Z is probably applicable) is considered by one of the judges as an infringement and by the other judge as a perfectly lawful activity. These decisions would therefore be incompatible between them.[24]

The Court of Justice has ruled, in *Roche Netherland*, that the condition of the same factual situation was not met.[25] According to the Court each branch operated in a separate country and the details of the patent infringement were different in each country. The infringing activity was also performed in different countries by each defendant. In other words, there was no joint activity in a particular country, and there were no overlapping infringing activities or defendants. There were purely parallel factual situations, territorial and national. In addition, the Court argued that this case was not even subject to the same law, because the European patent consists of a number of national patents and is granted as such. Each of these patents is subject to national patent law and these patents are independent from each other. This is certainly the case when patent infringement is expressly covered by national law.[26]

If we are ready to follow the analysis of the Court on this point, there is no question of irreconcilable judgments. Every defendant must answer for her deeds in a specific factual and legal situation. There is no factual situation involving several defendants jointly, and every form of overlapping is avoided. The need for claims 'closely connected' cannot be demonstrated despite the similarities among national cases, and Article 8(1) is not applicable because the conditions required by its text are not met.[27]

---

[23] Case C-539/03 above n 20 at para 26.

[24] See Ph de Jong, O Vrins and Ch Ronse, 'Evoluties in het octrooirecht' [2011] 11 RDC-TBH or Revue de droit commercial belge—Tijdschrift voor Belgisch handelsrecht and Zheng Sophia Tang, 'Multiple Defendants in the European Jurisdiction Regulation' (2009) 34 *European Law Review* 80.

[25] Case C-539/03 *Roche Nederland BV et al v Frederick Primus and Milton Goldenberg* [2006] ECR I-6535 para 27. See K Szychowska, 'Quelques observations sous les arrêts de la Cour de justice dans les affaires C-4/03 GAT et C-539/3 Roche' (2007) 5 *Revue de droit commercial belge—Tijdschrift voor Belgisch handelsrecht* 498–506.

[26] Case C-539/03 above n 20 at paras 29–31.

[27] ibid, para 33. See JJ Brinkhof, 'HvJEG beperkt mogelijkheden van grensoverschrijdende verboden' [2006] *Bijblad Industriële Eigendom* 319–22.

The 'spider in the web' doctrine argues that there is a supplementary factor to be considered, in addition to the web of coordinated activities: the planning by the spider. The *forum connexitatis* therefore is identified with the location where the spider is based. Given this additional factor, it is desirable to bring the cases before a single judge because of the close link resulting from the coordination by the spider. However, in the analysis of the Court there is no room for this supplementary step. The Court is not able to go this far and it does not apply the 'spider in the web' doctrine because the requirements of the wording of Article 8(1) are not met.[28]

It is fair to say that there have been cases since *Roche Nederland* that indicate that this rather inflexible approach may not be the final word on the matter. First of all, there was the *Freeport* case.[29] No intellectual property rights were involved, but the Court reconsidered its requirement that there had to be a single legal situation. In this case the matter against one defendant was approached from a tort perspective and against the other it was approached from a breach of contract perspective. That did not seem objectionable to the Court. Irreconcilable judgments remain the key point, but it is left to the national court to evaluate all the factors. Copyright entered this debate in the *Painer* case.

The least you can say is that the Court of Justice performs a peculiar analysis in the *Painer* case.[30] Here the *Freeport* doctrine is applied to a case concerning intellectual property rights, but this is not in itself very interesting. More interesting, on the contrary, is what is missing from the analysis of the Court in this case.

The factual situation in *Painer* is relatively simple. Ms Painer is a photographer and she takes pictures of children in schools. She keeps her copyright in the images that she sells. In this capacity, she took a picture of Natascha Kampusch before her kidnapping. After the kidnapping the Austrian police used the picture of Natascha Kampusch in their search and have therefore diffused the picture, which allowed a press photo agency to offer this picture to some newspapers after the escape of Natascha Kampusch, at a time when new pictures were not yet available.

Ms Painer claimed that the publication in the German and Austrian newspapers infringes her copyright. She sued both German and Austrian newspaper publishers before an Austrian court, on the basis of what is now Article 8(1) Brussels Ia. It should be noted that some German publishers were not active in the Austrian market, despite the fact that all publishers performed the same activity in relation to the picture, that is the publication of the picture obtained by the agency (retouched with the ageing software of the police).

The Court strongly emphasised that copyright law, which protects the picture at hand, has been harmonised by different EU directives. It is as if the Court sought to explain that the requirement of the same legal situation of *Roche Nederland* is almost met. However, immediately afterwards the Court cites *Freeport*, with the purpose of dismissing[31] some minor divergences between national copyright laws (of Germany and Austria), because an identical juridical basis is no longer necessary.[32]

---

[28] Case C-539/03 above n 20 at paras 34–35.
[29] Case C-98/06 *Freeport plc v Olle Arnoldsson* [2007] ECR I-8319.
[30] Above n 6.
[31] And since the difference is so negligible, this cannot become an important factor when the judge takes in consideration all factors.
[32] Above n 6, paras 72 and 82.

At first the Court has ruled on the basis that these are identical cases of copyright infringement. However, the national judge had indicated a potential problem in the different national juridical bases:

> By its first question, the referring court asks, in essence, whether Article 6(1) of Regulation No 44/2001 must be interpreted as precluding its application if actions against several defendants for substantially identical copyright infringements are brought on national legal grounds which vary according to the Member States concerned.[33]

This problem is dismissed with a strong reference to *Freeport:*

> In that regard, the Court has stated that, in order for judgments to be regarded as irreconcilable within the meaning of Article 6(1) of Regulation No 44/2001, it is not sufficient that there be a divergence in the outcome of the dispute, but that divergence must also arise in the same situation of fact and law (see Freeport, paragraph 40).

> However, in assessing whether there is a connection between different claims, that is to say a risk of irreconcilable judgments if those claims were determined separately, the identical legal bases of the actions brought is only one relevant factor among others. It is not an indispensable requirement for the application of Article 6(1) of Regulation No 44/2001 (see, to that effect, Freeport, paragraph 41).

> Thus, a difference in legal basis between the actions brought against the various defendants, does not, in itself, preclude the application of Article 6(1) of Regulation No 44/2001, provided however that it was foreseeable by the defendants that they might be sued in the Member State where at least one of them is domiciled (see, to that effect, Freeport, paragraph 47).[34]

The predictability for the defendant of the venue of the prospective litigation is one of the foundations of the Brussels I Regulation, and it is therefore always present. But it is nonetheless interesting to note that the Court links this aspect specifically to a discretional appreciation of the legal situation and to the absence of the requirement of an identical juridical basis. This discretional appreciation is somehow dependent on the predictability of the competent court by the defendant. This last aspect is almost a *conditio sine qua non* for the discretional application of Article 8(1).

The reduced importance of the requirement of the same juridical basis is, according to the Court, the result of the strong harmonisation of national legislation:

> That reasoning is stronger if, as in the main proceedings, the national laws on which the actions against the various defendants are based are, in the referring court's view, substantially identical.[35]

The more the national law is harmonised, the stronger are the arguments in favour of the application of Article 8(1). It is striking that the Court refrains from making any reference to *Roche Nederland* on this point. The analysis of *Roche* is not openly abandoned, but neither is it used to support the analysis in *Painer*. However, in consideration of the importance that the Court places on the harmonisation of national legislation in a scenario where a unique juridical basis is no longer an obligation, it is no longer possible to accept the argument in *Roche Nederland* that, despite a strong harmonisation, the infringement of a European patent is based on independent national laws, and that for this reason only irreconcilable judgments are impossible.

---

[33] ibid para 72.
[34] ibid paras 79–81.
[35] ibid para 82.

The Court further goes back to the fundamental requirement of the close connection between cases and to the risk of irreconcilable judgments:

> It is, in addition, for the referring court to assess, in the light of all the aspects of the case, whether there is a connection between the different claims brought before it, that is to say a risk of irreconcilable judgments if those claims were determined separately. For that purpose, the fact that defendants against whom a copyright holder alleges substantially identical infringements of his copyright did or did not act independently may be relevant.[36]

At this point, there is a notable addition. In *Painer* the question why it was necessary to examine the claims jointly if the defendants did not act in mutual agreement cannot be avoided. According to the narrative of the facts in the judgment, the publishers of different newspapers have decided in full independence to purchase the contentious pictures and to publish them without the authorisation of Ms Painer. This might suggest that the absence of every form of agreement or coordination, without mentioning the presence of a spider, is in itself sufficient to reject the application of Article 8(1), unless there is a common form of action. But not so in the analysis of the Court. The fact that the defendants have acted in an independent fashion is not decisive. The Court is satisfied with adding this argument, of a certain importance, to the list of the aspects that national courts have to consider to determine if there is a risk of irreconcilable judgments.[37]

One thing is clear. After *Painer*, neither the first nor the second condition established in *Roche Nederland* remains intact. If *Freeport* softened the second condition, *Painer* does the same thing to the first condition. Rather than two absolute requirements all now seems to come down to a single balancing act in which all factors can be taken into account. What remains the case is that mere divergence will not be sufficient and that the risk of irreconcilable judgments needs to be established.[38] But the high level of harmonisation of copyright law in the EU opens up perspectives for the use of Article 8(1) in copyright cases in an Internet context where there are several defendants.

D. Article 24(4)

From a historical perspective intellectual property rights that require registration, such as patents and trademarks, have a strong link with the intellectual property office, as a 'State organ', which grants these intellectual property rights and therefore indirectly also with the State concerned. This link becomes particularly dominant in a validity context where broadly speaking the argument is raised that a mistake was made when the intellectual property right was granted by the intellectual property office. Issues of registration and validity have therefore historically been subject to the exclusive jurisdiction of the courts of the State, or in an EU context of the Member State, where registration has been applied for or has taken place.[39] Copyright as an unregistered right is not affected by this rule whereas patents and trademarks as registered rights are.

---

[36] ibid para 83.
[37] ibid para 83.
[38] For a more detailed analysis see P Torremans, 'Intellectual Property Puts Art (6(1) Brussels I Regulation to the Test' [2014] *Intellectual Property Quarterly* 1.
[39] For a delicate analysis see *Chugai v UCB and Celltech R&D* [2017] EWHC 1216 (Pat).

An action alleging the invalidity of the right (or the application for such a right) will therefore have to be brought on a country by country basis when parallel rights in various Member States are involved. Arguably this is a logical consequence of the territorial approach and of the fact that an intellectual property office has a strong link to the State, a link that is so strong that it is inconceivable that foreign courts can be called upon to verify and judge the acts of such an intellectual property office. The application of the rule is on the other hand far less clear and obvious if the validity issue is merely raised as a defence in an infringement case. One could argue that the case is classified on the basis of its main point, ie infringement, and that one should not allow the defendant to take away the jurisdiction of the court, often in an Article 4 or 7(2) scenario a single court dealing with a cross-border scenario, by merely raising the validity point and then obliging the claimant to bring a separate case in each country where the intellectual property right concerned has been registered. There is a risk of abuse here, especially if one adds that raising validity is almost a standard defence in patent infringement cases. Nevertheless, this was the approach taken by the CJEU in the *Gat v Luk* case.[40] The Court argued that there was nothing in the Brussels I Regulation that allowed it to distinguish between the claim/counterclaim scenario on the one hand and the defence scenario on the other hand. Despite heavy criticism[41] the legislator has now enshrined the *Gat v Luk* approach in Brussels Ia where Article 24(4) now reads as follows:

> The following courts of a Member State shall have exclusive jurisdiction, regardless of the domicile of the parties:
>
> ...
>
> (4) in proceedings concerned with the registration or validity of patents, trade marks, designs, or other similar rights required to be deposited or registered, irrespective of whether the issue is raised by way of an action or as a defence, the courts of the Member State in which the deposit or registration has been applied for, has taken place or is under the terms of an instrument of the Union or an international convention deemed to have taken place. ...

It should therefore not come as a surprise that the CLIP group proposed an alternative approach, allowing the infringement court to continue to hear the case:

> Article 2:401: Registration and invalidity
>
> (1) In disputes having as their object a judgment on the grant, registration, validity, abandonment or revocation of a patent, a mark, an industrial design or any other intellectual property right protected on the basis of registration, the courts in the State where the right has been registered or is deemed to have been registered under the terms of an international Convention shall have exclusive jurisdiction.
>
> (2) Paragraph 1 does not apply where validity or registration arises in a context other than by principal claim or counterclaim. The decisions resulting from such disputes do not affect the validity or registration of those rights as against third parties.[42]

It is from that perspective encouraging to see that such an approach will also be taken, and *Gat v Luk* de facto departed from, in the context of the unitary patent. Inside the common

---

[40] Case C-4/03 *GAT v Luk* [2006] ECR I-6509.
[41] Fawcett and Torremans, above n 3, ch 7.
[42] European Max Planck Group, above n 16 at 138–52.

Unitary Patent Court the division before which the validity is raised during infringement proceedings will have the option to continue with the infringement case and rule on validity too.[43] The question does need to be raised whether it makes sense to keep the strict Article 24(4) rule for national patents and other registered intellectual property rights.[44]

III. Applicable Law

A. *De Lege Lata*

Of course, once jurisdiction has been established the question of the applicable law arises. Even a broad-brush introductory approach should make a distinction between the intellectual property right as such, and its infringement, on the one hand, and the contractual transfer on the other hand. Not only may different laws, such as the *lex loci protectionis* on the one hand and the *lex contractus* on the other hand, apply, but important issues of categorisation arise.

　In this context we focus on infringement. National treatment and the territorial approach of the intellectual property conventions led here too to a country by country approach. The *lex protectionis* or the law of the country for which protection is sought will apply on a country by country basis. In the EU this rule is accepted in Article 8 of the Rome II Regulation:[45]

Infringement of intellectual property rights

1. The law applicable to a non-contractual obligation arising from an infringement of an intellectual property right shall be the law of the country for which protection is claimed.

2. …

3. The law applicable under this Article may not be derogated from by an agreement pursuant to Article 14.

The outcome of all this is a patchwork of national copyright laws that are applied on a country by country basis when dealing with a copyright infringement case that crosses borders.[46] Whilst this may be feasible and workable in a scenario that covers a handful of countries, it becomes completely unworkable in an Internet context that potentially covers over 200 countries and national laws. And of course, the ubiquitous and automatic nature of copyright protection may also lead to the application of the laws of countries which the defendant did not target in any way.

---

[43] Art 33(3) UPC Agreement, see http://documents.epo.org/projects/babylon/eponet.nsf/0/A1080B83447CB9 DDC1257B36005AAAB8/$File/upc_agreement_en.pdf.

[44] See P Torremans, 'An International Perspective II: A View from Private international Law' in J Pila and C Wadlow (eds), *The Unitary EU Patent System* (Oxford, Hart Publishing, 2015) 161 at 171.

[45] Reg (EC) No 864/2007 of the European Parliament and of the Council of 11 July 2007 on the law applicable to non-contractual obligations (Rome II) [2007] OJ L199/40.

[46] For a more detailed analysis, see P Torremans, 'The Law Applicable to Copyright Infringement on the Internet' [2016] *NIPR (Nederlands Internationaal Privaatrecht)* 687.

B. *De Lege Ferenda*

The CLIP group has therefore proposed to deal with these problems by introducing a two-pronged approach. In a first stage there is an attempt to exclude the application of laws with which the conduct of the defendant is not linked:

Article 3:602: *De minimis* rule

(1) A court applying the law or the laws determined by Article 3:601 shall only find for infringement if

(a)   the defendant has acted to initiate or further the infringement in the State or the States for which protection is sought, or
(b)   the activity by which the right is claimed to be infringed has substantial effect within, or is directed to the State or the States for which protection is sought.

(2) The court may exceptionally derogate from that general rule when reasonable under the circumstances of the case.[47]

If, on the other hand, there is a truly ubiquitous case effective enforcement of copyright requires the application of a single law instead of the application of 200 plus national copyright laws:

Article 3:603: Ubiquitous infringement

(1) In disputes concerned with infringement carried out through ubiquitous media such as the Internet, the court may apply the law of the State having the closest connection with the infringement if the infringement arguably takes place in every State in which the signals can be received. This rule also applies to existence, duration, limitations and scope to the extent that these questions arise as incidental questions in infringement proceedings.

(2) In determining which State has the closest connection with the infringement, the court shall take all the relevant factors into account, in particular the following:

(a)   the infringer's habitual residence;
(b)   the infringer's principal place of business;
(c)   the place where substantial activities in furtherance of the infringement in its entirety have been carried out;
(d)   the place where the harm caused by the infringement is substantial in relation to the infringement in its entirety.

(3) Notwithstanding the law applicable pursuant to paragraphs 1 and 2, any party may prove that the rules applying in a State or States covered by the dispute differ from the law applicable to the dispute in aspects which are essential for the decision. The court shall apply the different national laws unless this leads to inconsistent results, in which case the differences shall be taken into account in fashioning the remedy.[48]

In short, a system is put in place to find the law with the closest connection on the basis of a number of factors. Once that is done the burden of proof switches to the defendant. It is up to the defendant to raise any exemption under a national copyright law on which the defendant may be able to rely.

---

[47] European Max Planck Group, above n 16 at 308.
[48] ibid at 314.

IV. Conclusion

Cross-border intellectual property litigation poses a particular challenge to the EU private international law framework. That framework contains suitable starting points but, as interpreted by the CJEU, it does not manage to deal adequately with the more complex aspects of intellectual property litigation. The CLIP principles contain a coherent set of proposals that could improve matters *de lege ferenda*. These improvements are particularly urgent for cases of ubiquitous infringement as the current rules render the intellectual property rights concerned de facto partially unenforceable. Effective remedies are not provided to rightholders, let alone on an efficient cross-border basis. Such an outcome is entirely unacceptable.

39

Private Enforcement
of Competition Law

JONATHAN FITCHEN

I. Introduction

For many years the European Union Commission has had a policy of trying to encourage the victims of breaches of EU competition law to privately enforce it. This policy has been connected with attempts to foster the more holistic and multi-level public and private competition law enforcement envisaged by the Commission's modernisation programme which led to Regulation 1/2003.[1] The proponents of the modernisation programme contemplated that victims of competition law infringements would bring private enforcement claims against the anti-competitive. They would do this either independently via stand-alone claims, or via follow-on claims brought in conjunction with public enforcement activities by either the European Commission or a national competition authority. Such a holistic approach to enforcement would, it was hoped, better deprive the anti-competitive of the gains and advantages derived from their illegal behaviour and thereby discourage others from emulating their anticompetitive activities. The modernisation policy recognised three basic points. First, that if anticompetitive activity is to be discouraged, the EU and the Member States could not merely rely on enforcement by the Commission. Second, that without an effective system of private enforcement infringers retain some or all of the benefits of their illicit actions while victims remain uncompensated. Third, that anticompetitive behaviour will continue in the Single Market to the prejudice of both consumers and competition itself. It has however, proven difficult to realise the modernisation policy on private enforcement in Member State legal systems.

Despite assistance from European Court of Justice (CJEU) decisions based on spasmodic preliminary references,[2] the private enforcement of EU competition law has not yet generated the necessary political will for a general EU legislative reform of the different legal topologies of Member State legal systems. Instead, legislative reforms have tended to be incidental at the EU level[3] or confined to given Member States, usually those that are most

---

[1] Council Reg (EC) No 1/2003 of 16 December 2002 on the implementation of the rules on competition laid down in Arts 81 and 82 of the Treaty, [2003] OJ L/1. Recitals 15, 21–22 and 34–35.

[2] Particularly, Case C-453/99 *Courage Ltd v Crehan* [2001] ECR I-6297; Cases C-295/04 to C-298/04 *Manfredi and Others* [2006] ECR I-6619; and Case C-352/13 *CDC Hydrogen Peroxide SA v Akzo Nobel NV*, EU:C:2015:335.

[3] Art 6(3)(b) of Reg (EC) No 864/2007 of the European Parliament and of the Council of 11 July 2007 on the law applicable to non-contractual obligations (Rome II) [2007] OJ L199/40.

popular with litigants.[4] In the meantime, claimants have often appeared to struggle as their cases founder on either local 'procedural' difficulties or, if more successful, seem to disappear into black-holes created by confidential settlement agreements.[5]

There are of course well-known difficulties attending any attempt to litigate a case based on an alleged infringement of a horizontally directly effective EU Treaty article if domestic procedural underpinnings necessary to facilitate the claim are of uncertain effect (or missing). These difficulties intensify if, as is common, the public enforcement infringement upon which the private claim is based, remains disputable for years before the EU's courts. Equally, it does not assist the claimant that even the information that he should legitimately be able to obtain (eg the non-confidential version of the Commission's Decision) is often held-up in negotiations between the Commission and the cartelists over the redaction of confidential information in the full Decision. A further basic point is that the typical defendant in a private enforcement action will be a large undertaking with access to the best legal advice. Though the point should not be misunderstood to indicate an inevitability, these defendants have previously sought, with considerable success, to exploit and hence to benefit from the abovementioned legal uncertainties and procedural deficits concerning the private enforcement of EU competition law. Even if such a defendant cannot fracture the case across different jurisdictions, or delay judicial consideration of the merits by raising a series of resource sapping and delaying preliminary issues, it normally benefits from the generally reasonable assumption of all domestic evidence laws that the claimant bears the burden of first proving its case. Furthermore, even if the legal proceedings reach the merits, the claimant must still demonstrate, quantify and then defend its computation of its alleged losses against the defendant's likely allegation that these should be substantially reduced, or wholly cancelled out, by the unpredictable operation of an emergent pass-on defence functioning in conjunction with both the CJEU's unfortunately expansive characterisation of the classes of potential victims, and with domestic ideas said to relate to the compensatory nature of claims heard before civil courts. To these difficulties, which derive from a much deeper, and as yet unresolved, tension between the desired relationship between public and private forms of competition law enforcement in the EU, could for many years be added further preliminary uncertainties arising from the operation of EU and national private international laws in the context of private competition law claims.

It is clear that the modernisation programme that led to Regulation 1/2003 did not itself materially reduce the private enforcement deficit summarised above. At the risk of over simplification, it seems as if many Member States were waiting for what they regarded as suitable initiatives from the EU, while at the same time the EU was hoping that the Member States (and their courts) would independently solve complex legal and procedural problems rooted in the fact that EU competition law was never designed to facilitate private enforcement. During this long and mostly unfulfilled period of mutual anticipation, the anticompetitive continued to enjoy relative safety from their victims inside the EU and therefore had a high probability of retaining illegal gains and benefits not removed by fines imposed by a public enforcer: this enforcement deficit was (and is) at its most egregious should the defendant receive 100 per cent leniency from the European Commission.

---

[4] The UK's Consumer Rights Act 2015 ss 81–82 and Sch 8.

[5] See BJ Rodger, 'Private Enforcement of Competition Law, the Hidden Story Part II: Competition Litigation Settlements in the UK, 2008–2012' (2015) 8(3) *Global Competition Litigation Review* 89.

Though the private enforcement deficit summarised above remains real, it must be noted that the majority of the systemic difficulties facing the private claimant are 'accidental'; they do not usually result from a considered policy choice to favour an anti-competitive business over its victim. Also it is neither the case that the legislative authorities in the EU are wholly neutral between the potential litigants nor that no progress has been made to resolve some of the abovementioned legal uncertainties.[6]

II. European Union Private International Law: Reducing Uncertainties by Reform and by Judicial Clarification of the Existing Law

As the private claims arising from the infringement of EU competition law are very likely to be international, matters such as the different venues available for the claim, and the law that each venue will apply, each have to be considered by the potential claimant. The value of, and prospects for, a private claim (or settlement) will depend on where and how the claim may be brought: in this context 'where' is determined by the meaning attributed to the jurisdictional provisions of the Brussels Ia Regulation,[7] while 'how' depends on the interaction of the relevant applicable law provisions[8] and the domestic civil procedure rules of the venue selected. As these issues are of great and immediate interest to both sides of the potential litigation, it is natural that an EU that wishes to facilitate the private enforcement of its competition law should intervene in various ways to try to promote this policy goal.

As the concretisation of a policy to promote the private enforcement of European competition law was significantly predated by the establishment of the EU's jurisdictional rules concerning civil and commercial claims (presently contained in the Brussels Ia Regulation), and as these jurisdictional rules can seemingly offer a reasonable variety of venues for such claims, there has been no significant political pressure to amend the existing EU legislation to create further jurisdictional opportunities specifically for a competition law claimant. Similar reasons have removed the need to make explicit legislative provision for competition law claimants in the determination of the applicable law for contractual obligations.[9] Matters were different however, for the determination of the applicable law for non-contractual obligations; thus the EU intervened with legislation to harmonise the

---

[6] See E Guinchard, 'L'espace judiciaire civil européen, révélateur d'une promotion timide et sélective du private enforcement du droit de la concurrence, La justice civile européenne en marche' [2012] *Thèmes et commentaires* 221.

[7] Reg (EU) No 1215/2012 of the European Parliament and of the Council of 12 December 2012 on jurisdiction and the recognition and enforcement of judgments in civil and commercial matters [2012] OJ L351/1.

[8] The applicable law concerning events in a private competition law claim arising before the EU's Rome II Reg is temporally applicable should be determined via the relevant domestic legislation in the Member State venue (eg in the UK by Pt III of the Private International Law (Miscellaneous Provisions) Act 1995). From the point at which the EU's Rome II is temporally applicable, the applicable law concerning any such event is to be determined via Reg (EC) No 864/2007 of the European Parliament and of the Council of 11 July 2007 on the law applicable to non-contractual obligations (Rome II) [2007] OJ L199/40.

[9] Reg (EC) No 593/2008 of the European Parliament and of the Council of 17 June 2008 on the law applicable to contractual obligations (Rome I) [2008] OJ L177/6.

determination of the applicable law for, inter alia, a private competition claim via the Rome II Regulation. This Regulation replaces the differing provisions of domestic private international law, that applied (and continue to apply) to events occurring prior to its temporal application.[10] Rome II harmonises the means by which a court determines the applicable law for events giving rise to a non-contractual competition law claim that is based on events occurring on or after the date of its temporal application. The Rome II Regulation provides a special applicable law provision for tort claims that is intended to simplify the determination of the applicable law in competition law cases. If the tort claim features multiple parties the law of the forum may, in certain circumstances, be allowed to apply to all of the cumulated claims. Though the routine application of the Rome II Regulation to competition claims is still awaited in the UK,[11] and though a range of concerns have been raised as to its probable operation in actual litigation,[12] there is no doubt that it represents a serious first attempt by the Commission and the Member States to improve the position of the private enforcer of competition law by, inter alia, reducing the uncertainties concerning the nature and the means of the determination of the applicable law for non-contractual competition law claims.[13]

Though there has not been a specific legislative intervention to reform or amend the jurisdictional rules concerning a private competition law claim, the CJEU has been able to effect substantial improvements for the private competition claimant in the recent *CDC* case. The Court clarified various disputed aspects of the interaction of the EU's Brussels I jurisdictional regime with cross-border competition law claims. The CJEU has clarified the subsequent legal effect of an exclusive choice of court/jurisdiction agreement between its parties once it has become clear that one such party has been part of a cartel. In such a case, a general choice-of-court agreement is not effective against a future competition law claim unless the drafting of the agreement indicates that such a claim was envisaged by the parties as being included within the choice-of-court clause at the point of its creation.[14]

The CJEU also clarified the meaning of the Brussels I Regulation's special jurisdiction rule for torts in the context of competition law torts. Though *CDC* saw the court offer many useful clarifications for the claimant in a competition law case, its explanation of the different venues potentially offered to the competition law victim by Article 7(2) is arguably the most valuable. It had previously been unclear how the Brussels I special jurisdiction for torts relating to a competition law claim based on secret agreements between the members of an international cartel that might have been created with the intent of evading the regulatory jurisdiction of the most effective venues for bringing private competition law claims and, or, may have then been operated across many different States causing actionable losses

---

[10] The Rome II Reg only applies to events occurring on or from its date of temporal application: 11 January 2009. If events happened earlier, domestic law applies to determine the applicable law until Rome II applies at which point it takes over to determine the applicable law for those events within its temporal scope.

[11] There is generally a considerable time lag in the litigation of the UK cases; as of 2016 the Rome II provisions have yet to 'take over' from domestic applicable law legislation.

[12] J Fitchen, 'Choice of Law in International Claims Based on Restrictions of Competition: Article 6(3) of the Rome II Regulation' (2009) 5 *Journal of Private International Law* 337 at 353 et seq and J Fitchen, 'The Applicable Law in Cross-Border Competition Law Actions and Article 6(3) of Regulation No 864/2007' in M Danov, F Becker and P Beaumont (eds), *Cross-Border EU Competition Law Actions* (Oxford, Hart Publishing, 2013) 297 at 323 et seq.

[13] Recitals 21–23 of the Rome II Reg.

[14] Case C-352/13 above n 2, paras 68–72.

and harm in either a deliberate or in a wholly fortuitous manner, should be fitted within the alternative possibilities now offered by Article 7(2) of the Recast Regulation. In other words, how was the place of the harmful event to be located if, in accordance with the orthodox law[15] on this point, it was to be considered to be alternatively located either in the place where the damage occurred, or, in the place of the event that gave rise to the damage? Now, thanks to the clarifications provided by the CJEU, the claimant can better understand how to locate the special jurisdiction provided by the Brussels Ia Regulation in such otherwise problematic competition law claims.[16]

The CJEU also offered an authoritative explanation of the legal effect of a settlement between the claimant and the so-called 'anchor defendant' on other defendants not domiciled in that Member State. An anchor defendant is relevant when the claimant has brought his action against multiple defendants, using Article 8(1) of the Brussels Ia Regulation to 'anchor' this litigation against all joined parties in the Member State in which that anchor defendant is domiciled. For some time it had been a defendant tactic to argue that if such a settlement occurred between claimant and the anchor defendant, the initial jurisdiction founded on the anchor defendant's domicile (and which had allowed the claimant to join other differently domiciled defendants to that single action heard in the anchor defendant's domiciliary Member State) would lapse and re-open the jurisdictional question concerning all of the other non-domiciled defendants who had not so settled. The CJEU rejected this reasoning.[17] If the initial claim is properly commenced[18] under Article 8(1) of the Brussels Ia Regulation (or under its forerunner Article 6(1) of the Brussels I Regulation) a later settlement with the anchor defendant does not re-open the jurisdiction question for the non-domiciled defendants who were joined at the point of commencement of the claim.

To the abovementioned reduction of legal uncertainties arising from aspects of private international law as noted above, may be added a more general legislative development that can seemingly operate in the claimant's favour, viz increased possibilities for private claimants to act and to claim collectively in certain Member States against infringers of EU competition law. The privately funded collective claims in question may involve consumers but are more likely, as in the *CDC* litigation, to involve 'high-level' commercial claimants,[19] quite possibly direct purchasers, and aim to present the competition infringer(s) with a collective claim that must be taken seriously and hence may possibly be resolved more quickly than the individual claims from which it is constituted.

When these pro-claimant developments are set against the unintended nature of the procedural advantages previously enjoyed by cartel defendants, it might be expected that, all other things remaining equal, competition law claimants will swiftly overturn the former

---

[15] As set out in Case 21/76 *Bier v Mines de Potasse* [1976] ECR 1735 at para 19.

[16] Case C-352/13 above n 2, the place of the causal event is set out by para 50 and the place where the damage occurred is set out by paras 51–54. The difficulty of *CDC* being possessed of a claim based on different consolidated claims is considered at para 55. See the analysis of this decision by Beaumont and Yüksel in Ch 33 above.

[17] ibid at para 33.

[18] The possibility of an abusive use of the possibility of joinder was also considered by the CJEU at paras 28–32, but it then stressed that only very clear evidence of abusive concealment would suffice. At para 32 the court expressly dismissed settlement negotiations as an example of 'abuse'.

[19] See case note by Polina Pavlova on the first application of the CJEU's *CDC* ruling by a Dutch Court, available from http://conflictoflaws.net/2015/first-application-of-ecjs-ruling-in-c-35213-cdc-hydrogen-peroxide-in-dutch-private-enforcement-proceedings/.

tendency for the law and its uncertainties to appear to assist the defendants. This assumption is however vulnerable to the objections that neither the enforcement goals nor the optimal relationship between public and private enforcement of competition law have yet been finally determined between the EU and its Member States. Most of the problems concerning private enforcement are ultimately attributable to this omission. If the EU and the Member States jointly decided how public and private enforcement should relate to each other (in other words, what form of private enforcement they wished to provide) and then decided which classes of claimant should be allowed to use it, and for what claimable losses, it would be a relatively small step to domestically facilitate the private claim and defences relating thereunto. The unresolved political issues cause the legal problems to remain and hence the improving trend for claimants, though real, may be somewhat weaker than might otherwise be assumed.[20] The issues considered below are consistent with a trend towards the encouragement of private enforcement within the European Union, but they also demonstrate various weaknesses attributable to unresolved political issues.

This chapter now considers two issues that are suggestive of a slow but detectable tendency towards promoting the European Union's policy goal of allowing an effective enforcement of EU competition law via private litigation. Though neither of the issues now considered is an example of what would classically be regarded as a purely private international law issue, each is relevant to the litigation of the private competition claims that EU private international law and domestic civil procedure attempt to facilitate. The first issue to be considered is the Damages Directive and its provisions; the second issue concerns the EU's tentative attempts to develop the possibilities and the law concerning 'low-level' collective redress mechanisms.

A. The Damages Directive

The Commission's desire to create a legislative instrument with which to facilitate private enforcement is of long-standing but has encountered various political obstacles which, for reasons of space, will not be considered in detail.[21] It suffices to say that the Commission has, since the time of Commissioner Kores, determinedly attempted to secure the support of the Member States to allow it to advance a legislative provision that could facilitate the private enforcement of competition claims by harmonising aspects of their legal systems concerning an EU damages remedy. This Commission policy reflects the importance of the damages remedy as a motivator for private claims. If the claimant cannot reasonably predict a damages liability for the defendant of a size sufficient to justify the risks and the resources that he must 'invest' to make that claim, he will not litigate to reclaim financial losses. That said, there is a basic illogicality in the decision to only address the remedy of Damages throughout the proposed Directive. Why assist a claimant in his claim for damages but not in his joined claim for 'injunctive' or declaratory forms of relief? Even if one speculates that certain Member States may possibly not allow types of remedy other than damages,

---

[20] See Guinchard, above n 6 at 225–26 and Fitchen, above n 12, 'The Applicable Law', 297.

[21] The DG Comp website shows the chronology of the efforts by the Commission and also of the reports and green and white papers that it piloted concerning the future of competition enforcement in the EU http://ec.europa.eu/competition/antitrust/actionsdamages/documents.html.

it is surprising that, at certain points,[22] the articles could not have been worded to include all existing remedial options. Such remedial narrowness is all the more surprising given that the Commission was criticised since the 2004 Ashurst Study for excluding injunctive relief from its scope.[23] The criticism of narrowness continues however even in relation to the scope of the proposed Directive: the private claim it seemingly envisages concerns a follow-on claim based on a cartel infringement, other forms of infringement were barely addressed.

As events were however to demonstrate, even with such a narrow scope and remedial focus it is one thing to know what needs to be done and quite another to succeed in garnering the necessary political support to do it. The introduction by the Commission into the laws of the EU's Member States of an effective private damages remedy for breach of EU competition law, based on the content of its 2008 White Paper, would best have been achieved by a Regulation. It is telling that the less intrusive legislative form of a Directive was selected. It is also telling that the Commission's 2008 White Paper proposals managed to be condemned both for timidity, by those involved in bringing cartel damages claims, for unnecessary intrusion by certain Member States, and even for administrative high-handedness by the European Parliament. The Member States and the European Parliament questioned the need for such provisions and also the authority of the Commission to introduce them. A particular concern for some Member States was that provisions in the draft Directive[24] disclosed a potential to 'pervert' civil compensation claims (as they were understood in their legal systems) by importing what were seen as negative 'American-style' concepts, such as class actions, into domestic legal systems that would thereby risk overcompensating victims and hence 'over-punishing' the anticompetitive who might—as well as facing public fines from the European Commission or a National Competition Authority (NCA)—also be sued by any party capable of connecting a financial loss to the actions of the cartel.[25] The awkwardly timed leaking of a draft 2009 Commission Proposal and Directive that not only included an opt-*out* collective redress provision (differing from the opt-in proposal in the White Paper) but also, surprisingly, nominated the exclusive use of Article 83 EC (now Article 103 Treaty on the Functioning of the European Union (TFEU)) as its intended legal base, led to further controversy and, a few days before the official publication date in Autumn 2009, the Commission decided not to publish its proposal and draft Directive, but instead to withdraw and to re-examine it.

It was not until June 2013 that the proposal document and draft Directive officially emerged, the idea of using only Article 103 TFEU as a legal base (thereby excluding the European Parliament) was dropped and other controversies were minimised by some toning-down of the provisions retained while an exercise in dépeçage was performed on

---

[22] The provisions on the disclosure of sensitive forms of evidence and also on limitation being two obvious examples.

[23] For the Study see http://ec.europa.eu/competition/antitrust/actionsdamages/economic_clean_en.pdf and for reasoned criticism supported by empirical data showing the greater importance of injunctive relief over damages in Germany see S Peyer, 'Myths and Untold Stories—Private Antitrust Enforcement in Germany' (2010) CCP Working Paper 10–12 at 69.

[24] In 2009 there was a leak of a draft Commission Proposal and Directive; it has not officially been published but the reader should understand references to the 2009 Proposal/Directive to refer to this document.

[25] The issues are well summarised in, J Kortmann and C Swaak, 'The EC White Paper on Antitrust Damage Actions: Why the Member States are (Right to Be) Less than Enthusiastic' (2009) 8 *European Competition Law Review* 340.

some of the more controversial aspects of the earlier 2009 draft.[26] Thus the proposal was accompanied by a separate Commission Recommendation on collective redress,[27] and a Commission Communication on the quantification of harm[28] plus an advisory practical guide on how to so quantify such harm.[29] This compromise version of the Damages Directive was formally adopted, with the involvement of the European Parliament, in 2014.[30]

The political compromises that led to the passage of the 2014 Directive (hereafter 'the Directive') are detectable in the more nuanced and conciliatory approach it takes to the reform of aspects of private enforcement in Member State legal systems. The Directive leaves out various matters of general importance to competition claims, which therefore continue to be regulated by the law of each Member State, except insofar as it refers to general EU legal principles of effectiveness and equivalence as set out in Article 4 of the Directive.[31] Even when the Directive specifically concerns itself with Member State laws, it only sets minimum standards for the Member States (to be in place by 27 December 2016) and implicitly permits stricter domestic laws if they are consonant with its provisions.[32] For example, though according to Article 3(1) full-compensation (as explained by Article 3(2) to include damages and claims for loss of profits plus interest) must be available in each Member State, the earlier concerns of some Member States concerning overcompensation are then allayed by Article 3(3) which forbids overcompensation, 'whether by means of punitive, multiple or other types of damages'. This third paragraph is not however merely conciliatory; it also should prevent a Member State from implementing stricter rules on *any* competition law damages award if such rules would lead to overcompensation by exceeding the possibilities envisaged in Article 3(2). It is not that the EU seeks via Article 3(3) to forbid a Member State from using a named type of damages (eg punitive damages), but rather that it forbids damages that overcompensate (or *do not* fully compensate) the claimant. Member State compliance with Article 3 therefore will depend upon more than the name, or assumptions, appended to a given type of damages. The subtler issue is whether any such damages will fully compensate the claimant or will impermissibly overcompensate him.

---

[26] European Commission, 'Proposal for a Directive of the European Parliament and of the Council on certain rules governing actions for damages under national law for infringements of the competition law provisions of the Member States and of the European Union' COM(2013) 404 final.

[27] Commission Recommendation of 11 June 2013 on common principles for injunctive and compensatory/collective redress mechanisms in the Member States concerning violations of the rights granted under Union law [2013] OJ L201/60.

[28] Communication from the Commission on quantifying harm in actions for damages based on breaches of Arts 101 and 102 of the Treaty on the Functioning of the European Union [2013] OJ C167/07.

[29] European Commission, 'Practical Guide: Quantifying Harm in Actions for Damages Based on Breaches of Article 101 or 102 TFEU of the Treaty on the Functioning of the European Union accompanying the Communication from the Commission on quantifying harm in actions for damages based on breaches of Article 101 or 102 of the Treaty on the Functioning of the European Union' (Working Document) SWD (2013) 205.

[30] Dir 2014/104/EU of the European Parliament and of the Council of 26 November 2014 on certain rules governing actions for damages under national law for infringements of the competition law provisions of the Member States and of the European Union Text with EEA relevance [2014] OJ L349/1.

[31] See also Recital 4 linking effective procedural remedies to Art 19 TEU and Art 47 of the Charter of Fundamental Rights of the European Union.

[32] The national progress to implementation of this Dir is chronicled at http://ec.europa.eu/competition/antitrust/actionsdamages/directive_en.html.

The Directive also makes some attempt to address issues left unclear by Regulation 1/2003 concerning the relationship between the public and private enforcement of EU competition law in the post-modernisation legal environment. In particular, Chapter II of the Directive includes an attempt by the Commission to clarify its view of the nature of the relationship between public and private enforcers of competition law in the recently controversial context of applications by private claimants for disclosure of confidential information and evidence held by public enforcers in connection with leniency applications. The controversies associated with this aspect of the public private enforcement debate became acute in light of the CJEU's decisions in *Pfleiderer*[33] and in *Donau Chemie*.[34] Article 5 provides a general obligation on the Member States to ensure that evidence disclosure to the claimant shall normally be possible via a reasoned and justified application to the national court for disclosure that accords with considerations of proportionality and necessary confidentiality: something similar to this approach was advocated by the CJEU in the *EnBW*[35] case as it appeared to reconsider unintended consequences flowing from *Pfleiderer* and *Donau Chemie*. Article 8 sensibly requires the Member States to ensure that there shall be effective penalties available to national courts to ensure compliance of any parties, third parties or legal representatives concerning the provisions of Chapter II. In Article 6 the Commission takes the opportunity to restrict routine access to the competition authority's file[36] or access during ongoing competition proceedings.[37] The Directive effectively instructs the Member States to override the possibility of *any* disclosure of evidence to a private litigant if his disclosure request arises in the specific context of a leniency application or a settlement submission.[38] Article 7 then imposes strict limits on the admissibility of evidence obtained solely through access to the file of a competition authority.[39]

These provisions indicate a strong desire by the Commission, and by the Member States, to safeguard the operation of public enforcement mechanisms and hence the continuing attractiveness of EU and national leniency programmes. The Directive ensures that leniency applicants and settlement candidates are protected from any disclosure of their submissions to private claimants and others who might sue them on the basis of their admissions made during these procedures. This is an instance of the collective interest in the public enforcement of competition law being justifiably prioritised over the individual interest of a private enforcer. The overwhelming trend for the private enforcement of EU competition law to follow-on from decisions by competition authorities, based on evidence secured via leniency motivated confessions, surely places the correctness of this policy decision beyond any doubt. It may also be noted that the restrictions imposed by Chapter II only affect one aspect of the evidence that a private claimant might wish to employ. A claimant is not debarred from suing a leniency applicant if he uses *admissible* evidence to support his

---

[33] Case C-360/09 *Pfleiderer AG v Bundeskartellamt* [2011] ECR I-5161.

[34] Case C-536/11 *Bundeswettbewerbsbehörde v Donau Chemie AG and Others* EU:C:2013:366.

[35] Case C-365/12P *Commission v EnBW Energie Baden- Württemberg AG* EU:C:2014:112.

[36] Art 6(9) only allows access from an authority if no party or third party can reasonably provide it.

[37] Art 6(5).

[38] Recital 26 and Art 6(6)(a)–(b) of the Dir and the limited form of examination permitted by Art 6(7) to allow the court to ascertain that the evidence in question is actually covered by Art 6(6).

[39] Art 7(1) treats matters under Art 6(6) as inadmissible; Art 7(2) prevents admissibility while the proceedings by the competition authority are ongoing; and Art 7(3) limits the use of any admissible Art 7 evidence to the applicant and those who succeed to his rights and claim.

claim. To this end, Chapter III of the Directive requires each Member State to ensure that final decisions made by *their* national competition authorities, or by *their* review courts, are deemed to be irrefutably established as a matter of evidence for the purposes of a damages action heard in their national courts.[40] In something of a watering down of the evidential value of such a decision, the Directive clarifies that if such a decision is produced in another Member State, the Member State in receipt of the 'foreign' EU final decision must treat it as at least prima facie evidence that an infringement of the relevant competition law has occurred.[41]

The application of domestic limitation periods to private competition claims is addressed by Article 10. This issue has often been problematic for those who would bring private claims: not only are there considerable variations in the nature and operation of limitation periods across the Member States, but it also can be difficult to know when time actually begins to run if a private claim is based on actively contested public enforcement. It is also difficult to know how limitation and the running of time are affected if public enforcement proceedings are commenced *after* the private claim begins. Article 10 clarifies that a minimum of five years must be offered as a limitation period for the damages claim, and also that Member States are required to provide limitation rules that determine the duration of their limitation period, the points at which time begins to run, and the events that will interrupt or suspend time so running.[42] The freedom of the Member States on this matter is somewhat constrained by Article 10(2) which makes the *initial* running of time conditional on both the cessation of the infringement, *and*, on the claimant knowing (or being reasonably expected to know) of the behaviour and also of the fact that it constitutes a competition law infringement by an identified infringer that has caused it harm.

Limitation is to be suspended in the event that either an Article 18 consensual dispute resolution process is begun, or, according to Article 10(4) if a competition authority should undertake investigatory action or 'proceedings in respect of an infringement of competition law to which the action for damages relates'.[43] The wide drafting of Article 10(4) concerning such suspensions may be expected to generate a number of references to the CJEU when and if the Member States attempt to render it into their domestic laws: eg it is unclear from the Directive whether the limitation period concerning a potential claim by 'A' against 'B' in France will be suspended by a decision by the Bulgarian authorities to investigate domestic aspects of the implementation of the same cartel. It should however be noted that the last line of Recital 36 appears to contemplate that Member States may choose to retain general limitation provisions, rather than introducing newly formulated ones, if the retained provisions do not make the right to full compensation unduly difficult or nugatory. It remains to be seen whether the Member States will implement Article 10 properly, but the fact that it only applies to claims for damages, and not to claims for other forms of relief, is an enduring weakness of the Directive. It may be doubted whether the limitation issues concerning a claim for damages plus an injunction is made simpler if the claimant has two different sets of limitation rules to navigate for the two remedies he would pursue.

---

[40] Art 9(1).

[41] Art 9(2); the final Dir has somewhat reduced the evidential status of foreign infringement decisions from the 2013 Proposal.

[42] Art 10(1) and (3).

[43] Art 10(4). The suspension of limitation continues for at least one further year from the end of the event that triggered the initial suspension.

A similar sense of a political compromise in operation may be experienced when considering Article 11 on the joint and several liability of undertakings that have behaved so as to jointly infringe competition law. The basic principle is that joint infringers are all and each to be treated as being liable jointly and severally to a competition law claimant until he has been fully compensated.[44] Thus the claimant can, in theory, sue any single cartel member for the entirety of its own losses attributable to the joint behaviour of the cartel members from which it purchased goods. A cartel member that has been required to pay for joint behaviour has a right of contribution against the rest of the cartel.[45] At this point however there are two potential complications which could themselves interact to further reduce the actual extent of joint and several liability for damages claims brought by private claimants. First, the application of these rules is varied if the target infringer is an 'immunity recipient'. In an attempt to protect a leniency recipient, it *usually* only has liability to its own direct and indirect purchasers, except when injured parties are unable to obtain full compensation from the other joint infringers, when it has to act as the long-stop defendant. The second complication takes the form of a different type of derogation from general joint and several liability that applies if a small or medium sized enterprise (SME) that has neither led the infringement nor coerced others into it, and has not previously infringed competition law, and which had a market share of less than five per cent at any time during the infringement, should be the defendant.[46] Such a comparatively 'innocent' SME need only fully compensate its own direct and indirect purchasers (and has no long-stop liability) if it should be that the usual application of joint and several liability would, 'irretrievably jeopardise its economic viability and cause its assets to lose all their value'.[47] It will be interesting to see whether, and if so how, these two exceptions will be implemented by domestic laws so as to be capable of successive or cumulative application in the context of a given cartel involving both an immunity recipient and a qualifying SME.

Article 12 of the Directive deals with the contentious issues of passing-on, and does so with reference to each of the two legal aspects of this concept. First, as a defence intended to prevent overcompensation of a claimant purchaser who has actually passed-on some (or all) of the cartel over-charge, and hence some or all of his losses, to his indirect purchasers. Second, as means of establishing the losses that will, in theory, empower successive classes of indirect purchaser to also found their claims for an appropriate percentage of the full compensation that Article 3(1) indicates is payable by the cartel to all levels of supply. It is clear that the dominant view of the pass-on concept in the CJEU, in the EU's institutions, and in its Member States, is currently that the pass-on concept is essential to prevent overcompensation and to facilitate private enforcement at all levels of the supply chain. For better or worse, the Damages Directive is drafted to follow this view.[48]

---

[44] Art 11(1) and Recital 37.

[45] Art 11(5) and Recital 38.

[46] Art 11(2)–(3). SME is defined with reference to Commission Recommendation 2003/361/EC of 6 May 2003 [2003] OJ L124/36.

[47] Art 11(2)(b).

[48] The pass-on defence can alternatively be argued to be an invidious legal concept by which cartel members are allowed to undermine the strongest private enforcement claims (brought by direct purchasers) to allow for an abstract possibility of further litigation (by successive classes of indirect purchasers) which may never materialise. The negative view of pass-on holds that it is cynically deployed to shield cartelists from the adverse consequences of being caught after they have voluntarily taken a decision to deliberately and illicitly act to obtain money and associated benefits from their unwitting victims. On this view, the cartel member should not be afforded the

In truth, any attempt to develop private enforcement of EU competition law by deducing horizontal direct effect from the bald provisions of Articles 85 and 86 EEC, and then to construe from them a private damages claim, would struggle to find any textual basis in these provisions to exclude *locus standi* for indirect purchasers. The private enforcement of EU competition law presently comes with an inbuilt propensity towards empowering indirect purchasers and hence both aspects of pass-on. The legal systems of the Member States also seem generally receptive to the defensive aspect of pass-on. It thus holds out a welcome potential to preserve domestic legal certainties in the face of the arrival of exotic foreign competition law concepts potentially leading to problematic litigation directed at domestically located undertakings[49] that might otherwise be over-punished by the overcompensation of litigants inspired by the rather over-stated likelihood of developing a US-style claims culture within their legal system.

The Directive treats pass-on in Articles 12–16 of Chapter IV. The Member States are required to ensure that any victim, whether a direct or an indirect purchaser, can claim its correct share, and no more, of the full compensation that the infringer must provide. So seriously is the danger of overcompensation taken that Article 12(2) imposes a positive obligation to set in place procedural rules to prevent it, while Article 12(5) requires that the Member States must provide their national courts with the legal power and the procedures to allow them to estimate any overcharge.[50] Article 13 specifies that the infringer must have the ability to wholly or partly defend against a claimant's damages claim by using the pass-on defence. The Directive very sensibly reverses the normal burden of proof by obliging the defendant who would invoke the pass-on defence to himself prove that the overcharge was actually passed on by the claimant.[51] This reversal goes some way towards a necessary equalisation of the burdens on the claimant and defendant when the defendant invokes pass-on for his own benefit. Logically enough, there is no such reversal if the pass-on is instead to be used by an indirect claimant to establish its *locus standi* to bring a damages claim against the defendant cartelist. In this circumstance it is the claimant (as alleged indirect purchaser) who must, according to Recital 41 on a prima facie basis, prove the fact of the pass-on of the overcharge to it from the direct or otherwise superior purchaser.[52] The three requirements that the indirect claimant must satisfy to prove that a cartel overcharge has been passed on to it are set out by Article 14(2)(a)–(c): these requirements may however be rebutted if the defendant can 'demonstrate credibly to the satisfaction of the court that the overcharge was not, or was not entirely, passed on to the indirect purchaser'.[53]

The Directive's use of the pass-on concept to determine the competent classes of indirect purchasers, and also its perennial horror of overcompensation of a direct or indirect claimant, each potentially necessitate additional EU coordination of the legal and evidential

---

opportunity to argue pass-on, and should instead be liable to return the whole overcharge and other benefits illicitly extracted, but only to his direct purchaser (indirect purchasers being prevented from bringing a claim). This view tolerates the abstract possibility of over-compensation of the direct purchaser because this will speed the litigation or settlement of the dispute, deprive the cartelist of *all* benefits and thereby discourage other cartels.

[49] See Art 12(2).

[50] Art 16 requires the Commission to issue guidelines on how to estimate the share of the overcharge passed on to indirect purchasers.

[51] Art 13 second sentence and Recital 39.

[52] Art 14(1).

[53] Art 14(2).

abilities of the national courts who must hear such damages claims and must establish whether the burden of proof concerning direct and indirect claimants have been satisfied. Article 15 is expressly directed against the dangers of either overcompensation or under-compensation in such cases. Article 15(1) requires that national courts must be allowed to take due account of any relevant information in the public domain that concerns the public enforcement of competition law, and also to take due account of any ongoing damages claims and final judgments at other levels of the supply chain that are related to the same competition law infringement as the instant claim.

The meaning of, 'to take due account of' in this context is somewhat elucidated by refer-ences in Article 15(2) and in Recital 44 to the discretionary stays allowed by Article 30 of the Brussels Ia Regulation. Though Article 15(2) of the Directive declares that Article 15 is to operate without prejudice to the rights and obligations of national courts under Article 30 of the Brussels Ia Regulation, Recital 44 makes plain that the drafters contemplate the need for the court hearing the damages claim to be domestically equipped with an ability to con-sider other domestic or even cross-border claims in order to estimate the nature and scale of the overcharge concerning a direct or indirect purchaser with accuracy. If some form of technical joinder of parties is required to allow the court in a given Member State to engage in such a consideration, Recital 44 appears to approve of the implementing Member State providing for this possibility (without prejudice to Article 30 of the Brussels Ia Regulation). Though there is no mention of this possibility in the text of Article 15(1), the qualification in Article 15(2) is meaningless without it.

The complex issue of how to quantify the harm caused to a given claimant by the infringe-ment of EU competition law so as to establish his damages is unfortunately one that, due to the lack of any EU rules on the subject, Article 17 of the Directive is only able to deal with in outline rather than in detail. For the present the detail is to be found in the laws of the Member States and in the general principles of equivalence and effectiveness exhorted by Article 17 and Recital 46. Thus Article 17(1) requires that Member States shall ensure that neither the burden of proof nor the standard of proof necessary to quantify harm will render the exercise of the right to damages either practically impossible or excessively difficult. It is however usefully added that, assuming that it has first been established that the claimant has suffered some harm, the Member States should ensure that their national courts are able to *estimate* the amount of harm that a claimant has suffered if more precise calculation of the harm is practically impossible or excessively difficult from the evidence available.[54] Even the welcome presumption stated by the first sentence of Article 17(2), that cartel infringements cause harm, has had to be balanced by the following sentence allowing for the possibility of the infringer exercising what the Directive refers to as his 'right' to rebut the presumption of harm.[55] Article 17(3) obliges the Member States to ensure that in a competition damages claim, the court may request an NCA to assist it in quantifying the amount of damages and, if the NCA considers it appropriate to offer such assistance, that it may do so.

The substantive provisions of the Damages Directive draw to a close with its provisions in Articles 18 and 19 concerning alternatives to litigation; 'consensual dispute resolution'.[56]

---

[54] See however Recitals 45–47.

[55] Also Recital 47.

[56] Recital 48 non-exhaustively describes this concept as including: 'out-of-court settlements (including those where a judge can declare a settlement binding), arbitration, mediation or conciliation.'

It is clear from Recital 48 that the use of alternatives to litigation over competition damages claims are very much encouraged and will, in future, be actively promoted.[57] To this end Article 18 clarifies the obligation of the Member States under the Directive to ensure that the pursuit of such alternatives to litigation should produce suspensive effects on limitation periods for the parties involved, and should also allow a national court seised with a competition law damages claim to suspend that proceeding for up to two years if the parties to that claim are involved in such a consensual dispute resolution procedure. Article 19 makes provision for the basic legal consequences of a consensual settlement on an existing damages claim or on further litigation. The settlement must be discounted from any unresolved part of the existing claim and must normally bar the claimant from continuing it as far as the settling infringer is concerned.[58]

B. Collective Redress

Collective redress, and its role in allowing all classes of competition law victims to recover their losses via private enforcement, remains a controversial issue in EU competition law.[59] The theoretical need for a collective redress mechanism flows from the EU policy of requiring competition law infringers to also pay full compensation to indirect purchasers. If the infringement is one that may be passed on, the actionable losses may therefore be diffused along the supply chain until the end consumer is reached. Those at the lower levels of the supply chain will probably be reluctant to risk the costs of suing to only recover the relatively small losses they are likely to individually be entitled to.[60] Accordingly, a likely (if unintended) consequence of allowing indirect purchasers to claim can be that infringers are de facto able to retain substantial parts of the illicit benefit that is deemed to have been passed on to those who do not sue individually. One way to resolve this conundrum is to promote an EU form of collective redress designed to empower 'low level' victims to seek effectively the compensation that they are due, and thereby to deprive the infringers of the illicit benefits they would otherwise retain. Considered in this sense, collective redress is

---

[57] Art 18(3) suggests that a competition authority may regard the payment of compensation that arises from a consensual settlement, and is also prior in time to its own decision imposing a fine, to be a mitigating factor. In similar vein, Art 19(4) makes the payment of a settlement a relevant factor in setting the amount of contribution between co-infringers.

[58] Art 19(3) contemplates the possibility (which may—and hence presumably always will—be excluded by the terms of the settlement agreement) of further liability for a settling infringer if the outstanding claim against its co-infringers is litigated and, at the point the damages are awarded, the non-settling co-infringers cannot pay them.

[59] The literature on collective redress as it affects the EU and its Member States is considerable. The most recent and significant publications include: S Weber Waller and O Popal, 'The Fall and Rise of the Antitrust Class Action' (2016) 39(1) *World Competition* 29; BJ Rodger, 'The Consumer Rights Act 2015 and Collective Redress for Competition Law Infringements in the UK: A Class Act?' (2015) 3(2) *Journal of Antitrust Enforcement* 258; A Andreangeli, *Private Enforcement of Antitrust: Regulating Corporate Behaviour through Collective Claims in the EU and the US* (Cheltenham, Edward Elgar, 2014); BJ Rodger (ed), *Competition Law: Comparative Private Enforcement and Collective Redress across the EU* (Alphen aan den Rijn, Kluwer, 2014); P Buccirossi and M Carpagnano, 'Is it Time for the European Union to Legislate in the Field of Collective Redress in Antitrust (and how)?' (2013) 4 *Journal of European Competition Law & Practice* 3; A Andreangeli, 'Collective Redress in EU Competition Law: An Open Question with Many Possible Solutions' (2012) 35(3) *World Competition* 529.

[60] See Buccirossi and Carpagnano, ibid at 5 discussing the 2006 action by *UFC Que Choisir* and the 2007 action by *Which* against JJB.

an important part of the private enforcement of EU competition law. When, however, the practical requirements of introducing a system of collective redress into Member State legal systems are considered, controversy is rarely far behind.[61]

Existing collective redress mechanisms, especially the sometimes effective and claimant friendly ones used in the USA, trigger deep-rooted anxieties in the EU and particularly in certain Member States.[62] US antitrust law and its collective redress mechanisms reflect a fundamentally different privately-led enforcement ethos to the publicly-led EU and Member State conceptions of the enforcement of EU competition law. For the EU, the predominant need to create collective redress mechanisms is to remedy problems posed by identified classes of litigants who are otherwise reluctant to sue. There is neither the desire (nor presently the legal ability) to use collective redress mechanisms to supplant public enforcement or other private enforcement possibilities. As is clear from events following the publication of the Commission's 2008 White Paper, various Member States also strongly opposed the idea of importing what they regard as foreign collective redress mechanisms into their legal systems. The enduring nature of this opposition may be induced from the fact despite work by the Commission since 2005 to promote collective redress[63] and a 2012 Study for the European Parliament[64] and its Resolution of the same year calling for the establishment of a coherent framework for collective redress for EU consumers,[65] the 2014 Damages Directive does not include any provisions on collective redress.[66] Indeed, references to collective redress were cut from the 2013 Directive Proposal and it was relegated to a non-binding Recommendation drafted in terms considerably wider than might be required for the particular purposes of EU competition law.[67]

The Commission Recommendation is indeed wider in scope than the Damages Directive, as well as covering other remedies it also cuts across a range of different Directorate General competencies covering: consumer protection; environment protection; protection of personal data; financial services legislation; investor protection, and competition. The stated aim of the Recommendation is, 'to facilitate access to justice in relation to violations of rights under Union law' and thus it recommends that, 'all Member States should have collective redress systems at national level that follow the same basic principles throughout the Union, taking into account the legal traditions of the Member States and safeguarding against abuse.'[68] A recurring issue in the Recommendation is the importance of avoiding

---

[61] Member State legal systems have typically been established with different conceptions of the correct means by which a claimant should bring his own claim; relate to and pay his legal representatives; conduct his case; and, be compensated only for his proven losses.

[62] In particular, opt-out class actions financed by contingency fees and potentially yielding triple damages.

[63] See Commission Green Paper on Consumer Collective Redress, COM(2008) 794 final, and, Commission Staff Working Document, Public Consultation: Towards a Coherent European Approach to Collective Redress, SEC (2011) 173 final.

[64] Collective Redress in Antitrust (2012) IP/A/ECON/ST/2011-19 PE 475.120 available from www.europarl. europa.eu/RegData/etudes/etudes/join/2012/475120/IPOL-ECON_ET(2012)475120_EN.pdf.

[65] Resolution of 2 February 2012 on 'Towards a Coherent European Approach to Collective Redress' EUR. PARL. DOC. P7_TA(2012)0021 (2012).

[66] The only reference to collective enforcement in the Damages Dir is found in Recital 13, second sentence, which records, 'This Directive should not require Member States to introduce collective redress mechanisms for the enforcement of Articles 101 and 102 TFEU'.

[67] Commission Recommendation of 11 June 2013 on common principles for injunctive and compensatory collective redress mechanisms in the Member States concerning violations of the rights granted under Union law [2013] OJ L201/60.

[68] Recital 10.

what it repeatedly characterises as 'abusive'[69] aspects of collective redress. Abuse is to be avoided by imposing tight forms of Member State regulation for any collective redress mechanisms put in place, or reformed, in line with the Recommendation. Such regulation includes restrictions on: the designated or certified private bodies that may bring such an action, and how they may lose the right to maintain an action;[70] the judicial verification of admissibility of the claim or its dismissal;[71] publicity provisions that protect the reputation of the putative defendant prior to a finding of its liability by an authority;[72] a 'loser-pays' principle concerning costs, but made subject to national rules;[73] an open-door opt-in basis for collective redress;[74] a ban on contingency fees or equivalent inducements to litigation or settlement;[75] an obligation on the claimant to declare the origins of its funding to the national court that then assesses any conflict of interest while also considering its extent and sufficiency to either fund the claim or the costs of losing it;[76] restrictions on private third party funders to prevent them influencing procedural decisions or settlement regarding the claimants or from funding claims against their own business rivals or from charging excessive interest;[77] and, a (wholly unnecessary) ban on punitive damages.[78]

With respect, it seems fair to describe the contents of the Recommendation, as they are intended to affect the development of collective redress mechanisms for competition law claims, as a counsel of perfection. The Recommendation pays too little attention to the practical issues of making privately funded collective redress function in the context of competition law claims: eg the need to cover the considerable pre-action costs[79] incurred in identifying and building the class (or classes) of claimants, and calculating potential damages, or of then administering the claim in search of a financially viable settlement or remedy plus costs. These practical issues are not complicated to conceptualise and reveal, with brutal honesty, whether or not a claim is financially worth bringing.[80] If the political will to reform the collective redress of competition law claims can ever be achieved in the EU it would be advisable to start from the practical economic determinants of this type of litigation rather than from entirely abstract notions of its alleged potential to be abused. At present too much attention seems to be paid to the overblown, and to a degree insulting, fears of certain Member States concerning a clumsy and insensitive imposition of a gruesome caricature of the US system upon their 'delicate' legal systems. In the meantime, low-level litigants continue uncompensated and cartel members retain significant parts of the benefit of their illicit actions.

---

[69] Recitals 10, 11, 13, 15, 19, 20 refer to preventing 'abuse': Art 1 echoes this, as do many specific provisions.
[70] Arts 4–6. Empowering a public authority is contemplated by Art 7.
[71] Arts 8–9.
[72] Arts 10–11.
[73] Art 13.
[74] Arts 21–24.
[75] Arts 29–30 and 33.
[76] Arts 14–15.
[77] Art 16.
[78] Art 31.
[79] See D Geradin, 'Collective Redress for Antitrust Damages in the European Union: Is this a Reality Now?' (2015) 22(5) *George Mason Law Review* 1079 at 1094–96 considering claims attempted by French and UK Consumer associations.
[80] ibid, 1096–98 with worked examples.

As ever, the absence of true political agreement between the legislative parties in the EU and in the Member States is the main obstacle to the EU's progress towards a more effective form of collective private enforcement for its competition law. It should not however be assumed that every Member State has an equal horror of collective redress mechanisms. Indeed, the main progress towards actual collective redress in various legal situations (including collective claims concerning competition law victims) has come from EU Member States that are well-disposed towards the concept of collective redress for claimants at every level. Such national provisions, some of which pre-date the Recommendation, indicate a wide range of different ways of addressing the particular problems of collective redress in given Member States.[81]

With respect to all of those who have worked in admittedly difficult circumstances to produce the 2013 Recommendation, it is suggested that a deeper and more strategic investigation of existing collective redress options, including (but not limited to) high-level private collective systems such as that offered by CDC and its rivals, the UK's new collective action regime plus its judicially supervised opt-out settlement system, and, in particular, the continuing trend towards the development of a more convincing form of collective action by the Netherlands,[82] should be undertaken before the EU or the Commission attempt to propose further hard or soft law measures concerning collective redress that could apply to competition law claims.[83]

III. Conclusion

As well as addressing the difficulties arising from the need to maintain the primacy of an effective and explicitly envisaged public enforcement of EU competition law, this chapter has demonstrated that the private enforcement of EU competition law continues to depend upon both a series of legal sophistications necessary to maintain a viable private law claim before Member State legal systems (eg horizontal direct effect of Articles 101 and 102 TFEU and the principles of effectiveness and equivalence). The chapter has also addressed the additional complexities arising from the contestable effects of the provisions of EU private international law that are required to locate the said claim in a Member State legal system

---

[81] Considerations of space prevent discussion of these national collective regimes but see: R Gaudet, 'Turning a Blind Eye: the Commission's Rejection of Opt-out Class Actions Overlooks Swedish, Norwegian, Danish and Dutch Experience' (2009) 30(3) *European Competition Law Review* 107; Buccirossi and Carpagnano, above n 59; Rodger, 'The Consumer Rights Act', above n 59.

[82] Concerning not only the well-established option of a mass collective settlement system (See XE Kramer, 'Enforcing Mass Settlements in the European Judicial Area: EU Policy and the Strange Case of Dutch Collective Settlements (WCAM)' in C Hodges and A Stadler (eds), *Resolving Mass Disputes. ADR and Settlement of Mass Claims* (Cheltenham, Edward Elgar, 2013) 63) but also the new draft Dutch Bill on collective actions (which seeks, inter alia, to accommodate the ruling of the CJEU in Case C-375/13 *Kolassa* EU:C:2015:37, to tighten up the eligibility requirement of the claimant, and to allow greater oversight of the claim). The draft Bill was presented to Parliament on 16.11.2016 by the Dutch Ministry of Justice see note by I Tzankova at http://conflictoflaws. net/2016/new-dutch-bill-on-collective-damages-action/.

[83] For example, the linkage between the offender attempting to compensate its victims to reduce its fine liability might be considered see J Bourgeois and S Strievi, 'EU Competition Remedies in Consumer Cases: Thinking Out of the Shopping Bag' (2010) 33 *World Competition* 241.

with jurisdiction over the claim and also to provide a means of determining the applicable law(s) in the complex factual situations associated with the illicit conduct of anticompetitive activities. It has been argued that, despite various forms of progress, the private enforcement of EU competition law has, in default of decisive legal reform of the private law claim, been too dependent upon the vicissitudes of international commercial litigation and the possibility that the EU law concerning the instant claim, including the EU private international law concerning that claim, might be developed during that litigation by the CJEU in the event that it should be presented with a suitable preliminary reference.

Though the international enforcement of the private law rights of private 'victims' that are only known to exist at all because of explanations by the CJEU of the latent potential of the European treaty provisions concerning competition law can scarcely be expected to be other than a complex area of law, this chapter has noted the difficulties facing the EU legislators in attempting to reform the private enforcement of their competition law. These difficulties have been attributed not only to the absence of a clear treaty provision establishing the private law claim, its purpose and its claimants, but particularly to a general reluctance by the Member States to reform effectively the laws and civil procedures of their legal systems to assist the claimant(s). This chapter has demonstrated, in the context of both the Damages Directive and the Collective Redress Recommendation, that for there to be any progress towards legislation from the EU to facilitate the private enforcement of competition law, the EU must persuade deeply conservative Member States that the benefits of facilitating private enforcement outweigh enduring concerns that this will 'open the floodgates' to wasteful litigation tending to unjustly enrich the claimant (and his lawyers) by requiring the defendant to make additional payments on top of the very high administrative fines already often imposed by the European Commission in the course of the public enforcement of EU competition law. It has been argued throughout this chapter that many Member States are too conservative, or too anxious of imagined dangers and theoretical abuses of legal procedure, while also being too sanguine about the effectiveness of bare public enforcement to deter anticompetitive business activities in an effective and just manner. This chapter has welcomed the recent progress towards the strengthening of the legal position of the claimant by the development of EU private international law by the explanations offered by the CJEU in the *CDC* case and also by the legislative reforms represented by the Rome II Regulation and by the new Damages Directive. It has however also been argued that the EU and the Member States must either reconceptualise the nature of the private claim or reconcile themselves to further and bolder EU legislative intervention concerning both single and collective claims if private enforcement is ever to perform its intended and complimentary function of assisting public enforcement by routinely deterring the potentially anticompetitive from acting to infringe EU competition law.

40

The Relationship Between Litigation and ADR: Evaluating the Effect of the EU PIL Framework on ADR/ Settlements in Cross-border Cases

MIHAIL DANOV AND STEFANIA BARIATTI

I. Introduction and Some Preliminary Remarks: ADR/Settlements and Cross-border Litigation

As already noted,[1] the empirical data demonstrates that cross-border litigation is a result-driven undertaking, presupposing a cost-remedy analysis.[2] This is reflected in the Brussels I (Recast) Regulation which aims to provide parties with effective access to remedies in disputes with an international element. An issue is that these disputes are characterised with a higher level of complexity which means greater litigation expenses by the parties in cross-border cases. This might have a negative impact on a party's decision whether to litigate because it is well established that this decision will be 'strongly influenced by beliefs about the likelihood of achieving the desired outcome.'[3] The problems would be exacerbated if the EU private international law (PIL) instruments do not effectively achieve their objective to provide an optimal level of legal certainty which is necessary to minimise the litigation costs and facilitate the parties' access to remedies.[4]

The EUPILLAR project[5] indicates that the outcome in a cross-border case may depend on the effectiveness/ineffectiveness of the EU PIL regime which could also impact the parties' decision whether/where to issue proceedings. In particular, a number of factors will have an effect on the litigants' strategies and the outcome of a dispute with an international element. First, the value and strength (or the relative strength) of the claimant's claim would be determined by the applicable law/s. Second, since the experience of judges to deal with cross-border cases and procedural laws (which are closely linked with costs and cost-shifting rules) varies across the EU, parties' access would depend on the place of

---

[1] Ch 35.
[2] Ch 5—England and Wales; ch 6—Belgium.
[3] H Genn, 'Understanding Civil Justice' (1997) 50 *Current Legal Problems* 155, 173.
[4] See ch 35.
[5] ibid.

litigation which leaves no doubt that the rules allocating jurisdiction will play a major role.[6] It is important for the purposes of this chapter to note that if the EU PIL framework is not functioning effectively, any resulting uncertainty/ambiguity about the outcome of litigation will have a bearing on alternative dispute resolution (ADR)/settlements. In keeping with the purpose of this project (which is to evaluate the effectiveness of the EUPILLAR Regulations), the aim of this chapter is to consider the relationship between litigation and ADR in cross-border cases.

Before defining ADR for the purposes of this chapter, it should be outlined that the EUPILLAR project demonstrates that the impact of the EU PIL framework on ADR/settlements negotiation could be significant.[7] A good example is the court-first-seised rule which has had a major impact on the stages when the parties will start considering out-of-court settlements in cross-border cases. As a part of an analysis of the relationship between ADR and litigation in a domestic context, Roberts made the following observations:

> alternatives themselves are as much about devoting new energy and attention to familiar phases in dispute processes preceding the resort to judgment as about the emergence of novel modes. These interventions converge upon three separate moments: the private efforts of parties to reach agreement at a point before resorting to specialist legal help; upon attempts to 'settle' somewhere along the path to the court once 'litigation' has formally commenced; and upon what happens in lawyers' offices.[8]

These observations, however, are not entirely consistent with the practice in disputes with an international element. Indeed, due to the court-first-seised rule, it would be increasingly unlikely for parties to negotiate and try to settle amicably unless an EU Member State court had been first seised within the meaning of Brussels Ia, IIa or Maintenance. A party who starts out-of-court settlement negotiations with another party, without seising the court which s/he considers appropriate to hear and determine the dispute, faces a real risk to have to defend in a pre-emptive strike (eg seeking a non-liability declaration)[9] initiated by the other party before another EU Member State than the one he intends to litigate in. This means that in disputes with an international element one of the parties normally seises a court first and only then do the parties engage in ADR/settlements. This will be particularly so in cross-border disputes which do not fall within the scope of an exclusive choice-of-court agreement between the parties.[10] Therefore, the implications of the EU PIL regime fly in the face of Lord Woolf's 'approach to civil justice ... that disputes should, wherever possible, be resolved without litigation. Where litigation is unavoidable, it should be conducted with a view to encouraging settlement at the earliest appropriate stage.'[11] The impact of

---

[6] See chs 5, 32 and 35.

[7] See chs 5, 32 and 35.

[8] S Roberts, 'Alternative Dispute Resolution and Civil Justice: An Unresolved Relationship' (1993) 56(3) *Modern Law Review* 452, 453.

[9] eg *Cooper Tire & Rubber Company v Shell Chemicals UK Limited* [2009] EWHC 2609 (Comm); *Cooper Tire & Rubber Company Europe Limited & Others* [2010] EWCA Civ 864; *McGraw-Hill International (UK) Limited v Deutsche Apotheker—und Arztebank EG, Uniqa Alternative Investments GMBH, Uniqa Capital Markets GMBH, Stichting Ratings Redress, The Royal Bank of Scotland NV* [2014] EWHC 2436 (Comm).

[10] See Art 31(2) of Brussels Ia.

[11] The Right Honourable the Lord Woolf, *Access to Justice—Final Report to the Lord Chancellor on the Civil Justice System in England and Wales* (HMSO, 1996) 107.

the EU PIL framework on the pattern of out-of-court settlements is most noticeably felt in cross-border matrimonial disputes in relation to financial remedies.[12] The point was clearly made by one interview respondent from England and Wales who stated:

> I would be negligent in a divorce case to encourage a client to consider ADR [-] if my client does not file in the right country where she will get more money, usually England. ... ADR has no place within Brussels IIa and divorce because of the way the Regulation is drafted ...[13]

This is a good example of how the PIL framework impacts the stages when a party may start considering ADR in cross-border cases which arise in the EU context. If one of the parties' advisers are less experienced (than those of his/her opponent), then carefully designed litigants' strategies may have a major influence on the ADR/settlement and ultimately remedies in cross-border cases.

Therefore, there is a strong case that the court-first-seised rule is shaping the litigants' strategies, impacting indirectly the outcome of ADR/settlement negotiations. An analysis of the way the current EU PIL framework impacts on ADR/settlements can indicate what other aspects (apart from the court-first-seised rule) might need to be revised with a view to improving the effectiveness of the EU PIL regime and facilitating litigants' access to remedies in cross-border cases. Since this book evaluates the effectiveness of the EU PIL framework in the light of the gathered qualitative data,[14] the authors will analyse the relationship between the EU PIL framework and ADR (including any settlement negotiations between the parties) in cross-border cases.

An important preliminary issue is about the definition of ADR and the scope of this chapter. The adoption of the Mediation Directive is strongly indicative that mediation as a form of ADR will need to be considered. Mediation, of course, may consist of 'a wide range of strategies, from passive to highly directive and evaluative.'[15] That said, mediation is not the only ADR mechanism. It is well established that '[t]here are several forms of alternative dispute resolution: arbitration, conciliation, mediation, negotiation, or combined ADR mechanisms like med-arb or mini-trial.'[16] One report shows that '[c]ross border mediation stand for less than 0.05%'[17] of the commercial disputes in the EU but a more recent study[18] concludes that:

> The research carried out in Austria, Germany, France, Scandinavia and the UK has revealed that mediation ... is definitely not only the most popular but also the most widely established and by far the most popular and frequently used form of dispute resolution process to be subsumed under the umbrella term ADR.[19]

---

[12] *S v S* [2014] EWHC 3613 (Fam); Case C-489/14 *A v B* EU:C:2015:654 discussed already in ch 5 above.

[13] EUPILLAR—England and Wales—Interview Transcript No 16.

[14] See chs 1 and 32 above.

[15] H J Brown and A Marriott, *ADR Principles and Practice* 3rd edn (London, Sweet & Maxwell, 2011) 154.

[16] C Esplugues, 'Civil and Commercial Mediation in the EU after the Transposition of Directive 2008/52/EC' in C Esplugues (ed), *Civil and Commercial Mediation in Europe* Vol II (Mortsel, Intersentia, 2014) 485, 491.

[17] V Tilman, 'Lessons learnt from the implementation of the EU Mediation Directive: the business perspective', www.europarl.europa.eu/document/activities/cont/201105/20110518ATT19584/20110518ATT19584EN.pdf, 4. See also Esplugues, ibid 492.

[18] E Filler, *Commercial Mediation in Europe: An Empirical Study of the User Experience* (Alphen aan den Rijn, Kluwer Law International, 2012).

[19] ibid 332.

These research findings, however, fly in the face of the 2016 edition of the *Jackson ADR Handbook* which states that 'negotiation remains the most common form of dispute resolution'[20] in England and Wales. In view of the high number of settlements in a domestic context, one could argue that an equally significant amount of cross-border disputes settle in England and Wales.[21] This is reflected in the English Civil Procedure Rules (CPR) Practice Direction—Pre-Action Conduct and Protocols.[22] The latter Practice Direction goes further to state:

> 8 ... the parties should consider whether negotiation or some other form of ADR might enable them to settle their dispute without commencing proceedings.

> 9. Parties should continue to consider the possibility of reaching a settlement at all times, including after proceedings have been started ...[23]

Hence, an important aspect, which must be considered in this chapter, concerns the fact that 'ADR has a symbiotic relationship with litigation and negotiation.'[24] Brown and Marriott have submitted that:

> It is self-evident that the facilitated negotiations processes that comprise ADR could not exist in the absence of negotiation. ADR's synergic relationship with litigation is, however, sometimes less acknowledged, as some proponents of consensual procedures promote these over litigation: the stark fact is that mediation would not be effective in most cases without the backstop of litigation or some form of adjudication.[25]

Indeed, it is well established that litigation tactics may force settlements.[26] There is a strong case that, in disputes with an international element, the litigants' strategies (which are devised under the current EU PIL framework) would have an impact on ADR/settlement dynamics. In particular, the specific nature of the cross-border disputes means that abusive litigation tactics may be devised by litigants to unduly benefit from the inefficiencies of the national judicial system and/or ineffectiveness of the EU PIL framework. Therefore, there is a need to evaluate the effect of the EU PIL framework on settlements in cross-border cases.

The authors' approach to include parties' negotiated settlements in their analyses of the relationship between EU PIL and ADR in cross-border cases is consistent with the view that the ADR 'process may or may not involve an independent third party.'[27] This is further in line with Andrews's observations, made in a similar vein as the view expressed by the authors of the *Jackson ADR Handbook*, that 'party-to-party negotiation leading to settlement ... is the most common way in which a dispute or claim is terminated'[28] in

---

[20] S Blake, J Browne and S Sime, *Jackson ADR Handbook* 2nd edn (Oxford, Oxford University Press, 2016) 17.
[21] See ch 5.
[22] See S 10 of CPR Practice Direction—Pre-Action Conduct and Protocols.
[23] Ss 8 and 9 of CPR Practice Direction—Pre-Action Conduct and Protocols.
[24] Brown and Marriott, above n 15 at 18.
[25] ibid, 18–19.
[26] Woolf, above n 11 at 107.
[27] Blake, Browne and Sime, above n 20 at 2.
[28] N Andrews, *The Three Paths of Justice: Court Proceedings, Arbitration and Mediation in England* (New York, Springer, 2012) 187; N Andrews, *Andrews on Civil Processes: Mediation* Vol II (Mortsel, Intersentia, 2013) 6.

England and Wales.[29] The relevant negotiation 'process may involve a very simple exchange between parties and/or lawyers, or a more structured settlement meeting including the parties.'[30]

Given that settlements in England and Wales have been widely promoted by the CPR rules for a number of years, an analysis of the effect of the EU PIL framework on ADR/settlements negotiations may be important for the EU policy-makers who have promoted the use of ADR in cross-border cases.[31] Since '[e]very settlement emerges from a negotiating process',[32] it will be particularly important to evaluate the impact of the EU PIL framework on the process of negotiation which is the foundation of the ADR process. The qualitative interview data is very helpful for making this analysis because '[a] critical feature of all forms of ADR is that they are dispute resolution processes conducted in private. Both the process and outcome of the procedures are generally confidential to the parties.'[33]

Bearing this in mind, it should be noted that the authors do not intend to make any 'attempts to weigh and evaluate the successes and failures of ADR processes',[34] but rather our purpose is to assess the impact of the EU PIL framework on ADR/settlements negotiations. The thrust in this paper will be on the way the EU PIL instruments and the current institutional framework may influence the litigants' access to effective remedies in cross-border civil and commercial law cases. To this end, the paper will first outline the relevant EU legislative framework which is shaping the EU landscape with regard to ADR. The EU policy-makers' objectives and the various challenges they face will be considered in this context by taking into consideration the Report of the European Commission on the application of the Mediation Directive. Then, the authors will consider the relationship between litigation and ADR in cross-border cases.[35] Finally, the impact of the current EU PIL framework on ADR/settlements negotiations will be considered in light of the gathered empirical data.

II. A Level of Harmonisation—The EU Legislative Framework

The EU legislator has adopted several instruments concerning the out-of-court resolution of civil and commercial disputes. In particular, a level of harmonisation in the area

---

[29] H Genn, *Judging Civil Justice* (Cambridge, Cambridge University Press, 2010) 21. See the Civil Justice quarterly statistics, www.gov.uk/government/statistics/civil-justice-statistics-quarterly-april-to-june-2016. H Genn, 'Why the privatisation of justice is a rule of law issue' *36th F A Mann Lecture*—Lincoln's Inn, 19 November 2012, www.laws.ucl.ac.uk/wp-content/uploads/2014/08/36th-F-A-Mann-Lecture-19.11.12-Professor-Hazel-Genn.pdf, 1.

[30] Black, Browne and Sime, above n 20 at 17. See also S Lewis, *Structured Settlements: The Law and Practice* (London, Sweet & Maxwell, 1993); D Foskett, *The Law and Practice of Compromise with Precedents* 7th edn (London, Sweet & Maxwell, 2010).

[31] See S II of this chapter below.

[32] Foskett, above n 30 at 216.

[33] H Genn, S Riahi and K Pleming, 'Regulation of Dispute Resolution in England and Wales: A Sceptical Analysis of Government and Judicial Promotion of Private Mediation' in F Steffek and H Unberath (eds), *Regulating Dispute Resolution: ADR and Access to Justice at the Crossroads* (Oxford, Hart Publishing, 2013) 447, 452.

[34] CJ Menkel-Meadow, 'Dispute Resolution' in P Kane and H Kritzer (eds), *The Oxford Handbook of Empirical Legal Research* (Oxford, Oxford University Press, 2012) 597, 600.

[35] Roberts, above n 8 at 452.

has been achieved through Directive 2008/52 on certain aspects of mediation in civil and commercial matters (Mediation Directive),[36] Directive 2013/11 on alternative dispute resolution for consumer disputes (ADR Directive),[37] and Regulation 524/2013 on online dispute resolution for consumer disputes (ODR Regulation).[38]

The Mediation Directive reflects the EU objective to 'enabl[e] the appropriate development and operation of extrajudicial procedures for settlement of disputes in civil and commercial matters so as to simplify and improve access to justice.'[39] The adoption of the Directive was fostered by the European Council at the Tampere meeting in 1999, which called for alternative and extra-judicial procedures with a view to facilitating further access to justice. The EU legislator's intention to promote ADR is justified by the following rationale:

> [M]ediation can provide a cost-effective and quick extrajudicial resolution of disputes in civil and commercial matters through processes tailored to the needs of the parties. Agreements resulting from mediation are more likely to be complied with voluntarily and are more likely to preserve an amicable and sustainable relationship between the parties. These benefits become even more pronounced in situations displaying cross-border elements.[40]

The EU developments are somewhat in line with what has already happened in England and Wales after Lord Woolf's reform of the civil justice system[41] One of Lord Woolf's objectives was 'to promote more, better and earlier settlements.'[42] That said, the Directive does not provide any specific conditions for the functioning of the mediation process which means that national laws may differ in many respects. Although the Directive applies only in cross-border cases, the Member States could decide to extend its provisions to internal mediation processes. Since England and Wales has already adopted a system which promotes ADR/settlements, an analysis of the way in which the EU PIL framework impacts on settlements in high value cross-border disputes brought there would be informative for any reform of the EU PIL framework.

Notwithstanding, an entirely different set of problems may arise in disputes involving consumers. The need for ensuring effective access to remedies for consumers through ADR is considered by EU policy-makers as an important objective because high litigation costs could be a deterrent for consumers in cross-border cases. Lord Justice Jackson has noted that:

> Costs are a major factor in every case. Sadly, costs sometimes exceed the sum which is in issue in litigation. Thus, the rules governing the incidence and assessment of costs are just as important as the rules governing the assessment of damages.[43]

This deduction is signified by the ADR directive which intends to 'offer ... a simple, fast and low-cost out-of-court solution to disputes between consumers and traders.'[44] The objective

---

[36] [2008] OJ L136/3.
[37] [2013] OJ L165/63.
[38] [2013] OJ L165/1.
[39] Recital 3 to the Mediation Dir.
[40] Recital 6 to the Mediation Dir.
[41] Woolf, above n 11.
[42] ibid, 104.
[43] Lord Justice Jackson, 'Foreword' in P Hurst, *Civil Costs* 5th edn (London, Sweet & Maxwell, 2013) vi.
[44] Recital 5 to the ADR Dir.

to provide an effective path for consumers who need remedies in cross-border cases is echoed in the ODR Regulation which intends to provide a cost-effective dispute resolution mechanism for consumers in disputes arising out of 'cross-border online transactions.'[45] The ADR Directive and the ODR Regulation apply to both cross-border and domestic disputes between consumers and traders, in order to provide a level playing field within the internal market.

Given the very few actions initiated by consumers (or on behalf of consumers) in England and Wales,[46] there are some specific issues to be addressed in such cases. It is well established that '[i]nformation and decision deficits as well as rational ignorance can affect consumers as regards the choice and conduct of dispute resolution.'[47] In his analysis of the EU legislative developments in the area of consumer redress, Cortés[48] restates the assumption that 'ODR is generally the best (and frequently, the only) option for increasing individual consumer redress'.[49] But could ADR/ODR on its own be an effective solution? One could be sceptical because, if the EU civil justice system is not effectively dealing with this type of cases, then traders might offer a significantly discounted compensation in cross-border cases. A consumer, faced with no other viable alternative to the trader's proposed discounted compensation, would have to accept the settlement offer. The point was captured by an interview respondent, a judge from England and Wales, who made the following observation:

> Broadly speaking I would say [ADR] probably does help [consumers] in terms of making it cheaper to get to a result. On the other hand, there may be an absence of knowledge on their part regarding how strong their claims might be. And therefore it can create opportunities for a defendant with a weak case to buy off the claims more cheaply than ought to be the result.[50]

Nonetheless, the EUPILLAR project suggests that lower litigation costs could incentivise consumers to bring cross-border claims.[51] In this context, the consumers could benefit from the rules protecting the weaker parties in cross-border civil and commercial cases—Section 4 of the Brussels I (Recast) Regulation and Article 6 of the Rome I Regulation. The European Small Claims Procedure may also have a role to play in cases where the value of the claim is less than EUR 2000.[52] But, ADR/ODR for consumers could be effectively incentivised only after the consumer litigation costs and funding issues are thoroughly addressed in the various Member States.[53] Admittedly, however, it is too early to analyse and assess the effects of the ADR Directive and the ODR Regulation: the former had to be implemented by the Member States by 9 July 2015, while the latter applies from 9 January 2016.

---

[45] Recital 8 to the ODR Reg.

[46] See chs 5 and 32.

[47] F Steffek et al, 'Guide for Regulating Dispute Resolution (GRDR): Principles and Comments' in Steffek and Unberath (eds), above n 33, 73, 117.

[48] P Cortés, 'A New Regulatory Framework for Extra-judicial Consumer redress: Where we are and How to Move Forward' (2015) 35(1) *Legal Studies* 114, 115.

[49] ibid 115.

[50] EUPILLAR—England and Wales—Interview Transcript No 4.

[51] See chs 9, 11 and 35.

[52] Reg (EC) No 861/2007 of 11 July 2007 establishing a European Small Claims Procedure [2007] OJ L199/1.

[53] XE Kramer and EA Ontanu, *The Dutch Perspective on Cross-Border Small Claims Litigation: Guarded Optimism and Pragmatism. A Normative and Empirical Approach* https://papers.ssrn.com/sol3/papers.cfm?abstract_id=2257729.

The time has come to analyse the application of the Mediation Directive.[54] Two years after publishing an extended study on the implementation of Directive 2008/52 on certain aspects of mediation in civil and commercial matters,[55] the European Commission has recently issued a report on the application of this important instrument in the Member States ('the 2016 Report').[56] The Study shows that, from the point of view of transposition, the legal systems of the Member States comply with the Directive, with a few minor remarks.

As far as the quality of implementation is concerned, however, the 2014 Study considered (a) relevance, consistency and complementarity; (b) effectiveness; (c) efficiency, in terms of (i) costs and financial aspects of mediation; (ii) information about mediation; (iii) the quality of mediation and training of mediators; and (iv) utility.[57] Although the Commission report suggests that there is a lack of comprehensive and reliable data, it concludes that the Mediation 'Directive has provided EU added value by raising awareness amongst national legislators on the advantages of mediation, introducing mediation systems or triggering the extension of existing mediation systems ...'[58] The Report further underlines that the Directive has had a significant impact on the Member States' legal systems. That said, the Commission goes on to identify the main factors which could impair the effectiveness of ADR:

> [T]he lack of a mediation 'culture' in Member States, insufficient knowledge of how to deal with cross-border cases, the low level of awareness of mediation and the functioning of the quality control mechanisms for mediators. A number of respondents in the public consultation argued that mediation was not yet sufficiently known and that a 'cultural change' is still necessary to ensure that citizens trust mediation. They also stressed that judges and courts remain reluctant to refer parties to mediation.[59]

Therefore, different problems may need to be addressed in the diverse EU. In some jurisdictions, judges would regularly suggest to the parties to attempt mediation and temporarily stay the proceedings for that purpose.[60] In Croatia, however, the parties prefer judge-mediators to other mediators since the court-assisted mediation is free of charge, while other entities providing mediation request payment for their services.[61] The Austrian report highlights another problem concerning the quality of mediation services which may involve not particularly sophisticated mediators, if mediators' fees are not attractive enough.[62] This appears to be an issue in Austria despite the fact that the mediators are recorded in special lists administered by the Government.[63]

---

[54] See Art 11 of the Mediation Dir.

[55] European Commission—DG Justice, *Study for an evaluation and implementation of Directive 2008/52/EC—the 'Mediation Directive'* (Final Report, October 2013) www.observatoiredesmediations.org/Asset/Source/refBibliography_ID-37_No-01.pdf. This study was updated in 2016 (https://e-justice.europa.eu/content_cross-border_family_mediation-372-en.do.

[56] The Report of the European Commission on the application of Dir 2008/52/EC of the European Parliament and of the Council on certain aspects of mediation in civil and commercial matters, COM(2016) 542 of 26 August 2016.

[57] European Commission, above n 55 at 11–13.

[58] ibid 11.

[59] ibid 4.

[60] See ch 13.

[61] ibid. In Austria (ch 11), recourse to ADR may be subsidised by the State.

[62] Austria (ch 11), where the report underlines that often parties with a migration background with no or low income and with poor knowledge of German might not receive the service they may expect.

[63] Ch 11.

Although the 2016 Report demonstrates that mediation can play an important role in commercial law disputes as well as in family law disputes,[64] it fails to consider the impact which the EU PIL framework may have on the effectiveness of mediation in cross-border cases. The authors aim to examine how the effectiveness of the EU PIL framework affects ADR/settlements which may impact the parties' effective access to remedies in cross-border cases. The issues are important because the EUPILLAR national reports indicate that, in some EU Member States, mediation is perceived as an appropriate pathway[65] to remedies in cross-border cases. This is very much so in consumer cases due to lack of proportionality between litigation costs and the claims' amounts.[66] In the context of consumer disputes, certain Member States have supported mediation in the banking and financial sector,[67] but the results appear to be somewhat diversified. With this in mind, it is important to note that the data from England and Wales indicates that court proceedings may provide a fairer environment which allows consumers to obtain effective remedies, with one interviewee submitting that:

> [ADR] could be a better solution [for consumers], but again, it's equality of arms; if you are a consumer turning up to a mediation to take on an EU giant, then you're going to feel rather intimidated, and … it will probably be better through a court, where you could hide behind court proceedings.[68]

Another issue might be that the defendant may not necessarily agree to participate in ADR. For example, it has been reported that, in a recent collective redress action against Master-Card brought on behalf of all consumers in the UK, the defendant was invited 'to consider resolving this—out of court—through ADR but it has not responded to that offer.'[69] This might suggest that the effectiveness of any ADR mechanism would be dependent on the effectiveness of the judicial system in a particular country.

Before evaluating the impact of the EU PIL framework on ADR/settlements negotiations, it is necessary to define what the relationship is between litigation and ADR in such cases.

III. The Relationship Between Litigation and ADR in Cross-border Cases

The PIL literature[70] has evaluated the EU PIL rules without properly considering the relationship between cross-border litigation and ADR/settlements. As a result, the way in which cross-border litigation proceedings—based on the EU PIL framework—impact

---

[64] COM(2016) 542, p 4.

[65] Andrews, *The Three Paths of Justice*, above n 28.

[66] Ch 9.

[67] See eg ch 25, but see ch 9—Spain (where, however, the number of settlements in this area is apparently low).

[68] EUPILLAR—England and Wales—Interview Transcripts No 12.

[69] Quinn Emmanuel—Firm News, 'MasterCard Facing Claim of up to £14 Billion Damages from UK Consumers in Landmark Collective Action' www.quinnemanuel.com/the-firm/news-events/firm-news-mastercard-facing-claim-of-up-to-14-billion-damages-from-uk-consumers-in-landmark-collective-action/.

[70] See the recent books published by the OUP Series of Private International Law.

on out-of-court dispute resolution, promoting and shaping the ADR negotiations and settlements dynamics has not been addressed. In domestic cases, there is a view that

> the current justification for mediation in civil cases derives primarily from the deficiencies of litigation, and *if it is* succeeding it does so within the context of an expensive and stressful litigation system. Without the pressure of mounting legal costs the stimulus for compromise may be lacking. The parties' 'interests today' largely comprise the interest in avoiding further litigation.[71]

This poses the question how the effectiveness (or ineffectiveness) of the EU PIL regime and the institutional architecture impacts on ADR/settlements in cross-border disputes.

Similarly, the growing number of comparative research studies concerning ADR[72] do not consider how the ADR/settlement negotiations relate to the EU PIL framework. It is well established that '[a] negotiating process of some kind may take place at many stages as a dispute is settled'.[73] If the negotiations run in parallel to the litigation proceedings, then the effectiveness of EU PIL may not only shape the litigants' tactics at different phases of cross-border disputes, but it would also directly impact on any out-of-court negotiations which would affect the outcome of the ADR proceedings in cross-border cases. In the US context, Menkel-Meadow has submitted that:

> The field of ADR (originally known as 'alternative' dispute resolution in the United States) has more recently been called 'appropriate' dispute resolution, or just dispute resolution. ... the field has become quite institutionalized and renamed 'appropriate' dispute resolution to connote the importance of the availability of a variety of processes for 'resolution' of legal, and more broadly, social, political, and interpersonal disputes and conflicts.[74]

Is the picture the same in the EU? Is ADR being considered in the high value cross-border disputes across the EU? Is ADR being considered in consumers' disputes? Whilst—in domestic cases—'the link between procedure and outcome is crucial',[75] there is a strong case that the effectiveness of the EU PIL framework will affect both parties' entitlement to remedy (ie rules about applicable law) the parties' access to remedies (rules about jurisdiction).[76] The EU PIL framework does shape the EU legal landscape in cross-border cases which may have an impact on the effectiveness of the litigation and any remedies ultimately awarded in ADR proceedings. The role of PIL will be significant in this context because the litigation is an important pathway[77] (if not the main pathway) to remedies in disputes with an international element. Therefore, the questions concerning the relationship between the cross-border litigation and ADR needs to be considered when assessing the effectiveness of the EU PIL regime.

The indicative list of interview questions, which were discussed with legal practitioners and judges, included questions concerning all types of ADR (including arbitration). The qualitative interviews, however, were conducted only in Belgium, England and Wales, Germany, Italy, Poland, Scotland and Spain. Although the outcome appears to be only

---

[71] Genn, above n 3, 184–85—the emphasis is in the original.
[72] eg Filler, above n 18; Steffek and Unberath (eds), above n 33; KJ Hopt and F Steffek (eds) *Mediation and Regulation in Comparative Perspective* (Oxford, Oxford University Press, 2013); Esplugues, above n 16.
[73] Blake, Browne and Sime, above n 20 at 139.
[74] Menkel-Meadow, above n 34, 597.
[75] Genn, above n 3, 179.
[76] Ch 32.
[77] Andrews, *The Three Paths of Justice*, above n 28.

partially reflecting what it is going on across the EU, the qualitative data was further complemented by national reports from nearly all the Member States. The following observations can be made. Mediation in civil and commercial matters is not a popular choice in some Member States,[78] but it is considered a useful tool in others,[79] particularly in cross-border cases.[80] It is worth noting the increasingly important role of settlements in the cross-border civil and commercial disputes in some of the leading EU jurisdictions such as England, Germany and the Netherlands.

The relationship between ADR and litigation in cross-border cases is nicely reflected in the international law firms' dispute resolution strategies. In particular, the qualitative interview data from England and Wales indicates that litigators 'use ADR on nearly all ... cases as part of the process, not as an alternative to court proceedings or arbitration, but as part of it at the appropriate juncture—... mediation or another form of ADR'[81] will be considered. In other words, the cross-border litigation and ADR are forming part of the cross-border adjudication services which are intended to provide remedies for private parties in cross-border cases. The point was reiterated by another interview respondent who noted:

> [L]itigation is just another weapon [to ...] use as a negotiating tactic. Very seldom do they use it for the purpose of going to trial. So it is always for a commercial purpose. ... A tactical device to enhance their negotiating strategy at the end.[82]

In the light of a high rate of settlements in cross-border cases in England and Wales, settlements are clearly an integral part of the cross-border litigation process. The fact that ADR and litigation are both part of the cross-border adjudication services which a particular judicial system offers, is also reflected in another phenomenon—the increasing 'privatisation'[83] of the civil justice system. A specific feature of the EU judicial system is that it consists of a number of national legal systems which are all 'providers of dispute adjudication services'.[84] The EU Member States will be providing both cross-border litigation services and ADR services as part of their cross-border dispute resolution amenities. This means that in the light of the current EU PIL regime and the relevant institutional architecture, the parties' access to remedies would depend on the talent of the lawyers (who may be very creative in exploiting the weaknesses of the current PIL) as well as on the experience of the judges and efficiency of the local courts in a particular jurisdiction.[85]

---

[78] Chs 6, 18, 22, 29 and 30. See I Verougstraete, 'Regulation of Dispute Resolution in Belgium: Workable Solutions?' in Steffek and Unberath (eds), above n 33, 318.

[79] Chs 7, 8, 11, 25 and 30. According to the Dutch report (ch 25), around 50 per cent of commercial disputes are settled after the start of the proceedings in first instance. See also PG Mayr and K Nemeth, 'Regulation of Dispute Resolution in Austria: A Traditional Litigation Culture Slowly Embraces ADR' in Steffek and Unberath (eds), above n 33, 223; B Hess and N Pelzer, 'Regulation of Dispute Resolution in Germany: Cautious Steps Towards the Construction of an ADR System' in Steffek and Unberath (eds), above n 33, 696; G De Paolo and AE Oleson, 'Regulation of Dispute Resolution in Italy: The Bumps in the Road to Successful ADR' in Steffek and Unberath (eds), above n 33, 797; M Pel, 'Regulation of Dispute Resolution in the Netherlands: Does Regulation Support or Hinder the Use of ADR?' in Steffek and Unberath (eds), above n 33, 973.

[80] Ch 25. According to the Austrian report (ch 11), cross-border mediation cases are increasing.

[81] EUPILLAR—England and Wales—Interview Transcript No 3.

[82] EUPILLAR—England and Wales—Interview Transcript No 7.

[83] See R Kulms, 'Privatising Civil Justice and the Day in Court' in Hopt and Steffek (eds), above n 72, 205. Genn, *36th F A Mann Lecture*, above n 29.

[84] Kulms, ibid, 205.

[85] Ch 35.

The qualitative interview data suggests that ADR is now part of the cross-border litigation (rather than an alternative to it). On this basis, it is reasonable to suggest that arbitration is still the main alternative to traditional court proceedings. This is clearly noted in several national reports.[86] Reasons to choose arbitration in cross-border disputes may be summarised as follows: an arbitrator may be from a country other than that where the parties to the disputes are domiciled; the proceedings can be conducted in English; arbitrators are specialised adjudicators; the admissible forms of evidence are wider than under domestic procedural law; and that the enforcement of arbitral awards is swifter and more comprehensively available globally than the enforcement of foreign judgments. The data from England and Wales indicates that the last factor is particularly important, if the other party is based outside of the EU[87] which clearly shows how the relevant framework (or the lack of one) could affect the way the parties would draft their contracts. Confidentiality is also mentioned as a major advantage for parties who wish to arbitrate.

That said, arbitration is often very expensive and not necessarily quicker than litigation. The high costs of arbitration might make it a less desirable mechanism with regard to some types of cross-border disputes. This was clearly noted by one interviewee from England and Wales who submitted:

> You can, of course, have an arbitration clause. In my experience that in itself has some significant costs attached to it. And you don't want to tie yourself down to arbitrating every single dispute no matter … what the value is …; because that actually … can mean that one party behaves unfairly; but they know that because it's a series of very small claims that actually you never arbitrate because of the disproportionate costs of going to arbitration.[88]

Therefore, various factors may impact the parties' decisions whether to litigate or arbitrate their cross-border dispute. Although this echoes the fact that arbitration may well be the main alternative to litigation, choosing to arbitrate (rather than litigate) does not necessarily mean that any other forms of ADR are excluded. Indeed, one respondent from England and Wales clearly submitted:

> [T]here is generally a recognition that arbitration does not mean the end of negotiations. It's simply a separate track. And negotiations settle most arbitrations; very few of them actually end up getting to contested hearings. But most claimants and respondents that I work for are legally advised at an early stage in disputes. They will have tried various forms of ADR and other negotiations. Those will have been unsuccessful. The parties will enter into arbitrations; will battle the arbitration some way down the line—perhaps, as far as experts' reports or some other stage. And, at that point, will generally settle.[89]

This means that ADR is now an integral part of the dispute resolution process in civil and commercial disputes with an international element. In other words, ADR is not really regarded by litigators as an alternative to litigation (and/or arbitration), but increasingly litigation and ADR are both seen as a part of the same pathway which intends to provide parties with access to remedies in cross-border cases. In view of this, it is important to consider the following questions. How are the expectations of the parties about the outcome

---

[86] Chs 6 and 30.
[87] EUPILLAR—England and Wales—Interview Transcripts No 3 and 17.
[88] EUPILLAR—England and Wales—Interview Transcript No 15.
[89] EUPILLAR—England and Wales—Interview Transcript No 17.

of a cross-border dispute affected by litigants' strategies under the EU PIL framework? How does this impact on parties' decisions whether to continue with the process of litigation or settle out-of-court?

IV. Assessing the Effect of the EU PIL Framework on ADR and Settlements

The EUPILLAR research findings strongly indicate that the EU PIL framework affects the parties' strategies in disputes with an international element, shaping the pattern of cross-border litigation. On the one hand, there is a case that, if the EU PIL framework is functioning effectively, then this will be factored into the settlement negotiations. A good example is the effective EU policy ensuring the free circulation of the EU Member States courts' judgments across the EU. Since the EU PIL framework is generally functioning well in this context, there would hardly be any problems with regard to settlements. The enforcement of court settlements is strengthened by Brussels Ia and the Maintenance Regulation.[90] Although recording a court settlement accordingly will be important in this context,[91] the qualitative interview data suggests that enforcement is rarely an issue under Brussels I, with one interview respondent noting that:

> [Enforcement of foreign judicial decisions in England] has become even more straightforward. … It is just basically an administrative thing. You would also be surprised how seldom you need to go to actual enforcement in practice. Those needs are quite low, at least in commercial cases. Because what generally happens in litigation: 97 or 98% of the cases get settled; the 3 or 4% that go to trial by the time you go on there and you have got a judgment, enforcement is not always a massive problem. … Sometimes you have got a recalcitrant defendant who won't pay and then you have got to enforce but it is really the minority of cases.[92]

On the other hand, if there are some aspects of the EU PIL framework which are not functioning effectively, then their ineffectiveness may be exploited by one of the parties in order to gain a negotiating advantage or adversely affect the other party's expectations about the outcome of litigation. This is likely to affect the amount at which the parties agree to settle. Therefore, the analysis of the relationship between the EU PIL framework and ADR/settlements is important because our research findings concerning the way EU PIL is functioning in a variety of EU Member States indicate that there may be various problems for parties to disputes with an international element in the different EU Member States.

The relationship between litigation and settlements/ADR in cross-border civil and commercial cases under the EU PIL framework may be less than effective in some EU Member States,[93] where the real issue appears to be insufficient experience of judges and litigators to deal with cross-border cases. Badly devised litigation tactics may mean that proceedings could be initiated in the wrong court which means that several months and/or years could

---

[90] See Art 59 of Brussels Ia and Article 48 of the Maintenance Reg. See also: CPR 74.11.
[91] Blake, Browne and Sime, above n 20 at 245–51.
[92] EUPILLAR—England and Wales—Interview Transcript No 7.
[93] See chs 12 and 32.

be lost which might impact on the claimant's expectation about the outcome. For example, in Bulgaria, there were a number of cross-border non-contractual disputes[94] in which the Bulgarian court was not competent under Brussels I because the defendants (or the first defendant on one occasion when the case was remitted to the lower instance court)[95] were not locally domiciled and the harmful event occurred abroad.[96] This indicates that the claimants were poorly advised in bringing their claims in Bulgaria. In such circumstances, even if the injured parties had a very strong claim (or even a relatively strong one), the claimants' lack of awareness of the EU PIL rules meant that any settlement would be hard to achieve. More importantly, after such a jurisdictional battle had been lost, a claimant with a strong claim could be willing to accept a significantly discounted compensation (ie a defendant could buy off a claim more cheaply than he should have been able to).

In other cases, foreign laws could be ignored completely[97] or misapplied. As already noted elsewhere,[98] in *Sheraleen Boyd Munro v Ian Munro*,[99] English law would have to be applied to the merits of the dispute between the parties, irrespective of where they had litigated. However, in the course of the jurisdictional battle before the English courts, Mr Justice Bennett noted that 'the husband's attitude may be driven by tactical considerations, namely either to wear down the wife and/or in an expectation that a Spanish judge would award the wife significantly less financial provision than an English judge.'[100] This could mean that if the parties were to litigate in Spain the wife's expectations about the outcome could be adversely affected, making her willing to accept a discounted compensation irrespective of the fact that English law would still apply in Spain. Following this line of reasoning, one could argue that the experience of the judges in applying a foreign law would certainly have a bearing on settlements under the current EU PIL framework.

The relationship between the cross-border litigation arising under the EU PIL regime and the settlements/ADR may further be impacted by the various deficiencies in the way the national judicial systems are functioning in the EU Member States.[101] In cases where the parties have no choice-of-court agreement, the existence of a rigid court-first-seised rule means that some real problems for parties could be caused by the excessive delay of these Member States' courts to deal with a cross-border dispute.[102] The point was made by an interview respondent from England and Wales who shared the following experience with us:

> I have had a similar situation in Greece where, in fact, it was quite a valuable claim; but again the Greek lawyers charged an awful lot of money to go to repeated hearings; and there was never

---

[94] Ruling No. 495 of 2012 of the Supreme Court of Cassation, Civil Chamber, 1st panel on private civil case No 456/2012; Ruling No 886 of 9.11.2011 of the Supreme Court of Cassation, Commercial Chamber, 2nd panel, on private commercial case No 130/2011; Ruling No 39 of 24.01.2015 of Peshtera District Court on civil case No 750/2008 aff'd Ruling No 328/13.05.2015 of Pazardzhik Regional Court, Civil Chamber, 2nd panel on private civil case No 430/ 2015. All the Bulgarian cases were kindly identified for us by Anton Petrov and Teodora Tsenova. See more in ch 12 above.
[95] Case No 130/2011, ibid.
[96] See ch 12.
[97] See ch 32.
[98] See M Danov and P Beaumont, 'Measuring the Effectiveness of the EU Civil Justice Framework: Theoretical and Methodological Challenges' (2015/2016) 17 *Yearbook of Private International Law* 151, 158–59.
[99] *Sheraleen Boyd Munro v Ian Munro* [2007] EWHC 3315 (Fam).
[100] ibid [5–6].
[101] eg chs 8 and 18.
[102] Case C-116/02, *Erich Gasser v MISAT* [2003] ECR I-14693.

any clarity about exactly where in the process we were; and what was going to happen next. ... eventually that claim was dropped; even though it was quite a significant value.[103]

This example demonstrates that the inflexibility of the EU PIL instruments to allow for proceedings to be transferred to an effectively functioning and appropriate jurisdiction may be a real issue which may occasionally encourage abusive litigation tactics, impairing litigants' access to effective remedies through litigation and/or ADR in cross-border cases.

The relationship between the EU PIL regime, on the one hand, and settlements and ADR, on the other hand, may also be affected in the EU jurisdictions[104] where litigants' tactics may be devised to take advantage of the weaknesses of the EU PIL instruments. This could be an issue in dominant jurisdictions like England and Wales, where the courts are dealing with a significant number of cross-border disputes, allowing the legal practitioners to develop a highly advanced knowledge and understanding about the nuances of the EU PIL rules.[105] This puts them in a good position to exploit the ambiguities of the current EU legal landscape in relation to PIL,[106] which may well affect ADR/settlement negotiations.

The impact of the various litigation tactics, devised to unduly benefit from the ineffectiveness of the EU PIL framework, on settlements/ADR could be significant. The problems will be illustrated by looking at the way in which the current EU PIL framework impacts on the settlement dynamics in England and Wales where settlements/ADR have been actively promoted since Lord Woolf's reform was implemented. To this end, the psychology of settlement negotiations in cross-border cases needs to be outlined. We can helpfully rely on an empirical study on commercial mediation in Europe.[107] As part of this study, Filler inter alia aimed to assess the effectiveness of the mediation by engaging with the relevant empirical data, submitting:

> [O]ne of the British commercial mediators in an attempt to accurately describe the psychology of dynamics in mediation, would compare the rules of the game with the ones found in the TV game shows like 'Who wants to be a millionaire?' where the candidates can win a lot of money ... if they have the correct answers, however, they will lose everything if they give the wrong answers: Whereas at the outset of a dispute the chance of reaching an agreement based on consensus usually is far away which is why launching legal action seems to be the better option. However, the closer a possible outcome that meets one's expectations gets, the more it becomes a question of conscience whether you reject the chance. There is no difference in mediation processes, there is also a point when people at strife realize this is now the best they can get that is apt to satisfy their sense of honour and bring all the grief to an end.[108]

In domestic cases, it is well established that '[s]ettlement negotiations take place in a climate of uncertainty in which the balance of evidence is important, but so is the ability to wait for an outcome, to endure exhaustion, and to withstand costs pressures.'[109] As already noted,[110] the interplay between the cost-shifting rules, on the one hand, and the outcome

---

[103] EUPILLAR—England and Wales—Interview Transcript No 15.
[104] eg ch 5.
[105] See more in ch 5.
[106] See more in chs 32 and 35.
[107] Filler, above n 18.
[108] ibid 271–72.
[109] Genn, above n 3, 178.
[110] See chs 32 and 35 above.

of a cross-border dispute, on the other hand, may be even more complex if there is uncertainty about issues of jurisdiction and/or choice-of-law.[111] There is a strong case that the cross-border implications of a given dispute will increase the level of uncertainty, inflating the litigation costs. This would normally be so because, for example, parties' evidence may need to be collected in different jurisdictions. As one legal practitioner from England and Wales noted, '[i]t is more complicated to run cross-border cases just because your witnesses are all over the place and you sometimes spend a lot of time getting your facts together.'[112]

These difficulties explain why the EU legislator has set the objective for EU PIL to enhance the level of legal certainty and predictability about the outcome of cross-border disputes. Therefore, the question is: how does the EU PIL framework and its implementation affect out-of-court settlement negotiations? Some of our interview respondents do indicate that the EU PIL framework does not have a direct impact on such settlements.[113] But, if the EU PIL framework does not directly impact settlements could it impact them indirectly? An interview respondent from England and Wales canvassed the way in which ADR operates by submitting:

> [T]ypically in a mediation 30% of the time will be spent on the merits. And then the merits of the case are put to the side. So you can have the best legal arguments in the world but the other side will say 'Short of a trial you are not going to persuade me'. And most often people are very fixed to their belief about the merits. What gets them to settle is the psychology; an assessment of the risk factors and a dynamic that happens in a settlement negotiation. So you are generally under the umbrella or the shadow of the law, but the law is not really the thing that drives settlement. You can't say it is irrelevant, but what happens is what I was saying earlier. By the time settlement takes place, generally you have isolated all of the legal issues down to four/five issues in dispute. And you are fighting about those and you are not going to persuade each other about them. But everybody is worried that they might lose one or two of these. And that is when settlement takes place.[114]

There is a case that the EU PIL framework indirectly impacts ADR/settlements negotiations, which will be conducted in 'the shadow of the law'.[115] The academic literature[116] embraces the view that, in the course of out-of-court settlement, '[t]he psychological effects operate through the expectations of the players.'[117] Our argument is that, in cross-border cases, any legal uncertainty about issues of jurisdiction, applicable law and recognition and enforcement will directly impact upon parties' expectations about the outcome (ie their effective access to desired remedies in cross-border cases). A lower level of expectancy about the achievable remedies would directly affect the outcome of the ADR/settlements negotiations. Indeed, there is a strong case that the properly advised parties

---

[111] See HSE Graville, 'The Efficiency Implications of Cost Shifting Rules' (1993) 13 *International Review of Law and Economics* 3; CF Beckner III and A Katz, 'The Incentive Effects of Litigation Fee Shifting When Legal Standards Are Uncertain' (1995) *International Review of Law and Economics* 205.

[112] EUPILLAR—England and Wales—Interview Transcript No 7.

[113] eg EUPILLAR—England and Wales—Interview Transcripts No 7 and 12.

[114] EUPILLAR—England and Wales—Interview Transcript No 7.

[115] R Cooter and S Marks with RN Mnookin, 'Bargaining in the Shadow of the Law: A Testable Model of Strategic Behavior' (1982) 11(2) *Journal of Legal Studies* 225.

[116] ibid. See also R N Mnookin and L Kornhauser, 'Bargaining in the Shadow of the Law: The Case of Divorce' (1979) 88 *Yale Law Journal* 950.

[117] Cooter and Marks with Mnookin, above n 115, 246.

will factor everything in during the course of out-of-court settlements, with one interview respondent from England and Wales, making the following observation:

> [T]he clients we act for are very sophisticated organisations and every conceivable factor will be factored in. … there's a cost benefit analysis that is always done by the clients, it factors in merits. Included in merits would be all the legal issues, including arguments about jurisdiction, arguments about proper law, arguments about service, and arguments about enforcement. So all the legal issues, not only substantive issues, but procedural issues, are part of it, the length of time is a part of it, the legal cost is a part of it. The risk of having to bear the other side's costs are undoubtedly a part of it.[118]

A strategic party may increase the level of complexity by exploiting the ambiguity of the nuances of the current EU PIL rules,[119] in order to cause delay and inflate the costs significantly which may increase the pressure over the other party to settle. On the one hand, the high litigation costs in the light of a rule that 'the unsuccessful party will be ordered to pay the costs of the successful party'[120] may mean that a level of legal uncertainty concerning the applicable substantive law[121] in cross-border cases may raise the pressure on the defendants to settle or engage with ADR proceedings. This would be particularly so in cases where the defendant considers it important to minimise the litigation costs.

On the other hand, a level of legal uncertainty about the courts' competence to deal with the case may have a significant impact on the claimant's willingness to continue with litigation or engage in ADR proceedings.[122] In particular, a party's expectations about the outcome of the litigation may be deflated by litigants' strategies which are intended to raise the level of complexity by challenging the court's jurisdiction and/or by initiating parallel proceedings somewhere else, in order to make it less attractive for the other party to continue litigating.[123] This could put a strain on the claimant's financial resources and make settlements or the various ADR mechanisms attractive options, offering a quicker path to remedies. In other words, various delaying strategies devised under the current EU PIL framework may adversely affect parties' effective access to desired remedies in cross-border cases.[124]

Furthermore, in some complex cases, defendants may even go further raising issues about the applicable law, so that they can—by exploiting the level of uncertainty—make it increasingly difficult (and costly) for claimants to access any available remedies. One interview respondent from England and Wales submitted that:

> [Applicable law] is often an issue. It hasn't been resolved yet; but it is certainly something where defendants see it as an opportunity for making life difficult for the claimants; because they will have started their proceedings here, they will have an English law team and if they suddenly find they have got to apply German law to their claim; this will be a problem for them.[125]

---

[118] EUPILLAR—England and Wales—Interview Transcript No 18.
[119] See chs 32 and 35.
[120] See English Civil Procedure Rule ('CPR') 44.2(2). See also N Andrews, *Andrews on Civil Processes: Court Proceedings* Vol I (Mortsel, Intersentia, 2013) 526–29.
[121] See chs 32 and 35.
[122] See ch 32.
[123] See ch 5, highlighting the high number of jurisdictional challenges in England and Wales. See also ch 32.
[124] See ch 35.
[125] EUPILLAR—England and Wales—Interview Transcript No 11.

This will obviously depend on the type of dispute (and may not always be available as a strategy), but it simply shows that there may be a number of tactics which could be employed by one of the parties with a view to forcing the other to settle on terms which he otherwise would not. All this may be factored in the out-of-court settlement negotiations which would then impact the other party's decision to accept (or decline) a settlement offer. The point was nicely captured by one interview respondent from England and Wales who stated:

> [T]he psychology of dragging out a case and causing difficulties; you are not sure which step is going to cause the other side, the claimant, to lose interest. But the harder you make them work, and the longer you make them work, the more chance that they are going to lose belief in some way which will lead to a more conducive framework for settlement.[126]

Therefore, it could well be argued that the weaknesses of the EU PIL framework may be exploited by strategic litigants, affecting parties' access to remedies by means of ADR/settlements. If the EU PIL regime and the institutional framework are not adjusted to effectively deal with any abusive litigation strategies, then litigants' access to remedies may be impaired in any out-of-court settlements. This may fly in the face of the EU objective to promote the use of ADR as a means to resolve cross-border disputes. In other words, a case can be made that, in the absence of an effectively functioning EU civil justice system, the use of ADR mechanisms can lead to significantly discounted compensation in cross-border cases. That said, the qualitative interview data show that any settlement is by its nature a fair deal between the parties, with one interviewee noting that:

> By definition ADR, because it's a settlement agreement ultimately, and it's an agreement between the parties, gives the claimant usually, in most cases, less than the claimant wanted when it made its claim. Like any settlement you don't get 100% of what you want. It's likely that ADR will result in less than the full claim … I don't see the fact that ADR produces a result as anything more than a fair agreement between two parties who have come to a closure as agreeing something that suits.[127]

Nonetheless, the same respondent did agree with the proposition that a level of legal uncertainty in relation to PIL may mean that the national courts could take longer, even to establish jurisdiction. This would most probably be factored in any form of out-of-court dispute resolution. In other words, if the EU civil justice system is not functioning effectively—taking a significant amount of time to even establish jurisdiction, then the discount in the out-of-court settlements could be significant. Therefore, there is a strong case that the EU PIL framework and the relevant institutional framework would be a major influence on ADR in cross-border cases. In particular, any ambiguity in the EU PIL rules could be exploited by strategic litigants to cause further delay and raise the level of legal uncertainty. This will directly impact the parties' expectations about the outcome of their dispute with an international element. The change in the parties' expectations will have a bearing on any form of out-of-court dispute resolution.

---

[126] EUPILLAR—England and Wales—Interview Transcript No 7.
[127] EUPILLAR—England and Wales—Interview Transcript No 18.

V. Conclusion

Litigation and ADR form part of the cross-border adjudication services provided by the different EU Member States in the market for cross-border litigation services. The relationship between the EU PIL regime and ADR may be shaped differently in the various EU jurisdictions, where litigants' tactics may be devised to take advantages of the weaknesses of the EU PIL instruments and/or deficiencies of the national judicial system. Given the fact that the current EU model of administration of justice in cross-border cases provides litigants with some choice as to where they initiate their claim, the relationship between litigation and ADR in cross-border cases may be another important factor in the forum selection process. The fact that the parties' access to effective remedies will depend on where the parties are suing may provide a better explanation (than Hartley's argument that the choice-of-law issues are less important) of 'why the parties will fight tooth and nail on jurisdictional issues'.[128]

Nonetheless, there is a good case that, even in dominant jurisdictions, ineffectiveness of EU PIL would affect the parties' access to remedies which may often depend on the talent of the lawyers who may be very creative in exploiting the weaknesses of the current PIL. Although the prevailing view is that the EU PIL framework would not directly impact out-of-court settlements, there is a strong case for an indirect impact. In particular, a level of legal uncertainty about PIL issues will deflate parties' expectations about the outcome which can affect their willingness to accept (or decline) settlement offers in cross-border cases.

Therefore, an EU civil justice system, which is less than effective in providing remedies for private parties in cross-border civil and commercial law cases,[129] reduces the effectiveness of ADR in cross-border cases. An EU reform improving the effectiveness of the EU PIL framework would facilitate the parties' effective access to remedies through out-of-court dispute resolution mechanisms.

[128] TC Hartley, *International Commercial Litigation* 2nd edn (Cambridge, Cambridge University Press, 2015) 5–6.
[129] See ch 35.

Part IV

Litigating Cross-border Family Law Disputes—A Europe of Law and Justice

41

Court of Justice of the European Union's Case Law on Family Law Matters Under Brussels IIa and Maintenance

PAUL BEAUMONT AND KATARINA TRIMMINGS

I. Introduction

This chapter examines to what extent the Court of Justice of the European Union (CJEU) deals appropriately with harmonised private international law (PIL) rules provided for in the Brussels IIa and Maintenance Regulations. The chapter is based on data gathered from the preliminary rulings on these two Regulations decided by the CJEU between March 2002 and December 2015. The data on case law derives from 24 cases in total (22 cases concerning Brussels IIa and two cases concerning Maintenance).[1]

The purpose of the analysis is to determine whether the CJEU has faithfully interpreted the Regulations in line with the EU legislature's intentions. In doing so a number of factors will be considered where relevant: the help given to the Court by the Advocate General (AG) in that case; consistency of the decision with the underlying international conventions and their explanatory reports; consistency with other EU legislation; using party autonomy to facilitate the integration with other EU legislation where possible; the interrelationship with the EU's Charter of Fundamental Rights; and the use of other international instruments. In some cases consideration will be given to how the case referred to the CJEU was handled after its ruling. Where appropriate consideration will be given to how the Commission has reacted to a decision of the CJEU in its Proposal for the Recast of Brussels IIa.

II. Brussels IIa Regulation

The dataset includes 22 CJEU cases concerning the Brussels IIa Regulation, all of which will be analysed in this section.

---

[1] All cases are available in the EUPILLAR Database at https://w3.abdn.ac.uk/clsm/eupillar/?_ga=1.57393827.8 60536064.1207048627#/home.

A. Scope and Definitions (Articles 1 and 2)

i. Scope (Article 1)

The case of C^2 was referred to the CJEU in the context of an appeal brought by Ms C, the mother of the children A and B, against the decision of the Administrative Court of Oulu (Finland) confirming the decision of the Finnish police ordering the handing over of her children to the Swedish authorities. The main question was whether a public law decision related to child welfare, such as taking children into care and placing them with a foster family, fell within the definition of 'civil matters' in Brussels IIa. The CJEU held that the Regulation applied to the enforcement of a decision ordering a child to be taken into care and placed in a foster family. Such a decision, although adopted in the context of public law rules relating to child protection, is covered by the term 'civil matters' in the Regulation. Although taking a child into care does not feature expressly amongst the matters listed as relating to parental responsibility, it is clear from Recital 5 that the Regulation covers all decisions on parental responsibility, including measures for the protection of the child. 'Civil matters' as used in the Regulation is an autonomous concept which must be interpreted purposively in accordance with the objectives of the Regulation. Consequently, the term 'civil matters' must be interpreted as covering measures that are classified as public law by the legal system of a particular Member State. Otherwise, the purpose of mutual recognition and enforcement of decisions in matters of parental responsibility would be compromised. The national court also asked whether the Regulation was to be interpreted as applying *ratione temporis* in a case such as that in the main proceedings. The CJEU held that by Articles 64(1) and 72, the Regulation applied only to legal proceedings instituted after 1 March 2005. However, Article 64(2) provides for the recognition and enforcement of judgments given after 1 March 2005 in proceedings instituted before that date but after the entry into force of the original Brussels II Regulation,[3] if jurisdiction was founded on rules which accorded with those contained in Chapter II of the Brussels IIa Regulation or in the Brussels II Regulation or in a convention concluded between the two Member States concerned if that convention was in force when the proceedings were instituted. In this case, the decision the enforcement of which was at issue was given on 3 March 2005, ie after the date on which the Brussels IIa Regulation came into force. The proceedings in Sweden were initiated in autumn 2004, ie before Brussels IIa applied but after the entry into force of Brussels II (1 March 2001). Finally, the jurisdiction of the Swedish courts was exercised on the basis of national law (ie residence of the children in Sweden when care proceedings were initiated) and these jurisdictional rules accorded with those provided for by the Brussels IIa Regulation. Consequently, all three conditions contained in Article 64(2) were fulfilled. The Court therefore held that, subject to factual assessment (which is a matter for the national court alone), the Regulation was to be interpreted as applying *ratione temporis* in this case. This is an important decision as it determines that the Brussels IIa Regulation applies in cases where children subject to care orders are moved from one Member State

---

[2] Case C-435/06 *C* [2007] ECR I-10141 (Grand Chamber).
[3] Council Reg (EC) 1347/2000 of 29 May 2000 on jurisdiction and the recognition and enforcement of judgments in matrimonial matters and in matters of parental responsibility for children of both spouses [2003] OJ L160/19.

to another. Hence, in respect of matters related to parental responsibility, the Regulation is not restricted to private law proceedings but covers also public law decisions relating to child protection. The extensive scope of the Regulation in this regard is consistent with its 'parent' in relation to parental responsibility issues, the Hague Convention of 19 October 1996 on Jurisdiction, Applicable Law, Recognition, Enforcement and Co-operation in Respect of Parental Responsibility and Measures for the Protection of Children (the 1996 Hague Child Protection Convention or the 1996 Hague Convention).[4]

The case of *A*[5] was referred to the CJEU in the course of an appeal brought by Ms A, the mother of children C, D and E, against the decision of the Administrative Court, Kuopio (Finland) confirming the decision by which the Basic Welfare Committee took the children urgently into care and placed them in a childcare unit. The CJEU interpreted several provisions of Brussels IIa in this case. As regards Article 1, the CJEU held, confirming its judgment in Case C-435/06 *C*, that an order that a child be immediately taken into care and placed outside his original home, which was adopted in the context of public law rules relating to child protection, was covered by the term 'civil matters' in Article 1(1) of Brussels IIa.

Health Service Executive v SC and AC[6] was referred to the CJEU in proceedings between the Health Service Executive (the HSE) and a child and her mother, concerning the placement of that child in a secure care institution situated in England. The CJEU interpreted several provisions of Brussels IIa in this case. As regards Article 1, the CJEU was asked whether a judgment of a court of a Member State which orders the placement of a child in a secure institution providing therapeutic and educational care situated in another Member State and which entails that, for her own protection, the child is deprived of her liberty for a specified period, is within the material scope of Brussels IIa. The CJEU held that 'placement in institutional care' (Article 1(2)(d)) had to be interpreted as covering placement in a secure care institution. Consequently, the judgment was within the material scope of the Regulation. Otherwise, vulnerable children would not be able to benefit from the Regulation which would be contrary to its purpose of ensuring equality for all children (Recital 5). The CJEU noted that only 'measures taken as a result of criminal offences committed by children' (Article 1(3)(d)) were expressly excluded from the scope of the Regulation and this did not apply as the detention of the child was not for committing a criminal offence.

Marie Matoušková[7] concerned a request for a preliminary ruling from the Czech Supreme Court in proceedings brought by Ms Matoušková in her capacity as court commissioner, in order to determine jurisdiction to approve the agreement on the sharing-out of the estate concluded by the guardian ad litem on behalf of minor children. The referring court asked the CJEU whether, if an agreement on the sharing-out of an estate concluded on behalf of a minor by his or her guardian ad litem required the approval of a court in order to be valid,

---

[4] See Opinion of Advocate General Kokott, paras 48–49. Hague Child Protection Convention (1996) Art 3. See, generally, N Lowe and M Nicholls, *The 1996 Hague Convention on the Protection of Children* (Bristol, Jordan Publishing, 2012); P McEleavy, 'The 1996 Hague Convention and the European Union: Connection and Disconnection' in Permanent Bureau of the Hague Conference (ed), *A Commitment to Private International Law: Essays in Honour of Hans van Loon* (Mortsel, Intersentia, 2013); and M Gration, I Curry-Sumner, D Williams QC, H Setright QC and M Wright, *International Issues in Family Law: The 1996 Hague Convention on the Protection of Children and Brussels IIa* (Bristol, Jordan Publishing, 2015).

[5] Case C-523/07 *A* [2009] ECR I-02805 (Third Chamber). See also n 20 and 51 below.

[6] Case C-92/12 PPU *Health Service Executive v SC and AC* EU:C:2012:255 (Second Chamber).

[7] Case C-404/14 *Marie Matoušková* EU:C:2015:653 (Third Chamber).

that decision on the part of the court was a measure within the meaning of Article 1(1)(b) or a measure within the meaning of Article 1(3)(f) of Brussels IIa. The Third Chamber agreed with AG Kokott's observation,[8] that legal capacity and the associated representation issues must be assessed in accordance with their own criteria and are not to be regarded as preliminary issues dependent on the legal acts in question. The appointment of a guardian for the minor children and the review of the exercise of her activity are so closely connected that it would not be appropriate to apply different jurisdictional rules, which would vary according to the subject matter of the relevant legal act. Therefore, the fact that the approval at issue in the main proceedings has been requested in succession proceedings cannot be regarded as decisive as to whether that measure should be classified as falling within the law of succession. The need to obtain approval from the court dealing with guardianship matters is a direct consequence of the status and capacity of the minor children and constitutes a protective measure for the child relating to the administration, conservation or disposal of the child's property in the exercise of parental responsibility within the meaning of Article 1(1)(b) and 2(e) of Brussels IIa. Such an interpretation is supported by the Lagarde Report on the 1996 Hague Child Protection Convention,[9] the scope of which corresponds with regard to parental responsibility to that of Brussels IIa. While explaining that successions must, in principle, be excluded from that Convention, the Report states that if the legislation governing the rights to succession provides for the intervention of the legal representative of the child heir, that representative must be designated in accordance with the rules of the Convention, since such a situation falls within the area of parental responsibility. That interpretation is also confirmed by the EU Succession Regulation,[10] not applicable *ratione temporis* in the case in the main proceedings, which, in accordance with Recital 9 thereto, was adopted in order to cover all civil law aspects of succession to the estates of a deceased person. Article 1(2)(b) thereof excludes from its scope the legal capacity of natural persons. That Regulation governs only the aspects relating specifically to the capacity to inherit, under Article 23(2)(c) thereof, and the capacity of the person making the disposition of property upon death to make such a disposition in accordance with Article 26(1)(a) thereof. The CJEU ruled that the Regulation had to

> be interpreted as meaning that the approval of an agreement for the sharing-out of an estate concluded by a guardian *ad litem* on behalf of minor children constitutes a measure relating to the exercise of parental responsibility, within the meaning of Article 1(1)(b) of that regulation and thus falls within the scope of the latter, and not a measure relating to succession, within the meaning of Article 1(3)(f) thereof, excluded from the scope thereof.

It is encouraging to see the CJEU acknowledging that in some respects, including scope, Brussels IIa follows the 1996 Hague Child Protection Convention, and expressly referring to the Explanatory Report on that Convention for guidance following the excellent advice of AG Kokott.[11]

---

[8] Opinion of Advocate General Kokott EU:C:2015:428, para 41.

[9] P Lagarde, 'Explanatory Report on the 1996 Hague Child Protection Convention' (1996), available at https://assets.hcch.net/upload/expl34.pdf.

[10] Reg No 650/2012 of 4 July 2012 on jurisdiction, applicable law, recognition and enforcement of decisions and acceptance and enforcement of authentic instruments in matters of succession and on the creation of a European Certificate of Succession, [2012] OJ L201/107.

[11] See Opinion of Advocate General Kokott EU:C:2015:428, paras 46–49.

The CJEU also gave good unsolicited advice on the possible relevance of Article 12(3) of Brussels IIa. The Third Chamber, without any advice from the AG on this point, went beyond the question referred by the Czech Supreme Court to give some practical advice on the jurisdiction rules in Brussels IIa. According to Article 12(3) of Brussels IIa, the courts of a Member State have jurisdiction in relation to parental responsibility in proceedings where, first, the child has a substantial connection with that Member State, in particular by virtue of the fact that one of the holders of parental responsibility is habitually resident in that Member State or that the child is a national of that Member State, and, second, the jurisdiction of the courts has been accepted expressly or otherwise in an unequivocal manner by all the parties to the proceedings at the time the court is seised and is in the best interests of the child. In this case Article 12(3) is capable of founding the jurisdiction of the court dealing with the matters relating to succession to approve the agreement on the sharing-out of the estate, even though that court is not the court of the child's habitual residence, as long as the abovementioned conditions are fulfilled. This encouragement of party autonomy permitted by Brussels IIa to make coherent jurisdiction between parental responsibility and succession is greatly to be welcomed.

Vasilka Ivanova Gogova v Ilia Dimitrov Iliev,[12] involving three Bulgarian nationals (father, mother and child) who all resided in Italy albeit that the mother and father lived apart, concerned the renewal of the child's passport. The CJEU was asked to interpret different provisions of Brussels IIa. As regards Article 1, the CJEU was asked whether an action in which one parent asks the court to remedy the lack of agreement of the other parent to their child travelling outside his Member State of residence and a passport being issued in the child's name was within the material scope of Brussels IIa. The CJEU noted that the concept of parental responsibility was given a broad definition in Article 2(7) of the Regulation— 'all rights and duties relating to the person or the property of a child which are given to a natural person by' law. The present action clearly fell within that definition. The CJEU said that the Regulation applies even to decisions which relate only to a 'particular aspect of parental responsibility' but does not apply to a decision on the award of a passport. This case was dealt with in five months by the CJEU because it was decided under the expedited procedure. This can be a suitable option for cases that are not so urgent as to require the PPU system which takes about eight to 12 weeks in the CJEU.

ii. Definitions (Article 2)

J McB v L E[13] was referred to the CJEU in appeal proceedings brought before the Irish Supreme Court by Mr McB, the father of three children, against the judgment of the Irish High Court, on the ground that the latter court had dismissed his application seeking a decision or determination declaring the removal of the children to the United Kingdom in July 2009 by Ms E, their mother, to be wrongful within the meaning of Article 2(11) of Brussels IIa and declaring that the father of the children had rights of custody on the date of that removal. The CJEU was asked to determine whether Brussels IIa, whether interpreted

---

[12] Case C-215/15 *Vasilka Ivanova Gogova v Ilia Dimitrov Iliev* EU:C:2015:710 (Fourth Chamber).
[13] Case C-400/10 PPU *J McB v L E* [2010] ECR I-08965 (Third Chamber).

pursuant to Article 7 of the Charter of Fundamental Rights of the European Union (the Charter) or otherwise,

> precludes a Member State from requiring by its law that the father of a child who is not married to the mother shall have obtained an order of a court of competent jurisdiction granting him custody in order to qualify as having 'custody rights' which render the removal of that child from its country of habitual residence wrongful for the purposes of Article 2(11) of that Regulation.[14]

The CJEU said that 'rights of custody' is an autonomous concept but that the identity of a person holding such rights (see Article 2(9) and (11)) is entirely dependent on the existence of rights of custody conferred by the relevant national law (ie the law of the Member State where the child was habitually resident immediately before the removal or retention). The father, however, submitted that such interpretation of the Regulation could violate his Article 7 of the Charter and Article 8 of the European Convention on Human Rights (ECHR) rights (ie right to respect for private and family life) or the rights of the child guaranteed by Article 24 of the Charter. He argued that for the purposes of Brussels IIa, 'rights of custody' should be interpreted as meaning that 'such rights are acquired by a natural father by operation of law in a situation where he and his children have a family life which is the same as that of a family based on marriage' (so called 'inchoate rights'). The CJEU held that the fact that, under Irish law, an unmarried father did not automatically acquire custody rights within the meaning of Article 2 of Brussels IIa, did not affect his right to private and family life, as long as he had the right to apply to the national court for an order awarding him custody rights. This interpretation applied also in cases where the father did not apply for custody rights prior to the removal of the child by the mother who, at the time of the removal, was the only custody rights holder, and was exercising her right to freedom of movement and her right to determine the child's place of residence. Hence, to accept the possibility that an unmarried father has rights of custody under Article 2(11) of Brussels IIa, although no such rights are conferred on him under national law, would be incompatible with the requirements of legal certainty and with the need to protect the rights of the mother. Accordingly, the Regulation must be interpreted as

> not precluding a Member State from providing by its law that the acquisition of rights of custody by a child's father, where he is not married to the child's mother, is dependent on the father's obtaining a judgment from a national court with jurisdiction awarding such rights to him, on the basis of which the removal of the child by its mother or the retention of that child may be considered wrongful, within the meaning of Article 2(11).

The CJEU, in *J McB v L E*, also took account of the rights of the child under Article 24 of the Charter and recognised that it is compatible with those rights for a State to decide that unmarried fathers must go to court in order to get parental responsibility in relation to their child. This was a wise decision by the CJEU on the interpretation of the Charter allowing States to protect children against automatic conferral of parental responsibility on an unmarried father who in an extreme case could be a rapist. It is however, very doubtful whether the Charter is at all relevant to the question of who is entitled to have custody rights because this is not a matter within the scope of EU law but is rather 'entirely' dependent on national law in the CJEU's own words.

---

[14] ibid, para 25.

B. Jurisdiction (Articles 3–20)

i. *Divorce, Legal Separation and Marriage Annulment (Articles 3–7)*

The CJEU has interpreted Article 3 of Brussels IIa in two cases.

Kerstin Sundelind Lopez v Miguel Enrique Lopez Lizazo[15] was referred to the CJEU in divorce proceedings brought by Mrs Sundelind Lopez against Mr Lopez Lizazo. The CJEU was asked where the respondent in a case concerning divorce is neither resident in a Member State nor a citizen of a Member State, whether the case may be heard by a court in a Member State which does not have jurisdiction under Article 3, even though a court in another Member State may have jurisdiction by application of one of the rules on jurisdiction set out in Article 3. The CJEU held that Article 6 did not prohibit a respondent who was neither habitually resident in nor a national of a Member State from being sued in a court of a Member State under national rules of jurisdiction in accordance with Article 7(1). This was, however, possible only where no court of a Member State had jurisdiction under Articles 3–5 of the Regulation. Consequently, it could not be said that Article 6 had laid down a general rule that in all cases involving a respondent not habitually resident in nor a national of a Member State, jurisdiction was to be based on domestic law—including cases where another Member State had jurisdiction under Article 3. To assume such a general rule would be tantamount to ignoring the clear wording of Articles 7(1) and 17, the application of which does not depend on the position of the respondent but exclusively on whether a court of a Member State has jurisdiction under Articles 3–5 of the Regulation. To sum up, Articles 6 and 7 of the Brussels IIa Regulation are to be interpreted as meaning that where, in divorce proceedings, a respondent is not habitually resident in a Member State and is not a national of a Member State, the courts of a Member State cannot base their jurisdiction to hear the petition on their national law, if the courts of another Member State have jurisdiction under Articles 3–5 of that Regulation. This decision helpfully clarifies the approach that should be taken by Member States' courts in proceedings involving respondents who are not habitually resident in or nationals of a Member State. In cases involving such respondents, national rules of jurisdiction can be relied on in accordance with Article 7 only where no court of a Member State has jurisdiction under Article 3. This was such a straightforward case that the Third Chamber was able to reach its decision without asking the Advocate General to give an Opinion.

Laszlo Hadadi (Hadady) v Csilla Marta Mesko, épouse Hadadi (Hadady)[16] was referred to the CJEU in proceedings between Mr Hadadi (Hadady) and Ms Mesko regarding the recognition by the French courts of a judgment of Pest Court (Hungary) granting their divorce. The CJEU was asked whether Article 3(1)(b) was to be interpreted as meaning that, in a situation where the spouses hold both the nationality of the State of the court seised and the nationality of another Member State, the nationality of the State of the court seised must prevail. It was also asked whether Article 3(1)(b) was to be interpreted as meaning that, in order to determine the court which has jurisdiction in respect of the divorce of persons having the same dual nationality, only the nationality of the Member State with which those

---

[15] Case C-68/07 *Kerstin Sundelind Lopez v Miguel Enrique Lopez Lizazo* [2007] ECR I-10403 (Third Chamber).

[16] Case C-168/08 *Laszlo Hadadi (Hadady) v Csilla Marta Mesko, épouse Hadadi (Hadady)* [2009] ECR I-6871 (Third Chamber).

persons have the closest links—the 'most effective' nationality—is to be taken into account, so that the courts of that State alone have jurisdiction on the basis of nationality, or, on the contrary, both nationalities are to be taken into account, so that the courts of those two Member States can have jurisdiction on that basis, allowing the persons concerned to choose the Member State in which to bring proceedings. The CJEU ruled that where the court of the Member State addressed had to verify, pursuant to Article 64(4), whether the court of the Member State of origin of a judgment would have had jurisdiction under Article 3(1)(b), the latter provision precluded the court of the Member State addressed from regarding spouses who each hold the nationality both of that State and of the Member State of origin as nationals only of the Member State addressed. That court must, on the contrary, take into account the fact that the spouses also hold the nationality of the Member State of origin and that, therefore, the courts of the latter could have had jurisdiction to hear the case.[17] The Court further held that where spouses each held the nationality of the same two Member States, Article 3(1)(b) prevented the jurisdiction of the courts of one of those Member States from being rejected on the ground that the applicant did not invoke other links with that State. On the contrary, the courts of those Member States of which the spouses held nationality had jurisdiction under that provision and the spouses could seise the court of the Member State of their choice. To sum up, where spouses have dual nationality of the same Member States, the courts of either of those States have jurisdiction to hear matrimonial proceedings and each spouse can seise the court of the Member State of his or her choice. The spouse who seises the court first will win the battle of jurisdiction due to the *lis pendens* rule in Article 19.[18] This is a wise decision by the CJEU. The CJEU pointed out that under Article 64(4) of Brussels IIa the recognising court can review the jurisdiction of the court of origin because it is expressly allowed to do so in such transitional cases but reminded everyone that normally the recognising court is prohibited from reviewing the jurisdiction of the court of origin by Article 24 of Brussels IIa.[19]

ii. Parental Responsibility (Articles 8–15)

a. General Jurisdiction (Article 8)

In the case of *A*,[20] the CJEU interpreted the concept of 'habitual residence' under Article 8(1). It held that the concept of habitual residence in Article 8(1) must be interpreted as meaning that it corresponds to the place which reflects some degree of integration by the child in a social and family environment. It is for the national court to establish the habitual residence of the child, taking into account all the circumstances specific to each individual case. The following factors in particular have to be taken into consideration: the duration, regularity, conditions and reasons for the stay on the territory of a Member State and the family's move to that State, the child's nationality, the place and conditions of attendance at school, linguistic knowledge and the family and social relationships of the child in that State. This decision is significant for a number of reasons. First, it is the first judgment of the CJEU that gives guidance on the interpretation of the concept of habitual residence

---

[17] ibid, paras 32–43.
[18] See ibid, para 56.
[19] See ibid, para 33.
[20] Case C-523/07 *A* [2009] ECR I-02805 (Third Chamber).

for the purposes of the Brussels IIa Regulation and it points out that the interpretation of that concept is not to be borrowed from other areas of Union law but rather is unique to Brussels IIa. Although it is a factual test, the CJEU acknowledges that the intention of the holders of parental responsibility to settle 'permanently' with the child in another State can be an indicator of the transfer of the habitual residence of the child.[21] The Court did not adopt the 'centre of interests' test suggested by AG Kokott.[22]

b. Jurisdiction in Cases of Child Abduction (Article 10)

Doris Povse v Mauro Alpago[23] was referred to the CJEU in proceedings between Ms Povse and Mr Alpago where the issue was the return to Italy of their daughter Sofia, who was in Austria with her mother, and rights of custody in respect of that child. The CJEU interpreted several provisions of Brussels IIa in this case.[24] As regards Article 10(b)(iv), the CJEU was asked whether a 'judgment on custody that does not entail the return of the child' was to be understood as meaning a provisional measure awarding in particular the right to determine the place of residence to the abducting parent pending the final judgment on custody. The CJEU held that a provisional measure did not constitute a 'judgment on custody' and could not be the basis of a transfer of jurisdiction to the courts of the Member State to which a child had been unlawfully removed.

Barbara Mercredi v Richard Chaffe[25] was referred to the CJEU in proceedings between the father, Mr Chaffe, and the mother, Ms Mercredi, of a female child, concerning rights of custody in respect of that child, who was at the time of proceedings with her mother on the island of Réunion (France). The English Court of Appeal sought a preliminary ruling from the CJEU on the following three questions: 1) the appropriate test for determining the habitual residence of a child; 2) whether the court was an 'institution or other body' to which rights of custody could be attributed; and 3) whether Article 10 of Brussels IIa had a continuing application after the courts of the requested State had rejected an application for the return of the child on the basis that Articles 3 and 5 of the Hague 1980 Convention were not made out. In relation to question two the CJEU noted that it was agreed that the removal of the child was lawful and it followed that Article 10 of the Regulation did not apply. It was therefore unnecessary to reply to the second question. In relation to questions one and three the CJEU ruled as follows: a) as a preliminary issue, under Article 16 of the Regulation, a court can be deemed to be seised only if a document instituting proceedings was lodged with that court. Accordingly, the English court was not seised when the father made his telephone application but only three days later when he made his application in writing; b) habitual residence has to be determined at the date the court is seised. In this case that was four days after the child arrived in Réunion. Such residence corresponds to the place which reflects some degree of integration by the child in a social and family environment. The environment of a young child is essentially a family environment determined by reference to the person(s) with whom the child lives (in this case the child had lived only with the mother from one week after she was born). The factors to be taken into

---

[21] ibid, para 40.
[22] Opinion of Advocate General Kokott, para 38.
[23] Case C-211/10 PPU *Doris Povse v Mauro Alpago* [2010] ECR I-06673 (Third Chamber).
[24] See below n 28 and 78.
[25] Case C-497/10 PPU *Barbara Mercredi v Richard Chaffe* [2010] ECR I-14309 (First Chamber).

consideration included, first, the duration, regularity, conditions and reasons for the stay in the State where the child is present and for the mother's move to that State and, second, with particular reference to the child's age, the mother's geographic and family origins and the family and social connections which the mother and child have with that Member State. It was for the national court to establish the habitual residence of the child, on the basis of the specific circumstances of the individual case; c) If the application of the test for habitual residence were to lead to the conclusion that the child's habitual residence could not be established, jurisdiction would have to be determined on the basis of the child's physical presence (Article 13); d) The Court noted that the English court had been seised in matters of parental responsibility before the Réunion court, therefore, pursuant to Article 19 of the Regulation (*lis pendens*), the English court must determine whether it has jurisdiction based on Article 8 of the Regulation. This urgent procedure case was dealt with by the CJEU in just over two months but it is important to note that the case was only referred to the CJEU when the child was already 14 months.

In *Mercredi*, the CJEU dismissed question two, however, AG Cruz Villalón suggested that it be answered as follows:

> Article 2(7), (9) and (11) and Articles 10 and 11 of Regulation No 2201/2003 must be interpreted as meaning that a court of a Member State may be an 'institution or other body' within the meaning of those provisions, to which rights of custody may be granted for the purposes of the provisions of that regulation, in so far as the legislation of that Member State provides for the grant of those rights of custody by operation of law.[26]

When the case returned to the English Court of Appeal,[27] it decided that even if the English courts had jurisdiction based on the child's habitual residence in England four days after she arrived in Réunion, the English court should, of its own motion, have applied Article 15 of Brussels IIa and transferred the case to the French courts in accordance with the best interests of the child. This was a wise and very pragmatic decision given that the child was not going to return from Réunion to the UK and the only live issue between the parents was how to secure access for the father to the child.

c. Return of the Child (Article 11)

In *Povse*,[28] one of the questions that the CJEU dealt with was whether a return order issued by a court falls within the scope of Article 11(8) even if the basis of that return order is not a final custody judgment delivered by that court. The CJEU held that a judgment of the court with jurisdiction ordering the return of a child fell within the scope of Article 11(8), even if not preceded by a final judgment of that court relating to rights of custody.

The Commission in its proposal for a Recast of Brussels IIa has suggested reforming the second ruling of the CJEU in *Povse* relating to the interpretation of Article 11(8)[29] and Article 26(4) of the proposed Recast, by allowing a return order to be made by the courts of the habitual residence of the child only after they have considered what is in the best

---

[26] View of Advocate General Cruz Villalón, para 147.

[27] *Mercredi v Chaffe* [2011] EWCA Civ 272.

[28] *Povse*, above n 23.

[29] See Commission (EC), 'Proposal for a Council Regulation on jurisdiction, the recognition and enforcement of decisions in matrimonial matters and the matters of parental responsibility, and on international child abduction (recast)' COM(2016) 411 final, 13.

interests of the child. This reform had been advocated inter alia by Beaumont, Walker and Holliday[30] and the same authors have welcomed this aspect of the Commission's Proposal.[31]

C v M[32] was referred to the CJEU in the context of legal proceedings brought by C against M concerning the return to France of their child who was in Ireland with her mother. The Supreme Court of Ireland referred the following questions to the CJEU:

1) Does the existence of the French proceedings relating to the custody of the child preclude, in the circumstances of this case, the establishment of habitual residence of the child in Ireland?; 2) Does either the father or the French courts continue to maintain custody rights in relation to the child so as to render wrongful the retention of the child in Ireland?; 3) Are the Irish courts entitled to consider the question of habitual residence of the child in the circumstances where she has resided in Ireland since July 2012, at which time her removal to Ireland was not in breach of French law?[33]

The CJEU held that Articles 2(11) and 11 of Brussels IIa had to be interpreted as meaning that, where a child had been removed lawfully in accordance with a judgment which was provisionally enforceable and was later overturned on appeal by a judgment granting custody rights to the left-behind parent, the courts of the requested State had to determine whether the child was still habitually resident in the requesting State immediately before the alleged wrongful retention. The CJEU did not determine the date of the alleged wrongful retention, correctly leaving this to the national court (presumably it is the day after the mother became aware of the French appeal court decision). Only if the child was, immediately before the retention, habitually resident in the requesting State, could an application for return be granted. The determination of the child's habitual residence has to be undertaken through an assessment of all the factual circumstances specific to the individual case. As a part of this assessment it was important that account be taken of the fact that the French judgment authorising the removal of the child was provisionally enforceable and that an appeal had been brought against it. The CJEU said those factors were not 'conducive' to a finding that the child's habitual residence had changed to Ireland by the time of the French appeal decision eight months later but the CJEU acknowledged other factors could point towards a change of habitual residence to Ireland and left the decision to the Irish courts.

The CJEU decision, in *C v M*, gives weight to non-factual considerations in determining habitual residence in a way neither consistent with its earlier case law nor the View of Advocate General Szpunar in this case. However, it wisely left the decision on habitual residence to the Irish courts. The Irish Supreme Court[34] decided that the child's habitual residence was in Ireland by the time of the alleged wrongful retention.[35]

---

[30] See P Beaumont, L Walker and J Holliday, 'Conflicts of EU Courts on Child Abduction: the Reality of Article 11(6)–(8) Brussels IIa Proceedings Across the EU' (2016) 12 *Journal of Private International Law* 211, 226–27.

[31] See P Beaumont, L Walker and J Holliday, 'Parental Responsibility and International Child Abduction in the Proposed Recast of Brussels IIa Regulation and the Effect of Brexit on Future Child Abduction Proceedings' [2016] *International Family Law* 307. The latest version of this paper is available as Centre for Private International Working Paper No 2016/6 at www.abdn.ac.uk/law/research/working-papers-455.php.

[32] C-376/14 PPU *C v M* EU:C:2014:2268 (Third Chamber). See ch 37 above for a short, sharp critique of the Court's decision in this case.

[33] ibid, para 32.

[34] *G v G* [2015] IESC 12.

[35] See a more in-depth analysis of the CJEU and Irish decisions in this case in P Beaumont and J Holliday, 'Recent Developments on the Meaning of "Habitual Residence" in Alleged Child Abduction Cases' Working Paper No 2015/3, available at www.abdn.ac.uk/law/research/working-papers-455.php. The final version is published in

In *David Bradbrooke v Anna Aleksandrowicz*,[36] the CJEU was asked whether Article 11(7) and (8) of Brussels IIa precluded a Member State from assigning jurisdiction to a specialist court to consider situations of parental child abduction, where a court or tribunal was already seised in substantive proceedings regarding parental responsibility with respect to the child. The CJEU noted that Brussels IIa did not seek to establish uniform substantive and procedural rules. Nevertheless, it was vital that such national rules did not impair the effectiveness of Brussels IIa and were compatible with the child's fundamental rights contained in Article 24 of the Charter (in particular, the right of the child to maintain on a regular basis personal relationships and direct contact with both of his or her parents), and the objective that procedures should be expeditious. Accordingly, the CJEU held that Article 11(7) and (8)

> must be interpreted as not precluding, as a general rule, a Member State from allocating to a specialised court the jurisdiction to examine questions of return or custody with respect to a child in the context of the procedure set out in those provisions, even where proceedings on the substance of parental responsibility with respect to the child have already, separately, been brought before a court or tribunal.

The CJEU could and perhaps should have followed the reasoning of the AG[37] and the Commission in commending the good practice of concentration of jurisdiction in specialised courts in parental child abduction cases rather than just saying that in principle it does not impair the effectiveness of the Regulation.[38] It is encouraging that the Commission has proposed concentration of jurisdiction for Hague 1980 return cases in the Brussels IIa Recast but, sadly, not yet for the Brussels IIa override cases.[39]

d. Prorogation of Jurisdiction (Article 12)

E v B[40] was referred to the CJEU in proceedings between Mr E ('the father') and Ms B ('the mother'), in relation to the jurisdiction of the courts of the United Kingdom to hear and determine, in particular, the usual place of residence of their child S and the rights of access of the father. The CJEU was asked the following two questions: 1) where there has been a prorogation of the jurisdiction of a court of a Member State in relation to matters of parental responsibility pursuant to Article 12(3) of the Regulation, does that prorogation of jurisdiction only continue until there has been a final judgment in those proceedings or does it continue even after a final judgment has been made?; 2) does Article 15 of the Regulation allow the courts of a Member State to transfer a jurisdiction in circumstances where there are no current proceedings concerning the child? The CJEU held that the grounds of jurisdiction in matters of parental responsibility established in the Regulation were

---

P Beaumont and J Holliday, 'Recent Developments on the Meaning of "Habitual Residence" in Alleged Child Abduction Cases' in M Župan (ed), *Private International Law in the Jurisprudence of European Courts—Family at Focus / Međunarodno Privatno Pravo u Praksi Europskih Sudova—Obitelj u Fokusu* (Osijek, Faculty of Law JJ Strossmayer University of Osijek, 2015) 37–56.

[36] C-498/14 PPU *David Bradbrooke v Anna Aleksandrowicz* EU:C:2015:3 (Fourth Chamber).
[37] See View of Advocate General Jääskinen, paras 62–66.
[38] See *Bradbrooke*, above n 36, para 51.
[39] See Proposal for a Council Regulation 2016, above n 29, and Beaumont, Walker and Holliday, above n 31, 308. For the full title of the Hague 1980 Convention see n 53 below.
[40] Case C-436/13 *E v B* EU:C:2014:2246 (Second Chamber).

shaped in the light of the best interests of the child,[41] and any prorogation of jurisdiction in accordance with Article 12(3)(b) had to be in the light of those interests. Such a prorogation, however, does not necessarily remain in the child's best interests beyond the end of the proceedings. The jurisdiction of the court therefore must be reviewed in each specific case where a court is seised of proceedings in matters of parental responsibility. Consequently, a prorogation of jurisdiction is valid only in relation to specific proceedings. That jurisdiction ceases, in favour of a court of a Member State with general jurisdiction under Article 8(1), following a final judgment in the proceedings from which the prorogation of jurisdiction derives. The CJEU further held that in the view of this conclusion, it was not necessary to rule on the second question. The reasoning of the Court in this judgment is coherent and fully in line with the principle of the best interests of the child on which the jurisdictional rules in matters of parental responsibility in the Brussels IIa Regulation are based. This was a straightforward case as seen by the fact that it was decided to proceed to judgment without receiving a View from the AG.

L v M[42] was referred to the CJEU in proceedings between Ms L, the mother of the children R and K, and Mr M, the father of those children, concerning the custody of those children. The children were with their mother in Austria, whereas the father lived in the Czech Republic. The CJEU was asked whether Article 12(3) of Brussels IIa must be interpreted as establishing jurisdiction over proceedings concerning parental responsibility even where no other related proceedings (ie 'proceedings other than those referred to in paragraph 1') are pending; and in the affirmative, whether Article 12(3) must be interpreted as meaning that 'acceptance expressly or otherwise in an unequivocal manner' includes also the situation in which the party who has not initiated proceedings makes a separate application for the initiation of proceedings in the same case but immediately on doing the first act required of him objects that the court lacks jurisdiction in the proceedings previously started on the application by the other party. The first question was answered in the affirmative. Article 12(3) must be interpreted as allowing, for the purposes of proceedings in matters of parental responsibility, the jurisdiction of a court of a Member State which is not that of the child's habitual residence to be established even where no other proceedings are pending before the court chosen. Any other interpretation would infringe the effectiveness of the provision. Indeed, to limit the possibility of utilising Article 12(3) to cases in which the proceedings in matters of parental responsibility were related to other proceedings would exclude the possibility of having recourse to prorogation under Article 12(3) in numerous cases, including situations where the prorogation of jurisdiction might be in the best interests of the child concerned. In answer to the second question, Article 12(3)(b) must be interpreted as meaning that it cannot be considered that the jurisdiction of the court seised by one party to proceedings in matters of parental responsibility had been 'accepted expressly or otherwise in an unequivocal manner by all the parties to the proceedings' within the meaning of that provision where the defendant in those first proceedings subsequently brings a second set of proceedings before the same court and, on taking the first step required of him in the first proceedings, pleads the lack of jurisdiction of that court.

The Third Chamber considered dealing with *L v M* under the urgent preliminary ruling procedure but decided not to after hearing the AG.[43] Instead, the case was dealt with as a

---

[41] See Brussels IIa Reg Recital 12.
[42] Case C-656/13 *L v M* EU:C:2014:2364 (Third Chamber).
[43] It is disappointing that there is no Opinion from the Advocate General in this case.

priority reference pursuant to Article 53(3) of the Court's Rules of Procedure but the priority was not very great as the CJEU took 11 months to give a judgment. The Third Chamber correctly decided that a court which has jurisdiction under Article 12(3) of Brussels IIa 'will, in principle, also have jurisdiction to hear an application for maintenance which is ancillary to the parental responsibility proceedings pending before it'.[44] By clarifying, against the views of the Commission and with no AG's Opinion, that Article 12(3) of Brussels IIa creates the opportunity for choice of court in parental responsibility proceedings beyond those linked to matrimonial proceedings, the Third Chamber is confirming a jurisdiction not found in the 1996 Hague Child Protection Convention. The EU is permitted in intra-EU matters to create such a new jurisdiction by Article 52(4) of the 1996 Hague Convention.

In *Vasilka Ivanova*,[45] one of the issues was whether the jurisdiction of the Bulgarian courts may be founded upon Article 12 solely because the court-appointed legal representative of the father did not contest the jurisdiction of those courts. The CJEU correctly regarded this question as being on the interpretation of Article 12(3)(b) of Brussels IIa. The CJEU noted that as the provision embodied an exception to the basic jurisdictional rule contained in Article 8(1), it had to be interpreted strictly. The acceptance of jurisdiction in terms of Article 12(3)(b) presupposed that the defendant was at least aware of the proceedings taking place. It was therefore unacceptable that the wishes of the defendant be deduced from the conduct of a legal representative appointed by the court in the absence of the defendant. Accordingly, Article 12(3)(b) had to be interpreted as meaning that the jurisdiction may not be regarded as having been 'accepted expressly or otherwise in an unequivocal manner by all the parties to the proceedings' solely because the legal representative of the defendant, appointed by those courts of their own motion in the defendant's absence, has not pleaded the lack of jurisdiction of those courts. This is an uncontroversial decision giving an expansive interpretation to the concept of 'parental responsibility'. This is to ensure that, through the application of the jurisdictional rules contained in the Regulation, the best interests of the child are protected in as varied situations as possible. The ruling wisely gives expression to the principle of party autonomy by requiring real and not imposed consent by both parties.

iii. Common Provisions (Articles 16–20)

a. Seising of a Court (Article 16)

A v B[46] concerned the divorce of a French couple who had got married in France and then moved to the UK. The husband petitioned for judicial separation in France. Two months later, the wife petitioned for divorce in England. The English court declined jurisdiction on the basis of Article 19 because the French court was already seised. The CJEU was asked to interpret Article 19 of Brussels IIa. The Third Chamber noted that in order to determine when a court is first seised under Article 19, it is necessary to refer to Article 16. It is apparent from the wording of Article 19(1) that, contrary to the rules in Article 27(1) of Brussels I,[47]

---

[44] *L v M*, above n 42, para 35. For the use of Art 12(3) to enable the choice of the forum where succession proceedings were pending see *Matoušková*, above n 7, as discussed at 715 above.

[45] See *Vasilka Ivanova*, above n 12.

[46] Case C-489/14 *A v B* EU:C:2015:654 (Third Chamber).

[47] Brussels Ia Reg, Art 29(1).

in matrimonial matters applications brought before the courts of different Member States are not required to have the same cause of action. As AG Cruz Villalón noted, while the proceedings must involve the same parties, they may have a different cause of action, provided that they concern judicial separation, divorce or marriage annulment.[48] The Court's interpretation of Article 27 of Brussels I applies equally to Article 19(1) of Brussels IIa. Thus, in order for the jurisdiction of the court first seised to be established within the meaning of Article 19(1), it is sufficient that the court first seised has not declined jurisdiction of its own motion and that none of the parties has contested that jurisdiction before or up to the time at which a position is adopted which is regarded in national law as being the first defence on the substance submitted before that court. Where that jurisdiction is deemed to be established under the rules in Article 3 of Brussels IIa, the court second seised is to decline jurisdiction in favour of the court first seised, in accordance with Article 19(3). However, in order for there to be a situation of *lis pendens*, it is important that the proceedings brought between the same parties and relating to petitions for divorce, judicial separation or marriage annulment be pending simultaneously before the courts of different Member States. Where two sets of proceedings have been brought before the courts of different Member States, and one set of proceedings expires, the risk of irreconcilable decisions, and thereby the situation of *lis pendens* within the meaning of Article 19, disappears. It follows that, even if the jurisdiction of the court first seised was established during the first proceedings, the situation of *lis pendens* no longer exists and, therefore, that jurisdiction is not established. That is the case following the lapse of the proceedings before the court first seised. In that situation, the court second seised becomes the court first seised on the date of that lapse. The CJEU held that since the proceedings before the French court first seised lapsed, the English court was the court first seised of the dispute. The conduct of the husband, notably his lack of diligence, and the existence of a time difference between the Member States concerned, which would enable the courts of the first Member State to be seised before those of the second Member State, in the particular circumstances of the present case, were not relevant.

As the whole litigation in France and England, in *A v B*, had dragged on for four years, the High Court wanted the CJEU to apply an expedited procedure under Article 105(1) of the CJEU's Rules of Procedure but the President of the Court refused this request and instead gave it priority over other references pursuant to Article 53(3) of the Rules of Procedure.[49] This prioritisation yielded modest gains in terms of time with the ruling being delivered in 11 months. It is a happy outcome that by sheer good fortune the wife's English divorce application went in a few days earlier than her legal advisers wanted (ie before the French legal separation proceedings were due to cease rather than immediately thereafter), and, therefore, inadvertently the English court became the court first seised of the divorce proceedings. No doubt the wife had been advised by her English lawyers during the French judicial separation proceedings not to exercise her right (which she could have used any time after the first three months of the husband lodging those proceedings) to turn those proceedings into divorce proceedings because she preferred the divorce to proceed in England. This was no doubt partially a convenience issue because both parties and the

---

[48] Opinion of Advocate General Cruz Villalón, para 76.
[49] ibid, para 32.

children were still resident in England but no doubt also because she wanted the English courts to apply English law to the financial provisions on divorce (which are known to be relatively generous to wives compared to other systems in the EU), rather than allowing the French courts to proceed on the application of French law. Although this case worked out well for the wife by a fluke it does highlight the need to create a transfer provision whereby divorce and legal separation cases could be transferred to the most appropriate forum to deal with them within the EU (the courts of the common habitual residence should trump the courts of the common nationality in most if not all cases) but, sadly, for political reasons, no such proposal has been made by the Commission in its Brussels IIa Recast Proposal. The Commission is reluctant to open up the provisions in relation to marriage and separation for fear of the issue of same-sex relationships causing a block to the adoption of the revised Brussels IIa in the Council given the need for unanimity in that institution.

b. *Lis Pendens* and Dependent Actions (Article 19)

Bianca Purrucker v Guillermo Vallés Pérez[50] was referred to the CJEU in proceedings between Ms Purrucker and Mr Vallés Pérez concerning rights of custody in respect of their son Merlín. The German referring court was faced with the issue whether a court seised solely for the purpose of making provisional measures (in this case, a Spanish court) should be regarded as the court 'first seised' for the purposes of Article 19(2). Another problem the German referring court encountered was that no information was forthcoming from the Spanish court as to whether it considered itself to be seised also of substantive custody proceedings. The CJEU ruled as follows: first, the provisions of Article 19(2) are not applicable where a court of a Member State first seised is seised only for the purpose of making provisional measures within the meaning of Article 20. Second, the fact that a court of a Member State is seised in the context of proceedings to obtain interim relief does not necessarily preclude the possibility that, subject to the national law of that Member State, there may be an action as to the substance of the matter which is linked to the action to obtain interim measures, and in which there is evidence to demonstrate that the court seised has jurisdiction. Third, where the court second seised has made unsuccessful efforts to obtain relevant information, and is therefore unable to determine the cause of action of proceedings brought before the court first seised, and where the interest of the child requires the handing down of a judgment which may be recognised in Member States other than that of the court second seised, it is the duty of that court, after the expiry of a reasonable period in which answers to the enquiries made are awaited, to proceed with consideration of the action brought before it. Provisional measures made under Article 20, since they are not capable of recognition in another Member State within the meaning of Article 21, cannot give rise to *lis pendens* within the meaning of Article 19(2). However, proceedings pending before a court whose jurisdiction is based on Articles 8 to 14, and which is first seised of an action relating to parental responsibility over a child, irrespective of the characterisation of the proceedings according to the national law of that Member State, and irrespective of whether the measure is sought on a provisional basis or whether it is sought for a definite or indefinite period, prevent a court in another Member State from ruling on the same cause of action until the court first seised has established that it has jurisdiction. Nevertheless, the

---

[50] Case C-296/10 *Bianca Purrucker v Guillermo Vallés Pérez* ECR [2010] I-11163 (Second Chamber).

best interests of the child principle requires that there is a limit as to how long the court second seised should be expected to wait for the information from which it can determine whether it can assume jurisdiction. Although this approach enables the court second seised to end the stalemate in the proceedings, there is a risk that, eventually, conflicting judgments emerge from the proceedings.

c. Provisional, Including Protective, Measures (Article 20)

In the case of C-523/07 *A*,[51] the CJEU also interpreted the operation of Article 20. The CJEU held that a protective measure (including taking a child into care) may be taken by a national court if the measure is urgent and provisional and is taken in respect of persons in the Member State concerned. There is no obligation for the national court that has taken the provisional measure to transfer the case to the court of another Member State which has jurisdiction but, as far as required by the child's best interests, it should inform that court. Finally, where the court of a Member State has no jurisdiction over the substance of the matter and does not consider any provisional measures under Article 20 to be necessary, it must declare so on its own motion and inform the court of another Member State which has jurisdiction. The court with no jurisdiction is not required to transfer the case to another court. This is a significant decision that clarifies the requirements that must be met before the power to take provisional measures under Article 20 can be exercised by national courts.

Jasna Detiček v Maurizio Sgueglia[52] was referred to the CJEU in the course of proceedings between Ms Detiček and Mr Sgueglia concerning custody of their daughter Antonella. The CJEU was asked whether Article 20 should be interpreted as allowing a court of a Member State to take a provisional measure in matters of parental responsibility granting custody of a child who is in the territory of that Member State to one parent, where a court of another Member State, which has jurisdiction under Brussels IIa as to the substance of the dispute relating to custody of the child, has already delivered a judgment provisionally giving custody of the child to the other parent, and that judgment has been declared enforceable in the territory of the former Member State. The CJEU reiterated the three conditions for the application of Article 20, ie that the measures in question must be urgent, relate to persons or assets in the Member State seised, and be provisional in nature. The concept of urgency relates to the situation of the child and the impossibility in practice of bringing the parental responsibility application before the court with jurisdiction as to the substance. If a situation of urgency for the purposes of Article 20 could arise from a change in circumstances resulting from a child's integration into a new environment, then any delay in the enforcement procedure in the requested Member State would contribute to creating the circumstances that would allow the court of the requested State to block the enforcement of the judgment that had been declared enforceable. Such an interpretation would go against the principle of mutual recognition. In addition, as the circumstances in the present case resulted from an abduction, the Regulation's aim of deterring wrongful removals and retentions would also be undermined. The Court also referred to the geographical element of Article 20 (ie the requirement that the provisional measures must relate to persons or assets

[51] *A*, above n 5.
[52] Case C-403/09 PPU *Jasna Detiček v Maurizio Sgueglia* [2009] ECR I-12193 (Third Chamber).

in the Member State seised). A provisional measure ordering a change of custody of a child is a measure taken not only in respect of the child, but also in respect of the left-behind parent (in this case the father who was not present in Slovenia). Finally, the Court highlighted Article 24(3) of the Charter of Fundamental Rights of the European Union, on a child's right to maintain on a regular basis a personal relationship and direct contact with both parents, and held that Article 20 could not be interpreted in a manner which disregarded that right. The Court concluded that Article 20(1) did not allow, in the circumstances such as these, a court of an EU Member State to take a provisional measure in matters of parental responsibility, granting custody of a child who was in the territory of that Member State to one parent, where a court of another Member State, which had jurisdiction under the Regulation as to the substance of the dispute relating to the custody of the child, had already delivered a judgment provisionally giving custody of the child to the other parent, and that judgment had been declared enforceable in the territory of the former Member State.

It was positive in *Detiček* that the CJEU defended the principles and the rules of the 1980 Hague Child Abduction Convention[53] and the Brussels IIa Regulation that combat the wrongful removal of children. However, the interpretation of the geographical element of Article 20 by the Court seems unconvincing as, taking this to the extreme, there could then never be any interim orders in respect of a child where one parent is in another country.

Bianca Purrucker v Guillermo Vallés Pérez[54] was referred to the CJEU in German proceedings brought by Ms Purrucker, the mother of the children Merlín and Samira Purrucker, against the decision of a German court so far as it ordered the enforcement of a judgment of the Juzgado de Primera Instancia Number 4 of San Lorenzo de El Escorial (Spain) awarding custody of those children to their father. The referring court asked the CJEU whether the provisions of Article 21 et seq of Brussels IIa on recognition and enforcement of decisions of other EU Member States, in conjunction with Article 2(4), also apply to enforceable provisional measures, within the meaning of Article 20 of that Regulation, concerning the right to child custody. It is to be noted that the relevance of that question was challenged, first, on the ground that the provisional measures concerned in the main proceedings did not fall within the scope of Article 20 of the Regulation, since they were taken by a court which had jurisdiction as to the substance of the matter (it was not clear from the Spanish judgment on which ground the Spanish court had assumed jurisdiction), and, second, on the ground that even if those measures had been taken by a court which did not have jurisdiction as to the substance of the matter, they could not in any event fall within the scope of Article 20 in so far as they related to the boy who was not in Spain when the court delivered its judgment. The CJEU ruled that the provisions laid down in Article 21 et seq of Brussels IIa on recognition and enforcement do not apply to provisional measures, relating to rights of custody, falling within the scope of Article 20. The CJEU accepted a suggestion by AG Sharpston that other international instruments or national legislation might be used to secure the recognition of such provisional measures. The CJEU noted that it was not clear from the Spanish court's judgment how it had applied the jurisdictional rules of the Regulation to the particular facts of the case. The court of a Member State hearing an application concerning parental responsibility must determine whether it has jurisdiction having

---

[53] Hague Convention of 25 October 1980 on the Civil Aspects of International Child Abduction.
[54] Case C-256/09 *Bianca Purrucker v Guillermo Vallés Pérez* [2010] ECR I-07353 (Second Chamber).

regard to Articles 8 to 14 of Brussels IIa. It must be clearly evident from the judgment that the court concerned had intended to respect the directly applicable rules of jurisdiction, or that the court had made its ruling in accordance with those rules. Where this clarity is lacking, it may be inferred that the judgment was not adopted in accordance with the Regulation's jurisdictional rules. Although the courts of other Member States must not review the assessment made by the first court of its jurisdiction (Article 24), this does not prevent an examination of the judgment determining whether it falls within the scope of Article 20. Indeed, to make such a determination is not to review the jurisdiction of the court of origin but merely to ascertain the basis on which that court considered itself competent. The CJEU held that the person affected by provisional measures must be given the opportunity to bring an appeal against the judgment without this being viewed as an acceptance of the substantive jurisdiction of the court that ordered the provisional measures.

This judgment, although providing a simple answer to a clear question, gives important guidance on the application of the jurisdictional rules of the Regulation. Specifically, it is vital that the court asserting jurisdiction under the Regulation, demonstrates clearly the basis on which it does so. There are some very important observations on the relationship between Brussels IIa and the 1996 Hague Child Protection Convention (in particular Article 11 thereof) by the Second Chamber[55] and by AG Sharpston.[56] Provisional measures under Article 11 of the 1996 Hague Convention do obtain recognition in other Contracting States to that Convention.[57] The Commission is proposing in the Recast of Brussels IIa to bring the provision on provisional measures in Brussels IIa within the jurisdiction chapter and therefore such measures could benefit from the recognition and enforcement provisions under the Regulation.[58]

C. Recognition and Enforcement (Articles 21–52)

i. Recognition (Articles 21–27)

a. Recognition of a Judgment (Article 21)

In *Health Service Executive*,[59] one of the questions that the CJEU dealt with was whether a judgment of a court of a Member State ordering the compulsory placement of a child in a secure care institution situated in another Member State must, before it can be enforced in the requested Member State, be recognised and declared to be enforceable in that Member State, and whether such a placement order has legal effects in the requested Member State prior to its being declared to be enforceable. The CJEU held that Brussels IIa had to be interpreted as meaning that a judgment of a court of a Member State providing for the compulsory placement of a child in a secure care institution situated in another Member State must, before its enforcement in the requested Member State, be declared to be enforceable

---

[55] ibid, paras 88–90 and 92.

[56] Opinion of Advocate General Sharpston, paras 174 and 176–77. See the analysis of this issue in Beaumont, Walker and Holliday, above n 30, 219–21.

[57] Lagarde, above n 9, para 72. See also Hague Conference on Private International law, 'Practical Handbook on the Operation of the 1996 Hague Child Protection Convention' (2014), para 6.12.

[58] See Beaumont, Walker and Holliday, above n 31, 313–14.

[59] See *Health Service Executive*, above n 6. On recognition of provisional measures see the discussion of *Purrucker* above at 728–729.

in that Member State. The CJEU however, pointed out that the decision of the court of the requested State had to be made with particular expedition and appeals against such a decision must not have suspensive effect.

b. Grounds of Non-Recognition for Judgments Relating to Parental Responsibility (Article 23)

In *P v Q*,[60] concerning rights of custody relating to two children of Lithuanian parents, the CJEU was asked by a Swedish court whether Article 23(a), notwithstanding Article 24, permits the refusal of recognition of a judgment of a court of another Member State which had ruled on the custody of that child. The CJEU recalled that Recital 21 required that the grounds for non-recognition be kept to a minimum. Accordingly, Article 23 had to be interpreted strictly. The CJEU therefore held that Article 23(a) should be interpreted as meaning that, having regard to the best interests of the child, in the absence of a manifest breach of a rule of law regarded as essential in the legal order of a Member State or of a right recognised as being fundamental within that legal order, that provision did not allow a court of that Member State which considered that it had jurisdiction to rule on the custody of a child to refuse to recognise a judgment of a court of another Member State which has ruled on the custody of that child. In other words, the public policy of the Member State where recognition is sought cannot be raised as an obstacle to the recognition or enforcement of a judgment given in another Member State solely on the ground that the Member State of origin failed to comply with the rules on jurisdiction contained in Brussels IIa. This is because Article 24 of Brussels IIa prohibits the review of the jurisdiction of the court of origin, even if that court relied erroneously on Article 15 (not specifically treated as a non-reviewable ground under Article 24 but deemed by the CJEU to be so), the transfer ground, as the basis of jurisdiction. The CJEU went further in instructing the national court that it could not use Article 23(a), despite saying that 'it is not for the Court to define the content of the public policy of a Member State', in this case because

> even if a difficulty concerning the wrongful retention [query was this not a wrongful removal case?] of a child were to arise in the case in the main proceedings, that difficulty would have to be resolved not by a refusal of recognition on the basis of Article 23(a) of Regulation No 2201/2003 of a judgment such as that of the [Lithuanian Court] ... but, if necessary, by recourse to the procedure laid down in Article 11 of that regulation.

The logic of this finding is that if the left-behind parent wants custody of their child, they have to seek a return order under Article 11(8) Brussels IIa even if they just want a joint custody order where the child spends most of the time with the abducting parent in the country where the child was abducted to. The judgment was delivered in 12 weeks and it was in line with the View of AG Wathelet.

It was significant in *P v Q* for AG Wathelet[61] that the father could have brought a further appeal in the Lithuanian courts, arguing that they did not have jurisdiction under Brussels IIa to decide on the custody of the children. Furthermore, AG Wathelet[62] and the Fourth Chamber[63] emphasised that the Swedish courts did not exercise their power, on the basis

---

[60] Case C-455/15 PPU *P v Q* EU:C:2015:763 (Fourth Chamber).
[61] View of Advocate General Wathelet, paras 75–76.
[62] ibid, paras 78–86.
[63] *P v Q*, above n 60, paras 48–52.

of Article 11(8) of Brussels IIa, to overturn the Lithuanian non-return order granted under Article 13 of the 1980 Hague Convention.[64] Sadly, it is not clear from either the AG's View or the CJEU's judgment what was the ground under Article 13 of the 1980 Hague Convention by which the Lithuanian courts refused to return the children to Sweden. Indeed, the AG simply adds more confusion by suggesting that the Lithuanian courts actually decided that the removal of the children from Sweden by the mother was not 'wrongful' because, at the time of the removal, the father was prohibited by Swedish law from having any contact with the children.[65] If this was indeed the reason for the Lithuanian judgment and the refusal to return the children was based on Article 3 of the 1980 Hague Convention, not Article 13(1)(a), then the Article 11(8) Brussels IIa override scheme would not be applicable.

ii. Decision of the Court in the Application for a Declaration of Enforceability (Article 31)

Inga Rinau,[66] concerned proceedings between Mrs Rinau and Mr Rinau regarding the return to Germany of their daughter Luisa, who was being retained in Lithuania by Mrs Rinau. The CJEU held that in so far as Article 31(1) provides that neither the person against whom enforcement is sought, nor the child is, at this stage of the proceedings, entitled to make any submissions on the application, is not applicable to proceedings initiated for non-recognition of a judicial decision if no application for recognition has been lodged beforehand in respect of that decision. In such a situation, the defendant, who is seeking recognition, is entitled to make such submissions. It is to be noted that AG Sharpston would have given a literal interpretation to Article 31(1) of Brussels IIa,[67] and therefore the contrary judgment of the Third Chamber on this point can be contested in a future case relying on AG Sharpston's arguments.

iii. Enforceability of Certain Judgments Concerning Rights of Access and of Certain Judgments which Require the Return of the Child (Article 42)

In *Rinau*,[68] the CJEU also interpreted Article 42. It stated that although intrinsically connected with other matters governed by Brussels IIa, in particular rights of custody, the enforceability of a judgment requiring the return of a child following a judgment of non-return enjoyed procedural autonomy, so as not to delay the return of a child who has been wrongfully removed to or retained in a Member State other than that in which that child was habitually resident immediately before the wrongful removal or retention. The procedural autonomy of the provisions in Articles 11(8), 40 and 42 and the priority given to the jurisdiction of the court of origin, in the context of Section 4 of Chapter III of the Regulation, are reflected in Articles 43 and 44, which provide that the law of the Member State of origin is to be applicable to any rectification of the certificate, that no appeal is to lie against the issuing of a certificate and that that certificate is to take effect only within the limits of the enforceability of the judgment. The CJEU held that once a non-return

---

[64] See *P v Q*, ibid para 19 and View of Advocate General Wathelet, para 26.
[65] See View of Advocate General Wathelet, para 82.
[66] Case C-195/08 PPU *Inga Rinau* [2008] ECR I-05271 (Third Chamber).
[67] View of Advocate General Sharpston.
[68] *Rinau*, above n 66.

decision had been taken and brought to the attention of the court of origin, it was irrelevant, for the purposes of issuing the certificate pursuant to Article 42, that that decision had been suspended, overturned, set aside or, in any event, had not become *res judicata* or had been replaced by a decision ordering return, in so far as the return of the child had not actually taken place. Since no doubt had been expressed as regards the authenticity of that certificate and since it was drawn up in accordance with the standard form set out in Annex IV to the Regulation, opposition to the recognition of the decision ordering return was not permitted and it was for the requested court to declare the enforceability of the certified decision allowing the immediate return of the child. Once an order implying the return of the child has been issued and certified by the State of origin under Article 42, it is not possible to seek non-recognition of that order in the requested State. Otherwise, the objective of the immediate return of the child would remain subject to the condition that the redress procedures allowed under the domestic law of the Member State in which the child is wrongfully retained have been exhausted. The Court further concluded that, except where the procedure concerned a decision certified pursuant to Articles 11(8) and 40 to 42, any interested party could apply for non-recognition of a custody decision, even if no application for recognition of the decision had been submitted beforehand.

The CJEU, in *Rinau*, clarified that the Articles 11(8) and 42 Brussels IIa procedure will be triggered if a non-return order based on Article 13 of the Hague Convention is made in the State where the child is present even though, on appeal, a return order is made by a court in that State. It is excellent that the AG's View is now always made available before or at the same time as the Court's judgment in the urgent preliminary ruling procedure (PPU) cases because quite a long time after the CJEU judgment in *Rinau* came out, AG Sharpston's View was still not available to the general public (even though the AG made it clear that her View was available to be published).[69]

Joseba Andoni Aguirre Zarraga v Simone Pelz[70] was referred to the CJEU in proceedings between Mr Aguirre Zarraga and Ms Pelz where the issue was the return to Spain of their daughter Andrea, who was in Germany with her mother. The German referring court asked the CJEU to determine whether, in circumstances such as those in the main proceedings, the German courts could oppose the enforcement of a judgment issued by the Spanish court which had been certified by that court on the basis of Article 42 of the Regulation as stating that it had fulfilled its obligation to hear the child before handing down its judgment, even though no such hearing had taken place. The CJEU ruled that the court with jurisdiction in the Member State of enforcement could not oppose the enforcement of a certified judgment, ordering the return of a child who has been wrongfully removed, on the ground that the court of the Member State of origin which handed down that judgment may have infringed Article 42, interpreted in accordance with Article 24 of the Charter of Fundamental Rights of the European Union, since the assessment of whether there had been such an infringement fell exclusively within the jurisdiction of the courts of the Member State of origin. This is a highly controversial decision but at least it was still possible to challenge the Spanish decision in the Spanish courts.[71] The CJEU gave guidance to

---

[69] The regrettable nature of this fact was noted in P Beaumont, 'The Jurisprudence of the European Court of Human Rights and the European Court of Justice on the Hague Convention on International Child Abduction' (2008) 335 *Hague Recueil des Cours* 9, 91.
[70] Case C-491/10 PPU *Joseba Andoni Aguirre Zarraga v Simone Pelz* [2010] ECR I-14247 (First Chamber).
[71] See ibid, para 72.

the Spanish courts that it is not enough to rely on the courts in the country where the child is present having heard the child.[72] The Spanish courts must give the child a 'genuine and effective opportunity to express' her views making use of the instruments of international judicial cooperation including Regulation 1206/2001.[73]

The CJEU was right to insist that in *Zarraga* the Spanish courts should hear the child themselves before overriding the non-return order of the German courts based on the wishes of the child under Article 13(2) of the 1980 Hague Convention.[74] In this case the child was never returned because the German court was able to say that it would not enforce a domestic custody order in similar circumstances because the child was old enough and, independently of her mother, made it clear to the German enforcement agencies that she refused to go back to her father in Spain.[75] It is good that in the Brussels IIa Recast the Commission is now proposing a limited public policy exception to the absolute duty on the courts where the child is present to regard the overriding return order from the courts of the habitual residence of the child as enforceable without any exceptions.[76] The Commission's Proposal to introduce this public policy exception was influenced by the Centre for Private International Law's Nuffield Foundation study on Conflicts of EU Courts in Child Abduction cases.[77]

iv. Enforcement Procedure (Article 47)

In *Povse*,[78] the CJEU also interpreted some issues relating to enforcement. The CJEU was asked whether a judgment delivered by a court in State A (the State of enforcement) and regarded as enforceable under the law of that State, by which provisional custody was awarded to the abducting parent, precluded the enforcement of an earlier return order made in State B (the State of origin) under Article 11(8), in accordance with Article 47(2) of Brussels IIa, even if it would not prevent the enforcement of a return order made in State A under the 1980 Hague Convention. The CJEU was also asked whether State A can refuse to enforce a judgment in respect of which a court in State B has issued a certificate under Article 42(2) of Brussels IIa if, since its delivery, the circumstances have changed in such a way that enforcement would now constitute a serious risk to the best interests of the child, or whether the opposing party must invoke that change of circumstances in State B, thereby allowing enforcement in State A to be stayed pending the judgment in State B. The CJEU held that a judgment delivered subsequently by a court in the State of enforcement, awarding provisional custody rights, and regarded as enforceable under the law of that State, could not preclude enforcement of a certified judgment delivered previously by

---

[72] Contrary to the view of AG Bot, see the *Zarraga* judgment, ibid paras 67–68 compared to the View of AG Bot, 7 December 2010, para 106.

[73] Reg No 1206/2001 of 28 May 2001 on cooperation between the courts of the Member States in the taking of evidence in civil or commercial matters, [2001] OJ L174/1.

[74] See P Beaumont, 'The European Court of Justice Prioritises the Abolition of *Exequatur* over Fundamental Rights in *Zarraga*' in J Díez-Hochleitner, C Martínez Capdevila, I Blázquez Navarro and J Frutos Miranda (eds), *Recent Trends in the Case Law of the CJEU (2008–2011)* (Madrid, La Ley, 2012) 621–34.

[75] See P Beaumont and M Danov, 'The EU Civil Justice Framework and Private Law "Integration through (Private International) Law"' (2015) 22 *Maastricht Journal of European and Comparative Law* 706–31, fn 90.

[76] See Beaumont, Walker and Holliday, above n 31, 311–13.

[77] See Beaumont, Walker and Holliday, above n 30, 254–58, and email correspondence between those authors and the Commission officials primarily responsible for the Commission's Brussels IIa Recast Proposal (on file with those authors).

[78] See *Povse*, above n 23 and 28.

the court with jurisdiction in the Member State of origin, ordering the return of the child (Article 47(2)). It also held that enforcement of a certified judgment could not be refused in the State of enforcement because of welfare concerns. Any application to suspend enforcement of its judgment must be pleaded in the State of origin.

In relation to this point of the *Povse* ruling, the Commission is also proposing a limited public policy exception to enforcement about which Beaumont, Walker and Holliday say:

> The proposal suggests that the enforcement should only be refused if enforcement would be manifestly contrary to the public policy of the Member State of enforcement. Nothing about this is controversial, public policy is one of the grounds for refusal of enforcement in the Brussels I (recast), prior to that it was a ground for refusal of recognition and enforceability in Brussels I, and it has previously been used to protect fundamental rights (*Krombach v Bamberski* (Case C-78/98) [2000] ECR I-10239). The recommendations highlighted in our working paper also suggest that the decision should be reviewable on fundamental rights grounds (Beaumont et al, 2016a, p 249). However, it is controversial that the court of enforcement will only be allowed to invoke its public policy if the breach of public policy is caused 'by virtue of a change of circumstances since the decision' was given in the state of origin. The proposal states the only two bases on which a violation of public policy can be found. First, the child now being of sufficient age and maturity objects to such an extent that the enforcement would be 'manifestly incompatible with the best interests of the child'. Secondly, 'other circumstances have changed to such an extent since the decision was given that its enforcement would now be manifestly incompatible with the best interests of the child'. The first effectively reverses one point in *Zarraga* where the German referring court asked the CJEU if they could refuse enforcement where enforcement would breach the rights of the child, in particular the right of the child to be heard under Art 24 of the Charter (*Zarraga* [37]). (However, the proposal does not permit review of the certificate in the state of enforcement, regardless of whether the certificate and decision comply with the requirements in the certificate. The certificate is subject to review only in the state of origin ...). This fits with the general approach of the proposal which seeks to give more weight to children's rights, in particular the child's right to be heard and have their opinions taken into account. The second ground is in stark contrast to the CJEU decision in *Povse*, where the court precluded a review in the state of enforcement because of a change in circumstances even if the enforcement was manifestly incompatible with the best interests of the child (*Povse* [83]). The proposal may help in cases like *Povse*, where the father had initially visited the child in the state where the child was abducted to but stopped doing so shortly after the abduction (*Povse v Austria*, 18 June 2013 Application no 3890/11 (... discussed in Beaumont et al, 2015a, pp 56–61). By the time the case was heard by the ECtHR, 4 years after the abduction, the child no longer knew her father and did not have a common language with him. However, there were two decisions, requiring return, given by the Italian court. The second which required the child to reside with her father was given after there had been a complete breakdown in the relationship between the child and her father and the loss of a common language. Although there had been a change of circumstances between the first decision and the second decision, and enforcement of this second decision would be incompatible with the best interests of the child partly because it did not require that contact was re-established in an appropriate way before the child was returned to Italy, there was not necessarily a change of circumstances between the issuing of the second Italian order and its enforcement. Therefore, it is not clear whether the second ground would work in such a case (the first ground might as the child clearly objected, bringing an application before the ECtHR). The provision could conceivably have been applied in some cases though (see, for example, French CA No 207DE2010, in Beaumont et al, 2016b, p 156).[79]

---

[79] See Beaumont, Walker and Holliday, above n 31, 312–3. Please consult the source to understand the shorthand citations in the quotation.

Christopher Bohez v Ingrid Wiertz[80] primarily concerned the interpretation of Articles 1 and 49 of Brussels I[81] and of Article 47(1) of Brussels IIa. It was referred to the CJEU in proceedings between Mr Bohez and Ms Wiertz concerning the enforcement in Finland of a penalty payment imposed by a decision given by a Belgian court in order to ensure compliance with the rights of access granted to Mr Bohez in respect of his children. The CJEU stated that Brussels I's scope was limited to 'civil and commercial matters' determined essentially according to the factors characterising the nature of the legal relationships between the parties to the action or the subject matter of the action. Regarding interim measures, the CJEU noted that this was determined not by their own nature but by the nature of the rights that they served to protect. It considered that the penalty payment in question was ancillary to the principal obligation which served to protect a right not falling within the scope of Brussels I, but rather within that of Brussels IIa. The CJEU held that Article 1 of Brussels I must be interpreted as meaning that that Regulation did not apply to the enforcement in a Member State of a penalty payment which was imposed in a judgment, given in another Member State, concerning rights of custody and rights of access in order to ensure that the holder of the rights of custody complied with those rights of access. In relation to Brussels IIa, the CJEU held that a penalty which the court of the Member State of origin, that gave judgment on the merits with regard to rights of access, had imposed in order to ensure the effectiveness of those rights, formed part of the same scheme of enforcement as the judgment concerning the rights of access. Therefore, the penalty must be declared enforceable in accordance with the rules laid down by Brussels IIa but only if the amount of the payment has been finally determined by the courts of the Member State of origin. The judgment was given in 20 months.

The First Chamber, following the advice of AG Szpunar, decided in *Bohez* to apply Article 49 of Brussels I to Brussels IIa by analogy on the ground that the legislature had not properly considered how to deal with penalty payments in relation to access orders when agreeing on Brussels IIa. As a matter of principle on a sensitive issue like 'actual enforcement' of judgments the CJEU should not have ruled that the matter is governed by Brussels IIa unless that Regulation expressly provided that this is the case. In the absence of such an express transfer of power over enforcement, from the national law of the State of enforcement to the national law of the State granting access, the CJEU should have ruled that the matter remained governed by the former.

D. Cooperation between Central Authorities in Matters of Parental Responsibility (Articles 53–58)

In *Health Service Executive*,[82] one of the questions that the CJEU dealt with was whether, where a judgment providing for the placement of a child for a specified time in residential care in another Member State is renewed for a further specified time, the Article 56 consent of the other Member State must be obtained upon the occasion of each renewal, and whether

---

[80] Case C-4/14 *Christopher Bohez v Ingrid Wiertz* EU:C:2015:563 (First Chamber).
[81] Brussels Ia Reg Art 55.
[82] See *Health Service Executive*, above n 6.

the judgment must be declared enforceable in that other Member State upon the occasion of each renewal. The CJEU held that where consent to placement under Article 56(2) had been given for a specified period of time, it did not apply to orders extending the duration of the placement. A judgment on placement made in a Member State, declared to be enforceable in another Member State, could be enforced in that other Member State only for the period stated in the judgment on placement.

The Irish High Court, in *Health Service Executive*, requested that this case be dealt with by the CJEU under the urgent procedure and its request was granted. This meant the CJEU gave a ruling in under 10 weeks. The CJEU noted that Article 56(3) gives discretion to Member States as to which body is competent to give consent to the placement of a child from another Member State in a secure institution but as 'a general rule' it must be an 'authority governed by public law'[83] and cannot be an institution 'which admits children in return for payment'.[84] In this case the UK secure care institution that gave the consent was managed by the local authority and therefore the consent was validly given under Article 56.[85] This was only clarified due to the UK Government intervening in the hearing and such Member State interventions by the States involved are strongly to be welcomed even in the urgent procedure. Whilst waiting for the declaration of enforceability to be granted in the State where the child is being placed in a secure institution, the child can be protected by the courts in that State putting in place protective measures under Article 20 of Brussels IIa.[86]

III. Maintenance Regulation

The EUPILLAR dataset includes two cases concerning the Maintenance Regulation.

Joined cases *Sophia Marie Nicole Sanders v David Verhaegen* and *Barbara Huber v Manfred Huber*,[87] the first preliminary ruling request that the CJEU received on maintenance, concerned the interpretation of Article 3(a) and (b). Both cases were maintenance claims brought before the applicant's local court for her place of residence in Germany against a debtor resident in Belgium and Barbados respectively. Two German courts referred the two cases to the CJEU. They were concerned that the German implementing legislation for the Maintenance Regulation had incorrectly decided that the court of the habitual residence would be the court of first instance (Amtsgericht) which has jurisdiction for the seat of the Regional Court of Appeal (Oberlandesgericht). So, in the two cases the maintenance creditors had to bring their cases in Düsseldorf rather than Mettmann and in Karlsruhe rather than Kiehl. In the first case the distance is 25 km (20 minutes by train) and in the second case the distance is 75km (55 minutes by train). The CJEU joined the cases and considered Article 3(b) as only this provision was relevant to the present case, ie the

---

[83] ibid, para 84.
[84] ibid, para 88.
[85] ibid, para 94.
[86] ibid, paras 130–32.
[87] Cases C-400/13 *Sophia Marie Nicole Sanders v David Verhaegen* and C-408/13 *Barbara Huber v Manfred Huber* EU:C:2014:2461 (Third Chamber).

legal proceedings were brought against the debtor by the maintenance creditor before the court for the creditor's place of habitual residence. The CJEU noted that Article 3(b), which conferred jurisdiction on 'the place where the creditor is habitually resident', determined both international and territorial jurisdiction. Consequently, it found that the correct interpretation of Article 3(b) is that it precludes national legislation which establishes a centralisation of judicial jurisdiction in matters relating to cross-border maintenance obligations in favour of a first instance court which has jurisdiction for the seat of the appeal court. It underlined that the only exception is where that rule helps to attain the objective of a proper administration of justice and protects the interests of maintenance creditors while promoting the effective recovery of such claims. It added that it is for the referring court to verify whether the exception applies.

This guidance provided by the CJEU appears to be rather vague. Indeed, there remains significant scope for subjective considerations as to whether the exception of 'achieving the objective of a proper administration of justice and protecting the interests of maintenance creditors while promoting the effective recovery of such claims' applies.

The judgment is not in line with the Opinion of AG Jääskinen.[88] The AG focused on the fact that Article 3(b) of the Maintenance Regulation centred on 'the court for the place where the creditor is habitually resident' and suggested to the CJEU that this should be the local court where the maintenance creditor resides. The AG rejected any notion of centralisation of jurisdiction (argued by Germany and the EU Commission) to create specialisation for practitioners and judges and thereby improve the 'proper administration of justice'. He elevated 'protection of the weaker party' and 'proximity' to the top of the goals of the Regulation. The CJEU was more balanced in finding that a) 'proximity' is one of the objectives of the Regulation;[89] b) the 'interests of maintenance creditors' and 'proper administration of justice' are the other objectives;[90] and c) all three objectives can be promoted by a degree of centralisation.[91] However, at that point the CJEU lost its way. In paragraphs 46 and 47, it suggested that it was for the national courts to decide whether the centralisation of jurisdiction in the German legislation was lawful. It did not indicate any kind of presumption that the German legislature's balancing of the objectives of the Maintenance Regulation should be respected unless clearly wrong. Rather, in the ruling it starts with the idea that centralisation of jurisdiction is wrong 'except where [it] helps to achieve the objective of a proper administration of justice and protects the interests of maintenance creditors while promoting the effective recovery of such claims, which is, however, *a matter for the referring courts to verify*.'[92] It is hoped that common sense and subsidiarity will prevail. The will of the German legislature should be respected by the German courts because 'specialisation' brought about by 'concentration' of jurisdiction is a good thing in international family law. The distance for maintenance creditors to travel is not huge and well within the discretion of the national legislature. Indeed, in many other countries the nearest local court would be further than 45 miles away anyway (eg the distance to the nearest sheriff court in the Highlands in Scotland could be longer).

---

[88] See Opinion of Advocate General Jääskinen, 4 September 2014, EU:C:2014:2171.
[89] See *Sanders v Verhaegen and Huber v Huber*, above n 87, para 40.
[90] ibid, para 44.
[91] ibid, paras 44 and 45.
[92] Emphasis added.

C-184/14 *A v B*[93] on the interpretation of Article 3(c) and (d) of the Maintenance Regulation was referred to the CJEU in Italian proceedings concerning an application filed in Italy relating to maintenance obligations in respect of the parties' two minor children habitually resident in England and Wales, concurrently with proceedings for the parents' legal separation. AG Bot was of the opinion that the Italian courts did have jurisdiction to rule on child maintenance issues as an 'ancillary matter' in a legal separation case under Article 3(c) of the Maintenance Regulation.[94] However, for reasons of compliance with the EU Charter of Fundamental Rights,[95] to secure the best interests of the child consistent with the principle of 'proximity', AG Bot stated that the Italian courts must decline jurisdiction in favour of the courts of the habitual residence of the children (the English courts in this case).[96] This is a surprising interpretation of the Maintenance Regulation because it does not create any space for a system of 'declining' to exercise jurisdiction. The Third Chamber found a more convincing legal route to arrive at its judgment by focusing on what constitutes 'ancillary matters' under Article 3(c) and (d). It said that 'ancillary matter' must be given an autonomous and uniform interpretation throughout the EU.[97] Influenced by the fact that the courts of the habitual residence of the child are better placed to tailor child support to the custody/access arrangements they make,[98] the CJEU decided that where one court in the EU is seised of divorce or legal separation issues and another court in the EU is seised of parental responsibility issues then it is only the latter proceedings in which child maintenance issues are an 'ancillary matter'. The CJEU did not decide that the courts with jurisdiction to deal with divorce or legal separation can never deal with child maintenance as an 'ancillary matter'. This interpretation means that if one of the parents brings an action for parental responsibility in the courts of the habitual residence of the child, then the divorce/separation court cannot deal with child maintenance as an 'ancillary matter'. Does that encourage a parent to thwart the divorce/separation proceedings on child maintenance at the last minute before judgment by bringing parental responsibility proceedings in the court of habitual residence? Only if that parent contested the jurisdiction from the first stage in the proceedings, otherwise that parent is caught by submission.[99] It is good from the point of view of legal efficiency and party autonomy that the divorce court can still deal with spousal and child support where the parties are content for all these matters to be decided in that court.

IV. Conclusion

The CJEU has done very well to deal with urgent cases (PPU) swiftly and accurately within two to three months of receiving them. This is a testament to the dedication and skill of the Legal Secretaries, Advocate Generals and Judges who have been involved in those cases.

---

[93] Case C-184/14 *A v B* EU:C:2015:479 (Third Chamber).
[94] See Opinion of Advocate General Bot, EU:C:2015:244.
[95] [2012] OJ C 326/391.
[96] See above n 94, para 64.
[97] See above n 93, para 31.
[98] ibid para 43.
[99] See Art 5 of the Maintenance Reg.

Generally, the CJEU has interpreted the Brussels IIa cases very well. There are only a few particularly strong examples of good interpretation taking proper account of the international context of Brussels IIa (many of its provisions owe their origins to the 1996 Hague Children Protection Convention and can be understood better by reading the *travaux préparatoires* on that Convention, notably the Lagarde Report)[100] and promoting the enhanced party autonomy allowed by Brussels IIa: C-256/09 *Purrucker* and *Matoušková*.

There are several cases (about a quarter of the cases on Brussels IIa and Maintenance) where we disagree with the CJEU's interpretation: *Detiček, Zarraga, Povse, Bohez, C v M* and *Sanders and Huber*.

In only two cases do we believe that the AG's View should have been given more weight, *C v M* and *Bradbrooke*, and in only three cases do we think the AG should have done significantly better in his View, *Zarraga, Sanders and Huber* and *A v B*. In one other case the advice given by the CJEU that the Article 11(8) Brussels IIa override system could have been used in that case is not convincingly demonstrated in the judgment and seems impossible from the AG's View (*P v Q*). The fact that AG's Views are published in PPU cases is greatly to be welcomed after the bad start by the CJEU in this matter in the *Rinau* case.

The CJEU's interpretations should be modified or reversed in relation to several cases if the Council adopts the Commission's Recast Proposal in relation to Brussels IIa (*Povse* and *Zarraga*). The purely internal effect of protective measures in parental responsibility cases because of the weakness of Article 20 of Brussels IIa, highlighted in *Purrucker*, will be reduced if the Commission's Proposal is successful. It is a pity that a transfer provision has not been put forward for divorce proceedings in the Commission's Brussels IIa Proposal. Such a provision could minimise the harm from the race to the court illustrated by the facts in *A v B*.

---

[100] Lagarde, above n 9.

42

Habitual Residence: The Factors that Courts Consider

THALIA KRUGER

I. Introduction

Habitual residence is an important basis of jurisdiction and connecting factor for applicable law in the Regulations that were the subject of EUPILLAR's work. It transpires from the national reports that giving content to this concept, based on the facts of the different cases, is an issue that often arises before the courts.

The Hague Conference on Private International law has often used 'habitual residence' as a connecting factor in its conventions. The Conference deliberately chose a concept that is not burdened by legal technicalities but dependent upon fact.[1] The European Union (EU) legislator has followed this approach in its Regulations in the field of Private International Law.[2]

This chapter will consider the Regulations that were analysed in the EUPILLAR project: Brussels I, Brussels IIa, Maintenance, Rome I and Rome II. All these Regulations use the concept of habitual residence to a greater or lesser extent.[3] Rome III and the Succession Regulation were outside the scope of EUPILLAR's work. While this chapter will not contain case law on these two Regulations, they are relevant for some of the discussions.

---

[1] L Collins (ed), *Dicey, Morris and Collins on The Conflict of Laws* 14th edn (London, Sweet & Maxwell, 2006) 168; SI Winter, 'Home is where the Heart is: Determining "Habitual Residence" under the Hague Convention on the Civil Aspects of International Child Abduction' [2010] *Washington University Journal of Law and Policy* 351 at 355.

[2] Collins, ibid at 168; A Briggs, *Private International Law in English Courts* (Oxford, Oxford University Press, 2014) 76.

[3] Brussels Ia uses 'habitual residence' in Art 15 on insurance, Art 19 on consumers, and Art 72 on the continued use of older conventions on the enforcement of judgments from third States. Art 21 on employment contracts uses the concept of habitually carrying out work, which is an entirely different notion. Brussels IIa uses 'habitual residence' more frequently: in recitals 12, 17 and 18 and in Art 2 in the definitions of 'rights of access' and 'wrongful removal or retention', Art 3, 6 and 7 on jurisdiction in divorce and marriage annulment, Arts 8–13 on jurisdiction in matters of parental responsibility, Art 15 on transfer of jurisdiction, Art 18 on the examination of admissibility, Art 23 on grounds for non-recognition of judgments in parental responsibility matters, Art 29 on the jurisdiction of local courts, Art 33 on the appeal against a decision of enforceability, Art 42 on the enforcement of return decisions, Art 51 on security, bonds and deposits, Art 57 on the working method of central authorities, Art 61 on the relationship with the Hague Child Protection Convention of 1996, and Art 66 on Member States with more than one legal system.

The comparison of case law in this chapter is based on the national reports as published in this book. In many instances the original material was not available to the author or not accessible in an understandable language. The chapter focuses on the law in the EU. There have been interesting developments in the case law of the US (especially the circuit courts), but that falls outside the ambit of this chapter.[4]

II. The Autonomous Interpretation of a Factual Concept

As a starting point, concepts in EU law have an autonomous interpretation. In the case of habitual residence, one cannot really speak of a 'definition', but rather of the way in which the concept is used. This autonomous interpretation, based on facts, is the same as in the Hague Conventions.[5] Habitual residence is factual and should not be tied to legalistic concepts.[6] None of the Regulations studied in EUPILLAR contain a comprehensive definition of habitual residence. Such definition would indeed deprive the concept of its essential factual nature. The Rome I and II Regulations do contain some explanation of habitual residence, especially for legal persons.[7] The Succession Regulation, however, contains a set of factors which courts can take into account when assessing habitual residence.[8] This is useful in a context where the person whose habitual residence is at stake is deceased.

The Maintenance Reg uses the term in recitals 15, 17 and 32, Art 3 containing the general rule on jurisdiction, Art 4 on choice of court, Art 8 on limits to proceedings in respect of States party to the Hague Maintenance Convention of 2007, Art 11 on the examination of admissibility, Art 27 on the jurisdiction of local courts, Art 32 on the appeal against a declaration of enforceability, and Art 45(d) on legal aid and costs.

Rome I makes use of 'habitual residence' as its main connecting factor. It is present in recitals 19, 21, 25, 28, 39, Art 4 on the applicable law in the absence of choice, Art 5 on carriage contracts, Art 6 on consumer contracts, Art 7 on insurance contracts, Art 10 on material validity, Art 11 on formal validity, and Art 19 containing a definition of habitual residence. Here again Art 8 on employment contracts uses the idea of habitually carrying out work.

In Rome II 'habitual residence' is not the main connecting factor as in Rome I, but has an important subsidiary place. It is employed in recitals 18, 20, 33, Art 4 containing the general rule, Art 5 on product liability, Art 9 on industrial action, Art 10 on unjust enrichment, Art 11 on *negotiorum gestio*, Art 12 on *culpa in contrahendo*, and Art 23 containing a definition of habitual residence.

[4] See G Zohar, 'Habitual Residence: An Alternative to the Common Law Concept of Domicile' (2009–10) 9 *Whittier Journal of Child & Family Advocacy* 169; A Weiner, 'Home is Where the Heart is: Determining the Standard for Habitual Residence under the Hague Convention based on a Child-centric Approach' (2014–15) 11 *Seton Hall Circuit Review* 454. T Heine, 'Home State, Cross-border Custody, and Habitual Residence Jurisdiction: Time for a Temporal Standard in International Family Law' (2011) 17 *Annual Survey of International and Comparative Law* 9 discusses both US and European case law. E Gallagher, 'A House is Not (Necessarily) a Home: a Discussion of the Common Approach to Habitual residence' (2014–15) 47 *New York University Journal of International Law and Policy* 463 compares Canadian, US and English cases.

[5] This was correctly confirmed by the judgment of the Finnish Supreme Court of 17 November 2008, KKO 2008:98; see ch 16 above.

[6] In *Re J (a minor) (Abduction: Custody Rights)* [1990] 2 AC 562 Lord Brandon of Oakbrook stated that 'the expression is not to be treated as a term of art with some special meaning, but is rather to be understood according to the ordinary and natural meaning of the two words which it contains.' See also *In the matter of A (Children)* [2013] UKSC 60.

[7] Art 19 Rome I; Art 23 Rome II. This is discussed in more detail below.

[8] Recitals 23–24 Succession Reg No 650/2012 [2012] OJ L201/107. See also I Rohová and K Drlicková, 'Habitual Residence As A Single Connecting Factor Under The Succession Regulation' (2015) 1 *International Journal of Law and Politics* 107–17.

The European Court of Justice has given guidance in the fields of social security and parental responsibility.[9] National courts have to follow the interpretations given by the Court of Justice, even though 'habitual residence' has to be determined on the basis of the facts of each individual case. There is a certain degree of tension between the factual nature of the concept and the guidance that the Court of Justice has given and which national courts have to follow.[10] The courts generally seem to follow this factual approach and autonomous interpretation.[11]

This concept is different from the more formal 'domicile'. This is indeed a concept that is burdened by legal technicalities, exactly of the kind that the Hague Conference and European Union legislator aimed to avoid. In some countries the difference is stark. For instance in Belgium, 'domicile' means the formal place where a person has his or her registered address in the population register. 'Habitual residence' on the other hand is a factual concept for which various circumstances are taken into account. This distinction is also clearly made in the Belgian Code on Private International Law.[12] In other countries confusion arises and the terms are used interchangeably. Bulgarian law does not contain a definition of 'domicile'. This has led to an inconsistent approach: some courts use the permanent address, others the current address and some use the definition of 'habitual residence' taken from their domestic law. The Regulations require courts to use their national law to determine domicile.[13] The authors of the Bulgarian report in this book suggest that there is a need for national legislation or an interpretative decision by the Supreme Court on the issue. This should clarify that the terms domicile and habitual residence have distinct meanings.[14] Polish courts sometimes misinterpret the concept of 'habitual residence' as being equal to that of the permanent residence.[15] The reporters however indicate that the awareness of the autonomous interpretation is growing in the Polish courts. A Finnish case provides a good example of the use of an autonomous definition. Both spouses were domiciled (in the sense of formally resident) in Helsinki, but neither of them had their habitual residence there. The court considered the habitual residence to be in Cyprus and decided it did not have jurisdiction on the basis of Brussels IIa.[16]

There are two more observations that should be made about the autonomous interpretation of the factual concept in national courts.

The first concerns the relationship between the approach to 'habitual residence' in EU law and in national law. When the concept of 'habitual residence' is used in national law, courts are not bound by the interpretations of the Court of Justice. However, it does not make sense to use different approaches to habitual residence under EU and national law.[17] National courts are influenced by interpretations by the Court of Justice and give the same meaning to the term whether applying a Regulation, Convention or domestic law.

---

[9] Discussed in more detail in sections III and V below.

[10] See on this tension Briggs above n 2 at 76–79.

[11] *Director of Department for Social Welfare Standards v Sharon Rose Roche*, Malta Court of Appeal (17 May 2016), as quoted in ch 24 above.

[12] Art 4 Belgian Code on Private International Law (2004).

[13] Art 59 Brussels I; Art 63 Brussels Ia.

[14] See ch 12 above.

[15] See ch 10 above.

[16] Helsinki Court of Appeal on 8 June 2012, Case S12/750, quoted in ch 16 above.

[17] Briggs, above n 2 at 78.

The United Kingdom Supreme Court has found in *A v A* that it was highly desirable that the same test be adopted for all these cases.[18]

Second, the interpretation of this factual concept by the courts of various Member States should not diverge, even though this is sometimes the case.[19] Even if courts acknowledge the factual nature of the concept, the interpretation in particular cases can cause difficulties.[20] The solution to the question as to how to deal with divergent case law is not by adding definitions about the concept in EU legislation. Rather, it is finding the factors that courts have used and that have been helpful. It is only through a comparative analysis and publication of case law on the concept of 'habitual residence' that we can prevent divergent interpretations.

III. Habitual Residence of Adults

The habitual residence of an adult is the place where he or she has the centre of his or her interests.[21] The Court of Justice of the EU has not yet had the opportunity to rule on the concept of the 'habitual residence' of adults in the field of private international law. However, we do find guidance in case law from other fields, especially staff cases.[22] In these cases the Court of First Instance, the Civil Service Tribunal, and on appeal the Court of Justice have had to consider the habitual residence of EU officials. Their habitual residence elsewhere than the place where they work for an EU institution determines their right to an expatriation allowance. The Court has held that

> the place of habitual residence is that in which the official concerned has established, with the intention that it should be of a lasting character, the permanent or habitual centre of his interests. However, for the purposes of determining habitual residence, all the factual circumstances which constitute such residence must be taken into account.[23]

Similarly, in social security cases, the Court of Justice has defined habitual residence as the 'habitual centre of their interests.' It added:

> In that context, account should be taken in particular of the employed person's family situation; the reasons which have led him to move; the length and continuity of his residence; the

---

[18] *A v A and another (Children: Habitual Residence) (Reunite International Child Abduction Centre intervening)* [2013] UKSC 60 at paras 35 and 54.

[19] See ch 9 above.

[20] See ch 29 above, in which the author mentions the interpretation of habitual residence as one of the issues with which courts have the most problems in the application of Brussels IIa.

[21] Report on the Brussels II Convention by A Borrás; *L-K v K* [2007] EWHC 3202; *Marinos v Marinos* [2007] EWHC 2047 (Fam); *O'K v A* [2008] IEHC 243; *Williamson v Williamson*, Sheriff Court (Tayside, Central and Fife) (Kirkcaldy) [2009] Fam LR 44, [2009] *G.W.D.* 14–220, [2009] ScotSC 18 (Sheriff AG McCulloch). See also chs 5 and 20 above.

[22] Advocate General Kokott in her Opinion for the CJEU case C-523/07, *A*, EU:C:2009:39 stated at paras 34–36 that it is not appropriate to transpose this case law when assessing the habitual residence of a child. In her view the family law context was different. This is certainly true for children. However, the guidance can be useful if not directly applicable to the habitual residence of adults in family disputes.

[23] Case C-452/93P *Magdalena Fernández v Commission of the European Communities*, EU:C:1994:332 at para 22; see also the judgments in this field by the Court of First Instance: T-60/00 *Liaskou v Council of the European Union*, EU:T:2001:129 at para 53; T-298/02, *Herrero Romeu v Commission of the European Communities*, EU:T:2005:369 at para 51; and by the Civil Service Tribunal: F-129/06, *Salvador Roldán v Commission of the European Communities*, EU:F:2007:166 at para 48; F-33/09 *Tzvetanova v European Commission*, EU:F:2010:18 at para 39; and F-6/12 *Bourtembourg v European Commission*, EU:F:2012:175 at para 28.

fact (where this is the case) that he is in stable employment; and his intention as it appears from all the circumstances.[24]

This judgment and others in this field are useful for several reasons. First, they deal with the concept specifically with respect to adults. The Court of Justice has ruled on the 'habitual residence' of children, but as will become apparent in the discussion of various cases below, the factors for children and adults cannot be entirely equated. Second, in the staff cases, the Court of Justice and the Civil Service Tribunal apply the law to the facts rather than giving only an interpretation of the law and leaving it to national courts to apply it to the facts.

The reference to 'centre of interests' is useful. This entails a mix between objective and intentional elements.[25] However, the EU courts seem to place more weight on the intention of adults: they are independent agents who organise their lives as they wish. The place of exercising a profession is an important indicator of the habitual residence of an adult.[26] Linked to this, the EU Civil Service Tribunal has considered the place where a person pays national insurance contributions and taxes as relevant.[27] The address that a person uses for professional contacts is also relevant.[28] Even secondary work is a relevant factor.[29] Temporary employment does not indicate a person's intention to permanently move the centre of his or her interests to this place.[30] The Civil Service Tribunal has also held that the fact of having many family members and relatives in a place does not in itself prove the establishment of a habitual residence.[31] Maintaining contact with family members and relatives in one's native country is considered normal and not an indication that a person has maintained his or her habitual residence there.[32] This is a nuanced difference from the situation of children, for whom the location of family, certainly the family members on which they are dependent, might be of greater pertinence in the finding of their habitual residence (see section V below).

Registration at a particular municipality may indicate a person's intention to move the centre of his or her interests to this place, but such registration may also be the result of other motives.[33] If for instance a person made such registration for purposes of entry to the European Union, it would not serve to indicate an intention of habitual residence.[34] Similarly, retaining registration in a municipality might indicate that the person did not have the intention to move the centre of his or her interests away from this place.[35] The Court has also held that the place of origin is in itself not relevant to establish a person's habitual residence. Rather, it took into account the duration of the stay and other factual circumstances.[36]

---

[24] Case C-90/97, *Swaddling v Adjudication Officer*, EU:C:1999:96 at para 29.

[25] F-129/06, above n 23 at para 56 the Civil Service Tribunal states that 'the concept of residence implies, irrespective of the purely quantitative element of the time spent by the person in a particular country, not only the actual fact of living in a given place, but also the intention of thereby achieving the continuity which stems from a stable way of life and from the course of normal social relations.'

[26] T-298/02, above n 23 at paras 54–58; F-6/12, above n 23 at para 39.

[27] F-129/06, above n 23 at para 51.

[28] ibid at para 52.

[29] T-60/00, above n 23 at para 60.

[30] F-6/12, above n 23 at para 40.

[31] ibid at para 38.

[32] T-60/00, above n 23 at para 64.

[33] F-6/12, above n 23 at paras 42–43.

[34] F-33/09, above n 23 at para 56.

[35] F-120/05, *Kyriazis v Commission of the European Communities*, EU:F:2007:202 at para 53.

[36] Case 201/88 *Palmerini v Commission of the European Communities*, EU:C:1989:365.

The Court does not seem to attach great importance to nationality, although it has admitted that this can be a relevant element.[37] However, when a person obtains an EU nationality for the purpose of having access to free movement, this cannot be seen as an intention to establish a habitual residence in the country of the new nationality.[38] Retaining ties in a country of citizenship, such as car registration, participation in elections, bank accounts, life assurance policies, medical treatment and ownership of property does not necessarily indicate a habitual residence in that State.[39] A brief period of absence would not lead to the person losing his or her habitual residence.[40] On the other hand, a sole intention not matched by the objective reality is insufficient to establish a habitual residence.[41] The intention to leave a particular country is not relevant if this intention was never put into practice.[42] In the same vein, searching for a job in a particular country does not make one habitually resident there.[43] It can, however, be relevant to indicate that the person did not wish to establish the centre of his or her interests in the place where he or she was (ie a place other than where he or she was searching for employment).[44] Studying somewhere does not per se indicate an intention to move the centre of one's interests,[45] although this is a relevant element.[46] Moreover, such intention might manifest from the fact of staying in the country of studies after completion thereof.[47] Ownership of or having at one's disposal immovable property is relevant.[48]

Some national courts have used the Court of Justice of the European Union (CJEU)'s case law on the habitual residence of children as a guideline for finding the habitual residence of adults in family law matters. English courts have turned to the CJEU case law on the habitual residence of adults outside the scope of Brussels IIa. They have, however, indicated that employment cases focus on a different element than cases on divorce.[49] For employment cases, of course the place of employment plays an important role, while the centre of a person's family life (relevant in divorce cases) does not necessarily correspond with his or her place of employment. The Italian Court of Cassation in a divorce case for instance referred to 'the place where the person has established, on a fixed basis, his permanent habitual centre of interests and where he or she carries out most of his or her personal and eventually professional life'.[50] In coming to this conclusion, the court considered the intention of the person, and whether he considered the move to be permanent or temporary, as a non-essential element in the assessment.[51] Although it is

---

[37] F-114/12, *Jelenkowska-Luca v European Commission*, EU:F:2014:3 at para 26.
[38] ibid.
[39] T-60/00 above n 23 at para 63; T-298/02, above n 23 at paras 59–61; F-129/06, above n 23 at para 59.
[40] *ABC v DE*, Civil Court (Family Section) (30 June 2015), as quoted in ch 24 above.
[41] F-28/10 *Mioni v European Commission*, EU:F:2011:23 at para 29 (this judgment was confirmed on appeal: T-274/11, EU:T:2011:719.)
[42] F-120/05, above n 35 at para 55.
[43] ibid at para 56.
[44] F-33/09, above n 23 at para 53.
[45] ibid at paras 49–50; Case 201/88 *Palmerini v Commission of the European Communities*, EU:C:1989:365 at para 11; F-114/12 *Jelenkowska-Luca v European Commission*, EU:F:2014:3 at para 25; F-61/15 *Proia v European Commission*, EU:F:2016:2 at paras 49–50.
[46] T-60/00 above n 23 at para 55.
[47] F-33/09, above n 23 at paras 49–50; Case 201/88 above n 45 at para 11.
[48] F-120/05, above n 35 at para 50; F-129/06, above n 23 at para 50; F-61/15 above n 45 at paras 55–56.
[49] *Marinos v Marinos* [2007] EWHC 2047 (Fam).
[50] Corte di Cassazione Sezioni unite, No 3680 of 17 February 2010; Corte di Cassazione Sezioni Unite, No 15328 of 25 June 2010; as quoted in ch 8 above.
[51] ibid.

difficult to transpose to adults the factors that the CJEU has identified as relevant to children, intention should indeed be *an* element. Probably intention should play a more important role in disputes about adults than in disputes about children, because in the case of children it is not their own intentions that are at stake but those of the persons upon whom they are dependent.[52] Adults, on the other hand, are free actors and can follow their own intentions to a larger degree. The Dutch courts have also sought inspiration from the CJEU cases about children's habitual residence.[53] In Bulgaria, when assessing the habitual residence of adults in order to determine jurisdiction for divorce, courts analyse the relevant facts comprehensively.[54] The England and Wales High Court has explained that considering the factors requires a qualitative rather than a quantitative assessment.[55]

The Family Division of the England and Wales High Court has struggled with the question of whether an adult can under Brussels IIa have two habitual residences simultaneously.[56] Again the Court took caution to interpret the Regulation autonomously and not to follow the situation under English law.[57] The Court came to the conclusion that the Brussels IIa Regulation allows only one habitual residence at any given time. However, it is possible to be habitually resident in one State and resident in another State at the same time.

A Portuguese court established a person's residence on the basis of the place of service instead of seeking the habitual residence (in a divorce case).[58] This does not seem a sufficient factor.[59] Table 1 shows factors considered relevant and irrelevant in national case law for the determination of the habitual residence of adults.

Table 1:

Factors considered relevant in national case law:
— Certificate of residence (Italy)
— Residence permit (Italy)
— Tax returns (Italy, Belgium, Scotland)
— Medical care (Belgium and Scotland)
— Social integration, including friends, language skills (Scotland)
— Ownership of immovable property (Belgium and Scotland)
— Ownership of a car (Scotland)
Factors not considered relevant in national case law:
— Fact that person worked at Embassy (Finland)

[52] See s V below.
[53] See ch 25 above.
[54] See ch 12 above.
[55] *Marinos v Marinos* [2007] EWHC 2047 (Fam) at para 56.
[56] ibid, followed on this point in *Munro v Munro* [2007] EWHC 3315 at para 47 (Fam); and *V v V* [2011] EWHC 1190 (Fam).
[57] Under English law the Court of Appeal has ruled that a person can be simultaneously habitually resident in more than one place: *Ikimi v Ikimi* [2001] EWCA Civ 873.
[58] TRC 28-06-2011 Case 255/09.5TBFZZ.C1, discussed in ch 26 above.
[59] See ch 26 above where the authors criticise the approach of the court.

Article 3(1)(a), fifth indent of the Brussels IIa Regulation has led to some confusion: it refers to the habitual residence of the plaintiff if he or she has resided there for at least six months. The question is whether this refers to a different standard than the 'habitual residence'.[60] The English courts have dealt with this question several times, but the uncertainty is not yet entirely cleared up.[61] The Family Division of the High Court of England and Wales in *Marinos v Marinos*[62] and *V v V*[63] took the view that the word 'residence' did in fact refer to something different from 'habitual residence'. To come to this conclusion the judges relied on the literal wording of the provision, indicating that if the legislator had meant 'habitual residence' it would have used that wording. In *Munro v Munro*[64] the Family Division took a different view. Bennett J relied heavily on the purpose of the provision, as explained in the Borrás Report.[65] In all these cases, though, the conclusion would have been the same on both interpretations. Finally, the Court of Appeal of England and Wales addressed the issue, but did not rule on it, as it was not considered necessary in the case.[66] Interestingly, Aikens J introduced a third possible reading of the provision: 'residence' of the required time proves habitual residence at the timing of instituting the proceedings.[67] The question has not been solved and conceivably it could remain so for some time, as cases in which residence can be proved for the relevant period but habitual residence cannot, are rare.

IV. Habitual Residence of Legal Persons

Also on the concept of the habitual residence of legal persons there is no guidance as yet from the Court of Justice of the EU. Rome I and Rome II provide some assistance.[68] Rome I and II also provide that the habitual residence of a company can be at the place of the branch of the company.[69] This is the case if the contract was concluded in the course of the operations of a branch or if performance is the responsibility of the branch[70] or if the event giving rise to the damage or the damage occurs in the course of operation of a branch.[71] Relevant factors to regard the place of the branch as the habitual residence of the company are the fact that the company had the obligation to and did in fact execute the performance, that the branch received payment in its bank at the place of the branch and it had a VAT number in that country.[72]

---

[60] See ch 8 above.

[61] On this topic, see also M Harding, *Conflict of Laws* 5th edn (Abingdon, Routledge, 2014) 26–29; P Rogerson, 'Habitual Residence: the New Domicile?' (2000) 49 *International and Comparative Law Quarterly* 86.

[62] [2007] EWHC 2047 (Fam).

[63] [2011] EWHC 1190 (Fam).

[64] *Munro v Munro* [2007] EWHC 3315 (Fam).

[65] At paras 50–53.

[66] *Tan v Choy* [2014] EWCA Civ 251.

[67] At para 30.

[68] Art 19(1) Rome I provides that the 'habitual residence of companies and other bodies, corporate or unincorporated, shall be the place of central administration. The habitual residence of a natural person acting in the course of his business activity shall be his principal place of business.' Art 23 Rome II contains the same provision.

[69] Art 19(2) Rome I; Art 23(1) Rome II.

[70] Art 19(2) Rome I.

[71] Art 23(1) Rome II.

[72] These elements have been used by the Maltese First Hall Civil Court: see ch 24 above.

V. Habitual Residence of Children

The Court of Justice of the EU has issued three judgments on the habitual residence of children in the field of private international law.[73] In these cases the Court set out factors that national courts should consider when determining the habitual residence of a child. In the first case, *A*, the Court set out a number of factors that courts should use to establish the habitual residence of a child. These are

> the duration, regularity, conditions and reasons for the stay on the territory of a Member State and the family's move to that State, the child's nationality, the place and conditions of attendance at school, linguistic knowledge and the family and social relationships of the child in that State.[74]

Looking at these factors, one detects a mix of objective and intentional elements, as for adults.[75] School and linguistic knowledge are clearly objective factors. The reasons for the stay incorporate an intention. It is important though that a mere intention is not sufficient to establish a habitual residence for a child. It must be borne in mind that the intention is not that of the child: most often the child cannot decide freely where to live.[76] The parents or persons responsible for the child decide. The objective reality plays a more important role than intention.[77]

This case law of the Court of Justice is well-known and used by national courts. However, in Bulgaria the approach varies: sometimes courts carry out a full analysis of the facts related to the child in order to establish his or her habitual residence and at other times they limit the discussion to a consideration of the child's permanent and current addresses.[78] English courts have adapted English law to be in line with the case law of the CJEU.[79] The UK Supreme Court has emphasised that habitual residence is a question of fact and not a legal concept,[80] in which the parents' intent plays only a limited role.[81] It is no longer considered a rigid rule that the habitual residence of a child cannot be changed absent joint parental intent.[82] The UK Supreme Court has also adopted a child-centred approach,

---

[73] Case C-523/07, *A*, EU:C:2009:225; Case C-497/10, *Mercredi v Chaffe*, EU:C:2010:829; Case C-376/14, *C v M*, EU:C:2014:2268. See also the discussion of these cases in ch 41 above.

[74] Case C-523/07, para 44 and 72.

[75] On this mix, see also R Lamont, 'Habitual Residence and Brussels II *bis*: Developing Concepts for European Private International Family Law' (2007) 3 *Journal of Private International Law* 261. See also R Schuz, 'Policy Considerations in Determining the Habitual Residence of a Child and the Relevance of Context' (2001) 11 *Journal of Transnational Law and Policy* 101; R Schuz, 'Case Commentary. Habitual Residence of the Child Revisited: a Trilogy of Cases in the UK Supreme Court' (2014) 26 *Child & Family Law Quarterly* 342; Heine, above n 4.

[76] See also *In the matter of A (Children)* [2013] UKSC 60 at para 38; Briggs, above n 2 at 82; Advocate General Kokott in her Opinion for C-523/07, *A*, EU:C:2009:39 at para 36.

[77] Finnish Supreme Court, 17 November 2008, KKO 2008:98, discussed in ch 16 above. In the US, the tension between objective and subjective factors is also clearly felt: Weiner, above n 4.

[78] See ch 12 above.

[79] See also P Torremans, A Mills, K Trimmings and C Heinze, Cheshire, North & Fawcett, *Private International Law* 15th edn (Oxford, Oxford University Press, 2017).

[80] *Re J (a minor) (Abduction: Custody Rights)* [1990] 2 AC 562; *In the matter of A (Children)* [2013] UKSC 60 at para 54.

[81] *KL (Abduction: Habitual Residence: Inherent Jurisdiction)* [2013] UKSC 75 at para 23; *AR v RN* [2015] UKSC 35 at para 17; *In the matter of B (A Child)* [2016] UKSC 4 at para 38.

[82] *AR v RN* [2015] UKSC 35 at para 17; *In the matter of B (A Child)* [2016] UKSC 4. See also D Hill, 'The Continuing Refinement of Habitual Residence: *R, Petitioner*' (2016) 20 *Edinburgh Law Review* 82 at 84. The matter is still alive in the US, where there is a circuit split: Weiner, above n 4; Heine, above n 4; Winter, above n 1.

looking at the children's views and their perception of reality.[83] One of the elements that should be considered is the duration of the stay. There is no cut and dried time that would be sufficient to establish a habitual residence for a child. An Austrian court has deemed six months sufficient, in combination with other factors.[84] Greek courts have found that a child can have a new habitual residence as of the day of the legal move.[85]

The situation of infants is not simple. The *Mercredi* case of the CJEU concerned the habitual residence of an infant who was a few months old. In this case the Court held that the same factors are relevant, but that the national court has to consider 'the family origins and the family and social connections' of the person of whom the infant is dependent.[86]

The French Court of Cassation has followed a different approach from the Court of Justice. It placed more emphasis on the common intention of the parents about where the child would be living.[87] The English courts have also struggled with this question.[88] Lady Hale was reluctant to find that an infant could have his habitual residence in a country where he has never physically been.[89] However, she refrained from ruling on this point, and also from referring the question to the CJEU, since the English courts would also have jurisdiction if the child were not habitually resident in England.[90] In a later case she said: 'The proposition ... that a young child in the sole lawful custody of his mother will necessarily have the same habitual residence as she does, is to be regarded as a helpful generalisation of fact, which will usually but not invariably be true, rather than a proposition of law'.[91]

Table 2 shows factors considered relevant and irrelevant in national case law for the determination of the habitual residence of children.

Table 2:

Relevant objective factors according to national case law:
— family ties (including with the parents)
— social ties (including language capabilities)
— duration
— school
— parental responsibility (sole or both parents) (Ireland)

(continued)

---

[83] *Re KL (Abduction: Habitual Residence: Inherent Jurisdiction)* [2013] UKSC 75; *In the matter of LC (Children)* [2014] UKSC 1. See also R Schuz, 'Case Commentary', above n 74.

[84] OGH 28 August 2014 no 6 Ob 116/14y; see ch 11 above.

[85] Athens FIC Case No 713/2015, Thessaloniki FIC Case No 13063/2015, Thessaloniki FIC Case No 22101/2011, Kavala FIC Case No 24/2009; see ch 18 above.

[86] Case C-497/10, *Mercredi v Chaffe*, EU:C:2010:829 at para 56 and in the operative part of the judgment (para 72).

[87] Fr Cass 26 October 2011 (première chambre civile). See also A Fiorini, 'The Habitual Residence and the Newborn—A French Perspective' (2012) 61 *International and Comparative Law Quarterly* 530.

[88] Fiorini, ibid 533–34.

[89] *In the matter of A (Children)* [2013] UKSC 60.

[90] On the basis of the residual jurisdiction, for which Art 14 Brussels IIa refers to national law, the English courts would have jurisdiction. See *In the matter of A (Children)* [2013] UKSC 60 at paras 59–76. See also Schuz 'Case Commentary', above n 74 at 350–53.

[91] *KL (Abduction: Habitual Residence: Inherent Jurisdiction)* [2013] UKSC 75 at para 21.

Table 2: *(Continued)*

— dependency of the child upon parents (Ireland)
— trips to country
Factors that are doubtful according to national case law:
— Serving documents (used by a Portuguese court, but criticised)
— legality (Austrian courts found this not to be relevant,[92] although the Court of Justice referred to the 'regularity' of the stay as a relevant factor);
— need for psychiatric treatment (used by a Finnish court)

A. Legality of Habitual Residence

The wrongful removal or retention of a child does not eliminate the jurisdiction of the courts of the habitual residence of the child before the abduction, unless the child has acquired a habitual residence in the new State and certain other conditions are met.[93] This does not mean that the habitual residence can never be established in the new country, even if the child was taken there illegally.[94] The Austrian courts have found the legality of the residence irrelevant.[95]

According to the case law of the Court of Justice of the EU, it is however not completely irrelevant. In *A* and *Mercredi* the Court found that the 'regularity' of the residence was relevant. The Court reiterated this in *C v M*.[96] In this case the CJEU ruled that the fact that the mother knew that the French judgment which had granted her permission to move to Ireland was subject to appeal and could be reversed (which it subsequently was) was a factor pointing away from the establishment of the child's habitual residence in Ireland. This, the Court said, is one of the factors that can be taken into account alongside the other factors specified in the earlier cases.[97] When this case returned to the Irish Supreme Court, it found that the child's habitual residence was in Ireland.[98] The Court took into account the pending French appeal at the time of the move, but also other relevant factors, such as the child's ties with her parents, her relatives in Ireland and her language capabilities.

In another Irish case, the Court of Appeal did attach weight to the fact that the father, who had parental authority according to French law, had not granted permission for the move.[99] The child was born in France and had previously lived there with both parents. The mother then took the child to Ireland. The father's intention was that the stay in Ireland would only be temporary, but when he ultimately requested the return of the child

---

[92] OGH 28 August 2014 no 6 Ob 116/14y and OGH 19 December 2012 no 6 Ob 217/12y; see chapter 11 above.

[93] Art 11 Brussels IIa and Art 7 Hague Child Protection Convention (1996).

[94] See for instance OGH 29 August 2013 no 1 Ob 136/13a; see ch 11 above.

[95] OGH 28 August 2014 no 6 Ob 116/14y and OGH 19 December 2012 no 6 Ob 217/12y; see ch 11 above.

[96] At para 52.

[97] At paras 55–56. For criticism of the CJEU ruling in this case, see P Beaumont and J Holiday, 'Recent Developments on the Meaning of "Habitual Residence" in Alleged Child Abduction Cases', Centre of Private International Law, University of Aberdeen Working Paper No 2015/3, available at www.abdn.ac.uk/law/research/working-papers-455.php.

[98] *G v G* [2015] IESC 12, discussed by Beaumont and Holliday, ibid and by M Harding in ch 20 above.

[99] *DE v EB* [2015] IECA 104 discussed by Harding, ibid.

to France, the mother argued that the child was habitually resident in Ireland. The Court of Appeal found that the child was habitually resident in France. In coming to this conclusion, the Court took account of all the circumstances related to the child, such as her social and family ties, and her trips back and forth. It also paid attention to the fact that the move to Ireland had happened without the consent of the father.

B. Dishonest Intentions

The Irish Appeal Court case discussed above shows a problem often encountered: that of the parent moving first temporarily and then making the move permanent. In this case it was quite clear from the facts that the mother had had the intention to stay in Ireland while she left the father under the impression that the stay was temporary. She had even resigned from her job in France without telling the father. Such a gradual move in order to change the habitual residence and then place the other parent before a *fait accompli* is problematic.

Similarly, parents can use mediation or settlement efforts dishonestly to allow for the passage of time and thus establish a new habitual residence.[100] Dishonest intentions should not be addressed by minimising the factual nature of the habitual residence criterion. Rather it is for practitioners and judges to be alert, especially in family law matters where proceedings must be swift and efficient. By acting with appropriate care and vigilance, practitioners and judges should not allow the passage of time to benefit a parent with dishonest intentions.

C. Dual Habitual Residence of Children?

A question that has come up in the assessment of the habitual residence of children is whether a child can simultaneously have more than one habitual residence. A Belgian first instance court has ruled that this is possible.[101] The case concerned children that lived alternately in Belgium and in Germany. The Finnish Supreme Administrative Court that had to apply the Court of Justice of the EU's ruling in *A* similarly found that the families lived in Finland and Sweden alternately.[102] The Finnish court then went further, taking into account the children's identity and social and cultural ties. It found that these were more closely connected to Finland. Interestingly, the Court also took into account the fact that the children needed psychiatric treatment in Finland (which would moreover be in Finnish). This was only one of the factors that lead the Finnish court to consider the habitual residence to be in Finland. Viewed on its own this factor can be doubtful: mutual trust would mean that courts have confidence that psychiatric care would be as good in Sweden as in Finland. Viewed in the light of all the circumstances, including the children's language abilities, this factor can be accepted as one among others. The court could also have issued provisional measures for treatment if the children were habitually resident in Sweden.

---

[100] See ch 7 above: 'settlement procedures sometimes seem to be protracted intentionally in order to establish a party's habitual residence.'
[101] See ch 6 above.
[102] 30 June 2009, KHO 2009:68; see ch 16 above.

D. Relevant Moment to Determine Habitual Residence

For children the habitual residence has to be determined as at the moment of the institution of the proceedings.[103] In child abduction cases, the relevant moment is immediately before the alleged wrongful removal or retention.[104] For adults, the moment can be different, for instance a previous habitual residence in divorce cases.[105] The Rome I and II Regulations do not mention a point in time. The problem with the time element for children is that circumstances might have changed between the institution of the proceedings and the time when the court (or even court of appeal) hears the case. This has led courts to also take into account factors that date from after the relevant moment.[106] On the other hand, some courts are careful to consider the pertinent moment when assessing the habitual residence.[107]

The Brussels IIa Regulation provides that the jurisdiction of the court where the child was habitually resident perpetuates.[108] This is different from the rule under the Hague Child Protection Convention, which provides for the loss of jurisdiction when the child's habitual residence changes.[109] The way in which courts deal with the issue under Brussels IIa is through the mechanism of the transfer of jurisdiction.[110] On this aspect, improvement might be on its way. The Commission's Proposal for the Recast of Brussels IIa removes the rule on perpetuation.[111] It does so by adding the words '[w]here a child moves lawfully from one Member State to another and acquires a new habitual residence there, the authorities of the Member State of the new habitual residence shall have jurisdiction' to the rule that the habitual residence determines jurisdiction.[112] (The Proposal retains the rule that a judgment on access rights can be amended within three months by the court of the former habitual residence.[113] This provisions only applies if there has been a judgment and if the dispute after the move concerns access rights: it therefore has a limited application.) The new wording would bring the Regulation in line with the Hague Child Protection Convention. It would also enhance the principle that courts close to the child should decide on the merits. Moreover, it would make it unnecessary in those cases for courts to revert to the mechanism of transfer to comply with the principle of proximity.

---

[103] Art 8 Brussels IIa.

[104] Art 11(1) Brussels IIa; Art 3a) Hague Child Abduction Convention (1980). The CJEU confirmed this moment in Case C-376/14 *C v M*, EU:C:2014:2268.

[105] Art 3 Brussels IIa; Art 8 Rome III.

[106] Ch 25 above specifically refers to courts that have done so. It is conceivable that this also happens in other countries, as the judges assess the facts in front of them.

[107] See for instance the Irish Appeal Court case of *DE v EB* [2015] IECA 104.

[108] Arts 8–10 Brussels IIa.

[109] Art 5(2) Hague Child Protection Convention (1996).

[110] Art 15 Brussels IIa. See chs 6 and 25 above.

[111] Proposal for a Council Reg on jurisdiction, the recognition and enforcement of decisions in matrimonial matters and the matters of parental responsibility, and on international child abduction (recast), COM(2016) 411, 30 June 2016.

[112] Art 7 of the Commission's Proposal. See also Recital 15 of the Proposal, clarifying that '[t]his should apply where no proceedings are yet pending, and also in pending proceedings.'

[113] Current Art 9 Brussels IIa; Art 8 of the Proposal.

VI. Conclusion

When assessing EU and national case law on 'habitual residence', the most important conclusion is that this is and remains a factual concept. It is possible to distil factors that courts use in order to make their assessment, but not to produce a perfect formula that will work in all cases. What the assessment does show is that both objective and subjective factors are of importance. For adults the subjective (or intentional) dimension plays a bigger role than for children. Adults can decide freely while children are physically and legally dependent on other persons. For adults their jobs and places where they pay taxes are important but not decisive. It is important to be conscious of the context in which habitual residence is being used, for instance in an employment dispute, or in a family dispute. In a family dispute (such as a divorce case), the centre of the family's interests is important, and these can be at a different place than the workplace. For children, objective elements such as the school are important. The intention of the bearers of parental responsibility is also relevant, but only as one of the factors amongst others. The factual situation and social and family integration of the person on whom the child is dependent is relevant in the case of infants.

It is encouraging to notice that the national judgments tend to follow the interpretations given by the Court of Justice of the EU. They do so also if the case law is different from previous constructions of 'habitual residence' under national law (as is seen clearly in the law in the UK). The result is the creation of a truly EU concept. Uniformity in this matter will reduce disputes about jurisdiction and enhance mutual trust at the recognition and enforcement stages. There are aspects which have not yet been crystallised. One of these is the question whether 'residence' in the fifth and sixth indents of Article 3(1)(a) of Brussels IIa has a different meaning to 'habitual residence'. Another is the extent to which manipulation (such as an apparent but dishonest promise to engage in mediation) can influence the habitual residence. Yet another is the question of whether a person (adult or child) can simultaneously have more than one residence. There have been national judgments on this issue, but they diverge. Moreover, it is not clear whether the answer should be the same for adults and for children.

Thus, there is more work to be done even though much has been done already.

43

No Deal Better than
a Bad Deal—Child Abduction
and the Brussels IIa Regulation

AGNIESZKA FRĄCKOWIAK-ADAMSKA

I. Introduction

International parental child abduction is regulated at the global level by the Convention of 25 October 1980 on the Civil Aspects of International Child Abduction[1] (the Hague Convention or Convention), which now has 97 Contracting States.[2] The Convention does not concern the merits of custody issues[3] but its aim is 'to establish procedures to ensure … prompt return [of abducted children] to the State of their habitual residence'.[4] It provides that the decision on the return is taken by the authority of a Contracting State to which the child has been removed or in which it has been retained.[5] The principle is that the authority shall order the return of the child forthwith except in exceptional cases.[6]

The European Union, desiring to support the Convention system and at the same time to complement it,[7] has adopted Regulation 2001/2003 concerning jurisdiction and the recognition and enforcement of judgments in matrimonial matters and the matters of parental responsibility[8] (the so-called Brussels IIa[9] Regulation). Even though the Regulation takes precedence over the Convention,[10] it does not deviate from the system established by the

---

[1] Entered into force on 1 December 1983. Full text: www.hcch.net/en/instruments/conventions/full-text/?cid=24.

[2] See www.hcch.net/en/instruments/conventions/status-table/?cid=24.

[3] Art 19 of the Convention: 'A decision under this Convention concerning the return of the child shall not be taken to be a determination on the merits of any custody issue.'

[4] Recitals and Art 1(a) of the Convention.

[5] Art 11.

[6] See Arts 12(2), 13 and 20.

[7] See Recital 17 to the Council Reg (EC) No 2201/2003 of 27 November 2003 concerning jurisdiction and the recognition and enforcement of judgments in matrimonial matters and the matters of parental responsibility, repealing Reg (EC) No 1347/2000, [2003] OJ L338/1.

[8] For commentary see U Magnus and P Mankowski (eds), *Brussels II bis Regulation* (Munich, Sellier, 2012). Child abduction is mentioned in Recitals 17–18 and 23–24 of the preamble and regulated in Arts 10, 11, 40, 42–45. The CJEU has adopted 23 judgments and two orders interpreting the Brussels IIa Reg, see ch 41 above.

[9] Or Brussels II bis Reg.

[10] Art 60 of Brussels IIa. See also Case C-400/10, *McB*, EU:C:2010:582, para 36.

latter but seeks to make it more efficient in the intra-Union context inter alia by setting a time limit for the courts and limiting the way in which the grounds for a refusal of return apply.[11] It aims to ensure the right of the child and the person who requested the return of the child to be heard.[12]

The Regulation, while respecting the Convention mechanism based on the right of the courts of the Member State which the child has been wrongfully removed to or retained in (the 'Member State of abduction') to order a non-return of the child, provides for the possibility of overturning such judgments by a subsequent decision of the courts of a Member State where the child was habitually resident before the abduction.[13] If the subsequent decision entails a return of the child, it will, under certain conditions, benefit from the special path of automatic recognition and enforceability without any possibility to refuse it in the Member State of abduction.[14] The so-called 'second chance mechanism' or 'overriding mechanism' introduced in Articles 11(6)–(8) and 42 Brussels IIa is a good example of the truth that a compromise is sometimes the worst possible outcome. The desire to apply the Hague Convention and have more efficient EU rules at the same time resulted in a system which is highly complex and unclear for litigants and courts.[15] Moreover, an absolute enforceability, unfortunately supported by the Court of Justice of the European Union (CJEU) and European Court of Human Rights (ECtHR), seems to be contrary to the principles of mutual trust and proportionality.[16]

The EU noticed the problems and on the 30 June 2016 the Commission published a proposal for the revision of Brussels IIa.[17] The issue of child abduction was one of the most heavily discussed during the preparatory works. Its importance is reflected in the title of the draft regulation in which 'international child abduction' appears as a separate issue from 'parental responsibility'. The proposal does contain a number of valuable amendments but does not solve the essence of the problem—the multitude of proceedings. A much

---

[11] Art 11(3)–(4) Brussels IIa.

[12] Art 11(2) and 11(5) Brussels IIa.

[13] Recital 17.

[14] According to Recital 23, it seeks to fulfil Tampere guidelines 'that judgments in the field of family litigation should be "automatically recognised throughout the Union without any intermediate proceedings or grounds for refusal of enforcement"'. See Recital 23 Brussels IIa. This system applies also to judgments on rights of access—see Arts 40–41 Reg 2201/2003.

[15] For similar criticism see national reports for Austria, Germany, Ireland ('interaction between substantive proceedings, orders for return and enforcement of existing child custody order is not well understood. This leads to multiplication of legal proceedings and delays for the parents involved'), and Slovakia ('the regulation of return proceedings is one of the most problematic aspects of the application of the Brussels IIa Regulation'). Those national reports are available in chs 11, 7, 20 and 28 above. See also s III.B.iii of this chapter.

[16] A Frąckowiak-Adamska, 'Time for a European "Full Faith and Credit Clause' (2015) 52(1) *Common Market Law Review* 191.

[17] Proposal for a Council Reg on jurisdiction, the recognition and enforcement of decisions in matrimonial matters and the matters of parental responsibility, and on international child abduction (recast), COM 2016/411 final. For an in-depth analysis see P Beaumont, LWalker, J Holliday, 'Parental Responsibility and International Child Abduction in the proposed recast of Brussels IIa Regulation and the effect of Brexit on future child abduction proceedings', Aberdeen CPIL Working Paper No. 2016/6, www.abdn.ac.uk/law/research/working-papers-455.php. See also *Nederlands Internationaal Privaatrecht* 2015/1 dedicated to the then upcoming revision of the Brussels IIa Reg, including Th M de Boer, 'What we *Should Not Expect* from a Recast of the Brussels IIbis Regulation' (2015) 1 *Nederlands Internationaal Privaatrecht* 10–19, available at www.nipr-online.eu/upload/documents/20150331T124932-NIPR%202015-1_De%20Boer_sample%20copy.pdf. Results of a public survey on Brussels IIa: https://ec.europa.eu/eusurvey/publication/BXLIIA.

better solution, in the opinion of the author, would be to utilise Article 36 of the Hague Convention in intra-EU situations to hand over the control of the return of the child to the courts of the habitual residence of the child before the abduction.

This chapter briefly describes the Hague mechanism, the provisions of Brussels IIa devoted to child abduction and their interpretation by the CJEU, practice of national courts as revealed by national reports prepared in the framework of the EUPILLAR project and reforms proposed by the Commission on 30 June 2016. Finally, it proposes an alternative solution.

II. The Hague Abduction Convention Mechanism

The Convention aims 'to protect children internationally from the harmful effects of their wrongful removal or retention'[18] and 'is based on a presumption that, save in exceptional circumstances, the wrongful removal or retention of a child across international boundaries is not in the interests of the child'.[19] The principle is thus such that the court of the Contracting State of abduction shall order the return of the child forthwith unless one of the exceptions in Articles 12, 13 and 20 applies. These exceptions which must be interpreted strictly[20] are: the commencement of the proceedings later than one year after the abduction and the settlement of the child in its new environment;[21] the lack of exercise of the custody rights by the child's caregiver or his/her consent to or acquiescence in the removal;[22] 'a grave risk that his or her return would expose the child to physical or psychological harm or otherwise place the child in an intolerable situation';[23] objections of a (sufficiently mature) child to being returned;[24] and the return would not be permitted by the fundamental principles of the requested State relating to the protection of human rights and fundamental freedoms.[25] The most frequently relied on important ground for refusal to return is a 'grave risk of harm' contained in Article 13(1)(b). The Convention states that the authorities of the State of abduction 'shall act expeditiously in proceedings for the return of children' and mentions the (non-obligatory) six-week time limit.[26]

---

[18] Recitals to the Convention.

[19] HCCH, Outline of the Hague Child Abduction Convention available at https://assets.hcch.net/docs/e6a6a977-40c5-47b2-a380-b4ec3a0041a8.pdf.

[20] See ECtHR Grand Chamber judgment in *X v Latvia* (see *X v Latvia* [GC], no 27853/09, §§ 93–102, 107 ECHR 2013) and 'the harm referred to in Article 13 (b) of the Hague Convention cannot arise solely from separation from the parent who was responsible for the wrongful removal or retention. This separation, however difficult for the child, would not automatically meet the grave risk test'. See the analysis of this case in PR Beaumont, K Trimmings, L Walker and J Holliday, 'Child Abduction: Recent Jurisprudence of the European Court of Human Rights' (2015) 64 *International and Comparative Law Quarterly* 39. See also *GN v Poland* (no 2171/14), para 61 and the case law quoted there.

[21] Art 12.

[22] Art 13(1)(a).

[23] Art 13(1)(b).

[24] Art 13(2).

[25] Art 20.

[26] However see s III.A.i below.

In some countries the jurisdiction for Hague Convention cases is centralised in one (eg Czech Republic and Netherlands) or several (Slovakia) courts; in others it is not (eg Slovenia and Poland).[27] According to the EUPILLAR reports the most serious problems with the application of the Convention are delays in proceedings[28] and differing interpretation by national authorities. Courts in some countries interpret Article 13(1)(b) of the Convention rather restrictively (German report), whilst courts in other countries take a more liberal approach. It happens that instead of verifying whether there is 'a grave risk that his or her return would expose the child to physical or psychological harm or otherwise place the child in an intolerable situation', courts analyse what the child's best interests are, including examining the merits of the custody rights.[29] The ECtHR has recently condemned this practice.[30]

III. Brussels IIa Regulation

Brussels IIa refers to child abduction in different provisions: in the Recitals stating that one of the main aims of the Regulation is to deter child abductions between Member States and, in cases of abduction, to obtain the child's return without delay,[31] in provisions enhancing the Hague Convention procedure,[32] governing the jurisdiction,[33] and the recognition and enforcement of judgments.[34]

A. Enhancing the Efficiency of the Hague Child Abduction Convention

i. Time Limits

The Regulation states in Article 11(3) that in deciding about the return a court in the Member State of abduction 'shall act expeditiously in proceedings on the application, using the most expeditious procedures available in national law'. It sets a precise time limit of

---

[27] See also *The Judges' Newsletter* on International Child Protection - Vol XX / Summer-Autumn 2013. Concentration of jurisdiction under the Hague Convention of 25 October 1980 on the Civil Aspects of International Child Abduction, www.hcch.net/en/publications-and-studies/details4/?pid=6090.

[28] See s III.A.i below.

[29] See for example the Greek report, in ch 18 above: 'In a limited number of child abduction cases, the Greek courts have decided also on the rights of custody and access by ignoring the fact that the return of a child should be decided separately and autonomously'.

[30] The ECtHR recently found that Poland was in breach of Art 8 of the ECHR because of an incorrectly broad interpretation of Art 13(1) (b) and awarded the father over €23,000 in respect of non-pecuniary damages and expenses—*GN v Poland* (no 2171/14).

[31] Recital 17 'In cases of wrongful removal or retention of a child, the return of the child should be obtained without delay'. Case C-195/08 PPU, *Rinau*, EU:C:2008:406, para 52 and Case C-211/10 PPU, *Povse*, EU:C:2010:400, para 43.

[32] Art 11.

[33] Art 10.

[34] Arts 11(6–8), 40(1) and 42(1).

six weeks[35] for the adoption of the decision but provides for no sanction for exceeding it. The national reports show that this time limit is often not respected.[36] Commission statistics indicate that to conclude an application which was appealed takes on average 154 days (and in extreme cases 324 days).[37] As there are no sanctions in EU law, it seems that the same time limit suggested by the Hague Convention is more effective, as, even if non-obligatory, it can lead to a condemnation of the State by the ECtHR.[38]

ii. Adequate Arrangements

The Hague Convention mentions the possibility of providing by the Central Authorities 'such administrative arrangements as may be necessary and appropriate to secure the safe return of the child'.[39] The Brussels IIa Regulation states in Article 11(4) that 'A court cannot refuse to return a child on the basis of Article 13b of the 1980 Hague Convention if it is established that adequate arrangements have been made to secure the protection of the child after his or her return'. This provision can be seen as an expression of mutual trust between Member States—if one of them puts in place adequate arrangements, another one cannot refuse the return. The purpose of Article 11(4) is to limit the possibility of refusing the return on the basis of Article 13(1)(b) of the Convention. The provision thus seeks to make the Convention more effective; however, as it is very general (for example, it does not state who shall organise the arrangements), it poses problems.[40] These difficulties arise in particular from differences in national laws or an unwillingness or inability (due to insufficient resources) to cooperate by Central Authorities in some Member States,[41] an overly narrow interpretation of Article 11(4),[42] a conviction of the courts that adequate arrangements cannot be made by definition[43] or the failure to respect orders securing the return of the child.[44] The lack of arrangements can be a motive for ordering a non-return.[45]

---

[35] Art 11(3) 'the court shall, except where exceptional circumstances make this impossible, issue its judgment no later than six weeks after the application is lodged'. In practice there are also doubts whether this term applies per instance or includes appeals—see Staff Working Document Impact Assessment, SWD (2016) 207 final, point 3.1.

[36] Expressly stated for example in the Belgian (ch 6), British (ch 5), Czech (ch 15), Latvian (ch 21), Portuguese (ch 26) and Slovenian (ch 29) reports. The problem, however, concerns all Member States.

[37] See Commission Staff Working Document Impact Assessment Accompanying the document Proposal for a Council Regulation on jurisdiction, the recognition and enforcement of decisions in matrimonial matters and the matters of parental responsability, and on international child abduction (recast), SWD/2016/0207 final, p 36.

[38] See eg *GN v Poland* (no 2171/14), paras 66–68, in which proceedings took almost one year and five months.

[39] Art 7(h) of the Hague Convention.

[40] See K Trimmings, *Child Abduction within the European Union* (Oxford, Hart, 2013) 136–61 and 242–46 and P Beaumont, L Walker and J Holliday, 'Conflicts of EU Courts on Child Abduction: the Reality of Article 11(6)–(8) Brussels IIa Proceedings across the EU' (2016) 12 *Journal of Private International Law* 211 at 218–19 and 221.

[41] Czech report (ch 15 above).

[42] Swedish report (ch 30 above).

[43] Latvian report (ch 21 above) which states that it happens if the 'abductor mother announces that she is not willing to return and based on psychological reports the Court establishes that the child cannot be separated from his or her abductor mother otherwise it will expose the child to physical or psychological harm or otherwise place the child in an intolerable situation'.

[44] An extreme example is quoted in the Czech report, ch 15 above: 'appellate court ordered the return of the child to Greece with some conditions and safeguards, including the right of the mother to stay with the child after the return. These safeguards, however, were not respected by the Greek authorities and immediately after the return (at the airport), the child was removed from the mother.'

[45] Maltese report (ch 24 above).

iii. Protection of the Right to be Heard of the Child and the Person who Requested the Return of the Child

Article 11(2) states that '[w]hen applying Articles 12 and 13 of the 1980 Hague Convention, it shall be ensured that the child is given the opportunity to be heard during the proceedings unless this appears inappropriate having regard to his or her age or degree of maturity'. Article 11(5) provides that '[a] court cannot refuse to return a child unless the person who requested the return of the child has been given an opportunity to be heard'. Some national reports[46] reveal that the requirement of the hearing of a child causes some problems in court practice but other studies show that these problems are much more apparent in Brussels IIa override cases than in Hague return cases, perhaps because in the former the child is not present in the State where the court is sitting.[47]

B. Jurisdiction

i. General Outline of Jurisdictional Rules

Jurisdiction in matters of parental responsibility is 'shaped in the light of the best interests of the child, in particular on the criterion of proximity',[48] and is governed by Articles 8–14 of Brussels IIa. General jurisdiction in matters of parental responsibility is granted according to Article 8(1) to the courts of a Member State where a child is habitually resident[49] at the time the court is seised. There are four exceptions to this rule. One of them[50]—Article 10—provides for the retention of jurisdiction by the court of the Member State where the child was habitually resident before the abduction even if, in certain circumstances, the child acquired habitual residence in the new Member State. The underlying rationale is that abduction, in itself, does not create a change in the jurisdiction to determine parental responsibility.

However, it is quite common that the abducting parent seeks to convince the courts of the Member State where he/she resides with the child after the abduction to decide on the merits of parental responsibility. He/she counts on the advantage of being present in the jurisdiction (thus having the opportunity to present his/her arguments), and on the benefit of common culture and language as usually it is the state of his/her nationality.

---

[46] eg Slovakian report (ch 28 above).

[47] Trimmings, above n 40 at 181–236 and 246–47, reported that Art 11(2) of Brussels IIa was increasing the tendency to hear the child in Hague child abduction cases within the EU and was ahead of the trend in major non-EU jurisdictions in Hague cases. However, in the context of the Brussels IIa override provisions in Art 11(6)–(8) a Nuffield Foundation funded study revealed serious concerns about how well the children are being heard by the courts of their habitual residence prior to the abuction, see Beaumont, Walker and Holliday, above n 40 at 232–41 and 258–59.

[48] Recital 12 Brussels IIa.

[49] This is an autonomous notion of EU law. See Case C-497/10 PPU *Mercredi* EU:C:2010:829, para 45. For a definition see also Case C-523/07 *A* EU:C:2009:225, paras 30–44.

[50] The other three exceptions are: retaining of a jurisdiction during a three month period following the lawful move of the child from one Member State to another and acquisition of a new habitual residence—for the purpose of modifying a judgment on access rights issued in that Member State before the child moved (Art 9); prorogation of jurisdiction (Art 12); and cases where a child's habitual residence cannot be established—the courts of the Member State where the child is present shall have jurisdiction.

The provisions of Brussels IIa which sometimes are used for this purpose are: Article 11, which governs the jurisdiction for the Hague Convention return procedure (which should be limited to a decision on return); Article 15, which provides for the mechanism of transferring the jurisdiction to another court; and Article 20, which permits the courts of a Member State not having jurisdiction as to the substance of the matter to adopt provisional measures in urgent cases.

Brussels IIa provides for an automatic recognition of judgments and a prohibition of a review of jurisdiction of the court of origin. It means that the courts of another Member State cannot refuse to recognise a judgment even if it was adopted in breach of rules of jurisdiction.[51] It is therefore extremely important that courts apply jurisidictional rules properly.[52]

ii. Article 10—Retention of Jurisdiction by the Courts of the Member State where the Child was Habitually Resident Immediately Before the Wrongful Removal

Article 10, whose aim is to deter wrongful removal or retention of children between Member States, contains a special provision on jurisdiction concerning the merits of parental responsibility in cases of child abduction. The abduction, even if followed by the change of habitual residence of the child, does not automatically change the jurisdiction.[53] According to Article 10 in cases of abduction the courts of the Member State where the child was habitually resident immediately before the abduction retain their jurisdiction. The jurisdiction changes to another Member State only if the child has acquired a habitual residence there and one or more of the following has occurred: each person or body having rights of custody has acquiesced in the abduction; or the child has resided there for at least one year, is settled in his or her new environment and at least one of the following four conditions is met: no request for return was lodged in the Member State of abduction within this one year; a request for return has been withdrawn and no new request has been lodged; after a non-return of the child was ordered by the Member State of abduction, no submissions on the question of custody of the child were received within three months by the court of the Member State where the child was habitually resident immediately before the abduction; or the courts in the Member State where the child was habitually resident immediately before the abduction issued a judgment on custody that did not entail the return of the child.[54]

---

[51] Art 24. Moreover the breach of jurisdiction cannot be taken into consideration within the public policy test, which is the most general ground for refusal of recognition of a judgment.

[52] The problem in this context is also that legal aid may not be available (Czech Republic, see ch 15 above) or may be granted only to the left-behind parent, without any investigation of means or merit. (England/Wales, see ch 5 above).

[53] See Case C-455/15 PPU *P v Q* EU:C:2015:763, para 44: 'the unlawful removal of a child should not, in principle, have the effect of transferring jurisdiction from the courts of the Member State where the child was habitually resident immediately before removal to the courts of the Member State to which the child was taken, even if, following the abduction, the child has acquired a habitual residence in the latter Member State'.

[54] The last condition was interpreted by the CJEU in Case C-211/10 PPU *Povse* EU:C:2010:400, in which it stated at para 50 that 'a provisional measure does not constitute a "judgment on custody that does not entail the return of the child" within the meaning of that provision, and cannot be the basis of a transfer of jurisdiction to the courts of the Member State to which the child has been unlawfully removed' and in para 46 that 'a "judgment on custody that does not entail the return of the child" is a final judgment, adopted on the basis of full consideration of all the relevant factors, in which the court with jurisdiction rules on arrangements for the custody of a child who is no longer subject to other administrative or judicial decisions.'

Article 10 is a compromise between the aim to deter child abduction between Member States and the criterion of proximity (that jurisdiction should lie with the Member State of the child's habitual residence). The final condition mentioned above, that the courts of the Member State where the child was habitually resident immediately before the abduction have issued a judgment on custody that does not entail the return of the child, must be interpreted strictly and does not arise when the judgment was only provisional.[55]

iii. *Article 11—Jurisdiction to Order the Return of the Abducted Child*

Pursuant to Recital 17 to Brussels IIa, 'the Hague Convention of 25 October 1980 would continue to apply as complemented by the provisions of this Regulation, in particular Article 11'. According to the Hague Convention, a decision on return shall be taken by a judicial or administrative authority of the Contracting State where the child has been wrongfully retained or removed to.[56] The legal basis for the proceedings on return is the Hague Convention and Article 11 of Brussels IIa[57] but courts in some Member States rely only on the Convention without making any reference to the Regulation.[58]

Article 11 also imposes an obligation on the court which has issued an order on non-return pursuant to Article 13 of the 1980 Hague Convention to transmit within one month a copy of the decision and of the relevant documents to the court with jurisdiction or the Central Authority in the Member State where the child was habitually resident immediately before the wrongful removal. This court or Authority must notify the parties and invite them to make submissions to the court within three months of the date of notification so that the court can examine the question of custody of the child. If no submissions have been received by the court within the time limit the court shall close the case. If the child has resided there for at least one year, and is settled in his or her new environment, in such a case the jurisdiction is transferred to the new Member State.[59]

If a submission was made to the court where the child was habitually resident immediately before the wrongful removal or retention within the three month limit, or the courts of this Member State have already been seised, any judgment which requires the return of the child adopted subsequent to the non-return order shall be enforceable in accordance with Section 4 of Chapter III.

The Hague Convention proceedings and the proceedings on the merits of custody (in the Member State of habitual residence) can be conducted at the same time independently. The CJEU stated that there can be no *lis pendens* between such actions as a Hague Convention

> 'action, whose object is the return, to the Member State of origin, of a child who has been wrongfully removed or retained in another Member State, does not concern the substance of parental responsibility and therefore has neither the same object nor the same cause of action as an action seeking a ruling on parental responsibility.[60]

In this context an important question arises as to whether the issue of return can be judged only in the context of the Hague Convention mechanism (ie by the Member State of

---

[55] *Povse*, ibid, para 45.
[56] Ch III of the Hague Convention.
[57] See also Case C-376/14 PPU *C v M* EU:C:2014:2268, para 43.
[58] See for example the Greek report, ch 18 above.
[59] Art 10(b)(iii)—see s III.B.ii above.
[60] Case C-376/14 PPU *C v M* EU:C:2014:2268, para 40.

abduction) or also by the Member State of habitual residence in the context of proceedings on the merits (including interim measures) instead of the Hague proceedings or parallel to it. There is no answer in the Convention[61] or in Brussels IIa.[62] It thus seems that it is up to the left-behind parent whether to initiate Hague Convention proceedings or regular proceedings on parental responsibility in the Member State of habitual residence of the child and ask for the return as an interim measure. But courts in some Member States think that 'according to Article 11 of the Regulation, jurisdiction to order the return of the child is to be determined under the 1980 Hague Convention', which means that a decision on the return of the child is in the exclusive competence of the Member State of abduction. The courts in the Member State of habitual residence are not obliged (or even competent) to adjudicate on the issue.[63]

iv. Article 15—Transfer of Jurisdiction to a Court of Another Member State

Article 15 provides for a means of cooperation supplementing the rules of jurisdiction,[64] 'by which a court of a Member State which has jurisdiction to hear the case under one of those rules may, by way of exception, transfer it to a court of another Member State which is better placed to hear the case'. However, occasionally courts use this provision incorrectly. In particular, courts in a Member State of abduction quote it as a legal basis for jurisdiction even if there was no request from the courts of a Member State of habitual residence of the child before abduction or no answer from those courts to a request for transfer made by the courts of the State of abduction.[65] Moreover it is not clear whether this provision can be used in the case of child abduction. Some courts declare that Article 15 cannot be used to legitimise child abduction.[66]

v. Article 20—Provisional Measures in Urgent Situations

Article 20 allows the court of a Member State not having jurisdiction as to the substance of the matter[67] to adopt 'such provisional, including protective, measures in respect of persons or assets in that State as may be available under the law of that Member State' if 'three

---

[61] Art 16 of the Convention concerns only the judicial or administrative authorities of the Contracting State to which the child has been abducted: 'After receiving notice of a wrongful removal or retention of a child in the sense of Article 3, the judicial or administrative authorities of the Contracting State to which the child has been removed or in which it has been retained shall not decide on the merits of rights of custody until it has been determined that the child is not to be returned under this Convention or unless an application under this Convention is not lodged within a reasonable time following receipt of the notice.'

[62] The Reg addresses only the situation when following the Hague proceedings the courts in the Member State of habitual residence adopt a judgment—see point on enforcement.

[63] This is the view of the Italian Supreme Court—see the Italian report (ch 8 above): 'No infringement of Regulation occurred in relation to the fact that the Italian court seised by the father for the decision on parental responsibility over his daughter—habitually resident in Italy before her mother took her to Poland without his consent, completely preventing him from seeing her—took no decision on the return of the child, as the competence over return issues in cases of child abduction involving EU Member States lies, pursuant to Articles 9, 10 and 11 of the 1980 Hague Convention on the civil aspects of international child abduction, with the central authority of the State where the child is, after the wrongful removal'.

[64] Case C-455/15 PPU *P v Q* EU:C:2015:763, para 44.

[65] See the Polish and Czech Reports (chs 10 and 15 above). See also Case C-455/15 PPU *P v Q* EU:C:2015:763, para 24.

[66] See the Belgian report (ch 6 above).

[67] Case C-256/09 *Purrucker I*, EU:C:2010:437, para 63.

cumulative conditions are satisfied, namely that the measures concerned must be urgent, must be taken in respect of persons or assets in the Member State where those courts are situated, and must be provisional'.[68] This provision is an exception to the system of jurisdiction laid down by the Regulation and must be interpreted strictly.[69] The CJEU also clarified that, as Article 20 does not determine substantive jurisdiction,[70] measures within its scope do not qualify for the system of recognition and enforcement established by Brussels IIa.[71] This does not prevent the recognition or enforcement of those measures in another Member State on the basis of international instruments or national legislation.[72]

Abducting parents sometimes try to use Article 20 to regulate questions of parental responsibility. Even if measures are only temporary and limited to the territory of one Member State they can be useful as they prolong the situation of residing in this State legally. The situation gets complicated if the court having jurisdiction as to the substance of the matter (the Member State of habitual residence of a child before the abduction) also adopts measures in relation to the same child. The CJEU stated that a judgment falling within the scope of Article 20 may, 'in the Member State of the court which has adopted the judgment, prevail over an earlier judgment adopted by a court of another Member State which has substantive jurisdiction'.[73] The situation is, however, different in the case of custody rights. In *Detiček* it was decided that Article 20 did not allow

> a court of a Member State to take a provisional measure in matters of parental responsibility granting custody of a child who is in the territory of that Member State to one parent, where a court of another Member State, which has jurisdiction under that regulation as to the substance of the dispute relating to custody of the child, has already delivered a judgment provisionally giving custody of the child to the other parent, and that judgment has been declared enforceable in the territory of the former Member State.[74]

Another solution 'would amount, by consolidating a factual situation deriving from wrongful conduct, to strengthening the position of the parent responsible for the wrongful removal.'[75]

C. Recognition and Enforcement

i. Two Paths to Recognition

The Brussels IIa Regulation provides for two different mechanisms[76] for the recognition and enforcement of judgments. The first is provided for in Articles 21–39 and is available for all cases falling within the scope of the Regulation, including judgments adopted in

---

[68] Case C-403/09 PPU, *Detiček*, EU:C:2009:810, para 39. See also Case C-523/07 A EU:C:2009:225, para 47.
[69] *Detiček*, ibid, para 38.
[70] Case C-296/10 *Purrucker v Vallés Pérez*, EU:C:2010:665 (*Purrucker II*), para 70.
[71] *Purrucker I*, above n 67, para 87.
[72] ibid, para 92.
[73] ibid, para 81.
[74] *Detiček*, above n 68, para 61.
[75] Additionally, it would run counter to the aim of the Reg to deter the wrongful removal or retention of children between Member States (*Detiček*, above n 68, para 49).
[76] Case C-195/08 PPU, *Rinau*, EU:C:2008:406, para 61 'the Regulation organises the recognition and declaration of enforceability of judgments in two parts (Articles 21(1) and (3), 11(8), 40(1) and 42(1))'.

the context of child abduction. It is similar to the mechanism of Brussels I,[77] and provides for automatic recognition (with the possibility of refusal) and the necessity of obtaining a declaration of enforceability (*exequatur*) to enforce the judgment in another Member State. The second mechanism is provided for in Articles 11(6–8), 40(1) and 42(1), and embodies automatic recognition and enforceability (without the need for *exequatur* and the possibility of refusal) available to the plaintiff on an optional basis[78] for two types of cases: certain judgments on rights of access to the child and certain judgments requiring the return of the child. The focus of this chapter is on the special mechanism provided for in Article 11(8).

ii. Automatic and Absolute Recognition and Enforceability—Article 11(8)

The special mechanism can be used only if the left-behind parent first uses the Hague Convention procedure,[79] and the return is refused pursuant to Article 13 of the Convention. Article 11(8) Brussels IIa states that:

> Notwithstanding a judgment of non-return pursuant to Article 13 of the 1980 Hague Convention, any subsequent judgment which requires the return of the child issued by a court having jurisdiction under this Regulation shall be enforceable in accordance with Section 4 of Chapter III below in order to secure the return of the child.

This provision must be read together with other provisions of the Brussels IIa Regulation. In order for the special mechanism to be used, the following conditions must be fulfilled:

— A child must have a habitual residence[80] in one Member State and be abducted to another Member State;
— a person or a body actually exercising the custody[81] must make on the basis of the Hague Convention an application for return to the Member State where the child had habitual residence immediately before[82] the wrongful removal or retention;
— the application was refused[83] on the ground of Article 13 of the Hague Convention[84] (the later fate of this decision is irrelevant);[85]

---

[77] Reg 44/2001.
[78] See Art 40(2) Brussels IIa: 'The provisions of this Section shall not prevent a holder of parental responsibility from seeking recognition and enforcement of a judgment in accordance with the provisions in Sections 1 and 2 of this Chapter'.
[79] Art 11(1) and (8) Brussels IIa.
[80] As Brussels IIa is silent on this issue, habitual residence is defined in case law of the CJEU: Case C-523/07 *A* EU:C:2009:225, paras 37–44; Case C-497/10 PPU *Mercredi* EU:C:2010:829, paras 47–56; and Case C-376/14 PPU *C v M* EU:C:2014:2268, paras 50–53 and 56.
[81] As defined in Art 2(11) Brussels IIa.
[82] Case C-376/14 PPU *C v M* EU:C:2014:2268, para 48: paras 2 to 8 of Art 11 do not apply if the child was not habitually resident in the Member State of origin immediately before the removal or retention.
[83] Case C-195/08 PPU, *Rinau*, EU:C:2008:406, para 59: 'a certificate cannot be issued pursuant to Article 42 of the Regulation unless a judgment of non-return has been issued beforehand'.
[84] The procedure of Art 11(8) is not triggered if the refusal is based on other provisions of the Hague Convention (for example Art 20). The Belgian report, ch 6 above, indicates that in practice 'figuring out on which legal ground a decision is based can be tricky, especially if it is based on more than one article (simultaneously on Articles 13 and 3 or 20)'.
[85] Case C-195/08 PPU, *Rinau*, EU:C:2008:406, para 89: 'once a non-return decision has been taken and brought to the attention of the court of origin, it is irrelevant, for the purposes of issuing the certificate provided for in Article 42 of the Regulation, that that decision has been suspended, overturned, set aside or, in any event, has not become *res judicata* or has been replaced by a decision ordering return, in so far as the return of the child has not actually taken place'.

— a court[86] of the Member State of habitual residence of the child prior to the wrongful removal or retention adopted a subsequent 'judgment which requires the return of the child'[87] and the following conditions of Article 42(2) were met: the child was given an opportunity to be heard, unless a hearing was considered inappropriate with regard to his or her age or degree of maturity; the parties were given an opportunity to be heard; and the court has taken into account in issuing its judgment the reasons for and evidence underlying the order issued pursuant to Article 13 of the Hague Convention (however, the verification of these conditions is carried out only by the court in the Member State of adoption of the judgment); and

— this judgment is enforceable and has been certified in accordance with Article 42 of Brussels IIa.

If all these conditions are met such a judgment 'shall be recognised and enforceable in another Member State without the need for a declaration of enforceability and without any possibility of opposing its recognition'.[88] It shall be enforced in the Member State of enforcement under the same conditions as if it had been delivered in that Member State. The only situation when it cannot be enforced is if it is irreconcilable with a subsequent enforceable judgment.[89] In *Povse* the CJEU clarified that this provision related only to judgments subsequently handed down by the courts with jurisdiction in the Member State of origin (ie not the Member State of enforcement).[90]

Both the CJEU and the ECtHR have supported the mechanism established by Article 11(8). In *Zarraga* the CJEU stated that the court in the Member State of enforcement cannot oppose the enforcement of a certified judgment, ordering the return of a child, even on the ground that the court of the Member State of origin infringed fundamental rights 'since the assessment of whether there is such an infringement falls exclusively within the jurisdiction of the courts of the Member State of origin'.[91] The CJEU gave the supremacy to the effectiveness of the system set up by the Regulation over the protection of fundamental rights.[92]

Both aspects of this mechanism seem to be wrong. The idea that the decisions on non-return could be replaced by a subsequent decision of the court of the Member State of

---

[86] It can be a court deciding on substance of parental responsibility or even a court specialised in parental child abduction with respect to the procedure provided for in Art 11(7)–(8) (even where a court or tribunal has already been seised of proceedings concerning the substance of parental responsibility in relation to the child)—see Case C-498/14 PPU *Bradbrooke* EU:C:2015:3, para 54.

[87] According to Case C-211/10 PPU *Povse*, EU:C:2010:400, paras 51–67 it does not have to be a final judgment on rights of custody but any subsequent judgment (including provisional measures) adopted by the courts of the Member State where the child was previously habitually resident.

[88] Art 42(1) Brussels IIa.

[89] Art 47(2).

[90] Case C-211/10 PPU *Povse* EU:C:2010:400, para 78. Other solutions would amount to circumventing the system set up by S 4 of Ch III of the Reg and would deprive Art 11(8) of the Reg of practical effect.

[91] Case C-491/10 PPU *Aguirre Zarraga* EU:C:2010:828, para 75.

[92] For a critique of this judgment see eg P Beaumont, 'The European Court of Justice Prioritises the Abolition of Exequatur over Fundamental Rights in *Zarraga*' in Diez-Hochleitner, Martinez Capdevila, Blazquez Navarro and Frutos Miranda (eds), *Recent Trends in the Case Law of the Court of Justice of the European Union (2008–2011)* (Buenos Aires, La Ley, 2012) 621; Frąckowiak-Adamska, above n 17; J Kuipers, 'The (Non) Application of the Charter of Fundamental Rights to a Certificate for the Return of a Child' (2012) 17 *European Human Rights Law Review* 397; and L Walker and P Beaumont, 'Shifting the Balance Achieved by the Abduction Convention: The Contrasting Approaches of the European Court of Human Rights and the European Court of Justice' (2011) 7(2) *Journal of Private International Law* 231.

habitual residence of the child prior to the abduction[93] is contrary to mutual trust (if one court resolved the case, how could another make a better decision?) and to common sense.[94] An absolute recognition and enforceability of the judgment fulfils the Tampere conclusions 'that judgments in the field of family litigation should be "automatically recognised throughout the Union without any intermediate proceedings or grounds for refusal of enforcement"'.[95] However, this mechanism is contrary to the principle of mutual trust and proportionality.

IV. Conclusions and Proposals

A. Conclusions

The current provisions on child abduction in Brussels IIa are not efficient. They are complex and give the possibility of many proceedings which can overlap. The multitude of possible proceedings—Hague Convention return proceedings; parental responsibility proceedings in the Member State of habitual residence of a child before the abduction (potentially complemented by interim measures which can be adopted in both sets of proceedings); and proceedings on interim measures on the basis of Article 20—leads to considerable confusion not only for the parties but also the judges. This is clear not only from the CJEU's case law quoted above but also from the national reports prepared in the framework of the EUPILLAR project—Czech,[96] Irish,[97] Greek[98] or Latvian.[99] The Slovakian report states that:

> [R]egulation of return proceedings … places a burden on the courts and encourage courts with jurisdiction under Article 10 not to decide on parental rights and obligations until proceedings on

---

[93] Recital 18.

[94] According to the Scottish part of the British report it 'tends to leave children in a prolonged state of uncertainty' (see ch 5 above).

[95] Recital 23 states that 'The Tampere European Council considered in its conclusions (point 34) that judgments in the field of family litigation should be "automatically recognised throughout the Union without any intermediate proceedings or grounds for refusal of enforcement". This is why judgments on rights of access and judgments on return that have been certified in the Member State of origin in accordance with the provisions of this Regulation should be recognised and enforceable in all other Member States without any further procedure being required.'

[96] See ch 15: 'A lot of problems in practice occur while concurrent proceedings are commenced. In some cases where the child was abducted, courts dealt with concurrent proceedings in another Member State, where *lis pendens* (Article 19(2)) should be applied. It happens that the first seised court, although not internationally competent, does not declare its non-competence immediately, but waits for the result of the return procedure, which seldom is finished in six weeks and often issues a preliminary order on custody for the abducting parent till the final decision on return'.

[97] See ch 20: '[t]he interactions between the different processes of enforcement, return and substantive order following an order of non-return do not seem to be well understood by litigants and cause delays. [There is] confusion as to how the mechanisms for return affect the determination of substantive issues.'

[98] See ch 18: '[i]n a limited number of child abduction cases, the Greek courts have decided also on the rights of custody and access by ignoring the fact that the return of a child should be decided separately and autonomously'.

[99] See ch 21: '[f]rom the experience of the Latvian institutions, courts in some of the Member States proceedings in accordance with Article 11 (6–8) consider as review of the non-return judgments of the Latvian Courts, not proceedings as regards parental responsibility, as a result of which it may or it may not request the return of the child'.

return are concluded as decisions issued in Member States with jurisdiction under Article 10 prior to the conclusion of the proceedings on return cannot be certified under Article 42 and enforced without the need for proceedings on *exequatur*.[100]

Sometimes the parties understand the decision on non-return as a substantive one. In Ireland, 'in many cases, the order for non-return is determinative of the substantive issue and no submissions are made following transmission of documents'.[101]

Moreover, the Article 11(6)–(8) procedure is not efficient in practice. It is used only exceptionally,[102] or even ignored by the courts.[103] Even if used, despite the unqualified enforceability of judgments introduced by Article 11(8), their actual enforcement often poses problems.[104]

B. Commission Proposal of 30 June 2016

In the process of the preparation of the proposal for the recast of the Brussels IIa Regulation, the European Commission considered five options[105] for improving provisions on child abduction:[106] (1) maintaining the status quo; (2) codification of the current interpretation based on available guidelines and the CJEU case law; (3) introduction of measures increasing efficiency and improving the functioning of the overriding mechanism; (4) deleting the overriding mechanism and returning to the Hague Convention; and (5) revoking the current system of Article 11 by concentrating the jurisdiction for return proceedings in the Member State of origin and enforcing the return order in the Member State of refuge. The Commission chose option three.

The 30 June 2016 proposal decided to follow the current philosophy. The Commission proposed to keep the application of the Hague Convention and overriding mechanism, but to eliminate absolute enforceability of judgments adopted on the basis of Article 11(8). As the proposal is for the abolition of *exequatur* for all judgments within the scope of application of the Regulation (with the possibility of refusal in exceptional cases), the judgments enacted in the framework of Article 11(8) will be enforced by means of the new general rules.

The rejection of absolute enforceability is a very good solution. The proposal, however, does not solve the essence of the problem—the multitude of proceedings.

C. Alternative Proposal

According to the author it would be better if the EU invokes Article 36 of the Hague Convention and introduces its own solution for intra-EU cases based on the exclusive jurisdiction

---

[100] Ch 28.

[101] Ch 20.

[102] Inter alia Belgian, Italian and Spanish reports (chs 6, 8 and 9 above). Staff Working Document Impact Assessment, SWD (2016) 207 final, point 3.2 indicates that there are annually up to 1800 cases of parental child abduction within the EU and the overriding mechanism is applied in only about 20 cases per year. See also Beaumont, Walker and Holliday, above n 40.

[103] Luxembourg report, ch 23 above.

[104] Polish report, ch 10 above and Beaumont, Walker and Holliday, above n 40.

[105] Staff Working Document Impact Assessment, SWD (2016) 207 final.

[106] Deter abductions and ensure swift and safe return of the child to his or her State of habitual residence. See Staff Working Document Impact Assessment, SWD (2016) 207 final, point 3.4.

of the courts of the Member State of habitual residence before the abduction. Proposing the disapplication of the Hague Convention system to intra-EU cases is tantamount to sacrilege,[107] but there are at least two important arguments—a systemic and a pragmatic one for this solution.

A systemic question is whether the taking of the child from one Member State to another could at all be called an 'international abduction'. Is it not against the spirit of EU integration to treat other Member States as foreign countries for the purpose of child abduction while they are not treated in this manner for the purposes of the free movement of goods, people, services and capital and, even more importantly, the free movement of judgments? Moreover is it not an unfair solution in cases when a 'good parent' escapes? If he/she must leave home because of violence, it is natural to seek help from parents and friends in his/her own Member State. If one parent moves with a child from Paris to Montpellier without the consent of the other parent, the Hague Convention is not used. If we have a common EU area of freedom, security and justice maybe it would be better to elaborate the rules similar to those applied to domestic situations.

A pragmatic argument relates to simplicity and time saving. The Regulation differentiates between the matters of merits of parental responsibility which shall be decided by the Member State where the child was habitually resident before the abduction, and the matter of the return of an abducted child to the Member State of habitual residence. Such a division of competences seems to be artificial and confusing not only for parties but also for the courts. It is also time consuming. If time is everything in cases of separation of a child from one parent, the most important thing is to eliminate double proceedings in different Member States and leave only one set of proceedings. This means the elimination either of the Hague Convention proceedings or the proceeding in the Member State of the habitual residence of a child. It is not contested that in general the courts of the State where the child was habitually resident before the abduction are best placed to decide on custody issues.[108] With the proposed solution all the decisions on a child (including the one on the need for return) should be done by the court with jurisdiction as to the substance of parental responsibility—on the basis of interim measures.[109] The situation would be clear—the courts of Member States of abduction should not have the right to make any assessment of the situation of the child.[110] The Central Authority or courts in this State could, however, be

---

[107] See eg the very different views of some of the other participants in the EUPILLAR project: T Kruger, who with L Samyn, stated recently that: 'Our proposal is to abolish the second chance procedure and return to the delicate balance struck by the Hague Child Abduction Convention. This will recover the same treatment of abducted children whether in or outside the EU. It will reiterate the approach of reverse subsidiarity' in T Kruger and L Samyn, 'Brussels II bis: Successes and Suggested Improvements' (2016) 12 *Journal of Private International Law* 132 at 159; Beaumont, Walker and Holliday, above n 40, at 258, also argued for the repeal of the override mechanism and return to the operation of the Hague 1980 Convention in intra-EU cases. See also Trimmings, above n 40, for another hostile view of the Brussels IIa override scheme and a support for the existing Hague Convention system with possible improvements at the global level.

[108] This idea is the backbone of the Hague Convention. However, the exceptions in Arts 12, 13 and 20 are there to deal with the exceptional cases where it would be best for the long term custody of the child to be determined in the courts of the place where the child is present after the abduction.

[109] Alternatively, it could be the courts of the Member State of abduction—the same which are competent to hear Hague Convention cases but in intra-EU cases the return will be automatic.

[110] If we give the court of the new Member State the right to assess the need for return, it should also have the jurisdiction for the substance of the case.

useful to locate the child, serve documents from the court of the Member State of habitual residence and enforce the judgment.[111]

It is not contested that the EU should support the Hague Convention system but it does not mean that it has to apply it in internal EU relationships. In order to promote the Convention at the global level, it is enough that the EU (or all Member States) are party to the Convention and apply it in their relationships with other Contracting Parties. Trying to apply the Hague Convention and the EU Regulation at the same time is a good example of a bad deal.

---

[111] Though it must be acknowledged that one of the problems with the Brussels IIa override system is how few judgments, of the courts of the habitual residence of the child before the abduction which order the return of the child to that place, are actually enforced in the State where the child has been abducted to, see Beaumont, Walker and Holliday, above n 40, at 212–31 and 254–59.

44

New (and Old) Problems
for Maintenance Creditors Under
the EU Maintenance Regulation

LARA WALKER

I. Introduction

The EU Maintenance Regulation is designed to enable creditors to easily obtain a mainte-nance decision which will be automatically enforceable in another Member State without any further formalities.[1] From the outset the Commission aimed to simplify the recovery of maintenance for creditors and guarantee enforcement. The main objective of the Commis-sion's proposal was to 'accelerate and simplify enforcement of decisions, in order to guar-antee the effective recovery of maintenance.'[2] On 15 December 2005 the Commission sent a proposal for a Maintenance Regulation to the Council.[3] The ambition of this proposal was to 'eliminate all obstacles which still today prevent the recovery of maintenance in the European Union.'[4] The final text of the Regulation was adopted in December 2008 and it covers all the aspects dealt with in the Commission's 2005 proposal, apart from applicable law, which is governed by the Hague Protocol.[5] The Commission was also unable to fully achieve the objective to abolish the *exequatur* procedure,[6] which remains for decisions that originated in a Member State that does not apply the Hague Protocol.[7] The Commission set out to create law and justice in the area of cross-border maintenance, however it is questionable whether these goals have been met and if creditors can now easily obtain a

---

[1] Council Reg (EC) 4/2009 of 18 December 2008 on jurisdiction, applicable law, recognition and enforcement of decisions and cooperation in matters relating to maintenance obligations [2009] OJ L7/1 (Maintenance Reg) Recital 9.

[2] Staff Working Document, Annex to the Proposal for a Council Regulation on Jurisdiction, Applicable Law, Recognition and Enforcement of Decisions and Cooperation in Matters relating to maintenance obligations—Impact Assessment, SEC/2005/1629, s 3.

[3] COM(2005) 649 final, 2005/0259 CNS, Proposal for a Council Reg on jurisdiction, applicable law, recognition and enforcement of decisions and cooperation in matters relating to maintenance.

[4] ibid s 1.2.

[5] Hague Protocol of 23 November 2007 on the law applicable to maintenance obligations.

[6] Staff Working Document, Annex to the Proposal for a Council Reg on Jurisdiction, Applicable Law, Recogni-tion and Enforcement of Decisions and Cooperation in Matters relating to maintenance obligations—Impact Assessment, SEC/2005/1629, s 3.

[7] Maintenance Reg, Arts 30–34 (UK and Denmark).

maintenance decision which can be automatically enforced effectively. In some cases this is directly related to the Regulation itself and in other cases this is caused by the incorrect implementation of the Regulation into national law. This chapter will focus on recent decisions under the Maintenance Regulation in the context of jurisdiction and enforceability, in order to highlight some difficulties that may arise for litigants in this area.[8] It will also make some suggestions as to how the Regulation could be reformed in the future to further facilitate access to justice in cross-border maintenance disputes.

II. Jurisdiction

There have been two interesting cases on jurisdiction under the Maintenance Regulation arising from England and Wales to date. One related to the ancillary provisions, in a dispute relating to England and Italy, where the Italian courts requested a ruling from the Court of Justice of the European Union (CJEU).[9] The other considered three of the jurisdictional provisions in detail.[10] This section will lay out all the jurisdictional bases in Articles 3–7 of the Regulation, with the focus being on the interpretation given to the relevant provisions by the case law. There are a number of options available under the Maintenance Regulation for a creditor seeking a maintenance decision in a cross border case. First, they can sue under any of the general jurisdictional rules of the Regulation.[11] The rules provide that a court will have jurisdiction if either the defendant[12] or the creditor is habitually resident in that State.[13] These provisions are pro-claimant, as the creditor can sue in either the State of their habitual residence or the State of the defendant's habitual residence, whereas the defendant can only sue in the State of the creditor's habitual residence.[14] This is designed to protect the maintenance creditor, the purported weaker party. In maintenance disputes creditors can be considered to be the weaker parties because they are reliant on debtors to pay maintenance, or perform the obligation,[15] which is meant to meet the creditor's needs or allow the creditor to be self-supporting.[16] In addition, the creditor's habitual residence is generally considered to be the most appropriate forum for the trial, since a court there is best able to gauge the creditor's needs. There are two other general provisions and these relate to ancillary proceedings. First, the court, which according to its own law has jurisdiction to hear proceedings on the status of the person if that matter relating to maintenance is ancillary to those proceedings, unless that jurisdiction is based solely on the domicile or nationality of one of the parties.[17] No definition is

---

[8] For a fuller analysis of the text of the Maintenance Reg, the Hague Protocol and the Hague Convention, see L Walker, *Maintenance and Child Support in Private International Law* (Oxford, Hart Publishing, 2015).

[9] *EA v AP* [2013] EWHC 2344 (Fam) and C-184/14 *A v B*, EU:C:2015:479.

[10] *B v B* [2014] EWHC 4857 (Fam).

[11] Art 3.

[12] Art 3(a).

[13] Art 3(b).

[14] Subject to the special rule on modification in Art 8.

[15] G Rühl, 'The Protection of Weaker Parties in the Private International Law of the European Union: A Portrait of Inconsistency and Conceptual Truancy' (2014) 10 *Journal of Private International Law* 335, 345.

[16] C-220/95 *Van den Boogaard v Laumen* [1997] ECR I-1147.

[17] Art 3(c) and Art 2(3).

provided in the Maintenance Regulation of proceedings concerning status, but this will cover proceedings for divorce, nullity or judicial separation. So, a court in a Member State will be able to make a maintenance order against a respondent habitually resident in another Member State if the court has jurisdiction over the main proceedings under certain provisions of Brussels IIa.[18] Second, the court, which according to its own law has jurisdiction to hear proceedings on parental responsibility,[19] has jurisdiction if the matter relating to maintenance is ancillary to those proceedings, unless that jurisdiction is based solely on the domicile or nationality of one of the parties.[20] In most, if not all cases, this ancillary jurisdiction will be determined by the jurisdiction rules in Brussels IIa, which focus on the habitual residence of the child.[21]

A question that has been raised is whether the two ancillary provisions are mutually exclusive in a case where spouses are divorcing and making applications for child maintenance and spousal maintenance, or whether they are two separate and independent ancillary claims. This problem arose in an English-Italian case, where the spouses were Italian nationals who had lived in England for the majority of their married life and the children had been born and raised in England.[22] The father initiated divorce proceedings in Italy on the basis of the parties' common nationality,[23] but it was clear that issues relating to parental responsibility had to be decided by the English courts.[24] The question therefore was which court should deal with the maintenance question.[25] The CJEU considered that the scope of the concept of ancillary matter could not be left to the discretion of national courts, and instead an autonomous and uniform application was required.[26] The Court pointed out that a literal interpretation of the Maintenance Regulation indicated that proceedings on status and parental responsibility were to be distinguished from one another,[27] and that Brussels IIa also separates parental responsibility proceedings from divorce proceedings.[28] The purpose of this separation was to ensure the protection of the best interests of the child on the basis of proximity.[29] The court also considered that the valuation of child maintenance was intrinsically linked to parental responsibility,[30] therefore decisions on child maintenance could only be ancillary to parental responsibility proceedings and not divorce proceedings where the two provisions resulted in conflicting jurisdictions.[31] Further it is unclear how in this particular case Article 3(c) could apply to the children

---

[18] Council Reg (EC) No 2201/2003 of 27 December 2003 concerning jurisdiction and the recognition and enforcement of judgments in matrimonial matters and the matters of parental responsibility (Brussels IIa), Art 3.

[19] 'Parental responsibility' is the neutral term used by Brussels IIa, and has generally been taken to mean any proceedings relating to the care and upbringing of the child, which includes parental responsibility.

[20] Art 3(d) and Art 2(3).

[21] Brussels IIa, Art 8.

[22] *EA v AP* [2013] EWHC 2344 (Fam).

[23] Brussels IIa, Art 3(b).

[24] Brussels IIa, Art 8.

[25] C-184/14 *A v B*, EU:C:2015:479.

[26] ibid [30]–[31].

[27] ibid [32].

[28] ibid [36].

[29] ibid [37]. This is based on the approach taken by Brussels IIa, see Rec 5 and 12.

[30] ibid [40]. Art 3(d) has been used by the Brussels Court of Appeal to combine cases on parental responsibility and maintenance, see ch 6.

[31] ibid [48]. The Italian Supreme Court of Cassation followed the decision of the CJEU, see ch 8.

anyway as there was no question of *status* in relation to these particular children.[32] The outcome is consistent with Brussels IIa and makes sense in relation to the protection of the child. However it will not assist maintenance creditors where the other party has brought divorce proceedings, and proceedings for financial relief,[33] in another Member State and both parents then have to pay for proceedings in two Member States. This will not protect creditors, particularly litigants in person, who will have to find their way around two different legal systems.

In addition to the general provisions, there are several other special jurisdictional rules found in the Maintenance Regulation. Article 4 introduces a choice-of-court clause, but the provision limits the parties' choice. Under Article 4 the parties can select a court, or courts, in a Member State where one of the parties is habitually resident,[34] or court(s) in a Member State where one of the parties is domiciled or a national.[35] Where the maintenance obligation relates to spouses or former spouses, they can also designate the court which has jurisdiction to determine their matrimonial disputes, or the court of the Member State where they had their last common habitual residence, provided that that residence lasted for at least a year.[36] A choice-of-court clause does not apply to any maintenance proceedings concerning children under the age of 18.[37] Any agreement must be in writing,[38] however in *B v B* Parker J held that a choice-of-court agreement does not have to be explicitly stated and it can be inferred.[39] In this case the agreement was clearly inferred from the prayers in the divorce petition.[40] It is unclear whether the CJEU would have taken the same approach as the English courts if the question was posed to it. The Regulation simply states that the agreement should be in writing, which includes any durable record, but it does not give any indication of whether the agreement should be explicit, or follow a particular format.[41] Although Mr B indicated in the prayers at the end of his divorce petition that he would initiate maintenance proceedings in England, it is questionable whether this should be considered as a choice-of-court 'agreement'.[42] Limits placed on party autonomy in relation to choice-of-court agreements are generally intended to protect the weaker party.[43] In order to ensure this happens in maintenance disputes, where the Regulation generally aims to protect the weaker party, it is arguable that an agreement in writing should be a written

---

[32] Emphasis added, and see Walker, above n 8, 63.

[33] In accordance with Art 3(c).

[34] Art 4 (1)(a).

[35] Arts (4(1)(b) and 2(3).

[36] Art 4(1)(c).

[37] Art 4(3) and see *B v B* [2014] EWHC 4857 (Fam) [62], where the choice-of-court agreement could not apply to child maintenance.

[38] Art 4(2).

[39] *B v B* [2014] EWHC 4857 (Fam) [45].

[40] ibid. The husband had seised the English court for divorce proceedings on the basis of his domicile, under s 5(2)(b) of the Domicile and Matrimonial Proceedings Act 1973. This is because no court had jurisdiction under Brussels IIa and Art 7(1) provides that national law should apply in such circumstances.

[41] Art 4(2).

[42] In national English cases, at least, it is common practice to tick all the boxes in the prayers at the end of a divorce petition regardless of whether the litigant actually brings these proceedings. This has generally been seen as an administrative exercise. Going forward however, it would be unwise for a litigant to tick the boxes in the prayers in an international case, unless the litigant was clear that they wanted to bring maintenance proceedings in England, in case this is perceived as a choice of court agreement. In Belgium, less controversially, a court in Brussels found a choice of court agreement on the basis of letters between counsel (*S.—R v R* Brussels 18 February 2013).

[43] See Rühl, above n 15.

agreement signed by both parties, akin to a contract. Conversely in *B*, Parker J held that the indication in the prayers constituted a choice-of-court agreement in order to protect the weaker party. Although the approach worked in this case, it may not have the desired outcome in every case and it is a rather inflexible precedent.[44]

Article 4 departs from the previous system where the provisions on prorogation of jurisdiction permitted the parties to select any court and covered child maintenance.[45] This is supposed to protect children as the weaker party, possibly because they would not understand the consequences of the agreement.[46] However given that the Regulation limits the parties' choice to certain courts it is questionable whether it is necessary to automatically exclude child maintenance from choice-of-court agreements.[47] Where the parties have carefully selected a court, which they have a connection to, and it is clear that both parties agree that that court should determine the outcome of their maintenance dispute, it would have been simpler if that court could also determine child support where there are children who resulted from the marriage, to ensure that any order is coherent and consistent.[48] The Regulation could be reformed to include an escape clause where the judge in the chosen court can transfer the dispute on child maintenance to the State of the child's habitual residence if that is appropriate and in the best interests of the child in that particular case.[49] This would have allowed parties to designate a court to determine their whole maintenance dispute, including child support, while ensuring that the best interests of the child are protected.

Jurisdiction can also be based on the defendant's submission. Article 5 provides that if 'the defendant enters an appearance before a court, and the appearance is not to contest jurisdiction, then that court will be considered to have jurisdiction for the purposes of the Regulation.'[50] The provision prevents the defendant from contesting jurisdiction at a later date, thus preventing delays, in cases where it appears that the defendant has already accepted the jurisdiction. In *B v B* the husband acceded to a maintenance pending suit order which required him to file a record of his means for the purpose of a maintenance hearing. This was deemed sufficient to meet the requirements in Article 5.[51] The judge also indicated that the husband had failed to challenge this order within 14 days.[52] German and Italian case law also shows that this basis can be met relatively easily.[53] The policy behind the

---

[44] This is in contrast to the outcome in relation to Art 7 (discussed below) which is still left to be determined on a case by case basis at the judges' discretion.

[45] Art 23 Brussels I and see *M v V* [2010] EWHC 1453 (Fam) where a jurisdiction agreement in relation to a child was upheld by the High Court.

[46] Rühl, above n 15, 346. See also M Hellner, 'The Maintenance Regulation: A Critical assessment of the Commission's Proposal' in K Boele-Woelki and T Sverdrup (eds), *European Challenges in Contemporary Family Law* (Mortsel, Intersentia, 2009) 343, 349, who argues that the exclusion of children is not necessary.

[47] Although this is in line with the decision of the CJEU in C-184/14 *A v B*, EU:C:2015:479 and the desire for the decision on child maintenance to be made by the court with the closest proximity to the child, it is not consistent with Art 12 Brussels IIa.

[48] This was not the case in *A v B* where the parties were in disagreement as to which court should determine their dispute.

[49] For example Art 15, Brussels IIa.

[50] Art 5.

[51] *B v B* [2014] EWHC 4857 (Fam) [53]–[54].

[52] ibid [54]. This 14 day requirement relates to service. Under English law the 14 days runs from the filing of acknowledgement of service (Art 11 CPR). This rule is to be applied restrictively (see *B v B* [2014] EWHC 4857 (Fam) [49]).

[53] See ch 8 (for Italy) and OLG Koblenz, 18.3.2015—13 UF 825/14; OLG Stuttgart, 17.1.2014—17 WF 229/13 (summaries available from the EUPILLAR database). In contrast this has not been the case in Poland, where the

jurisdiction is party autonomy, as it is effectively 'consent based jurisdiction'.[54] Unfortunately this can disadvantage weaker parties, such as litigants in person, who do not consult a legal professional before entering an appearance. This is in contrast to the general approach of the Regulation which is designed to protect the weaker party, allowing for creditor-based jurisdiction under Article 3. However, Article 26(2) of the Brussels Ia Regulation, which offers a model of a more nuanced submission provision designed to protect weaker parties requiring that the defendant is informed of the consequences of entering an appearance, could be followed in a revised Maintenance Regulation.[55]

The remaining two provisions extend the scope of the Regulation so it can apply to parties not habitually resident in the EU, and there is no geographic limitation in the Maintenance Regulation. Where no court has jurisdiction under Articles 3, 4 and 5 (so neither the defendant nor the creditor is habitually resident in the EU) and no court of a State, that is not a Member State, has jurisdiction under the Lugano Convention the courts of the Member State of the common nationality of the parties shall have jurisdiction.[56] There is also a *forum necessitatis* rule, which applies, on an exceptional basis, where there is no jurisdiction under Articles 3, 4, 5 and 6, and if proceedings cannot be brought in a third State with which the dispute has a closer connection.[57] It is not clear from the text of the Maintenance Regulation what is meant by 'exceptional basis'. The relevant recital appears to give two separate indications with two completely different thresholds. On the one hand the recital indicates that an exceptional basis may be deemed to exist where it is impossible to bring proceedings in a third State due to civil war.[58] On the other hand the recital indicates that there may be an exceptional basis where 'an applicant cannot reasonably be expected to initiate or conduct proceedings'[59] in the third State. The first is an extremely high threshold and the jurisdictional basis would be virtually useless if it only applied in cases of civil war. For example, in regard to the current civil war in Syria, in many cases the whole family attempts to migrate together. If the whole family has migrated together it seems conceivable that they will be able to attain a new habitual residence in the host State.[60] Further if the whole family managed to make it to the same host State then the question becomes an internal matter. If the family became separated, with one half in Greece and the other half in Germany, the creditor could still conceivably get an order under the Regulation on the

courts have thrown out cases because there was no jurisdiction under Art 3. The result being that the defendant had not been notified so was unable to submit. This approach is more favourable to parties but it is not the approach envisaged by the Reg. The misunderstanding was corrected on appeal (X Cz 134/14 (SO w Bydgoszczy); III Cz 417/13 (SO w Gliwicach) (summaries available from the EUPILLAR database).

[54] P Beaumont, 'International Family Law in Europe—the Maintenance Project, the Hague Conference and the EC: A Triumph of Reverse Subsidiarity' (2009) 73 *Rabels Zeitschrift* 509, 534.

[55] Reg of the European Parliament and of the Council of 12 December 2012 on jurisdiction and the recognition and enforcement of judgments in civil and commercial matters [2012] OJ L351/1.

[56] Art 6.

[57] Art 7. This provision means that the Maintenance Reg will always apply in maintenance disputes heard in a Member State and there is no geographic limitation. If one party is domiciled in, or a national of, an EU Member State and the other party is domiciled in a third State, the Maintenance Reg does not provide for jurisdiction on this basis so a Member State court can only have jurisdiction if this can be found under Art 7. Subsequently national laws which provide for jurisdiction on the basis of sole domicile or nationality are no longer applicable (unless the defendant submits to the jurisdiction, by virtue of Art 5) even in non-intra EU cases.

[58] Recital 16.

[59] ibid.

[60] See, for example, *In the matter of B (A Child)* [2016] UKSC 4 [46].

basis of Article 3, particularly if the creditor sues in their own State and that is the intended destination of the family group. It is also important to take into account the fact that in most cases the families will be destitute when they arrive in the host State, therefore the creation of a maintenance obligation will not be practical in most cases. It could be practical and necessary if one of the parties successfully gains employment, however employment would also be an indication that the party had gained a habitual residence in the host State as it is evidence of integration into the social environment, or that the place is the habitual centre of their interests.[61] Where the debtor travels to a host State and the creditor remains in Syria, it is unlikely that the creditor will have any knowledge of the Regulation. If they do it is likely that the above arguments would still apply in relation to the debtor in the host State. Where the debtor has remained in Syria, it might be possible to rely on Article 7 to get an order (if the creditor has not become habitually resident in the host State), but there is virtually no chance of that order ever being enforced in Syria, at present, so the provision is of very limited use to someone who has fled civil war. However the second statement relating to reasonable expectations is a much lower standard and it seems conceivable that there might be situations which could be deemed as exceptional on this basis and therefore Article 7 would be applicable.[62] The provision is only applicable where the dispute has a sufficient connection with the Member State of the court seised.[63]

In *B v B* the court considered Article 7 as an alternative jurisdiction and held that it would be applicable if Articles 4 and 5 were not.[64] The English court was seised for divorce on the basis of the husband's domicile which was considered to be a 'sufficient connection'. The husband also intended to seek a residence order, in relation to the child,[65] in England which would create an even closer connection.[66] Parker J suggests that 'exceptional' means by way of exception, rather than extraordinary.[67] She goes on to conclude that proceedings cannot be brought in Dubai, as Mrs B no longer had a residence visa, and could not obtain entry without one,[68] and there was not a sufficient connection with Indonesia so proceedings could not be brought there.[69] There was a connection with Ethiopia, but the connection was no closer than the connection with England, and as the wife had already committed herself to the proceedings in England it would not be reasonable for her to be compelled to re-litigate in another jurisdiction.[70] Parker J held that jurisdiction was established under Article 7 because proceedings could not reasonably be brought in a third State for the reasons outlined above. So the interpretation of 'exceptional situation' was based on the expectations of the parties in light of the husband's behaviour, at least in relation to Ethiopia,[71] rather than whether or not it was possible

---

[61] C-497/10 PPU *Mercredi v Chaffe* EU:C:2010:829; C-372/02 *Adanez-Vega* [2004] ECR I-10761.

[62] Such as *B v B*, discussed below.

[63] ibid.

[64] *B v B* [2014] EWHC 4857 (Fam).

[65] Under s 8 of the Children Act 1989 (this is now known as a child arrangements order).

[66] *B v B* [2014] EWHC 4857 (Fam) [59].

[67] ibid [55].

[68] ibid [57].

[69] ibid [58].

[70] ibid [59].

[71] ibid [60]–[61]. The husband chose to seise the English court for divorce and child arrangements. It seems ridiculous that he should be able to avoid that jurisdiction for maintenance, given that it is impossible to bring proceedings in Dubai the country with the closest connection to the marriage.

to bring proceedings.[72] This seems to coincide with the second threshold in the sense that the wife cannot be reasonably expected to bring proceedings in Ethiopia,[73] given the amount of time, money and effort she has already put into the proceedings in England. One benefit of this approach is that courts can get around the sole domicile problem. The English courts previously had jurisdiction for a maintenance dispute, under English law, where one party was domiciled in England.[74] Now, because the Maintenance Regulation does not provide for residual jurisdiction,[75] this jurisdictional rule cannot apply even in non-intra-EU cases.[76] The decision to exclude residual jurisdiction from the Regulation was apparently taken to protect the weaker party,[77] but in this case it had the opposite effect. In any event it is unclear how the jurisdictional provisions can really protect the creditor, who may not seek legal advice prior to entering an appearance, when the submission provision can always apply. Further even when Mrs B gets an order from the English courts, she will have difficulty enforcing that order in Indonesia, or wherever the husband is residing at the time that the wife seeks to enforce the order, as the recognition and enforcement provisions in the Regulation will not apply.[78]

Another difficulty with *B v B* is that the jurisdictional provisions in the Maintenance Regulation apply in the alternative, rather than cumulatively. The judge indicated that she was using them in the alternative,[79] but it creates a rather odd result particularly when Article 4 can only apply to part of the case, not child maintenance, and Article 7 should only be engaged on an exceptional basis when jurisdiction cannot be founded on any other ground. It is likely that the judge presumed that the father would appeal the decision,[80] and therefore ruled that there could be jurisdiction on the basis of several grounds in order to limit the father's chance of a successful appeal because in order for jurisdiction not to be found, he would have to argue that the judge had reached the incorrect conclusion on all three grounds rather than just one. The father did apply for leave to appeal, however the judge rejected his application and considered that all the findings of Parker J were legally sound.

---

[72] A German court assumed jurisdiction under Art 7 on the basis that it was doubtful that an American court would hear the case. This assumption was based on the fact that American procedural law works on the principle of 'continuing exclusive jurisdiction' and the German courts had previously ruled on the case (BGH, 14.10.2015—XII ZB 150/15), and see ch 7.

[73] See Recital 16.

[74] J Carruthers and J Fawcett, *Cheshire, North and Fawcett: Private International Law* 14th edn (Oxford, Oxford University Press, 2008) 1055. Further the old intra-EU law, under Brussels I, allowed for jurisdiction based on the sole domicile of the defendant. (Council Reg No 44/2001 of 22 December 2000 on jurisdiction and the recognition and enforcement of judgments in Civil and Commercial matters (Brussels I) Art 2).

[75] Compare with Art 7 Brussels IIa which provides that national law should apply where no court has jurisdiction under that Reg.

[76] This is subject to Art 5, submission.

[77] Recital 15.

[78] The *lis pendens* and related actions provisions only apply between Member States, so even though the English courts have held that there is jurisdiction for the purpose of the proceedings, the father can still bring maintenance proceedings in a third State and the rules in the Reg cannot prevent this. The only safeguard might be the application by the third State of the Hague Maintenance Convention 2007 with its restriction in Art 18 on where debtors can bring proceedings.

[79] *B v B* [2014] EWHC 4857 (Fam) [62].

[80] 'I have come to the view that this husband will run any argument, and employ any tactic, to avoid his responsibilities to his wife and child, and that he has deliberately sought to engage in these proceedings so as to starve her of litigation funds.' *B v B* [2014] EWHC 4857 (Fam) [2], [47] and see [61].

The decision of the CJEU in *A v B* gives clarity to what should happen in cases where the ancillary provisions are invoked. The Regulation operates on the basis of the proximity to the child in cases which relate to child maintenance, and this is also consistent with the decision of the drafters to exclude child maintenance from choice-of-court agreements. This approach is based on Brussels IIa which allocates jurisdiction for parental responsibility proceedings on the basis of proximity.[81] The decision in *B v B* however, was obviously intended to get the right outcome for the creditor but it might have set a difficult precedent for later cases in relation to Article 4 and it is questionable whether the judge was correct to find jurisdiction on three different grounds, albeit in the alternative. The use of Article 7 was correct on the facts of the case, and the wider interpretation given to exceptional circumstances makes Article 7 a viable and useful provision for creditors.

III. *Lis Pendens*

The Maintenance Regulation aims to prevent irreconcilable judgments arising in two different Member States. It does this by putting in place a mechanism which is clear and effective in order to resolve all situations of *lis pendens*.[82] The Regulation requires that proceedings before the court second seised, of a dispute brought by the same parties and involving the same cause of action, should be stayed until the court first seised has decided whether to hear the case.[83] Therefore as long as the court second seised simply stays proceedings and does not throw out the case the dispute remains pending before the court second seised. This becomes interesting if the proceedings before the first court expire, because then the court second seised effectively becomes the court first validly seised.[84] The English court raised this before the CJEU in a case where the wife had initiated divorce proceedings in England on the basis that the French proceedings were soon to expire, whilst the husband waited for the French proceedings to expire before seising the French courts.[85] Therefore was this an abuse of process, on the part of the wife, because the English court had been unable to dismiss the proceedings given the short timeframe, or did it not matter that the

---

[81] See Recitals 5 and 12 Brussels IIa.

[82] Arts 12 and 9.

[83] Art 12.

[84] C-489/14 *A v B* EU:C:2015:654 [37].

[85] The other question, which the court did not respond to adequately, primarily because it was not relevant to the outcome of the case and therefore a hypothetical question (C-244/80 *Foglia v Novello* EU:C:1981:302), was; in a case where both parties had waited for the French proceedings to expire at midnight on 16 June and were both to 'lodge' proceedings the next morning at the first opportunity, when the courts opened at 9am, the French proceedings would always be first in time because 9am in France is only 8am in England so the French courts would always be seised first. Therefore in all similar proceedings parties living in England are always at a disadvantage because mainland Europe is (at least) one hour ahead. The court states that 'the time difference is not in any event capable of frustrating the application of the rules of *lis pendens* in Article 19 of Regulation No 2201/2003, which, taken in conjunction with the rules in Article 16 of that regulation, are based on chronological precedence.' (C-489/14 *A v B* EU:C:2015:654 [44]). This seems to indicate that it is a litigant's bad luck if they want to bring proceedings in England and each party seises a different court at 9am local time and the time is an hour ahead in the State in which one of the courts is located. This gives litigants who want to bring proceedings in the UK even more reason to act tactically in order to ensure that their proceedings are lodged, but not dismissed, at the time that the earlier proceedings expire.

wife had acted in this way? The CJEU responded to the question as if the answer were obvious and took no account of the fact that the wife might have been trying to abuse the system.[86] Although systematically this provides an obvious and clear solution that can be easily applied going forward, it is likely to lead to even more tactical behaviour by litigants in order for the court of their choice to be first seised. In cases where the court in Member State A is seised for separation proceedings, a clever litigant can seise the courts in State B for divorce proceedings shortly before the proceedings expire; when the proceedings in State A expire then the court in State B becomes first seised and has jurisdiction for divorce proceedings.[87] This can have a knock-on effect for maintenance proceedings if the litigant also chooses to seise the court in State B under Article 3(c) Maintenance Regulation at the same time. Further if the litigant ticks the boxes in the prayers at the end of the divorce petition then it could also be found that there is a choice-of-court agreement in place.[88]

IV. Recognition and Enforcement

The Maintenance Regulation requires that maintenance orders given in one Member State are recognised in another Member State without any special procedure being required.[89] There are two systems for enforceability dependent on whether the decision originated in a Member State bound by the Hague Protocol or not. Where the decision originated in a Member State bound by the Hague Protocol, it is not possible to oppose the recognition of the decision,[90] and the decision is automatically enforceable.[91] There is a very limited right to apply for a review, 'in order to guarantee compliance with the requirements of a fair trial.'[92] A defendant who did not enter an appearance in the Member State of origin can apply for a review, in that State, where it was not possible for him to challenge the decision, because either he did not have sufficient time to arrange a defence or he was prevented from contesting the claim due to extraordinary circumstances without any fault on his part.[93] If it was possible for the defendant to challenge the decision and he did not do so, then the defence is unavailable.[94] The grounds for review represent a minimum standard and may not guarantee a fair trial in all circumstances.[95]

---

[86] C-489/14 *A v B* EU:C:2015:654 [40].

[87] The *lis pendens* provisions in the Maintenance Reg are equivalent to those in Brussels IIa so this case could also encourage more tactical behaviour in relation to maintenance proceedings.

[88] *B v B* [2014] EWHC 4857 (Fam).

[89] Ch IV Maintenance Reg. This applies to all maintenance orders given after 18 June 2011. Orders established before that date can, in some circumstances, be recognised and enforced in accordance with Brussels I (Art 75 Maintenance Reg).

[90] Art 17(1).

[91] Art 17(2). It is possible to request a declaration of enforceability, but this is not required. No review on grounds of public policy is permitted. See Walker, above n 8, 105–28 and I Viarengo, 'The Enforcement of Maintenance Decisions in the EU: Requiem for Public Policy?' in P Beaumont et al (eds), *The Recovery of Maintenance in the EU and Worldwide* (Oxford, Hart Publishing, 2014) 473.

[92] Rec 29.

[93] Art 19 (1) Maintenance Reg.

[94] ibid.

[95] G Cuniberti and I Reuda, 'Abolition of Exequatur—Addressing the Commission's Concerns' (2011) 75 *Rabels Zeichshrift* 285 and see P Beaumont and L Walker, 'Recognition and Enforcement of Judgments in Civil

The authorities in the Member State of enforcement can refuse to enforce a maintenance decision, or suspend enforcement, on the grounds of refusal of enforcement under the law of that Member State.[96] Enforcement can also be refused if the right to enforce the decision is extinguished by the effect of prescription or limitation, under either the law of the Member State of origin or enforcement, the law which provides the longer limitation period should be applied.[97] On application of the debtor, the Member State can refuse enforcement where the decision is irreconcilable with a decision given in that State, another Member State or a third State (if it is enforceable in the State where enforcement is requested), and where the competent court in the State of origin has been seised of an application for review under Article 19.[98] The streamlined procedure does not necessarily mean that maintenance obligations will be enforced.[99] There are still procedural problems that lead to delays in proceedings, and sometimes authorities in the enforcing State do not respond to requests and there is no method to force them to cooperate.[100] Member States must apply this procedure to all decisions coming from a Member State except those originating in the UK and Denmark. Therefore the UK courts should apply this procedure to all maintenance orders given in another Member State, apart from orders arising in Denmark. However the English and Welsh implementing legislation has created some uncertainty in this area.[101] The implementing legislation suggests that an application should be made to the family court,[102] but this is subject to paragraph 4(2), which indicates that the application should be transferred to the family court by the Lord Chancellor.[103] It has been argued that the effect of this provision is that 'all applications for enforcement under the Maintenance Regulation have to be presented to the Family Court by REMO.'[104] It is unlikely that this procedure constitutes a simplified mechanism for enforcement as envisaged by the Maintenance Regulation, nor does it mean that intra-EU orders are treated in the same way as national orders. In *EDG* Mostyn J considered that the provision was ambiguous and argued that there was a mistake in the provisions and individuals should have a right to direct enforcement.[105] In the case of *MS* Roberts J decided to request a ruling

---

and Commercial Matters in the Brussels I recast and lessons from it and recent Hague Conventions for the Hague Judgments Project' (2015) 11 *Journal of Private International Law* 31, 46–54, for an analysis of why the public policy defence is more effective at protecting the procedural right to a fair trial than more the limited default defence.

[96] Art 21(1).
[97] Art 21(2).
[98] Art 21(3).
[99] See chs 6 and 10. For evidence that the abolition of *exequatur* does not secure enforcement in child abduction cases see P Beaumont, L Walker and J Holliday, 'Conflicts of EU Courts on Child Abduction: the Reality of Article 11(6)–(8) Brussels IIa Proceedings Across the EU' (2016) 12 *Journal of Private International Law*, 211, 229–31.
[100] See ch 10. Ch 8 highlights that there is some scepticism about the procedure in Italy, and ch 19 indicates that the Greek courts have reviewed the substance of maintenance decisions despite the fact that the Reg prohibits this.
[101] See *MS v PS* [2016] EWHC 88 (Fam), *EDG v RR* [2014] EWHC 816 (Fam) and *AB v JJB* [2015] EWHC 192 (Fam). See also B Hess and S Spancken, 'The Effective Operation of the EU Maintenance Regulation in the Member States' in P Beaumont et al, above n 91, 385 for an analysis of implementing legislation in the context of EU PIL Regs.
[102] Civil Jurisdiction and Judgments (Maintenance) Regs 2011/1484 Sch 1, para 4(1)(a).
[103] ibid, para 4(2)(a), as inserted by Crime and Courts Act 2013 (Family Court: Consequential Provision) (No 2) Order 2014/879 Pt 2 art 128(b).
[104] *MS v PS* [2016] EWHC 88 (Fam) [34]. REMO is the designated Central Authority for England and Wales.
[105] *EDG v RR* [2014] EWHC 816 (Fam) [15]–[16].

from the CJEU in order to determine in what circumstances a direct right to enforcement is necessary, and if each Member State must provide a direct right to enforcement.[106] It is of course certain that the CJEU will find that a Member State must provide a direct right to enforcement,[107] any other interpretation conflicts with the provisions in the Regulation,[108] but this step should provide more certainty for applicants seeking to enforce a decision in England and Wales.[109] It is unfortunate that Roberts J felt that it was necessary to request a ruling from the CJEU when the answer seems to be obvious (or *acte clair*).[110] The Regulation provides two routes for enforcement, a direct route and an alternative route through the Central Authority. The alternative route through the Central Authority can be seen as providing some benefits. This is because the applicant can pass the burden to the Central Authority who would then have to ensure that the order was transmitted to the relevant Central Authority in the enforcing state, or transmit the order for enforcement.[111] The Central Authority should also provide additional assistance in relation to applications which go through them such as facilitating the ongoing enforcement of maintenance obligations and providing legal aid if necessary.[112] In fact this provision of legal aid is only required for child support applications which go through Central Authorities. If the application does not go through the Central Authority there is no requirement to provide legal aid, and a means and merits test applies instead.[113] The distinction provided in Article 46 makes it clear that two routes are envisaged; a direct route, and an indirect route through the Central Authority. Given that Central Authorities are supposed to be heavily involved and provide relevant assistance in all cases that go through them,[114] it is strange that REMO have argued that all orders must go through them.[115] Views presented in the case suggest that REMO have not been meeting the requirement to provide legal aid nor assisting applicants with the case after the file has been transmitted.[116] Therefore not only has making an application through the English and Welsh Central Authority been described as a 'second class system',[117] because it is much slower than a direct application for enforcement, and because the money is not paid directly to the creditor when the order

---

[106] *MS v PS* [2016] EWHC 88 (Fam), Annex.

[107] Since this paper was written the CJEU has confirmed that a direct right to enforcement was indeed necessary (C-283/16 *M.S v P.S*, 9 February 2017 ECLI:EU:C:2017:104).

[108] 'It seems to me to be inconceivable that the Secretary of State could have intended to have imposed more restrictive measures of enforcement by virtue of the 2011 Regulations, in circumstances where Articles 17 and 41 expressly forbid that. Therefore, I have no hesitation in concluding that … the mother here is entitled to issue her application for general enforcement in the Principal Registry.' (*EDG v RR* [2014] EWHC 816 (Fam) [17]).

[109] The Scottish legislation, correctly, provides for direct enforcement (*MS v PS* [2016] EWHC 88 (Fam) [25]).

[110] See 283/81 *Srl CILFIT and Lanificio di Garvardo SpA v Ministry of Health*, EU:C:1984:91.

[111] See Art 51.

[112] ibid.

[113] Arts 46–47.

[114] Walker, above n 8 at 205–25.

[115] *MS and PS* [2016] EWHC 88 (Fam) [6] and [39]. It is also peculiar that REMO have been asked their opinion on the interpretation of the law when there are no lawyers working in the department, the Government lawyers are based in the Ministry of Justice, and REMO should refer any legal questions to them (see Walker, above n 8, 202). In contrast to the opinion provided by REMO, evidence from the DIJuF Forum for Expert Debates indicates that there is nothing in the Reg which requires applicants to go through Central Authorities. (*MS and PS* [2016] EWHC 88 (Fam) [24]).

[116] *MS and PS* [2016] EWHC 88 (Fam) [40].

[117] ibid [35].

is enforced;[118] it appears that the Central Authority is not meeting the requirements in Chapter V of the Regulation,[119] begging the question, why should litigants be required to use this system when they are not even getting the benefits they are entitled to?

A requirement to transmit all applications through the Central Authority does not facilitate access to justice and does not necessarily help to ensure the order is enforced.[120] In order to ensure the effective recovery of maintenance and the simplification of enforcement proceedings it is essential that litigants have a direct right to enforcement. Although there are obvious benefits to direct enforcement, many litigants need additional support and therefore will want to go through the Central Authority system. The litigants that choose to utilise the system should be fully supported by their Central Authority in accordance with Chapter V, in order to ensure that they have access to justice[121] and the aims of the Maintenance Regulation are also met in these cases. The cost of enforcement and the delay that can be caused by Member States not providing streamlined procedures is problematic for litigants particularly where the maintenance decision to be enforced is for a relatively low sum, and this problem has been identified in several Member States.[122] It has been indicated that litigants often abandon maintenance cases when they discover that the cost of enforcement, or indeed legal proceedings in general, might negate the money they hoped to receive.[123]

In contrast all outgoing orders given in the UK or Denmark are subject to a different procedure in the receiving Member State. Maintenance orders established by a court in the UK or Denmark can be refused recognition if an interested party makes an application for recognition.[124] Recognition must be refused where the recognition would be manifestly contrary to the public policy of the State addressed,[125] where it was given in default of appearance and it was not possible for the defendant to challenge the decision,[126] if the decision is irreconcilable with a decision given in a dispute between the same parties in the State where the recognition is sought,[127] or if the dispute is irreconcilable with a decision given in another Member State or a third State, involving the same cause of action and the same parties.[128] Both the public policy and the irreconcilable judgments' defence could be problematic in this area. Public policy is problematic because unlike under the Protocol

---

[118] ibid [31] and see *EDG v RR* [2014] EWHC 816 (Fam) [6].

[119] For an earlier analysis of the efficiency of Central Authorities under the Reg see Walker, above n 8, 225–36.

[120] It is recognised that in some cases the use of the Central Authority will help individuals to gain access to justice, particularly where they do not have the funds to seek independent legal advice. For further information on legal aid and access to justice see, for example, S Cobb, 'Legal Aid Reform: its Impact on Family Law' (2013) 35 *Journal of Social Welfare and Family Law* 3. Some administrative bodies working as Central Authorities function very effectively, and can help individuals secure enforcement of their orders, but unfortunately this is not always the case.

[121] As required under Art 47 of the European Charter of Fundamental Rights. See also ch 9 where it is acknowledged that the cost of maintenance proceedings is too high. In Greece the debtor must pay the creditor's fees in advance of the proceedings (see ch 18) this will create problems for debtors who do not have extensive funds.

[122] See for example, chs 6, 9 and 18.

[123] See ch 6.

[124] Arts 23 and 24. Such an application is not necessary.

[125] Art 24(a) and see (C-7/98) *Krombach v Bamberski* EU:C:2000:164, for the application of this provision under Brussels I.

[126] Art 24(b) and see (C-283/05) *ASML Netherlands BV v Semiconductor Industry Services GmbH* EU:C:2006:787.

[127] Art 24(c).

[128] Art 24(d).

track, where recognition of the maintenance decision does not imply recognition of the family relationship that gave rise to the decision,[129] Member States may refuse to recognise a maintenance decision on grounds of public policy under the non-Protocol track because they do not want to recognise the family relationship underlying the decision.[130] Certain Member States, particularly Poland, may refuse to recognise maintenance obligations arising out of civil partnerships or same-sex marriages. It might also be possible for courts in Member States to refuse to recognise high value maintenance obligations relating to lump sum payments, where the national law of that State does not provide for such high maintenance payments. Irreconcilable judgments could arise because there is no clear definition of 'maintenance'. This could be particularly problematic in the context of spousal maintenance on divorce where there are a number of alternative bases of jurisdiction available and parties could select different courts to deal with divorce,[131] maintenance and matrimonial property.[132] Irreconcilable judgments could arise where one court characterises a payment as maintenance and another as matrimonial property, particularly in relation to lump sum payments.[133] If money has already been allocated in relation to property then it could be difficult to enforce a lump sum maintenance order. A decision awarding an interim payment on divorce could also conflict with a final maintenance order. Irreconcilable judgments could also arise in relation to maintenance decisions made in third States, because the *lis pendens* and related actions provisions only cover proceedings in another Member State.[134] In *Hoffmann v Krieg* it was held that a German award for spousal maintenance was irreconcilable with a later decision on divorce, between the same parties, given in the Netherlands.[135]

V. Conclusion

It is clear that creditors may still face some difficulties when seeking a maintenance order in one Member State and then getting that order enforced in another Member State, or even

---

[129] Art 22. See also *Virtudes vs. Heraclio.Roj*: SAP B 7594/2013—ES:APB:2013:7594, where the Spanish court refused to reduce child maintenance payments on the basis of 'unofficial fatherhood' (summary available from the EUPILLAR database).

[130] Art 22 falls under S1 of Ch IV—'Decisions given in a Member State bound by the Hague Protocol'. There is no directly equivalent provision in S 2—'Decisions given in a Member State not bound by the Hague Protocol', therefore courts can refuse recognition and enforcement of a decision on this basis. Art 37 does allow for partial enforceability but this does not guarantee that Member States will recognise a maintenance decision where they consider that the relationship underlying the decision violates public policy.

[131] Under Brussels IIa.

[132] The proposal on Matrimonial Property and the proposal on the property of registered partners were rejected by Council on 3 December 2015. These proposals are now going ahead under the enhanced cooperation scheme. See Council Decision (EU) 2016/954 of 9 June 2016 authorising enhanced cooperation in the area of jurisdiction, applicable law, and the recognition and enforcement of decisions on the property regimes and the property consequences of registered partnerships ([2016] OJ L159).

[133] For further information on problems of characterisation see C Nagy, 'Love and Money: Problems of Characterisation in Matrimonial Property and Maintenance Matters in the European Union' in Beaumont et al, above n 91, 411; M Torga, 'Drawing a Demarcating Line between Spousal Maintenance Obligations and Matrimonial Property in the Context of the New Instruments of European Union Private International Law' in Beaumont et al ibid, 425, 436–41 and Walker, above n 8, 40–45.

[134] Maintenance Reg, Arts 12 and 13.

[135] 145/86 *Hoffmann v Krieg* [1988] ECR 645. See also *R v West London Magistrates' Court* [1994] 1 FCR 421 and *Macaulay v Macaulay* [1991] 1 WLR 179.

a third State. The submission provision should be less severe to prevent unwitting litigants submitting to a jurisdiction prior to seeking legal advice. The decision to extend the jurisdictional provisions with no geographical limits seems unnecessary. It is unclear why the EU sought to protect creditors resident in third States in this inflexible way, and the rule will not necessarily protect creditors in any event. Refusing courts in Member States the opportunity to hear cases on the basis of one party's domicile or nationality, in situations where neither party is habitually resident in a Member State, there is no choice-of-court agreement and there is no dual nationality (or domicile) in a Member State, is questionable when there is unlikely to be any link with EU law in these cases. Therefore courts should be able to revert to national law in such circumstances.

The interpretation given to the English implementing legislation by REMO has prevented creditors from being able to automatically enforce an EU maintenance decision in England and Wales. It is unclear whether there is a similar practice in other EU Member States, but the national reports indicate that there are problems with recognition and enforcement, appeals are made against enforcement or cases are sent for a declaration of enforceability when this is not required. Sometimes these applications are thrown out by national courts as they are not compatible with the Regulation, but on other occasions the arguments are accepted. National legislation or national practices which require non-national creditors to jump additional hurdles than national creditors do not comply with the Regulation, and hinder access to justice for maintenance creditors. Where creditors do choose to utilise their Central Authority, governments should ensure that Central Authorities are functioning as effectively as possible in order to ensure that maintenance creditors have suitable assistance so they can obtain orders and have them enforced successfully.

45

Mediation in EU Cross-border Family Law

RUTH LAMONT*

I. Introduction

Private international family law was once the preserve of national, technical rules adjudicated on by courts. Increasing migration by families between countries has affected the workability of this approach and led to the promotion of alternative methods of international dispute resolution. In mediating a dispute, parties meet with an independent third party mediator, not necessarily legally trained, to discuss issues arising from the breakdown of their relationship including financial and caring arrangements affecting their children. Mediation represents a shift away from the value of law in managing cross-border relationships to private, individualised resolution. It permits the parties to exercise autonomy over the process and outcome to reach an individualised agreement responding to their personal circumstances. Mediation has been encouraged by the European Union (EU) as a desirable form of dispute resolution supported by the adoption of the Mediation Directive 2008/52.[1]

This contribution will focus on mediation in cross-border cases involving children to examine the concept of autonomy underpinning mediation. This approach conceives of the family as a private institution, consisting of autonomous individuals making rational decisions about their family arrangements.[2] The impact of autonomy following relationship breakdown has been examined in relation to domestic family law but not fully considered in the context of private international law. Autonomy has value in EU private international law in removing cases from courts, potentially reducing the cost of proceedings and providing flexibility in the agreement. In family law, autonomy promotes respect for individuality and equality within the family. Despite these benefits, this contribution will argue that promoting autonomy in international family law carries assumptions about the nature of family life and its impact on equality, and risks to the protection of the rights of children. Interrogating the underpinning concept of autonomy permits an exploration of the limitations of the regulatory framework of the Directive in ensuring that mediation is conducted

---

* I am grateful to Neville Harris for his comments and insights in developing this contribution.
[1] Dir 2008/52/EC of the European Parliament and of the Council of 21 May 2008 on certain aspects of mediation in civil and commercial matters [2008] OJ L136/3 (Dir 2008/52).
[2] Alison Diduck, 'Autonomy and Family Justice' (2016) 28 *Child and Family Law Quarterly* 133.

in a way that takes account of the interests of those affected by the outcome of the agreement, particularly children. This contributes further to our understanding of the development of international family law and the potential weaknesses of adopting autonomy as a guiding principle.

Section II considers mediation as an aspect of EU private international law to identify the value of the concept of autonomy underlying the adoption of the Mediation Directive. Using analysis of autonomy in domestic family law, the impact on international family law will be considered, particularly in relation to the protection of children's rights and the inclusion of the child's views in mediation. Section III addresses whether the Mediation Directive responds effectively to identified concerns in regulating family mediation to ensure a fair process.

II. Mediation: Expression of Autonomy

Mediation is defined by the Directive as: 'a structured process whereby two or more parties to a dispute attempt by themselves on a voluntary basis, to reach an agreement on the settlement of their dispute with the assistance of a mediator.'[3] The court may invite the parties to mediation under Article 5, or the parties may agree to mediation, or be obliged to attempt mediation under national law. Alternative, extra-judicial procedures are regarded as providing for access to justice.[4]

Mediation of disputes has been identified as having a desirable role in both private international law and in family law specifically. The promotion of autonomous decision-making by individuals through this process in family law has been increasingly questioned, yet in the context of international family law it is actively pursued. In this section the claims made for the desirability of mediation in family law will be further examined, focusing specifically on the adoption of mediation and autonomy in EU law, and the concerns this may raise in the specific context of international family law.

The central aspect of mediation is to enable the parties to reach a decision for themselves without the formal decision of a court, representing an expression of autonomy. Diduck describes this as 'autonomy of process', aimed at providing a form of individualised justice determined by the parties for themselves away from the pre-determined procedure and rules of the court.[5] Providing scope for autonomy of decision-making away from the court has been a developing aspect of European private international family law. Mediation has been encouraged in family law for a number of reasons including speed of dispute resolution, cost saving in avoiding court proceedings, flexibility of procedure and confidentiality.[6] The Directive suggests that mediation

> can provide a cost-effective and quick extra-judicial resolution of disputes through processes tailored to the needs of the parties. Agreements resulting from mediation are more likely to be

---

[3] Dir 2008/52, Art 3(a).
[4] Dir 2008/52, recital 2.
[5] Diduck, above n 2, 134.
[6] ibid 142.

complied with voluntarily and are more likely to preserve an amicable and sustainable relationship between the parties.[7]

A. Promoting Autonomy in EU Private International Family Law

The EU's approach to civil private international law rules adopted for commercial and family law matters under Article 81 Treaty on the Functioning of the European Union (TFEU) (ex Article 65 EC),[8] has been based on strict rules of jurisdiction and recognition and enforcement of judgments stemming from the principle of mutual trust between Member States, with more flexibility in choice-of-law rules. Alongside strict rules, there has been a developing emphasis in policy on enabling the autonomy of the parties to determine certain matters for themselves. Traditionally, private international family law rules were linked to state norms respecting the family, for example, relying on the *lex fori* for decisions over family status. Permitting greater autonomy to individuals in this context has been advocated as a way of developing respect for individual identity.[9]

Mediation is regarded as a method for facilitating access to justice in accordance with Article 47, Charter of Fundamental Rights of the European Union.[10] Particularly in cross-border family law matters, this has given rise to questions over the extent to which parties should be able to agree questions of jurisdiction and choice-of-law for themselves, and when such agreement should be qualified.[11] The use of party autonomy as a determining principle, for example in identifying the choice-of-law governing a divorce under Article 5, Rome III Regulation,[12] delivers certainty to the parties and identifies the most appropriate law to govern the dispute from the perspective of the parties themselves. This is in accordance with the wider EU private international law principles of legal certainty and predictability.

The Mediation Directive takes the promotion of party autonomy further, by providing scope for the parties to take decisions not only over private international law issues such as choice-of-law, but in resolving the entirety of the substantive dispute and making the decision enforceable. Recital 19 states that: 'Mediation should not be regarded as a poorer alternative to judicial proceedings in the sense that compliance with agreements resulting from mediation would depend on the good will of the parties'. An agreement concluded through mediation rendered enforceable in one Member State may subsequently be enforced

---

[7] Dir 2008/52, recital 6.

[8] [2012] OJ C326.

[9] Sharon Shakargy, 'Marriage by the State or Married to the State? On Choice of Law in Marriage and Divorce' (2013) 9(3) *Journal of Private International Law* 499, 525.

[10] European Union Agency for Fundamental Rights, 'Access to Justice in Europe: An Overview of Challenges and Opportunities', [2010] OJ C83/401, www.fra.europa.eu/sites/default/files/fra_uploads/1520-report-access-to-justice_EN.pdf.

[11] Janeen Carruthers, 'Party Autonomy in the Legal Regulation of Adult Relationships: What Place for Party Choice in Private International Law' (2012) 61 *International and Comparative Law Quarterly* 881, 887.

[12] Council Reg (EU) 1259/2010 of 20 December 2010 implementing enhanced cooperation in the area of law applicable to divorce and legal separation [2010] OJ L343/10.

in another under the Brussels IIa Regulation.[13] It is clearly intended that a mediated settlement may have the same status in EU private international law as a court determined judgment. This potentially avoids the need for court proceedings in any Member State, beyond those for ensuring enforcement of the agreement as a judgment.

Negotiated settlements in cases affecting children have been formally promoted in cases of parental child abduction since the adoption of the Hague Convention on the Civil Aspects of International Child Abduction 1980. The Convention creates a remedy of returning the child to their habitual residence if they have been unlawfully removed or retained abroad. A court may order the return of the child to their habitual residence under Article 12. Under Article 10, all appropriate measures should be taken to obtain the voluntary return of the child to their habitual residence. Voluntary returns are regarded as preferable to judicial proceedings, saving court time and costs, and potentially resulting in better communication between the parents. Lowe identified that the voluntary return of the child was achieved in 1999 in 18 per cent of cases globally and in 22 per cent of cases in 2003.[14] In 2008, 19 per cent of returns were voluntary compared to 27 per cent of judicially ordered returns.[15] Voluntary returns without a court order tended to be settled more quickly than returns requiring an order.[16] Significant differences in attitudes in different countries applying the Convention towards negotiating voluntary returns have been identified. For example, the courts in England and Wales have been criticised for favouring judicially court ordered return compared to other countries where a higher rate of voluntary return has been identified.[17]

A German-French Mediation Project was specifically designed to provide professional bi-national mediation in cases of child abduction. Specific support has been provided by the EU through the appointment of a European Parliament Mediator for International Parental Child Abduction. Their role is to find mutually acceptable solutions where the child is taken by one of the parents, providing coordination and suggested outcomes in specific cases. Discussions are convened outside of the legal process for return of the child 'in order to save children and parents the emotional and psychological strain arising from legal proceedings.'[18] In the Stockholm Programme, mediation in cases of child abduction is identified as desirable and a way of securing the rights of the child to be heard and

---

[13] Council Reg (EC) 2201/2003 of 27 November 2003 concerning jurisdiction and recognition and enforcement of judgments in matrimonial matters and the matters of parental responsibility [2003] OJ L338/1 ('Brussels IIa' or 'Reg 2201/2003') Arts 28 and 41 for judgments and 46 for agreements between the parties that are enforceable in the Member State in which they were concluded. If the mediated agreement is not enforceable in national law, it cannot be made enforceable under foreign law.

[14] Nigel Lowe and Katarina Horosova, 'Operation of the 1980 Hague Abduction Convention: A Global View' (2007) 41 *Family Law Quarterly* 59, 76.

[15] Including judicial returns with consent. Hague Conference 'A Statistical Analysis of applications made in 2008 under the Hague Convention on the Civil Aspects of International Child Abduction: Global Report 2008', www.hcch.net/en/publications-and-studies/details4/?pid=6224&dtid=57.

[16] Lowe and Horosova, above n 14, 87.

[17] Sarah Armstrong, 'Is the Jurisdiction of England and Wales Correctly Applying the 1980 Hague Convention on the Civil Aspects of International Child Abduction?' (2002) 51 *International and Comparative Law Quarterly* 427, 432.

[18] European Parliament Mediator for International Parental Child Abduction, www.europarl.europa.eu/atyourservice/en/20150201PVL00040/Child-abduction-mediator.

have decisions taken in their best interests.[19] Mediation can provide the parties a broader spectrum of possible outcomes beyond securing the return of the child,[20] and therefore greater control of the process.

The Mediation Directive potentially applies to all forms of cross-border parental responsibility disputes. Context will strongly influence the nature of the decision-making by the parties to the mediation. Determining a short-term outcome following an abduction may be different to identifying the substantive outcome of a dispute over residence and contact where the welfare of the children in the long term may need extensive consideration. Identifying exactly the scope of the dispute subject to mediation, including the governing legal principles, will be important to the success and viability of any mediated agreement.

Cross-border family law disputes involving two different national legal systems may be very complex, raising both procedural conflicts and potential conflicts of substantive law on children. The role of the law in a dispute resolved by mediation is not to directly govern the outcome. It may be a background factor, providing the contextual framework for determining issues like the relevant governing law and general principles such as the best interests of the child.[21] The mediated agreement, in the absence of a choice-of-law by the parties, will generally be subject to the statutory provisions of the law where it was concluded.[22] Under the terms of the Mediation Directive, the parties cannot determine any rights that they are not free to decide under the relevant applicable law.[23] This may cause difficulties in specific cases, for example if there is no provision in national law for awarding parental responsibility to a same-sex partner despite their factual parental role in caring for a child conceived through donor insemination. In avoiding litigation, the law will not necessarily be tested by the courts, potentially preventing development in understanding of the legal framework.

The agreement reached through mediation of a dispute may not be the same as a decision reached by a court after litigation. Mediation may take considerations outside the legal framework into account in reaching an agreement, and contemplate a broader range of outcomes. Individualised justice is potentially desirable for the parties, but also raises questions over the public and protective role of the court in proceedings affecting children. Legal proceedings are sometimes cited as harmful in cases involving children, but as McGregor suggests: 'courts play a symbolic and legitimizing role and are trusted by parties and the public to administer justice as well as distilling what is meant by the "essence" of judicial remedies.'[24] Promotion of mediation to the detriment of judicial proceedings is potentially harmful to the parties, but also to the wider justice system. The law in relation to children and the family has an important protective purpose, and it also provides an important statement regarding the social expectations of 'doing family' and the conduct of

---

[19] European Council, 'The Stockholm Programme—An Open and Secure Europe Serving and Protecting the Citizens' 16, [2010] OJ C115/01.

[20] Eberhard Carl, 'Cross-border Family Mediation: Challenges, Experience, Perspectives: a Report from Germany' [2012] *International Family Law* 56. For an in-depth analysis see Sarah Vigers, *Mediating International Child Abduction Cases* (Oxford, Hart Publishing, 2011).

[21] Michael Bartlet, 'Mediation Secrets: In the Shadow of the Law' (2015) 35 *Civil Justice Quarterly* 112.

[22] Mauro Rubino-Sammaartano, 'Domestic, Transnational, Foreign and International Mediations: Legal Issues' (2015) 81 *Arbitration* 381, 384.

[23] Dir 2008/52, Art 1(2).

[24] Lorna McGregor, 'Alternative Dispute Resolution and Human Rights: Developing a rights-based approach through the ECHR' (2015) 26 *European Journal of International Law* 607, 629.

family disputes.[25] Promo ting private resolution may hide socially useful functions of court proceedings in highlighting the nature of disputes arising and testing the value of the way in which the law resolves them.

As McGregor suggests, the public expects the courts to administer 'justice' and achieve an outcome of fairness between the parties. In pursuing autonomy, this is not necessarily the function of mediation.[26] Autonomy grants the freedom to make bad, as well as good, decisions that may remain private and untested in court. The quality of the decision-making process is left to the parties, as is determining the outcome, with some scope for external accountability mechanisms such as a further application to court.[27] The discussion surrounding the desirability of mediation of cross-border family cases in the EU has not explored these concerns of procedural and substantive justice in the context of personal autonomy. Mediation has been advocated without fully questioning whether the underlying purpose of mediation is to achieve some form of justice, or whether autonomy and empowerment of the parties is more important. These underpinning theoretical questions of the value of law and court proceedings need further consideration particularly since the value of pursuing 'autonomy' in the context of the family may be regarded as problematic.

B. Autonomy in the Family

Mediation may facilitate personal autonomy but there remain structural and social issues with potential for a significant impact on the conduct of any mediation, and which should not be ignored in the practice and regulation of family mediation. The extent to which family members can be truly regarded as individual actors free of influence in making choices and decisions about the future when a relationship breaks down may be questioned. Mediation represents a strong endorsement of personal autonomy in family law, but its potential effects in shaping cross-border disputes require closer examination to establish the limitations on its role in dispute resolution.

The Mediation Directive covers mediation of cross-border disputes in both commercial and family law contexts, making little distinction between the two processes,[28] though they may give rise to different concerns in reality. Family mediation can be defined as:

> A process in which those involved in family breakdown employ an impartial third person to assist them to communicate better with one another and reach their own agreed and informed decisions concerning some or all of the decisions relating to separation, divorce, children, finance or property by negotiation.[29]

Mediation in family law disputes will not necessarily finalise or terminate obligations and relationships between the parties but shape them for the future, for example to manage

---

[25] Diduck, above n 2, 134.

[26] Above n 24. See also Helen Stalford, 'Crossing Boundaries: Reconciling Law, Culture and Values in International Family Mediation' (2010) 32 *Journal of Social Welfare and Family Law* 155, 161.

[27] Neville Harris et al, *Resolving Disputes about Educational Provision* (Farnham, Ashgate, 2011) 41.

[28] Distinguishing only where an agreement would not be enforceable under the law of the country where it was made under Recital 21, and in the rights and obligations that cannot be determined by the parties in family and employment relationships under Recital 10.

[29] UK Family Mediation Council Code of Practice 2010, art 1.2, www.familymediationcouncil.org.uk/us/code-practice/definitions/.

contact and access with children and ongoing maintenance. Family relationships do not have the 'at arms-length' quality of commercial relationships, and the experience of the previous relationship between the now-disputing parties can affect the conduct of mediation. Mediation disputes involving children, where an ongoing relationship is likely to be maintained between the parties, raises specific considerations regarding perceptions and reality of autonomous 'rational' decision-making. In cross-national relationships, this may be further complicated by cultural expectations and practical constraints such as physical distance between the parties at the mediation, but also in shaping the long-term care arrangements for children.

Barlow has identified that, in modern family law, there is an increasing tendency to regard adult relationships as equal partnerships where each partner can exercise their autonomy.[30] Respecting such autonomy is an expression of formal equality in that each party has identical rights and powers over their own decisions affecting the relationship. No distinguishing factor is drawn on the basis of gender or expected roles; individuals are able to determine their roles for themselves on an equal footing. Herring states that autonomy is resonant of individual choice, liberty and self-sufficiency and holds a 'sacred status' in the modern law.[31] Conceiving of family life as a partnership of autonomous equals is attractive since equality and autonomy are regarded as empowering concepts permitting the free exercise of individual rights.[32]

This conception of the family has a significant impact on how family relationships are organised by the law. It means that parties to any relationship can expect to have a measure of control over the management and effects of the relationship. Rather than regarding decisions taken by family members as for the wellbeing of the family, decisions taken are exercised in joint autonomy by the adult parties to the relationship. After the relationship has ended, each party is regarded as capable of exercising their own autonomy to rationally identify and secure their own interests in relation to financial implications and arrangements for their children in the future. Mediation keeps matters of an intensely personal relationship to be resolved between the parties away from the public sphere of the court.[33] The law may influence the overall framework of individual decisions made between the parties, but it does not govern the private family space. The role of the law then is to be facilitative in shaping private decision-making, rather than be determinative.

This conception of family life identifies each party to the relationship as individualised autonomous actors, as 'parties' rather than former partners. Yet in its pure form, exercising personal autonomy fails to account for the social realities of human relationships. Individuals rarely live lives entirely detached from emotional relationships that have the capacity to affect their judgment and rationality. As Herring suggests: 'People do not understand their family lives as involving clashes of individual rights or interests, but rather as a working through of relationships.'[34] These relationships are an essential social part of living but are also a constraint on individualised choice and action. Irrational decisions may be taken

---

[30] Anne Barlow, 'Solidarity, Autonomy and Equality: Mixed Messages for the Family?' (2015) 27 *Child and Family Law* 223.

[31] Jonathan Herring, 'Relational Autonomy and Family Law' in J Wallbank, S Choudhry and J Herring (eds), *Rights, Gender and Family Law* (Abingdon, Routledge, 2010) 257–275, 267.

[32] Barlow, above n 30, 225.

[33] Diduck, above n 2, 133.

[34] Herring, above n 31, 266.

against self-interest based on an emotional commitment of care. The emotions of relationship breakdown may also result in other behaviours, which may be regarded as aggressive or, in some circumstances such as child abduction, as a response to perceived abuse. The emotional ties created by intimate relationships of love and care are valuable for the functioning of normal society, and cannot be ignored. Even once the intimate relationship between adult partners has ended, there will be emotional ties that continue, and where there are children of the intimate relationship, unless there are circumstances that indicate to the contrary, the former partners should maintain relations to some degree through their joint relationship with their child(ren).

The negotiation involved in mediating decisions at the end of an intimate relationship are an acknowledgment of those past emotional ties and the reality of a relationship of a different familial and financial nature continuing into the future. Whilst autonomy may be exercised in this process, it is by its nature affected and influenced by the surrounding emotions, relationships and resources.[35] The emotional impact of an intimate relationship may be particularly evident where there has been abuse of one partner by another. In these circumstances, mediation will not be appropriate because the dynamics of the former relationship are damaging. The Directive contains no specific provision to this effect, instead leaving the issue of determining when mediation is appropriate to national law. Article 5(1) of the Directive states that a court 'may, when appropriate and having regard to all the circumstances of the case, invite the parties to use mediation.' National law can make mediation compulsory or subject to incentives.[36] This does not guarantee that mediation will be prevented where violence and abuse has been part of the relationship, despite the concern of the EU to combat the effects of violence in intimate relationships.[37] The failure to include such guarantees in the Directive demonstrates the impact of linking family mediation with mediation of other civil and commercial disputes.

Diduck has argued that the promotion of autonomy means that only those deemed 'vulnerable' are worthy of the procedural protections of a formal legal process, and excluded from mediation because their autonomy in decision-making is compromised.[38] However, a person deemed autonomous might still be vulnerable in various ways for reasons of financial security or health. Particularly in cross-border cases a formal court hearing may be necessary where circumstances other than family abuse are present because of the complexity of the issues raised and the impact geographical distance may have in restricting movement or resistance between the parties. Categorisation of cases suitable for mediation must be nuanced to be effective and to avoid the unrealistic assessment of the pressures exerted on the parties. Assessment of suitability for mediation will depend on national legal frameworks on mediation in family law and will vary in approach.

The pursuit of autonomous decision-making in family law is underpinned by the assumption of equality between the parties to the mediation. However, the conduct of family life remains heavily influenced by structural inequalities and gendered social norms, particularly in relation to parenting practices and participation in paid work after the birth

---

[35] ibid 268.

[36] Dir 2008/52, Art 5(2).

[37] Ruth Lamont, 'Beating Domestic Violence? Assessing the EU's Contribution to Tackling Violence Against Women' (2013) 50 *Common Market Law Review* 1787, 1805.

[38] Diduck, above n 2, 147.

of children. In the EU as a whole, women are more likely than men to work part time or not at all and adopt the primary carer role, undertaking the majority of household chores.[39] For women, the tax burden and childcare policies have a significant impact on labour market participation. The gender pay gap remains with women paid 16 per cent less than men for an hour of work.[40] The nature of caring patterns and labour market participation does vary between the Member States. In countries such as Italy, where the employment rate of women is low, the gender pay gap is low. In other countries, such as the Czech Republic and Germany, the labour market for women is highly segregated or dominated by part time work but participation is higher, as is the gender pay gap.[41]

The assumption that the partners are equal in terms of financial and caring resource at the end of the relationship is flawed. Pursuit of autonomy should dictate that the parties live with the decisions made during the relationship regarding their relative roles,[42] but this ignores the fact that these decisions would have been shaped by factors beyond the partners' control such as relative earning capacity and availability of childcare. Logically the rational choice is often that women would adopt the primary caring role for any children. Alongside these 'rational' factors, the social norm in most Member States still favours women as the primary carers of children creating further expectations regarding the adoption of traditional gender roles in relation to caring for children.

These structural inequalities inevitably undermine the assumption of equality underpinning the use of mediation in family law generally, but have particular impact in cross-border cases. Women migrants are far less likely to participate in their host labour market than male migrants; the male breadwinner model of economic migration is effectively maintained between the Member States.[43] In reporting on the state of gender equality in the EU the European Commission has identified that: 'Migrant women have even fewer opportunities and resources than male migrants and are more likely to face multiple discrimination.'[44] This means that if a mother has migrated with a father within the EU and she wishes to work, then returning to her home State will provide better opportunities, but her caring obligations and the need to maintain a relationship between the child and the father may restrain her from this option on relationship breakdown.[45] Her economic position is likely to be significantly weaker than her partner's, and economically weaker than a non-migrant mother.

Using mediation to resolve cross-border family disputes may have some advantages over litigation if it allows the parties to avoid the structural inequalities of one law. For example, if the law of a Member State favours one gendered partner as primary carer, the parties could mediate a different arrangement more suitable to their needs. However, structural inequalities may further affect the actual conduct of the mediation in two ways. First, the

---

[39] European Commission 'Report on Equality Between Women and Men 2015' 11 (Report on Equality), http://ec.europa.eu/justice/gender-equality/files/annual_reports/2016_annual_report_2015_web_en.pdf.

[40] ibid 16.

[41] ibid 52.

[42] ibid 231.

[43] Louise Ackers, *Shifting Spaces: Women, Citizenship and Migration in the European Union* (Bristol, Policy Press, 2009) 45.

[44] European Commission, *Report on Equality* (above n 39) 15.

[45] Ruth Lamont, 'Free Movement of Persons, Child Abduction and Relocation within the European Union' (2012) 34 *Journal of Social Welfare and Family Law* 231, 232.

nature of the relationship prior to the breakdown in relation to paid work and the care of children is likely to heavily influence the outcome of the mediation in terms of the arrangements reached. In migrant families, the likelihood is that in an opposite-sex relationship the mother is the primary carer for the children and the father is the primary breadwinner. If this is the arrangement before a relationship breaks down, it is unlikely to be fundamentally changed through mediation, although it may be formalised. This limits access to the labour market for women and can lead to poverty in single parent households across the EU.[46]

Second, structural inequalities affect the resources available to the parties in terms of accessing information and appropriate legal advice. Mediation directs cases away from the court, but it does not mean that lawyers will not be involved in the process of providing advice.[47] The parties are rarely equal, risking power imbalance and inequality of arms:

> [A] party may feel pressurized to settle on less favourable terms than the case merits because of final need, the leveraging of access to children and/or a lack of resources to proceed to litigation where legal aid is unavailable.[48]

If one party is significantly better advised and financially supported than the other, they will be able to articulate their best position during mediation. These costs are likely to be exacerbated in cross-national cases given the potential complexity of the arrangements for the mediation, the private international law issues of choice-of-law and enforceability, and the range of substantive issues that may need resolving. Financial resource to access specialist legal advice can be a serious problem in cross-border family litigation; it will remain an issue even where a dispute is mediated. Inequality of arms and potential power imbalances are potentially exacerbated where the negotiation is private, without the protective oversight of the court.

C. Party Autonomy and Inclusion of Children in Mediation

The emphasis on party autonomy within mediation assumes that the children of any adult relationship will be the focus of the parents' decision-making. The parents, in negotiating with one another and exercising their autonomy, are expected to seek arrangements that secure the best interests of their child. The focus on the autonomy of the adults to make decisions potentially eclipses the interest of the children in the decisions reached over arrangements affecting their welfare. This underlying assumption has to be tested for its utility in cross-border cases to ensure mediation, despite being a private individualised process, has the capacity to respect for the child's right to be heard and have decisions affecting them made in their best interests.

Recital 27, Directive 2008/52 states that: 'This Directive seeks to promote fundamental rights, and takes into account the principles, recognised in particular by the Charter of Fundamental Rights of the European Union.' In seeking to secure the fundamental rights of individuals involved in cross-border litigation, the focus has been on Article 47 and access to justice. However, for family proceedings, other provisions of the Charter will be highly

---

[46] European Commission, *Report on Equality* (above n 39) 15.
[47] Diduck, above n 2, 142.
[48] McGregor, above n 24, 613.

relevant. Under Article 24(2) of the Charter, in all actions relating to children by public authorities or private institutions the best interests of the child must be a primary consideration. Article 24(1) protects the right of the child to be heard and have their views taken into consideration on matters that concern them, in accordance with their age and maturity. These rights reflect the rights expressed in the UN Convention on the Rights of the Child 1990 (UNCRC)[49] and should be taken into account by the institutions of the EU and by the Member States when implementing EU law.[50]

The UNCRC has been signed by all EU Member States, and all Member States are bound by their obligations under the European Convention on Human Rights and Fundamental Freedoms 1950, which provides protection for the welfare of children under Article 8. To implement these obligations, the Council of Europe has adopted a Recommendation on the Participation of Children and Young People[51] which seeks to ensure that children can exercise their right to be heard. As part of this recommendation, children's right to participate should be taken into account in legislative measures, and the Council of Europe suggests that parents and carers should be encouraged to respect the child's human dignity, rights, feelings and opinions. States should also ensure that providers of services to families and children support children to participate in service delivery, and this could include mediation services. The family is the primary site for developing child participation in everyday decision-making, enabling a child's sense of self and autonomy as they grow up to adulthood. This aspect of child participation is hidden in legal principles focused on formal modes of participation in court to ensure a child is effectively heard in proceedings.

In implementing these obligations to protect and promote the welfare of children, each Member State will have its own arrangements to enable participation of children in court proceedings, and hearing children in decisions affecting the child. In cross-border proceedings affecting children, the Brussels IIa Regulation reinforces this obligation on Member States, for example by requiring that a child of appropriate age and maturity be heard in return proceedings following international child abduction.[52] This obligation does not arise if a dispute is mediated. In mediated disputes, there are no formal court processes or compulsion to ensure that the child is heard.[53] The privacy of mediation and the ability of the parties to organise the process as they choose in exercising their own autonomy means that they can effectively limit the extent to which the child participates in the process.

In relation to English practice on mediation, Ewing et al have identified the risk that: 'the fact that only the adults are participants creates an inevitable tendency for all processes to become dominated by adult agendas and for children's voices to be marginalised.'[54] Mediation of disputes gives rise to the question of how the child's views are brought into the process. Underpinning the family with the concept of party autonomy should highlight the child's own autonomy and interest in the outcome of mediation. Yet, rather than hearing

---

[49] Particularly Arts 3, 9, 12 and 13 UNCRC, Explanatory Note on Art 24, [2007] OJ C303/17.

[50] Charter of Fundamental Rights, Art 52.

[51] Council of Europe, 'Recommendation CM/Rec[2012] 2 of the Council of Ministers to Member States on the Participation of Children and Young People under 18', 28.3.2012. www.coe.int/en/web/children/participation.

[52] Reg 2201/2003, Art 11(2).

[53] Grainne Dennison, 'Is Mediation Compatible with Children's Rights?' (2010) 2 *Journal of Social Welfare and Family Law* 169, 170.

[54] Jan Ewing et al, 'Children's Voices: Centre-Stage or Side-Lined in Out-of-Court Dispute Resolution in England and Wales?' (2015) 27 *Child and Family Law Quarterly* 42, 59.

the child directly in the process, parents may be regarded as representing the interests of their children and may be actively resistant to having the child involved in the mediation or meeting the mediator, often on the grounds of protecting the child. The mediator may be concerned over possible effects of coaching by one parent and the difficulties feeding back on the child's opinion to each parent.[55]

The role of mediators themselves and their training and ability to secure child inclusiveness is highly important, potentially adding to the expense of mediation. Ewing et al found that mediators tended to focus on decision-making to secure the child's welfare, rather than on child-inclusive mediation that includes the child in the process of making the decision.[56] In cross-border mediation, access of the child to the process is likely to be even more limited, and cost and time considerations may further limit the extent of their participation. Whilst this is compliant with Article 24(1) of the Charter, since only public and private institutions have to make provision to hear the child in decisions affecting them, it does not respect the wider principle of child participation or, if autonomy is desirable, promote the child's autonomy.

Determining whether an agreement reached through mediation should meet the standard of securing the best interests of the child is unclear. Article 7(1)(a) of the Directive permits the confidentiality of proceedings to be breached where the best interests of the child require the release of information. In cross-border proceedings, cultural understandings of indeterminate concepts like 'best interests of the child' can cause additional difficulties in providing both a source of conflict, and a relative standard.[57] In the exercise of their autonomy, some parents will have difficulty in separating the child's interest from their own, particularly where there are strong emotions involved in the breakdown of their relationship with the other parent. Both parents may insist they are seeking to secure their child's best interests in pursuit of their own personal interests.[58] Relying on the parents to represent their child's perspective encourages the child's parents to listen to the child's opinion and give weight to it in their own decisions, but it also gives rise to the risk that the child's best interests will be determined, without examination, solely by adults.[59] The decision of a court is the decision of adults, but Article 24, Charter requires that there should be a formalised process by which the child is heard and can contribute to a decision made to secure their best interests.[60]

Protection of human rights and children's rights particularly is a relatively new consideration in private international law[61] and the EU has been central to increasing the profile of children's rights in cross-border proceedings.[62] In the context of mediation, where there exists a clear risk that the interests of the child may be lost in a private process, the EU has

---

[55] ibid 52.

[56] ibid 49.

[57] Stalford, above n 26, 163.

[58] Ewing et al, above n 54, 58–59.

[59] Michael Freeman, 'The Best Interests of the Child? Is the Best Interests of the Child in the Best Interests of Children?' (1997) 11 *International Journal of Law, Policy and the Family* 11, 58.

[60] R Lamont, 'Article 24: The Rights of the Child' in S Peers et al (eds), *The Charter of Fundamental Rights: A Commentary* (Oxford, Hart Publishing, 2014) 661, 667.

[61] James Fawcett, 'The Impact of Article 6(1) ECHR on Private International Law' (2007) 56 *International and Comparative Law Quarterly* 1, 2.

[62] H Stalford, *Children and the European Union: Rights, Welfare and Accountability* (Oxford, Hart Publishing, 2012) 41.

not provided protection for these rights. A dissatisfied party to the mediation always has the option to petition the court for a formal resolution of the dispute, but in most cases the child does not have that option. If the child is not included, they become the object of the mediation, rather than part of the process, and expressions of their opinion risks being limited in expressions of parental autonomy.

III. Mediating Decisions Affecting Children Under Directive 2008/52

Consideration of the concepts underpinning mediation in cross-border family disputes has identified concerns over the promotion of autonomy and the desirability of generalised use of private negotiation in cases involving children. Directive 2008/52 requires further examination to interrogate whether this framework is effective to regulate mediation across two countries and family law cultures, issues of equality and protection of children's rights. This will shed light on the circumstances in which mediation is an appropriate method of dispute resolution, and how the role of the mediator is being regulated within the EU to protect the rights and interests of the people involved in a mediated dispute.

A. Role of the Mediator

The role of the mediator has been identified as central to addressing the interests of the parties to the mediation and including and representing the interests of others involved in the outcome, particularly children. Article 4 of the Directive states that the Member States should encourage adherence to voluntary codes of conduct and provide systems for quality control of mediation services, including the provision of training for mediators. Whilst this is directed at ensuring quality mediators, there is currently no standard 'quality mark' for training or qualifications across the EU for mediators with an international specialism.

The European Commission developed a Voluntary Code of Conduct for Mediators[63] that addresses four principles: competence of the mediator, independence of the mediator, conduct of the mediation, and confidentiality. It states that the mediator should be both competent and knowledgeable of the process of mediation, be independent of the parties and act impartially between them. The mediator must terminate the process if the agreement reached is likely to be illegal or unenforceable, and keep the existence and processes of the mediation confidential. These guidelines are general and not specific to family law, designed instead to cover all procedures in civil and commercial cross-border disputes within the scope of the Mediation Directive. The expectation is that the Member States will develop their own processes for regulating mediators and provide specific training. One of the limitations identified in the development of mediation practice following the adoption

---

[63] European Commission, 'Voluntary Code of Conduct for Mediators', 2004. http://ec.europa.eu/civiljustice/adr/adr_ec_code_conduct_en.pdf.

of the Directive is the existence of significant mismatches in the accreditation of mediators between the Member States and the level of training required of a mediator.[64]

Mediation of international family disputes has been recognised as a specialised form of mediation practice.[65] Specific mediation projects have adopted methodologies involving bi-lingual mediators from both countries involved in the dispute with different specialisms, including knowledge of the legal framework.[66] Mediators in international family law require specialist knowledge and flexibility in the conduct of the mediation to account for circumstances including the parties and the child being at a physical distance.[67] To improve the standard of international mediation services, the Commission has sponsored training provision for mediators through bodies such as the Centre for Effective Dispute Resolution.[68] Non-governmental organisation (NGO) services support the training of mediators and the provision of international mediation services, such as those provided by www.crossbordermediator.eu and the University of Leuven in Belgium. The International Social Service provides information to mediators and is working on a project to develop an international charter of professional conduct for cross-border mediators.[69]

Whilst the availability of training is good, the number and range of projects indicate the diversity of training and lack of common standards in mediation practice, including availability of insurance.[70] Given the specialist skills required of international mediators and the pivotal role identified for the mediator in addressing some of the concerns identified in mediation of family disputes, this is problematic. In using a Directive, the EU has permitted diversity of practice without common standards surrounding family mediation, the promotion of fundamental rights, and knowledge of the law to ensure enforceability of any agreement, limiting the effectiveness of EU intervention on mediation.

B. National Difference in Mediation Practice

The Mediation Directive leaves much for the individual Member State to structure and regulate, and as a result a Council of Europe Commission has found that:

> [V]arious obstacles prevent the development of mediation, namely, lack of awareness, high cost of the procedure and disparities, both in training and qualifications of mediators as in the scope and guarantees of confidentiality. At present an overview on family mediation in Member States still shows a significant diversity concerning Member States' national specific legal framework and standards, organisational structure, financial support, procedures, training, codes of conduct and outcome.[71]

---

[64] European Parliament, 'Lessons learnt from implementation of the Mediation Directive, the Judges' Point of View', 2011, www.europarl.europa.eu/thinktank/en/document.html?reference=IPOL-JURI_NT(2011)453169.

[65] Stalford, above n 62 at 63.

[66] See Carl, above n 20.

[67] European Parliament, 'The Current State of Family Mediation in the European Union', 2010, www.europarl.europa.eu/thinktank/en/document.html?reference=IPOL-JURI_NT(2010)432732 (State of Family Mediation).

[68] www.cedr.com.

[69] www.iss-ssi.org/images/Conf-MFI/guides/Guide_EN.pdf.

[70] Simone White, 'Directive 2008/52 on Certain Aspects of Mediation in Civil and Commercial Matters: A New Culture of Access to Justice?' (2013) 79 *Arbitration* 52, 60.

[71] European Parliament, above n 67 at 15.

Mediation is heavily used to resolve family disputes in some Member States, such as Belgium, France, Spain and Ireland. In other countries such as Greece and Cyprus it is not a recognised method of dispute resolution. The adoption of the Mediation Directive has developed the use of mediation in Latvia, Lithuania and Romania. To address the issue of diversity in practice, it has been suggested that the use of mediation should be promoted by Central Authorities involved in cross-border family disputes and that training at European level should be further developed, harmonising standards through a cross-border family mediators' network.[72]

One of the most significant differences in mediation practice between the Member States is whether the parties may be compelled to consider mediating a dispute rather than litigating. In cases such as those identified above where there has been family violence as part of the relationship, mediation should never be compulsory. However, in other types of cases, consideration of mediation is required by some EU Member States such as Italy. Article 5(2) makes it clear that the provisions of the Directive are without prejudice to national differences in this regard. The Court of Justice considered whether compelling mediation represented a breach of Article 6(1), European Convention on Human Rights (ECHR), the right to a fair trial, in a commercial dispute, *Rosalba Alassini v Italia Telecom*.[73] The Court held that the Member States were free to adopt legislation making mediation compulsory and considered that mediation was beneficial. It did not examine the empirical evidence on the use of mediation or fully analyse the value of compelling the parties to mediate. Compulsory mediation weakens the voluntary aspect of mediation practice,[74] undermining the central value of autonomy. McGregor argues that to be compliant with Article 6(1), schemes of compulsory mediation must be able to demonstrate the benefits of mediation over litigation, and have clear standards of justice associated with this form of dispute resolution.[75] These are not yet in evidence in relation to cross-border mediation of family disputes.

The protection of the fundamental rights of the parties through the process of mediation is an under-developed aspect of the EU's framework on cross-border family mediation. More thorough consideration of integrating child participation into the mediation process should be considered as part of mediation training. One of the most difficult aspects of mediation as a form of international dispute resolution is in ensuring that the agreement is portable to different legal systems.[76] The role of public policy in policing agreements reached by mediation has also been highlighted as a specific area of diversity in practice between the Member States.[77] The use of public policy can be an important check to protect the fundamental rights of the parties affected by the agreement, particularly the child, if considered as a factor when making the agreement enforceable.

---

[72] ibid 20–24.
[73] Case C-317/08 *Rosalba Alassini v Italia Telecom* [2010] ECR I-02213.
[74] White, above n 70 at 56.
[75] McGregor, above n 24 at 629.
[76] Hague Conference, 'Report of the Experts' Group meeting on cross-border recognition and enforcement of agreement in family matters involving children', Prel Doc No 5 of January 2016, www.hcch.net/en/projects/legislative-projects/recognition-and-enforcement-of-agreements.
[77] European Parliament, above n 64.

IV. Conclusions

The Mediation Directive has had limited impact on mediation practice, but across the EU, Council of Europe and Hague Conference on Private International Law, there is enthusiasm for the promotion of mediation as a desirable form of cross-border family dispute resolution. This contribution has highlighted the changing conception of the family underpinning the promotion of mediation, based on autonomy and self-determination of private disputes. The wider questions regarding the nature of justice achieved through the exercise of autonomy in international family disputes deserves further examination if mediation is to be further encouraged. Awareness of the limitations of party autonomy and the risks posed to the representation of children at the heart of these disputes should be central to the development of mediation regulation and training, and to the promotion of mediation. Whilst mediation may be flexible and responsive to circumstances, it can also lack the oversight and process guarantees of fundamental rights that are a highly desirable aspect of court proceedings. Focus on procedure and promotion of mediation in any review will limit consideration of these crucial issues, and the conception and realities of cross-border family life should underpin the approach of the EU to any further intervention in this field.

46

Matrimonial Matters Under the Brussels IIa Regulation[1]

KATARINA TRIMMINGS

I. Article 1: Material Scope

Article 1(1) of Brussels IIa provides that '[t]his Regulation shall apply, whatever the nature of the court or tribunal, in civil matters relating to … divorce, legal separation or marriage annulment.'[2] Pursuant to Recital 8, the Brussels IIa Regulation 'should apply only to the dissolution of matrimonial ties and should not deal with issues such as the grounds for divorce, property consequences of the marriage or any other ancillary measures.'[3] The national reports have revealed a level of ambiguity as to the interpretation of 'matrimonial matters', in particular whether the term should be interpreted in a more liberal way to include same-sex marriage and registered partnership.[4] For example, Dutch case law and academic literature embody the view that same-sex marriage falls within the scope of Brussels IIa, although registered partnership does not.[5] Portuguese courts agree that Brussels IIa does not apply to the dissolution of registered partnerships, however, the applicability of the Regulation to the dissolution of same-sex marriage 'remains an open

---

[1] See generally Algeria Borrás, *Explanatory Report on the Convention on Jurisdiction and the Recognition and Enforcement of Judgments in Matrimonial Matters*, OJ C 221, 16/07/1998, paras 27–34 ('Borrás, *Explanatory Report*'); Maire Ní Shúilleabháin, *Cross-Border Divorce Law* (Oxford, Oxford University Press, 2010); U Magnus and P Mankowski, *Brussels IIbis Regulation* (Munich, Sellier European Law Publishers, 2012); European Commission, Practice Guide for the Application of the New Brussels II Regulation, 2014, paras 2.1–2.56, see http://ec.europa.eu/justice/civil/files/brussels_ii_practice_guide_en.pdf; and D Hodson, 'What is Jurisdiction for Divorce in the EU? The Contradictory Law and Practice Around Europe' [2014] *International Family Law* 170–74.

[2] Member States are under no obligation to provide all three forms of matrimonial relief. See Ní Shúilleabháin, ibid at 103–04. Indeed, until October 2011, divorce was not available in Malta; marriage annulment is not available in Sweden or Finland; and a number of Member States do not provide for legal separation. European Commission, Annex to the Green Paper on applicable law and jurisdiction in divorce matters, COM (2005) 82 final. Nevertheless, Member States are obliged to recognise all divorce, legal separation and marriage annulment judgments even if the particular relief is not available within the given jurisdiction. Ní Shúilleabháin, ibid at 105.

[3] Interestingly, Italian courts apply the Reg also to a specific type of proceedings termed '*richiesta di addebito*' which concern legal separation on fault grounds and involve a declaration as to the attribution of fault for the separation (Art 151(2) of the Italian Civil Code). Italy (ch 8). The report explains that 'such a request … is considered to be so closely related to the application for separation that it cannot be decided separately.' Italy (ch 8).

[4] See eg the Netherlands (ch 25); and Portugal (ch 26). For an in-depth analysis of this question see Ní Shúilleabháin, above n 1 at 105–19.

[5] eg M Bogdan, 'Registered Partnerships and EC Law' in K Boele-Woelki and A Fuchs (eds), *Legal Recognition of Same-Sex Couples in Europe* (Mortsel, Intersentia, 2011) 171–77, per the Netherlands (ch 25).

question' in Portugal.[6] In contrast, more conservative Member States, where no formal recognition is afforded to same-sex relationships, interpret 'matrimonial matters' including for the purposes of Brussels IIa as pertaining solely to heterosexual couples.[7] In the UK, it is largely agreed that divorce of same-sex marriages and dissolution of civil partnerships fall outside of the scope of Brussels IIa.[8] This view is supported by the fact that special provision is made for the jurisdiction of the English and Welsh courts to entertain, in relation to same sex marriages, proceedings for divorce, judicial separation and nullity.[9] Similarly, the domestic law provides jurisdictional rules for the dissolution or annulment of a civil partnership, or for the legal separation of civil partners.[10]

Another point of uncertainty is the applicability of the Regulation to status-declaration proceedings, and third-party and posthumous nullity proceedings.[11] This issue was raised in only one national report (Slovakia), and the relevant passage reads as follows:

> Slovak law recognises proceedings on divorce, proceedings on declaring a marriage void and proceedings on declaring a marriage non-existent. The Slovak legal theory currently agrees that all of the proceedings listed above fall within the scope of the Regulation, although there had been some doubts as to whether including the proceedings on declaring a marriage non-existent within the scope of the Regulation was suitable. The reason for this was that in such proceedings persons other than the husband or wife may act as the petitioner, meaning that the jurisdiction criterion related to the petitioner's habitual residence may create exorbitant jurisdiction.[12]

II. Article 3: Jurisdictional Grounds

By virtue of Article 3, jurisdiction in divorce, legal separation and marriage annulment shall lie with the courts of the Member State:

(a)   in whose territory:
  — the spouses are habitually resident,[13] or

---

[6] Portugal (ch 26).

[7] See eg Slovakia (ch 28), stating that '[t]he Brussels IIa Regulation in Article 1(1) uses the term "marriage". This term is defined in Article 41(1) of the Constitution of the Slovak Republic as a unique bond between a man and a woman.'

[8] See eg P Torremans, A Mills, K Trimmings, U Grusic and C Heinze (eds), *Cheshire: Private International Law* 15th edn (Oxford, Oxford University Press, 2017 forthcoming); Lord Collins of Mapesbury, J Harris, A Dickinson, D McClean, P McEleavy, C McLachlan, R Aikens, V Ruiz Abou-Nigm and F Toube (eds), *Dicey, Morris and Collins: The Conflict of Laws* 15th edn (London, Sweet & Maxwell, 2012) para 18–027, and J Hill and M Ní Shúilleabháin (eds), *Clarkson and Hill: Conflict of Laws* 5th edn (Oxford, Oxford University Press, 2016) para 8.54. See also Ní Shúilleabháin, above n 1, at 106 where this point is acknowledged, however, the author argues that 'this orthodox view is not necessarily justified' and gives a detailed discussion at 106–19.

[9] Domicile and Matrimonial Proceedings Act 1973, Sch A1, para 1(a). Additionally, jurisdictional provision is made for proceedings for an order which ends a same-sex marriage on the ground that one of the couple is dead, and proceedings for a declaration of validity of a same-sex marriage. ibid, para 1(b) and (c) respectively.

[10] Civil Partnership (Jurisdiction and Recognition of Judgments) Regs 2005.

[11] See Slovakia (ch 28).

[12] For a detailed discussion of this problem see Ní Shúilleabháin, above n 1, at 119–23. On the developing concept of 'non-marriage' in England see *Cheshire* (above n 8), Ch 20.

[13] See Borrás, *Explanatory Report*, para 31. For analysis of potential downsides of this provision in certain factual scenarios see Ní Shúilleabháin, above n 1 at 134–35. cf A Richez-Pons, 'Habitual Residence Considered as a European Harmonization Factor in Family Law (Regarding the "Brussels II-*bis*" Regulation)' in K Boele-Woelki (ed), *Common Core and Better Law in European Family Law* (Mortsel, Intersentia, 2005) 357, stating the positive aspects of this jurisdictional ground.

— the spouses were last habitually resident, insofar as one of them still resides there,[14] or

— the respondent is habitually resident,[15] or

— in the event of a joint application, either of the spouses is habitually resident,[16] or

— the applicant is habitually resident if s/he resided there for at least a year immediately before the application was made,[17] or

— the applicant is habitually resident if s/he resided there for at least six months immediately before the application was made and is either a national of the Member State in question or, in the case of the United Kingdom and Ireland, has his/her domicile there;[18]

(b) of the nationality[19] of both[20] spouses or, in the case of the United Kingdom and Ireland, of the domicile[21] of both spouses.

The Article 3 jurisdiction grounds are 'based on the principle of genuine connection between the person and a Member State',[22] and reflect political compromise based on the inclusion of the grounds as they exist in various national legal systems across the EU.[23] As can be seen, there is a level of overlap amongst some of the grounds.[24] The relative frequency of the use of the individual grounds appears to vary among the Member States. For example, Article 3(1)(b) is the most common ground for assuming jurisdiction by Bulgarian courts,[25] whereas habitual residence appears to be the most frequently relied on connecting factor in Italy.[26] The application of Article 3 appears to be unproblematic in some Member States;[27] however, serious shortcomings seem to arise in other Member States. In particular, the Greek national report narrates:

> The European legislator uses the word 'or' to indicate that the grounds provided in Article 3(1)(a) are established alternatively. However, it does not use 'or' between Article 3(1)(a) and

---

[14] See Ní Shúilleabháin, above n 1 at 135.

[15] This ground corresponds to the principle of *actor sequitur forum rei*. Borrás, above n 13 at para 31. For examples of relevant English cases see *Armstrong v Armstrong* [2003] EWHC 777, [2003] 2 FLR 375; *L-K v K (No 2)* [2006] EWHC 3280 (Fam); and *Tan v Choy* [2014] EWCA Civ 251.

[16] For an in-depth discussion of this jurisdictional ground see Ní Shúilleabháin, above n 1 at 137–41.

[17] See Borrás, above n 13 at para 32 and Ní Shúilleabháin, above n 1 at 141–44. For examples of relevant English cases see *Sulaiman v Juffali* [2002] 1 FLR 479; *Olafisoye v Olafisoye* [2010] EWHC 3539 (Fam); *V v V (Divorce: Jurisdiction)* [2011] EWHC 1190 (Fam); *Vardinoyannis v Vardinoyannis* [2011] EWCA Civ 1369; *Chai v Peng (Jurisdiction: Forum Conveniens)* (No 2) [2014] EWHC 3518 (Fam); and *Tan v Choy* [2014] EWCA Civ 251.

[18] See Ní Shúilleabháin, above n 1 at 144–46.

[19] See ibid 73–77 and 146–47. eg *L-K v K (Brussels II Revised: Maintenance Pending Suit)* [2006] EWHC 153 (Fam), [2006] 2 FLR 1113.

[20] Some states had wanted the condition to attach to one spouse only, but that was rejected on the ground that it would amount to pure '*forum actoris*': Borrás, above n 13 at para 33.

[21] For the purposes of Brussels IIa, 'domicile' has the same meaning it has under English common law. See *Re N (Jurisdiction)* [2007] EWHC 1274 (Fam Div); *Chandler v Chandler* [2011] EWCA Civ 143; *Ray v Sekhri* [2014] EWCA Civ 119; and *Divall v Divall* [2014] EWHC 95 (Fam).

[22] Borrás, above n 13 at para 30.

[23] ibid, para 30.

[24] For a criticism of this aspect of the provision see eg T de Boer, 'Jurisdiction and Enforcement in International Family Law: A Labyrinth of European and International Legislation' (2002) 49 *Netherlands International Law Review* 307, 316. See also *Cheshire*, above n 8, Ch 21; and Ní Shúilleabháin, above n 1, 133.

[25] Bulgaria (ch 12).

[26] Italy (ch 8).

[27] See eg Bulgaria (ch 12), stating that '[t]he Bulgarian courts correctly interpret and apply the criteria under Art. 3 as alternative grounds for international jurisdiction in matrimonial matters.'

Article 3(1)(b). Therefore, the Greek courts, by following a strict textual interpretation of Article 3, cumulatively apply one of the grounds of habitual residence and the common nationality of the spouses in determining their jurisdiction.[28]

A. Habitual Residence

The principal connecting factor—'habitual residence'—is not defined in the Regulation. Thus far, the Court of Justice of the European Union (CJEU) has interpreted 'habitual residence' for the purposes of Brussels IIa only in the context of parental responsibility.[29] In the absence of a CJEU decision on 'habitual residence' for the purposes of Article 3,[30] some EU Member States' courts have taken a rather mechanical approach towards the determination of habitual residence by relying on criteria such as 'the certificate of residence, the stay permit and the income tax return'[31] or 'the place of service'.[32] Such an approach is clearly incorrect as it disregards the factual nature of habitual residence. Nevertheless, other courts have adopted a more plausible approach of following relevant CJEU guidelines given in the context of parental responsibility proceedings.[33]

In England and Wales,[34] courts have experienced difficulties in interpreting the text of indents five and six of the provision[35] where the connecting factor of 'habitual residence' is coupled with the connecting factor of 'residence'.[36] It was disputed whether the two expressions were to be considered as two distinct concepts,[37] or whether 'residence' was to be read as meaning 'habitual residence'.[38] The Court of Appeal addressed this ambiguity in *Tan v Choy*[39] where Aikens LJ suggested that there were (at least) three possible constructions of the provision,[40] proposing thus an interpretation additional to the two approaches that

---

[28] See ch 18. See also above comment about the incorrect application of Art 3(1)(b) in Greece.

[29] Case C-523/07 *A* [2009] ECR I-02805 (Third Chamber); Case C-497/10 PPU *Barbara Mercredi v Richard Chaffe* [2010] ECR I-14309 (First Chamber); and Case C-376/14 PPU *C v M* EU:C:2014:2268.

[30] For a discussion concerning the interpretation of 'habitual residence' for the purposes of Art 3 see eg Ní Shúilleabháin, above n 1 at 35–66; and Kruger, 'Habitual Residence: the Factors that Courts Consider' ch 42 of this volume. For examples of relevant English case law see *L-K v K (Brussels II Revised: Maintenance Pending Suit)* [2006] EWHC 153 (Fam), [2006] 2 FLR 1113; and *Z v Z (Divorce: Jurisdiction)* [2009] EWHC 2626 (Fam). Bulgarian courts 'conduct full analysis of the relevant facts to determine the state of habitual residence.' Bulgaria (ch 12). See also Italy (ch 8).

[31] Italy (ch 8), referring to the practice of Italian lower courts.

[32] Portugal (ch 26), referring to a decision of a Portuguese appellate court in the case TRC 28-06-2011 Case: 255/09.5TBFZZ.C1.

[33] eg Dutch courts and the Italian Supreme Court. Per the Netherlands (ch 25) and Italy (ch 8) respectively.

[34] See also Italy (ch 8), noting the same problem.

[35] See *Cheshire*: above n 8, Ch 21.

[36] The French national report notes that '[t]he determination of residence remains problematic, since the diversity of definitions under EU law in different contexts is clearly confusing.' France (ch 17).

[37] *Marinos v Marinos* [2007] EWHC 2047 (Fam), per Munby J (*obiter*). Hence two elements have to be present: '(i) habitual residence on a particular day and (ii) residence, though not necessarily habitual residence, during the relevant immediately preceding period.' ibid, at [46]. cf Collins, above n 8, para 18-006.

[38] *Munro v Munro* [2007] EWHC 3315 (Fam), per Bennett J (*obiter*), suggesting that indents five and six imposed a single condition of habitual residence of at least one year (indent five) or six months (indent six), at the date of the presentation of the petition. ibid, at [45]–[53]. Also *V v V (Divorce Jurisdiction)* [2011] EWHC 1190 (Fam), per Jackson J.

[39] [2014] EWCA Civ 251. Specifically, the case concerned the interpretation of indent five.

[40] ibid, at [30].

had been identified previously. First, that the person seeking to establish jurisdiction shows that he was 'habitually resident' in the territory concerned at the date the proceedings began and that he has 'resided' there for at least a year before the relevant proceedings started. Second, that he was 'habitually resident' there for one year prior to the start of the proceedings. Third, that 'habitual residence' is proved by establishing that he had resided in the territory for at least a year immediately before the proceedings started. It was, however, not necessary in the present case to resolve this 'doctrinal dispute' as the finding that the husband was 'habitually resident' in England for the relevant period, satisfied any of the three possible constructions of the provision.[41] It is suggested here that the two terms—'habitual residence' and 'residence' as referred to in indents five and six—should be considered as two separate concepts, as suggested by Munby J in *Marinos*.[42] This interpretation has the advantage of simplicity and 'can be justified by reference to the precise language of the text'.[43] Indeed, as suggested by Jackson J, it 'reflect[s] a plain reading' of Article 3(1)(a).[44]

B. Domicile and Nationality

The connecting factors of domicile and nationality are not excluded completely. There is no autonomous definition of 'domicile' for the purposes of Brussels IIa; rather, the connecting factor has the same meaning it has under English and Irish common law. In relation to nationality, in the past, problems occasionally arose in interpreting Article 3(1)(b) in relation to spouses holding the same dual nationality.[45] In particular, the issue was whether jurisdiction in respect of the divorce of such spouses lied with the courts of both Member States, or only with the courts of the Member State with which those persons had the closest links ('the effective nationality'). The ECJ resolved this ambiguity in *Hadadi v Mesko*[46] by wisely[47] holding that the strength of the parties' connections with the jurisdiction was irrelevant, and thus allowing the persons concerned to choose the Member State in which to bring proceedings. The spouse who seises the court first will win the battle of jurisdiction due to the *lis pendens* rule in Article 19.[48]

The national reports have revealed that, despite the decision of the ECJ in *Hadadi*, national courts continue to adopt divergent approaches. For example, Greek courts 'on their own motion decline jurisdiction where one of the two nationalities of the wife is common with the nationality of the husband'[49] whereas French and Slovakian courts

---

[41] ibid, at [31]. On the findings of fact, the trial judge had correctly decided that it was not necessary to make a reference to the CJEU to resolve the question of the interpretation of indent five of Art 3(1)(a)—per Aikens LJ at [36].

[42] Ní Shúilleabháin, above n 1 at 143, notes that this appears to be the 'predominant' view.

[43] *Cheshire*, above n 8, Ch 21.

[44] *V v V (Divorce Jurisdiction)* [2011] EWHC 1190 (Fam), at [47].

[45] Slovakia (ch 28); Italy (ch 8); France (ch 17); and Greece (ch 18). See Ní Shúilleabháin, above n 1 at 74–76; and Borrás, above n 13 at para 33.

[46] *Hadadi v Mesko* (Case C-168/08) [2009] ECR I-6871. See Beaumont and Trimmings, 'Court of Justice of the European Union Cases on Brussels IIa and Maintenance' ch 41 of this volume.

[47] cf Ní Shúilleabháin, above n 1 at 82, noting an increased scope for forum shopping as a potentially negative consequence of the judgment.

[48] *Hadadi v Mesko* (Case C-168/08) [2009] ECR I-6871, at [56]. See s 'Article 19—*Lis Pendens* and Dependent Actions in Matrimonial Matters' below.

[49] eg Athens CoA Case No 2712/2011, per Greece (ch 18).

correctly follow the '*Hadadi*' approach.[50] This seems to be the case also in Italy where case law (although infrequent) tends to disregard 'national provisions such as Article 19 of the Law No 218/1995', which allows for the common nationality to prevail and thus ensure 'equal treatment in all the Member States.'[51]

III. Articles 6 and 7: Residual Grounds of Jurisdiction

The interrelationship between 'Brussels IIa jurisdiction' and 'residual jurisdiction' in matrimonial matters is governed by Articles 6 and 7 of the Regulation. Article 6 states that where a spouse is habitually resident in a Member State, or is a national of a Member State, or, in the case of the UK and Ireland, has his or her domicile there, he or she may only be sued in another Member State in accordance with Article 3.[52] Article 7(1) provides that residual grounds of jurisdiction[53] can be availed of only where no court of a Member State has jurisdiction pursuant to Article 3.[54] Article 7(2) seeks to ensure equality of treatment of EU nationals[55] by allowing a Member State national who has become habitually resident in another Member State to take advantage of the residual grounds of jurisdiction conferred on the nationals of that Member State where the respondent is not habitually resident and is not a national of a Member States (or, in the case of the UK and Ireland, is not domiciled there). The interplay between Articles 3, 6 and 7, which undoubtedly is rather complex,[56] was the subject of the European Court of Justice (ECJ) decision in the case of *Sundelind Lopez v Lizazo*.[57] In particular, the ECJ was faced with the question as to what extent the national rules of residual jurisdiction of one Member State could be utilised to trump the potential exercise by another Member State of Article 3 jurisdiction.[58] The ECJ confirmed the precedence of Article 3 grounds over residual grounds of jurisdiction by ruling

---

[50] See eg Cass civ 1, 17 February 2010, No 07-11.648, per France (ch 17) which notes that '[w]hile double nationality has always been a sensitive issue, the case-law post-*Hadadi* seems to be well settled.' See also Slovakia (ch 28), stating that the Slovakian courts had consistently taken this approach even prior to the ECJ decision in *Hadadi*.

[51] Italy (ch 8).

[52] Any reference to Art 3 in this section covers also the derivative grounds contained in Arts 4 ('Counter-claim') and 5 ('Conversion of legal separation into divorce'). For a detailed examination of these provisions see Ní Shúilleabháin, above n 1 at 148.

[53] Most commonly, in continental Member States residual grounds of jurisdiction are based on single-party nationality. See A Nuyts, 'Study on Residual Jurisdiction (Review of the Member States' Rules Concerning "Residual Jurisdiction" of Their Courts in Civil and Commercial Matters Pursuant to the Brussels I and II Regulations): General Report', September 2007, available at http://ec.europa.eu/civiljustice/news/docs/study_residual_jurisdiction_en.pdf.

[54] cf the Netherlands (ch 25), noting a decision of the Court of Appeal of The Hague in a case involving Malta where the Dutch court based its jurisdiction on the ground of Art 9(b) of the Dutch Code of Civil Procedure (*forum necessitatis*) regardless of the fact that Brussels IIa was applicable. The reason was that Maltese law (at that time) did not allow for divorce. Hof Den Haag 21 December 2005, (2006) *NIPR* 101. The same approach was taken in a case involving Malta by German courts, see BGH NJW-RR 2013, 641, per Germany (ch 7).

[55] Borrás, above n 13 at para 48.

[56] See eg Portugal (ch 26); Luxembourg (ch 23); and Germany (ch 7). For an in-depth analysis of this issue see Ní Shúilleabháin, above n 1 at 158–62.

[57] *Sundelind Lopez v Lopez Lizazo* (Case C-68/07) EU:C:2007:740. See Beaumont and Trimmings, above n 46.

[58] See *Cheshire*, above n 8, Ch 21.

that residual jurisdictional bases could not be relied on where another Member State had jurisdiction under Article 3. In particular, the Court held:

> Articles 6 and 7 of the Regulation are to be interpreted as meaning that where, in divorce proceedings, a respondent is not habitually resident in a Member State and is not a national of a Member State, the courts of a Member State cannot base their jurisdiction to hear the petition on their national law, if the courts of another Member State have jurisdiction under Article 3 of the Regulation.

Rather worryingly, it appears that, in some Member States, the above interpretation tends to be misapplied,[59] or even blatantly ignored by the national courts.[60] In order to avoid the negative effects of the complexities inherent in Articles 6 and 7, some national reporters expressed the view that no jurisdictional grounds should be left to national law,[61] or that common residual grounds of jurisdiction should be introduced into Brussels IIa.[62]

IV. The Bigger Picture: Fragmentation of Jurisdiction[63]

The national reports revealed concerns over the complexity of EU private international law instruments in the area of family law[64] and the fact that their application has to be 'fitted around' various domestic rules. For example, under Czech law, parental responsibility and divorce cannot be combined in one action as parental responsibility (and maintenance) must be judicially resolved before a divorce can be granted.[65] In contrast, domestic law in other EU jurisdictions requires that divorce, parental responsibility and maintenance proceedings (or a combination of any two of these) are joined in one action. For illustration, under Lithuanian and Polish laws, divorce cannot be resolved separately from parental responsibility and maintenance.[66] These issues have to be joined in one action, although they are covered by different sets of jurisdictional rules contained in Brussels IIa (divorce and parental responsibility) and the Maintenance Regulation (maintenance). A negative effect of this fragmentation of jurisdiction is that, often due to the lack of expertise,[67] judges

---

[59] See eg Portugal (ch 26).

[60] See eg Luxembourg (ch 23), stating that '[t]he Luxembourgish courts do not follow the approach set by the CJEU in *Sundelind*. Therefore, there might be cases where the Luxembourgish courts apply domestic grounds of jurisdiction whereas in fact the Brusells IIa grounds are relevant.'

[61] Portugal (ch 26).

[62] Luxembourg (ch 23).

[63] See Ní Shúilleabháin, above n 1 at 171, discussing the advantages of 'unity of proceedings' or 'alignment of jurisdiction'.

[64] See eg Germany (ch 7), referring to the problem of 'plurality of legal sources'.

[65] Czech Republic (ch 15). This domestic rule leads to 'uncertainties in the application of Article 12(1).'

[66] Lithuania (ch 22) and Poland (ch 10). The Polish national report notes that, where under domestic law divorce and parental responsibility proceedings have to be conducted jointly, spouses with common nationality can be prevented from obtaining divorce in their 'home' jurisdiction if Art 8 Brussels IIa points to a different forum for parental responsibility proceedings and prorogation under Art 12(1) is not forthcoming.

[67] On the EUPILLAR findings concerning this aspect of the application of EU private international law see K Trimmings and B Yüksel, 'Diversity in Applying EU Private International Law' in V Ruiz Abou-Nigm and MB Noodt Taquela, *Diversity & Integration: Exploring Ways Forward: Essays on Private International Law in Europe and the Americas* (forthcoming in 2017).

in some Member States tend to misapply the jurisdictional rules, for example, by incorrectly extending the material scope of Brussels IIa to maintenance obligations and automatically applying the Brussels IIa regime of jurisdiction in parental responsibility also to the issue of maintenance.[68] Alternatively, where all three causes are joined in one action, judges may correctly base the jurisdiction in divorce on the Brussels IIa Regulation, but automatically link this issue with parental responsibility and maintenance, without examining whether they can indeed establish jurisdiction in these matters in accordance with Article 12(1) of the Brussels IIa Regulation[69] and the Maintenance Regulation.[70] Problems may arise also in situations where under domestic law divorce and parental responsibility proceedings have to be conducted jointly, leading to spouses with common nationality being prevented from obtaining divorce in their 'home' jurisdiction where Article 8 Brussels IIa points to a different forum for parental responsibility proceedings and prorogation under Article 12(1) is not forthcoming.[71]

V. Article 19—*Lis Pendens* and Dependent Actions in Matrimonial Matters

The grounds of jurisdiction in Article 3 are set out as alternatives; there is no hierarchy among them.[72] In the absence of a hierarchy within the Article 3 grounds, jurisdiction will often be conferred on the courts of more than one Member State in respect of a particular dispute. This may lead to concurrent proceedings in two different jurisdictions, with the added financial cost and stress for the parties, legal uncertainty and the possibility of conflicting judgments at the end of the proceedings.[73] Article 19 seeks to prevent such a situation by laying down the rule that the spouse who seises the court first will win the battle of jurisdiction. The positive aspects of Article 19 are outweighed by the fact that the provision encourages a 'race to court' between the parties[74] and thus diminishes attempts at mediation and reconciliation.[75] Unlike parental responsibility proceedings under Brussels IIa, matrimonial proceedings cannot be transferred from one Member State to another.[76] In particular, Article 19(1) provides:

> Where proceedings relating to divorce, legal separation or marriage annulment between the same parties are brought before courts of different Member States, the court second seised shall of its

---

[68] Greece (ch 18). eg Grevena FIC Case No 96/2013 and Athens FIC Case No 2995/2010. See Case C-184/14 *A v B*, EU:C:2015:479, Beaumont and Trimmings, above n 46.

[69] Slovakia (ch 28) and Poland (ch 10). In Luxembourg, 'the litigants tend to rely on Article 12 while not fulfilling the strict conditions therein, especially the condition of an express agreement between the parties.' Luxembourg (ch 23). In Lithuania, the courts 'do not appreciate the prorogation option in Article 12 and they do not take advantage of it.' In contrast, Bulgarian courts 'often rely on Art 12'. Lithuania (ch 22) and Bulgaria (ch 12) respectively.

[70] Slovakia (ch 28).

[71] Poland (ch 10). See also Lithuania (ch 22). cf Ní Shúilleabháin, above n 1 at 166, suggesting that 'Brussels II bis achieves a reasonable level of harmony between parental responsibility and divorce jurisdiction.'

[72] See Borrás, above n 13, paras 28 and 44.

[73] See European Commission, above n 1, para 2.4.

[74] Germany (ch 7).

[75] See *Wermuth v Wermuth* [2003] EWCA Civ 50, at [3]; and *Cheshire*, above n 8, Ch 21.

[76] cf Art 15 Brussels IIa which enables the courts of a Member State having jurisdiction in parental responsibility proceedings to transfer the case, in limited circumstances, to courts of another Member State. The UK Supreme

own motion stay its proceedings until such time as the jurisdiction of the court first seised is established.

According to Article 19(3), 'where the jurisdiction of the court first seised is established, the court second seised shall decline jurisdiction in favour of that court.'

The Practice Guide explains that Article 19 covers two scenarios: first, where proceedings relating to the same subject matter and cause of action are brought before courts of different Member States (eg spouses each raise divorce proceedings in two different Member States);[77] and second, where proceedings which do not have the same cause of action but which are 'dependent actions' are brought before courts of two different Member States (eg one spouse raises divorce proceedings in one Member State and the other raises annulment proceedings in another Member State).[78]

The rule as to the time at which a court is seised for the purposes of Article 19 is laid down in Article 16. Depending on the procedure applicable in the Member State concerned, the court shall be deemed to be seised either at the time when the document instituting the proceedings or an equivalent document is lodged with the court,[79] provided that the applicant has not subsequently failed to take the steps he was required to take to have service effected on the respondent,[80] or if the document has to be served before being lodged with the court, at the time when it is received by the authority responsible for service (provided the applicant has not subsequently failed to take the steps he was required to take to have the document lodged with the court). As the steps which the petitioner has to take to lodge a document with the court or with the authority responsible for service vary from State to State, the 'race to court' may be 'run on unequal terms'.[81] The time zone offset may be an additional obstacle to equality.[82]

Court has recently set out its first analysis of Art 15 in *Re N (Children) (Adoption: Jurisdiction) (AIRE Centre and others intervening)* [2016] UKSC 15 before the CJEU gave its first interpretation of Art 15 in Case C-428/15, *Child and Family Agency v J D*, EU:C:2016:819. It has been suggested that the provision is applied much less frequently in continental Europe than it is in the UK. M Gration, I Curry-Sumner, D Williams QC, H Setright QC, and M Wright, *International Issues in Family Law: The 1996 Hague Convention on the Protection of Children and Brussels IIa* (Bristol, Jordan Publishing, 2015) 71.

[77] eg *LK v K (No 3)* [2006] EWHC 3281 (Fam) where divorce proceedings were initiated in France and England on the same day.

[78] European Commission, above n 1, para 2.4. eg *MH v MH* [2015] IEHC 771 (referred to the CJEU: Case C-173/16 *MH v MH* EU:C:2016:542, per Ireland (ch 20).

[79] See Case C-173/16 *MH v MH* EU:C:2016:542. The Sixth Chamber concluded that: 'Article 16(1)(a) of Regulation No 2201/2003 must be interpreted to the effect that the "time when the document instituting the proceedings or an equivalent document is lodged with the court", within the meaning of that provision, is the time when that document is lodged with the court concerned, even if under national law lodging that document does not in itself immediately initiate proceedings.' (at para 29).

[80] However the CJEU has clarified that this proviso is to avoid an abuse of process and therefore: 'for the purposes of checking compliance with that condition, account would not be taken of delays caused by the judicial system applicable, but only of any failure of the applicant to act diligently (order of 16 July 2015 in *P*, C-507/14, not published, EU:C:2015:512, paragraph 34).' (*MH v MH* EU:C:2016:542 at para 27).

[81] See *Cheshire*, above n 8, Ch 21. The French national report in this context refers to the problem of the 'chronology of seising'. France (ch 17). See also Poland (ch 10), noting that '[d]ue to the lack of harmonised procedural rules, each Member State uses its own procedural system and practical problems arise in the area of ... the seising of the court ....' (Additionally, the report notes 'the exchange of letters and notifications' and 'the participation of legal representatives in the proceedings' as examples of other problems that arise from the lack of harmonised rules of procedure.).

[82] See eg *S v S (Brussels II Revised: Articles 19(1) and (3): Reference to ECJ)* [2014] EWHC 3613 (Fam). See also Ní Shúilleabháin, above n 1, 194.

A court may have to determine whether it has indeed been seised of matrimonial proceedings for the purposes of Article 19.[83] This may not always be straightforward. For example, the Maltese national report contains the following example. Maltese domestic law requires that separation proceedings commence with an attempt at mediation, which is to precede contentious separation proceedings before a court.[84] Maltese courts have held that the filing of a request for mediation with the registry constituted seisin for the purposes of Article 19. Accordingly, in *AB v CB*,[85] where mediation was commenced prior to the institution of divorce proceedings in the UK but formal separation proceedings in Malta were filed two days after the UK proceedings, the Maltese court held that it had been first seised to hear the case.

The court second seised may have to determine whether, and when, a foreign court has been seised. This is to be determined by taking account of the domestic law of that foreign Member State.[86] In England, practical problems have arisen in this respect especially regarding Italy, where judicial separation is a necessary precursor to divorce.[87] In particular, in *C v S*[88] the wife's petition for judicial separation in Italy was declared void by the Italian court due to a non-appearance of the petitioner. The petition was then archived but remained revivable. Hedley J held that the Italian decision had brought the matrimonial proceedings in Italy to an end, with the effect that the Italian court could no longer be regarded as being seised under Articles 16 and 19 Brussels IIa. His Lordship rightly suggested that Article 19 had to be read purposively, meaning that for a court to remain seised, there must be existing proceedings before it. Any other interpretation would 'make a nonsense' of the provision by a 'court being seised of a matter about which it can do nothing unless a party revives it.'[89] In contrast, however, in *Ville De Bauge v China*,[90] it was held that the Italian court that had been seised of separation proceedings did not lose the seisin after the ending of the separation proceedings but before the expiry of a 30 day appeal period. As the Italian court remained seised of the matter during the appeal period, both parties were precluded from issuing Italian or English divorce proceedings until the expiration of the appeal period at which the husband issued formal divorce proceedings in Italy.[91]

---

[83] See eg *Rogers-Headicar v Rogers-Headicar* [2004] EWCA Civ 1867; and *Weiner v Weiner* [2010] EWHC 1843 (Fam).

[84] The Maltese national report further explains: 'After the end of mediation proceedings and where an agreement has not been reached between both parties, either party may file a law suit for marital separation, if the law suit is not filed, then separation proceedings are deemed to have been abandoned. However, if a law suit is filed within the specified time period as per regulation 7 of LN397/2003, then the separation process is considered to be an ongoing one.' Malta (ch 24).

[85] Civil Court (Family Section) (31 May 2016), per Malta, ibid.

[86] See Cheshire, above n 8, Ch 21, citing *W v W* (Preliminary Issue: Stay of Petition) [2002] EWHC 3049, [2003] 1 FLR 1022, citing *Overseas Union Ltd v New Hampshire Co* [1992] 1 QB 434; *C v C* (Brussels II: French Conciliation and Divorce Proceedings) [2005] EWCA Civ 68, [2005] 1 WLR 469; *L-K v K* (Brussels II Revised: Maintenance Pending Suit) [2006] EWHC 153 (Fam), [2006] 2 FLR 1113. See also Ní Shúilleabháin, above n 1, 193.

[87] This point was made also by the Italian national report (see Italy ch 8) referring to 'the so-called "false *lis pendens*"' between legal separation and divorce proceedings, and explaining that '[s]ince under Italian law legal separation is the first step in a two-tier procedure of divorce, it is rather common that an application for separation is lodged first in Italy, whereas an application for divorce is lodged afterwards in another Member State.'

[88] [2010] EWHC 2676 (Fam). See *Cheshire*, above n 8, Ch 21.

[89] ibid, at [20].

[90] [2014] EWHC 3975 (Fam).

[91] ibid, per Nicholas Cusworth QC, at [17].

The meaning of the word 'established' for the purposes of Article 19[92] arose as the central issue in the case of *S v S (Brussels II Revised: Articles 19(1) and (3): Reference to ECJ)*.[93] The conflict resulted in Hedley J staying the proceedings and making a reference for a preliminary ruling to the CJEU. The factual scenario was as follows: the husband issued judicial separation proceedings in France. The wife then filed for divorce in England but her application was dismissed by consent on the basis that the jurisdiction of the French courts had been established under the Brussels IIa Regulation. Later, the husband filed a divorce petition in France but this was also dismissed, because the French judicial separation proceedings were still alive. The husband, however, took virtually no steps to progress those proceedings. Under French law, the judicial separation suit would lapse after 30 months following the first court appointment and whilst these proceedings were ongoing, neither spouse could initiate divorce proceedings. In the present case, the judicial separation proceedings lapsed at midnight on 16 June 2014. Nevertheless, prior to that, on 13 June 2014, the wife had again seised the English court of divorce proceedings.

Hedley J asked the CJEU whether in the case of judicial separation and divorce proceedings brought between parties before the courts of two Member States, Article 19 of Brussels II bis should be interpreted as meaning that where proceedings before the court first seised had expired after the second court in the second Member State has been seised, the jurisdiction of the court first seised should be regarded as not being established.[94]

The CJEU held that once the judicial separation proceedings before the French court lapsed as a result of the expiry of the legal time limit, the jurisdiction of the French court was no longer established, and, accordingly, criteria for *lis pendens* were no longer fulfilled.[95] Consequently, since the proceedings before the French court first seised lapsed, only the English court remained seised of the dispute.

VI. Declining Jurisdiction in Favour of a Third Country: Implications of *Owusu v Jackson*[96]

In *Owusu* the ECJ ruled that where an English court had jurisdiction under Article 2 of Brussels I, that court could not rely on the common law doctrine of *forum non conveniens* to decline jurisdiction in favour of a more closely connected third country. It is suggested here that, by analogy, the decision in *Owusu* would be likely to preclude a court in a Member State from declining jurisdiction conferred upon it by Article 3 of Brussels IIa, on the ground that the court of a third country represents a more appropriate forum.[97]

---

[92] See also Romania (ch 27) referring to a decision of the Ploieşti Court of Appeal which concerned *lis pendens* concerning a Spanish court. Ploieşti Court of Appeal (1st Civil Chamber), Case No 2824, decision dated 15 October 2013.

[93] [2014] EWHC 3613 (Fam).

[94] *A v B* (Case C-489/14) at [26]. See Beaumont and Trimmings, above n 46.

[95] *A v B*, ibid at [45].

[96] Case C-281-02, [2005] ECR I-1383.

[97] See also *Cheshire*, above n 8, Ch 21; Crawford and Carruthers, *International Private Law—A Scots Perspective* 4th edn (London, Sweet & Maxwell, 2015) paras 12–16, and I Karsten QC, 'The State of International Family Law Issues: A View from London' [2009] *International Family Law* 35.

In *JKN v JCN*,[98] however, the English High Court held the opposite view, ie that the *Owusu* principle does not apply to Brussels IIa. The case concerned a couple who married in New York, however, they lived in London for most of their marriage. Nevertheless, by the time they separated, they were both living in New York. The wife, after having been advised that she did not satisfy the residence requirement for New York jurisdiction, issued divorce proceedings in England, relying on Article 3 of the Brussels IIa Regulation. The husband filed an acknowledgement of service confirming that he did not intend to defend the proceedings in England but stated that New York was the appropriate forum. He then issued divorce proceedings in New York, and sought to stay the wife's English proceedings. The wife argued that it was not open to the court to grant a stay of her English petition since, by analogy with the decision in *Owusu*, where jurisdiction was founded on Article 3 of Brussels IIa, there was no power to grant a stay of English proceedings under the Domicile and Matrimonial Proceedings Act 1973. Theis J held that it was 'neither necessary nor desirable to extend the *Owusu* principle in cases where there were parallel proceedings in a non-member state.'[99] If the *Owusu* principle applied to Brussels IIa, there would be a risk of irreconcilable judgments as both sets of proceedings would continue.[100] Alternatively, the principle was inapplicable to Brussels IIa as there was no 'direction connection' between the Brussels I and the Brussels IIa Regulations, and although it was possible to refer to Brussels I in interpreting Brussels IIa where the language was identical, the respective provisions of the Regulations were different in several material respects.[101] Accordingly, the English court retained a discretion to stay its proceedings where there were proceedings pending in a non-EU Member State,[102] and, as New York was the more appropriate forum,[103] the wife's English proceedings were stayed in favour of the husband's proceedings in New York on the ground of *forum non conveniens*. The dicta of Theis J in *JKN v JCN* was approved by the Court of Appeal in the case of *Mittal v Mittal*.[104] Lewison LJ, with whom Rimer and Jackson LLJ agreed, confirmed the first instance decision of Bodey J that the English court had jurisdiction to stay the wife's English divorce proceedings on the ground of *forum non conveniens*, in favour of divorce proceedings commenced earlier by the husband in India. His Lordship held that the dicta in *Owusu* had 'little to do' with the present case, and did not apply to Brussels IIa for a number of reasons.[105] Paragraph 37 of the judgment lists six reasons, the final being that the policy underlying Brussels I has itself changed: the Brussels Ia Regulation recognises a discretionary power to stay proceedings where there are parallel proceedings in a non-Member State. Accordingly, if Brussels Ia had applied to the present case, the English court would have been permitted to stay the English proceedings.[106]

---

[98] [2010] EWHC 843.

[99] ibid at [149].

[100] ibid. This point is not very persuasive. Indeed, the risk of irreconcilable judgments is equally undesirable in the context of matrimonial proceedings as it is in the commercial law context. See also Crawford and Carruthers, above n 97, paras 12–16.

[101] [2010] EWHC 843 at [149].

[102] ibid at [150].

[103] ibid at [158].

[104] [2013] EWCA Civ 1255 (also known as *AB v CB (Divorce and Maintenance: Discretion to Stay)*). The decision was welcomed by the legal profession—see eg B Frankle, 'It Is OK to be Inappropriate: *Mittal v Mittal*' [2014] *International Family Law* 17. See also I Bantekas, 'The Pitfalls of Lis Pendens in Transnational Matrimonial Jurisdiction Disputes Before English Courts' [2014] *International Family Law* 30.

[105] See [2013] EWCA Civ 1255, at [37].

[106] ibid at [40]. See Brussels Ia Reg, Arts 33 and 34 and Recitals 23 and 24.

As expressed by the present author elsewhere, the approach adopted by the High Court in *JKN v JCN* and the Court of Appeal in *Mittal v Mittal* 'seems to be at odds with the latest European developments'[107] for the following reasons:[108]

> The recently published Proposal for a Council Regulation on jurisdiction, the recognition and enforcement of decisions in matrimonial matters and the matters of parental responsibility, and on international child abduction (recast)[109] makes it clear that no changes to Article 19 of the Regulation are contemplated as a part of the ongoing Brussels IIa review process.[110] This means that, in respect of parallel proceedings, the Brussels IIa (Recast) Regulation will not be following the Brussels I (Recast) Regulation. To confirm this, in a document accompanying the Proposal,[111] the Commission expressly refers to the judgment in *Owusu* by stating: 'As the Court of Justice has ruled that Member States are not allowed to use any discretion which may exist under their national law to transfer jurisdiction established by EU Regulations.'[112] Contrary to the reasoning of Lewison LJ in *Mittal v Mittal*, the Commission adds that, although *Owusu* concerned the Brussels I Convention, 'the overwhelming majority of courts and academics applies this statement also to other EU instruments such as the Brussels I Regulation and the Brussels IIa Regulation, as far as matrimonial matters are concerned.'[113]

This is in line with the view advocated earlier in this chapter.[114]

VII. Concluding Remarks: Time for Reform?

As a part of the ongoing review of the Brussels IIa Regulation,[115] in April 2014, the Commission adopted a Report on the application of Council Regulation (EC) Number 2201/2003 concerning jurisdiction and the recognition and enforcement of judgments in matrimonial matters and the matters of parental responsibility, repealing Regulation (EC) Number 1347/2000. The Report identified three underlying shortcomings of the jurisdictional rules of the Regulation in relation to matrimonial matters. First, the alternative (as opposed to hierarchical) grounds of jurisdiction encourage the 'rush to court' behaviour. Second, the Regulation lacks provision for at least a limited party autonomy in matrimonial matters. By not allowing spouses to agree on the competent court, Brussels IIa fails to follow the trend in recent EU regulations in civil matters to permit at least a certain level of party autonomy, and hinders the objectives of legal certainty and predictability. Finally, Article 6 which reiterates the exclusive nature of the jurisdiction determined under Articles 3, 4 and 5 of Brussels IIa can 'create confusion' and is 'superfluous' as Articles 3, 4 and 5 state when a court has exclusive jurisdiction.

---

[107] *Cheshire*, above n 8, Ch 21.
[108] ibid.
[109] COM(2016) 411 final.
[110] ibid, p 42.
[111] SWD (2016) 207 final.
[112] ibid, Pt II.
[113] ibid, fn 49.
[114] See above p 813.
[115] See eg J Borg-Barthet for the European Parliament, 'Jurisdiction in matrimonial matters—Reflections for the review of the Brussels IIa Regulation' 2016, at www.europarl.europa.eu/RegData/etudes/STUD/2016/571361/IPOL_STU(2016)571361_EN.pdf.

On 30 June 2016, the Commission published a Proposal for a Council Regulation on jurisdiction, the recognition and enforcement of decisions in matrimonial matters and the matters of parental responsibility, and on international child abduction (recast).[116] Very surprisingly, however, as regards matrimonial matters, the Proposal departs entirely from the 2014 Report. It claims that due to 'limited evidence of existing problems' it was not possible to identify the scale of the issues or to establish 'the need to intervene'.[117]

This failure to act is highly regrettable. As expressed by the present author elsewhere:[118]

> [T]he Brussels II *bis* recast will become a missed opportunity to rectify at least some of the issues that were justifiably highlighted in the 2014 Report, in particular the 'race to court' problem,[119] and the lack of party autonomy in relation to jurisdiction in matrimonial matters. The 'race to court' problem could have been resolved either through establishing a hierarchy of jurisdiction, or through a transfer provision which would have allowed a Member State to transfer proceedings to the court of a Member State with the closer connection.[120] With regard to party autonomy, as a minimum, spouses should have been allowed to enter into a choice of court agreement opting for either the courts of the Member State of their habitual residence, at the time the agreement is concluded; the courts of the Member State of their last habitual residence, provided that one of them still resides there at the time of the agreement; or the courts of the Member State of the nationality of either spouse at the time of the agreement.

---

[116] COM(2016) 411 final. See also Commission Staff Working Document, Impact Assessment Accompanying the Document Proposal for a Council Reg on jurisdiction, the recognition and enforcement of decisions in matrimonial matters and the matters of parental responsibility, and on international child abduction (recast) (SWD (2016) 207 final, 30 June 2016).

[117] COM(2016) 411 final, p 3.

[118] *Cheshire*, above n 8, Ch 21.

[119] The Commission believes that the 'rush to court' problem was already addressed by the harmonisation of the rules on the law applicable to divorce in the Rome III Reg. SWD (2016) 207 final, Pt II. However, Rome III is an enhanced co-operation instrument which does not apply in all Member States.

[120] See eg Hedley J's comments in *S v S (Brussels II Revised: Articles 19(1) and (3): Reference to ECJ)* [2014] EWHC 3613 (Fam), where he expressed a strong criticism about Brussels IIa 'seemingly inflexible jurisdiction rules in relation to divorce' which may lead parties to engage in 'extensive, expensive and futile manoeuvres', at [17]. His Lordship rightly suggested that such undesirable situation could be prevented if powers were available to achieve a transfer of jurisdiction to a 'court which is better placed to hear the case or otherwise is a more convenient forum', as available with regard to parental responsibility cases by virtue of Art 15 of the Reg, ibid. For a detailed analysis of the policy options that were considered by the Commission see SWD (2016) 207 final, s II.

Part V

Conclusion

47

Cross-border Litigation in Europe: Some Theoretical Issues and Some Practical Challenges

PAUL BEAUMONT, MIHAIL DANOV,
KATARINA TRIMMINGS AND BURCU YÜKSEL

I. Factors Impairing Parties' Access to Effective Remedies: A Case for Reform

The EUPILLAR data suggest that cross-border litigation is a result-driven undertaking. This is indeed in line with Brussels Ia's objective to safeguard the litigants' right to an effective remedy in disputes with an international element.[1] The analysis of the data indicates that the strength of the claimant's claim and the remedy (which is being sought) will both impact the litigants' decisions where/whether to initiate their cross-border claims and the defendants' strategies. It seems that parties would be less prone to delay the resolution of disputes which involve children; so too judges would aim to resolve such cross-border disputes as soon as possible. That said, the fact that there appears to be a tendency for the parties to use delaying strategies in high value commercial disputes strengthens the deduction that the desired remedy affects litigants' strategies. In addition, once a claim had been initiated, the defendants' strategies would be determined by a number of additional factors which include the strength of the claim, the litigation venue and the current EU private international law (PIL) framework. For example, if the claim is weak, then the defendant will have no incentives to delay the resolution of the dispute.

The delaying tactics are much more common if the claim is relatively strong. In turn, this indicates that a strong defendant's strategy, which is devised under the current EU PIL, could help a litigant gain a negotiating advantage. An analysis of the litigants' tactics with regard to jurisdiction and choice-of-law helps us to identify the weaknesses of the EU PIL framework. The litigants' strategies in this context and the EU PIL legislative developments, which have formed the foundation of the EU civil justice system, indicate that the EU concept of justice in cross-border private cases would need to be broadened in order to cover certain procedural aspects which are dealt with in the EU PIL instruments. The EUPILLAR paradigm is that any analysis of the factors which impair the parties' effective access to

---

[1] Recital 38 to Brussels Ia.

remedies in cross-border cases must consider how strategic litigants exploit the weaknesses of the current EU PIL framework and the deficiencies of the institutional architecture in which the relevant PIL is set to be applied.

The EUPILLAR research demonstrates that the triangular relationship between the relevant set of jurisdiction rules (identifying procedural law), the choice-of-law rules (ascertaining the governing substantive law) and the desired legal remedy may well be among the primary considerations which are affecting the parties' litigation tactics and settlement dynamics in cross-border cases. In other words, the need for the parties to obtain an effective remedy in such cases may be determinative of the parties' decision where to sue as well as of parties' strategies regarding governing law. This appears to signify the important role of PIL rules for private parties' access to justice in cross-border cases. There is no doubt that achieving a desirable outcome in cross-border disputes often depends on three important factors, which the EU PIL instruments systematically deal with: the place where the proceedings are taking place (ie jurisdiction would pre-determine the relevant procedural rules and associated costs); the applicable law/s (ie determining parties' liability); and the recognition and enforcement of any rendered local judgment in the state where the judgment-debtor's assets are. Disputes on issues of jurisdiction, choice-of-law and recognition and enforcement of judgments raise the level of complexity. This is especially so in high value claims where the lawyer and litigants may be extra-creative in exploiting the ambiguities of the EU PIL instruments. As a result, the litigants' strategies will inflate the litigation costs and cause a level of delay which may affect litigants' access to remedies in cross-border cases.

It can be concluded that, on the one hand, the triangular relationship (ie the allocation of jurisdiction—identification of governing law—available remedy) has a significant impact on the litigants' strategies and any settlement dynamics in cross-border cases within the EU. This would ultimately impact on the private parties' access to remedies in such disputes. However, on the other hand, this triangular relationship is affected by the institutional framework which is the foundation of the EU model of administration of justice in cross-border cases. Therefore, there is a strong case that, when it comes to the administration of justice in the EU, the theoretical framework for data analysis must consider how the EU PIL institutional framework impacts on the triangular relationship, shaping the litigants' strategies and affecting the settlement dynamics in cross-border cases. On the basis of this data analysis, the researchers were in a position to identify the weaknesses of the EU civil justice systems.

The EUPILLAR theoretical framework for data analysis identifies two important aspects which need to be considered when evaluating the effectiveness of the current PIL framework. The first feature is that the parties' entitlement to an effective remedy depends on the applicable law. In view of this, EU PIL is set to ensure that, regardless of where the parties litigate, the same law is to be applied in civil and commercial cases with an international element.[2] The significance of this principle reflecting 'conflicts justice'[3] theory may

---

[2] Recitals 6 to Rome II and Rome I.

[3] G Kegel, *Internationales Privatrecht* 6th edn (Munich, Beck, 1987) 186–87, 193 cited in FK Juenger, *Choice of Law and Multistate Justice* (Leiden, Martinus Nijhoff Publishers, 1993) 69. See also M Danov and P Beaumont, 'Measuring the Effectiveness of the EU Civil Justice Framework: Theoretical and Methodological Challenges' (2015/2016) 17 *Yearbook of Private International Law* 151–80.

be reinforced by pointing out that an entirely different litigation pattern is adopted in cross-border matrimonial cases where the applicable law is not harmonised for all EU Member States.[4] The Brussels IIa Regulation promotes a rigid court-first-seised rule which may lead to forum shopping, creating incentives for the parties to issue proceedings in England and Wales where the courts always apply forum law to such cases.

As Danov and Beaumont have noted,[5] there is a need for a better solution which would allow judges to take account of the law of different countries in line with Von Mehren's proposal for 'special substantive rules for multistate problems'.[6] The importance of applicable law for the parties' choice of jurisdiction clearly demonstrates that it is misconceived to claim that 'the outcome of a case depends much more on jurisdiction than choice of law.'[7] It is true that the defendants tend to raise jurisdictional issues more often, aiming to delay the resolution of the dispute. However, this does not mean that choice of law is not important. On the contrary, as already noted, there is a strong case that any delaying tactics would be considered by only one of the parties if his/her opponent has a relatively strong claim. The questions, how strong the claimants' claim is and whether he/she is entitled to a remedy, would be dependent on the applicable law to be determined under Rome I and Rome II. This is clearly an important element.

The second aspect of the EUPILLAR framework for data analysis, which needs to be considered in assessing the effectiveness of the EU PIL framework, concerns parties' access to effective remedies. It is very important that parties' entitlement to remedy as well as parties' access to remedy are carefully analysed when assessing the effectiveness of the PIL rules. An important aspect of our theoretical framework is that the applicable law issues are not less important than the jurisdictional issues in cross-border cases, but it is rather that the claimant's access to a remedy (to which he is entitled under the relevant applicable law/s) is often more directly dependent on the place where the parties litigate, which is to be determined under the relevant jurisdictional rules. This is why the parties in cross-border cases often heatedly argue about the issues of jurisdiction. The EUPILLAR theoretical model might better explain why 'in England today there are far more reported cases on international jurisdiction and procedure than on choice of law.'[8] Consequently, the litigants' access to effective remedies is often contingent on jurisdiction being established before an

---

[4] Council Reg (EU) No 1259/2010 of 20 December 2010 implementing enhanced cooperation in the area of the law applicable to divorce and legal separation (Rome III Reg) [2010] OJ L343/10 applies to Belgium, Bulgaria, Germany, Greece, Spain, France, Italy, Latvia, Lithuania, Luxembourg, Hungary, Malta, Austria, Portugal, Romania and Slovenia. In relation to the financial consequences arising from divorce the applicable law is not harmonised for all Member States. The maintenance issues are governed by the Hague Protocol on Applicable Law, which all EU Member States apart from Denmark and the UK are bound by (see Council Decision of 30 November 2009 on the conclusion by the European Community of the Hague Protocol of 23 November 2007 on the Law Applicable to Maintenance Obligations [2009] OJ L331/17). The matrimonial property issues have very recently been harmonised on an enhanced co-operation basis for some Member States, see Council Reg (EU) 2016/1103 of 24 June 2016 implementing enhanced cooperation in the area of jurisdiction, applicable law and the recognition and enforcement of decisions in matters of matrimonial property regimes [2016] OJ L183/1 (which applies to Belgium, Bulgaria, the Czech Republic, Cyprus, Germany, Greece, Spain, France, Croatia, Italy, Luxembourg, Malta, the Netherlands, Austria, Portugal, Slovenia, Finland and Sweden).

[5] Danov and Beaumont, above n 3.

[6] AT von Mehren, 'Special Substantive Rules for Multistate Problems: Their Role and Significance in Contemporary Choice of Law Methodology' (1974–75) 88 *Harvard Law Review* 347.

[7] TC Hartley, *International Commercial Litigation* 2nd edn, (Cambridge University Press, 2015) 5.

[8] ibid 5–6.

appropriate EU Member State court that can effectively and efficiently dispense justice. This means that the place where the proceedings are initiated may frequently be central to parties' effective access to a desirable legal remedy in cross-border cases. The point was put forward by one interview respondent from England and Wales who noted that:

> one of the big differences … is the disclosure because, under the English system, we get disclosure; and continental systems, … you ask for core documents, but you have to know what they are before you ask for them. And documents tend to win cases.[9]

It is well established that Brussels Ia and Brussels IIa aim to unify[10] the relevant jurisdictional rules and make them highly predictable.[11] That said, the EU model of administration of justice provides claimants with a choice where to initiate certain cross-border claims on the basis of some of the special/alternative jurisdictional rules.

It can be further concluded that the current EU PIL institutional framework may be regarded as promoting a level of adjudicatory competition in respect to high value disputes with an international element.[12] The court-first-seised rule does play a central role in encouraging parties to quickly issue proceedings in one Member State rather than another. The EUPILLAR framework for data analysis considers the following variables which many selective parties[13] appear to factor in when deciding where to sue: the ability of the Member States' judges to deal with cross-border disputes; diverse procedural rules; efficiently (or inefficiently) functioning national judicial systems; costs and cost-recovery rules. This means the effectiveness of the EU PIL framework could be impaired not only by the inexperience of some national judges and/or slowness of national judicial systems, but also by the delaying litigation strategies[14] which inflate the litigation costs.[15] There appears to be a strong case that the current EU model of administration of justice is not suited to be applied in a diverse legal landscape dominated by the above mentioned variables. This means that the EU PIL framework is less than effective in ensuring access to remedies for litigants in cross-border cases.

An analysis of the way the current EU civil justice framework affects the selectiveness of the parties, in terms of choosing whether to litigate their claim in one jurisdiction rather than another, helpfully indicates the factors which impair the litigants' access to effective remedies in cross-border cases. In theory, Danov and Beaumont[16] have noted that the triangular relationship (ie allocation of jurisdiction—identification of governing law—the available remedy) would be influenced by the ability of the EU Member States' judges to effectively deal with cross-border cases. This may be strengthened by the EUPILLAR data analysis, which shows that the lack of experience of some national judges and lawyers to deal with complex cross-border cases may be a cause for concern in some of the new Member States. There is data which leave no doubt that the question whether the judges in

---

[9] EUPILLAR—England and Wales—Interview Transcript No 12.

[10] Recital 4 to Brussels Ia and Recital 12 to Brussels IIa.

[11] Recital 15 to Brussels Ia.

[12] See E Lein et al, 'Factors Influencing International Litigants' Decisions to Bring Commercial Claims to the London Based Courts ('BIICL Report')' < www.gov.uk/government/uploads/system/uploads/attachment_data/file/396343/factors-influencing-international-litigants-with-commercial-claims.pdf.

[13] See Ch 35.

[14] Recital 22 to Brussels Ia.

[15] Recital 26 to Brussels Ia.

[16] Danov and Beaumont, above n 3, 168.

a particular jurisdiction are knowledgeable and competent is an important consideration affecting a claimant's choice of forum in cross-border cases.[17] An *argumentum a contrario* is that the inexperience of the judges in dealing with cross-border cases and the slowness of the decision-making process may impair parties' access to effective remedies in cross-border cases. This is not to say that the national courts do not deal appropriately with harmonised PIL instruments. Indeed, the national reports[18] do indicate that the Member States' courts generally correctly apply the EU PIL regulations.

However, there are some examples,[19] which indicate that the lack of familiarity of national judges and lawyers with EU PIL, may be an important issue in some of the newer Member States and potentially in all Member States in relation to new PIL instruments. It is a real problem how to identify such cases. A major issue appears to be that both judges and parties (including their lawyers) may be unaware of the implications of the PIL instruments.[20] Also, the issue about the possible variations concerning the interpretation of Brussels IIa in a diverse Union was noted by one interview respondent from England who said:

> It is very evident that most Member States come at these sort of cross-border disputes from their own perspective. And I have found very considerable variation in the approach amongst the Member States. … It gives rise to a lot of problems that don't necessarily make their way into the law reports.[21]

The problems would be more visible in cases where the issues have been raised but the judges have addressed them very briskly, without really developing their reasoning and failing to address very complex PIL issues.[22] Another example about the possible variation across the EU is to be found in an English judgment,[23] in which Mr Justice Wood expressed a level of concern about a gross misapplication of Brussels IIa by another EU Member State court's judge. In this case, a Greek court wrongfully assumed jurisdiction, without even considering to 'declare of its own motion that it ha[d] no jurisdiction'.[24] It is indeed surprising that the jurisdiction was exercised, despite the fact that the Greek judge had established that the child was habitually residing in England.[25]

Given the level of diversity across the EU, an important objective was for the EUPILLAR Project to consider how high the risk was for national judges to inconsistently apply the PIL instruments. The issues were considered important because it was felt that, if the risk was high, this would have undermined the effectiveness of the PIL framework. Some examples from the case law do confirm that there is a level of risk especially in the new Member States where judges may have less experience in applying the PIL framework. The deduction concerning the risk of inconsistent application of the PIL instruments appears to receive some

---

[17] See the BIICL report above n 12. See also EUPILLAR—England and Wales—Interview Transcript No 1.

[18] See Pt II.

[19] eg Decision 248 of 24.04.2014, Provincial Court of Pernik, case No 427/2013; Ruling of 13.03.2013 of Varna Appellate Court, Commercial Chamber on commercial case No 96/ 2013. See ch 32.

[20] Decision 248 of 24.04.2014, Provincial Court of Pernik, case No 427/2013. See more in ch 32.

[21] EUPILLAR—England and Wales—Interview Transcript No 10.

[22] Ruling of 13.03.2013 of Varna Appellate Court, Commercial Chamber on commercial case No 96/ 2013. Compare: *Kleinwort Benson v Glasgow City Council* [1999] 1 AC 153 (HL); Case C-366/13, *Profit Investment Sim SpA* EU:C:2016:282; Case C-102/15, *Gazdasági Versenyhivatal v Siemens Aktiengesellschaft Österreich*—Opinion of AG Wahl, EU:C:2016:225. See more in ch 32.

[23] *Re: S (A Child)* [2014] EWHC 4643 (Fam).

[24] Art 17 of Brussels IIa.

[25] *Re: S (A Child)* [2014] EWHC 4643 (Fam) [82].

support in the qualitative data. However, the national reporters share the view that the PIL instruments are overall interpreted correctly by the EU Member States' judges. The work of the national judges appears to have been facilitated by the Court of Justice of the European Union (CJEU) which has already addressed many issues about the interpretation of the PIL instruments.

That said, the EUPILLAR data analysis shows that the litigants' strategies are the most dynamic element (and complex aspect) which shapes the triangular relationship in cross-border cases. The national reports clearly outline that there may be some complex issues which the courts will have to deal with in cross-border cases. In particular, jurisdictional challenges are often raised in the EU Member States. There appears to be a level of ambiguity with regard to the nuances of the PIL instruments which could pose difficult questions about the interpretation of the relevant provisions. Strategic defendants may well be exploiting the uncertainties/ambiguities of the current EU PIL framework by raising jurisdictional challenges, in order to increase the complexities in cross-border cases. This may have an impact on both judges and claimants. First, some of the EU Member States judges' willingness to assume jurisdiction may be affected as they may seek to avoid dealing with the difficult cases.[26] Second, this may have an impact on the claimants' decision whether to continue with the proceedings or accept a discounted compensation as a result of settlement negotiations. Indeed, any dispute about jurisdiction will raise the litigation costs and cause delay. A level of uncertainty about the courts' competence may lead to a significant drop in the value of a prolonged litigation for a claimant faced with a rising level of litigation costs.

Moreover, the ambiguity about the interpretation of Brussels Ia may encourage strategic litigants to issue proceedings in one jurisdiction rather than another. The problems could be exacerbated by the implication of the court-first-seised rule for the litigants' strategies in a diverse Union. If there are deficiencies in the functioning of a national judicial system,[27] then the court-first-seised rule may effectively be used to impair the litigants' access to remedies. In particular, the slowness of some of the national judicial systems may be exploited by strategic litigants. In other words, given the fact that it will take several years for an action to be heard in Greece,[28] the parties may seise a Greek court. This would inevitably have an effect on claimants' willingness to continue with the cross-border proceedings in Greece. At the same time, the inflexible nature of the court-first-seised rule means that any second-seised-court would have to stay its proceedings under the current EU PIL regime. This may adversely affect litigants' access to remedies.

The problems were spectacularly highlighted in the *Erich Gasser* case, which was already discussed above.[29] Some common law scholars seised the opportunity to criticise the functioning of the EU PIL regime and the work of the CJEU.[30] Although the *Erich Gasser* issue

---

[26] eg Germany (ch 7). See more in ch 35.

[27] eg Greece (ch 18).

[28] ibid. See also ch 32 and 35.

[29] Ch 35.

[30] eg T Hartley, 'The European Union and the Systematic Dismantling of the Common Law of Conflict of Laws' (2005) 54 *International and Comparative Law Quarterly* 813 and J Harris, 'Understanding the English Response to the Europeanisation of Private International Law' (2008) 4 *Journal of Private International Law* 347.

was addressed by Brussels Ia, the broader issue of a rigid jurisdictional system permitting abusive litigation tactics can still cause problems in cases where there is no choice-of-court agreement or where there are different dispute resolution clauses between the same parties. In other words, it is still possible for a non-bona fide party to deploy abusive litigation tactics. Therefore, an appropriate solution is for the EU policy-makers to devise rules which provide some flexibility, allowing judges to 'do justice in individual cases'.[31]

Even further delay will be generated if a preliminary ruling is sought from the CJEU, where the proceedings will take on average 15 months. The ineffectively functioning institutional framework strongly suggests that the EU PIL framework is not able to pursue its objectives to 'mak[e] cross-border litigation less time-consuming and costly',[32] and 'avoid abusive litigation tactics'.[33] This will effectively restrict litigants' access to effective remedies in cross-border cases. Therefore, there is a strong case for an institutional reform which allows EU Member States' courts to effectively deal with litigants' strategies that may impede parties' effective access to remedies in cross-border cases. But, a real challenge is how to provide the necessary flexibility that will enable EU Member States' judges to defeat abusive litigation tactics under the EU PIL framework. Before making a case for reform in relation to the institutional architecture, some specific aspects in relation to cross-border family law cases will be highlighted.

II. Some Specific Aspects in Relation to Cross-border Family Law Disputes

The national reports have highlighted the complexity of the EU PIL regime in the family law area. Divorce and/or parental responsibility and/or maintenance are commonly joined in one action[34] although they are covered by different sets of jurisdictional rules contained in Brussels IIa (divorce and parental responsibility) and the Maintenance Regulation (maintenance). Such fragmentation of jurisdiction[35] creates confusion[36] and, in extreme cases, leads to a misapplication of the instruments.[37] Moreover, the application of the jurisdictional rules has to be 'fitted around' various domestic laws which may be inconsistent

---

[31] Recital 14 to Rome II.

[32] Recital 26 to Brussels Ia.

[33] Recital 22 to Brussels Ia.

[34] In some Member States this is required by domestic law, eg Lithuania and the Czech Republic. See Lithuania (ch 22) and the Czech Republic (ch 15) respectively. The Czech national report notes the negative consequences of a potential inconsistency between the Czech law and the law of another Member State in situations where the child is habitually resident abroad. The same point is made by the Lithuanian report.

[35] See Luxembourg (ch 23).

[36] France (ch 17). See also the Czech Republic (ch 15).

[37] Eg by incorrectly applying the Brussels IIa regime of jurisdiction on parental responsibility also to the issue of maintenance (see eg Greece (ch 18)), or, where all three causes are joined in one action, by correctly basing the jurisdiction on divorce on Art 3 of Brussels IIa but automatically linking this issue with parental responsibility and maintenance, without examining whether jurisdiction can indeed be established in these matters in accordance with Art 12(1) of Brussels IIa and the Maintenance Reg (see eg Slovakia (ch 28)).

across Member States to the level that serious negative consequences ensue.[38] The problem of fragmentation of jurisdiction is exacerbated by the fact that judges in some EU jurisdictions lack sufficient knowledge and expertise in the application of EU PIL,[39] which in turn is caused by the relatively infrequent occurrence of cross-border cases, especially in small jurisdictions,[40] and an insufficient level of concentration of jurisdiction for cross-border family law cases across EU Member States.

In order to remedy the above problems, the national reports noted the need for a better coordination of the EU PIL instruments in the area of family law.[41] To address the problem of the lack of expertise, suggestions were made for the provision of workshops and training sessions on the relevant EU regulations for national judges.[42] Ideally, this should be preceded by concentration of jurisdiction for cross-border family law cases[43] or at least specialisation of judges for cross-border family law issues,[44] to ensure that the training sessions are directed at the relevant group of judges who in turn have the opportunity to develop a requisite level of expertise in handling cross-border cases. It was also suggested that practical guides to the application of the regulations be made available in local languages.[45] Finally, proposals were made for an increased level of interaction among judges from different Member States,[46] and wider accessibility of national case law on EU PIL regulations in civil law jurisdictions.[47] In the context of Brussels IIa's provisions on matrimonial matters, the project findings revealed differences in the characterisation of 'marriage' as some Member States regard same-sex unions as falling within the scope of the Regulation whereas other Member States reject such an approach.[48] Similarly, in the absence of a binding interpretation of habitual residence of adults for the purposes of Brussels IIa, divergent approaches are likely to emerge in this respect.[49] Problems have arisen also in relation to the definition

---

[38] See eg Czech Republic (ch 15), noting that under Czech law, custody and child maintenance must be judicially resolved before a divorce can be granted by Czech courts. Where the child is not habitually resident in the Czech Republic, the Czech courts may have jurisdiction for divorce but not for parental responsibility as prorogation of jurisdiction under Art 12(3) may not be forthcoming. If the law of the habitual residence of the child does not allow for parental responsibility proceedings to be conducted separately from divorce, the parties will be prevented from obtaining a divorce in the Czech Republic.

[39] See eg Slovenia (ch 29), Spain (ch 9), and Bulgaria (ch 12). The problem of the lack of expertise is particularly acute for first instance judges. See eg Poland (ch 10).

[40] See eg Portugal (ch 26). However, compare for example Luxembourg (ch 23) explaining that despite limited case law, 'the practice of Luxembourgish courts is not isolated' as they tend to rely on French case law. Consequently, decisions in particular from the Court of Appeal and the Supreme Court 'are very didactic with regards to EU PIL application'.

[41] See eg the Netherlands (ch 25), Luxembourg (ch 23), Ireland (ch 20), France (ch 17), and Spain (ch 9).

[42] See eg Greece (ch 18), Spain (ch 9), and Bulgaria (ch 12). The Austrian national report notes the active role played by the Austrian Central Authority in this respect, see Austria (ch 11).

[43] See eg Spain (ch 9). As a minimum, jurisdiction should be concentrated for child abduction cases, see eg Slovenia (ch 29). For examples of concentrated jurisdiction for child abduction see Slovakia, the Netherlands, Latvia and the Czech Republic (chs 28, 25, 21 and 15 respectively). It is encouraging that the European Commission Proposal for the Recast of the Brussels IIa Reg contains a suggestion to this effect, at least in relation to child abduction cases. See Proposal for a Council Reg on jurisdiction, the recognition and enforcement of decisions in matrimonial matters and the matters of parental responsibility, and on international child abduction (recast), COM(2016) 411 final, Recital 26 and Art 22.

[44] See eg Poland (ch 10) and Spain (ch 9). See also Italy (ch 8).

[45] Poland (ch 10).

[46] See eg Bulgaria (ch 12) and Poland (ch 10).

[47] See eg Romania (ch 27), Sweden (ch 30), Luxembourg (ch 23), Czech Republic (ch 15), and Poland (ch 10).

[48] See eg Trimmings, ch 46.

[49] See eg the Netherlands (ch 25), Italy (ch 8) and Bulgaria (ch 12). See also Kruger (ch 42).

of seising under Article 16 of Brussels IIa,[50] leading to a proposal for a certain level of procedural harmonisation.[51]

In relation to Brussels IIa's provisions on parental responsibility, including child abduction, it was pointed out that significant divergences existed among national practices concerning the hearing of the child for the purposes of the Regulation, demonstrating a need for common minimum standards to ensure a higher level of uniformity.[52] The Brussels IIa approach to child abduction is perceived as too cumbersome[53] and prone to non-uniform application, for example due to differing views of Member States' courts on the sufficiency of protective measures for the purposes of Article 11(4) of the Regulation.[54] It was also noted that courts of some Member States struggled to meet the six week time limit set out in Article 11(3) of Brussels IIa.[55]

The Maintenance Regulation appears to have generated only a limited amount of case law, whilst particular problems seem to have arisen in relation to recognition and enforcement.[56] The project findings also highlighted the need for well-functioning Central Authorities and their effective cooperation.[57]

III. Case for Reform: Institutional Architecture and Remedies in Cross-border Cases

There is a strong case that the inability of the institutional framework to defeat abusive litigation tactics poses real hurdles for parties seeking to obtain effective remedies in cross-border cases. An ineffectively functioning EU PIL framework, which does not provide the tools for the EU Member States' judges to effectively cope with abusive litigation tactics, cannot provide litigants with access to justice in individual cross-border cases. Such a system is not able to achieve its objective to provide certainty and predictability about the outcome of the dispute because strategic litigants may exploit the various ambiguities in the interpretation of the PIL provisions by tactically raising issues of jurisdiction and choice of law. This inflates the litigation costs even further, effectively restricting the litigants' effective access to remedies. Therefore, the various delaying strategies are even more of an issue for parties with no access to finance.

An appropriate reform presupposes a revision of the institutional architecture. This is important in order to enable the EU PIL framework to develop in a way which provides legal certainty about jurisdiction and choice-of-law as necessary pre-conditions for effective remedies in cross-border cases. In the view of the high number of jurisdictional challenges

---

[50] See eg Ireland (ch 20) and Great Britain (ch 5). See also Trimmings (ch 46).
[51] eg Spain (ch 9).
[52] See eg Slovenia (ch 29).
[53] See eg Frąckowiak-Adamska (ch 43).
[54] See Czech Republic (ch 15).
[55] See eg Portugal (ch 26), noting in particular situations involving appeals, and Greece (ch 18).
[56] Walker (ch 44). See also Greece (ch 18) and Latvia (ch 21), describing the general application of the Maintenance Reg in those jurisdictions as 'incorrect' and 'poor' respectively.
[57] See Poland (ch 10) and Walker (ch 44).

under the Brussels I regime which inflate litigation costs and cause delays, a case for a level of harmonisation at EU level can be made. The need to do so may be sustained by noting that the claimants' and defendants' tactical behaviour with regard to establishing/challenging jurisdiction may adversely affect effective access to remedies in cross-border disputes. Whereas a level of harmonisation with regard to the jurisdictional challenges is needed at EU level, some exceptions to the rigid court-first-seised rule are highly desirable, justifying some legislative amendments. Indeed, there is a strong case for the policy-makers to revise the court-first-seised rule, as a part of such a comprehensive reform aiming to provide litigants with access to effective remedies in cross-border cases. This deduction may be reinforced by the data and its analyses[58] which suggest that the Brussels Ia and IIa Regulations do not deal effectively with parallel proceedings,[59] promoting a race to the court and encouraging abusive litigation strategies.

A case for reform may be strengthened by noting that, as already mentioned, an attempt was made by the Commission to provide more flexibility in cases where 'the court first seised [did not] establish its jurisdiction within six months'.[60] The fact that the issue was left unaddressed by the EU legislator indicates that the review of the court-first-seised rule should be put on the legislative agenda again with a view to thoroughly tackling the problems in the next revision of Brussels Ia.[61] A transfer of proceedings, from one Member State court to another without considering which is the court first seised, may be seen as an appropriate solution to the problems of parallel proceedings. A legislative intervention, which allows for transfer of proceedings in cases where it is necessary for the proper administration of justice, may also tackle any litigation tactics which abusively benefit from the delay generated by some of the inefficiencies of national judicial systems. An appropriately drafted provision could be modelled on Article 15 of Brussels IIa and Articles 30 and 33 of Brussels Ia. In particular, a new provision could state that:

1. By way of exception, the courts of a Member State having jurisdiction as to the substance of the matter may, if they consider that a court of another Member State, with which the dispute has a close connection, would be better placed to hear the case, or a specific part thereof, and where this is necessary for the proper administration of justice:
   (a) stay the case or the part thereof in question and invite the parties to introduce a request before the court of that other Member State; or
   (b) request a court of another Member State to assume jurisdiction.
2. The courts of a Member State having jurisdiction as to the substance of the matter may, upon application of a party, and where related actions are pending in the courts of different Member States, stay the case or the part thereof in question and request a court of another Member State to assume jurisdiction.
3. The courts of that other Member State may, where due to the specific circumstances of the case, where this is necessary for the proper administration of justice, accept jurisdiction within six weeks of seizure.

A case for reform may be further strengthened by noting that Article 15 of Brussels IIa appears to be working very well in parental responsibility proceedings before English and

---

[58] See chs 5 and 35.
[59] Recital 21 to Brussels Ia.
[60] Art 29(2) of the Commission Proposal Brussels I Recast COM(2010) 748 final.
[61] Art 79 of Brussels Ia.

Welsh courts.[62] Furthermore, when considering whether to make a transfer request in cases where related proceedings are pending in different EU Member States' courts, the following factors, which are relevant for the purposes of Article 30 of Brussels Ia, may be taken into account by national judges: 'the extent of the relatedness and the risk of mutually irreconcilable decisions; ... the stage reached in each set of proceedings; and ... the proximity of the courts to the subject-matter of the case.'[63] As a part of the proper administration of justice test in the proposed new provision, the time period—within which a final judgment will be rendered in the respective fora—may be considered.

There is a case for revising the rigid rule which assumes that the first seised court is always appropriate and capable to dispense justice in cross-border cases. An additional challenge is how to adjust the current institutional framework for such a rule to function effectively, considering the diverse nature of the EU. The diverse nature of the Union makes any reform of the PIL instruments extremely difficult because any new provision may bring fresh uncertainty. This will be even more of an issue if the provision provides a level of flexibility and discretion. This poses particularly difficult questions about the way the institutional framework should be devised. Whereas it is beneficial that a significant number of national PIL cases and all CJEU cases are available on the EUPILLAR database, there are some challenges which need to be addressed in order to improve the effectiveness of the current EU PIL.

The EUPILLAR research findings indicate that the litigants and judges across the EU do not always face the same problems in applying the PIL regulations. As already noted,[64] in some EU Member States,[65] judges and lawyers appear to be less than experienced in dealing with cross-border disputes. This may adversely affect their ability to apply (or respectively advise on the application) of the EU PIL instruments in these countries. In other Member States,[66] the judges have gained significant experience in applying the EU PIL regulations. The lawyers in these jurisdictions have developed advanced levels of understanding which allow them to exploit every nuance in the application of the EU PIL instruments. Hence, this knowledge taken together with their sophisticated tactical skills puts them in a good position to gain advantage from every ambiguity by raising it, in order to adversely affect their opponent's expectations about the outcome of the cross-border case,[67] whilst causing delay and inflating the litigation costs.

It has been suggested that in relation to PIL 'there should be specialised seminars for all judges at least once every year, covering the newest trends in national and CJEU case law.'[68] National judges' lack of familiarity with EU PIL instruments and/or the insufficient reasoning of their judgments in applying them should be addressed by providing further training. As already noted,[69] there is a level of variation in respect of the EU Member States' judges' qualifications and experience. This is another critical aspect which may influence

---

[62] See ch 5.
[63] Case C-129/92, *Owens Bank Ltd v Fulvio Bracco and Bracco Industria Chimica SpA*—Opinion of AG Lenz EU:C:1993:363 [76].
[64] ch 32.
[65] eg ch 12 above.
[66] eg ch 5 above.
[67] ch 40.
[68] ch 12 above.
[69] ch 35.

the effectiveness of any harmonised EU PIL instrument. The process of recruitment of qualified judges and the criteria for their promotion may be equally important[70] for the development of an EU civil justice system which relies on national judges to dispense justice in cross-border cases. This is a particularly important aspect because the Union has been very successful in ensuring that the judgments given in one Member State are swiftly recognised and enforced in the other Member States.[71]

However, it would be very resource-intensive to provide seminars for all the judges across the EU. It is a relatively safe assumption that the value added by so many seminars would be insignificant in comparison to the costs. Furthermore, if a significant number of judges handle only one or two PIL cases per year, then it will be difficult for all the judges to have an optimal number of cases which should allow them to achieve a level of effectiveness and efficiency in dealing with them. This will significantly inflate the 'societal costs',[72] whilst improving only marginally (if at all) litigants' access to effective remedies in cross-border cases.

The effectiveness of any training as a viable policy option without any other reform may be questioned on the basis of the suggestion that the EU PIL instruments may be given different interpretations even by judges in the same Member State. Therefore specialisation of judges and concentration of jurisdiction to deal with cross-border cases is to be welcomed when done unilaterally by individual Member States. Sometimes it may be appropriate to mandate it in EU legislation as is being proposed for child abduction in the Commission's Proposed Recast of Brussels IIa.[73]

When revising the court-first-seised rule by introducing a new rule that provides a level of flexibility/discretion, such a solution may bring fresh uncertainty in cross-border cases unless appropriate safeguards are put in place. In this context, as already noted, it is a real issue that the procedure for obtaining a preliminary ruling from the CJEU is less efficient than it ought to be due to the length of the procedure and the number of dubious decisions. There is a strong case for an institutional reform, providing a specialised chamber in the CJEU devoted to PIL issues which would be supported by a specialist Advocate General and specialist referendaires. The judges and Advocate General in this specialised chamber would host workshops of leading PIL academics and national judges and practitioners who deal with PIL cases in Luxembourg on a regular basis. It is also suggested that all major EU PIL Regulations be accompanied by an expert explanatory report along the lines of those prepared in the Hague Conference on Private International Law.[74]

Therefore, an evidence-based law reform approach is strongly recommended for all the reforms concerning the EU PIL Regulations and their application in a cross-border context. The need to do so is strengthened by the findings of the EUPILLAR research project which appear to suggest that the litigants' effective access to remedies may be restricted by litigation strategies which exploit the ambiguities of the EU PIL regime. In other words, there

---

[70] RA Posner, *Economic Analysis of Law* 8th edn (Alphen aan den Rijn, WoltersKluwer, 2001) 709.

[71] Recital 4 to Brussels Ia and Recital 21 to Brussels IIa.

[72] J Bronsteen, 'Some Thoughts About the Economics of Settlement' (2009) 78 *Fordham Law Review* 1129, 1133.

[73] See above nn 43 and 44 and the text accompanying those notes.

[74] For the EU institutional issues, see B Yüksel, An Analysis of the Effectiveness of the EU Institutions in Making and Interpreting EU Private International Law Regulations' Ch 3 above.

is a strong case that the EU legal landscape impacts the triangular relationship, affecting litigants' access to remedies by its inability to defeat abusive litigation tactics concerning disputes about jurisdiction and choice-of-law. Consequently, there is a case for revamping the institutional architecture, so that it enables the EU Member States' judges to deal with the constantly evolving litigants' strategies. The decision of the UK, as one of the leading EU jurisdictions, to leave the Union, could spur an institutional reform with a view to making the remaining EU jurisdictions more competitive in the market for cross-border litigation, enabling the EU Member States' judges to efficiently and effectively provide access to appropriate legal remedies in cross-border cases.

There is a case for reform which should aim to overhaul the way the EU PIL framework is functioning. In this context, the EU policy-makers should consider how the EU Member States' courts can enhance their ability to provide effective remedies for litigants in cross-border cases. Such a reform should also aim to help some of the EU Member States' courts in establishing themselves as leading litigation centres which can successfully compete with English courts in the market for high-value cross-border cases.

IV. Revising the EU Legal Landscape and the BREXIT Implications: Could There be Even More Adjudicatory Competition?

The EU model of administration of justice, which is based on the EU PIL instruments, has successfully promoted adjudicatory competition in high value cross-border disputes, driven by the law firms and litigation funders (who take investment decisions whether to fund litigation in certain jurisdictions). Although some jurisdictions appear to be attracting a high volume of disputes with an international element, these are predominately in relation to low value claims (driven by domestic policies and local litigation fees) which have little or no effect on the market for cross-border litigation services.

That said, the UK's decision to leave the EU may leave a significant gap in the market for cross-border legal services with regard to disputes arising in the EU context. It is now imperative for the EU policy-makers to consider how the EU legal landscape should be developed. In this context, the following questions should be addressed: how can the EU Member States' courts enhance their ability to provide effective remedies for litigants in cross-border cases? How can some of the EU Member States' courts establish themselves as leading litigation centres which can successfully compete with English courts in the market for high value cross-border cases?

The theoretical framework developed under the EUPILLAR project, which has evaluated the effectiveness of the EU PIL framework, could be used to analyse the relevant policy options with a view to mending the EU civil justice system, making it suited to defeat abusive litigation tactics. A challenge is that, whilst the EUPILLAR project sought to find out how the EU PIL framework was shaping the litigants' strategies, an evidence-based law reform will need to define the design of the institutional architecture by collecting data about the litigators' expectations. An analysis of the empirical data will indicate how to design the EU legal landscape considering how the different policy options may impact the litigants' strategies and any settlement dynamics in different types of cross-border cases. A central aspect in the analysis should be the question how to design the EU institutional architecture, in order to provide legal remedies for litigants in cross-border cases, enhancing the competitiveness of the EU Member States' courts in a global context.

The three criteria, which should be used to identify the optimal policy options for revising the EU PIL framework are: *relevance, effectiveness* and *efficiency*.[75] A policy option will be regarded as relevant, if it is successful in providing effective remedies for litigants in cross-border cases and in defeating the abusive litigation tactics (and be adjustable to defeat any new delaying tactics). There is a strong case for an appropriately designed research project to carefully consider how the institutional architecture should evolve. In this context, it is worth discovering anticipated and actual changes in litigants' tactics under the different policy options which should indicate how best EU policy-makers should design the institutional architecture.

The effectiveness of the various policy options will be determined by considering the following two elements of an effective remedy. First, as already noted, it is well established that the potential claimant would consider the remedy, which (even if declaratory or injunctive in nature) would normally have a monetary value[76] in commercial cases with an international element. The claimant's entitlement to such a remedy and the scope of the defendant's liability would both be determined by the governing law/s. Second, there is a strong case that any access to a remedy would depend on establishing jurisdiction before an appropriate court. It has been demonstrated that the litigants' access to effective remedies in legal proceedings may be restricted by litigants' strategies which cause further delay by exploiting the ambiguities of the EU PIL legal landscape. For example: service may be an issue; jurisdictional challenges may be raised; parallel proceedings may be initiated in another EU Member State. These litigants' strategies inflate the litigation costs and reduce the value of litigation with a view to forcing a significantly discounted settlement. Therefore, an analysis of the collected data will indicate the policy options which would be most efficient (ie cost effective)[77] in defeating these delaying tactics.

Adjudicatory competition could be further promoted in Europe because the UK may design its own PIL legal landscape. It will be important for UK policy-makers to consider how the PIL legal landscape should be adjusted, so that the UK courts continue to provide effective legal remedies for litigants in cross-border cases and can remain a leading litigation centre in respect to high value cross-border disputes.

---

[75] F Varone, B Rihoux and A Marx, 'A New Method for Policy Evaluation? Longstanding Challenges and the Possibilities of Qualitative Comparative Analysis (QCA)' in B Rihoux and H Grimm (eds), *Innovative Comparative Methods for Policy Analysis* (New York, Springer, 2006) 213, 215.

[76] Chs 5 and 7 above.

[77] Varone, Rihoux and Marx, above n 75, 215.

INDEX

Lightning Source UK Ltd.
Milton Keynes UK
UKHW051017160822
407360UK00004B/164